W9-CTW-257

Contemporary
Literary Criticism

Guide to Gale Literary Criticism Series

For criticism on	Consult these Gale series
Authors now living or who died after December 31, 1959	*CONTEMPORARY LITERARY CRITICISM (CLC)*
Authors who died between 1900 and 1959	*TWENTIETH-CENTURY LITERARY CRITICISM (TCLC)*
Authors who died between 1800 and 1899	*NINETEENTH-CENTURY LITERATURE CRITICISM (NCLC)*
Authors who died between 1400 and 1799	*LITERATURE CRITICISM FROM 1400 TO 1800 (LC)* *SHAKESPEAREAN CRITICISM (SC)*
Authors who died before 1400	*CLASSICAL AND MEDIEVAL LITERATURE CRITICISM (CMLC)*
Black writers of the past two hundred years	*BLACK LITERATURE CRITICISM (BLC)*
Authors of books for children and young adults	*CHILDREN'S LITERATURE REVIEW (CLR)*
Dramatists	*DRAMA CRITICISM (DC)*
Hispanic writers of the late nineteenth and twentieth centuries	*HISPANIC LITERATURE CRITICISM (HLC)*
Native North American writers and orators of the eighteenth, nineteenth, and twentieth centuries	*NATIVE NORTH AMERICAN LITERATURE (NNAL)*
Poets	*POETRY CRITICISM (PC)*
Short story writers	*SHORT STORY CRITICISM (SSC)*
Major authors from the Renaissance to the present	*WORLD LITERATURE CRITICISM, 1500 TO THE PRESENT (WLC)*

Volume 96

Contemporary Literary Criticism

Excerpts from Criticism of the Works
of Today's Novelists, Poets, Playwrights,
Short Story Writers, Scriptwriters, and
Other Creative Writers

Deborah A. Stanley
EDITOR

Jeff Chapman
Pamela S. Dear
Daniel Jones
John D. Jorgenson
Aarti D. Stephens
Polly A. Vedder
Thomas Wiloch
Kathleen Wilson
ASSOCIATE EDITORS

GALE

DETROIT • NEW YORK • TORONTO • LONDON

STAFF

Deborah A. Stanley, *Editor*

Jeff Chapman, Pamela S. Dear, Daniel Jones, John D. Jorgenson, Aarti D. Stephens,
Polly A. Vedder, Thomas Wiloch, and Kathleen Wilson, *Associate Editors*

John P. Daniel, Christopher Giroux, Joshua Lauer, Janet Mullane,
Annette Petrusso, Linda Quigley, and John Stanley, *Contributing Editors*

Marlene S. Hurst, *Permissions Manager*
Margaret A. Chamberlain, Maria Franklin, and Kimberly F. Smilay, *Permissions Specialists*
Diane Cooper, Edna Hedblad, Michele Lonoconus, Maureen Puhl, Susan Salas, and Shalice Shah, *Permissions Associates*
Sarah Chesney and Jeffrey Hermann, *Permissions Assistants*

Victoria B. Cariappa, *Research Manager*
Julia C. Daniel, Tamara C. Nott, Michele P. Pica, Tracie A. Richardson,
Norma Sawaya, and Cheryl L. Warnock, *Research Associates*
Laura C. Bissey, Alfred A. Gardner I, and Sean R. Smith, *Research Assistants*

Mary Beth Trimper, *Production Director*
Deborah L. Milliken, *Production Assistant*

Barbara J. Yarrow, *Graphic Services Manager*
Sherrell Hobbs, *Macintosh Artist*
Randy Bassett, *Image Database Supervisor*
Robert Duncan and Mikal Ansari, *Scanner Operators*
Pamela Hayes, *Photography Coordinator*

Library of Congress Catalog Card Number 76-46132
ISBN 0-7876-1060-7
ISSN 0091-3421

Printed in the United States of America
10 9 8 7 6 5 4 3 2 1

Contents

Preface vii

Acknowledgments xi

Preface

A Comprehensive Information Source
on Contemporary Literature

Named "one of the twenty-five most distinguished reference titles published during the past twenty-five years" by *Reference Quarterly,* the *Contemporary Literary Criticism (CLC)* series provides readers with critical commentary and general information on more than 2,000 authors now living or who died after December 31, 1959. Previous to the publication of the first volume of *CLC* in 1973, there was no ongoing digest monitoring scholarly and popular sources of critical opinion and explication of modern literature. *CLC,* therefore, has fulfilled an essential need, particularly since the complexity and variety of contemporary literature makes the function of criticism especially important to today's reader.

Scope of the Series

CLC presents significant passages from published criticism of works by creative writers. Since many of the authors covered by *CLC* inspire continual critical commentary, writers are often represented in more than one volume. There is, of course, no duplication of reprinted criticism.

Authors are selected for inclusion for a variety of reasons, among them the publication or dramatic production of a critically acclaimed new work, the reception of a major literary award, revival of interest in past writings, or the adaptation of a literary work to film or television.

Attention is also given to several other groups of writers-authors of considerable public interest—about whose work criticism is often difficult to locate. These include mystery and science fiction writers, literary and social critics, foreign writers, and authors who represent particular ethnic groups within the United States.

Format of the Book

Each *CLC* volume contains about 500 individual excerpts taken from hundreds of book review periodicals, general magazines, scholarly journals, monographs, and books. Entries include critical evaluations spanning from the beginning of an author's career to the most current commentary. Interviews, feature articles, and other published writings that offer insight into the author's works are also presented. Students, teachers, librarians, and researchers will find that the generous excerpts and supplementary material in *CLC* provide them with vital information required to write a term paper, analyze a poem, or lead a book discussion group. In addition, complete bibliographical citations note the original source and all of the information necessary for a term paper footnote or bibliography.

Features

A *CLC* author entry consists of the following elements:

- The **Author Heading** cites the author's name in the form under which the author has most commonly published, followed by birth date, and death date when applicable. Uncertainty as to a birth or death date is indicated by a question mark.

- A **Portrait** of the author is included when available.

- A brief **Biographical and Critical Introduction** to the author and his or her work precedes the excerpted criticism. The first line of the introduction provides the author's full name, pseudonyms (if applicable), nationality, and a listing of genres in which the author has written. To provide users with easier access to information, the biographical and critical essay included in each author entry is divided into four categories: "Introduction," "Biographical Information," "Major Works," and "Critical Reception." The introductions to single-work entries—entries that focus on well known and frequently studied books, short stories, and poems—are similarly organized to quickly provide readers with information on the plot and major characters of the work being discussed, its major themes, and its critical reception. Previous volumes of *CLC* in which the author has been featured are also listed in the introduction.

- A list of **Principal Works** notes the most important writings by the author. When foreign-language works have been translated into English, the English-language version of the title follows in brackets.

- The **Excerpted Criticism** represents various kinds of critical writing, ranging in form from the brief review to the scholarly exegesis. Essays are selected by the editors to reflect the spectrum of opinion about a specific work or about an author's literary career in general. The excerpts are presented chronologically, adding a useful perspective to the entry. All titles by the author featured in the entry are printed in boldface type, which enables the reader to easily identify the works being discussed. Publication information (such as publisher names and book prices) and parenthetical numerical references (such as footnotes or page and line references to specific editions of a work) have been deleted at the editor's discretion to provide smoother reading of the text.

- Critical essays are prefaced by **Explanatory Notes** as an additional aid to readers. These notes may provide several types of valuable information, including: the reputation of the critic, the importance of the work of criticism, the commentator's approach to the author's work, the purpose of the criticism, and changes in critical trends regarding the author.

- A complete **Bibliographical Citation** designed to help the user find the original essay or book precedes each excerpt.

- Whenever possible, a recent, previously unpublished **Author Interview** accompanies each entry.

- A concise **Further Reading** section appears at the end of entries on authors for whom a significant amount of criticism exists in addition to the pieces reprinted in *CLC*. Each citation in this section is accompanied by a descriptive annotation describing the content of that article. Materials included in this section are grouped under various headings (e.g., Biography, Bibliography, Criticism, and Interviews) to aid users in their search for additional information. Cross-references to other useful sources published by Gale Research in which the author has appeared are also included: *Authors in the News, Black Writers, Children's Literature Review, Contemporary Authors, Dictionary of Literary Biography, DISCovering Authors, Drama Criticism, Hispanic Literature Criticism, Hispanic Writers, Native North American Literature, Poetry Criticism, Something about the Author, Short Story Criticism, Contemporary Authors Autobiography Series,* and *Something about the Author Autobiography Series.*

Other Features

CLC also includes the following features:

- An **Acknowledgments** section lists the copyright holders who have granted permission to reprint material in this volume of *CLC*. It does not, however, list every book or periodical reprinted or consulted during the preparation of the volume.

- Each new volume of *CLC* includes a **Cumulative Topic Index,** which lists all literary topics treated in *CLC, NCLC, TCLC,* and *LC 1400-1800.*

- A **Cumulative Author Index** lists all the authors who have appeared in the various literary criticism series published by Gale Research, with cross-references to Gale's biographical and autobiographical series. A full listing of the series referenced there appears on the first page of the indexes of this volume. Readers will welcome this cumulated author index as a useful tool for locating an author within the various series. The index, which lists birth and death dates when available, will be particularly valuable for those authors who are identified with a certain period but whose death dates cause them to be placed in another, or for those authors whose careers span two periods. For example, Ernest Hemingway is found in *CLC,* yet F. Scott Fitzgerald, a writer often associated with him, is found in *Twentieth-Century Literary Criticism.*

- A **Cumulative Nationality Index** alphabetically lists all authors featured in *CLC* by nationality, followed by numbers corresponding to the volumes in which the authors appear.

- An alphabetical **Title Index** accompanies each volume of *CLC*. Listings are followed by the author's name and the corresponding page numbers where the titles are discussed. English translations of foreign titles and variations of titles are cross-referenced to the title under which a work was originally published. Titles of novels, novellas, dramas, films, record albums, and poetry, short story, and essay collections are printed in italics, while all individual poems, short stories, essays, and songs are printed in roman type within quotation marks; when published separately (e.g., T. S. Eliot's poem *The Waste Land),* the titles of long poems are printed in italics.

- In response to numerous suggestions from librarians, Gale has also produced a **Special Paperbound Edition** of the *CLC* title index. This annual cumulation, which alphabetically lists all titles reviewed in the series, is available to all customers and is typically published with every fifth volume of *CLC*. Additional copies of the index are available upon request. Librarians and patrons will welcome this separate index: it saves shelf space, is easy to use, and is recyclable upon receipt of the next edition.

Citing *Contemporary Literary Criticism*

When writing papers, students who quote directly from any volume in the Literary Criticism Series may use the following general forms to footnote reprinted criticism. The first example pertains to material drawn from periodicals, the second to material reprinted in books:

[1]Alfred Cismaru, "Making the Best of It," *The New Republic,* 207, No. 24, (December 7, 1992), 30, 32; excerpted and reprinted in *Contemporary Literary Criticism,* Vol. 85, ed. Christopher Giroux (Detroit: Gale Research, 1995), pp. 73-4.

[2]Yvor Winters, *The Post-Symbolist Methods* (Allen Swallow, 1967); excerpted and reprinted in *Contemporary Literary Criticism,* Vol. 85, ed. Christopher Giroux (Detroit: Gale Research, 1995), pp. 223-26.

Suggestions Are Welcome

The editors hope that readers will find *CLC* a useful reference tool and welcome comments about the work. Send comments and suggestions to: Editors, *Contemporary Literary Criticism,* Gale Research, Penobscot Building, Detroit, MI 48226-4094.

Acknowledgments

The editors wish to thank the copyright holders of the excerpted criticism included in this volume and the permissions managers of many book and magazine publishing companies for assisting us in securing reprint rights. We are also grateful to the staffs of the Detroit Public Library, the Library of Congress, the University of Detroit Mercy Library, Wayne State University Purdy/Kresge Library Complex, and the University of Michigan Libraries for making their resources available to us. Following is a list of the copyright holders who have granted us permission to reprint material in this volume of *CLC*. Every effort has been made to trace copyright, but if omissions have been made, please let us know.

COPYRIGHTED EXCERPTS IN *CLC*, VOLUME 96, WERE REPRINTED FROM THE FOLLOWING PERIODICALS:

African Literature Today, n. 6, 1973 for "Okot p'Bitek Two Songs: 'Song of a Prisoner' and Song of Malaya" by Bahadur Tejani. Copyright 1973 by Heinemann Educational Books Ltd. All rights reserved. Reproduced by permission of the author.— The African Studies Review, v. 28, December, 1985. © 1989 African Studies Association. All rights reserved. Reproduced by permission.—*America,* v. 122, May 23, 1970. © 1970. All rights reserved. Reproduced with permission of America Press, Inc., 106 West 56th Street, New York, NY 10019.—*The American Book Review,* v. 14, February-March, 1993. © 1993 by The American Book Review. Reproduced by permission.—*Ariel: A Review of International English Literature*, v. 6, April, 1975 for "Daphne's Metamorphoses in Janet Frame's Early Novels" by Jeanne Delbaere-Garant; v. 25, October, 1994 for an interview with Caryl Phillips by Carol Margaret Davison. Copyright © 1975, 1994 The Board of Governors, The University of Calgary. Reproduced by permission of the publisher and the respective authors.—*Australian Literary Studies,* v. 11, October, 1983 for "An Infinite Onion: Narrative Structure in Peter Carey's Fiction" by Teresa Dovey; v. 12, October, 1986 for "American Dreaming: The Fictions of Peter Carey" by Graeme Turner. Both reproduced by permission of the publisher and the respective authors.—*Best Sellers,* v. 26, July 15, 1966. Copyright 1966, renewed 1994, by the University of Scranton. Reproduced by permission.—*Black American Literature Forum,* v. 14, 1980 for "'I Wish I Was a Poet': The Character as Artist in Alice Childress's Like One of the Family" by Trudier Harris; v. 24, Summer, 1990 for "W. E. B. Du Bois's 'Autobiography' and the Politics of Literature" by William E. Cain. Copyright © 1980, 1990 Indiana State University. Both reproduced by permission of Indiana State University and the respective authors.—*The Bloomsbury Review,* v. 14, May-June, 1994 for "First Indian on the Moon" by Carl L. Bankston III; v. 15, July-August, 1995 for "Reservation Blues" by Abigail Davis. Copyright © by Owaissa Communications Company, Inc., 1994, 1995. Both reproduced by permission of the author.—*Book World—The Washington Post,* August 2, 1987; July 31, 1988; April 28, 1991; September 27, 1992; October 17, 1993 © 1987, 1988, 1991, 1992, 1993 Washington Post Book World/Washington Post Writers Group. All reproduced with permission.—*Books and Bookmen,* n. 364, February, 1986 for "Like a River in Summer" by Adewale Maja-Pearce. Copyright © Adewale Maja-Pearce 1986. Reproduced by permission of the author.—*Boston Review,* v. XIX, June-September, 1994 for a review of "Crossing the River" by Farah Jasmime Griffin. Copyright © 1994 by the Boston Critic, Inc. Reproduced by permission of the author.— *Callaloo,* v. 14, Summer, 1991. Copyright © 1991 by Charles H. Rowell. All rights reserved. Reproduced by permission.— *Chicago Tribune—Books,* October 18, 1992. © copyrighted 1992, Chicago Tribune Company. All rights reserved. Used with permission.—*Children's Literature Association Quarterly,* v. 13, Summer, 1988. © 1988 Children's Literature Association. Reproduced by permission.—*The Christian Science Monitor,* August 19, 1987. © 1987 The Christian Science Publishing Society. All rights reserved. Reproduced by permission from *The Christian Science Monitor.*—*CLA Journal,* v. XXXIII, June, 1990. Copyright, 1990 by The College Language Association. Used by permission of The College Language Association.— *Critia Hispanica,* v. VII, 1985. Reproduced by permission.—.*Essays on Canadian Writing,* n. 29, Spring, 1984. © 1984 Essays on Canadian Writing Ltd. Reproduced by permission.—*Freedomways,* v. 20, second quarter, 1980. Copyright © 1980 by Freedomways Associates, Inc. Reproduced by permission of *Freedomways.*—*Hispania,* v. 65, May, 1982 for "Woman's Triumph Over Man in Rene Marques's Theater" by Thomas Feeny. Copyright © 1982 The American Association of Teachers of Spanish and Portuguese, Inc. Reproduced by permission of the publisher and the author.—*Journal of Black Studies,* v. 2, March, 1972. Copyright © 1972 by Sage Publications, Inc. Reproduced with permission of Sage Publications, Inc.—*Journal of Commonwealth Literature,* v. XV, August, 1980 for "Modes of Freedom: The Songs of Okot p'Bitek" by Anne Marie Heywood; v. XXIX, 1993 for "Historical Fiction and Fictional History: Caryl Phillips's Cambridge" by Evelyn O'Callaghan. Copyright by the respective authors. Reproduced by permission of Hans Zell Publishers, an imprint of Bowker-Saur Ltd.—*Kliatt,* v. 28, May,

COPYRIGHTED EXCERPTS IN *CLC,* VOLUME 96, WERE REPRINTED FROM THE FOLLOWING BOOKS:

PHOTOGRAPHS AND ILLUSTRATIONS APPEARING IN *CLC,* VOLUME 96, WERE RECEIVED FROM THE FOLLOWING SOURCES:

Sherman Alexie
1966-

Spokane/Coeur d'Alene poet, short story writer, and novelist.

The following entry provides an overview of Alexie's career through 1995.

INTRODUCTION

Alexie, a Spokane/Coeur d'Alene Indian, is one of the most prominent Native American writers of his generation. In his critically acclaimed poetry and fiction, he tells of the hardships and joys of contemporary life on an Indian reservation. Alexie's works are celebrated for their detailed descriptions of the psychology and environment of the reservation; the humor and wit that are displayed in the face of the intense poverty and the ravages of alcohol abuse that are part of reservation life; and their broad, universal messages of hope and perseverance.

Biographical Information

Born in 1966 on the Spokane Indian Reservation in Wellpinit, Washington, Alexie was raised in an environment often characterized by depression, poverty, and alcohol abuse. Alexie's mother supported the family by selling her hand-sewn quilts and working at the Wellpinit Trading Post, while his father, an alcoholic, was often absent from the house. Alexie was an exemplary student in elementary school—he read every book in the Wellpinit school library—and in high school. In 1985 he was admitted to Gonzaga University in Spokane. There, under intense pressure to succeed, he began abusing alcohol. Eventually he transferred to Washington State University and began writing poetry and short fiction. A selection of his work was published in *Hanging Loose* magazine in 1990. This early success provided Alexie with the will and incentive to quit drinking and to devote himself to building a career as a writer. In 1991 Alexie was awarded a Washington State Arts Commission poetry fellowship, and in 1992 he won a poetry fellowship from the National Endowment for the Arts. He continues to live on the Spokane Reservation in Wellpinit, Washington. Reflecting on his life experiences, Alexie asserted in *The Lone Ranger and Tonto Fistfight in Heaven* (1993): "[Indians] have a way of surviving. But it's almost like Indians can easily survive the big stuff. Mass murder, loss of language and land rights. It's the small things that hurt the most. The white waitress who wouldn't take an order, Tonto, the Washington Redskins."

Major Works

Alexie's debut collection of poetry and short fiction, *The*

Business of Fancydancing (1992), grew out of the first writing workshop Alexie attended at Washington State University. Focusing on "Crazy Horse dreams"—a metaphor for aspirations, either far-fetched or close-at-hand, that succeed or fail without any apparent logic—*The Business of Fancydancing* introduces a broad range of characters, many of whom have continued to appear throughout Alexie's prose and verse. Typically, these characters evoke the despair, poverty, and alcoholism that often pervade the lives of Native Americans on reservations. Personalities like Thomas Builds-the-Fire, Seymour, Junior Polatkin, Lester FallsApart, and Victor—who engage in reservation basketball tournaments, fist fights, and visits to the local tavern—developed into the characters that populate such later works as *The Lone Ranger and Tonto Fistfight in Heaven* and *Reservation Blues* (1995). *The Lone Ranger and Tonto Fistfight in Heaven*, a collection of short stories with frequent autobiographical overtones, takes survival and forgiveness as its major themes. Alexie explores these issues both on the reservation and in Anglo-American-dominated Spokane. Similarly, Alexie's first novel, *Reservation Blues*, studies the life experiences of Native Americans. The novel describes the successes and failures of "Coyote Springs," an all-Indian rock-and-roll band, as its members travel and perform concerts with a guitar that belonged to legendary blues musician Robert Johnson. *Reservation Blues* extends Alexie's literary use of the locale and inhabitants of the Spokane reservation, reiterating his focus on the conditions of life on the reservation and the hardships faced by many Native Americans. His most recent novel, *Indian Killer* (1996), is set in the Pacific Northwest and is, in part, a mystery about a killer who scalps his victims. Alexie has also published three books of poetry, *I Would Steal Horses* (1992), *First Indian on the Moon* (1993), and *Old Shirts & New Skins* (1993). Like Alexie's fiction, these collections evoke sadness and indignation but leave the reader with a sense of respect and compassion for characters who are in seemingly hopeless situations. Involved with crime, alcohol, or drugs, they struggle to survive the constant battering of their minds, bodies and spirits by white American society and by their own self-hatred and sense of powerlessness.

Critical Reception

Alexie has won a strong following for his works and is recognized as a major emerging literary voice. He is especially noted for his keen insights into the plight of Native Americans living on reservations. In discussing *The Business of Fancydancing*, Andrea-Bess Baxter described Alexie's work as "at once painful and compelling yet somehow balanced with humor and hope." Leslie Marmon Silko, referring to *The Lone Ranger and Tonto Fistfight in Heaven*, found Alexie's writing to "dazzle with wicked humor, lean, fresh language, and deep affection for his characters." Alexie's work has also garnered attention for its descriptive qualities and its intense connection to life on an Indian reservation. According to Silko in an essay on *Reservation Blues*, "the power of his writing rises out of the Spokane River and the Spokane earth." She concluded, "on this big Indian reservation we call 'the United States,' Sherman Alexie is one of the best writers we have."

PRINCIPAL WORKS

I Would Steal Horses (poetry) 1992
The Business of Fancydancing (short stories and poetry) 1992
First Indian on the Moon (poetry) 1993
The Lone Ranger and Tonto Fistfight in Heaven (short stories) 1993
Old Shirts & New Skins (poetry) 1993
Reservation Blues (novel) 1995
Indian Killer (novel) 1996

CRITICISM

Alex Kuo (essay date 1992)

SOURCE: "Introduction," in *The Business of Fancydancing:*

Stories and Poems by Sherman Alexie, Hanging Loose Press, 1992, p. v.

[*In the essay below, Kuo describes the wide range of cultural references in Alexie's prose and verse.*]

Sherman Alexie's territory, as he describes in these forty poems and five stories [in ***The Business of Fancydancing***], ranges from the All-Indian Six-Foot-And-Under Basketball Tournament to ESPN to the politics of geography and family to powwows to Indians "not drinking enough." Alexie's work has escaped the pervasive influence of writing workshops, academic institutions and their subsidized intellect, and has instead focused on reservation and border realities in his eastern section of Washington state.

Central to this landscape inhabited by family, friends, and a wild coterie of reservation cops, seers, Buffalo Bills, Crazy Horses, and of course, fancydancers, is the absence of self-indulgence. The characters in Alexie's work have actual identities whose faces have shadows that suggest other histories. The visionary Seymour and Simon, for example, travel forward and backward in time with dreams that sustain the narrator—often, they are Crazy Horse dreams and do not work, but sometimes they do, in a fancydance that suggests an existence beyond the survival of life's pain and contradictions.

Throughout this collection, there is an emphasis on balancing carefully, and a willingness to forgive, as in the subsistence forays into the sestina in **"Spokane Tribal Celebration, September, 1987,"** and **"The Business of Fancydancing."** The history these stories and poems remember goes beyond the individual; it is the healing that attends the collective space and distance of both writer and reader, which will hopefully "make everything work / so everyone can fly again." Here, on a long jumpshot arcing into the distance, there is enough light to push back the darkness for several generations to come.

Publishers Weekly (review date 1 February 1993)

SOURCE: A review of *Old Shirts & New Skins*, in *Publishers Weekly*, Vol. 240, No. 5, February 1, 1993, p. 87.

[*In the following review of* Old Shirts & New Skins, *the critic praises Alexie's verse for "capturing the full range of modern Native [American] experience."*]

[In ***Old Shirts and New Skins,*** Alexie] emerges as a Native poet of the first order. He captures the full range of modern Native experience, writing both with anger and with great affection and humor. Detailing the continuing deprivation and colonialism, the poet pointedly asks, "Am I the garbageman of your dreams?" and defines Native "economics": "risk" is playing poker with cash and then passing out at powwow. Focusing on the Leonard Peltier case, Alexie exposes the ineffectualness of both white Indian-lovers and some Native leaders in **"The Marlon Brando Memorial Swimming Pool"**: "Peltier goes blind in Leavenworth . . . / and Brando sits, fat and naked, by the Pacific ocean. *There was never / any water in the damn thing."* General Custer is allowed to give an accounting of himself, as Alexie links genocide of America's indigenous peoples with Vietnam, the Triangle Shirtwaist Factory fire and other acts of warfare and destruction. Alexie writes comfortably in a variety of styles. Many of the poems turn on grim irony, putting the author himself in the traditional role of the trickster. Adrian Louis provides a powerful foreword, and Elizabeth Woody's moody illustrations add to the volume's impact.

The New Yorker (essay date 10 May 1993)

SOURCE: "Fancydancer," in *The New Yorker,* Vol. LXIX, No. 12, May 10, 1993, pp. 38-40.

[*In the following essay, the critic explores the impact of Alexie's life experiences on his literary works.*]

Why the nondescript Northwestern city of Spokane was chosen as the site of the 1974 World's Fair is difficult to understand. The "attractions" are almost gone now, except for one that was there all along. Perhaps Expo '74's greatest legacy, or perhaps its only one, was to reveal a roaring stretch of the Spokane River by tearing down an inner-city rail yard that had obscured it from view for more than seventy years.

For centuries, the falls were a spiritual center for the Spokane, a nomadic American Indian tribe whose name means "children of the sun." The Spokane came here in the spring from their winter villages to camp in tepees by the riverbank, lured by the salmon that once ran from the Pacific up the Columbia River into this river. The tribe's first rite of spring was to fast and don beaded, feathered regalia for ceremonial dances to thank the Great Spirit for the salmon, their summer sustenance and their currency of sorts when they began to trade with the *suapi,* Spokane for "white man."

About a century ago, the *suapi,* in the form of the American government, sent the Spokane tribe upstream to a reservation sixty miles northwest of the city, in Wellpinit. After the Second World War, when the Indian war veterans came home to Wellpinit, they "modernized" their traditional dancing to reflect more of what they'd seen in the wider world. "Fancydancing" was the name they gave to the flashier, more improvisational version of their dance.

The Haleposey clan, pronounced roughly "Alepsie," was given a new name, too, but well before the Second World War. Russian fur traders who stopped by Wellpinit found the name indecipherable and rechristened the clan "Alexie" in their ledgers. Almost every afternoon, Sherman Alexie,

twenty-six, one of the youngest generation of the Haleposey descendants, returns to the sacred site of his ancestors, where he shoots hoops on the basketball courts of the Spokane Y.M.C.A. It's how he caps off a morning spent at his kitchen table doing his own version of "fancydancing," which is the name he has given to his writing. This writing-and-basketball routine has gone on for the past five years, and so far it has spawned three small-press books, a poetry fellowship from the National Endowment for the Arts, and, this past January, a six-figure, two-book contract for a short-story collection and a novel from Grove/Atlantic Monthly Press. "Salmon-travelling," evoking the salmon's sometimes bloody fight upstream, hurling itself over falls and rocks to spawn, is a word one finds sprinkled through Alexie's writing. It is also a word that describes Alexie's own journey. Alexie's obstacles were the joint inheritance of poverty and alcoholism. His mother supported the family by working at the Wellpinit Trading Post or selling quilts she sewed during the long evenings when her husband was drinking.

Alexie shut out this world by devouring books. By the time he was in fifth grade, he'd read the entire Wellpinit school library, auto-repair manuals included. At twelve, he announced to his family that he was going to Reardan High School, thirty-two miles down the road from the reservation. He started there in eighth grade.

Alexie isn't quite sure what drove him to join every possible club and become the captain of the school's basketball team— called, to his family's amusement, the Reardan Indians. Nonetheless, his overachieving gained him admittance to the Jesuit Gonzaga University, in Spokane. Gonzaga had a derailing effect on Alexie, who until that point had never tasted alcohol. There, he discovered its numbing effect, and, after his long struggle to get to college, it soothed his increasing terror about what could or should come next. Rescue was provided by his high-school girlfriend, who was going off to Washington State University. Alexie transferred there with her after two years at Gonzaga. Although he continued to drink uncontrollably, he also began to write.

In 1989, from Washington State, he sent a few poems and short stories to *Hanging Loose* magazine, a Brooklyn-based literary biannual he'd seen while he was hanging around the university's library. He was first published in the magazine in 1990, and later a poetry-and-short-story collection, ***The Business of Fancydancing,*** was published by the ancillary Hanging Loose Press.

Until 1992, Alexie had never been east of Missoula, Montana, but now sixty readings have taken him, and his sense of guilt and wonder, all over America. "There were as many opportunities for me to fail as to succeed," he says. "I know a hundred other stories of people on my reservation who failed. I'm amazed that I've made it, and feel guilty because I've left some people behind. Why do doors keep swinging open at the right time?" he asks. The answer must be all that fancydancing.

His latest and longest jump shot has been onto the national literary scene. Grove/Atlantic Monthly Press has made *The Lone Ranger and Tonto Fistfight in Heaven* its lead book for the fall. Alexie recently came to New York for a reading at New York University's Loeb Student Center. He wore a special mugger's wallet he'd invented for the trip, and saw his first Broadway show. He met his agent and his publisher, but not for drinks: he won the struggle against drinking three years ago. When Indians succeed in the *suapi* world, Alexie says, "we can all hear our ancestors laughing in the trees."

Sybil S. Steinberg (review date 19 July 1993)

SOURCE: A review of *The Lone Ranger and Tonto Fistfight in Heaven,* in *Publishers Weekly,* Vol. 240, No. 29, July 19, 1993, p. 235.

[*In the following review of* The Lone Ranger and Tonto Fistfight in Heaven, *the critic lauds Alexie's short stories as exemplary products of the author's potent imagination.*]

Known primarily as a poet, [Sherman] Alexie (*Old Shirts and New Skins*), a Spokane/Coeur d'Alene Indian, offers [in *The Lone Ranger and Tonto Fistfight in Heaven*] 22 extremely fine short stories, all set on or around the Spokane reservation in Washington state. Characters flow from one tale to the next; many involve Victor, who grows from a small child watching relatives fight during a New Year's Eve party ("**Every Little Hurricane**") to a dissolute man sitting on his broken-down porch with a friend, watching life pass him by (**"The Only Traffic Signal on the Reservation Doesn't Flash Red Anymore"**). The author depicts with fierce determination all the elements of modern Native American life, from basketball and alcoholism to powwows and the unexplained deaths of insignificant people. Humor and tragedy exist side by side, and stories often jump back and forth in time and space, recounting two narratives that ultimately prove to be skeins of the same tale. Alexie writes with simplicity and forthrightness, allowing the power in his stories to creep up slowly on the reader. He captures the reservation's strong sense of community and attitude of hope tinged with realism as its inhabitants determine to persevere despite the odds. In "**Imagining the Reservation**" (a title that evokes John Lennon's song "Imagine") he writes, "Survival = Anger x Imagination. Imagination is the only weapon on the reservation"—a weapon this author wields with potent authority.

Andrea-Bess Baxter (review date August 1993)

SOURCE: A review of *The Business of Fancydancing,* in *Western American Literature,* Vol. XXVIII, No. 2, August, 1993, pp. 161-62.

[*Below, Baxter comments on the themes of isolation and alienation in* The Business of Fancydancing.]

Sherman Alexie's remarkable debut, *The Business of Fancydancing,* is an outstanding collection of poetry, prose, vignettes and epigrams that will surely launch him firmly into the Native American literature scene.

A spontaneous combustion propels the reader into the complex density of the modern Indian world, on and off the reservation, at once painful and compelling yet somehow balanced with humor and hope. Alexie's razor-sharp irony races toward unexpected twists and turns.

His stark portraits are vivid and disturbing: house fires, sin and forgiveness, Crazy Horse dreams (the kind that don't come true), Buffalo Bill opening a pawn shop, pow wows and fancydancers like Vernon WildShoe (Elvis in braids), Crazy Horse just back from Vietnam in the Breakaway Bar, Lester FallsApart translating the directions on a commodity can of soup, Chief Victor, two hundred winter beers wide, still sinking jump shots from thirty feet and beyond.

Alexie grew up in Wellpinit on the Spokane Indian reservation. He speaks of his connections to and isolation within, not only white America, but his own tribe. His writing hits hard because it comes directly out of his own experiences. Comic relief provides an element of surprise. And throughout we encounter the theme of forgiveness. In **"Pow Wow"** we read of the usual hustle and bustle, humorous incidents and the inevitable encounters with whites, all taking place in the present and past. The poem ends:

> still, Indians have a way of forgiving anything
> a little but more and more it's memory lasting
> longer
> and longer like uranium just beginning a half-life.

The threads of isolation and alienation that weave through these stories all sum up what Gerald Vizenor terms the "cultural schizophrenic," who has the impossible task of living in two worlds, always questioning where he or she belongs. In **"Distances"** we are told that "There is nothing as white as the white girl an Indian boy loves." And "I do not speak my native tongue. Except that is, for the dirty words. I can tell you what I think of you in two languages."

Sherman Alexie's powerful voice exemplifies how imagination and the power of words, native or not, can be the most potent weapon of all. His writing challenges the reader to listen and listen well and to confront an honest portrait of the contemporary Indian world, a world where, all too often, "suddenly, nothing happens." It is exactly this kind of truthfulness and insight that leads to triumph in battle. *The Business of Fancydancing* is guaranteed to provoke, amaze and remove those rose-colored glasses from idealistic non-Indians by revealing the hard realities of the present-day Native American world.

Brian Schneider (review date Fall 1993)

SOURCE: A review of *The Lone Ranger and Tonto Fistfight in Heaven,* in *The Review of Contemporary Fiction,* Vol. 13, No. 3, Fall, 1993, pp. 237-38.

[*In the following review of* The Lone Ranger and Tonto Fistfight in Heaven, *Schneider briefly examines Alexie's narrative voice.*]

Each of the twenty-two stories in Sherman Alexie's collection **The Lone Ranger and Tonto Fistfight in Heaven** examines the modern problems and contradictions of reservation life. Most of the stories are situated on the Spokane Indian Reservation, which Alexie's lyrical voice describes through stories that examine not only the real problems of alcoholism or unemployment but also happier moments: romance, basketball, and dancing. Alexie's voice is strongest when the real problems collide with the lighter moments—in these instances his prose is brutally honest and depicts the horrible strains of poverty, alcoholism, and violence—but also shows the flip side: the tribe continues to exist in its language, myth, and culture (Alexie's own stories) even in the face of what at times seem like insurmountable odds.

The collection is loosely linked through Alexie's narrative voice, a voice that resonates whether operating in first or third person with a passion that sees the irony in the flower power movement's co-opting of mostly American Indian values (**"Because My Father Always Said He Was the Only Indian Who Saw Jimi Hendrix Play 'The Star-Spangled Banner' at Woodstock"**) and captures the personal and national feelings of alienation American Indians face as their numbers dwindle, but also the sense of duty and honor they hold for one another (**"This Is What It Means to Say Phoenix, Arizona"**). Alexie's remarkable collection deserves a wide audience because of his original narrative voice, which mixes mythmaking with lyrical prose and captures the nation-within-a-nation status of American Indians and the contradictions such a status produces, and more importantly, the survival of a people through mythmaking rooted in their everyday lives.

Reynolds Price (review date 17 October 1993)

SOURCE: "One Indian Doesn't Tell Another," in *The New York Times Book Review,* October 17, 1993, pp. 15-16.

[*Below, Price commends Alexie's ability to portray the sufferings of Native Americans but suggests that the author's rapid publication of his work may be affecting its quality.*]

Sherman Alexie was born in 1966. Victor, the central character and sometime narrator of at least half of these 22 short stories [in **The Lone Ranger and Tonto Fistfight in Heaven**], is the same age. Like Mr. Alexie, Victor is a member of the Spokane Indian tribe and continues to live in the state of Washington. But where Victor has no diversions more effective than alcohol from the bleakness of his reservation life, Sherman Alexie has a striking lyric power to lament and praise that same crucial strain of modern American life—the oldest and most unendingly punished strain, the Native American, as it's been transformed for many Indians through a long five centuries of brutal reduction to powerlessness and its lethal companions: alcoholism, malnutrition and suicidal self-loathing.

There are three stories here that could stand in any collection of excellence—**"The Trial of Thomas Builds-the-Fire," "Jesus Christ's Half-Brother Is Alive and Well on the Spokane Indian Reservation"** and **"Witnesses, Secret and Not."**

Young as he is, though, Mr. Alexie has employed his gift briskly. The present volume is his first full-length work of fiction, but last year he published **The Business of Fancydancing,** a widely praised collection of poems and sketches, and there are earlier collections of poetry, **Old Shirts & New Skins, I Would Steal Horses** and **First Indian on the Moon**. Though the themes, the tones of voice and the names of characters are often identical in the two most recent volumes, **The Business of Fancydancing** consists mostly of verse—laconic and grim but often humorous free-verse responses to the same world that underlies all Mr. Alexie's work.

The Lone Ranger and Tonto Fistfight in Heaven is entirely in prose, its tales ranging in length from fewer than five pages to more than 10. Each part is named promisingly—the title piece is a good example—yet a majority of the pieces quickly dispense with the common reader's expectations of short narrative. There is very little plot in any of them—plot in the sense of consecutive action with emotional outcome. Little human conflict is witnessed in present time; almost no attention is paid to whatever visible world surrounds the vocal line of narration, though there are frequent generic references to HUD housing, crowded saloons and powwows enriched by the omnipresent Indian fry bread. With those sparse hints, the reader is expected to perform a number of jobs that are generally assumed by the writer. Anyone impelled to enter Mr. Alexie's world must conspire with the sound of his fictional voices to create a new world, to people it and then to feel along with a set of characters about whom we're told little more than their names and a few slender facts about their age and health.

Knowledge of the immensely imposing and varied body of recent fiction by American Indians—from N. Scott Momaday and James Welch to Leslie Marmon Silko—will suggest that there's nothing especially typical of Native Americans in Mr. Alexie's limited angle of vision and in the kinds of dense filters he interposes between the reader and the world implied. In a terse three sentences in his beautiful closing story, however, the narrator seems to claim otherwise. He says: "One Indian doesn't tell another what to do. We just watch things happen and then make comments. It's all about reaction as opposed to action."

However unpromising a creed that would seem to be for a fiction writer who hopes to be read by a culturally assorted audience, its offhand claim defines the motive force of these pieces. The great surprise is that given such narrow bounds, Mr. Alexie's strength proves sufficient to compel clear attention through sizable lengths of first-person voice (the hardest voice to make compelling, given all our dread of the first-person bore; and most of Mr. Alexie's voices resemble one another closely). The skills by which he lures us on through the quickly familiar atmosphere are a stark lucidity of purpose and an extreme simplicity of cast and action (there are seldom more than two characters present in any scene). Above all, he lures us with a live and unremitting lyric energy in the fast-moving, occasionally surreal and surprisingly comic language of his progress.

Passages as lively as the following are not infrequent, and go a good way toward lifting the stingy minimalist gloom that might otherwise sink more of these sketches than the two or three that actually founder:

> In the outside world, a person can be a hero one second and nobody the next. Think about it. Do white people remember the names of those guys who dove into that icy river to rescue passengers from that plane wreck a few years back? Hell, white people don't even remember the names of dogs who save entire families from burning up in house fires by barking.

However exhilarating such vitality proves to be throughout the volume, a sympathetic reader may finally dwell on a serious question—and it's a question that arises in the presence of any writer who not only is very young but who is also publishing rapidly. Has Sherman Alexie moved too fast for his present strength? A youthful prodigy is far scarcer in narrative writing than in any other art. There have been great poems from teenagers, great pieces of music and admirable paintings; but there's no sizable body of impressive fiction by any writer much under 30. The power to dredge up useful narrative lumber from the packed unconscious mostly requires long years of mute waiting while the mind flows over and reshapes its memories into public objects of arresting interest and wide utility.

Despite his extraordinary powers, in the quick succession of two books in two years Sherman Alexie has plumbed a number of obsessive themes and relationships as deeply as they

permit; and moments of gray, unrevealing monotony are too common. Though no one can tell a writer—least of all a young one—where to look and how to see, the reader who admires Mr. Alexie's plentiful moments of startling freshness and his risky dives into unmapped waters can wish for him now that he discovers a new and merciful rhythm that will let him find new eyes, new sights and patterns in a wider world, and a battery of keener voices for launching his urgent knowledge toward us.

Anne Goodwin Sides (review date 17 October 1993)

SOURCE: "Making It Against the Odds," in *Book World— The Washington Post,* October 17, 1993, p. 6.

[*In the following review of* The Lone Ranger and Tonto Fistfight in Heaven, *Sides examines how Alexie uses storytelling to help rescue his tribe and his culture from oblivion.*]

Reading Sherman Alexie's **The Lone Ranger and Tonto Fistfight in Heaven** is like leaning out the side window of a speeding car, watching the world slip in and out of focus faster than you can sort the future from the present from the past. The world, in this case, is an American Indian reservation. Keeping time like the staccato thumping of a nail stuck in a tire are drumbeats, blaring televisions, dancing, fighting, nightmares, visions and the small explosions of beer bottles thrown from a car driving in no particular direction.

Maybe from all that thumping, the narrators of most of the 22 stories in **The Lone Ranger** are insomniacs. One of them, Victor, is at least part Sherman Alexie. Both grew up on the reservation for the Spokane/Coeur d'Alene tribe, a government ghetto where dogs won't eat the "commodity" (government-issue) beef and cheese, but people do. That and potatoes, every day. Victor's sisters save a few quarters to buy food coloring to dye the potatoes red, green and blue, helping them imagine that the starchy whiteness is anything else. There are days when Victor's family is so hungry they fantasize eating "oranges, Pepsi-Cola, chocolate, deer jerky." Life in this American Soweto is so suffocating that drinking Sterno or sniffing rubber cement and gas fumes is a rite of passage as innocent as a child's first kiss. "I remember my brother stretched out over the lawnmower, his mouth pressed tightly to the mouth of the gas tank . . . everything underwater . . . Stare up at the surface, sunlight filtered through water like fingers, like a hand filled with the promise of love and oxygen."

And there are the constant humiliations Indians suffer off the "rez": A couple is pulled over for no reason by a cop who extorts money. A young man with dark skin and long black hair is watched like a thief for walking into a 7-11 to buy a Creamsicle.

The Lone Ranger is a collage of dreams, journal entries, quotes from other native writers, archival letters, fictional Kafkaesque court transcripts, tribal newspaper reports, drug trips, and basketball games. In Alexie's fiction, basketball is a weapon and therapy for negotiating the straits between an impoverished Indian world and a suspicious, secret-coded white one. Basketball is also a white man's invention that's been appropriated as the reservation game every Indian plays.

In real life, according to recent articles about him, Sherman Alexie begins his day writing at the kitchen table and rewards himself with a sweaty game on the Spokane YMCA court after lunch. It's a ritual that may have saved his life. Three years ago, when the small literary journal *Hanging Loose* first published a few of Alexie's unsolicited poems and short stories, he stopped drinking. His writing only got better. At 26, he has already published a collection of short stories and poetry, *The Business of Fancydancing;* and two books of poetry. Atlantic Monthly Press reportedly offered Alexie a six-figure contract for two more books: this one and a novel to follow.

In the title story, the narrator admires a white basketball player who "could play . . . Indian ball fast and loose." The author himself has parlayed his gift for writing poetry into fast, loose prose. At intervals, Alexie so loses himself in his imagery that his prose unravels into a succession of modern sonnets with jarring, sardonic codas. The story **"Indian Education"** is structured like a diary documenting the first seven years of Victor, the protagonist, at school on the reservation and the next five years at the white farm-town high school. In second grade, the missionary teacher gives the class a spelling test. But she singles Victor out, giving him a test for junior-high students. When he gets all the answers right, she crumples up the paper and makes him eat it. "You'll learn respect," she says, mocking him before the class by calling him "Indian, Indian, Indian." This part of the story ends with Victor saying, "*Yes, I am. I am Indian. Indian, I am.*"

The Lone Ranger can be read either as a long poem, an experimental novel or a collection of short stories. The same characters keep appearing either as narrators or subjects. Alexie uses a rough-cut documentary style, as though he were holding a video camera, interviewing childhood friends and relatives and recording their stories in brief, disjointed scenes, then turning the camera on himself at different points in his life. The result is a many-faceted picture, like a mosaic of broken glass.

The unnamed narrator of the story **"Imagining the Reservation"** actually tapes shattered pieces of a mirror all over his body, the shards reflecting his reservation life. The effect is both dreamy, like stepping into a Salvador Dali, and shockingly real—too true to be fiction. Alexie lulls his reader with passages of lush elegiac prose-poetry, only to break off the reverie with an act of unspeakable cruelty. In one scene, U.S. cavalrymen play polo with an Indian woman's head. In an-

other, a woman holds her newborn son while, unknown to her, the doctor ties her tubes.

Most of the characters in *The Lone Ranger* are collaborators with a white world that has stripped them of everything but their supply of liquor, collaborators in a centuries-old plot to tear away, bit by bit, every scrap of Indian land, culture, character. At a carnival midway Victor sees Dirty Joe, passed out from "too much coat-pocket whiskey . . . I stood over him, looked down at his flat face, a map for all the wars he fought at the Indian bars." As a cruel joke, Victor gives a carny 20 bucks to put Dirty Joe on a roller coaster for the grotesque entertainment of the white crowd. After the carny chucks Joe down the steps head-first into the crowd for emptying his stomach on the platform, Victor flees to the funhouse. There, wracked with guilt, he examines his own distorted features in the funhouse "crazy mirrors" and sees "the Indian who offered up another Indian like some treaty."

Given the pervasive bleakness he finds around him, it's remarkable that Sherman Alexie has survived at all. There is something hopeful in the very fact that he is writing, examining what hurts most, and healing ancient wounds. But there's also an urgency bordering on desperation in his voice. Alexie seems to be telling stories to save himself from the bottomless depression of the bottle, to rescue his tribe and his culture from oblivion, and to force a complacent white reader to look out the window, maybe even stop the car, and witness the crime that is an American Indian reservation.

Publishers Weekly (review date 8 November 1993)

SOURCE: A review of *First Indian on the Moon,* in *Publishers Weekly,* Vol. 240, No. 45, November 8, 1993, p. 70.

[*In the following review, the critic praises Alexie's use of the metaphor of fire in* First Indian on the Moon.]

Reading [*First Indian on the Moon,* the] latest offering of poetry and short prose pieces from Native American writer Alexie (*The Lone Ranger and Tonto Fistfight in Heaven*), it's easy to see why his work has garnered so much attention. Working from a carefully developed understanding of his place in an oppressed culture, he focuses on the need to tear down obstacles before nature tears them down. Fire is therefore a central metaphor: a sister and brother-in-law killed, a burnt hand, cars aflame. Tongue in cheek, Alexie inserts images from popular songs and movies, and catalogues aspects of traditional reservation life that have been sacrificed in America's melting pot. "After 500 years of continuous lies / I would still sign treaties for you," he says in one of this volume's many love poems—a love so powerful it threatens to engulf readers as well. Alexie renews the nearly forgotten sense of language equaling power. And the language in these sequential works is flawless, each section picking up from and expanding upon the previous one, poetry and prose working naturally together. "[I]magination is all we have as defense against capture and its inevitable changes," he writes. And he proves his point.

Frank Allen (review date 15 November 1993)

SOURCE: A review of *First Indian on the Moon,* in *Library Journal,* Vol. 118, No. 19, November 15, 1993, pp. 77-8.

[*In the following review, Allen discusses cultural and personal influences on Alexie's verse in* First Indian on the Moon.]

Outraged pride, broken promises, and the scourge of alcoholism are the burden of [***First Indian on the Moon***'s] sharp-edged, high-impact poems, prose poems, mini-essays, and fragments of stories woven together in a tapestry of pain about death by fire and survival by endurance on the Spokane Indian Reservation. Memories of great Indian chiefs, "fancydancers," powwow campfires, and "some Crazy Horse dreams," set against cruelty toward Native Americans, reveal "what went wrong with our love." Caught between alien white and disintegrated Native American cultures, "homeless and hopeful," Alexie uses the "magic and loss" of song and story to forge an "entire identity" out of anger and the nightmare of racism. Despite pain, this moving work celebrates something that can't be killed by cavalry swords, Thunderbird wine, "fake ceremonies," or "continuous lies": there is "nothing more beautiful than snow fallen onto the dark hair and braids of these Spokane Indians."

Joseph Bruchac (review date Winter 1994)

SOURCE: A review of *First Indian on the Moon,* in *Small Press,* Vol. 12, No. 1, Winter, 1994, p. 86.

[*In the following review of* First Indian on the Moon, *Bruchac explores Alexie's evolution as a writer.*]

Few young writers have burst onto the scene with as much praise as Sherman Alexie. His first book, [***I Would Steal Horses,***] published in 1992, was called "wide-ranging and dexterous" with "an astonishing range of voice and emotion." ***First Indian on the Moon,*** his second volume of poems published by Hanging Loose Press, is further evidence that such praise was truly warranted.

In some ways, this book is more unified than his first, for it can almost be read as a cycle of poems—about Native loves and losses and fires—set against the backdrop of the Spokane Reservation. The double-edged theme of fire appears again and again in his pictures of an Indian family so cursed by conflagrations that "When the Tribal Cop heard on his radio / that a car was burning down at Little Falls Dam, his first thought / was *Those damn Alexies and their goddamn cars.*" That kind of humor, understated at times and broader than burlesque at others, is so typical of contemporary Na-

tive life and so seldom caught in print that I found myself holding my breath as I raced from poem to poem with titles, such as **"Reservation Drive-In," "The Alcoholic Love Poems," "Tiny Treaties,"** and **"Seven Long Songs Which Include the Collective History of the United States."** The mirror he holds reflects us all, Native and transplant American alike.

There is enough love, heartbreak, and ironic intelligence in this small book to fill an encyclopedia. Although Alexie may sometimes lean a little too far towards repetition, it simply means there is room for growth at the start of what bodes to be a long, meaningful career. There is the kind of spiritual strength in his work that speaking the most painful truths can bring. ***First Indian on the Moon*** is strong medicine—but a medicine needed by us all.

Alan R. Velie (review date Spring 1994)

SOURCE: "Native American," in *World Literature Today,* Vol. 68, No. 2, Spring, 1994, p. 407.

[*In the review below, Velie describes* The Lone Ranger and Tonto Fistfight in Heaven *as "powerful and lyrical."*]

Although it is highly uncommon for American writers to be successful at both poetry and fiction, it is the rule rather than the exception for American Indian novelists. Scott Momaday, James Welch, Gerald Vizenor, Louise Erdrich, Leslie Silko, and Linda Hogan have published both novels and collections of verse. The latest to join the list is Sherman Alexie. He initially achieved notice for his poetry collections ***I Would Steal Horses, Old Shirts & New Skins,*** and ***First Indian on the Moon,*** and gained a measure of prominence when his 1992 collection of prose and verse, ***The Business of Fancydancing,*** was selected by the *New York Times* as one of its Notable Books of the Year. His latest work, ***The Lone Ranger and Tonto Fistfight in Heaven,*** somewhere between a novel and a collection of short stories, à la Louise Erdrich's *Love Medicine,* establishes him not only as one of the best of the Indian writers but as one of the most promising of the new generation of American writers.

Alexie is Spokane and Coeur d'Alene, and ***The Lone Ranger*** is about growing up Indian on the rez in eastern Washington. A major theme of the book is the feeling of despair, guilt, and helplessness that overcomes Indians as they and their friends and relatives give up on life and lapse into unemployment and alcoholism. The story here is not a bleak one, however; it is leavened with humor, and the writing is powerful and lyrical enough to transmute the dross of Spokane existence into something fascinating.

Alexie introduces us to a colorful cast of characters: Lester FallsApart, David WalksAlong, Thomas Builds-the-Fire, and Frank Many Horses, among many others. More than most ethnic groups, Indians have a strong sense of history; they think constantly of their glamorous past of mounted warfare. They are painfully aware that the days of stealing horses and making war are over, but they are not sure what to replace those activities with. The chief substitute is basketball, a game that reservation Indians love as much as urban blacks do. Unfortunately, whereas blacks commonly use sports as a way out of the ghetto, Indians, though they are often as gifted, are so tied to tribal life that it is extremely rare for them to make it to college as athletes or scholars.

Words that recur frequently in **The Lone Ranger** are *survival* and *forgiveness*. Survival is a constant concern in what Alexie describes as "the generation of HUD house, of car wreck and cancer, of commodity cheese and beef." The self-destructiveness of the characters is appalling: alcoholism and its related catastrophe, the car wreck, are pandemic. Indians are sensitive rather than callous, however, "the most sensitive people on the planet," and so they feel terrible guilt and constantly seek forgiveness.

Louise Erdrich portrays a similar bunch of scuzzy lumpen types in *Love Medicine* and, through compassion and humor, transforms them into characters we care about. Alexie does this for his crew, and adds an element of the exuberant magical realism Gerald Vizenor employs in his Griever books. For instance, [in **"Family Portrait"** in] **The Lone Ranger** he writes:

> In the summer of 1972 or 1973, or only in our minds, the reservation disappeared. . . . Just like that there was nothing there beyond the bottom step. . . . My father was happily drunk and he stumbled off the bottom step before any of us could stop him. He came back years later with diabetes and a pocketful of quarters. The seeds in the cuffs of his pants dropped to the floor of our house and grew into orange trees.

Like Erdrich and Vizenor, Alexie has turned the lives and dreams of the people of his reservation into superb literature.

James Beschta (review date May 1994)

SOURCE: A review of *First Indian on the Moon,* in *Kliatt,* Vol. 28, No. 3, May, 1994, p. 23.

[*Below, Beschta surveys Native American themes in* First Indian on the Moon.]

[**First Indian on the Moon**] opens with **"Influences,"** a poem of the survival of young Indian children in the face of the alcoholism that dominates their parents, their reservation, their world. That theme of Indian survival in a hostile environment is constant throughout the book, as is the alcoholism, depression and poverty of the reservation system. Through varying situations and scenes, these pieces are connected by

their reaction to the establishment which has systematically abused Native Americans. Not so long ago, this would have been labeled "protest poetry" in its reaction to a perceived political agenda.

> Children, the enemy reads us
> the news
> at 6 o'clock every night.

Yet this book rises above this simplistic categorization. It does so because of its lyricism;

> . . . Here I offer what I own:
> this crown of flame, this skin scarred
> and blistered, this sinner curled
> like blackened leaves
> in the hands of an angry god.

and it does so because of its intellectual perception;

> Often, in this poetry, we steal words, gather
> kindling,
> twist newspaper, circle rocks, and wait for the
> flame. We
> create metaphors to compensate for what we have
> lost.

and it does so in its pride and optimism;

> but every once in a while
> we can remind each other
> that we are both survivors and children
> and grandchildren of survivors.

The theme here is limited but sincere. The writing is skillful and effective. This book serves both as social conscience and art.

Carl L. Bankston III (review date May-June 1994)

SOURCE: A review of *First Indian on the Moon,* in *The Bloomsbury Review,* Vol. 14, No. 3, May-June, 1994, p. 15.

[*In the following review of* First Indian on the Moon, *Bankston notes that while Alexie's recent verse resembles his previous efforts, his work has not become "hackneyed."*]

We know what to expect from poet and short-story writer

Sherman Alexie. In his first three volumes of poetry and in his recent collection of stories, he focused intently on modern Native American life in the Northwest, employing the same characters to explore the themes of the bleakness of reservation life, of alcohol as the only readily available release from this bleakness, of powerlessness as the pervasive reality of contemporary tribal existence. In verse and prose, he has expressed this uncompromising vision with a spare, minimalist style, paring his words down to the bone. Comic moments appear suddenly and unexpectedly on this harsh landscape, so that irony twists despair into a peculiar kind of faith.

Alexie's new book [*First Indian on the Moon*] will be familiar in its characters, style, themes, and atmosphere to all of his readers. He is not exploring new territory. But he is reworking the old ground productively, like a gardener who sticks to his own backyard.

As in the author's previous works, a distinctive personality underlies the poems. While the writing may not be strictly autobiographical, it has the intimacy and the particularity of confessional literature. True, it often employs generic images of the modern Native American reservation as ghetto (HUD housing, fry bread, alcoholism), but the voice that lingers over small moments and the poems' powerful sense of self salvage these images from sociological abstraction.

Alexie appears to be keenly aware of his tendency to dwell, almost obsessively, on certain themes and images, and he frequently uses this tendency as a means of organizing his poems into chapters. In the section entitled "A Reservation Table of the Elements," for example, fire—both the air-fire of flame and fire-water—intertwines with memories of reservation existence. The first lines of the poem **"Genetics"** proclaim:

> Fire
> follows my family
> each spark
> each flame
> a soldier
> in the U.S. Cavalry.

The fire is a symbol, but it's also a series of actual tragic and tragicomic events in the speaker's past. A childhood attic fire has burned up all the family possessions except

> . . . a family portrait
> singed
> curled at the edges
> all of our dark skin
> darkened
> by ash and smoke damage.

A trailer fire kills the speaker's older sister and her husband. A series of electrical fires destroys three cars in separate incidents: "When the Tribal Cop heard on his radio that a car was burning down at Little Falls Dam, his first thought was *Those damn Alexies and their goddamn cars*."

The poem **"Fire Storm"** is one of the most intense and moving pieces of the book, shifting between verse and prose poem in a series of reflections on the fire that killed the older sister. Alexie follows mundane detail with simple but impassioned language, ending in an offertory funeral speech reminiscent of passages from Ginsberg's *Kaddish*. Death and life are close in this and other poems, and Alexie shows a gift for standing by the line that separates them and looking in both directions.

The poems in the section "Tiny Treaties" revolve around another of Alexie's recurrent themes: the contradictions and difficulties of having dark skin and inhabiting a white-skinned world. This emotional tangle, which one writer has referred to as the "cultural schizophrenia" of minority members, has occupied a dominant place in all of Alexie's writings. The "treaties" of love and friendship made with whites are continually plagued by tentativeness and doubt:

> Sometimes when an Indian boy loves
> a white girl and vice versa
> it's like waking up
> with half of the world
> on fire. You don't know
> if you should throw water
> onto those predictable flames
> or let the whole goddamn thing burn.

In writing about the twisted relationship between Indian and Anglo, Alexie slips from the intimately personal to the categorical. The fourth song of **"Seven Love Songs Which Include the Collective History of the United States of America"** evokes two lovers, one apparently native and the other apparently white:

> Suddenly, we are all arms and legs
> and it's summer and too hot to make love
> but we do anyway on the kitchen floor
> near the refrigerator with its door open.

In the next song, these two individuals have become racial categories: "I was a fisherman for 15,000 years / before you stumbled onto my shore / your legs sea-heavy and awkward." This continual tension between Alexie's autobiographical voice and his concern with the social and historical forces that shape biographies gives the poems a unique quality of being socially aware without being propagandistic, and of presenting a world from the perspective of the first person without being egocentric.

As he balances between the personal and the historical, Alexie also balances between song and ideas. "All I Wanted to Do Was Dance" proclaims the title of one of the book's sections, and readers can almost dance to the rhythm of the lyrics, but they won't lose themselves in the music. Alexie is always thinking while he's singing or dancing, always trying to come to terms with himself and provoke others to come to terms with themselves. Many of the poems close on notes of celebration:

> Believe me, the warriors are coming back
> to take their place beside you
> rising
> beyond the "just surviving"
> singing
> those new songs
> that sound
> exactly
> like the old ones

But the dominant mood is dark and contemplative:

> Sometimes, I think I love you
> because it's always easiest
> to love the unloved
> to dream about the dreamless
> to watch an Indian woman
> just this side
> of beautiful
> slow dance
> to a sad song
> and never have to worry
> about making her any promises

The poems create an impression of somber, introspective requiems that constantly verge on breaking into triumphal marches, the cartoon movements of Merrie Melodies, or reservation fancydancing.

Sherman Alexie's new songs sound a lot like his old ones. But the songs haven't become hackneyed, and the poet still has his gift for lifting his readers above "just surviving."

Andrea-Bess Baxter (review date November 1994)

SOURCE: A review of *Old Shirts & New Skins, First Indian on the Moon,* and *The Lone Ranger and Tonto Fistfight in*

Heaven, in *Western American Literature,* Vol. XXIX, No. 3, November, 1994, pp. 277-80.

[*In the review below, Baxter discusses elements of realism and imagination in Alexie's* Old Shirts & New Skins, First Indian on the Moon, *and* The Lone Ranger and Tonto Fistfight in Heaven.]

Many Native Americans have been proclaiming recently that their new weapons for the future will be their art. The proliferation of these weapons is vital, not only for the survival of traditional cultures, but for exposing the hard truths of their lives, which is the first step in instigating change. Activist or not, Sherman Alexie, a Spokane/Coeur d'Alene Indian from Wellpinit, Washington, is a natural-born warrior quite adept at shaking things up.

In [***Old Shirts & New Skins, First Indian on the Moon,*** and ***The Lone Ranger and Tonto Fistfight in Heaven,***] he continues his themes, from two previous books of poetry, of exploring the paradoxes of living on and off the reservation, of home and family, love affairs, sorrow and loss, helplessness and forgiveness. Some of his stories are full of despair; others are downright bleak. His direct honesty prevails and we are required to think and listen and think again even as we smile and laugh. He will not let us forget, well aware that without memory, stories will die.

Alexie has the power of a riveting storyteller, along with pivotal timing at using humor at the exact moment we need it most and expect it least. Throughout his work there's a stubborn insistence on living by his creed: "Survival = Anger x Imagination." His writing is deceptively minimalist and lucid in its simplicity, but there is nothing "easy" here. He refuses to allow us to relax.

In ***Old Shirts & New Skins*** his irony is honed to a sharp edge. This book is full of poetry, vignettes and little lessons. His talent for frequently turning history upside down is illustrated when Crazy Horse, who is often resurrected, finds himself in ludicrous situations. In **"Indian Education"** we learn that

> Crazy Horse came back to life
> in a storage room of the Smithsonian,
> his body rising from a wooden crate
> mistakenly marked ANONYMOUS HOPI MALE

In **"Postcards to Columbus"** he writes that "this history and country / folded over itself like a Mobius strip. . . . Christopher Columbus, you are the most successful real estate agent / who ever lived, sold acres and acres of myth." He also issues a warning: "Columbus, can you hear me over the white noise / of your television set? Can you hear the ghosts of drums approaching?"

History, movies, politics, cable TV—his penchant for discovering the irony in these areas is notable. All are thrown without mercy into **"The Marlon Brando Memorial Swimming Pool"**: "I can't believe it. This late in the 20th century and Dennis Banks / and Marlon Brando are eating / finger sandwiches out by the swimming pool. This must be fiction. But, wait, / whatever happened to AIM? / Did they all drown because Marlon refused to pay for a lifeguard?" He reiterates that "There are no mistakes on the reservation. The 20th century warrior relies / on HBO for his vision / at three in the morning." At this point, it's not too difficult to "Imagine Coyote accepts the Oscar for lifetime achievement" nor to "Imagine the reservation metaphors: . . . pour whiskey into the pool / until it smells like my kidney; . . . / Imagine the possibilities. / . . . Imagine how our lives will change."

A well-meaning yet useless monument, a typical swimming pool, becomes a symbol for dashed hopes and dreams, whose illusionary lure is ruinous. The only person who remains somewhat intact is Vine Deloria, Jr., who has insisted all along that *"there was never any water in the pool."*

First Indian on the Moon, a volume of poetry and prose, continues to expose so many fraudulent illusions that tempt us all in America today. The filmmaking industry is again hard-hit with the fast-punching prose of **"The Native American Broadcasting System."** We are alerted to a news bulletin that Hollywood has "announced the establishment of a new category for this year's Academy Awards: Best Performance by a Non-Native in a Native American Role. Nominees this year include Burt Lancaster, Charles Bronson, Trevor Howard, Burt Reynolds, and Kevin Costner." Are we still seeing Indians as romantic symbols, not as real human beings? The current trend of interest in everything Indian has yet to prove otherwise.

In both volumes of poetry, Alexie perfects an intriguing style, of his own making I believe, in which a prose-sonnet uses fourteen stanzas and carries a word or two from the last line of the previous stanza to the first line of the next. It creates a curious flow, almost like automatic writing, surprising the reader and even the writer himself. **"Captivity"** (the title refers to the narrative of Mrs. Mary Rowlandson, who was taken captive by the Wampanoag of Massachusetts in 1676) employs this style, in which stanzas seven, eight, and nine illustrate a kind of subconscious reasoning:

> 7.
>
> Piece by piece, I reassemble the house where I was born, but there is a hole in the wall where there was none before. "What is this?" I ask my mother. "It's your sister," she answers. "You mean my sister made that hole?" "No," she says. "That hole in the wall is your sister." For weeks, I searched our architecture, studied the walls for imperfections. Listen: imagina-

tion is all we have as defense against capture and its inevitable changes.

> 8.
>
> I have changed my mind. In this story there are words fancydancing in the in-between, between then and now, between walls in the alley behind the Tribal Cafe where Indian boys smoke old cigarettes at half-time of the all-Indian basketball game. Mary Rowlandson, it's true, isn't it? Tobacco and sugar are the best weapons.

> 9.
>
> The best weapons are the stories and every time the story is told, something changes. Every time the story is retold, something changes. . . .

A memorable character, Lester FallsApart, appears—and disappears—like an existential anti-hero throughout Alexie's books. He is perpetually caught in the "in-between" and always amazed at how or why he gets stuck there, between the Anglo and Indian worlds. And he somehow always survives his mishaps, drinking binges, house fires, jumping off rooftops onto an Indian girl's teardrop, singing, sleeping outside on the reservation, waking up in the city in the wrong house. No matter what happens, he remembers. He shows up here and there to tell his latest story and to remind us that "no one will believe this story so it must be true."

The Lone Ranger and Tonto Fistfight in Heaven, a collection of twenty-two short stories, and his first book by a major publishing house, continues the now-familiar themes and characters. Yet this work is more personal, autobiographical at times. He is still imagining, still believing in forgiveness, though "travelling heavy with illusions." Satire rescues Alexie from sliding into self-absorption or pontification. Perhaps he is telling us that one way Indians have survived has been to perfect the art of gallows humor.

This kind of humor is gloriously exalted in **"The Approximate Size of My Favorite Tumor."** Jimmy Many Horses drives his wife, Norma—the world champion fry bread maker—away with his unrelenting gallows humor concerning his impending death from cancer. "Actually my favorite tumor looks just like a baseball," he announces, calling himself Babe Ruth. Fed up, Norma makes good on her threats to leave him, even though they shared a certain kind of laughter which kept them from feeling the pain too strongly: "Humor was an antiseptic that cleaned the deepest of personal wounds." Months after she'd gone, Jimmy was still at it, telling his doctor that, after a few more zaps of useless radiation treatments, "I'll be Superman." "Really?" the doctor said. "I never knew that Clark Kent was a Spokane Indian."

Norma eventually realizes that not only will she inevitably feel his death deeply and privately, she will also have to deal with her fear that "every one of our elders who dies take a piece of our past away. And that hurts more because I don't know how much of a future we have." Whether or not she realizes she is also referring to her husband, we don't know. But she leaves the powwow circuit to come home. She is "a warrior in every sense of the word" and she returns home to help Jimmy "die the right way. And maybe because making fry bread and helping people die are the last two things Indians are good at." And they both laugh when Jimmy responds, "Well, at least you're good at one of them."

There is no typical plot in Alexie's prose and stories, no easy linear events to follow with a beginning, a middle and a neatly-wrapped ending. Things don't change rapidly, nor does hope always triumph over despair after a moment of understanding or a summer of sobriety.

By wielding the weapon of imagination skillfully and passionately, Sherman Alexie exposes a gritty realism of Indian life today. He creates history, past and present, a new mythology that re-interprets fiction and fact and introduces unforgettable characters, full of irony, pain and confusion, and an inexhaustible wit. He writes about real people and real places and that makes him a tremendously accessible writer. We are invited to share in this mythology of his own making, for he tells us in **"Breaking Out the Shovel"**:

> Friend, this is a strange journey, digging
> for hours, then days, through generations of need
>
> and it is better not to know how much farther
> the digging needs to go, but I want you to know
>
> I often stop for rest, ask directions . . .
>
> . . . I move through history
>
> and my story and your story, gathering
> into our warmth, this heart changing by halves.

Leslie Marmon Silko (review date 12 June 1995)

SOURCE: "Big Bingo," in *The Nation,* New York, Vol. 260, No. 23, June 12, 1995, pp. 856-58, 860.

[In the following review, Silko studies characterization in Reservation Blues.]

When N. Scott Momaday won the Pulitzer Prize for his novel *House Made of Dawn* in 1969, book reviewers fretted that the experience of Indian reservations was too far out of the "American mainstream" for most readers; by now, such expressions of concern should seem quaint. Since 1969, the "global economy" has brought changes; now a good deal of urban and suburban United States has begun to resemble one giant government reservation—clear-cut, strip-mined then abandoned not just by Peabody Coal and General Motors but by Wal-Mart too—where massive unemployment and hopelessness trigger suicide and murder. As the good jobs have gone the way of the great herds of buffalo, the United States has become a nation of gamblers. Suddenly Indian writers are not "writing from the margins" of U.S. culture, they are writing from the center of the front page.

Thanks to Bishop Landa and his thugs, who burned the great libraries of the Americas in 1540, we know very little about the early literatures of the Americas. But it is clear from oral narratives that lengthy "fictions" of interlinked characters and events were commonplace. So it should come as no surprise that voices such as Linda Hogan, Betty Louise Bell, Ray Young Bear, Greg Sarris and Adrian C. Louis are emerging.

Another of these writers, Sherman Alexie, has swept onto the publishing scene with poems and short stories that dazzle with wicked humor, lean, fresh language and deep affection for his characters. His collection of interlinked short stories, ***The Lone Ranger and Tonto Fist Fight in Heaven,*** won a number of prizes, including the PEN/Hemingway Award for best first book. My favorite story in that collection is titled **"Because My Father Always Said He Was the Only Indian Who Saw Jimi Hendrix Play 'The Star-Spangled Banner' at Woodstock."** In ***The Business of Fancydancing,*** Alexie's characters from the Spokane reservation stop off in Reno. With their last dollars they hit the jackpot and live it up for about twenty-four hours before they lose it all again. The old American Dream: Hit the jackpot, win the lottery, bingo big.

Now Alexie's first novel, ***Reservation Blues,*** focuses on the American Dream and the price of success. All over the world in rural communities, young people share similar dreams, stirred by the same images beamed in by satellite TV and by the same lyrics of rock and roll music. Youth in this "global village" share similar discouragement too—unemployment, hunger and aborted attempts to escape their hopeless situation.

The characters in ***Reservation Blues*** have been out of high school for a few years. Their home is a small Indian town on the Spokane reservation with dead-end jobs and shared poverty and sadness to look forward to. The Spokane people still watch out for one another like one big family, except sometimes this big family seems a bit dysfunctional. (Of course, a dysfunctional family is still better than no family at all.) But for the rural landscape and the strong sense of tribal identity, Alexie's Spokane Indian town of Wellpinit could be a neighborhood in East L.A. or the Bronx; except the Spokane people use car wrecks and cheap wine, not drive-by shootings and crack, to make their escape. Reservation housing and inner-city housing are quite similar:

> Thomas still lived in the government HUD house where he had grown up. It was a huge house by reservation standards . . . however, the house had never really been finished because the Bureau of Indian Affairs cut off the building money halfway through construction. The water pipes froze every winter, and windows warped in the hot summer heat.

So while Alexie writes about the "Spokane Indian reservation," the reader begins to realize that poverty in the United States has common denominators. Take the powdered milk that connects poor rural communities and poor urban areas all over the country:

> No matter how long an Indian stirred her commodity milk, it always came out with those lumps of coagulated powder. There was nothing worse. Those lumps were like bombs, moist on the outside with an inner core of dry powdered milk. An Indian would take a big swig of milk, and one of those coagulated powder bombs would drop into her mouth and explode when she bit it. She'd be coughing little puffs of powdered milk for an hour.

But Sherman Alexie doesn't limit his world to a single, corporeal dimension; Shakespeare and Henry James use ghosts, and he does too. Blues guitarist Robert Johnson walks into Wellpinit, having faked his death by poison years before so he could find out how to undo the deal he made with the old "Gentleman," the Devil got up as a well-dressed white man. He's been told there is a large woman on a mountaintop somewhere who can help him. Thomas Builds-the-Fire gives Johnson a ride up the sacred mountain where Big Mom lives; Big Mom is part of God but she's not God herself.

Later, Thomas notices that Johnson left behind his guitar in the van. When his friend Victor touches the guitar, it makes wonderful music despite his lack of skill. Victor "wanted to resist all of it, but the guitar moved in his hands, whispered his name. Victor closed his eyes and found himself in a dark place. 'Don't play for them. Play for me,' said a strange voice." This is the Devil's guitar; by the time Victor stopped playing, "his hair stood on end, his shirt pitted with burn holes and his hands blistered."

The Devil guitar seduces them, and Thomas, Victor and Junior, with Chess and Checkers as backup, form a rock and roll band named Coyote Springs. They dream of modest success—to open for Aerosmith at Madison Square Garden and make a little money; here the "American Dream" has been downscaled. This being an Indian reservation, everyone has an opinion about Coyote Springs: Christian churchgoers call their efforts Devil music (which in this case is literally true);

the tribal chairman is jealous and yearns to find any excuse to arrest them. But "gossip about the band spread from reservation to reservation. All kinds of Indians showed up: Yakima, Lummi, Makah, Snohomish, Coeur d'Alene. Thomas and his band had developed a small following before they ever played a gig."

With the sounds from the Devil guitar, Coyote Springs wins a battle of the bands in Seattle, and record company executives pounce on them with a recording contract and studio time in New York City. These New York record company executives are named Sheridan and Wright—names of the two U.S. Army generals who fought the Spokane people and slaughtered thousands of Spokane horses in cold blood. Chess and Checkers, the young backup singers from the Flathead reservation, begin to have their doubts about the price Coyote Springs may have to pay for success, but Thomas, Victor and Junior know only that rock and roll stardom is calling them. They've got only one more number to go and they'll "bingo big"; all they have to do is make the demo tape in New York! Suddenly the pressure is on:

> We have to come back as heroes. They won't let us back on this reservation if we ain't heroes. Unless we're rock stars. We already left once, and all the Spokanes hate us for it. . . . What if we screw up in New York and every Indian everywhere hates us? What if they won't let us on any reservation in the country?

Alexie may use an image from Indian culture, the gambler's sticks, but the meaning is clear: "If an Indian chose the correct hand, he won everything, he won all the sticks. If an Indian chose wrong, he never got to play again. Coyote Springs had only one dream, one chance to choose the correct hand."

The atmosphere of the recording studio, however, leaves a lot to be desired. The fiery Sheridan says of Coyote Springs and their music: "They don't need to be good. They just need to make money. I don't give a fuck if they're artists. Where are all the executives who signed artists? They're working at radio stations now, right?" Not even the Devil guitar can endure this. Coyote Springs is playing along just fine when suddenly Robert Johnson's haunted guitar twists itself out of Victor's hands and spoils the take. Victor loses his temper and tears apart the recording studio. Coyote Springs is finished and so is the dream.

With guys like Sheridan and Wright running the music business, the Devil guitar probably does these young Indians a favor by breaking up the recording session. But this is one area of the novel that is a bit fuzzy. There is ambivalence throughout toward the guitar, toward a talent or gift that consumes individuals and calls them away from the community. Alexie's version of Robert Johnson, on the run to escape the music, his hands burned and scarred by the guitar, casts an ominous light on talent. A gift for making music or for writing sets you apart from others, family and friends, whether you want this distance or not. Alexie wrestles with the conundrum: Did their gift for music kill Jimi Hendrix and Janis Joplin or did the music sustain them and lengthen their time in this world? Is it better to throw away your guitar or word processor and live an ordinary life? Will you be happier?

Coyote Springs' members return to the Spokane reservation, but everything has been changed by their brush with success. Junior commits suicide, as he probably always meant to. His ghost visits Victor and says he just got tired of living. The ghost helps Victor throw away the liquor bottle, but when Victor tries to get a job to save himself, his own uncle, the pompous tribal chairman, writes him off. Victor seems bound to join Junior in the other world. Only Thomas and Chess, who are in love, and Checkers, who loves them, survive the crushed dream. Again there is a whiff of ambivalence about success in the "mainstream" world. Big Mom hadn't wanted them to go to New York in the first place—the implication being that music should be made for people, for the community, not for record companies.

Yet it is clear that having a shot at success means a great deal. Thomas is infuriated when he learns that the only musicians who get a big recording contract and realize the American Dream are the two young white women, Betty and Veronica, who once sang backup for Coyote Springs. The record company executives Sheridan and Wright decided they needed "a more reliable kind" of Indian. "Basically, we need Indians such as yourselves," they tell the two young white women, who reply, "But we ain't that much Indian." "You're Indian enough, right? I mean, all it takes is a little bit, right? Who's to say you are not Indian enough? . . . What it comes down to is this. You play for this company as Indians. Or you don't play at all. I mean, who needs another white-girl folk group?" When Betty and Veronica send Thomas a copy of their first album, he furiously destroys the tape.

Yet Alexie's characters are young, still learning; with the blessing of Big Mom and the citizens of Wellpinit, the remaining former members of the rock band decide to leave the reservation for a while. The town of Spokane isn't far from the reservation, and the phone company is hiring—just as it might be. If we Indians do not "represent" our communities as we see them, then others, the likes of Sheridan and Wright, will concoct fantasies that pass for truth. Unlike the bucolic idylls of small-town America pawned off by, say, Garrison Keillor, Alexie's portrayal of the reservation town of Wellpinit and its people is in the tradition of communities evoked in *The Scarlet Letter, Babbitt, Sanctuary* and *The Last Picture Show.* These small towns are like the old cat who eats her kittens.

It is difficult not to imagine **Reservation Blues** as a reflection of the ambivalence that a young, gifted author might have about "success" in the ruthless, greed-driven world of big publishing, where executives very much resemble cavalry generals. He may feel the same pressure the members of Coyote Springs felt to come home to the reservation a "hero." At the same time, small communities, Indian and non-Indian alike, are ambivalent about the success of one of their own. There is bound to be a bit of jealousy, and maybe even those who mutter that they prefer anonymity for their community.

Make no mistake: Alexie's talent is immense and genuine, and needs no Devil's typewriter. The power of his writing rises out of the Spokane River and the Spokane earth where it is sweetened with the music of Robert Johnson, Hank Williams, Elvis Presley, Janis Joplin and Jimi Hendrix. On this big Indian reservation we call "the United States," Sherman Alexie is one of the best writers we have.

Frederick Busch (review date 16 July 1995)

SOURCE: "Longing for Magic," in *The New York Times Book Review,* Vol. C, No. 29, July 16, 1995, pp. 9-10.

[*In the following review of* Reservation Blues, *Busch comments on narrative structures in the work.*]

To read about Native American reservation life is usually to read about illness and despair. Fiction originating from that life is also, of course, capable of wild happiness and celebration; but the darkness is a fact of life and art. James Welch, in his superb novel *Winter in the Blood,* observes his characters' suffering from the corner of his narrative eye; Reynolds Price, in his moving novella *Walking Lessons,* confronts the sorrow directly. Sherman Alexie, whose 1993 collection, ***The Lone Ranger and Tonto Fistfight in Heaven,*** was justly applauded, writes about characters who are squarely in the middle of reservation life but who report it to us from a point of view that is simultaneously tangential to the mainstream of that life as well as part of its sad, slow rhythms.

Here, for example, from his first novel, ***Reservation Blues,*** is Mr. Alexie's description of the Indians' mythic coyote "a trickster whose bag of tricks contains permutations of love, hate, weather, chance, laughter and tears, e.g., Lucille Ball." He catches the ancient and the contemporary, the solemn and the self-mocking, at once; he evokes dreary days of watching black-and-white television reruns in a place of "poverty, suicide, alcoholism," where "Indian Health only gave out dental floss and condoms." When Mr. Alexie writes at his best, he creates stinging commentary, and he shows his determination to make you uncertain whether you want to laugh or cry.

His characters long for a traditional magic that is endangered, crushed under hundreds of years of bad faith and bad luck and bad management. As Thomas Builds-the-Fire, in ***Reservation Blues,*** reports to us, "Nobody believed in anything on this reservation." "More than anything," Mr. Alexie says of Thomas, "he wanted a story to heal the wounds, but he knew that his stories never healed anything." Mr. Alexie's humor, like Thomas's, is a shield against aggression from within and without. Like Mr. Alexie, Thomas dreams and tells deeply moving domestic stories. And he insists upon bearing witness, in quiet, powerful ways, to the sad, diminished life of so many of the Spokane and other American Indians. Like Thomas, Mr. Alexie wants "the songs, the stories, to save everybody."

Mr. Alexie means *everybody*. He writes of love affairs and marriages between Indians and whites. He salutes the very un-Indian Franz Kafka in a short story about Thomas Builds-the-Fire included in *The Lone Ranger and Tonto* by using as its epigraph the opening lines of *The Trial*. And when you read *Reservation Blues,* you will think of Kafka, perhaps his stories "The Bucket Rider" and "The Judgment." You might also be reminded of the character Milkman Dead in Toni Morrison's novel *Song of Solomon* and those little, light-footed Jews of Bernard Malamud and Marc Chagall. All are capable of suggesting to us dreamy flight while reminding us of the great specific gravity of their world.

Reservation Blues takes many characters from *The Lone Ranger and Tonto,* as well as characters we've not met before, and connects their stories of Spokane reservation life. Thomas Builds-the-Fire may be said to be the protagonist, but it is his people who are at the center of the narrative and, indeed, no chapter is carried by a single character's consciousness. One moves from the point of view of Thomas to that of his friend Victor to that of Chess, the woman he loves, to that of Father Arnold, the doubting reservation priest, to that of Robert Johnson, the great African-American bluesman, who has faked his death to escape the Gentleman—the Devil, to whom he sold his soul for the ability to make great music—and who seeks the wisdom of Big Mom, who is the reservation's repository of Indian lore. (She can even make 200 pieces of fry bread from 100, a good equivalent to the parable of fishes and loaves.) Johnson abandons his guitar, and Victor takes it up and plays it wonderfully; so Victor, Thomas (who sings) and their friend Junior (who plays the drums) form Coyote Springs, a rock-and-roll band. Mr. Alexie provides the lyrics of their songs, which aren't any better or worse than other rock songs, although their subject matter is Indian life.

The story connects dozens of smaller stories about these characters. Also connecting the fragments are dreams. "Indians were *supposed* to have visions and receive messages from their dreams," Junior says. "All the Indians on television had visions that told them exactly what to do." At his best, Mr. Alexie refuses to be pious or to pretend that he is writing anything other than sad reflections on a people's loss. He is funny, he is perceptive and he knows how to stir us in large and small ways.

When he goes wrong, it is because he tries to suggest that a rock band can bear the metaphorical weight of an entire culture—not even Roddy Doyle's novel *The Commitments* sustained such a concept—and because he uses repetition as a substitute for narrative structure. Early in the novel, we are given a story about Big Mom, who is magically alive 134 years before we meet her and who witnesses a terrible slaughter of Indians' horses by the United States Cavalry. We are told that a colt "fell to the grass of the clearing, to the sidewalk outside a reservation tavern, to the cold, hard coroner's table in a Veterans Hospital." If referred to once in a story in that way, such an image provides an awful and telling moment, and the event can support the burden of suggestion. Mr. Alexie, either not trusting that we will understand the significance, which he has already underscored, or believing that the metaphorical value will increase with repetition and will serve as structure, has the slaughtered horses screaming many times, often as the sole event in a paragraph—"The horses screamed"—but the freighted words carry no additional weight, and they don't connote more than they did earlier. A couple of white singers named Betty and Veronica—get it?—sell out with ease to a recording company, but Coyote Springs has far more difficulty. Executives of the company, named Sheridan and Wright by Mr. Alexie, after men who planned and executed the genocide of American Indians, call for liquor to celebrate their discovery of the band: "The horses screamed." We do get it.

Though there is wonderful humor and profound sorrow in this novel, and brilliant renditions of each, there is not enough structure to carry the dreams and tales that Mr. Alexie needs to portray and that we need to read. His talent may be for the short form. But the talent is real, and it is very large, and I will gratefully read whatever he writes, in whatever form.

Abigail Davis (review date July-August 1995)

SOURCE: A review of *Reservation Blues,* in *The Bloomsbury Review,* Vol. 15, No. 4, July-August, 1995, p. 16.

[*Below, Davis praises the universality of Alexie's literary works.*]

This first novel by Sherman Alexie [*Reservation Blues*] comes as close to helping a non-Native American understand the modern Indian experience as any attempt in current literature. The reader closes the book feeling troubled, hurt, hopeful, profoundly thoughtful, and somehow exhausted, as if the quest of the characters had been a personal experience.

Alexie, a 28-year-old Spokane/Coeur d'Alene Indian raised on the Spokane Indian Reservation, is a powerfully prolific writer whose earlier works have received much attention. *The Business of Fancydancing* (1992), a collection of poems and stories, was named a *New York Times* Notable Book for 1992; Alexie is a citation winner for the PEN/Hemingway Award for Best First Book of Fiction and winner of the 1994 Lila Wallace-Reader's Digest Writers' Award.

Reservation Blues chronicles the career of an Indian rock group called Coyote Springs. The three male members, Thomas Builds-the-Fire, Junior Polatkin, and Victor Joseph, are from the Spokane Indian Reservation in Wellpinit; two women vocalists, Chess and Checkers Warm Water, are members of the Flathead tribe. When, for a brief time, two white groupies (who are into Indian men rather than musicians) join the band as backup singers, all hell breaks loose. The group evolves rather than forms, and with little or no direction or planning moves from playing reservation bars to a club in Seattle to a potential recording contract in New York. Readers of Alexie's previous collections of poems and stories—***The Lone Ranger and Tonto Fistfight in Heaven*** (1994), ***First Indian on the Moon*** (1994), and ***The Business of Fancydancing*** (1992)—will recognize some familiar characters, and will most significantly be alert to Alexie's unmistakable narrative voice, which, as always, is laced with humor and anger and driven by great intelligence.

As musicians, Coyote Springs puts the "a" in amateur. Their burgeoning skills and subsequent success are due to a mystical guitar—clearly a tool of the devil—that was once owned by blues legend Robert Johnson, who was said to be murdered in 1938. Johnson allegedly sold his soul Faust-style for his talent, and his appearance as a living character in Alexie's story is significant. Johnson is still trying to "lose" the guitar and escape its grip. In Alexie's version of the Faust legend, the devil tells Johnson that he has to give up "whatever you love the most" in exchange for superhuman musical ability. Johnson sacrifices his freedom (*not* his soul), and until the guitar finds a new "owner" (in this case, Victor Joseph, lead guitarist for Coyote Springs), Johnson is trapped. Alexie gives the theme of evil as a pandemic and enduring force a new twist when Victor cuts his own deal with the devil and, presented with the same choice as Johnson, sacrifices his best friend. Unlike those who addressed the theme before him—authors Marlowe and Goethe, composers Berlioz and Liszt—Alexie seems to find the loss of freedom and friendship more serious and dangerous than the loss of one's own soul; or perhaps we are meant to understand that the three are intrinsically interconnected, symbiotic, and that the human experience is more complex than even Goethe thought.

Alexie is a plot magician, and the actual story of the musical escapades of Coyote Springs is but a fraction of this complex book. The narrative contains traditional dialogue along with songs and poems, dreams, visions, newspaper excerpts, charismatic characters, an Indian (and, to my mind, improved) version of the Faust legend, several well-placed whacks at missionary and Catholic Christianity, as well as some riotously funny scenes. The collective impact of these various narrative devices is startling; layer after layer, we are pulled into the fractured experiences and spiritual lives of the characters. We (and here I speak as an outsider to the experiences

that Alexie writes about so vividly) are jarred into any number of acknowledgments: that reservation life includes a cruel Catch-22, whereby the people who leave the reservation to break the cycle of dependency on the U.S. government are considered traitors by those who stay; that prejudices between tribes are just as virulent and hostile as the racist attitudes that infect other areas of American society; that life for mixed-blood children is the same hell on the reservation as it is in most other places for most races. *"Your son will be beaten because he's a half-breed,"* Chess says to a vision of a white woman and half-Indian child.

> No matter what he does, he'll never be Indian enough. Other Indians won't accept him. . . . Don't you see? . . . Those quarter-blood and eighth-blood grandchildren will find out they're Indian and torment the rest of us real Indians. . . . [They] will get all the Indian jobs, all the Indian chances, because they look white. Because they're safer.

Alexie casts a wide net, and in ***Reservation Blues*** his narrative style is a highly effective combination of all the prose forms. In chronicling the pain and progress of one five-person, mixed-tribe rock band, Alexie has, miraculously, managed to speak to all of us.

FURTHER READING

Criticism

Bankston, Carl L., III. "Weaving the Line of the Spirit." *The Bloomsbury Review* 12, No. 6 (September 1992): 7.
> Discusses characterization in *The Business of Fancydancing,* finding that Alexie's poetry appears "unexpectedly" from the themes of everyday life.

Lambert, Pam. Review of *Reservation Blues*, by Sherman Alexie. *People Weekly* 43, No. 18 (8 May 1995): 35.
> Favorable assessment of *Reservation Blues*, praising the way Alexie "explores the place where dreams and down-and-dirty reality collide."

Review of *Reservation Blues*, by Sherman Alexie. *Publishers Weekly* 242, No. 18 (1 May 1995): 42-3.
> Laudatory assessment of *Reservation Blues*, stating that the novel is "hilarious but poignant" and "filled with enchantments yet dead-on accurate with regard to modern reservation life."

Reardon, Patrick T. "Life on the Reservation Yields Never-Ending Losses." *The Chicago Tribune* (27 September 1993): 3.
> Argues that *The Lone Ranger and Tonto Fistfight in Heaven* is comparable in scope and significance to Richard Wright's *Native Son.*

Roraback, Dick. Review of *The Lone Ranger and Tonto Fistfight in Heaven*, by Sherman Alexie. *Los Angeles Times Book Review* (28 November 1993): 6.
    Praises Alexie's sense of humor and depth of theme in *The Lone Ranger and Tonto Fistfight in Heaven*.

Sowd, David. Review of *Reservation Blues*, by Sherman Alexie. *Library Journal* 120, No. 10 (1 June 1995): 158.
    Brief review of *Reservation Blues*, focusing on the novel's principal theme: the "tragedy of reservation life."

Throm, Lindsay. Review of *The Lone Ranger and Tonto Fistfight in Heaven*, by Sherman Alexie. *Booklist* 90, No. 1 (1 September 1993): 31.
    Praises *The Lone Ranger and Tonto Fistfight in Heaven* for its powerful narrative voice.

Additional coverage of Alexie's life and career is contained in the following sources published by Gale Research: *Contemporary Authors,* **Vol. 138;** *DISCovering Authors Modules: Multicultural Authors;* **and** *Native North American Literature.*

Peter Carey
1943-

Australian novelist and short story writer.

The following entry presents an overview of Carey's career through 1995. For further information on his life and works, see *CLC*, Volumes 40 and 55.

INTRODUCTION

Praised for his inventive mixture of the fantastic, the comedic, and the ordinary, Carey often creates detailed, realistic settings into which he introduces surreal and fabulous events. Usually set in Australia, Carey's works address themes of nationhood and history as he satirizes contemporary social values, explores the illusory nature of reality, and self-consciously examines the art of fiction. Robert Towers has stated that "Carey's prose can hold the ugly, the frightening, and the beautiful in uncanny suspension. It is this gift, among others, that makes him such a strong and remarkable writer."

Biographical Information

Carey was born in Bacchus Marsh, Victoria, Australia, on May 7, 1943. After attending Monash University, he worked in advertising from 1962 to 1988. Carey's first major publication, the short-story collection *The Fat Man in History,* appeared in 1974; he published *Bliss,* his first novel, in 1981. Carey's works have received numerous awards in both Australia and England. *Illywhacker* (1985) for instance, was nominated for the Booker Prize in 1985; *Oscar and Lucinda* (1987) was awarded the Booker Prize in 1988. Carey has also taught writing at New York University and Princeton University.

Major Works

Most of the stories in *The Fat Man in History* depict individuals who experience sudden anxieties when they encounter surreal events in commonplace situations. In others, Carey satirizes the effects of technology and foreign influences on Australian culture and society. In *Bliss,* Carey centers on Harry Joy, a man who dies for nine minutes and has an out-of-body experience through which he observes family members and friends involved in unseemly activities. Carey uses black humor and satire to examine hypocrisy, identity, and moral poverty in contemporary society. He also analyzes the function of stories and story-tellers in a community, as the novel embeds a number of stories within the larger structure of the

novel. While much of the novel is related in straightforward, realistic detail, the allegorical plot transports Carey's protagonist from the "hell" of suburban life to a mental hospital and ultimately to a blissful life in a rain forest. *Illywhacker* is an expansive comic novel that relates the adventures of Herbert Badgery, a man who claims to be 139 years old. The novel's title is an Australian slang expression variously defined as "taleteller," trickster," "con man," and "liar," all of which describe Badgery's main talents. The central focus of *Illywhacker* is the art of lying; Badgery lies constantly in order to survive and improve his life, and Carey employs lying as a metaphor for writing fiction. The picaresque adventures of Badgery are related to Australian historical themes: Badgery was born near the time of Australia's independence from Great Britain, and the book's epigraph is a quote by Mark Twain: "Australian history does not read like history, but like the most beautiful lies. . . ." While introducing many characters and events and developing an intricate series of symbolic references involving animals, Carey explores such themes as colonization, technology, and human relationships. *Oscar and Lucinda* delineates the odd romance between Carey's eccentric title characters who are drawn together by their passion for gambling. The novel begins with Oscar's childhood in rural nineteenth-century Devon, England, where he lives with his father, a renowned naturalist and a preacher in the fundamentalist Plymouth Brethren sect. Gambling on what he believes is a sign from God, the adolescent Oscar reluctantly rebels against the teachings of his father and joins the Anglican Church. Later, at Oxford University Oscar relies on earnings from wagering on horse races to pay for his living expenses and tuition. The narrative also relates events in Lucinda's sheltered childhood in rural Australia, which ends at age eighteen with her mother's death. She uses her inheritance to purchase a glass factory and relocate to Sydney. Lucinda's brusque country manners and active management of her factory make her an outcast in Sydney, and gambling provides her only social outlet. After failing to engage in a more active social life during a stay in England, Lucinda meets Oscar on her return by boat to Australia, where he plans to begin a ministry. Oscar and Lucinda become involved in a strange, tragicomic love affair beset by frequent farcical misunderstandings, culminating with Oscar undertaking a horrific river journey through the Australian outback with materials for building an elaborate glass church. *Oscar and Lucinda*'s expansive narrative is composed of more than one-hundred short chapters, gradually unfolding plot details, odd bits of information, direct addresses to the reader, and frequent use of glass and water imagery. The narrative also features a plethora of well-developed minor characters and authentic descriptions of nineteenth-century London, Sydney, Oxford, and rural New South Wales. As in *Illywhacker,* Carey endeavors in *Oscar and Lucinda* to reimagine Australian history. Set in Sydney, Australia, *The Tax Inspector* (1991) centers on the Catchprice family and Maria Takis, an investigator from the Australian Taxation Office, who has been sent to review the records of the Catchprice's auto dealership. The Catchprice family includes a bizarre group of characters: Granny Frieda Catchprice, who reported her children to the tax authorities because she feared she was going to be sent to a nursing home, is half-senile and carries explosives in her pocketbook; Frieda's middle-aged daughter Cathy dreams of becoming a country-western singer; and Frieda's 16-year-old grandson Benny believes he is an angel. *The Unusual Life of Tristan Smith* (1995) concerns themes of national and cultural identity. The novel's protagonist is a citizen of Efica, an imaginary island nation that loosely resembles Australia. Efica has been colonized and exploited by Voorstand, a colossal world power which resembles the United States. Like those of Carey's previous works, the plot for *The Unusual Life of Tristan Smith* is highly convoluted; Carey also provides an extensive historical background for Efica as well as a glossary of Efican dialect. At the center of the story is the Eficans' struggle to retain their cultural identity, which the Voorstanders attack through a high-tech, semi-religious entertainment spectacle known as the Sirkus. The principle characters in the Sirkus—Broder Mouse, Oncle Duck, and Hairy Man—bear close resemblance to the Walt Disney icons Mickey Mouse, Donald Duck, and Goofy. Hor-

ribly deformed at birth, the novel's narrator and title character searches for love and acceptance, which he finds after disguising himself in a Broder Mouse costume.

Critical Reception

Commentators have often described Carey's works as metafictional; two of his novels, *Bliss* and *Illywhacker,* for instance, deal explicitly with telling stories and the relationship between truth and fiction. The use of fiction—lies, as Carey calls them—to support and justify social existence is an important theme in many of Carey's works. Scholars have noted that Carey typically attacks the reader's sense of narrative coherence, order, time, and sequence by providing conflicting versions of his narratives. Arguing that Carey views history as an act of selection, Graeme Turner has stated that Carey's "fantastic, alternative worlds . . . can always be seen as alternative perspectives on an historical world, questioning it and exposing its constructed, arbitrary nature." This line of thought also influences the direction Carey takes in his exploration of individual characters. Turner has suggested that Carey's novels and stories "do not examine what lives mean as much as they examine how lives are constructed in order to produce their meanings." Carey's talents for placing extraordinary events in mundane contexts and for exposing the absurd and corrupt aspects of everyday life have drawn extensive praise from critics and comparison to such writers as Franz Kafka, Gabriel Garcia Marquez, Samuel Beckett, and Jorge Luis Borges. Critics have noted Carey's interest in themes of nationhood, cultural identity, entrapment, and colonialism as well. Summarizing Carey's writing, A. J. Hassall has stated: "Like Beckett and Kafka, . . . and also like Swift, Carey defamiliarizes the stories from which 'reality' is constructed, exposing absurdities and corruptions so familiar that they customarily pass unnoticed and unchallenged."

PRINCIPAL WORKS

The Fat Man in History (short stories) 1974
War Crimes (short stories) 1979
The Fat Man in History, and Other Stories (short stories) 1980; also published as *Exotic Pleasures,* 1981
Bliss (novel) 1981
Illywhacker (novel) 1985
Bliss: The Screenplay [adaptor, with Ray Lawrence; from Carey's novel] (screenplay) 1986; also published as *Bliss, the Film,* 1986
Oscar and Lucinda (novel) 1987
The Tax Inspector (novel) 1991
Collected Stories (short stories) 1994
A Letter to Our Son (nonfiction) 1994
The Big Bazoohley (juvenilia) 1995
The Unusual Life of Tristan Smith (novel) 1995

CRITICISM

Teresa Dovey (essay date October 1983)

SOURCE: "An Infinite Onion: Narrative Structure in Peter Carey's Fiction," in *Australian Literary Studies,* Vol. 11, No. 2, October, 1983, pp. 195-204.

[*In the following essay, Dovey remarks on the mythic qualities of Carey's fiction, focusing her analysis on* Bliss.]

It is a common practice of current literary critics to reveal how the subject matter of various literary works is in fact narrative itself, and from the structuralist perspective the process of creating the narrative is the only subject matter there can be. The increasing self-reflexiveness of post-modernist novels deals with the nature of narrative in a largely explicit manner, but Todorov claims [in *The Poetics of Prose,* 1977] that even the earliest narrative, the *Odyssey,* has as its theme 'the narrative forming the *Odyssey'*. So when I say of Peter Carey that his novel and his stories are concerned with the nature of narrative, and with the forms and functions of fiction, I am claiming nothing new, either for myself or for Carey. And **Bliss** makes it evident that Peter Carey claims nothing new for himself. Harry Joy becomes the storyteller at Bog Onion Road but, the narrator tells us, 'He never thought of what he did as original. It wasn't either. . . . He was merely sewing together the bright patchwork of lives, legends, myths, beliefs, hearsay into a splendid cloak that gave a rich glow to all their lives.'

This passage might be said to describe the process whereby Carey creates *his* fictions, and to define his role not as creator, but as re-creator. As in traditional narrative, Harry Joy's stories have been passed 'from one recognized "owner" to his heir'. [In *The Nature of Narrative,* 1966] Scholes and Kellogg equate traditional narrative with myth, and in this context the structure of **Bliss** can be described as mythic, in a way which recalls the sacred origins of myth in the rituals enacting the cyclical processes of nature. The plot pattern follows the seasonal pattern of mortification, purgation, invigoration, and jubilation, which corresponds to Harry Joy's first death, period of purgatory in his imagined hell, restoration to self and to the society of Bog Onion Road, and the final joyful reunion with Honey Barbara. That Carey is concerned with myth is evident in the story **'Do You Love Me?'** where the results of the annual census are 'the pivot point for the yearly "Festival of the Corn" (an ancient festival, related to the wealth of the earth)'. The juxtaposition of gross materialism and sacred ritual here constitutes an ironic comment on modern ritual.

In the case of traditional narrative, Scholes and Kellogg claim that 'newly invented stories must be only somewhat less rare than accurate historical narrative'. Likewise, the narrator of **Bliss** makes the point that, with one exception, Harry Joy's stories are not original. If the stories cannot be original in themselves, then it is in the process of telling that the capacity for originality resides; this is the essence of Alex Duval's words to Harry 'You were a good talker Harry. That's what made you, you know that? Not what you said, no . . . It was the damn way you said it' (**Bliss**). The foregrounding of the art of the narrator is one of the features of the mode described by Robert Scholes [in *Fabulation and Metafiction,* 1979] as fabulation:

> The fabulator is important to the extent that he can rejoice and refresh us. And his ability to produce joy and peace depends on the skill with which he fabulates. Delight in design, and its concurrent emphasis on the art of the designer, will serve in part to distinguish the art of the fabulator from the work of the novelist or the satirist. Of all narrative forms, fabulation puts the highest premium on art and joy.

Both the title of the novel and the name of the protagonist testify to Carey's concern with these aspects of fiction.

The 'art of the designer' is foregrounded at different levels of the narrative structure. The mythic framework, filled in with stories told, heard, written, and acted out, places all narrative within the all-encompassing bounds of myth. Scholes says 'myth tells us that we are all part of a great story' and

> Just as the realistic novel was rooted in the conflict between the individual and society, fabulation springs from the collision between the philosophical and mythic perspectives on the meaning and value of existence, with their opposed dogmas of struggle and acquiescence. If existence *is* mythic, then man may accept his role with equanimity. If not, then he must struggle through part after part trying to create one uniquely his own.

The conflict between the fictions within which people live, and the fictions which they create, is central to Carey's meaning in both the novel and the short stories. The narratives which make up **Bliss** are Vance Joy's stories, ranging from folklore through parable to anecdote; Harry's stories, which are Vance's stories, with one notable exception; David's lies and dreams; Alex Duval's reports; the 'wreckers yard of words' in which Bettina spent her childhood; Honey Barbara's folk literature, which consists of Cancer Maps and 'the Dream Police (a legendary squad of psychiatrists) and the whole cast of Cosmic Conspirators, the CIA, flying saucers, multinationals with seed-patents'; the old man in Alice Dalton's institution, writing down his last memories before shock therapy destroys them; the little boy scouts making notes, who drop their pitiful notebook and pencil as they are carried, screaming, from the institution. There are other stories, and there are the non-verbal forms of narrative, the signs and systems which are either personal or social constructs: New York, which

Vance Joy says will become 'after the next flood, a splendid book read by all mankind with wonder', the language of advertising, and the death scenarios of Bettina, Joel and David.

The conflict between the fictions within which people live, and the fictions which they create, is central to Carey's meaning in both *Bliss* and the short stories collected in *The Fat Man in History* and *War Crimes*.

—Teresa Dovey

At the centre of them all, right inside the infinite onion (which is Harry's vision of hell), is the circus elephant episode. When Harry's car is squashed by a circus elephant he becomes the subject, or the object, of a worn-out joke, he is in someone else's story. It is characteristic of Carey, who refuses absolutes, to place in the mouth of Billy de Vere, the foolish, jovial circus man, the words of Oscar Wilde, 'Life imitating art'—modified somewhat by his afterthought, 'Or should I say . . . life imitating bullshit'. The proposition is made, and simultaneously undermined. We perceive reality through the lenses of preconstructed fictions which, depending on the value or the validity of the fictions, can be seen as life imitating art, or life imitating bullshit. In other words, you are in someone else's story, and all that you can do about it is to tell your own story.

At the police station, where he is taken as a result of the circus elephant joke, Harry extemporizes 'the only original story he would ever tell. In fear of punishment, in hope of release, glimpsing the true nature of his sin, he told a story he had never heard about people he had never met in a place he had never visited'. At this point Harry is like Scheherazade in the *Arabian Nights,* who 'lives exclusively to the degree that she can continue to tell stories' (Todorov). Here 'Narrative equals life; absence of narrative, death' (Todorov). On the way home from the police station, the taxi takes Harry over a river 'black as the Styx' (*Bliss*): as a reward for originality Harry has been released from the underworld. If narrative is the subject of Carey's novel, so is death and, by extension, life. The deaths of the various characters constitute the major articulations of the novel, and the first words we read are 'Harry Joy was to die three times'. By giving us the ending in the beginning, the narrator is saying that there *is* only one possible ending to the narrative of life, and so gives the lie to any fictions which would disguise this fact. And once again he is saying that it is not the tale which is important, but the telling. To quote from David Lodge [in *The Modes of Modern Writing: Metaphor, Metonymy, and the Typology of Modern Literature,* 1977], who is quoting from a story by Leonard Michaels (the infinite onion of the world of criticism!), 'Fictions, whether literary, theological, philosophical or political, can never make

death acceptable or even comprehensible, yet in a world "incessantly created of incessant death" . . . we have no other resource'. It is precisely this resource, the capacity for telling stories, which gives Harry a God-like stance and a temporary immunity from death, and it is significant that his resemblance to Krishna is referred to several times in the novel.

Neither David, nor Bettina and Joel have this capacity. They are 'blind-worms pushing forward, entwining in the dark. One could, unfairly perhaps, imagine them as the instruments of someone else's pleasure' (*Bliss*). They live frustrated, thwarted lives and die violent, meaningless deaths. Bettina lives according to the fiction of the Great American Dream. David is trapped within the fictive constructs of Vance Joy's stories, passed on by Harry, doomed to act them out because he cannot interpret them and retell them in his own way. It is tempting to interpret the actions of David in Freudian terms: he tries to get rid of his father, by placing him in a mental institution, and makes love to Honey Barbara, his father's lover. The oedipal struggle has been translated into literary terms by Harold Bloom [in *The Anxiety of Influence: A Theory of Poetry,* 1973], with the father standing for the literary predecessors of any particular poet. Bloom claims that 'True poetic history is the story of how poets as poets have suffered other poets, just as any true biography is the story of how anyone suffered his own family—or his own displacement of family into lovers and friends' and that 'Poetry is the enchantment of incest, disciplined by resistance to that enchantment'. David cannot resist that enchantment and his actions within the family can be taken as a means of signifying his failure as a storyteller. At the level of the imagination his relationship with the father remains one of pure plagiarism: he orchestrates his life and his death according to Vance's stories. However, the meaning of the novel as a whole discourages this kind of interpretation by reduction through reminding one that the theories of Freud and Bloom are just two more fictive constructs.

David's mock heroic death is a sign that the use or function of fiction is 'not as the "representation of an action", but as an imaginative construct' (Scholes). Similarly, the stories related by Carey's narrator are not to be taken as absolutes. He tells the stories of a particular culture; they are a conglomerate of the signs and systems of meaning by which we attempt to live and to interpret the world. They are myths in the other, smaller sense of the word, the network of beliefs and fears which constitute our perception of the world: the myth of America, of money, of power, of success, of the world of drugs, of cancer, of eating habits, of 'dropping-out'. Even Harry's retreat to the seemingly idyllic existence at Bog Onion Road is undermined by the cowardly way in which he does it, and by his violent reception in 'paradise' at the hands of Clive and Daze. If the novel is didactic—and the didactic quality is characteristic of fabulation—it is so only in terms of what it has to say about the relationship between life and fiction. As Scholes says, the value of fiction is its effect on the life of the imagination. For that reason one has to give something for a story, as Vance Joy says; what one gives is the exercise of the imagination to interpret, to re-create what the narrator has given.

This concern with the relationship between life and fiction is central to the mode of fantasy. According to Todorov

> the fantastic text is not characterized by the simple presence of supernatural phenomena or beings, but by the hesitation which is established in the reader's perception of the events represented. Throughout the tale, the reader wonders (in the same way that a character often does, within the work) if the facts reported are to be explained by a natural or a supernatural cause, if they are illusions or realities. This hesitation derives from the fact that the extraordinary (hence potentially supernatural) event occurs not in a marvelous world but in an everyday context, the one most familiar to us. Consequently the tale of the fantastic is the narrative of a perception. . . .

I have quoted at some length from Todorov because this description is particularly appropriate to the world of **Bliss** and of the stories. The opening sentence of **Bliss**, 'Harry Joy was to die three times' places the events of the novel within the context of the supernatural, but what follows is more or less naturalistic. Carey himself has said 'My novel is a love story, and it's pretty naturalistic' [Peter Carey quoted by John Maddocks in 'Bizarre Realities: An Interview with Peter Carey', *Southerly* (1981)]. Within the novel Harry wonders whether he is in hell or whether he is mad. The context is crucial: if the setting is supernatural then the behaviour of his friends and family is 'natural'; if the setting is the natural world then their behaviour is extraordinary, and he is mad. **Bliss** is truly a 'narrative of perception.'

Carey has also said 'The writer I probably most liked in retrospect was Gabriel García Márquez—his ability to blend elements of fantasy and reality on a big scale, with some complexity' (Maddocks interview). With the novel's emphasis on the impossibility of originality it seems legitimate to seek out his literary sources. The similarities between Carey's novel and Márquez' major novel, *One Hundred Years of Solitude,* are mainly centred around the use of fantasy. For both writers fantasy is an expression of freedom, in the sense that one liberates oneself from cultural 'lies' by telling one's own stories. More specifically, both novels express a cyclical concept of time, and locate their origin not in the author himself, but in the timeless world of myth. Márquez' novel is supposedly written by Melquíades, a magical, mythical figure who resists death, and whose status to some extent resembles that of Harry Joy. There is also the fairly direct parallel between the episode in which the citizens of Macondo write labels for objects as they begin to lose their memory, and the episode in which the old man buries his written memories in the grounds

of the institution. They both signify that all we can retain of past reality is words and that these in fact have a very tenuous relationship with that 'reality'.

These similarities point outwards to certain parallels in the socio-historical context of these two writers. Australia and Colombia are both post-colonial societies, and both novels make it clear that the former colonizers have merely made way for more insidious cultural and economic colonization by America. In this context it seems fairly certain that Carey's choice of Bogota as the locale of David's final scenario was influenced by the significance of Bogota in *One Hundred Years.* There it represents modern, Western civilization—Thomas Wolfe's statement that you can't go home transformed into 'You can't leave home any more?' Western 'civilization' is ubiquitous (almost), hence Miquel Fernandez, who reluctantly shoots David, and looks forward to opening a bookshop near the university in Medelin where he would 'sell Stevenson in translation but also in English' (**Bliss**).

If the stories the narrator tells, and tells of, comment upon the narrating act, so does his omniscient stance towards the narrative. This omniscience is evident from the outset in the twice-quoted opening lines, and in the unabashed use of prolepses throughout the narrative. [In a footnote, Dovey states: "[See] Gérard Genette, *Narrative Discourse,* trans. Jane E. Lewin (Oxford: Basil Blackwell, 1980), p. 40. I use Genette's terminology here. *Prolepsis* signifies 'any narrative manoeuvre that consists of narrating or evoking in advance an event that will take place later' and *analepsis* signifies 'any evocation after the fact of an event that took place earlier than the point in the story where we are at any given moment'."] These range from brief pointers, such as 'Bettina would certainly grow in leaps and bounds over the following year' (**Bliss**), to the longer sections telling of David's death and of the coming cancer epidemic, both of which constitute external prolepses. That important opening sentence 'Harry Joy was to die three times' is the equivalent of what Todorov calls a 'plot of predestination' in his discussion of primitive narrative, and so constitutes yet another link with the mythic origins of narrative. As in folklore, the narrative conforms largely to chronological order but it is interesting to note that the few analepses that there are also convey a sense of predestination. They refer to the childhood of Harry, Bettina and Honey Barbara in a way which suggests that the roles of these characters are to some extent determined in advance.

The narrator's direct address of the reader is an important source of meaning in the novel. He does this in different ways. The first is simply another example of his omniscience: 'It was not a question that would have occurred to Harry, who had never seen his family as you, dear reader, have now been privileged to' (**Bliss**). The next is more significant: 'The rewards of originality have not been wasted on him and if he is, at this stage, unduly cocky, he might as well be allowed to enjoy it. So we will not interfere with the taxi driver, who is prolonging his euphoria by driving him the long way home'. Genette discusses this narrative figure, which classical rhetoricians called *author's metalepsis,* in some detail. Metalepsis here has the sense of 'taking hold of (telling) by changing level', and the figure 'consists of pretending that the poet "himself brings about the effect he celebrates".' As such it is an important device for foregrounding the narrating act and, although the figure is not used extensively in *Bliss,* I am going to quote at some length from Genette, as his discussion of the figure is highly relevant to Carey's novel:

> All these games, by the intensity of their effects, demonstrate the importance of the boundary they tax their ingenuity to overstep, in defiance of verisimilitude—a boundary that is precisely the narrating (or the performance) itself: a shifting but sacred frontier between two worlds, the world in which one tells, the world of which one tells. Whence the uneasiness Borges so well puts his finger on [in *Other Inquisitions*]: 'Such inversions suggest that if the characters in a story can be readers or spectators, then we, their readers or spectators, can be fictitious'. The most troubling thing about metalepsis indeed lies in this unacceptable and insistent hypothesis, that the extradiegetic is perhaps always diegetic, and that the narrator and his narratees—you and I—perhaps belong to some narrative.

The narrator again oversteps this boundary between the world of which one tells and the world in which one tells, in the closing sections of the book: 'But now, the last story, and the last story is our story, the story of Harry Joy and Honey Barbara, and for this story, like all stories, you must give something, a sapphire, or blue bread made from cedar ash' (*Bliss*). He claims the role of traditional narrator, passing the story on to his heirs. It is our story both because we must read it and because, as Harry Joy's children, we are fated to tell it: we can only tell what has been told before. One is aware of a fairly complex narrative effect here, which can be illuminated by Todorov's concept of 'embedding'. An embedded narrative is one told by a second (or third, or fourth) narrator, within another narrative, as occurs in the *Arabian Nights.* Several of Vance Joy's stories, and Harry's story at the police station, are embedded in *Bliss,* which is thus the embedding narrative. Todorov describes the significance of embedding as being the 'articulation of the most essential property of all narrative. For the embedding narrative is the *narrative of a narrative.* . . . The embedded narrative is the image of that great abstract narrative of which all the others are merely infinitesimal parts as well as the image of the embedding narrative which directly precedes it'. If *Bliss* in turn, becomes embedded in the story of the reader, the narrative of the novel is doubly enclosed: by the tradition out of which it grows, and the tradition which it creates.

Carey's use of Bogota is evidence of the foregrounding of the intertextual aspect of the narrative, and there are other examples of this, such as the Meursault wine which Harry asks for in Milanos restaurant. Aldo says 'There is no Meursault'. This use of the name of Camus' protagonist in *L'Etranger* may be interpreted as a subtle denial of the position Camus' heroes adopt in an absurd universe. Discussing black humour (and Carey can be considered a black humorist), Scholes says 'The best, in fact, that Camus found to offer humanity as a response to the human condition was 'scorn' . . . . What man must learn is neither scorn nor resignation, say the black humorists, but how to take a joke'. In *Bliss* it is obvious that the way to take a joke is to tell a joke, or a story.

Another example of the foregrounding of intertextuality is the title of the novel, which is surely taken from Katherine Mansfield's story of the same name. The protagonist of that story is also Harry, but there it is his wife who, having mistakenly assumed that she is living in a state of domestic and marital bliss, has her illusion shattered by the sudden discovery of her husband's infidelity. The stories in Katherine Mansfield's collection, *Bliss and Other Stories,* are about modes of perception, about how people live within their own cosy fictions, which often bear no relationship to the way things are. Which makes them very similar, at a profound level, to the stories in Carey's two collections, *The Fat Man in History* and *War Crimes.* Harry Joy's stories are described as 'new constructions' (*Bliss*), and the recurrence of ingenious constructions in the stories has been noted. The constructs, whether they be of the mind, or whether they are concrete, physical structures, such as the Kristu-Du in the story of that name or Gleason's model town in '**American Dreams**', stand for the various attempts of characters to 'narrate' their own world. The ending of the story then reflects back upon the validity or, in most cases, the *in*validity of these constructs as ways of perceiving or acting in the world.

The stories correspond fairly closely to Eikhenbaum's definition of the genre in his essay on O. Henry and the theory of the short story [*O. Henry and the Theory of the Short Story,* trans. I. R. Titunik, 1968]: 'The story must be constructed on the basis of some contradiction, incongruity, error, contrast, etc. But that is not enough. By its very essence, the story, just as the anecdote, amasses its whole weight *toward the ending'.* In almost all cases, Carey's stories follow this pattern: an expectation or an hypothesis—which varies from the concreteness of a well worked out plan to the vagueness of an undefined fear—is set up by one or more of the characters, only to be frustrated or proven invalid by the ending, which reveals some 'contradiction, incongruity, error, contrast'. Thus Crabs' fantasy about leaving the Drive-In, which has become the world, is thwarted when the road out leads back to the way in, and he is locked out; the narrator in '**Peeling**' has his anticipation of the slow exploration of the girl who visits him, the prospect of discovering her layer by layer, episode by episode, turned back on himself when he peels everything away only to reveal a small, broken, white doll. Carey has said of this story that it has 'many, many meanings', and that one of the things it is saying is that 'there was a mystery at the end and it was the mystery you saw in the first place. Dolls— . . .' (Maddocks)—another 'infinite onion', and a demonstration of the attempt to interpret mocked yet again; the train-trip scenario of **'The Journey of a Lifetime'** turns from dream into nightmare as the narrator is served tangible evidence of the true nature of his venture in the form of ice blocks from a refrigerated cadaver; the architect in **'Kristu Du'** bases his scenario for the justification of his life's work on the false evidence of the corrupt Mr Meat—and finally his dream is thwarted by his own error in planning. And so on.

The endings do not constitute a revelation concerning the psychology of the characters. In fact character is a secondary consideration with Carey who has outlined the way he sets about writing a story: 'Yes, well I suppose that how I've worked is to be interested or intrigued by a particular situation. In thinking about that situation I've had to find people to flesh it out and be part of it' (Maddocks). If the stories are characterized by a surprise ending, this is not a hollow device of emplotment, but one of the major ways of establishing meaning. If we compose and interpret the world by means of fictions, then surprise is inevitable as they are inevitably exposed as such. This is clearly a more negative view of the human capacity to 'narrate one's world' than that expressed in *Bliss.* Stories such as **'The Puzzling Nature of Blue'** and **'The Rose'** are evidence that creativity may have evil sources and consequences, and have been described by Carey [in an interview with Philip Nielsen entitled "Tell Me what Colour You Think the Sky Is," *Australian Literary Studies* (1981)] as 'the signs of a crime made physically manifest'. 'Originality, without Goodness . . . is nothing, of no worth' says Alex Duval in *Bliss.* In true Carey fashion these words have been placed in the mouth of a somewhat suspect character, which undercuts their significance in the total context of meaning. In the light of the portrayal of Harry's experience, with the warping of his perceptions following his two 'deaths', it seems safer to say that creativity without awareness is nothing. Whereas in the beginning he did not understand Vance's stories and so 'transmitted them imperfectly', by the end 'he told them better because he now understood them'.

On the other hand, another group of stories shows that if personal fictions are often invalid, so are the public fictions, the myths, beliefs and cultural assumptions which are taken as reality. **'Conversations with Unicorns'** belongs to this group, and reveals the human origins of a belief system. Similarly, **'The Puzzling Nature of Blue'** shows how signs, such as blue extremities in the story, are cultural constructs, arbitrary and absurd in their origins, and not 'natural' at all, as modern myths would have one believe. In **'The Fat Man in History'** the meaning of 'fat' varies according to the socio-historic context. This story further suggests that any form of investigation is a projection of one's personal construct onto the world and that this construct has the power to change the

structures which one seeks to interpret. Nancy Bowlby's relationship with the fat men provides her with the opportunity to study their behaviour, but it becomes the *cause* of their behaviour, of the 'Revolution in a Closed Society': a marvelous demonstration of the structuralist position.

Whence back to the fallibility of interpretation, something one is constantly aware of when writing about Carey. The tendency of postmodernist fiction is to defy criticism, and Legasse has placed Carey within the context of postmodernist writers: 'His music is more international . . . and echoes the upbeat rhythms of the three B's: Borges, Barth and Barthelme' [Jim Legasse, review of *War Crimes,* by Peter Carey, *Westerly*]. However, as David Lodge points out, with reference to Beckett (another 'B'): 'The often-asserted resistance of the world to meaningful interpretation would be a sterile basis for writing if it were not combined with a poignant demonstration of the human obligation to attempt such interpretation'.

In alphabetical order, C comes after B, Carey comes after the three (or more) B's. While his work is informed by similar issues, it provides a highly pleasurable narrative experience, which is often not the case with his predecessors. Carey has said 'I'd like to write for as broad an audience as possible . . . . I really believe very, very firmly in the possibility of popular art that's good in anybody's terms' (Maddocks), and he has most certainly achieved this goal. If one has to give something for a story, it is a pleasure to do so, for Carey's stories engage one's interest on so many levels and, to use the words of Robert Scholes, they have the power to rejoice and refresh. And so, for what it is worth, here is my sapphire, or blue bread made from cedar ash.

Graeme Turner (essay date October 1986)

SOURCE: "American Dreaming: The Fictions of Peter Carey," in *Australian Literary Studies,* Vol. 12, No. 4, October, 1986, pp. 431-41.

[*In the following essay, an earlier draft of which was presented at the conference of the Association for the Study of Australian Literature in July 1986, Turner outlines the major characteristics of Carey's fiction and discusses Carey's use of "American" formal devices to create literature with Australian themes.*]

Arguments around the concepts of nationalism and internationalism are familiar presences in discussions of Australian literature and other areas of cultural production, such as Australian film. Within such discussions, the internationalist position recommends itself as a kind of sophistication, a smoothing over of the rough edges of parochialism, and the embodiment of wider, even universal, standards of achievement. Peter Carey has been hailed as an international writer. *The Sydney Morning Herald* review of *Bliss* [October 10,

1981] is representative in its typing of Carey as a writer who 'finally brings Australia out of the last stubborn crannies of provincialism' and into a 'new universality and sophistication.' Reviewers may divide on such issues as the 'Australian-ness' of *Illywhacker,* but sophistication is a word which occurs regularly in accounts of Carey's fiction. Most often, this sophistication is seen to be primarily stylistic or formal— a product of Carey's use of the modes of black humour, metafiction, or fabulation, and his employment of popular sub-genres like science fiction. Although few go so far as to deny that there are important correspondences between the worlds depicted in Carey's fiction and Australian society, the fact that such correspondences are not usually literal—they reside at the level of interpretation—makes it possible to talk of his works as universal or, conversely, un-Australian. Such judgements may be partial, but they do highlight an important feature of the reception of Carey's fiction: that is, its distinctiveness is first apprehended as a distinction of form rather than of meaning or theme. Such a separation cannot, of course, be maintained, and in this discussion I wish to make some connections between Carey's use of international forms— specifically, American forms—and his generation of Australian meanings in order to outline what I see as important constituents of his fiction.

Although I wish to examine the relationship between Carey's fiction and American forms and meanings, it must be admitted that they are not the only international influences perceptible in his work. It is possible, for instance, to draw quite precise parallels between Carey and Marquez. As writers from post-colonial cultures they stand in similar political relations to the dominant literary forms and establishments, and have close stylistic and thematic affinities; the issue of colonialism, too, is prominent in both bodies of fiction. However, it is the Marquez who has been appropriated by American traditions who will make the occasional appearance in this discussion, as it is the American connections with which it is most concerned. The ways in which Carey and Marquez might form the basis for a discussion of post-colonial writing and the dominance of American literary culture must be deferred for future explorations.

That qualification made, it is clear that there is a strong American influence on Carey's work. It has become customary to see his fiction in the context of American black humour, metafiction, or fabulation. (Metafiction is 'fiction about fiction', self-consciously addressing and exposing its constructed nature; fabulation is defined, unhelpfully, by the coiner of the term, Robert Scholes [in *Fabulation and Metafiction,* 1979], as 'ethically controlled fantasy', revealing the contemporary 'plunge back into the tide of story'.) Such terms are conventionally used to characterise the dominant mode of contemporary writing in the United States, although it must be added that they are as representative of American appropriation of external influences as of exclusively indigenous traditions. Fabulation is more applicable to Borges and

Marquez than to any American writer—hence the appropriation of these two writers into any discussion of American metafiction or fabulation. American fiction has been particularly adept at absorbing influences from elsewhere (in addition to Borges' fabulation, for instance, Camusian absurdist thought dominates post-war American comic fiction). Such absorption does not, however, disqualify its objects from incorporation and transformation into American traditions and ideologies. The orthodox view of the dominant stylistic characteristics of modern American fiction may be as constructed as any other form of orthodoxy but it serves as an important reference point for readers, and for Carey's reviewers.

The grounds for placing Peter Carey within an American context are essentially stylistic, but style is more than decoration. It is the product of a theory of 'the real', a view of the function of fiction, and thus of the status of the writer. The adoption of a style is also potentially the adoption of that theory of 'the real', and of the making of fictions, which produces it. Peter Carey's fiction *is* like much American fiction in that it uses its forms to expose and interrogate its fictional status. While relatively infrequent in Australian fiction, the adoption of formal strategies which have foregrounded the making of the fiction and its self-reflexivity has occurred in American fiction since Melville and almost conventionally since the 1960s. In recent American fiction, mimesis has been displaced while fantasy and romance have prospered; the recovery of the primacy of plot and design paradoxically coexists with reminders of their constructed and arbitrary nature.

This may look abstract, but it can take place at the most basic levels of narrative organisation. For example, in *The World According to Garp,* John Irving uses the past historic tense as his 'base tense', but breaks it up by intrusions of the future tense. The consequent dispelling of any illusion of the story 'telling itself' exposes and foregrounds the storytelling process rather than attempting to bury it in a realist narrator. Carey has used a similar method: beginning with the present, often dropping into the past as his base tense, and continually alluding to the future. This happens in many of his stories and is basic to the narrative organisation of *Bliss* and *Illywhacker.* Like Irving and other contemporary American writers, Carey also generalises from this *formal* problematic of fictionality, adopting a *thematically* metafictional view of the importance of fiction, of lies, to support social existence. In Kurt Vonnegut's *Slaughterhouse Five,* Billy Pilgrim overhears Rosewater say to a psychiatrist, 'I think you guys are going to have to come up with a lot of wonderful new lies, or people just aren't going to want to go on living'. It is a warning the Peter Carey of *Bliss* would understand.

The above quotation is not only about fiction, it is also about those fictions we call history. The interest in fictionality in modern American writing, the use of fantasy, and the consequent questioning of the real, has inevitably proposed the fictionality of history. This proposition is not confined to

American writing; the work of Borges and Marquez in South America and of Fowles in the U.K. are important here. But, as Richard Poirier has remarked [in *A World Elsewhere: The Place of Style in American Literature,* 1967], 'Americans have always regarded reality as their own construction', and so American metafictionists such as John Barth, in *The Sot-Weed Factor,* or Robert Coover, in *The Public Burning,* are representative in their exploitation of the tension between the historical and the fantastic in their novels. The aim in such novels is to dissolve any easy distinction between the fictional and the historical; in *The Public Burning* the fantastic most often employs documentary, historical modes of representation, while *The Sot-Weed Factor* constructs its absurd world with all the apparent deference to history typical of the historical novel. In *Slaughterhouse Five,* again, the destruction of Dresden during World War II is represented as being as fantastic (that is, as difficult to believe) as the visit from the aliens of Tralfamadore. The point is not that the destruction of Dresden did not actually occur, but that history's silence on it has made it impossible to believe it occurred. History is revealed as a selection, a compositional act, and thus a fictional account of the real.

Peter Carey has admitted an interest in this view of history. In an interview with Philip Neilsen ['Tell Me What Colour You Think the Sky Is'; published in extract, *Australian Literary Studies,* (1981)] he talked of his admiration for Marquez' combination of fantasy and history, and its magical, mythic effects. Carey's fantastic alternative worlds, like those of Barth, Coover, Vonnegut, and Marquez, can always be seen as alternative perspectives on an historical world, questioning it and exposing its constructed, arbitrary nature. Even *Illywhacker,* which begins uncharacteristically in an almost social realist style—a style which privileges history—eventually modulates into the fantastic—a style which is able to see history as a construction. As is the case with *The Public Burning* and *One Hundred Years of Solitude,* the mythic quality of *Illywhacker* proceeds from this modulation and the tension it produces. For Carey, and, incidentally, for Marquez, the interrogating of history as myth and the proposition of fiction as an alternative has a special significance within the literature of a post-colonial, but still colonised, culture.

The preceding remarks underline how difficult it is to describe formal narrative strategies independently of their cultural context. The description usually implies a history. More importantly, any consideration of formal properties must progress towards a consideration of the view of the world and of fiction they represent. So, a formal interest in fantasy and in science fiction can also be a thematic interest in the forms and construction of experience. The novelist's seizing of the opportunity to play with non-realist forms can nevertheless be directed towards a point of view on the real or on history. In Carey's work such linkages are rarely made systematically, as in allegory for instance, but exist as correspondences with or inferences towards Australian society and

mythology. Such correspondences and inferences are made essential components of one's reading of Carey's fiction through the characteristic oscillations between the fantastic and the historical, something which is skilfully controlled and a key source of the reader's pleasure in both the novels and in such stories as **'American Dreams'** and **'A Windmill in the West'**.

One of the benefits of Todorov's book on the fantastic [*The Fantastic: A Structural Approach to a Literary Genre,* 1973] was his localising of the sensation of 'hesitation'. A definitive component of the fantastic, this occurs when the reader is caught between the explicable and the inexplicable (what Todorov calls the 'uncanny and the marvelous') as they read. It is the point where logical, natural explanations do not suffice, but where overtly supernatural explanations have not been explicitly invoked. At such moments, possibilities multiply and the real and fantasy worlds have either to be explicitly reconciled (as in a scientific explanation of an apparent ghost) or convincingly held apart (as a mystery, a dream, or, harder still, a plausible fantasy). This speculative pleasure is often brief and encapsulated. At the end of a supernatural thriller like *The Hound of the Baskervilles,* for instance, order is restored, fantasy consigned to its proper place in the shade of mimesis, and the hesitation is no more than a passing titillation, *frisson* in the pleasure of the text.

> **Carey's fantastic alternative worlds, like those of Barth, Coover, Vonnegut, and Marquez, can always be seen as alternative perspectives on an historical world, questioning it and exposing its constructed, arbitrary nature.**
>
> —*Graeme Turner*

Carey, and he is by no means alone in this, tends not to resolve or dispel hesitation in this way. Rather, he tends to employ it as a method of closure. **'Peeling',** for instance, or **'Exotic Pleasures',** are stories where the possibilities of speculation are released rather than encapsulated by the end of the tale. A story such as **'Crabs'** makes sufficient correspondences with the real world to enable the story to be seen as an alternative perspective on it. The ending then challenges the reader's determination to make a more systematic connection between the fantasy of the text and the real. (What does the drive-in mean? Is it an image of modernity at the end as it is at the beginning? Or does it sharpen into an image of totalitarianism, the destruction of the individual? Does Crabs' turning into a machine at the end have a social and critical function?) In the most characteristic stories, the tension this creates is not easily resolvable, and the reader 'hesitates'—neither wishing to see the story as allegory nor as ethically uncontrolled. The *meaning* of the fiction is typically elusive, dominated by the structure, the design of the narrative itself.

In many of Carey's stories, the design of the narrative, and the thematic function of storytelling itself, is crucial. Harry Joy uses language as ritual, to reconstruct his world; Herbert Badgery ultimately accepts few effective distinctions between truth and lies. Reality is seen as something one constructs rather than apprehends objectively, and one's own constructions of it are no less legitimate for being just that. Conversely, since history is a fiction too, our commonsense understandings of existence are only more familiar versions of the delusions suffered by Carla in **'The Chance',** or the fat men's hopes of a counterrevolution in **'The Fat Man in History'.** The foregrounding of fictionality in the formal organisation of the narratives is thus paralleled by the thematic proposition that all lives are constructions, all accounts are fictions, all explanations are partial or motivated.

This is not to claim too much for Carey as a metaphysician or ideologue. His stories do not try to explain existence. In my view, Carey is not much interested in the metaphysical. His fiction's most basic structural situation is enclosure, entrapment, and he *is* interested in that. But he is less interested in these traps as political structures—as fuel for a social critique, for instance—than as material *forms;* he seems drawn to examine their complexity, their symmetry, their completeness. Carey's fictions do not examine what lives mean as much as they examine how lives are constructed in order to produce their meanings. And stories, lies, fantasies, are not the only kind of formal constructions in his fictions which are employed to generate meaning. Other kinds of constructions abound. We have the dome in **'Kristu Du'**; the pet shop and Herbert's compulsive house-building in **Illywhacker**; the working with the wood and hammer in **'Williamson's Wood'**; the prison door in **'The Chance'**; the hole for the barbecue in **'The Fat Man in History'**; the fence dividing Australia in **'A Windmill in the West'**; the model of the town in **'American Dreams'**; the penthouse within the factory in **'War Crimes'**; the conversion of the drive-in to a refugee camp in **'Crabs'**. Like fictions, these constructions are contingent and no matter how physically substantial they might be, they rarely have the desired effect of imposing stability or finality on the characters' lives.

Such are some of the connections which can be made between Carey's fiction and that of his formal models. It is understandable if such connections support claims for his internationalism, for his belonging to the world rather than Australia, and for displacing his Australian-ness.

As I said earlier, the appropriation of a formal strategy takes on more than its stylistic attributes; literary form is not innocent of ideology nor is it easily separable from the mythology of the cultural context which produced it. Black humour,

for instance, can legitimately be seen as a peculiarly American form, composed of a blend of French existentialism and American pragmatism John Barth labelled 'cheerful nihilism'. [In a footnote, Turner adds: "The label is used in Barth's *End of the Road,* 1962, and is developed into a theoretical argument in Richard Boyd Hauck's *A Cheerful Nihilism: Confidence and the Absurd in American Humorous Fiction,* 1971."] It has more than a touch of American romanticism, which means that its version of the absurd incorporates a contradictory element of individualism. Our fiction tends not to be romantic in the same ways; nor is it absurdist or individualist. American fiction, unlike ours, supports the individual, seeing them as morally prior to the society, able to survive its impositions and, like Huck Finn, 'light out for the territory' without dying in a cave like Heriot, being eaten by aboriginals like Voss, or being disappeared by a hanging rock. Such differences between the two narrative traditions have to be negotiated, not only formally but also thematically and ideologically. In Carey's case, this negotiation occurs by way of his thematic preoccupation with colonialism and colonisation, essentially a nationalist position which views Americans with genuine suspicion as threats to an authentic Australian culture.

Carey's fiction regularly depicts isolated individuals or fragmented communities confronting an exploitative system. This system is usually powerful, inscrutable, and insensitive to the indigenous culture it has colonised. Often this indigenous culture is recognisable as Australian by the fact and details of its colonisation. In both **Bliss** and **'American Dreams'** we know the place we are reading about is Australia *because* it is the subject of American colonisation. And although some of Carey's fictional societies are colonised from other sources— the Japanese in **Illywhacker,** the extra-terrestrial Fastalogians in **'The Chance'**—it is the Americans who are most often the oppressors, the seducers, the invaders.

The Americans are overthrown by the revolution in **'The Fat Man in History'**; the ground of the story is the slippage between the view of all Americans as fat, greedy and grotesque and its application to indigenous, defensibly glandular, fat men like Alex. In **'American Dreams',** the ideology of American capitalism has colonised the indigenous community's subconscious: 'we all have dreams of the big city, of wealth, of modern houses, of big motor cars: American dreams, my father calls them'. In Carey's stories America has colonised the myths and forms of modernity itself: Crabs has 'American dreams' in Frank's luxurious '56 Dodge; **'The Report from the Shadow Industry'** offers us the latest frightening consumer item from America; and Nathan Schick lures even the nationalistic Charles with the promise of the 'best pet shop in the world' in **Illywhacker. In Bliss,** the combination of the glittering forms of advertising and the myth of success, with their metonym of New York, goads Bettina to self-destruction and is the antithesis of the values advocated through Honey Barbara. The novel's central, and entirely traditional, opposition between Nature and Society is articulated through the conflict between indigenous Australian values—the bushman at the end—and the American 'imported shit', represented with the concentration of metaphor in the examples of petrol, cancer, and advertising.

Such a view of America is not without ambivalence, however. As Herbert Badgery in *Illywhacker* says, 'no matter how much he hated Henry Ford, he always loved Americans'. Nathan Schick, the provocation for this observation, is both exploiting and engaging:

> Schick could talk a line of bullshit like I never heard before, and in this had the distinct advantage of being an American and therefore never hesitant about expressing an opinion. Australians, in comparison, lack confidence, and it is this, not steel mills or oil wells, that is the difference between the two nations.

Although it is Nathan who eventually develops 'the best pet shop in the world' to turn Australia into a theme park for American tourists, the puritanical Leah Goldstein 'loved Nathan Schick's vulgar suit and ringed hands':

> She liked the garrulous checks, like leftover material from a Silly Friends party. Even as he had walked across the saloon bar, stepping over the snake so carelessly, even as he opened his gold-filled mouth to expose her for fraud, she liked him.

In *Bliss,* advertising is American. Bettina's love affair with America is negotiated through advertising, overheated by the myth of New York, and sufficiently strong to survive her affair with Joel. Her ads are brilliant, testimony to her complete adsorption of her American advertising annuals. The narrator's description of the ads she creates, displayed in a magic circle around their living room and provoking an immediate erection from Harry, is not without relish.

> A comped-up ad is not a final ad. It is, technically, a rough. It is the sort of rough that is done when a client has no imagination or, more often, when the person doing the ad is too much in love with it to show it in any way that is really rough and does everything to make it appear finished, taking 'rough' photography and getting colour prints, ordering headline type and sticking down body copy in the exact type face (if not the correct words), carefully cut to give the appearance of the final paragraphs. And over all of this is placed a cell overlay, so that a comp. ad, framed with white, mounted on heavy board, covered with its glistening cell overlay, looks more precious to its maker than it ever will again.

Here and elsewhere in *Bliss,* the appeal of the ads and their magical power is enjoyed and savoured. As with Henry Ford

and Nathan Schick, Carey's narrator might deplore the ideology but he loves the forms.

Such is probably a fair description of the relationship between Carey's fiction and its American models. If his resistance to American domination does not inhibit either his narrator's enthusiasm for advertising or Carey's own adoption of American narrative strategies, his use of American forms in his fiction does not simply recycle an anachronistic American ideology to an Australian audience. Instead he appropriates and transforms his models, adapting them to local use as the colonised strike back. As indicated earlier, individualism is easily supported by such formal models but Carey's fiction is ambivalent about the individual as well as critical of society. Its view of the natural world is romantic and in many ways reminiscent of the naive preference for the natural we see in American fictional traditions; however, there is also a strong post-romantic preference for nature in the Australian tradition. Further, while we can see the influence of fabulatory models in *Illywhacker,* we can also see the influence of Furphy's *Such is Life.* Tracing this relationship may be a project for someone in the future; for the purposes of this discussion, I wish to conclude by addressing two important effects of the processes I have been describing—effects which may be central to an understanding of Carey's fiction. The first is the way his fiction seems to be producing a new kind of popular readership; the second is its serving, in an unusually self-conscious manner, the cultural function of narrative.

Peter Carey does enjoy a wide readership in Australia. If one's conversations with one's students have any empirical value, it does seem that many have come to his fiction as their first experience of contemporary Australian writing; for some, it is their first experience of any Australian writing. Carey's reputation has spread beyond literary culture; I am encouraged in this view, if I can be forgiven recourse to anecdote, by a conversation I had with an airline clerk while returning from the conference where I presented an earlier version of this article: he told me he had enjoyed my paper on Carey and engaged me in a discussion about the relative merits of *Bliss* and *Illywhacker.* This is not a normal experience for those of us who labor in the groves of academe and, while hardly representative, is yet another indication that Carey is tapping a new, often younger, audience for Australian fiction. I believe there may be explanations for this in the formal properties of his work.

Since the 1890s, fiction in Australia has moved progressively away from its popular audience. This has not been so generally the case in the U.S.A., and American writers have traditionally been more comfortable with popular forms and popular culture than their Australian counterparts. The hip, counter-culture vernacular of a Vonnegut, a Brautigan, or a Tom Robbins, is contemporary evidence of this and it finds its Australian version in Peter Carey. Like them, he announces his adventurousness and displays himself as a writer, not by drawing on the avant-garde or the literary as much as by drawing on popular forms such as science fiction, and popular fashions and mythologies such as those which inform **'Crabs'**. In this he differs from, say, a Frank Moorhouse, whose observations, while perceptive, are nevertheless made from a position outside popular culture and through literary forms which reject plot or sensation—the stuff of popular entertainment. There is a sense in which Carey's writing is anti-literary, hence his uneasy relationship with the academic world. Patricia Waugh has suggested [in *Metafiction: The Theory and Practice of Self-Conscious Fiction,* 1984] that by incorporating popular forms as Carey does, the writer undermines and shifts dominant constructions of 'good' literature, the role of the author, and the use of fiction itself. Literariness is not necessarily part of Carey's initial appeal to my students; they find him accessible and familiar before they find him original and demanding. His fiction's clear foregrounding of plot, of story, can be seen as a shifting of the dominant constructions of 'good' literature; it also enables the stories and the novels to be read within a number of reading conventions and at a number of levels—something that is not true of, for instance, David Malouf's fiction.

Another effect of this dominance of plot—the level of display in the narrative design which foregrounds the storyteller in the inventiveness of the plot itself, let alone its constitutive discourses—is that it enunciates the author as a figure, as a visionary in his or her own right. The mythologising of Kurt Vonnegut in the U.S.A., the ease with which his Mark Twain-like cracker-barrel philosophising has found an audience, is an image of the potential for the writer to become not just part of the literary culture, but part of popular culture. Carey's involvement with film, through *Bliss,* (1985) and *Dead-End Drive-In* (1986), and popular music, through the rock-opera *Illusion* (1985), seems to be exploiting that potential. Such factors may be affecting the nature of his readership.

More important, however, is Carey's fiction's fulfilling of the cultural function of narrative. Elsewhere, [*National Fictions: Literature, Film and the Construction of Australian Narrative,* 1986], I have talked about this—the largely post-structuralist argument that all narrative (film, fiction, myths) serves comparable functions for its culture; crudely, that of helping to make sense of experience within that culture. (Such a view of narrative and culture also informs Robert Dixon's discussion of the historical novel [in 'Rolf Boldrewood's *War to the Knife:* Narrative Form and Ideology in the *Historical Novel*' (1986)] in *Australian Literary Studies*). Narrative has the potential to both produce and reproduce mythologies, to question or legitimate the culture's explanations of itself, to resolve its contradictions. It seems essential, inasmuch as while not all cultures have novels, all cultures have narrative. Developments in narrative theory have suggested that narrative is an epistemological category; this is not to make the conventional claim that 'we make up stories in order to understand the world', but rather that 'the world comes to us

in the shape of stories' [William C. Dowling, *Jameson, Althusser, Marx: An Introduction to the Political Unconscious,* 1984].

Clearly, for the cultural function of narrative, myth is of central importance. Peter Carey's work has been celebrated for its mythic quality, its facility for creating stories which have a fable-like significance. In a story such as **'American Dreams',** a myth is proposed; one of resistance to colonisation, to domination from outside the culture. Such a myth is presumably more powerful within and appropriate to an Australian cultural context than either British or American contexts. One of the ways in which it articulates itself is through the image of the 'American dreams' of its characters—the colonising of their dreams by another culture. The image is rich, and its appropriateness is emphasised by the fact that it has occurred elsewhere in Australian cultural production, within a similarly resistant argument. In 1958, Tom Weir wrote an article [published in Albert Moran and Tom O'Regan, eds., *An Australian Film Reader,* 1985] calling for support for an Australian film industry, in which he argued for the dissemination of Australian images and mythologies through the narrative feature film. He called his article 'No Daydreams of Our Own: The Film as National Self-Expression', and both his and Carey's image of a colonised subconscious are mobilised to attack the influence of foreign mythologies, and to argue for the need to buy back the mythological farm.

In Carey's fiction, this endeavour is specific at the literal and the thematic levels. His thematic emphasis on story, together with his sensitivity to the indigenous culture and its vulnerability to colonisation, proposes fiction-making as an activity that is constitutive of the community and is thus essential to it. His most detailed depiction of this is through Harry Joy at the end of *Bliss*:

> And he also gave value to a story so that it was something of work, as important in its way, as a strong house or a good dam. He insisted that the story was not his, and not theirs either. You must give something, he told the children, a sapphire, or blue bread from cedar ash. And what began as a game ended as a ritual.

> They were the refugees of a broken culture who had only the flotsam of belief and ceremony to cling to, or sometimes, the looted relics from other people's temples. Harry cut new wood grown on their soil and built something solid they all felt comfortable with. They were hungry for ceremony and story. There was no embarrassment in these new constructions.

Here fiction and myth elide into each other as the stories are possessed by their audience, becoming the rituals and ceremonies which bind the community together.

It is, perhaps, at such moments in Carey's fiction where the emphasis on fictionality is so clear, that his American influences are most obvious. However, these influences are put to nationalist use by these 'refugees of a broken culture'. In *Bliss,* Carey is arguing the necessity of constructing stories to live by, stories which emerge from and are given value by the community itself, rather than from the importation of American dreams. Harry Joy's eventual function within this new community in *Bliss* can be regarded as a kind of model for the writer within the Australian culture, providing fictions, Australian dreams, for a culture 'hungry for ceremony and story'.

Tony Thwaites (essay date September 1987)

SOURCE: "More Tramps at Home: Seeing Australia First," in *Meanjin,* Vol. 46, No. 3, September, 1987, pp. 400-09.

[*In the following excerpt, Thwaites argues that* Illywhacker *is a self-referential text in the tradition of Samuel Beckett's novels.*]

Many reviewers (here, and in England and the United States) have treated *Illywhacker* relatively unproblematically as either a realist text or a contemporary version of older genres, such as the tall tale. It obviously has much in common with various pre-modernist types of narrative: for a start, it is dominated by a first-person narrative from a narrator who seems to tell the story from a position of relative omniscience.

Herbert Badgery is a story-teller of immense gusto and confidence. Doubtless, Badgery would like to be thought of as a masterful narrator. The first two pages of the novel are full of self-sung praise for his storytelling abilities: 'lying is my main subject, my specialty, my skill'. But then, on the other hand, the very first paragraph also lets us know that something, somewhere along the line, has gone very wrong: 'It is hard to believe you can feel so bad and still not die'. Badgery is a captive, to an extent that will only be fully revealed almost 600 pages later. If his narration seems masterful, little else about him does: he is resentfully old, decrepit, unable even to die. The confidence seems a trick, the gusto disgust.

The question of his mastery of his own situation is bound up with that of his mastery of his story. As we learn from the long narrative that separates Badgery's two appearances in his cage, he survives here because of his storytelling alone. He is an exhibit in grandson Hissao's Pet Emporium, where all of Australia is arranged by type for the tourist eye—'shearers . . . lifesavers, inventors, manufacturers, bushmen, aboriginals'. We are not told the label on Badgery's cage, perhaps because that would be superfluous: there it is, 'neatly printed on a chart not three feet from where I lie', on the front cover of the book. Not only is his life one of telling stories, as a profession: it is now nothing more than a story, both

diegetically (he is alive because he tells stories) and literally (text and character bear the same label). Badgery's stories are his survival and his captivity: a decrepit old body barely alive, its voice its sole vigour, he has collapsed into his own story, is now no more than his own tale, true or false. The sign on the cage is the sign on the book. Imprisoned in writing, a voice talks on long after the proper time of its death, like that of Poe's M. Valdemar: a narrating 'I' as insubstantial as paper, a voice all but without source.

It is worth looking more closely at this 'I'. The elision of text and speaker makes it impossible to treat the pronoun as simply the sign of a character, let alone the hallmark of a well-constituted, confident and basically realist character. A decrepit old man, isolated beyond death, recounting his gaps-and-all story into a void to pass the time: what does this suggest if not the Beckettian narrator? The 'I' of Beckett's prose becomes less and less of a character, and becomes instead the very effort of the text itself to construct a subject, one which remains hesitant, preliminary, riddled with silences in a perpetual freefall of collapse; the pronouns mark the voice(s) with which the text speaks ultimately of *itself* in its interminable movement towards subjectivity. Take, almost at random, *The Unnamable:*

> . . . it's I am talking . . . no need of a mouth, the words are everywhere, inside me, outside me . . . I hear them, no need to hear them, no need of a head, impossible to stop them, impossible to stop, I'm in words, made of words, others' words, what others, . . . I'm all these flakes, meeting, mingling, falling asunder, . . . this dust of words, with no ground for their settling, no sky for their dispersing, coming together to say, fleeing one another to say, that I am they, all of them, those that merge, those that part, those that never meet, and nothing else . . .

What if one reads the opening and closing pages of *Illywhacker* in this self-referential way? What if this novel, in many ways apparently so old-fashioned, this text which moves so close to certain models of Australian realist and genre writing and to certain national stereotypes—what if *Illywhacker* is capable of a *double* reading? If its first-person pronoun not only refers to the history and present situation of *an* illywhacker, Herbert Badgery, a fictional construct evoking a past era of novel-writing—but also if it refers, in the very same words, to the history and present situation of this *Illywhacker,* the text, and of the genres and traditions it draws on, sums up, and speaks through? It is not at all difficult to read the framing narrative of *Illywhacker* in this way: indeed, virtually every sentence of it offers such a double reading. This modernist *Illywhacker* inserts itself into the traditionalist or genre one, speaking with its voice, in its words; it enacts the protracted death throes of such traditionalisms. In its opening and closing pages, the Great Australian Novel (that summation of realist or genre forms) dies in a slow fall in the very midst of being staged as domestic and international spectacle.

'I am a hundred and thirty-nine years old and something of a celebrity', says Badgery; 'They come and look at me and wonder how I do it'. Perhaps the date is a lie. Nevertheless, 139 years before *Illywhacker* is published, James Tucker has just written *Ralph Rashleigh,* and on Norfolk Island Rufus Dawes is about to have his name cleared. By 1919, Badgery is 'already dragging out too many hairs with my comb each morning': Joyce is working on *Ulysses,* Eliot on *The Waste Land,* and in Australia Henry Handel Richardson is working on the second volume of *The Fortunes of Richard Mahoney,* already old-fashioned in its naturalism. If the dates are somewhat arbitrary, they're also apt.

After an anti-intellectual past, Badgery says, he could now 'invent a library':

> I could fill up bookcases carelessly, elegantly, stack volumes end to end, fill the deep shelves with two rows of books, leave them with their covers showing on the dining-room table . . .

If lying, or fictionalising, has always been Badgery's 'main subject'—or if the tall-story has always been seen as one of the dominant genres of Australian fiction—then, as he declares,

> It is a great relief to find a new use for it. It's taken me long enough, God knows, and I have not always been proud of my activities.

All but immobile, Badgery has been 'poked . . . and prodded' by 'independent experts' (of which this paper would no doubt be one), who are fascinated with his longevity (or morbidity) but also with 'my foul-smelling mouth', 'my legs', 'my dick . . . as scabby and scaly as a horse's'—speech, mobility, dissemination. All that keeps him alive, he says, is the curiosity 'to see what my dirty old body will do next'. Even his obsession with his bodily functions is not simply a matter of naturalism, any more than it is in Beckett.

Not only does Badgery provide a commentary on certain streams of Australian fiction: he also provides commentary on commentary, giving advice to his readers, critics and reviewers and at the same time prefiguring what will be (has been) said about this very text:

> But now I feel no more ashamed of my lies than my farts (I rip forth a beauty to underline the point). There will be complaints, of course. (There are complaints now, about the fart—my apologies, my fellow sufferers.) But my advice is not to waste your time with your red pen, to try to pull apart the strands of lies and truth, but to relax and enjoy the show.

And there are, of course, complaints—about the farts, and about the lies. Undoubtedly the most frequent complaint about *Illywhacker,* echoed in nearly every review, has been that it is really only a series of episodes, most of them individually quite marvelous, but somewhat lacking in coherence when strung together into a fiction of this size. A few examples:

> Each story should be there, each one has something to say and says it well. But the stories don't listen to each other. (John Hanrahan, *Age Saturday Extra,* 6 July 1985)

> . . . for most of the time the novel has an air of lurching on with a kind of desperate improvisation from one situation or fancy to the next. (Laurie Clancy, *Australian Book Review,* 73, 14-15)

> There is a strong whiff of . . . laboriousness of invention sometimes, an overfertility of metaphor, one dragon and one traveling Australian illusionist too many. (Howard Jacobson, *New York Times Book Review,* 17 November 1985)

> *Illywhacker* has many brilliant moments but in the end it overreaches itself. (Andrew Hislop, *Times Literary Supplement,* 3 May 1985)

The perception is accurate enough in the terms implied by the reviews. If we assume that it is a text just like those it mimics—a realist or genre form—and that it should conform to classical expectations of closure and unity, then *Illywhacker* is certainly something less than tidy. Without organic unity, it becomes distended; without economy in its production of meaning, it becomes laborious; without firm underlying plan, it improvises; unrestrained, it overreaches.

But then might that not be the point? As I have suggested, it is possible to read *Illywhacker* another way altogether—as a *doubled,* reflexive, metalinguistic text. Its untidiness can be read as an intense and prolific crisis of meaning, a perpetual excess where the narrative hovers on the verge of collapse, one of whose effects is an oscillation among text (*Illywhacker* as genre novel), metatext (as comment on genre novels) and meta-metatext (as comment on received criticism of genre novels). It is this tendency to overspill boundaries that the various reviewers above have missed entirely yet at the same time named quite precisely.

Under this doubled reading, the 600 pages that separate the two brief appearances of the caged Herbert Badgery start to look very different from the realist and genre forms they mimic so closely. They more resemble the stories Beckett's Malone tells himself alone in his room, or those increasingly fragmented tales with which the Unnamable passes the interminable time. Carey's narrator, of course, does not work on the edge of panic that informs Beckett's protagonists in ever greater degree throughout the trilogy, the *Texts for Nothing* and *How It Is*. Badgery is to the last a showman, after all. His façade of control is all but complete. He very rarely lets his confidence (trick) slip to reveal weariness or despair. But it is precisely the long-delayed approach to the ending of the book that makes the futility of Badgery's stories evident. The more they tell, the more they repeat the progress of Badgery's decline and their part in his downfall, the closer they bring Badgery the character to his final position, as Badgery the old and powerless narrator: the only distance between the two is that created by a reservoir of story ever closer to exhaustion. They attempt to create a past, the honourable past of folklore; but all they create is a present, and a captivity.

Like the Pet Emporium, *Illywhacker* is full of the types of a nationalist literature: the spruiker, the inventor, the entrepreneur, the dilettante, the man on the land . . . And mingling throughout the text's host of stories also, like these stereotypes, are all sorts of heterogeneous literary genres, which the narrative raids for its elements: the tall story; the historical novel (Les Chaffey and Robert Menzies, by their simple presence, act as 'independent experts' who attest to the veracity of the illywhacker's narrative); the political novel (the Goldstein sections); or the *Bildungsroman* of an unsentimental education. In Beckett, there is always only one story, whose endless variation only serves to underline its moribundity. Badgery's host of stories and genres can do no more.

Where Beckettian syntax and stories stumble and halt like their crippled protagonists en route to immobility, the tales Badgery tells are nearly always exactly evocative, researched, as glossy as a television mini-series and as seductive as the photography of a 1970s Australian film (though it plays a negligible role in the events of the novel, cinema—that recent Australian cultural export *par excellence*—haunts *Illywhacker*). In their attention to detail and their meticulous reconstruction of a past, they become a sort of hyperrealism, outdoing even their ostensible models. Compare, for example, Carey's treatment of the Chinese with that of Furphy in *Such is Life; Illywhacker* is fiction for and from the multicultural 1980s.

However dazzling its surface, though, *Illywhacker* is never more than a simulacrum of the 'genuine article'. It is incessantly aware of the decrepitude written under its gloss: 'behind' the tales, there is always the caged Herbert Badgery, verging on but never achieving death, forced into more tales and more digressions, unable to let go. *Illywhacker* disorders and discomforts its own realist and genre affinities by bringing them to sustained crisis; and this crisis is one which Badgery's storytelling can neither repair (as its only tools are precisely those which have brought it to crisis) nor force beyond this impasse of the already-written, into the death of its rationalist speaking subject. The crisis is one of the stories themselves—or, as these are an illywhacker's stories, of lies.

The liar, of course, is a received figure of fiction, and the tall story a received genre. But what makes *Illywhacker* interrogate these forms is a further twist, which deflects all questions of truth and falsity.

This begins with Badgery's now-notorious opening whopper about being a hundred and thirty-nine years old. Almost immediately after this, he warns that he is 'a terrible liar' and then swears blind that whatever else he might be lying about, he isn't lying about his age. And yet, two pages on, he states that he was 33 years old in 1919. Is he, then, narrating the entire thing from around the year 2025? It appears not: as the book progresses, Badgery seems to be approaching a narrative present in the quite near future at most, not one in the third millennium. At last, two pages from the end of the book, Badgery reveals that his age was a lie all along, a spruik for the customers:

> The chart on my door says I am a hundred and thirty-nine years old. It also says I was born in 1886, but there are no complaints. The customers are happy.

In quite a classic way, the text has set up an enigma that arches over the entire span of the book. But it is revealed as nothing more than a false lead, a teaser to keep the reader reading. That it is patently false, or even contradictory, is of no consequence at all. It still works perfectly well in the only way that matters—as a spiel.

From a purely formal point of view, the paradox here is that of the Cretan liar: can one afford to believe or (deadlier still) *not* to believe a self-proclaimed liar? But form is not the point. The point is that the paradox works. *Illywhacker* is not concerned with deconstructing the spiel so much as with its pragmatics.

That concern has already been figured in the first epigraph, from Twain's *More Tramps Abroad*:

> Australian history is almost always picturesque; indeed, it is so curious and strange, that it is itself the chiefest novelty the country has to offer and so it pushes the other novelties into second and third place. It does not read like history, but like the most beautiful lies; and all of a fresh sort, no mouldy old stale ones. It is full of surprises and adventures, the incongruities, and contradictions, and incredibilities; but they are all true, they all happened.

The tone of this passage is of interest here, rather than questions of truth versus falsehood. It is pure tourism. In Twain's Michelin guide, with its search for the picturesque, the novel, Australian history gets five stars. The passage is addressed to those Tramping Abroad, not to the inhabitants: it is Australian history as spectacle, just like the history *Illywhacker* stages—a diorama of politics and empire builders, the rural, the urban, the illywhackers and their marks. Tall tales and true from the legendary past. As epigraph, the Twain passage sets up a closed system of mediation: this is Australia for the outside eye, which then in a trans-oceanic leap (or loop) mediates the spectacle for domestic consumption.

That looping is everywhere in *Illywhacker.* It makes even Badgery's speech not his own but something that belongs elsewhere, always elsewhere. His speech is what is demanded of him by his audience: that is, on the one hand by the overseas visitors who come to see 'the chiefest novelty the country has to offer,' and on the other, by those natives who can 'afford the entrance money' to see this mediated tourist Australia. In other words, its customers have no choice but to see Australia through foreign eyes, as tourists. And these customers, who have paid the admission, read the title *Illywhacker* on the door of Badgery's cage, heeded the *caveat emptor* and stayed for the stories, include, of course, the readers of the book.

Badgery's grandson Hissao, the proprietor of this Best Pet Shop in the World, has 'put so many of his fellow countrymen and women on display' that the display is almost all-encompassing: 'Who could possibly compete with it?' How could Australian visitors possibly not recognise themselves? The display can no more be false than it can be true: all that matters is that it be exhaustive. Debunking it is useless, because there is no truth it hides, no falsehood to do the hiding, only a spectacular machinery of attraction where truth and falsehood are effects and come-ons. The sign on Leah Goldstein's door says 'Melbourne Jew'; she 'spends a lot of time explaining that she is not a Jew, that the sign is a lie, that the exhibition is based on lies; but visitors prefer to believe the printed information.' Within Hissao's 'masterpiece', even political contestation is just part of the display, the spectacle of controversy. Hissao himself is powerless, proprietor in name only, absorbed into the merchandise:

> It would be of no benefit for him to know that he is, himself, a lie, that he is no more substantial than this splendid four-storey mirage, teetering above Pitt Street, no more concrete than all those alien flowers, those neon signs, those twisted coloured forms in gas and glass that their inventors, dull men, think will last forever.

If the present and the immediate future belong to the gaze of tourism, with the proud traditions of illywhacking and independence simply another product to be consumed by others (or by Australians as others), then the past too has always been a series of lies, as the opening paragraph of M. V. Anderson's 'history' suggests:

> Our forefathers were all great liars. They lied about the lands they selected and the cattle they owned. They lied about their backgrounds and the parentage

of their wives. However it is their first lie that is the most impressive for being the most monumental, i.e., that the continent, at the time of first settlement, was said to be occupied but not cultivated and by that simple device they were able to give the legal owners short shrift and, when they objected, to use the musket or poison flour, and to do so with a clear conscience. It is in the context of this great foundation stone that we must begin our study of Australian history.

Badgery has never really been the even precarious master of his own lies: they have always been somebody else's lies. The voice that asserts itself with such individuality, individualism and independence is always at risk of dissolving out into other voices, or forever talking itself into a corner, or a cage. It is a voice that is its own dispossession, a fabric of voices from elsewhere.

It's this that Badgery tries to keep at bay with his insistent irony: there are, he acknowledges, other voices in this story— a large part of the text, after all, may be Leah Goldstein's, and that too may be no more than lies. Badgery tries to deny that these voices are anyone's but his. When this is not possible, he tries to circumscribe them, in effect to place quotes around them to show where they begin and end, to minimise their invasion of his text, and to distance himself from them with scorn. (Much of that scorn is directed at the reader: the very act of reading turns one into the spieler's mark. More importantly, the voice Badgery has to speak in is none other than his audience's: it's a question of giving the customers what they want.)

But it doesn't and can't work. Badgery cannot close off the quotation marks, and mark off what definitively remains his utterance, because the property and propriety of his language are not his in the first place. Attempting to ironise, he instead becomes ironised himself. The speaking subject haemorrhages out into a spoken subject, spoken from somewhere else. The subject can no longer separate itself from what comes from without and constitutes it as imaginary and dislocated; and yet, in the same movement, it can no longer be anything but that speech of the other, captive, its barest residue, on the garrulous verge of silence.

Badgery's tales not only draw on certain traditions of Australian writing; they are themselves a writing of 'Australian traditions', whether these be fictional or metafictional and critical. 'Tradition' is here no longer something as idealist as the expression of a national individualism, a voice which essentially, necessarily, unstoppably speaks from an entire nation. It is rather the very means by which the idea of such a 'national individualism' is constructed, and involves all the apparatuses of production, consumption, propagation, staging and spectacle, as summed up in the dominant metaphor of the Pet Emporium.

Under the noise and dazzle of the birthday celebrations [1988 marked the bicentennial of English settlement in Australia] that are almost on us, and the rising hum of traditions being summed, Herbert Badgery grumbles on about myths of servitude.

Helen Daniel (essay date 1988)

SOURCE: "Lies for Sale: Peter Carey," in *Liars: Australian New Novelists,* Penguin Books, 1988, pp. 148-84.

[*Daniel is an Australian critic. In the following excerpt, she provides an overview of Carey's works through* Oscar and Lucinda.]

Illywhacker opens with the Liar's paradox: 'I am a terrible liar and I have always been a liar.' Herbert announces this early 'to set things straight'. He urges us not to waste time trying to 'pull apart the strands of lies and truth, but to relax and enjoy the show'. He is a liar and a showman, and he is also a salesman. He gives fair warning to the buyer, but he is a good salesman, his goods are glossy, and the *caveat* becomes a forgotten small-print clause. Herbert is a used-car salesman and, with his 'salesman's sense of history', he is also selling us used-history, second-hand history. So who is the previous owner of this history Herbert Badgery is selling? What kind of deal have they got going between them? Badgery is the go-between in the business of the Lie, the showman in the showroom, the previous owner, Peter Carey. As Herbert sells us second-hand history, Carey is outside the showroom, Carey-Escher watching Herbert Badgery's hands drawing each other. The Liar is Carey, the reader is the buyer, and the real business deal is the Lie of fiction. *Caveat emptor.*

Herbert Badgery is not only negotiating with the reader to sell us Carey's Lie. He is also the narrator, the *Spieler* go-between, the entrepreneur between the characters and the writer, and he is not an honourable intermediary: some of the history he is selling us has been stolen from Leah Goldstein. Outraged, Leah accuses Herbert of the theft:

> A hundred things come to me, things that amused me at the time, touched me—and now I see they were only excuses to thieve things from me. And even then you have not done me the honour of thieving things whole but have taken a bit here, a bit there, snipped, altered and so on. You have stolen like a barbarian, slashing a bunch of grapes from the middle of a canvas.

But who is the barbarian? Leah blames Herbert but she does not suspect the existence of the Pig Tyrant Carey.

At the start of *Illywhacker,* Herbert is beached, 'like some old squid decaying on the beach'. In Carey's story, **'Concerning the Greek Tyrant'** [from *The Tabloid Story Pocket Book,* edited by Michael Wilding, 1978], Homer's characters are beached too, waiting on the beach because Homer is tossing in a fever, afraid he cannot cope with the next episode, afraid Odysseus will accuse him of mismanagement, afraid of mutiny. Odysseus reminds him sharply that it is worse for the men waiting on the beach. Echion is a battle-scarred veteran, questioning the reason for his terrible sufferings, and so is a dangerous character who could start the mutiny Homer dreads. Suspicious of Odysseus, Echion reads his papers and finds they are not navigational but verse—and contain a plot to kill him. Angry, Echion resolves to escape but Homer, a man he did not know existed, intervenes and ties him up. Echion manages to free himself and escapes—only to die in exactly the way Homer had plotted. But Echion's death was for nothing. Homer scrubbed the episode. We are left with a strange pity for Echion—Echion who is only a possibility Carey sees in Homer's story, a possible character, not even a real character. Before he died, Echion scrawled in the dust, 'KILL THE PIG TYRANT HOMER WHO OPPRESSES US ALL'. What of Carey whose existence Echion never suspected? Echion dies ignorant of the existence of the real Pig Tyrant, Carey. Carey is Echion's killer—and gets off scot free, while Echion lies bleeding in the dust. Behind Homer is the Pig Tyrant Carey.

So who stole Leah Goldstein's story? Who is the barbarian who did the slashing? Herbert or Carey? Who killed Harry Joy and sent a Good Bloke to Hell? Who stole Herbert's daughter, broke up his marriage, sent him to prison, made him live for 139 years and left him beached like an old squid? The Pig Tyrant Carey. But then being written up is no novelty to Herbert, in fact it is one of his weaknesses. So he has some good business deal with the Liar, who is outside the showroom where Herbert is trying to sell us his used-history. So sit back, relax and buy. Lies for sale.

Bliss is a novel built on an Escher double vision of heaven and hell, life and death, bliss and despair. But it is not so simple as double vision: Carey writes of 'the infinite onion of the universe' and of peeling back layers and layers of reality. A Godelian layering runs throughout his work, up and down a Tangled Hierarchy. One of his best known stories is **'Peeling'**, where layer after layer is peeled away from the woman revealing first her marginal selves, and finally a white doll. Underneath the layers of reality, which Carey peels away one by one, is the white doll, an absurdist truth.

> I like to write like a cartoonist—I look at things that exist and push them to their ludicrous or logical extension . . . When you push far enough, you can find yourself in some strange and original places. [Peter Carey in an interview with Janet Hawley, in *The Age* (26 September 1981)]

This is a Liar's push, 'ludicrous or logical' extensions of things, reminding us at every step of his own strategies and artifice. In **'The Fat Man in History'**, Carey comments on Alexander Finch.

> He enjoys himself with these theories, he has a love of such constructions, building ideas like card houses, extending them until he gets dizzy and trembles at their heights.

Thus does Carey build his fictions, like card houses, which leave the reader dizzy and trembling at their heights. Often Carey begins with the seemingly familiar, then suddenly jolts us into the surrealistic or the absurd. Often he works through a shift in our temporal or spatial bearings, disorienting the reader. His characters are sliding identities, who suddenly slip into a new marginal self or into a different time scale. Carey has a wonderful sense of play, enjoys playing with those incongruous aspects of reality that blur and trick, events that are no longer innocent but deceptive and devious. The Liar flaunting his Lie.

Born in 1943, Peter Carey grew up in Bacchus Marsh, Victoria, where his father ran the family car business. He attended Geelong Grammar for seven years, then studied science for one year at Monash University, drawn to chemistry as a magical world, 'transmuting one element into another' [Carey in an interview with Alison Summers, in *The National Times* (1-7 November 1985)]. In a way which recalls Foster, Carey found magic in

> organic chemistry—which I never understood—but it was the alchemy of it that fascinated me, things changing into other things. So perhaps whatever it was I was looking for in organic chemistry I finally found in fiction. [Carey in an interview with Candida Baker, in *Yacker: Australian Writers Talk about Their Work,* 1986]

He then joined an advertising agency, where he worked with Barry Oakley, Morris Lurie and Bruce Petty. He lived in Melbourne until 1967, then he went to London and, in 1968, wrote a novel, 'this very maniacal and highly mandarin novel which out-Becketted Beckett and out-Robbe-Grilleted Robbe-Grillet' [Carey in an interview with Frank Moorhouse, in *Australian Literary Studies* (October 1977)]. Now he mocks the obscurity of it and, believing firmly in 'the possibility of popular art that's good art in anybody's terms' [Carey in an interview with John Maddocks, in *Southerly* (March 1981)], he prefers to write for as broad an audience as possible. He returned to Australia and advertising, which he wrote about in **'War Crimes'**.

> The story is actually just like real life, like working in an advertising agency. It pushes things to extremes a bit—people are shot rather than fired. But that's just the logic of business anyway . . . That's my business story.

His first collection of short stories, *The Fat Man in History,* was published in 1974 and in 1980 the second, *War Crimes,* which won the New South Wales Premier's Award. A combined collection of his stories was published as *Exotic Pleasures* and his stories have been translated and published in Japanese, German, Dutch and Swedish.

Written while Carey lived in a Queensland commune and commuted to a Sydney advertising agency, his first novel, *Bliss,* won the New South Wales Premier's Award and the Miles Franklin and national Book Council Awards. Critics at the Cannes Film Festival were not enthusiastic about the film *Bliss,* but in 1985, it won the Australian Film Institute Awards—Best Film, Best Director, best Script (written by Carey and Ray Lawrence). His second novel, *Illywhacker* (1985) won *The Age* Book of the Year Award, The National Book Council Award, the Barbara Ramsden Award of the Victorian Fellowship of Australian Writers and was shortlisted for the 1985 Booker Prize. First published in 1988, Carey's third novel, *Oscar and Lucinda,* is a dazzling Lie set in the eighteen-sixties. Carey suggests,

> A lot of it's to do—I think—with Christianity and Christian stories and their effect on our culture. I'm interested in that; I grew up with it around me, but the tales seem to have gone now, just the last echoes of them are around . . . [interview with Baker]

Shades of the storytelling in *Bliss,* which is itself a 'post-Christian' novel. In a shimmering play of light and dark, *Oscar and Lucinda* is also about the molten mysteries in the manufacture of glass—and the manufacture of the Lie.

Carey's literary kin include Borges, Barthelme, Brautigan, Vonnegut, and in some ways Marquez whom Carey much admires for 'his ability to blend elements of fantasy and reality on a big scale, with some complexity'. Other writers he enjoys include the French new wave writers (Sarraute, Robbe-Grillet, Butor), Kosinksi (especially *The Painted Bird*), Faulkner, Kerouac, Joyce and Nabokov 'who really loved setting little rabbit snares'. Carey's stories bring to mind Borges' idea of the 'secret plot', the arcane element in narrative. Borges' theme of a man caught in a trap he has himself unwittingly constructed is Carey's theme in the story **'Kristu Du'** as well as *Bliss,* but it runs throughout his work. Like Borges' stories, Carey's are often built on precise, substantiating detail which brings a weird air of probability to the fantastic and the bizarre, a disturbing vision of the unknown and the nightmarish emerging from inside the known.

In **'Crabs'**, Carey moves from the apparently familiar into the sudden futuristic or surrealistic world where the Karboys prowl and plunder, while Crabs himself, a nervous daredevil trying to escape from his own fears, finds himself plunged into the drive-in nightmare. The drive-in theatre is in part a refugee-camp, where he is stranded, being stripped of hope as his car is stripped first of two wheels, then of generator, carburetors, distributor, battery. He plots against his loss, struggling to reconstruct his hopes with the car, but under the bonnet are gaps, holes, emptinesses. Trucks arrive bringing other crippled cars, further distorting his hopes of escape. He decides that 'to be free, you must be a motor car or vehicle in good health' (*The Fat Man in History*), and so becomes one. When he moves freely outside the fence, he finds only a deserted world, and is left looking through the fence at the lights, the movement, the people inside the theatre boundaries. Carey himself has commented,

> he spends all his time escaping from something which he finds unsatisfactory only to realise finally that what he's trying to escape from is the world, and there he is outside the fence.

He is left trapped in the wasteland outside the fence.

In **'Peeling'**, the narrator is contemplating the prospect of unhurried exploration of the woman, Nile, preferring 'to know these things, the outside layers, before we come to the centre of things'. Their relationship, he insists, is 'beyond analysis', his sense of time is stilled—'Normally it seems to be late afternoon'. He is content to contemplate change as a slow process, in slow motion, disappointed when she hastens it, and finds her behaviour promiscuous. His slowness is very deliberate, a practised discipline of eking out pleasures, for fear of emptiness, of nothing to do. In a world of white and her white dolls stripped of feature, where he would prefer more colour, 'more character about it', he contemplates 'moving layer after layer, until I discover her true colours'. He finds first the other marginal selves she contains, the young male, the woman beneath the male, but then as a stocking is unrolled, a limb disappears, until she is exposed as nothing, only the fragments of a small white doll without features. The more he tries to discover her true self, the more tightly he is embroiled in a surreal nightmare: the threads unravel and reveal nothing. **'Peeling'** is a brilliant, surrealistic fiction of the fear that, if we peel back the layers of the infinite onion of the universe, there will be nothing, or only an image, without features.

Like Borges' stories, Carey's are often built on precise, substantiating detail which brings a weird air of probability to the fantastic and the bizarre, a disturbing vision of the unknown and the nightmarish emerging from inside the known.

—*Helen Daniel*

Two stories hinge on absurd contradiction, an existential paradox. In **'Life and Death in the South Side Pavilion'**, Carey creates a Kafkaesque predicament, in which the narrator, Shepherd 3rd Class, is engaged in an absurd activity, employed by The Company to prevent the horses falling into the swimming pool and drowning. He feels bound to remain in his job until they all drown, which it is his job to prevent. When he deliberately allows them all to drown, so that he will be free and able to leave the Pavilion with Marie, replacement horses are delivered by The Company the next day. **'A Windmill in the West'** has a similar absurdity but is more elaborate. The American soldier stands at his post on the line of electrified fence, which shimmers away into the distance, dividing east and west, one side designated the United States, the other Australia. His duty, to prevent unauthorized people from crossing, is to be carried out in ignorance of the length, shape, status and function of the line. In isolation, ignorant of what the line divides, encircles or contains, he loses all orientation, confusing east and west, inside and outside. In the absence of categories, he tries to devise his own measurements and definitions, killing scorpions in order to calculate the area of desert now free of scorpions. The spatial dislocation extends to a dislocation of his sense of self, a loss of connection with his own reflected image.

> He can see his face in the shaving mirror, like the surface of a planet, a photograph of the surface of the moon in 'Life' magazine. It is strange and unknown to him. He rubs his hands over it, more to cover the reflected image than to feel its texture.

Unable to determine the significance of the aeroplane, he finally shoots it down. He acts distantly, as if observing his own actions and he has no categories by which to assess the significance of his action. Within a surrealistic structure, this is a marvelous Kafkaesque fiction of disorientation and loss of the categories by which we define and determine our actions.

'American Dreams' turns on the notion of the real and the artifice co-existing, the scale model the means of both realizing and destroying the dreams of the real country town. The idea of building, which runs through **'Kristu Du'** and later *Illywhacker,* is part of Carey's transmutation of things as well as people. The story builds up the mystery of Gleason's actions, and speculates on his motives. The townspeople's dreams of the big city, wealth, modern houses and big motor cars, their American dreams, are realized through the model town. But the town is stilled too, stopped on the knife-edge of its self-consciousness, transfixed in the past. The narrator is left feeling guilty and, like the townspeople generally, bereft of his dreams. Unlike the slow, suspenseful building in **'American Dreams'**, **'Report on the Shadow Industry'** immediately proclaims its central fiction of an industry, with factories, all the encumbrances of industrial technology and commercial marketing—of which the product is shadows. Shadows have different value, good and bad, beautiful and despairing, but, without shadows, there is 'the feeling of emptiness, that awful despair that comes when one has failed to grasp the shadow'. At the end, the narrator admits

> My own feelings about the shadows are ambivalent, to say the least. For here I have manufactured one more: elusive, unsatisfactory, hinting at greater beauties and more profound mysteries that exist somewhere before the beginning and somewhere after the end.

Carey turns the fiction round to comment on itself and the manufacture of shadows, without which there is only emptiness.

In **'The Fat Man in History'**, the revolution spawns a new notion of fat men as greedy oppressors and, somehow American, grotesque enemies of the people. Alexander Finch is the secretary of the clandestine 'Fat Men Against the Revolution', living communally with its leader Fantoni and four others in a slum ghetto, their only trusted link to the outside world, Nancy Bowlby. The story builds to the fantastic notion of eating her as a political protest, which in Finch's formal rationale becomes an act of consummation by which the Fat Men will purify the revolution. But it is Fantoni himself whom they devour, when the man-who-won't-give-his-name kills Fantoni and assumes his role. The unexpectedly chilling end is the discovery that the whole sequence is part of a continuing experiment, a study of revolution in a closed society in which Nancy always precipitates change and the heir-apparent, the-man-who-won't-give-his-name, always supplants the Fantoni.

These are unforgettable fictions, the kind which lodge in your mind ineradicably and open up new strange territories of the real. Reality smudges across into the fabulous and the fantastic, as these fictions construct their own points of reference and then suddenly offer us new bearings on an old reality. Out of this exploration of the dark myths comes a new perspective on the real. All the stories in *The Fat Man in History* have what Carey has called a 'cool, hard surface', pared down, precise, with a finely tuned logic by which he elaborates the central absurdity or fabulous notion.

As a collection of short stories, *The Fat Man in History* I think is unsurpassed in Australian literature, even by *War Crimes* which is another brilliant collection. Carey has commented that, although his characters tend to be defeated, in *War Crimes* 'the characters are starting to win' because it is 'a more complex battle and a more complex defeat'. In *War Crimes,* Carey explores collective fears and imaginings of the future. Vast and awful possibilities loom up out of the present, which the mind finds intolerable and shuns. Carey takes us into these possibilities, makes us examine them, recognize and work out our choices.

In the title story ["War Crimes"], the narrator insists he is one of us.

> And I am not mad, but rather I have opened the door you all keep locked with frightened bolts and little prayers. I am more like you than you know. You have not inspected the halls and attics. You haven't got yourself grubby in the cellars. Instead you sit in the front room in worn blue jeans, reading about atrocities in the Sunday papers.

He knows he will, in the end, be judged, by people who 'have supported wars they have not fought in, and damned companies they have not had the courage to destroy'. He will be judged a tyrant, a psychopath, an aberrant accountant, but, in this war, he insists his conduct is no aberration, but a more deliberate version of the normal and accepted conduct of business in our world. This is the norm of commercial war, their methods of motivating salesmen 'historically necessary'. He and Bart have become 'the Andy Warhols of business', and the story has, at moments, a macabre humour, with Bart strutting in his cowboy boots and waving his gun menacingly at top executives. The story has truly a black absurdist humour, full of menace and horror, which owes much to the cool, elaborating detail by which Carey relentlessly convinces us of its truth. It is set in the bitter disenchantment of the future, in a world in which there are roving gangs of vagabond unemployed and apocalyptic sects preach millennial doom, a future which is railing at its own disarray and 'surely, the Last Days'. The multitudinous unemployed camp around the boundaries of the food factories, executing the executive who appears outside its gates until they are themselves the victims of atrocities carried out by an army of workers under the orders of the accountant who watches from his window.

> As I watched men run through the heat burning other men alive, I knew that thousands of men had stood on hills or roofs and watched such scenes of terrible destruction, the result of nothing more than their fears and their intelligence.

In the interests of business, Bart's hatred is diverted to the unemployed, by day obscure grey figures in a drab landscape, by night a menace licking at the face of darkness.

Some stories in *War Crimes* hinge on a central paradox, such as **'The Journey of a Lifetime'**, in which all the mystique and wonder of the train journey, so long anticipated, is sullied and corrupted by its purpose, a journey of execution and death. In **'The Uses of Williamson Wood'**, the grim, cruel reality of sexual assault smears across the girl's fantasy world, which becomes also the domain of her rebellion and revenge. Carey sustains the two worlds finely, as they blur into each other. Some longer stories are constructed out of a central absurdist notion, which Carey elaborates into an image of a futuristic society. In **'Do You Love Me?'**, he begins with the wondrous notion that parts of the country are becoming less real. Then he traces the beginnings of dematerialization, first of the neglected nether regions of the land, then of buildings and finally of people.

In **'The Chance'**, one of the best of Carey's stories, he sets up a futuristic world in a post-American era, where people undergo grotesque change in the Genetic Lottery. Social institutions are breaking down, abandoned ferries rust away, gangs of unemployed rove through the streets, people plunder and devastate isolated by fear and self-interest, religious sects are spawned—all through 'the total embrace of a cancerous philosophy of change'. The narrator begins to rediscover some of the moral values and categories of the remembered past but cannot avert the girl's grotesque change into an old hag so she can be part of the Hup revolutionary vanguard. In the Genetic Lottery, 'a new shrill current of desperate selfishness' is carelessly fostered by the exploiting Fastalogians and the people are the blind accomplices to their own ruin. With each change, the self gains a new outer cladding and loses a little of the remembered past. The story grows from absurd notions of change and beauty, which twist around into ugly people in an ugly society. Underneath the blindness of the people is Carey's sense of an aesthetics of the real.

Throughout *War Crimes,* the notion of aesthetics recurs in fantastic ways. The narrator in the title story ["War Crimes"] is horrified by factories which are for him monstrous yawning caverns in which terrible mutilations are carried out, but he is horrified too at the idea that factories might be less ugly, less brutal. In **'Exotic Pleasures'**, the superficial beauty of the silken blue Pleasure Bird blinds Lilly to its menace so that she becomes an accomplice to its ultimate 'complicated and elegant victory' over Earth. In **'Kristu-Du'**, the aesthetics of an ideal blinds the architect to the ugliness and horror of the tyrant for whom he constructs his beautiful gleaming dome. Employed by a mass murderer but anaesthetized by his dream of Kristu-Du, the architect has an almost mystical faith in its saving power, 'an immense benevolent force capable of overthrowing tyrannies and welding tribes into nations'. He abrogates all moral values and categories in pursuit of his dream, but is left only with the twisting irony of an architectural error. Through all of these, as in **'The Chance'**, Carey suggests that an aesthetic which owes no allegiance to the real and the moral is a destructive force which threatens the future of our world.

In **'War Crimes'**, Carey says of Bart:

> His mind was relentless in its logic, yet fanciful in style, so the most circuitous and fanciful plans would always, on examination, be found to have cold hard bones within their diaphanous folds.

Carey's stories too have cold hard bones within their diaphanous folds. Carey has suggested,

> The stories themselves ask questions. They say 'What

if?' You look at the way people live their lives, and ask if they have to live like that; what happens if they organise themselves another way?

Pushing the hypothetical through to horrifyingly logical limits, he speculates on what happens if the new shrill self-interest is unchecked, if unemployment is a matter of indifference, if the Americans stay, if the Americans go, if we pursue beauty according only to glossy phantoms of it and without regard for the beauty of the real world. He speculates on self-interest as the basis of ethical and political systems, watches the world begin to dematerialize, watches it taken over by exotic birds and plants which destroy it, watches it submit to an alien power in pursuit of an absurd notion of change and beauty. His fictions shock and jolt the reader, startling him out of conventional attitudes and perhaps out of an apathy which is complicity and assent to a grotesque future.

The caretaker who was the last to leave the I.C.I. building, just as it was dematerializing in **'Do You Love Me?'**, looked almost translucent and claimed he had been able to see 'other worlds, layer upon layer, through the fabric of the here and now'. In all Carey's stories, there is a translucency, through which we glimpse the infinite onion of the universe, with all its layers of reality. Carey sets up extravagant worlds which reflect a fantastic mirror image of reality and peels back layers in the Godelian hierarchy of existence. In *Bliss,* Harry Joy also discovers 'that there were many different worlds, layer upon layer, as thin as filo pastry'. His first death lasts for nine minutes, during which time ecstasy touches him and he finds he can slide between the spaces in the air. He recognizes 'the worlds of pleasure and worlds of pain, bliss and punishment, Heaven and Hell'. At the very start of the novel, Carey sets up the double notions that are our landmarks, the points from which we take our bearings as we move through strange new territory. Life and death, pleasure and pain, Heaven and Hell, bliss and punishment, embodiment and disembodiment—these are the poles the novel offers at the start, as Harry Joy slides between the spaces in the air above the earth peering down at the body lying below. These familiar landmarks are complicated and blurred through the novel. Like Harry, Carey is a cartographer, beginning with the known before exploring and mapping out a strange new territory, the double vision of the Lie.

Harry himself is a familiar figure at the outset: a Good Bloke, a conventional family man, living in a conventional house and style, in a conventional job. He is blind to the faults in others and to the injustices of the world which is surely conventional too. He is 'not particularly intelligent, not particularly successful, not particularly handsome and not particularly rich'. His vision will be complicated, he will stumble into strange new territories of his own life. He, who inhabits the middle ground of existence, will be thrust into the extraordinary and the extreme.

He was like someone who has lain in bed too long eating rich food: within his soul there was suddenly a yearning for tougher, stronger things, for ecstasies, for the thrill of goodness perfectly achieved, to see butterflies in doorways in Belize, to be part of the lightning dance, to quiver in terror before the cyclone.

Instead of being 'not particularly' anything, Harry Joy wants to feel the sharp edges of experience; he yearns for the bliss and the terror. In a Borgesian way, he finds both inside his own existence, when he peels back the surface layer with which he has been content and discovers new layers of his own existence, new perceptions of 'a universe made like an infinite onion'.

Harry has been 'suckled on stories' in the innocent world of childhood, imbibing a world which was fresh and green:

> Dew drops full of visions hung from morning grass and old Clydesdales stood silently in the paddock above the creek. Crickets sang songs and everything had meanings. The sky was full of Gods and Indians and people smiled at him, touched him, stroked him, and brought him extraordinary gifts from the world outside where there were, he knew, exotic bazaars filled with people in gowns, strange fruits piled high, the air redolent with spices, and Jesus Christ, and the Good Samaritan, always dressed in his dusty grey robe with its one red patch on the left sleeve, and the soldier offering the dripping red sponge of wine to Jesus, and there were small boiled sweets and white sheets and the smell of bread, and floor polish and, far away, New York, its glass towers trembling in an ecstasy of magic which was to become, his father said, one day, after the next flood, a splendid book read by all mankind with wonder.

Bliss opens with a gathering of myths, myths of innocence and purity, myths that no longer hold. These myths, religious, moral, political and national, social and existential, are the myths of Harry Joy's time, which is our time. The opening of the novel is closely tied to narrative and storytelling, the inherited stories, the myths of Good and Evil and Clydesdales, of crickets and the smell of bread and floor polish, of moral landmarks lighting up the map of existence. In Harry's childhood, lit by the glow of the Vision Splendid, he received the myths. When Harry himself becomes the storyteller, passing on his heritage to his family, he transmits the stories imperfectly, without understanding them, and they take on different meanings. Vance Joy's stories have

> drifted like groundsel seeds and taken root in the most unlikely places. They had rarely grown in the way he would have imagined, in that perfect green landscape of his imagination, intersected with streams and redolent of orange blossom.

In certain climates they became like weeds, uncontrollable, not always beautiful, a blaze of rage or desire from horizon to horizon.

At the outset of the novel, Carey establishes the notion of a heritage received, transmitted without understanding and thereby changed, become weedlike, choking growth. It is a heritage of meaning, which in Harry Joy's time has been lost.

Vance's stories of New York contain apocalyptic visions and conflicts between Good and Evil, but like his other stories they have changed in Harry's telling. Amid the stories of Harry's childhood, always New York, New York, 'the most beautiful and terrible city on earth. All good, all evil exists there'. Now, dreaming of New York, Bettina is marooned in one of the outposts of the American Empire. Subscribing to the articles of the American Faith, she believes in,

> the benevolence of their companies, the triumph of the astronauts, the law of the market-place and the twin threats of Communism and the second-rate, although not necessarily in that order.

The townspeople are more ambivalent than Bettina, envying American power but 'wishing to reject it and embrace it all at once', at once attracted and repelled. Set, according to the Liar, on the edge of the American Empire, *Bliss* plays with the talismanic myth of New York, the dream of its gleaming towers.

In a novel which is a post-Christian fable of our times, Harry tries to conceive a new eschatology, a new god, new myths for our time. He makes a list of all religions and, to the Reverend Desmond Pearce, announces his decision that they are all wrong. He ponders on the notion of a new god.

> Maybe it's a god like none you've ever thought of. Maybe it's a 'they' and not a he. Maybe it's a great empty part of space charged with electricity. Maybe it's a whole lot of things in a space ship and flying saucers are really angels . . . I will tell you two things: the first is that there is an undiscovered religion, and the second is that there definitely is a Hell.

Harry begins an ontological quest for meaning, a post-Christian quest for salvation, in a post-Christian novel where salvation and damnation are not clear, untrammelled opposites but conjoined, twin modes like the concave and the convex of an Escher vision.

As Harry begins to move beyond the Christian landmarks, to map out the new territory he discovers in the universe, the god-like narrator becomes our guide and commentator. Like the disembodied Harry registering with sharp clarity the body lying down below, Carey's narrator watches from above, from outside, observing all that is played out in the narrative and

commenting on it. He plays with time and sequence, anticipating future developments, retracing earlier events, disrupt-
ing the lines of his narrative and fracturing our sense of time.
He watches Aldo in the restaurant, murmuring 'It would be
another minute before he would know . . .'. He comments in
collusive asides to the reader, nudging at us: 'It was not a
question that would have occurred to Harry, who had never
seen his family as you, dear reader, have now been privileged to.' Like some literary deity, he knows all, sees and
hears all, knows the past of all the characters, their dreams
and delusions, can tell their stories in fragments, setting them
in motion inside the story of Harry. He stands back, detached,
grave, sometimes gently tolerant, sometimes wryly amused.
Then he steps forward to comment, elaborate, dislocate and
remind us of his artifice. He already knows where Harry is
going, is already familiar with the territory, has already heard
the story.

Harry Joy is trapped in a Hell which he has himself constructed. After his second death, Harry knows he is in Hell.
He conducts periodic tests of his own sanity, making notes
and observations on his own behaviour, and he amasses formidable evidence that this is Hell. On his white map of this
'unknown continent', he begins pencilling in marks, which
are crude and inexact at first, 'but surely even Livingstone
must have become lost occasionally and needed some high
ground to see the lay of the land'. He is not only an explorer
in the unknown territory of his life but also a zoologist devising keys and codes for classifying the creatures he finds in
this new territory. It is an Orwellian classification and similar
to [Australian novelist David] Ireland's terms of freedom and
captivity in *A Woman of the Future.* But in **Bliss** the captivity
is another face of freedom, the double modes of sly actors.
Harry learns how to identify the Actors employed by Those
In Charge to persecute the Captives.

> On his walks, he saw ugliness and despair where once
> he would have found an acceptable world: goitrous
> necks, phlegmy coughs, scabrous skin, lost legs, wall
> eyes, dropping hair, crooked spines, lost hope, and
> all of this he noted.

But this dark vision of ugliness and deformity, an existential
horror, is shifted suddenly, with Carey's usual incongruity,
into Harry's unexpected boredom. He shrugs it off with a
quick new optimism, only to have both the optimism and his
car crushed by an elephant. This wonderfully parodic sequence culminates in Harry's testing out storytelling, preliminary lies, to save himself from the police, a comic anticipation
of his own salvation at Bog Onion Road—and a quick glimpse
of Herbert Badgery waiting in the wings, eager to start whack-
ing the illy.

Released by the police, Harry Joy crosses the river Styx.

> Barges carried their carcinogens up river and neon
> lights advertised their final formulations against a
> blackening sky.

> Harry Joy, his face ghastly with hives, his suit filthy,
> his chest bleeding, his back sore, lounged sideways
> in the back seat, drugged with sweet success. The
> buildings of Hell, glossy, black-windowed, gleam-
> ing with reflected lights, did not seem to him uncon-
> querable. It seemed that a person of imagination and
> resources might well begin to succeed here, to re-
> main dry, warm, and free from punishment.

He resolves to be Good, trying out self-abasement and humility, but that too shifts suddenly when, with residual doubt,
he determines on One Last Test because the evidence so far
he finds 'insufficient to justify this terrible, risky strategy of
Goodness'. In the tree scene which is a fine parody of the
Tree of Knowledge, Harry conducts the Final Test and at the
windows of Hell, he discovers the full family horror—
Bettina's infidelity with Joel, his children's incestuous com-
merce. Having discovering the infernal truth of his family,
his friends and the products marketed by his agency, he re-
coils from it to the relative safety of the Hilton Hotel. As a
diversion from 'the razor-blade tortures of Hell', he fires his
clients, Krappe Chemicals, and standing in the epicentre of
Hell, he studies the cancer map. The whole sequence in the
Hilton Hotel and the beginnings of Harry's education by his
new mentor, Honey Barbara, 'pantheist, healer, whore', all
culminate in David's financing his father's committal to the
hospital. When, by the intervention of chance and contingency, Alex Duval is taken to the hospital in Harry's place,
Harry enters the depths of his Hell and experiences a new
horror, loss of identity, which is the climax of the novel and
its double vision.

The hospital scenes have a splendid mixture of absurdity and
horror as well as tightening the intellectual tensions of the
novel. Until the outside intervention of the formidable wife
of Alex Duval, Harry is steadily dispossessed of his own identity, stripped down to a residual self which is somehow not
his own. The centre of his private gravity shifts and his deter-
minations are no longer his own, but taken over by Alex.
Harry contends not only with the institution but also with the
constant presence of a rival claimant to the disputed commodity of Harry Joy's identity. The rival is actively resentful
and reproachful at Harry's attempts to retrieve his own identity. It becomes wonderfully absurd, a kind of titanic struggle
between them, each one tugging at the name and the identity
of Harry Joy—the right to dress, walk, talk, behave, the right
to be Harry Joy. It becomes a nightmare of dispossession,
with Carey outside the frame delighting in the paradoxes, as
the two Escher hands struggle for possession of Harry Joy's
identity. This is classic Carey, with the companion figure of
Nurse burying his memories in the garden for safe-keeping
and periodically digging them up to see which ones have been
stolen from him by shock treatment. Harry accompanies Nurse

round the garden to check his store of memories, with the marvelous notion that one can lose one's whole identity by institutional theft or by the takeover bid of an old mate.

Through Alex, Carey exploits the notions of role-swapping and sliding identities, in which the self, whatever is left of it, is marginal, vestigial. Harry is upset in puzzling, contradictory ways by the changes in Alex as Alex grows into the role of Harry, and disconcerted by watching Alex/Harry's behaviour. It becomes a kind of split identity which they share, both marginal selves watching the shared self of Harry on which they both make claims. Harry begins to feel the pain of the people around him, developing a sympathy for the plights of others which is far removed from the figure at the start of the novel who was blind to other people and blind to the injustices of the world. But there is more to come: when Alex prevails upon Harry to accept that he should play Alex, not only does Harry quickly begin 'to embrace the pale, shuffling unhappiness of an Alex', but as Harry/Alex his whole status in the community changes radically. He ponders on the folly of seeking 'salvation by giving away the trappings of power', that is, the privilege of being Harry Joy, and realizes the consequences:

> While he had still been the legitimate Harry Joy some power was attached to him . . . But once he was an Alex everyone knew he was a crumpled thing, a failure, defenceless. Three silk shirts were stolen from him and were worn, brazenly, in his presence . . .

> They had authority over him. They made him sweep the concrete paths and he did it. They tried to feed him like an Alex. They did it for sport. For their amusement. They brought him big doughnuts and laughed at him when he pulled faces.

At Nurse's insistence, he writes everything he learned from Honey Barbara, particularly about food, in the book for burial in the garden, for fear of losing that too. While the new Harry Joy confers with Alice in her office and orders the old men about, the new Alex hears him and is jealous, envying the loud happy laugh of Alex/Harry, envying his peace of mind. The masterly touch here is that after all Harry's deliberations on Actors playing out roles, the novel reaches this climactic sequence of role-playing and role-swapping, in which Alex and Harry become actors playing each other. They impersonate each other, identities sliding to and fro between them, the way Heaven and Hell have been impersonating one another, sliding to and fro throughout the novel. It is the climactic pitch of the double vision on which the entire novel is built, but unfortunately the novel now begins to falter and grow frail as Carey relaxes the doubleness.

It is ironic that happiness is much more difficult to represent than misery and pain, that bliss is much more elusive than horror. In ***Bliss,*** this is a particularly pungent irony. Once the

novel actually tackles bliss and salvation, it does not have the same impact or intensity as the earlier part. Honey Barbara and the idyllic existence in Bog Onion Road never manifest the same energy as the account of Harry's descent into Hell. The scenes of Honey Barbara as part of the household in Palm Avenue and the events leading to Bettina's death in the Mobil explosion, then the death of Joel, as well as the interpolated narrative of David's mock-heroic death, are all narrated briskly. But Harry himself is elusive at this stage, his motives enigmatic. Drawn to the feel of silk and money, his commercial energies are quickened again by Bettina's ability and her renewed vision of herself as a hot-shot on the way to New York. The notion of Hell recedes and Harry is content to regard himself as 'a prisoner with special privileges'.

The theme of cancer which has been sustained through the novel in moral, economic, health and political terms, develops into a futuristic vision of anarchy, against which Carey tries to set the Bog Onion Road version of salvation. It is an unequal battle and the supposedly idyllic existence of the community at Bog Onion Road does not stand up against the earlier black absurdity. In part Harry's salvation is story-telling, telling Vance's stories with new understanding.

> And when he told stories about the trees and the spirits of the forest he was only dramatizing things that people already knew, shaping them just as you pick up rocks scattered on the ground to make a cairn. He was merely sewing together the bright patchworks of lives, legends, myths, beliefs, hearsay into a splendid cloak that gave a richer glow to all their lives . . . He insisted that the story was not his, and not theirs either. You must give something, he told the children, a sapphire or blue bread made from cedar ash. And what began as a game ended as a ritual.

Through the ritual retelling of the myths, Harry Joy regains his lost heritage and retrieves the sustaining myths which he shares with the whole community of refugees hungry for ceremony and story. When he addresses the ritual words to the circle of trees where he will build his house, they are Vance's words, with Vance's pantheism. After his third death, he is a sigh in the trees and his heritage handed down to the children of Honey Barbara and Harry Joy.

Bliss examines the myths by which we live, the myths which have failed, the myths we have lost. With a splendid absurdity, it explores the existential horror lying just below the surface of the ordinary life of a Good Bloke. Yet just as it is built on double vision, flipping from heaven to hell, from freedom to captivity, from one Escher hand to the other, so it is a work of contrary energy and paradoxical affirmation, which insists that Harry Joy is not finally trapped in Hell but can discover and explore new territories of his own existence within the layers of the 'infinite onion' of the universe. ***Bliss*** is Carey's storytelling, with Carey's narrator actually playing out the themes of the novel. It is also about storytelling with the storyteller quietly reminding us of the artifice and strategies of his own telling. It is a gentle strumming on the notion of lies and truth. In *Illywhacker,* no more quiet strumming, lies are the show, Herbert Badgery's subject, his specialty, his skill.

> ***Bliss*** **is about storytelling with the storyteller quietly reminding us of the artifice and strategies of his own telling. It is a gentle strumming on the notion of lies and truth. In *Illywhacker,* no more quiet strumming, lies are the show, Herbert Badgery's subject, his specialty, his skill.**
>
> —*Helen Daniel*

Let's relax and enjoy the show. We are in the hands of a Liar, and a showman, offering the best in entertainment, but a salesman too, working for a Liar and selling us Peter Carey's Lie, a conman.

'An illywhacker,' Leah Goldstein said loudly like someone fearful of burglars who descends the stairs, flashlight in hand, in the middle of the night.

'What's an illywhacker?' said Charles.

'Spieler,' explained Leah, who was not used to children. 'Eelerspee. It's like pig Latin. Spieler is ielerspe and then iely-whacker. Illywhacker. See?'

'I think so,' Charles said.

'A spieler . . . A trickster. A quandong. A ripperty man. A con-man.'

Herbert is 139 years old, born in 1886, and so the novel opens in the year 2025 A.D., unless he is lying—which he is. He is like some ancient prophet, an androgynous seer, turning into a woman, growing tits and giving suck. Now beached by time 'like some old squid decaying on the beach', he is also master of ceremonies, promising 'plenty of hanky-panky by and by relating to love of one sort or another'. His advice is 'to not waste your time with your red pen, to try to pull apart the strands of lies and truth, but to relax and enjoy the show'. From the opening proposition of the Liar's Paradox, *Illywhacker* is a play on truth, fiction, lies, spun by Herbert inside Carey's own web. The lies cling, adhere and trail behind us as Herbert spins his tales and whacks the illy, luring us deep inside his fictions, stopping only to remind us suddenly that he is a liar. And this he does with a true 'salesman's sense of history', exquisitely playing with time and fiction

and the passage of the reader's credibility, and selling us not only lies which are his own and therefore his to sell, but also lies of our own, lies we already own. Spinner of tales and webs, illywhacker and deceiver, spieler, conman, distorter of truth and fabricator of fiction—this is the showman and narrator on whose word we, the readers, the believers and self-deceivers, the dupes, will always depend. Forget the finer points of truth, forget its boundaries and its lines of demarcation. Don't worry about who owns the Lies. The Lies are for sale. Just relax and enjoy the show.

Illywhacker is a constant delight, spinning splendid new fictions at every turn, lies which are beautiful and noble, some subsistence lies, some mean and ignoble, snivelling things, noisome, some simply bullshit. There are lies too which are political, some public and national, some historical. And there are lies which are personal, guises and disguises of the self. And some Lies which are literary, artifices of fiction. [In "Weaving a Tangled Web of Lovely Lies," *The Weekend Australian* (6 July 1985)] Adrian Mitchell calls it 'an aesthetics of the lie', and certainly some are more beautiful than others, some ugly, some glossy, some tawdry, some makeshift put-up jobs, some made of sturdier stuff. But perhaps rather than aesthetics, *Illywhacker* is about the calibrations of the Lie and so about the calibrations of truth. What calibre suits our needs? How much truth do we really want? In the opening quotation from Mark Twain, Carey raises not only the notion of beauty and truth, but of novelty. Rich pickings for the Liar in the 'novelty' of history.

> Australian history is almost always picturesque; indeed, it is so curious and strange, that it is itself the chiefest novelty the country has to offer and so it pushes the other novelties into second and third place. It does not read like history, but like the most beautiful lies; and all of a fresh new sort, no mouldy old stale ones. It is full of surprises and adventures, the incongruities, and contradictions, and incredibilities; but they are all true, they all happened.

How much novel truth do we want about our history? Behind the lies is not only Herbert's specialty, 'The role of lies in popular perceptions of the Australian political fabric', but also a truth full of splendid incongruities and incredibilities, which we can buy if we want to from our own history. Herbert is selling us used-Australian history, second-hand history. It's a novelty but it's all true. *Caveat emptor.*

What is a 'salesman's sense of history'? It is timing, a quick sale before events run on or your buyers run off.

> I do not mean about the course of it, or the import of it, but rather its scale of time, its pulse, its intervals, its peaks, troughs, crests, waves. I was not born in some Marxist planet out near Saturn where the days last a year and the inevitabilities of history take a

century to show. I am from Venus, from Mars, and my days are short and busy and the intervals on my whirling clock are dictated by the time it takes to make a deal, and *that* is the basic unit of my time. And even if I have boasted about how I was a patient man when I sold Fords to cockies, shuffled cards, told a yarn, taught a spinster aunt to drive, I was not talking about anything more than a day or two of my life, and *then* off down the road with the order in my pocket.

Carey's salesman's sense of Australian history is like that of the other great Australian salesman, Peter Mathers—it has the pulses and intervals and crests of history, a history which is chaotic and yet continuous, full of bizarre twists and turns, tenuous connections and absurd lines of continuance. The fantastic and the bizarre are embedded in the stubbornly substantial and convincing. Characters come and go apparently at random, slipping off the edge of the narrative, like Phoebe and the schemer Nathan Schick, only to re-appear later. The narrative slithers in complex traces across the page, inside skins likely to be sloughed off at any moment. Like the snakes slithering through *Illywhacker,* the narrative itself is serpentine and sinuous, uncoiling its snake lines as if never-ending, until it tapers and finally reveals the sub-caudal scales of the tail. The tip of the Liar's tale.

In contemporary Australian fiction, *Illywhacker* is closest to Mathers' novels and like them, it is a form of picaresque novel, a narrative that proliferates through time and space, in which the protagonist takes on a series of roles and guises, partly because reality palls and partly because it is the only way to deal with reality—then off down the road. Like Percy Wort, whose guises sprawl through the parody family saga, Herbert plays a series of roles, changing with his chaotic passage through history. Bow-legged, blue-eyed, head shaved bald for twenty-one years, Herbert is variously Aviator with Morris Farman Shorthorn; an illiterate who learns to read in his fifties, correspondence student and later graduate; manipulator, using frailty and decency as a prisoner; used car salesman selling T-models to cockies; child assistant cannon vendor; trickster; nationalist; herpetologist; thespian; walker who favours the Gentleman's Stroll; bigamist; purloiner of church hall; architect and builder of flimsy structures with improbable materials. He is also one-time resident of Mallee hole in ground; wanderer of Western District, nomad across the face of Victoria; paternal conman with son with snake trick; hatcher of schemes; master of his own visibility; urger and enthusiast in general. But there is more: he is also a dealer and trafficker in lies, forger swapping notions of himself for accommodation, lies his currency; a thief and plagiarist, filcher of Leah's writings; and finally 139-year-old androgynous patriarch and concocter of family saga of the 'fatally flawed Badgerys'; writer, with the callused writing finger, 'the liar's lump'; and above all, spieler, the storyteller addressing a spellbound audience.

At the start of his tale, with the exquisite sense of timing of a dealer and an illywhacker, Herbert assures us there is little he looks forward to as much as the story of November 1919, when he was thirty-three (mythically speaking, just the right age). We are hooked, snared, thrust right into the middle of the show, as Herbert lands in Balliang East, in the middle of a lie about a snake, in the middle of the lives of the McGrath family, to whom he delivers value, swapping lies and fictions for free accommodation. As he counts the day of his revenge on his father on the Punt Road hill as the day of his birth, so he counts this day of landing in Balliang East as the start of his adult life. And with the true storyteller's timing, while he unfolds his tale, Herbert keeps interrupting his own narrative, to anticipate, darting head to hint at the exciting developments awaiting us there, or to retrace, darting back to an earlier episode to draw out the storyteller's connections, so that the narrative proliferates sideways and backwards as well as running ahead. Out of it grows a sense that behind every yarn, every vignette, every thread, lies another story and another and another. The forward movement of the narrative is constantly disrupted as though the narrative is conical or cuneiform and only the tip is showing: the further one delves, the more the story enlarges, deepening and complicating in a tangled hierarchy.

One of the extraordinary features of *Illywhacker* is the range of its settings and times. The snake narrative uncoils through the Western District, across Balliang, Geelong, Anakie, Terang, Bendigo, the Ballarat area, moving to Melbourne and the Maribyrnong house, Woodend, Jeparit and the Mallee, Bacchus Marsh and the Underhill family, then wends its way through Victoria, a few passages to Queensland, before coiling itself into Sydney—only to uncoil again for some overseas scenes in Rome and Japan. It slithers across the face of Australian history, from the Lambing Flat riots, the shearers' strike of the 1890s, the colonial era where Imaginary Englishmen strut across society, through the period of the Wobblies, the rise of aviation, the 1930s, the Depression, the Second World War and the influx of Americans, the 1950s and on into the 1970s, from there to the putative future. Herbert's 139 year life encompasses all this, either in truth or in the artifice of lie. His childhood was nomadic, his father a wandering cannon salesman, with rounds of ammunition for sale to squatters to ward off marauding shearers. He sloughs off that life with revenge on the Punt Road hill and enters the life with Goon Tse Ying, which offers him the gift of invisibility—a lie which underlies Sonia's disappearance and is later contested in the struggle over Goon's Book of Dragons. He wanders then, marries, nearly marries in Nambucca Heads until foiled by a corgi, sells cars, becomes an aviator, until his debut, when he drops down from the skies to Vogelnest's paddock.

From the moment he lands in Balliang East, Herbert is trapped inside his own snake-lie, driven to ingenious concoctions to substantiate it until the snake strikes and, killing Jack, kills off the future Herbert had devised. To Jack McGrath who is dreamer and visionary, Herbert delivers value by offering the 'gift' of the richly packaged lie of his aviator self.

> I was an Aviator. That was my value to them. I set to work to reinforce this value. I propped it up and embellished it a little. God damn, I danced around it like a bloody bower-bird putting on a display. I added silver to it. I put small blue stones around it.

When others contribute 'creamy coats of credibility' to his lie, then it becomes beautiful, the nasty speck of grit transformed into the lustrous pearl and the dream of an aircraft factory. Jack McGrath becomes Herbert's straight man, the willing dupe on the other side of Herbert's lie: 'There was nothing to protect us from each other. We were elements like phosphorus and air which should always be kept apart'. The liar and the self-deceiver, the salesman and his willing customer, in idyllic union until the snake strikes. There is a snake biding its time, waiting to strike the other dupe too, the one duped by the other Liar, Carey—the reader of *Illywhacker.*

But a lie, though a tenuous thing in constant need of support and embellishment, is also a version of the self, a cloak.

> It was the trouble with the world that it would never permit me to be what I was. Everyone loved me when I appeared in a cloak, and swirled and laughed and told them lies. They applauded. They wanted my friendship. But when I took off my cloak they did not like me. They clucked their tongues and turned away. My friend Jack was my friend in all things but was repulsed by what I really was . . . could only like the bullshit version of me.

Impatient with the confines of reality, Phoebe loves the liar: 'You have invented yourself, Mr Badgery, and that is why I like you. You are what they call a confidence man. You can be anything you want'. Her vision of their lives together is simple: 'We will invent ourselves'. In Maribyrnong, Herbert's inventions are more architectural and domestic, a matter of scavenging for things timber. Phoebe takes a poetic turning, writing poems Herbert cannot read. Now he looks back:

> But now I know a poem can take any form, can be a sleight of hand, a magician's trick, be built from string and paper, fish or animals, bricks and wire.
>
> I never knew I was a hired hand in the construction of my wife's one true poem. I knew only, in the midst of its construction, that Horace would puzzle me with his sympathetic eyes which would not hold mine when I confronted him.

On the edge of the novel, Horace is another marvelous Carey character: mid-wife, devotee of Phoebe, poet, housekeeper,

epileptic, frequenter of strange literary rooming houses, faithful companion and itinerant Rawleigh's man, a man of many faces and roles, an incipient Herbert without the lies. Phoebe, self-indulgent and preening like a caged budgie, is in the mainstream of the first book of the narrative, until she slips over to the wings to wait for the third book, there to re-appear as a free spirit, combining her literary aspirations with her powers of sexual persuasion, playing the role of one of the great characters and hostesses of Sydney.

When Phoebe flies out of the cage she perceives as Herbert's life, he is comforted by Molly McGrath for a year, until he enters the itinerant phase again, this time complete with Charles, Sonia and the Dodge, roving Victoria in quest of survival, until he meets Leah Goldstein. Thespian now, for six or seven years, Herbert becomes part of Badgery and Goldstein (Theatricals) and Pet Suppliers, with detours into political acts which culminate in the glorious battle (and Pyrrhic victory) with John Oliver O'Dowd and his bully boys. Nathan Schick, schemer, entrepreneur, vanguard of the Americans, enters the narrative with his flashy show in Ballarat, until the departure of Leah to tend the injured Izzie and begin spinning her inventions, then the disappearance of Sonia. Herbert's encounter with Goon Tse Ying in Grafton and the bizarre severing of Goon's finger bring him to Rankin Downs Prison and, with his new literacy, to a B.A. by correspondence and new inklings of political lies.

By the third book, the centre of gravity has shifted to Charles, first amid the plague in the Mallee staring in comic bafflement and consternation at his dismantled bike, then, oblivious of all omens, launching into his marriage to Emma and the opening of his pet shop. From here the development of the pet shop itself holds the centre of the stage. As Carey weaves a vast pattern of time and place, with interpolations, crosscurrents of narrative, silvery trails of related tales that could have been told, its main forward thrust through the Badgery family and through a hundred years of history is to the Pet Emporium, into which the fortunes of all the main characters are finally subsumed. Herbert's role shifts with it, from itinerant and thespian, to prisoner living on the 'perfumed razor blades' of Leah's inventions, to patriarch and finally writer. As he writes and records, still spinning lies and fabrications, the narrative shifts forward again into the next generation, with Hissao taking charge of the family fortunes.

Herbert's role is apparently more passive in Book 3, perhaps the reason that some reviewers of *Illywhacker* found that part less successful than Books 1 and 2, feeling the narrative palls and the interest wanes. I find, on the contrary, that the narrative begins to tighten and intensify here, because it is at this point that Carey's conception of his illywhacker is expanding: Herbert moves steadily out of the lies of his own existence into the political and national lies of Australia, without diminishing the artifice of his own role. His role changes throughout the novel, but the major change is revealed in the sudden disclosure of the lies of his version of events. In her 'book-keeping', which, amid the dullness of her life with Izzie, has become her sacred time, Leah's letters have offered Herbert the salvation of invention. He decides 'There was nothing left for me but to teach myself to be an author. It was the only scheme available'. In a succinct and skilful sequence, Carey shifts our perspective on Leah and Herbert and the whole status of the narrative, when Leah complains that Herbert has stolen her material and stolen it like a barbarian. What follows is a contestant version of Herbert's narrative, not only alleging that his version is a concoction of stolen fragments of her writings but with specific disclaimers of details and challenges to his interpretation and representation of specific incidents. They share the same publisher, Doodles Casey, and, according to Leah, have already collaborated on other books, notably 'Gaol Bird', but Herbert regards the real subject of Leah's writings as 'not the people but the landscape and its roads . . . the raw optimistic tracks that cut the arteries of an ancient culture before a new one had been born'. Placed at a critical point in the novel, this whole sequence is crucial to our perception of Herbert's role in exposing the lies of Australia.

The lies of *Illywhacker* have such convincing substance that the issue of their truth fades and retreats, but the man with 'the liar's lump', the callused writing finger, keeps reminding us of the Lie. This is the content and the movement of the novel, and this final reminder through Leah is the culmination of the Lie of the novel. After Herbert's luminous discovery (through M.V. Anderson) that a liar might be a patriot, his last scheme is Carey's scheme, the big Lie, the all-encasing one of *Illywhacker*. Carey weaves the web of historical lies into his narrative, the lies of settlement and Aborigines, the lies of English colonization, the lies of whole eras, as in the 1930s.

> Lies, dreams, visions—they were everywhere. We brushed them aside as carelessly as spider webs across a garden path. They clung to us, of course, adhered to our clothes and trailed behind us . . .

As well as the lies that cling and entrap, Herbert knows all too well the allure of lies, their soft, warm comfort:

> It is why we believed the British when they told us we were British too, and why we believed the Americans when they said they would protect us. In all these cases, of course, there is a part of us that knows the thing is not true, and we hold it closer to ourselves because of it, refusing to hold it out at arm's length or examine it against the light.

The lies of Australia, its history, its society, its independence, its economy, its architecture, are finally exposed amid Sydney, the city of trickery and illusions. The lies include the lie of 'Australia's Own Car' which is 'one more element in an old-pattern of self-deception', the lie of the Holden which is at the centre of [Australian novelist Murray] Bail's *Holden's Performance*. All these are inside the vast Lie of Carey.

The Pet Emporium, which to Herbert and Hissao always is like stepping into a vision, every edge sharp, every colour intense, steadily becomes ever more bizarre and absurd: Mr Lo conducting ferocious arguments with an imaginary umpire, Emma practising courtesan arts in her cage with its pink venetian blinds, Herbert architecturally engaged in demolition work, then, after Charles' death, at his window amid the neon sign, enthroned high above Pitt Street while angels or parrots trill attendance. Through the schemes of Major Nathan Schick, the juggler with a myriad schemes arcing through the air, The Best Pet Shop in the World thrives in war-time and the 1940s, fed by Americans. In time it becomes dependent on smuggling of Australian animals, and bribery of customs officials, then a financial disaster, then a rusting slum until, following the absurdist death of the last recorded golden-shouldered parrot, it is reborn with Japanese investment. Like his grandfather and mentor, Hissao is an architect, building 'like a liar, like a spider—steel ladders and walkways, catwalks, cages in mid-air, in racks on walls, tumbling like waterfalls.' His features inexplicably Japanese, Hissao is the putative future, given suck by Herbert as he waits for revolution.

Illywhacker abounds with pets, animals—snakes, parrots, goannas—generally caged and entrapped. From Herbert's first being entrapped in his own snake-lie, to the image of Phoebe as a trapped parrot, from Leah's snake-dance to Charles' instinctive skill with snakes and his peculiar impulse to tell the whole snake truth, down to the last sub-caudal scales, the pattern of snakes and snake images slithers through the narrative. When Herbert learns to read, he is transformed. 'I was an old python with his opaque skin now shed, his blindness gone, once again splendid and supple, seeing the world in all its terrifying colours.' Amid the images of cages and entrapment, amid the lies coiling and uncoiling through the novel, the narrative sheds a succession of opaque skins, until we glimpse an image of the future, splendid and supple, with the world in all its terrifying colours. Australia, The Best Pet Shop in the World, becomes a human museum, its caged exhibits an endangered species, Australians: shearers, manufacturers, lifesavers, inventors, masons, Aborigines, bushmen, artists and writers, Leah a Melbourne Jew and Herbert the 139-year-old exhibit, who cannot die 'because this is my scheme. I must stay alive to see it out.' In the vast human museum of Australia, 'the very success of the exhibit is their ability to move and talk naturally within the confines of space', as though real, as though not just exhibits of a historical lie, displaying their own capacity for self-deception. Herbert and Hissao are left amid 'this splendid four storey mirage', in the land of the lie.

Illywhacker is an extraordinary blend of comic vignettes,

absurdist notions, zany fictions and convincing images of time and place rich in corroborative detail, which have an ineradicable, stubborn substance constantly challenged by the artifice of the novel. It is a vast and generous novel in which wondrous scenes abound, some of them fugitive, fleeting scenes, sharp with Carey's quick sense of a single, telling detail; some more sustained with collusive character and circumstance: Leah's emu dance when Herbert first meets her; the car selling sequence in Woodend; the battle with John Oliver O'Dowd and his bully boys; Father Moran's tale of seeing a fairy; the sergeant's thrusting the bottled finger at Herbert; the dismantling of Charles' bike by Les Chaffey, where it occurs to Charles that he has fallen among mad people; Emma's retreat to the goanna cage and the nurturing of the goanna foetus; Herbert's period of imprisonment; Sonia's fascination with the insubstantiality of things. Obsessed with truth in all its endless detail, Charles is 'a poor salesman . . . because the truth told thus, is of no interest to the average punter'. With his 'salesman's sense of history', Herbert's telling of it is in the true illywhacker style, playing on all its high points, teasing out its tangles where major strands knot together, interrupting the narrative to go back to some earlier episode or run ahead to anticipate some later development, telling yarns within yarns, running off at tangents and detours when they promise richer tales, but never losing the way back. Episodes spread tentacles which run on into the future or, at the most climactic moments, take a sudden dramatic turning, are left open, hanging. We are left baffled, bewildered, impatient to know, captive and waiting for explanations, which Carey withholds with a true storyteller's timing.

Herbert's story is an Australian family saga, with the family legacy of lies bequeathed to his children and to theirs. 'Spawned by lies, suckled on dreams, infested with dragons', their family history is the Australian history of lies, of self-deception, of dreams and visions preferred to truth—the calibrations of self-deception which leaves Australia a human museum, a pet shop. Throughout *Illywhacker,* Carey bares and flaunts his own artifice, with a rich canvas of fictions, within the marvelous strategies of the Liar and his character, liars together, partners spinning their webs of lies which cling and adhere and trail around the reader.

Like *Illywhacker,* Carey's third novel, *Oscar and Lucinda,* is a vast and teeming Lie which conjures up marvelous images at every flick of the Liar's hand. Set in the 1860s, it is an absurdist novel about the passage of Christian stories to Australia and about the stakes in the Christian bet on God. But *Oscar and Lucinda* is more than the myriad past behind the Gleniffer church in the present, more than the passage of dreams across the face of the 1860s. It is also a dazzling Lie about the manufacture of glass—and the manufacture of the Lie.

Behind the Prince Rupert Glassworks in Sydney, there is another factory, the 'fancy-factory' of the mind, where Lucinda and the Reverend Oscar Hopkins manufacture their dreams. And behind this is Carey's own 'fancy-factory', the Liar's workshop with its own molten mysteries, where the Lie is manufactured. As the narrator writes, he holds in his left hand a Prince Rupert's drop, 'not the fabled glass stone of the alchemists, but something almost as magical'. Formed by dropping molten glass into water, a Prince Rupert's drop seems unbreakable but, if the slender tail is nipped with pliers, it bursts into a myriad fragments, scattering grains of glass. A spectacular moment of 'fireworks made of glass. An explosion of dew. Crescendo. Diminuendo. Silence.' A Liar's moment. With his pliers, the Liar grips the tail of the past. In one dazzling movement, all the slivers of time and chance are spread out before us. An explosion of word and image. Crescendo. Diminuendo. Silence.

Oscar and Lucinda is a Liar's Prince Rupert's drop, one which shines and dances with a shimmering play of light and dark, the luminous, magical fireworks of the Lie.

Lucinda discovers the wonder of Prince Rupert's drops as a child and so learns

> glass is a thing in disguise, an actor, is not solid at all, but a liquid . . . invisible, solid, in short, a joyous and contradictory thing, as good a material as any to build a life from.

Entranced by the molten mysteries of Prince Rupert's Glassworks and delighting in the construction of fancies, Lucinda dreams of building a structure of glass, a pyramid, a tower, an arcade of glass spun like a web, until she conceives the fabulous image of a glass church. When the lives of Oscar and Lucinda lock together, Oscar, like Lucinda, becomes entranced with the manufacture of glass. He too is captivated by the image of the glass church, dancing around it like a brolga, seeing 'light, ice, spectra'. He sees that glass is the gross material closest to the soul, free of imperfection, an avenue for glory. An actor, a contradiction, glass is a Liar's substance. *Oscar and Lucinda* is the Liar's brolga dance through the light and spectra of the Lie.

Oscar appears a praying mantis, a scarecrow, with wild red hair, a neat triangular face and a luminous innocence. He has a reedy, fluting voice and flapping hands, and knees which click when he runs, a nervous scuttling motion. He is a superb ungainly creature, angular, but also light, airy, 'made from the quills of a bird'. A man of 'holy profligacy', who lacerates himself with his paradoxes, Oscar is a very moving figure, from the start in Hennacombe, where he is trapped in his own bewilderment and grief. For Oscar the toss of the tor in the hopscotch game reveals the will of God, commanding him to emigrate to New South Wales, as the earlier toss commanded him to leave Theophilus and become Anglican. He receives Wardley-Fish into his life as a spiritual messenger, an agent of the Lord sent to reveal the wonders of the race-track and the proper religious activity of backing horses. In the spiritual conundrum on which the novel turns, Oscar sees his passion for gambling as vile, but his notebooks of betting data as diaries of his communion with God.

The delightful Wardley-Fish, with his awkward kindness and enduring love for Oscar, recognizes that Oscar is 'one of those trick drawings in *Punch* which have the contradiction built in so that what seems to be a spire one moment is a deep shaft the next.' This is the *trompe l'oeil* of Oscar's Escher self, the spire soaring up into dazzling light, and the shaft reaching down into the darkness of hell. The whole novel is lit by this Escher vision of spire and shaft, light and dark, the shimmering light and mysteries of glass, yet the nightmarish images of darkness and hell.

For Oscar and Lucinda, existence is gloriously random, life the play of chance, the roll of the dice—and the dividend, 'We are *alive* . . . We are alive on the very brink of eternity'. Spurning all the structures of safe passage through their lives, Oscar and Lucinda choose the exquisite knife-edge of risk. Both reject the vouchsafed life inside accepted boundaries of religious, social and moral codes, and, for Lucinda, 'The Glass Lady', the life inside the conventional roles of women in colonial society.

In colonial New South Wales, Lucinda Leplastrier is a contained creature, with,

> a clean, starched stillness. But the stillness was coiled and held flat. Like a rod of ebony rubbed with cat's fur, she was charged with static electricity.

Two gamblers on an arc towards each other, Lucinda and Oscar are partners, two players across hemispheres, looking for a game. Lucinda is alienated from colonial society by her dress, her spinsterhood, her aloofness, her gambling—and her dreams. She pits herself passionately against male voodoo, determined to manufacture her dreams at her Prince Rupert's Glassworks. Yet her life is split between the glass dream and the circle of card players at D'Abbs' house, the circle which is for her an abstraction of human endeavour, the electric edge of life. Forever in search of a game, she prowls across Sydney to the Chinese fan-tan room, as she later prowls through the *Leviathan,* in search of the electric ecstasy of the game.

The novel abounds in images of safety, vouchsafed lives, with edges dulled. Against this, Oscar and Lucinda choose the risk and place their bets.

Like working out the odds, Carey scatters chance circumstances over the face of the novel: the Christmas pudding which turns Oscar away from Theophilus; the chance death of Lucinda's father on Palm Sunday; the chance that Wardley-

Fish took Oscar to Epsom the first time; the chance of the sermon on Christmas Day, which disposed Oscar and Lucinda to accept Jeffris' proposal of leading the expedition; the chance that Wardley-Fish, who might have saved Oscar, was robbed and forced to return to Sydney; Oscar's chance encounter with Miriam Chadwick, who becomes the narrator's great-grandmother. A vast array of marginal figures press forward into the novel, from the Reverend Dennis Hasset, entranced by Lucinda's coiled stillness, to the preening d'Abbs in his habitat, from the stern fundamentalist Theophilus with the trembling hymnal soul, to the thin brittle soul of Melody Clutterbuck. As contingent character and chance event flow around them, Oscar and Lucinda play out the gamble and wager everything.

Giddy with fear of the water, Oscar's journey on board the *Leviathan* is a nightmare the hopscotch will of God has demanded of him. While up above, there is phosphorescence, the sea studded with sparkles of light, a luminescent sea of globes of fire, Oscar is below, a creature of dark, caught in the web of his own phobia, 'a sad and ugly creature in a fairy tale, one forever exiled from the light and compelled to skulk, pale, big-eyed, sweat-shiny in the dark steel nether regions.' Searching for a game, Lucinda journeys through the innards of the Gargantuan *Leviathan* to a nightmare of some monstrous creature pouring black effluent up from its stomach into the sky.

In a triumph of contingency, with the Liar waiting eagerly for the moment, the two lives come together, Oscar and Lucinda in a moment of joyous conjunction, discovering a partner. Oscar is in a cloud of electricity, Lucinda both enchanted and appalled by his innocence. When Lucinda confesses her gambling Oscar articulates the notion on which the novel turns, that gambling is noble, part of the divine design. Religious faith is a wager, a bet on the existence of God, in which we stake our lives on a structure of fancies.

> 'Our whole faith is a wager, Miss Leplastrier, We bet . . . we bet that there is a God. We bet our life on it. We calculate the odds, the return, that we shall sit with the Saints in paradise.'

> 'I cannot see,' he said, 'that such a God, whose fundamental requirement of us is that we gamble our mortal souls, every second of our temporal existence . . . It is true! We must gamble every *instant* of our allotted span. We must stake *everything* on the unproveable fact of His existence.'

In this splendidly Dostoyevksian proclamation, the Reverend Oscar Hopkins insists gambling is a part of the divine scheme of things. Later Lucinda proudly asserts 'We are gamblers, in the noble sense. We believe all eternity awaits us.' We bet on the spiritual dividends.

At the Glassworks, Oscar becomes Lucinda's tangle-legged

usurper, until she reveals her precious dream of the glass church. Now the moment of conjunction—glass and gamble become one. Now the splendid leap of the Lie—the glass church becomes their bet, in which Oscar and Lucinda are one, the glass church their progeny.

Born of Christian thinking, the glass church and its delivery to the Reverend Hasset is 'a knife of an idea, a cruel instrument of sacrifice, but also one of great beauty, silvery curved, dancing with light'. Oscar bets on the benefits of sacrifice in hope of winning Lucinda's heart through the prism of the church. Both are betting their inheritance—Lucinda her fortune, Oscar his faith. The period they spend together in the cottage at Longnose Point is a coda period in the novel, a touching period of haven for them both, but quickened by the lure of the bet on the glass church. As the expedition leaves, Lucinda feels the absurdity of the whole venture, the packaged glass church not 'the crystal-pure, bat-winged structure of her dreams', but a heavy folly.

Like Lucinda's nightmarish drive through Sydney at night, on the way to the Chinese gambling den, Oscar's journey is a longer and more horrific nightmare, a hellish journey into the heart of darkness. The passage of the church across unmapped territory is a dark emblem of the cost of their fancy and the cost of the Christian fancy. Adrift and besmirched inside a laudanum nightmare, Oscar is trapped under the tyranny of Jeffris, and, during the massacre of the Aborigines, tied to a tree, he becomes a horrified, wailing witness. At Bellingen, under the crushing weight of evil, Oscar is gaunt and scraped out, haunted by his complicity in the massacre, until, in the evil heart of the land, he is driven to the murder of Jeffris. A black and absurdist Christ figure, still bearing the rope burns from the time of the massacre, Oscar becomes a man afire, burning and dancing in his own firelight, as he constructs the glass church for its final passage on the water.

Out of all the patterning of light and dark, it is the hellish darkness with which the novel ends, culminating in Oscar's death, inside his own nightmare. He wins the bet with Lucinda on the glass church, and loses the bet on God. As the glass church slides down its tilting ramp, the fractured panes of glass open to admit his ancient enemy. The flying foxes close on the river seem 'like angels with bat wings. He saw it as a sign from God. He shook his head, panicking in the face of eternity'. He dies screaming, caught in the sheetfolds of a nightmare, realizing, Like Lucinda, the glass church is 'a product of the Deuce's insinuations into the fancy-factory of his mind', a terrible folly.

If the novel is Conradian in its journey into the heart of darkness, it is also Dostoyevksian in its reach of dark and light, its religious themes of risk and gamble. In a wry literary joke, Carey even posits a link with George Eliot through Lucinda's mother which Lucinda herself disclaims when she finds Eliot out of sympathy. There are other nineteenth-century literary shadows. The style is sometimes Dickensian, wonderfully comic, with quick sketches like Mrs Stratton's walking at an angle for carrying books, thus revealing her donnish nature, or Mrs Williams' hairbrushing; or Bishop Dancer's vision of Sydney as 'an orphan's party with a dressing-up box', with maids donning tiaras, piemen dressed up as gentlemen. Or the image of the d'Abbs house, like a ball of string, a grand expensive tangle in which the pristine d'Abbs dances. In spite of all the literary play which conjures up nineteenth-century literary kin, the flickering shadows of Dickens and Eliot, the darker presence of Conrad and Dostoyevsky, yet here is unmistakably a contemporary Australian Lie.

Oscar and Lucinda is a post-Christian novel, an absurdist black comedy of the life of Reverend Oscar Hopkins, a man of burning faith, playing the hopscotch game of God's will. There is a dark absurdity in the scene of Oscar's standing among the lettuces at the Stratton house and declaring himself a theological refugee, 'called' to the Anglican faith; or the scene of Oscar, blindfolded, caught inside his own fear, being loaded in a cage by crane on to the *Leviathan,* a man of faith obedient to his God. This is the man who brought the Christian stories up the river with him, the stories which have vanished now as the Gleniffer church has vanished, replaced by thistles. No sign now of what the church has meant to the narrator's family: Palm Sundays, resurrections, water into wine, loaves and fishes, 'all those cruel and lofty ideas'. The narrator hears the echoes, feels the brush of ghostly presence and wonders. The great-grandson searches for an explanation of the vanished stories, meditating on the shadowy presences.

Oscar is a creature manufactured out of slivers of gospel stories: Jonah and the Whale and the parting of the waters are transmuted into the massive ship, the *Leviathan* where Oscar huddles below in the dark. Jesus' walking on the water becomes translated into Oscar's terror of water and death in water. No Lazarus here either, only the death of Stratton, the murder of Jeffris and the massacre of Aborigines. No miracles of driving out demons here, only the voracious gambling monster which must be fed. God spoke from the Burning Bush but here there is a fiery light and burning fire of Oscar assembling the glass church. The river that turned to blood, the story of Jesus rising from the dead and ascending to heaven— these become in the hands of the Liar, Oscar pulled down into the river waters surrounded by bat-winged figures, a sacrifice offered up to the limits of his own dream. New stories start here, handed down to Kumbaingiri Billy by his aunt, Oscar's Aboriginal Mary Magdalen, on the day Jesus came to Bellingen to construct the glass church and reach Boat Harbour by Good Friday.

In this post-Christian novel, Australia is not a Christian landscape.

You could feel it in the still shadows along watercourses. She felt ghosts here, but not Christian ghosts, not John the Baptist or Jesus of Galilee. There were other spirits, other stories, slippery as shadows.

Oscar finds his Randwick flock 'creatures of their landscape',

> Sydney was a blinding place. It made him squint. The stories of the gospel lay across the harsh landscapes like sheets of newspaper on a polished floor. They slid, slipped, did not connect to anything beneath them. It was a place without moss or lichen, and the people scrabbling to make a place like troops caught under fire on the hard soil.'

The narrator marvels that, in this ancient landscape, as his great-grandfather drifted up the Bellinger River, inside the glass church, Oscar saw nothing.

> The country was thick with sacred stories more ancient than the ones he carried in his sweat-slippery leather Bible. He did not even imagine their presence. Some of these stories were as small as the transparent anthropods which lived in puddles beneath the river casuarinas. These stories were like fleas, thrip, so tiny that they might inhabit a place (inside the ears of the seeds of grass) he would later walk across without even seeing. In this landscape every rock had a name, and most names had spirits, ghosts, meanings.

The glass church, with ice-walls of light, drifting down the river through the ancient landscape, with the black-suited figure inside, is a superb image of the incongruity of Christian faith in this landscape. The church cracks and crazes, into ice-knives hanging over Oscar's head, with jigsaw edges refracting a spectrum of colours over his hands. Up above, the sky is blemished, or curdled, and the glass so splintered it is almost opaque. Christianity cracks like glass, breaking up in the face of the ancient landscape.

But what of the Liar's fancy-factory, with its molten mysteries? No folly this, no insinuations of a literary Deuce here. This is a splendid unforgettable Lie, which dances with light and dark, an Escher vision of spire and shaft, light and dark, the shimmering light and mysteries of glass and nightmarish images of darkness and hell. The reader has only to break the tail of this magical Prince's Rupert's drop, open *Oscar and Lucinda,* and the spectacular vision begins, an explosion of magical words.

A. J. Hassall (essay date Winter 1989)

SOURCE: "Telling Lies and Stories: Peter Carey's *Bliss,*" in *Modern Fiction Studies,* Vol. 35, No. 4, Winter, 1989, pp. 637-53.

[*Hassall is an Australian educator and critic. In the following essay, he provides a thematic analysis of* Bliss.]

There are many stories in Peter Carey's *Bliss* and not a few lies, but there is one story that enjoys a special, privileged status. This is the story of Little Titch that Harry Joy invents under duress and tells to Constable Box and Sergeant Hastings, "the only original story he would ever tell." I want to examine the story of Little Titch, and the sequence of other stories in which it is embedded, as a point of entry into Carey's larger "story" in *Bliss,* the bildungsroman of Harry Joy's mid-life crisis, his fall into hell, and his eventual attaining of "bliss." A story about telling stories, *Bliss* is postmodern in its awareness of the problematic nature of trying "to grasp reality through a fictitious construct" [Elizabeth Wright, "Modern Psychoanalytic Criticism," in *Modern Literary Theory,* edited by Ann Jefferson and David Robey, 1986], and yet it uses such problematic stories to make narrative sense of extra-fictional experience.

The story of Daniel or Little Titch is a double parable of survival in a brutal world. Titch's mother survives, despite her diminutive size, by displaying her disability—notably in the 1909 Queenscliff competition for *The Shortest Woman,* which she wins. Little Titch, who admires the silver cup his mother won at Queenscliff, develops his own strategy for survival, attaching himself to the lashing rear leg of the vicious gelding Billy-boy, the only place where his persecutors—his father and his older brothers—are afraid to approach him. [In a footnote, Hassall adds: "The victimization of a weaker younger brother by a brutal father and more robust older brothers recurs in the childhood of Herbert Badgery in Peter Carey's *Illywhacker.*"]

At the end of Little Titch's story, the teller is "as perplexed (who was Little Titch?) and as embarrassed" as his audience; but—perhaps instinctively, or as in a dream—his narrative images both his own immediate need to escape the brutality of the police station and also his larger need to devise a strategy for survival in the hell in which he has just discovered that he is living. The Little Titch section is thus a microcosmic version of the story of *Bliss* as a whole. It also enjoys the dual status of being an invention, that is, in some sense a lie, and yet in another sense true to Harry's experience, because in telling it, the author informs us, he is "glimpsing the true nature of his sin." And after telling the story and being released from custody, Harry feels rejuvenated, experiencing "the rewards of originality." It is, however, his only original story, and he cannot invent another for his wife Bettina.

Harry's only original story is embedded in a series of other stories, some of which are self-evidently highly fictive. Harry is at the police station, for example, as a result of an earlier, very unoriginal story—the elephant that allegedly sat on his red Fiat 500, mistaking it for the red box on which it was (supposedly) trained to sit (it may be a subtextual pun that one of the policemen who pick up Harry is a senior Constable Box). The elephant story has acquired the status of an urban legend, and a variant of it is used, for example, in the television advertisement for AAMI Car Insurance in which an elephant stands on a car. The story is first told to Harry at Milanos Restaurant by Aldo and Billy de Vere from the circus, and the narration stresses its fictive status:

> "What happened?" Harry asked. . . .
>
> "Drink first . . . or you'll think I'm lying. . . ."
>
> "It is almost the same as the original story" . . . "No . . . in the original . . . it was a red Volkswagen" . . . "No . . . it was a Fiat. . . ."
>
> "Life," Billy de Vere raised his glass, "imitating art. Or should I say . . . life imitating bullshit."
>
> "Do you know the story about the Elephant, Mr Joy?" Aldo said. "Because very soon you are going to have to tell it to your insurance company."
>
> Aldo and Billy de Vere roared laughing.

Very soon Harry has to tell it to Constable Box and Sergeant Hastings, who pull him over for driving his crushed Fiat, decide he is either "a smart arse or a looney," and take him to the police station for a little interrogation. The car is certainly crushed, but the reader—like Harry—never learns whether an elephant was really responsible or whether Billy de Vere imposed the "bullshit" story on a quite different set of circumstances. The "truth" of the story cannot be ascertained and is not important—what matters is its narrative appeal, its humor, and its credibility with the police and the insurance company.

But when Harry offers the story to the police, they refuse to accept it, despite the evidence of the crushed Fiat: "If you're going to tell stories to the police, tell us something original. Don't come and tell us old elephant stories, and if you do, get the car changed. The car in the story was a Volkswagen." Contrary to the supposed laws of evidence, then, the police do not want the truth—they prefer a good story. If the story is old, however, they insist, with the pedantry of children hearing a favorite bedtime story, that the details not be changed. Harry is thus doubly the victim of the elephant story and its dubious, legendary status. His beloved Fiat is crushed, while everyone laughs instead of sympathizing; and when he repeats the story he has been told, the guardians of evidence question it as fiction instead of as fact.

Under threat of physical assault, then, and a charge for possession of the marijuana that Aldo has forced upon him, Harry tells another victim story, the only original story of his life, "a story he had never heard about people he had never met in a place he had never visited." [In a footnote, Hassall adds that in "An Infinite Onion: Peter Carey's Fiction," *Australian Literary Studies* (1983) "Teresa Dovey aptly compares Harry at the police station to Scheherazade telling stories to save her life."] Perhaps because it is not constrained by awkward "facts" or "evidence," it has the desired effect on its audience: "There was a silence in the room and the two policemen looked the way people look when the lights come on in the cinema. . . . 'I think you better piss off now,' Hastings said quietly to the story-teller." If Harry's story is an inspired lie—and it is not factual—it nonetheless serves its purpose—his audience is satisfied and Harry is released—and it therefore has a kind of fictive validity. Later, at the end of the book, Harry, who tells stories and who can rewrite his own narrative, survives; whereas his wife Bettina, his son David, and his partner Joel, who are trapped in other people's stories, all kill themselves. Harry had learned early from his father, Vance, that you must pay *with* a story (if you are a story-teller), and that you must pay *for* a story (if you want to hear one); and these ritual laws of barter are observed by the police. In his earlier, prelapsarian life, Harry had used his story-telling skill to earn a living by writing advertising and to win his wife Bettina with his father's stories of mythical New York. Harry is later to enjoy a brief period as one of "Those in Charge" when he sells Bettina's advertisements, which are also fictions and which are better than his. Later again he adapts his stories, or rather his father's stories, to the less sophisticated but no less appreciative audience at Bog Onion Road:

> He never thought of what he did as original. It wasn't either. He told Vance's old stories, but told them better because he now understood them. He retold the stories of Bog Onion Road . . . he was only dramatizing things that people already knew, shaping them just as you pick up rocks scattered on the ground to make a cairn.

And when Honey Barbara objects: "[S]o the man's got some nice stories. They're not his stories anyway. They're his father's. He even stole his *stories*," his audience is uninterested in such legalistic distinctions, as the police were, one of them responding, "I don't see that that matters."

What clearly does matter is the way a story is told and the emotional investment of the teller in the story: "[W]hen you talk about trees," Paul Bees says to Harry, "it sounds like you want a fuck." And this revealing comment follows a passage in which Harry finds himself experiencing a timeworn cliché with an Adamic sense of wonder:

> Everybody has pointed this out to everybody else before. They have made films about it and called them "Miracle of Life" and so on. He may even have seen them, but when Harry Joy squatted on his haunches and contemplated a pea growing it did not matter a

damn to him (it did not even occur to him) that his experience was not new. He was not interested in newness.

The "miracle of life" story evokes an intense response in Harry, and that, for him, is the ultimate test of its value.

Much earlier in the book Harry's retelling of Vance Joy's story of the Beggar-King is embedded in a complex pattern of "true" and fictive stories, tellers, and listeners. His son David has been exposed for telling lies at school. David's mother Bettina, however, is unconcerned, referring to David's "lies" as "stories": "he is like his father, always telling stories." When David then listens to Harry's story, however, it is "with his mother's ears" because "the dreams that shone most brightly in his imagination were often gathered from his mother." The author, who is also listening to the story, and interrupting to comment on its narration, observes that Harry tells "the exact words" of the story but ignores its "political implications," forgets the "lovely, ice-thin malice" of Vance Joy's voice, and does not, like his father, enact the "unbeggarly strut" of the king masquerading as a beggar. Because of this hybrid narration—word perfect but poorly enacted—which Carey has described as "brainless" transmission, the story in Harry's hands became "[A] poor directionless thing, left to bump around by itself and mean what you wanted it to, although it was not without effect and young David Joy sat silently before its sword-sharp edges." This is one of the very few Vance and/or Harry Joy stories that are actually told in *Bliss,* and presumably it is told to contrast its shape and integrity with Harry's defective telling of it. As Helen Daniel points out in *Liars,* the deracinated Harry of the beginning of the book has lost the meaning of the stories he has inherited and cannot tell them properly.

By the time he retells Vance's story "Journey to the Sunshine" in the fifth section of the book, however, Harry has learned its meaning, and so the emphasis there is on his telling of the story, the words of which "could be of no use to anyone else. The words, by themselves, were useless." Presumably that is why this story is not retold—although there is a brief précis—and instead the author celebrates the telling, likening it to "the skill of . . . the craftsman more than the artist."

Harry's ultimate skill as story-teller to the forest community at the end of the book seems to consist of finally understanding the stories of his father that he has been hearing and telling—with increasing skill—all his life, giving artistic form and expressive rendition to stories that he finds lying about, and knowing which stories are appropriate to the occasional needs of his listeners.

Like an epic poet, then, he "makes" the tales of his adopted tribe from inherited stories of the old cultures and the ordinary circumstances of the people's lives, drawing eclectically

from the Hopi Indians, "New York," and Bog Onion Road. He realizes that it is the function of the stories, not their status as "true" or "false," original or unoriginal, that is important, and he emphasizes the value of a story to its audience:

> He gave value to a story so that it was something of worth, as important, in its way, as a strong house or a good dam. He insisted that the story was not his, and not theirs either. You must give something, he told the children, a sapphire or blue bread made from cedar ash. And what began as a game ended as a ritual.

> They were refugees of a broken culture who had only the flotsam of belief and ceremony to cling to or, sometimes, the looted relics from other people's temples. Harry cut new wood grown on their soil and built something solid they all felt comfortable with. They were hungry for ceremony and story.

In this lyric account of the myth-making role of the story-teller in the "broken culture" of Bog Onion Road, Carey is clearly offering an ambitious interpretation—[in Philip Neilsen's "Waiting for the Barbarians: An Interview with Peter Carey," *Literature in North Queensland* (1987)] he has called it "a writer's wish-fulfilment"—of both the personal value to the story-teller, and the cultural value to the community, of local stories and story-telling, particularly in a colonized culture like Australia's. But he does not retell Harry's stories, which remain only as embedded absences, and it is therefore Harry's own story which must serve as an enabling myth for its teller and for the larger Australian culture outside Bog Onion Road.

The relationship between the reader and the stories that make up *Bliss* is not, however, as uncomplicated, or as serviceable, as the previous quotation might suggest. Like García Márquez, whose work he admires—he has described *One Hundred Years of Solitude* as "a beautiful, fantastic, perfect book" ["Building the Fabulist Extensions: An Interview with Peter Carey," *Makar* (1976)]—Carey writes with a disturbing, surreal clarity, in which the recognizably quotidian mingles unnervingly with the actualized terrors of the subconscious, leaving the reader sensitized and disoriented. The first sentence of the book is typical: "Harry Joy was to die three times, but it was his first death which was to have the greatest effect on him, and it is this first death which we shall now witness." Like the beginning of Kafka's *Metamorphosis,* this sentence is deceptively lucid in its abrupt defamiliarization and in its dream-like multiplication of death by three, which simultaneously diminishes and increases its menace.

The opening further disconcerts the reader by using a traditional, fulsomely authorial story-teller, "which we shall not witness"—a technique retained, although in much reduced form, and with Harry as the narrator, in the film version. The reader does not learn until the other end of the book—literally the last line—that "we" are "the children of Honey Barbara and Harry Joy." This unexpected identification of the previously uncharacterized, extradiegetic and seemingly omniscient story-teller/s, refocalizes their relationship with the reader and qualifies the status of the story. It does not render *Bliss* unreliable in quite the same way that Herbert Badgery's confession at the beginning of *Illywhacker* traps the reader in the problematics of the Liar's Paradox: "I am a terrible liar and I have always been a liar. I say that early to set things straight. *Caveat emptor*" (*Illywhacker*). But it does indicate to the reader that what she or he has just read is the story of Harry Joy as told by his children: it has no other, privileged authority.

Carey foregrounds the fictional status of *Bliss* in a number of ways, including using "its forms," as Graeme Turner observes [in "American Dreaming: The Fiction of Peter Carey," *Australian Literary Studies* (1986)], "to expose and interrogate its fictional status." The triple death announced in the first sentence of the book serves, as we have seen, to alert the reader that this is not a "true" story. The reader is later reminded of the privileged status she or he enjoys: "It was not a question that would have occurred to Harry, who had never seen his family as you, dear reader, have now been privileged to." This address to the "dear reader" is not repeated by Carey—as it is by those eighteenth-century novelists like Sterne and Fielding from whom he borrows it—although there are a number of other asides. These give the reader of the fiction access to privileged information which, as Fielding suggests [in *Tom Jones,* 1749], would have been denied in a parallel situation in "real life" outside the text.

There are other occasions when the narration gives the reader privileged information that presumably could not have been derived from Harry, as, for example, when Harry takes a taxi home from the police station: "The rewards of originality have not been wasted on him and if he is, at this stage, unduly cocky, he might as well be allowed to enjoy it. So we will not interfere with the taxi driver, who is prolonging his euphoria by driving him the long way home." It is difficult to see how Harry's children could know this—and presumably they made it up, for the sake of their story. There are then slippages, as well as a degree of self-consciousness, in the position from which the story is narrated, and these also serve to foreground its fictiveness.

Like Beckett and Kafka, writers he admires, and also like Swift, Carey defamiliarizes the stories from which "reality" is constructed, exposing absurdities and corruptions so familiar that they customarily pass unnoticed and unchallenged. And his satiric purpose, like Swift's, is unmistakable. The accounts of the carcinogenic products of Krappe Chemicals and of the conduct of Alice Dalton's Free Enterprise Hospital are the work of an author determined to extrapolate from his fictional text to the cultural texts that surround it and to work some change upon them. Like its even more disturbing

predecessors, *The Fat Man in History* and *War Crimes, Bliss* employs an unsettling combination of postmodern form and traditional satiric indignation.

Carey is also a poet of anxiety and neurosis, like Kafka, and he generates an intensity of fear and repulsion that transgresses both the ordinary boundaries of the text and the self-referentiality of much postmodern writing. David Foster [in "Satire," *The Phoenix Review* (1988)] has likened the satirist to a streetfighter "overendowed with aggressive impulses, living in a society in decline, and conscious of his own damnation." Carey, who coincidentally gives a streetfighter's body to the protagonist of his story **"The Chance"** (*War Crimes*), certainly attacks and upsets his audience, as was graphically demonstrated when the film version of *Bliss* was shown on ABC television in 1987, creating a storm of protest from viewers. It is therefore not surprising to find that he has written about the mimesis of terror, and the contradictory audience response to it, in **"The Last Days of a Famous Mime"**: "They fled their seats continually. Only to return again. . . . The audience devoured the terror like brave tourists eating the hottest curry in an Indian Restaurant" (*War Crimes*).

Like García Márquez, Carey writes with a disturbing, surreal clarity, in which the recognizably quotidian mingles unnervingly with the actualized terrors of the subconscious, leaving the reader sensitized and disoriented.

—A. J. Hassall

Suspicion of—and fascination with—fiction like Carey's, which seems to distort and yet to imitate life unnervingly, is of course at least as old as Plato, who wanted the truth, not the lies of poets, in his Republic. Defoe defined novel-writing bluntly as lying like the truth. And Mark Twain captured the shifting and ambiguous relationship between art and life with typical wit in a passage much admired by Carey—perhaps because it is a precise albeit anachronistic definition of magic realism—and used as an epigraph to *Illywhacker*: "Australian history . . . does not read like history, but like the most beautiful lies; . . . but they are all true, they all happened." In more recent times, Saussure has effected a divorce between the sign and the referent, and Derrida has proclaimed the separation of the signifier and the signified, which, if true, would reduce all lies and (hi)stories, satires and truths to the status of mere texts. [In a footnote, Hassall states: "Jacques Derrida's assertion that: 'there is no "outside" to the text (il n'y a pas de hors-texte)' (*Of Grammatology*) is a classic—if disputed—statement of the poststructuralist denial of referentiality."] Carey himself canvasses the alternatives drily in his story **"Report on the Shadow Industry,"** which adroitly links the shadows on the television screen and those on the wall of Plato's cave:

> There are those who say that the shadows are bad for people, promising an impossible happiness that can never be realized and thus detracting from the very real beauties of nature and life. But there are others who argue that the shadows have always been with us in one form or another and that the packaged shadow is necessary for mental health in an advanced technological society. There is, however, research to indicate that the high suicide rate in advanced countries is connected with the popularity of shadows and that there is a direct statistical correlation between shadow sales and suicide rates. This has been explained by those who hold that the shadows are merely mirrors to the soul and that the man who stares into a shadow box sees only himself, and what beauty he finds there is his own beauty and what despair he experiences is born of the poverty of his spirit. (*The Fat Man in History*)

Carey is a child of his time, and he plays elegant metafictional games with his readers, as Teresa Dovey has pointed out; but he does not, in the postmodern manner of David Malouf's *Child's Play,* abandon the referential world that appalls and terrifies him for its textual, self-referential, and finally hermetic alternative. As David Foster observes, satire is not postmodern but "essentially modernistic"; as it juggles the old and the new it "moves towards decadence, but retains a fundamental sympathy with classicism."

Carey's classic, unfashionable concern with morality, and with the corrective function of satire, is evident in his enthusiastic use of the traditional iconography of heaven and hell in Harry's story. As the title *Bliss* and names like Joy and Honey Barbara indicate—not to mention Krappe Chemicals and Detective Herpes—*Bliss* is an allegory, indeed a religious allegory. It is, however, situated in a late-twentieth-century, post-Christian outpost of the "American Empire" that, while recognizably Australian, is also resolutely nonspecific—a deliberate conflation of Sydney, Brisbane, Townsville, and Cairns. It can therefore also serve as an allegorical Everywhere in which his latter-day Everyman enacts a twentieth-century *Divine Comedy,* with its progressive dream journey through the circles of the underworld, purgatory, and heaven.

The Australian dimension of the setting is especially appropriate because as far as its European inhabitants are concerned, Australia began life as a hell on earth for transported convicts, and the imagery of hellish imprisonment has figured large in its literature and its cultural self-images ever since. Ironically enough, the other dominant myth of Australia has been as a paradise, a new world, a virgin continent, a south land of the holy spirit, a social laboratory, where the ills of the old European world might be put to right. Carey draws on this specifically Australian tradition of hell and heaven, as well as on the larger Christian tradition in *Bliss.*

Like a middle-aged version of Blake's *Infant Joy,* then, Harry falls from a world of innocence—he is the archetypal "Good Bloke"—to a world of experience, which he explores extensively, before he can graduate to the state of higher innocence in the forest world of Bog Onion Road. His first death is presented as a fall from primal, albeit suburban, innocence: "And indeed he thought himself happy, and why shouldn't he? He had a wife who loved him, children who gave no trouble, an advertising agency which provided a good enough living." The innocence from which Harry falls is the belief that there is only one world, the one that he mistakenly believes he inhabits: "later . . . he discovered that there were many different worlds, layer upon layer, as thin as filo pastry." Before this initiation Harry shared his innocence around:

> He exhibited a blindness towards the faults of people and the injustices of the world which should have been irritating but which seemed to have almost the opposite effect: his very blindness reassured those around him and made them feel that their fears and nightmares were nothing but the products of their own overwrought imaginations.

Harry's fall into the nightmare world of experience involves a major deconstruction of the stories he has been telling himself about his business and his family. Confined at home, he soon discovers that in their different ways Bettina, David, and Lucy are all frustrated, trapped in the socially-approved roles he has imposed upon them, seething with restlessness, alienated, nasty, and selfish. And when he does finally go back to work, he finds Alex Duval writing "alternative" conference reports that document the dark, carcinogenic underside of Harry's advertising business.

His disillusionment is complicated by his initial naïveté about the practices and discourses of hell, which he documents clumsily in his notebooks, and by the difficulty of effecting so major a deconstruction of the thinking of half a lifetime. It is rendered complete, however, when he carries out his "Final Test" in the tree outside his home and witnesses the adultery of his wife with his partner and the incest of his children. The family's response to Harry's discovery of the knowledge of good and evil is to incarcerate him in a mental hospital, that last resort of totalitarian regimes for dealing with dissidents. Although they could live with Harry as a Good Bloke, they cannot tolerate his newfound knowledge of their true natures and his enthusiasm for Goodness, which is not at all the same as being a Good Bloke.

Images of imprisonment recur obsessively throughout Carey's work, and it is therefore not surprising to find that Harry—and Alex Duval—are literally as well as metaphorically imprisoned. Alex is an alter ego of Harry, and it is not entirely a comic mistake when he is substituted for Harry and given Harry's identity in Alice Dalton's asylum. Like Harry's family, Alex and the staff of the Agency have relied on Harry's innocence, "his bleeding, blind optimism." By contrast Alex has been imprisoned in hell, at work and at home, long before Harry joins him. He explains to Harry that his alternative "true" conference reports are his punishment "for what we do here," that is, the lies in the official agency reports. Alex is not an innocent, like Harry, but a failed "man of principle" who eases his conscience by voting for the Communist Party and writing his alternative reports:

> He was not so mad as to not know he was mad. He knew, almost exactly, how mad he was. But he also allowed himself the 1 per cent chance that he was taking a useful precaution, and so his Saturday morning sessions had continued. Later, going down in the lift, he would feel the damp sour shame of a perversion finally practised, a lust satisfied . . . he would feel at once self-hatred and a strange sense of superiority.

The paragraph from which this quotation is taken is a good example of Carey's ability to tell a character's story with unnerving insight in a few sentences, as García Márquez characteristically does.

When the newly moral Harry decides to act on Alex's alternative report, however, and to fire Krappe Chemicals, because "we're going to be good," Alex feels betrayed: "I need a job." He has learned to keep his personal stories—his nighttime reading of "Rousseau and Pascal, Bertrand Russell and Hegel, Marx and Plato"—separate from his income-earning lies as account director for Krappe. He may understand the issues better than the naïve, newly-converted Harry, who "did not read books," but he is not willing to enact his moral convictions, and indeed he agrees to take the Krappe account to another agency that offers to make him a director. Later on, of course, Harry also backslides into advertising: its allurements are considerable.

Images of entrapment and incarceration pervade the domestic as well as the business lives of Harry/Alex. After a tragicomic exchange of beds worthy of Fielding's *Joseph Andrews*, Alex finds himself identified as Harry and imprisoned in Alice Dalton's hospital instead of at Ogilvy's agency. He enjoys being in the asylum, however, because it frees him from the worse prison of his marriage, which is imaged in one of Carey's unforgettable nightmare visions:

> Alex Duval had this dream. . . . There is a plush green carpet and a svelte grey cat with silky fur. On the cat's back is a large crayfish, about the same size as the cat. The crayfish is digging its sharp claws into the cat's body. There is a crackling sound. It is the cat tearing off those of the crayfish legs it can reach with its mouth. Alex Duval is watching. He believes at first that the crayfish will die, but then it occurs to him that this is stupid—dream-logic—and that the crayfish is in agony and cannot scream. The noise of the legs in the cat's mouth is the same noise you hear when you bite a cooked crayfish leg.

> It was a portrait of his marriage. Who was the cat? Who was the crayfish? He didn't know.

As might be expected, Alex's asylum in the asylum is short-lived, despite his conscientious efforts to live up to the identity of Harry Joy—so fortuitously thrust upon him—even to the point of telling Harry Joy-type stories. Like Emma Badgery in *Illywhacker*, Alex's wife Martha has "devoted her life to paying him back for having once left her"; and not even the formidable Alice Dalton is going to deprive her of her husband.

Alex's situation—so powerfully conveyed in this "story"—parallels Harry's, and the exchange of identity between them is feasible, as well as bizarre and threatening, exploring, as Helen Daniel observes [in *Liars: Australian New Novelists,* 1988], "the marvelous notion that one can lose one's whole identity by institutional theft or by the takeover bid of an old mate." Carey is fascinated by threats to and exchanges of identity, as stories like **"The Chance"** (*War Crimes*) illustrate so hauntingly. Both Alex and Harry are triply imprisoned in marriage, in advertising, and in the asylum. Alex, however, is a lifer, and when he leaves the asylum, he submits himself again to the yoke of his own identity and his marriage. Harry, on the other hand, uses Honey Barbara's understanding of the system and his own newly-discovered anger to shake off the schmuck self-image of Alex, which has been colonizing his own personality, and to escape—first from the little hell of the asylum, and finally from the larger hell outside.

Whereas ***Bliss*** contains many kinds of true and false stories, the alluring fictions of advertising occupy a position of special privilege as the brilliant, decadent *fleurs du mal* of late, decaying capitalism. It is the power of advertising that frees Harry from the asylum. Bettina bails him out on condition that he sell her advertisements. He sets up a new agency with Bettina and Joel, which is an altogether more professional, "American," and successful operation than his earlier, relatively innocent business, which lifts the Joys from the comfortable regions of the upper middle class to the intoxicating heights of "Those in Charge," and which rewards Harry, with ironic appropriateness, with the position of Trustee of the State Gallery. The artworks that lift the new agency out of the ruck are not Harry's, however, but Bettina's, although she still needs Harry to sell them for her. Hell is not yet liberated, and the fallen Harry, who still retains some of the brightness of the Good Bloke, is a formidable salesman who can sell Bettina's advertisements to clients even less able than he is to recognize just how good they are: "Gone was that dozy lethargic Harry Joy, the old tell-us-what-you-want-and-I'll-do-it-for-you pragmatist. In his place was a man who felt he must not fail, a cunning, slightly angry personality who hid his aggression behind the natural blanket of his charm." Honey Barbara does not like Harry's newly acquired "fear and anger," and even Bettina resents his "shallow nasty sort of skill" in winning her clients. But his dextrous blend of fear, charm, and anger works extremely well in hell.

The conflict for Harry's soul between Bettina and Honey Barbara is most intense at this point, and Harry is genuinely divided. Contrary to his initial expectations, Bettina's advertisements are brilliant. When he first sees them, he is both repentant and excited: repentant that he has not allowed her to work in the agency before as she has repeatedly requested, and excited by the access to money, fame, freedom, and power that her advertisements represent:

> What he saw in those advertisements, in their shimmering reflections, was the possibility of safety. With advertisements like that you could make a lot of money. You could be rich and even, in a limited way, famous. You would be undeniably Harry Joy and there would be no one to take it from you. No one was going to steal your shirts or suits or shoes. If anyone tried to give you Therapy you could give them money. The principle was so simple it delighted him.

Like the *ingénu* Gulliver, Harry is alternately the vehicle and the object of his author's satire and sometimes, as in this deliciously simplistic passage, both simultaneously.

Bettina's advertisements are described as "decadent," as having "black magical powers," and the dinner ceremonies at which their success is ritually celebrated are a kind of witches' sabbath. But decadent or not, advertising is an art form of which Carey is both a practitioner and a connoisseur. And Bettina is a genius:

> Few people in the world could see, perhaps fifty in England, eighty in America. Most of the people who made advertisements for a living could not see. Even Harry could not see what Bettina saw: the combination of all the complexities of a product, a market, competing forces, the proposition, the image, this writhing, fluxing, struggling collection of worms all finally stilled, distilled and expressed in its most perfect form, which, to Bettina's taste, was in one big picture and one single line of type running underneath it . . . Bettina . . . sought, as the apotheosis of her endeavours, something as unbearably perfect as the English Benson and Hedges advertisements, which had, against all possibility of government regulation, produced a totally new language with no words, only pictures.

As English society had broken slowly apart it had produced these wonderful flowers which grew amongst the rubble. But Bettina had never seen the rubble, merely these flowers, as exotic as anything stolen from a landscape by Rousseau.

Bettina is good partly because she covets with a fierce, uncomplicated passion the delights, the "cargo," that an advertising-driven society aspires to and exalts. It is therefore both appropriate, and cruelly ironic, when she discovers that she has cancer—caused by inhaling benzine fumes throughout her childhood—just at the moment when her career is set to take off for the *ne plus ultra* of New York. In a semiotically brilliant murder-suicide, she petrol-bombs the board of Mobil for whom she wrote her finest advertisement and whose product has poisoned her—as Aldo is poisoned, and Adrian Clunes' wife is poisoned, and a high proportion of all the people who live in the inner circles of the cancer map will be poisoned in the looming cancer epidemic. When Bettina receives her death sentence from the doctor, she realizes, in a moment of illumination that matches Harry's moment of truth in the tree outside his home, that her "whole life had been built on bullshit." The fictions that have seduced Bettina, and to which she has herself contributed with great distinction, are beautiful lies, cultural myths that threaten a fate far worse than self-deception. Bettina's realization comes too late for her to survive and to substitute alternative fictions; but Harry is given the chance to adapt his story-telling talents to creative, not destructive use, to tell stories and not lies. As Carey's postmodern Everyman, he represents the only escape from death that remains open.

The *auto da fé* of the Mobil board symbolically anticipates the looming self-immolation of the entire twentieth-century military-industrial culture. It is a significant part of this deliberate composition that the only flower surviving in the rubble is Bettina's last and most personal advertisement: "Petrol killed me." The dry authorial humor of the paragraph that records its survival distances the violence into symbolism:

> Only one advertisement survived that inferno (certainly no people did) and beneath its bubbled cell overlay one could read the headline, set in Goudy caps and lower case: "Petrol killed me," it said and it is an interesting reflection on the art of advertising that it was four hours before anyone bothered to read the body copy and learned that the death in the headline was a death by cancer.

> So when the police interrogated Harry for the first time . . . there was only one motive he could think of.

> "They must have rejected her ads," he said.

It is, as Bettina intends, a fitting epitaph: for herself, and for the culture that betrays her. It is the nearest she gets to telling—indeed to having—her own original story; but she cannot escape the tragic script that was written for her by the "bullshit" culture of New York.

The pastoral has not been an easy form to practice in the post-Nietzschean twentieth century, as we grimly wait for the barbarians, shoring fragments against our ruin. It has survived, however, like a flower in the rubble, perhaps because of the centrality of the garden myth in Western culture, and despite a determined attempt in the eighteenth century by writers like Johnson (in *Rasselas*) and Crabbe (in *The Village*) to ridicule it once and for all out of existence. Lawrence is one modern writer who argues that Western society has to go back to a simpler, more innocent, preindustrial culture, one in harmony with the natural rhythms of life. But his own attempts at twentieth-century pastoral, in *Lady Chatterley's Lover* for example, are not entirely convincing.

Carey's version of pastoral in **Bliss** has also been attacked as unrealistic, sentimental, and "a cop-out"; but he resists the charge and emphasizes that "the whole book stands or falls" on the last (pastoral) chapter, "Blue Bread and Sapphires," and that "I did wish to celebrate the human spirit" [*Beautiful Lies: Peter Carey* (videocassette), 1987. In a footnote, Hassall adds that Carey "has also suggested that his own preferred title for the book was *Waiting for the Barbarians* and that '**Bliss** sometimes has been misinterpreted' (Neilsen)."] The ending of the novel certainly offers Harry, and the reader, a deliberate moral choice between the city and the forest, Sydney and the bush. These alternative myths have a long literary history; but they also have a particular application in Australia, a country whose European beginnings consisted of a series of convict settlements surrounded by a hostile and unfamiliar bush that offered both danger and the only possibility of freedom. It was a pretty dubious version of the pastoral myth to European-trained eyes, and that ambiguity remains part of the cultural inheritance that informs **Bliss.**

Harry Joy and Honey Barbara are both divided in their feelings about the choice they have to make, and not only because—when they meet and fall in love—Harry "lives" in the city and Honey Barbara "lives" at Bog Onion Road (a name, incidentally, which hardly evokes an Edenic paradise). Honey Barbara visits the city every year to make money as a prostitute, and her memories of the city contradict her experience when she is there:

> She always forgot the fear when she remembered the
> city afterwards . . . each year when the wet ended she
> found herself looking forward to it again. . . . She
> remembered the bars and restaurants and movies and
> even the junk food seemed tasty in her memory and
> the businessmen didn't seem so bad and she remembered the good times and ones who danced.

She likes city plumbing, she learns to like expensive wine, and she is aware that the forest is not necessarily morally superior:

> She did not forget . . . bad things . . . the bloated body
> of an unknown man hanging from a casuarina above
> the falls. . . . Witchcraft was practised in the bush
> and the head of a sheep, or a pig, writhing with maggots, lay often in the path of Honey Barbara's horse,
> and the night was a less innocent place than it had
> once been.

For his part, Harry is addicted to the pleasures of "success," the bitch goddess, even after he realizes that he is living in the city of hell. He likes money, silk shirts, American Express, restaurant meals, and being elected a trustee of the state gallery. On the other hand he does not like cancer, asylums, police inquiries, and family life in Palm Avenue. The drunken dinners at Palm Avenue focus the conflicting claims of city and bush, and they raise to an artform attempts at "taking the piss" out of these alternative styles of living. Typical is Bettina's inspired suggestion for the ultimate Monsanto product, which also ridicules Honey Barbara's beliefs—"Organic Poison." Although Harry's family life does not quite equal the nightmare of Alex Duval's marriage, it is grim enough: his son David, for example, seduces Honey Barbara and pays $5,000 to have Harry certified and imprisoned. Harry must escape from this family or die. Still, the vortex of money, success, corruption, and unhappiness holds him, even after Honey Barbara leaves in despair, realizing that her values have been compromised and marginalized, and that she is losing the battle for Harry's allegiance to Bettina, advertising, and the city.

After the Mobil holocaust, however, the collapse of Joy, Joy and Davis, and the visitations of the police, Harry steals David's money and Ken's Cadillac and flees the Dickensian wen of the city for the forest Bog Onion Road. He has not undergone a conversion from the values of late capitalism to pastoral communalism but simply wants to survive at any cost, like Little Titch, and is willing to abandon one narrative and to enter into another. Perhaps because of his backslidings and betrayals, he is obliged to serve a long apprenticeship in the forest before he is fully accepted as a story-teller by the community and as a lover again by Honey Barbara. The final section of the book is certainly lyric—brilliantly so—but it offers no over-easy answers, just a tantalizing story about a possible way to escape from the maelstrom of the late twentieth century into "a quiet eddy of time" (*Beautiful Lies*).

In his two earlier volumes of short stories, Carey charts the lives of a collection of physical and/or psychological pygmies who seek to master "the system" but end up instead as its inmates and victims or on display as its clowns. Harry begins as a licensed clown, a good bloke, who was "suckled on stories" and who went on to tell approved lies about Krappe

Chemicals for a living. Like many of his predecessors, Harry undergoes an arbitrary metamorphosis—dying—and experiences, also like them, the nightmares of being unemployed, solitary, imprisoned, and powerless. But Harry's end is different. He is the first of Carey's victims to break out of the circle, to escape from the prisons of city and family, to metamorphose positively from telling the lies of advertising to telling the ritual, life-enhancing stories of the forest.

This change in Harry represents, I believe, a significant turning point in Carey's career. Although he remains intensely aware of the problematic status of fictional narratives, as **Illywhacker** demonstrates, he also wants to celebrate the functions that good and well-told stories may serve, particularly in a colonized and half-formed culture, one that is hungry for its own enabling myths, for native stories to displace imported stories, and to valorize what the original inhabitants would call its dreaming. The story of Harry Joy, which Carey has told, and I have retold, addresses the ambitious task of substituting an Australian dreaming for a colonial dreaming—whether English, American, or Japanese.

Graham Huggan (essay date Spring 1990)

SOURCE: "Is the (Günter) Grass Greener on the Other Side? Oskar and Lucinde in the New World," in *World Literature Written in English,* Vol. 30, No. 1, Spring, 1990, pp. 1-10.

[*In the following essay, Huggan compares Carey's* Oscar and Lucinda *to Günter Grass's* The Tin Drum, *arguing that Carey's novel is an allegorical critique of colonialism.*]

By the final stages of Günter Grass's notorious novel *The Tin Drum,* first published in 1959, the rebellious dwarf Oskar and his counter-rhythmical drum have achieved cult status. "What we cured best of all," gloats Oskar, "was loss of memory. The word 'Oskarism' made its first appearance, but not, I am sorry to say, its last." No doubt Oskar would be perversely delighted to know that "Oskarism" is still alive and well, with disciples all over the post-colonial world. For Grass's novel has held a particular fascination for post-colonial writers, among them Salman Rushdie, whose aberrant symbolic child Saleem Sinai in the 1981 novel *Midnight's Children,* like Grass's Oskar, incorporates the contradictions of his age; and Nuruddin Farah, whose ambivalent narrator Askar in the 1986 novel *Maps* is first glorified, then vilified, as "the 'epic' child of the modern times."

At once rebellious against and complicitous in the socio-political divisions of their respective countries, Saleem and Oskar counteract their involuntary engagement in history by devising allegorical narratives which register an alternately self-justifying and self-incriminating escapism. But if allegory is the site for an apparent dislocation from history, it also provides the reader with a means of relocating the text in history against the narrator's wishes. So the allegorical narratives of

Midnight's Children and *Maps,* like that of *The Tin Drum,* are characterized by a complicated process of entanglement and disentanglement involving the alternate de- and reconstruction of historical events. George Lukacs has suggested [in "The Ideology of Modernism," in *Realism and Our Time,* 1962] that the main features of allegorical representation: its shift of emphasis from the personal to the abstract, its palpability of form, its implication of distance or distortion, makes it "that aesthetic genre which lends itself par excellence to a description of man's alienation from objective reality." Lukacs claims support from Walter Benjamin, who asserts that the portrayal of history in modern allegory does not involve "the gradual realization of the eternal, but . . . a process of inevitable decay." Now if we can accept that, in the process of allegorical representation, the materiality of the world—its rootedness in history—undergoes a significant alteration in which "every person, every object, every relationship can stand for something else," then we are in a position to consider allegory as a profoundly *anti*-historical gesture which, like Oskar's narrative, registers both an outcry *against* the times involving the attempt to escape from or militate against history and a statement *of* the times in which history is viewed as a process of decay.

The pertinence of this view to as deeply disillusioned a novel as *The Tin Drum* is clear enough; but it is less clear why post-colonial writers, many of whom ally the general process of historical reinscription to their own specific projects of cultural recuperation, should be attracted towards an apparently "anti-historical" mode. An alternative way of considering allegory within the post-colonial context, however, is as a form of counter-discourse in which the structural fracture inherent in the allegorizing process is exploited as a means of laying bare inconsistencies or contradictions within a dominant discourse or discursive mode. This is the approach taken, for example, by Stephen Slemon [in "Monuments of Empire," *Kunapipi* (1987)], who demonstrates the particular utility of allegory as a mode of post-colonial counter-discourse. Slemon first illustrates the complicity between the self-privileging gestures of colonialism and the subordinating practices of allegorical alteration in which an "other" or series of "others" are construed as a means of effecting and reinforcing a subject construction of self already prefigured by the dominant discourse. Slemon then goes on to show how "the horizon of figuration upon which a large number of post-colonial literary texts seek to act is this prefigurative discourse of colonialism, whose dominant mode of discourse is that of allegory." Thus, concludes Slemon, "allegory becomes a site for the discursive manifestation of . . . a cultural form of struggle . . . a site upon which post-colonial cultures seek to contest and subvert colonialist appropriation through the production of a figurative opposition or textual counter-discourse." Slemon's comments are clearly relevant to writers such as Rushdie and Farah whose narratives cut across received colonialist versions of history. I shall now go on to demonstrate their relevance to the allegorical narratives of another post-colonial writer: the Australian Peter Carey.

Carey's work, like Rushdie's and Farah's, is much indebted to Grass. In his first novel *Bliss* (1981), Carey includes in his offbeat parable of The American Dream the exemplary story of a recalcitrant dwarf whose perceived deformity and consequent social stigmatization become symptoms of the twisted yet paradoxically conformist world of contemporary multinational capitalism. And in his next novel *Illywhacker* (1985), Carey puts the responsibility for retelling the history of twentieth-century Australia in the altogether unreliable hands of used-car salesman and compulsive liar Herbert Badgery, whose narrative deceptions expose the fraudulent myths of a self-glorifying national consciousness. The focus of this paper, however, will be on Carey's most recent novel *Oscar and Lucinda* (1988) which, set in the mid-nineteenth century, engages in a subtle allegorical critique of the 'foundation' and subsequent colonization of the "New World."

Oscar and Lucinda relates the parallel stories of hypersensitive English vicar Oscar Hopkins, ironic mirror-image of Grass's malevolent anti-Christ, and feisty Australian libertarian Lucinda Leplastrier, who are drawn together but eventually disgraced by their fatal attraction for gambling. The scandal surrounding their relationship forms the focus of the novel and acts as a catalyst for Carey's subtle exploration of the fragile nature of spiritual, emotional and intellectual faith. It also explicitly recalls the 'scandalous' novels of Grass and Schlegel. The influence of Grass's Oskar and Schlegel's Lucinde on the two protagonists of Carey's novel is considerable; more interesting, perhaps, is the implied influence they have on one another, for Grass's heavily ironic portrayal of a faithless age in *The Tin Drum* is delicately counterbalanced by Schlegel's invocation of a mystique of love in *Lucinde,* first published in 1795 and itself a highly controversial novel of its time. Carey's portrayal of the heartwarming but fated relationship between Oscar and Lucinda combines these elements of ironic disillusion and mystical enlightenment: on the one hand, Schlegel's envisioning in *Lucinde* of the ideal union between spiritual and physical love is ridiculed by analogy with Oskar's perverse Third Reich Trinity in *The Tin Drum* (for "faith, hope, love" read "barbaric, mystical, bored"); but on the other hand, the unconsummated Schlegelian relationship between Carey's Oscar and his first love Lucinda produces a cathartic effect on the reader which transcends the memory of his destructive German predecessor.

Carey's exploitation of the allegorical mode in *Oscar and Lucinda* similarly reflects a paradoxical alliance between, rather than a mutual destruction of, these two apparently opposing tendencies. In *The Tin Drum,* as I suggested, the choice of allegory as a primary discursive mode allows for an enactment of the narrator's insistent, though doomed, attempts to dissociate himself from history. In *Lucinde,* the bizarre "alle-

gory of impudence," primarily an attack on the then fashionable quality of prudery, provides the means for a critique of hypocritical virtue while allowing for the possibility of a union between the sexes based on values which transcend social acceptability. In the first instance, allegory is conceived of as an instrument of individual alienation; in the second, as a prerequisite for interpersonal union. In Carey's novel, these tendencies towards dissociation and reassociation are used as contrapuntal structuring devices for the ambivalent alliance between Britain and Australia and for the establishment of a counter-discourse which works both within and against the predominantly binary structures informing colonial discourse.

To demonstrate more fully what I mean, I shall focus initially on the structural agent which operates in the novel as a metonymy for the allegorizing process: *glass.* In *The Tin Drum,* glass functions primarily as a medium of expression for the disillusioned Oskar, whose glass-shattering voice, like his counter-rhythmical drum, is directed not so much against Nazism or any other single form of authority as against the ways in which prevailing ideologies are assumed, and assume themselves, to be truthful. In *Oscar and Lucinda,* however, glass is rather that contradictory medium which reveals the transparency of illusion and the facticity of the illusion-making process; thus Lucinda, purchasing the ill-fated Prince Rupert's Glassworks in Sydney,

> did not have to be told . . . that glass is a thing in disguise, an actor, is not solid at all, but a liquid . . . that even while it is as frail as the ice on a Parramatta puddle, it is stronger under compression than Sydney sandstone, that it is invisible solid, in short, a joyous and paradoxical thing, as good a material as any to build a life from.

But glass also cuts; so while it is the medium that brings Oscar and Lucinda together, it also brings about their mutual destruction. The paradoxical figure for this union/disruption is the fabulous glass church which, intended for the man Oscar mistakenly believes Lucinda loves, becomes both the symbol of their own fated love and a solitary reminder of the misguided idealism which attended the 'founding' and forming of the new crown colony of Australia. Losing Lucinda her fortune and Oscar his life in a crazy venture which dramatizes the contradictions and deceptions involved in the development of colonial Australia, the church is the novel's all-encompassing embodiment of risk, encapsulating the hopeful but unprincipled industrialism of Lucinda's glassworks, the ambitious but imprisoning materialism of the giant transoceanic liner *The Leviathan* on which she and Oscar meet for the first time, and the calculated but, by its very nature, contingent gambling of Oscar. Like the glassworks, the ship, and the various ludic devices employed by Oscar as "structures for divining the will of God," the church is finally recognized, however, to be a "devil's trick," an instrument of deception which belatedly indicates to Lucinda the folly of her ambitious dreams and to Oscar the tyranny of his obsession with form. Nurtured by a stuffy English education which reinforces social and class differences, a narrow religious formation which only exchanges one set of pseudo-certainties for another, and by a weakness for gambling which remodels rather than rejects the rigid classificatory systems of his father's profession (zoology), his family and social background, and his Victorian culture, Oscar's obsession proves to be his eventual ruin; for he fails crucially to understand that all of his belief-structures are inherently flawed.

Like Grass, Carey uses a series of defective, incomplete or unstable metonymic structures as self-parodic analogues for the textual system. Probably the most succinct of these is the Prince Rupert's drop, a tiny teardrop of glass which, strong enough to withstand blows of sledgehammer intensity, explodes when nipped with pliers "as if you have taken out the keystone, removed the linchpin, kicked out the foundations." The apparent strength but actual fragility of the exquisite drop make it an apt metaphor for the imperilled relationship between Oscar and Lucinda and for the fundamental instability of Carey's finely-crafted text. There is a further implication, however, behind Carey's depiction of an analogous series of flawed systems; for The System was, of course, the euphemistic term used to denote the infamous penal system of early colonial Australia. Thus another metonymic structure, the ship *The Leviathan,* which features a three-tiered division between a vast but scarcely habitable first class, a more comfortable but somewhat uncouth second class, and the infernal nether-regions of the engine-room, becomes the site of Carey's witty parody of a transplanted colonial culture based on rigid social stratification, equal measures of snobbery and vulgarity, and an underlying viciousness by no means confined to its convict workforce. And Carey's choice of name for the ship suggests more; for incorporated into *The Leviathan* is an equally subtle critique of the political theory of the rationalist thinker Thomas Hobbes. Subtle, because although Carey clearly satirizes Hobbes's politics, specifically the latter's championing of the cause of a monarchist commonwealth which conveniently glosses over class differences, he seems less averse to Hobbes's philosophy, and would appear in particular to subscribe to an extreme version of Hobbesian nominalism in which the supposedly systematic classification of things into kinds is demonstrated to be wholly arbitrary. By cleverly turning Hobbes's philosophy against his politics, Carey is able to suggest not only the inherently contradictory nature of the newly formed Australian society but also the equally contradictory nature of the colonial discourse which serves it. And this discourse, as I have suggested in accordance with Slemon, finds expression in an allegorical mode which allows both for the symbolic enactment of formal differences and for the embodiment of internal flaws or inconsistencies within a dominant or "governing" system.

Two parallel incidents in the novel serve to illustrate. In the first, the young Oscar designs a symbolic cross, ironically but not wholly inaccurately mistaken by his father for a set of witches' markings from his largely pagan neighbourhood in England's West Country. The cross features a set of squares inlaid with symbols arbitrarily representing the various systems of belief Oscar has superficially encountered in his as yet short and inexperienced life. The confused Oscar wishes to ask God which system he should choose; but significantly, he leaves the top square blank in what he imagines to be a token of reverence. The implication is that the model is not only arbitrarily conceived, but necessarily incomplete. A parallel mock-pagan ritual in Australia confirms this suspicion. The young Lucinda, having taken her favourite doll into the unfamiliar territory of the "back creek," proceeds to submit it to a bizarre aboriginal transformation intended to confirm both her love for the "old Australia" and her hatred of the new Anglo-Saxon colony which has supplanted it. On opposite sides of the world, Lucinda and Oscar simultaneously intuit that the landscape and its original dwellers are not Christian: Lucinda's apparently harmless transgression into the forbidden "blackfellow" territory which the polite society of New South Wales disclaim to the point of non-existence, like Oscar's seemingly innocuous inscription of a blank space into his religious model, is therefore perceived to provide the missing link which subverts an entire social and theological system. Again, the analogy with Grass is instructive. Towards the end of *The Tin Drum,* a sequence is unveiled which leads inexorably to the indictment of Oscar although, with typical ambivalence, it is for a crime which the evidence suggests he may not have committed. The sequence: drumstick, scar, cartridge case, ring finger, connects the novel's earlier leitmotifs and associates them with the parodically accusatory finger of the murdered nurse Sister Dorothea which Oscar, believing it his right to keep, has adoringly preserved in a glass pickle-jar. The jar in turn recalls the test-tubes which Oscar had petulantly shattered with his "gifted" voice during a childhood visit to the office of Dr. Höllatz, thereby releasing the latter's unsavory collection of reptiles and human embryos. The implications of guilt and retribution, not just for Oscar's but for Germany's unwholesome past, are clear. So too in Carey's novel, where Lucinda's transmogrified doll, itself emanating from a (birthday) jar, implicates both the colonial project which has wilfully dispossessed the Australian aborigines of their land and, by analogy with Oscar's naturalist father's painstakingly bottled specimens, the combinations of cold-hearted rationalism and religious intolerance which form Australia's unprepossessing colonial inheritance.

The most striking example of a non-recognition of aboriginal codes which lays bare the structural flaw in and prefigures the eventual collapse of the colonial project is Oscar's horrific journey through the unmapped territory of the Australian interior towards the remote outpost where the glass church is to be reassembled and delivered to the undeserving Rev. Hasset. Allegorizing the so-called "discovery" of the inland continent, a discovery based of course on the misconception that the land was previously uninhabited, or that even if it was inhabited, then its benighted inhabitants somehow "did not count," Carey draws inspiration here less from Grass than from the apocalyptic parables of fellow-Australians Patrick White and Randolph Stow and, particularly, from a story widely used by twentieth-century Australian writers, Franz Kafka's "In the Penal Colony." In this latter work, an ironic adaptation of the Biblical parable in which the Kingdom of heaven is likened to a man travelling into a far country, a foreigner is initiated into the strange and brutal rituals of a régime whose social and ethical codes he cannot decipher but which, it is suggested, he may know better than he claims to understand. The parable, which other post-colonial writers (notably the South African J.M. Coetzee) have found appropriate to the ironic demonstration of imperial prerogatives, is turned by Carey into a parodic revision of European heroic and purgatorial myths. Oscar fails the test, goaded into the tragicomic murder of the demented expedition leader Jeffris and falling even further from glory when he succumbs at the hands of the seductive Miriam to the temptation of lust. The disastrous mission takes place within the allegorical framework of colonial expansionism, whose two opposing aspects are represented in the novel by the gentle but hopelessly unadapted Oscar, whose education, social background and conceptual vocabulary are incompatible with the "sawtoothed savagery" of his new surroundings and with the often indelicate sensibilities of his new colleagues; and by the megalomaniac Jeffris, a Leichhardt/Voss surrogate determined to imprint his own name, at whatever cost, on the face of the continent. Both fall victim to their obsessions: Oscar gambles once too often, and Jeffris's brutality is turned against himself; but although the expedition ends in disaster, Oscar's school friend Wardley-Fish later discovers that the wider colonial mission, through a combination of deceit and destruction, has reaped its undeserved rewards:

> [There was] not so much as a clue as to what passions had brought his friend to inhabit this damp and sorry place . . . the only brightness on that long peninsula came from Borrodaile's shiny red surveyor's stakes which dotted the earth as regularly as pegs upon a cribbage board.

Borrodaile's surveyor's stakes, symbols of colonialist territorial appropriation, recall the rigid demarcations of Oscar's native English landscape, where "he had as firm a sense of territory as a dog, and when he moved across the terrain outside his map . . . he moved jerkily, running, his knees clicking, out of breath, with a pain in his side." The map provides one metaphor for the imposition of a set pattern upon a landscape which it inevitably falsifies; the cribbage board another which, through its introduction of the factor of chance, implicitly controverts the perfectionist rationale behind, and therefore undermines the authoritarian claims of, the map. Both are metonymies for the text and for the colonial system it exemplifies: the map allegorical, precise but depersonalized

and limiting, the cribbage board parodic, designed to perfection but regulated by chance. Borrodaile's stakes bring the two together, suggesting at once the sacrifice of life in the colonial acquisition and expansion of territory and the wager which, though lost by Oscar and Lucinda, is won by the scheming Borrodaile and his colonialist minions at their expense. Thus, as in *The Tin Drum,* the formation of a corrupt society is shown to rest on the twin foundations of violence (the accusatory scars on Herbert Truczunski's back in Grass's novel; the embattled landscape of the Australian interior in Carey's) and opportunism (the abuse of talent and/or good fortune in both the joyous yet perilous construction of one's life as a house of cards, a game of skat or cribbage).

It is above all Oscar's death, drowned when the glass church of his dreams collapses with him trapped inside on the flimsy lighter which had been used to transport it, which provides a clue as to the relation between Grass's and Carey's novels and as to the counter-discursive nature of the latter's allegorical narrative. Oscar's ineffectual scream as he realizes he is about to die ironically inverts the arrogantly destructive screams of Grass's self-glorifying protagonist high up on the Danzig Stockturn. The tower does not stand tall this time, but totters; the glass is not shattered *at* but *against* will. It is as if the dream, taking on a maleficent life of its own, has returned to haunt, and eventually to engulf, the dreamer. The desanctification of the Rev. Oscar Hopkins, it would appear, is complete; but what about the implicit denunciation of his sacrilegious predecessor? Is Carey suggesting here that the death of his Oscar, unlike the inconclusive committal of Grass's, provides some sort of cathartic release induced by an awakening to moral and social responsibilities for a reprehensible past? The implicitly recuperative function of Schlegel's *Lucinde* in Carey's text would certainly appear to palliate the negativity he associates with *The Tin Drum,* but while it is possible to see in the collapse of Oscar and Lucinda's church the metaphorical *sub*mergence of a nefarious colonial heritage, it would no doubt be too simplistic to deduce from this the parallel *em*ergence of an emancipated post-colonial Australia. For a start, the marks of the colonial project are inscribed, if not indelibly, then at least enduringly, into the land; in addition, the miserable fate of the libertarian Lucinda, forced into drudgery after being cheated out of her fortune, suggests both the continuance in Australia of a patriarchal society which impedes the freedom of women and the historical complicity between the repressive practices of *patriarchal* and *colonial* discourses. And in any case, the emergence of a supposedly "authentic" Australian nation would seem very like a perpetuation of precisely the *colonialist* rhetorical model, based on fallacious notions of unity and completeness, that Carey resists in **Oscar and Lucinda,** as elsewhere in his work.

To seek working alternatives to this falsely essentialist model, it becomes necessary to return to the notion of allegory as a counter-discursive mode. In Carey's, as in many other post-colonial texts, allegory functions as an exemplary device for the internal erosion or fracture of the dominant discursive system. Thus, far from reconfirming the colonialist project of "building a new nation"—for allegory, as I mentioned before, is a mode which lays bare the palpability of form—Carey undermines it from within by exposing the structural flaws inherent in colonial discourse which belie its pretensions to ideological coherence. This notion of ideological rupture is usually associated with the work of the European Marxist critics Pierre Macherey and Terry Eagleton, but I think it is best expressed in the post-colonial context by the Australian critic Helen Tiffin [in "Post-Colonial Literatures and Counter-Discourse," *Kunapipi* (1987)]. In discussing the contestatory position often taken up by post-colonial writers and critics, Tiffin takes care to distinguish between what she sees as their primarily *subversive* manoeuvres and the construction of *essentially* national or regional discursive formations. This leads her to claim, correctly in my view, that "post-colonial literatures/cultures are constituted in counter-discursive rather than homologous practices [which implement] counter-discursive strategies to the dominant discourse." And, she adds pointedly, "the operation of post-colonial counter-discourse is dynamic, not static: it does not seek to subvert the dominant with a view to taking its place, but . . . to evolve textual strategies which continually consume their own biases at the same time as they expose and erode those of the dominant discourse." A counter-discursive allegorical mode, in this context, is instrumental in the process of cultural decolonization precisely because it avoids the fallacy of self-constitutive essentialism, recognizes the need for constructive self-critique, and opens itself to the possibility of a plurality of intra- and inter-cultural perspectives.

It is here, I would argue, that Carey, like Rushdie and Farah, diverges from Grass. But not, certainly, because Grass's allegory is not contestatory (it is) or because he supports an essentialist doctrine (he doesn't) but because he seems to remain trapped within the context of a Eurocentric ideology which may "consume its own biases" but which ultimately fails to seek alternatives beyond itself. Rushdie already hints at this in *Midnight's Children* by distinguishing between Saleem Sinai's grandfather Aadam Aziz and his anarchic German friends Oscar (again) and Ilse; for at medical school in Heidelberg Aadam had learnt that "India—like radium—had been discovered by the Europeans; even Oscar was filled with admiration for Vasco da Gama, and this was what finally separated Aadam Aziz from his friends, this belief that somehow he was the invention of their ancestors." Carey similarly dissociates himself from this position: first, by parodying the rhetorical strategies implemented by the "first" European explorers and settlers, thereby effecting an "undiscovery" of the "New World" which leads to the rematerialization in its supposedly blank spaces of the suppressed discourses of aboriginal culture; and, second, by propelling his protagonist into the self-destruction which awaits those who are congeni-

tally unable to distinguish between their life and their dreams. So Carey's Oscar, more sympathetic if less dynamic than his German counterpart, is finally made to confront, rather than to predict, his nemesis, and is denied the "ideal" relationship he had always coveted. By analogy, Carey avoids the allegorical extremes of an idealized union between Britain and Australia or of a simplistic disabusal of the legacy of European colonialism. Carey's clear-eyed account of Australia's colonial past, funny, shocking and poignant by turns, shows that the Grass can be just as green on the other side. But Carey, no doubt, would beg to differ; for, in his ongoing critique of cultural prejudice, which "side" is to be construed as "other"?

Robert Ross (essay date 1990)

SOURCE: "'It Cannot *Not* Be There': Borges and Australia's Peter Carey," in *Borges and His Successors: The Borgesian Impact on Literature and the Arts,* edited by Edna Aizenberg, University of Missouri Press, 1990, pp. 44-58.

[*In the following essay, Ross focuses on Carey's short stories as he speculates on the influence of Argentine writer Jorge Luis Borges's works on Carey's artistic development.*]

> *You're quite right when you suggest that it might be difficult to say exactly how Borges may have influenced me, also right to suggest that the influence is/ was there. . . . It is there, it cannot not be there.*
> —PETER CAREY, letter

On first reading Peter Carey's writing, I found it different from other Australian literature, and I resolved this encounter with the unexpected by making broad and perhaps obvious comparisons: Carey belongs more to the world tradition than to the Australian; more specifically, his work suggests South American writers, such as Borges and García Márquez, or North Americans like Barth, Barthelme, Vonnegut, and Kesey, or Europeans like Kafka and Camus—all facile enough parallels to draw. In fact, Australian reviewers had already said much the same about Carey's work, one observing, for example, that "his music is more international . . . and echoes the upbeat rhythms of the three B's: Borges, Barth and Barthelme" [Jim Legasse, review of *War Crimes* by Peter Carey, *Westerly* (June 1980)]. The Australian critic Brian Kiernan noted in a letter to me that reviewers in Australia often make such sweeping statements about Carey, but critics there fail to develop these generalizations because comparative literature is not generally pursued in Australian universities either as a field of study or as an avenue of criticism, except to a limited extent, comparing Australian writing with American, British, and other English-language literatures. Thus there exists no body of criticism on which to rely.

Instead I turned to Peter Carey himself and in a letter asked the questions one would often like to pose when setting out on a comparative study: had he in truth read Borges? If so, what part, if any, had Borges played in his own development as a writer? Carey replied [in a letter to the critic dated October 22, 1986], in the words of the headnote above, then elaborated:

> I remember the name of the friend who introduced me to Borges, remember the Melbourne bookshop where the first book (*Ficciones*) was purchased. . . . The bookshop was The Whole Earth Bookshop (God, could it *really* have been called that?) and its Hippy-poet proprietors ignored all the publishers' ideas on how the world of literature must be divided up and (illegally) imported paperbacks direct from the U.S. (Up until that time we could only read what London publishers decided.) . . . I shudder to imagine how the works of an erudite blind librarian might have been understood, misunderstood, as they were gulped down by a twenty eight year old Australian—recently embarked on the adventure of reading—who, I am sure, took them in long impatient draughts, better suited to simple spring water than such fragrant and delicate distillations.

Agreeable to further question-answering, Carey concluded: "I look forward to the inquisition." [In a footnote, Ross adds: "To Peter Carey, I am grateful for his clear replies to my sometimes muddled questions. I have quoted at length from Carey's response to 'the inquisition.' Perhaps foolishly I ignored his admission in one letter: 'Is what I am saying the truth? Was this really the attraction [to Borges's writing] or am I simply trying to build an answer that will make us both happy?' But such are the hazards of the comparative enterprise, especially with the author looking over one's shoulder."] Whether he used "inquisition" intentionally remains speculative, yet one cannot help but think of Borges's first book of essays, which he called *Inquisiciones* (1925), as well as of the later volume, *Otras Inquisiciones* (1952). Another of Carey's remarks, when read in a Borgesian light, suggests that image so much a part of Borges's world picture: the universe as a library, maybe even a bookshop. Did his first encounter with the great South American really occur in a store called "The Whole Earth Bookshop," Carey asks, seeming to hint at the irony involved in such a name.

A young writer, Carey has published two volumes of short stories, *The Fat Man in History* and *War Crimes,* and three novels, *Bliss, Illywhacker,* and *Oscar & Lucinda.* [In a footnote, Ross states: "In a study of this length, it was not feasible to take up Carey's novels. First published in Australia, they have been issued in the United States by Harper & Row. *Bliss* is a richly comic novel about Harry Joy who survives a heart attack but discovers in the process that he has been living in hell. On one level more realistic than the short stories, *Bliss* continues to break down the barriers between fiction and life. In *Illywhacker* Carey reshapes Australian history,

which Mark Twain called 'the most beautiful lies.' The narrator described himself as an *illywhacker,* an Australian slang term for a professional trickster or con artist. Certainly, Borges would have appreciated and approved of such a name for the storyteller. Not without its shadow of Borges, *Illywhacker* brings to mind more fully Gabriel García Márquez's *One Hundred Years of Solitude,* thus showing once again how Borges, on whom García Márquez in part relied, helped to establish modern Latin American literature and its international reputation. *Oscar & Lucinda,* which depicts a minister (Oscar) who is an inveterate gambler and thinks it is appropriate because believing in God is the biggest gamble of all, also has its Borgesian touches."] With the publication of *The Fat Man in History,* he established himself, first at home and then abroad, as a highly original figure in Australian literature. In a review of that first book Frank Moorhouse, another innovator of Australian fiction, praised Carey's inventiveness and the freshness he had brought to Australian literature: "For some time now there has been a vacancy in the Sophisticated Fantasy Section of the Short Story Industry. It is my pleasure to announce that Peter Carey, 30, of Melbourne has been appointed to fill that position. He will also do allegories, fables, and astonishing tricks" [Quoted in Don Anderson, ed., *Transgressions, Australian Writing Now,* 1986].

Like Borges, Carey had inherited a national literature dominated by social realism. Before Carey's writing appeared another Australian, Patrick White, had altered irrevocably, through a series of impressive novels, the course of Australian fiction, which White himself early on described [in "The Prodigal Son," *Australian Letters* (April 1958)] as "the dreary, dun-coloured offspring of journalistic realism." Like White, who looked to the European tradition and wrote as though Australian fiction before him did not exist, Carey searched elsewhere for his models. That Carey's first book appeared in 1974 is significant, for a year earlier White had received the Nobel Prize for Literature, the first time an Australian had been so honored. Of course, White had been writing for nearly twenty-five years without much recognition from Australian critics who too often considered his metaphysical handling of Australian materials a violation of the social realism, bush humor, and other established conventions they admired. Once recognized by so prestigious a prize, White's work soon became acceptable to the most reluctant of his critics—at least publicly. So did other writing that broke away from the stock and often hackneyed accounts of such seasoned matter as life in the bush, family struggles on a sheep or cattle station, mateship, pioneering, and the labor movement. Gene Bell-Villada concludes [in *Borges and His Fiction,* 1981] that "Borges's best stories contribute a new praxis and sensibility" to Latin American fiction, and he praises this "fruitful artistic mode that breaks away from psychology and realism, which for some two hundred years have been the fundamental materials of prose narrative." In regard to Australian literature, much the same could be said of White, then of Peter Carey and the others who emulated White in his rejection of literary custom, and in their own ways let ripen in Australia a "fruitful artistic mode" resembling the one Bell-Villada saw take hold in Latin America.

Not many years ago, the question was frequently asked: Is there really an Australian literature? As a result of White's reception abroad, even before he received the Nobel Prize, and the international recognition accorded Australian writers in recent years, the faraway continent's distinctive literary voice now speaks with such clarity that the once scornful question has lost its edge. For instance, Tom Shapcott, director of the Literature Board of the Australia Council, has reported that during 1986 publications in the United States reviewed more books from Australia than from any other foreign country except Great Britain. Scores of Australian books, most often fictional works but occasionally a volume of poetry, now appear on major American publishers' lists each year, many of them faring well in the marketplace. According to editors and agents, the competition for Australian books has become keen among publishers in the United States.

This literary zest, stemming in part from government subsidy administered by the Literature Board of the Australia Council, has benefited Carey and his generation of writers, as have changes in worldwide publishing practices that make the books of international writers, especially those in translation, accessible to young Australians, who can now mature on a cosmopolitan literature. "I grew up in almost total ignorance of literature, the literature of my own country in particular," Carey recalls. When he began to read seriously he says that he did not turn to "the fiction written in, by, or about Australia" but became, as he described himself in a letter [to the critic dated April 6, 1987],

> a denizen of one of Borges' libraries—a great circular building crammed with unindexed books, its bulging shelves occasionally interrupted by tall thin windows through which one could see a brilliant ultramarine sky, dust from road works or quarries, a society founded by convicts where even those who now had big houses and expensive cars still carried, not the values of their apparent bourgeois status, but the values and prejudices of convicts. The society outside the library did not value writers, artists, singers, story tellers. It was a society that valued men who were good with their hands.

Yet it is about this society that Carey most often writes, recording his vision of it not in the "dun-coloured" tinge of the realist but in the broad and vivid strokes of the mythmaker, the fabulist, the visionary, the metaphysician.

In his twenties, during Australia's involvement in the Vietnam War, Carey left Australia, which he then considered "a Client State . . . of the American government." Abroad, he imagined himself "a citizen of the world": "In Europe (Brit-

ain in particular) I had come 'home.' I had returned to the culture from which I and two generations before me had been exiled. I cannot tell you what a delight it was to see the electric green grass between Dover and London or, for that matter, to hold a copy of the Sunday *Times*—complete with colour supplement—on my lap." He came back to Australia, though, a country that he admits he has always held a "great love" for but at the same time "feared and loathed." After returning, he worked as an advertising copywriter, lived part of the time in a commune, and started to write the fiction that is neither Australian nor non-Australian, just as Borges's work is neither Argentine nor non-Argentine. For both, although inhabitants of the world library, are firmly grounded in their own particular countries whose reality they enhance by traveling abroad in the country of the mind, the country that Patrick White describes through Laura Trevelyan's confession in *Voss*: "Knowledge was never a matter of geography. Quite the reverse, it overflows all maps that exist. Perhaps true knowledge only comes of death by torture in the country of the mind."

This young Australian, growing up in "a society where," he says, "artists were not only not valued but, often despised," found "a book called *Ficciones*" and years later remembers that first reading when he discovered "within its covers—stories of a potency . . . never dreamed possible. The stories were magical, hermetic, creatures of the library. They posited a world where books had power, where artists had power, where story-telling mattered." In retrospect, though, how do we determine the ways this journey into the country of the mind affected Carey's writing? Like Borges, Carey demonstrates a strong sense of nationality, for he makes full use of the peculiar materials his country offers—its history, social oddities, geography; its people and their folklore—along with autobiographical and family matter. On the other hand, like Borges, Carey can turn to any part of the world and call it his own within that particular fiction. Yet for both writers the components of a story—setting, plot, dialogue, character—derive their strength not from faithful rendering of locale, not from the sources on which they draw, not from strong character delineation, not from the virtuosity of their prose, but from "truths painfully arrived at," as Carey defines the ancient art of story making.

[In *Jorge Luis Borges: A Literary Biography,* 1978] Emir Rodríguez Monegal describes *Ficciones* as "perhaps the single most important book of prose fiction written in Spanish in this century." To make such a claim for Carey's *The Fat Man in History* (1974) in relation to Australian fiction may be debatable, but certainly this book of twelve stories brought a singular newness to the Australian short prose narrative. Carey had presented himself as being "international," a label with which Australian critics often dub a writer who breaks the mold. Exactly what they mean by that appellation—at times complimentary, at times derisive—remains somewhat obscure, but I rather imagine they intend to suggest that the writer has looked to European and American literary figures, especially those considered postmodern, for his or her artistic mode, rather than to the Australian classic writers like Henry Lawson and Joseph Furphy, whose stature is comparable to that of Mark Twain and Bret Harte in the literature of the United States.

To return now to the original proposition—that Carey's work from the outset led me (and other readers) to think of Borges and those authors often associated with him; let us then ask, in what ways does Carey's fiction recall the Argentine master's? This is an obvious question in light of the knowledge that Carey has admitted to reading Borges and considering this literary experience an important element in his own formation as a writer. If it were possible, I would present here an impressive and all-encompassing list of characteristics to define the qualities that make Borges's fiction distinctive, then methodically apply them to Carey's writing. But no matter how thorough the search, first through the fiction itself, then through the abundant commentary on it, no such ordered list emerges. [In *The Cardinal Points of Borges,* edited by Lowell Dunham and Ivar Ivask, 1971] Donald A. Yates attempts just such a feat in his essay "The Four Cardinal Points of Borges." While admitting that "to ascribe to Borges's artistic world four key aspects, four cardinal points, is, to be sure, arbitrary," Yates hopes that with "any luck" his scheme will be "in some way telling." And luck rides with him, as he compares the cardinal points to those of the compass and thereby provides an ordered way to look at Borges's work.

South on this compass stands for Borges's deep sense of Argentine nationality, not only in the way he makes use of indigenous materials but also in his absorption and synthesis of borrowings from diverse sources—an easy assimilation Yates ascribes to the special type of Argentine *criollismo* that Borges represents. Carey, a third-generation Australian, is also a *criollo,* born of European parents transplanted in the Southern Hemisphere. Bound to Australia, but ambivalent in his sentiments toward it, Carey, like all his countrymen of European descent, has always looked to the Northern Hemisphere and taken from it those elements required to complement his intellectual and artistic development. To call either Borges or Carey "Europeanized" or "international" may be a legitimate appraisal but not a disparaging one, as an examination of the next point on the compass will prove.

North, according to Yates, takes language and literature as its orientation. Borges has often said that the most significant feature of his childhood was his father's library of English books, which helped direct him toward a life of literature. Because Borges's writing makes use of other literatures, he admits to influences without hesitation, Yates notes, and then concludes, "Language . . . continues in [Borges's] later years to be a point to which he is oriented, a north by which he still guides himself." Carey, too, recalls a library whose "bulging shelves" transported him to a world far beyond the one that

"interrupted" through the "tall thin windows" of that "great circular building" in Australia (an apt description of the Victoria State Library in Melbourne). Like Borges, Carey does not hesitate to grant those books a place in his own writing, admitting easily that his eclectic reading led him into literary experiments of his own, some successful, others not. With many creative years ahead of him and with his literary success freeing him of other responsibilities, Carey now lives a life of language, derived in large part from "a north by which he still guides himself." In **Bliss,** Carey describes the talent of a great storyteller who gave to language a meaning that only his handling of it could impart: "The words of the story could be of no use to anyone else. The words, by themselves, were useless. The words were an instrument only he could play and they became, in the hands of others, dull and lifeless, like picked flowers or bright stones removed from underwater." Thus the north of the compass alone would be useless, an observation that introduces the next point.

East on this literary compass is the cardinal point that represents what Yates calls the most "distinctive feature" of Borges's writing: "It could be described as a fascination with philosophical and metaphysical questions that manifests itself, in part, in the incorporation of these problems as elements of his prose fiction." Drawn more to the abstractions of infinity and identity than to the palpable substance of daily life with which he clothes these larger concerns, Borges has admitted that he is "quite simply a man who uses perplexities for literary purposes." [In a letter to the critic dated April 6, 1987] Carey recalls how, on discovering Borges's work, he had found storytelling that mattered, that gave artists power. No such phenomenon, Carey notes, had occurred in his country (where the tale and its teller mattered little) since the time, a century ago, when Australians took to their hearts Henry Lawson and his accounts of bush life. But Carey finds suspect even Lawson's fabled reception, and he wonders if the popular reports of "shearers and bushworkers reading Lawson by lanternlight may be the wishful thinking of city intellectuals." Similarly, Borges found noteworthy that the literature celebrating the exploits of Argentine gauchos, the equivalent to Lawson's tales of bushmen, was in truth the creation of city writers—those urban intellectuals who claimed to speak in the style and voice of the gauchos. Lawson, like his Argentine counterparts, much preferred the comforts and relatively cosmopolitan atmosphere of Sydney to the bush he extolled. For both Borges and Carey, the storyteller and the story *matter*—their power is derived not from the faithful yet artificial recording of national myth but from the painful seeking of truth. This belief in the power of story is the province of the final point.

West on Borges's compass Yates considers to be "the strong, ever-present narrative ingredient of drama." This element he describes as assuming the form of vivid color, melodrama, mystery, tight plotting—those features that stand in for the psychological probing or exposition generally absent in

Borges's work. Likewise, Carey's stories are well constructed from a narrative standpoint, never employing the tricks of tedious psychological probing or dreary internal meandering. Instead, their dramatic events emerge swiftly in dazzling and mysterious ways. For one thing, both Borges and Carey show a penchant for depicting violence, a tendency Yates attributes in part to Borges's fondness for western films, gangster movies, and detective fiction. Carey, an Australian growing up in the fifties, most likely saw his share of American crime films and westerns. Both come from countries where violence has always played a significant role in everyday life. "I grew up in a country town," Carey explains, "where disagreements were always resolved physically," much in the same way, one might suppose, that Borges's *guapos* and *compadritos*—Argentina's native toughs—settled disputes and defended their honor. Another element of their narrative mode is comedy, a device that merges into the story as unobtrusively as it does in real life, sometimes intentionally, at other times accidentally. The first-person narrator, who so often appears in both writers' works, beholds the goings-on around him in a manner detached, ironic, and amused. He then reports his version of what he has seen, in tales that lack narrative pretensions and structural artifice but that display instead a self-disguised plotting and an enviable control of dramatic tension.

The four metaphorical points of the compass may now be transformed into the list of characteristics, albeit abbreviated, that I sought earlier. Both writers display a sense of nationality along with an awareness of the larger world. Their work reveals a broad reading, which they have incorporated. They take up the perplexities that trouble them and their fellows. And they both accomplish this through adherence to the rules that have always governed effective storytelling, so that their readers finish the fiction and are affected by it: remembering it, marveling at its power, and, because of its many-layered thematic texture, finding in it diverse, new, and private meanings.

For both Borges and Carey, the storyteller and the story *matter*—their power is derived not from the faithful yet artificial recording of national myth but from the painful seeking of truth.

—Robert Ross

With this compass in hand, let us venture into the literary territory of Borges and Carey, beginning with one of the stories from Carey's first volume, possibly the best known among them, **"American Dreams."** Set in a small Australian town during the fifties, the events unfold in a matter-of-fact way, recounted as a young male narrator's reminiscences. He tells

how a respected townsman named Mr. Gleason one day orders his Chinese laborers to build ten-foot-high walls around nearby Bald Hill and then orders them to top the walls with broken glass and barbed wire and to build a mysterious construction inside. The years pass and the inhabitants of the town (which closely resembles those bush settlements depicted in countless stories from earlier Australian realistic literature) still do not find out what is hidden behind those walls; nor does the reader. Eventually Mr. Gleason dies and his widow orders the walls destroyed to reveal what the narrator calls "the most incredibly beautiful thing I had ever seen in my life." At first he only "breathed the surprising beauty of it," then he realizes that "it was our town," scaled down and "peopled," so that the townsfolk find themselves in familiar places performing daily tasks, their mundane, earthly lives caught in a miniature stroke of eternity.

Although the town council soon asks Mrs. Gleason to destroy the model town "on the grounds that it contravened building regulations," their action comes too late, for the city newspapers discover the marvel, and the minister for tourism declares the site a tourist attraction, promising that "the Americans would come,... take photographs and bring wallets bulging with dollars. American dollars." And they do arrive, the narrator reports, to examine and photograph the model town, then to compare it to the real one through telescopes, eventually leaving the miniature and descending into the life-size original to take additional photographs for which they pay a dollar each. But "having paid the money," the narrator concludes, "they are worried about being cheated. They spend their time being disappointed and I spend my time feeling guilty, that I have somehow let them down by growing older and sadder." As the story opens, the narrator, who reveals what has happened after the fact, believes that the townspeople somehow offended Mr. Gleason, thus causing him to go to such lengths to settle his score with them. His revenge was to make them immortal; even worse, he forced them to look at their eternal selves while growing mortally "older and sadder."

"American Dreams" brings to mind any number of other literary works—Edward Albee's *Tiny Alice,* for one, in which a miniature of a house rests within that house, holding yet another replica, and so on. The wall that encloses Mr. Gleason's secret also has its parallels in the labyrinths that figure so often in Borges's fiction. The title, too, plays on and then perverts the tradition of the American dream. Once transferred to the bush town, the dreams turn materialistic and shoddy in their secondhand state, speaking only "of the big city, of wealth, of modern houses, of big motor cars," the wrong sort of dreams for people to use as vehicles for escape from their "poor kind of life" (as Borges describes the existence of people who are too sure about reality). In an interview [from Richard Bargin's *Conversations with Jorge Luis Borges,* 1969], Borges observes, "If you're a materialist, if you believe in hard and fast things, then you're tied down by reality, or by what you call reality." Carey's townsfolk had tied themselves to such a reality even in their dreams, despite the fact that dissolving reality (which, Borges says, "is not always too pleasant") can mean that people "will be helped by . . . [the] dissolution."

The picture of the tiny, disembodied townspeople caught in perpetuity, while time takes its toll on those whose lives served as models, brings to mind another of Borges's perplexities: what if man were immortal? Commenting on his story "The Immortals," Borges notes, "Such an idea as immortality would, of course, be unbearable. In 'The Immortals' we are face to face with people who are only immortal and nothing else, and the prospect, I trust, is appalling" [*The Aleph and Other Stories 1933-1969,* 1970]. Like don Guillermo's son or Dr. Narbondo's "immortals," the residents of the Australian bush town go on living in their own world, detached from the past, alienated from the present, impervious to the future. Carey has treated the same philosophical question that Borges often debated, and he has done so in a manner reminiscent of Borges by grounding his story in reality, then spreading over it a transparent covering woven from the strands of fantasy. In both cases, out of the remembrances of first-person narrators come stories that insist on their believability, for the narrators of **"American Dreams"** and "The Immortals" have, as Ana María Barrenechea says of Borges [in *Borges: The Labyrinth Maker,* 1965], erased "the boundaries between life and fiction," indeed the boundaries between story and metaphysical inquiry. Extraordinary events have occurred, yet they seem altogether ordinary, set as they are in very commonplace contexts.

Each of the stories in Carey's first volume gains resonance when read in the light of this commonality of philosophical concerns and narrative structure, even when the relationship is limited to a single element of Borges's fiction: the labyrinth. In **"Crabs"** the labyrinth evolves into a drive-in movie theater where Crabs and his girl friend find themselves trapped—their captivity an outcome that is natural enough in the real yet fantastic world they inhabit. Another instance of a physical structure figuring prominently in relation to the story's metaphysical framework arises in **"Life & Death in the South Side Pavilion."** The narrator relates how he has been assigned to watch the horses living in the pavilion, both he and the horses being prisoners in this place of unexplained confinement. That the pavilion represents the narrator's mental labyrinth becomes evident once he tells of drowning the horses and describes them floating in the pool where they "bumped softly into one another like bad dreams in a basin." The fat men in the title story of the collection [**"The Fat Man in History"**] find themselves shunned by a society that refuses to tolerate obesity. They are imprisoned not only in their fat but also in a bleak and colorless structure amid "high blocks of concrete flats and areas of flat waste land where dry thistles grow." For Carey, the metaphor of the labyrinth emerges not only as a metaphysical structure that turns inward and de-

vours itself but also as a physical entity, a concept realized in another of the stories, **"Peeling."** Here the narrator relates how he undresses a female companion and accidentally pulls a zipper that removes another layer to reveal a male body hiding beneath, and then another female body; finally "with each touch she is dismembered, slowly, limb by limb" until he loses hold and she falls to the floor, making a "sharp noise, rather like breaking glass." He discovers among the fragments "a small doll, hairless, eyeless, and white from head to toe."

Carter Wheelock stresses [in *The Mythmaker,* 1969] that "Borges' much-noticed labyrinth, his symbol for the universe, is not the objective universe but the human mind." Both Borges and Carey suggest that once men discover they are lost in a mental labyrinth, entrapped and encircled by its mysteries, afloat in its chaos, helpless in its enclosure, they attempt to provide explanations. The traditional writer or the philosopher will form grave hypotheses to explain away the "Great Labyrinth," whereas Borges "stands above this attempt to account for the universe; his truth does not depend on the things that can be called true but on the assumption that nothing can be so called. For him the goal of thought is not knowledge, but distraction." Extending this critical comment to Carey adds dimension to his stories, which repeatedly explain away mystery with distraction. Both writers derive one aspect of their comedy from this quality of distraction, by eschewing seriousness in the unraveling of the perplexities they behold.

Borges and Carey share another aspect of narrative structure, their handling of time. Most often Borges sets his tales in the past, but he narrates them from an immediate point of view as though recollecting the events as he records them. On the other hand, Carey's stories often occur in a hazy, remote future. Yet, like Borges, Carey relates the happenings from a past perspective, with an immediacy established to contrast with the vaguely defined past of the future about which he is talking. George R. McMurray, in his discussion of Borges's manipulation of time [in *Jorge Luis Borges,* 1980], concludes, "In the end, at the center of the labyrinth, inexorable lineal time prevails." Both writers embrace this inexhaustible time, stretching backward and forward, and turn the past into immediacy, the future into long ago, the now into the infinite.

Much has been said about Borges's half-formed characters, a criticism that gains legitimacy only in light of the criteria for social realism. Borges, in an interview [with Burgin], talks about books that take characters as their focus (such as the work of Dickens), but he admits to admiring fiction in which "there are no characters," a judgment that he makes concerning the work Franz Kafka and then applies to Henry James: "While if I think of James, I'm thinking about a situation and a plot. I'm not thinking about people, I'm thinking about what happened to them." Borges's stories do not conjure up the likes of Emma Bovary or David Copperfield, all flesh and blood; nor does any piece of Carey's short fiction. In spite of the adventurers, intellectuals, historical figures, murderers, wanderers, outsiders, and criminals of all sorts that inhabit Borges's and Carey's narratives, few, if any, stand out as characters. Instead, they stand as metaphors for ambiguous beings caught in a meaningless universe where they wander, trying to make some sense of its contradictory nature.

Let us look in particular at the wanderer, the picaresque figure found in earlier Spanish literature and, for that matter, in Australian literature. The role such a hero plays in Borges's and Carey's stories is exemplified by the narrator of "The Babylon Lottery" [from Borges's collection *Ficciones*]. He opens his tale: "Like all men in Babylon I have been a pro-consul; like all, a slave; I have also known omnipotence, opprobrium, jail." He goes on to recount other exploits, making known finally that he owes "this almost atrocious variety to an institution which other republics know nothing about, or which operates among them imperfectly and in secret: the lottery." A capricious game dictates the destinies of the Babylonians, subjecting each to the disorder that chance sets in motion. The wanderer, leaving his life to such an unreliable determiner, evolves into everyman facing the vicissitudes of fortune through the ages.

Carey's **"The Chance,"** which appears in *War Crimes,* provides a similar handling of the wanderer who also falls victim to the lottery's whimsical dictation of men's affairs. In a distant yet lineal time, as far in the future as Babylonia lies in the past, the narrator of **"The Chance"** opens his account of "the Genetic Lottery" three summers after the Fastalogians have arrived, succeeding the Americans, the previous occupants of this unnamed but perpetual "Client State." He explains that "for two thousand inter-galactic dollars (IG\$2,000) we could go in the Lottery and come out with a different age, a different body, a different voice and still carry our memories (allowing for a little leakage) more or less intact." A large part of the story develops the relationship between the narrator and a girl he meets. He fails to prevent her appointment with "the Genetic Lottery" and loses her, along with the illusion of permanency they have created amid the lunacy and fragmentation prevailing in those days. "So long ago. So much past," he concludes, describing himself as "a crazy old man, alone with his books and his beer and his dog. I have been a clerk and a pedlar and a seller of cars. I have been ignorant, and a scholar of note. Pock-marked and ugly I have wandered the streets and slept in the parks. I have been bankrupt and handsome and a splendid conman." "Because Babylon is nothing but an infinite game of chance," as Borges ends his story, the eternal wanderer remains helpless, whether he is the plaything of "the Company" or of "the Fastalogians."

Outlaws and desperadoes have long taken a dominant role in both Argentine and Australian literature, their exploits belonging, as Borges says in the opening of "The Challenge" [*The Aleph and Other Stories 1933-1969*], "to legend or to history or (which may be just another way of saying it be-longs to legend) to both things at once." The gauchos from an Argentine past fascinate Borges, and he puts them to use not as traditional characters whose deeds he celebrates for their own sake but as representations of those whose "manly faith" and "chivalric passion" was "in all likelihood . . . no mere form of vanity but rather an awareness that God may be found in any man." Their stories, he says, helped "men who led extremely elementary lives—herders, stockyard workers, drovers, outlaws, and pimps"—rediscover "in their own way the age-old cult of the gods of iron."

Similar figures have found their way into the legends or history of Australia, namely the bushrangers, whose defiance of fate allowed them an escape from "elementary lives." To hardworking, often poor and dissatisfied, farmbound or citybound Australians, tales of the bushrangers' challenging of established order helped these ordinary folk discover for themselves "the age-old cult of the gods of iron." In **"War Crimes,"** the title story of his second volume, Carey has found a new use for the paradigm of the bushranger, by transforming him into the ultimate capitalist, the one who sees that "BUSINESS MUST GO ON." As the narrator of **"War Crimes"** gloats over his ruthlessness, he considers his code of honor not unlike the "manly faith" and "chivalric passion" that set apart the gauchos and bushrangers. Once more, Carey has placed **"War Crimes"** in a far-off time when business must go on, even if its continuation depends on wandering capitalistic bushrangers who overcome all obstacles with violence. The narrator flaunts the peculiar religion created by the demands of capitalism, boasting to those whose "elementary lives" prevent them from similar action: "I am not mad, but rather I have opened the door you all keep locked with frightened bolts and little prayers." They lack courage, he tells them: "you sit in the front room in worn blue jeans, reading about atrocities in the Sunday papers." Carey's modern-day bushranger, ironically cast in his futuristic role as the capitalist run amok, does, at the end of the story, hint that he, as Borges says of the gauchos, acted out of "no mere form of vanity" but behaved more from "an awareness that God may be found in any man": "I wished I had been born a great painter. I would have worn fine clothes and celebrated the glories of man. I would have stood aloft, a judge, rather than wearily kept vigil on this hill, hunchbacked, crippled, one more guilty fool with blood on his hands." But like the gauchos and bushrangers of Argentine and Australian history, he cast himself in the role of the outsider who cultivated violence and developed by necessity a code of courage that placed him above ordinary men: one part of him noble, standing aloof from his fellows; the other part, guilty and bloody, even a little bit foolish.

The stories contained in *The Fat Man in History* and *War Crimes* proved, as Frank Moorhouse said of the first collection, that Carey could do "astonishing tricks," learned in part, as we have seen, from Borges. Returning again to Yates's metaphor of the compass, we find that Carey followed the call of its four points. He proceeded in one direction to track his own ambivalent "Australianness"; then he traveled on another course through books that took him far beyond the provincial society where he only half belonged. Thus he prepared himself for further exploration: to investigate the perplexities he encountered and to chart unmapped territories in his native literary landscape.

The new generation of Australians, so much less restricted in national literary choices than their predecessors, greatly admires Carey's sophisticated fantasy. The widespread acceptance of this fantasy, in a literature once dominated by social realism, might make it possible someday to study Carey's effect on the Australian short story and demonstrate how he helped to alter its course. That traces of Borges's genius "cannot *not* be there," at least in the work of one writer, should assure that Australia's fiction will, as Moorhouse puts it [in *The State of the Act: The Mood of Contemporary Australia in Short Stories,* 1983], "'go too far' and resist blandness." The new work now appearing, much of it "international" in both mode and publication, suggests that Australian writers have taken up that challenge, just as Carey did a decade before.

Edmund White (review date 30 August 1991)

SOURCE: "Recognizing Jack," in *The Times Literary Supplement,* No. 4613, August 30, 1991, p. 21.

[*White is an American novelist, short story writer, and critic. Below, he favorably reviews* The Tax Inspector.]

Peter Carey has an approach to the novel destined to make him one of the most widely read and admired writers working in English. His characters are well motivated but not all shade and nuance. Instead, they are drawn with a firm bounding line and they quickly leave an indelible mark on the memory. His language is straightforward but supple enough, semantically and syntactically, to be fully expressive. His plots unfold chronologically. There are no tedious post-modernist high jinks undermining the authority of the text. He has a strong sense of place—in this book [*The Tax Inspector*] a decaying garage like something out of an Edward Hopper painting. Indeed, his visual sense, the novelist's most essential gift, is astonishingly clear; his people are never just voices nattering on in the dark, as is so often the case in commercial fiction. They are always well lit and about to do something strange and suitable.

The Tax Inspector (a title that makes one think of Gogol's *The Government Inspector* with its comic and religious overtones) is about the sudden appearance of a handsome Greek woman, Maria Takis, who has come to examine the fraudulent books of a family below reproach, the Catchprices. They own the moribund garage and automobile showroom in a no longer safe neighbourhood. Old Mrs Catchprice receives the Tax Inspector as though she were a long-lost daughter and

never lets her get a word in. It turns out that Mrs Catchprice, the family matriarch, is the one who has denounced her children to the tax department because she fears they want to pack her off to an old people's home:

> "Mrs Catchprice. Are you Mrs F. Catchprice?"
>
> "Frieda," said Mrs Catchprice. "I've got the same name as the woman who was involved with D. H. Lawrence. She was a nasty piece of work."
>
> "There's no other Mrs F. Catchprice in your family?"
>
> "One's enough," she laughed. "You ask the kids."
>
> "So you are the public office and also the one with the anomalies to report?"
>
> "Me? Oh no, I don't think so." Mrs Catchprice folded her arms across her chest and shook her head.
>
> "You didn't telephone the Taxation Office to say you were worried that your business had filed a false tax return?"
>
> "You should talk to Cath and Howie. They're the ones with all the tricks up their sleeves. All this talk about being a professional musician is just bluff. She's an amateur. She couldn't make a living at it. No, no—what they want is to set up a motor business of their own, in competition to us. That's their plan—you mark my words. But when you look at the books, you take my word, you're going to find some hanky-panky. I won't lay charges, but they're going to have to pay it back."

Frieda Catchprice's husband is dead, her daughter is a middle-aged would-be Country and Western singer, one son is an urbane, successful lawyer and art collector, the other an erotomane and incompetent used-car salesman. The grandsons, however, are the real prizes—a bald, saffron-robed Hare Khrisna devotee named Vish who never stops mumbling prayers, and a psychotic blond sixteen-year-old who has taken assertiveness training ("Affirmations and actualizations") and who now believes he is an angel.

Carey's triumph is that he doesn't ever turn his eccentrics into grotesques. We experience everything so intimately from several points of view that we scarcely judge anyone at all, any more than we ordinarily judge ourselves in the usual moments of just being. This suspension of moral discrimination is brought to our appalled attention only at the end of the book; the climax makes us recognize that we've dangerously misplaced our sympathies.

Along the way we get a vivid picture of the make-up of contemporary Sydney. Maria Takis is a second-generation Greek who resents arrogant, *nouveau riche* Aussies and the shocking social inequities all around her. A Mafia leader intimidates or buys off everyone. Sarkis Alaverdian is an Armenian hairdresser who instantly sizes up Mrs Catchprice: "He could smell the meat-fat smell then, from that far away, the Aussie smell, as distinctive as their back yard clothes-lines with their frivolous flags of T-shirts, board shorts and frilly underwear, so different from Armenian washing which was big and practical—sheets, rugs, blankets, grey work trousers and cotton twill shirts."

Sarkis and the Catchprices live in Franklin, a Sydney suburb that was once beautiful countryside; now it is a burnt-out wasteland filled with murderous teenagers. Mrs Catchprice remembers an earlier, rural Australia, where, as the wild daughter of defeated parents, she had claimed her independence by walking out on them armed with sticks of dynamite carried about her person.

Her son Jack has escaped the burnt-out Franklin and family feuds to become a cultured, sensitive lawyer (all ironies intended). Jack meets Maria, the Tax Inspector, when she is pregnant and he is hungry for her baby. He wants to marry her so he can raise her child and he is far more attentive to her pre-natal care than she herself is. He is the sort of man, in any event, who drinks herbal tea from a raku teapot, whose designer house opens up to cabbage tree palms populated by lorikeets, who knows how to order a good Haut Brion—you know the type. Curiously enough, one really does feel one recognizes Jack.

His wealth troubles Maria. As she tells him, "I'm a very Tax Office sort of person. I hate all this criminal wealth. This state is full of it. It makes me sick. I see all these skunks with their car phones and champagne and I see all this homelessness and poverty. Do you know that one child in three in Australia grows up under the poverty line?"

In an earlier novel, *Bliss,* and in his stories, *The Fat Man in History,* Carey explored urban blight, greed, youth, violence, ecological disaster. In *Oscar and Lucinda,* set in the nineteenth century, he created two mythic figures at once at odds with their fellow Australians and emblematic of their diversity and sheer stamina. *Oscar and Lucinda* and the earlier *Illywhacker* were national epics in the tradition of *One Hundred Years of Solitude*—dense with characters, breathlessly paced, visionary (who will ever forget the picture of a glass church floating up a river in *Oscar and Lucinda*?)

In *The Tax Inspector,* a shorter if no less ambitious book, Carey has rescored his big symphonies for a smaller, more articulate, crisper instrument—a harpsichord, say. In fact, if the novel made me think of Gogol's mixture of social satire and mysticism, it also reminded me of De Falla's eerie harpsichord concerto in which modern music is played on a classical instrument.

Richard Eder (review date 29 December 1991)

SOURCE: "Titans of the Junkyard," in *Los Angeles Times Book Review,* December 29, 1991, pp. 3, 8.

[*An American critic and journalist, Eder received the Pulitzer Prize for criticism in 1987. In the review below, he remarks on the characters in* The Tax Inspector.]

Three generations of Catchprices run a failing General Motors dealership in the slummy outskirts of Sydney, Australia. Frieda, the octogenarian matriarch, interferes, sulks and carries gelignite in her pockets as another woman might carry Mace. Cathy, her husky daughter, runs the business end but belts out country-and-Western ballads, and yearns for stardom. Her brother, Mort, a mild, hairy man, runs the shop while dreaming of a quiet little garage of his own. Jack, the other brother, has broken away to become a rich downtown developer.

As for the grandchildren, Mort's sons: Vish is a Hare Krishna, but keeps getting dragged into the family's stormy councils; 16-year-old Benjamin, glittering and deranged, has a prophetic determination to turn the crumbling business into a dazzling money-spinner.

But it is not simply an eccentric family that Peter Carey has created in *The Tax Inspector.* The Catchprices are a race of ramshackle Titans, the Gods' doomed predecessors. Monstrous, deformed and often very funny, they threaten to pull in anyone who comes near their collapsing universe.

Maria Takis doesn't simply come near; she marches right in. She is the tax inspector of the title, and when she drives up to Catchprice Motors one day and asks for books, she brings the whole structure of family secrets, madnesses and wild improvisations crashing down quite as surely as if she'd ignited the explosives in Grandmother Catchprice's pockets.

Before the end, the gelignite will, in fact, be set off. By that time, the Grand Guignol will seem almost an anticlimax, so spectacular have been the schemes and confrontations that Carey has introduced.

The Tax Inspector, written with considerable brilliance, is not so much a novel as a modern mythology. Its larger-than-life figures—the Catchprices and, less obviously, Maria—suggest personifications for the unmanageable forces at loose in the world. Unlike the old mythologies, here it is not a matter of thunderbolts, sea-storms and other threats of an unmastered Nature, but rather the different and equally unmanageable threats of a world where Nature is mastered, and the masters are disintegrating.

All the principal characters follow vehement and often nutty purposes, only to be yanked oppositely by equally odd and vehement cross-purposes. When Maria arrives, she is all business and evidently prepared to sink the whole disreputable Catchprice enterprise. But it is not so simple.

For one thing, she is eight months' pregnant. Her impregnator is Alastair, her boss. He is a charismatic idealist; he sees tax collection as a noble mission. It is the means by which the disgusting profits of land speculators and money artists will be channeled into schools and old-people's homes. Maria, along with her colleagues, is inflamed by the vision. Her immigrant mother was abused all her life by arrogant bosses; now Maria can make them pay.

The Tax Inspector, written with considerable brilliance, is not so much a novel as a modern mythology. Its larger-than-life figures—the Catchprices and, less obviously, Maria—suggest personifications for the unmanageable forces at loose in the world.

—Richard Eder

Alastair, however, is a skunk as well as an idealist. Maria's condition irritates him. In order to pressure her into quitting, he assigns her such dead-end tasks as going after the Catchprices. They may be crooked, but they are clearly no profiteers. The dealership, economically speaking, is a junkyard.

So Maria's sense of mission is undermined from the start. And the Catchprice strategy—masterminded by Benny—to show her their human side undermines her further. Eventually, while attempting to conduct her auditing by day, she breaks into the tax office at night to try to cancel the Catchprice file out of the computer.

The original tip, after all, was lodged by Frieda, who is convinced that Cathy and her husband are stealing money to launch her singing career. And all the Catchprices behave in equally unsettling ways. Mort, who wants to get away, urges Maria to find evidence of fraud. Cathy arrives at Maria's house late one night, toting her guitar, and tears off a ballad. If they are fined, she urges, she will never be able to get away to sing.

The highly flavored brawl of Catchprice manias through which Maria wanders has a fearful line of force running through it. Frieda contributed one part of it. Her outsized energy and a fanatical determination snagged her a quiet, music-loving husband, Cacka, and then put together, first a

chicken farm, and then the dealership for him to run until his death.

Cacka's own contribution was a curse. He sexually abused both Cathy and Mort as children. Mort, in turn, abused Benny as a baby. Coming upon the scene, Mort's wife shot him and missed; the bullet hit Benny, leaving a blue scar on his shoulder.

It is like the mark of Cain. Benny is the gleaming, driven end-product of his family heritage of zeal and perversity. He dyes his hair blond, shaves his body, buys a gleaming white suit and a set of self-actualization tapes, proclaims himself the Angel of Plagues, Ice and Lightning. Angelically, he tries to pursue his mad vision of turning the decrepit business into a model of capitalism on hallucinogens, a car agency that will make millions not by the sale of cars but by pyramiding credit and insurance rake-offs on the side. He doesn't manage to get started or sell a single car; instead, he turns his blazing urgency on his family, or takes it to the dank basement where he has built a machine to inflict abusive sex.

There are all manner of side excursions, notably a love affair between Maria and Jack, the only Catchprice who seems to have escaped the family vortex. It is tender, sensual and, since Maria is eight months pregnant, astonishing. But gradually, the book centers on a confrontation between Benny and Maria. The contenders take on archetypal configurations: Maria as a type of struggling humanity, and Benny as humanity transformed by pride into the fallen angel, Lucifer. The end is grisly.

Carey is powerfully good at creating his odd Titans, and his success accounts for the book's excitement and allure. He is not nearly as good at giving a sense of what they stand for, or of linking them to the mythology he is trying to suggest. This may account for a queasy feeling of letdown, of intoxication followed by hangover. In fiction, to be alive can be just about enough; to be larger-than-life, you need a purpose.

Robert Towers (review date 25 June 1992)

SOURCE: "House of Cards," in *The New York Review of Books,* Vol. 39, No. 12, June 25, 1992, pp. 35-6.

[*Towers was an American educator, novelist, and critic. In the following review, he surveys Carey's previous novels and remarks favorably on* The Tax Inspector, *praising the novel's arresting prose and elaborate yet coherent structure.*]

The Australian writer Peter Carey is little known in the US, although for the last few years he has been living in New York and teaching at New York University. His lack of following is as mystifying as it is regrettable, since his novels contain scenes so powerfully visualized and characters so various in their eccentricity, willfulness, goodness, and depravity that it is hard not to mention Dickens or Balzac when one is writing about them. Carey has a wide readership in both his native Australia and in Britain, where his third novel, *Oscar and Lucinda,* won the Booker Prize in 1988. American readers are not likely to be put off by Carey's sexual frankness (and occasional scurrility) or by his taste for sudden violence. Can it be that they find something boring in reading about Australia, where (they may think) banal vestiges of a British colonial heritage coexist with a brainless Californian hedonism? Nothing could be further from the grotesque yet eerily familiar world of Carey's novel [*The Tax Inspector*].

Indeed, it has taken Carey some time to find the fictional form to contain his peculiarly turbulent imagination. His first novel, *Bliss* (1981), begins with a wonderfully hallucinatory account of the out-of-body experience of *un homme moyen sensuel*— a "Good Bloke" named Harry Joy, who has just had a heart attack and is lying on the green grass of his suburban lawn, a cigarette smoldering between his fingers. In the nine minutes that elapse before he can be revived by the doctors and ambulance crew, Harry is touched by ecstasy.

> He found he could slide between the spaces in the air itself. He was stroked by something akin to trees, cool, green, leafy. His nostrils were assailed with the smell of things growing and dying, a sweet fecund smell like the valleys of rain forests. It occurred to him that he had died and should therefore be frightened.

> It was only later that he felt any wish to return to his body, when he discovered that there were many different worlds . . . and that if he might taste bliss he would not be immune to terror. He touched walls like membranes, which shivered with pain, and a sound, as insistent as a pneumatic drill, promised meaningless tortures as terrible as the Christian stories of his childhood.

> He recognized the worlds of pleasure and worlds of pain, bliss and punishment, Heaven and Hell.

> He did not wish to die. For a moment panic assailed him and he crashed around like a bird surrounded by panes of glass.

After this experience, Harry concludes that the life he has been leading, and the life to which he returns after an open heart operation, is really Hell. There is much to confirm this conclusion. Harry's bitchy wife is unfaithful, his son deals drugs, his daughter performs oral sex on her brother, and his advertising clients manufacture carcinogenic products. Unfortunately the novel degenerates and turns shapeless. While Carey's gift for fresh and arresting imagery remains everywhere in evidence, his powers of invention become hyperac-

tive, so to speak. Characters and scenes are multiplied to the point where the reader begins to feel suffocated, and nothing is allowed to stay in place long enough to have much impact.

Carey's second novel, *Illywhacker* (1985), is even more distracted than *Bliss*—problems exacerbated by the book's six-hundred-page length. Its narrator, Herbert Badgery, is one hundred and thirty-nine years old. An inveterate liar and teller of tall tales, he has been a wanderer, a con man, a car salesman, a pioneer aviator, and a bigamist. Ranging in time from 1917 to roughly the present, *Illywhacker* incorporates a considerable amount of modern Australian history and is packed with nearly every variety of Australian life—the shearers and squatters and diggers, the Irish, the Chinese, and the Jews, as well as fauna, including birds, marsupials, and a giant three-legged monitor lizard, or "dragon." As with *Bliss,* there are many good scenes and much vigorous writing, which the reader hardly has time to savor before being rushed on to something else equally vivid or fantastic. Although picaresque in its intentions, *Illywhacker* lacks the kind of consistently imagined anti-hero—whether adventurer, waif, thief, or soldier of fortune—which picaresque novels from *Gil Blas* to *Roderick Random* to *The Confessions of Felix Krull* have relied on to impose a semblance of unity on a highly episodic structure. For considerable stretches of the novel, Herbert Badgery is absent altogether, and the author's interest seems diverted into many different channels, like a river lost in its delta. One finishes the novel with an impression of abundant talent prodigally wasted.

With *Oscar and Lucinda* Peter Carey at last produced the coherent narrative that was absent in the two earlier works. A long historical novel set in mid-Victorian England and Australia, and teeming with characters and scenes and an abundance of historical details, *Oscar and Lucinda* might seem to invite the sprawl and antiquarian excess characteristic of the genre. In fact, the book moves steadily along, never once veering from the main story. Carey not only invents two distinctive eccentrics but involves them so intensely in the events of the story that the reader follows their headlong course with mounting excitement and apprehension. Oscar, a young Anglican clergyman with dead white skin, red hair, a chicken neck and spindly frame, is one of nature's victims, a hapless misfit and an ignorant prude in sexual matters: he is shown also, believably, to be a compulsive gambler, an ardent Christian, an agonized lover, and a man who, at the lowest point of his degradation, is capable of splitting the skull of his tormentor with an axe. Lucinda, the teen-age Australian heiress who impulsively invests her inheritance in a glass-works, has eyes that were "gateways to a fierce and lively intelligence. They were like young creatures who had lost their shells, not yet able to defend themselves." She, too, is a gambler, addicted to poker; willful and courageous, she defies the conventions of her society and is more than willing to pay the price.

Beginning with Oscar's childhood in rural Devon, Carey devotes alternating sections of the novel to each of his two characters, bringing them together in Sydney and launching them on a joint enterprise that fully engages their oddities and their idealistic naiveté. The goal he devises for them is one worthy of the age of Joseph Paxton and the Crystal Palace: to prefabricate a church made of glass and to transport it overland in crates to a remote station in the Outback. Once the goal is in prospect, the action undergoes a kind of epic heightening, though the events of the expedition itself are almost unbearable in their sordidness and brutality. Carey understands very well the uses of sustained suspense and last-minute surprise. In scenes involving Oscar's unintended fathering of an heir and his own death by drowning, he brings this luminous novel to a conclusion so ironic as to cheat our sentimental expectations while dazzling us with its virtuosity—and rightness.

"Luminous" is not a term easily applied to **The Tax Inspector.** The story concerns four increasingly catastrophic days in the life of the Catchprices, a radically "dysfunctional" family whose members own a General Motors dealership in Franklin, a once independent town that has now been absorbed into greater Sydney. The family members live above, behind, and, in one case, below the various components—showroom, workshop, spare-parts department, and lube bay—of Catchprice Motors.

> Time-switched neon lights lay at their centre. The odours of sump oil and gasoline sometimes penetrated as far as their linen closets. They were in debt to the General Motors Acceptance Corporation for $567,000.

With loving and often pitiless detail, Carey animates his little collection of losers and freaks. The dominant figure among them is the eighty-six-year-old Frieda Catchprice. Half-senile but still spirited, she is struggling to maintain her precarious hold over her crumbling domain.

> She liked to smoke Salem cigarettes. When she put one in her mouth, her lower lip stretched out towards it like a horse will put out its lip towards a lump of sugar. She was not especially self-critical, but she knew how she looked when she did this—an old tough thing. She was not a tough thing. She made jokes about her leaking roof but she was frightened there was no money to fix it.

For many years she has been carrying a salami-shaped stick of nitroglycerine and fuses in her handbag; the reader knows, of course, that, like the pistol in the Chekhov play, it will have to go off before the novel ends.

The rest of the family consists of Granny's forty-five-year-old daughter, Cathy, who dresses as a cowgirl and would love to escape both the dealership and her mother's clutches in order to sing with a rock band; Cathy's sleazy husband, Howie,

who has "a pencil-line moustache, a ducktail, and a secret rash which stopped in a clean line at his collar and the cuffs of his shirt. He had the ducktail because he was a Rock-a-Billy throwback . . ."; Cathy's brother Mort, a wide and burly man with "kissy" lips, who exudes an air of seedy depression and guilt; and Mort's two sons, Johnny (known as Vishnabarnu—"Vish"—since he joined the Hare Krishnas) and Benny, who at sixteen is by far the strangest of the lot. Another Catchprice remains offstage until late in the novel— he is Jack, Granny's favorite son, who has escaped from the falling House of Catchprice to become a successful real-estate developer in Sydney.

Cathy has just fired Benny from his job in the spare-parts department. Benny is an unprepossessing, unclean youth in a cut-out Judas Priest T-shirt, with dark fuzz on his lip, a Marlboro in his mouth, and a Walkman on his head. Attention is drawn to his "bright blue cat's eyes full of things he could not tell you."

> Those eyes were like gas jets in a rust-flaked pipe. They informed everything you felt about him, that he might, at any second, be ringed with heat—a peacock, something creepy.

Two days later, he is transformed. His hair has been dyed "pure or poisonous" white and "swept upwards with clear sculpted brush strokes, like atrophied angel wings." His body, treated with wax, is now completely hairless, and, as we learn a little later, he has had an angel's wing tatooed on his back, running over his shoulder all the way from his collarbone to his buttocks. As a result of a course in "self-actualization" that he is taking, the boy now sees himself as a figure of enormous power, a fallen angel.

At once pathetic and dangerous, Benny lives in a cellar under the motor works. Carey's description is characteristic of the heightened detail that he gives his settings:

> "Welcome to the Bunker," Benny said.

> It was worse than anything Vish could have imagined. The air was as thick as a laundry. The concrete floor was half an inch deep in water. It was criss-crossed with planks supported by broken housebricks. A brown-striped couch stood against one end, its legs on bricks. The bricks were wrapped in green plastic garbage bags. Electric flex was everywhere, wrapped in Glad Wrap and bits of plastic with torn ends like rag. . . . Two electric radiators stood on a chipped green chest of drawers, facing not into the room but towards the walls where you could see the red glow of two bars reflected in what Vish, at first, thought was wet floral wallpaper. It was not wallpaper. It was handwriting, red, blue, green, black, webs of it, layer on layer. In the corner . . . was a white fibreglass

object, like a melted surfboard in the shape of a shallow "n."

The "melted surfboard" is, we learn, a sexual contraption rigged with straps designed to hold a victim motionless for whatever purposes the boy has in mind.

Peter Carey's prose can hold the ugly, the frightening, and the beautiful in uncanny suspension. It is this gift, among others, that makes him such a strong and remarkable writer.

—Robert Towers

Such is the Australian gothic world in which Maria Takis, a healthy, good-hearted young woman, arrives to audit the books of Catchprice Motors. Maria is a Greek immigrant who works for the Australian Taxation Office and is eight months pregnant by a man who cannot marry her. Her arrival interrupts the proceedings Cathy has set in motion to commit Granny Catchprice to a nursing home. A friendship soon develops between Maria and the old woman, and Maria determines not only to save Granny from the nursing home but to have the audit of the obviously vulnerable Catchprice Motors called off. At the novel's conclusion Maria, who has meanwhile fallen in love with Jack (the only Catchprice with a future), is subjected to a terrifying ordeal in Benny's cellar. In what may be a remote allusion to "The Fall of the House of Usher," this scene occurs at the very moment when, thanks to Granny Catchprice's nitroglycerine, the walls of Catchprice Motors come literally tumbling down.

Carey has created a fairly elaborate structure that can, without losing coherence, accommodate all sorts of bizarre juxtapositions, excursions into family history, and sudden shifts in location (including Greece in one extended flashback). The seemingly disparate parts are carefully interrelated; they do not fly off centrifugally as they tend to do in *Illywhacker.* Some reviewers have been disconcerted, even offended, by the shifting tone of *The Tax Inspector*—the wild leaps between the comic, the sensationally perverse, the sentimental (as in Maria and Jack's love affair), and the horrific. But these juxtapositions and disparities seem entirely justified in the updated gothic atmosphere Carey has created.

It should also be pointed out that the hard, brilliant surface of Carey's prose and the unsparing objectivity with which he records the behavior of the Catchprices by no means reflects a lack of sympathy for them. As in the case of Mary Shelley's monster, we are exposed to the yearnings and sorrows of misbegotten or hopelessly thwarted characters. We learn that Granny Catchprice as a young woman had wanted to own a

flower farm, but instead after her marriage she had to help run a chicken farm and then a car dealership, both of which she hated. The explosives she carries were once intended to blow up the tree stumps on the acreage to be cleared for growing flowers.

Benny longs to be beautiful and admired. When his father tells him, after his "transformation," that he looks like a "poof," Benny feels like crying.

> He wanted to tie his father up and pour water over his face until he said he was sorry. He felt like a snail with its shell taken off. He was pink and slimy and glistening. Even the air hurt him. He felt like dying. It was not just his father. It was everything. He could feel depression come down on him like mould, like bad milk, like the damp twisted dirty sheets in the cellar. He wanted to go to the cellar and lock the door.

We learn a little later that Benny has been sexually molested by his father since the age of three and that both Mort and Cathy in turn had been similarly molested by their father. In a subsequent scene, graphically described, Benny scornfully seduces his father, who has been aroused by the hairlessness of his son's body. To know all is by no means to pardon all, but at least some pathos has been introduced into this bizarre mix, a curious one that has something in common with the lyrical "decadence" of a novel like Ian McEwan's *The Cement Garden.*

Still another image for the effect produced by *The Tax Inspector* can be found in the novel itself. At an elegant party in Sydney to which Jack takes Maria, the conversation turns to a de Kooning painting for which one of the dinner guests has just paid $23 million. Maria is glad to hear that the painting in question is not one of de Kooning's "women." "'He's such an extraordinary painter,' she said. . . . 'I love his work, but the women always frighten me.'" A moment later she adds, "'He's so lyrical and beautiful. . . . I mean, it's like I'm giving my heart to him and then I walk into the next room and feel I'm in the power of a serial killer.'"

Peter Carey's prose can hold the ugly, the frightening, and the beautiful in uncanny suspension. It is this gift, among others, that makes him such a strong and remarkable writer.

Jonathan Coe (review date 22 September 1994)

SOURCE: "Principia Efica," in *London Review of Books,* Vol. 16, No. 18, September 22, 1994, p. 5.

[*Coe is an English journalist, novelist, nonfiction writer, and critic. In the following review, he discusses* The Unusual Life of Tristan Smith, *praising the novel as a successful investigation of cultural imperialism and national character.*]

Like his near-namesake, Tristram Shandy, the unlikely hero of Peter Carey's new novel [*The Unusual Life of Tristan Smith*] begins the story of his life at the very beginning. While he doesn't go into quite as much detail about the moment of his conception, he appears to have a very clear memory of the minutes leading up to his delivery. As his mother leaves her theatre (where she has been rehearsing the Scottish Play) and sets out for the hospital,

> things started happening faster than she had expected. Oxytocin entered her bloodstream like a ten-ton truck and all the pretty soft striped muscles of her womb turned hostile, contracting on me like they planned to crush my bones. I was caught in a rip. I was dumped. I was shoved into the birth canal, head first, my arm still pinned behind my back. My ear got folded like an envelope. My head was held so hard it felt, I swear it, like the end of life and not its glorious beginning.

From then on, there is little that is glorious about Tristan's life. As with Sterne's luckless protagonist, sadness is embedded in his name and he is destined to embark upon 'a set of as pitiful misadventures and cross accidents as ever small HERO sustained'. He is born horribly deformed. The obstetrician takes his mother aside to advise her, quietly, that it might be best to kill him. At birth he is 'a gruesome little thing . . . small, not small like a baby, smaller, more like one of those wrinkled furless dogs they show on television talk shows'. His pale eyes 'bulge intensely in his face'. He has 'shrunken twisted legs, bowed under him' and 'no lips, but a gap in the skin that sometimes shows his toothless gums'. Revulsion is the initial response of all those who set eyes on him, even the enlightened members of his mother's small, politically active theatre group. A few years later, he will find himself climbing down the outside wall of a hospital while a crowd looks on, and will realise that these spectators see him as 'something like snot, like slime, like something dripping down towards them from which they wished to take their eyes and which, the clearer and closer it became, produced in their own eyes and lips such grotesque contortions that I knew—properly, fully, for the first time in my life—I was a monster.' *The Unusual Life of Tristan Smith* is not, however, a book about disability. It's a subtly but intensely political novel about imperialism, cultural hegemony and the ambivalent relationship between small, weak countries and the larger, stronger ones which both oppress and inspire them. Peter Carey currently lives in New York and there is every indication that he is attempting here to resolve his own very contradictory feelings about America, even though that country is not mentioned once in the novel.

Tristan Smith is born and grows up in an invented country called Efica, a diffident chain of '18 little islands between the tropic of Capricorn and the 30th parallel', whose inhabitants are both fiercely nationalistic and 'abandoned, self-doubting'.

The first half of the book is set in Efica, the second in the much more powerful country of Voorstand. These nations have been imagined in some detail: all the dates in the novel are given according to the Efican calendar (making it hard to tell whether the narrative takes place in the present or future); maps are provided; and Carey has devised more than a hundred new dialect words for the languages of each country, listing them in a lengthy glossary at the end of the book. The imaginative world of the novel is both consistent and self-contained. No reference is made to places or events outside Efica and Voorstand; even the publisher's blurb sustains the pretence that these countries exist and declines to come clean by explicitly puffing the virtues of the book as a parable or allegory.

This is perhaps just as well, because it's a difficult novel to discuss in such terms without doing violence to the extreme delicacy with which Carey cloaks a whole range of possible political meanings beneath his narrative. It's not clear, for instance, that Voorstand should be identified directly with America, although the two countries have many things in common, the most obvious being the popular mythologies which they export so ruthlessly. Carey posits a believable dystopia in which sophisticated technology (holograms, gigantic video screens, computer-controlled life-size puppets) co-exists with a whimsical, almost infantile folk culture: the three key figures are a dog, a duck and, most important, a cheerful, wily, lovable mouse known as 'Bruder Mouse'. Any resemblance to Goofy, Donald and Mickey is no doubt intentional. The image of Bruder Mouse comes to dominate the book, becoming emblematic of everything that is most sinister and at the same time most irresistible about Voorstand. Tristan's mother, a Voorstander by birth, loathes the mouse and just about everything it stands for, but when her son makes it clear that, despite all his physical shortcomings, he too wants to become an actor, she indulges him by presenting him with a Bruder Mouse mask. This gives rise to some powerful imagery: Tristan refuses to take the mask off and wears it even while watching the television screen on which his mother, embarking on her short-lived political career, makes a strong anti-Voorstand speech, evoking 'the sharp-toothed blue-coated Mouse as a paranoid—its white-gloved finger hovering above a button which might destroy the planet'.

The first half of the book, then, offers a series of different and constantly surprising takes on the theme of cultural imperialism, the notion of art as a political weapon whether in the hands of the oppressor or the oppressed. A realistic, highly detailed depiction of the workings of a small theatre group jostles with our sense of disorientation on finding ourselves in the midst of Efica's unfamiliar landscape, and this somehow creates a space in which the weightlessly symbolic is able to flourish. The Eficans function as a metaphor for every downtrodden nation, with 'their small population, their geographic isolation, their lack of natural riches, their tiny GNP' and Tristan himself becomes the underdog's underdog: and it's no surprise that to someone so appalled by his own physical appearance, and so undernourished by the small-scale, low-budget theatrical entertainments he has grown used to, his first sight of authentic Voorstand popular culture should come as a revelation. The Voorstand Sirkus which tours Efica is a high-octane, high-risk entertainment featuring jugglers, acrobats and astonishing technological effects, and Tristan's first glimpse of it provides the descriptive highlight of Book One:

> There was no slow build-up in this show. The pace, from the first drum beat, was extraordinary. It was like being accelerated into the stratosphere. The jokes and the tricks followed each other at a dizzying speed. It was like being tickled. You could not bear the thought that what you were laughing at would be intensified, although it surely would be, and would be again, as tumbling High-Hogs flew across the stage chasing tumbling panicking holographic Bruders.

Tristan's exhilaration, or something like it, must have been felt by many young people when watching a big-budget, feelgood American movie after years of exposure to their own downbeat national cinema or television. Even the hardened 'Voorphobe' who escorts Tristan to the Sirkus is moved to tears, and comes out declaring: 'They're a great people . . . That's what a show like this teaches you. Theirs was a country that was founded on a principle.'

From here on, however, the thrust of the novel is to expose the more threatening side of the Voorstanders' triumphalism. Tristan's mother, on the verge of an election victory which would involve the renegotiation of Efica's treaty with Voorstand, is assassinated. Years later, Tristan himself travels to Voorstand, along with his guardian and his nurse, to try to locate his father, who has long ago abandoned the smallscale Efican theatre and made a name for himself as a performer in the Voorstand Sirkus. Pursued by operatives of the Voorstand Intelligence Agency (the VIA—one of the novel's more obvious political signposts), they make their way to Saarlim, the capital city, infiltrate the upper echelons of Voorstand society and find that the infantilism and regressive puritanism of the culture is here well advanced, as they learn of a plan to turn the whole city into a gigantic heritage theme park or 'Ghostdorp'.

From even this cursory attempt to summarise aspects of its plot, you will gather that *The Unusual Life of Tristan Smith* is a pretty extraordinary book. On two previous occasions—in *Illywhacker* and *Oscar and Lucinda*—Carey has shown himself capable of using the novel as a basis for the investigation of national character, an enterprise normally fraught with hubris and presumption. This novel is even riskier, being very specific in its treatment of individual characters while at the same time asking the reader to take a good deal on trust. That we buy into it at all is a tribute less, perhaps, to the

discipline of Carey's imagination than to the unanswerable plainness of his prose, which, like the Efican landscape—and the Australian, for that matter—is characterised above all by 'an emptiness, a refusal to charm'.

No doubt this plainness is the result of endless paring down and re-drafting; without it, we would probably think of Carey as a very difficult writer indeed. Certainly it's rare for anyone to have sustained such a wide international readership while making, in his last two books, such minor concessions to the conventional novelistic pleasures. In *Illywhacker,* where the fake, the fabulous and the bizarre were at the heart of the book both thematically and technically, and in *Oscar and Lucinda,* where a terrific pastiche of 19th-century writing gave us a good substitute for solidity of character, it was possible to ignore some facts which *The Tax Inspector* and *The Unusual Life of Tristan Smith* have since brought to the light. There's an almost terminal bleakness in Carey's presentation of human relations, for instance—a bleakness which can sometimes combine with his disinclination for stylistic adornment to make the process of entering his fictional worlds (both real and invented) a positively spartan experience. There's the question, too, of his pronounced taste for the grotesque, which in this novel is taken to new extremes. Carey's image of a glass church sailing down the river in *Oscar and Lucinda* was not only a powerful one, but it was also rigorously argued for in the preceding narrative; here, on the other hand, there's very little to prepare us for the freakish peculiarity of the closing scenes, where the folksy, childlike mythology of Bruder Mouse collides with Tristan's emerging sexuality. I was reminded at this point of William Wharton's *Franky Furbo*—the only other novel I can think of where a writer has so daringly appropriated the language and imagery of children's literature and deployed it to adult ends. To say that Carey's is the harder-edged book is not necessarily to offer it unqualified praise. Finally, in fact, *The Unusual Life of Tristan Smith* left me hoping that next time around his 'refusal to charm' would not be quite so adamant.

Richard Eder (review date 5 February 1995)

SOURCE: "An E-Ticket Ride," in *Los Angeles Times Book Review,* February 5, 1995, pp. 3, 8.

[*In the review below, Eder comments favorably on* The Unusual Life of Tristan Smith, *but finds the second half of the novel less compelling than the first.*]

If the 17th-Century Dutch hero, Admiral Tromp, had used a bigger broom—he attached it to his mast to signal that he was about to sweep the English from the seas—perhaps our world would have resembled the one set out in Peter Carey's prickly futurist fantasy. In *The Unusual Life of Tristan Smith,* the era's dominant military, economic and cultural empire resembles the United States in a number of ways, except that its heritage, like that of white South Africa, is not British but Dutch.

The empire is called Voorstand. It is a vast continental realm, run by a moneyed class that speaks a kind of Dutch-Afrikaans patois and pays lip service to a tradition of sturdy God-fearing settlers, while living in high-tech luxury and treating the slum-dwellers in its decaying capital as fourth-class citizens. It uses cash, guns and an intelligence service to protect its interests around the world.

A few of these interests—an underground naval-communications network and a nuclear-waste dump—reside in the fragile island nation of Efica, somewhere in the South Atlantic. The Eficans, descended from French and English settlers, are down-at-the-heel and, as Carey puts it, "laconic, belligerent and self-doubting." Their capital, Chemin Rouge, is "a small, slightly rancid port city."

Nonetheless, Efica possesses a scruffy human charm. Though the Voorstand version of the CIA works with the local intelligence service to keep the right-wing Reds party in power and sabotage the midly radical and anti-Voorstand Blues, the place is too insignificant to have its local particularities obliterated. When the book begins, for instance, work has only just started on the country's first Sirkus.

Sirkuses are Voorstand's great cultural weapon, and Carey's parodic equivalent of Disneyland. They are spectacular displays of holographic images coupled with real-life acrobatics that have the distinction of leaving the performers frequently dead or maimed. Like Disneyland, they have two trademark characters: Broder Mouse and Oncle Duck. It is worldwide junk-food entertainment: irresistible, and shriveling all merely local and particular cultural endeavors.

Tristan is born, hideously deformed, into one such endeavor. His mother, Felicity, runs the Feu Follet (Will o' the Wisp) theater company, which tours the islands putting on avant-garde versions of the classics. The downfall of the company, Felicity's subsequent fatal entry into politics as a Blue—she is murdered by Voorstand agents—Tristan's injured youth, and his pilgrimage to Voorstand form the plot of Carey's gaudy satirical exercise.

The Unusual Life of Tristan Smith is elaborate and parodically referential in strict and, in this case rather sterile, post-modern fashion. Tristan, crippled, lipless, dwarfish and with a raging need for love and justice, inevitably calls to mind *The Tin Drum's* Oskar, rat-tat-tatting his way through a grotesque and unpredictable world.

Wearing a Broder Mouse mask as a child and the entire outfit while adventuring in Voorstand, he is used as other contemporary writers have used cartoon heroes: Jay Cantor with Krazy Kat, Frederic Tuten with the Belgian Tintin and Robert Coover with Pinocchio. Such use declares a malevolent impenetrability and unreality in modern life, so pervasive that only as a cartoon can heroism or even simple emotion be credible.

In fact, Carey, author of *Oscar and Lucinda* and *The Tax Inspector,* has written something of a hybrid. Tristan and the other characters go back and forth between human and cartoonish, particularly in the first part set in Efica. Here the book's prevailing tone—an extravagant but flat hyper-reality—is tempered by moments of imaginative intimacy. Its structure, which toward the end is inhabited mostly by the games played in it, shows signs of human occupancy.

Felicity, beautiful, high-strung and combative, is an impressive figure, although more of a force, perhaps, than a person. Her two lovers, either of whom could be Tristan's father, are more abstract; Carey has designed them but he has not really built them. One is Bill, an actor in the Feu Follet company, who emigrates to work in a Voorstand Sirkus. The other is Vincent, a wealthy businessman who launches the opposition campaign that will end up with Felicity hanged in her own theater.

Much livelier are Wally, the theater manager, who loves Felicity unsuccessfully and ends up taking care of Tristan and accompanying him to Voorstand, and Roxana. She arrives on the scene with cratefuls of pigeons; Wally, instantly besotted with her, buys them. It is a comic and ultimately melancholy courtship. Beautiful, ambitious and childlike, Roxana is also mad.

The madness—she is a pyromaniac and ends up trying to poison Tristan—is more than a sign of the times or metafictional gesturing. It is a human gap through which the endearing love that she and Wally eventually find for each other will sadly drain away. When it does, and she disappears, she takes with her the enticing quirkiness that Carey has managed to suggest for the Efican world. The book goes into hyper-real overdrive.

Tristan, now 22 but still only three feet tall, sails to Voorstand with Wally, who has grown old and cranky, and a nurse who goes under the name of Jacques. He (or perhaps she) is in fact someone else and, at the end, an unlikely hero/heroine.

The trek to Voorstand's capital is full of difficult adventures; among others, the robbery at gunpoint of Tristan's money, which he has earned playing the stock market via computer. There are encounters with spies from Voorstand and Efica who try to kill him, and with a robot Broder Mouse, which Jacques eviscerates so that Tristan can hide in it. As Mouse, he enjoys enormous success with Voorstand's rich and powerful, particularly with a millionairess who provides him, despite some zipper trouble, with his first sexual experience. Finally, there is escape to freedom with Jacques and Bill, the father whom Tristan rediscovers. Their route leads across the Arctic Circle. Carey conveniently bends it, pretzel-like, so that Voorstand can be both polar and subtropical.

Some of these things are diverting and quite a few are clever. We can note their satirical lessons; the noting is rather detached, though. Tristan's adventures in Voorstand have the approximate relation to human adventures that Warhol's soup cans have to soup. Tristan, who back in Efica often was as real as soup—he suffered the extravagant pain of his young life and, more often than not, we felt it along with him—has turned into an airy cartoon. He leaves no pain behind.

Carol Shields (review date 12 February 1995)

SOURCE: "Voorstand, Go Home!," in *The New York Times Book Review,* February 12, 1995, p. 7.

[*An American-born Canadian novelist, poet, playwright, and critic, Shields won a Pulitzer Prize and a Governor General's Award for her novel* The Stone Diaries (1993). *In the review below, she remarks favorably on* The Unusual Life of Tristan Smith.]

Peter Carey has always been a novelist of size. Previous novels like **The Tax Inspector** and **Oscar and Lucinda** were big books constructed around large ideas. Now, with **The Unusual Life of Tristan Smith,** he gives his readers a new big novel, his most ambitious to date. The word "unusual" in the title is a tossed pebble of understatement. Tristan Smith's life is brimful of extravagant sorrows and conflicting loyalties, of self-hatred and well-tended hubris. His voice, which dominates the narrative, is the intelligent, freakish voice of an actor miscast in the world and in his body.

Tristan's journey toward disillusionment begins in parable— the tale of an ugly, half-orphaned child—then lurches in its second half toward full picaresque flamboyance. Finally, in the closing chapters, amid a chaos of greed and compromise, Tristan arrives at a post-modern world as bleak as any we've seen in contemporary fiction. This is a novel crowded with incident—also with excrement, urine, blood and drool—but it is, in the end, a sustained meditation on the folly of imperialism.

An Australian by birth and upbringing, Mr. Carey is attentive to literary as well as political echoes. We're meant to notice the novel's kinship with Laurence Sterne's *Tristram Shandy,* and the fact that sadness is buried within Tristan Smith's name. But Mr. Carey stirs his bowl of allusive soup with a new spoon of social acuity. Both the oppressed and the oppressors in this novel are damaged by imperial design.

Our hero is hideously deformed at birth, looking less like a baby than like "one of those wrinkled furless dogs they show on television talk shows." His hair grows "queerly thick," his

eyes bulge and his face is severely triangular, lipless, insufficient in flesh. His speech is halting, his legs twisted and shrunken. Even his mother's politically fastidious theater group finds him repulsive.

The boy grows up in the invented country of Efica, an 18-island geographical entity (a map is provided) populated by rebellious and nationalistic people who have been colonized for generations by the much larger nation of Voorstand, another invention. The Voorstanders store their chemical wastes in Efica's northern islands and ruthlessly export their popular culture, particularly a trio of monstrously cute creatures who bear more than a passing resemblance to the Disney menagerie, Goofy, Donald and Mickey. Mr. Carey is shrewd enough to scramble his allegorical equivalencies, but it seems not unlikely that Voorstand gestures toward contemporary America, where he now lives.

Besides maps, Mr. Carey provides glossaries of the Efican and Voorstand languages, complete with etymological details. National mythologies, so difficult to pin down when they are attached to real countries, are here fully furnished, solidly rooted and plausible. The Eficans, with their low gross national product and secondhand culture, are repelled and made self-righteous by Voorstand values. At the same time, they are mesmerized by Voorstand's dynamic high-tech entertainment offerings, the traveling troupes of acrobats and jugglers tricked out with electronic dazzle. Young Tristan, whose mother is a leader in Efica's purist agitprop theater movement, is bewitched by his first sight of Voorstand theatrics: the glittering stars, the extraordinary special effects and the noisy celebration of a once-glorious history.

The second half of the novel takes place in Voorstand, where Tristan, like many a young colonial before him, makes the ritual journey "home." There he finds a nation spiritually eroded, clinging nostalgically to the myths of its founding principles. Voorstand highways are unsafe. Crime abounds. A repressive puritanism has taken hold of the culture. The infrastructure of the main center of Saarlim (New York?) is broken beyond repair, although there are citizens so obscenely wealthy they can dream of turning whole cities into theme parks.

Mr. Carey makes clear that imperialism is not limited to nation-states. The healthy colonize the weak and deformed; parents hold hegemony over their children; everyone is drugged by a bland, pervasive popular culture, which is mindlessly conceived but expertly transmitted.

This serious novel is full of incidental pleasures, little side trips into arcane avenues like pigeon fancying, theories of acting, the mystery of masks and disguises, all brought forward with authority and with what is clearly Mr. Carey's own delight in authentic detail. It is tempting, when reading about the novel's two invented countries, to reach for an atlas, checking the imagined against the possible.

The first two pages are enough to tell us we're in the hands of a master storyteller. "Please sit in your seats," Tristan, the narrator, begs, "while I have you understand exactly why my heart is breaking." This irresistible invitation is characteristic of the whole novel, which is both intimate and theatrical in tone and supple and surprising in its cadences.

The Unusual Life of Tristan Smith is laid out with a tough, spare, considered language, and Mr. Carey knows when and how to put a torque on a sentence so that it strikes precisely at all that is fake or fatuous. His chapter endings and beginnings bite down on each other like sets of teeth, giving dramatic energy to the page and a discordant, but oddly pleasing, music to the ear.

If Peter Carey refuses to charm his reader with easy reconciliations, it may be because he is at heart an old-fashioned utopian trapped in a dystopian universe. The elaborate phantasmagoria of his narrative chess game clears again and again to reveal the hard emotional truth that neither the weak nor the strong have been able to make themselves a safe home in the world.

Richard B. Woodward (review date 28 February 1995)

SOURCE: "Out of Efica," in *The Village Voice,* Vol. XL, No. 9, February 28, 1995, p. 59.

[*In the following review, which also includes comments from an interview with Carey, Woodward discusses themes in and the inspiration for* The Unusual Life of Tristan Smith.]

Like many strangers in this strange land, Peter Carey found himself beguiled against his will on his first visit to that cradle of American postmodernism, Disneyworld. For the Australian novelist, the sight of Mickey and Minnie greeting well-wishers along the vacuumed streets of their Potemkin village was like walking into Baudrillard's wet dream.

"They were like royalty, like Ron and Nancy," says Carey, sounding cheerfully appalled on half a bottle of lunchtime wine. Fifty-one, with an unruly, clownish thatch of hair and a lopsided grin that leaves deep ripples in his cheeks, he is genial soul whose comic tone often oxidizes on the page into something dark and strange. His seriousness sneaks up on you.

"I started to wonder how these creatures could inhabit a society, the way that Santa Claus does," he says. "I wanted to invent their moral roots in America. What was the Christian idealism that led to this tacky, tawdry business?"

Carey's new novel, *The Unusual Life of Tristan Smith,* is being read and celebrated in the Southern hemisphere as a wicked Candide-like allegory about American cultural imperialism as seen through the eyes of the colonized. The title character and narrator is a native of the tiny archipelago of Efica, "a country so unimportant that you are already confusing the name with Ithaca or Africa."

Young Tristan has grown up in a radical theater collective that prides itself on reconstructions of Shakespeare and Chekhov. But he longs to make his way to the vast, brutal, fun-crazed nation of Voorstand so that he may taste the forbidden pleasures of a spectacle called the Sirkus. The two chief elements of this laser-lighted, computer-animated, socioreligio rite are a simulated mouse and duck. Any similarity to the cartoon cash cows of a famously litigious entertainment empire is stoutly denied by the author.

"I'm not satirizing America or Disney," insists Carey. "I also carry some baggage with me: the incredible love of the small culture for the big culture, at the same time the feeling of being unnoticed and interfered with and used."

Voorstand dominates Efica, peddling the Sirkus to its citizens and meddling in its politics to the point of assassinating troublemakers. Readers may be reminded of American attempts to undermine Gough Whitlam's Labor government in the '60s and '70s, still a flash point of controversy where Carey comes from. "There were all sorts of instances in the last 20 years of serious intrusions by the U.S. into Australian politics," he says with raised voice. "When the labor government recognized China, the CIA went ape shit. We had a prime minister who during Vietnam actually said, 'We're all the way with LBJ.'"

But the novel is modeled more along the lines of *Satanic Verses* than *Penguin Island*: an exploded allegory that seeks to establish grounds for its own credibility and sabotages neat correspondences between fictional states and their real counterparts. "Once I found that something was cutely or patly equivalent, it seemed boring," says Carey. "Whenever there was an opportunity to emphasize something that wasn't equivalent, I took it." Written with a zest for spurious scholarship à la Tristram Shandy, the book comes with bogus footnotes and a glossary that approximates the motley origins and vulgar, efflorescent slang of the English vocabulary (e.g., "rikiki: the little finger, an undersized person, a 4 fl. oz. glass of beer. Corruption of French *riquiqui*.")

After five thick and increasingly audacious novels, Carey has become a literary contender on three continents, competition for Patrick White and Thomas Keneally in the heavyweight division of Aussie novelists. A talkshow celebrity at home, followed by documentary film crews, he has won every major award the country has to offer. And since 1984, when his novel *Oscar and Lucinda* won the Booker Prize (a rare unanimous choice and in the fastest decision time in history), he has been well-read and reviewed in London as well. Along with his pal Salman Rushdie, and younger novelists like Ben

Okri and Vikram Seth, he has been lumped into the camp of writers who in the mid '80s reinfused the English novel and language from the boundaries of a defunct Empire.

Each of Carey's novels has broken radically with the style of its predecessor, as though he needed constantly to test his authority and the good wishes of his readers. The critically acclaimed *Oscar and Lucinda,* his ode to the repressed desires of a pair of Victorian misfits and lovers, was followed by *The Tax Inspector,* a sordid tale about a family of small-time car dealers in contemporary Sydney. Hard-bitten and close to the bone, with large doses of slapstick involving a grandmother and sticks of lignite, it couldn't be more different from the arch cleverness and gentle fantasy of *The Unusual Life of Tristan Smith.*

"Australians have a habit of writing about worlds that they don't know about," says Robert Hughes, a longtime fan of Carey's. "They tend to pick up subjects ad hoc. I wouldn't go so far as to call it a national characteristic. But intelligent Australians when they hop out into the world are tremendously curious about what they find and what they leave behind. Efica is a terrific invention. But maybe you have to be Australian to understand the sense of coercion, that edge of resentment. Peter did it brilliantly."

The Unusual Life of Tristan Smith, is being read and celebrated in the Southern hemisphere as a wicked Candide-like allegory about American cultural imperialism as seen through the eyes of the colonized.

—*Richard B. Woodward*

The new novel is the first to bear the imprint of Carey's time in New York. The loudness of Voorstand suggests that he has spent long, hot summer evenings in the city. The physical appearance of Tristan, a lipless dwarf who hides his monstrous deformities inside a mouse suit, was inspired by a stroll along Bleecker Street.

"I was reading *Beauty and the Beast* to my children, and I found myself incredibly moved by the story," says Carey. "The next day I was walking along Bleecker and I saw this man in a wheelchair, terribly misshapen, and I had to look away. It was one of those moments when you flinch, as though you'd been cut with a knife. I thought: 'You really haven't learned very much from *Beauty and the Beast,* have you?' And then I thought: 'But you've found a good psychological reason why a man would want to hide out in a mouse suit.'"

Carey has the unvarnished manner of a guy who flunked out of university, and labored hard to absorb the craft of fiction. He wrote four unpublished novels over 10 years, supporting himself by writing ad copy. His parents, "dead, totally dead," ran a car business near Melbourne now owned by his brother and sister. He is the first to admit that he is not especially well-read.

"My friends have always been far better educated than I," he says. "I had no idea what arena I would be competing in. I was stupid and enthusiastic. If I had been charming I probably would have been wildly successful."

Carey's long apprenticeship has kept him humble about the need for narrative pleasure. Like John Irving, he has a weakness for the grotesque and the picaresque and for extended, leisurely, 19th-century form. In *Bliss* and *The Tax Inspector,* he managed to make comic hay out of incest and child abuse. He gets away with it because of the tenderness he shows toward even the vilest of characters and because he writes sentences suavely balanced and aerated with wit. "No one has ever messed with my sentences," he says. "Ever."

The new book's split sense of place—it is broken into Efican and Voorstand halves—reflects Carey's own state of being. He has lived in New York with his wife and two children for five years, earning a green card by teaching writing at NYU and Princeton. But he gets edgy when asked if he is staying.

"I don't want to go back tomorrow," he says. "But I have this general anxiety that I'm not at home. Having arrived here not accidentally but lately, and being very happy to be here, I now find myself more and more obsessed with my Australianness. Why are we like this, why are you like that?"

He launches into a cherished theory about the two continents. "We always say we're so much alike. The big difference is that we've got a defeat culture and you've got a success culture. We're suspicious of big dreams. We think it's ludicrous to take ourselves seriously. If that attitude were prevalent in America, it would be attractive because America could do with a bit of that. In Australia, it's a little crippling." The feisty anti-imperialist sentiments of the new novel have put Carey back in the good graces of his native land again. Feelings had been bruised by *The Tax Inspector.* "They took it personally," says Carey. "They thought I didn't like my country." (One critic described it as "a lump of shit on a well-crafted plate.") *Tristan Smith,* on the other hand, has been called his best book and won him another round of awards.

Carey's standing in his adopted land may be less secure. (He refers to himself as "another goddamn foreign writer"; his critical renown and lack of wider visibility thwart his populist yearnings.) But he is not foolish enough to ignore his good fortune. Most of the time, he appears to be that rare creature in New York City: the blissful, bourgeois family man.

"As I become more connected to this society, I feel more and more how strange and not me it is," he says. "I feel that my own country is uncharted, unmapped, unknown to itself, unknown to me. We don't even recognize our own history. I'd like to go home some day. But I have two sons with American accents who go to school around the corner. My wife is working happily in New York theater. I have lots of good friends. I'm feeling those sorts of passions."

Back in his apartment, in the tiny upstairs aerie where he writes, he plays me some old Australian prison ballads and tries not to cry, his typical reaction. They are research for his new novel, "a reworking of the first Australian to go home and not be welcome," says Carey.

From the Macintosh on his desk he can look down at a cluster of Village backyards while on the wall behind him hangs a Rousseau-like painting of a farm in New South Wales where he once lived. As the doleful music fills the room, the voices singing of prolonged isolation and madness—the Ur-story of white Australia—he traces his finger across the painting where a river called Never-Never runs through the fields. For the moment, anyway, he looks like a man happily displaced, in two places at once.

Michael Heyward (review date 10 April 1995)

SOURCE: "Parallel Universes," in *The New Republic,* Vol. 212, No. 15, April 10, 1995, pp. 38-41.

[*In the review below, Heyward examines themes of cultural and national identity in* The Unusual Life of Tristan Smith.]

Peter Carey knows that the novelist's greatest freedom is the freedom to invent. He is an artificer, a fabulist whose work, with its gestures toward fantasy and science fiction, has always had the spectacular credibility and the irrevocable logic of dreams. When his short stories, with their hapless characters trapped in eerie, claustrophobic landscapes, began to appear in Australia in the 1970s, one thing was obvious: anything could happen in them. A man could become a truck. Aliens might invade and introduce a genetic lottery. People found their hands turning blue. Carey's imagery was vivid, surreal, scary. Australian fiction was never like this.

As Carey grew more confident, the short story became insufficient for his purposes. In the longer stories and in the novels that followed—*Bliss* (1981), *Illywhacker* (1985), *Oscar and Lucinda* (1988), *The Tax Inspector* (1991)—he learned how to stitch one incident into another to create the sensation of an unstoppable plot. He never abandoned the clean, lean prose of the early work. It was if he suspected that the trappings of art would interfere with the drive to communicate his fictional universe. This clarity and raciness, combined with the obvious ambition in Carey's work, also made him stand out in an antipodean context in which the longing for work

that can be taken seriously has often produced the effect of brocade: writing that is ornate, heavy, self-consciously literary. By the end of the 1980s, once readers had access to *Illywhacker* and *Oscar and Lucinda,* it was clear that one of the obvious points of reference for Carey's work was the Victorian novel, with its supposition of an enthralled, page-turning reader. Both *Illywhacker* and *Oscar and Lucinda* had intricate, gargantuan plots that gave readers a continent enlarged under the glass of Carey's imagination. They were received in Australia with the kind of excitement that Patrick White's novels generated in the 1950s.

From the outset, Carey's work introduced readers to a gallery of freaks, losers and fast-talking rogues. The idea of the misfit who wins our confidence and makes us believe in his humanity runs through much of his writing. *Illywhacker* begins with this dazzling confession:

> My name is Herbert Badgery. I am a hundred and thirty-nine years old and something of a celebrity. They come and look at me and wonder how I do it. There are weeks when I wonder the same, whole stretches of terrible time. It is hard to believe you can feel so bad and still not die. I am a terrible liar and I have always been a liar. I say that early to set things straight.

Carey prefaced *Illywhacker* with Mark Twain's wonderful observation, made in 1897 after his tour of the colonies, that Australian history "is itself the chiefest novelty the country has to offer" and "does not read like history, but like the most beautiful lies; and all of a fresh sort, no mouldy old stale ones. It is full of surprises and adventures, incongruities, contradictions and incredibilities; but they are all true, they all happened." You could not find a better gloss for the way Carey set about constructing an imaginary Australia that is indisputably strange and strangely plausible. If Carey is a magical realist, it is in part because he has been obsessed by questions of nation and history, by the need for the writer to believe that his work can define how these issues are imagined and discussed. "I think the writer has a responsibility to the truth," Carey once said, "not to shy away from the world as it is."

Carey always knew his nationality was an advantage, precisely because it gave him the opportunity to make indelible images in a country still coming to grips with the antiquity of its indigenous culture, and the novelty of its transplanted European culture. Perhaps the appropriate point of comparison for the development of Australian writing in the past fifty years is with mid-nineteenth-century America, with Melville, Whitman and later Twain himself as they collectively helped to build a national literature. "With sheer will and determination and enthusiasm you can make something that's going to affect the whole history of your country," Carey once said. "We're really so privileged to be able to be working with Australian literature at this time." He fulfilled these ambitions with *Oscar and Lucinda,* a love story that concludes with the indelible image of a glass cathedral—"a prism, a cube, a steeple of light sliding into the green shadows"—floating down the Bellinger River in an 1860s Australia. This was indeed a beautiful lie.

Carey's new book is also obsessed by the idea of national and cultural identity. *The Unusual Life of Tristan Smith* quite explicitly devotes itself to the construction of an imaginary world that hauntingly resembles the actual world. The contours of this fascinating allegory are more reminiscent of Carey's early short fables than any of the intervening work. Here again we enter an intimidating high-tech world, this one defined by vids and zines and simis and voice patches. (The latter allow their wearers to talk underwater.) Once more we find ourselves in the heart of a menacing, labyrinthine environment, in which the lives of the characters are governed by shadowy powers stronger than they are, and which seems to operate according to systems to which only a few have the key. In this book Carey locates these powers directly in the sphere of international espionage. The novel is a picaresque fable that ultimately assumes the shape of a political thriller, though its overriding preoccupation is with cultural power. This is a world in which arguments about culture can break up relationships and incite murder.

Carey has pushed his imaginative prowess to the limit. He has not simply intuited the possibilities of national history or character, he has invented an entire geography, and two new species of English patois. *The Unusual Life of Tristan Smith* is a tale of two nations: the Republic of Efica, a small provincial country, a cluster of eighteen islands "between the tropic of Capricorn and the thirtieth parallel"; and Voorstand, a powerful hub of cultural and economic activity that throws its long shadow over almost everything that happens in Efica, even though it's thousands of miles away, with part of its territory lying within the Arctic Circle.

Efica is a former penal colony, settled several centuries previously by the French and the English. The Efican Calendar dates from the foundation of the country, and the action of the book begins in the year 371EC. Efican English is deeply influenced by its French roots, and it has a lively vernacular. A "bride" is a pint of beer. "Mollo mollo" tells its hearer to relax. The wet season is called the "Moosone." A "turnboy," we learn, was "originally a chauffeur, but later a mechanic." To understand Efica, we are told, you need to read books such as *Efica: From Penal Colony to Welfare State,* published by Nez Noir University Press in 343EC. One of Efica's writers, a certain Jacqueline Bardwell, grew famous by writing a book called *A Long Way from Anywhere.*

Carey's Eficans are self-deprecatory, ironic, open, practical people. They are "laconic, belligerent, self-doubting." "No one can even tell me what an Efican national identity might be," someone says in exasperated despair.

We're northern hemisphere people who have been abandoned in the south. All we know is what we're not. We're not like those snobbish French or those barbaric English. We don't think rats have souls like the Voorstanders. But what are we? We're just sort of "here." We're a flea circus.

Carey's Eficans are faced with the inherent provincial dilemma of how to reconcile themselves to the fact that the metropolis knows next to nothing about how they live, may not even know where their country is. The great wide world about which they dream is not wide enough to include them. "My name is Tristan Smith," the novel begins. "I was born in Chemin Rouge in Efica—which is to say as much to you, I bet, as if I declared I was from the moon." With its huge ultramarine skies and its semitropical air, Efica might be a Caribbean island, though for Australian readers it is more precisely the kind of place Australia might be if it were imagined as a Caribbean island. You will not find the word Australia mentioned once in the book, but for Australians that is all the evidence they need. *Tristan Smith* is an obsessive parable of national identity.

Voorstand—"2,000 miles from north to south, 865 lakes, 10,000 towns, ninety-three major cities"—is a more dangerous and more contradictory place by far. It is both effortlessly self-confident and driven by a nostalgia for a time when it was a better, simpler country. "You hold the red passport with the phases of the moon embossed in gold," Tristan tells the nameless Voorstandish reader to whom the book is addressed. "You stand with your hand over your heart when the Great Song is played, you daily watch new images of yourself in the vids and zines." Like Efica, Voorstand is a country of the new world but its colonizers, and the shapers of its English, were Dutch.

Thus a skyscraper is a "wolkegrabber," explained in Tristan Smith's glossary as "a cloud-grabber." A rollerblader is called a "wheel-squirrel." Voorstanders perfume themselves with "odeklonje." Carey's intuition of the dialectics of Efica and Voorstand is one the novel's prime imaginative feats. The words his characters use become a key indicator of cultural difference. In context their speech is never unintelligible, but provides the fictional equivalent to that sensation of strangeness we all have when we hear foreigners speaking our language but using words we never would. We know what they mean but would say it differently. At the back of *The Unusual Life of Tristan Smith* you will find glossaries for Efican and Voorstand English, but as you read on you will find yourself flipping to these to confirm what you have already understood.

If Voorstand seems very like the United States, then Saarlim, the great metropolis that dominates Voorstandish life, is a version of New York, with its lavish private wealth and public decrepitude. "Saarlim City was littered with abandoned papers, cans, bottles, cars, mattresses, stuffed furniture." But Saarlim, as one of its inhabitants describes it, is also the "Arts and Leisure capital of the world." Its stories are told "in every corner" of Efica, and Eficans dream about it the way children do Narnia. Tristan remarks that

> it is hard for some Ootlanders to accept that they are not attuned to the soul of Saarlim. They may never have visited Voorstand but they know the names of the steegs, the kanals, the parks, the bars, the Domes. . . . But they do not live in Saarlim and therefore there is much that they do not understand.

Voorstand's cultural dominance of Efica is the natural outcome of its political influence in the smaller country. The two nations are allies but Voorstand exploits Efica for defense purposes, interferes in its elections and murders its citizens when the status quo is threatened. "That is the paradox," Tristan grumbles when he meets a man in Saarlim who has never heard of his homeland. "We are important enough for you to bring down our government, but you have never heard of us. You could see this gjent had no damn idea where Efica was."

This highly suggestive relationship between the two nations is focused on the outlandish figure of Tristan Smith himself. He was born in 371EC; by the novel's end, he is in his early 20s. He is raised by his mother Felicity, a Voorstander who has adopted Efica as her own and identifies with its creative ambitions. "We have a whole damn country to invent," she tells another actor in the small, left-wing, avant-grade theater company she runs. Tristan's father, Bill Millefleur, is an Efican who later migrates to Voorstand. Tristan himself is the ugly duckling of this international union.

> a gruesome little thing. He is small, not small like a baby, smaller, like one of those wrinkled furless dogs they show on television talk shows. His hair is fair, straight, queerly thick. His eyes are pale, a quartz-bright white. They bulge intensely in his face. He has a baby's nose—but in the lower part of his severely triangular face there is, it seems, not sufficient skin. His face pulls at itself. He has not lips, but a gap in the skin that sometimes shows his toothless gums.

This deformed mouse-like boy grows into a man "three foot six inches tall, bandy-legged, club-footed, rag-faced," but his consciousness and his intelligence form the moral heart of the book. When the adult Tristan eventually makes the long, hazardous and tiring journey to Voorstand himself, he undergoes an astonishing transformation that turns Carey's theme of cultural domination into something grotesque, compelling and finally irresistible. The wild (Efican?) ironies of the novel's concluding events on the streets of Saarlim and, in the velvety confines of a plush "trothaus" (apartment) there,

derive directly from the possibilities created by Tristan's deformities. Carey makes the most of having his innocent Efican abroad. Along the way Tristan is robbed, intimidated, and ultimately put in extreme danger of his life. He might be so ugly as to disgust casual bystanders in the street, but there is something indestructible about him, too, perhaps because he is guileless, generous and good.

Before all this can happen, however, Tristan becomes a not-very important activist against the alliance between Efica and Voorstand. The whole political mood of the novel is reminiscent of Australia in the early- to mid-1970s, the period of the Vietnam War and the sacking of Gough Whitlam as prime minister, when anti-American sentiment reached fever-pitch in some quarters of Australian society. (Voorstand goes to war against Burma, with Efican support.) Many people of Carey's generation absorbed American culture with their mother's milk, but they were also suspicious about the extent of its influence. Australia, some thought, had become the "Coca Colony." When the Whitlam government, which had pulled Australian troops out of Vietnam and sought to formulate an independent foreign policy, was sacked in 1975, some detected the hand of the CIA, up to its old tricks. These sorts of echoes help explain why this book seems to reach back to the atmosphere of Carey's early work. In part it fictionalizes the political context in which he began to publish. (For the record, Tristan Smith dates his autobiography with the year 426EC, which puts him in his mid-50s at the time of writing. Carey himself is in his early 50s.)

The dominant cultural form in both Voorstand and its satellite Efica is the Sirkus, Voorstand's "thrilling, spectacular, addictive, but also heartless" brand of mass entertainment, sometimes seen live and sometimes on vid, as Tristan would say. Its impact in Efica, we are to understand, is comparable to the influence of Hollywood and American television in Australia today. But the Sirkus has its own traditions and rituals that are inseparable from the mainstream values of Voorstand itself, where mice have souls, and it is supposedly taboo to kill any animal. Behind the Sirkus is an elaborate Franciscan ideal, introduced to Voorstand by those "brave Dutch heretics," the "Settlers Free," who were intent on a "Sirkus Sonder Gevangene"—a circus without "prisoners," that is, one without animals.

The idea has now been corrupted at the same time as the long-dead Settlers Free, with their folksy values, shining eyes and simple lives, have been elevated into the misty realms of the Great Historical Past, when Voorstand was a kinder, gentler place. It matters not that "grey furry Bruder Mouse with his iridescent blue coat, his white silk scarf, his cane" is now "nothing more than a logo-type, the symbol for an imperialist, mercantile culture." The global power of the Sirkus increases regardless, even though, as Tristan notes, "in its celebration of the individual, in its inequitable rewards for luck, in its invitation to have the audience be complicitous in the not infrequent death of performers, it ran counter to everything we Eficans held so dear."

Voorstandish readers of this book will detect in Carey's account of that nation's cultural and religious pieties a compelling parody of the uses to which Christian fundamentalism can be put, and a cool insight into the way that nostalgia for a sanitized past can intensify the confusion of the present. "We were decent people then," laments Mrs. Kram, a denizen of Saarlim City. "Bruder Mouse was not a clown. We knew him when we saw him. . . . We did not have all these codicils and revisions to the old laws. We ate beans and rice and raagbol pudding. We did not rape and murder. We did not thieve. We were better then."

The Mouse, the Duck and the Dog, Sirkus stars all of them, fill the heads of Carey's characters. Donald, Mickey and Goofy were never so palpable as the appalling creatures Tristan encounters on his voyage to Saarlim. If all the world is not a stage now but a themepark, we really are destined to become the residents of Voorstand and Efica. Could there be anything worse, Carey seems to be asking, than a situation in which practically everyone espoused the values of mass culture, especially in societies that did not create them? Tristan might know what's wrong with the Sirkus, and he might even, by seeming to be a part of it, have his final revenge on the Sirkus; but the Sirkus will continue to expand, like the universe itself. Driving [*The Unusual Life of Tristan Smith*] is the savage irony of the provincial who has learned that the metropolis is merely a larger and more powerful province than his own. "All art is provincial," Felicity declares, but her son Tristan, berating his reader from Voorstand, provides the rider that perhaps inspired Peter Carey to write the novel in the first place. "You have no idea of your effect on those of us who live outside the penumbra of your lives."

FURTHER READING

Criticism

Adam, Ian. "Breaking the Chain: Anti-Saussurean Resistance in Birney, Carey and C. S. Peirce." In *Past the Last Post: Theorizing Post-Colonialism and Post-Modernism,* edited by Ian Adam and Helen Tiffin, pp. 79-93. University of Calgary Press, 1990.
    Compares Earle Birney's narrative poem "David" and Carey's story "Do You Love Me?," focusing on the father-figures in the stories and their Oedipal relations.

Daniel, Helen. "'The Liar's Lump' or 'A Salesman's Sense of History': Peter Carey's *Illywhacker*." *Southerly,* No. 2 (June 1986): 157-67.
    Describes *Illywhacker* as an "extraordinary conception of the nature of truth and reality."

Glover, Douglas. "Australia on My Mind." *Chicago Tribune* (19 February 1995): 5.
    States that *The Unusual Life of Tristan Smith* is "about the place where nation, myth and the personal intersect."

Grimes, William. "An Australian Novelist with a Full-Tilt Pace and Ferocious Humor." *New York Times* (28 January 1992): C11, C15.
    Includes a review of *The Tax Inspector* as well as comments from an interview with Carey.

Hensher, Philip. "Heaven, Hell and Disneyland." *Guardian Weekly* (23 October 1994): 28.
    Favorably reviews *The Unusual Life of Tristan Smith,* finding it "new and surprising at every turn, even to a reader steeped in Carey's previous novels."

Kellaway, Kate. "Every Man Is a Theatre." *The Observer Review* (11 September 1994): 18.
    Reviews *The Unusual Life of Tristan Smith* and incorporates comments from an interview with Carey.

Koenig, Rhoda. "Taxes and Death." *New York* 25, No. 2 (13 January 1992): 62.
    Mixed review of *The Tax Inspector.* Koenig praises Carey's prose but finds the people comparable to "brightly colored cartoon characters."

Korn, Eric. "Entertaining Empires." *Times Literary Supplement* (2 September 1994): 10.
    Favorably reviews *The Unusual Life of Tristan Smith.*

Marx, Bill. "Dystopia Down Under." *Nation* 254, No. 10 (16 March 1992): 346-48.
    Reviews *The Tax Inspector,* arguing that the characters in the novel lack any "sense of redemption."

Prose, Francine. "Would You Buy a Used Car from This Family?" *New York Times Book Review* (12 January 1992): 3, 26.
    Favorably reviews *The Tax Inspector,* noting the beauty of Carey's prose in particular.

Ryan-Fazilleau, Suzan. "One-Upmanship in Peter Carey's Short Stories." *Journal of the Short Story in English,* No. 16 (Spring 1991): 51-63.
    Examines several of Carey's techniques for subverting "the traditional relationship between author and reader" and discusses the story "War Crimes" in detail.

See, Carolyn. "A Magic Tale of Spectacle." *Washington Post* (17 February 1995): F7.
    Favorably reviews *The Unusual Life of Tristan Smith.*

Shone, Tom. "Wild Ride." *New Yorker* (6 March 1995): 124-25.

Comments favorably on *The Unusual Life of Tristan Smith,* focusing on Carey's characters.

Tate, Trudi. "Unravelling the Feminine: Peter Carey's 'Peeling'." *Meanjin* 46, No. 3 (September 1987): 394-99.
    Analyzes themes relating to gender relations and gender identity in Carey's short story "Peeling."

Turner, Graeme. "Nationalising the Author: The Celebrity of Peter Carey." *Australian Literary Studies* 16, No. 2 (October 1993): 131-39.
    Discusses critical and popular reaction among Australians to Carey's works.

Additional coverage of Carey's life and career is contained in the following sources published by Gale Research: *Contemporary Authors,* **Vols. 123, 127;** *Contemporary Authors New Revision Series,* **Vol. 53;** *Contemporary Literary Criticism,* **Vols. 40, 55; and** *Major 20th-Century Writers.*

Alice Childress
1920-1994

American dramatist, screenwriter, novelist, prose writer, editor, and author of children's books.

The following entry provides an overview of Childress's career. For further information on her life and works, see *CLC,* Volumes 12, 15, and 86.

INTRODUCTION

Childress is considered a pivotal yet critically neglected figure in contemporary black American literature. Because she wrote about such topics as miscegenation and teenage drug abuse, some of Childress's works have been banned from schools and libraries in various regions. In her dramas as well as in her novels for children and adults, Childress drew upon her own experiences and created relatively normal, everyday protagonists. She explained in a 1984 essay entitled "A Candle in a Gale Wind": "My writing attempts to interpret the 'ordinary' because they are not ordinary. . . . We are uncommonly and marvelously intricate in thought and action, our problems are most complex and, too often, silently borne."

Biographical Information

Childress was born in Charleston, South Carolina, but grew up in Harlem in New York City. She was raised primarily by her grandmother, who was an early influence on her writing. Childress noted in a 1987 interview: "[My grandmother] used to sit at the window and say, 'There goes a man. What do you think he's thinking?' I'd say, 'I don't know. He's going home to his family.'. . . When we'd get to end of our game, my grandmother would say to me, 'Now, write that down. That sounds like something we should keep.'" Childress attended high school for two years but left before graduation. She held several jobs while acting as a member of the American Negro Theatre in Harlem; as part of the company, she performed in *A Midsummer-Night's Dream* and other works. Childress was also in the original cast of *Anna Lucasta* on Broadway, yet she found acting unfulfilling. She commented: "Racial prejudice was such that I was considered 'too light' to play my real self and they would not cast light-skinned blacks in white roles. I realized I had to have some other way of creating." She began to write dramas, later attributing this decision in part to her grandmother. "I never planned to become a writer, I never finished high school," she wrote in her 1984 essay. "Time, events, and Grandmother Eliza's brilliance taught me to rearrange circumstances into plays, stories, novels, scenarios and teleplays."

Major Works

In 1949 Childress's first play, *Florence,* was produced. The setting is a railway station waiting room divided into a "white" and a "colored" section. Mama sits on the colored side; she is going north to retrieve her daughter, Florence, who is trying unsuccessfully to act in New York City. Mrs. Carter is a white woman in the other section who tries to show Mama that she is not racist. Mama finds this claim to be false when she asks Mrs. Carter to use her influence to help Florence, only to have Mrs. Carter volunteer to ask one of her friends, a stage director, to hire Florence as a domestic. *Trouble in Mind* (1955) is a play about a group of actors rehearsing *Chaos in Belleville,* a fictional drama with an anti-lynching message. One of the black performers, Wiletta Mayer, refuses to obey the director, who wants Wiletta's character to put her own son into the hands of a crowd that is sure to lynch him. Wiletta contends that the director is forcing her character to act illogically, thus reinforcing a negative image of blacks. Wiletta's challenge to the director causes most of the troupe to question their own roles in *Chaos in Belleville.* In one version of the drama, Wiletta leads a cast walkout and the director demands a script revision in the finale; in another, Wiletta loses her part. Although *Trouble in Mind* was optioned for Broadway, Childress would not consent to the changes that producers wanted to make in the script, and it was never produced there. *Wedding Band* (1966), which focuses on South Carolina's anti-miscegenation laws and an interracial love affair, was both controversial and difficult to produce. Despite praise accorded to its initial 1966 production in Michigan, *Wedding Band* did not reach a wider audience until 1973, when it was performed in New York. In the play, Julia, a thirty-five-year-old black seamstress, celebrates the ten-year anniversary of her common-law marriage to Herman, a forty-year-old white baker. He gives her a wedding band to wear on a chain around her neck until they can be legally married in another state. They are never married, for Herman contracts influenza. In *Wedding Band,* Childress revealed racism in all characters, not just against blacks but also against Germans, Chinese, and others. *Wine in the Wilderness* (1969) is about intraracial hostilities and prejudices. In it Tomorrow-Marie, called Tommy, affirms that she is not a "messed-up chick" as artist Bill would like to paint her, but the "wine in the wilderness," his image of the majestic "Mother Africa." Although Childress devoted most of her career to drama, she was also a noted author of children's literature. She wrote two plays and three novels for children, including *A Hero Ain't Nothin' but a Sandwich* (1973) and *Rainbow Jordan* (1981). By far her best-known work, *A Hero Ain't Nothin' but a Sandwich* is the story of thirteen-year-old Benjie Johnson's emerging addiction to heroin. His story is told from many points of view, including those of his stepfather, teachers, and pusher. *Rainbow Jordan* is another unflinching look at adolescence, from the point of view of a fourteen-year-old girl trying to create stability in her turbulent life. Childress's last published work was another children's novel, *Those Other People* (1989), concerning a young boy's coming to terms with his homosexuality and its impact on his family.

Critical Reception

Childress was instrumental in the genesis of black theater in America and throughout her career remained a vital, uncompromising force in contemporary drama. Her plays and children's books have received much praise, yet many critics believe her work deserves even more attention and recognition. Elizabeth Brown-Guillory asserted in *Phylon* that Childress's plays "beg for scholarship" and described Childress as "a playwright whose dramaturgical advances have paved the way for women in the theatre." Although *Florence* was produced on a small scale in Harlem, the critical praise it received launched Childress's career. With *Gold through the Trees* (1952), she became the first black woman to have a play professionally produced on the American stage, and with *Trouble in Mind* she was the first woman to win an Obie Award for best original off-Broadway play. *A Hero Ain't Nothin' but a Sandwich* was Childress's most controversial work and accounted for the majority of her critical attention. Despite overwhelming praise for its realistic treatment of a

sensitive issue, several school districts banned *A Hero Ain't Nothin' but a Sandwich,* apparently on the grounds that the theme of the work was inappropriate for young readers. Childress encountered similar resistance to her plays as well; for instance, the state of Alabama refused to air *Wine in the Wilderness* when it was produced for television. Childress commented on the reception of her works in her 1984 essay: "I do not consider my work controversial, as it is not at all contrary to humanism."

PRINCIPAL WORKS

Florence (drama) 1949

Just a Little Simple [adaptor; from the short story collection *Simple Speaks His Mind* by Langston Hughes] (drama) 1950

Gold through the Trees (drama) 1952

Trouble in Mind (drama) 1955

Like One of the Family: Conversations from a Domestic's Life (prose) 1956

Wedding Band: A Love/Hate Story in Black and White (drama) 1966

The Freedom Drum (drama) 1969; also performed as *Young Martin Luther King,* 1969

String [adaptor; from the short story "A Piece of String" by Guy de Maupassant] (drama) 1969

Wine in the Wilderness: A Comedy Drama (drama) 1969

Wine in the Wilderness (screenplay) 1969

Mojo: A Black Love Story (drama) 1970

A Hero Ain't Nothin' But a Sandwich (novel) 1973

Wedding Band (screenplay) 1973

When the Rattlesnake Sounds (drama) [first publication] 1975

Let's Hear It for the Queen (drama) [first publication] 1976

*Sea Island Song (drama) 1977

A Hero Ain't Nothin' But a Sandwich (screenplay) 1978

A Short Walk (novel) 1979

String (screenplay) 1979

Rainbow Jordan (novel) 1981

Moms: A Praise Play for a Black Comedienne (drama) 1987

Those Other People (novel) 1989

*This work was also produced as *Gullah* in 1984.

CRITICISM

Rosemary Curb (essay date Winter 1980)

SOURCE: "An Unfashionable Tragedy of American Racism: Alice Childress's *Wedding Band,*" *MELUS,* Vol. 7, No. 4, Winter, 1980, pp. 57-67.

[*In the following essay, Curb explores Childress's portrayal of women in her dramas, particularly* Wedding Band.]

Alice Childress, a serious contemporary playwright whose work has received little scholarly recognition, has been working in American theater for four decades. Born a decade before Lorraine Hansberry, Alice Childress produced her first play, *Florence,* ten years before Hansberry's *A Raisin in the Sun.* Childress was, in fact, the first black woman to have a play produced on the professional American stage, and she is still writing successful drama in the 1980s. Not only has she had eight serious plays produced, but she has also published two children's plays, two novels, a nonfiction collection of interviews with black women who work as domestics, and an anthology of scenes from plays by black Americans as exercises for black actors. Like Hansberry, Childress has affirmed a deep commitment to social and political causes that promote human rights for black people and women. Unlike Hansberry, however, Childress features black women as protagonists in her fiction and drama.

As an early troupe member of the American Negro Theatre in Harlem, Alice Childress performed leading roles for many years before she wrote *Florence* in 1949. The one-act play, set in a Jim Crow railroad station in the deep South, features an encounter between a black woman and a white woman across a little fence separating them. The white woman attempts to demonstrate her cordiality and lack of prejudice toward Negroes by recounting the plot of her brother's best-selling novel about a "tragic mulatto" girl (a favorite black stereotype for white writers of the thirties and forties) but she unmasks her racist condescension. Angered, the black woman changes her plans to go to New York to retrieve her daughter Florence, who is struggling with little success to become a professional actress. She sells back her train ticket and wires the money to Florence with the message: "Keep trying."

Following successful performances of two other short plays featuring humble characters, Childress initiated Harlem's first all-union Off-Broadway contracts recognizing the Actor's Equity Association and Harlem Stage Hand Local Union. Based on her own backstage struggles as a professional actor, director, and playwright, Childress presented *Trouble in Mind,* her first full-length play, in 1955, at the Greenwich Mews Theatre in New York. The play ran for 91 performances and won the *Village Voice* Obie Award for the best original Off-Broadway play of the 1955-56 season.

Like *Florence, Trouble in Mind* uses an interracial cast but features the struggles of a lone middle-aged black woman in the face of subtle racism from white liberals and the woman's final heroic affirmation of black pride. As the play opens, veteran Wiletta Mayer arrives for the first rehearsal of *Chaos in Belleville,* her first leading role in a serious Broadway play. Although the play purports to be an accurate treatment of racial tension in the deep South, in fact, it reinforces the same demeaning black stereotypes Wiletta has been trying to escape throughout her career in the theater. After the white director forces a method acting technique on her, Wiletta drops

her mask of "Tommish" hypocrisy, which she has always used when working with white directors, and admits that she finds the character impossible; the mother she plays would not send her son out to face a lynch mob. To emphasize the faulty characterization, she asks the director if he would send his son out to be killed. He snaps back at her: "Don't compare yourself to me." Having unmasked the liberal director's hidden racism, Wiletta leads a cast walk-out even though it is clear that her heroism may result in professional suicide.

Early in the sixties Childress wrote her second full-length serious drama, *Wedding Band: A Love/Hate Story in Black and White,* about the tragic results of anti-miscegenation laws and what Childress calls "anti-woman" laws in the South after Reconstruction, and still in force in the first decades of the twentieth century. Born in Charleston, South Carolina in 1920, the playwright witnessed the suffering of women legally isolated and restricted by the inhumane laws. In essence, the laws which Childress found especially noxious freed the fathers (black and white) of the children of black women from any responsibility for their offspring, and disinherited black women and their children from property rights. Not only was sexual mixing of races strictly prohibited by law, but simply the birth of a mulatto child was proof of the mother's guilt and justified her conviction. Black and white women both suffered under such laws, and each suffered alone, since a woman's testimony about the paternity of her child was not considered valid.

Wedding Band dramatizes the anguish and repercussions surrounding an interracial love affair in Charleston, South Carolina, in 1918. Julia Augustine, a thirty-five-year-old black seamstress with an eighth grade education, has violated both state anti-miscegenation laws and the common mores of the working class by continuing a monogamous love relationship with a white man for ten years. Childress considers the play to be a vigorous political statement protesting the denial of black women's rights during a period of American history rarely featured in current literature about racial struggles. Childress has remarked:

> *Wedding Band* dealt with a black woman and a white man, but it was about black women's rights. I took Herman as an understanding, decent human being. But he could not give her [Julia Augustine] protection in a society where the law is against them. He couldn't marry her. I didn't give him a last name because if Julia couldn't have it, I felt no need to give it. No one has questioned this. The woman is the one most denigrated in such situations. I wrote the play because the only thing I saw about such things was the wealthy white man and his black mistress. But most of the interracial couples then and now didn't come from the wealthy but from working class people. So I took a seamstress and a baker, and this made it an unpopular topic for a lot of people who

prefer the portrayal of upper strata whites. The play shows society's determination to hold the black woman down through laws framed against her. There are similar laws framed against white women, and, of course, unwritten laws. I never run out of subject matter for writing about women's rights particularly black women, but white women too, which I have included in *Wedding Band*.

As the play opens one Saturday morning in summer 1918, Julia Augustine greets her first full day in a working-class ghetto populated by a variety of ethnic groups. Her immediate neighbors are all black women surviving more or less alone. Julia's landlady, Fanny, self-appointed representative of the black race, seems delighted with her new tenant, the only one who has paid in advance. She pries mercilessly into Julia's meager material goods. Eagerly Fanny relays gossip about the other renters: that Mattie worked in a "sporting house," and that Lula adopted a son after she "killed" her natural one. Mattie appears to be a boisterous, high-spirited woman so destitute that she scolds her eight-year-old daughter, loud enough to wake the neighborhood, just after the opening curtain, for losing a quarter.

Lula wins Julia's sympathy by confiding rather than prying initially. Because Lula had suffered such abuse from her husband that she sought consolation from a friend, she tells Julia, she neglected to watch her son, who wandered out and got killed on the railroad track. Her adopted son, Nelson, now full grown, is home on leave from the army. Fanny considers it "unnatural" for Lula to live alone with such a handsome muscular boy, not her blood kin, but fails to recognize or acknowledge her own attraction for him. Nelson rebuffs Fanny's unsubtle advances, but he flirts with Julia and begs her for a date.

Pursued by Nelson and probed by Fanny, Mattie, and Lula, Julia breaks down at the end of the scene and reveals that she cannot marry the man she has "been keepin' company with" because he is white. As a prelude to Julia's shocking revelation, Mattie flatly states, "Man that won't marry you thinks nothin' of you. Just usin' you." Mattie's rigid judgment is ironic in the light of her subsequent revelation that she is not legally married to October, the man with whom she has shared most of her adult life. Mattie tells Julia that her first husband left her after years of habitual battering and verbal abuse. Even though she and October were married in a religious ceremony on Edisto Island eleven years ago, the state of South Carolina only recognizes her first marriage. After Julia's confession, Mattie concludes that Julia is carrying on the affair for money: "You grit your teeth and take all he's got; if you don't, somebody else will. . . . Rob him blind. Take it all. Let him froth at the mouth. Let him die in the poorhouse—bitter, bitter to the bone."

Relentlessly, but compassionately, Childress characterizes

Julia's neighbors as petty and narrow-minded in their racist assumptions and defensive obsessions about their need for social status. If an all-pervasive racism has conditioned the women to be suspicious of white cordiality, it has also toughened them with the stamina necessary for survival. By characterizing Mattie as ruthlessly greedy and conniving, Childress succeeds in illuminating a significant truth of American social history: desperately impoverished and overpowered black women have so long been used as commodities by white men that the only relationship Lula and Mattie can imagine between a black woman and a white man is one of exploitation. They simply advise Julia to exploit the man as much as he is exploiting her. Childress dramatizes the assumption early in the scene by having the poor white bell man, who sells linens to black women, proposition Julia and offer to pay her for sexual favors with stockings. She drives him out, raging: "Beneath contempt, that's what you are. . . . I wish you was dead, you just oughta be dead, stepped on and dead." Her fury ironically foreshadows her driving Herman and his family from her house at the end of the third scene.

When Julia tries to explain to her neighbors that she and Herman love each other, even though he is not rich or prominent, the other women judge her crazy or a fool. What sticks in Julia's mind at the end of the scene is a phrase she read aloud from October's letter to illiterate Mattie: "Two things a man can give the woman he loves . . . his name and his protection." Sadly Julia realizes that Herman can provide neither as long as they stay in the South.

Herman, a poor forty-year-old baker, makes his first entrance at the beginning of the second scene, set that evening. When Julia's neighbors eye his shabby appearance with scorn, Julia scolds him for not wearing his good suit. The scene richly exhibits both the tenderness and beauty as well as the ordinariness of Herman and Julia's love. Herman brings Julia an elaborately decorated wedding cake to celebrate their tenth anniversary and a gold wedding band, which she has long desired as a symbol of their commitment, to wear on a chain around her neck until they can be legally married. Eagerly they make plans to sail on the Clyde Line to New York, where anti-miscegenation laws will not thwart them. Herman voices chagrin that they must wait until he sells his bakery and pays back a loan to his mother. Their delays seem also to be influenced by their reluctance to leave the familiar city and by apprehension about the challenge which life in the North presents. Their dialogue provides exposition about Herman's family, work, financial situation, and the homey intimacy of their relationship; Herman does not even know his own size in socks or where to buy them because Julia has been taking care of his clothes for years. (Childress frequently selects unerringly accurate details which succeed in illuminating the intimate nature of a relationship better than a speech peppered with flowery protestations of devotion.)

The scene also reveals that Julia and Herman tread gently on racial issues. Julia has a tendency to make generalizations about "white folks" and Herman thinks Julia is one of "the good kind of colored folks"—implying that he thinks most are not good. A racist slur which Herman's mother once uttered to hurt her son, he had incautiously mentioned to Julia, who has never forgotten it. Herman's mother, a woman with social aspirations, always out of reach, once remarked to her daughter: "Annabelle, you've got a brother who makes pies and loves a nigger." Recalling the remark in the context of their current stalemate situation, Julia complains to Herman: "Sometimes I feel like fightin' . . . and there's nobody to fight but you. . . ."

Just as Childress characterizes Julia's neighbors as narrowly cautious, she exhibits the pair of star-crossed lovers as flawed. They are not heroic crusaders for sexual liberation, civil rights for minorities, or racial equality. They show neither a desire for martyrdom nor for masochism. However, although they are not battling for social justice, their situation has opened their eyes to the narrowness of their lives and the pettiness of those who restrict them. Herman says, "My mother is made out of too many . . . little things . . . the price of carrots, how much fat is on the meat . . . little things make people small. Make ignorance—you know?" As in her other plays, Childress dramatizes the daily frustrations and minor crises that tempt the impoverished to despair and self-hatred. She demonstrates that maintaining personal dignity and hope for the future in the midst of destitution and social rejection can be heroic. In fact, all of the characters who appear in *Wedding Band* merit admiration simply for surviving. Considering the hostility of Herman's family and Julia's neighbors, it is remarkable that Julia and Herman never doubt each other's love.

At the end of the first act, Herman is stricken with influenza. Childress skillfully interweaves two historical catastrophes here. The influenza epidemic, which swept the country in 1918 and left eleven million dead, provides the moral dilemma which creates the plot. The anti-miscegenation laws force Julia to face impossible choices. She could call a doctor, not only risking their arrest but also endangering the property and reputation of the landlady and the livelihood of everyone who lives in these rental houses. She could hire somebody to transport Herman to a doctor, but he might die on the way. In any case, she could be arrested for transporting a white man under suspicious circumstances. She could patiently wait for Herman's recovery. But the statistics are against her; most influenza victims are dying, and she knows it. If Herman dies in her house, Julia faces the same legal charges from the coroner that a doctor might present. She decides to send for Herman's mother and sister, who can take Herman to a doctor, even though she knows that she faces their hatred and scorn. She also faces prosecution for violating the law which demands that influenza victims be kept under quarantine. For fear of the laws, even Herman's mother chooses to wait until dark to transport him. Thus his life is jeopardized by unjust laws.

By the opening of the second act, Julia's situation has reached a crisis which tightens the tension leading to her climax of rage and anguish at the end of the scene. Fanny refuses to let Julia call a doctor: "They'll say I run a bad house." Fanny knows well the difficulty with which she has won her social and economic position:

> Julia, it's hard to live under these mean white folks . . . but I've done it. I'm the first and only colored they let buy land 'round here. . . . When I pass by they can say, "There she go, Fanny Johnson, representin' her race in-a approved manner" 'cause they don't have to worry 'bout my next move. I can't afford to mess that up on account-a you or any-a rest-a these hard-luck, better-off-dead, triflin' niggers.

Childress portrays Fanny as a black woman with white-identified values, but she is even more harsh in her characterization of Herman's mother and sister, poor white women who lamely glean what little dignity they can from bolstering their belief in white superiority and condemning Herman for lowering himself to love a black woman. Both white women secretly envy Julia who has known love and passion in a way they have not and probably will not. The sister says to Herman, "Most excitement I've ever had was takin' piano lessons." Later Herman's mother also mentions the emptiness of a life confined to duty and service to other people's needs and pleasures: "I put up with a man breathin' stale whiskey in my face every night . . . pullin' and pawin' at me . . . always tired, inside and out." Childress does not invite her audience to mock white sexuality but to pity the pathetic anguish of a tired old woman.

In her compassion for all her genteel but poor characters, Childress describes the indignities suffered by even the least desirable characters. Although she portrays Herman's mother and sister, the only two white women who appear in any of her plays of the sixties, as racists, she analyzes their motivations within the context of their own suffering. Childress has called Herman's mother thus:

> A victim of terrible circumstances. No one was able to sit down with her and take her hands in theirs and explain anything. No one was able to say, "We thank you for what you've done. We understand what you've been through." But rather a series of detestations goes on. I treat her with compassion as a woman. I feel that my liberation is not to become as unjust as those who deny my rights. My liberation is not to change places with those who have practiced racism against me.

Herman's mother clings desperately to meager symbols of respectability. Because Annabelle once played a concert in a church, she calls her daughter a "concert pianist." From her first entrance, Herman's mother insults Julia. She makes the same assumptions Lula and Mattie did: Julia is Herman's whore out to exploit him. As Julia's fury mounts, Herman's mother demands to have all of Herman's things that are at Julia's house so that she can burn them. She prompts the delirious Herman to recite a racist speech by John C. Calhoun, which she had whipped him to memorize when he was five, for the Knights of the Gold Carnation (a white supremacist group similar to the Ku Klux Klan). Crazed with fever, Herman grasps the porch post and begins to recite the speech. Julia explodes.

The scene erupts into name calling—the climax of the action:

> HERMAN'S MOTHER. Nigger whore . . . he used you for a garbage pail . . .
>
> JULIA. White trash! Sharecropper! Let him die . . . let 'em all die . . . Kill him with your murderin' mouth —sharecropper bitch!

Julia orders Herman and his family out and continues to scream wildly even after they have gone.

Julia's temporary insanity rages through most of the last scene. Wearing the wedding dress she had been keeping carefully packed away in her hope chest, Julia scatters the rest of the chest's precious contents around the room in a drunken furor. Then Mattie appears and the sudden recognition that she is not the lone victim of legal injustice sobers her somewhat. Mattie tearfully laments that she cannot get any family benefits from the Merchant Marines since she has no state marriage license. The anti-woman state law forbidding divorce punishes Mattie just as the anti-miscegenation laws restrict Julia's freedom and happiness.

Herman arrives, clutching two tickets for the "black deck" on the steamboat to New York. When Herman staggers into the house, Julia gives the tickets and her wedding band to Mattie. She locks out Herman's mother and sister when they come. As the final curtain falls, Julia holds Herman in her arms, imagining that they are riding the steamer to New York. Julia's firm stand—taking Herman in and locking his mother and sister out—dramatically demonstrates her assertion of her rights, even though such a gesture lacks any public effect or crusading zeal. Furthermore, Julia's moment of self-awareness and recognition of her fate is tinged with hysteria.

The two plays which follow *Wedding Band* in Childress's career feature similar strong women. *Wine in the Wilderness* portrays black characters separated by class, education, and political/cultural conditioning. Childress wrote the play for WGBH television in Boston as the first drama in the series, *On Being Black,* in 1969. In the play Tommy-Marie, a factory worker in her thirties wearing mismatched clothes and a cheap wig, and fleeing from the ravages of a race riot, agrees to model for a black artist. What she does not realize at the outset is that Bill and his two friends—snobbish, college-educated, and self-consciously Afro-American—actually hold Tommy in contempt as their image of a "messed-up chick." When she recognizes their scorn, her rage fuels her self-assertion. She uncovers the hypocrisy of their affectations by pointing out their self-hatred: "You don't like flesh and blood niggers. . . . You comin' on 'bout how we ain' never together. You hate us, that's what! *You hate black me.*" The clusters of images which Childress carefully arranges contrast Bill's artificial and exotic ideal with the real live Tommy, that familiar woman on the streets of Harlem, as has been pointed out by Janet Brown.

In *Mojo: A Black Love Story,* first presented in 1970, Irene pays a visit to her former husband, Teddy, before entering the hospital for serious cancer surgery. She tells him that she always loved him even though she finds it difficult to express her feelings, and that they have a daughter. Irene shares with Teddy her newly discovered black pride and her need for blackness as a psychic shield against the whiteness of surgery. However Irene's self-assertion and sense of affirmation have occurred before the play opens and merely manifests itself through her courageous revelations to Teddy.

In the seventies Childress devoted her talent and energy to writing fiction and drama for children and adolescents. *A Hero Ain't Nothin' But a Sandwich* won the Jane Addams Honor Award in 1974 as a young adult novel and the Lewis Carroll Shelf Award from the University of Wisconsin in 1975. In 1977 the film version won the Virgin Islands Film Festival Award. In 1979 Childress published *A Short Walk,* a novel for adults featuring the life story of a spunky and courageous black woman from the beginning of the century to her death in the seventies. The character has both the earthy grit and assertive energy of Childress's dramatic heroines.

Through essentially solitary struggles, Childress's strong women forge through barriers not only of race and sex, but also class, education, and age which threaten to keep them poor and powerless to a recognition of personal worth. Jeanne-Marie Miller comments: "Childress's women characters not only transcend their predicaments but often function as catalysts for change in those whose lives they touch."

Although all of Childress's published work deserves to be read, *Wedding Band* is her finest and most serious piece of literature and deserves comparison with the most celebrated American tragedies. Like Childress's other plays, it features an ordinary black woman past her prime. What we have here is that Julia's soul-searching in the midst of her moral dilemmas takes place on stage; her confusion is fully dramatized. The problems which face Julia are complicated by a convergence of historical and political dilemmas with which a woman of her education and conditioning is ill-prepared to cope. That she and the other flawed women in *Wedding Band* survive is tenuous but believable.

Childress's mode of characterization is unflinching realism. Earthy dialogue and crude figurative language characterize the "nitty-gritty" characters who populate her plays as bursting with vitality and a fully realized sensuality. No saints or villains clutter Childress's *dramatis personae*. In *Wedding Band,* racism and the desire for respectability obsess both black and white characters. Every ethnic minority suffers insults. Herman is angered when someone with an excess of patriotism writes, "Krauts . . . Germans live here," on the side of his house. Suffering from the racist jeers of others does not, however, prevent Herman's mother from calling Julia, "Dirty black nigger," or Julia from calling her, "Kraut, knuckle-eater, redneck." In an earlier scene, the black and white children together, Teeta and Princess, jump rope to the racist rhyme: "Ching, ching, Chinaman eat a dead rat. . . . Knock him in the head with a baseball bat." Later when they make fun of the "Chinamerican" man down the street, Mattie tells them, "If he ketches you, he'll cook you with onions and gravy." Fanny accuses the sign painter of being a "black Jew" when he refuses to return her money after he misspells a word in her sign.

Name-calling and racist insults bolster the fragile dignity of the member of any ethnic minority desperate to be thought respectable or at least higher on the ladder of social respectability than someone else. Clinging to symbols of respectability is the only way to survive the rejection of the larger society. In a similar way, Fanny brags about her silver tea service, her English china, and her Belgian linen; Julia keeps her hope chest. In an absurd attempt to conceal Julia's indiscretion from the children, Mattie tells them that Herman is Julia's husband—"a light colored man."

The antagonist of *Wedding Band* seems to be the whole system of government-sanctioned oppression and the conservative *status quo* fearful of change. However, Childress's uneducated characters lack the ability to understand the nature of the enemy or to articulate their own victimization. Herman and Julia are not presented as the American version of Romeo and Juliet, although their plight invites comparison. They lack the requisite youth and beauty, social prominence and wealth, romantic perfection. They are weak, confused, superstitious, lonely, and impatient; no empires crumble when catastrophe strikes them. Herman's death and Julia's madness create nothing to nurture the healing of racial hatred. However, despite their insignificance, they are brave and honest enough to carry on a love affair threatened by criminal penalties because they know instinctively that love is stronger than unjust laws.

Wedding Band dramatizes more than a tragic love affair. It presents the social, economic, moral, religious, legal, political, historical, psychological context in which a black woman like Julia Augustine makes independent decisions that affect her life and the lives of everyone she touches.

Despite its literary merits, *Wedding Band* has been largely ignored by producers as well as scholars. Early in 1965 Loften Mitchell wrote:

> *Wedding Band* had a rehearsed reading in 1963. Immediately after that it was optioned for a Broadway showing. To date it has changed hands at least five times. Yet, *Wedding Band* is, to all who have heard it, an exceptionally well-written, humorous dramatic piece, positive in its approach and fully-deserving a first-rate production.

The University of Michigan gave *Wedding Band* a full production in 1965. It took seven years more for the play to reach a larger recognition. In November 1972, Joseph Papp produced it at the New York Public Theatre. In 1973 the American Broadcasting Company presented a televised version of the play on prime time. Ruby Dee, who played the leading role in both the Public Theatre and television productions, comments:

> There is a tragedy here that cannot be underestimated. Alice Childress is a splendid playwright, a veteran—indeed, a pioneer. She has won awards, acclaim, and everything but consistent productions. It is difficult to think of a play by a white writer earning the reviews that *Wedding Band* earned in 1965 and then having to wait until 1973 to reach the New York stage.

> It proves one thing: We may salute and savor the glory of the black theatrical pioneer, but in a land where materialism is all-important, the real salutes take longer.

Exactly why it took so long for *Wedding Band* to reach large American audiences can only be guessed. Childress herself guesses that the content was unpopular. However, no producer told her directly: "We just don't do serious plays featuring middle-aged black women," or "We'll only consider an interracial love story if it's scandalous, violent, and terribly romantic." Nobody refused to produce it because the historical period play was out of vogue. Nevertheless, it seems inevitable that a play such as *Wedding Band* was doomed to be passed over in the sensational sixties and early seventies because it offers an unbloody plot with unglamorous characters, in an unfashionable setting, in an unflinchingly realistic style. No wonder one opening night New York theater critic dismissed it as "an appealing but inconsequential little period play about miscegenation . . . ready for a Jerome Kern score." Another belittled it as "a romantic play that does not entirely escape the charge of sentimentality . . . a sweet old love story about hard, dusty times in a hard, dusty place." One can only conclude that the critic, Clive Barnes, had more of an eye to his own prejudices and expectations than to the play on stage. No careful reader would give the play the following judgment: "The writing is rather old-fashioned in its attempt at Ibsenite realism, and neither the situation nor the characters really change from the beginning of the play to the end."

Far from being "old-fashioned," the writing in *Wedding Band* offers the authenticity of the regional dialect in the diction of the period. Necessarily, the dialogue sounds stilted to a contemporary ear. Although Childress's realism owes much to Ibsen and Chekov, it cannot for that reason be dismissed as out-of-date. After all, realism has proved to be a successful mode for most of what are considered the great American tragedies. However, it is no doubt true that *Wedding Band* failed to win popular acclaim for the very reason that it deserves to be re-read and re-evaluated by serious scholars: it is an authentic portrait of American racism in a rarely dramatized historical period with credible characters.

Geraldine L. Wilson (review date 1980)

SOURCE: "A Novel to Enjoy and Remember," *Freedomways,* Vol. 20, No. 2, 1980, pp. 101-02.

[*In the following review, Wilson praises Childress's rich characterization and dialogue in* A Short Walk.]

Alice Childress has written a remarkable book [*A Short Walk*] that takes its title from the answer given by protagonist Cora James' father to the question "What is life?"—which she asks him at age five while watching a minstrel show. Life, he responds, is "a short walk from the cradle to the grave . . . and it sure behooves us to be kind to one another along the way." On the same occasion, when a storm threatens to erupt out of a black performer's impromptu musical discourse on oppression, Cora's father counsels, "Let all run that wants to run, Cora. We stay put where we are, so's not to get trampled."

Deeply influenced by her relationship with her father (which relationship, incidentally, displays our child-rearing system in one of its most satisfactory variations), Cora develops into a kind, loving adult who stays put a good deal and is adept at dealing with those problems that present themselves. From her father she has taken a strong will, a deep love for her people and their culture, a critical eye and a strong sense of responsibility for herself and those close to her.

In Cora James' odyssey from the Low Country of South Carolina to the Big Apple, we see reflected those legions of black folk who made the journey and poured their energies into creating Harlem, U.S.A. Thoughtful, womanly, strong, responsible, tough, resilient and stubborn, Cora is at once uniquely herself and every black woman "that's ever had to stand squarefooted and make her own way." Author Childress sees to it that we come to know and understand the whole Cora and that we take special note of her solitariness, that pronounced aloneness which often goes unrecognized in the lives of so many black women. Cora's blood mother, we learn, had suffered such aloneness to a tragic degree at a very young age.

We also realize, after reading what it was like for Cora to come to a big city and survive, that her struggle is the same forty or fifty years later and will probably be the same forty years from now. So you check back through the pages of *A Short Walk* to note again just what it was that kept her going.

In her relationships with men, Cora seeks some justice, comfort and understanding, *and she struggles for them*. The man, Cecil, whom she deeply loves, she loves through the long haul though she is pained because "he cannot see himself at all as I see him." She realizes that the reverse is also true. The male characters are dramatic and memorable, each for different reasons; and though not all are strong, entirely admirable people, none is caricatured.

Perhaps it is the author's playwrighting skills which account for the novel's superb dialogue—a veritable celebration of the black community's use of language. And not only the dialogue but the descriptive passages as well are rich, both in imagery and adroitly used proverbs.

Through the author's masterful juxtapositions of tragedy and humor, sorrow and joy, cruelty and kindness (sometimes in the same person), readers are led to deal with her juxtaposition of African/African-American culture and cultural repression in stunning ways. There are political elements which invite family discussion—you will recognize them. You will be energized by this book, and you will be surprised from time to time—nobody's predictable, certainly not Cora. You will remember *A Short Walk* and think about your own.

Trudier Harris (essay date 1980)

SOURCE: "'I Wish I Was a Poet': The Character as Artist in Alice Childress's *Like One of the Family*," *Black American Literature Forum,* Vol. 14, 1980, pp. 24-30.

[*Harris is an educator. In the following essay, she discusses Mildred, Childress's narrator in* Like One of the Family, *and her position in oral and written African-American literature.*]

When they are creating their works, black American writers can draw upon two equally strong traditions. They have available to them the rich European and American written tradition and the equally rich African and Afro-American oral tradition. They can incorporate the written forms representative of the best of Shakespeare or Henry James as well as the oral forms of the anonymous slaves who told their tales to each other at the ends of many fourteen-hour days of picking cotton. Written and oral forms both have their distinct features, and when they are combined, they evolve into a similarly distinct product.

In traditional written literature, metaphorical language and expected forms dominate. A poet is expected to use the sonnet form or couplets or free verse and incorporate similes and metaphors in their appropriate iambic or trochaic feet. A short story writer or novelist is expected to provide setting and use symbols in his presentation of the exposition, development of conflict and climax, and in the resolution of his tale. In the purest and most traditional of the written forms, then, the teller becomes subordinate to his tale. He creates a work of art, an object, that can be interpreted, explained, criticized, or dismissed. He offers a work which, once having been read, can become the stimulus for further reflection and meditation. The form itself does not necessarily require that the reader do anything to it or for it *as he is in the process of reading*. The author, object, and reader remain three entities which can, but are not required to, act upon one another.

The oral tradition, on the other hand, *demands* audience attention, participation, and response. An audience can approve, applaud, or correct the action related while the teller *is in the process of telling his tale*. Oral tradition presupposes an interaction between teller and audience; therefore, the teller and his tale are inseparable. The teller can be held accountable for knowledge about and ordering of events he relates, and the audience functions to insist upon that knowledge and ordering. For example, when Zora Neale Hurston was collecting for *Mules and Men*, she related the episode of a black man in Florida who, when asked to tell a tale, responded: "'Oh, Ah don't know it well enough to say it. Ah jus' know it well enough to know it.'" The informant "clearly understands his role," Robert Hemenway points out . . . , "as a passive tradition-bearer [listener, audience], a self-correcting force who will ensure that the active bearer—the tale teller—will not violate too extensively the community's expectation of a given performance." Both the active and the passive tradition bearers are central to the oral culture. Those who tell are appreciated by those who listen, and those who listen and applaud are needed by those who tell.

Consider also the case of the black folk preacher to illustrate the point about tellers, tales, and audience. When the text of a folk sermon appears in print, as in Bruce Rosenberg's *The Art of the American Folk Preacher*, it is lifeless and essentially formless. It can certainly be discussed, but it has little meaning as a form when it is on a page. It acquires life and meaning in the mouth of the preacher. When he delivers the sermon, he provides rhythm and substance through the process of delivery. He has individuality, or style, within the performance, but his audience can also detect when he deviates and skips a card in the "Deck O' Cards" sermon or say amen when he delivers it to agreement with their expectations. The preacher cannot be separated from his sermon; the teller is tied to his tale; art is performance.

Black writers who combine the oral and written forms, then, create works that are not simply objects to be read and reflected upon, but works which allow participation during the act of reading. And the oral tradition which provides this participation brings with it the idea that literalness is often not expected. Audiences which heard tales of John outwitting Old Master, or of the single shot that killed six quail, a deer, seven blackbirds, a bear, and a snake, did not assume that the teller told a literal truth. The truth he might have revealed could refer to the universal desire for freedom, as exemplified by John, or to the human need for entertainment or for transcendence of difficult situations, as exemplified by the hunting lie.

By using features from both written and oral traditions, Alice Childress is one black American writer who succeeds in adding a unique dimension to her work. In her collection ***Like One of the Family*** . . . Childress makes use of traditional metaphoric language and written form, but she uses the storytelling forms of black folk tradition to give Mildred, her major character, the means for telling her own stories and interacting with the audience. Usually in literary works in which the author relinquishes the reins of narration to a character, there is still a sense of an authorial presence. An author will create a semblance of removal for the purpose of evoking a particular response from readers, but they may still sense a direction for their sympathies. In such cases, an author's ostensible absence from a scene suggests that the character has a life of his or her own, and a consciousness uncontrolled by the author. However, Childress's knowledge of folk forms allows her to succeed to a greater extent than most authors because she totally effaces herself from the narrative, and Mildred indeed seems to have a consciousness of her own.

Obviously we know that Alice Childress wrote a book called ***Like One of the Family***. Beyond the title and the author's name, however, we never see the presiding presence of Childress. Once a reader opens the book, he or she ceases to be a reader and becomes a part of an audience. As members of that audience, we are never allowed to verbalize the fact that the author, Childress, is in control of the volume. We are simply confronted with a character, whose name we later learn is Mildred. We are never introduced to her or given any background information about her or presented with another character who tells us anything about her. The form of the collection allows us to see Mildred and no reality beyond that. We meet her, interact with her, and must rely upon her for whatever we experience in the book. As a character, Mildred completely controls her storytelling environment as well as the *form* in which her stories are presented. Mildred is not only the principal actor in the story, though; she quickly assumes the role of artist by embroidering the series of events in which she acts or has acted. She does her own kind of mythmaking without any apparent manipulation from Childress. While Mildred manages to incorporate forms of black folk storytelling, she nevertheless keeps her stories within the broad guidelines of the conscious creation of literature.

Mildred is a maid who does day work in New York. She is a thirty-two-year-old woman who, during the early 1950s, has worked for a succession of white women in the New York area. *Like One of the Family* is a collection of short conversations between Mildred and her friend Marge about Mildred's many day work experiences with white women and men. However, we get only Mildred's part of the conversations. Ellipses are used to allow us to infer when Marge has presumably made a comment. The conversations are all related *after* Mildred's adventures, and the technique of monologue, which is employed throughout, creates a sense of immediacy. The conversations, though well-ordered, draw upon devices from oral tradition to simulate casualness and spontaneity, so that Mildred's seeming artlessness is not so.

"I wish I was a poet," Mildred says in one conversation, and that desire for a metaphorical language ties her to traditional written forms just as the legendary substance of her tales and her aphoristic and folk expressions tie her to oral forms. When she makes statements such as "what kicks some people just bugs me" and "if you throw all your troubles in a bag, there's no tellin' which one will jump out first" or uses expressions such as "right nice," "indulgin' my feelin's," "let the cat out of the bag," "enjoyin' myself no end," "too devilish much," "took a lick at a snake [meaning to work]," "wear my nerve-cells pretty near the breaking point," and other dialectal forms, Mildred comes close to kinship with Hurston's informants in *Mules and Men* and to black folk communities generally. Her use of the monologue, which expresses a need for hearing as well as reading, also suggests a closeness to oral forms. The fact that the monologues are called conversations is also important. The audience is privileged, Mildred implies, to share the intimacy of her confidences. We can sit in her presence and share her experiences as if we are all gathered on a summer evening telling tales.

Mildred also sets forth, fairly early in the volume, her theory of artistic expression. Creation begins with observation, and Mildred certainly has the potential to see beyond the obvious, to look beneath the surface of things. Consider the instance in which she explains to Marge that, although she might get tired of being a house servant, "everyone who works is a servant." Then she tries to make Marge "see" some of the work that people don't usually think about:

> Take that chair you're sittin' on. . . . Can't you see the story behind it? The men in the forests sawin' down the trees . . . the log rollers . . . the lumber-mill hands cuttin' up the planks . . . people mixin' up varnishes and paints . . . the artists drawin' the designs . . . all the folks drivin' trains and trucks to carry 'em . . . the loaders liftin' them off and on . . . all the clerks writin' down how many there are and where they're goin'—and I bet that's not half of the story.

> Now Marge, you can take any article and trace it back

like that and you'll see the power and beauty of laboring hands.

> This tablecloth began in some cotton field tended in the burning sun, cleaned and baled, spun and bleached, dyed and woven. Find the story, Marge, behind the lettuce and tomato sandwich, your pots and pans, the linoleum on the floor, your dishes, the bottle of nail polish, your stove, the electric light, books, cigarettes, boxes, the floor we're standin' on, this brick building, the concrete sidewalks, the aeroplanes overhead, automobiles, the miles of pipe running under the ground, that mirror on the wall, your clock, the canned goods on your shelf, and the shelf itself. Why, you could just go on through all the rest of time singin' the praises of hands.

The interest in the story, in making things come unexpectedly to life, is what defines Mildred as a budding artist. Her imagination has not been dulled by housework, and she will use it often in her conversations. For those who would question a maid becoming an artist, this passage suffices to combat such objections. A short way from the statement that everyone who works is a servant is also the suggestion, by inference, that any servant can become an artist. Similarly, when we question Mildred's presentation of material, we have already been warned that the substance of her artistry is that which is beneath the surface. Things should not be taken literally, but metaphorically.

When we get to reconciling art with truth, or, more precisely, to examining the extent to which Mildred joins her folk ancestors in creating a legend of herself, Mildred has prepared us for her approach to artistic creation and for the metaphorical interpretation over the literal one. The critical problem becomes apparent as Mildred relates her incredible and controversial escapades in the white world. There may be an unbridgeable chasm dividing what Mildred has actually done and what she relates; however, the audience is locked into Mildred's world and must attempt to evaluate for itself the distinction between the experiential and the created in what Mildred recounts. Our own ordering of human experiences might make us question Mildred, but in the absence of Childress, Mildred is all we have; therefore, we *must* trust her reliability as artist even when we suspect that Mildred as character is unreliable. It is the nature of the artist to reorder human experiences, and that is precisely what Mildred the artist does. As creator of experience, the artist manipulates the audience through language. And, just as folk audiences responded to tales during the process of telling, Mildred's audience must similarly respond during the process of storytelling. Here, the audience, along with Mildred, must make sense of experience. In "knowing not to say it, but to know it," the audience, in an effort to grasp "the truth," must constantly reinterpret information with which it is presented. By using its imagination just as Mildred uses hers, the audience comes to an understanding of Mildred both as character and as artist.

The audience shares Marge's position in the conversations. We have not been with Mildred in the specific situation in the white world and therefore cannot see objectively what Mildred has been involved in, yet we know enough of that world through our own experiences to join Marge in questioning Mildred's actions at points, expressing shock, dropping our pans of beans at times, and generally reacting when credibility as we know it has been strained. Yet, because we have been incorporated as a special part of the play between teller and tale in its folk context, our role conforms to that of an ideally created audience. In spite of our response to the *literalness* of what Mildred relates, we are sympathetic to her position as that of the weaker character overcoming obstacles provided by the stronger adversary. That ideal audience would also appreciate wit, humor, the art of performance (storytelling), and the overtones of individual and racial triumph represented in the conversations. As part of that audience, we are drawn into the play about Mildred and her employers, and into that between Mildred and Marge.

What Mildred accomplishes through the conversations is what Childress might have been less able to accomplish in omniscient narration. The literary climate that would deter an author from using a didactic, propagandistic approach to the racial situation in the mid-1950s would not exert the same influence on a character who speaks her own mind and who experiences so intensely the problems she relates. Thus Mildred relieves Childress of a certain amount of responsibility for what the character says. The distance between author and character is increased even more at those points at which Mildred most resembles folk storytellers. The suggestion is that Mildred's particular kind of storytelling has been going on so long and it is so traditional that it certainly transcends Alice Childress.

Folk storytellers, through the use of the "intrusive I," often assume identity with the personalities and tales they relate; Mildred follows a similar pattern. Mildred, the legendary maid who has told off a white mistress or given her advice about raising her children, serves as the content level of the conversations. Mildred, the neighbor and friend to Marge, who chats over tea or coffee, represents the creative genius who gives form to the experiences and identifies with Mildred the maid. Mildred transforms herself, through her own artistic creation, into Supermaid, THE domestic who champions the causes of morality and decency in all such personalized relationships. Through the shaping force of art, Mildred becomes Brer Rabbit, John, and John Henry all transformed into a single personality.

When Mildred says she wishes she were a poet, that tendency to creativity is realized again and again. She doesn't want to be famous, but she does wish to be a poet "because some-

times there are poetry things that I see and I'd like to tell people about them in a poetry way." She proceeds to sketch out very sensitively the love she has witnessed between a poor old white couple. In a later conversation, after listening to bored and boring dissertations from the whites attending a dinner party of their trips to foreign countries, she sketches the freshness of taking an early morning or late afternoon train ride through the countryside in South Carolina:

> "I've never had a more wonderful feelin' than lookin' out of the train window in the first early hours of the mornin'. There's a deep misty haze hangin' just a few feet above the ground, the sky is streaked with red and gold against gray, everything is quiet and still-like and it seems as though there's not a livin' soul in the world.

> "The brown-wood lean-to houses look like livin' things standin' along the side of the track and watchin' the train whizz by. If you can get to the diner and have a cup of coffee at that exact time, well, you'll find that coffee tastes better at that minute than any other time. You feel cozy and close to your own thoughts, yet lookin' out the window makes you think of how big and strange the world is and how small you are."

> "Yes," she [Mrs. G] said, "I do recall that feelin' slightly although I never paid too much attention at the time." "But," I says, "that's not all. You have to look sharp if you want to get the *good* out of a trip. Be sure and watch for early twilight-time and you'll really be in luck if there's a little rain happenin' at the same time. You'll see the tall cornstalks noddin' and wavin' in the fields, you'll see a horse shakin' his head and strollin' in little circles. I've always wondered why the horse pays the train no mind. And right about then the train engineer blows his whistle 'too-whoo-whoo-whooooo,' and all of a sudden I smile to myself . . . not about a joke or even anything I can describe. No, I can't name the feelin', but I smile or laugh a little to myself and it feels good to get up and rock and sway down the aisle and drink a cup of icewater out of one of those paper cups."

Mildred truly enjoys the experience of her trip while the white women have simply catalogued the places they have visited that make them a part of an in-crowd. The sensuousness and vividness with which Mildred conjures up memories of the train ride, and her ability to evoke a mood, illustrate her tendency toward the creative and the creativity that becomes questionable in the conversations in which she sketches her more controversial interactions with white women and men. Even in the description of the train ride, Mildred shows an awareness of contrast. France and India recede into the background in the face of the winning description of a place so physically and emotionally close to home. Riches and privilege diminish, and it is the white employer, Mrs. G, who ends up with a mouth-watering desire to experience that inviting train ride.

Mildred's awareness of effective dramatic ordering and timing of narrative events is evident in the description of the train ride as well as in the many other tales she relates. She consciously manipulates details which control Mrs. G's, Marge's, and the audience's responses; all are presented with actions and sensations they can experience vicariously. Mildred's sense of irony and understatement help shape the form of her tales. The insight and crispness with which she recounts events are also especially noteworthy. Most important of Mildred's techniques, however, is the device of turning the tables. It puts the bottom rail on top by allowing the presumably ignorant black maid to get the moral upper hand. Like the tellers of the tales of John confronting Old Master, Mildred creates a set of circumstances in which the triumph of the weaker character/teller over the more powerful adversary carries the weight of psychological, if not logical, conviction. Complexity is undone by simplicity, and book learning gives way to mother wit.

Conversations such as "The Pocketbook Game," "The Health Card," "Mrs. James," "Interestin' and Amusin'," and "Let's Face It" are excellent examples of the very creative Mildred getting the best of her white employers. A look at "The Health Card," one of the shorter conversations, will serve as an illustration. Mildred tells about an incident that could have been embarrassing, but she manages to retain her dignity by turning the messy situation back on the white woman:

> Well, Marge, I started an extra job today. . . . Just wait, girl. Don't laugh yet. Just wait till I tell you. . . . The woman seems real nice. . . . Well, you know what I mean. . . . She was pretty nice, anyway. Shows me this and shows me that, but she was real cautious about loadin' on too much work the first morning. And she stopped short when she caught the light in my eye.
>
> Comes the afternoon, I was busy waxin' woodwork when I notice her hoverin' over me kind of timid-like. She passed me once and smiled and then she turned and blushed a little. I put down the wax can and gave her an inquirin' look. The lady takes a deep breath and comes up with, "Do you live in Harlem, Mildred?"
>
> Now you know I expected somethin' more than that after all the hesitatin'. I had already given her my address so I didn't quite get the idea behind the question. "Yes, Mrs. Jones," I answered, "that is where I live."

> Well, she backed away and retired to the living room and I could hear her and the husband just a-buzzin'. A little later on I was in the kitchen washin' glasses. I looks up and there she was in the doorway, lookin' kind of strained around the gills. First she stuttered and then she stammered and after beatin' all around the bush she comes out with, "Do you have a health card, Mildred?"
>
> That let the cat out of the bag. I thought real fast. Honey, my brain was runnin' on wheels. "Yes, Mrs. Jones," I says, "I have a health card." Now Marge, this is a lie. I do not have a health card. "I'll bring it tomorrow," I add real sweet-like.
>
> She beams like a chromium platter and all you could see above her taffeta housecoat is smile. "Mildred," she said, "I don't mean any offense, but one must be careful, mustn't one?"
>
> Well, all she got from me was solid agreement. "Sure," I said, "indeed *one* must, and I am glad you are so understandin', 'cause I was just worryin' and studyin' on how I was goin' to ask you for yours, and of course you'll let me see one from your husband and one for each of the three children."
>
> By that time she was the same color as the housecoat, which is green, but I continue on: "Since I have to handle laundry and make beds, you know . . ." She stops me right there and after excusin' herself she scurries from the room and has another conference with hubby.
>
> Inside fifteen minutes she was back. "Mildred, you don't have to bring a health card. I am sure it will be all right."
>
> I looked up real casual kind-of and said, "On second thought, you folks look real clean, too, so . . ." And then she smiled and I smiled and then she smiled again. . . . Oh, stop laughin' so loud, Marge, everybody on this bus is starin'.

The stereotypes inherent in this seemingly innocuous piece are decidedly vicious. Mrs. Jones draws conclusions about Mildred because of race and community. Filth, which Mrs. Jones associates with black people, especially those who live in ghettos, is prominent in her mind. The gap she envisions between Harlem and downtown, black and white, urges her to see Mildred as a part of a black blob, not as an individual; however, Mildred has shown her individuality again and again in the conversations, and she shows it here. By forcing the white woman to see her in a new light, Mildred simultaneously forces a level of mutual humanity into the relationship. Mildred is not some filthy woman come to clean house; she is as concerned about the personal hygiene of those whom she would serve as they are about hers.

So we conclude from the sketch Mildred gives us. But what really happened with Mrs. Jones? Had Mildred been as cool as she suggests to Marge? After all, the insinuation of disease and uncleanliness is enough to daunt the strongest personality. Has Mildred withstood it all, unscathed? And would a white woman in 1956, even in the North, have been so timid in making demands of her "colored help"? Would she have given in so easily, as Mildred would have us believe? The suggestion is definitely that the woman has learned her lesson and won't be so quick to relegate the next maid to dirt and filth. Our objections, however, have already been prepared for. Mildred succeeds in convincing her audience to accept her position because metaphoric truth subverts the literalness of the situation presented. She convinces us by putting her extra bit of creativity to work and by involving us in the tale as she tells it.

Let's consider the circumstances under which the tale is recreated. A hard day's work has just ended, and Mildred and Marge are riding home together on a bus. White threat, indignation, and insult are absent. Mildred and Marge are in a reasonably relaxed situation. Mildred has the catalyst of Marge's presence, and what can prod the storyteller more than an appreciative audience? Thus Mildred performs; she recreates *whatever* has happened with Mrs. Jones and gives it vitality and additional meaning. Her purpose in the presence of Mrs. Jones might have been to save her job or assert her humanity or exercise her tricking ability. With Marge and the audience, didacticism recedes and entertainment becomes prominent. Mildred is on stage as artist and as performer. By telling her tale to a sympathetic audience, she may relieve further whatever anxiety she may have felt at the point of occurrence of the incident, and she scores an additional victory when Marge and the audience laugh. She is appreciated twice—for putting Mrs. Jones in her place and for providing a pleasant release from the world that Marge must also encounter.

As artist, Mildred is well aware of the impact her tale will have. Even if she stretches the truth of her actions at the content level, what she accomplishes through the form of the tale is not necessarily untrue. Certainly persons who work as domestics want to be treated as human beings; it is this level of truth that Marge cannot deny even if she questions the actions used to convey the truth. Mildred frames her story nicely; in a tone of voice that we can only imagine, she succeeds in evoking the response, laughter, that she will later desire more fully of Marge and of the audience sharing Marge's position. She then introduces a situation, proceeds to a development of conflict, delays climax sufficiently to peak interest, goes immediately to resolution, and closes the frame with an intensification of the reaction she initially evoked from Marge.

Mildred is able to control the physical level of her role in the

tale without losing the individuality of her characterization. She has achieved a certain amount of aesthetic distancing from the event at the point of contact with Mrs. Jones to the event as it is told. Distancing has been effected by time lapse between action and telling as well as by material removal from the presence of Mrs. Jones. The soothing effect of Marge's presence and the bus ride contribute to the most important distancing—that of real or expected emotional involvement in the situation. By allowing things to cool down, the artistic ordering necessary for the artful performance can take place with quieter inspiration. Mildred has taken events that were probably not at all reassuring or entertaining and has made them so. Marge laughs heartily, but she can also identify vicariously with a maid who stood up for her humanity even if Marge would be unable to do the same thing in a similar situation.

Notice, too, that Mildred is thoroughly aware that she is creating. She introduces her tale with an opening frame and closes it with another. She moves into the world of imagination and steps back from that world when the tale is finished. The admonition to Marge to stop laughing because everybody on the bus is staring is a return to the here and now. It lets us know that Mildred is aware that she has been creating and is in control of that creation. As artist, she essentially says: "A tale has just been told. Now we are people again and no longer characters." This closing can also be compared to the formulaic endings many black storytellers use to separate the world of the story from the world outside the story; significantly, devices such as these are still part of the interplay between tellers and audience.

The fact that Mildred carries the monologue so well is another indication of her artistic abilities. The tone is light and confident; it almost belies the seriousness of the content of the situation. Mildred's ability to control tone and sustain interest in the monologue is presented perhaps a bit more vividly in "The Pocketbook Game" than in "The Health Card," although Mildred is equally as economical in selecting details and just as effective in ordering them. Circumstances are equally conducive to the telling of the tale, which also concerns stereotypes:

> Marge . . . Day's work is an education! Well, I mean workin' in different homes you learn much more than if you was steady in one place. . . . I tell you, it really keeps your mind sharp tryin' to watch for what folks will put over on you.
>
> What? . . . No, Marge, I do not want to help shell no beans, but I'd be glad to stay and have supper with you, and I'll wash the dishes after. Is that all right? . . .
>
> Who put anything over on who? . . . Oh yes! It's like this. . . . I been working for Mrs. E . . . one day a week for several months and I notice that she has

some peculiar ways. Well, there was only one thing that really bothered me and that was her pocketbook habit. . . . No, not those little novels. . . . I mean her purse—her handbag.

Marge, she's got a big old pocketbook with two long straps on it . . . and whenever I'd go there, she'd be propped up in a chair with her handbag double wrapped tight around her wrist, and from room to room she'd roam with that purse hugged to her bosom. . . . Yes, girl! This happens every time! No, there's *nobody* there but me and her. . . . Marge, I couldn't say nothin' to her! It's her purse, ain't it? She can hold onto it if she wants to!

I held my peace for months, tryin' to figure out how I'd make my point. . . . Well, bless Bess! *Today was the day!* . . . Please, Marge, keep shellin' the beans so we can eat! I know you're listenin', but you listen with your ears, not your hands. . . . Well, anyway, I was almost ready to go home when she steps in the room hangin' onto her bag as usual and says, "Mildred will you ask the super to come up and fix the kitchen faucet?" "Yes, Mrs. E . . . ," I says, "as soon as I leave." "Oh, no," she says, "he may be gone by then. Please go now." "All right," I says, and out the door I went, still wearin' my hoover apron.

I just went down the hall and stood there a few minutes . . . and then I rushed back to the door and knocked on it as hard and frantic as I could. She flung open the door sayin', "What's the matter? Did you see the super?" . . . "No," I says, gaspin' hard for breath, "I was almost downstairs when I remembered . . . *I left my pocketbook!*"

With that I dashed in, grabbed my purse and then went down to get the super! Later, when I was leavin' she says real timid-like, "Mildred, I hope that you don't think I distrust you because . . ." I cut her off real quick. . . . "That's all right, Mrs. E . . . , I understand. 'Cause if I paid anybody as little as you pay me, I'd hold my pocketbook too!"

Marge, you fool . . . look out! . . . You gonna drop the beans on the floor!

How Mildred deals with the stereotype of thieving blacks adds to her creativity as performer and as storyteller. By confronting the white woman and forcing her to see her faults, Mildred again becomes THE black maid in the quest for decency and mutual consideration. And she obviously enjoys her role in Mrs. E's comeuppance. She is not the timid black maid who cringes at insinuation, but a confident, creative woman who consciously plans and executes a confrontation. She allows herself room to act, and the retelling of the tale allows her the double pleasure of appreciating her own performance. It simultaneously allows Marge and the audience to appreciate the performance. Any questions about the truth of the action are offset by the essential rightness of the assertion of humanity.

The audience and Marge laugh with Mildred because the comic tale contains a gem of truth. And it is the nature of comedy effectively presented to evoke a positive, identifying response from the audience. Mildred's punchline is old, and it has the ring of folk tradition to it, but these are precisely the qualities that win audience approval for Mildred. We identify with the way in which she orders the old and the traditional for a new situation and succeeds in making them work.

Perfect control of tale telling is also exemplified here. Mildred starts off with a general statement on the educational value of [a] day's work and proceeds to a specific illustration of that statement. The effect she has on Marge, which, to some extent, is also *a part of the tale,* is gauged by the references to the beans. Marge's mishandling of the beans, as a result of intense interest in and laughing reaction to the nearly incredible parts of Mildred's tale, is again a key to audience response. Mildred dares to violate an expected sense of place, much in the fashion of John the slave in his bouts with Old Master, and she succeeds in doing so just as John succeeds. She orders details of that violation where they will provide most for the tale she tells. She proceeds to the climax and denouement of the incident and provides the closing frame to the story, a closing which is again an intensification of an earlier reaction by Marge.

The tale also contains Mildred's specialty, her favorite technique of turning the tables on an adversary; here, too, she is much like Brer Rabbit and John in black folk tradition. Her tale is appropriately called "The Pocketbook Game"; "game" offers connotations of opponents and winning, and it might be said that Mildred wins, or tricks her opponent, in this confrontation. The word is also relevant because the player least expected to win the game actually wins it. Mildred turns the tables on Mrs. E just as she has on the woman who requested the health card and on the widely-traveled ladies. The underprivileged becomes privileged and the bottom rail again promotes itself to the top. Mildred's awareness of the ranges of the tables-turned technique, both physically and psychologically, enables her to shape her tales for the best possible effect. She makes the negative become positive, and she turns stereotypic traits into assets. This feature of her artistry also ties her to storytellers in black folk tradition, in which stereotypic traits are often turned into virtues and in which the distinction between characters in the tales and the tale tellers is sometimes blurred. Consider the stories about Staggolee: In many versions of them the teller will often use exaggerated notions of black sexual prowess to advantage, and he will often slip into calling Staggolee's exploits his own. Roger Abrahams documents this phenomenon of identifying with heroes in *Deep Down in the Jungle: Negro Narrative Folklore from the Streets of Philadelphia.* . . . Abrahams calls this tendency the "intrusive I." Instead of telling the story or toast in the third person, the teller immediately shifts into first-person narration. He *becomes* the legendary Staggolee. Three versions Abrahams collected from toast tellers all have this feature:

> Back in '32 when times was hard
> I had a sawed-off shotgun and a crooked deck of cards.

> Back in '32 when times was hard
> Had a sawed-off shotgun with a crooked deck of cards.
> Had a pin-striped suit, old fucked-up hat,
> And a T-model Ford, not a payment on that.
> I had a cute little whore, throwed me out in the cold.
> When I asked her why, she said, "Our love is growing
>   old."

> In 1938 when things was hard
> I had a crooked pair of dice and a stacked deck of cards.
> I waded through water and I waded through mud.
> Until I came to a place called the "Bucket of Blood."

And each of the tellers proceeds to relate Staggolee's sexual and shooting exploits as if they were his own.

An audience listening to the toast would not question the validity of the teller's transference. They would become involved in the events as related—sexual prowess, defiance of the law, the "tombstone disposition, graveyard mind" frame of reference. Similarly, Mildred's audience becomes involved in the tales she relates and responds to her on that basis; questions fade into the background.

By adapting a traditional one-person-in-control formula, Mildred is able, like the tellers of the tales of Staggolee, to command all that Marge and the audience know about her adventures. She has the added advantage that her tales are not popularly known, as are those of Staggolee. Therefore the measure of her heroic exploits and one level of the vicarious reliving of them are peculiarly her own. She, like tellers of the Staggolee toasts, becomes an active tradition bearer, but *of her own experiences*. The total blurring of identities of actor and storyteller is accomplished. The tale as it happens becomes the material that Mildred the artist and near folk storyteller reshapes for identification with the legendary character about whom she "converses." The fact that oral transmission, talking, is chosen over another means of communication, enhances the folk aura of Mildred's conversations. As a literary technique, it also serves to authenticate the narrative, to make it both spontaneous and sincere; and, finally, it persuades.

Mildred's occupation is ultimately a point to consider in the folk analysis as well. Mildred is a maid, one of millions, just as Abrahams' narrators were perhaps mere faces among the many black men he met in Philadelphia. By giving herself a distinctive identity, Mildred emerges from the crowd just as good toast tellers stand out from the crowd. She is herself an example of the unexpected becoming important, of the politically powerless becoming politically potent. Mildred is poet and artist; she negates the stereotype of the intellectually dull and submissive black maid, and she emerges as a talented individual who is able to shape and control experience. From the confined position of domestic, she rises to the height of release in artistic expression. She provides the character for her own escape just as the toast tellers defy the law with Staggolee. But Mildred not only provides the character; she *is* the character. And what she is able to accomplish psychologically on the road from maid to artist surpasses the usual exorcising function that much folklore serves.

The combination of art forms allows Mildred a wider range of creativity than would relying upon either one or the other. She is doubly able to take over the reins of narration from Childress and is thoroughly able to converse in her own right. By consistently staying out of the conversations, Childress succeeds in granting to Mildred a total independence. Throughout the conversations, Mildred is consciously and effectively the character as artist. In the final analysis, Mildred even goes as far as to turn the tables on Childress by transcending her creation and saying much more than the absent author perhaps intended initially.

Elbert R. Hill (essay date 1983)

SOURCE: "A *Hero* for the Movies," in *Children's Novels and the Movies,* edited by Douglas Street, New York: Frederick Ungar Publishing Company, 1983, pp. 236-43.

[*In the following essay, Hill compares the strengths and weaknesses of Childress's book* A Hero Ain't Nothin' but a Sandwich *with those of the film version of the novel.*]

The important differences between novels and films become particularly apparent when the same author treats a story in both media, as Alice Childress did when she wrote the screenplay for *A Hero Ain't Nothin' But a Sandwich,* based on a novel she had published five years earlier.

Like other novels directed at an adolescent audience, the story has an adolescent, Benjie Johnson, as its central character. Benjie, who lives in Harlem with his mother Rose, with his grandmother, and sometimes with his "stepfather" Butler, has a heroin habit. The novel follows him through his, initially, casual flirtations with drugs, his insistence that he can always kick the habit—that he, in fact, does not really have a habit—his grudging recognition of his addiction, to an indeterminate but hopeful ending in which he has at least a good chance of getting off drugs. The story is told in a series of first-person narratives, several by Benjie himself, and others by ten other characters, including members of his family, his teachers and friends. Newspaper clippings regarding events mentioned by the narrators follow the appropriate chapters and lend accent or emphasis.

The mood of the novel is stark, and the reader shares Benjie's hopelessness. He does not know where his real father is and agonizes over this fact. Because his mother is busy with her job and her new love, he feels excluded from her life. Butler makes efforts to be a father to him, but Benjie is unable to relate to him and feels that he has stolen Rose's love from him.

In school, Benjie encounters such diverse role models as Nigeria Greene, a fiery black nationalist who makes racial pride the main study in his classes; Bernard Cohen, a Jewish teacher who worries about the decline of traditional learning in general and about the influence of Greene's teaching methods in particular; and the principal, who is just trying to hold on until his retirement three years hence.

Besides narratives by these characters, we also find various other points of view represented. Benjie's grandmother believes that her particular brand of religion-superstition is the answer to his problem; a neighbor woman has designs on Butler and thinks Rose is foolish to let Benjie or anyone else come between her and such a fine man; a pusher, Walter, denies that he is doing anything particularly bad and maintains that if he didn't supply his customers someone else would. Several boys Benjie's age are portrayed in the book, including his only real friend, Jimmy-Lee, who has broken the dope habit, and with whom Benjie must then break if he is to rationalize his own heroin dependence. There are also some "dope friends," Carwell and Kenny, and another pusher, Tiger.

The first-person narration form is particularly effective in bringing out the uncertainty and ambiguity the various characters feel about their own identities; their stories provide an effective parallel to Benjie's own confusion and uncertainty.

The book is extremely powerful, and Benjie is a character we care about. Though he indulges in considerable adolescent self-pity, he is not without saving graces. His fear of allowing himself to look up to anybody lest he later be disappointed is expressed in the title statement: "A hero ain't nothin' but a sandwich."

We also care about Rose, who longs to express her love for her son but finds herself only able to criticize, and about Butler, who sincerely loves Rose and is fond of Benjie but who though he works hard to support both them and Benjie's grandmother is keenly aware that he has no official status in their lives.

The novel's ending offers no easy solutions to Benjie's prob-

lems, but it leaves us hopeful. As Butler waits for Benjie to show up at the Drug Rehabilitation Center, he says: "Come on, Benjie, I believe in you. . . . It's nation time. . . . I'm waiting for you." We do not know for sure that Benjie will actually come, but the understanding that he and Butler have begun to achieve suggests that he has at last begun to have a hero in his life, and it strongly implies that if he does not come that day he will come soon.

Both the problem portrayed and the characters are clearly realistic, and what might easily have been a preachy or sentimental book becomes in Childress's hands a sensitive, honest view of life, the way things are today. Because of her skillful use of first-person narrations, the characters—and not just the problem (drugs)—are important. This is not always true of "problem novels" for young readers.

The film based on the book is a Robert Radnitz production, directed by Ralph Nelson and released by New World Pictures. The character of Benjie is played by Larry B. Scott, with Cicely Tyson as the mother, Paul Winfield as Butler, Glynn Turman as Nigeria, and David Groh as Cohen.

The first change one notices is that the setting has been changed from Harlem to Los Angeles, presumably because it was cheaper to film location shots near the Hollywood studio. Obviously, a drug problem such as Benjie's might as easily be found in Los Angeles as in Harlem since no locale or level of affluence is immune from drugs today, but, the effect of moving Benjie from what is clearly an ugly, threatening environment, as portrayed in the novel, to the movie's world of beautifully landscaped parks, palm trees, and beachfront, is to mute the dreariness that characterizes Benjie's environment in the book. In addition, Benjie's home as depicted in the movie, while not elegant, is clearly no tenement. It is comfortable and livable, and there is even one scene of Benjie and Butler talking in the back yard, with the sky showing through the leaves of a vine arbor overhead.

Even more significant than the shift in setting, however, is the change from the multiple first-person narration form of the book to the dramatic objective viewpoint of the camera eye. The power of the novel in illuminating the characters' inner frustrations and confusions is largely lost through this change. Nowhere is this more evident than in the characters of Nigeria and Cohen, who seem much weaker in the film than in the novel. The very sharp, deep conflict between them and their values—as well as the genuine concern for their students that forms a mutual bond between them—is reduced in the film to a superficial playground confrontation that does little except establish the fact that there is a school drug problem something already apparent to the viewer. In the case of Benjie and Butler, however, the characters are both so well developed that we do not miss having their first-person narrations.

The roles of some characters are given either greater or lesser emphasis in the film than in the novel. Rose seems more of a real person in the film than in the novel, where she was a rather shadowy figure. The principal does not appear in the film, and we do not particularly miss him. The grandmother and her religion are given somewhat less prominence in the movie, the neighbor woman is completely eliminated; both changes work well in the film. The four characters of Benjie's dope world acquaintance are effectively combined into two in the movie, each being given enough of a role to make him seem real.

Butler's role is significantly increased in the film—so much so that he seems almost equal in importance to Benjie. This may give the movie a real problem with respect to its intended audience. The book is clearly aimed at young adolescents who—to use the filmmakers' term—would be "pre-sold audience," the carryover audience from a popular book. The movie, with its "PG" rating, is apparently trying to appeal to the whole family, thus the greater emphasis on Butler and Rose and their problems. However, a young adolescent would likely not be able to relate to Butler's problem of establishing his role as the father, for instance. The movie is almost *too* much Butler's story, and there is a mild schizophrenia in point of view. The book, in spite of the multiple first-person narration from, is very clearly Benjie's story.

One of the outstanding points about the movie is the excellent quality of the acting. Larry B. Scott as Benjie successfully conveys the adolescent vulnerability hidden beneath a superficial teen-age swagger. Cicely Tyson captures Rose's full range of emotions, from her girlish excitement about a night on the town with Butler to her despair over Benjie's drug problem. The scene in which Rose desperately tries to wash Benjie's drug problem away in the indigo bath is one of the most touching in the movie. Winfield's portrayal of Butler has quiet strength and great sensitivity. In fact, from the very beginning of the film Butler seems so clearly concerned about Benjie that it is difficult for the viewer to understand why the boy holds him at arm's length for so long. In the book, this side of Butler is far less apparent until late in the story.

The plot of the novel moves more or less straight forward in normal chronology, though there are some overlaps in time because of the changes in narrators, who frequently comment on the events already mentioned and commented on. In the book, this effectively brings out the various viewpoints and is not really distracting or confusing to the reader. Nevertheless, the movie's straightforward presentation may be somewhat easier for young people to follow.

There are several changes in the sequence of events from novel to film. For instance, the encounter between Benjie and Jimmy-Lee in which the latter declares that he is not going to use dope any more because "I got somethin' better for a dollar to do," takes place early in the book. This is a signal to the reader that despite his protestations to the contrary Benjie is becoming so addicted to heroin that he prefers to break off this important relationship, since Jimmy will no longer join him in his habit. In the movie, this scene appears almost at the very end and therefore only indicates that Benjie is continuing in what we already know is a serious drug habit. Its usefulness in helping us follow Benjie's descent into drugs is lost in the movie.

In fact, the movie never makes it sufficiently clear how or why Benjie becomes addicted to drugs. To show that Benjie is becoming hooked, the filmmaker resorts to the device of repetitive scenes showing him using the drugs and earning money for this habit by delivering drugs. In the movie, the whole time lapse from Benjie's first use of marijuana to when we know that he is, in fact, unable to quit heroin, seems altogether too brief and unrealistically sudden. And the question of *why* Benjie takes drugs remains quite puzzling. Though bothered by the fact that he does not know where his real father is, he appears to have no other problem. Because of the shift in setting and some other changes as well, Benjie's environment seems neither hostile nor threatening. At home, he is surrounded by people who care about him, even though they have their own needs and preoccupations too. And in school he even seems to be something of a star. There is a scene in Nigeria's class in which Benjie is able to amaze the whole class, teacher included, with his knowledge about a particular black leader. And in Bernard Cohen's class, he is asked to read aloud a composition for which he is publicly praised and given an "A."

The scene is apparently used to show two things: first, assigned to write about a member of his family, Benjie has selected his mother, thus revealing her importance to him as his only remaining parent. Second, when as part of his praise Cohen says, "Keep this up and some day you'll be somebody," Benjie replies, "I'm somebody now." We are confronted with a common adolescent problem: the feeling that adults don't give them credit for being someone *now,* and focus too much on what they *may* grow up to be. The scene thus fulfills some valid functions in the movie, but combined with the scene in Nigeria's class it also suggests that Benjie's school provides a generally supportive atmosphere. In the book, the praise Benjie receives for the paper about his mother is said to be something that happened years before the time of the book, and it is not typical of his school career. There is no equivalent in the book of the scene in Nigeria's class.

In addition, the Benjie of the novel tells us several times that one of his problems is that he feels betrayed by Nigeria Greene, who, along with Cohen, has turned him in for drug use. Though the movie does show the two teachers taking him out of class when he is obviously stoned, it does not emphasize for us the importance that this betrayal has for

Benjie because it has not made sufficiently clear how he has idolized Nigeria.

A time shift that is even more troublesome than the one involving Benjie's encounter with Jimmy-Lee concerns the change in the relationship between Benjie and Butler. In the book, after Butler has saved his life, Benjie writes "Butler is my father" one hundred times. This indicates that Benjie finally realizes that Butler does indeed care for him, and suggests to the reader that the boy is accepting Butler's role in his life. Also, because Benjie slips this paper into Butler's coat pocket, where Butler is sure to find and read it, Butler is given more justification for taking off work to meet Benjie at the Drug Rehab Center. In the movie, Benjie writes "Butler is my father" much earlier, *before* Butler has saved his life—and so far as we know Butler never sees the piece of writing. Thus, the movie Benjie's motivation for trying to get off drugs—like his motivation for getting on them—is not fully clear, and the movie Butler does not have the same motivation to wait for Benjie at the Rehab Center.

Several scenes and elements in the movie do not appear in the book, and some of these are extremely effective. Although the encounter group scene in the hospital, in which other patients bombard Benjie with their views about drugs, seems to add little, Nigeria's oration at Carwell's funeral is touching and effective. The still photographs of Benjie as he goes through the various stages of withdrawal in the hospital are a brilliant directorial choice and heighten our horror at Benjie's predicament.

Moving pictures, however, are clearly better at vividly portraying some scenes than are either stills or word pictures. For instance, the rooftop scene in which Benjie's life is in danger gets our adrenalin flowing far better in the visual medium than in Childress's novel. Along with Benjie, we hang precariously by one hand as Butler strains to pull us up. The ending of the movie is revealing of the overall differences between the two forms. In the movie, when Butler waits for Benjie at the Rehab Center, the boy actually appears; in the book Butler only waits and hopes. The movie ending is weaker in consequence, but the change is necessitated by the differences in chronology and motivation mentioned earlier. The reader was led to believe that Benjie will appear, because this would be the logical result of his realization of Butler's love for him and of his acceptance of the older man as his hero. But since moviegoers have not had this clear motivation for Benjie to change, they need to be shown that the boy does indeed intend to change.

The experience of viewing a movie based on a book need not—cannot—be the same as that of reading the book. Whereas the book is more subtle in its portrayal of people and uncompromising in its presentation of the environment in which they live, the movie sharpens the individual portraits but softens the environment. However, we care deeply about the people in both book and movie, and that is one of the important tests of any story presentation, whether verbal or visual.

Elizabeth Brown-Guillory (essay date September 1986)

SOURCE: "Images of Blacks in Plays by Black Women," *Phylon,* Vol. XLVII, No. 3, September, 1986, pp. 230-37.

[*In the following essay, Brown-Guillory discusses the stages of Tommy's development in* Wine in the Wilderness.]

Alice Childress, born in 1920 in Charleston, South Carolina and reared in New York City, is an actress, playwright, novelist, editor, and lecturer. Claiming her grandmother, the Bible, Shakespeare, and Paul Laurence Dunbar as principal influences, Childress developed into an exceptional playwright. However, few are aware of the immense contributions that she has made to black playwriting in America in her 36 years of writing for the American stage. Consequently, the aim of this [essay] is twofold: (a) to demonstrate that Alice Childress, a black woman who has struggled against powerful odds to survive in the theatre, has made monumental contributions to black women's playwriting in America, and (b) to illustrate that Childress' heroine in **Wine in the Wilderness** survives whole, just as Childress has, regardless of seemingly impenetrable barriers.

Alice Childress has written twelve plays, some of which include **Florence; Gold Through the Trees** ([the] first play by a black woman to be produced professionally on the American stage); **Trouble in Mind** (first Obie Award to a woman for the best original Off-Broadway play of [the] 1955-56 season; the play also was produced by the BBC in London); **Wedding Band** (broadcast nationally on ABC); **Wine in the Wilderness** (presented on National Educational Television); **Mojo** (best known because of frequent productions); and **When the Rattlesnake Sounds** ([a] children's play about Harriet Tubman).

Alice Childress' plays, which Genevieve Fabre in *Drumbeats, Masks, and Metaphors* places in the category of "ethnic theatre of black experience" as opposed to "militant theatre of protest," have neither been produced nor critically written about to the extent that they deserve. Suffice it to say that the American stage, with its highly political infrastructures, has traditionally disregarded women playwrights generally, not to mention black women playwrights. However, Childress has continued to write for the American stage even when it has apparently looked upon her with blind eyes and turned to her with deaf ears. She is a driven playwright and her compulsion to write is evident in the following lines:

> Am working on two new plays. Why? Why? Why? I
> can't stop and the market being what it is—I should—
> How I wish I could stop. But there is an inner clock

that keeps ticking away and running the works in one direction.

Alice Childress is, indeed, a pioneer—a crucial link—in the development of black women playwriting. Forerunner of Lorraine Hansberry, Sonia Sanchez, Martie Charles, Adrienne Kennedy, Ntozake Shange, and others, Alice Childress has written plays which incorporate the liturgy of the black church, traditional music, African mythology, folklore, and fantasy. She has experimented by writing socio-political, romantic, biographical, historical, and feminist plays. It is no small matter that Alice Childress' striving to find new and dynamic ways of expressing old themes in an historically conservative theatre has opened the door for other black women playwrights to make dramaturgical advances. Her "firsts" invariably paved the way for a line of black women playwrights to insist upon craft and integrity over commercialism. Doris Abramson writes, "Alice Childress has been, from the beginning, a crusader and a writer who refuses compromise . . . She refuses productions of her plays if the producer wants to change them in a way that distorts her intentions." *Trouble in Mind* is a case in point; it was optioned for Broadway, but Childress refused when a producer attempted to "sharpen and delineate" so as not to offend sensibilities.

Because Alice Childress has made significant and innovative contributions to black women playwriting in America, in particular, and to theater, in general, her works merit serious critical treatment. One can not read very far into a Childress play without being impressed by her "good ear for dialogue and fine sense of characterization." Jeanne-Marie Miller observes, "Childress noted early that Black women had been absent as an important subject in popular American drama, except as an empty and decharacterized faithful servant." As a result of this awareness, Alice Childress has created as James V. Hatch states, ". . . The modern black woman . . . no longer is she depicted as the overly devout, hard-working, suffering matriarch, the prostitute, or the faithful (and/or dumb) servant; instead she emerges as a real human being of dimension, having needs and desires." In short, characterization is Childress' forte.

One of the few major playwrights of the 1950s without a college education, Alice Childress writes largely about poor women for whom the act of living is sheer heroism. In fact, Childress' own background resembles that of her heroines in *Florence, Mojo, Trouble in Mind, Wedding Band,* and particularly *Wine in the Wilderness*. In her recent essay **"Knowing the Human Condition,"** Childress makes the following observation:

> My great grandmother was a slave. I am not proud or ashamed of that; it is only a fact. . . . I was raised in Harlem by very poor people. My grandmother, who went to fifth grade in the Jim Crow school system of

South Carolina, inspired me to observe what was around me and write about it without false pride or shame. . . .

Indeed, her poor, dejected heroines are depicted as morally strong, sometimes vulnerable, but resilient. She portrays these women honestly as they fight daily battles not just to survive but to survive whole. Childress comments, "I attempt to write about characters without condescension, without making them into an image which some may deem useful, inspirational, profitable, or suitable. Listen to the poetry in common prose, a sensitive experience."

Childress' commitment to creating dimensional heroines who represent the large numbers of poor blacks in America is apparent when she makes the following assessment:

> But it is serious self-deception to think that culturally ignoring those who are poor, lost and/or rebellious will somehow better our "image." If we will not see them, we must also fail to see ourselves. The wrong is not in writing about them, but in failing to present them in depth, in denying their humanity, in making them literary statistics in social studies, and in using them in street stories as humor or relief. Black writers cannot afford to abuse or neglect the so-called ordinary characters who represent a part of ourselves, the self twice denied, first by racism and then by class indifference.

Wine in the Wilderness is the best illustration of Childress' superb handling of characterization. Captivating drama that exhibits suspense, plausible conflicts, swift repartee, meaningful and well developed dialogue, *Wine in the Wilderness* is perhaps Childress' finest play. The heroine of this play, Tomorrow Marie, who calls herself Tommy, epitomizes the typical heroine who peoples Childress' plays. Tommy is no defiled, broken, delicate woman who crawls off into some corner to suffer from a nervous breakdown and spend the rest of her life condemning men for her emotional and physical bruises. Instead, she steadily moves in the direction of wholeness. James V. Hatch says of Tommy, "Alice Childress has created a powerful new black heroine who emerges from the depths of the black community, offering a sharp contrast to the typically strong 'Mama' figure that dominates such plays as *Raisin in the Sun*."

In *Wine in the Wilderness,* Tommy is pitted against Bill Jameson, Cynthia, and Sonny-man, three middle-class blacks who despise their heritage and disassociate themselves from and castigate "grass roots" blacks. Hatch makes the following observation about the play and its heroine:

> The beauty of *Wine in the Wilderness* is in part due to the author's sensitive treatment of Tommy, 'a poor, dumb chick that's had her behind kicked until it's

numb,' but whose warmth, compassion, inner dignity, and pride make her more of a woman than Cynthia will ever be.

Regardless of the fact that her bourgeois acquaintances almost destroy her, Tommy moves to a state of completeness, i.e., develops a positive sense of self.

Tommy's odyssey or search for wholeness takes her through six stages: koinonia, logus, metanoia, kerygma, didache, and eucharistia. These are terms from Koine Greek, which was the marketplace or common man's Greek spoken during Hellenistic through Roman periods. Much of the New Testament is based upon Koine Greek. Interestingly, Alice Childress lists the Bible as one of her sources of inspiration and influences. It is important to note that these terms lend themselves to broad interpretations and will be defined in the context of this [essay].

These stages are comparable to the stages discussed by Joseph Campbell in *The Hero with a Thousand Faces,* wherein the archetypal journey of the hero is broken into three stages: the departure, the initiation, and the return. Additionally, Pearson and Pope in *The Female Hero* view the journey of the heroine as basically an exiting, an initiation, and a return to one's community as a whole person. However, the Koine Greek stages of growth far better describe the stages through which Childress' heroine journeys.

Tommy, by the time the play opens, has already experienced the first stage of growth, and it is through flashbacks that information about her koinonia is given. By way of definition, koinonia means fellowship, united in something deeply, family, to be inextricably bound by common grounds, a sharing of life's moments, a foundation, values imparted to a person via her community, a fellowship which helps to define and positively affirm a person's sense of self. Tommy's background is one of poverty, but it is apparent that she, as a child, had loved ones of whom she was proud and who made her feel worthy, loved, and rooted, as is seen in her conversation with Bill Jameson:

> TOMMY. I was born in Baltimore, Maryland and raised here in Harlem. . . . My Mama raised me, mostly by herself, God rest the dead. . . . Her father was a "Mason". . . . I had an uncle who was an "Elk". . . . Early in life I pledged myself to A.M.E. Zion Church. . . .

Tommy's comments demonstrate her strong ties to her family and community.

In short, the koinonia is a person's beginnings, and there can be no "exit" or "departure" that Campbell or Pearson and Pope speak of unless there is a koinonia. Rev. Victor Cohea contends that koinonia, as it applies to blacks in America, is a stage of growth which does not generally build in racial bias as a buffer; in other words, Cohea believes that parents of black children generally do not teach them about racism and, in fact, do their best to shield them from prejudice. Thus, according to Cohea, black children become very vulnerable when they go out into the real world which is inundated by racism.

Credence is given to Fr. Cohea's comments about blacks' vulnerability to racism because of what takes place in Tommy's second stage of growth, the logus. In the narrow sense, logus means "the word of Jesus" but in its broader interpretation logus can be defined as an awareness moment, a revelation which sets things in motion, a "loss of innocence." Logus parallels what Lindsay Patterson in *Black Theater* refers to as the "Nigger Moment." Patterson makes the following assertion:

> But there comes a time in life when one loses his innocence and is pushed boldly into the real world . . . I mean by lost innocence that specific moment when a black discovers he is a "nigger" and his mentality shifts gears and begins that long, uphill climb to bring psychological order out of chaos. It's not a moment, however, easily detected. All of black literature is more or less unconsciously preoccupied with precisely pinpointing and defining it. It is an elusive, complex moment, with complex reactions and can occur at four or forty, and its pursuit, I believe, will continue to occupy serious black writers for decades to come.

Thus, the logus or "Nigger Moment" serves to bring on confusion.

Tommy's logus or "Nigger Moment" occurs during her adolescence. Tommy comes to this as do the children in Margaret Walker's poem "For my People" who chant, ". . . We discovered we were black and poor and small and different and nobody cared and nobody wondered and nobody understood." She recalls in a touching conversation with Bill Jameson, a middle-class black with whom she is enamored, the moment she realized that blacks were oppressed in America. Tommy tells Bill of the painful moment in her life when her uncle and fifteen hundred blacks went to jail for wearing the "Elk" emblem on their coat lapel, an emblem which at that time only whites were allowed to wear. It is the moment which leads to her curiosity about black/white relationships in her community and her subsequent confusion about her place in America. Thus, the quest begins.

The metanoia, the third stage, is the turning away or turning around, a quest to understand and be saved from confusion, a struggle to cope with oppression, a coming to terms, an uphill climb accompanied by a series of trials and errors. From Tommy's conversations with her "cultured" associates, it is evident that she is a "woman alone," one who has struggled to make sense of the confusion in her life. She has not despaired over racial or social inequities; instead she has resiliently forged ahead as is indicated in her comment to Cynthia, "Tommy's not lookin' for a meal ticket. I been doin' for myself all my life . . . A black man see a hard way to go." Tommy's metanoia is further defined as she interacts with her bourgeois companions who subtly ridicule at every turn her speech, mannerisms, clothes, and values.

Tommy's quest or metanoia is further heightened by these haughty blacks who are as mean to her as some of the whites who have denigrated her. Tommy bends but doesn't break as she tries hard to emulate and be accepted by these supposedly sophisticated blacks. Determined to get their stamp of approval, Tommy lays bare her soul to the insensitive, insipid Cynthia:

> What's wrong with me, Cynthia? Tell me, I won't get mad with you, I swear. If there's something wrong that I can change, I'm ready to do it. . . . I come from poor people . . . Cynthia, I remember my mother tyin' up her stockin's with strips-a rag 'cause she didn't have no garters. When I get home from school she'd say . . . 'Nothin' much here to eat.' Nothin' much might be grits, or bread and coffee . . . . We didn't have nothin' to rule over, not a pot nor a window. . . . I'm so lonesome . . . I'm so lonesome . . . I want somebody to love. Somebody to say, 'That's alright,' when the world treats me mean.

Tommy's pain goes unassuaged, and she is no closer to a positive sense of self than before she met these "refined" blacks.

Perhaps the single most important impetus for Tommy's turning away, or metanoia, is her discovery from Oldtimer, an elderly "grass roots" black man, who inadvertently tells Tommy that she is to be represented on the triptych as the "dregs of society." Tommy is almost leveled by the blow, especially since the night before she had made love to the man, Bill Jameson, who was going to depict her as society's cast-off. Tommy's metanoia comes full circle in the following lines:

> OLDTIMER. And this is "Wine in the Wilderness" . . . The Queen of the Universe . . . the finest chick in the world.

> TOMMY. That's not me.

> OLDTIMER. No, you gonna be this here last one. The worst gal in town. A messed-up chick that—that—

> TOMMY. The messed-up chick, that's why they brought me here, ain't it? That's why he wanted to paint me! Say it!

At this point in Tommy's growth, she realizes that the people she wanted to be like are emotional and social cripples, and she completely reevaluates her earlier decision to try to emulate these "wine-sampling" blacks.

The kerygma generally follows the metanoia. This stage of growth centers around the heroine's compulsion to speak, when she lashes out and, in effect, says "I can't and won't stand the way I'm being treated, and I will make it stop." Kerygma suggests explosion, sometimes verbal but oftentimes physical. Pearson and Pope in *The Female Hero* contend, "The hero who is an outsider because she is female, black, or poor is almost always a revolutionary." Though Tommy is triply disadvantaged, her explosion is a calculatedly verbal one.

Tommy clearly moves into the [fourth] stage, kerygma, when she snaps, stops accommodating, and explodes when it is confirmed that she is merely being studied like a guinea pig. Tommy's wrath is evident in the following lines:

> Trouble is I was Tommin' to you, to all of you . . . "Oh, maybe they gon' like me." . . . I was your fool, thinkin' writers and painters know more'n me, that maybe a little bit of you would rub off on me.

When Bill tells Tommy not to refer to herself as "nigger," she becomes even more enraged:

> If a black somebody is in a history book, or printed on a pitcher, or drawed on a paintin', . . . or if they're a statue, . . . dead, and outta the way, and can't talk back, then you dig 'em and full-a so much damn admiration and talk 'bout "our" history. But when you run into us livin' and breathin' ones, with the life blood still pumpin' through us, . . . then you comin' on 'bout how we ain' never together. You hate us, that's what! You hate the black me!

The didache, the fifth stage, is a summation, the bottom line of a formal message that the heroine passes on to the naive blacks who have yet to learn what she has learned. A stronger, more confident Tommy is emerging as she tries to enlighten those "pseudo-intellectuals" about what she has just been able to piece together because of their treatment of her. Her epiphany manifests itself when she comments:

> You treat me like a nigger, that's what. I'd rather be called one than treated that way . . . When they [whites] say "nigger" just-dry-long-so, they mean educated you and uneducated me. They hate you and call you "nigger," I called you "nigger," but I love you.

She proceeds to tell them that if blacks are so untogether it is because the ones with education have forgotten what it is to be black and have joined forces with those whites who castigate blacks. Her message, or didache, serves as a catalyst for them and catapults her into her final stage of growth.

The eucharistia, stage six, is a combining of inner wholeness with outward community. This wholeness or completion leads the heroine back to her community which reaffirms her newfound positive sense of self. Eucharistia is a celebration of the commonness that the community shares; it is a celebration of self, of life, and of community wholeness. Fr. Cohea points out, "There can be no eucharistia if there is no koinonia."

Tommy wades into eucharistia when she firmly resolves that she will not let anyone make her feel small, half-human again. In this stage of growth, she realizes that her "Nigger Moment" was a hoax, that she is not a nigger, i.e., inferior in any way. All of her past wounds are healed once she asserts herself. For some, a positive experience brings them into wholeness, into humanity, but Tommy's eye-opener stems from negative treatment by blacks who themselves are not whole. A strong, whole woman emerges as Tommy speaks the following lines to her transfixed and transformed would-be-friends.

> I don't have to wait for anybody's by-your-leave to be a "Wine in the Wilderness" woman. I can be it if I wanta . . . and I am. I am. I am. I'm "Wine in the Wilderness" . . . alive and kickin', me . . . Tomorrow-Marie, cussin' and fightin' and lookin' out for my damn self 'cause ain' nobody else round to do it, dontcha know . . . And, Cynthia, if my hair is straight, or if it's natural, or if I wear a wig, or take it off, . . . that's all right; because wigs . . . shoes . . . hats . . . bags . . . what you call acess. . . . accessories. Somethin' you add on or take off. The real thing is takin' place on the inside . . . that's where the action is. That's "Wine in the Wilderness," . . . a woman that's a real one and a good one. And ya'll better believe it.

Tommy's wholeness or celebration of self is infectious; the once "phoney niggers" join in and affirm Tommy's metamorphosis. Together they celebrate the cessation of Tommy's quest, a journey which has, presumably, benefited them as much as her. Hatch aptly comments on Tommy's wholeness and its impact on her associates: "When she undergoes a metamorphosis before his eyes, he suddenly becomes aware that she is the source of inspiration that he and the others so desperately needed to find themselves, and their blackness." Thus, Tommy does become that wine, with its Biblical resonances, which will revive, nourish, and nurture her black counterparts.

Jacqueline Fleming, author of *Blacks in College,* recently stated that "People are the sum total of the conditioning they've been given." Her point was that negative conditioning breeds failure. However, she stressed that there are some cases where people survive and succeed without the benefit of positive reinforcement. Childress, through her characterizations, concurs with Dr. Fleming. Tommy, for example, metaphorically gives birth to herself in order to survive whole.

C. W. E. Bigsby in *The Second Black Renaissance* points out that Childress' work is less caustic than that of Ed Bullins and Charles Gordone, but what Bigsby doesn't acknowledge is that Childress' plays are every bit as relevant and powerful because as Loften Mitchell observes, "Her characterizations are piercing; her observations devastating." Childress' heroines, especially in **Wine in the Wilderness,** survive whole, not as fragmented, irreparably wounded, delicate, caustic women. Others like Tommy pass through the stages of growth, koinonia, logus, metanoia, kerygma, didache, and eucharistia, making sure not to be destroyed by the psychological and social minefield through which they must journey. Childress' heroines, in general, are at once courageous, discerning, vulnerable, insecure, and optimistic. In short, they are human, real.

Childress' twelve plays beg for scholarship. A playwright whose dramaturgical advances have paved a way for women in the theatre, Childress is that new thought, that breath of fresh air, that possibility. More than just a wine in the wilderness, Alice Childress is the bread and the song.

Alice Childress with Elizabeth Brown-Guillory (interview date 1 May 1987)

SOURCE: "Alice Childress: A Pioneering Spirit," *Sage,* Vol. 4, No. 1, Spring, 1987, pp. 66-8.

[In the following excerpt from an interview conducted May 1, 1987, Childress discusses her background and motivation as an author.]

Alice Childress, born in 1920 in Charleston, South Carolina, and reared in New York City, is an actress, playwright, novelist, editor, and lecturer. Childress is the only Black American woman whose plays were written and professionally produced over a period of four decades. . . .

Though Childress admits that she is not a "public" person, she graciously talked to me about childhood memories, her writing process, her struggle to carve a place for herself on the American stage, and several high points of her life. The interview took place at the University of Massachusetts on May 1, 1987. . . .

[Brown-Guillory:] Most artists can recall that "significant other" who served as a source of inspiration and who gently prodded them into telling truths about life. Is there someone who gave you a gentle push? Who influenced you to become a writer?

[Childress:] My grandmother, more than anyone else, inspired me to write. She wasn't just a typical grandmother. She was a well read person who made me interested in storytelling. She used to sit at the window and say, "There goes a man. What do you think he's thinking?" I'd say, "I don't know. He's going home to his family." She'd say, "Well, how many children does he have?" I'd say, "Three." My grandmother would ask, "Is his wife nice?" I'd say, "No, I don't like her." When we'd get to the end of our game, my grandmother would say to me, "Now, write that down. That sounds like something we should keep."

You speak with such reverence for your grandmother. Are there other memories of her that have sustained you?

She had seven children and was very poor. There wasn't any time to do anything, except try to keep the children in clothing and someway fed. Always running out of everything. When I came along, all of her children were grown. We were together all of the time. Her name was Eliza. She was named for Eliza who crossed the ice in Harriet Beecher Stowe's book, *Uncle Tom's Cabin.* My grandmother's maiden name was Campbell. Her mother was a slave who was freed very early . . . like at fourteen or fifteen. She was turned out in the middle of Charleston, South Carolina downtown. They drove off in a horse and buggy and left her standing there. A white woman named Mrs. Campbell stopped and asked her why was she crying. She said, "Folks just left me." Mrs. Campbell said, "Well, I don't have much but would you like to come live with me? I have a cottage with five rooms." My great-grandmother went. She didn't have anywhere else to go. And, Mrs. Campbell's son became my grandmother's father. Then he went off to sea and never came back. He was a merchant seaman. Mrs. Campbell's name was Ann or Anna and my great-grandmother's name was Annie. It was Mrs. Campbell who named her grandchild Eliza. I put so much emphasis on my grandmother, Eliza, because my father and mother were separated when I was very little. I vaguely remember him. My mother was always working and on the go. My grandmother was a very fortunate thing that happened to me.

Are there particular experiences that you and your grandmother shared that shaped your writing?

We used to walk up and down New York City, going to art galleries and private art showings. She used to say to the people in charge, "Now, this is my granddaughter and we don't have any money, but I want her to know about art. If you aren't too busy, could you show us around?" Then she'd quiz me when we'd get home. She'd take me to different neighborhoods to explore. I was storing up things to write about even then. She took me to an Italian neighborhood and said, "Now, what's that smell?" I remember the smell of escargot. My grandmother was a member of Salem Church in Harlem. We went to Wednesday night testimonials. Now that's where I learned to be a writer. I remember how people, mostly women, used to get up and tell their troubles to everybody. Just outright tell it! "My son's in jail," or "My daughter's sick," or "I don't have any money, and my rent is due." Everybody rallied around these people. I couldn't wait for person after person to tell her story. One woman told of a suicide in her family; he had jumped off the roof. Everybody went over to hug her and tell her it would be all right. It was kind of frightening. But, that's where I got my writing inspiration.

Were there others who inspired you?

I learned to read in Baltimore in a Jim Crow class. I had a teacher named Miss Thomas. Now, she was a source of inspiration. She said to us on the first day of class, "You're going to learn to read in my class or stay in here until you're twenty-one." I spent one year in Baltimore, but it was a very telling year. I was in the third grade and my teacher told us that everybody was going to go out reading and reading well. All we did all day was practice and did reading homework.

Although they deserve it, we usually don't credit our early teachers with playing significant roles in our lives. Miss Thomas gave you a special gift. She empowered you to read about many of the things in life that your grandmother wished for you to know.

A high point in my life was when I got my library card. I believe I was in the fifth grade in Harlem at the time. My teacher took us to the library and they explained to us that we could draw out two books a day . . . free! I went to the library everyday and took two books and read them at night. I read incessantly.

I'm sure you were a star pupil. You obviously had a solid foundation in the basics.

What changed everything in life for me was that I never finished high school. I had two years of high school. My grandmother died. My mother died. And I had to go to work. But I had that foundation with grandmother of studying.

You have a steady list of publications in several genres, including essays, novels, stage plays, teleplays. I've read and thoroughly enjoyed your novels, **A Hero Ain't Nothin' But a Sandwich, A Short Walk, Rainbow Jordan,** *as well as all of your plays. Which form is your favorite?*

Plays are my favorite form. But, theatre is the hardest business at which to make a living.

How did you become involved with the theatre?

I was in some plays in school. But later I joined the American Negro Theatre. I joined in 1941 and was there for eleven years. After about seven years, I was personnel director for a year while Fred O'Neal went abroad. I learned to direct plays at the American Negro Theatre, and I began writing. We needed things. We needed good writing. I was an actress in the American Negro Theatre. I was in a working situation. I was doing. It's like working in a factory that makes paint; it's different from reading about paint than mixing paint. You learn how to do it by doing it. As an actress, I was able to get on-the-job training. We also had to coach other actors who were coming in. We had to do some of everything in the theatre. The American Negro theatre is one of the best, if not the best. Newspaper accounts said that we studied like the martial arts schools. We had no money, but we worked hard. If you were late two or three times in a row, you were dropped. If you weren't in a production, you still had to be there four times a week to work on make-up, costumes, props, stage managing, sets, etc. I did everything there is to be done in the theatre.

The kinds of experiences that you talk about are so very crucial to anyone who aspires to be a playwright. Your comments have proven that a playwright needs to be attached to a theatre in order to develop craft. Your writing plays, then, was a natural outgrowth of working in the theatre and seeing a need for accurate images of Blacks. Your first play, **Florence,** *treats the issue of stereotyping. I understand that you wrote* **Florence** *overnight.*

Yes, I did. I had a talent for writing. Sidney Poitier was in the house when I began writing it that night.

How would you describe your writing process?

I learned by trial and error. As I wrote, I learned. I began to sense what didn't quite work. You learn to ask yourself all sorts of questions as you write, like "Why is it too slow or too long or boring?"

In the fall of 1986, my play Snapshots of Broken Dolls *was produced at the Lincoln Center in New York City. During an interview with a journalist from the* New York Amsterdam News, *I credited you as one of my favorite writers. You are a master craftswoman. Did you read plays by other authors?*

I felt inspired to write from reading. Anything that you read or anything that you talk to people about shapes your writing. But it wasn't like I picked out a playwright and read and started writing. I began reading other people's plays after I was writing. I became interested in craftsmanship. I found instinctively that I knew a lot about craft. I liked Shakespeare. I also belonged to a group in Harlem that was doing only Shakespeare.

Did you take any professional writing courses?

I never had a writing course. Ever. I probably would have enjoyed one very much. Today, too many writers don't re-

spect craft. They write thirteen pages today and want to send it off to MGM tomorrow. They don't treat writing as an art. Just as music is an art, so is writing. A good musician has to practice a lot. My husband [Nathan Woodard] has a degree in music, and he teaches music. I see the patience he has with studying music. I think it's important for writers to keep developing craft, to keep studying and to keep writing.

You were able to develop your craft during a two-year tenure, between 1966 and 1968, at Radcliffe/Harvard.

The Radcliffe/Harvard appointment was a high point in my life. It was Tillie Olsen who recommended me for this appointment. Everybody who participates in this program has a doctorate. I was honored to be chosen, especially since I had not finished high school. I wrote **Wedding Band** and other pieces during my appointment. I was awarded a graduate medal from Radcliffe/Harvard for the writing I did. I'm not sure who judged my work, but Lillian Hellman was connected with the program at the time.

The Radcliffe/Harvard medal is symbolic of the possibilities if one works at fine-tuning her craft. Many can only dream of such an affirmation of one's skills in the theatre. Did you always dream about becoming a writer?

I didn't dream about anything. I didn't plan or plot, as people say, to be this, that, and the other. I was too busy happening all the time. I was in the middle of happening. The things that really make me want to write are those things that happen to me, not those things I read when I pick up a book. I might go to a ballet and feel inspired to write.

Record has it that your play, **Trouble in Mind,** *was the first play by a Black woman to be professionally produced, meaning it was performed by equity actors.*

Actually, the American Negro Theatre's production of **Gold Through the Trees** in 1952 in Harlem was done with paid actors before the media picked up on the off-Broadway professional production of **Trouble in Mind** in 1955.

How do you view the host of "firsts" that have been attached to your name?

I never was ever interested in being the first woman to do anything. I always felt that I should be the 50th or the 100th. Women were kept out of everything. It almost made it sound like other women were not quite right enough or accomplished enough, especially when I hear "the first Black woman." When people are shut out of something for so long, it seems ironic when there's so much going on about "the first."

Thanks to you, though, some doors have been opened for other women playwrights. It is up to critics and scholars to point out the many contributions you've made to American theatre.

The very first review I ever received was from Lorraine Hansberry. We both worked at Paul Robeson's newspaper, *Freedom*. She did reviews and covered *Gold Through the Trees*. I still have that review. She just signed it L.H.

What are you working on now?

I'm writing my autobiography. I'm also working on two novels. This past January, my play *Moms*, based on the life of Moms Mabley, was produced in New York City.

Elizabeth Brown-Guillory (essay date Fall 1987)

SOURCE: "Black Women Playwrights: Exorcising Myths," *Phylon*, Vol. XLVIII, No. 3, Fall, 1987, pp. 229-39.

[*In the following essay, Brown-Guillory discusses the depiction of black characters in the plays of Childress, Lorraine Hansberry, and Ntozake Shange.*]

Alice Childress, Lorraine Hansberry, and Ntozake Shange, three outstanding contemporary black women playwrights, are crucial links in the development of black women playwriting in America. These three playwrights, whose perspectives and portraits are decidedly different from those of black males and white playwrights, have created images of blacks which dispel the myths of "the contented slave," "the tragic mulatto," "the comic Negro," "the exotic primitive," and "the spiritual singing, toe-tapping, faithful servant."

Childress, Hansberry, and Shange have created credible images of blacks, such as "the black militant," "the black peacemaker," "the black assimilationist," "the optimistic black capitalist," "the struggling black artist," and "the contemporary black matriarch." However, three images which appear most frequently in the plays of these black women are "the black male in search of his manhood," "the black male as a walking wounded" and "the evolving black woman."

The black male in search of his manhood, a product of the ambivalence fostered mainly by the continued disinheritance of blacks after World War II and the Korean War, is a major new image in contemporary literature. Functioning in this role, the black male struggles to realize who he is and what his function in life is to be. In his essay, "Visions of Love and Manliness in a Blackening World: Dramas of Black Life from 1953-1970," Darwin T. Turner states:

> Ironically, as black dramatists examine their characters more critically, often they seem less polemical and more compassionate because, in the black world, they perceive not only individuals searching for manhood and love but even more pathetic figures too impotent to search for manhood or to achieve a relationship of love. . . .

Plays by Childress substantiates Turner's claim because the image of the black male in search of his manhood is shown either as a creature who is in the process of becoming a mature human being or one who is too incapacitated to search for manhood. His insecurity of his own identity and values renders him generally passive. He vacillates between integration and separatism. He has yet to establish a philosophy about how to succeed or cope in American society.

As he strives to overcome personal problems and to achieve responsible maturity, the confused black male may castigate blacks and opt to align himself with whites who he feels will validate his manhood. Though he may reject his ethnicity during the search, he reaches maturity when he realizes that his manhood does not hinge upon his acceptance by anyone but himself.

John Nevins, a black male in search of his manhood, appears in Childress' 1955 Obie award-winning drama, *Trouble in Mind*, a play which centers around the frustration blacks feel because of the limited and demeaning roles available to them on the American stage. John, in his early twenties, hopes to prove his manhood by becoming a successful actor. A novice among his veteran-actor co-workers, John dreams of making money regardless of what must be sacrificed. When the white director, Al Manners, appears, John immediately becomes a "yes-man," indicating that he is neither assertive nor self-respecting.

Nevin's self-effacement is apparent during the rehearsal of *Chaos in Belleville*, Childress' play within a play, a device which she learned from Shakespeare, one of her principal influences. When Al Manners asks John if he can object in an artistic sense to the word *darkies*, John placatingly replies:

> No I don't object. I don't like the word but it is used, it's a slice of life. Let's face it, Judy wouldn't use it, Mr. Manners wouldn't . . .

John eagerly compromises his opinions to keep his role in *Chaos in Belleville* in order to "make it" in the theatre and, thus, define his manhood.

When his black co-workers display anger at his "Tomish" remarks, John aligns himself with one of the white actresses, Judy, hoping that she will validate that he is a man. Not only does he seek approval or direction from Judy, but he also turns to Al Manners. However, Manners, during an argument over interpretation, unthinkingly makes the mistake of implying that John could not be compared to his son because John is black and his son is white. Angered by this remark and encouraged by his black co-workers to assert himself, John examines his values and decides that racial pride means more to him than success in a play that degrades blacks. Boldly he declares, "They can write what they want but we don't have to do it." John moves in the direction of maturity as his black peers help him to become whole.

Whereas John Nevins eventually asserts himself, Sheldon Forrester, one of John's co-workers, typifies the image of the black who is too impotent to search for manhood. Sheldon chooses to sacrifice dignity for minor roles on the American stage. He has no self-respect, and he chastises those blacks who affirm themselves. Sheldon has been worn down and perceives that it is futile for a black male to try to function as a man in American society. Ironically, Sheldon defines his manhood in terms of success at projecting that he is not a man among white men. He brags that his denial of self has helped him to survive in the world and says that blacks ought to "take low" in order to keep whatever jobs are issued out to them. The audience sees Sheldon's spinelessness when he aims his remarks at his co-worker, Millie:

> I hope the wind blows her away. They gonna kick us until we all out in the street . . . unemployed . . . get all the air you want then. Sometimes I take low, yes, gotta take low. Man say somethin' to me, I say . . . "yes, sure, certainly." That ain't tommin', that's common sense. You and me . . . we don't mind takin' low because we tryin' to accomplish somethin' . . . Well, yeah, we all mind . . . but you got to swaller what you mind. . . .

Sheldon has neither the courage nor the determination to become a whole person.

Like Sheldon, Teddy is a black male in search of his manhood in Alice Childress' *Mojo: A Black Love Story,* a play which deals with the need for black men and women to be supportive of each other both in and out of love relationships. At the beginning of the play, Teddy is searching for his manhood in his relationship with his white girlfriend, Berniece. He wants very much to please her so that she, as he says, will make him feel like a man. Teddy's devotion to his status symbol is apparent when he makes the following comments: "Aw, baby, I aint callin you white folks, you wild, yallerheaded, fine thing, you! They all white folks but you . . . you somethin else. I'll be there. . . ."

Later when Teddy argues with his black ex-wife, Irene, he displays insecurity and his need for affirmation from a white woman:

> TEDDY. Git offa my back, Reeny . . . that's one thing bout that simple Berniece . . . she make me feel like a man. She's white but she make you feel like. . . .
>
> IRENE. Feel like . . . feel like . . . I been hearing that all my days. . . sound like my poppa . . . "I wanta feel like a man." You wanta be a man . . . forget that feel like . . . feel like. . . .

> TEDDY. If you wasn't on your way to the hospital I'd knock the hell out of you, for underminin me. Berniece knows how to make you feel pleasant.

Towards the end of the play Teddy, with the help of Irene, does begin to insist that he is a man, not a child needing approval. His growing confidence in himself is demonstrated when he lovingly reaches out to comfort Irene who is soon to be hospitalized.

Childress' sensitive treatment of the black male in search of his manhood reflects her vision that black men and women can become whole only when they not only join forces but resources as well. Childress' Teddy represents those black males who refuse to let poverty and had luck keep them from growing into fine black men who accept responsibility for their families.

Unlike the black male in search of his manhood is the black male as a walking wounded. Whereas the former struggles for direction and identity, the latter knows exactly who he is and is painfully aware of the fact that he is oppressed in American society. He not only survives but survives whole. Though physical and/or emotional blows are heaped upon him, he is neither fragmented nor abusive to his women. He is fully aware of his roots and is proud of his heritage.

The black male as a walking wounded insists that he be treated like a human being. A contented slave he is not; instead, he struggles to free himself and others from oppressive forces. Because of a positive sense of self, he can and does reach out to others. He especially has a strong sense of family togetherness, a trait which his African fathers brought with them to America. In short, this character, which is diametrically opposite to the image of the incorrigible black beast that dominated the American stage for so many decades, refuses to be anybody's sacrificial lamb and boldly keeps going in spite of his wounds.

Though Childress, Hansberry, and Shange have created credible images of black men, the females in plays by black women have much more dimension and are more finely tuned than the males. These black women characters are not sexually insatiable like Karintha and Carma in Jean Toomer's *Cane* or Bessie Mears in Richard Wright's *Native Son.* Nor do they resemble the countless "black mammies" who were created to represent black womanhood, such as Dilsey in Faulkner's *The Sound and the Fury,* Berniece in Carson McCullers' *The Member of the Wedding,* Addie in Lillian Hellman's *The Little Foxes,* or Ella Swan in William Styron's *Lie Down in Darkness.* Doris Abramson in *Negro Playwrights in the American Theatre 1925-1959* includes the following Hansberry quote which demonstrates her rejection of the then popular images of blacks:

> One night, after seeing a play I won't mention, I sud-

denly became disgusted with the whole body of material about Negroes. Cardboard characters. Cute dialect bits. Or swinging musicals from exotic sources.

Additionally, Cynthia Belgrave in "Readers' Forum: Black Women in Film Symposium," comments on the inaccurate and narrow images of black women on the American stage:

> If you're strong and stoical you're a matriarch, and if you're weak and sensual, you're a whore. Of course there are no equitable gradations in between . . . The Black woman is at the mercy of everybody. When we finish kicking people, let us kick the Black woman again.

Childress, Hansberry, and Shange do not limit themselves to the deity and/or slut syndrome. In her essay, "Images of Black Women in Plays by Black Playwrights," Jeanne-Marie A. Miller contends that the images of black women are not only peripheral in plays by whites, but the portraits of black women in plays written by black men are, generally, radically different from the images of black women in plays by black women:

> In the plays written by Black males, Black women's happiness or "completeness" depends upon strong Black men. Thus, Black women playwrights bring to their works their vision, however different, of what Black women are or what they should be.

In short, Miller calls for an inclusion of the caricatures of black women playwrights when the images of black writers are the subject of discussion.

Mary Helen Washington in *Black Eyed-Susans: Classic Stories By and about Black Women* makes a strong case in the following lines for studying black women writers:

> What is most important about the black woman writer is her special and unique vision of the black woman. . . . One of the main preoccupations of the black woman writer has been the black woman herself—her aspirations, her conflicts, her relationships to her men and her children, her creativity. . . . That these writers have firsthand knowledge of their subject ought to be enough to command attention.

Childress, Hansberry, and Shange view black women from a special angle. One image which dominates their plays is "the evolving black woman," a phrase which embodies the multiplicity of emotions of ordinary black women for whom the act of living is sheer heroism. This creature emphasizes understanding and taking care of herself. Not always a powerhouse of strength, the evolving black woman is quite fragile. Her resiliency, though, makes her a positive image of black womanhood. Self respecting, self-sufficient, assertive, these women force others around them to recognize their adulthood. . . .

Florence in Alice Childress' *Florence,* may be classified as an evolving black woman. As the play opens, Florence's mother, Mrs. Whitney, and her sister, Marge, discuss Florence, who has moved to New York because she views the South as too confining for a black woman desirous of improving her lifestyle. Characteristically, Florence strives to survive in a hostile world. Placed in the position of supporting herself and her son because her husband was killed by whites in the South, Florence dreams of becoming an accomplished actress. She chooses to relocate in order to fulfill those dreams.

Though Florence has not met with much success, except for the several times that she has played the part of a maid in plays, she is determined to find a way to make a name for herself in the theater. Florence is a positive image of black womanhood; she refuses to use racism as an excuse for not trying to improve her lifestyle. She represents those black women who refuse to despair in the sight of seemingly insurmountable obstacles. Instead of applying for public assistance, she sets out to become self-sufficient in a profession that she considers dignified. It is her determination to succeed after her husband's death which makes her a character truly to be admired.

The evolving black women in Childress' *Wine in the Wilderness* and Ntozake Shange's *For Colored Girls Who Have Considered Suicide/When the Rainbow is Enuf* are preoccupied with themselves because they have been disappointed by the men who have come into their lives. These are women who have had their share of "deferred dreams" and are no longer willing to play the role of "woman-behind-her-man" to men who appreciate neither their submissiveness nor their docility. These women rebel and claim that no man is ever going to oppress them again. They are not women who give up on men or feel that all men are insensitive beasts; instead, they are women who have become independent because of their fear of being abused physically and/or emotionally in subsequent relationships.

The image of the black woman in these two plays is that of a woman who has to "sing the blues" before she is able to make some sense out of the chaos in her life. Though black women who are abandoned in Childress' and Shange's plays bewail their losses, emphasis is placed on their ability to survive in a world where they are forced to care for themselves. The evolving black women in these plays fight back after they have been bruised, and they work toward improving their lifestyles.

Tommy Marie in Alice Childress' *Wine in the Wilderness* is an evolving black woman. When a young, black, middle-class artist, Bill Jameson, chooses to include Tommy in his triptych, she gets the impression that he is interested in starting a relationship with her. However, though Bill seduces her, he merely intends to use her to capture the image of, as he describes it, "the dumb chick whose had her behind kicked until it's numb."

When Cynthia, a bourgeois friend of Bill, tries to tell Tommy that she is not good enough for Bill and that she must not look upon him as a possible provider, Tommy Marie flaunts her independence:

> Tommy's not lookin' for a meal ticket. I been doin' for myself all my life. It takes two to make it in this high priced world. . . . I have a dream too. Mine is to find a man who'll treat me just half-way decent . . . just to meet me half way is all I ask, to smile, to be kind to me. Somebody in my corner. Not to wake up by myself in the mornin' and face this world alone . . . I'm so lonesome . . . I want somebody to love. Somebody to say . . . "That's alright," when the world treats me mean.

Tommy typifies the evolving black woman in that she dreams of finding a man who will love and share with her, but it is apparent in her comments that she has equipped herself to survive alone if she must.

When Tommy discovers, after she has made love with Bill, that she is to represent the "lost womanhood" in his painting, Tommy's assertiveness and resiliency are apparent:

> I don't have to wait for anybody's by-your-leave to be a "Wine in the Wilderness woman." I can be it if I wanta, . . . and I am. I am. I am. I'm not the one you made up and painted, the very pretty lady who can't talk back, . . . but I'm "Wine in the Wilderness" . . . alive and kickin' me . . . Tomorrow-Marie, cussin' and fightin' and lookin' out for my damn self 'cause ain' nobody else around to do it, dontcha know. . . . That's "Wine in the Wilderness," . . . a woman that's a real one and good one. And yall just better believe I'm it.

Tommy's message to Bill Jameson is that he is a "phoney nigger" who talks about black brotherhood only because it is in vogue. She tells him that he has treated her like a "nigger," but that she will go right on with the business of living because she has always had to take care of herself.

James V. Hatch contends that Tommy Marie is a positive image of black womanhood because she is honest, and she is not living under the illusion of false reality. Hatch suggests that she is a survivor who refuses to despair:

> True, Tommy "hopes" that Bill will seriously fall for her, but if he doesn't, she is prepared to move on.

She is a sensible woman without pretense. The beauty of *Wine in the Wilderness* is in part due to the author's sensitive treatment of Tommy whose warmth, compassion, inner dignity, and pride make her more of a woman than Cynthia will ever be. Alice Childress has created a powerful, new black heroine who emerges from the depths of the black community.

At the end of the play, Tommy is confident that if Bill Jameson does not see her worth and beauty, another male will. What is important to note is that Alice Childress has created an image of a woman whose inner strength will protect her as she searches for a stable relationship in which there is reciprocity. . . .

Alice Childress, Lorraine Hansberry, and Ntozake Shange are contemporary black women playwrights whose visions or perspective[s] are different from black males or white writers. To exclude black women playwrights as a source for examining black life is to omit a large piece of the human puzzle. These three major women writers are important because they, too, like black women writers in other genres, supply America with plausible, and in some cases unique, images of black men and women.

Some have dared to ask, "Do black women playwrights really depict black life?" Unequivocally, they do, but these images must be viewed in conjunction with the images created by black males in order to create an accurate picture of black life. Others have asked, "Do black women playwrights represent the majority of blacks?" These selected playwrights do not create images which represent the majority of blacks; no two or three writers can, or should have to try. However, these three women playwrights present a vital slice of life, and it is up to many more black writers to capture the multitude of images of blacks.

Perhaps, the most important question to be asked is "Will society be different after meeting the characters in the plays of black women?" The answer is yes, significantly so. When blacks turn to theater for better ways to live, Childress, Hansberry, and Shange offer them a multiplicity of options via black characters who come from the heart of the black community. Contemporary black women playwrights uniquely give to the American stage a view from the other half.

Sandra Y. Govan (review date Summer 1988)

SOURCE: "Alice Childress's *Rainbow Jordan:* The Black Aesthetic Returns Dressed in Adolescent Fiction," *Children's Literature Association Quarterly,* Vol. 13, No. 2, Summer, 1988, pp. 70-4.

[In the following review, Govan explores the role of the Black Aesthetic in Childress's novel Rainbow Jordan.*]*

In 1988, twenty years beyond the period and in an age enamored of political voyeurism as opposed to political participation, it is decidedly unfashionable to speak favorably of the Black Aesthetic. As critical literary theory the Black Aesthetic was, after all, an overtly political doctrine, an artistic manifesto of the militant "revolutionary" 1960s. Nowadays, art from this period which adhered to a Black Aesthetic is shunned for its stridency or militancy; the aesthetic credo itself is now largely ignored or discredited. Yet curiously, I find that in order to discuss Alice Childress's **Rainbow Jordan,** I must also discuss the Black Aesthetic because for me, the one most decidedly evokes the other.

Briefly then, let me indicate the principal spokespersons and basic tenets of what was once proudly trumpeted as the Black Aesthetic. Its chief architects were Larry Neale, Hoyt Fuller, Julian Mayfield, Addison Gayle, Carolyn Gerald, and Ron Karenga. For Julian Mayfield, in "You Touch My Black Aesthetic . . . ," the new critical credo could be distilled as "our racial memory and the unshakable knowledge of who we are, where we have been, and springing from this, where we are going." For Carolyn Gerald in "The Black Writer and His Role," the Black Aesthetic fell upon the artist as a concrete responsibility. The artist was to be a "guardian of image; the writer [was] the myth-maker of his people." Gerald went on to argue that there was a "sense of power" derived from a "mythic consciousness based on a people's positive view of themselves" which was also inherently part of the then emerging critical code. Poet Mari Evans crystallized many of these sentiments in her "Speak Truth to the People." Evans demanded that artists:

> Speak Truth to the people
> Talk Sense to the people
> Free them with reason
> Free them with honesty
> Free the people with Love and Courage, and Care
> for their
> Being
> Spare them the fantasy
> Fantasy enslaves

By far, however, the best known, most provocative proponent of the Black Aesthetic was Maulana Ron Karenga, a Black nationalist. Karenga's "Black Art: Mute Matter given Force and Function" presents the most codified requirements for both Black artists and Black art.

Karenga argued bluntly that "black artists and those who wish to be artists must accept the fact that what is needed is an aesthetic, a Black aesthetic, that is a criteria for judging the validity and/or beauty of a work of art." Karenga proposed to judge art from two perspectives, the social and the artistic. For him, "artistic considerations" while necessary for any art, were by themselves insufficient. What finalized any artistic endeavor was its social dimension, the "social criteria for judg-ing art." This was the most crucial criterion for, in his terms, "all art must reflect and support the Black Revolution, and any art that does not discuss and contribute to the revolution is invalid." Strong statements alone, but Karenga further augmented them by borrowing from traditional African art three guiding characteristics which became the cornerstone of the Black Aesthetic. Black art was to meet these essential tenets: it must be "functional," that is "useful"; it must be "collective," that is, it must emerge from and return or speak to the people; it must be "committing" or committed. This meant Black art must "commit us to revolution and change," commit us to a new and different reality.

It is time to call the question—what precisely does **Rainbow Jordan,** a contemporary adolescent novel considered "outstanding" (Nilsen & Donelson) in its field, have to do with an avowedly political, although now apparently unpalatable approach to art? The answer is a great deal. On **Rainbow Jordan**—on its narrative mode, its themes, and most particularly its characters—is imprinted the stamp of a conscientiously Black literary/political agenda. While Alice Childress is not wedded to a concretized notion of what Black art "must do," this novel, as do her other novels and plays, has embedded—refashioned and redressed, to be sure—the substantive core of what was the Black Aesthetic. Not a strident text, **Rainbow Jordan** nevertheless reflects these values: it is functional, it is collective, it is committed.

When a theory has been discarded and rejected largely for its vehemence and the seeming rigidity of its proscriptions, it could be dangerous or perhaps presumptuous to try to link a particular artist and her work to it. And had not Childress consistently reiterated her own ideas about literary politics, ideas which sometimes seem in conflict but which are, on balance, not that distant from the political motives of the Black Aesthetic, I would not even attempt it. For instance, in **"A Candle in a Gale Wind,"** Childress illuminates her literary stance. She acknowledges "bending" her writing "to most truthfully express contents, to move beyond the either/or of 'artistic' and politically imposed limitations." This pronouncement seemingly undercuts my initial premise; yet, if what is accented is her commitment to "truthfully express content," the argument saves itself. Truth, after all, and truth tied to knowledge emerging from the unique perspective of the Black writer who observes and records it, is the greatest demand "imposed" on the Black artist. Within this essay Childress outlined her methods, goals, and intentions. Rejecting the premise that the writer's duty was to compose inspirational tracts about Black high achievers—large heroic figures who surmounted the barriers of racism and economic deprivation—she chose to focus on illustrating the "have nots in a have society"—those who seldom receive attention unless as targets of "derogatory humor and/or condescending clinical and social analysis." "Politically," wrote Childress, "I see my Black experience, my characters, and myself in very special circumstances." In depicting the powerlessness inherent in that "special circumstance," in showing the complexity of frustrated dreams, frayed hopes, yet persistent determination Childress finds her calling. As she put it: "I continue to write about those who come in second, or not at all—the four hundred and ninety-nine and the intricate and magnificent patterns of a loser's life." As if anticipating and deflecting the shopworn charge of "universality," Childress forthrightly defines her philosophical commitment: "My writing attempts to interpret the 'ordinary' because they are not ordinary. Each human is uniquely different. We are uncommonly and marvelously intricate in thought and action, our problems are most complex and, too often, silently borne."

Clearly, Childress's concern is for the people, for showing them as they are. She is not concerned with constructing necessarily better or "positive" images of poor or "ordinary" Black folk. In fact, image-building for its own sake becomes an empty symbolic gesture devoid of substance. There is no inherent value in "self-deception," or in ignoring those "who are poor, lost, and/or rebellious" merely in the service of proper "image" (**"The Human Condition"**). When we refuse to see the poor, Childress argues, "we also fail to see ourselves. The wrong is not in writing about them but in failing to present them in depth, in denying their humanity, in making them literary statistics. . . ." Further, Childress asserts that her goal is to write "about characters without condescension, without making them into an image which some may deem more useful, inspirational, profitable, or suitable" (**"Human Condition"**). This last statement is certainly an unqualified rejection of the image-as-symbol school and possibly a reaction to any critical ultimatum specifying that the artist adopt a set didactic approach to the question of Black "images." In Childress's realm, "images" are not essential; rather, characters are the focal point.

And yet ironically, me thinks the artist doth protest too much. As surely as any sensitive reader digests **Rainbow Jordan,** that reader will be unable to leave the novel without some sense of [the] more "positive" images of particular people/characters resonating in the imagination. And, that reader will be unable to put the novel down without some sense of admiration—inspired by the unassuming almost stoic heroism of characters facing hard choices and hard compromises daily. Childress's characters have all their foibles showing; it is in watching them recognize and reevaluate their weaknesses and their strengths that readers may see conflict as a way of testing or molding "character," as a way of recasting image. Without excluding any sensitive reader, **Rainbow Jordan** successfully becomes an attractive version of the Black Aesthetic redressed because it is myth-making at work for younger audiences. By focusing on the Jordan family and Rainbow's alliance with her adult mentor, it is also illustrative of "racial memory," racial identity—of "where we have been . . . and where we are going" (Mayfield). And to reiterate, because Childress chooses to present truth, as she witnesses it, **Rainbow Jordan** reflects those three essential characteristics defining the Black Aesthetic; that is, it is functional, collective, committed.

Obviously, most adolescent readers of **Rainbow Jordan** have never heard of the Black Aesthetic. It's likely that neither have their teachers. And that's okay. It isn't necessary to know about the Black Aesthetic in order to enjoy and appreciate the novel at its first level. Teachers like the novel because it is well written, discusses significant issues, and treats realistic conflicts sensitively. Youngsters who enjoy reading like the book because it addresses them. The novel features a fourteen year old heroine with whom teens can easily sympathize or identify. It treats subjects—stressful parent-child relationships, peer pressure, sex education and teen pregnancy, friendships beyond family—teenagers respond to. It has familiar themes in contemporary cloth. Most importantly, Rainbow Jordan, the protagonist, speaks frankly to adolescents at their level. Although Childress uses a modified variation of the *Rashomon* shifting narrative structure technique—or what she calls "monologue style" first and second person storytelling (**"A Candle"**)—when Rainbow speaks, her voice remains consistent, never breaking for authorial intrusion or comment. When Rainbow speaks, it is as a child, albeit a woman-child carrying far too much responsibility on her young shoulders.

Rainbow's voice is the first voice heard in the novel. Since she is the central protagonist and it is largely her story, she narrates more often than any other character. Initially, Rainbow confides that she has heartaches and that there are good reasons for her woes. Her mother is missing; a social service caseworker is due any moment to remove Rainbow from the apartment she and her mother share; she will be placed, for the third time, in an "Interim Home," that is, foster care. In addition, she has research papers due for school and she has no real communication with her boyfriend. Under the circumstances, Rainbow has ambivalent feelings about her mother and about the life they both live. She realizes that her 29-year-old mother is often irresponsible ("What else is it but abandon when she walk out with a boyfriend, promise to come home soon, then don't show"), immature ("My mother taught me to call her by first name . . . Kathie for Katherine. I never had a mama and a daddy. I got a Kathie and a Leroy"), and occasionally abusive ("Some of the best presents I ever got was the day after a beatin. Truth is, she was not beatin on me every minute. Sure wouldn't hear about any outsider givin me a bad time"). Nevertheless, Rainbow loves her mother fiercely, has lied for her repeatedly, and would much rather remain at home and wait for her than go to a foster home. But even she doesn't know where Kathie is or when she will return. "Life," in her words, "is complicated." The complications multiply when she is forced to make painful critical assessments of Kathie's virtues and failings, then live her life accordingly—shielding the disruptive pattern of the small family's life from the prying eyes of peers, school officials, and social service agents. The frustrated love for Kathie remains, but it is driven inward and Rainbow, often forced to cope with the outside world alone, becomes an introspective, self-contained, "difficult" child who pulls a protective shell around her sensibilities, daring anyone to knock.

The second dominant voice in the novel belongs to Josephine Lamont, Miss Josie, the "Interim Parent" who takes Rainbow into her home. Anticipating cute and cuddly children (as a result of T.V. images) when she first undertook the responsibilities of foster parenting, Josephine has learned to accept with good grace the chip-shouldered, silent, often sullen teenaged youths sent to her for nurturing. Normally, Miss Josie offers hugs and affection warmly for she believes all profit by hugging. This time, however, when Rainbow returns, Miss Josie almost grudgingly gives of herself, resignedly accepting the burden of Rainbow and her shell. It seems Josephine is busily constructing one of her own. She, too, has heartaches which she imagines Rainbow cannot fathom. A sturdy, gentle, hard working seamstress and an attentive, gracious homemaker in her fifties, Miss Josie attempts to conceal her wounds from Rainbow—her marriage is disintegrating; Harold, her husband, is now more visitor than helpmate.

With her own emotional center destabilized, Josephine must still make room for Rainbow. Casting herself in the role of the martyred woman who must remain the mature responsible adult, Josephine sees in Rainbow merely a defiant child in need of guidance. Completely devaluing Rainbow's attempts to maintain her pride, Josephine perceives only arrogance: "not directly rude but walks around with her nose slightly in the air . . . as if she's superior and is merely allowing me to handle her situation. She is a definite case of child neglect but puts on like it's all some kind of misunderstanding." Of course, Miss Josie considers herself the "superior" partner in this match. She plays several roles including surrogate parent, guardian, teacher, and mentor "exposing" Rainbow to traditional middle-class values and culture, to multi-cultural perspectives, to the "gray" areas between right, wrong, and hard societal "rules." However, as the novel progresses and both Rainbow and Josephine tell their respective stories and share their observations and perceptions about each other, it becomes quite apparent that Josephine sadly underestimates Rainbow and overplays her role as stoic mentor.

Kathie's is the third narrative voice in the novel. Appropriately, as she is an absentee parent, we do not hear from her often nor are her comments as thoughtful or as perceptive as Rainbow's or Josephine's. Kathie focuses most often on her own dilemma; her daughter's is often an afterthought. Here is a cautionary tale. She was a teenaged parent; she now has a teenaged child whose very presence reminds her that time passes. An attractive woman, Kathie attracts men; but, invariably, the kind with little to give her except physical love and/or physical abuse. Stymied by her inability to do more than barely provide, Kathie vacillates from one stance to an-

other: from firm responsible parent, to negligent abusive parent, to self-centered irresponsible parent. Stranded eighty miles away when a "gig" or job is cancelled, Kathie thinks that with her boyfriend she "could really have a good time except for worryin about Rainbow. No way to forget her with rent due and me stranded . . . pleasant as a strand might be." Receiving only haphazard child support and not content with the small ADC (Aid to Dependent Children) check, Kathie seeks work to supplement her minimal income. But with no education and no training, the only jobs she finds available are as a go-go dancer, a precarious occupation at best.

Kathie's most earnest attempts at introspection or self-analysis fail miserably; she becomes willing accomplice, participating in her own victimization. Lacking the courage of her daughter or Miss Josie, Kathie capitulates to fear and violence. Once her ill-tempered violent boyfriend falls asleep, Kathie reflects: "No matter how hard I try to do the right thing . . . I always mess up. I can't love Burke as much as he loves me . . . maybe can't love anybody else either. Not a man in this world is takin care of me . . . except this clown, Burke." Yet when Burke awakens and offers her a drink, Kathie's mask is fixed in place. "Okay, sweetie," she replies. "Thank you, Burke. Just a small one . . . sugar pie." With this, Kathie abdicates any further responsibility for her own life or for Rainbow's; thereafter, she virtually disappears from the novel.

Oddly, although she is neither heroic nor admirable, rather, merely a callow young woman perpetually the Peter Pan, Kathie's capsulized story is strangely compelling and threatens to steal the novel. Indeed, she is the novel's most tragic character though her flaws are not entirely of her own making. But that is another subject; suffice it to reiterate here that hers is a cautionary tale which Childress asks her readers to ponder.

At this first level of *Rainbow Jordan* we are asked to ponder or consider a great deal. We see a 14-year-old struggling alone to preserve her equilibrium, to maintain her grades, to maintain both her integrity and her identity in the face of powerful peer pressure, to build relationships with adults beyond the parent-child bond. While considering what it means to be rejected or abandoned, Rainbow must also think about her homework and of how to obtain parental permission (with her mother gone) to attend sex education class. Rainbow is a concerned student; and unlike a young Alice Childress who resisted such topics and directives to write on them, Rainbow willingly writes papers on Black high achievers and receives high marks for them. But she recognizes clearly that knowing the "Accomplishments of Black People in America" or the history of "The Black Family in America" or about Black millionaires or celebrities or even about the lives of Black martyrs like Martin Luther King and Medgar Evers will not help ease her immediate problem of survival with her soul intact.

We are witnesses, watching Rainbow make the painful passage from child to adult. Her initiation is not easy; but, because Rainbow is perceptive beyond her years, her insights are both useful and keen. Rainbow knows, for instance, that though she is lonely, family "business" is never confided to friends or outsiders. The continual absences of her mother are linked to death. After a class discussion about death and saying goodbye to the dying, Rainbow makes this analogy: "When my mother is away if feel like death; but when she's back it's like life again." Rainbow must cope with her boyfriend Eljay's constant pleas for sex. He resurrects some *old* lines ("If you love me you'd be willin to give up somethin. What you savin it for?") to assault her position. Eventually, when her alienation from her peer group means confronting humiliation daily, Rainbow does waver and actually plans her first liaison. Fortunately, however, Rainbow discovers that her sense of self worth is not dependent on Eljay and thus, she is able to reexamine her sense of values and reinstate them at the core of her soul.

True, by taking her key and returning home alone to await Eljay, Rainbow has betrayed Miss Josie's trust. Yet having won a painful moral victory, Rainbow is willing to atone for this betrayal if Josephine is willing to listen and try to trust again. But emotionally battered by Harold's desertion—which she has denied and kept hidden—Josephine is unprepared or unable to hear about trust or truth from a child. In that accusatory manner the newly vindicated can adopt, Rainbow uncovers and somewhat painfully points to Josephine's own conceits and deceitfulness. Honest Josephine is not 50 but 57; she uses, kept hidden in a drawer, bleaching cream, false eye lashes, and hair dye; Harold Lamont is not assisting sick relatives as Josie has said but has left for another, younger, woman. Josephine then recognizes they have more in common that a simple "interim" relationship. Finally Josephine notices that Rainbow is not simply a difficult child but is an observant, maturing womanchild. And Rainbow learns to see Josephine as more than a perfect "role-model"—she is a decent middle-aged woman with her private vanities, dashed hopes, and heartaches, just like countless other women. It is an extraordinarily poignant moment when these two isolated individuals face each other honestly, each stripped of pretense or hostility. The reader unmoved is carved from stone.

But moving readers, and demonstrating that her characters are indeed human and not mere symbols, statistics, images, or stones, is clearly a part of Childress's multi-layered strategy, part of the function of her art.

And when we examine the novel at its second level, we see Childress being attentive not only to function but to the other considerations of the Black Aesthetic as well. If, for instance, the function of Black art is to accent racial identity—who we are and where we are going; or if it is to make myths and render the ordinary extraordinary—Childress achieves this

"function" and yet accomplishes this in her own singular fashion. Unlike a Mildred Taylor or a Toni Cade Bambara, writers known for their creation of sassy or tough young female protagonists, in *Rainbow Jordan* Childress makes her heroine, and each of her other characters, walk the high wire in a solo balancing act, alone and unsteady until they learn first to reach inward for self-validation and strength, then outward to touch others who themselves are authentic and thus willing to reach out.

The usual or traditional community support structures typically illustrative of Afro-American life and culture play virtually no role in *Rainbow*. The Black church, a staple symbol in much Afro-American literature, is notable by its absence. In fact, Josephine's Quaker neighbor teaches Rainbow the Quaker concept of "centering down" rather than prayer to help face a problem. The strong nurturing community with neighbor helping neighbor, a recurring motif in much Afro-American literature, especially that set in the South, is also absent. Rather, Childress unabashedly depicts the divisive, splintered, often antagonistic communities which are, regretfully, a truism of contemporary urban living.

Rainbow's awkward family situation stands as ironic counterpoint to the dominant Afro-American literary tradition that paints a strong cohesive family, either nuclear or extended, as central element in the formation of character. Here we have a portrait of family disintegration, again an all too frequent truism of modern urban life. Authentic female bonding among peers, such as that which occurs in Toni Morrison's *Sula* (1973) or Paule Marshall's *Brown Girl, Brownstones* (1959), is also missing. Of course, Rainbow and Josephine "bond" but 14 and 57 is hardly the same peer group. Instead, Rainbow painfully learns the wisdom of that deathless folk pronouncement, "Everybody who say they your friend, ain't." Intriguingly, the one remaining traditional symbol or cultural ritual which Childress permits is a very subtle bow to the blues. Both Rainbow and Josephine suffer from heartache; and heartaches are, as every mature reader knows, a staple of the blues. Even Kathie has heartaches, but she is essentially a "good time girl," another kind of staple blues figure. Heartaches, of course, don't last always and by novel's end, Rainbow and Josephine have hardened their will, left the "low-down" men in their lives behind, and walked away. They suffer still, but they've experienced the catharsis the blues afford.

Because of the skill with which they are invoked, both Rainbow (and certainly the name is weighted with obvious symbolic intent) and Josephine become, despite any intent to the contrary, symbols of survival. They are also powerful images of what it can mean to "hold fast" to one's dreams, as Langston Hughes has said, and to live with integrity and dignity. Childress's commitment to depicting the lives of people within the working-class and middle-class Black communities provides us with, as Trudier Harris says, a "sensitive readable book which entertains quietly and teaches without being overly didactic." Thus, the call for a "functional" art is satisfied at a variety of levels.

"Function" is probably the most significant cornerstone of the Black Aesthetic. The parallel calls for "collectivity" and "commitment" can be addressed summarily. The idea of art "emerging from" and "returning or speaking to the people" translates to a question of audience. Naturally, any novelist hopes that her work will have a large general audience capable of following both the broad sweeping moments in the text and its subtle nuances as well. Though Childress conceptualizes her books as theater pieces, particularly as she stages the settings and the "visual, staged scenes and live actions" (**"A Candle"**), the voices in the novel call loudly to a Black audience attuned to the inflections, rhythms, structural patterns, and nuances of urban Black folk speech. We see through the voice characters clearly identified with or emerging from a familiar Black experience. We see them operate and function almost totally within the confines of that experience. Childress accents the intraracial community; very little energy is expended on noting interracial tensions. Thus, the reader examines an enhanced segment of Black life with characters who function as guides to various components of the community Josie bridges the working class and the middle class; Kathie "represents" the bottom rung, the hand-to-mouth existence so many endure. Rainbow struggles to keep her feet on the right road; her aim, troubles not withstanding, is to march on to victory.

Committed or committing art calls for a commitment to revolution and change. That "directive" which grates so harshly on the celebrated freedom of the artist, is nonetheless imprinted on the thematic structure of the novel. The revolutions Childress speaks to, however, are revolutions of habit and heart and mind rather than violent large scale social revolutions. Her revolutionary call to arms is embodied in the dictum: each one, reach one, teach one. Rainbow and Josephine learn from each other; each also teaches the other something significant about facing life's complexities. Kathie is something of the "counter-revolutionary" character. She is a conservative reactionary who refuses to change, refuses to accept responsibility for her own life, preferring the worn illusion of female dependence on dominant men. Rainbow and Josephine survive because adversity has taught them resiliency and toughness. Theirs is a strength which emerges through the process of change, by a "revolution" if you will, in their approach to life. They will march on until the victory is won.

Consistently, just as Mari Evans demanded, Alice Childress in **Rainbow Jordan** speaks "truth to the people." The novel "talks sense" to us; it "frees" readers with any awareness at all to see the honesty, reason, love, courage and caring interwoven as part of its message. Coincidentally or not, in **Rainbow Jordan** Childress has redressed the Black Aesthetic and

given it a daring new look with a vivid splash of contemporary color.

Catherine Wiley (essay date 1990)

SOURCE: "Whose Name, Whose Protection: Reading Alice Childress's *Wedding Band*," in *Modern American Drama: The Female Canon,* edited by June Schlueter, Fairleigh Dickinson University Press, 1990, pp. 184-96.

[*In the following essay, Wiley offers a feminist reading on the relationships among the female characters in* Wedding Band.]

In the first act of **Wedding Band,** a scene of reading and performance occurs that lies at the center of a feminist interpretation of the play. Mattie, a black woman who makes her living selling candy and caring for a little white girl, has received a letter from her husband in the Merchant Marine and needs a translator for it. Her new neighbor, Julia, the educated outsider trying to fit into working-class surroundings, reads the sentimental sailor's letter aloud. After her performance, in which the women listening have actively participated, Mattie tells Julia that, in addition to his love, her husband gives her what is more important, his *name and protection*. These two standards of conventional love are denied Julia because her lover of ten years is white; and even Mattie learns that because she never divorced her first husband, she is not now legally married and cannot receive marital war benefits. Neither woman enjoys a man's name or his protection, in part because the chivalry implied in such privilege was unattainable for blacks in the Jim Crow society of 1918 South Carolina. The women in **Wedding Band** learn to depend on themselves and each other rather than on absent men, a self-reliance born painfully through self-acceptance.

Wedding Band received mixed reviews when it opened off-Broadway in 1972. It was described both as "the play about black life in America that isn't a 'black' play" and too much "like a story wrenched from the pages of what used to be known as a magazine for women." Interesting for their racist and sexist connotations, these comments betray the reviewers' uncritical assumptions about who constitutes a theater audience. The play doesn't look "black" because its integrationist subtext surfaces only occasionally and its political urgency is dressed safely in realistic period costume. New York theater patrons of 1972 applauding the drama as entertainment alone could assure themselves that the play's World War I setting depicted a reality long past. The first reviewer assumes that a "black" play, one that speaks primarily to a black audience, is implicitly alien and uninteresting to a white audience. Representations of so-called minority lives told from a minority point of view cannot interest the rest of us, if we are white. Likewise, the pages of a women's magazine would bore us if we were men, because they focus on the small, private issues of home and heart. And although none of the liberal reviewers profess any shock over the play's important theme of miscegenation, no New York producers would touch **Wedding Band** until 1972, six years after it was written and first performed, attesting to the subject's unpopularity.

My reading of the play argues that its subject is less interracial heterosexual relations than the relations between black women and and white women in World War I-era South Carolina. That said, I must add that I perceive a certain danger in trying to read feminist rather than racial politics into Alice Childress's play. White feminists must take care not to offer our own invaluable "name and protection" to black women writers who do not need them. For a feminist criticism that is not limited to the privileged location of many of its practitioners, it is crucial that white feminists read the work of black women, especially those like Childress who have been all but ignored in academic theater. We might read in the same spirit of canon disruption inspiring the informal creation of a women's literary counter-canon, recognizing that in the same way white women writers were denied membership in the old canon on the basis of "greatness," we may be guilty of blocking black women writers for the same reason. The value of a literary text cannot be defined out of context. White readers should try to decentralize our historically majority context—to see ourselves, for once, in the margins with respect to the Afro-American women's literary tradition. I recognize with dismay the truth of Hortense J. Spillers's statement: "When we say 'feminist' with an adjective in front of it, we mean, of course, white women, who, as a category of social and cultural agents, fully occupy the territory of feminism." But does including Afro-American women writers in the canon, which seems to be my project in writing for this book, imitate a colonizing gesture? Am I offering the protection of the cannon to Alice Childress, protection on the canon's (and for now, white women's) terms? Instead of attempting to answer these questions now, I can only say that I am beginning to learn to read black women's plays in the same way many feminists ask men to read women's texts. Rather than seeing myself reflected in their work, I want to understand why my difference makes these plays a challenge to read.

Difference has become a feminist catch-word, complicated by its dual usage as what makes women different from men as well as that makes women different from each other. Teresa de Lauretis and Linda Gordon have argued recently that the first definition, which makes women's primary characteristic the fact that we are not men, risks becoming a substitute for women's opposition to men's discriminatory practice. This opposition, however, has always differed from one group of women to another, because our discrimination as women has always differed. The various ways we have resisted male practice through history define women as much as what we have in common biologically. It is not enough for white feminists merely to tolerate women of color or invite them to join our canon, but to understand how we are different, to understand differences among women as differences within women.

Because, in de Lauretis' words, "not only does feminism exist despite those differences, but . . . it cannot continue to exist without them."

Many of these differences, especially between black women and white women in the United States, have been constituted historically. As Childress writes in the *Negro Digest* of April 1967, her newest play, **Wedding Band,** serves as a reminder of the many promises made in 1918 that are still unkept in 1967. During the gap between the play's initial production in 1966 at the University of Michigan and today, most of the promises of integration have been fulfilled legally; however, we still have much to learn of the limits of the successes of the civil rights movement. Although the *Negro Digest* article refers specifically to the Jim Crow laws prohibiting intermarriage, Childress's play can be read today as a history lesson pointed at white women to remind them and us, in 1966 or now, that our vision of sisterly equality has always left some sisters out. Until the Civil War, the women's rights movement was essentially inseparable from the abolitionist movement. As Angelina Grimke, the southern white abolitionist, wrote in 1838:

> The discussion of the rights of the slave has opened the way for the discussion of other rights, and the ultimate result will most certainly be the breaking of *every* yoke, the letting the oppressed of every grade and description go free, an emancipation far more glorious than any the world has ever yet seen.

But the interests of women fighting for decades to assure themselves a voice in the political process could not be reconciled to those of white politicians eager to take advantage of black men's votes. Despite their political training as abolitionists, most of the white suffragists were quick to forgo interracial solidarity as their own movement foundered in the Reconstruction era.

Black women's frustration heard an echo a century later as the civil rights movement shifted from its origins in the rural south to the industrialized north. Hundreds of black women in the south led the grass-roots movement for desegregation and voter registration in the late 1950s, and in the early 1960s they trained younger white women who had come down from northern colleges to take part in the Freedom Rides. The early civil rights movement had been affected most dramatically by an army of nameless women: black women who honed their leadership skills in the only place available to them, their churches. But in 1964, an anonymous paper about women's position in the Student Nonviolent Coordinating Committee (SNCC) circulated at the Waveland Conference, although assumed to be written by a black woman, was written by two white women who were trying to inject the civil rights movement with theories of women's liberation. Although these white women had learned invaluable skills, including the courage to withstand jailings, beatings, and death threats, from the black women, their influence in the overall movement dwindled in the mid-60s, partly because of their sexual liaisons with black men. The Waveland Conference position paper, which criticized the assumption of male superiority at work in SNCC by comparing it with white superiority, marked the move of white women out of the civil rights movement and into the women's movement. Sexual discrimination in the civil rights movement forced white activists to confront their differences from black women in a way they had not since the struggle over voting rights a century earlier. The result of this confrontation, according to many historians, was the same: white women abandoned Afro-American liberation to pursue a goal closer to home, that of a race- and class-specific women's liberation.

Set chronologically midway between the poles of Reconstruction and civil rights, *Wedding Band* describes an era when lynching presented one answer to demands for equality in the south, while Harlem flowered as a mecca for black culture in the north. In the 1960s, white women and black men's sexual relations generated tension in the black community, but miscegenation as the white master's rape of his slave retains deeper historical ramifications for black women. Childress's drama, subtitled "a love/hate story in black and white," takes place on the tenth anniversary of Julia and her white lover in the small backyard tenement to which Julia has moved after being evicted from countless other houses. Determined to get along with her nosy but well-meaning neighbors, Julia seems to have won a guarded acceptance until her lover, Herman, visits her. He has brought her a gold wedding band on a chain, and they plan to buy tickets on the Clyde Line to New York, where Julia will proudly and legally bear Herman's name. But Herman succumbs to the influenza epidemic, and in the second act he lies in Julia's bed waiting for his mother and sister to take him to a white doctor. Julia's landlady has refused to help because it is illegal for Herman to be in Julia's house, and she cannot appear to sanction Julia's immoral behavior. Herman's mother sides with the landlady in preserving respectability even at the cost of her son's life, and she will not carry him to the doctor until it grows dark enough to hide him. In the last scene, Herman returns to Julia with the boat tickets, which she refuses to take because his mother has convinced her that blacks and whites can never live together. Finally she appears to relent so that Herman can die believing that Julia, even without him, will go north.

The secondary characters, however, more than the two lovers, underscore the drama's didactic politics. They are types, but not stereotypes, and their separate dilemmas and personalities describe the injustices blacks have endured in the south. The landlady, Fanny, the neighbors Mattie and Lula, Lula's adopted son, Nelson, and the abusive white traveling salesman give the stage community a historical idiosyncrasy missing from Julia and Herman's relationship. Fanny has proudly joined the middle class by acquiring property and exploiting her tenants (in 1918 a relatively new possibility for black women) in the name of racial uplift. As homeworkers, Mattie and Lula exist bound to a variety of semi-skilled, low-paying jobs to feed their children. Nelson, as a soldier in the newly desegregated United States army, assumes that when the war is over he will be given the rights of a full citizen, even in South Carolina. He is a forerunner of the militant youth who would later provide the impatient voice to the nascent civil rights movement of the late 1940s, and whose dreams of integration would be realized only partially in the 1960s.

These characters who inhabit Miss Fanny's backyard tenement underscore the vexed issue of difference as explored by the feminist scholars cited above. Julia's problem throughout the play is less her white lover than her reluctance to see herself as a member of the black community. Although a mostly white theater audience would see her as a different sort of heroine because of race, her black neighbors perceive her as different from them for issues more complex than skin color. She assumes that her racial transgression with Herman will make her unwelcome among the women she wishes to confide in, but her aloofness from their day-to-day interests also serves as a protective shield. In this, Julia is similar to Lutie Johnson in Ann Petry's *The Street,* written in 1946. Both characters are ostensibly defined by their unequal relations with men, but their potential for salvation lies in the larger community that depends on the stability of its women. Lutie Johnson is so determined to move off "the street" in Harlem she thinks is pulling her down that she refuses to join the community Harlem offers her, a community that in some ways defies the white society keeping it poor. Neither poor nor uneducated, Julia finds herself defying the black community by asserting her right to love a white man, but this self-assertion is, in a larger sense, a more dangerous defiance of the white community. She wants her love story to be one of individual commitment and sacrifice, but it is that only in part. Julia's refinement in manners, education, and financial independence, which are middle-class, traditionally white attributes, make her and Herman available to each other. But theirs is, as the subtitle insists, a "love/hate" story, in which interracial love cannot be divorced from centuries of racial hate.

As *Wedding Band* opens, Julia sleeps on her bed in the new house while a little girl enters her yard weeping about a quarter she has lost. Her mother, Mattie, chases the girl, threatening to whip her unless she finds "the only quarter I got to my name," the quarter that was to buy the ingredients to make the candy she sells. Julia tries to sleep through this scene, but she cannot hide from either the noise or the predicaments because the coin has rolled under her porch and Mattie is trying to knock it down to get at the money. When Julia tries to escape back into her private room after giving Mattie a quarter, Fanny follows her to discern whether or not the new tenant is "quality." In Fanny's eyes, Julia's ability to give quarters away without a second thought is an indication that her boarding-house business is improving. She gossips about the other women and says Mattie was low-class enough to have worked once washing "joy-towels" in a white whorehouse. Another neighbor, Lula, has her grown-up adopted son living with her, although the arrangement is in Fanny's eyes "'gainst nature." Unmarried herself because she has to "bear the standard of the race" and "colored men don't know how to do nothin' right," Fanny's notions of sexuality are as puritanical as they are ignorant. But according to the Bell Man who sold it to her, she is the first and only black woman in the country to own a silver-plated tea service, a symbol of her single-handed effort to improve the appearance of her race in the eyes of the white community.

The first white character to appear in the play is the Bell Man, a foil to Herman, who pedals dime-store merchandise in the poor neighborhood using the insidious installment system, "fifty cent a week and one long, sweet year to pay." Recognizing Julia from another neighborhood, he comments sardonically that she moves a lot, invites himself into her bedroom, and bounces on the bed. "But seriously, what is race and color?" he asks. "Put a paper bag over your head and who'd know the difference." When Julia chases him out with a wooden hanger, he calls her a "sick-minded bitch" because she refuses to play the historical role of the master's sexual toy, already bought and paid for on the slave market. Like the landlady, who also has pushed herself unwanted into Julia's rented room, the Bell Man objectifies Julia into a representative of her race. If for Fanny the proper black woman is to be asexual, for the salesman she is to be a body with a paper bag over her head, hiding not only her race but her existence as an individual with a face and a name. Fanny's attitude constitutes one legitimate response to centuries of white men's sexual abuse of black women. Julia's relationship with Herman should not leave her open to the insults of a traveling salesman, but in his eyes, and perhaps in Fanny's, that relationship makes her another black woman who "prefers" white men.

This scene points to the inseparability of racism and sexism, an issue that cannot be isolated from the historical relationship of the civil rights and women's movements. The fallacy of *sisterhood* as the word was used in the women's liberation movement of the 1960s lay in its assumption that oppression was universal. The signal white women's liberationists sent to black women echoed the one suffragists had sent to their abolitionist sisters a century earlier: your race matters less than your gender. As Bell Hooks puts it, "If we dared to criticize the movement or to assume responsibility for reshaping feminist ideas . . . our voices were tuned out, dismissed, silenced. We could be heard only if our statements echoed the sentiments of the dominant discourse." If a black woman is to be a feminist, it appears she must cease to be black. Julia's treatment by Fanny and the salesman effects the opposite but equally insidious contradiction: she can be a member of the black race, but as such she cannot be an individual woman.

In stark contrast to the private and commodified vision of sexuality the salesman offers Julia, in which he fixes a price for his use of her body, Mattie's letter from her husband reminds Julia that human love also involves a community. Knowing that Mattie can't read the letter herself, Fanny snatches it from her and offers to read it aloud for a dime, but Mattie objects saying, "I don't like how you make words sound. You read too rough." She would rather not hear the words at all than receive them through an unsympathetic voice, as the words themselves only partially represent the layers of meaning contained in the letter. Fanny would have excluded Mattie from her own letter by turning the reading of it into a business transaction. Julia's reading of it is inclusive, not exclusive, and brings out several dramatic levels in the text. One level is the author, October, writing a love letter from his ship in the middle of the ocean. He writes that he wishes he had a photograph of his wife and daughter to show the white men around him, to prove that although he looks different from them he's as good as they are and has a family to miss as much as they do. As Julia reads October's words about loving and missing his wife, Mattie responds in kind, as though he were beside her. Mattie embodies the spectator willing to suspend her disbelief; even third-hand, October's words are enough to bring him into her presence. When Julia reads, "Sometimes people say hurtful things 'bout what I am, like color and race," Mattie replied "Tell 'em you my brown-skin Carolina daddy, that's who the hell you are."

The words Julia reads remind her of what she does not have with her lover: the social legitimation of the public bond racism denies them. Julia carries October's message to Mattie in her voice; her enactment of his text and Mattie's reactions to it reconfirm Julia's own insecurity. The irony of the women's voices turning a private, written text back into a communal text that is orally conveyed is completed later in the play when we learn that October's papers do not "match up" and Mattie cannot receive his benefits. The other significant missing papers are the divorce paper legally freeing Mattie from an abusive husband and the marriage paper realizing her bond with October. All of these legal documents are, of course, controlled by white institutions hostile not only to women's needs but to the Afro-American community historically barred from them. As Susan Willis argues, the southern rural tradition that most contemporary black women writers refer back to depends on oral communication and storytelling. Willis describes this as, unlike writing, a "noncommodified relationship to language, a time when the slippage between words and meaning would not have obtained or been tolerated." Because the paper containing October's letter is marked with her name, Mattie owns it and the words inscribed in it, although she can't read it. Papers she has or does not have control her life, like the laws on "the books" of South Carolina keeping Julia and Herman from marrying.

At the close of his letter, October assures Mattie that he will be home as soon as he can: "Two things a man can give the women he loves . . . his name and his protection . . . The first you have, the last is yet to someday come." For Mattie, "name and protection" ensure a man's responsibility toward his wife; otherwise she just lets him use her. In other words, a woman's options are limited to a heterosexual union sanctioned by a piece of paper enforcing not the man's responsibility but her connection to him. In Mattie and October's case, however, he cannot offer her the financial protection of his war benefits because he has never legally given her his name. The bonds of sisterhood, on the other hand, offer no name, but an unspoken, and, more importantly, unwritten protection.

In response to Mattie and Lula's warm reception of her letter-reading, Julia feels compelled to confess her sin of "keeping company" with a man for ten years without being married, and Mattie and Lula prescribe folk remedies to tie him down. Learning that Herman is white, the two women are initially shocked but cannot believe that Julia really loves him. As Mattie says about whites, "They're mean, honey. They can't help it: their nose is pinched together so close they can't get enough air." But when Julia insists that she feels about Herman the way Mattie feels about October, she loses her sympathetic audience. Having entered their company by reading October's letter, Julia tries to forget the class difference she had earlier imagined separated her absolutely from Lula and Mattie, but the women will not allow her love for a white man to be the same as their love for their own men. Sisterhood is threatened by a traditional loyalty to men whether the men are present or not. One thing besides race that these women hold in common is their status as single women: whether by choice or circumstance they are independent, a situation shared by the two white women who appear in the second act, Herman's mother and sister. Although independence and the complications of sustaining legal heterosexual relationships carry different valences for black and white women, especially in the Jim Crow era, the failure of these relationships for all of Childress's characters can serve as a locus of understanding between them.

In act 2, Julia must face the consequences of Herman's illness and her estrangement from her neighbors. Fanny will not permit her to call a doctor for Herman because she knows the repercussion such publicity would have on everyone. She tells Julia sarcastically, "No, you call a doctor, Nelson won't march in the parade tomorrow to go back in the army, Mattie'll be outta work, Lula can't deliver flowers. . . ." Fanny's pragmatism comes through what initially sounds like selfishness, but when Herman wakes up and Fanny is described as "very genial" in the stage directions, addressing him as "Sir" and "Mr. Herman," her desire not to make waves changes its tone. She dons the mask of the happy slave here, a mask of subservient self-protection echoed by Lula in scene 2 as she tells Julia how she saved Nelson from the chain gang. On her hands and knees, she says she "crawled and cried, 'Please white folks, yall's everything. I'se nothin, yall's everything.' The court laughed—I meant for 'em to laugh. . . ." Julia responds

with pity that a lady is not supposed to crawl, but Lula reminds her that she was saving her son's life. A black woman cannot afford the luxury of ladylike behavior when her son is treated like an animal, but no one should have to crawl. Fanny and Lula recognize, and Julia is learning to recognize, that dignity finds its limits in the respect accorded it by others. The doubleness of black women's existence that gets enacted through the play, the flexibility of demeanor needed to survive in a society in which an unguarded facial expression could kill you, is what Julia thinks she can escape in the north.

White women, however, need no acting ability to get by. Herman's sister, Annabelle, does not mask her discomfort entering the strange world of Fanny's backyard, wondering aloud if the little white girl in Mattie's charge and Mattie's daughter might be her brother's illegitimate children. Although she tells Julia "you look like one-a the nice coloreds" and cannot call the other woman—her figurative sister-in-law—by her name, she admits to Herman her envy of his ten-year love affair. As dominated by their mother as her brother is, Annabelle blames Herman for not showing more solidarity with her on the one occasion she invited her sweetheart home. "You didn't even stay home that one Sunday like you promised . . . Mama made a jackass outta Walter. You know how she can do. He left lookin' like a whipped dog." Like Julia, she only wants to escape the south and go to Brooklyn to marry the sailor she loves, but, like Herman, she cannot break her mother's apron strings.

The audience discovers the desire and disappointment Julia and Annabelle share as Annabelle confesses curiosity about the other woman to Herman, but Julia's real lack of difference from her black neighbors is articulated when Herman's mother faces her and insists that she can never escape the history she shares with all black women. Julia's neighbors may perceive her difference in terms of class, but to Herman's mother, and initially to Annabelle as well, black women are indistinguishable from each other. After throwing Julia out of her own house, the mother addresses her son privately:

> There's something wrong 'bout mismatched things, be they shoes, socks, or people.
>
> HERMAN. Go away, don't look at us.
>
> HERMAN'S MOTHER. People don't like it. They're not gonna letcha do it in peace.
>
> HERMAN. We'll go North.
>
> HERMAN'S MOTHER. Not a thing will change except her last name.
>
> HERMAN. She's not like others . . .

The mother is perhaps typecast as an ignorant, dangerous

"cracker," but she is right that integration did not abolish racism in the north. When Herman insists that Julia is not like the others, he belies his feeling that other black women are as bad as his mother describes them. Herman's response to his mother, telling her not to look, is as naive as Julia's desire to escape her problems in New York. He cannot make her hatred disappear, and it finally reminds him of his own. As he leaves, supported by his mother and sister, Julia shouts that she will scrub her home with hot water and lye, to "clean the whiteness outta my house," that they should leave her "to [her] own black self!"

Julia's crisis is precipitated by her belated understanding that love does not allow Herman to transcend his racism. Made delirious by the pain medicine the women have been pouring down his throat, he spouts a speech he had recited at a Klan picnic as a little boy, a moment of which his mother has always been proud, although she whipped him into memorizing it: "It is a great and dangerous error to suppose that all people are equally entitled to liberty . . . It is a reward to be earned, a reward reserved for the intelligent, the patriotic, the virtuous and deserving; and not a boon to be bestowed on a people too ignorant, degraded and vicious. . . ." Far from enacting the language of inclusion, as Julia's reading of October's letter does, this spectacle reinforces centuries of exclusion based on bigotry. The speech works two ways given the anti-German sentiment of the World War I period. First, it reveals to Julia and the audience the depth of Herman's ambivalence over his love for a black woman, and, secondly, it points to the historical specificity of prejudice. Herman's mother's embarrassment over her first name, Frieda, prompts her to introduce herself to Fanny as "Miss Thelma." She has also planted a red, white, and blue flower garden and has posted a sign in her window announcing: "We are American Citizens." Although the effects of racism cannot be compared to a few decades of anti-German feeling, Herman's mother's ethnic vulnerability exacerbates her own racial hatred. Julia counters the white woman's accusations of "Black, sassy nigger" with "Kraut, knuckle-eater, and red-neck," but the name-calling effectively ends with Frieda's pronouncement that "White reigns supreme . . . I'm white, you can't change that."

The urgency of integration as a method of combatting such ingrained hatred marks Julia's turning point in the play. After Herman and his family are gone, she must face her own difficult reintegration into the community of Fanny's backyard. As the women prepare to escort Nelson to his proud participation in the soldiers' parade, the air of festivity inspires Lula and Julia to perform an impromptu strut dance to the music of Jenkin's Colored Orphan Band. They discover a small common space in the mutual performance of a *"Carolina folk dance passed on from some dimly-remembered African beginning."* Later, to send Nelson on his way, Lula begs Julia to give him a farewell speech telling him "how life's gon' be better when he gets back . . . Make up what

should be true," whether Julia believes in her performance or not. Julia makes a speech proclaiming the abolition of the "no-colored" signs after the war and the new lives of respect awaiting Nelson and October after their return home. Although the stage directions do not specify this, according to reviews of the play, she addresses these words directly to the audience. Edith Oliver, writing for the *New Yorker,* called the speech "dreadful . . . like something out of a bad Russian movie," in part because by addressing the audience Julia moves the issue of racism north of the Mason-Dixon line. Breaking the fourth wall of realism brings the drama out of its historical context of 1918 into the present and makes Julia's words about integration harder for a northern audience to ignore.

At the end of the play, Julia gives her wedding band and boat tickets to Mattie and her daughter, finally admitting that "You and Teeta are my people . . . my family." But the gesture is compromised by its implication that the only choice for Afro-Americans is to leave their homes in the South. It was still illegal for blacks and whites to marry in South Carolina in 1966, but, despite the laws, by that time blacks had already begun to reclaim their homes. As Alice Walker argues in her essay "Choosing to Stay at Home," one thing Martin Luther King gave his people was the possibility of returning to the South they or their parents or grandparents had left. The civil rights movement recreated the South as a site of militant resistance, resistance enacted equally by black women and men. Set in South Carolina and staged in Michigan and New York, **Wedding Band** provides a site of resistance like the political movement from which it grew. Julia's decision to stay at home, to keep her own name, makes the spectator witness to her new-found ability to celebrate, as she says, her "own black self."

Despite her helplessness regarding her mother, Annabelle, the literal "white sister" in the play, is a character who, like Julia and Nelson, embodies hope for the future in the South. Like the audience, she witnesses Julia's articulation of her newly-won independence. Julia's curtain speech with Herman dying in her arms escapes sentimentality only through the staging of Annabelle's mute participation in it. Julia and Herman remain inside Julia's house, after she simply but irrevocably bars Annabelle, Herman's mother, and Fanny from entering. Everyone leaves the stage except for Annabelle, who moves toward the house, listening to Julia's words to her brother. Without entering the house, to which the black woman has denied her access, she hears the other woman's words and so manages to share silently the loss of Herman without translating it into white terms. As Julia comforts Herman by describing their pretend journey north on the Clyde Line Boat together, she says, "We're takin' off, ridin' the waves so smooth and easy . . . There now . . . on our way. . . ." Julia and Herman are not on their way, but perhaps Julia and Annabelle will someday be on *their* way to mutual respect. I can only read these words as a directive to the audience of college students at the University of Michigan in 1966, empassioned with the growing fervor of the anti-war and women's liberation movements and prepared in their innocence to change the world. They cannot do it, *Wedding Band* gently but firmly insists, as gently and firmly as Julia closes her door on the other women, without a renewed commitment to civil rights for all people in the United States, in the South as well as in the North. Sisterhood, especially from the point of view of white women learning to understand black women, begins with listening, not to what one wants to hear but to what is being said.

FURTHER READING

Criticism

Brown, Janet. "Wine in the Wilderness." In her *Feminist Drama: Definition & Critical Analysis,* pp. 56-70. Metuchen, N.J.: The Scarecrow Press, Inc., 1979.

> Feminist analysis of Childress's *Wine in the Wilderness* in which the critic analyzes associational clusters and pattern of symbolic action.

Clurman, Harold. Review of *Wedding Band,* by Alice Childress. *The Nation* 215, No. 5 (13 November 1972): 475-76.

> Generally positive review of Public/Newman Theatre's staging of *Wedding Band.*

Karlin, Barbara. "To Grow On." *The Los Angeles Times* (25 July 1982): 9.

> Brief, positive review of *A Hero Ain't Nothin' but a Sandwich.*

Kaufmann, Stanley. Review of *Wedding Band,* by Alice Childress. *The New Republic* 167 (25 November 1972): 22, 36.

> Generally negative review of the Newman Theatre's staging of *Wedding Band.* Kaufman attacks both the script and the direction of Childress and producer Joseph Papp.

Oliver, Edith. Review of *Moms,* by Alice Childress. *The New Yorker* LXIII, No. 1 (23 February 1987): 105.

> Positive review of the Hudson Guild's staging of *Moms.*

Rogers, Norma. "To Destroy Life." *Freedomways* 14, No. 1 (First Quarter, 1974): 72-5.

> Review that provides a plot summary of *A Hero Ain't Nothin' but a Sandwich.*

Simon, John. "No Thanks for the Memory." *New York* 20, No. 8 (23 February 1987): 127-28.

> Generally laudatory review of Childress's *Moms.*

Tait, Marianne Pride. Review of *Those Other People,* by Alice Childress. *The Booktalker* 1, No. 1 (September 1989): 14-15.

> Short review providing a plot summary of *Those Other People.*

Additional coverage of Childress's life and career is contained in the following sources published by Gale Research: *Authors and Artists for Young Adults,* **Vol. 8;** *Black Literature Criticism; Black Writers,* **Vol. 2;** *Children's Literature Review,* **Vol. 14;** *Contemporary Authors,* **Vols. 45-48, 146;** *Contemporary Authors New Revision Series,* **Vols. 3, 27, 50;** *Contemporary Literary Criticism,* **Vols. 12, 15, 86;** *Dictionary of Literary Biography,* **Vols. 7, 38;** *DISCovering Authors Modules: Dramatists, Multicultural, Novelists; Drama Criticism,* **Vol. 4;** *Junior DISCovering Authors; Major Authors and Illustrators for Children and Young Adults; Major 20th-Century Writers;* **and** *Something about the Author,* **Vols. 7, 48, 81.**

W. E. B. Du Bois
1868-1963

(Full name William Edward Burghardt Du Bois) American essayist, journalist, historian, novelist, biographer, poet, playwright, nonfiction writer, speech writer, critic, and autobiographer.

The following entry provides an overview of Du Bois's career. For further information on his life and works, see *CLC,* Volumes 1, 2, 13, and 64.

INTRODUCTION

Du Bois was a major force in twentieth-century society who helped define African-American social and political causes in the United States. Alternately considered a leader and an outcast, Du Bois espoused controversial opinions about race and politics and was regarded by many as a prophet. He is widely remembered for his conflict with Booker T. Washington over the role of blacks in American society—an issue that he treated at length in the essays collected in *The Souls of Black Folk* (1903). A writer of important works in many genres, Du Bois is particularly known for his pioneering role in the study of black history. According to Herbert Aptheker, however, Du Bois was above all a "history maker," and his works and ideas continue to attract attention and generate controversy.

Biographical Information

Du Bois had an almost idyllic childhood in Great Barrington, Massachusetts. Class and race distinctions were negligible in the small town of 5,000, where Du Bois's family was part of a community of fifty blacks. When his mother died soon after his high school graduation, some residents of the town gave Du Bois a scholarship on condition that he attend Fisk University, a southern school founded for the children of emancipated slaves. Du Bois accepted the scholarship and in 1885 traveled to Fisk in Nashville, Tennessee—his first journey to the southern United States. "No one but a Negro going into the South without previous experience of color caste can have any conception of its barbarism," Du Bois wrote in *The Autobiography of W. E. B. Du Bois* (1968). Yet he was "deliriously happy" at Fisk, where he met students of his own race, excelled at his studies, and during summers taught young blacks who lived in destitute rural areas of Tennessee. After graduating with honors from Fisk, Du Bois entered Harvard in 1888. There he met several professors who would provide lifelong inspiration, particularly William James, who became a mentor and friend. After receiving a bachelor's degree, Du Bois studied for two years at the University of Berlin. In 1896 he received his doctorate from Harvard—the first black

American to do so—and published his dissertation *The Suppression of the African Slave-Trade to the United States of America, 1638-1870.* Du Bois's efforts at finding a teaching position, however, proved frustrating. The University of Pennsylvania, for instance, commissioned Du Bois to do a sociological study of the city's black population but did not offer him a faculty position. Du Bois eventually found a position at Atlanta University, where he taught from 1897 to 1910 and 1934 to 1944. In 1905 Du Bois formed the Niagara Movement, the first black protest movement of the twentieth century. Du Bois helped institute a more lasting movement in 1909 when he became the only black founding member of the National Association for the Advancement of Colored People (NAACP). From 1910 to 1934 Du Bois served as the organization's director of publicity and research, and as editor of *Crisis,* the official publication of the NAACP, which became one of the most prominent journals directed at a black audience. Du Bois contributed editorials condemning lynching and disenfranchisement, and his discussion of arts and letters in *Crisis* has been credited as a catalyst for the Harlem Renaissance literary movement. Du Bois's popularity as a leader of black America began to decline in 1918 with the publication of the editorial "Close Ranks," which urged support for American involvement in World War I, and his conflict with Marcus Garvey, the popular Jamaican leader of the Universal Negro Improvement Association and "back-to-Africa" movement. Du Bois's position in the NAACP also became tenuous and strained. He was removed from the organization twice for ideological differences, once after opposing the NAACP's idea of integration, and later for supporting Progressive Party candidate Henry Wallace for president in 1948 while the NAACP's executive secretary unofficially campaigned for Harry Truman. In 1951 Du Bois was indicted as an unregistered "agent of a foreign principal" because of his involvement in the "subversive" Peace Information Center, an organization that sought to inform Americans about international events and to abolish the atomic bomb. Although Du Bois was acquitted, his passport remained in the custody of the United States government. Awarded the International Lenin Prize in 1958, Du Bois became a member of the Communist Party of the United States in 1961, shortly before renouncing his American citizenship. He died at the age of ninety-five in Accra, Ghana.

Major Works

Du Bois's works spread across a wide range of genres and subjects including history, sociology, fiction, biography, and autobiography. His most celebrated work, *The Souls of Black Folk,* is a collection of fourteen essays that comment on the state of blacks in America. According to Arnold Rampersad, *The Souls of Black Folk* became "perhaps the most influential work on blacks in America since *Uncle Tom's Cabin.*" In the essay "On Mr. Booker T. Washington and Others," Du Bois praised Washington for preaching "Thrift, Patience, and Industrial Training," but condemned his apologies to those in power, maintaining that Washington "does not rightly value the privilege and duty of voting, belittles the emasculating effects of caste distinctions and opposes the higher training of our brighter minds." Other essays were largely autobiographical and discussed the "twoness" of being both American and black—"two warring ideals in one dark body, whose dogged strength alone keeps it from being torn asunder." *The Philadelphia Negro* (1899) is a systematic, sociological study of Philadelphia's black population. Commissioned by the University of Pennsylvania, the study includes data gathered from approximately 5,000 interviews and pioneered the scholarly study of black Americans. Du Bois's historical works include *The Gift of Black Folk* (1924), which examines the contributions blacks have made to civilization; *Black Reconstruction* (1935), a revisionist interpretation that employs a Marxist perspective and focuses on the role blacks played in Reconstruction; and *Black Folk, Then and Now* (1939), in which Du Bois outlined the history of blacks in Africa and America. In addition to his nonfiction, Du Bois also published five novels during his career. *The Quest of the Silver Fleece* (1911) centers on a young black man who, after gaining some education, travels North, where he becomes involved in politics and then returns to the South to further the struggle of blacks for education and a better life. *Dark Princess,* published in 1928, concerns a young black man who, embittered by racism, leaves America for Europe, where he becomes involved in politics and a plot against colonialism. *The Black Flame* (1976) trilogy includes *The Ordeal of Mansart* (1957), *Mansart Builds a School* (1959), and *Worlds of Color* (1961). The trilogy centers on the life of a black man who strives to serve his race as a teacher. Though not gifted intellectually, the protagonist is honorable and through his story, Du Bois dramatizes the major events of black history in America and the culture of the American South. Capitalism is depicted in a negative fashion in the novels whereas socialism is portrayed in a positive light.

Critical Reception

Much of the commentary on Du Bois has centered on his controversial political views, particularly his turn toward Communism and support for Stalinism. His fiction, for example, has been largely ignored. Nevertheless, many of Du Bois's works are considered ground-breaking. *The Philadelphia Negro,* for example, was the first systematic study of an urban black population, while *The Souls of Black Folk,* scholars contend, remains one of the most profound and succinct delineations of the dilemma of black Americans. "The problem of the twentieth century is the problem of the color line," declared Du Bois to the Pan-African Congress in 1900, and his famous statement, which became the introduction to *The Souls of Black Folk,* has been hailed as prophetic. Despite the controversy that surrounded his ideas and actions throughout his lifetime, Du Bois continued to fight for equality between races. Arnold Rampersad wrote: "Far more powerfully than any other American intellectual, [Du Bois] explicated the mysteries of race in a nation which, proud of its racial pluralism, has just begun to show remorse for crimes inspired by racism."

PRINCIPAL WORKS

The Suppression of the African Slave-Trade to the United States of America, 1638-1870 (dissertation) 1896
The Philadelphia Negro: A Social Study (essay) 1899
The Souls of Black Folk: Essays and Sketches (essays) 1903
The Negro in the South, His Economic Progress in Relation to His Moral and Religious Development; Being the William Levi Bull Lectures for the Year 1907 [with Booker T. Washington] (lectures) 1907
John Brown (biography) 1909
The Quest of the Silver Fleece (novel) 1911
The Star of Ethopia (drama) 1913
The Negro (history) 1915
Darkwater: Voices from within the Veil (poems, essays, and sketches) 1920
The Gift of Black Folk: The Negroes in the Making of America (history) 1924

Dark Princess: A Romance (novel) 1928

Africa: Its Geography, People and Products (history) 1930

Africa: Its Place in Modern History (history) 1930

Black Reconstruction: An Essay Toward a History of the Part Which Black Folk Played in the Attempt to Reconstruct Democracy in America, 1860-1880 (history) 1935

Black Folk, Then and Now: An Essay in the History and Sociology of the Negro Race (history) 1939

Dusk of Dawn: An Essay Toward an Autobiography of a Race Concept (autobiography) 1940

Color and Democracy: Colonies and Peace (essay) 1945

The World and Africa: An Inquiry into the Part Which Africa Has Played in World History (criticism) 1947

In Battle for Peace: The Story of My 83rd Birthday (memoirs) 1952

*The Ordeal of Mansart (novel) 1957

*Mansart Builds a School (novel) 1959

*Worlds of Color (novel) 1961

†Selected Poems (poetry) 1964

The Autobiography of W. E. B. Du Bois: A Soliloquy on Viewing My Life From the Last Decade of Its First Century [edited by Herbert Aptheker] (autobiography) 1968

W. E. B. Du Bois Speaks: Speeches and Addresses [edited by Philip S. Foner] (speeches) 1970

The Emerging Thought of W. E. B. Du Bois: Essays and Editorials from "The Crisis" [edited by Henry Lee Moon] (essays) 1972

W. E. B. Du Bois: The Crisis Writing [edited by Daniel Walden] (essays) 1972

The Education of Black People: Ten Critiques, 1906-1960 [edited by Herbert Aptheker] (essays) 1973

*These works were published as *The Black Flame* in 1976.

†The publication date of this work is uncertain.

CRITICISM

Stanley Brodwin (essay date March 1972)

SOURCE: "The Veil Transcended: Form and Meaning in W. E. B. Du Bois' *The Souls of Black Folk*," in *Journal of Black Studies*, Vol. 2, No. 3, March, 1972, pp. 303-21.

[*In the essay below, Brodwin examines theme and structure in* The Souls of Black Folk *and remarks on Du Bois's presentation of black consciousness.*]

No student of black culture in American can escape the melancholy conclusion that, amid the wide range of human tragedy slavery and racism have inflicted on an entire race, black men of talent and genius have had to suffer in more complex ways than their less-gifted brothers. Apart from the general agony he shared with his brethren, the black artist or intellectual has always been forced to channel his natural abilities

and personal aims into political and social arenas where they could best be used to achieve civil rights and human dignity. Black intellectuals had to accept the sacrifice of personal ambition, recognizing that there were issues and causes that transcended individual goals. The spiritual compensations for such sacrifice could be great, as DuBois himself pointed out: "And to themselves in these days that try their souls, the chance to soar in the dim blue air above the smoke is to their finer spirits boon and guerdon for what they lose on earth by being black." But the price still had to be paid in order to soar above the smoke. The price was particularly heavy in literature, for no black writer could escape the racial imperative thrust on his work or person. Even the colonial poetess, Phillis Wheatley, whom Richard Wright described as being "at one" with her American culture and who carefully kept militant racial themes out of her work, was made the subject of racial controversy. Important nineteenth-century black writers such as William Wells Brown, James Madison Bell, David Walker, Frederick Douglass, Martin R. Delany, Frances E. W. Harper, Paul Laurence Dunbar, and Charles Waddell Chesnutt all had to turn their literary efforts into attacks against slavery, disenfranchisement, or cultural stereotyping, using a variety of strategies in their works to do so.

Novelists like Sutton Griggs (and Chesnutt) finally turned away from fiction as a weapon with which to break down racial injustices. In the twentieth century, the writers of the "Harlem Renaissance" struggled to reconcile the claims of art and propaganda, a problem debated by such contemporary figures as James Baldwin, Ralph Ellison, LeRoi Jones (Imamu Baraka), and Eldridge Cleaver. But in the whole spectrum of black writing from the colonial period until today, W. E. B. DuBois stands out as the one acknowledged genius who poured his energies into almost every literary form available to him. Indeed, he lived his thesis that the Negro is "primarily an artist." Today, however, despite his image as a propagandist, his academic reputation rests rightly on his great sociological and historical works, beginning with **The Suppression of the African Slave-Trade to the United States of America, 1683-1870** (1896). Yet he wrote a small body of effective poetry, five novels, an autobiography, and several volumes of what can only be called poetic essays which mix autobiographical and sociological matter. Out of all this work, **The Souls of Black Folk** (1903) alone has reached a wide audience, in more than twenty editions. In the burgeoning Black Studies programs throughout the country, it is required reading, and is now—belatedly—included in American history and literature courses in some universities. James Weldon Johnson, who himself was a fine writer and scholar, wrote that **The Souls of Black Folk** has had "a greater effect upon and within the black race in America than any other single book published in this country since *Uncle Tom's Cabin*." In short, the work has become an established part of American literary culture and history. However, apart from an occasional appreciative glance at the literary aspects of this unified collection of essays, the book has received no extended criticism.

When it is examined, it is nearly always in terms of DuBois' radical break with Booker T. Washington's accommodationism and its evocation of a new spiritually militant mood from the black intelligentsia. The book's most famous line, "The problem of the twentieth century is the problem of the color-line" is invoked as DuBois' central insight, though DuBois later revised this idea in terms of a more general Marxist orientation. And there is no doubt that the book was in the vanguard of a social revolution that was soon to create, under DuBois' aegis, first the Niagara Movement and then the NAACP. It is only when *The Souls of Black Folk* is studied as a literary phenomenon, however, that its true meaning emerges. For beyond the clear sociological analysis of the black man's plight during the nineteenth century, DuBois presents an intensely personal vision of how one man confronted and transcended the complex tragic life generated in living behind the veil of the color line. To this end, DuBois employed a variety of literary techniques handled with skill: rhetorical tropes, allegory, symbolic patterns, personal confession, biography, and musical motifs from the sorrow songs or spirituals. Using all these elements to create his organic vision, DuBois structured fourteen essays in the form of a neo-Hegelian dialectic whose stage of synthesis carried him—and by extension, all those who would follow—into a spiritual realm of historical and racial understanding that does not merely rend, but transcends the veil of color. This literary strategy is at once relevant to both black and white man, giving the work its universal dimension.

DuBois recognized the fact that the black community could not, with its weak power base, achieve a social revolution completely on its own. He was able to see the symbiotic relationship between white and black in America, and he strove to enlighten his white audience as to the specific psychological and economic tensions and bonds that affected both races. Therefore *The Souls of Black Folk* had to be not only a force in awakening black pride, but also a spiritual guidebook for whites, most of whom had little awareness of the genuine strivings and psychic realities in black folk. Like many black writers, DuBois had to speak to audiences of two different mental and cultural dispositions, and bridge the gap between them. He had to integrate the "protest" or propaganda aspects of the work with the purely descriptive and personal. And beyond both of these tasks—intrinsic to the very nature of black writing in America—DuBois had to reconcile the "twoness" within himself, if only to give personal validity to his larger social and spiritual aims.

All this DuBois sketches in for the reader in "The Forethought." He will talk about the spiritual strivings of blacks and the effect of emancipation upon them; he will talk of "the two worlds within and without the Veil," and the "central problem of training men for life." Finally, he will speak

of the "deeper recesses" of black souls. What this structure actually does is to delineate three major phases of black history and strivings. The first phase is that of revolt and freedom—the whole Civil War complex—the second phase is that of moral, intellectual, and economic adjustment, attendant with all the temptations of the white man's values for blacks, passivity in the face of white power, and the effect of personal tragedy on DuBois' own striving; the third phase deals with the necessity to affirm life in the face of tragedy as seen through Alexander Crummell, "John Jones," and the sorrow songs themselves.

Throughout this pattern runs the thread of DuBois' spiritual autobiography. In the first chapter, "Of Our Spiritual Strivings," DuBois tells us how, as a young man growing up in New England, he discovered the Veil between himself and his fellow white students, and how he "held all beyond it in common contempt, and lived above it in a region of blue sky and great wandering shadows." Here we have a passive transcendence which will gradually develop over the years into a dynamic and intellectual action. But this passive transcendence enabled DuBois to reflect upon his own inner life and that of his race. Reflection yielded two spiritual poles around which the whole work revolves: self-consciousness and culture. Indeed, it would not be an oversimplification to say that these two concepts embodied the values implicit in DuBois' whole life. For he saw that the Negro—"born with a Veil"—lived in a world which "yielded him no true self-consciousness, but only lets [sic] him see himself through the revelation of the other world." A black man "ever feels this twoness—an American, a Negro; two souls, two unreconciled strivings." Therefore, the "history of the American Negro is the history of this strife—this longing to attain self-conscious manhood, to merge his double self into a better and truer self." This "truer self" admits of no subordination of one side to another. Although DuBois did push his American identity aside in order to affirm his being a Negro when he came to Fisk University, at this point he wishes only to make it possible "to be both a Negro and an American." The result of this synthesis is to allow the Negro to be a "co-worker in the Kingdom of culture." DuBois knows, too, what the pitfalls will be before one can reach such a synthesis. For in his attempt to be a coworker, the Negro may actually find himself slipping backward instead of going forward. Indeed, as DuBois asserts: "real progress may be negative and actual advance be relative retrogression." To dramatize the Negro's problem in this respect, DuBois employs the Greek myth of Atalanta and Hippomenes:

> Perhaps Atlanta was not christened for the winged maiden of dull Boeotia; . . . swarthy Atalanta, tall and wild, would marry only him who outraced her; and how the wily Hippomenes laid three apples of gold in the way. She fled like a shadow, paused, startled over the first apple, but even as he stretched his hand, fled again; hovered over the second, then,

slipping from his hot grasp; flew over river, vale and hill; but as she lingered over the third, his arms fell around her, and looking on each other, the blazing passion of their love profaned the sanctuary of Love, and they were cursed. If Atlanta be not named for Atalanta, she ought to have been.

DuBois was troubled that the growth of industrialism in the South would gradually brutalize the last vestiges of a Southern humanistic tradition though feudal myths might still linger in them. The goal of wealth was replacing the Platonic ideals of "Truth, Beauty, and Goodness" and posing a genuine spiritual threat to the "Black World beyond the Veil." In a vivid image, DuBois sees "this young black Atalanta" infected with "mammonism," degenerating into an economic miscegenation with the South: "lawless lust with Hippomenes."

It is this condition—or temptation—that makes the Negro peer into himself "darkly as through a veil." Here the allusion to St. Paul's message to the Corinthians carries the double suggestiveness as to what black salvation is in the dark veil-mirror of existence, and as to what might be the depth of black guilt if the race cannot penetrate to spiritual values instead of material ones. For the black man may see himself, as all others, darkly, *affirmatively,* and save himself for himself. "So," DuBois writes "dawned the time of *Sturm und Drang"* within the black soul. The storm and stress is, of course, also within the whole structure of black adjustment to emancipation and the economic stresses that soon followed. These problems are studied carefully in the essay on Booker T. Washington, whose compromising speech at the Atlanta Exposition in 1895, according to DuBois, set back the black struggle for manhood and civil rights. And in the essays **"Of the Wings of Atalanta"** and **"Of the Training of Black Men,"** DuBois formulated his doctrine of the "Gospel of Sacrifice," insisting that young, dynamic blacks "learn of a future fuller than the past, and hear the voice of Time: 'Entbehren sollst du, sollst entbehren.'" Like Goethe's Wilhelm Meister [the protagonist of the play of the same name from which the preceding German quote was taken], they must learn to renounce, and renounce they must. DuBois is grateful to the Freedmen's Bureau for what it was able to accomplish for Negro education during Reconstruction, though it failed to fulfill its purposes entirely; he is grateful for the New England "schoolmarms" who came down South to teach blacks; but the Negro intellectual elite, the Talented Tenth, was not being reached. Under the control of Southern white money, Negro schools were kept basically industrial and second-rate, blunting the drive toward a genuine higher education blacks so desperately needed, but which seemed to threaten white supremacy. The question of higher education was DuBois' *idée fixe,* and he strove to be a living example of black intellectual accomplishment. DuBois wrote of the universities that they must be the "Wings of Atalanta" which will bear the Negro past the "temptation of the golden fruit." The university was central for the movement that would lead blacks into a meaningful synthesis between self-consciousness and culture:

> The function of the Negro college, then, is clear: it must maintain the standards of a popular education, it must seek the social regeneration of the Negro, and it must help in the solution of problems of race contact and cooperation. And finally, beyond all this, it must develop men. Above our modern socialism and out of the worship of the mass, must persist and evolve that higher individualism which the centers of culture protect; there must come a loftier respect for the sovereign human soul that seeks to know itself and the world about it; that seeks a freedom for expansion and self-government; that will love and labor in its own way untrammeled alike by old and new.

This is a statement that derives from DuBois' immersion in New England intellectual life as well as his own firsthand knowledge of black needs; it is a statement that consciously evokes the values and rhetorical language of Emerson and William James. For we must not forget that DuBois studied with James at Harvard and held him in supreme regard.

The Souls of Black Folk has to be not only a force in awakening black pride, but also a spiritual guidebook for whites, most of whom had little awareness of the genuine strivings and psychic realities in black folk.

—Stanley Brodwin

At the end of this chapter, DuBois brings his personal dialectic to its climax. His blackness (thesis) and his Americanness (antithesis) have been bridged by learning, teaching, and confronting the duality within himself; then, bearing himself past the temptation of the golden apples which threatened to destroy any spiritual reconciliation, DuBois is at last able to penetrate to his own self-consciousness and culture (synthesis):

> I sit with Shakespeare and he winces not. Across the color line I move arm in arm with Balzac and Dumas, where smiling women glide in gilded halls. From out the caves of evening that swing between the strong-limbed earth and tracery of the stars, I summon Aristotle and Aurelius and what soul I will, and they come all graciously with no scorn nor condescension. So, wed with Truth, I dwell above the Veil.

Here DuBois has replaced the lure of the golden apples with

the lure of the knowledge that transcends color; in so doing, he has made himself the incarnation of the ideal which perceptive white, as well as black, men cherished. A meeting ground is established for both races, but it is a ground which implicitly flatters and inspires each at the same time.

While a dialectic progression to a high synthesis was perhaps DuBois' most important strategy of form, he did not ignore other techniques. One of the most important of these is thematic imagery. As a man "who probably felt much more poetry than he wrote," DuBois was well aware of the powerful impact vivid imagery makes in any kind of literature. At least two of his poems, **"The Song of the Smoke"** (1899) and **"A Litany at Atlanta"** (1906) are notable for their remarkable images and have become indispensable to any study of black poetry in America. *The Souls of Black Folk* contains a wide range of imagery which derive from four main sources: war, the Bible, Greek mythology, and nature. DuBois speaks of the "advance guard" of young black students climbing toward their "Canaan"; of the need to use the ballot as a "weapon" against gradual disenfranchisement and economic rape; of the need for the white man to know that if "your heart sickens in the blood and dust of battle," for a young black boy "the dust is thicker and the battle fiercer." There is the necessary warning that the black will grasp at a "gospel of revolt" if his conditions are not ameliorated. DuBois said clearly that "the doctrines of passive submission embodied in the newly learned Christianity" and wielded by that all-important life-phenomenon for the black—his church—were creating "a note of revenge" in the souls of his people genuinely seeking freedom.

Biblical imagery and allusions appear constantly in *The Souls of Black Folk,* and I have already alluded to a few of them. DuBois accepted—as a basic metaphor, if nothing else—the traditional black identification with the Children of Israel and the search for their Promised Land. DuBois' language often takes on biblical rhythm and syntax as when he cries "Why did God make me an outcast in mine own house?" After speaking of his being "wed with Truth," DuBois asks America: "Are you so afraid lest peering from this high Pisgah, between Philistine and Amalekite, we sight the Promised Land?" Then there is the religious "awakening," when "the pent-up vigor of ten million souls shall sweep irresistibly toward the Goal, out of the Valley of the Shadow of Death, where all that makes life worth living—Liberty, Justice, and Right—is marked 'For White People Only.'" The universal biblical image of death is repeated, most poignantly, in the chapter on the death of his son, "Of the Passing of the First-Born." The "Shadow of Death" covers his child, who was born within the Veil. DuBois had struggled to transcendence through sacrifice and knowledge, but his child achieved it through death:

> Are there so many workers in the vineyard that the fair promise of this little body could lightly be tossed away? The wretched of my race that line the valleys

of the nation sit fatherless and unmothered; but Love sat beside his cradle, and in his ear Wisdom waited to speak. Perhaps now he knows the All-love, and needs not to be wise. Sleep, then, child—sleep till I sleep and waken to a baby voice and the ceaseless patter of little feet—above the Veil.

Yet, in the following chapter, "Of Alexander Crummell," he uses the same imagery with a note of affirmation. For Alexander Crummell, a remarkable black clergyman who spent many years in Africa as well as America fighting for black dignity and culture, triumphed over the "temptation[s] of Hate . . . Despair . . . and Doubt, that ever steals along with twilight. Above all, you must hear of the vales he crossed, — the Valley of Humiliation and the Valley of the Shadow of Death." We immediately think of Bunyan's *Pilgrim's Progress,* as DuBois wishes us to do, and to see in Crummell a black Christian who will one day sit with a King: "a dark and pierced Jew, who knows the writhings of the early damned, saying, as he laid those heart-wrung talents down, 'Well done!' while round about the morning stars sat singing."

Along with biblical patterns and images, DuBois exploited the Greek tradition in Western culture. The myth of Atalanta and Hippomenes was used to penetrate the dilemma young black intellectuals found confronting them. In the chapter "Of the Quest of the Golden Fleece," DuBois uses another myth to illuminate the plight of the black worker and sharecropper. The essay is a brilliant analysis of the economic conditions in the ante- and postbellum South and the role cotton played in shaping them. Land values, rent, crops, and the economic heritage of slavery are all discussed, and it is made clear how the black man was forced into unending debt and peonage. The golden fleece of cotton now covers a "Black and human sea" in America, far from its mythical home in Asia Minor, the Aegean and Black Sea lanes where . . . "one might frame a pretty and not far-fetched analogy of witchery and dragon's teeth, and blood and armed men, between the ancient and the modern quest of the Golden Fleece in the Black Sea." The wry pun on the Black Sea gives the passage a glint of bitter humor, but the conception as a whole makes startlingly vivid the transformation of the past's noble and imaginative mythology into the dehumanizing Southern myth of King Cotton and the pseudo-aristocratic plantations built on serf-black labor. Indeed, the city of Atlanta, Queen of The Cotton Kingdom, had already been dubbed by DuBois as the "new Lachesis, spinner of web and woof for the world." DuBois well knew he was struggling against a system which seemed to most blacks fate itself.

Finally, one passage may be used to illustrate DuBois' frequent use of nature imagery in vivifying his narrative. He is imagining Crummell's confrontation with Bishop Onderdonk, a corpulent white clergyman who has rejected the idea of Negro representation in his Church convention:

I seem to see the wide eyes of the Negro wander past the Bishop's broadcloth to where the swinging glass doors of the cabinet glow in the sunlight. A little blue fly is trying to cross the yawning keyhole. He marches briskly up to it, peers into the chasm in a surprised sort of a way, and rubs his feelers reflectively; then he essays its depths, and, finding it bottomless, draws back again. The dark-faced priest finds himself wondering if the fly too has faced its Valley of Humiliation, and if he will plunge into it—when lo! it spreads its tiny wings and buzzes merrily across, leaving the watcher wingless and alone.

The imagery that DuBois employed in *The Souls of Black Folk* was the kind familiar to most intelligent readers at that time. DuBois used such imagery not only because he was imbued with traditional nineteenth-century notions of literary culture, but because the imagery created an esthetic commonality between himself and his white reader. At the same time, his display of well-earned erudition and easy familiarity with the cultural signs of the white world helped to elevate the image of the black mind in many reader's eyes.

It is the chapter "Of the Coming of John," however, that best reveals the peak of DuBois' art in *The Souls of Black Folk*. Here is a section that can easily stand as a self-contained short story and which contains all the lineaments of that genre. Description of locale, characterization, plot, and imagery all combine to make it a paradigm of DuBois' tragic vision which remained darkly at the back of his thrust be transcendence. The bare outline of the story suggests a racial tragedy more reminiscent of Richard Wright's early tales in *Uncle Tom's Children* than what we would expect from DuBois' profound sociological genius. Young "John Jones" is a "long, straggling fellow" forever late for his classes at a preparatory school in Georgia, but a constant source of high merriment to this schoolmates. A good-natured but lazy student, he gets suspended, only to work his way back to school and college. Now filled with the seriousness of life, John returns to his hometown, Altamaha by the sea, in Southeastern Georgia. His family and the black community await his coming in joy and trepidation. At the same time, the son of the town's white judge arrives from Princeton. The two boys had met at a performance of Lohengrin, and the black John had to give up his seat to the white John, who could not acknowledge the black youth he had known as a playmate. The black John, now a chastened young man of profound depths, returns home to teach according to the Judge's rule of preventing "fool ideas of rising and equality" coming into his people's minds. But John begins to teach "dangerous" notions—in particular, the ideas of the French Revolution. His school is, of course, closed. After the judge's decision, the white John, himself now aimless, drifts off into the woods where he meets and attempts to seduce a Negro kitchen maid. The black John, having decided to leave Altamaha and to follow the "North Star," also wanders into these same woods, brooding on his

defeat. Seeing "his dark sister struggling in the arms of a tall and fair-haired man," he silently picks up a fallen limb and kills him. Then, as in a daze, he remembers his early prankish school days and the discovery of his identity while the melodies of Lohengrin pass through his mind. He sits and waits for the lynch mob to get him, but can only feel pity for the "haggard white-haired man" with the rope. His eyes closed, John turns toward the sea, "and the world whistled in his ears."

The character and destiny of John Jones are clearly a merging of two symbolic types; he is in the first instance the embodiment of the tragic fate implicit in the black man's striving to get beyond the debased heritage of slavery. When John comes to talk at his Church, he reflects only on "what part the Negroes of this land would take in the striving of the new century." His sister can only ask him, "does it make every one—unhappy when they study and learn lots of things?" His answer can only be that it does. As a sign of her own awakening depth and response to John, she too now wishes to be unhappy. The irony is that racism will not even allow the Negro the luxury of his unhappiness, an unhappiness born out of his newfound but stifled awareness of identity and world culture. Such frustration, DuBois makes clear, can and does create an inner resentment and despair so deep that violence becomes the last meaningful action. In the end, John—and the Negro—nevertheless achieve a moral dimension denied to the white and a pure, though isolated, relation to "The great brown sea" of nature. Second, John is a black John the Baptist preparing a way in the wilderness for salvation through knowledge. At the Church, John can only scold the bickering Baptists and Methodists:

> "Today," he said, with a smile, "the world little cares whether a man be a Baptist or Methodist . . . so long as he is good and true. What difference does it make whether a man be baptized in river or washbowl, or not at all? Let's leave all that littleness, and look higher." Then thinking of nothing else, he slowly sat down. A painful hush seized that crowded mass. Little had they understood of what he said, for he spoke an unknown tongue, save the last word about baptism; that they knew, and they sat very still while the clock ticked.

He is another voice crying in the wilderness. But this black John, emancipated from the fundamentalist traditions of his fathers, has no Savior to turn to, unless it is the freedom of the mind itself. And though he kills in the end, that inner freedom is not lost, though it is rendered impotent to change the world. John is lynched—America's version of crucifixion—but there seems little hope that its meaning will be recognized. There is only vengeance and countervengeance. Throughout the story there runs the poetic motif of the sea which gives a rich and universal quality to its mood. John Jones "came to us from Altamaha . . . where the sea croons to the sands and the sands listen till they sink half drowned beneath the waters, rising only here and there in long, low is- lands." And when he goes to New York after his graduation, the hurried masses remind him "of the sea . . . so change- lessly changing, so bright and dark, so grave and gay." Most significantly, John drifts into a vision of his home, his mother, and his sister as he listens to the music of Lohengrin: "And his heart sank below the waters, even as the sea-sand sinks by the shores of Altamaha, only to be lifted aloft again with that last ethereal wail of the swan that quivered and faded away into the sky." This is the sea toward which he turns his closed eyes at the end of the story, the sea whose movement from ebb to flow symbolically drowns and then regenerates his heart's needs. For John belongs to Altamaha and its rice fields, the natural beauty of the earth he is heir to, the tragedy of the black man in the midst of it all; yet he is also heir to that mystic world of the knights of the Holy Grail whose quest in his own way he emulates. Indeed, DuBois may well have meant to suggest symbolic parallels between John and Lohengrin. Both characters are charged with mystically con- ceived missions; Lohengrin must keep his identity a secret in order to do good; John must find his identity; both meet treach- ery. But Lohengrin can return to the Knights of the Holy Grail having freed Gottfried from being a swan; John frees a sister and faces a lynch mob with only a dream of the sea beyond in his mind. The reality of the black man in the American South and the high mystic romanticism of Wagner symbolize two contradictory states of being, but for DuBois the contradic- tion can be resolved by the capacity of the mind to synthesize and transcend experience. John begins as stereotype and ends as a doomed but self-conscious and cultured hero. He is at once an individual and "collective" hero. In him reside the souls of black folk. Sociology and poetry are harmoniously merged.

DuBois chose to end *The Souls of Black Folk* with an im- passioned analysis and appreciation of Negro spirituals, or "sorrow songs." Beginning with "Nobody Knows de Trouble I See," in the first essay, he prefaces a bar of music from various spirituals to each succeeding essay, thereby giving the reader a chance, musically, to *feel* the particular pathos so fundamentally part of the black's "soul beauty." Many of the great spirituals are represented: "Swing Low, Sweet Chariot," "Roll, Jordan, Roll," "My Way's Cloudy," "Steal Away to Jesus," and others. Each spiritual, as DuBois carefully points out was chosen to make a musical comment on the chapter it prefaced. But what DuBois centers on, despite his clear pride and exultation in the Fisk Jubilee Singers and their contribu- tion to American music, is the way the sorrow songs reflect a primal and vital African past. He sees clear differences among the songs, differences which again demonstrate cultural vari- ety and growth: "The first is African music, the second Afro- American, while the third is a blending of Negro music with the music heard in the foster land. The result is . . . distinc- tively Negro . . . but the elements are both Negro and Cauca- sian." DuBois feels that the sorrow songs in themselves are cultural proof as to how deep the black man's spirit has pen-

etrated white America's. This is yet another synthesis that, if rightly appreciated, describes the "soul" of black folk. Here is yet another key to transcendence:

> Even so is the hope that sang in the songs of my fa- thers well sung. If somewhere in this whirl and chaos of things there dwells Eternal Good, pitiful yet mas- terful, then anon in His good time America shall rend the Veil and the prisoned shall go free.

In terms of DuBois' overall strategy in *The Souls of Black Folk,* the sorrow songs fulfill a vital stylistic function. Their profound and direct emotionalism conveyed through the im- ages of a folk spirit, help to balance and soften DuBois' own literarily sophisticated stance. Images like "There's a little wheel a-turnin' in a-my heart," and "I know moonrise, I know star-rise / I walk in the moonlight, I walk in the starlight / I'll die in the grave and stretch out my arms," stand in striking contrast to DuBois' own intense rhetoric often saturated with alliteration: "Even so is the hope that sang in the songs of my fathers well sung." DuBois frequently uses inversions and lapses, occasionally, into language like "Lo," "anon," and "hark!" He employs archaic biblical forms such as "Hast thou." His prose is often "purple" and even quaint: "I have seen a land right merry with the sun, where children sing, and rolling hills lie like passioned women wanton with harvest." But the final poetic effect with which DuBois wishes to leave us is captured in the concluding spiritual, "Let us cheer the weary traveller / Along the heavenly way."

With all of DuBois' mighty efforts to affirm life and tran- scend the Veil, critics were still struck by a "note of pessi- mism" running throughout *The Souls of Black Folk.* And necessarily so. For DuBois saw the spiritual havoc the Veil played upon his race. The "double life . . . must give rise to double words and double ideals, and tempt the mind to pre- tence or revolt, to hypocrisy or radicalism." In 1903, DuBois saw "two groups of Negroes, the one in the North, the other in the South, represent these divergent ethical tendencies, the first tending toward radicalism, the other toward hypocritical compromise." DuBois' hope then was that the "deep religious feeling of the real Negro heart" would save blacks from such choices. And while radicalism and compromise have taken on new connotations in the contemporary scene, the rise of Martin Luther King and other black religious leaders perhaps gives credence to DuBois' view—despite the assassinations— and the still turbulent racial strife in America. Yet *The Souls of Black Folk* must be studied and read not only as political prophecy but as spiritual scripture. As Alvin F. Poussaint points out, "the whole concept of . . . black consciousness found its beginnings in the mind of DuBois." The real task of DuBois in *The Souls of Black Folk* was to render that con- sciousness palpable, as it were, and to invoke it so power- fully that it would have inspirational effect on black and white alike. His strategy was to translate social and historical "facts" into the perceptual framework of an ideal. Specific analyses or predictions might come in time to be revised, or even rejected, but the ideal—the "good, the beautiful, and the true"—had to be established in the hearts and minds of his readers. This DuBois achieved through an art form and style which made it possible to glimpse his own soul constantly striving to transcend the Veil.

Arlene A. Elder (essay date December 1973)

SOURCE: "Swamp Versus Plantation: Symbolic Structure in W. E. B. Du Bois' *The Quest of the Silver Fleece*," in *Phylon*, Vol. XXXIV, No. 4, December, 1973, pp. 358-67.

[*In the following essay, Elder discusses the themes of class, race, and morality in Du Bois's novel* The Quest of the Silver Fleece.]

Although in the past commentators on the writing of W. E. B. DuBois have concentrated upon his historical and sociological works, some recent critics are intrigued by his fictional presentation of the black adventure in America. Most of this new critical interest centers upon his trilogy, *The Black Flame* (1957-1961), a historically based saga of the Mansart family. DuBois' first novel, *The Quest of the Silver Fleece* (1911), is, nonetheless, equally interesting in its artistic presentation of the economic, political, and social forces shaping black life. It is a crowded and complex work, shifting its action from the rural South to Washington, D.C. and back again, and achieves its unity of plot and statement through a carefully constructed framework of contrasting symbols. *The Quest of the Silver Fleece* is structured upon the clash of two opposing world views, that of the Swamp and that of the Plantation. The Swamp represents all that is free, wild, joyful, and loving, the Plantation, all that is self-serving and exploitative.

DuBois successfully avoids the obvious trap of simplistically equating the Swamp with black life and the Plantation with white. While his main concern in the book is to demonstrate the physical and mental serfdom which trapped blacks even after Emancipation and to suggest effective courses of action to overcome this kind of slavery, he recognizes that some whites, too, were oppressed by economic and political conditions and that some blacks knowingly profited from the subservience of their people. Therefore, he presents self-sacrificial whites, like Miss Smith, the Northern schoolteacher who devotes her life to educating Southern blacks, and Afro-Americans like Caroline Wynn, who have capitulated to the world's injustice and wish only to manipulate it to their own advantage. Plantation and Swamp morality, then, have more to do with the tone of the soul than with the color of the skin.

Nor does DuBois paint the Swamp mentality as all good and the Plantation view as all evil. Primitivism, which is the weaker side of Swamp life, he shows as insufficient to advance a people in an industrial economy. Primitivism consists of limiting qualities, historically generated in blacks, such as the subservience, ignorance, and acceptance of degradation found in the swamp witch, Elspeth, which must be eliminated before blacks can compete with whites. Moreover, for all its inhumane aspects, the Plantation viewpoint does encourage ambition and a thirst for knowledge, which DuBois considers essential for any group's success. Racial, class, and even human advancement, then, rest for DuBois in the development of the best qualities of both philosophies.

The actual swamp in the book is an area a short distance from the white-dominated town and farms. It is both ugly and beautiful, a source of nightmares as well as dreams, of despair as well as hope, a spot where black exploitation has traditionally festered as well as the place where black self-determination could ultimately flourish.

Its first description suggests the danger, despair, and loss of vision which it represents: "Night fell. The red waters of the swamp grew sinister and sullen. The tall pines lost their slimness and stood in wide blurred blotches all across the way, and a great shadowy bird arose, wheeled and melted, murmuring, into the black-green sky." Deep in the darkness of the swamp is the hut of Elspeth, "an old woman—short, broad, black and wrinkled, with fangs and pendulous lips and red, wicked eyes." It is in this hut that local white men gather at night to drink and carry on the ante-bellum tradition of sexually exploiting black women.

Zora, the wild, ignorant "elf-girl," was born in the swamp and knows it intimately. Hating Elspeth, her mother, and the sordid life at the hut, she lives in a private world of fantasy, conjuring up creatures symbolic of both the beauty and ugliness she sees around her. "And over yonder behind the swamps," she imagines, "is great fields full of dreams." Zora's dreams, spawned by the contrasts she observes, hang "like big flowers, dripping dew and sugar and blood." The inhabitants of her dream-land reflect both the hope and despair of her life:

> "And there's little fairies there that hop about and sing, and devils—great ugly devils that grabs at you and roasts and eats you if they gits you! . . . Some devils is big and white, like ha'nts; some is long and shiny, like creepy, slippery snakes; and some is little and broad and black. . . ."

Many of the blacks of the region bedevil themselves and participate in the creation of their own hell by rejecting the education Miss Smith offers and forgetting any dreams they once had of escaping the oppressive conditions of tenant farming. Because they cannot read the contracts they are required to sign, they ignorantly bind themselves for life to the wealthy white Cresswells. At first, they even reject the chance for self-determination which Zora offers them with her plan for a black-run farming commune. They cling, instead, to the old gospel of happiness-in-the-hereafter fed to them by the self-serving Preacher Jones. Ignorance, fear, jealousy of each other, despair, and hopeless acquiescence in their own debasement are the self-defeating qualities which the hag, Elspeth, and the terrible "gray and death-like wilderness" of the swamp represent.

There is, however, a beautiful, joyous, vibrant aspect to the swamp which is reflected in the souls of some of the black and white characters. Zora, "black, and lith, and tall, and willowy," with her music, her poetry, and her dreams is DuBois' most striking representative of good Swamp qualities. Despite the area's general gloom, at times the "golden sun" pours "floods of glory through the slim black trees," and "the mystic sombre pools [catch] . . . and [toss] . . . back the glow in darker duller crimson." The intensity of this description is reflected in Zora, her "heavy hair" bursting from its fastenings and lying "in stiffened, straggling masses, bending reluctantly to the breeze, like curled smoke." She recognizes in herself the pent-up aspirations of her people and dreams eventually not of her childhood devils and dripping blood but of the escape from Elspeth which Miss Smith and the world beyond the swamp offer to her.

Her plans for escape are dependent upon the Silver Fleece, the special crop of cotton which she and Bles grow on her island deep in the swamp. From its sale, she intends to finance her education. DuBois extends the symbol of the Fleece to include all the cotton grown in the South and uses it to reveal the close relationship Southern blacks feel with the soil and the difference between this kinship and the Plantation mentality's emphasis upon property and profits.

"I don't like to work," Zora once confided to Bles. "You see, mammy's pappy was a king's son, and kings don't work. I don't work; mostly I dreams. But I can work, and I will—for the wonder things—and for you." As a matter of fact, she works until her hands are raw and bleeding, clearing the island to plant the magic cotton seeds. She even comes close to losing her life in a flood, building dikes to protect her young crop. The tender, young cotton sprouts become her new "dream-children, and she tended them jealously; they were her Hope, and she worshiped them."

It is thematic that it is Elspeth who provides the seed, "wonder seed sowed with the three spells of Obi in the old land ten thousand moons ago," and sows it herself in a ritual during the dark of the moon. Its product is magnificent, but neither its inherent value nor Elspeth's magic is sufficient to guarantee Zora's success in an exploitative society.

Although Zora's relationship to the Silver Fleece is intensely personal, her love of the land and complete involvement in the creative process of growth is representative of the attitude of her people. Bles rapturously describes the sprouting cotton to Mary Taylor, his Northern-born teacher: " . . . we

chop out the weak stalks, and the strong ones grow tall and dark, till I think it must be like the ocean—all green and billowy; then come little flecks there and there and the sea is all filled with flowers—flowers like little bells, blue and purple and white." Other blacks, "huge bronze earth-spirits," who harvest the crops do so joyously, although they know that most of the profits from their labor will fatten the pockets of the Cresswells: "The cry of the Naked was sweeping the world, and yonder in the night black men were answering the call. They knew not what or why they answered, but obeyed the irresistible call with hearts light and song upon their lips—the Song of Service."

DuBois recognizes worldwide economic forces at work in the production and sale of Southern crops. The blacks, most directly responsible for the cotton, however, know next to nothing about supply and demand or fair profits and wages. This ignorance, the author suggests, is one of the major reasons for black entrapment. Even when coupled with child-like joy in the harvest and pride in the land, black ignorance can only result in black powerlessness. Nevertheless, DuBois appreciates the richness of the workers' natural, creative relationship with the land and describes it lyrically: "All the dark earth heaved in mighty travail with the bursting bolls of the cotton while black attendant earth spirits swarmed above, sweating and crooning to its birth pains."

The Plantation viewpoint is most clearly distinguished from that of the Swamp by its purely economic attitude toward the cotton crop: ". . . the poetry of Toil was in the souls of the laborers. . . . Yet ever and always [*sic*] there were tense silent white-faced men moving in that swarm who felt no poetry and heard no song. . . ." To the white Southern landowners and their counterparts, the Northern speculators, the cotton sings only of profits. Plantation mentality, North or South, is paternalistic, exploitative, self-deceptive, and, ultimately, cruel.

Recognizing Zora's crop as the most valuable ever produced on their land, Harry Cresswell, nevertheless, denigrates it as "extra cotton," worthy only to be turned into lint, and through dishonest financial manipulation manages to cheat her of the entire crop and even to place her twenty-five dollars in his debt. Zora's loss is common. The blacks all find themselves deeper in debt after each year's toil. They are kept at their labor by false promises of freedom, cheated by contracts "binding the tenant hand and foot to the landlord," and threatened with being sold out and put in the chain-gang if they resist.

Nor is this exploitation aimed solely at blacks. Southern poor whites, employees in the mills which Northern capitalization brought with it, are as over-worked, cheated, and trapped as the black tenant farmers. In the third part of the novel, when it appears that the oppressed of both races might combine and, through their superior numbers, overwhelm the wealthy landlords, John Taylor, the Northern speculator, remarks, "even if they do ally themselves, our way is easy: separate the leaders, the talented, the pushers of both races from their masses, and through them rule the rest by money." Although the blacks, because of racial bigotry and their historical position as serfs in the South, are the primary victims of men of Plantation mentality, any member of a powerless minority is in danger.

Furthermore, the Plantation morality is no respecter of social rank. Not only poor whites, but Southern "aristocrats," as well, are in danger of becoming victims if they are ignorant of the economic complexities affecting them. The prospect of a poor cotton crop and the persuasive arguments of John Taylor convince Colonel Cresswell to forget his "southern honor" and to entangle his fellow cotton planters in a business deal from which he stands to make two million dollars in five years. When Taylor announces his plan to form an "All-Cotton combine" and corner the year's market, the Colonel asks, "And the other planters?":

> "They come in for high-priced cotton until we get our grip."
>
> "And then?"
>
> "They keep their mouths shut or we squeeze 'em and buy the land. We propose to own the cotton belt of the South."

At this revelation, Colonel Cresswell automatically starts from his seat and indignantly sputters something about betraying "southern gentlemen" to Northern interests. But the chance for tremendous profits quickly outweighs the sense of honor by which he likes to believe he lives, and he agrees to the scheme.

Taylor, as well as the Cresswells, is obviously a Plantation type. The only difference that DuBois recognizes between Northern and Southern manifestations of the attitude is the degree of self-deception Southerners have traditionally allowed themselves. In most matters involving other whites, Colonel Cresswell is much more honest than John Taylor. "But there was one part of the world which his code of honor did not cover," and this was the part inhabited by blacks. Despite the fact that he, himself, has a mulatto granddaughter, he still looks upon blacks as inherited property. As long as they remain "faithful niggers" like Johnson and Preacher Jones, the Colonel ignores them, cheating them periodically in the comfortable, time-honored way, content to be oblivious to their existence. When blacks try to break out of the rigid class-race structure of Plantation economics, however, as Zora does with her Silver Fleece, or when she attempts to buy the swamp for her farm commune, he is willing to per-

jure himself and others to maintain the status quo. "The uninitiated," DuBois explains,

> . . . cannot easily picture himself the mental attitude of a former slave-holder toward property in the hands of a Negro. Such property belonged of right to the master, if the master needed it; and since ridiculous laws safeguarded the property, it was perfectly permissible to circumvent such laws. No Negro starved on the Cresswell place, neither did any accumulate property. Colonel Cresswell saw to both matters.

It is this fractured concept of honor which John Taylor most dislikes about his Southern father-in-law and business partner, and it his refusal to cooperate in cheating Zora of the swamp which leads to the destruction of their relationship. No less self-serving than Cresswell, Taylor, nevertheless, is a genuine admirer of talent and ambition, whether they belong to a white or a black. "The weak and the ignorant of all races he despised and had no patience with them." The able, he respects. And it is only the able, DuBois insists, who can hope to undermine Southern paternalism and overcome Northern indifference.

Throughout the first part of the novel, the story of Jason and the Golden Fleece appears as a mythic referent for DuBois' Plantation-Swamp dichotomy. The story is first alluded to by Mary Taylor, who, responding to Bles's lyrical description of the growth of the cotton, murmurs, "The Golden Fleece—it's the Silver Fleece!" Pleased by the opportunity to "uplift" one of her charges, she tells the boy of Jason and the Argonauts and is startled and puzzled by his response:

> "All yon is Jason's." He pointed with one sweep of his long arm to the quivering mass of green-gold foliage that swept from swamp to horizon. "All yon golden fleece is Jason's now," he repeated.
>
> "I thought it was—Cresswell's," she said.
>
> "That's what I mean." . . .
>
> "I am glad to hear you say that," she said methodically, "for Jason was a brave adventurer—"
>
> "I thought he was a thief."
>
> "Oh, well—those were other times."
>
> "The Cresswells are thieves now."

To Mary Taylor, the Jason myth embodies the values of ambition, daring, and heroism; to Bles, the "stealing" of the Fleece represents an immorality basic to an outlook which values property and power over people. The cotton means only gold to those Northerners and Southerners who maintain and enforce the Plantation system, rather than the bounty and beauty of the earth, as it does to Bles and his people.

The Jason story is also employed, however, to reveal the shortcomings of Swamp mentality. When Bles tells Zora of Jason and Medea, she asks,

> "Do you s'pose mammy's the witch?"
>
> "No; she wouldn't give her own flesh and blood to help the thieving Jason."
>
> She looked at him searchingly.
>
> "Yes, she would, too."

By maintaining her cabin for the pleasures of the local whites, Elspeth has sold Zora and others into a moral slavery. Her nonresistance increases her own helplessness and is reflective of the general condition of her people.

Weakness and ignorance, the dark sides of Swamp life, are qualities which both Zora and Bles realize that they and their race must outgrow. Both travel North in the second part of the novel in quest of personal development. What they find there is a political version of the Plantation morality which they hoped to leave behind in the South.

In his picture of Northern blacks, DuBois suggests that the victims of exploitation frequently adopt the very techniques which were used against them. The members of Washington's black middle class seem to Bles "at times like black white people—strangers in way and thought." Caroline Wynn, a confidante of white politicians and an influential force in black social circles, is cynical about the promises of the democratic system and is willing to compromise with the whites in power to mislead the black electorate if it means her own security and advancement.

"I use the world," she explains; "I did not make it; I did not choose it." Sophisticated in the intricacies of political manipulation, she undertakes to mold Bles into a charismatic, but controllable, racial leader. Her goal is not the elimination of the injustices of a racist society, but a secure foothold for herself within that society. She schemes to have Bles appointed Register of the Treasury and envisions herself, not as Mrs. Bles Alwyn, but as the wife of the new Register of the Treasury.

Bles's refusal to defend the Republican Party, after it has capitulated to Southern pressure and abandoned a racially important education bill, seals his political and personal fate.

The enraged Republicans drop him as quickly as they dropped the piece of legislation and fill the position of Register with Samuel Stillings, a "shrewd" black man who has jealously plotted against Bles all along. Just as rapidly, Caroline Wynn agrees to become Mrs. Stillings.

While DuBois clearly rejects the opportunism which determines Carrie Wynn's choices, he understands her, just as he understands Colonel Cresswell. Her youthful ambition to be recognized as an artist was quickly thwarted by the racial realities of Washington, D.C.: "she found nearly all careers closed to her." Even her job as a teacher is precariously dependent upon political circumstances. Her early disappointment, moreover, is daily reinforced by the insults of the jim crow city in which she must live. Her decision that idealism and honesty are commodities too dear and self-deceptive for Afro-Americans, DuBois realizes, stems from years of social and economic injustice.

Within the tensions of Caroline's and Bles's relationship, then, DuBois subtly reinforces the structural symbolism of the earlier part of the book. As a spokesman for the simple, hopeful members of his race, Bles insists upon absolute honesty in his dealings with both races in Washington. As a spokesman for those blacks who, because of disillusionment and a desire for wealth and power, have accepted the tactics of the Plantation, Carrie Wynn considers deception the only useful tool for the Afro-American. "Honesty," she tells Bles, is "a luxury few of us Negroes can afford." Limited by her desire for social acceptance and material advancement, she rejects Bles as an anomaly: "that good Miss Smith has gone and grafted a New England conscience on a tropical heart, and—dear me! —but it's a gorgeous misfit." This suggestion, that in order to succeed, blacks must continue the tradition of deception foisted upon them in slavery days, is every bit as destructive of racial progress as the particular kind of debasement practiced in Elspeth's cabin. Caroline Wynn wishes Bles to deceive other blacks about the intentions of the Republicans, thereby personally securing the Party's patronage. Elspeth receives free rent from the Cresswells for her services.

The third segment of the novel returns DuBois' protagonists to the South. Like Bles, Zora has encountered the power politics of Northern life and, through her betrayal by Mrs. Vanderpoole, has learned that self-reliance is the only solution for her people. Moreover, she has spent her time in the North well, educating herself through literature and observation to the complexities of the world at large. She returns to the swamp not as the defeated "elf child" who left it, but as a woman, worldly-wise, and dedicated to leading her people out of their morass of powerlessness.

What Zora learned in the North was the necessity of maintaining in her people the best values of the Swamp—their honesty, joy, and reverence of the land—while infusing them with cleverness and ambition, the best aspects of the Plantation. As she demonstrates in her handling of Colonel Cresswell when he attempts to cheat her out of the land she has purchased from him, she has become cognizant of the political changes which accompanied the industrialization of the South and understands the regional psychology well enough to predict local reactions to her efforts. She informs Bles that she intends to take Cresswell to court and believes that she stands a good chance of winning because the men in power in the town are no longer the landowners, but the rising lower class of whites who share, to some degree, her class concerns. Moreover, after studying the laws governing her land purchase, she intends to conduct the case against the Colonel herself: "as a black woman fighting a hopeless battle with landlords, I'll gain the one thing lacking . . . the sympathy of the court and the bystanders." When Bles replies incredulously, "Pshaw! From these Southerners?" she explains:

> "Yes, from them. They are very human, these men, especially the laborers. Their prejudices are cruel enough, but there are joints in their armor. They are used to seeing us either scared or blindly angry, and they understand how to handle us then, but at other times it is hard for them to do anything but meet us in a human way."

Like Caroline Wynn, Zora realizes the necessity of knowing the people with whom she must deal, recognizing their weaknesses and strengths, and turning them to her own use. Unlike her Northern counterpart, however, Zora intends to deceive no one, and her only selfishness is her ambition for her people. Furthermore, by the close of the book, she has moved beyond strictly racial concerns and sees her struggle as one in behalf of the oppressed class of both races.

It is fitting, in terms of DuBois' dichotomies, that Zora, not Bles, develops into the far-seeing political leader. Bles's defeat in Washington is predictable and demonstrates the powerlessness of ignorant idealism in the face of entrenched corruption. His defeat is an honorable one, of course, but does nothing toward advancing social justice. Zora's success, on the other hand, depends largely upon her perception of political realities. She is not tricked by traitorous blacks or manipulative whites because she sees her situation clearly and does not rely on either of these groups for help. The worst quality of the Swamp is the powerlessness and ignorance which fester in it; Bles, despite his training at Miss Smith's, demonstrates these traits in Washington. Zora moves from her sure knowledge of white values and laws and with the strength of black farmers committed to working with and for each other.

Even the love story between the two main characters can be understood in terms of DuBois's symbols. Bles's attitude toward Zora "had always been one of guidance, guardianship, and instruction. He had been judging her and weighing her from on high, looking down upon her with thoughts of uplift and development." This is, obviously, the same attitude as that of the most benevolent Southern whites towards blacks, one of superiority and paternalism. Bles rejects Zora because he discovers that life in Elspeth's cabin has left her "impure." He is concerned only with not appearing a fool in others' eyes and reveals himself finally insensitive to the realities of the master-slave relationship. Unlike Zora, he has been affected by the conventional standards of Mary Taylor; significantly, it is she who tells him of Zora's past. It is only when he suffers, himself, and realizes the insufficiency of his past training and returns to the swamp that he is enlightened enough to appreciate Zora's true worth.

Zora, even after she becomes a student in Miss Smith's school, resists Mary Taylor's instruction. Mary Taylor forfeits any claim she might have to moral superiority over her ignorant charges by despising the black students and eagerly becoming Mrs. Harry Cresswell in order to escape from her dark-skinned pupils to "the lighter touches of life . . . new books and periodicals and talk of great philanthropies and reforms." Echoing the sentiments of Booker T. Washington, DuBois's antagonist, and of most of the whites in the novel, she "believed it wrong to encourage the ambitions of these children to any great extent; she believed they should be servants and farmers, content to work under present conditions until those conditions could be changed; and she believed that the local white aristocracy, helped by Northern philanthropy, should take charge of such gradual changes." Zora becomes and remains a protegé of Miss Smith, who is frequently exasperated and outraged by her young, white colleague.

In *The Souls of Black Folk* (1903), the work for which he is most widely known, DuBois comments on the valuable contribution which the culture of Afro-Americans could make to American society: "all in all, we black men seem the sole oasis of simple faith and reverence in a dusty desert of dollars and smartness." "Smartness," nevertheless, is a quality he deems essential for his people and, despite his reservations about the effectiveness of the Freedman's Bureau, credits it with "best of all . . . inaugurat[ing] the crusade of the New England schoolma'am." Because of the nation's unwillingness to commit itself morally and financially to the development of the newly freed blacks, the Bureau eventually failed, and in 1903, DuBois could look around him and see that "in well-nigh the whole rural South the black farmers are peons, bound by law and custom to an economic slavery, from which the only escape is death or the penitentiary."

The Quest of the Silver Fleece is the fictional working out of this problem in American racial history. Its understandings are long-held concerns of DuBois; its symbolic structure is his attempt at an artistically effective framework for presenting his convictions about social, political, and economic tensions, North and South, black and white.

Irving Howe (essay date 1979)

SOURCE: "W. E. B. Du Bois: Glory and Shame," in *Celebrations and Attacks: Thirty Years of Literary and Cultural Commentary,* pp. 170-79. New York: Horizon Press, 1979.

[In the essay below, Howe contends that Du Bois's commitment to Communism and Stalinism at the end of his life "was soiled both morally and intellectually."]

If the name "Du Bois" means anything at all to most Americans, it is probably linked in their minds with those campus sects—the Du Bois clubs—that speak for Moscow-style Communism. Richard Nixon, with his special gift for parodying native follies, once suggested that the campus Communists were trying to capitalize on the phenotic kinship between the Du Bois clubs (*dew boys*) and the Boys Clubs (*da boys*). Actually, the Communists were quite within their rights, for in the last decade of his remarkable life—he died in 1963 at the age of ninety-five—William Edward Burghardt Du Bois had become a loyal and, it must be added, a courageous spokesman for Stalinism.

Most of his life Du Bois was something decidedly better. He was the first American Negro in the twentieth century to gain national recognition as intellectual, tribune, and agitator. Prickly, gifted, endlessly articulate, Du Bois was both sufficiently self-aware to see how his unavoidable embattlement had forced him, as he said, into a "twisted life" and sufficiently principled to keep right on battling. He taught, he exhorted, he prodded and shamed American Negroes into their climb from passivity to militancy. He was a scholar of some importance, both as sociologist of urban Negro life and historian of Black Reconstruction. He kept hammering away at the thick hide of American conscience, and by his example made ridiculous the racist nonsense in which Americans indulged themselves. Above all else, he was a formidable antagonist, tough in polemic, fierce with a phrase, impatient toward fools.

Hardly a tendency in Negro politics today, but it owes something to Du Bois. In the course of his long life he tasted the repeated defeats of the American Negroes and, with the energy of despair, kept changing his views, sometimes to place his stress on absolute integration and sometimes to fall back on a kind of segregated nationalism. His experience sums up almost every impulse and opinion among American Negroes. Yet this remarkable man is barely known today—we Americans are not very strong when it comes to historical memory.

Du Bois wrote two incomplete autobiographies, **Darkwater** at fifty and **Dusk of Dawn** when past seventy. The first shows Du Bois at the point in his career, surely the most interesting, when he had fought a hard battle against Booker T. Washington's creed of accommodation; the second shows Du Bois at a point when he had in effect turned his back on American society and accepted a quasi-nationalist view of the Negro struggle, which in some respects was similar to

that of Washington himself. The book now issued as his **Autobiography** was completed in 1960, when Du Bois was past ninety, and together with an account of his life in the Negro movement, every page of which is valuable, it includes sections on his travels in Russia and China and his harassment as a political suspect during the McCarthy years, every page of which is predictable.

International Publishers, the Communist house that has issued this book, fails to make clear that the **Autobiography** is by no means an entirely new piece of work; when it comes to commercial caginess, it has little to learn from bourgeois publishers. Nevertheless, the **Autobiography** is a work of considerable importance. Parts of it, dealing with Du Bois's youth and early years, form a classic of American narrative: composed in a lovely if old-fashioned formal prose, rich in portraiture of late nineteenth-century New England, and packed with information and opinion about the early years of Negro protest. Other parts read as if they came from a mimeograph machine.

The classical outcry of Negro autobiography in America is probably Richard Wright's *Black Boy,* a record of suffering so extreme and anger so harsh as to be almost beyond bearing and sometimes beyond belief. Claude Brown's *Manchild in the Promised Land* follows roughly in the same tradition. By way of contrast and correction, Ralph Ellison's scattered memoirs stress the inner strength and occasional joy of American Negro life; Ellison rejects the notion that all has been deprivation and insists upon the capacity of a people to create its own values and improvise its own pleasures. Nothing written by these or other gifted American Negroes prepares one, however, for the opening autobiographical pages of Du Bois, an account of his youth that seems quintessentially American in its pastoral serenity:

> I was born by a golden river and in the shadow of two great hills, five years after the Emancipation Proclamation, which began the freeing of American Negro slaves. The valley was wreathed in grass and trees and crowned to the eastward by the huge bulk of East Mountain, with crag and cave and dark forests. . . . The town of Great Barrington, which lay between these mountains in Berkshire County, Western Massachusetts, had a broad Main Street, lined with maples and elms, with white picket fences before the homes. The climate was to our thought quite perfect.

The black Burghardts had been living in this area since the late eighteenth century, part of a tiny enclave that hardly knew segregation or hostility. When the elder Du Bois, a man of mixed blood, came to Great Barrington, he joined a clan of Negroes who lived by farming, minor crafts, and service jobs: a world relatively comfortable and enjoying the stiff democracy of the New England town. All the traits we associate with New England—the Puritan stress upon work, the inbred life of the family, the personal styles of reticence and rectitude—seem to have been absorbed by these Negroes obscurely nestling in Western Massachusetts. And when Du Bois writes about his boyhood, he presents himself not so much as a Negro but as an American of an older and more virtuous age:

> The schools of Great Barrington were simple but good, well-taught; and truant laws were enforced. I started on one school ground, and continued there until I was graduated from high school. I was seldom absent or tardy. . . . We learned the alphabet; we were drilled vigorously on the multiplication tables and we drew accurate maps. We could spell correctly and read with understanding.

This was not, nor could it be, an untarnished idyll. Negroes, even when living in comfort, had an awareness of limited opportunities. Still,

> The colored folk were not set aside in the sense that the Irish were, but were a part of the community of long-standing; and in my case as a child, I felt no sense of difference or separation from the main mass of townspeople.

Bright in school, the boy found encouragement among the townspeople; once he bought Macaulay's *History of England* in five volumes, in 25-cent weekly installments; and when the time came for him to go to college, the local whites raised a purse, a sort of community scholarship.

What grips one in reading these pages is the story of a life that on almost every outward level follows the pattern of American industry and ambition yet must carry within itself the certainty of frustration, the doom of rage which American brutality toward the Negro still evokes. Young Du Bois seems to have sensed all this himself: he was class orator when he was graduated from school in 1884, but the address he gave was a celebration of Wendell Phillips, the Abolitionist leader. It is as if that "twisted life" about which decades later he would speak so bitterly had enforced itself upon his consciousness from the very start.

Yet the boy had never moved beyond the protected circle of Negro life in Western Massachusetts. He knew little or nothing, at first hand, about the life of American Negroes in the terrible years when the white South had reestablished itself through terror and the white North had sunk back into indifference. When the idea came up that he should go to Fisk University, a Negro school in Nashville, Du Bois's family objected strongly, for *they* must certainly have understood what their darling would encounter on a journey south. But their darling went, and it changed his life forever.

"Henceforward I was a Negro."

Some of the finest pages in the *Autobiography* describe Du Bois's work as a summer teacher in Eastern Tennessee, where he was greeted by the Negro farmers with a touching and absolute faith:

> I travelled not only in space but in time. I touched the very shadow of slavery. I lived and taught school in log cabins built before the Civil War. My first school was the second held in the district since Emancipation. . . .

Despite his difficulties in opening himself to other people—perhaps because of them—Du Bois proved to be a good teacher:

> I loved my school, and the fine faith the children had in the wisdom of their teacher was truly marvelous. We read and spelled together, wrote a little, picked flowers, sang, and listened to stories of the world beyond the hill.

Exposure to the post-Reconstruction South brought crucial lessons: "No one but a Negro going into the South without previous experience of color caste can have any conception of its barbarism." After Fisk, Du Bois was lucky enough to get into Harvard for graduate work, and as one of the very few Negroes then to be admitted there, he slipped still more deeply into the schizoid way of life from which, it now seems clear, he really had no escape: half pampered prodigy, half despised nigger. He studied with William James (who was genuinely kind) and Santayana; the years in the South had prepared him psychologically for the mixture of icy correctness and subtle segregation he would find in Cambridge; and he turned, by way of defense, into "a self-centered 'grind' with a chip on my shoulder." But meanwhile he was learning how to shape his life: he was learning to live inwardly, tensely, at a high emotional price but also from the incomparable resources of his pride. "I had my 'island within' and it was a fair country."

Picture him now at twenty-six: a young scholar who had done graduate work at Harvard and spent time in further study abroad; a bit of a dandy flashing a Van Dyke beard, elegant gloves, and a cane; yet stonebroke and glad to take a teaching job at Wilberforce University, a Negro denominational school, for $800 a year. In these years he commanded "a terrible bluntness of speech that was continually getting me into difficulty." Between his grating iconoclasm and the fundamentalist pieties of the Negro college at the turn of the century, there could be no lasting truce.

As Du Bois struggled through academic life—with a happy thirteen-year stay at Atlanta University, one of the few Negro schools that deserved to be taken seriously—he slowly carved out his special role. He would be both scholar and tribune, both a dispassionate student of the socioeconomic situation of Philadelphia Negroes and the leading spirit among those Negro intellectuals who set themselves the goal of the outer liberation and inner regeneration of their people. This was then, as now, an overwhelming task, for it required Du Bois to confront both white domination and black demoralization.

Atlanta was poor but hospitable. It gave Du Bois freedom to begin serious sociological studies of Negro life, to build a lively community of Negro scholars and intellectuals, and to hold his annual Conferences where the programmatic bases would be worked out for the Negro movements of tomorrow. The one thing modern history seems to bear out is that every movement for liberation requires first of all a totally committed intelligentsia, a vanguard of visionaries—and this Du Bois helped create. Living now in the Deep South, however, he could not work in isolation or without disturbance. Very soon he had to confront—which meant, unavoidably, to clash with—Booker T. Washington, then the dominant figure in American Negro life and one of the canniest politicians ever to operate in this country. Nothing in Du Bois's life, nothing in the history of twentieth-century American Negroes, is more important than this clash.

The standard "enlightened" view of Washington runs something like this:

When Booker T. Washington made his famous 1895 Address at the Atlanta Exposition, he offered the white South a *detente* which in effect meant a surrender. According to Washington, the Negroes would cede their claims to equal citizenship and would repress their struggle for political power, civil rights, and higher education. In return for this recognition of the supremacy it had just wrested through terror, the South would call a halt to lynching and wanton brutality, and would help the Negroes gain vocational training, so that they could find employment in crafts and new light industries.

White and Negro labor (I continue to summarize Washington's scheme) would be taken out of competition, by strict segregation in work and by granting the whites a near-monopoly of skilled employment. Negroes would be left with farm and unskilled labor. As a sweetener for this arrangement, Northern white philanthropy would enter the picture by providing financial help, so that the Southern Negroes could establish their craft and industrial training schools. Disfranchised and resigned to second-class status, the Southern Negroes would at least find a peace of sorts and be able to achieve some economic improvements.

For the militant Negro intellectuals led by Du Bois, this strategy seemed little short of a sellout. Du Bois opened the attack:

The black men have a duty to perform . . . a forward

movement to oppose a part of the work of their greatest leader. So far as Mr. Washington preaches Thrift, Patience, and Industrial Training for the masses, we must hold up his hands and strive with him. . . . But so far as Mr. Washington apologizes for injustice, North or South, does not rightly value the privilege and duty of voting, belittles the emasculating effects of caste distinctions, and opposes the higher training and ambition of our brighter minds . . . we must unceasingly and firmly oppose him.

Years later an authoritative Negro historian, J. Saunders Redding, would continue in the vein of Du Bois:

Having raised [Washington] to power, it was in white America's interest to keep him there. All race matters could be referred to him, and all decisions affecting the race would seem to come from him. In this there was much pretense and, plainly, not a little cynicism. There was pretense, first, that Washington was leader by sanction of the Negro people; and there was the pretense, second, that speaking in the name of his people, he spoke for them.

But what if, like it or not, Washington *did* speak for them? And still more painful, what if Washington's strategy was the only workable one for Southern Negroes at the turn of the century? These were questions that radicals, liberals, and militant Negroes never thought to ask—and for perfectly understandable reasons. During recent decades it has been necessary above all to break from the psychology of acquiescence which Washington had encouraged. But now that time has passed and some historical perspective is possible, we can see that the Du Bois-Washington battle was far more complex than we had supposed.

Booker T. Washington was in effect *the leader of a conquered people,* and a conquered people is never quite free to choose its own leaders. He was, if you like, the Pétain of the American Negroes, but far shrewder and far more devoted to his people than Pétain to the French. The evidence also suggests that Washington was sometimes a surreptitious de Gaulle, deeply involved in a quasi-underground resistance.

Professor August Meier, a historian whose sympathies are wholly with the civil-rights militants, has printed in the *Journal of Southern History,* May 1957, a fascinating account of the Washington-Du Bois struggle in which he presents a large amount of evidence to show that the issues between the two men cannot be reduced to acquiescence *vs.* militancy. Du Bois was an intellectual whose obligation it was to think in terms of long-range ends; Washington was a leader who had to cope with immediate problems. The white South had just achieved a counterrevolution in which Negroes had been reduced to near-slavery; in fact, as Washington made clear in his still-impressive autobiography *Up from Slavery,* the Negroes were in many respects worse off than before the Civil War. They were frightened, demoralized, and economically helpless. Simply to come to them and cry out for militant struggle in behalf of political enfranchisement or full integration, would have elicited no response from them, would have been of little help to them, and would have provoked ghastly retaliation from the white South.

Washington had therefore to maneuver from day to day, making the best he could out of an all but total defeat. He spoke deprecatingly of political rights in order to assuage the whites whose money and toleration he needed; but in practice, as Professor Meier shows, he covertly tried to preserve the Negro franchise and kept supplying funds for test cases in the courts.

Washington was an extremely skillful leader. He built up a network of semi-visible agents throughout the country, whom he kept under strict control by means of subsidies and shrewd tactical advice. He maintained close connections with the Republican party and especially Theodore Roosevelt, serving as its central agency for dispensing patronage (such as it was) to Negroes. He was friendly with some of the richest and most reactionary white industrialists. Professor Meier concludes: "Washington was surreptitiously engaged in undermining the American race system. . . . The picture that emerges from Washington's correspondence is distinctly at variance with the ingratiating mask he presented to the world."

Yet when Du Bois launched his fierce assaults upon Washington, he was clearly speaking to the point. For it was true that in large measure Washington had pledged the Negroes to the humiliations of Jim Crow. It was true that officially he had made peace with the reigning powers. It was true that he felt strong hostility toward the handful of Negro intellectuals who distrusted his political machine, his dictatorial methods, and his wily rhetoric.

Washington was not an attractive figure; he was a remarkable leader who helped sustain the morale of a broken people. And to the extent that he succeeded, he prepared the way for his own removal. Du Bois was a brilliant intellectual who insisted that only a program of unconditional equality could be acceptable to enlightened Negroes and who proposed as a major immediate task the training of a Negro elite, "the Talented Tenth," which might lead the black masses into struggle. In a recent biography of Du Bois, Mr. Francis Broderick provides a vivid sketch of their differences in personality and style:

> Washington, thick-set and slow-moving, had the assurance of a self-trained man. A shrewd, calculating judge of people, he had the soft speech and accommodating manners that made him equally at home among sharecroppers and at the President's table. A master of equivocation, he made platitudes pass as

earthly wisdom. . . . Du Bois, slight, nervous in his movements, never forgot for a moment his educational background. Proud and outspoken, he held aloof from the Negro masses, but felt at home with a small company of his peers. . . . Washington had the appearance of a sturdy farmer in his Sunday best; Du Bois, with his well-trimmed goatee, looked like a Spanish aristocrat. . . .

In the short run, there can be no doubt that Washington offered the Southern Negroes more than Du Bois possibly could, if only because Washington had an economic program which might slowly yield visible benefits. But Du Bois, in part because he lacked Washington's deep roots in Southern life and in part because he worked from a truly national perspective, opened the way for the decades of struggle that were inevitable. He might not be able to compete with Washington at the moment—what could he offer an industrious Negro hoping to learn carpentry?—but he was right in saying that even if Washington's entire program were realized it would not begin to solve the problems of the American Negroes. For as the historian Vann Woodward has remarked, "Washington's individualistic doctrine never took into account the realities of mass production, industrial integration, financial combination, and monopoly. . . . His training school . . . taught crafts and attitudes more congenial to the pre-machine age than to the twentieth century. . . ."

We see here one of those utterly tragic situations in which two enormously talented men are pitted against each other in ferocious struggle, each clinging to a portion of the truth, each perceiving a fraction of necessity, but neither able to surmount those objective barriers which the triumphant whites place before all Negroes, acquiescent or rebellious. The more men like Du Bois and Washington were penned in as Negroes, the more they were driven as Negro leaders to fight with one another. Yet from that war, at unmeasured cost, there emerged the Negro movement as we have come to know it. In 1905 Du Bois and a handful of intellectuals started the Niagara Movement, which put forward, with stirring bluntness, a program for unconditional equality. From the Niagara Movement there soon emerged the NAACP, in which Du Bois would spend a large portion of his life, as editor of its journal *Crisis,* as its main spokesman to the world at large, and as a hard battler within its ranks for whatever his ideas happened at a given moment to be.

The final years were somewhat less than glorious. Du Bois, whose whole life had been devoted to a restless experiment in unorthodoxy and rebellion, ended his life by lapsing into Stalinism, that dismal orthodoxy of the once rebellious. His pages about the Soviet Union show not the slightest trace of discomfort, even though they were written after the Khrushchev revelations. On the Hungarian revolution: "I was glad when the Soviet Union intervened and thus served notice on all reactionaries . . ." etc., etc. On China: "envy and class hate are disappearing." On Russia: "the overwhelming power of the working class . . . is always decisive."

What troubles one is not merely that such remarks are inane, but that Du Bois surrendered all those critical attitudes he had spent a lifetime sharpening. And this cannot be explained by senility; he kept his powers to a remarkable extent. I see, then, two ways of grappling with the problem, either of which could form a conclusion:

W. E. B. Du Bois suffered every defeat and humiliation of his people, and he kept changing his views because none seemed able to gain for American Negroes what should simply have been their birthright. Is it not entirely understandable that in his ultimate despair he should have turned to the ideology of Stalinism? That he should have ignored its repressions and murders, so long as it seemed to champion the rights of black men? What is surprising is not that Du Bois turned toward a totalitarian outlook but that so few Negroes joined him. To judge the octogenarian Du Bois is to display a failure in sympathy concerning the emotions of the oppressed.

To understand is one thing, to justify another. The explanation just offered for Du Bois's acquiescence in totalitarian politics may be quite correct, yet that does not remove the fact that he, so long a victim of injustice at home, became an apologist for injustice abroad. After all, there were other Negro leaders, equally militant, who found it possible to fight against Jim Crow in America without becoming apologists for dictatorship in Europe and Asia.

> **W. E. B. Du Bois suffered every defeat and humiliation of his people, and he kept changing his views because none seemed able to gain for American Negroes what should simply have been their birthright.**
>
> —*Irving Howe*

Which of these conclusions shall we accept? For me, at least, there can be no doubt. To refrain from saying that Du Bois's final commitment was soiled both morally and intellectually is to indulge in precisely the sort of condescension he had always scorned. Better to fight it out than "make allowances" because his skin was black. And besides, he wasn't the kind of man who needed allowances—not from anyone.

Walter C. Daniel (essay date June 1990)

SOURCE: "W. E. B. Du Bois' First Efforts as a Playwright," in *CLA Journal,* Vol. 33, No. 4, June, 1990, pp. 415-27.

[*In the essay below, Daniel remarks on Du Bois's first drama,* The Star of Ethiopia.]

By the time he arrived in New York City in 1910 to assume duties as director of research and publicity for the newly established NAACP, W. E. B. Du Bois was well on his way to becoming America's most prominent black scholar. Fifteen years earlier he had earned his Doctor of Philosophy degree at Harvard University and had studied in Germany with some of Europe's pioneer sociologists and distinguished German philosophers. He had conducted a study, ***The Philadelphia Negro,*** for the University of Pennsylvania, where he held a one-year appointment as a researcher, and had taught briefly at Wilberforce University in Ohio, where the black classics scholar William Sanders Scarborough was president. Leaving Wilberforce was a fortuitous move for both Du Bois and Scarborough, for the two of them could hardly find their own space in so small and so poor an institution. With all his promise as a dominating force in American academia, rigid racial segregation simply did not permit Du Bois the freedom which his superior abilities merited. Moving to Atlanta University in 1897 at the invitation of the president of that American Missionary institution that had become the capstone of black higher education in the deep South already for a quarter of a century, Du Bois came to full flower. He took charge of the sociological studies which the president had already initiated and which became the famous Atlanta University Publications. In the meantime he pursued another interest of his. Since his high school days in Great Barrington, Massachusetts, and his undergraduate years at Fisk University in Nashville, Tennessee, Du Bois had written news stories and features for periodicals. In the days before formal degrees in journalism, one expected university graduates to write for publication. Du Bois went further than writing. He published a "precious" magazine which he called *The Illustrated Moon* in Memphis from December 1905 until July 1906; and *Horizon: A Journal of the Color Line* in Washington, D.C., from January 1907 to July 1910. Although he had no part in the financial or editorial duties of the *Voice of the Negro* that was issued from Atlanta, Georgia, from January 1904 to October 1907, he became a regular contributor to it and inveigled its editor, Jesse Max Barber, to ally the magazine with the Niagara Movement.

When he came to his new position in the NAACP, Du Bois knew he would establish a magazine. In doing so, he would find a way to continue his interest in writing and editing. His ***Souls of Black Folk*** (1903) had already created uncommon attention in the nation. Its series of essays had become an "autobiography of the race" and had challenged Booker T. Washington's role as the premiere spokesman and power broker for black Americans. *The Crisis,* the NAACP's journal, became a critical element in Du Bois' rise to prominence. Members of the fast-growing NAACP received the magazine with their enrollment in the organization. At long last, the editor found a financial base far more secure than the precarious ones available to him in his other magazine ventures. Moreover, his new position placed him at the center of the American financial and publishing worlds. Wealthy white liberal philanthropists, joined with black intellectuals, made the support base for the NAACP. Within a few years after its first issue appeared, *The Crisis* became the best known and longest living black magazine in America. Du Bois edited it for 24 years.

Details of his long and distinguished career are fairly common knowledge. Less familiar is Du Bois' attempts to establish himself as an American playwright. When he was in graduate school at Harvard, he interacted with the black community in Boston. At one time, he directed a performance of Aristophanes' *The Birds* at the Charles Street African Methodist Episcopal Church. In later years he must have known about Henry Hugh Proctor's pageant *Up from Freedom* that was presented in August 1912 at the Atlanta Auditorium under the auspices of Proctor's Congregational Church. Both Proctor and Du Bois had been favorably impressed with the rise of the pageant at theatres in Europe. Formerly a member of the famous Fisk Jubilee Singers during his undergraduate student years at that institution, and the writer of a thesis on the theology of the songs of the American slaves for his graduate degree at Yale Divinity School, Proctor was a significant figure in the cultural and political life of Atlanta during the time that Du Bois worked at Atlanta University. Because Negroes were not permitted to attend the concerts that brought prominent metropolitan stars and other performers to the city, Proctor's church organized the Atlanta Colored Music Festival that presented its own festivals at the city auditorium. Proctor had also been one of the leading personalities in seeking to bring about racial harmony in the city following the devastating race riots in 1906. He was a close friend to Booker T. Washington. In fact, he had been Washington's official escort at the time the Tuskegeean delivered his historic "Atlanta Exposition Address" there. But Proctor was hardly a "Bookerite." He was not a complete devotee to either Du Bois or Washington during the years of their often-publicized controversy. He believed both in self-improvement and in good race relations. Unfortunately, little is known about any significant relationship between Du Bois and Proctor, perhaps because there was little. One can hardly help concluding, though, that the two men were aware of each other's thoughts about the pageant as a vehicle for educating Negroes about themselves and for addressing the ubiquitous Negro problem to the nation in a new key.

In a memorandum which he prepared for the NAACP Board of Directors in 1915, Du Bois wrote: "Four years ago, at a time of financial distress on the part of the Association, I wrote a pageant and presented it to the officers as a means of raising funds. After some consideration the officers decided that the plan was not feasible." His interest did not end with the Board's decision, however, for his active interest in writing for the stage continued for the next thirty years and yielded

some 25 or 30 scripts and sketches that make up some of the most interesting parts of his *Papers*. Beginning in 1913 and ending in 1923, he produced his historical pageants—the first in New York in 1913; the second in Washington in 1915; the third in Philadelphia; and the last one in Los Angeles in 1923. They were related to historical commemorations among black Americans in each of those cities; and they were a means of amplifying Negro achievements from ancient Africa to the contemporary milieu. They were also attempts to establish a black national theatre that was written by blacks about blacks and acted by blacks. His efforts antidated the Broadway successes written on Negro subject matter by Ridgeley Torrence, Eugene O'Neill, Paul Green, and Dorothy and DuBose Heyward. With NAACP chapters, *The Crisis,* and the theatrical stage, Du Bois anticipated a concerted national movement that would accomplish goals which the Niagara Movement had failed to bring to fruition. Simultaneously, he would replace Booker T. Washington as the major force in black America. Scientific study of sociology no longer interested him as it had in his work at Atlanta University. Through press and stage he would accomplish his personal, political, and artistic aspirations. How he would actually come to enter his not-very-successful career as the impresario of his own historical pageants has not been dealt with previously by scholars. Yet, his "Ethiopianism" plays are important documents of Afro-American cultural history.

Although many persons had spoken informally about the necessity for a national celebration for the fiftieth anniversary of the issuance of the Emancipation Proclamation, first formal efforts came through a letter to Booker T. Washington from a Professor E. L. Blackshear of Prairie View State College in Texas. Blackshear's letter was written to the *Star of Zion* newspaper of the A.M.E. Zion Church and reprinted in the *New York Age.* Richard R. Wright, Sr., president of black Georgia State Industrial College; Dr. J. W. E. Bowen, a member of the faculty of Gammon Theological Seminary in Atlanta and a former associate editor of the *Voice of the Negro;* and Robert R. Moton, then an official at Hampton Institute in Virginia who would succeed Washington as head of Tuskegee Institute, had presented the idea to the Executive Committee of the National Negro League, a vital organization established by Washington that was operating with chapters in some thirty states. That committee considered the matter and released its suggestions to the black press. The committee felt that because Congress had failed to appropriate funds for a national exhibition for this purpose, as had been called for by President Taft in his message to Congress in 1912, and inasmuch as 1913 was rapidly approaching, making it infeasible for an appropriate national exhibition to be planned and executed, the following action should be taken: (1) the third week in October 1913 should be set aside for the celebration and should be known as Fiftieth Anniversary Week; (2) instead of a central exhibition, schools and churches and all other societies and organizations in each community should unite and cooperate for the purpose of holding local celebrations that would exhibit the progress in commercial, professional, moral, intellectual, and religious directions that the race had made in these communities; (3) where it was convenient to do so, these commemorations should be held in conjunction with regular dates for holding county and state fairs; (4) special effort should be made to secure, in addition to the physical exposition, a program or appropriate speeches and other literary features; and (5) should the Congress make the appropriation that was being requested, it should be apportioned among the states to be expended under the control of the governor or some other state authority, in proportion to the number of Negroes residing in the different commonwealths.

This plan anticipated raising the county and state fairs into a semicentennial celebration. Negroes living in most Southern states were accustomed to holding these annual exhibitions that demonstrated farm products, particularly, that had been grown by black privately owned farms in the areas. President R. R. Wright of the Georgia State College for Negroes had been the executive officer for the state fair for Negroes in Georgia. It had been for several years a notably successful venture. In all cases, the exhibitions accentuated the products of industrial education as espoused by Washington and Wright. The plan outlined here would have been executed, no doubt, if Congress had actually funded the money. The debate over the enabling legislation in the United States Senate is particularly interesting and revealing of the terror of the times and some of the seldom-understood tensions between the followers of Washington's industrial education disciplines and Du Bois' advocates for higher education.

Senate Bill 180, passed by the 62nd Congress, 2nd session, April 2, 1912, literally launched W. E. B. Du Bois' limited career as a playwright. For introducing that legislation, titled "Anniversary Celebration of the Semicentennial Anniversary of the Act of Emancipation and for other Purposes," enabled Du Bois to produce his pageant, *The People of Peoples and Their Gifts to Men.* It was performed October 22-31, 1913, at the 12th Regiment Armory in New York City. During the previous year, 1911, a group of Negroes led by President Wright petitioned Congress to make an appropriation to support the project. Senate Bill 180 underwent several revisions during deliberation over its provisions in the Senate. It had been referred to the Committee on Industrial Expositions [on] February 2, 1912. When the measure reached the floor for final debate, its language read as follows:

> That whenever the President of the United States shall be satisfied that the Semicentennial American Emancipation Exposition Co., a corporation organized under the laws of the State of Georgia, has made provision for an exposition to be held during the year 1913, to illustrate the history, progress, and present condition of the Negro race, and to celebrate the fiftieth anniversary of the proclamation of emancipation by President Lincoln, on the 1st day of January,

> 1863, and that said corporation has raised and secured money or property to the amount of not less than $50,000 for the purposes of such exposition, the President is authorized and respectfully requested to make proclamation of the time and place and purpose of such exposition and celebration, of such other information in relations thereto as he may deem expedient.

Du Bois appeared before the subcommittee in order to explain the bill and to answer any questions the senators might want to raise. Most of them—even those who were favorable to the request—spoke of the opportunities that industrial education offered to the Negro. Some praised the race's progress. But few saw any virtue in an appropriation of a quarter of a million dollars for the celebration. National publications wrote glowingly of the accomplishments Negroes had made in the fifty years since the Emancipation Proclamation. Despite the rather wide support which the measure gained in the public press, Congress never appropriated the money for the national exhibition. State Representative John J. Fitzgerald from Brooklyn presented a bill to fund the Negro Exhibition in commemoration of the fiftieth anniversary of the Emancipation Proclamation in the New York State legislature. It provided $25,000 for that purpose. Governor William Sulzer appointed a local commission—all Negroes—to plan and carry out the celebration. The nine members were James D. Carr, an assistant corporation counsel in New York City; Robert N. Wood, a printer and member of Tammany Hall, the Democratic political organization in New York City; John R. Hillary, a chiropodist in Harlem; William A. Byrd, a Presbyterian minister; James H. Anderson, editor of the *Amsterdam News;* George H. Sims, a Baptist minister; J. B. Clayton, owner and operator of an employment agency in Harlem; J. H. Taylor, an A.M.E. Church pastor; and Du Bois. Conflict arose immediately over the format for the celebration and the names of persons who would be honored in the exhibits. Clearly, the Washington Du Bois controversy was present in the commission's deliberations.

By late September of 1913 plans for the exhibition had been announced. It was referred to as a "Negro congress." The state appropriation of $25,000 had been augmented by private gifts. Du Bois had won over the Washington forces. The exhibition was not to be one more of the county fair models. These affairs had highlighted industrial education. This one would consist of a series of floats, each depicting a scene typical of a phase of development of the race. The first would illustrate Negroes living in the Valley of the Nile and their contact with the Egyptians, and the last would be an allegorical tableaux suggesting "Hope and Encouragement for the Future." Between the two would come floats showing the intermediary stages of Negro development. This was the essence of the press releases Du Bois sent to the *New York Times.* Du Bois used *The Crisis* to explain his aspirations for the exhibition and to publicize it. He wrote in his "Along the

Color Line" monthly column that the affair should be distinctly and impressively educational. It would stress religious, economic, and cultural advances and concerns. Actually, Du Bois had planned a series of pageants for the exhibition. Each would represent a special feature of the commemoration. He wanted the event to cover ten days, including special emphases on Governor's Day, Douglass Day, and Lincoln Day. The exhibits would comprise thirteen separate divisions. They would follow roughly the subjects of the Atlanta University Publications. They would be housed in a small central temple designed by a black architect that would contain sculpture and a library of black newspapers and books. It would replicate the Paris Exposition of 1900. The Afro-American collection there had pleased Du Bois.

Du Bois titled his pageant *The People of Peoples and Their Gifts to Men.* He considered the New York Exhibition the national event he had envisioned once he saw a way to become personally involved in this celebration. His pageant began with a Prelude that was in the form of heraldry. With the lights of the Court of Freedom ablaze, a trumpet blast is heard and four heralds, "black and of gigantic stature," appear with silver trumpets and standing at the four corners of the temple of beauty say:

> Hear year, hear ye! Men of all the Americas, and listen to the tale of the eldest and strongest of the races of mankind, whose faces be black. Hear ye, hear ye, of the gifts of black men to this world, the Iron Gift and Gift of Faith, the Pain of Humility and the Sorrow Song of Pain, the Fight of Freedom and of Laughter, and the undying Gift of Hope. Men of the world, keep silent and hear ye this!

Each Gift was dramatized into what Du Bois called Episodes of the drama. The first three Gifts were expressed in terms of the political, military, and cultural history of black Africa. But for the "humblest and mightiest of the races, the Gift of Humility would show how men can bear even the Hell of Christian slavery and live." In this Episode, the Mohammedans force their slaves forward as European traders enter. The Negroes refuse gold but are "seduced by beads and drink." Chains rattle. Christian missionaries enter, but the slave trade increases. Out of this rendering of the African slave trade, known intimately by Du Bois owing to his doctoral dissertation on the suppression of that Dance of Death and Pain, follows the Gift of Struggle Toward Freedom. In it is the story of Alonzo, the Negro pilot in Columbus' fleet; Stephen Dorantes, who discovered New Mexico; the brave Maroons and valiant Haytians; and Crispus Attucks, George Lisle and Nat Turner. Suddenly King Cotton arrives, reminding the audience that had the cotton gin not been invented, slavery in the United States might well have ended early in the nineteenth century. But with King Cotton come Greed, Vice, Luxury and Cruelty to seduce the slaveholders. The old whips and chains appear again. Nat Turner is killed for his rebel-

lion, and slaves drop back into silence and work silently and sullenly.

The next Episode comes through the works of William Lloyd Garrison, John Brown, Abraham Lincoln, and Frederick Douglass, and through the marching of black soldiers to the Civil War. Sojourner Truth asks Frederick her famous question, "Frederick, is God dead?" and a mighty chorus of voices take up the question and chant it. Douglass answers: "No, and therefore slavery must end in blood."

This pageant of speaking and dancing and singing has traced the history of the black man in the world, particularly his life in America. It has included the symbolic figures of the Laborer, the Artisan, the Servant of Men, the Merchant, the Inventor, the Musician, the All-Mother, who begins as the Veiled Woman, who is now unveiled in her chariot with her dancing brood and with the bust of Abraham Lincoln at her side. Appropriately, the trumpets blast and the voices sing triumphantly while the Heralds sing:

> Hear ye, hear ye, men of all Americas, ye who have listened to the tale of the oldest and strongest of the races of mankind, whose faces are black. Hear ye, hear ye, and forget not the gift of black men to this world—the Iron Gift and Gift of Faith, the Pain of Humility and Sorrow Song of Pain, the Gift of Freedom and Laughter and the undying Gift of Hope. Men of America, break silence, for the play is done.

And the banners announce, "The play is done!"

The historian-playwright has interpreted the Negro to America. With his pageant he has ordered their experiences on two continents and their progeny have made their statement.

When the Exhibition closed, Du Bois wrote in *The Crisis* that it was "perhaps the largest single celebration which colored people have had in the North." He said the total attendance was over 30,000; that the order of the crowd was perfect; that not a single arrest was made. There were relatively few exhibits, he admitted—not nearly so many as he had planned. Each was significant, he wrote. Greatest of all, to him, was the historical pageant. Its performance had been his principal motivation for working to bring about the commemoration. He said that it engaged 350 actors. Charles Burroughs, a local elocutionist who specialized in putting on dramatic production in black churches, directed the pageant with the help of other black New York artists, who trained the dancers and singers. Burroughs became Du Bois' associate in the three other presentations of *The Star of Ethiopia,* the name he gave to the other three productions of his pageant. With this 1913 event, Du Bois began his serious work as an author of dramatic works. To some extent his dramas were part of the NAACP's new plan to use drama as a weapon in the fight for social uplift—particularly against the increasing plague of lynching. One has to remember that Angelina Grimke, a young black high-school teacher at the time in Washington, D.C., wrote her play *Rachel* as a part of this NAACP thrust. It was staged in Washington in 1916. Most persons who write about early black drama in the United States mention Grimke's play, although they usually call it "propaganda." Strangely, they almost never mention Du Bois' *The Star of Ethiopia,* although it received a far wider and more sympathetic viewing than did Grimke's. Fannin S. Belcher, Jr., tossed *Rachel* aside as little more than a sermon against lynching in his monumental history of black stage plays, but even he ignores Du Bois's drama.

Du Bois' own statement about his efforts in this respect seemed unduly modest when he wrote: *The Star of Ethiopia*—with a thousand actors—that was given for Negroes by Negroes in three great cities to audiences aggregating tens of thousands—but the white world heard of it despite the marvelous color and drama." No doubt he exaggerated when he spoke of the "thousand actors" and of the "tens of thousands" of audience members. But he should be permitted an embellishment, especially since practically no one gave him the honor of forerunner in establishing black American drama.

William E. Cain (essay date Summer 1990)

SOURCE: "W. E. B. Du Bois's *Autobiography* and the Politics of Literature," in *Black American Literature Forum,* Vol. 24, No. 2, Summer, 1990, pp. 299-313.

[*Cain is an educator. In the essay below, he focuses on Du Bois's decision to join the Communist Party and leave the United States for Ghana.*]

During the course of his long career, W. E. B. Du Bois produced superb work in many genres. His Harvard dissertation *The Suppression of the African Slave Trade* (1896) was a pioneering, minutely detailed analysis of the growth and eventual elimination of the slave trade to the Unites States; his absorbing rendering of African culture and African-American history *The Negro* (1915) served as "the Bible of Pan-Africanism"; and his later historical book *Black Reconstruction* (1935) bitingly challenged the traditional view of the post-Civil-War period as a time of white suffering and Negro abuses and abominations. His studies of the black family and community, especially *The Philadelphia Negro* (1899), remain valuable; his countless essays and reviews, not only in *The Crisis* but in other academic journals and popular magazines and newspapers, are impressive in their scope and virtuosity; and his numerous articles on education, labor, and the Pan-African movement further testify to his national and international vision of the development of colored people. He also wrote novels, stories, and poetry, and invented mixed genres of his own, as the sociologically acute and lyrical *The Souls of Black Folk* (1903) demonstrates.

Du Bois's many autobiographical writings, notably *Dusk of Dawn* (1940) and his posthumous *Autobiography* (1968), are also rewarding texts that situate the life of the writer within the complex trends of the late-nineteenth and twentieth centuries.

As a premier man of letters, Du Bois has few rivals in this century. Yet with the exception of *The Souls of Black Folk,* his writings are infrequently taught and rarely accorded in literary history the credit they deserve. In part this results from the fertile ways in which Du Bois's writings cross and exceed generic and disciplinary categories. Who should teach him? Where should he be taught? Du Bois's astonishing range has possibly worked to his disadvantage, particularly in the academy, leaving the majority of his books unstudied because it is unclear to whose departmental terrain they belong. "His contribution," concludes Arnold Rampersad, "has sunk to the status of a footnote in the long history of race relations in the United States."

Another, more commanding reason for Du Bois's uneven and troubled reputation is that he wrote politically: He always perceived his writing, in whatever form or forum, as having political point and purpose. As he noted in a diary entry on his twenty-fifth birthday, "'I . . . take the world that the Unknown lay in my hands and work for the rise of the Negro people, taking for granted that their best development means the best development of the world'" (*Autobiography*). Du Bois assembled knowledge, fired off polemics, issued moral appeals, and preached international brotherhood and peace in the hope of effecting differences in the lives of the lowly and oppressed. He stood for equality and justice, for bringing all men and women into "the kingdom of culture" as co-workers (*Souls*). So much was this Du Bois's intention that he was willing to use the explosive word *propaganda* to accent it. Viewing himself as, in everything, a writer and an artist, he affirmed that "all art is propaganda and ever must be, despite the wailing of the purists. I stand in utter shamelessness and say that whatever art I have for writing has been used always for propaganda for gaining the right of black folk to love and enjoy" (**"Criteria for Negro Art"**).

Du Bois's blunt deployment of art as "propaganda" makes plain the reason that he has proved an awkward figure for literary historians, yet it still remains curious that he is undertaught and undervalued. William James, Nathaniel Shaler, Albert Bushnell Hart, George Santayana, and others praised Du Bois during his student days at Harvard. Hart later said that he counted him "'always among the ablest and keenest of our teacher-scholars, an American who viewed his country broadly'" (cited in *Autobiography*). Some of America's most gifted novelists, poets, and playwrights admired him. Eugene O'Neill once referred to Du Bois as "ranking among the foremost writers of true importance in the country." Van Wyck Brooks commended him as "an intellectual who was also an artist and a prophet," a man "with a mind at once passionate, critical, humorous, and detached" and "a mental horizon as wide as the world." Even earlier, no less an eminence than Henry James termed him "that most accomplished of members of the Negro race." It was William James who sent his brother a copy of *The Souls of Black Folk*, referring to it as "a decidedly moving book."

A commanding reason for Du Bois's uneven and troubled reputation is that he wrote politically: He always perceived his writing, in whatever form or forum, as having political point and purpose.

—William E. Cain

The Souls of Black Folk is indeed a landmark in African-American culture. James Weldon Johnson, in his autobiography, stated that the book "had a greater effect upon and within the Negro race in America than any other single book published in this country since *Uncle Tom's Cabin.*" Rampersad has summarized its significance even more dramatically: "If all of the nation's literature may stem from one book, as Hemingway implied about *The Adventures of Huckleberry Finn,* then it can as accurately be said that all of Afro-American literature of a creative nature has proceeded from Du Bois's comprehensive statement on the nature of the people in *The Souls of Black Folk.*"

But while *The Souls of Black Folk* has loomed large within the African-American intellectual community and, to an extent, within the white one as well, it has not generated a more extensive interest in Du Bois's autobiographies and writings in other genres. In part, Du Bois has received relatively little scrutiny because his race has worked against him in the dominant culture: His black skin bars him from reaching the stature that he had, by rights, attained through his publications and activities. But Du Bois remains an outcast as much, if not more, for ideological reasons. His standing has suffered— and he suffered literally in his life—because of his leftist/socialist sympathies and eventual membership, in 1961, in the Communist Party. As not only a black man but, by February 1963, a Communist citizen of Nkrumah's Ghana, Du Bois has been excluded from the main literary and historical register of scholarship and canon formation.

The *Autobiography,* the last of Du Bois's works, is crucial not only for its review of the formidable span of his career, but also for the ideological positions that it conveys, positions that help account for Du Bois's problematical reputation inside and outside the academy. The *Autobiography* begins with an intense account of Du Bois's extremely favorable impressions of the Soviet Union and China, and it concludes with ample sections on his "work for peace," in-

dictment and trial for allegedly subversive behavior (he was eventually acquitted), and zealous support for Pan-Africanism and Communism. To be sure, we must attend carefully to the *Autobiography* as an interestingly structured work of autobiographical art. But at this juncture, we need particularly to engage and reexamine the ideologically charged parts of Du Bois's book, acknowledging his errors and misjudgments where these exist but also perceiving how his Communist views, as he understood them, stemmed from his lifelong commitment to brotherhood and peace. His decision near the end of his life to become a Communist seemed treasonous during the Cold War, and it strikes many as luridly aberrant today, as the Communist countries of Eastern Europe and the Soviet Union undergo sweeping transformations. But this decision was one that Du Bois weighed carefully. It is important to grasp its origins and not allow it to blind us to his achievement, integrity, and intellectual conscience. The basic case for Du Bois as an exemplary intellectual and one of America's major writers has yet to be satisfactorily made, and the place to begin, artistically and politically, is with the *Autobiography*.

Not all readers, it should be noted, have felt comfortable about the status of the *Autobiography* as a text. The editor of the book, Herbert Aptheker, tells us that Du Bois wrote the first draft in 1958-59 (when he was 90 years old), and then revised it somewhat in 1960. According to Aptheker, Du Bois took the draft with him to Ghana in late 1961, and it was first published, in an abbreviated form, in China, the USSR, and the German Democratic Republic in 1964-65. Shirley Graham Du Bois, the author's widow, fortunately managed to rescue the manuscript after the military coup that occurred in Ghana in late 1966; and Aptheker reports that he prepared it for publication in its entirety, making only a few minor corrections such as fixing a date or providing a complete name. But when the *Autobiography* appeared in 1968, some scholars testily wagered that Aptheker had probably played a more active role. Truman Nelson, for example, queried the inclusion of the long opening section on Du Bois's travels in, and enthusiastic support for, the Soviet Union and the People's Republic of China. Maintaining that this section did not appear in a carbon copy of the manuscript in his own possession, Nelson implied that it might have been stitched into the manuscript by Aptheker. Rayford Logan and others have similarly questioned Aptheker's involvement, noting many resemblances between passages in the *Autobiography* and much earlier writings by Du Bois (Logan and Winston 196). Aptheker has steadfastly denied that he significantly modified or adjusted the manuscript. In his 1973 *Annotated Bibliography* of Du Bois's writings, he repeated that he had merely made "technical" changes.

For the literary and historical record, it is obviously imperative to know as best we can the condition of the manuscript that Du Bois himself wrote. One needs also to tally the affinities between parts of the *Autobiography* and material previously published in *The Souls of Black Folk, Dusk of Dawn, In Battle for Peace,* and other texts. Yet, in another sense, the controversy about the text of the *Autobiography* simply dramatizes issues of authorship and authority familiar to us from many African-American autobiographies. Who is the real author of the text? Was it actually produced, in part or whole, by a black or white author, co-author, or editor? What is the relation between the manuscript and the published book? These questions, often raised about slave narratives in the nineteenth century, have also figured in discussion of auto-biographical writings by Booker T. Washington, Zora Neale Hurston, Richard Wright, and Malcolm X. Such questions, and the difficulty of answering them cleanly, constitute a vexed central feature of the tradition of African-American autobiography.

Often such questions arise because some readers frankly doubt or object to what the text itself says. They do not readily believe in a text that advances a self-representation that is at odds with their own understanding of the author's self and with the historical and political truths that they have embraced. In the case of Du Bois's *Autobiography,* many readers have doubtless discounted this text as much on political as on scholarly and bibliographical grounds. They would prefer, it sometimes seems, to regard the ardently pro-Communist thrust of the book, and its hugely uncritical attitude toward Soviet state power, to be somehow not "really" present in Du Bois's text—as though these sentiments were more a faithful reflection of Aptheker (a Communist Party member himself) than of Du Bois, who, a tired old man of 90, could not have deeply meant his own words even if he did indeed write them.

The *Autobiography* is a flawed and disappointing book in certain respects, but we can only make sense of it (and of the life and career to which it attests) if we confront how its words—however much we might disapprove of them—tellingly accord with crucial facts about Du Bois. By the mid-1940s, he was adamantly hostile to the conduct of American foreign policy, and, in the midst of Cold War repression in the United States, he sought to establish connections to and alliances with the Soviet Union. In 1958-59, when he drafted the *Autobiography,* he traveled extensively in the Soviet Union and China; and, in 1961, his manuscript now finished, Du Bois joined the Communist Party of the United States.

As the *Autobiography* reveals, the foundations for Du Bois's decisive act of 1961 were laid even earlier than the 1940s. He first became absorbed in Marxism at the time of the Russian Revolution, journeyed to the Soviet Union in 1926, and, after his resignation from the NAACP and return to Atlanta University in 1934, began to teach a graduate course there on Marxism. In *Dusk of Dawn,* published in 1940, Du Bois speaks skeptically about Communism, rebuking the misguided forays of the Party in America and declaring, "I was not and am not a communist." Yet he also boldly praises Marx,

touts the extraordinary importance of the Russian Revolution, and aligns himself with the struggle for socialism in his statement of the "Basic American Negro Creed." Though he claims that he spurns the revolutionary pitch of Communism, he also says openly that "Western Europe did not and does not want democracy, never believed in it, never practiced it and never without fundamental and basic revolution will accept it." Du Bois's belief in Communism did not descend upon him suddenly, nor did it result from world weariness. He knew where he stood—he was not "mindless"—and clearly gauged what he was doing when he at last became a Party member.

The *Autobiography* not only contains explicit statements of Du Bois's homage to Communism, but also furnishes prophetic signs of the emergence and development of the views he came devoutly to hold in his last years. When he first visited the Soviet Union in the 1920s, what impressed him about the Russian people was their vital, energizing "hope." All of life, he states, "was being renewed and filled with vigor and ideal." Everywhere he looked, he approvingly noticed a dedicated striving to modernize education, abolish poverty, and end the reign of destructive myth and superstition. Nowhere did he detect evidence of race hatred. Returning to the Soviet Union in 1958-59, he saw that the hopes of the Russian people (and his own as well) had taken inspiring form: "The Soviet Union which I see in 1959 is power and faith and not simply hope." Once again, too, he did not sight in the Soviet Union the harrowing fact of bigotry that informed his excruciating vision of America and Europe: "The Soviet Union seems to me the only European country where people are not more or less taught and encouraged to despise and look down on some class, group or race. I know countries where race and color prejudice show only slight manifestations, but no white country where race and color prejudice seems so absolutely absent." Free from the scarring presence of race hatred, the Soviet Union seeks always, Du Bois insists, to lend its support to liberation movements and the worldwide fight against racism, imperialism, and colonialism.

Du Bois's celebration of the Soviet Union is difficult to appraise because it complicatedly blends the country (and ideology in action) that Du Bois actually glimpsed with the country he longed to locate, one that would be constructed according to reason and scientific principle and that would foreground a better, and manifestly attainable, alternative to the oppressive situation in America. The *Autobiography* can hardly be said to supply readers with a rounded, dispassionate account of the Soviet system. For Du Bois, intolerance and injustice, brutality, imprisonment, and murder do not exist under Communism. To allege that these do exist, or to fasten upon the apparent immorality and human price for converting Communist theory into rigorous, coherent practice, signals political blindness and bad faith, Du Bois believes. Such a critique of the Soviet Union misleadingly and unfairly stresses the "ethics" of the "methods" employed to secure

Marxist socialism rather than sympathetically observing the workings of the thing itself.

Du Bois's perspective on the Soviet Union is skewed, but it does reflect an honorable, if exasperating, consistency. It derives from his own bitter disappointment in, and alienation from, the American scene, which seemed to him in the 1950s still to be ravaged by racism despite his own and others' decades of struggle. From one angle, his strangely distanced remarks about the Soviet purge trials of the 1930s, his affirmation of the rightness of the Soviet invasion of Hungary, and similarly meager, muted statements about the limits of Communism likely strike us as absurd. Yet it may be missing the point somewhat to label Du Bois in his *Autobiography*— as does Irving Howe—a dismal apologist for Stalinism "whose final commitment was soiled both morally and intellectually." In large measure, Du Bois's grand endorsement of Communism represents his own implacable verdict upon America; and his refusal or inability to articulate the evils of Communism bears unremitting witness to his desire to preserve a leftist point of view untainted by the U.S.'s Cold War rhetoric. Like Howe, we are inescapably drawn to indict Stalinism, as are now the Soviet people themselves, encouraged by Mikhail Gorbachev's new spirit of openness and reexamination of the past. But Du Bois, in the 1940s and 1950s, regarded attacks on Stalinist Russia as always deflecting the gaze away from America's own history and crimes in the present and, furthermore, as weakening the already marginalized American left. Du Bois judged, I think, that when people on the left assailed Communism under Stalin, they recklessly played into the hands of the McCarthyite right; by so self-righteously criticizing an apparently pro-Stalinist left, they threatened to discredit the left in general.

The *Autobiography* therefore places exacting political pressure on its readers, who face a potent array of pro-Soviet claims. But the book does provide rewards not tied to the ideological strife of the Cold War, including precise accounts of Du Bois's boyhood in Great Barrington, Massachusetts; his education at Fisk, Harvard, and the University of Berlin; his work as a teacher and scholar at Wilberforce, the University of Pennsylvania, and Atlanta University; and his opposition to Washington's program for Negro uplift, his leadership of the Niagara movement, and his leading role in the organization of the NAACP. The *Autobiography* is, however, regrettably silent or restrained on many key aspects of Du Bois's life. He says nothing at all about his five novels and very little about his other written works, especially such historical studies as the epic volume *Black Reconstruction*. While he mentions his estimable labor for *The Crisis,* the NAACP magazine he edited from 1910 to 1934, he offers few details. He omits altogether his relation to the writers and artists of the Harlem Renaissance, and refers in a sketchy manner to his ferocious feud with Marcus Garvey. With so much of the beginning of the book taken up with an account of Du Bois's travels to the Soviet Union and China, and with so much space

toward the end occupied by Du Bois's work for peace and his indictment and trial in the 1950s, there are inevitably missed opportunities, and much personal, professional, and sociopolitical material is left unexamined.

Du Bois is also guarded about his inner life. He refers to his "habit of repression," hints at the "self-protective coloration, with perhaps an inferiority complex," that marked his life at Harvard, and alludes to his reserve and inhibitions. But these statements are few and fleeting, and do not serve as occasions for deeper probing and meditation. Even the chapter titled "My Character," though surprisingly candid about Du Bois's own sexual disappointment during his first marriage, is rather formal and stiff. Du Bois does not seem at ease with sustained self-scrutiny, finding a chapter on his "character" to be necessary to certify the autobiographical "picture" as a "complete" one but not meeting the assignment with real curiosity or earnest intent.

The cost of Du Bois's relative inattention to his inner life bears upon the politics of his book. It is not just that many readers have heatedly disputed Du Bois's Communism, but that they also cannot clearly perceive its intellectual, emotional, and psychological appeal for him. He exhibits the external conditions in the Communist state that gratify him, yet fails to clarify the human needs that such a state functions to fulfill. When one reads Richard Wright's *American Hunger* or his essay in *The God That Failed,* one can apprehend why Communism so attracted Wright and crucially assisted him in forging his identity as a writer. Even as he recants his affiliation with the Party, his prose still testifies compellingly to his gratitude to it for its constructive lessons. In their different ways, the autobiographies of the African-American Communists Hosea Hudson and Harry Haywood also achieve something that Du Bois's book does not. Filled with detail about arduous educational and organizational work, these texts enable readers to appreciate the concrete meaning of Communism for many black Americans, particularly during the 1930s, as they dramatize the powerful feelings of solidarity along race and class lines that both men experienced.

Du Bois's own proud, prickly temperament partially explains the absence of personal inquiry in his *Autobiography;* he did not view this potential of the genre as one that kindled his writerly interest. In this respect, his term for his autobiographical act in this book—he calls it a "soliloquy"—is admittedly absorbing on a theoretical level but is an inappropriate guide to the nature of what he has actually achieved. *Soliloquy* implies a 'speaking to oneself,' a disclosing of one's innermost thoughts and feelings unmindful of an audience. It connotes, too, a theatricalized or dramatic posture and pose, a vividly prosecuted, intellectually dense and complex form of speech that highlights self-reflection and risks unanticipated kinds of self-exposure. Du Bois's *Autobiography* does not really take such a cast or tone. It is less a soliloquy than an elaborate lecture or, better still, the prolonged testimony of an unyielding conscience that accosts America with truths that this nation, in Du Bois's appraisal, was too imprisoned in Cold War defensiveness and guilt to discern itself: "I sit and see the Truth. I look it full in the face, and I will not lie about it, neither to myself nor to the world. . . . I see this land not merely by statistics or reading lies agreed upon by historians. I judge by what I have seen, heard, and lived through for near a century."

Du Bois suggests that he has earned the right to pronounce this stern sentence through long years of demanding, systematic, progressive "work." *Work* is, in fact, the key word of the *Autobiography*. Du Bois uses it many times, nearly always in the context of the building or shaping of a whole "life" in terms of a carefully chosen, determinedly pursued form of work. Preparing to begin his studies at Harvard, Du Bois stresses that he "above all believed in work, systematic and tireless." Later, having finished his advanced training at the University of Berlin, he returned to America to earn his living as a scholar and teacher: "I just got down on my knees and begged for work, anything and anywhere. I began a systematic mail campaign" to find work. Seizing upon an opportunity for an appointment at the University of Pennsylvania, he avidly professes that he was "ready and eager to begin a lifework, leading to the emancipation of the American Negro."

These passages and others similar to them show that Du Bois conceives of his life, as represented in his *Autobiography,* as highly dedicated "work." He undertakes work with a mission, and according to a specific plan: "The Negro problem was in my mind a matter of systematic investigation and intelligent understanding. The world was thinking wrong about race, because it did not know. The ultimate evil was stupidity. The cure for it was knowledge based on scientific investigation." The word *work* is aligned with a group of related words—system, knowledge, fact, basis, truth, plan, organization—and the *Autobiography* as a whole contains a number of proposals and schemes for mammoth research projects on the condition of the Negro. Writing in his ninetieth year, Du Bois realizes the limitations of his vision of work, especially as he formulated it in his early years as a scholar and educator. Everything he did, he now understands, presumed the willingness of Americans to ponder the conclusions that his work unequivocally disclosed and to *do* what the true facts mandated. Du Bois concedes that he was naïve about the ability of accumulated knowledge to speak for itself and impel certain reforms. But this by no means lessens his staunch conviction that one's life only matters when "work" defines it.

Du Bois's concern for "work," for visible achievement that ratifies the worth and rightness of life, possibly accounts for the reticence about personal feeling in his *Autobiography*. Deeds matter more than feelings, in Du Bois's calculation. The self knows how it feels by looking back upon and confi-

dently reckoning what it has done. Though commendable in most ways, such a program has its dangers, and, as Du Bois describes it, it is unduly abstract and theoretical. Indeed, one wonders whether Du Bois's extreme emphasis on resolutely organized work, systematic investigation, highly controlled scientific inquiry, and centralized authority and administration indicates to us why the Soviet state struck him so positively. Accenting everywhere its admirable central planning and scientific efficiency, he does not comprehend, let alone grapple with, the pain and devastation among the masses of men and women that Stalin's work of economic overhaul entailed.

Du Bois admits that his *Autobiography* is not an altogether reliable record of his life. It is, he observes, "a theory of my life, with much forgotten and misconceived, with valuable testimony but often less than absolutely true, despite my intention to be frank and fair." If the *Autobiography* fails or disappoints us, it may do so because of the intriguing inadequacy of the very "theory" of Du Bois's life and career that it propounds. Du Bois says clearly that he "believe[s] in socialism" and seeks "a world where the ideals of communism will triumph—to each according to his need, from each according to his ability. For this I will work as long as I live. And I still live." Even as he states his loyalty to the Communist ideal, however, and unflinchingly affirms the model for nationhood that he perceives in both the Soviet Union and China, he adheres to a myth of American exceptionalism and does not recognize the tension and conflict that he thereby introduces into his book—and into his theoretical conception of his life.

"I know the United States," Du Bois concludes. "It is my country and the land of my fathers. It is still a land of magnificent possibilities. It is still the home of noble souls and generous people. But it is selling its birthright. It is betraying its mighty destiny." Du Bois swears that he still loves America, yet how can his profession of faith in this nation stand alongside his passionate fidelity to Communism and the Soviet experiment? To put the question even more pointedly: What does Du Bois mean by his invocation of American destiny? This seems to be a puzzling term for him to employ at this stage of his book (and his career), since he had powerfully sought in his painstaking historical research to demonstrate how America's destiny, and its power and wealth, has been terribly entwined with slavery and racism. It is not as though Du Bois has forgotten these hard facts in his *Autobiography,* for he refers in his final pages to the tragic legacy of slavery in America. But he appears momentarily to need to lose sight of these facts in order to retain his sense of America as essentially a land of freedom and opportunity that has strayed from its destined path.

Some have said that Du Bois idealizes the Soviet Union, but he may idealize America just as much. In his final paragraph, he states that "this is a wonderful America, which the founding fathers dreamed until their sons drowned it in the blood of slavery and devoured it in greed." Yet Du Bois himself had noted, several pages earlier, that George Washington "bought, owned, and sold slaves"; he knows that the founding fathers compromised their "dream" from the very beginning, and that they, not their sons alone, carry the burden and guilt of slavery.

In his first book, *The Suppression of the African Slave Trade,* Du Bois spoke words that reverberate against the position to which he clings in these final pages of his last one. "We must face the fact," he stated in 1896,

> that this problem [of slavery] arose principally from the cupidity and carelessness of our ancestors. It was the plain duty of the colonies to crush the trade and the system in its infancy: they preferred to enrich themselves on its profits. It was the plain duty of a Revolution based upon "Liberty" to take steps toward the abolition of slavery: it preferred promises to straightforward action. It was the plain duty of the Constitutional Convention, in founding a new nation, to compromise with a threatening social evil only in case its settlement would thereby be postponed to a more favorable time: this was not the case in the slavery and slave-trade compromises; there never was a time in this history of America when the system had a slighter economic, political, and moral justification than in 1787; and yet with this real, existent, growing evil before their eyes, a bargain largely of dollars and cents was allowed to open the highway that led straight to the Civil War.

Though the *Autobiography* announces its acceptance of Marxist-Leninist ideology, it is *The Suppression of the African Slave Trade* that arguably shows greater insight into the relationship between politics and economics, and that more resourcefully demystifies pure notions of American destiny. Audaciously pro-Soviet and highly critical of American policies at home and abroad, the *Autobiography* nevertheless gives evidence of Du Bois's deep attachment to America and his inclination to idealize his native land even as he sagely and sometimes savagely criticizes it.

At one point, for example, Du Bois commends the "democratic" theory and practice of Soviet society, citing the frequent debates, consultations, and discussions of common events current there, and he adds that life under Communism thereby resonates with the same democratic rhythms as small-town America. The Soviet people, he says, "sit and sit and talk and talk, and vote and vote; if this is all a mirage, it is a perfect one. They believe it as I used to believe in the Spring Town Meeting in my village."

There is more detail about these town meetings in Du Bois's chapter on his boyhood in Great Barrington, where he tells of his respect for them. There was one old man who regularly attended these meetings, using them as an opportunity to rail against funds for the local high school.

> I remember distinctly how furious I used to get at the stolid town folk, who sat and listened to him. He was nothing and nobody. Yet the town heard him gravely because he was a citizen and property-holder on a small scale and when he was through, they calmly voted the usual funds for the high school. Gradually as I grew up, I began to see that this was the essence of democracy: listening to the other man's opinion and then voting your own, honestly and intelligently.

On the next page, Du Bois concedes that the democracy he admired was not truly democratic: "of course our democracy was not full and free. Certain well-known and well-to-do citizens were always elected to office—not the richest or most noted but just as surely not the poorest or the Irish Catholic." Du Bois shrewdly exposes the limits of the ideal he reveres, and he incorporates other de-idealizing devices elsewhere in his book, as when he observes that the "golden" river of his birth was golden "because of the waste which the paper and woolen mills poured into it and because more and more the river became a public sewer into which town and slum poured their filth." Yet he safeguards his exaltation of America's "dream" from irony, despite his own mustering of evidence that would seem to make the irony inescapable for him. In a word, Du Bois exempts America from the indictment that his own reading of our history would appear to demand. This pro-Soviet, anti-American text is, then, confusedly, movingly, and eloquently patriotic—a jeremiad that simultaneously blasts America for its contemptible sins and hymns its magnificent, if not yet achieved, destiny.

Near the center of his *Autobiography,* Du Bois reflects that his "thought" has long been characterized by a "dichotomy": "How far can love for my oppressed race accord with love for the oppressing country? And when these loyalties diverge, where shall my soul find refuge?" One could conceivably maintain that by the close of his life, as he sums it up in his book, Du Bois had chosen his race and rejected his country, becoming a believer in Communism and a supporter of the Soviet Union because America had come, for him, to stand for sheer intolerance, repression, and militaristic sponsorship of colonialism. But Du Bois never lost his fervent affection for his country. Even at the end, he declared his belief in a distinctive American message and mission, curiously suspending the ironic demystifications of the American dream that he had defiantly undertaken for many decades and that he had reiterated in the *Autobiography* itself. To say that Du Bois was a Stalinist apologist and, eventually, a Communist Party member registers truths about the life that he led and wrote about. But these explicitly recorded truths perhaps count for less than the queer beauty of Du Bois's lingering love for the America he told himself he had momentously abandoned.

Ronald A. T. Judy (essay date Summer 1994)

SOURCE: "The New Black Aesthetic and W. E. B. Du Bois, or Hephaestus, Limping," in *The Massachusetts Review,* Vol. XXXV, No. 2, Summer, 1994, pp. 249-82.

[In the following essay, Judy relates Du Bois's concept of black consciousness as expressed in The Souls of Black Folk *to the New Black Aesthetic.]*

> Such is Beauty. Its variety is infinite, its possibility is endless. In normal life all may have it and have it yet again. The world is full of it. . . . Who shall let this world be beautiful? . . . We black folk may help for we have within us as a race a new stirrings; stirrings of the beginning of the new appreciation of joy, of a new desire to create, of a new will to be; . . . and there has come the conviction that the Youth that is here today, the Negro Youth, is a different kind of Youth, because in some new way it bears this mighty prophesy on its breast, with a new realization of itself, with new determination for all mankind. (W. E. B. Du Bois)

In an ambitious 1989 essay, the novelist Trey Ellis tried to give a coherent expression to a way of thinking about authenticity emerging among an increasing number of young African American artists. The expression he found was New Black Aesthetic (NBA), an apt naming that performs a chief function of the way of thinking it refers to—parody. After all, the NBA is a way of thinking about artistic expression that while recognizing its indebtedness to the agitprop of the Black Arts Movement, and confidently employing the forms and themes of previous black arts, ironically parodies all claims of genealogical purity or continuity. Granted, as J. Martin Favor has recently argued, this parody still falls within the line of a particularly African American form of expression—signifying. Yet, as Favor also notes, this signifying is so thoroughly iconoclastic it problematizes any genealogy, compelling Favor to relate it to the postmodern practice of pastiche. This goes along with Ellis's characterizing the NBA as "cultural mulattos," who following in the steps of the "Third Plane" (artists like August Wilson, Richard Pryor, Toni Morrison, and George Clinton) expand and explode "the old definitions of blackness, showing us the intricate, uncategorizeable folks we had always known ourselves to be." The NBA is about understanding authentic blackness as a practice and not status. It is the practice of generating new signs that transgress dominant cultural norms, and recognizing that every new expression, no matter how subjective, is historically hybrid—it is related genealogically to all those utterances that came before it and are around it. This constitutes the collective enunciation of Black experience. In fine, being a cultural mulatto is being true to the black. Echoing Greg Tate, Ellis calls this a "postliberation aesthetic" that "somehow synthesizes . . . the Harlem Renaissance and the Black

Arts Movement," in its claim to be "'separate but better'" than the dominant culture. Ellis's expression of the NBA has gained currency, and his essay "The New Black Aesthetic," has become a manifesto of a new arts movement.

The synthesis of the Harlem Renaissance and the Black Arts Movement that Ellis refers to is that of avant garde modernism and Leftist vanguard agitprop, which Tate also claims as the basis for a popular black poststructuralism, in which "black consciousness and artistic freedom are not mutually exclusive but complementary." For both Ellis and Tate, "black culture" signifies a multicultural tradition of expressive practices, which is why the NBA "can feel secure enough about black culture to claim art produced by nonblacks as part of its inheritance." On the face of it, this is a New Black Aesthetic because it has given up trying to work according to modernity's understanding of sign-value; that is, it no longer conceives of the truth of experience as a totality. From this perspective everything can be reinvented. In the world of highly mediated networks of disciplinary institutions and sign-systems that is transnational capitalism, none of the old categories of experience have any explanatory force, or progenitive capacity, least of all nationalism. What is required is critical intervention in the process by which [transnational] capitalism is rationalized through mass culture and modernism. And in Tate's view such a viable non-cultural nationalist resistance is found in the "worldly-wise stoopidfresh intelligentsia of radical bups who can get as *ignant* as James Brown with their wings and stay in the black." Or, as Ellis puts it, the NBA.

Although neither Ellis nor Tate make explicit reference to W. E. B. Du Bois, the characterization of the NBA as a "postliberated aesthetic" bears a striking resemblance to Du Bois's conception of a liberated black art that makes use of all the methods of creation available to realize beauty without necessarily abandoning the quest for liberation. Indeed, Ellis fends off accusations of naive optimism and political timidity, by insisting that with NBA we are witness to a collective project of "disturbatory art" that will take us to the next plane. In this he echoes Du Bois's assertion that the artist is

> one upon whom Truth eternally thrusts itself as the highest handmaid of imagination, as one of the one great vehicle of universal understanding. . . . The apostle of Beauty thus becomes the apostle of Truth and Right not by choice but by inner and outer compulsion. Free he is but his freedom is ever bounded by Truth and Justice; and slavery only dogs him when he is denied the right to tell the Truth or recognize an ideal of Justice. Thus all art is propaganda and ever must be, despite the wailing of the purists.

I've quoted Du Bois at length to leave little doubt about how the pastiche of idioms from the black masses (Houston Baker's vernacular) and elites that define the NBA, and which prompted Eric Lott to claim it to be "one of the only postmodernisms with a conscience," recalls Du Bois's understanding of art as the expression at the nexus of thought and practice. It would appear, then, that what the NBA pulls off is just the sort of grounding of black social praxis in authentic black thought that Du Bois strove for. Insofar as this is so, then the NBA is certainly more of a flash of resistant subjectivity than it is a popular movement of resistance to transnational capital. In other words, it is a form of modernism, rather than postmodernism, in its understanding of culture as the callaloo producing the authentically liberated subject. This is, perhaps, a harsh critique, depending on one's understanding of the relationship between modernism and postmodernism. It is, however, an arguable claim. Making that argument will require more careful elaboration of the resemblance between Du Bois's thought and that of the NBA. What interests me most about Ellis's giving expression to a new way of thinking about black artistic work as being in the van of cultural production, however, is how it echoes W. E. B. Du Bois's project of thinking black thought. A brief exhibition of the unifying themes at work in Ellis's expression will make more accessible the reasons why the NBA prompts this interest in Du Bois's epistemology.

The principal themes of the New Black Aesthetic Movement discernible in Ellis's essay are: (1) "black culture" signifies a multicultural tradition of expressive practices, with a peculiar capacity for generating new signs that transgress dominant cultural norms; (2) the power of black expression to reinvent experience, and enunciate a new world; and (3) this post-liberation aesthetic is being realized by a new black intelligentsia that synthesizes the Harlem Renaissance and the Black Arts Movement. The first and second themes express the underlying necessary principle of the New Black Aesthetic, namely that human emancipation requires the recognition that democratic society is the work of humans, who are conscious of their institutive action. Or, in the language of critical theory preferred by Tate, "democracy creates itself through people's appropriation of their power of signification."

The third theme is what situates this principle in the intellectual genealogy that is of interest here. By recognizing both the Black Arts Movement and the New Negro Movement of the Harlem Renaissance as the foundational sources of the New Black Aesthetic, Ellis provides a direct link to the thinking of Du Bois. Both these movements were explicit in citing the significance of Du Bois's work for any attempt to think rigorously about African American cultural production. In his afterword to the Black Arts Movement manifesto, *Black Fire,* Larry Neal credits Du Bois with providing the inspiration for delineating the parameters of the Black Aesthetic. The particular manifestation of this revived Du Boisian spirit that so moved the Black Arts Movement was *The Souls of Black Folk,* published in 1903. Alain Locke credited Du Bois with producing the conceptual conditions through which the

New Negro Movement "gradually gathered momentum." It is also Du Bois who gets the last word in the movement's manifesto, *The New Negro,* contributing the last chapter, which rehearses the key pronouncement of *The Souls of Black Folk:* "And thus again in 1924 as in 1899 I seem to see the problem of the 20th century as the Problem of the Color Line." That such antagonistic movements could both find their legitimacy in the same book of Du Bois warrants regarding *The Souls of Black Folk* as the principal in a long line of texts that attempt to delineate the genealogy of authentic collective African American enunciation.

So it is no surprise at all that in its conception of a politically committed avant garde black art, the New Black Aesthetic appears to have rediscovered the most ambitious aspect of Du Bois's program of racial uplift: the attempt to establish materialist grounds for total human emancipation. What makes it interesting, on the other hand, is that along with that rediscovery comes a particular problem of agency that plagued this program. Du Bois's commitment to the conception of democracy as the work of human reason, and his effort to understand theory as a praxis, led him to view a political episteme as the only agency for achieving justice. His conception of social revolution organized around the work of a vanguard intelligentsia (the talented tenth) was not only elitist, but it was antinomic to the concept of pluralist democracy he espoused in that it derived from an abstract universalization of reason. Du Bois eventually recognized the antinomy entailed in a conception of democratic society founded on rationalism as the method for the universal production of truth. Even so, he remained bound to it by his conception of racialism. Yet, in between the lines of Du Bois's argument for a black intelligentsia there is a permanent reminder of the indeterminacy of knowledge as a necessary condition of democracy. That is to say, when one reads *The Souls of Black Folk* carefully, one finds a conception of the historical emergence of black consciousness as a contentious process of cognition that resists resolution.

Understandably, this might pose problems for those of us who hypostatize black subjectivity. Nevertheless, Du Bois arrived at his understanding of black subjectivity from assumptions he viewed as hypothesis—i.e., those postulated points of reference necessary for any teleological judgment. The interrogation of those assumptions is, I think, crucial to any reading of *The Souls of Black Folk* that tries to come to terms with how his conception of black subjectivity is antinomic to his commitment to pluralist democracy, and that tries to perceive the paralogism entailed in the play of figuration about the veil. In this regard, James Weldon Johnson's oft-cited description of *The Souls of Black Folk* as having "had a greater effect upon and within the Negro race in America than any other single book published in this country since *Uncle Tom's Cabin,*" proves to be insightful, because it draws attention to the specific features of literary form that make Du Bois's book a paradigmatic instance of African American cultural critique.

This is the cultural critique both Ellis and Tate claim for the NBA. At first glance, Du Bois's project was considerably more ambitious than that of the NBA. His stated aim in *The Souls of Black Folk,* after all, was to trace "the history of the American Negro;" while that of the NBA is to draw attention to the emergence of a new way of thinking about and making black art. More careful consideration of both projects will discover that the difference is not all that great. Du Bois's project, like Ellis's, is expressed in terms of three dominant themes: (1) the power of black expression to reinvent experience, and enunciate a new world, (2) intellectual, and cultural vanguardism, and (3) the repressive effects of capitalism. In combination, these three themes of *The Souls of Black Folk* define Du Bois's understanding of the function of art as intellectual work.

In pursuit of these three themes, let's recall that the focus of the following reading of *The Souls of Black Folk* is his concept of black consciousness as the presupposition of his understanding of intellectual vanguardism, and how that concept is antinomic to his commitment to pluralist democracy. Interrogating Du Bois's concept of black consciousness will make more accessible the claim that it is paradigmatic for the NBA. Moreover, taking care of the relation between this concept of black consciousness and the antinomy of intellectual vanguardism and pluralist democracy will, at least, offer a glimpse of some of the reasons why it is still possible for the NBA to identify black intellectual vanguardism with societal change. That possibility has to do with precisely what is meant by consciousness in the concepts black consciousness and black experience.

Along these lines, Du Bois's *The Souls of Black Folk*['s] significance stems from its being the most widely-read and definitive expression of what he took black consciousness to mean. Analyzing the text as a combination of philosophical, social, and quasi-religious discourses facilitates reading it as a strategic engagement with that order of knowledge called *Geistesgeschichte*. This interpretive arrangement of the text, although not reductive, draws attention towards the question of how black thought or consciousness is realized in the world as the paramount concern of Du Bois's book. Although the question of black consciousness is the frame of reference in *The Souls of Black Folk,* its explicit elaboration occurs chiefly in two chapters: "Of the Coming of John," which is the thirteenth, penultimate chapter; and "Of Our Spiritual Strivings," which is the opening chapter.

These two chapters represent the oldest and newest writings in *The Souls of Black Folk*. Among the fourteen essays composing the book, seven were written and published previously, and five were published for the first time in *The Souls of Black Folk*. Among the seven, "Of Our Spiritual Strivings" was the earliest, being substantially the same 1897 essay published in *Atlantic Monthly* as **"Strivings of the Negro People."** That essay was one of the earliest definitive public

formulations of what Du Bois meant by black consciousness. The only earlier, equally precise public expression of that meaning occurred in **"The Conservation of Races,"** delivered to Crummell's American Negro Academy in March of 1897, a piece we will have cause to consider later. By contrast, "Of the Coming of John" appeared for the first time in *The Souls of Black Folk,* and was Du Bois's first published generically fictional piece. The only such piece in the book, it is its most vivid portrait of double-consciousness. In fact, John Jones, the black protagonist in "Of the Coming of John," is Du Bois's archetypical figure of the traveler who is tragically caught up in the double-consciousness of being an American Negro. What is particularly pertinent about the story of John Jones is how double-consciousness appears to entail an unhappiness that renounces the intelligibility of human reality. But, it is imperative that a careful consideration of what is meant by double-consciousness be undertaken before grappling with this complicated question of renunciation. Such a consideration begins with a close reading and engagement with "Of Our Spiritual Strivings," where the concept of double-consciousness is first formulated in an oft-cited passage:

> After the Egyptian and Indian, the Greek and Roman, the Teuton and Mongolian, the Negro is a sort of seventh son, born with a veil, and gifted with second-sight in this American world,—a world which yields him no true self-consciousness, but only lets him see himself through the revelation of the other world. It is a peculiar sensation, this double-consciousness, this sense of always looking at one's self through the eyes of others, of measuring one's soul by the tape of a world that looks on in amused contempt and pity. One ever feels his twoness,—an American, a Negro; two souls, two thoughts, two unreconciled strivings; two warring ideals in one dark body, whose dogged strength alone keeps it from being torn asunder.

This passage is generally interpreted to mean that the African American is an essentially fragmented subject. Taken to the extreme, this reading construes the black body itself as a site of contestation and struggle between two heterogenous conceptual schemas that have it as their common percept. Here, the perception of the phenomenal black body is predicated on the dualism of mind (consciousness being understood as synonymous with mind) and body. The body may be something, but the mind is something else, and the givenness of the body as a meaningful object of consciousness is the act of the mind, which determines the possibilities of experience a priori. The difference between American consciousness and Negro consciousness is substantial, then. Not only are there two acts of perception, but each act is meaningful within and according to unique and different conceptual schemas: each perception-act entails the correlation object/subject, but each perception-act is also the correlate of a particular consciousness. This understanding of Du Bois's double consciousness, which lead Larry Neal and the Black Arts Movement of the 1970s to assert that there is something called black consciousness which is the correlate of black experience, is a sort of idealist psychology.

I propose another interpretation of Du Bois's double-consciousness as a particular (American Negro) instance of the fragmentation of subjectivity that is conterminous with modernity. In this reading, the difference is not between two incommensurate consciousnesses occurring in the same body, instead double-consciousness involves the awareness in one consciousness of being both a knowing subject and an abject object. In this reading, the "veil of the seventh son" functions as a "decoding" of the hierarchical structures that characterize the organization not only of society but of knowledge. That is to say, in *The Souls of Black Folk,* Du Bois seeks to decode the experiential facts of life as a specific order of knowledge in which the expression "I, a thinking black being," designates the object-matter of psychology.

Granted, the concept of two incommensurate consciousnesses occurring in one body was already an object of psychological study when Du Bois wrote *The Souls of Black Folk*. Arnold Rampersad refers to the work of Oswald Kulpe, as one of the possible sources in psychology for Du Bois's concept of double-consciousness. In addition to this there was William Palmer's analysis of Mary Reynolds as a case of such double-consciousness, published in the May 1860 issue of *Harper's New Monthly;* and Alfred Binet's *Alterations of Personality* (1896) went some way towards establishing the phenomena as a legitimate object of psychology. It is not at all evident that Du Bois was familiar with this work, or made use of it in formulating his concept of double-consciousness. Williams James, however, is generally credited with having had the more significant influence on Du Bois's formulation of the concept of the Negro's double-consciousness. The time during which Du Bois had been James's student (1888-1892) James was teaching the non-existence of consciousness, or rather that consciousness is a function of knowing and not an entity or substance. Even without any recourse to speculation of James's influence, there is good cause in the text of *The Souls of Black Folk* for reading Du Bois to understand consciousness as a function of knowing, and not as an entity.

Admittedly, at first glance, Du Bois's formulation of his concept of double-consciousness does lend itself to understanding that two incommensurate consciousnesses inhabit the same body. To some extent, this results from his careless use of terms in describing double-consciousness. He begins by describing double-consciousness as the lack of unified consciousness, or "true self-consciousness," resulting from having no subjective sense of oneself. Then, it is a feeling of being twoness—American and Negro, which are described as being two unreconciled striving thoughts in one body. The situation is not helped by his subsequently asserting that the

"history of the American Negro is the history of this strife [between two thoughts in one body],—this longing to attain self-conscious manhood, to merge his double self into a better and truer self."

What is at stake becomes more accessible when we recall that the description of double-consciousness in *The Souls of Black Folk* derives from Du Bois's autobiographical account of becoming aware that he embodied the Negro problem, and that this account is a first response to the suppositional question: "How does it feel to be a problem?" The awareness occurs at an unspecified age in childhood as a result of a specific rejection. Du Bois and his classmates decide to exchange visiting cards:

> The exchange was merry, till one girl, a tall newcomer, refused my card,—refused peremptorily, with a glance. Then it dawned upon me with a certain suddenness that I was different from the others; or like, mayhap, in heart and life and longing, but shut out from their world by a vast veil.

By itself, this passage equates the veil with social, and not conceptual difference. In fact, it explicitly remarks, in order to emphasize the traumatic pain, that up to and including the moment of rejection there was no difference of consciousness between Du Bois and his classmates. This emphatic portrayal of like consciousness is rhetorical. Du Bois introduces the experience of racial hatred from the perspective of a thinking feeling child, who up until the moment he is told he is different is unaware of this difference. In that first moment the child does not understand a difference in consciousness between him and his mates, only a sharp sense of unjust exclusion, an exclusion made all the more painful by the knowledge that he is conceptually the same as them. Not only is the world posited the same way for him as for them, but it is meaningful in the same way; it signifies the same things. The new awareness of difference is made all the more painful and traumatic, in that it doesn't entail a conceptual rupture.

> I had thereafter no desire to tear down that veil, to creep through; I held all beyond it in common contempt, and lived above it in a region of blue sky and great wandering shadows. The sky was bluest when I could beat my mates at examination-time, or beat them at a foot-race, or even beat their stringy heads. Alas, with the years all this fine contempt began to fade; for the worlds I longed for, and all their dazzling opportunities, were theirs, not mine. But they should not keep these prizes, I said; some, all, I would wrest from them.

It is noteworthy that Du Bois's experience of himself is chiefly conceptual—no reference is made to physical differences between Du Bois and his classmates (in subsequent versions of this same story it is made clear that this is not because he did not look different, but in *The Souls of Black Folk* it is purely so). He is conscious of himself as a "little thing, away up in the hills of New England"; a knowing subject in the world of things, this is a conceptual thing, not a percept. That is to say, the boy Du Bois has a concept but no perception of his self. Of course, read in this way, Du Bois's description of his childhood consciousness is a psychologism at best: he has a contentless, pure soul. This is, to a certain extent, part of the rhetorical ploy of portraying childish innocence. But it is also pivotal in understanding the move Du Bois makes from social to conceptual difference. What happens with the girl's rejection is not her establishing for Du Bois that, for her, he is simply a percept—some material thing in the world. He was already that, being a body; and he was a perceived body for himself as well. The text is quite clear, the trauma resulted from a judgment—contempt. The problem with that judgment is that it is apophantic. This is not because Du Bois now knows himself as that which it is predicative of: Du Bois suffers the contempt of his classmates, and reciprocates—if they think they are better than me, then I think I am better than them. In other words, the girl's rejection of him does not compel him to conceptually experience himself any differently than he had previously. Whatever predicable she has in mind is just that, a concept in her mind.

This is a significant point for two reasons. First, the Negro problem is not an object, but a proposition whose precondition is the distinction between reference and meaning—the Negro need not have a truth value (a reference) in order for it to be meaningful. Second, referential indeterminacy does not necessarily equate with semantic ambiguity, instead there is evidence of two incommensurate semantics of Negro. Accordingly, the split consciousness of the Negro is understood as a function of consciously experiencing this incommensurability. Yet, because the very precondition for this semantic incommensurability is the distinction of reference and meaning, whose own precondition is the possibility of object-ness— the positing of an object—it necessarily involves a synthetically unitary (transcendental) consciousness. Insofar as this unitary consciousness is meaningful only semantically (at the level of connotation), semantic incommensurability equates with incommensurate subjective consciousnesses. In other words, the Negro's split consciousness is a function of unfungible value—of having two meanings in incommensurate languages. What makes this incommensurability a crisis is the fact that both systems claim the same reference at the same time. The temporality of reference, however, raises the question of whether or not these unfungible values are indeed heterogeneous. That is, the "Negro problem" Du Bois draws our attention to is only at first glance that of confusing referentiality and meaning; on more careful consideration it becomes that of confusing knowledge about something with thinking on it.

After all, contempt is still not conceptual difference. On the contrary, it contains the risk of the afterthought: "suppose after all, the world is right and we [Negros] are less than men." Here is the rub, Du Bois is capable of having the same concept of himself that the girl has, and achieving the same apophantic judgment without forgetting his prior conceptual experience of himself. In reflecting on the rejection, Du Bois has come to understand that knowledge of self or consciousness is purely conceptual. Social difference becomes the index of conceptual difference. This interpretation, however, begs the question which Du Bois set out in his "Forethought" as the exploration with which he connects the fourteen essays in *The Souls of Black Folk:* What are "the strange meanings of being black?" It gets rephrased in the first chapter, "Of Our Spiritual Strivings" as: "How does it feel to be a problem?" The question of the problem is about what it means to be always at minimum object-plus-subjects. Yet, in beginning to address this question, we still need to know what Du Bois means by consciousness.

Du Bois somewhat carelessly equates consciousness with thought, and understands the latter as something in his "dark body." For both Du Bois and his classmates, his body is a complex percept. For Du Bois, prior to the girl's rejection, that percept was related to his consciousness as a correlate object of it: this is my body, he would state. The statement "I am American" is slightly more complicated, in that American as a concept is also a correlate object of consciousness, and at the same time it is the conceptual correlate of the perceptual body. After the girl's rejection of him, Du Bois still knew his body as a perceptual object of consciousness, but it was also now a correlate of the concept Negro, which in turn was a conceptual object of consciousness. The two correlations, body/American and body/Negro, are objects towards which consciousness is directed: their experiences are intentional experiences. At the same time, the two different concepts, American and Negro, correlate to the same perceptual object—the dark body. There are two concepts and one percept.

Now, every intention has a structure, whose components, while themselves intentional, act in a synthetically unified intentionality. In other words, difference in intentionalities may indicate different moments of consciousness, but these differences act to constitute a unified being—they are changes in orientation of perspective within one stream of consciousness, which is nothing more than the conjunctive relation that provides a continuous associative lineage within the flow of experience. Following this, in asserting that the same object is turned or directed towards two different consciousnesses, Du Bois is asserting that there are two different intentionalities, two different *cogitos*. That is simply to say that two minds can know one thing. If this, however, is what Du Bois means by the Negro's double-consciousness, then he is maintaining an absurdity. Or else, he understands the Negro to be definitionally a multiple personality.

If consciousness is nothing more than the conjunctive relation that provides a continuous associative lineage within the flow of experience, then both the American and Negro are experiences *of* consciousness, and not consciousnesses. At this point, it seems clear that what Du Bois means by consciousness is identity. What Du Bois calls double-consciousness in the same mind is more rigorously understood as two disjuncted identities experienced *within* the stream of one consciousness. Identities are conceptual objects of experience, regardless of how they refer to or terminate in particular percepts. As such they are functions of consciousness and not consciousness itself. Whereas two incommensurate consciousnesses in one mind is an absurdity, two incommensurate identities in one stream of consciousness is not. As conceptual objects the American and Negro need not have a truth value (they need not correlate with aggregates of percepts) to be meaningful—they constitute aggregates of concepts. This reading enables us to gain some significant insights into Du Bois['s] psychology. Du Bois's double-consciousness is now recognized as a serious attempt to think about the American Negro as a particular case of the possibilities of experience in modernity rather than as an object for analysis. Insofar as he succeeds in that attempt he enables us to conceive of black consciousness as a function of experience and not the ground for experience. Black consciousness is a subjective mode of thought.

The possibility of intersubjective (collective) black identity issues from the critical engagement with the tension between the objective conditions of blackness and the subjective consciousness of blacks: other thinking creatures who look like me and have analogous experiences to mine think as I do. Based on his understanding of this tension, Du Bois recognizes black consciousness as a surplus value in the dialectic of the Negro's material abjection and black self-consciousness. In other words, Black consciousness constitutes a collective (class) critical understanding of historical change. Du Bois's proposal to engage the "darker thought,—the thought of things themselves" rather than encouraging us to determine once and for all the fact of blackness, leads our understanding away from the "natural" attitude of beings whose life is involved in the world of things to the transcendental life of consciousness. Taking that into account, his concept of double-consciousness is concerned with the question of essential authentic being, that is, with the very possibility of experience. This question of authenticity is ontological, it is concerned with genuine self-possessedness.

Even though it is Du Bois's concept of double-consciousness that leads us to this question of ontological authenticity, it is not a question he is prepared to address in *The Souls of Black Folk*. Throughout most of the book, Du Bois considers the meaning of being black—i.e., double-consciousness—in terms of the structures and relations between beings. He focuses on particular sets of social and moral behaviors. In this way the meaning of blackness is ontical, and not a question of essential authentic being. In other words, Du Bois never

really does more than continually draw our attention to the "Negro problem" as a function of unfungible values, or referential indeterminacy, which legitimates his consideration of the meaning of being black, and not what the black is. Granted, his consideration is restricted to the ontical, but that is because what he strove to overcome was the positivist cynical disregarding of the Negro's conscious self in order to "gleefully count his bastards and his prostitutes." Du Bois strove to overturn positivist sociology's narrow understanding of the Negro as merely a social phenomena, something to be objectively tabulated and studied.

For Du Bois, the only appropriate way to react to the connotation of the Negro as thing-laborer is the application of thought, to turn away from the body as being, from black people in the world as the collocation of phenomena, toward the inquiry into the constitution of the thought of black subjectivity as the ground of being. The "history of the American Negro" traced in *The Souls of Black Folk* is the projection of Negro being in thought, striving to achieve the annihilation of double-consciousness. It is the history of the dialectic interplay between knowledge and power: black thought emerges in the opposition of Will to the ordering of Ideas. Du Bois's recognizing the Negro as a real ontical being, rather than merely an object for positive scientific analysis, was an extremely radical departure from the established way of thinking. Even though it is not yet there, his departure is towards thinking the question of authentic ontological being. What is lost in the exchange of the empirical black, who was the object of sociological analysis, for the thinking black subject is the ability to unproblematically talk about blacks in the world. What is gained is the ability to think the authentic possibilities of being—the *thetic*.

This is not to deny the fact that there are Negroes, a fact that the girl's rejection drove home for Du Bois. Instead, it is to deny that the fact of the Negro defines the authenticity of Negro being. For all the limitations of Du Bois's concept of double-consciousness, this is the challenge it draws us towards, the challenge to think the Negro authentically. Thinking the authentic being of the Negro requires the constructive bringing to view of Negro being by projecting the free possibilities of being out of its particular structures. This projection requires, in turn, the deconstruction of that thinking about Negro being that correlates the perceptual and conceptual objects. The proper pursuit of this line of thought would call for a rather rigorous phenomenology of the Negro, which is far more than can be done at this moment. Even though it is Du Bois's concept of double-consciousness that has enabled us to discover the question of authenticity, pursuing it any further along these lines will take us a bit too far from the concern with which we began. That concern was with Du Bois's concept of double-consciousness as the presupposition of his understanding of intellectual vanguardism, and how that is antinomic to his commitment to pluralist democracy.

Appreciating more clearly how Du Bois's understanding of the black intellectual vanguard presupposes his concept of the Negro as a real ontical being requires a more careful interrogation of his notions about the proper socio-political function of the black artist. Succinctly stated, that function was to create in different media as accurate as possible a representation of Blacks' unfailing moral strength in the face of the daily struggle with abjection at the hands of white America. Black artists should be ever mindful that given the historical, political, and social stakes of the division between black and white America, the relation of cultural object to group "being" matters. For Du Bois, artists, and especially literary artists, were ideologues, not as producers of false consciousness, but as the producers of a whole new body of knowledge derived from and constitutive of the lived experience of the Negro. Black art should serve black solidarity. Such a solidarity grounded in objective representation has to construe truth as correspondence to reality, requiring that there be formulated a special relation between belief and their objects, enabling the differentiation of true and false beliefs and thereby entailing the determination of specified procedures of justification of belief. Du Bois understood that relationship as duty: the obligation to know the difference between the best and the worst. Thus, artistic activity relies upon a determination of the nature of things; Du Bois's artist is a modern intellectual who requires that epistemology enable procedures of legitimation that are not merely social but apparently natural, issuing from the linking of human action to nature in general. Only those procedures of legitimation that lead to truth, to the correspondence of knowledge to reality, are truly legitimate under this view.

Furthermore, truth as the result of artistic/intellectual activity was an absolute to be pursued for its own sake, beyond the immediate desiderata and practical exigencies of one's self and/or community, which, again, should themselves derive from this understanding of the truth. As Anthony Appiah has observed, throughout his life Du Bois was concerned not just with the meaning of race but with the truth about race. Indeed, Du Bois's famous Atlanta Conferences were driven by the search after truth.

Prior to *The Souls of Black Folk,* Du Bois sought this truth in social positivism. As he argued in **"My Evolving Program,"** the "long term remedy [to racism] was Truth: carefully gathered scientific proof that neither color nor race determined the limits of a man's capacity or desert." Du Bois employed positivism to reveal the constructed and ideologically determined character of the "givenness" of Black inferiority. Du Bois's conception of the social sciences was that they were the theoretical understanding of existent social phenomena. On this view, science is instrumental, in the logical sense that its propositions are only conditionally heuristic or prescriptive and never absolutely so. This understanding of instrumental reason was the methodological basis for both his *Philadelphia Negro* and the Atlanta Conferences (1897-

1910). As a result of the problems encountered in interpreting and translating into a program of action the data collected by the Atlanta Conferences, however, he concluded that privileging scientific sociology was not the best means for achieving black liberation. Confronted with the "startling reality" of the black's oppression, which called for immediate action to prevent social death (i.e., lynching), Du Bois perceived that positivism's conception of knowledge entailed a dangerous disjunction between theory and its practical consequences.

This is not to suggest that Du Bois abandoned a notion of truth as such, but rather that he began to question the validity of any procedure of rational justification that claimed to derive its legitimacy from determinate knowledge. As far as the social condition of blacks was concerned, there just wasn't enough time to determine the comprehensive grounds for knowledge. Epistemology was useful only insofar as it entailed a theory of action. In Du Bois's thinking, the social interests informing technological progress were inseparably linked to the function of hypothesis-ordering entailed in scientific inquiry. In effect, then, the facts that are most fruitful, including those of the knowledge already possessed, are those that have practical application to given circumstances. Knowledge must constitute theory in an absolute way, as though theory was grounded in the inner nature of instrumental knowledge itself. Or else theory must be legitimated in some other ahistorical fashion, such as the actualization of instrumental interests in nature. At this point, Du Bois's whole attitude toward the function of theory in the social sciences had to change—in the study of human beings and their actions, there could be no divergence between theory and social praxis.

In the course of this celebrated turn from positivism to pragmatism, Du Bois started thinking about the historical emergence of black consciousness as a contentious process of cognition that resists resolution. Du Bois called this crucial irresolvable contention the "dialectic of progression," whose two terms are natural law (necessity) and chance (indeterminacy). Gaining insight into this dialectic required that sociology be reformulated as a philosophy of science, whose work was to determine the relationship of indeterminacy to law. It also required just the sort of elaboration provided in *The Souls of Black Folk* of how self-reflective subjectivity comes to consciousness through experience. Du Bois's gesture is a calculated one, in which he redirects sociology back toward Kant's anthropology. In his own words, the object of sociology becomes to measure the "Kantian Absolute and Undetermined Ego."

In this context the "veil" of black consciousness functions as the metonymic statement of the unthought in its unthinkableness, whose purpose is to expose thinking as generating complexities and complications in its density, rather than resolving difference in its translucence. This is a restating of our earlier reading of Du Bois's "history of the American Negro" as the dialectic between knowledge and power. Only in this restating, it is far more clear what is at stake in understanding this to mean that black thought emerges in the opposition of Will to the ordering of Ideas. It means black consciousness is truth. The consequent relativization of knowledge is meant to clear a space for the introduction of a theory of value capable of problematizing the material basis for theories of social determinism and their concomitant legitimation of racism. This shift to theory of value notwithstanding, Du Bois does not altogether abandon the conception of an ultimate truth. On the contrary, truth is recognized as a teleology that discovers the essential homogeneity of humanity through the universality of relative values. Truth is preserved as a question that is unanswerable, except in terms of its specific localized expression—i.e., the truth of black consciousness— it remains always as the essential Absolute in which the cultural frame of reference is grounded.

Thus far, I have found it useful to talk about *The Souls of Black Folk* as Du Bois's presentation of the history of the American Negro. I have also shown how, as such, it is exemplary of his treating the American Negro as the paradigmatic case in his attempt to describe the production of collective identity in terms of discursive effect. I have done so to underscore the extent to which his investment in reasserting the priority of the epistemological subject over and against the ascendancy of the positivist methodology of the social sciences is predicated on his commitment to pluralist democracy. The history of the American Negro outlined in *The Souls of Black Folk* is a demonstration that truly pluralistic democracy is instituted through people's appropriation of their power of signification. Positivism resists that appropriation; in its asserting that the foundations of the social are determined by objective conditions, independent of human will, it makes foundational knowledge the special province of scientific methodology.

> **Black consciousness, for Du Bois, is a function of experience and not the ground for experience. It is a mode of thought that emerges in interplay between knowledge and power. As such, the concern of Black consciousness is authenticity as genuine self-possessedness.**
>
> **—Ronald A. T. Judy**

Du Bois recognized that such an exalted methodology, whose theory derives from purely logical or methodological sources, takes the place of religion in its dogmatic refusal to put into question the legitimacy of the status of its knowledge. His dialectic of progress is the desacralization of this knowledge, in which natural law is reconceptualized as a constructed frame of reference marking objective reality, and interacting with

our indeterminate knowledge (which Du Bois at times refers to as being an autonomous dynamic). According to the dialectic of progress, liberating sociological analysis does not derive from purely logical or methodological sources, but can only be understood in the context of historical social praxes. Theory as intellectual work is a social praxis actively involved in the instituting of the social. In this way the dialectic of progression produces black consciousness as a principle of social democracy—i.e., the secularization of knowledge gets subjects who are conscious of their power of institution. In other words, whereas positivism saw sovereignty in the correct function of knowledge (i.e., methodology), Du Bois found it in the collective will, the consciousness of the folk.

Recall that in *The Souls of Black Folk* Du Bois displaces the Negro as an object of positive scientific analysis for the Negro as a self-conscious thinking ontical being. The concept of double-consciousness enables this displacement because it calls us to think the Negro authentically. Even though this concept of double-consciousness leads to the ontological question of authenticity it fails to address it. Instead, it serves two strategic (in fact rhetorical) functions. On the one hand, it enables Du Bois to exhibit the Negro as a self-conscious thinking subject. On the other hand, it is the figure of collective psychosis, resulting from social injustice. By the same token, double-consciousness establishes the heterogeneous origins of Negro and American identity. The psychosis of double-consciousness is not the result of a prior unified identity becoming fragmented, it results from the failure to merge two heterogeneous consciousnesses into one identity. At this point, Du Bois is quite clear that pluralistic democracy dictates the annihilation of double-consciousness: "The history of the American Negro is . . . this longing to attain self-conscious manhood, to merge his double self into a better and truer self." On the face of it, the argument is that pluralistic democracy requires the merging of the divided racial subject "into" the truer self of the American citizen. Yet, the very next sentence contradicts this, slipping from "into" to "with":

> He [the Negro] would not Africanize America, for America has too much to teach the world and Africa. He would not bleach his Negro soul in a flood of white Americanism, for he knows that Negro blood has a message for the world. He simply wishes to make it possible for a man to be both a Negro and an American.

This passage is one of the rare moments in *The Souls of Black Folk* where it's explicitly stated that the two juxtaposed consciousnesses are those of the Negro and the white, and not the Negro and the American. Even in *The Souls of Black Folk,* the Negro is a consciousness and American is an identity. Arguably, this is little more than Du Bois's revisiting the Jeffersonian idea of the difference between the private and public spheres. According to this concept polity is in the public sphere, and each and every citizen participates as an individual citizen in that sphere regardless of their affiliations or formations in the private sphere of culture or society. Participation in the public sphere does not require the renunciation of the citizen's private interests and affiliations; what guarantees access to the public sphere is the rule of law. The chief problem with this view is it fails to take sufficient care of the problems of movement between the two spheres. If any one corporate interest of the private sphere gains hegemony over the public sphere through its controlling the conditions in which the rule of law is interpreted, then the effectiveness of the distinction between the two spheres is lost. Of course, it was precisely such a hegemony Du Bois sought to problematize: the law defined the Negro as property in accordance with certain collective interests in the private sphere; that fact of law precluded the Negro's gaining direct access to the public sphere where, as free citizens, they could amend the law. The violent rupture of civil war precipitated the amendment of the law; yet since the war was principally a political, and insufficiently a private issue, the broader societal factors, the complex of private interests, that had enslaved the Negro legally, interpreted the law so as to maintain their hegemony.

In *The Souls of Black Folk,* Du Bois identifies the relationship between ideology and law when, writing about the failure of the Freedmen's Bureau to exercise its juridical function, he states: "Almost every law and method ingenuity could devise was employed by the legislatures to reduce the Negroes to serfdom,—to make them slaves of the state, if not of individuals." Or again, writing about the possibilities of the Negro's participation in the public sphere, he proclaims: "The laws are made by men who have little interest in [the Negro]; they are executed by men who have absolutely no motive for treating the black people with courtesy or consideration." This interrelationship between ideology and law creates, in Du Bois's view, the circumstances in which "the Negro is coming more and more to look upon law and justice, not as protecting safeguards, but as sources of humiliation and oppression." The rule of law has become the means by which the Negro is enslaved, the cause is in "the all-pervading desire to inculcate disdain for everything black, from Toussaint to the devil." Hence, the urgency with which Du Bois argues that the recognition and development of the Negro as a thinking subject as *the* prerequisite for complete democracy. For that matter, pluralist democracy is not possible in America as long as the racial subject is antinomic to the citizen. Merging the racial subject with the citizen is the solution called for in *The Souls of Black Folk,* the way of achieving this offered in **"The Conservation of Races"** is to formulate a legitimating collective narrative capable of transcending comprehensively the plurality of communities within the nation. That narrative is based on understanding the real meaning of race, which recognizes racial identity as a function of historical development towards the realization of absolute human spirit: "that one far off Divine event."

Recognizing that Du Bois thinks about race in terms of *Identitätsphilosphie* (identity-philosophy), is a *sine qua non* for understanding the idealism operating in his conception of race and its connectedness with his notion of social democracy. Race for Du Bois is *Gemeinschaft,* an assemblage of human beings according to common history, traditions and impulses, "who are both voluntarily and involuntarily striving together for the accomplishment of certain more or less vividly conceived ideals of life." The subject of race results from the authenticating genealogy or collective narrative of shared historical experience, giving rise to what Du Bois called culture. The conception of race as culture and not biology is fundamentally an argument for the discursive constitution of subjects. But in Du Bois's theory of the historical construction of collective identity, a fundamental and universal consciousness drives each collective identity in its specificity. Racial difference functions according to a dialectic of progression in which each race strives to realize the utopian movement in which the spirit of humanity will return to itself. As he puts it in **"The Conservation of Races,"** the "full complete Negro message of the whole Negro race" is to be given to the world through "the development of Negro genius, of Negro literature and art, of Negro spirit."

Understanding the subject of race to be a specific expression of the essential, or Absolute, human entails taking the exclusionary legitimation of the American citizen to be the annihilation of the human. As Du Bois pointed out in his *Suppression of the Atlantic Slave Trade,* and later in *Black Reconstruction,* where the American citizen is the subject selected as the legitimate custodian of political will, it is selected as such in exclusion of specific other subject-constructions, specifically blacks. When the state invests in such a narrow definition of the citizen as its sole legitimate subject, it cannot bring the collective human will into full effect. Du Bois's corrective for this was a program of intellectual activity that reaffirmed the subject of race as the sole legitimate space for socialization. The merger of the Negro's double-consciousness into a truer self called for in *The Souls of Black Folk* is not so much a merger as the accommodation of the political will to racial identity. Positing the universality of the subject of race as an abstraction, Du Bois discovers the psychology of the Negro as *the* case for thoroughly calculating the generation and effect of cultural representations, and displacing the speculative interests of social positivism with the figure of the racial subject as the legitimate grounds for organizing the social. Accordingly, black intellectuals are the legitimate representatives of the race—race-men. Their election, however, is based on a propriety of knowledge that presupposes rightful participation in a public sphere that already excludes the Negro from civil society (which Du Bois came to identify with economy). The principal function of the talented tenth, then, is to engender an order of publicity, aimed at the inclusion of the Negro in civil society (hence Du Bois's insistence that an additional function of the tenth is incorporation in economic co-operatives). In other words, the legitimate work of the black intellectual is to both represent the essential humanity of black folk, and to create the conditions in which that humanity is recognizable as valuable to civil society.

Du Bois's argument that the development of the Negro subject was a prerequisite for complete democracy notwithstanding, having race monopolize legitimate socialization is antinomic to democracy precisely because it disassociates the political will from the social in such a way that social authority is the determinant of legitimate accesses to the public sphere. In the case of the black intellectual, social authority is a function of racial authenticity, which is acquired by defining the grounds of legitimate folk expression. In the movement from racial subject to citizenship that characterizes the merging of the Negro's double-consciousness into a truer self, the public sphere is not produced by the continuous conscious spontaneity of action on the part of free individuals under the rule of law; instead, it is the sphere of struggle between organic collective constituencies. Even as indeterminacy points to the limitations of prescriptive natural law, it reveals the subjugation of the political subject (the citizen) to racial identity. The logic of racial emancipation in differentiation is, thus, discovered in the socioeconomic and political totalitarianism of a *patria*. Here is where the antinomy of race and democracy I spoke of earlier strikes. Establishing the universality of the subject of race as an abstraction is the first step towards achieving the annihilation of the political subject. Having engaged in an anti-foundationalist critique of sociology in order to recognize that a condition for democracy is the indeterminacy of knowledge, Du Bois reaffirms that the foundations of the social are determined by objective conditions after all: the almost mechanistic dialects of race and bloodline.

This careful retracing of the tortuous turns in Du Bois's critical theory was undertaken in order to understand how Du Bois's theory of intellectual vanguardism presupposed his concept of black consciousness, and how that concept is antinomic to his commitment to pluralist democracy. Simply put, the black intelligentsia are race-men, whose authority derives from their ability to define black consciousness as the only authentic mode of being in which the Negro can enter the public sphere. Such a consciousness is antinomic to pluralist democracy because it subordinates the political subject to the racial. The need to understand this was prompted by the New Black Aesthetics' offering us a return to racial vanguardism as the means of affirming social democracy. More is at stake here, however, than simply establishing that Du Bois's concept of black consciousness is paradigmatic for the NBA. The more crucial issue is how is such a conception of black consciousness as key to social change still possible, given the absurdity inherent in its formulation. As stated earlier, that possibility has to do with precisely what is meant by consciousness in the concepts black consciousness and black experience.

Black consciousness, for Du Bois, is a function of experience and not the ground for experience. It is a mode of thought that emerges in interplay between knowledge and power. As such, the concern of Black consciousness is authenticity as genuine self-possessedness. The thing is, in Du Bois's concept of double-consciousness, the question of authenticity is misconstrued. Rather than being the concern with genuine self-possessedness as the very possibility of experience, *The Souls of Black Folk* is concerned with the socio-political meanings of Black consciousness. What this means is that the question of authentic Black being is presupposed by the concept of double-consciousness, but never addressed. This failure to address authenticity proves critical, for in order to establish the Negro's consciousness Du Bois is compelled to ground it in an unsubstantiated notion of exceptionalism: "[The Negro] would not Africanize America, for America has much to teach the world and Africa. He would not bleach his Negro soul in a flood of white Americanism, for he knows that Negro blood has a message for the world."

The self-conscious parody and ironic signifying of Ellis's NBA—i.e., the idea of the "cultural mulatto"—is best understood as a form of this same exceptionalism, only with a deft modernist spin to it. Like Du Bois, the NBA understands culture as a field of human activity that although historically related to material economic conditions transcends those conditions. Again, as with Du Bois's thinking, the NBA defines black identity in terms of culture. Culture is not simply derivative of what used to be referred to as political economy; it does not represent the system of the material socio-economic relations that regulate the existence of individuals, but the imaginary relation of those individuals to the material socio-economic relations in which they live. That is to say, individuals live in the moment of their imaginary relations to the material, and this is culture.

There is an acute sense of the present as a constitutive element of aesthetic experience in Ellis's conception of the NBA as a postliberation aesthetic. This is underscored in his emphasizing its being the synthesis of past aesthetics (the Harlem Renaissance and the Black Arts Movement) that rearticulates them into a representation of the present. We have not adequately addressed the question of time in Du Bois's and Ellis's conceptions of aesthetics. A beginning gesture towards addressing this question—which is all there is time for in this closing summary of resemblance—would be to note the permanent parabasis (the stepping aside) prevalent in so much NBA work, such that it constitutes the narrative structure of Ellis's *Platitudes,* and Darins James's *Negrophobia,* as well as being expressed musically in sampling and scratching. Permanent parabasis, so Friedrich Schlegel defined irony, and irony, for Ellis, is a constitutive element of the NBA.

The idea of the cultural mulatto is, after all, the idea of the permanently self-conscious narrator, whose enunciations continually discover the temporal predicament of the "now": the mere coincidence of material reality and the reality of enunciation. There is a sense of Baudelaire's driven and harassed man (*imitant la toupie et la boule*) in Ellis's characterization of the New Black Aesthetic as *"neobarocco."* In other words, the cultural mulatto is caught up in an unrelieved vertigo, in which identification and stability exist only in the symbolic power of the mind. Thinking about irony in this way is to think, again, like Baudelaire, for whom irony was the absolute comedy in its tendency towards hyperbole.

To suggest that the New Black Aesthetic is a form of absolute comedy, is not to dismiss it, but, instead to remark on its relationship to Du Bois's Romantic idealism in its understanding of aesthetics. This is the end of an already complicated and conceptually burdened essay, and so it is not the moment to embark on an elaboration of the etymology of "aesthetics." What can be stated sensibly at this juncture is that in claiming for the NBA a transforming robust spirituality—Ellis calls it the attitude of liberalism—with global implications, Ellis understands aesthetics to be sentimental. This means that the disturbatory expression of the NBA is focused on the interiority of the new black, cultural mulatto consciousness. Hence, the overemphasis on formalism in Ellis's descriptions of what makes the NBA "new." Thing is, this understanding of aesthetics becomes the basis for a supremacist sense of black cultural difference. Ellis asserts that the NBA dominates popular culture because it is separate from and better than the dominant culture. This claim for the NBA catches it in a vexing dilemma. How can the NBA be an anti-aesthetic when it persists in seeing culture as the terrain of subjective formation? Auto-parody leads to a stasis of thought when the NBA can proclaim that "'that other culture is definitely spent,' while black people have yet to see the best days of our race," and still claim to be "an attitude of liberalism rather than a restrictive code." The notion of cultural exceptionalism is also intimated in Tate's arguing that it is the "worldly-wise stoopidfresh intelligentsia of radical bups" who embody the viable non-cultural nationalist resistance to transnational capitalism. Tate's parody of Du Bois's concept of the talented tenth keeps him caught up in Du Bois's concept of thinking humans as the agents of historical change. For the NBA, as well as for Du Bois, there are thinking subjects who collectively enunciate society.

To hold culture as the grounding of the triad culture/subject/society so that culture describes thought—as in black culture black thought—is to still work according to modernity's understanding of sign-value: to hold the truth of experience as a totality. Tate, more than Ellis, has some sense of this when he calls for a form of resistance that doesn't aim for transcendence of corporation into some mythical liberated zone of authentic identity, but for critical intervention in the process by which transnational capitalism is rationalized through mass culture and modernism. Doing this becomes possible, however, only by letting go of a certain way of thinking about thought in relation to society, an abandoning of the Hegelian dialectic of recognition lurking in the identification of beauty and truth with which this essay begins. This, of course, is an altogether different question of authenticity.

FURTHER READING

Biography

Broderick, Francis L. *W. E. B. Du Bois: Negro Leader in a Time of Crisis.* Stanford: Stanford University Press, 1959, 259 p.
> First book-length biography of Du Bois. Broderick made use of Du Bois's private papers at the University of Massachusetts until Du Bois closed them to the public after his 1951 indictment as an unregistered agent of a foreign power.

Du Bois, Shirley Graham. *His Day Is Marching On: A Memoir of W. E. B. Du Bois.* Philadelphia: J. B. Lippincott Company, 1971, 384 p.
> Biography and personal memoir by Du Bois's second wife.

Moore, Jack B. *W. E. B. Du Bois.* Boston: Twayne Publishers, 1981, 185 p.
> Biography concentrating on Du Bois's life and works.

Criticism

Baker, Houston A., Jr. "The Black Man of Culture: W. E. B. Du Bois and *The Souls of Black Folk.*" In *Long Black Song: Essays in Black American Literature and Culture,* pp. 96-108. Charlottesville: The University Press of Virginia, 1972.
> Discusses Du Bois's definition of "the black man of culture and his role in modern society."

Byerman, Keith. "Race and Romance: *The Quest of the Silver Fleece* as Utopian Narrative." *American Literary Realism* 21, No. 3 (Spring 1992): 58-71.
> Argues that the allegorical elements in Du Bois's *The Quest of the Silver Fleece,* as well as the necessities of narrative, undercut the novel's ideological message.

———. "The Children Ceased to Hear My Name: Recovering the Self in *The Autobiography of W. E. B. Du Bois.*" In *Multicultural Autobiography: American Lives,* edited by James Robert Payne, pp. 64-93. Knoxville: The University of Tennessee Press, 1992.
> Argues that a deep sense of anxiety pervades Du Bois's autobiography and concludes that Du Bois sought to create a "permanent portrait of himself as the ultimate American."

Downs, Robert B. "Black Protestant: William Edward Burghardt Du Bois's *The Souls of Black Folk.*" In *Books That*

Changed the South, pp. 197-207. Chapel Hill: The University of North Carolina Press, 1977.

    Examines the essays contained in *The Souls of Black Folk* and concludes that the book is "an impassioned black nationalist document, consciously directed toward the Negro people, and identifying with Africa, blackness, and the rural Negro."

Duberman, Martin. "The Autobiography of W. E. B. Du Bois." In *The Uncompleted Past,* pp. 195-202. New York: Random House, 1969.

    Reviews Du Bois's *Autobiography* and comments on his beliefs about racism in the United States.

Johnson, Dennis Loy. "In the Hush of Great Barrington: One Writer's Search for W. E. B. Du Bois." *The Georgia Review* XLIX, No. 3 (Fall 1995): 581-606.

    Provides a summary of Du Bois's life and discusses the controversy surrounding a memorial to him in his hometown of Great Barrington, Massachusetts.

The Massachusetts Review XXXV, No. 2 (Summer 1994): 166-332.

    Special issue devoted to Du Bois and his works.

McCarthy, Mary. "The Federal Theatre." In *Sights and Spectacles, 1937-1956,* pp. 30-38. New York: Farrar, Straus and Cudahy, 1956.

    Briefly reviews Du Bois's play *Haiti* along with several other plays.

Rampersad, Arnold. *The Art and Imagination of W. E. B. Du Bois.* Cambridge, Mass.: Harvard University Press, 1976, 325 p.

    Evaluation of Du Bois's intellectual influences and changing thought.

Rudwick, Elliotte. "W. E. B. Du Bois: In the Role of *Crisis* Editor." *The Journal of Negro History* XLIII, No. 3 (July 1958): 214-40.

    Analyzes Du Bois's stewardship of the NAACP's magazine *Crisis* from 1910 to 1934 and his relationship with the organization's board of directors.

Stepto, Robert B. "The Quest of the Weary Traveler: W. E. B. Du Bois's *The Souls of Black Folk.*" In *From Behind the Veil: A Study of Afro-American Narrative,* pp. 52-91. Urbana: University of Illinois Press, 1991.

    Examines the narrative structure and technique of *The Souls of Black Folk.*

Taylor, Councill. "Clues for the Future: Black Urban Anthropology Reconsidered." In *Race, Change, and Urban Society,* edited by Peter Orleans and William Russell Ellis, Jr., pp. 603-618. Beverly Hills, Calif.: Sage Publications, 1971.

    Analyzes various black urban anthropological studies, using Du Bois's *The Philadelphia Negro* as a model for comparison.

Additional coverage of Du Bois's life and career is contained in the following sources published by Gale Research: *Black Literature Criticism; Black Writers; Concise Dictionary of American Literary Biography, 1865-1917; Contemporary Authors,* **Vols. 85-88;** *Contemporary Authors New Revision Series,* **Vol. 34;** *Contemporary Literary Criticism,* **Vols. 1, 2, 13, 64;** *Dictionary of Literary Biography,* **Vols. 47, 50, 91;** *DISCovering Authors; Major 20th-Century Writers; Something about the Author,* **Vol. 42; and** *World Literature Criticism.*

Janet Frame

1924-

New Zealand novelist, autobiographer, short story writer, and poet.

The following entry presents an overview of Frame's works through 1992. For further information on her life and career, see *CLC*, Volumes 2, 3, 6, 22, and 66.

INTRODUCTION

Frame is one of New Zealand's most well-known contemporary fiction writers and has published numerous novels, stories, and poems, many of which are set in her native country. Much of her fiction is marked by a concern with death, language, poverty, and madness—conditions with which she became familiar while growing up during the Depression, and later when she spent several years in a mental institution after being diagnosed erroneously as a schizophrenic. Frame often explores misconceptions about insanity by juxtaposing madness and fantasy with reality. She also frequently employs figurative language in an effort to depict the ways in which people communicate—or fail to communicate. W. H. New explained that "for the patient reader of her fiction, the . . . reward derives from the aesthetic demands the author makes; to read Frame's stories is not merely to be invited to meet a set of characters and a range of strange events, but also to be drawn into framed narratives where the structures of the prose are themselves the means and the metaphors of perceptual understanding."

Biographical Information

Frame began writing as a child in an effort to liberate herself from what she termed "a background of poverty, drunkenness, attempted murder, and near-madness." During the Depression, her large family scraped out a living in a rural area of New Zealand and suffered several tragedies: two of her sisters drowned in separate incidents, and her younger brother suffered many seizures from epilepsy. Though she wanted to be a writer, Frame studied teaching in college but soon suffered a nervous breakdown that landed her in a psychiatric hospital and effectively ended her teaching career. She was forced to submit to hundreds of sessions of electroshock therapy, but despite this she continued to write and published her first book of short stories, *The Lagoon* (1951), while still a patient. Reflecting her abiding concerns for destructive familial relationships and the consequences of miscommunication between individuals and societies, Frame's writing addresses the social inequities of people who are perceived as being psychologically, physically, or intellectually inferior by those possessing political power.

Major Works

Frame's early novels are generally regarded as disturbing and powerful. These include *Owls Do Cry* (1957), which concerns a woman struggling to survive in a psychiatric hospital; *Intensive Care* (1970), a story about the creation of legislation that would rid the world of misfits; and *Scented Gardens for the Blind* (1963), an allegorical tale about the possible atomic destruction of Britain. Robert Osterman commented on Frame's early work: "No one can call Janet Frame an easy novelist to come to terms with. Her imagination is most comfortable with subjects like madness, personal dislocations in time and place, and the use of dreams and illusions to keep life at bay. And deep in all her fiction lies a passionate concern for language and the betrayals of human purpose it can be made to serve." Much of Frame's fiction contains autobiographical elements, but it was not until the publication of her three-volume autobiography in the 1980s that Frame revealed the details of her family life and the eight years she spent in and out of mental hospitals as a young woman. *To the Is-Land* (1982) traces Frame's poverty-stricken childhood in New Zealand and investigates some of the incidents that later led to a series of nervous breakdowns. In the second installment, *An Angel at My Table* (1984), Frame recounts her experiences as a student at a teacher's training college and the events that caused her to flee from an assignment when an inspector entered her class to observe her lesson. After this incident Frame attempted suicide for the first time, was diagnosed as schizophrenic, and sent to a mental hospital where "the squalor and inhumanity were almost indescribable." The narrative of *The Envoy from the Mirror City* (1985) begins after Frame was released from psychiatric care. Deciding to move to England to broaden her experience and to develop her talents as a writer, Frame visits a respected mental facility in London and discovers that the diagnosis of schizophrenia which had ruled her life for so many years was incorrect. Although unnerved by the implications of this discovery, Frame continues to rely upon the rejuvenating powers of writing to which she had always been drawn: "It is a little wonder that I value writing as a way of life when it actually saved my life." In 1989 New Zealand filmmaker Jane Campion brought Frame's story to the cinema in the award-winning film *An Angel at My Table,* which dramatizes many of the events in the three volumes of Frame's autobiography. Frame has continued to garner critical acclaim with her subsequent novels, most notably *The Carpathians* (1988), which won Frame a Commonwealth Literary Prize. *The Carpathians* takes place in the fictional town of Puamahara, New Zealand, where a local legend purports that a young Maori woman gained unusual knowledge of human history after tasting the fruit of an unknown tree. Mattina Breton, a wealthy New Yorker, travels to New Zealand to learn the source of the folktale from Puamahara's eccentric residents and becomes fascinated by reports of the Gravity Star, an astral phenomenon that—if real—would challenge common perceptions of time and space and destroy the world.

Critical Reception

Several critics, including Owen Leeming, have commented on how difficult Frame's novels can be to interpret. Narrators cannot be assumed to be truthful, and events cannot necessarily be taken as fact. Many critics have praised the lyrical, complex language and word games Frame employs in her fiction; the names of her characters are frequently symbolic, like Thera Pattern in *The Edge of the Alphabet* (1962), Vera Glace in *Scented Gardens for the Blind,* and Malfred Signal in *A State of Siege* (1966), but other critics have dismissed these tactics as a distraction from her thematic intentions. In addition, some critics have faulted *The Carpathians* for complex and interrelated elements of reality and fantasy, but have lauded her exploration of the relationships between language, conformity, and the mysteries of time and space. Jayne Pilling has commented: "As so often in Frame's novels, there's a curious, combustible mix of modes at work here. An apparently straightforward narrative is exploded from within by a mother-load of metaphor. . . . Yet its possibilities are so rich that Frame needs several different narratives, Chinese-box style, to contain them." Thomas Crawford has called her "our

most subjective writer," but her depictions of 1950s mental hospitals are considered by most to be a valuable insight into a system marked by abuse of power and neglect of the individual. One criticism of Frame's portrayal of social inequities is that she is quick to point out the shortcomings of the bourgeoisie, but she never proposes a solution; as Muriel Haynes has explained it, Frame is an "obsessed mourner" who is "steeped in nostalgia and, in her grief for man's betrayal of his sustaining myths, tends to slight present social and cultural complexities." Jeanne Delbare-Garant, in an essay regarding Frame's early novels, has praised the author's technical skill, stating that "Frame herself is, like Orpheus, the keeper of the lighthouse and the guardian of language, the torchbearer standing in the radiance of the perfect circle, the authentic *Dasein* through which being reveals itself and, like the wind in a tree, sends its message to the rest of mankind."

PRINCIPAL WORKS

The Lagoon (short stories) 1951
Owls Do Cry (novel) 1957
Faces in the Winter (novel) 1961
The Edge of the Alphabet (novel) 1962
The Reservoir: Stories and Sketches (short stories) 1963
Scented Gardens for the Blind (novel) 1963
Snowman, Snowman: Fables and Fantasies (short stories) 1963
The Adaptable Man (novel) 1965
A State of Siege (novel) 1966
The Pocket Mirror (poetry) 1967
The Rainbirds [published in the United States as *Yellow Flowers in the Antipodean Room*] (novel) 1968
Intensive Care (novel) 1970
Daughter Buffalo (novel) 1972
Living in the Maniototo (novel) 1979
To the Is-Land (autobiography) 1982
An Angel at My Table (autobiography) 1984
You Are Now Entering the Human Heart (short stories) 1984
The Envoy from the Mirror City (autobiography) 1985
The Carpathians (novel) 1988

CRITICISM

Aileen Pippett (review date 9 September 1961)

SOURCE: A review of *Faces in the Water,* in *Saturday Review,* September 9, 1961, p. 23.

[*Pippett is a British editor, biographer, and critic. In the following review, she finds that Frame expresses "an underlying truth about our common humanity" in* Faces in the Water.]

A prefatory note states that this book, [Janet Frame's *Faces in the Water,*] although in documentary form, is a work of fiction. This claim to be true in outline and essence is amply justified. As a report on mental hospitals in New Zealand it checks with accounts from many countries about similar conditions of overcrowding and shortage of adequately trained staffs. As a novel it carries conviction because the author has artistic integrity and intuitive understanding. She is firmly in control of her material and sure of her direction, as the unfortunate girl who here tells her own story of nine years of physical confinement and mental confusion so piteously was not.

The choice of the odd name of Estina Mavet for her hapless heroine is an indication of Miss Frame's skill, for it immediately suggests divergence from the normal, since no other character in the story, mad or sane, is so outlandishly identified. But Estina's apartness from her real self and from other people was not complete. At times reduced to almost subhuman level, she retained some awareness of her plight; she knew she was mad, in a madhouse, but she was not an idiot, a contented babbler.

Miss Frame can command the nightmare images of delusion but she uses them with restraint to increase their effectiveness. She never allows Estina to attempt an explanation or pretend a feeling beyond her limited capacity. Thus we are not told what caused the "great gap [which] opened in the ice floe" and cut Estina adrift from reality, though there are hints in the account of a confused love-hate attitude towards a nurse that point to the possible disturbing factor of an unresolved conflict with her mother and jealousy of a happily married sister.

However, we can only guess at explanations, for Estina seems to have had very little psychiatric help. Doctors flit hurriedly past, too busy to pay much attention to any one patient. Their orders are relentlessly enforced; protests are unavailing. Treatment, including electric shock, is therefore not understood as curative in purpose but as punishment for unknown offenses. Relaxation of stricter rules, removal from one category to another as the disease tightens or loosens its grip are equally inexplicable to a sufferer staggering under a self-imposed load of fear and guilt.

We do not know how Estina eventually regained her reason and her freedom, but we see the first glimmer of light in her darkness when she writes, "We all see the faces in the water" (that is, drowning people in need of help), "and sometimes we see our own face." Thus Miss Frame uses an illusion in a sick mind to express an underlying truth about our common humanity. Her novel by its objectivity and its coherence takes us through an inferno but releases us at last to sweet upper air.

Robert Pick (review date 8 October 1961)

SOURCE: "Ordeal at Cliffhaven," in *The New York Times Book Review,* October 8, 1961, p. 36.

[*Pick is an Austrian-born novelist, editor, and translator. In the following review, he discusses the literary device of allegory as it pertains to Frame's* Faces in the Water.]

When Miss Frame's first book, **Owls Do Cry,** appeared a year ago, it was hailed as the first important novel to come out of New Zealand. Her new novel [*Faces in the Water*] is an equally remarkable achievement. Presented as the memoir of a cured mental patient, its blend of on-the-spot observation and hindsight, far from weakening the immediacy of the writing, strengthens its power. A disturbing book, it grows confusing only when the author permits her apparent love of poetical metaphor to invade her prose, with the result that the reader is left wondering to which plane of experience these lyricisms belong.

The narrator of the story is Istina, a young woman and one-time teacher, who has spent several years behind asylum walls in her native New Zealand. Once she is "signed out of hospital" by her married sister against the advice of the doctors, but after six weeks finds herself back in Cliffhaven, in bed "in the observation dormitory and gazing with terror at the treatment room." Her remembrances spare the reader none of the horrors of that estranged world in its effect on the ill mind. Yet quite unlike most other such reminiscences, hers are free from the self-centered bent that narrows their scope. Fear-ridden, lost in her longing for the "world outside," Istina even then retains the faculty of grasping the motives of other people's behavior—grasping them while incapable of accommodating her own reactions or giving tongue to her feelings.

All this may of course be anything but novel to alienists. The lay reader is struck by the sophistication of the memoir writer:

> Unfortunately, I observed Sister Bridge too closely. This unself-conscious giving of herself to those in her care was a marvel worth watching, and it caused me great sadness when, one day, as I was standing quietly by, she noticed me and knew immediately that I had been marveling at her almost telepathic sympathy with the patients. From then on Sister Bridge showed her resentment towards me and seized every opportunity to hurt me. By an unintentional glance I had surprised her into surprising herself into an uncomfortable consciousness that seemed to amount to fear."

Cliffhaven appears to stand no less in need of reform than our own much-criticized state hospitals, but this author is not burning with reforming zeal. For all the heartbreak Istina recalls and despite the bitterness with which she thinks of the past, Miss Frame's talent as a novelist carries her beyond her own narrator's memories. She may even have aimed at bringing to life the precariousness of Istina's existence as an allegory of the insecurity of human relations at large. She is a very gifted writer.

Thomas Crawford (review date March 1963)

SOURCE: A review of *The Edge of the Alphabet*, in *Landfall*, Vol. 17, No. 1, March, 1963, pp. 192-95.

[*Crawford is a Scottish educator, writer, and critic. In the mixed review below, he praises Frame's* The Edge of the Alphabet *for its rhetoric and cadence, stating that Frame writes in a language "so eloquent that few of her contemporaries can equal it."*]

It is hard for the novelist of the lost childhood, the madhouse or the concentration camp to write about the so-called 'real' contemporary world. Janet Frame tries to do it in [*The Edge of the Alphabet*]; the result is part failure, part success.

Her failure is the inevitable consequence of pretending that the book is a manuscript 'found among the papers of Thora Pattern after her death, and submitted to the publishers by Peter Heron, Hire-Purchase Salesman.' It is a nineteenth century, even an eighteenth century device. None the worse for that, you may well say—but then the *personae* of Scott and the Gothic Novelists weren't in the habit of addressing their characters directly, nor were they so closely identified with their creator. Another trait reminiscent of early novels is the frequency with which essayistic comments on Life (presumably Thora Pattern's comments) are scattered throughout the book.

The novel about the writer composing a novel belongs to a more recent tradition than Sir Walter's. In this convention it is necessary that the novelist-character should be at least as convincing as the people he invents and, perhaps, that one of the book's main concerns should be the nature of the creative process itself. But we do not feel that Miss Pattern is in the least interesting or credible, and we don't learn much about how or why she writes, except that her motive is self-exploration; that the end of self-discovery is to arrive at the dead (why not at God? or at existence or essence? or at the contemplation of a universal dialectical process?); and that she belongs to a Chosen Race—the Unhappy Few who live 'at the edge of the alphabet'. Two of her characters—Toby Withers the epileptic from *Owls Do Cry* and Zoe the failed schoolteacher—also live at the edge of the alphabet, and Thora persists in trying to communicate with them directly—

> I hear your thoughts, Zoe. . . . Day and night, Zoe, I have walked in the market among the crowds and the cries, Lovely Oranges, Lovely Oranges, while the night-papers exhort Crucify, Crucify.

> Who are the Lost Tribe, Toby? Why do they lie hidden in your mind, like beetles under a stone? . . . They live, he says, behind a mountain approached through a secret pass.

Thora's irritating questions and apostrophes destroy our faith in the reality of Toby, Zoe and even Pat Keenan, the pathetic 'ordinary man' who tries to decoy the introverts into his spider's web of normality. We just aren't able to believe in them after Zoe's Berkeleyan remark to Toby at the ship's fancy-dress party:

> It doesn't make you afraid, does it, that you are fiction, that you are not really aboard the *Matua* sailing to England, that you exist only in someone's mind, some poor writer who cannot do better than bring forth the conversation of musicians, poets, mice?

Janet Frame does not seem altogether aware that Thora Pattern's attitudes and pronouncements are tinged with arrogance and spiritual pride. The blurb describes the novel as 'wise, compassionate, and infinitely tender'—but the wisdom appears pretentious, and the compassion too often like condescension: a sad falling off from *Owls Do Cry*. True, Chicks's diary in that novel is hardly motivated by generous sympathy; it is a masterpiece of savage irony that is more than a little unfair to the real Chicks's of this world because it fails to hint at the unrealized potentialities behind their petty suburbanite selfishness. Nevertheless, that is a minor blemish compared with the beautiful portrayal of young Toby and Daphne, and the fine evocation of the Withers's childhood world. In *The Edge of the Alphabet*, however, Thora Pattern seems to have acquired some of the characteristics of an introverted Chicks; there's a melancholy smugness that comes out in her glib scorn of 'pop' culture and common folk. Whether this is Miss Frame's intention or not, Thora cannot avoid displaying her sense that she is better than Pat and even Toby. Thora's greatest defect is a failure of tone, which could be demonstrated from almost every chapter. A small-scale example is provided by the placing of 'of course' in the following sentence: 'His early enthusiastic reading of love explained, of course, his facility in the translation of death: the alphabet, the grammar, are the same.' The implication is that such an idea is a truism to the Chosen Race; that you too, dear reader, are a member of a select band—though not ('of course') quite so select as Thora Pattern herself.

And yet, in spite of everything, the book's virtues outweigh its flaws. Miss Frame, our most subjective writer, is perhaps also our best writer of documentaries. *Faces in the Water* is a better rendering of mental hospitals than any social scientist could provide, and the present novel's handling of passenger life on a one class ship couldn't possibly be improved upon. When she keeps her eye on the object, she can do better than the realists. She is also a wonderful craftsman—mistress of pedal and keyboard, princess of the arpeggios and cadenzas of prose; and she has a nice sense of humour (seen at its best in her treatment of Mr and Mrs Kala and son, the family who come on board at Panama), which is all too often spoiled by Thora's solemn and wistful intrusions. It is precisely because of her great gifts, because words and phrasing, prose-rhythm and image patterns mean so much to her, that she has fallen into the trap of making her book a rhetorical construct rather than a novel, where Janet Frame, Thora Pattern, the characters they create, even the entire human race become fused into a single whole—or, if you like, they all fall into the same slough:

> How I am haunted by death and the dead! And by the division of humanity into so many people when one birth, one mind, one death would be enough to end the tributary tears that flow in every acre of the earth in the stone obstructions of the heart that are called stars. What mathematical trick has divided the whole into the sum of so many people, only to set working in our hearts the process by which we continually strive to reduce the sum once more to its indivisible whole—until millions in one city become for us two or three people and finally one person. We pass our mother fifty times in a few seconds in the street, and our father, and the only people we have ever really known; and if we love, everyone we meet is our lover.
>
> And what if the person who meets us for ever is ourselves? What if we meet ourselves on the edge of the alphabet and can make no sign, no speech?
>
> So it is the end of self-discovery. I have arrived at the dead.

What moving rhetoric! What beauty of cadence! And how arbitrary, really, since the reader feels that Thora's voyage of self-discovery isn't a genuine voyage. She does not convince us that her own death, or Zoe's for that matter, is inevitable; she merely tells us so in language so eloquent that few of her contemporaries can equal it.

Wilfrid Sheed (review date 8 August 1965)

SOURCE: "When the Spell Works It's Binding," in *The New York Times Book Review,* August 8, 1965, p. 4.

[*Sheed is a British novelist, editor, columnist, and critic. In the following review, he praises Frame's* The Adaptable Man, *considering the novel "comic, intense, [and] stylish."*]

The New Zealand authoress Janet Frame is a "witch-novelist" who stirs her plots under a full moon and has various magic powers, including a number-one witch's curse. Her prose style is a series of charms and incantations, passwords repeated in a baleful voice, which hex up the whole landscape, turning the vegetables into people and the people back into vegetables, or worse: into rock formations, soap advertisements or ancient ruins.

These alchemistic tricks are central to her new novel, [*The Adaptable Man,*] which concerns the urge of people and

things to adapt, to assume the right shapes for the 20th century. Each of her characters would like to become the human equivalent of a television antenna or a three-day deodorant or a really good museum piece. Under Miss Frame's curse, they become instead crystal radios, one-day deodorants, museum rejects.

Even the village they live in (one of those whimsical English ones well-known to mystery readers) is struggling to adapt—to become a jet airport or a thruway or a history reserve. A hundred local deities fuse in this effort, sprites of field and harvest and even gods secreted in the new farm-machines. For in Miss Frame's metaphor kingdom you never know what has a soul and who hasn't.

The human characters proper are introduced in a prologue which suggests that they are all basically the same person anyway, in a sequence of different attitudes. In a mythic novel of this type, the personality is nothing, the role is everything—i.e., it doesn't matter who is priest and who is victim, so long as the rite is performed. Each uses the same voice—the milkman, the clergyman, the village bore—passing the "I, I, I," back and forth and ending with "I, the earth,"—the earth being no more and no less a character than the others.

Each of these alleged characters has one foot inside his own century and one waving about outside. Russell Maude the dentist has barricaded himself behind a picket-fence of teeth, solid as tombstones: his strategy is to practice a modern science with outrageously out-of-date instruments. His wife has buried herself in vegetables, and fortifies herself with litanies of the latest plant diseases. Their son Alwyn seems to have stepped all the way into his own century, committing a senseless murder and feeling only two pages of guilt to 600-odd for Raskolnikov, but by the end of the book he has begun to look worried. And of course, to worry is to be unadapted, to lose your place in the lemming-rush.

Parts of this book could best be reviewed a page at a time, as a number of poems and essays stashed together—some pages of excellent nature writing, a few more of theologizing—and indeed, whenever plot-development threatens to dominate, Miss Frame determinedly changes the subject and goes off on a new ramble. When the magic is working, which is most of the time, the effect is spellbinding; when it isn't the brew tastes more like Campbell's toad soup, and you half wonder why such an earnest, talky woman should be a witch in the first place.

But this is probably the kind of trick you can expect from witches. When the juice is on, Miss Frame is undoubtedly the real thing. Her prose is haunting, and she can use it to lay a spooky atmosphere over anything she chooses, from a stamp album to a row of teeth. Occasionally she wrestles a metaphor too fiercely and winds up in a snarl of arms and legs, but few writers have ever used so many of them so successfully.

In general, she has done what every writer strives to do: find and perfect a form that fits over her ideas and dreams like a skullcap.

Now if she could just find an equally good proofreader, or wave a wand over her old one. But maybe these weird typos and open-ended parentheses are meant to add an extra Halloween touch. In any event, *The Adaptable Man* is an original novel, comic, intense, stylish, from one of the most interesting writers around.

H. T. Anderson (review date 15 July 1966)

SOURCE: A review of *A State of Siege,* in *Best Sellers,* Vol. 26, No. 8, July 15, 1966, pp. 149-50.

[*In the review below, Anderson praises Frame's* A State of Siege, *considering it "a truly singular reading experience."*]

The truly singular reading experience does not present itself very frequently in modern fiction. Janet Frame's latest novel, *A State of Siege,* affords just such a rare privilege. The book allows the reader a remarkably intimate intrusion into the subtly tragic life of Malfred Signal, retired art teacher whose entire being had been directed toward two things: teaching young girls how to draw and nursing a dying mother who "stayed so long that her role had become fictional."

The mother is dead and Malfred is left with that paradoxical bereaved elation known only to those suddenly released from a dying aged parent who had forced them by illness and circumstance to sacrifice a lifetime of opportunities to live themselves. At 53 Malfred retires, released at last to make one last attempt at life.

Malfred decides to sever all ties, in spite of the remonstrances from family and friends, and to move "up North" to the remote island of Karemoana, the fringe of New Zealand. Here in a small cottage she will attempt to live the answer to a question—"can release given by death, by her mother's death, promise a lifetime of bounty?" The novel is the answer.

Arriving at Karemoana, Malfred attempts to get familiar with people and terrain. She begins to discover that the envisioned tropical paradise is more alien and inflexible than anticipated. The carrier who brings her to the cottage ominously warns her to lock all doors since the island has its "element."

Perhaps the one thing from which Malfred was fleeing most desperately was Intrusion; ironically, it follows her to Karemoana. During her very first night in her new life and her home, Intrusion enters—with a tropical storm raging outside, there is a knocking, an incessant pounding on her door that plunges her into an endless night of terror. The phone dead, the neighbors distant and unknown, the "element" outside her door, there is no one to heed her desperate cries for help.

The situation becomes a "state of siege" against an unknown intruder attempting to gain entry into her house and her new life. During this terrifying, isolated experience—in her cabin plunged into darkness—Malfred's mind in a frantic attempt to find comfort in the familiar goes back to her father, her mother, and Wilfred, the love known but lost.

The time element in the novel is beautifully handled. During the one long sleepless night, the major portions of her life's contacts, purposes, desires, and disappointments are brought before the reader in a dream-like kaleidoscopic flashback, interrupted periodically and brought back to a present reminder of the immediate terror with a return to "the knocking."

A State of Siege is an extraordinary novel by a uniquely talented New Zealander. What the reader is confronted with is not a book but a canvas on which Janet Frame executes a portrait that captures with remarkable clarity the tragic figure of Malfred Signal. The novel is worth the experience just for the richness and color of the prose alone.

It is Malfred's story—not as she would have told it, but as she would have painted it. Malfred who suddenly realized what she had missed seeing in life by her dutiful habit of just looking; Malfred who longed to live at last by herself in "the little room two inches behind the eyes." Malfred who asked only that she be given the peace to live as she had decided to live without her mother, father, sister, brother, and lover. She wanted dignified isolation; she was not going to be allowed it. The Intrusion . . . "I wonder, now, what parts of me are being seized, held up to the light, snipped, trimmed, polished, gilded, reshaped, fouled, adorned by people I have known? How can I arm myself with a New View, a New Life, when my Self, the armory, is threatened not only by my past and its inhabitants but by these immediate presences that besiege me in my white house on the hill?"

Malfred fails and the novel ends in an enigmatic tragedy too cruel to be anything else but true. *A State of Siege* is a remarkable novel by a writer of genius who has something to say and who knows confidently how to say it. The result is magic.

Muriel Haynes (review date 19 April 1969)

SOURCE: "Nature as Status," in *Saturday Review,* April 19, 1969, pp. 41-2.

[*In the review below, Haynes offers a mixed assessment of* Yellow Flowers in the Antipodean Room, *finding in it a "virtuosity" that eventually "wears thin."*]

The New Zealand Novelist Janet Frame is an obsessed mourner at the grave of the ancient mysteries that once linked the individual and his group in a tradition of man's oneness with the universe. [*Yellow Flowers in the Antipodean Room*] seems intended as a parable of our grievous separation from the mythic past. Yet its hold on the form is shaky; I find it more satisfying when read as an inquiry—by a compulsively directed poetic imagination—into the darkness that lies beneath our supposed enlightenment. Story is not so much side-stepped as skewed to serve the author's preoccupations: reversals of symbolic meaning; contradictions in our perception of what is real (sanity, health) and what is illusion (madness, disease); death in life and its opposite.

The narrative derives from a rite of initiation. The adventurer crosses the threshold into the unknown and returns, radically transformed, to be reborn. The modern world, however, does not "permit" the regenerative cycle to be completed. The voyager's new knowledge threatens a temporal society that exalts utility above all, and he is cast out, for he has lost material value. "Everything could be worked out in money . . . it seemed easier to give all the responsibility of living and dying over to money. It's so hard to keep judging, weighing, testing, valuing what is invisible."

The man rejected is Godfrey Rainbird, a young, altogether unremarkable Englishman, a clerk in a tourist office, who has already moved, quite literally, to the other side of the world. Ten years earlier he had emigrated from London to New Zealand in search of warmth, space, and the life of salutary ease offered by a land of benign climate and fair shares for all. One night he is struck down by a car on the highway and, through a medical error, pronounced dead. When he awakens in the mortuary thirty-six hours later, Godfrey finds himself neither hero nor miracle, but an acute embarrassment to the normal world and, as time passes, an object of fear and finally contempt. He lives on, cut off from the sun's glow, in an icy purgatory of psychic arrest and split consciousness. Gradually his sphere as wage-earner, father, and husband is usurped and his domain shrinks to that of a cripple's chair.

> **Janet Frame is steeped in nostalgia and, in her grief for man's betrayal of his sustaining myths, tends to slight present social and cultural complexities**.
>
> *—Muriel Haynes*

Miss Frame's attitude toward her homeland shows traces of the resentment of the ousted proprietor. It is not just from New Zealand but everywhere that the gods have been routed, to be replaced by the banners of the secular, competitive nation-state described by Joseph Campbell, "where every last vestige of the human heritage of ritual, morality and art is in full decay." But, whereas Campbell looks ahead to envision

the task of the future hero, Janet Frame is steeped in nostalgia and, in her grief for man's betrayal of his sustaining myths, tends to slight present social and cultural complexities (for science and technology cannot be banished).

The author, however, freshens the now-familiar theme of spiritual impoverishment and infantilism by the sweep and sharpness of her observations of this part of the world she knows so thoroughly. No detail escapes her regarding the endless perversity by which nature's beneficence, its unifying religious presence, has been corrupted through a cult of Philistine pleasure-seeking and chauvinism. The "Antipodean room" of her title, the open stretch of an underpopulated physical paradise, translates to the smug isolation of one's own "section," the graveyard of community. "Where are the people?" wonders Godfrey's sister, arriving for the first time in Dunedin after leaving congested London. Hills, the expanse of harbor and sky, no longer whisper of eternity, but are objects of status, possessive pride in a view. Forests, weather, the profusion of flowers cater to an arrogant sense of superiority. "A healthy outdoor life" is the true blessedness and tourism its profitable end-product.

I dwell on this background because I find it more persuasive of Miss Frame's special view of the world and simply more interesting than the story she has placed against it. A parable must convince not just in its latent meaning, but on the objective level. Since *Yellow Flowers in the Antipodean Room* is necessarily set in the present day, its plot runs counter to certain logical expectations to which the times entitle us. The events are improbable. Like the characters, who are flatly symbolic, they are contrived to the author's purpose. So the pleasure to be found in this book is in another sense its handicap: the omnipresence of the author's voice conducting an insistent, ever-sifting, ever-shredding monologue. It is an essentially literary voice which speaks even for her characters, taking charge of their thoughts and dialogue, though Miss Frame has, and occasionally uses, gifts of mimicry. Sometimes this voice is brilliant, as in Godfrey's "icy spelling," an invention of ruefully comic puns. Then again it is just funny in a homely, everyday sort of way, as when Miss Frame rings changes on the word-traps that lie in wait for the conversationalist who tries to avoid allusions to death.

Still, in the end, even the virtuosity wears thin. The line between the serious and the self-parodic in such a feverishly driven work is dangerously fine. Miss Frame does not entirely surmount this risk.

Patrick Evans (review date June 1969)

SOURCE: A review of *The Rainbirds,* in *Landfall,* Vol. 23, No. 2, June, 1969, pp. 189-94.

[*In the review below, Evans finds that while* The Rainbirds *is occasionally threatened by "artistically gratuitous passages of authorial comment," it is exemplary of Frame's "immense verbal talent."*]

The newest inhabitant of Janet Frame's world is thirty-year-old Godfrey Rainbird, an English immigrant who has become a Dunedin clerk, and who has a wife, a house with a view, and two children. In *The Rainbirds*, Godfrey experiences death and resurrection in suburbia. He is taken lifeless to the morgue after being knocked down one night on the way home from a meeting. His wife, her parents, his children and sister smoothly assume the attitudes of grief expected and accepted by society; his older sister Lynley decides to emigrate from England in time for the funeral, and this ceremony is expensively, lavishly prepared without love but with a monogrammed coffin. But fate has cruelly tricked them all: Godfrey wakes from a coma, a sleep of death and not death itself, and all those who reconciled themselves so swiftly to his going find it impossible to reconcile themselves to his return. His 'corpseness' constantly repels his wife Beatrice; both now possess an unspoken awareness of the presence of death in life. She often thinks and speaks of him in the preterite, is aware of the coldness of his body and hands (which even civilization's latest electric blanket cannot cherish back to lively warmth), and perceives new meaning in the word 'sleep'.

But where she increasingly shies away from this alien morbidity, he is increasingly fascinated by it. He begins to see emblems of death all about him. Those all about him also begin to perceive death in this man who has died and returned. On the bus going in to his job at the Tourist Bureau he is treated with curiosity by his fellow passengers, and he has to get off early. When he does reach the Tourist Bureau it is to receive notice: a man who has been dead cannot promote tourism. People stare at him in the street; his story is wanted for television, for newspapers, and for sermons at Easter. His experience makes him a social cripple. In a society engaged in a festering pursuit of the material, the 'live' and the superficial—a chase which is a panic avoidance of everything abstract, eternal, or spiritual—Godfrey is a walking reminder of mortality.

His withdrawal into himself is a withdrawal from life and its practical problems. Excluded from suitable work, he is content to assemble electric plugs at home; he spends the rest of his time in idle contemplation. The neighbours begin to call him an irresponsible cripple, and their children to taunt the Rainbirds. Beatrice Rainbird, a dull suburbanite unarmed for such battles, succumbs, and, with stones thrown by the neighbours rattling on the Rainbirds' roof, she opens up her throat with a sharp silver knife. The last chapter surveys the Rainbirds' grave in Anderson's Bay Cemetery, and, with skimpy irony, outlines their posthumous fame and the successes of their children. Seen in this compressed form, *The Rainbirds* appears to be a scathing criticism of New Zealand society. Janet Frame's dark suburbanites are an undifferenti-

ated mass capable only of a dull collective evil against the Rainbirds, turning unseeing from the grain of sand which Godfrey holds up.

By inclination, Miss Frame favours interior exploration of her characters, and her technique has always aided her search. But in *The Rainbirds* she shows a desire to cast a cold eye also on the society in which she places her characters, and in which she perhaps sees herself as well. Her eye is often acute and perceptive.

> . . . Easter: the beach, the last supply of sun . . . Easter eggs, rabbits for the children; Good Friday changed to Dead Friday; death on the roads, in the mountains, the final drownings before summer came again. . . . Alternate wails and cheers from the churches: He is dead, He is risen. Then Anzac Day most solemn: khaki and poppies.

Here is the panoramic sweep and the compression of the social observer—of Janet Frame, almost tangibly present as author, no matter which character she drapes each remark over. And there's the rub: the further the novel proceeds at this social level, whatever the intrinsic value of the observations made at these heights, the greater is the damage done to the introspective aspects of the novel, the very area in which in the past the writer has gained and communicated her most significant insights. Despite initial appearances to the contrary, Janet Frame is at heart an omniscient narrator 'peering in' at her characters. Rather than being a genuine user of the stream-of-consciousness technique, she establishes the illusion of 'possessing' the consciousness of her characters. More and more in *The Rainbirds* she will speak—either directly, or at a slight remove from us, through characters—in her own voice, surprising us often with her urban drawl. And the more we hear of this civilized voice, the less we hear of that barbarous tongue with which we are accustomed to receive her messages from the darker regions she explores. It is for these messages, after all, that we go to her books; and the story of Godfrey Rainbird implies by its emphasis that its burden, too, will result from exploration rather than survey. In recording a journey of exploration Janet Frame employs here the language of a social diary, and the resulting uncertainty distorts the meaning of *The Rainbirds*.

Its force, too, is dissipated by fundamental troubles at the heart of the process of writing, in the matter of technique. Because of an unusual attitude towards her medium, Miss Frame often allows the force of her writing to be deflected. It is ironic that a writer with an almost Joycean reverence for words should on this occasion, instead of building surely, tend at times to go against the business of true creation through her use of them. Her aim as a writer has always been high, she attempts to lift the painted veil which those who live call Life. Her problem is that Shelley's veil, for her, has always had words painted on it, not people; and these words often distract her from telling us what lies beneath them. Janet Frame is more interested in the appearance, size, sound, and personal reverberations of each word rather than in its meaning. So we see this:

> —Have either of you noticed this? . . . —Why no, they said together and he could not tell if they spoke the truth or lied; liars; liar; fair fire.

At another point she follows the thought 'killed instantly' with the unnecessarily facile 'like coffee'; and the narrative pursues this until exhaustion sets in. Word association in interior monologue must have only a secondary place to verisimilitude set up in the novel. Reality must dictate meaning in the long run, whoever owns the consciousness that perceives both the reality and the meaning. But too often, the meaning of this book is dictated by the word associations—almost as if life is one of those interminable Oxford Debates which change direction with each new pun or change of key word. The degree to which Miss Frame sees life as words is indicated in her description of Beatrice Rainbird's realization that her parents are mortal: 'Then realizing that one day *their* tense would change . . .'. And when Godfrey, after his 'resurrection', sees life and society in the perspective of the grave, Miss Frame makes him turn over the thick surface of *words,* reversing them and turning them inside out:

> here in the creamtorium
> lie the dead
> radeye to be bunred.

Surely the resurrected should turn over ideas and values and concepts, and not just the words they are wrapped in?

That the author is preoccupied so often with the colour, sound and 'feel' of words at the expense of semantics again places the author constantly at the reader's side. Like Hopkins' Holy Ghost, Miss Frame broods over her bent world—and sometimes blinds us with the flash of those bright wings—but with a commitment to the inward lives of characters there should go an attempt to create the illusion that those words formed themselves upon the page, that no author was required to arrange them in that way. Miss Frame's constant 'presence' goes against this, and ultimately penalizes her creation of character—it drains them of any chance for integrity or uniqueness, for no characteristic is sacred, all traits are common and held in the presence of the author. The beautiful and often lyrical stream of consciousness which we have had from this writer in the past is now replaced too frequently by a kind of interpretation which puts us at a distance from the characters. Intimacy is lost. The voice which pervades the book is Janet Frame's, not those of her characters. She appears to inhabit her characters perfunctorily: it is only with an effort that we believe that Godfrey really did awaken from

that coma, and at no point does he, nor do any of his family, become 'alive' and true. This individuality in a character, whether in a conventionally-narrated novel or in one using some sort of 'interior' narration, is after all basically an illusion, created in the surface of the book. When the author remains 'outside' his character, he gives it depth by assigning to it certain traits of speech, actions and behaviour, which he excludes from other characters. The novelist who takes us on a voyage through the consciousness of his characters has a greater number of ways by which to foster this illusion of individuality in characters: he may give them different patterns of thinking, using distinctive symbols and images in their thoughts; at his best he will equip each character with his own rhetoric of thought and speech.

Virginia Woolf springs to mind here as a successful exponent of many of these methods, especially in *The Waves,* that book devoid of apparent author or narration, which sweeps us along in the six-fold stream of its characters' consciousness. But the Janet Frame of *Owls Do Cry* also has this ability and is able to voyage on the dangerous seas of the human mind armed with the discretion of fine objectivity. In *Owls Do Cry* Miss Frame disciplined her talents towards self-effacement, eliminating the artistically gratuitous passages of authorial comment which occasionally threaten to capsize **The Rainbirds.**

However, the immense verbal talent remains, always best when economical, concentrated into phrases and single words. Here is Beatrice, alone in bed after Godfrey has 'died': ' . . . she . . . felt . . . the cold lack, the unattended level and chill of his absence . . .'. Although the bold vision and insight which distinguished the earlier books, particularly **Owls Do Cry,** is still present, to find less than the full measure in this new novel is a disappointment.

Julian Moynahan (review date 3 May 1970)

SOURCE: "A Sort of Anzac Peter Ibbetsen and Family," in *The New York Times Book Review,* May 3, 1970, p. 4.

[*Moynahan is an American educator, novelist, essayist, and critic. In the review of* Intensive Care *below, he criticizes Frame for not answering the many questions she raises in the novel.*]

Janet Frame is a New Zealand novelist and poet who is not well known in this country and whose eighth novel, **Intensive Care,** is unlikely to win her many new converts among the novel-reading public. The book is sprawling and invertebrate, overwritten at times in a vein of capricious prose-poetry and actual poetry, indifferent to problems of construction and coherence raised by its episodic, disjunctive plot, simplistic and even careless with respect to the moral issues the lives of its principal characters fitfully reflect. Although it is arranged in three parts and employs the services of five narrators, these compositional tactics remain *pro forma* and never work together to create form and a controlling perspective upon a world one can take seriously.

Intensive Care opens promisingly when a sort of Anzac Peter Ibbetson named Tom Livingstone goes from Waipori City, N. Z., to England in search of a nurse originally encountered during the Great War and whom he has secretly loved for 50 years. But this adventure peters out and Tom dies, and the book shifts to consider the lonely aging and dying of Tom's brother, Leonard, a bibulous bachelor and war veteran who spent his last years in a shack near the home of the Tom Livingstones. The rankness and banality of the quotidian life of an ordinary lower-middle-class failure are fairly well rendered, but the book soon shifts again, taking up bits and pieces of the careers of Tom's children and their spouses.

One Livingstone daughter grows hugely fat and unhappy and does volunteer work for the Bruised Baby Society. The other wanders away but reappears in the story as the author of a number of nostalgic chapters, written in verse form and addressed lovingly to old Tom. A son-in-law, an accountant, falls obsessively in love with a 19-year-old girl, runs away with her to Australia, loses her, eventually goes mad and slaughters her, along with her parents and himself. However, the extremely emotional rendering of this "tragic" affair loses all effect, simply because the author never bothers to establish the man as any sort of real presence in the book.

The last part of *Intensive Care,* abandoning the Livingstones without ever having really dealt with them except randomly, takes up another Waipori family named the Galbraiths. The time is the future, perhaps late in the reign of the English King Charles, and society has come under the control of some university technocrats and computer buffs. Their scheme is to solve all demographic and political problems by killing off upon a certain day those persons whom the computer declares to be defective or otherwise unpromising. The book ends with this Final Solution accomplished and with the rather nervous reflections of one of the technocrats upon the results.

Most of the last part is narrated by Milly Galbraith, a 26-year-old who tells us that she is "doll-normill" and "oughtistic" and spends a lot of time under a pear-tree playing with her cat, sewing, and talking to an imaginary Reconstructed Man of gold until she is hustled off to die, together with the rest of the family, on the big day. Her report is couched in spelling reminiscent of "Daisy Ashford" and reminds me of those revolting "Uncle Eph" advertisements for Raymond's department store in Boston that were the plague of my youth; but its contents are merely sentimental and grossly repetitive.

At the end, Miss Frame leaves unanswered all those questions that her employment of doomsday and apocalyptic conventions raises in the reader's mind. Who is supplying the

muscle and the guns that enable the university technocrats, a feeble bunch as characterized, to carry out their deadly work? And what point, necessarily, is she making about actual New Zealand society? The designated victims go to the slaughter like a mob of sheep. Is that what New Zealand is like, or heading toward, nowadays? Out of respect for the memory of all those gassed and wounded veterans of foreign wars, like Tom Livingstone, with which the opening chapters are so tenderly concerned, she owes an answer. But apparently the author of *Intensive Care* couldn't care less.

Edward P. J. Corbett (review date 23 May 1970)

SOURCE: A review of *Intensive Care,* in *America,* Vol. 122, No. 20, May 23, 1970, pp. 565-66.

[*Corbett is an American educator, writer, and critic. In the review below, he approaches Frame's fiction ambivalently, stating that* Intensive Care *is "like no other novel I have ever read."*]

[*Intensive Care*] is a difficult book to describe or evaluate. It is like no other novel I have ever read; and having read this one, I am still uncertain whether I will ever be disposed to read any of Janet Frame's previously published seven novels.

Yet the quotes on the dust jacket are unstinting in their praise of the earlier novels—John Barkham on the first novel, *Owls Do Cry*: "The most talented novelist to have come out of New Zealand since Katherine Mansfield"; Stanley Hyman on her *Scented Gardens for the Blind*: "This amazing book is the most remarkable I have read in a long time. A brilliant and overwhelming *tour de force*." Any writer who can get a publisher to risk his capital on eight full-length novels and can elicit high praise from estimable critics has to be given a serious reading.

What makes my own reaction to this first serious reading of a Janet Frame novel so ambivalent is that I am baffled by her technique and puzzled about what she is trying to say. The novel presents a number of fleeting episodes, moving back and forth in time and interlarded with epigraphs of free-verse poetry, snatches of songs, flashes of dreams, glimpses of letters and diaries, and intonations of refrains ("All dreams lead back to the nightmare garden"). This kaleidoscopic structure is not so much ambiguous as it is incoherent, like a Fellini movie. Where are we now?

The first two-thirds of the novel concentrates on the fateful history of three generations of the Livingstone family in Waipori City, New Zealand: Tom Livingstone, his daughters Naomi and Pearl, his brother Leonard, his grandson Colin. The final hundred pages or so leap into the distant future, with an entirely different cast of characters and with the only link to the earlier part of the book being the pear tree that stands on what was once Livingstone property.

There are some vividly drawn characters, e.g., Peggy Warren, the wartime tart who in her declining years moves in on the widowed Tom with a view toward a belated marriage. There are some poignant incidents, like the tragic love affair between Colin and Lorna Kimberley. And there is the horrifying climax, related through the journal entries of the retarded girl Milly Gilbraith, in which those citizens of Waipori City who have been classified by the computer as being Animal rather than Human are marched off to be executed.

But what does it all add up to? Is the theme adumbrated in these words of the novel: "Is that how it was? Was that Tom Livingstone mad in love as all the Livingstones were, their passions, as generation succeeded generation, resembling an assortment of old Scottish ballads where to be a human relative was to be, inevitably, one of the murderers or the murdered?" If the author herself has to ask, rather than declare, the reader can hardly be blamed for wondering.

An excerpt from *An Angel at My Table*

In my state of alarm about my future, when I saw mother standing there at the entrance to the ward, in her pitifully 'best' clothes, her navy costume and her navy straw hat with the bunch of artificial flowers at the brim; with at hint of fear in her eyes (for, after all, I had been in a 'mental' ward) and her face transparently trying to adopt the expression *All is well*, I knew that home was the last place I wanted to be. I screamed at mother to go away. She left, murmuring her bewilderment, 'But she's such a happy person, she's always been such a happy person.'

I supposed, then, that I'd stay in hospital a few more days then be discharged, find a job in Dunedin, continue my University studies, renouncing teaching for ever. I did not realized that the alternative to going home was committal to Seacliff. No-one thought to ask me why I had screamed at my mother, no-one asked me what my plans were for the future. I became an instant third person, or even personless, as in the official note made about my mother's visit (reported to me many years later), 'Refused to leave hospital.'

Janet Frame, in her An Angel at My Table: An Autobiography, *George Braziller, 1984.*

Jeanne Delbaere-Garant (essay date April 1975)

SOURCE: "Daphne's Metamorphoses in Janet Frame's Early Novels," in *Ariel: A Review of International English Literature,* Vol. 6, No. 2, April, 1975, pp. 23-37.

[*In the essay below, Delbaere-Garant traces similarities between Daphne, the protagonist of* Owls Do Cry, *and the characters in Frame's novels* Faces in the Water, The Edge of the Alphabet, *and* Scented Gardens for the Blind.]

Owls Do Cry, Janet Frame's first novel, begins with a message in italics signed "Daphne from the deadroom." Other such mysterious and poetical messages by the same hand are scattered throughout the story which introduces us to Daphne as a child and tells us about the circumstances which led her to the madhouse. Daphne is the first version of a recurrent figure in Janet Frame's early novels which I propose to examine in the present article. The other versions are Istina Mavet in ***Faces in the Water,*** Thora Pattern in ***The Edge of the Alphabet*** and Vera Glace in ***Scented Gardens for the Blind.*** They form a complex pattern of overlapping features, cross-references and recurrent motifs which gradually completes itself and out of which a more or less complete image of the character as a whole finally emerges.

Daphne is one of the four Withers children. She has two sisters, Francie and Chicks, and a brother, Toby, an epileptic. One day, while the children are playing in the rubbish dump of Waimaru, looking for "treasures" thrown away by grown-ups, Francie falls into the fires lit by the council men to hasten the destruction of their material cast-offs and she dies. It is immediately after Francie's death that Daphne shows the first symptoms of insanity. The accident breaches the wall of her self and leaves her confronted with the basic situation of her human predicament. For the rest of her life she will remember the rubbish dump with "the sun shining through the sacrificial fire to make real diamonds and gold." But her "wonder currency" is not legal tender in the world of the grown-ups and her vision—the awareness of death which brings about a greater insight into life—is called madness by the "normal world." She must be cured and the vision be dimmed so as not to blind her: "Your eyes out, like Gloucester, to save your sight of the cliff."

Daphne lives in the "deadroom" where the transitoriness and negativity of all beings is revealed to her. She is not afraid of death because she sees it ontologically as part of life. When Flora Norris comes to inform her of her mother's death she knows the news before being told. She has given up the mere babble of the world and only speaks the true inspired language of the poet, the true language of being which passes through her like the wind through a tree. Her messages sometimes succeed in piercing the walls of Chicks' conformity so that strange reveries are let in and her sister wonders what spell has come over her. But society won't let Daphne knit for long the "unintelligible pattern of dream": they force her to conform and to become a useful citizen. A doctor practices a lobotomy on her brain which turns her into an exemplary factory-girl. She is then offered a watch with three diamonds inside it: the instrument in which time is safely caged again and the wonder currency of dream converted again into the fake values of the world.

Although she escapes the lobotomy and goes back with her old self to the normal world Istina Mavet, the narrator and protagonist of the next novel, *Faces in the Water,* is clearly another version of Daphne. She alludes to the visit of her father in terms that remind us of Tom Withers' visit to Daphne in *Owls Do Cry*: "my father journeyed up north to make the first visit he had ever made me in hospital." She stays for a while with her sister who, like Chicks, lives "up north," her mother is now "in a region of snow and ice" and with her face "like that of a witch with her nose meeting her chin." Istina's mother is obviously the Amy Withers described in almost the same words by Toby in the next novel.

Though *Faces in the Water* reads more like a documentary, images of holes and traps which had been used already in *Owls Do Cry* and will be used even more abundantly in *The Edge of the Alphabet* also appear here, sometimes under a scientific guise. Everything begins with "a great gap which opened in the ice floe between [the protagonist] and the other people" so that she remained "alone on the ice." The lobotomy is seen as a hole bored in people's skulls and E.S.T. —Electric Shock Treatment—a fall into a trap. This treatment is an extremely powerful metaphor for the way in which people are forced into the recognition of being in everyday life so that instead of "curing" the patients it leaves them even more alienated than before:

> I feel myself dropping as if a trap door had opened into darkness. I imagine as I fall my eyes turning inward to face and confound each other with a separate truth which they prove without my help. Then I rise disembodied from the dark to grasp and attach myself like a homeless parasite to the shape of my identity and its position in space and time.

The same is true of the injection of insulin after which the patients are overtaken by a double vision and confusion: they pass from the brilliant whiteness and intensity of snow to an utter blackness "like love which overstrains itself into hate, or like the dark side of our nature which we meet most suddenly when we believe ourselves to be journeying furthest from it."

The construction of the novel—Cliffhaven, Treecroft, Cliffhaven—indicates that Istina covers the whole distance from a more or less "normal" state to the last degree of schizophrenia and back. The word "cliff" contained in Cliffhaven is one of the minor motifs binding the first novels together. It appears in connection with King Lear in both *Owls Do Cry* and *Faces in the Water.* In the first novel Daphne compares herself to Gloucester forced to take out her eyes "to save her sight from the cliff." Here Istina alludes to the same scene:

> And I thought of the confusion of people, like Gloucester, being led near the cliffs,

> *Methinks the ground is even.*

> *Horrible steep . . .*

> *Hark, do you hear the sea?*

And over and over in my mind I saw King Lear wandering on the moor and I remembered the old men at Cliffhaven sitting outside their dreary ward, and nobody at home, not in themselves or anywhere.

In the next novel Zoe Bryce will plunge from her little cliff at the outskirts of communication.

Thora Pattern is clearly another of Daphne's metamorphoses. Unlike her, however, she plays no active part in the plot; she is the creator of three characters who exist only in her mind and like her live "on the edge of the alphabet." Neither really alive nor dead she dwells in a kind of no-man's land between being and non-being:

> And I, Thora Pattern, living—no! in a death-free zone

We know nothing about her except what can be deduced from the imaginary lives of Pat, Zoe and Toby. She herself is a void, unattached—"Am I plugged into the sky?"; surrounded with light—"Is it a waste of light out here?" and not far from the sea—"with the mauling sea so close." Actually she lives in a hospital somewhere in London, awaiting death in solitude and silence. We know nothing about the nature of her illness. It is the proximity of and familiarity with death, this permanent dwelling in what Heidegger [in his *Vorträge und Aufsatze*] calls the "shrine of non-being" which reveals to her and to the characters she creates the basic instability of all things including her own actions and existence.

The book largely deals with problems of identity. Who is Thora Pattern? Is she Zoe, Pat or Toby? Do these characters have no life of their own? Is she nothing but them? Again and again the reader, like the characters themselves, is confronted with lost boundaries, confusion, reflections in mirrors (another version of the "faces in the water"). Even the game played aboard the ship that takes Toby and Zoe from the antipodes to England is a search for identity: Toby is supposed to be Orpheus and must find his partner. His quest leads him to the ship's library where the officer in charge gives him a book on a war-ship of the same name as the legendary poet. Toby is completely lost. The death of his mother had already made a whole wall of himself tumble down but now he is full of confusion. Past, present and future blur, images of people, living or dead, superimpose themselves in his mind, people keep shifting "like lantern slides inserted when no one is looking" or like "panels or lantern slides or cards mysteriously removed and replaced and one person is another, and people do not stay."

It is not death but love—there is no difference: "the alphabet, the grammar are the same"—which opens a breach in the wall of Zoe Bryce's identity. She goes to the antipodes to forget her unrequited love but while she lies seasick on the ship's hospital bed she is kissed by an unknown sailor who does not even remember her the next day. The gap enlarges and the sea leaks in. Before the kiss—the first in her life— she believed that "people were separate with boundaries and fences and scrolled iron gates, Private Roads, Trespassers Will Be Prosecuted; that people lived and died in shapes and identities with labels easily recognizable, with names which they clutched, like empty suitcases, on their journey to nowhere." After the kiss she is frightened to realize that "people were all the time being extended, distorted, merged, melted . . . like pictures on a television set when the tube is broken or worn out and no one will repair or replace it."

Both Toby and Zoe engage in "private research" to escape dissolution. Toby wants to write a book on "The Lost Tribe" but never goes further than the three words of the title. Zoe wants to give shape to the little silver vision which the kiss has revealed to her. After she has finally done so by building a shape in the silver paper of an empty cigarette packet, she commits suicide. When he hears of Zoe's suicide Pat Keenan, the third character who had always wanted the other two to invest "in something clean and safe" decides to take a job in stationery because "one thing you learn in stationery is to keep things in their place; things and people." Pat does not engage in "private research" and reacts to the news of death by hiding his face even more deeply than before in the blue robe of our Lady or under the white wing of the mother swan.

It is not difficult to understand that the novel itself is Thora Pattern's little "private research," the "pattern"—her name is significant—which she imposes upon a world of confusion and lost boundaries, the silver shape or written message which she feels bound to deliver from her privileged place in the shrine of non-being. In the last pages of the book she stands alone, like Zoe Bryce on her little cliff, considering committing suicide and making "a little kite to follow the tides of death in the sky." Just as Zoe and Thora are often undistinguishable from each other these characters are in turn undistinguishable from Thora Pattern, their creator. A single example will suffice to illustrate this. Here is Thora Pattern soliloquizing in her "death-free zone":

> Cherish your interest, pursue your private research. My interest is in the maps of roads, underground cables, the terrible hoover that works here upon the stairs, sucking identities into the steel tube so that I watch floating and grasping vainly at the pegs and hooks and niches of air, the people I have known— Toby, Zoe, Pat, and others you do not know yet— and myself, and the creature, the member of the crew who stood apart like a god shaking the mixture of

fate and pouring out in that cool room your necessity.

Here is Zoe Bryce in the next chapter:

> I am interested now in traffic lanes, in byways, highways, in the terrible hoover at the top of the stairs, and the way my identity has been sucked in with the others so that in the dust and suffocation of the bag which contains us all I cannot tell my own particles, I am merely wound now with the others in an accumulation of dust—scraps of hair and bone welded in tiny golf balls of identity to be cracked open, unwound, melting in the fierce heat of being.

The demarcation line between Janet Frame's different novels is as blurred as the contours of her characters' identities. Toby is the Toby Withers of **Owls Do Cry,** Daphne's epileptic brother. He and Zoe Bryce have so much in common that they are said somewhere in the novel to be brother and sister. Since Zoe is a projection of Thora Pattern, the latter is also Toby's "sister" and hence another of Daphne's metamorphoses. The same is true of the most important images which recur from one novel to the next with only slight alterations. We have already mentioned the cliff. The rubbish dump is another of them. In **The Edge of the Alphabet,** which begins and ends with Thora Pattern's obsession with "the litter and refuse associated with human lives," it becomes the "terrible hoover at the top of the stairs," an appropriate metaphor for the confusion of people's identities whose individual particles of dust are finally reunited in the indivisible whole. The dust in turn becomes people ash in **Scented Gardens for the Blind,** the next novel.

Whereas Thora Pattern expressed herself through her creation while retaining a life of her own, Vera Glace is completely empty and has exploded into three "selves" which have no existence except as projections of herself. This the reader does not know before the last pages of the novel in which he suddenly realizes that Erlene, Edward and Vera have never existed in their worldly functions of daughter, husband and mother and that there is only one Vera Glace, a spinster of sixty, who has been silent for thirty years and whose sole companion is a Clara Strang on whom she seems to have grafted her life: "Two torn people grafted together in secret life and growth." She has never left her native town where she worked as a librarian until she was suddenly struck dumb at the age of thirty. This is the "objective," "scientific" reality as seen by two doctors who exchange reflections about her: a shrivelled creature, hardly human at all, given to posturing and to stereotyped and incomprehensible actions—a hopeless cause of schizophrenia.

But the novel tells us another story. It tells us about the secret silent dreams people like Vera Glace held inside themselves "like irremovable stones at the bottom of their minds, mixed with the sediments of their lives." And the reader who had already noticed a striking similarity between the three "characters" is forced to read the novel again to understand it properly. He then realizes more clearly that there is only one series of events which are seen differently by each of the three "selves" and there gradually emerges from the apparently fragmentary book the three-dimensional structure of Heidegger's *Dasein:* being-ahead-of-itself, already being-in-the-world and being-with represented respectively by Erlene (future), Edward (past) and Vera (present). Seen from inside the little schizophrenic of the last pages becomes the authentic *Dasein* looping the loop not only of her whole being but of the whole existence of the historical period in which she lives, standing in the maddening light of being, free from compromise, given to the silence of those who have given up talking in the hope of discovering the true message "placed between the layers of babble," holding herself open to a continual insecurity and anxiety and free from all worldly ties because she knows that these will vanish for ever with death, the ever-present possibility of her existence.

The first of Heidegger's existentials, facticity or already-being-in-the-world, is represented by Edward, a new, more articulate version of Toby in quest of the lost tribe. Edward plays with plastic soldiers and his behaviour is described in terms of tactics and strategy. The enemies against which he wages a pitiless war are time and change. He would like to believe that man is timeless and eternal and in order to prove this he traces the lineage of an ordinary family—the Strangs—hoping to find an uninterrupted line, a "private life belt which he dreams of throwing to the human race." But history presupposes the transitoriness of "history-making man" for it is the advent of being among beings which would not be possible if man were eternal. Everything is all right as long as Edward deals with the past Strangs: he can remain uncommitted and live "by remote control." But at the end of the line of Strangs he necessarily comes to the present and the living representatives and he can no longer escape contingency. His private research which had taken him to a remote past and to the antipodes ends in New Zealand with Clara Strang, the last of the line. In the room where he talks with her a sound can be heard in the distance as "of some thing raking and shuffling" and again the hero is confronted with the ineluctable and by now familiar Gloucester situation:

"The sea's near?" he asked.

"Down the road," Clara answered. "It's not for bathing, there's an undertow; you can hear the sea everywhere."

She seemed to be listening.

"Yes, it's close," Edward said.

"Oh yes, it's close," Clara affirmed.

The second of Heidegger's existentials, "existentiality" or being-ahead-of-itself is represented by Erlene, the mute "daughter" who wants to protect herself by an uninterrupted line of silence. Erlene is obsessed with death and like the opossums when she hears sniff-sniffing in the grass she feigns death in order to escape it. If she is already dead the soldiers who pass in twos in the night will not kill her and the hawks will not alight upon her, take away the embroidered cloth in which she wraps herself for the night and eat her inside. She feels that she can achieve some measure of safety by turning people into insects or animals and by transforming everything into its negative image. Thus she turns her mother into a sheep and Dr. Clapper into Uncle Blackbeetle who takes off his black apron each time he starts telling a story. One day she forgets herself and says aloud: "You speak like Dr. Clapper." These are the only words she utters in the novel and when the psychiatrist exclaims gladly: "But I *am* Dr. Clapper!" she runs home to find Uncle Blackbeetle cut in two on the windowsill: she has been discovered and recedes further back into herself.

Love, comprehension and language are dangerous because they would distract her from the only thing that really matters: her constant watchfulness in the face of death. She must not be taken by surprise. Language is replaced by "secret signals" which people are too busy to notice. Like Arnold's scholar-gipsy Erlene is waiting for the fire to fall from the sky. She knows, however, that it will not be the spark of love but of destruction, that it is "too late for fire, unless it was the kind which enables the soldiers to fill their sachets with people ash and disease, which forced her father to invent the Strang family in the wild hope that it would survive, as dreams may be known to do, when all else is destroyed, which confused her mother to the extent of inducing her to blackmail furniture and to weep by the grass-grown beds of rivers that consulting no one had changed their courses and without the usual patronage of willows, flax, rushes, were taking the unplanned lonelier route to the sea."

If Edward is obsessed with time and change, Erlene with death and silence, Vera is obsessed with light and guilt. She suggests the third of Heidegger's existentials, forfeiture or being-with. She assumes the role of the mother who is responsible for everything: "Which accident? Erlene wondered. There had never been an accident, except of birth." Just as Erlene plays possum in the hope of escaping death Vera pretends to be blind in order to protect herself against the dazzling light of being. When she was a child her parents used candles and kerosene lamps, a small, unobtrusive light which "did not search into far corners of each room." People still had private places, little crimes which were left out of the searching glow. Now things have changed, everything is plunged too suddenly into light so that no crime escapes detection and she is more and more oppressed by the radiance. Though we know nothing about what, at thirty, led her to the madhouse, we know that everything would have been different if she had never taken her magnifying glass and discovered, like Daphne, that the currency of time was counterfeit:

> It happened because somewhere at a certain moment one of us by chance picked up a genuine coin, judged it to be genuine, and thus could never recall the judgment. So the shining vision stays, expands, takes up room. The tiny threepenny truth melts and flows and silvers the entire view and runs down the edge of being, like moonlight; and all the time with the silver vision before us we judge, judge.

The keeper of the lighthouse on Waipapa beach is one of the central images of the novel. Each of Vera Glace's three "selves" remembers him in its own way. The mother, obsessed with light, remembers that she was picnicking on the beach when the man was taken to the madhouse and her father told her not to look at what did not concern her so that she never knew "whether the lighthouse keeper really changed to a bird, flying round and round under the sun." The daughter, obsessed with language, compares words with lighthouses "with their beacons roaming the seas to rescue the thoughts or warn them against perilous tides, cross-currents, approaching storms." The father, obsessed with strategy, remembers a man who built himself a throne on the beach and controlled the waves. Each of the three "selves" can be identified with the keeper who became mad for having lived too long with the light: Vera would like to be blind to escape from the dazzling glow of light, Erlene waits for the flash in the sky and the wax of Edward's wings has melted because, in his attempt to escape from his human predicament he has, like Icarus, "tasted the sun."

The world of *Scented Gardens for the Blind* is a world of silent expectation. Nothing happens except that change creeps in, that time leaks through the breaches in the walls of the citadel in which Vera Glace has immured herself in the hope of escaping death.

—*Jeanne Delbaere-Garant*

The world of ***Scented Gardens for the Blind*** is a world of silent expectation. Nothing happens except that change creeps in, that time leaks through the breaches in the walls of the citadel in which Vera Glace has immured herself in the hope of escaping death. But even if the line of Strangs is traced back as far as Adam it finally ends up in the present, even if she refuses to speak for fear of being comprehended, the boundaries of Vera's territory are gnawed and eroded day after day with the inexorable regularity of a tide. The light-

house keeper brings together the different threads of the novel as well as the different selves of the protagonist. He is a metaphor for authentic *Dasein,* the receptacle of being and the guardian of the house. But his fate indicates that the most complete authenticity is also the extreme limit of alienation. There had been some confusion in the minds of Toby and Zoe but here the divisions between people have vanished altogether: "the stirred smell of light [is] inseparable from dust." Vera Glace whose very name combines authenticity—*Vera*—and complete alienation—*Glace* or ice which is so clearly associated with madness in ***Faces in the Water***—bears the burden of the historical period in which she lives. She is the guardian of language and when the message finally comes out with extraordinary force on the last page of the novel, after the atom bomb has destroyed Britain, it is the cry of a new-born species negating all humanity and all civilization and starting anew from the primordial cleft of the world.

Daphne, Istina, Thora and Vera are clearly different facets of the same character. I have pointed to a few motifs and cross-references linking the four novels together. One of these might easily be overlooked though it is the essential key to the Daphne figure. In ***Faces in the Water*** Istina Mavet reads Rilke's *Sonnets to Orpheus* and quotes the first words of sonnet II, 12—"*Wolle die Wandlung*—Choose to be Changed"—in connection with the operation on the brain with which they threaten to change her personality. In ***The Edge of the Alphabet*** Toby is given the part of Orpheus in the identity game played aboard the ship. These two allusions are sufficient to remind us that Daphne, metamorphosed by the lobotomy at the end of ***Owls Do Cry*** is also the name of the nymph turned into a laurel at the end of Rilke's poem and that Vera was the name of the girl for whom the sonnets were written as a funeral monument.

Orpheus is the common denominator. Each of the different versions of Daphne possesses some of his features. Like him Istina wanders in the country of the dead. Thora imposes order on the confusion of the world, Vera turns the shelter into a temple and rescues language from complete annihilation. Like him they have visited the country of Eurydice and have come back alienated from the society of mankind and aware that the dead are as much part of their lives as the living. Like him—torn to pieces by the fierce Maenads—they have limbs loosely attached or are split into fragments of themselves—unifying and holding together by their very dispersion. Orpheus also helps us to understand the tree imagery which runs through the novels. Retrospectively we see better why Toby dreams that he is a tree or "an entire forest, with the Lost Tribe inhabiting him" and why the kiss is Zoe's "tiny precious berry from the one branch of a huge tree in a forest where the trees are numberless," why the central part of ***Faces in the Water*** is called Treecroft and why Edward cannot do without his genealogical tree of Strangs. Finally Orpheus also links Janet Frame herself with Rilke and Ovid and all the poets of the past whom she has assimilated and whose voice is part of her own.

All this, I hope, suffices to indicate that Rilke's *Sonnets to Orpheus* play a more important part in Janet Frame's early novels than might appear at first sight. They are inseparable from the intricate form she has devised to express her Heideggerian concept of man as thrown into an already existing world, incomplete in his basic structure and continually fulfilling himself by a series of metamorphoses until he comes to the final contact with being. Just as her novels never give us the last word on anything but continue all the time to illuminate each other in all directions Daphne is never fixed in a single attitude but she is continually in the making. There always remains something which she can become but is not yet. This is suggested by her reappearance in the four novels, each time under a different guise and each time confronted with a different "ending": the lobotomy (*Owls Do Cry*), the return to normal life (*Faces in the Water*), suicide (*The Edge of the Alphabet*) or incurable schizophrenia (*Scented Gardens for the Blind*).

Whatever the metamorphosis it is death that will put the last touch to the picture by making the final choice. But because she encompasses the whole network of existence and remains constantly on the watch Daphne-Istina-Thora-Vera, alias Janet Frame herself is, like Orpheus, the keeper of the lighthouse and the guardian of language, the torchbearer standing in the radiance of the perfect circle, the authentic *Dasein* through which being reveals itself and, like the wind in a tree, sends its message to the rest of mankind.

Carole Ferrier (essay date 1978)

SOURCE: "The Rhetoric of Rejection: Janet Frame's Recent Work," in *South Pacific Images,* edited by Chris Tiffin, South Pacific Association for Commonwealth Literature and Language Studies, 1978, pp. 196-203.

[*Ferrier is an educator and editor. In the following essay, she discusses thematic shifts in Frame's fiction from her earlier to her later works.*]

Through the carefully-woven patterns of imagery and symbolism which distinguish Janet Frame's novels runs a dominant theme—that of oppositions. These range from the antinomies of treasure and rubbish around which *Owls Do Cry* is organised, to the juxtaposition of 'this' and 'that' world, discussed by Frame in a well-known interview [in *Landfall,* 19, March, 1965.] In Frame's earlier novels, the opposition is between perceptions categorised as the opposition between the 'sane' and 'insane' views of one's society, and it is clear that for Frame the insane view has ultimate validity. As she continues writing through the sixties, her characters' consciousness of radical dissociation from their surrounding society increasingly finds its culmination in death after a loss

of touch with material reality. The emphasis shifts from mental to physical vulnerability, *A State of Siege* (1966) marking the point of greatest fusion of the physical and the psychological. We no longer know by the end of this novel if all of what is being recounted has in fact occurred; whether there is a violent storm going on outside Malfred's cottage on the island off the North Island of New Zealand and someone is knocking persistently on the door, or whether the storm and the knocking are simply an extended metaphor of her past and present beleaguered state of mind in which a symbolic situation appears to be actual, before being revealed to have been all in the mind (as with Golding's Pincher Martin whom we believe until the end of the novel of this name to be cast away on a rock in the ocean.)

The breaking in at the end of *A State of Siege* represents both an apparent attack on Malfred's physical self and the collapse of her mental defences. In the work which this discussion will focus upon—Frame's most recent novels, *The Rainbirds* (1967), *Intensive Care* (1970), and *Daughter Buffalo* (1972)—the expression of extreme and inevitable withdrawal, of saying 'no', is no longer insanity, a retreat into madness, but a retreat into death. The mental hospitals which provide the settings for part of *Owls Do Cry* and all of *Faces in the Water,* are replaced in *Intensive Care* by hospitals in which the elderly and diseased live out their last days, though the young too are not immune from the treachery of their bodies. The focus of breakdown has shifted from being mental to physical, and this shift implies a darkening of Frame's philosophical perspective, for there is no 'cure' for death, as there is for the divided self in the possibility of a different social system which would transform the relations of individuals within it. This paper will explore some of the implications of this development in Frame's fiction.

A central aspect of the expression of growing depression and despair in the novels is a preoccupation with the failure of communication, the collapse of language into silence. In Frame's novels in which the central characters confront the failure of their own language (particularly *A State of Siege* and *The Rainbirds* and the last part of *Intensive Care*) a contrast is clear between this verbal inability and Frame's own dazzling poetic expression in extended descriptive passages. The discourse of the main body of *Daughter Buffalo,* by contrast, is barren; Frame's consciousness of this being expressed in her insertion of a number of 'poems' into it that are a pale reflection of the lyrical passages that expressed Daphne's apprehension of the process of her life in *Owls Do Cry.* Godfrey Rainbird reads words he is presented with in an 'icy language' of anagram following his 'death' and subsequent revival after being knocked down by a car. This expresses the confusion of all his responses due to this event which has pushed him into a heightened consciousness of the absurdity of his existence. He loses any sense of having 'his personal control' on (over) his electric blanket for example, the dial of which appears to him to read, sinisterly, 'his responal clonrot'. When he receives his letter of dismissal from work, the 'cold spelling' again seems to Godfrey to express 'more truthfully' his sense of being lost, cast away.

> A hundred pounds is indeed a moth's jaws to help us face the work at the door. No doubt my name is Dogrey Brainrid of Feelt Drive, Resonsand Bay, Dunndie, Ogoat, Shuto Sanlid, Wen Lazeland, Rotusen he-mis-phere, the Drowl. Or the Unserve, the reathe as a plante in the sky among the rats, the noom, the comtes, all the dewnors of speac.

As Frame comments, 'Not a prepossessing address!' Her playing with orthography has in it, however, an element of regressiveness that goes beyond an appealing naïveté to being at times irritating, coy or over-contrived, particularly for example in the formula language of Milly Galbraith's monologue in the last section of *Intensive Care.* The 'cold spelling' in which Godfrey Rainbird reads everything seems to lack a dimension of psychological probability; seems at times more on the level of game than having any organic connection with the reality it endeavours to express. R.D. Laing, one of the most prominent members of the anti-psychiatry school in Britain in the late fifties and sixties comments [in his *The Divided Self*] on schizophrenic speech, 'A good deal of schizophrenia is simply nonsense, red-herring speech, prolonged filibustering designed to throw dangerous people off the scent, to create boredom and futility in others'. If this is the function of the distorted language that Milly Galbraith uses in *Intensive Care,* then it might be argued that Frame's own alienation has taken her to the point where the language of her novel becomes mystifying or alienating rather than expressive; that there has been a failure of art. We have moved from the deviance of Daphne that was expressed through poetic utterance in *Owls Do Cry* to a formulaic language of advertising jingles, knitting patterns and recipes—a superficial discourse inadequate to express the reality Frame seeks to embody. Language is moving towards being a closed system (without the internal consistency, albeit convoluted and almost undecodable of, say, *Finnegans Wake* and lacking that novel's virtuoso surety of touch). Eventually this can lead only to silence: any message that can come through to us from the author will be only that brought by the messenger at the end of Ionesco's *Les Chaises*: he opens his mouth and no words come out or, in the alternative ending, she writes on a blackboard in incomprehensible characters: the implication is that there is no point in trying to understand or communicate the meaning of experience. Significantly, at the end of the novel which preceded *The Rainbirds, A State of Siege,* the stone which Malfred Signal dies clutching in her fist has wrapped around it a piece of paper with 'last century's or tomorrow's news in verse . . . not in any language she had learned' and the words 'Help Help' scrawled across it in red crayon. The meaning of Malfred's experience has become incomprehensible and undescribable.

Frame's increasing despair seems to be produced by a capacity for apprehending but not for suggesting ways of transforming the conditions of life in the predominantly petty-bourgeois societies in which her novels are set—those of New Zealand, Australia, Britain and the United States. The hegemonic ideology of these societies asserts that characteristics such as acquisitiveness and greed (prominently displayed by all the characters who are part of 'this' world in Frame's earlier novels) are inherent in universal 'human nature' rather than being aspects of a particular transitional stage (that is to say, capitalism) of the historical development of such societies. Lucien Goldmann argues [in his *Introduction to the Problems of a Sociology of the Novel,*] that the homology which exists between works of art and the society in which they are produced can in bourgeois society be more clearly seen in the novel form than in any other. The controlling theme of Frame's fiction is the conflict between the inner life and the social life, that must inevitably be particularly pronounced under late capitalism; the increasing predominance of the inner life leads in Frame's work to an increasingly pessimistic view in which the individual resists but is gradually dragged under by social and institutional forces.

> **Frame's increasing despair seems to be produced by a capacity for apprehending but not for suggesting ways of transforming the conditions of life in the predominantly petty-bourgeois societies in which her novels are set—those of New Zealand, Australia, Britain and the United States.**
>
> **—Carole Ferrier**

This perspective having become dominant, a capitulation on the part of the author to the inevitability of fascism then becomes possible, and *Intensive Care* in fact concludes with a Human Delineation Act which determines who will be eliminated and who survive. The fascist mode of human relationships demands three main groups of participants — those who classify, those who are classified and a public called upon to accept or reject these classifications. Thomas Szasz has argued that throughout history different social groups, religious dissidents, witches, the 'mentally ill' and Jews, among others have been classified by the hegemonic groups and subsequently incarcerated or destroyed. In early Frame novels, the central character was frequently shut up in a mental hospital for part or all of the novel. In *The Rainbirds,* Godfrey Rainbird is classified as abnormal, a kind of walking reminder of the reality of death, and so he becomes an outcast. His wife Beatrice fantasises about escaping this by moving to another town, but the outcast brand is indelibly etched on their minds.

Relevant to this is Szasz's identification of the labelling of certain groups as a 'rhetoric of rejection' which involves the selection of some members of one's society for social stigmatisation. Frame both shows the operation of this in bourgeois society and tries herself to challenge the norms from which this labelling is conducted. But in parts of Frame's more recent novels this creation of a group of outcasts moves beyond being a social force which must be resisted; rather than a mental collapse which is hopefully temporary (though Daphne's becoming forewoman at the mill at the end of *Owls Do Cry* is hardly an achievement in Frame's terms), the inability to resist any longer is expressed through a physical collapse or decay which usually appears to be an irreversible process: there is little prospect of regeneration when you have cancer or a stomach ulcer like some of the characters in *Intensive Care* or *Daughter Buffalo*. Physical collapse can be read as a metaphor of profound despair in Frame's work. Her characters increasingly fail to resist and become subjected to the 'withering institutions' of society. A near hopelessness in the face of this is embodied in a vision such as that of the hospital in which most of the characters in *Intensive Care* live out their last days.

> People fastened like dead leaves to a blossomless tree, the incomplete bodies, the lost limbs, the icy paralysis, the slow reptilean or swift lush cancer growths nourished and sheltered by the old house as a forest accommodates its fungi; the amputation of limbs seeming as natural as the loss of limbs from the trees, the institutional withering of mind and body accepted as is the withering from time to time of healthy trees in a forest or orchard.

Perhaps one might argue that as R.D. Laing gradually rejected the social orientation of his work in *The Divided Self,* to the point where he could become for a time a monk in Sri Lanka, or as Doris Lessing gradually moved from her preoccupation with social action to a fascination with Sufism and futurology, writing in 1971 in the Preface to a new edition of *The Golden Notebook* of her certainty of coming apocalyptic collapse, so Janet Frame has, over time, gravitated towards one side of the opposition at the expense of the other, the dominant imagery patterns of treasure, darkness, death, and disintegration profoundly and pervasively embodying her thesis on a deeper level. There are striking correspondences between Frame's essential philosophy and Lessing's as expressed in her most recent novel *The Memoirs of a Survivor* (1974), and they are bleak philosophies that offer little prospect of social renewal. Relevant here is ["Self, Symptom and Society,"] an article by Peter Sedgewick which suggests in relation to Laing's development:

> Peaceful co-existence between the normal and the psychotic ideologies is impossible, and it follows that any person who accepts the psychotic vision as au-

thentic must at once declare war on the world-view of the normal consensus.

Does this rejection of 'the normal consensus' mean that Frame's writing lacks breadth, or 'universal validity'? While not in any way subscribing in the traditional criticism often levelled at women's writing that it is deficient since it portrays a circumscribed universe and a small and generally domestic compass and does not express general or 'important' conflicts or events, I would nevertheless agree that one can find in Frame a limitation of perspective that is perhaps a function of the naive anarchism that is the only identifiable political tendency of her work. An examination of the general direction of her writing shows that in her two most recent novels (despite the expansion of her range of characters beyond the types that she has habitually drawn) she presents a partial view that gives little hope of positive change, merely a dialectic of decay. Lucien Goldmann asserts that the hero of the novel, that literary form which embodies most centrally the dominant features of bourgeois society, must be 'mad or a criminal . . . a problematic character' in conflict with his or her surroundings. Increasingly, psychological conflicts associated with usually unsuccessful attempts to come to terms with sexuality and with death dominate the lives of her central characters. Almost invariably in Frame's work sexuality is associated with misunderstanding, thwarted love or desire, and death: in all her novels someone dies, but in her three most recent works death becomes the pervasive motif. (Evans argues that there is not this development, that 'death has been the common denominator of all her work'.) The mass slaughter at the end of *Intensive Care* represents to me the inevitable perhaps, but greatly intensified culmination of earlier tendencies. The world of work and action, present as an alternative to withdrawal into the self in *Owls Do Cry* is gradually replaced by the world of institutionalisation, usually in mental hospitals: in *Daughter Buffalo* Talbot Edelman *works,* but his work is the study of death. Murder and violent death are staple motifs in most of Frame's novels but become more and more pervasive, the New York setting of her most recent novel *Daughter Buffalo* being perhaps a rationale for this. And where, after all, could Frame go, after portraying her vision of the Human Delineation Programme and mass murder at the end of *Intensive Care*? If the characters are not dead, they exist in a living death like Godfrey Rainbird, or have amputated limbs, or are dying of cancer (like Ciss Everest, or Naomi, or Turnlung's Aunt Kate). Sexuality with its potential for fulfillment and regeneration provides no positive alternative in *Daughter Buffalo*; indeed it is explicitly connected with death: for Talbot and Lenore first make love after they 'share' the death of a child. The death of Edelman's dog Sally, to whom he is almost as devoted as if she were human, is the signal for Lenore to leave him. Turnlung's recollection of a scene of two copulating dogs and a linesman electrocuted above them is an almost medieval image of the terror of sexuality. Hold back, or you will be hurt, if not killed! This pattern can be observed in the earlier books. In ***Intensive Care*** the marriage of Peg and Tom never occurs because Tom dies of a stomach ulcer, while in ***Owls Do Cry*** Francie is burned to death on the rubbish dump at the onset of adolescence.

Frame's habit of drawing characters who are in the process of, or in an advanced state of retreat from their society has in a sense led her into a *cul de sac* from which there is little chance of escape. It would seem that in this *cul de sac* death is the only reality which matters and the life to which it is opposed lacks an equivalent force. Frame attempts in ***Daughter Buffalo*** to evade the implications of her own conclusions: we are asked to believe that the death of Turnlung has not actually occurred, because he is alive and well and writing the epilogue at the end of the novel; that the gaiety of the artist has 'transfigured all that dread.' But it can hardly be denied that Frame is given over almost entirely to 'that' world. The evidence of Frame's three most recent novels is that she has written herself into a dead end and perhaps only the development of an increased consciousness of the necessity of challenging the institutions and the power structures of 'this' world with a more valid base than individual resistance unto death can carry her out of this. She has published almost nothing for the past few years, and one wonders if she is grappling with, or is in fact submerged by, this central problem in her work.

P. D. Evans (essay date Spring 1981)

SOURCE: "'Farthest from the Heart': The Autobiographical Parables of Janet Frame," in *Modern Fiction Studies,* Vol. 27, No. 1, Spring, 1981, pp. 31-40.

[*In the following essay, Evans traces the parallels between themes, techniques, and metaphors in Frame's early stories to those in her later works.*]

No one approaches Janet Frame's writing for an evening of light entertainment. The atmosphere of her work is almost unrelievedly dark; its texture thick with imagery and allusion; its plots full of deceits engineered to trick the reader; its significance half-stated and often obscure, as if the process of writing has not fully released the impulses which have brought it about. It is this last quality which I wish to discuss in this essay: the sense gained by any copious reader of her work that it represents a recurring engagement with the business of writing itself, with the relationships of words and things, and with the limiting nature of the things we attempt to discuss with words, rather than being a process of steadily expressing a vision that is largely preconceived.

In discussing this, as will be evident, I have broken the rule which states that a writer's life has nothing to do with a writer's art. I break it because it does not fit the writer: Janet Frame seems to me to dictate a different critical approach because, as anyone familiar with the details of her life will know, she

constantly places herself at the center of her own writing. Like the Malcolm Lowry of *Under the Volcano,* for example, Frame is an extraordinarily egocentric writer who finds herself in everything and will empathize with her environment only in order to cannibalize it, so that the flesh of others may become the substance of her fiction. Knowing this does not lessen her stature, of course, any more than it will lead us to some kind of absolute interpretation of her work. Acknowledging her fundamental egocentrism simply reveals a concealed level of meaning in her writing and helps us to understand why she writes as she does.

To begin illustrating some of these claims, I have chosen what seems at first to be one of her slightest stories, **"The Linesman."** Very little happens in this story, whose narrator describes a few moments she has spent gazing through her window at an electrical linesman who has climbed a telegraph pole to make repairs to the wires in her street. She notices certain ironies: the fact that the safety harness which prevents him from falling to his death is also holding him up against wires that could fry him to a crisp; and the contrast between this dangerous position and the surrounding lassitude of an early spring day which is being celebrated with truly suburban anonymity by women pegging out billowing washing and youths sprawled in amatory postures beneath motorcycles. There is little else to be seen, but the narrator confesses that she is unable to pull herself away from the window—because, as she reveals in the final sentence of the story, she has been hoping to see the linesman fall to his death.

On the face of it, this story appears to reveal the writer herself turning from the typewriter in boredom and admitting to a desire for a little titillation. I would suggest that there is much more to the story than this, however, and that the crucial element in it is the electricity to which the linesman is so close. Frame underwent frequent electric shock treatment herself while in psychiatric hospitals between 1947 and 1953, and she seems to have had a special fascination with electricity ever since. One thinks of the frequent references in her writing to innocuous electrical devices (such as heaters in ***The Rainbirds***) and the dangers they represent; of the linesman in ***Daughter Buffalo*** who is burnt to death in mid-air; and, more substantially, the images of encircling fire that occur in some of the other novels. In ***Owls Do Cry*** the central symbol of the book, the rubbish dump with its "tickle of yellow toi-toi" round its edge, is specifically related by imagery to the encircling fires of electric shock treatment; a nuclear explosion ends the fourth novel, ***Scented Gardens for the Blind,*** and her next, ***The Edge of the Alphabet,*** concludes with the killing-off of most of its characters by a falling chandelier lit to celebrate the arrival of electricity in a small English village. For this writer, electrical power is secular power, a natural force which humans use to destroy and oppress.

Watching an electrical linesman at work, then, is no straightforward thing for such a writer, who immediately sees not an artisan but herself in a symbolic situation which represents her own predicament as she sees it. The equation she appears to make is roughly as follows: the linesman like the artist has special gifts of vision, his being literal (neighbors draw their curtains in case he looks down into their houses) and hers figurative (nothing can stop her imaginative insight into the lives of other people). But both pay a price for this vision, the linesman through his proximity to a voltage which may kill him, the artist through her proximity to a voltage which, through electro-convulsive therapy, might rob her of her imagination and leave her like Daphne after her leucotomy at the end of *Owls Do Cry*. Trapped in such a predicament—the artist has even less freedom than the harnessed linesman— one may well wish occasionally for the merciful release of a sudden fall.

What Frame is doing here is done to a certain extent by all artists, who turn the surrounding world into metaphors which embody their vision. But few so distinctively focus the metaphors on their own special plight; few operate such a gravitational pull on the objects of their fictional worlds, drawing everything towards a central sensibility but refusing subsequently to force them back out again much transformed. Her tendency to do these things in her writing is present from the first collection of short stories, *The Lagoon,* which was written during her early years in a hospital. The personal nature of these stories and their subsequent tendency towards autobiographical parable can only be explained by an understanding of the importance of the events that immediately preceded her admission to a hospital in the fall of 1947.

Frame entered the hospital voluntarily, with the aim of turning herself into a professional writer. The most interesting thing she tells us about herself during this time is that she carried a copy of Rilke's *Sonnets to Orpheus* with her wherever she went. These sonnets had been written in response to the death of the daughter of a friend, a talented dancer whose sudden demise Rilke attempted to understand and to accept in a long sequence of poems about art, life, and death that were based on the classical myth of Orpheus and Eurydice. What must have fascinated Frame was the similarity of Rilke's situation to her own: just before her entry to the hospital she had lost her younger and favorite sister, Isabel, who had drowned at Picton, the beach resort home of the Frames' maternal grandparents, during a late summer holiday taken with the writer.

Rilke, then, was more than just another writer; she chose to study him because he was approaching death by means of art, and in her situation art alone offered some means of coming to terms with a tragic bereavement. Like the poet, she would dedicate her writing to understanding her loss, and it was in this mood that she began to write her first mature stories.

The reader is immediately struck by her oblique approach to her task. Although no one could deny that the stories in *The Lagoon* are insistently about death, there is an equally undeniable sense in them of the writer circling about a subject that both fascinates and repels her. The title story of the collection, for example, is set at the scene of Isabel's death, but conceals fact with a layer of fiction. The way in which this is done is worth noting. **"The Lagoon"** begins with its young female narrator returning in late adolescence to the scene of her happy childhood holidays to find that the little township as well as her favorite lagoon on the beach are far smaller and shabbier than she remembered them. She recalls her beloved grandmother, who has recently died, and especially remembers the old woman's ability to weave stories about everything in Picton except the lagoon, which "never had a proper story." Now that the old woman has gone, the girl's aunt reveals the "proper story" at last: "Your great grandmother was a murderess. She drowned her husband, pushed him in the lagoon." The girl's grandmother never mentioned the murder, as the aunt explains, because, "The reason one talks farthest from the heart is the fear that it may be hurt."

This sentence is the most crucial in the entire collection. It draws attention to the dishonesty possible in storytelling, to the ease with which writers may manipulate facts and thereby control the responses of their readers. The process of storytelling is one of the things this story is about: the grandmother's ability to tell stories about things is one of its subjects, as is the ability (conjectured by the aunt later in the story) of Dostoevsky and popular journalists to do the same. Bringing the inventedness of fiction before the reader, particularly by means of a sentence which speaks of avoidance and hurt, inevitably draws attention to the inventedness of the story itself, and it invites the reader to plunge beneath its surface in order to examine the processes of fictionalization. Aware as we are of the actual events behind the story, we are better placed than most readers to see how Frame forms life into parable. Just as the lagoon is sullied by the invading seawater, she seems to say, childhood is sullied by adult life, especially by its diminution of the transforming imaginative power we have when we are innocent. But that is not all that pollutes the lagoon of childhood: violent death, a death in the family, has contaminated it too. This is the nearest the writer comes to mentioning the incident which has hurt her heart; this, and the clear reference to the invading seawater which in fact carried her sister's life away.

This process of "talking farthest from the heart" becomes a staple of Janet Frame's fiction, a technique in which actual events, and particularly this one event (which becomes melded from time to time with the almost identical loss of her older sister, also by drowning, in 1937), are turned into fiction, but in such a way that the reader is always made aware of the fictitiousness of the fiction. In the *Lagoon* stories and others of the period, she follows a rigid system: if the location of Isabel's death is confronted—the beach—then the loss is either suffered by someone else or is less than a loss of a sister.

If the doomed sister is mentioned openly (as in **"The Secret,"** where the threatened girl bears the name of Frame's older drowned sister, Myrtle), then the point of the story is that she is not going to die, after all. At no point do we find the death behind her fiction faced squarely, and at no point can we sense her retreat completely from it. Even in ***Daughter Buffalo,*** where she describes the drowning and the subsequent train journey from Picton with the coffin, she gives the experience to an anonymous friend of the narrator, Turnlung. She cannot avoid mentioning the topic, which is scarcely crucial to the story, yet she cannot bring herself to mention it fully. She conceals but teases, or reveals but turns away.

"The Lagoon" is the best brief example of Frame's curious behavior, but there are others that are little different. In **"Swans,"** we again find the child narrator taking us back to the beach and again find that all is not well. Because it is the middle of the week, their father cannot come with them, and the usual crowds are not there; and these absences not only rob the place of its former magic, but they fill it with darkness and a sense of threat that is disproportionate to the events which occur. When the children find a shell that looks like a cat's eye, death enters the story at last: they are reminded of the dying cat they have left at home.

But there is a coda to this story, as in **"The Lagoon,"** which focuses this image of death a little more sharply. As they make their way back up the beach at evening with their mother, the girls see another lagoon:

> It was dark black water, secret, and the air was filled with murmurings and rustlings, it was as if they were walking into another world that had been kept secret from everyone and now they had found it. The darkness lay massed as if you could touch it, soon it would swell and fill the earth. . . . They looked across the lagoon then and saw the swans, black and shining, as if the visiting dark tiring of its form, had changed to birds, hundreds of them resting and moving softly about on the water. Why the lagoon was filled with swans, like secret sad ships, secret and quiet. Hush-sh the water said, rush-hush, the wind passed over the top of the water, no other sound but the shaking of rushes and far away now it seemed the roar of the sea like a secret sea that had crept inside your head forever.

This is the same lagoon as before, once pleasant but now darkened by the birds which represent death; beyond it is the sound of the sea with its inescapable secret which only the writer knows.

The inevitable lagoon of **"The Reservoir"** is slightly different from the others in that it is man-made. The young children who are at the center of this story play frequently in their tiny local creek but are warned by their parents not to follow it inland to the reservoir which feeds it. The repetition of such warnings soon turns the reservoir into a symbol that contrasts with the innocence of the little creek: where the latter is safe, the former, as notices remind the children, is full of danger (or "ANGER," in the case of one slightly dilapidated notice). When the children decide to visit it after all, they are in effect visiting the adult life that lies ahead of each of them, but none of them is able to understand what the concrete lagoon represents, and they return home filled with complacent bafflement at their parents' earlier warnings.

The *real* story, as in **"The Lagoon,"** comes through implication, through the fact that the innocent mind of the child is being recreated by the experienced mind of an adult. The hidden threat of the journey to the reservoir and of the reservoir itself is revealed through images that are those of a fairy story that has gone wrong: there are "huge trees that lived with their heads in the sky, and their mazed and linked roots rubbed bare of earth, like bones with the flesh cleaned from them," and pines which make "the sound of speech at its loneliest level where the meaning is felt but never explained, and it goes on and on in a kind of despair." And the description of the reservoir has a similar feeling of inexplicable desolation:

> The fringe of young pines on the edge, like toy trees, subjected to the wind, sighed and told us their sad secrets. In the Reservoir there was an appearance of neatness which concealed a disarray too frightening to be acknowledged except, without any defence, in moments of deep sleep and dreaming. The little sparkling innocent waves shone now green, now grey, petticoats, lettuce leaves; the trees sighed, and told us to be quiet, hush-sh, as if something were sleeping and should not be disturbed—perhaps that was what the trees were always telling us, to hush-sh in case we disturbed something which must never be awakened?

The petticoat-waves are from a childhood story; the sense that they conceal something unspeakable sounds like a story from the Brothers Grimm. Here again is one of those secret seas that has crept inside the narrator's head and altered the perspective of everything she writes, making the children's final conviction that their parents have got the reservoir all wrong pathetic by contrast with the knowledge implied in the story.

Another ***Lagoon*** story, **"Keel and Kool,"** makes some important developments of the parabolic method. At first, in fact, autobiography appears to have triumphed over parable, because the story openly mentions the death of a beloved sister. Once again we are at the beach, once again we are in the hands of a child-figure, but the emphasis here is on the absoluteness of death, its complete unavoidability. Instead of returning Winnie, the bereaved girl, to childhood at the end of the story, Frame sends her into a lonely pine forest where the restrained lamentation of other stories is placed in the voice of a seagull circling high above the pines, "a seagull as white as chalk, circling and crying Keel Keel Come home Kool come home Kool. And Kool would never come, ever."

Does this story show Frame coming to terms with her loss at last, able to face it after the exorcising process of art? The fact that **"The Reservoir"** was written after **"Keel and Kool"** suggests that this is unlikely and that we should continue to look at her work as parable. The key to this story, in fact, seems to be in the gull's cry, which is not only onomatopoeic but also a pun: the gull flies above the girl as an ostensible emblem of the frankness of her despair and the completeness of her loss, but, as it does, its voice draws attention to a secret loss, of someone who has been *killed and cooled*—someone dead but, so to speak, frozen in memory. Once more, then, as in **"The Lagoon"** in particular, we have an apparent story (a girl comes to terms with her loss) and a "real" or "secret" story, implied by means of a special signal.

Two factors, then, seem inextricably involved in Janet Frame's art, to judge from these early stories: first, its devotion to a single historical event, and second, the increasingly complex and subtle way in which she signals this to the reader. There is a great distance between the tell-tale words and sentences of **"The Lagoon"** and the punning of the seagull in **"Keel and Kool."** The first draw attention to themselves and are fairly readily decodable; the second seems furtive and obscure, requiring special information to be recognized, let alone understood. Generally speaking, this tendency toward obscurity becomes a dominant trait of her later writing, developing into a curious and almost neurotic desire to manipulate the reader, to treat the inventedness of fiction as a means of breaking the conventions governing the relationship of writer and audience. There is a streak of this game-playing in two of the **Lagoon** stories, **"Dossy"** and **"Jan Godfrey,"** where the reader is given a specific perspective on the stories only to be told finally that this perspective is incorrect. The replacement of apparent narrators by "real" ones becomes a staple of some of her novels (I am thinking of **Scented Gardens for the Blind** and **Daughter Buffalo,** in particular), where personae split during the course of reading and where narrators are revealed to be concoctions of other, hidden, narrators, figures who are surrogates for the author, who have been "educated" by the experience of death and who lecture the reader on the essential processes of human existence.

In many of the novels, then, Frame seems to be deliberately attempting to devalue traditional fictive methods, to baffle and to confuse the reader, and to imply the existence of qualities and values that are concealed beneath the surface of her writing; these tendencies develop directly from her short initial fiction. To do justice to a generalization like this would be impossible, but I think a fair way to conclude this essay would be to look at the single work in which most aspects of that generalization come nearest to being true. In turning to

Scented Gardens for the Blind, I confront a novel whose considerable obscurity originates in that slight obfuscation we saw in **"The Lagoon,"** a work that is essentially a short story so encrusted with complications that it is no longer recognizable—but a work which, nevertheless, contains sufficient signals to enable the reader to decode it, to return to Frame's aboriginal "secret."

The most important character in this novel is not a human being but a black beetle which lives inside a dictionary from which it emerges through a hole between two words, *trichotomy* and *trick*. Frame is as wryly aware of the demands her writing places on her readers as anyone can be, and here she produces a parody of the reader of her own novel, caught up in a bewildering system of language from which he seeks a way out. Avid Frame readers will see immediately that the way out of **Scented Gardens for the Blind** is to recognize that its *trick* is that its narrator, Vera Glace, is a *trichotomy* of imagined characters (herself, a husband, and a daughter) whose task is to enact the novel's themes. Recognizing Vera as the "death-educator" of the work simplifies its structure and leads us immediately back to the controlling author.

Verbal tricks like this are no different in intention from those phrases in the **Lagoon** stories which remind the reader to look below the surface of the language; they are simply more compact, revolving round single words. But it is a further trick of this novel to persuade the reader that he has only one trick to solve and that once we have identified ourselves with the literary beetle and Vera with the other main human characters our work is done. We ought to recall the untrustworthy perspective of some of those stories and ask whether Vera Glace is the "true glass" her name seems to suggest. Within her own novel she is, in the sense that she is able to see what her author believes to be "true"; semantically she is not, in that her name suggests another pun ("true ice," *via* the French) which invites our gaze outside the work in which she appears by evoking that theme of killing and cooling that has appeared before. And it is not difficult to guess where we are supposed to focus our attention, since in the same year in which she produced this novel she also produced a long story called **"Snowman, Snowman."**

There can be no doubt, I think, that the writer means us to make this unusual transition from one work to another, because the story reads like a large fragment that has somehow fallen from the novel. Its form is much the same, with the novel's long conversations between Erlene Glace and the black beetle being paralleled by those in the story between the narrating snowman and a rather garrulous snowflake. The tone of these fabulistic elements is similar; images (parachuting snowflakes which fall from story to novel, beetleskins which are shed from novel into story) are common to both; and, above all, the themes of the story—principally concerning man's false evolution away from a healing language of communion and toward the violence that has disfigured the twentieth century—are simply consummations of those of the novel.

We could say that the "successful" reader of *Scented Gardens for the Blind* becomes a sort of graduate in verbal trickery whose growing awareness of the concealing power of language has admitted him to an experience not available to all. With such awareness the opening lines of **"Snowman Snowman"** can be seen to reveal more:

> People live on earth, and animals and birds; and fish live in the sea, but we do not defeat the sea, for we are driven back to the sky, or we stay, and become what we have tried to conquer, remembering nothing except our new flowing in and out, in and out, sighing for one place, drawn to another, wild with promises to white birds and bright red fish and beaches abandoned and then longed for.

> I never conquered the sea. I flew at midnight to the earth, and in the morning I was made into a human shape of snow.

> "Snowman, snowman," my creator said.

Here, quite openly, are the images of the first stories recreated more than a dozen years later: the beach, the unconquerable sea, the white birds above, the doomed girl (the child who makes the snowman is killed later in the story). And, more covertly, in the snowman himself are impounded further early images: wind and sea conspire to produce crystals of ice which the girl in turn conspires to turn into her snowman; two lumps of coal give it the "pine-forest eyes" that recall the dark trees that are part of the early imagery of bereavement. Containing evocations, surrounded by evocations, the snowman takes its place with Frame's other surrogates as one who has learned about mortality at first hand.

What we see at work between the novel and the story occurs perhaps a little too neatly to be wholly typical of Frame's other longer fiction, but it is the quintessence of her tendency to write about herself and her experiences as if she were writing about other things. In her other novels, the disguises vary, and the tricks of language are different; but they are still disguises and tricks, whose job is to conceal the same sensibility and experiences as before and then reveal them to a select few. However far from us in time the damaging but creative experience moves, the damaged creator seems to remain essentially the same, setting up verbal puzzles that repel the casual reader but draw the initiate down through layers of language to a truth which is always the same, to the death which, as the black beetle of *Scented Gardens for the Blind* says, is the common denominator of all things.

Pointing these things out as I have tried to do helps to explain why her writing is as it is; it does not explain away the diffi-

culties but it explains why they are there. Knowing their origin is an unavoidable part of any approach to Janet Frame. Whether we begin at the beginning or start with her most recent novels, *Daughter Buffalo* and *Living in the Maniototo,* we must acknowledge the writer's distinctive relating of death and language in a way that yields an *oeuvre* quite unlike any other in English. It confronts us with a limiting and obsessive self-absorption as well as the liberations of a language that has been set free from the everyday. If we ignore her limitations, her liberation seems feckless and unearned; if we turn away from her linguistic gifts, we are left with darkness and self-pity. Only by seeing one as a function of the other can we see the unity of all her fiction and glimpse with sympathy the experience which constrains it.

An excerpt from *The Carpathians*

If you walk in mid-afternoon through the streets of Puamahara you might suppose you walk through a neatly kept cemetery where the graves are more spacious than usual, with flowers and vegetable gardens, fences, concrete paths leading to the door of the family mausoleum. The silence, cavelike, may be entered. No sound of cars, trains, planes, radios, people, dogs; and just as you become certain that you walk in a cemetery, the sounds of the living intrude, the dream vanishes, and those whom you thought to be dead appear in the doorways with brooms and brushes and motormowers and hedge-clippers to perform the daily sweep and cut and snip, while others wheeling shopping trundlers, riding bicycles, driving cars, set out in search of substance to feed on, to sleep on, make love on, die on; to clean with, to look at, to spit on, to sigh over, to read, to admire, to wear: all to make certain of one more day of life, that is, to protect the habits of being human: housekeeping their lives.

Janet Frame, in her *The Carpathians,*
Bloomsbury, 1988.

Helen Bevington (review date 21 November 1982)

SOURCE: "The Girl from New Zealand," in *The New York Times Book Review,* November 21, 1992, pp. 14, 34.

[*Bevington is an American educator, poet, and critic. In the following review of* To the Island, *she notes that Frame's book, while part of a trilogy, can stand alone as an autobiographical work.*]

When the New Zealand writer Janet Frame was 7, she found in her school reader an adventure story, *To the Is-Land,* that she read as *To the Is-land.* Though corrected by her teacher, she accepted the word thereafter as meaning what it said, the

Land of Is, not the Was-Land, not the Future. In [*To the Is-Land,* the] first volume of her autobiography, which she calls "a selection of views of the Is-Land," it is the place of her childhood and adolescence.

Naturally, one question a writer faces in embarking upon a prolonged journey through his own life is whether there is adventure or philosophy enough in his earliest years to fill a book—a problem charmingly illustrated by Richard Steele when he reported in *The Tatler* the salient facts of his infancy: "I was bred by hand, and ate nothing but milk till I was a twelve-month old: from which time I was observed to delight in pudding and potatoes." Janet Frame, the author of 10 highly regarded novels and a volume of poetry, knows how to avoid the pitfalls of memory and keep her tale eventful. While she notes that, when young, she drank "mook," sang "God Save Our Gracious Tin" thinking she sang about a kerosene tin, called a bird a birdie and her baby sister "Iddabull" instead of Isabel, she is, it seems, reminiscing for the right person, as if to herself and for herself, as if carefully following a map of childhood to discover where it went.

It went from Dunedin, where she was born in 1924, to the small town of Oamaru on the coast of South Island. Her father, George, was a railway engineer who played the bagpipes. Her mother, Lottie, a former housemaid in Katherine Mansfield's home in Wellington, was a woman of wisdom and character who wrote poems, sold them from door to door during the Depression and became the local poet. Like Colette's mother, Sido, she made valid each flower or blade of grass she and her children passed, filling them with mystery. Like Sido she would cry "Look! Look!" commanding the children, five in all, to heed the magical world around them. But she spoke also in an "earthquake-and-lightning" voice to deal with disasters when they punctually occurred.

Janet's red hair was a frizzy tangle that grew straight up from her head: She had dimples, freckles, shabby clothes that affirmed the family's poverty, and she had "tics and terrors." To her teachers she was from the start different, a word she soon translated into peculiar or a little mad. Quite early she learned the deceit of words—permanent waves were not permanent, "True Stories" were not true, a shop called "The Self Help" didn't mean she could help herself to the merchandise. Words were part of the bewildering contradictions of life, since they were her joy as a source of truth, at least in books, the very essence of the poetry she loved. But on her fifth birthday, when she started school, she lifted fourpence and a farthing from her father's pocket and treated the children in her class to chewing gum. Both at home, where her father took the strap to her, and at school she was labeled Thief, a word to her unfair and untrue. She found a friend, Poppy, who taught her the names of things and lent her Grimm's Fairy Tales, but by imparting information about sex gave her forbidden words that she was punished by Dad for even knowing.

It is a wistful tale, honestly and believably told, of the puzzling encounters of childhood, the recognitions, the gain and the loss. In spite of their quarrels and Dad's thrashings, her family was a closely knit one from which gradually Janet grew apart, angered by her mother's unfathomable peacefulness and habit of waiting on others, of loving God and poetry. Her brother, Bruddie, whose epilepsy brought on episodes of violent rage increased by his father's mockery, sought escape in alcohol. One afternoon when Janet was 13, her older sister, Myrtle, a strong swimmer, was discovered drowned in the Oamaru Public Baths. Dad had been hardest on Myrtle, who wanted to be a film star, who was rebellious, daring, openly disobedient. At the news of her death, Miss Frame writes, "At first I was glad, thinking there'd be no more quarrels, crying, thrashings, with Dad trying to control her and angry with her and us listening frightened, pitying, and crying, too." Then came the realization of Myrtle's entire removal from the face of the earth. She had vanished, unreturning.

The last year of high school, in the Upper Sixth, was "a cruel year, the cruelest I had known." Still clad in her torn and patched school tunic, still without close girlfriends or any boyfriends, she sometimes felt a desolation she had no words for. "I'm going to be a poet," she wrote in her diary, but that summer she burned all her diaries and notebooks of poems. The story ends with a lonely, troubled girl traveling "south on the Sunday slow train to Dunedin and my Future"—to a new Is-land, the Dunedin Teachers' College, where she would prepare to become the teacher she didn't want to be. And one closes the book aware that if one is to know Janet Frame better, hear the rest of it, one must consent to follow her on her journey to as many Is-Lands as there are. Yet this vivid first volume is in a real sense complete, satisfying not merely as Chapter One but as an account of the making of a writer from the beginning possessed by words.

A. L. McLeod (review date Spring 1983)

SOURCE: A review of *To the Is-Land: An Autobiography,* in *World Literature Today,* Vol. 57, No. 2, Spring, 1983, p. 352.

[*McLeod is an Australian-born educator, poet, and critic. In the following review, he discusses Frame's autobiographical style in* To the Is-Land, *considering it unsatisfactory and lacking in discretion.*]

Herbert Spencer observed that the autobiographer "is obliged to omit from his narrative the commonplace of daily life," while Somerset Maugham noted that the writer of an autobiography often places too great an emphasis on matters that are more common than supposed. Certainly Janet Frame, in this first volume of her autobiography [*To the Is-Land*] (which ends with her acceptance to university), has not observed Spencer's dictum: almost every incident, observation, riposte or reaction has been recalled for inclusion, though not always of interest to the reader or of ready significance to her own psychological or literary development.

It is this lack of selectivity—of discretion, perhaps—that accounts for the failure of this work, even when compared with such an obvious (and not wholly satisfactory) recent example as Patrick White's *Flaws in the Glass.* Whereas White's book provides too little detail of his life, beliefs and interests, Frame's prolixity concerning ordinary experiences of early childhood and adolescence gives her work a private quality rather than a public one: it is as if she were writing her reminiscences for family use. Only rarely do we gain special insights to the New Zealand ethos or psyche, as when she notes "the everlasting preoccupation with blood in a country that based its economy on the killing and eating of farm animals." This national concern is particularized in Frame's detailed account of her own menstruation, perspiration and elimination, but it is unrelated to her general philosophy or her literary career—which is illumined only in part in the concluding chapters of *To the Is-Land* that reprint some of her early poetry.

There is no widespread disagreement that Janet Frame is the most important New Zealand writer of the past generation; but this volume might suggest that the special demands of biography are not within her compass, as they were for so many earlier writers of prose fiction. Unfortunately, the book is poorly edited.

W. H. New (essay date Spring 1984)

SOURCE: "The Frame Story World of Janet Frame," in *Essays on Canadian Writing,* Vol. 29, Spring, 1984, pp. 175-191.

[*New is a Canadian educator, essayist, editor, and critic. In the following essay, he discusses the theoretical structure and narrative framing devices commonly used by Frame in her writing.*]

Since 1951, when her first work, *The Lagoon,* appeared, Janet Frame has gathered a faithful international readership. At first noticed only in her native New Zealand, where as a short story writer she remained in Katherine Mansfield's shadow, she began to publish in the United States and England (with George Braziller and W.H.Allen) in the early 1960s. In 1960 Braziller reprinted her first novel, *Owls Do Cry* (published initially in Christchurch in 1957), and in a spate of creative energy, Frame produced nine more novels, two books of short stories, a children's tale, and a book of poems over the next nineteen years. Restless, introspective, sometimes lyrical and sometimes savagely ironic, her work as a whole explores a distinctive and often private world, which the author, in denser and denser metaphor, repeatedly strives to make clear and struggles to share. For the faithful reader, the aesthetic re-

wards are substantial. Frame is not only one of New Zealand's most forceful contemporary novelists, reflecting sharply on her own society's mores, but also one whose explorations of metaphoric distance—of madness, fear, femaleness, and death—transform her local landscape into a much larger one, involving the pressures and the imaginative restrictedness of forms of Western Civilization.

Frame's three books of short stories provide a place to begin an enquiry into her use of form, for the contrast between *The Lagoon* (1951) and the other two, *The Reservoir* and *Snowman Snowman* (each published in 1963), shows both her change in social horizon and the changes of form by which she contrived to express her developing perspective. In the twenty-four stories of *The Lagoon and Other Stories* (the title of the second edition, 1961) can be found many of the themes and images which she was later to develop. An invented portrait of a grandmother and glimpses of life in mental hospitals and factories, for example, were to reappear, more carefully honed, in *Owls Do Cry*; the repeated images of water, sunshine, and an expanding darkness were to develop into the metaphoric substance of the books of the late 1960s. But a reader is conscious more than anything else in *The Lagoon* of reading a kind of imitation Mansfield, slices of New Zealand life about children's capacity to enter dream worlds, in which the vignettes never give ample rein to the style, nor rely sufficiently on it. There are good phrases. There is a memorable moment in **"My Cousins who could eat cooked turnips,"** when we are told of children who do so while sitting "in cold blood." More importantly, there appear on occasions controlled breaks in formal pattern, as in **"Swans,"** when the deliberate run-on phrase "the sea roared in their ears it was true sea" sharply establishes the leap of understanding which, for these characters, distinguishes the world of appearances from another kind of world they "know" to be true. The difficulty of taking this leap is examined more fully in **"The Lagoon"** itself, where the stylistic contrast—between certainties ("were gone") and qualifications ("or if they were there," "especially if")—establishes affinities to two different notions of reality. For a character in a lesser story, **"The Pictures,"** empirical fact asserts its precedence; however attractive the "movie-house world might be," all that is "fact" (and therefore "something to be sure of") is that the film is seven thousand feet long. Such "facts" for Frame offer a deceptive safety, of a kind which her subsequent works expose.

The title story of *The Reservoir* is particularly effective in this regard. On the surface it is the story of children who collectively defy their parents' warning, visit a reservoir that they have been told is dangerous, get frightened themselves by darkness and their own imaginations, then return home to sunshine with a new pseudosophistication, lording it over the parents who they now think are afraid of the reservoir, the actual water, itself. As the story makes clear, the adults' fear has much to do with water and drowning, but much more to do with a sexuality which their puritan culture inhibits. They cannot *express* what they know. So they erect signs against the pressures they *are* willing to recognize, relying on the word DANGER, on the verbal threat of "infantile paralysis," on the orderly cliché of school composition language ("tired but happy"). This theme is picked up in other stories. When a girl in **"A Sense of Proportion"** complains that she can't draw *appearances,* we are told that *her* world was stripped of shadows, alone in light, whereas her teacher had been comforted by accepting tricks of the eye. In **"The Triumph of Poetry"** Frame writes that "Names . . . bestow space, keys, power on the nameless which encircle human lives, waiting their chance." In **"Obstacles"** she writes: "We are merely trying to ignore the notice DANGER, ANGER, and, with or without witnesses, to cross, the hard way, the unfathomable darkness between man and man." What is happening, through the anagrams and the syntactical breaks, is that Frame is trying to find a language to free language from its own constraints. In the less successful **Snowman Snowman** (subtitled *Fables and Fantasies*), she strives for an even more obvious break from "realistic" vignette. But it is a false lead, the allegorical fable proving to be an even more confining form, whereas with **The Reservoir** she had found a way to turn the local observations of **The Lagoon** into ampler reflections on the ties between language and social values.

In 1965, in an autobiographical essay called **"Beginnings,"** Frame suggested some of the particular influences in her life that spurred these reflections into being. A sympathy for the subtleties of language and an appreciation for insights that were not verbal, an understanding of both the power of language and the power that lay beyond and behind language, created tensions that affected her sense of her own relation with the world about her. What she calls "'this' and 'that' world" would not be reconciled. Efforts to belong only to "this" world—the practical, empirical one—accepting its demands to *adapt,* and "fitting in" to its *definitions* of reality resulted in bouts of illness; choosing "that" world made other demands. There is a sardonic cheerfulness about her declaration; she had tried to be a teacher, she writes, but "one day when the Inspector was visiting my class at school I said, — Excuse me, and walked from the room and the school, from 'this' world to 'that' world where I have stayed, and where I live now." Staying faithful to whatever her imagination realized, however, created other predicaments, not the least being those that faced her as a writer, trying to use "this" world's words to communicate "that" world's understanding. Tone in her writing, perhaps as a result, is always on an edge between terror and joy. Her children's story, **Mona Minim and the Smell of the Sun** (1969), and many of the poems of **The Pocket Mirror** (1967), such as one called **"The Farenheit Man,"** delight in play rhymes, for example—and play rhymes also appear in associative passages in novels like **The Rainbirds** (1968) and **Scented Gardens for the Blind** (1963)— but at the same time they speak of isolation and uncontrollable fear. In the novels from **Owls Do Cry** (1957) to **A State of**

Siege (1966), she explores these interconnections further, creates deliberate tensions between method and situation, and strives to reveal the meaning she finds in a world that established society has defined as chaotic and mad.

Owls Do Cry tells the story of the four children of the Withers family in Waimaru (compare her own hometown, Oamaru, South Island, New Zealand: Francie, who (just entering adolescence) dies; Daphne, who spends most of the novel undergoing electric shock therapy, and finally a lobotomy, in a mental institution; Toby, an epileptic, who feels more than others are aware he does but is unable to establish relationships with anyone; and Chicks (later Teresa), who flees into the security of a middle-class life and the clichéd language that passes there for intelligent conversation. The contrast between their childhood capacity for dreams and games and their barren or restricted adult lives reiterates the themes of sexuality and institutional sterility which the short stories raised. Francie is sacrificed in society's refuse, in the garbage of schools, hospitals, churches, and other social structures. The dump where the younger children find dream-treasure is something Francie thinks she has outgrown, but in a not-so-subtle symbolic gesture, it overcomes her; she dies in a rubbish-dump fire, becomes a social castoff at the moment of trying to assert her identity with normal society. The brittle comedy which presents Chicks' "solutions" conveys in another way a failure to abjure dreams and to "belong." Uncertainty (couched in indefinite pronouns) threatens both Francie and Chicks, but the language they strive to use is as deceptive as the safety they seek to ensure by it. Toby's language, too, is instructive. We are told early of his love for the fairy-tale book he finds at the dump, a book that "had been thrown away because it did not any more speak the right language, and the people could not read it because they could not find the way to its world." When later he asserts his belief in the truth of "child's stories," and in an uncharacteristically articulate moment adds "There's a giant bomber and a giant loneliness," he excludes himself further from society rather than explains himself to it. Over the course of time, he becomes a grasping, narrow man, also a failure. The sequence from one child to the next leads finally to Daphne, whose metaphor-rich and run-on "songs," sung mutely from the "dead room," the shock therapy centre, punctuate the novel and give it a third dimension, both linguistically (for her images of shell, glass, wind, darkness, seasons, and sun throw the language of the rest of the novel into relief) and thematically (for it is Daphne who sees, yet Daphne whose freedom—like Ariel's, alluded to by the title—is enchanted away). If she lives "*after* summer, merrily," Ariel's phrase suggests that the joy of singing her insights is held in tension with the terrors of the wintry dead room. At the end of the novel, the lobotomy, which gives her "normality," only deprives her of her singing; the dead room, transformed at least metaphorically into the woollen mill where she is allowed at last to work, remains, and becomes a definition of the world at large.

Frame moves in two directions from this work, variously taking madness or journeying as the central metaphor of the next novels. She tells Toby's subsequent story in *The Edge of the Alphabet* (1962). Toby goes *overseas* to England, pursues his dream ("Now there is in Toby's land . . . an affliction of dream called Overseas, a suffering of sleep endured by the prophetic, the bored, the retired, and the living who will not admit that it is easier and cheaper to die, die once and forever and travel as dust"). As much as anything, as the second section of the novel declares, it is a "lost traveller's dream of speech." Toby meets Zoe in London, whose "occupation is with boundaries, in a border country where people still carry their worn maps, trying to read them and knowing the directions are useless," but she also commits suicide, and Toby realizes, in a classically ironic antipodean image, that he has travelled "from Winter to Winter." Place becomes season, as, for the various narrators of *The Adaptable Man* (1965), travel becomes a matter of time: "The thought that he is not a migrating bird might make a man mad. Human beings have little to impel them from century to century." Violent events keep intruding on the ordinary lives of these characters, who live out ostensibly equable quests for their own growing space. But at the end of *The Adaptable Man* (after an extraordinarily melodramatic scene in which a falling cut glass chandelier kills off three of the main figures), one person is left altered, and the reader is offered a characteristically interrogative conclusion:

> The marvel was, everyone said, that Vic Baldry had adapted himself to a weatherless world that he could not reach or touch; to living his life in a mirror.
>
> But imposing our own weather, our own limits of reach and touch, our own star-shaped irreparable flaw, don't we all live in mirrors, for ever?

Society, that is, refuses to interpret Vic in any but its own self-perpetuating terms. To do otherwise, as the question makes clear, is to raise doubts about society's grasp of reality. It is not "safe."

For Vera Glace in *Scented Gardens for the Blind* (1963), space and time coalesce. Mute, in an asylum, Vera invents a mute daughter named Erlene who declares in the alphabet of her own mind that she lives "between *speech* and *spell*." Edward Glace, meanwhile, trying to grasp order through genealogy, is researching the history of the Strang family ("an ordinary family" in need of having its language recorded). Yet he comes to a conclusion that disrupts his order: "Strang, Strong, Strange, estrange, danger, . . . but were people anagrams after all?" And in due course we find out that Clara Strang is in the asylum with Vera. It is a novel played with mirrors, asserting (in an odd echo of *Owls Do Cry*) that "Madness is only Open Day in the factory of the mind." Such blitheness contrasts with the rejection elsewhere of the idea that madness is romantic poetry, but it reasserts the notion

that *The Rainbirds* later declares directly: "finally there is no Out or In, all is one territory, Out is merely the place where a man is afraid to go, a place that he therefore denies exists, but it is there, in him; it stays, as the sea and the land stay. . . ." The division temporary, the boundary at some point no longer a wall for keeping out but a gate for going in, the separation Frame had noted between "this" world and "that" transforms itself. Images of fragmented mirrors recur, finding an aural counterpart in the anagrammatic identities that the characters possess. The fluidity of Janet Frame's "reality" becomes clearer.

Faces in the Water (1961) and *A State of Siege* (1966) take madness as a direct subject. The first of these novels traces the moves that a woman, a former teacher named Istina Mavet, makes into and out of a hospital; the second details the progressive "insanity" and eventual death of a retired teacher named Malfred Signal when she moves from Central Otago to an isolated resort "'up north' in a foreign climate." Pressured by a knocking that she hears or fancies she hears, unaided by the calls she makes or fancies she makes to priest, doctor, and constable, Malfred Signal surrenders her defences when at least to her mind's eye the glass of her house shatters, the storm enters her room, and she finds a stone wrapped in paper bearing the words *"Help Help"* and a verse "that was not in any language she had learned." *A State of Siege* is not a particularly successful work, but the images of storm, shattered glass, foreign land, and foreign language all reflect the world of the earlier books. In *Faces in the Water,* a much more intense and moving novel, it is the visitors to the mental home who are "like tourists in a foreign land," the nursing sister is named Matron Glass (there is also a Dr. Trace, a Dr. Howell, a Sister Honey, a Sister Bridge); and phrases from the beginning and end of the book show how the context shifts from one involving personal choice to one involving social structure. Istina early avers: "I was not yet civilized; I traded my safety for the glass beads of fantasy"; and later the author interpolates: "Conversation is the wall we build between ourselves and other people, too often with tired words like used and broken bottles which, catching the sunlight as they lie embedded in the wall, are mistaken for jewels." The early ironic comment shows how the "safety" of "civilization" is dependent upon a rigid definition of what constitutes fantasy; the later comment adds to it, demonstrating how the society that considers itself sane, direct, and not fanciful, in fact mistakes itself daily, how the language it uses deceives, how values thereby become distorted, and how rigid distinctions, on close examination, blur. Istina at the end of the novel is going home to be "normal." In light of the shifts in perception that have preceded this assertion, the word "normal" asks for sympathetic interpretation. Face value is deceptive. Reflections move. These are "faces in the water" we have been shown, and the difficult recognitions that take place through "shattered" glass at the very least prove disconcerting.

Towards the end of *The Edge of the Alphabet* the writer/

narrator asks a question that highlights another facet of the discoveries these novels portray: "And what if the person who meets us for ever is ourselves? What if we meet ourselves on the edge of the alphabet and can make no sign, no speech?" The immediate contextual answer to the question is a promise of speech in the future and, in the meantime, mirrors. Taken as a more general guide to the novels, these observations underline the fracturing of personality that lies at the heart of them all. The social metaphors—New Zealand's hemispheric position, notions of foreigners and home, the genealogies, the language—all articulate the divided consciousness of an individual personality. The "madness" of the characters consists in their being unable to live with the separation or to reconcile the various divisions. Even more fundamentally, the concern for articulating the shattered selves derives from Frame's own sense of herself. Her essay **"Beginnings"** affirms as much. But the structure of the stories is an implicit declaration of the same understanding. One way or another they are all *frame-stories,* stories told within a framework which adds an extra dimension or distance to the central set of tales. *Owls Do Cry* opens with one of Daphne's private "dead room" songs and closes with an extrapolative, almost impersonal, generalizing epilogue. *Faces in the Water* is structured so that the mental hospital section, "Treecroft," is surrounded by the two experiences of "Cliffhaven." Towards the end of *Scented Gardens for the Blind* we discover that the story is being told by Dr. Clapper, the psychiatrist, not by Vera at all, but we make this discovery only to be taken further out of the story by yet another narrator, who talks of the atom bomb that has destroyed Britain and all the structures, including language, that Dr. Clapper has considered norms. And in *The Edge of the Alphabet,* Toby's story is contained within the papers of one Thora Pattern, and is submitted to a publisher by a Hire-Purchase salesman named Peter Herron. There is a brittle wit in this repeated device, and in the emblematic names that so many of the characters possess: Daphne Withers, Mona Minim, Malfred Signal, Sister Bridge, Thora Pattern, Matron Glass, Ed Glace; names that appear in the succeeding books too: Godfrey Rainbird, Turnlung, Colin Monk, Violet Pansy Proudlock. There is an obvious link between the names Pattern and Frame, and an obvious irony that it should be Vera and Clara in the asylum in *Scented Gardens for the Blind,* but the point of such names goes further than simple emblem and simple irony. We are asked throughout to consider the failure of communication—of existing signals, existing structures (Pattern, Bridge, the safety rules of **"The Reservoir"** and *Faces in the Water,* the children's learned litany of *Owls Do Cry*: "Everything in a glass case is valuable")—and yet we are asked at the same time to recognize the degree of relationship, the "illogical" logic, that binds and identifies one character with another. Individuals with their siblings and family connections, the nursing sisters with their wards, local people with the foreigners among them: they all confront each other, seeking the common language that will admit their identity. Each narrative "frame" provides a means of entering the "foreign"

world—one which the author designs deliberately for the reader's points of reference—but what the frame ultimately reveals is the extent to which the framing world and the framed world are one.

To come to this assertion is to declare the fluidity of "frame" and "pattern," and to deny the rigidity of the separation between "this" world and "that." The general trend of Frame's work to this point had been a personalizing one: solipsistic at times, but concerned with articulating and sharing her own consciousness. *Meaning* was lodged in *person,* so *person* had to be made intelligible. Finding a fluid form by which to declare the personality—and allegorical fable proved not fluid at all—provided the means, but at the same time it promoted a shift in direction. Divisions, and the notion of division itself, came to be questioned; existing rigidities—governing definitions of social progress, male and female roles, sanity and madness, and other "norms"—could be challenged because they were no longer accepted as mutually exclusive "opposites." And in her next four novels, *The Rainbirds* (1968), *Intensive Care* (1970), *Daughter Buffalo* (1973), and *Living in the Maniototo* (1979), Frame rejects a repeated reliance on dualities in experience, projecting now from her personal metaphors out to her interpretation of social conditions.

Many of the metaphors are familiar, of course. *The Rainbirds*—called *Yellow Flowers in the Antipodean Room* in its U.S. edition—picks up the foreigner and seasonal cycle references. *Intensive Care* intensifies all the earlier hospital images (turning the comfort of "care" into a threat of centralized social order) and engages them with the visions of holocaust that are adumbrated in *Faces in the Water, Scented Gardens for the Blind,* and *Snowman Snowman. Daughter Buffalo,* with its American setting, confronts the idea of death with as much directness as fable, newly used here, will allow. And *Living in the Maniototo* (1979), set in New Zealand and California, probes the nature of fiction itself and the power of the writer to command life, death, and words. But these stories tell finally not of outcasts unable to communicate, but of a time when the outcasts' visions are absorbed by the society that has excluded them. *The Rainbirds* opens when Godfrey Rainbird, British emigrant to New Zealand, successful travel agent, is struck by a car, taken to hospital, and *pronounced dead.* When in a few days he recovers from what had been only a coma, his society is unable to adjust. The plans that have been made in the interim and the fact of pronouncement take precedence over the human being. Pressures build; the family is disrupted. His job lost, Godfrey is advised to go home to his "own country," but he reflects: "everywhere's a place I don't recognize"—including language. Anagrams intrude, affecting—but sharpening—his understanding. The company's offer of "references" is transformed into the control of "re-refences"; "Rainbird" itself is turned into "Brainrid"; and the false comfort of the business cliché "we do assure you"—in a variant version of "Intensive Care"—

becomes the vague but unquestioningly threatening "we do arruse you, we do arruse you." The threats offer no comfort, and Godfrey's subsequent life can scarcely be called happy. It is at the end of the novel that the contrary movement surfaces. After his death, Godfrey's grave becomes a tourist site, accepted, though still objectified, even mythologized, by society. But then the novelist adds:

> The cemetery is beautiful in summer. The grave overlooks the sea and the long sweep of coast from St. Kilda to St. Clair and you can sit in the sun on the low rock wall surrounding the grave and look at the ocean breakers rolling in, or you can close your eyes and dream but do not dream too deeply in case, awakening, you discover that the yellow and gold flowers . . . have merged one with the other . . . to become a floating mass of red lilies; but that is only if you visit in summer; if you go there in winter you will have no help with your dreams, you will have to experience for yourself the agony of creating within yourself the flowers that you know will blossom there in summer.

The imagination can visualize beauty as well as holocaust, retrieve a reality from the past, grasp it from the future, allow it to enhance rather than just to upset life. An active commitment is required, however. The sea, as we are told in this novel, may be a "personal possession" of New Zealanders, kept—in one of the recurrent Mansfield echoes—"at bay" most of the time. But the point is that it alters. *Faces in the Water* had asserted that "Using tenses to divide time is like making chalk-marks on water." Here the author affirms a way of overcoming such division, and of making the fluidity of perception a power for life.

Yet to fix the outcome of kinetic process is illogical in such a world. Hence, as *Intensive Care* asserts, "all dreams lead back to the nightmare garden." Certainty limits growth. Fear returns. In a world used to expecting justice from law, lawyers go "about their business of translating common phrases into the legal syntax of death." At the end of *Intensive Care* (Frame's vision of the bureaucratic future and the not unrecognizable present), the Human Delincation Act is passed. People are classified. Those pronounced human are allowed to live; those judged inferior or different are not. It is a simple and powerful indictment of the essentially bureaucratic notion of turning people into categories. It also further praises the element within people that resists classification, for the act finally fails to take account of either human nostalgia or the "unsubduable animal in man" that repeatedly makes behavioural generalizations meaningless. That the "unhealthy," "deformed," "insane," "defective," and "outcast" should become the "new elite" in the supposedly perfect "delineated" society is an ironic commentary on the results of imposing rigid norms—and it offers a sardonic glimpse of the devious adaptability of any authority—but it is wholly in accord with Frame's attitude to social change and with the growing self-confidence of her rendering of the world.

Frame asks us to reflect on the impact of illusion on the mind, and to realize that *bizarre* and *fantastic* are simply verbal judgements we use in the face of the unfamiliar to reassure ourselves and maintain *our* illusion of safety.

—W. H. New

Collapsing the distinctions between here and there, between present, past, and future—or at least, because of the way the mind works and because of the antipodean perspective, asserting the simultaneity rather than the dualities of seasons, of time, of place—these novels bring Frame to a confrontation with the distinction between life and death. It is a theme she has repeatedly alluded to. In the stories of *The Reservoir,* and in **"The Mythmaker's Office"** (in *Snowman Snowman*) where two characters break the existing social code by saying to each other "Let's make Death," love and death are frequently intertwined. Deaths and allusions to death occur in all the novels, but in *Daughter Buffalo* death becomes the subject and the running metaphor. Fabular by nature, the novel comes perilously close in form to the *Snowman Snowman* pieces or *A State of Siege*. Ostensibly it is the story of the growing relationship between Talbot Edelman, who is an American graduate student, and a dying old non-American writer named Turnlung. The relationship develops because Edelman is a student of death—"A citizen of a country of death, with no death education?" Turnlung asks him—yet it finds its expression in the attachment they develop ("love" might not be too strong a word) for a young buffalo in the city zoo. They adopt her and declare their relationship with her. Thus repeated here are the implicit attacks on corporate social structures and the open celebration of animal vitality. If that were as far as it went, the notion would be unspectacular, the novel sterile. But integral to the novel is another recurrent theme, involving language, which loosens the allegorical features of the book and questions the distinction between occurrence and nonoccurrence. "Words," says Turnlung, "first words, are as traumatic as first love and first death." Getting past the word to the reality changes into the task of finding the word to convey the scope of reality. In true Frame fashion the shift is not casual. In the story Turnlung dies, Edelman contends with his death, and later becomes a respected, avoided, national figure in death education. "Man, Dog, Buffalo, Do You Know Your Name?" the chapter is called. But an epilogue follows, called "Yes I am an old man." Turnlung is the narrator; letters to Edelman are returned from the Dead Letter Office; what had seemed to be empirical dissipates. But something else remains. "Whether I dreamed,"

Turnlung reflects, " . . . does not matter. What matters is that I have what I gave." Creative acts, that is, however bizarre, however fantastically expressed, establish a reality all their own. By creating, artists strive to possess this reality, and so to possess that which is authentic about themselves and about their relation with other human beings.

These powers of artistic creativity are the open subject of **Living in the Maniototo** (1979). The Maniototo is a South Island plain, unforgettable (says the *New Zealand Encyclopaedia* entry which gives the novel its epigraph) and largely unknown: it is a metaphor for the wellspring or private landscape of any writer, and the "writer" in this case is the novel's narrator, many-named. She is a twice-married, twice-widowed woman (Mavis Furness/Barwell/Halleton) who identifies herself as other women as well: as Violet Pansy Proudlock ("You might think it strange that I choose to be a ventriloquist, to be in a narrow path on the margin of creation and recreation when I could go to the center, but I choose to be here, as an entertainer") and as Alice Thumb ("Instant traveler, like the dead, among the dead and the living; an eavesdropper, a nothingness, a shadow, a replica of the imagined, twice removed from the real"), and as others still. The complex plot takes the novelist from New Zealand to the U.S.A., and takes other characters on journeys from house to house, country to country, life to death, and sometimes back again. All lives and lies in perception, nothing is explained. As we come to see experience as a cumulative process, moreover, all perceptions become metaphors that are projected from inside the self. When an estate is being divided, Mavis "felt dismay. *I* had wanted the golden blanket. I knew I could still have it, as everything belonged to me, but to make an issue of it would be to reveal myself when I, too, had taken care to fix the view of myself which others might see." But to make an issue of self is also to objectify the self as thing and to put it on display and make it vulnerable—which is even less acceptable when one realizes that transformation rather than formation is the mode more suited to understanding the fluid subjective identity. Hence repeatedly in the novel the fixity gives way; the travels, the deaths, the returns, all disrupt a presumed tidiness of life, a tidiness which the world of words, of fiction, can no more render permanent than can life itself. Admitting to the evanescence, the narrator resolves at the end of the novel to return to her source, but in so doing she does not abandon her connection with "external" reality; she just recognizes clearly what it is and what relation it has with her versions of perception: "I, Violet Pansy Proudlock, Barwell, Halleton, Alice Thumb herself, would continue to live and work in the house of replicas, usefully, having all in mind— the original, the other, and the manifold."

The frame story technique, then, provides the author with a means to focus not just on dual possibilities (this world and that, the original and the other, the person who sees and the thing seen), but also on the multiplicity of point of perception. Just as there is a power to creativity, she argues, there is

also a personality, and it is these together that Frame seeks to express. The author asks us to reflect on the impact of illusion on the mind, and to realize that *bizarre* and *fantastic* are simply verbal judgements we use in the face of the unfamiliar to reassure ourselves and maintain *our* illusion of safety. That it is an illusion is reaffirmed by the speed of the changes that recurrently disrupt our safety and by the apparent ability we have to adapt, to erect new "safe" structures in the face of events that affect us. Grasping the significance of events, when the events themselves are so elusive, is therefore difficult. But for Frame, asking "Did an event happen?" appears to be both less appropriate and less consequential a question than asking "How did you see it happen?" There is a certain responsibility for seeing which Frame requires her readers to accept. We are asked not to construct monolithic philosophies but to understand what occurs at a moment of insight— not to shape a frame (for that is where we begin, angled on experience, safely distanced from it), but to comprehend what happens when the divisiveness of dualism itself breaks down, when the seer and the seen become one. In a further paradox still, this "one" is found to be "manifold"—which is not a denial of coherence but an affirmation of an imaginative or recreative, reconstructive process. Frame's early works depict characters whose creative powers were rejected by society, who found themselves excluded from order, and who surrendered to that external definition; the later works less celebrate the powers such characters possess than they express a determination to accept them, and by so doing to assert the validity of the mind's eyes. For Frame the later writings seem to be a way to connect the mind's imaginative percepts with the less "authentic replicas" that empirical life enacts and empirical words conceptualize. For the patient reader of her fiction, the greater reward derives from the aesthetic demands the author makes; to read Frame's stories is not merely to be invited to meet a set of characters and a range of strange events, but also to be drawn into framed narratives where the structures of the prose are themselves the means and metaphors of perceptual understanding.

A. L. McLeod (review date Summer 1985)

SOURCE: "New Zealand," in *World Literature Today,* Vol. 59, No. 3, Summer, 1985, pp. 488-89.

[*In the review of* An Angel at My Table *below, McLeod criticizes the kind of autobiographical information Frame includes in her work.*]

Two years ago Janet Frame brought out the first volume, **To the Is-Land,** of her projected three-volume autobiography: that installment concluded with her departure from home for university and city life; the second one, **An Angel at My Table,** ends with her departure from New Zealand for England and continental life, thus chronicling almost fifteen years of social, psychological, and literary struggle in which she was judged schizophrenic (and almost lobotomized), was adjudged winner of a small literary prize, and was adjudicated worthy of government support as a promising writer. Though she takes pains to deny her mental abnormality, she also takes pains to stress her insecurity at placing coins in a telephone, picking up a college newspaper, and submitting contributions to a university periodical.

As in the first volume, Frame dwells on odd behavior (keeping sanitary napkins with soiled clothes and chocolate wrappers in a chest of drawers), admits her general naïveté (of lesbianism, masturbation, homosexuality, and European literature), and details her disregard of personal cleanliness (clothing, rotting teeth, menstruation). Her eight years in a mental institution are, unfortunately, not well documented or discussed; an equal period as a waitress and housemaid is somewhat overtreated. Though *The Lagoon and Other Stories* is alluded to frequently, there is no account of its contents, genesis, themes, and reception; on the other hand, some of Frame's early poems, which she advises us "are best not remembered," are, oddly, reprinted before she tells us that they were destroyed. Together with these rather pedestrian matters and repetitious accounting of train trips throughout New Zealand, there are several—again, unhappily, not satisfactorily recounted—vignettes of writers she met and who encouraged her: Frank Sargeson is the principal mentor, and he is the "angel" whose early support clearly was crucial; but Greville Texidor, Charles Brasch, and Allen Curnow pass as mere phantoms about whom we would like to learn more.

Unfortunately, the book has a different typeface and trim size than its predecessor. Thus far, the autobiography has been poorly edited; though printed in the United States, British spelling is used.

Patrick Evans (essay date September 1985)

SOURCE: "Janet Frame and the Art of Life," in *Meanjin,* Vol. 44, No. 3, September, 1985, pp. 375-83.

[*In the following essay, Evans discusses Frame's career as it is explored in the first three volumes of her autobiography,* To the Is-Land, An Angel at My Table, *and* The Envoy from Mirror City.]

With the publication at sixty of the first three volumes of her autobiography (*To the Is-land,* 1983; *An Angel at My Table,* 1984; *The Envoy from Mirror City,* 1985), Janet Frame gives the impression of rounding out her long career as a writer. Her first published story appeared just after the Second World War; since then there have been five volumes of short fiction, one of poetry, ten novels, a children's book, and three volumes of autobiography. If the latter is in fact the end of things it will conclude one of the oddest and most distinctive bodies of writing in the history of English. While she is demonstrably a New Zealand writer and a writer of her time, she has also made her own rules and is directly influenced by

nobody. Least of all is she concerned, it seems, with any notion of penetrability; reading her fiction is like tangling in a thicket of words and illusions, constantly being moved away from the possibility of explanation or meaning. Hers is the novel (*Scented Gardens for the Blind,* published in 1963) in which a young girl has long conversations about death with a black beetle while her mother waits anxiously in the next room and her father plays with toy soldiers twelve thousand miles away in England. At the end the novel is revealed to have been hallucinated by a patient in a mental hospital.

The deceptive nature of fiction, particularly of the conventions of realism, almost obsesses Frame; in her tenth novel (*Living in the Maniototo,* published in 1979) a character is removed from the text by a household bleach, characters who die early in the novel reappear alive later in it, characters who seem alive prove imaginary, and the narrator's American host is bumped off for good measure as the book closes. The 'ficticides' of these novels are relatively jolly and arbitrary compared with the unremittingly tragic vision of the earlier writing. No consistent reading of Frame's writing leaves much sense of optimism for the human race.

Although the equating of life with art is far too deceptively simple to explain the nature of her writing, no account of her work can avoid the tragic aspects of her first thirty years of life. There is its provenance, for a start, in the dreary little coastal South Island town of Oamaru, where she lived for fifteen years from about 1930, the third of the five children of an impoverished railway worker. Her reconstruction of this period in *To the Is-land* is surprisingly sunny and bright, evoking the pleasures of family closeness and especially the richness of nature and the literature brought into the house by a well-read mother. Elsewhere, in the fiction and in interviews, we glimpse and sense a darker world marked by that special contempt a smug, conservative rural community reserves for those who are in any way different from the rest. But more than poverty, death disfigured the family twice: the oldest girl, Myrtle, drowned in the local swimming baths in 1937, and almost exactly ten years later the fourth child of the family, Isabel, drowned at the holiday resort of Picton, at the north of the South Island. Not long after Isabel died Janet was admitted to mental care, in which she stayed for eight years. She had already broken down and had a period in hospital, where she was classified as a schizophrenic, a diagnosis she has consistently rejected and, in the second volume of her autobiography, ridiculed.

Appalling as these events are they should not be seen as the sort of explanation that assumes that parachutists must write about the fall of man. Because all writing is in some way autobiographical (as all autobiography is fiction) details of her life appear frequently in her imaginative work; the deaths of her sisters are described in as late a novel as *Daughter Buffalo* (1973), while the unfortunate American host who dies in *Living in the Maniototo* bears a resemblance to her own friend and American host, Professor John Money of Baltimore. The autobiographical thread is clearest in the first three of her novels, published between 1951 and 1963. Effectively a trilogy, they follow the misfortunes of a family named Withers in a small New Zealand town named Waimaru, and compositely they address the question asked by Frank Sargeson in his fake Maori placename 'Waiamihea' (*I Saw in My Dream,* 1949): 'Why am I here, so far from European civilisation, writing in a tradition that has its roots elsewhere, in a country that does not value art?' It is the sort of question James Joyce addressed years before. The Withers trilogy, like Sargeson's novel and Robin Hyde's *The Godwits Fly* (1938), is a portrait of the artist.

The first novel, *Owls Do Cry* (1957) is a remarkable though depressing account of the loss of childhood, the commonest theme in New Zealand literature. There is no sense of the world as a place full of opportunities for pleasure, growth and fulfillment: society and the universe itself threaten to engulf the proletarian Withers family with a destructiveness that is as real as it is indefinite:

> and the world in one stride would walk in and take possession of them, holding them tight in its hand of rock and lava, as if they were insects and they would have to struggle and kick and fight to escape and make their way. And each time they made their way and the world had dropped them for a while to a peaceful hiding place, it would again seize them with a burning one of its million hands, and the struggle would begin again and again and go on and never finish.

This destructive force is in the world, represented particularly by imagery of winter, and it is hostile to all society; but somehow society transforms its power and makes it destructive of the individual.

The assumption here is basically romantic, that children possess a spontaneity of seeing and living that is dinned out of them as they grow older. As the novel develops the four Withers children move inexorably towards the sterility of their parents. Freedom for them is represented by the town rubbish dump, where amongst the usual discarded refuse of a society obsessed with puritan tidiness they find Grimms' fairy tales and a mildewed book of poems—the 'treasure' that is referred to in the title of the first section, 'Talk of Treasure' (the original title of the book). But it is in this same rubbish dump that the oldest child, the adolescent Francie, dies, falling into a fire lit by a council worker.

In a novel of such symbolic intensity no fire is simply a means of incinerating trash and careless children. Francie is destroyed literally, but in different ways the remaining children are destroyed by figurative fires. Toby, the slow, half-witted son, falls during his epileptic fits into a world of poetic and imaginative understanding, but as he grows older he betrays the

meaning of the rubbish dump by becoming a scrap merchant who sells the 'treasure'. The youngest child, Chicks, makes a successful marriage and lives in a house built on reclaimed land over the dump, her house full of the gadgets and conveniences the novel clearly labels as rubbish. Only the third child, Daphne, who narrates the novel, keeps herself clear of this destruction for a while. But as an adult with the eye and imagination of a child she is labelled 'insane' and locked away in a mental hospital. There she is given a lobotomy and returns to the work-force 'normal' and 'safe'. The novel's coda shows her as a mill forewoman being presented with a watch for long service.

A summary like this emphasises both the pessimism and the conservatism of Janet Frame's writing; she is not the first or the only writer to depict lost souls going nowhere, and the grimness of her world is typical of much New Zealand writing. But what makes *Owls Do Cry* stand out are its form and language. In her own life Frame claims to distinguish between what she calls 'this' world (the here-and-now with its tax returns, unwashed dishes, clamouring children, and so on) and 'that' world (the rich, private imaginary world in which she spends her life). That division is in the novel, which alternates passages in roman type for the narration of events with passages in italic that are lyrical and full of images:

> what use the green river, the gold place, if time and death pinned human in the pocket of my land not rest from taking underground the green all-willowed and white rose and bean flower and morning-mist picnic of song in pepper-pot breast of thrush?

'Sung' by Daphne from the 'dead room', these are her last utterances before the lobotomy which robs her of her power to 'sing,' and they provide a seed-bed of images which enrich and help us better understand the remainder of the work. Rather than gesturing at powers which distinguish the artist, this novel demonstrates them, making more poignant their final surgical demise.

The remaining novels in the trilogy that follows the lives of some of the Withers family lack the imaginative achievement of *Owls Do Cry,* but the second, *Faces in the Water,* has a power quite distinctive in Frame's writing. The question it briefly invites—whether its account of its heroine's time in mental hospitals is autobiographical—is unimportant; the renaming of the heroine (she is called Istina Mavet now) and the cool detachment of tone suggest a reworking of experience. Relentlessly foregrounded are the horrors of incarceration and the inevitability of the slow descent into insanity; it is only after a rereading that the book's true themes become quietly evident: the question of what constitutes insanity and whose faces its waters reflect, the question of what our society does to women in suburbia, the question of what is implied by Istina's ultimate—and sudden—recovery. The third 'Withers novel', *The Edge of the Alphabet,* lacks the imaginative power of the first and the force of the second. It appears to reflect some of the experiences of Frame's journey to Europe in 1956, giving these to the moronic Toby from *Owls Do Cry*. Although references to reality, illusion and the sacrifices required by the artist occur and recur throughout, the novel never transcends its dreary descriptions of loneliness, inadequacy and social decay. Its heroine, Zoe Bryce, ends the novel in suicide; Toby develops a sore on his chest and returns to New Zealand in defeat, and a novel about the demands of artistic inspiration closes by showing what happens when that inspiration is not there.

In the early 1960s when she was living in England, Frame seemed to write continuously. Within a year of publishing *The Edge of the Alphabet, Scented Gardens for the Blind* appeared. The central figures are Erlene, the mute girl, and the black beetle with whom she holds imaginary conversations on her windowsill. Its chapters move from Erlene to anxious mother to genealogist father and back to Erlene again, until the nuclear explosion which concludes it, along with the revelation that we have been tricked into believing that its one character, an old mute mental hospital patient called Vera Glace, is three people.

Scented Gardens for the Blind is in many ways the most important of her books. It gives us the way of seeing the world of old Vera Glace, who, in her loneliness and fear, particularly of the interrogating father-figure psychiatrist, Dr Clapper, has changed herself imaginatively into a child and the psychiatrist into the less threatening fairytale figure of the aproned black beetle who spins her stories and parables. These stories pass the day but they also provide clues to how the novel should be read. The beetle tells a story of another beetle who lives in a dictionary between the words 'trichotomy' and 'trick'. (The trick is that Vera is a trichotomy of characters.) Once attuned to these signals the reader can understand how the novel works, and realise its central message of the metaphoric power of language, its hidden power to direct and enrich. What concerns Frame here, as in her other fiction, is the inadequacy of language to bring people together in love, trust and understanding. When language fails—as it does in the everyday sections set in roman type in the first novel—humans drift apart, seek power over one another, make war, and destroy themselves. It is no accident that *Scented Gardens for the Blind* ends with nuclear destruction. Like Freud, Frame sees civilisation caught between Eros and Thanatos; but she sees in language the potential for love and harmony. In the novel language fails, and at its end the ancient Vera Glace utters the grunts that begin the evolution of a new, healing language.

Frame's period in England was enormously productive. During that time she wrote five novels and two collections of short prose. The last of these, *The Adaptable Man,* was written at the end of her time in England and published after she returned to New Zealand. It can be seen as a wry farewell to the demands of the English tradition. In my view the most underestimated of her novels, it also departs from the sombre tone of the earlier fiction. Set in a fictional Suffolk village it allows Frame to return, with a delight that is apparent, to the Anglo-Saxon origins both of language and of place:

> Say the names, then to yourself.
>
> Little Burgelstatham (a burgel was originally a burial place of the heathen). Tydd. Lakenthorpe. Murston. Segham. Colsea. Withigford. Say the names again and again, and soon there's no weetbox-coloured railway station . . . There's no village store . . . There's no Clematis Cottage . . . nothing but a dream of earliest praise, of sea-flooded inlets, lakes, marshes, sedge, willows and those birds, half-hidden, which walk tall, camouflaged as reeds, and sound, morning and evening, their lonely cries; water, birds, and now and again the soft rustle and wash and splash of the men, the Southfolk, guiding their boats through the inland seas.

This novel is a parable of misevolution; it sees the twentieth century as a time when, to use Henry Adams's phrase, 'the continuity stopped'. Its central figure, Alwyn Maude, is a man of the age, able to murder and fornicate without conscience or scruple; around him Frame forms a novel that politely thumbs the nose at the English tradition it imitates and satirises. With one hand she creates characters, spins plots, describes and contrives, and with the other she as skillfully pulls her own work down to show the arbitrariness of fiction within the arbitrariness of all things. Finally, after a display of nonchalant brilliance, she continues one of the larger scale ficticides in modern fiction by dropping a chandelier onto several of her characters as they sit round a dinner table. It is typical of Frame's control and skill in this novel that this moment also consummates its symbolism.

Her next two novels, written during years spent in the town of her birth, Dunedin, display a clear recession of her powers. It is as if the return from Europe to a place of earlier suffering (*An Angel at My Table* reveals the terrors of her student years in Dunedin) diminished the range of her thought and associations and forced her in on herself. Certainly, both *A State of Siege* (1967) and *The Rainbirds* (1969) can be seen as parables about herself as an artist and an outsider. The first is a competent enough work about the failure of an art teacher who retires to paint 'properly' but is destroyed by the growth of new, visionary powers. The second is the story of a man who becomes a pariah after being thought killed by a car; like the artist of the preceding book he too is killed by his apprehension of what lies beyond the here and now. Both these novels feel frustrated; essentially they rework Frame's earlier assertions about the trials and superiority of the artist, and they reveal how limiting she finds New Zealand. Her last three novels were written when she began to travel and to live and write in North America; all of them are freer, lighter in tone, and with her interest in experiment renewed.

Intensive Care (1970) is one of a small group of New Zealand novels that respond to New Zealand's minor involvement in the later stages of the Vietnam War. Like Karl Stead's *Smith's Dream* and Craig Harrison's *Broken October* it imagines New Zealand as Vietnam, divided and full of American troops. There is little that is thematically new here; reading its pages we are told again of the aridity of New Zealand life, its fear of the imaginative and the artistic and of the regimentation and suppressed violence of a society that is, in Kendrick Smithyman's phrase, a 'death-centred democracy'. But the imaginative transplantation of this country into another part of the world rekindles powers dormant for five years: Frame's portrait of the hideous adventurer, Peggy Warren, is unforgettably convincing, while the whole work is rich with the evocative strength of her symbolic imagination and is often nearer poetry than prose.

The settings of *Daughter Buffalo* (1972) and *Living in the Maniototo* are predominantly North American. The former is an extraordinary novel, again ultimately revealed as the hallucination of one of its actors, about an elderly New Zealand writer who 'mates' with a young Jewish doctor in New York; together this odd couple produces a 'daughter', a young buffalo they see while visiting a local zoo. Baffling if seen as realistic, *Daughter Buffalo* is best read as another parable about the predicament of the artist, the dying old man Turnlung representing Frame's New Zealand self, perhaps, and the young man, Edelman, a new, cosmopolitan self capable of fathering rough but authentic beasts that are not quite what we expect to come from human beings. Such an interpretation gives emphasis to Edelman's long ruminations on the American way of death that take up so much of the novel:

> When I set out toward the rivers, taking the cross-town bus part of the way, I found that there was no place to *be,* and this, within my waking dream of death, seemed ominous. The two rivers flow farther and farther from the streams of man and if a man can get to stand near them he realises that the water does not even grant him a shadow, nor does it grant a shadow to the city, while the sun itself cannot dredge from it a light-glimmer of gold. The city rivers, filled with death, have long ago given up speaking of seasonal irony; in springtime, they allow a green and yellow fire of grass and forsythia to break out along the riverbanks of the Hudson Valley, above the opaque polluted waters, flaunting the green and yellow life that bears the seeds of decay.

Anyone audacious enough to write a novel with a plot like this has obviously left the cares of traditionalism far behind, and it seems almost inevitable that her most recent work, *Living in the Maniototo,* should be openly and happily a

metafiction; that, after all, is where *The Adaptable Man* was leading her. The novel is like a survey of all her others: there is a section set in Baltimore that dwells on poverty, death and suffering, the surface of its language crackles with puns on which deeper structural meanings depend; and it is about what it is like to be a writer.

Its narrator, Mavis Halleton, opens the novel with a disquisition on the deceptiveness of language and the writer as a confidence trickster. She explores the way artists try to express their vision without departing wholly from the real world. Amongst the many metaphors for this, that of the hypotenuse triangle stands out, with a base that represents life and a vertical that represents art. Although this opening section, and a second set in Baltimore, are full of events, there is no larger narrative carrying the novel's meaning; rather, as in most of her novels, Frame relies on images to evoke the complicated and private ideas that animate her writing. Images of reflection, for example, occur, with their evocations of the mirroring of life by art: there are twins, as well as children called Binnorie and Lonnie, and a confidence trickster in Auckland has a duplicate in Baltimore, which in turn is twin city to Blenheim in Auckland.

It is in the final section of the novel, set in California, that Frame gets down to the business of demonstrating the power and the shortcomings of literature. Mavis moves into the opulent home of the Garretts, two wealthy art lovers who are off to Italy, in order to write. News arrives of their death in an earthquake and that their house is, surprisingly, willed to Mavis. Equally surprisingly, two couples, friends of the Garretts, arrive at the house to mourn its former owners; they each tell their stories, meticulously recorded in realistic prose by the writer, and then the Garretts, alive after all, return to reclaim their home. Mavis goes back to Baltimore and finds that her host there has died in her absence.

None of this of course can do justice to a novel that is both baffling and compelling. But old Frame hands will find their way clearer on the second and third readings that all her novels demand, and will see that the first two sections, with their meditations on the trials, aspirations and limitations of the artist, are a preparation for a third in which Frame sets about the business of illustrating these. Mavis is like the author, a writer overwhelmed by the difficulties of artistic communication; in the Garretts' house she is in an artist's 'garret' and the house of fiction itself. The four characters who enter it are indeed characters, inventions of the mind of the artist-within-the-novel, as real and as fake as characters in realistic fiction, their invented stories and the evocation of their psychological life as convincing as anything in literature.

In *Living in the Maniototo* Frame has it both ways, exploiting the limitations of traditional fiction to write in a way that is entertaining and curiously realistic, given the attacks on realism that her writing contains. For her, it seems, there is little distinction between life and art, for the process of shaping appears to begin with perception and not with a conscious act of creation. To write three volumes of autobiography, as she has after *Living in the Maniototo,* is not to alter her medium or her purpose or necessarily to signal the end of the fiction-writing process in her life. Indeed, there seems to be little alteration of emphasis, language or ideas in the move from 'art' to 'life', and to read these works is to be suspended again, magically and rather mysteriously, in a space that lies between the two.

> My memory is once again of the colours and spaces and natural features of the outside world. On our first week in our Glenham house on the hill, I discovered a place, *my place*. Exploring by myself, I found a secret place among old fallen trees by a tiny creek, with a moss-covered log to sit on while the new-leaved branches of the silver birch tree formed a roof shutting out the sky except for the patterned holes of sunlight. The ground was covered with masses of old, used leaves, squelchy, slippery, wet. I sat on the log and looked around myself. I was overcome by a delicious feeling of discovery, of gratitude, of possession. I knew that this place was entirely *mine;* mine the moss, the log, the secrecy.

From the first Frame's autobiography assumes its freedom, the lack of responsibility that the act of remembering gives, the way it releases the writer more than fictionalising does to explore the places which give rise to that fiction. Her first volume, with its pungent and yet delicate evocations of a childhood familiar to many New Zealanders, takes us into that frozen 'ice-land' of present memory which, one suspects, is the hinterland of all her art, the 'mirror city', glittering, distant, intimate, eternal, that gives the title of her third volume. Here, one suspects, she most happily belongs, safe from the blows of what has clearly been a demanding life and equally safe from the traditional demands to shape and mean.

Gina Mercer (essay date September 1985)

SOURCE: "Exploring 'The Secret Caves of Language': Janet Frame's Poetry," in *Meanjin,* Vol. 44, No. 3, September, 1985, pp. 384-90.

[*In the following essay, Mercer examines Frame's poetry in* The Pocket Mirror *as well as the more poetic passages of her novels, finding both to be "innovative and engrossing."*]

When she was sixteen, Janet Frame wrote in her diary, 'Dear Mr Ardenue, *they* think I'm going to be a schoolteacher, but I'm going to be a poet'. She has become a poet, but she is still beset by the problem of a 'they' who think she is, or ought to be, something else.

Janet Frame is repeatedly referred to as a 'novelist'. This,

despite the fact that ten of her twenty published books are not novels, but volumes of short fiction, poetry, autobiography and children's fiction. Of the ten remaining books, Frame calls only one a 'novel', to explicitly distinguish it from her other long fictions, which she calls 'explorations'. She eschews the label 'novel' and, one may assume, 'novelist', because of the restrictive expectations such labels engender. Yet she continues to be referred to as a 'novelist' by journalists and critics alike. Frame, though, is neither a 'novelist' nor a 'poet' exclusively. She is an explorer in language, boldly crossing forbidden borders of form and style. One of the most fixed and impassable borders in literature is that between poetry and prose, yet Janet Frame repeatedly traverses this border, writing poetic prose and including whole chapters of poetry in her fictional explorations. The punishment meted out to Frame for these 'transgressions' is neglect by the literary establishment. She has been publishing poetry, prose, and her subtle mixtures of both since the early 1950s, but the total body of literary criticism on Frame is small, and substantial appraisals of the poetic aspects of her work are non-existent. A few small, though positive, reviews of her volume of poetry, *The Pocket Mirror,* followed its publication in 1967. One unpublished thesis interestingly compares Frame's poetry with that of Anne Sexton, Sylvia Plath, and fellow New Zealander, Fleur Adcock, and there is a brief description of *The Pocket Mirror* in what is so far the major critical work on Frame, Patrick Evans' *Janet Frame* (1977), but that is it.

The same cursory treatment is apparent when it comes to discussion of the poetic sections in Frame's fiction. Most critics and reviewers gloss over, or simply ignore, her subversion of genre, and certainly do not discuss the anarchic implications of her disruptions of the novel form. They go on referring to her as a 'novelist', labelling her explorations 'novels', in spite of her obvious and repeated attacks on the very conventions which define that particular literary form.

In this article I want to look at Frame's poetry, both that published separately as poetry, and that published as part of her anarchic fictional explorations. In so doing, I do not want to reinforce the very genre distinctions she is working to subvert, but to focus on her important alterations of conventional form, and her fascinating, self-reflexive use of language.

The major focus of Janet Frame's work is upon the unlikely and often paradoxical structures on which our cultural perceptions are based. One of the most fundamental of these structures is language and, as one might expect of a writer concerned with exploration and subversion, Janet Frame repeatedly makes language itself the subject of her writing. She regards language with affection and admiration, but at the same time with trepidation, even terror. She is constantly aware of its power and paradoxical weakness. It has limitations and borders; a border defines and communicates a shape, that is its virtue. In so doing, however, it confines and restricts the communication of any other shape and that is its fearful power.

> In the dream in the dream
> the child played a poem
> protected by mild adjectives
> gentle verbs and the two
> pronouns teaching the
> division of earth and sky
> night and day
> object and show; and the separating
> personal eye.
>
> *Intensive Care*

> all along that ruined coast littered with language,
> . . . see-through words, glass words, bleaching,
>   indestructible synthetic words
> helping to complete the big . . . people-kill.
>
> *Daughter Buffalo*

These pieces reveal two of the varying attitudes to language which Frame explores. In the first, language has the power to nurture and teach, which is also a confining power. The language of the 'poem' described is 'gentle' and protective, but at the same time it is 'teaching the division'. This is a crucial aspect of language for Frame. Language can be comforting because of its familiarity, but ultimately its comfort is that of the straitjacket. It allows communication, just as a straitjacket allows movement, but it is communication of a very specific and limited kind. One of the most fundamental ways in which language restricts communication is through its 'division' of experience into exclusive and opposite halves: rational vs irrational; sane vs insane; novelist vs poet. These are prescriptive oppositions; not neutral transparent words allowing free communication, but value-laden terms which colour and constrain our thoughts as soon as we attempt to express them. It is *against* such oppositions that Janet Frame protests whenever she writes. She shows language to be a prime culprit in the perpetuation of this divisive, dichotomous system of perception. Thus the child, in playing with a poem (it could well be a nursery rhyme), is being taught the 'division' by 'gentle', 'mild', protective language.

This piece is the beginning of one of Janet Frame's most interesting fictions, *Intensive Care* (1970). It is a tri-partite work, a bizarre sort of family saga dealing with the past, present and future of an ordinary group of New Zealanders. Importantly though, the patriarchal, familial relationships between the characters are much less significant than the connections which develop through their common experiences. In the final section of the book, set in the future, Frame depicts a society where the divisions on which we base our language

and thought have been taken to terrifying extremes. The Government of this future New Zealand has passed a 'Human Delineation Act' under which people are arbitrarily divided into two exclusive groups labelled 'Human' and 'Non-Human'. The 'Humans' are immensely privileged and have absolute power over the others; the people classified as 'Non-Human' may be caged, killed, eaten, enslaved or experimented upon—that is, they may be treated as we presently treat all animals other than ourselves. Through this initial poem, Janet Frame subtly introduces the theme of the fundamental divisions inherent in language, a theme she describes as 'so basic it is embedded in the grammar and syntax of the language where it lies like a trap. She shows how early we learn the practice of 'division', and why it is so insidiously necessary and comforting for the poem-playing child who remains in all of us.

> **Janet Frame repeatedly makes language itself the subject of her writing. She regards language with affection and admiration, but at the same time with trepidation, even terror.**
>
> **—Gina Mercer**

The second piece of poetry comes from Janet Frame's next book, *Daughter Buffalo* (1972), which explores another fundamental division: life and death. One of the main characters is involved in death studies and finally becomes 'Head of the Department of Death Studies'. Frame explores the way people, most particularly modern Americans, reject death and attempt to exclude it from life. (This idea is more comically explored in Evelyn Waugh's *The Loved Ones,* which focusses especially on the way avoidance of death is manifested in language in the form of laughable, almost grotesque, euphemisms.) What makes this particular piece of poetry interesting is the way in which it likens words to a type of tideline flotsam, renowned for its resistance to decay. The words Janet Frame describes so vividly may bleach or break, but they will not disintegrate naturally, thus 'helping with the big . . . people-kill'. While the resulting pollution is an obvious aspect of this image, most importantly Janet Frame is suggesting the way in which 'Indestructible synthetic words' (words perhaps like 'global overkill' or 'strategic defence initiative' with their euphemistic, high tech. glossing over of unimaginable disasters) are pushing us steadily toward the 'big . . . people-kill'—the ultimate destructive pollution of nuclear war. She suggests that language, with its built-in oppositions, is fundamental to creating and sustaining the adversary mentality. At the end of one of her earlier explorations, *Scented Gardens For the Blind* (1964), she suggests that unless we find a new mode of language, a new way of communicating, we will be 'tasting people ash in [our] mouths' and reverting to the 'ancient rock and marshland', only able to communicate in grunts and groans.

These two pieces more or less represent the poles of Janet Frame's feelings toward language and the power of words. In between these poles of cautious affection and the prophecy of doom for the human race, lies a whole range of other attitudes. She explores many of them, speaking fearfully of 'hemlock syllables', admiringly of 'Words [which] . . . drop like pearls', and critically of the

> man of sin who without repentance
> could turn a comma from its comfortable sen-
> tence,
> could in cold language strangle a new-born
> thought.

Language then, is to be feared for its capacity to poison those who try to explore its liquid depths, admired for its translucent beauty, and hated for its deathly coldness. In another poem, **'Poets',** Frame describes, not language, but those who seek to explore and employ it

> And we are not fish rich nor poor
> and we can neither swim nor drown.

Such is the 'in limbo' position of the explorer of language.

In a recent interview, Frame said that she'd 'Never really discovered how to make words work for [her]', and described words as 'instruments of magic'. As with most magic, there are elements of mystery in Frame's poetry. At times she even creates a whole new mysterious language. In poems like **'La-ment For The Lakes'** (*The Pocket Mirror*) she speaks in this other language, somewhat reminiscent of James Joyce or Lewis Carroll:

> Barevolved craffhanded turbuked
> under driftices of berge
> damperly they have sultured
> mormed without crumbience or zone
> each tressled pave.

A first reaction to this may be to regard it as whimsy taken to extreme but, as part of her long-term enterprise to make us examine language carefully, poems like this have an appealing validity. By writing in an 'other' language Frame forces us to see how conventional language excludes the experience of the 'other', how it systematises the concept of 'other' experience (be it the 'otherness' of women or the disabled or

the insane) as experience which is not 'normal', and which therefore must be excluded. This is the most extreme of the various types of 'poetic fiction that . . . usefully allow a writer to explore varieties of otherwise unspoken or unacceptable feelings, thoughts and language'. Janet Frame uses the same technique in certain prose passages in *The Rainbirds* and *Intensive Care*. Though difficult passages to read because of our expectations, they function somewhat like the surreal images in a Luis Bunuel film. They are highly suggestive, and throw a questioning critical light on the 'norm' we so unthinkingly expect and accept.

Frame's relationship to language is intense and magical, but one which does not restrict her. She writes on all kinds of topics, many of them as taboo as the practice of genre jumping. [Critic Patrick Evans] has complained that the themes raised in her poetry are not 'inherently poetical'. This raises the question of the experiences which have traditionally been excluded from poetry, on moral, religious, or political grounds, all under the guise of 'aesthetic' consideration of the 'truly poetical'. But once again Frame is concerned with *inclusion* not exclusion, and writes with refreshing freedom on whatever she sees, even

> the sewage with its shaggy golden mane
> . . . adrift silently on the tides

She shows the same freedom in writing about other writers and their ideas. For example she transforms Kafka's beetle into

> . . . the dungbeetle
> sucking feeding upon the excrement of word.

And she performs a similar transformation when she allows a suicide note to become a bold declaration of a woman's right to choose, rather than the morbid, apologetic message usually portrayed in fiction:

> Tonight I devise my own simple time for dying,
> without rules or help from neighbouring factories,
> without the mid-week sustenance of pork-pie and
> penis

Frame is exploring the poetic possibilities of both form and content. She does not write 'inherently poetical' poetry. Rather she is writing against such restrictive notions. She writes as freely about individual problems like cancer in **'O Lung Flowering like a Tree'**, as she does about global problems in **'Instructions for Bombing with Napalm'**. Her poems are as often wry and humorous as they are dark and solemn. In **'Sunday Afternoon at Two O'Clock'** she describes Dunedin, where she was born:

> Having been to church the people are good, quiet,
> with sober drops at the end of their cold Dunedin
> noses,
> with polite old-fashioned sentences like Pass the
> Cruet,
> and, later, attentive glorying in each other's roses.

Later in *The Pocket Mirror* Frame reflects again on this subject, in another wry poem, **'Cat Spring'**

> At this time of year strangers lurk in my garden.
> Their cry gobbles the snow-encircled full moon,
> their alley-hunger makes a sexual slum
> of a city that is rumored to be clean. I
> never trust
> rumor.
> Beware, Dunedin!
> The cats are out of the bag at last.
> The chambers
> of night commerce are full to overflowing.
> It is spring.
> The gardens hold immeasurable loot of
> gold
> crocuses, silk—
> veined daffodils
> stained lust of
> tomcats'
> milk.

Even in a seemingly simple, descriptive poem like **'Pukeko'** Frame creates a twist, by sardonically adopting the fashion-writer's style.

> Pukeko, swamp hen
> unescorted
> is wearing junior navy
> a pillarbox beak
> burnt orange casual claws.
>
> If shadow violates
> will spear the dark
> the damp lonely dark swamp
> with hatpin scream
> —Cree Cree!

Frame's poetry can be sardonic, erotic, delicate and dark. Of course some poems are less effective than others, but generally she has the words, her chosen 'instruments of magic', under powerful control. Those who, early in Frame's career, criticised her for only expressing a 'dark vision of the narrow limitations placed upon human possibility', now seem almost self-reflexive in their comments. Frame creates 'dark visions' brilliantly, exploring and exposing limitations, especially those inherent in language. But she does much more. By revealing the limitations of judgement and exclusion built into our system of speech and thought, Frame is opening up new possibilities. She is opening up the possibility of *inclusion*. It is especially in her poetry that Frame focusses on the possibility that literature should include all experience, hence her subversion of the restricting literary conventions of form and content. She writes to challenge the sovereignty of the government of 'correct norm', and affirm the experience of the 'other'. The twenty volumes published so far, have firmly established Janet Frame as one of this century's most innovative and engrossing language artists. Through them she has demonstrated 'that the uses of poetry are endless but not always harmless'.

Carol Sternhell (review date 6 October 1985)

SOURCE: "In the Imagination's True Country," in *The New York Times Book Review,* October 6, 1985, p. 30

[*In the review below, Sternhell compares the third volume of Frame's autobiography,* The Envoy from Mirror City, *to the previous volumes,* To the Is-Land *and* An Angel at My Table.]

Even as a small child, Janet Frame believed that words were magic. She collected bright moments of language as other children might gather shiny marbles or seashells, protective totems against the crowded, puzzling world of home and school. She was not completely surprised, years later, when literature quite literally saved her—when a scheduled lobotomy was canceled at the last minute because her first book of short stories had unexpectedly won a prize. "It was my writing that at last came to my rescue," she told us quietly in *An Angel at My Table,* her second autobiographical volume, after detailing eight horrifying years spent in and out of mental hospitals. "It is little wonder that I value writing as a way of life when it actually saved my life."

"It actually saved my life." To Miss Frame, now one of New Zealand's best-known novelists, writing has always salvaged the past and promised the future; it has always offered a way out and a way in. The awkward, eager girl she described in *To the Is-Land* the first volume of her autobiography, lived as much in the world of English and French literature as in the small South Island town of Oamaru—her homemade school tunic, painfully tight after years of use, may have been spotted with patches; blood leaked embarrassingly through her bulky, homemade sanitary towels; one sister had drowned

and her brother, an epileptic, was seriously ill, but the teenage Janet wrote in her diary, "I'm going to be a *poet*."

The lonely young woman of *An Angel at My Table,* mistakenly diagnosed as schizophrenic and trapped in the back ward of Seacliff Hospital for "loonies"—a chilling experience Miss Frame recounts in her powerful second novel, *Faces in the Water*—never doubts her calling. "If I could not live within the world of writing books," she wonders, "then where could I survive?" And the adult novelist of Miss Frame's latest volume, living in London and typing eagerly in rented rooms, still seeks solace in the joy of words: "Language that had betrayed, changed, influenced, could still befriend the isolated, could help when human beings had withdrawn their help."

The Envoy From Mirror City is a memoir of travel and imagination. It opens with Miss Frame's seasick ocean voyage and her arrival in London on the day after her 32d birthday, in 1956, and ends eight years later after a seasick journey home—away from ancient Europe, which "was so much on the map of the imagination" with "so many layers of mapmakers," and back to a country where it was possible "to be a mapmaker for those who will follow nourished by this generation's layers of the dead."

The Envoy him- or herself is an imaginary traveler, "that watching self, who was already waiting to guide me to my fictional home," both a companion on the trail and the midwife of creation. Mirror City, "where everything I have known or seen or dreamed of is bathed in the light of another world," is the imagination's true country, "that wonderful view over all time and space, the transformation of ordinary facts and ideas into a shining palace of mirrors."

Because the real journey of Miss Frame's book, and of her life, is the passage to Mirror City, the daily events she meticulously records seem curiously insubstantial. It's not that nothing happens during these years. She travels to Ibiza and Andorra, marveling like any other tourist at the wonderful strangeness, "the colour of the olive trees and of the buildings thumbed and worn like old stone pages."

She loses her virginity after "waking one morning with a haunting thought that I (shy, in my thirty-third year, travelling overseas to 'broaden my experience') might never have another such experience."

She visits the Institute of Psychiatry at Maudsley Hospital and discovers that she never suffered from schizophrenia, a verdict she finds unexpectedly terrifying: "Oh why had they robbed me of my schizophrenia which had been the answer to all my misgivings about myself? Like King Lear I had gone in search of 'the truth' and I now had nothing." But all this eventfulness is a mere backdrop to the writing, to Mirror City; Miss Frame meets many brightly colored characters but

makes no friends. When she sails back to New Zealand she asks a librarian from the British Museum to see her off, "unable to face a solitary departure."

If *The Envoy From Mirror City* is less compelling than the earlier volumes of Miss Frame's autobiography, it may be because writing is less immediate a metaphor than childhood or madness—and perhaps because the discussions of her literary processes remain determinedly mystical, with Mirror City always gleaming over the horizon. It's difficult not to be charmed, however, by Miss Frame's luminous prose (she always knew that words were magic). And it's impossible not to be moved by this extraordinary portrait of a woman for whom art is life, a life well worth living.

Robert Ross (essay date Autumn 1987)

SOURCE: "Linguistic Transformation and Reflection in Janet Frame's *Living in the Maniototo,*" in *World Literature Written in English,* Vol. 27, No. 2, Autumn, 1987, pp. 320-26.

[*In the essay below, Ross analyzes Frame's use of language in* Living in the Maniototo, *concluding that Frame is able to transcend conventional narrative structures through the manipulation of language.*]

Janet Frame has travelled often to the "Is-Land," the "Table" where the angel hovers, to "Mirror City," then returned to tell the truth allotted her. But she owns only language to transform this "view over all time and space" into a coherent vision that reflects the "treasures" she beheld and touched during her travels. Often, she admits, "the medium of language" fails, for the revelations she attempts "have acquired imperfections . . . never intended for them . . . have lost meaning that seemed, once, to shine from them." Frame has, nonetheless, consistently demonstrated that the tradition-bound barriers of language need not constrict—in fact, demonstrated this so fully that she has invented a new kind of novel that contradicts its very form.

Those approaching Frame's work critically always note its non-novelistic tenor. For instance, Margaret Atwood says in a review of *Living in the Maniototo,* "Frame spurns plot except as a device for prodding the reader." To C.K. Stead the work "challenges its own genre, questions its own 'reality,' and finally collapses in upon itself." Carole Cook, reviewing *Living in the Maniototo,* observes that "Geography and language stand in for plot." Patrick Evans talks of how in Frame's work "the rigidities of characterization have crumbled"; and H. Winston Rhodes of how the "power" of "Frame's imagination" does not show itself in "plot structure, in the creation of character, nor even in her capacity for 'naming things.'"

Thus, bypassing the accepted requirements of fiction, Frame carries out in their place a linguistic process of transformation and reflection. That is, she engages language in such totality that her fiction transcends conventional narrative and turns instead into an often anguished, sometimes comic, private record made public, in which narrator, plot, character, setting and theme are subordinated to their determiner, language.

The struggle to harness language as a means to transform and to reflect experience overlies Frame's three autobiographical volumes, *To the Is-Land* (1983), *An Angel at My Table* (1984), and *The Envoy from Mirror City* (1985). Although concrete in their treatment of her life, these books—as their titles suggest—more accurately provide a gloss to the fiction which that life has engendered, recording as they do her growing awareness of language, its weaknesses, inadequacies, mysteries, strengths, elusiveness. "I was learning words, believing from the beginning that words meant what they said," she recalls in *To the Is-Land*'s opening pages devoted to early childhood, then tells how she read an adventure story titled *To the Island* but aloud called it *To the Is-Land*. Once corrected on pronounciation she "had to accept the ruling," but within herself "still thought of it as the Is-Land." So, early on, the vagary of language led her to entangle the outer world with the inner, a paradox central to her fiction. In *An Angel at My Table* she speaks of the private language which provides the substance for her writing: "My only freedom was within, in my thoughts and language most of which I kept carefully concealed, except in my writing."

Frame has continually sought the freedom this hidden language provides, a quest which has yielded astounding effects in her writing. Critics, on making passing reference to this phenomenon, have attempted to name it, albeit not always accurately or appropriately. It has been described as an "interest in communication," or by H. Winston Rhodes as "the gift of parabolic utterance"; by Margaret Atwood as a "voice" which is "quirky, rich, eccentric, nervous and sometimes naive," or by Carole Cook as "coy but militant solipsism," even by Patrick Evans as "esoteric experimentation." In grander terms, C.K. Stead has called this singular talent with language "the instrument of the imagination . . . the hawk suspended over eternity"; or as Frame herself says: " . . . the hawk suspended above eternity."

Although touching the edge of Frame's genius, such phrases fail to penetrate its core. In 1973 Patrick Evans observed that Frame may well be New Zealand's most successful contemporary novelist but one who "has reached this position, curiously enough, without the impetus of unified critical understanding"; the reason: " . . . the difficulty of sensing immediately where the centre of her work lies." As I see it, the centre, the core, lies in language for whose sake Frame has forfeited the conventions of prose narrative. Such has been the case to varying degrees in all her novels; but the one published just before the autobiographies, *Living in the Maniototo* (1979), shows that the linguistic transformation and reflection process has appropriated the fictional properties and made them its own.

Instances of that preoccupation with language as it emerges in some of the earlier works will serve to lay the groundwork for the fuller treatment of *Living in the Maniototo*. Frame's 1960 novel, *Owls Do Cry,* makes use of language in ways altogether original and suggested then—and continues to do so—that here is no ordinary piece of fiction. In it, for example, one of the characters tries to find words for her diary, a recurring device in the future novels which often include writing within writing. Stymied by the inflexibility of language, the character/writer in *Owls Do Cry* laments: "I should like to put in a simile, the way it is done by writers, to describe the loveliness of the blossoms in my old home. I can think of nothing to say except they are choking white." Similar frustrations with language appear in the succeeding novels, the writer either disguising herself as one of the characters or appearing openly to decry her talent to say things as she ought. In *The Edge of the Alphabet* (1962) Thora observes: "Home? The edge of the alphabet where words crumble and all forms of communication between the living are useless. One day we who live at the edge of the alphabet will find our speech." The continued loss of that speech provides the focus for the next novel, *Scented Gardens for the Blind* (1964); in it Vera decides not to talk to anyone, "because every time she opened her mouth to say something, her voice, in hiding, reminded her that there was nothing to say, and no words to say it."

By the time of *A State of Siege* (1966) Frame had introduced another of her devices to stress the fragility of language, this time scrambling the accepted signs to represent nothing while they appear to do so. A newspaper with a stone wrapped inside is thrown into a room, and Malfred reads its account of the news, although "not in any language she had learned." Pure nonsense, this "last century's or tomorrow's news in verse":

> Soltrin, carmew desse puniform wingering brime
> commern in durmp, a farom a ferinwise lumner,
> sturph, wolpe,. . . .

Across it in red crayon someone has scrawled *"Help Help."* Godfrey, whose return from the dead *Yellow Flowers in the Antipodean Room* (1969) tells, may have thrown the newspaper-wrapped stone, for language stands as the invisible barrier between his mistaken death and never-retrieved life. Why, he wonders, had he "ever trusted so obvious a deceiver as language". Some of Frame's other linguistic concerns also play freely in this work, such as the cliché, tense and the language of advertising.

But *Living in the Maniototo,* more than any of the previous novels, shows what happens when language is allowed to hold absolute sway over the conventions of fiction, thus exposing those conventions for the liars they are. Incorporating all the devices used in the earlier work and adding new ones, Frame has produced a novel that tells the whys and the how of its writing: to reveal truth about life and to depend on lies in doing so. For truth does emerge in spite of the conveyor's unreliability.

In criticism of fiction, questions concerning reliability usually arise, even if unconsciously. How reliable is the narrator? Is the plot convincing? Or does it depend too heavily on the tricks of coincidence or farfetched reversals? Are the characters consistent? motivated? "real"? Are they allowed their own lives? Or does the narrator manipulate them? undercut them? Does setting serve as background, or at times, as the instigator of action? Or does it provide the place for yet another deception? How does the author reveal the theme? Is the meaning too obvious, too much in the foreground, too didactic in its presentation? Or does the theme ridicule itself, making light of its own pretensions? If these elementary questions get the wrong answers, then the work's failure is likely to be assured. Yet, while *Living in the Maniototo* draws all the incorrect responses, it succeeds. So the concern changes to how Frame did not execute the demands, how she rejected the accepted dictums of her craft and turned the novel inside out to exhibit the seams and the lining and unsightly stitches that hold together the fabric woven from words.

For one thing, the identity of the first-person narrator in *Living in the Maniototo* remains uncertain. She calls herself a "'writer'", and has published a novel and a volume of poems. She might be Mavis Furness Barwell Haleton, or the "penultimate Mavis," or "Alice Thumb" or one of a dozen or so other persons made real by names, or even "Violet Pansy Proudlock, ventriloquist." That a novelist might be a ventriloquist suggests how far she has removed herself from the original, feeding words to the dummy whose lip movements and voice form a linguistic deception the public accepts. Even though the narrator has already published, she enrolls in a creative writing course, there learning about what she once called the "I-book." Disagreeing with her teacher's view that first person relies on perfection, on the turning of "the writer into a god or goddess with perfect vision", she forms her own definition:

> A writer taking on the "I," takes a straight line that can be turned upon itself to become a circle or curved to become a hook or left alone as a prelude to infinity or have its back broken into the hypotenuse, the opposite, the adjacent.

Such, then, becomes the approach of this "'I' writer," whose straight line language comprises, a line that turns on itself, circling, curving, twisting, finally serving "as a prelude to infinity."

Because this novel relies on the first person narrator—whoever she may be—it should probably tell her story and those events familiar to her. Mavis—so she will be called for the time being—begins to do just that, revealing first how events

in her life conspire to make her socially acceptable through language's magic; for now in public she can say "I've buried two husbands, you know", thus gaining the immediate regard of others while standing in bus lines, shopping, or walking along the street. The burial of the second husband also allows her the freedom to travel and write, for no longer a housewife in Blenheim, Auckland's "young new suburb," she takes up a new life, first in Baltimore, then in Berkeley. The outward action, although easy enough to summarize, still suggests little to indicate the intensity of the inner action, at which even the table of contents only hints:

PROLOGUE: Naming people and places.

PART I: Paying Attention to Husbands, Dead Writers, the Blue Fury, Debtors and Debt Collectors.

PART II: Paying Attention to The Ice Pick, the Diamond Account Book, a Family Heirloom and an Invitation.

PART III. Attending and Avoiding in the Maniototo.

PART IV: Avoiding, Bound By the Present Historic.

PART V: Avoiding and Paying Attention to Keepsakes and Shelter and the Withering of a Tongue Blossom.

Language, this peculiar assortment of topics promises, is to play the central role, as an often undetermined feminine "I" takes up the subjects outlined in the contents and makes them her own. But before long she turns into a second narrator, equally evasive in identity, and creates situations that the initial narrator undoes, showing them to be the artifice of fiction, not the stuff of real life. Fully realized incidents and their participants vanish in a reversal of words; they existed, after all, as mere replicas, as reflections of the real, false as the prints of the paintings on the walls of the house Mavis sublets in Berkeley.

The characters, shown to be made not of flesh and blood but of nouns and verbs, function ultimately to represent the novel's concern with language. This creates a circular proposition, considering that language brings them to life and, in turn, often kills them. Some die and stay dead; others die, then come back to life, always at the will and convenience of their linguistic manipulator. The two husbands, for example, she remembers mainly in light of their verbal oddities and tells little else about them, except their deaths. The first husband, Lewis, after his stroke, no longer possessed the ability to name things, only to give definitions and wait for his wife to feed him the words. This loss strikes Mavis as the saddest part of his ten-year illness: "Lewis had been struck by lightning that burned great holes in his language and scorched the rest so as to make the pattern unintelligible; he had no more sustenance or warmth from language." A few years later she remarries, this time to a French teacher, Lance, who soon sets aside the refinements of French grammar for the cruder rhetoric of debt collecting, a profession he pursues with dedication and vigor. When she pleads with him to return to "the humanities," to "language which never harmed anyone," he responds: "I've known more rape and murder and debt in language . . . Suicide too! This is what partly persuaded me to give up teaching language." She realizes that his changed attitude "could be blamed on words;" then, defending her work as a novelist, she insists that "a novel doesn't prosecute or haunt anyone," to which Lance replies, "I wouldn't be too sure." In the simplest terms, when Mavis writes that "language in itself may be a force to prompt behaviour," she has summed up her approach to characterization.

Through selective detail, the novel's "I" draws graphic pictures of the three cities she inhabits. Blenheim in New Zealand she calls a "disinherited suburb-city where the largest, most impressive building is not a cathedral, a community hall, concert hall or theatre, but a shopping mall" built in the architecture of North America. The Baltimore she creates is one of "grey asphalt and red brick and black iron of gratings and windowbars," a place where time is not measured by blossoming flowers but from the blossoming of robberies and murders, where the drifts are not of flower petals but of litter. She captures the decaying eastern city in more concrete terms as well, showing how she can through language transform and reflect the substance of experience which Mirror City has provided her:

> . . . the Roxy, the strip-tease club where you could watch porn movies and see a middle-aged strip-tease artist making her breasts dance, and throwing lace handkerchiefs (wiped between her legs) to the men in the front rows; past the market, the stale goods bake shops, bargain stores, Five and Dime, the Salvation Army, the veterans, Volunteers of America, Purple Hearts, the launderettes with their half-dozen Speed Princess machines, mostly out of order, where the old man used to go, without any laundry, pay a quarter, and watch the water whirling around as the machine completed its cycle. For company.

To the gentler and more natural landscape of Berkeley and the San Francisco Bay area she gives kinder treatment, and landmarks such as the Golden Gate Bridge she considers "a memory-marvel," something she had known years earlier from American films seen in New Zealand.

However vivid the three cities beginning with the letter "B," though, the novel takes for its only valid setting the imagination, represented by the plain of Maniototo. Such a place indeed exists in the interior of New Zealand's South Island, a high plain, cold, distant and rarely visited, not even in the novel which bears its name. Mavis tells about a New Zealand

writer named Peter Wallstead, largely unknown until after his death, then more recognized for "living in the Maniototo" than for writing. "Goodness knew what he had discovered on that secret plain," Mavis exclaims. Or in Mirror City, she might have said, for the Maniototo has its replica, as surely as Blenheim and Baltimore and Berkeley reflect one another. The Maniototo, which Mavis never visits except in the imagination, stands as the source of experience and its understanding, whose transformation and reflection Mavis records through language in her "manifold," another name for the narrator/character's diary that so often figures in Frame's earlier work. "A writer," Mavis observes, "will hoard scraps from the manifold and then proceed to gnaw obsessively." While living in the cities of the three Bs and setting the action and characters within their confines—as any first-person narrator would do—this "I-writer" shows how the replicas she has constructed depend on a single source for their fictional reality: the Manifold, drawn from Mirror City atop the Maniototo's plain of experience.

Although the theme emerges, as it should, from the plot, characters and setting, the narrator—whether in the voice of Mavis or any of the other shifting personas—expounds endlessly on language theory. Through revealing the workings of the fiction-making process, the novel's "I" proves how unreliably art treats the truth it supposedly serves. The purpose of the novel Mavis and her replicas deny, for she/they have turned the novel against itself and destroyed all that it has set out to do: to name, to pay attention, to attend and to avoid. In their hands the novel, the "Tongue Blossom," has withered. Or has it?

Certainly, if judged in conventional terms, ***Living in the Maniototo*** could only be called a withered replica of the real thing. It goes about everything in the wrong way: the narrator is admittedly unreliable; the characters wander into fictional exile, experience death and rebirth; the setting shifts about in its "house of replicas"; the theme of language intrudes, resembling at times a textbook treatise on diction or syntax.

But how petty and worthless these complaints when set against the originality, the depth, the immensity of Frame's talent to transform and to reflect the keenest truth about the human condition, which she sees as the pawn of language. Like her questionable narrator in ***Living in the Maniototo,*** Frame proves: "I decided to break the rules, not because I felt my writing would even approach the shadow of perfection, but because nothing in art is forbidden. By critics and teachers, yes. By the painters, writers, composers, sculptors, no."

Ruth Brown (essay date September 1990)

SOURCE: "*Owls Do Cry*: Portrait of New Zealand," in *Landfall,* Vol. 44, No. 3, September, 1990, pp. 350-58.

[*In the following essay, Brown comments on the way in which*

Frame analyzes New Zealand society in her novel Owls Do Cry.]

Janet Frame emerged in 1954 after eight years in hospital to join a literary academy which had strong views about society's shortcomings. New Zealand was held to be narrow, bourgeois, puritanical, philistine, boring and materialist. Two influential articles in *Landfall:* Pearson's 'Fretful Sleepers' (1952) and Chapman's 'Fiction and the Social Pattern' (1953) elaborated a perception of New Zealand which by that time had transcended the status of opinion and become accepted as fact. The fringes of the perception were open to modification—Pearson predicted that puritanism was about to be replaced by shallow and sneering hedonism, while Chapman concentrated on explaining why New Zealand society was so puritanical—but no-one suggested that the central tenets of the theory were all wrong. New Zealand was fixed in literary perception as a land materially prosperous and culturally poor. The perception did not include consideration of the nature of global consumer capitalism and New Zealand's part in it: it just insisted that life should have been different and blamed New Zealanders for having failed to make it so.

Owls Do Cry, first published in 1957, verifies and strengthens criticisms of New Zealand society. As exemplified by Waimaru, society is so materialist and so powerfully inimical to the creative spirit that no-one can prevail against it. Nothing can ever help.

The most obvious explanation for Janet Frame's representation of New Zealand corroborating existing literary views is that everyone was right: New Zealand really was like that.

But there is another possibility, which is that Janet Frame made sense of her past and of New Zealand's past by fitting them both into an existing framework of meaning. This framework of meaning, which found New Zealand society to be materialistic, boring and so on, had its uses and served certain purposes, but was not necessarily right.

Recollection is a selective process. From the moment we experience an event we use the meanings of our culture to make sense of it. Memories are painful if they do not conform with public norms or versions of the past, and so there is a tendency for private memory to filter out or subdue those strands which contradict the accepted version.

In ***Owls Do Cry,*** Janet Frame filtered out memories which conflicted with the norm so that her perception of New Zealand corresponded with received opinion. This process is illustrated in the way wealth and poverty are perceived.

Waimaru is represented in such a way as to suggest that prosperity is both general, and linked with cultural poverty. All the indicators of civic progress—the begonia house, the Freezing Works set in its own garden and fancy flower beds, the Woollen Mills, the chocolate factory, the butter factory and the flower mill are taken by the people of Waimaru to mean 'prosperity and wealth in a fat-filled land.' As readers, we are asked to accept that material prosperity is a fact, and that it obscures more essential values. When the Waimaru councillors worry that if the town does not expand on to the bush clad hills it will be left behind while Northern towns go ahead, the narrator asks, 'Left behind from going where?'

The question invites readers to stop and think about the validity of material progress. We are not invited to wonder how far material prosperity is shared, nor are we given space in which to ponder on the implicit proposition that because material prosperity means inauthentic living, the way to authenticity must be via poverty.

Waimaru is prosperous: only the Withers are poor. 'Francie Withers is dirty. Francie Withers is poor. The Withers haven't a weekend bach nor do they live on the South Hill nor have they got a vacuum cleaner nor do they learn dancing or the piano or have birthday parties nor their photos taken at the Dainty Studio to be put in the window on a Friday.'

> In ***Owls Do Cry,*** **Janet Frame filtered out memories which conflicted with the norm so that her perception of New Zealand corresponded with received opinion. This process is illustrated in the way wealth and poverty are perceived.**
>
> —*Ruth Brown*

Having a weekend bach and other material advantages is made to sound like the norm. Material living standards in the 50s had doubled since the 20s, according to [W.B. Sutch in his *Colony or Nation?*] but this does not mean that everyone was prosperous. There was never a time when nearly everyone had a weekend bach. And if ***Owls Do Cry*** has a connection with Janet Frame's childhood experiences, it goes back to the depression when poverty was widespread. Oamaru was particularly hard hit. Futile and badly paid jobs were devised upon which men worked for alternate weeks; children ready to leave school were forced to remain there until the very schools themselves were threatened with closure. On this basis, far from being exceptionally poor, Francie Withers is one of the lucky ones because she has a job to go to.

In ***To the Is-land,*** Janet Frame admits that for a long time she failed to notice that her family's poverty was not unique. 'Toward the end of my years at school I emerged from a shocked concentration on the turmoil of being in Oamaru, the state which received so much blame for so much that had happened to us, to a realization that many other girls had not even reached high school because their parents had not been able to afford it or made the sacrifices to afford it as our parents undoubtedly did. I thought of the family of seven children up Eden Street who went barefoot, not always by choice, and of how I'd seen them running to school on a frosty morning, their feet mottled blue with cold; and of the family in Chelmer Street who lived only on soup made from pork bones from the bacon factory.

These memories refer not only to the depression, but to the time towards the end of her years at school, that is, from 1940-42.

Janet Frame is not the only New Zealand writer to have thought at one time that her family were unique because they were poor. Sylvia Ashton-Warner also came from a very poor family but it was years before she realised that they could not have been the only ones. 'We couldn't know then, as I know now, that ours was not the only family after the war wandering the face of the country, hungry, homeless, jobless, divided.'

It would appear that the perception of New Zealand as a prosperous, fat-filled land was so pervasive that memories were adjusted to conform to the generally accepted view. If anyone remembered being poor, the memory was filtered so that poverty was recalled as an exceptional state of affairs. *Owls Do Cry* remembers a New Zealand past in which everyone apart from the Withers family had access to the 'false treasures' of material well-being.

What is the origin of the perception of New Zealand as a prosperous, fat-filled land? Richard White observes in his book *Inventing Australia,* 'When we look at ideas about national identity, we need to ask not whether they are true or false, but what their function is, whose creation they are, and whose interests they serve.'

Some answers to these questions are provided within a popular history of New Zealand, *The Long White Cloud* by W. P. Reeves, first published in 1898. Reeves may not have invented the idea of a prosperous New Zealand but he certainly was responsible for its proliferation, and he provided an authentic-sounding basis for a perception adopted by the education system and the media. His history established the view that although old-world industrial conditions may have been reproduced in New Zealand before 1890, the legislation of the Liberal government eliminated all that and set everyone on the road to prosperity. Reeves claims, 'A very brief study of statistics would show that between 1890 and the present time (1898) the volume of trade, production, and private wealth has swelled in a very remarkable way.' Reeves also found New Zealand to be intellectually dull. 'New Zealanders appeared to distrust distinction, dislike brilliancy, and doubt originality.'

There are no statistics given about increased wealth and its distribution, no explanation of how and against whom New Zealanders' attitudes were being measured. Reeves 'history' of New Zealand is a generalised impression, written, as the preface makes clear, with the British reader in mind. Consciousness of what other nations must think of us continued to shape ideas about national identity. When John A. Lee wrote in *Children of the Poor* (1934) about a New Zealand with class divisiveness and widespread poverty, one reviewer was appalled. 'There is no hint to the overseas reader that the conditions described were out of the ordinary.' As Patrick Evans comments, there is a two-fold message here: Lee's New Zealand cannot exist, and the reason it cannot exist is that it is a betrayal of an overseas view of New Zealand.

The perception of New Zealand as materially prosperous which was so widely held in the 1950s is contestable. It very possibly derives from an image which was found in 1898 to be acceptable 'overseas', and thus to attract immigrants and investment, but which was never seriously examined.

The other part of the perception, that New Zealand was particularly impoverished culturally, probably goes back further than William Pember Reeves. De Tocqueville authoritatively established in *Democracy in America* (1835) that the 'new' world was more egalitarian, but less cultured than the old. This is another idea which has transcended the status of opinion and become established as fact, and New Zealand as a 'new' country was automatically included in it. Samuel Butler noted that New Zealand was an egalitarian society, but not one in which to talk about Bach or the pre-Raphaelites. (Is there a country where most people talk about Bach?)

But after 1945, the cultural deprivation of New Zealanders appeared to increase or to become more noticeable, as the early pages of *Landfall* show. If we follow Richard White's suggestion, and ask not whether this idea about national identity is true or false, but what its uses are, we can see that it served a particular function in relation to post-war Britain.

After 1945, Britain was undergoing the simultaneous traumas of post-war recovery and Imperial decline. Political centrality was noticeably passing to the United States. The outflow of skilled and professional talent outnumbered an influx of largely unskilled labourers. Protestations of philistinism from Australasians (and Australian literati were as vociferous as New Zealanders in condemning the shallow materialism of their society) served to re-assure Britain that she was both cultured and central despite the loss of political power. Barry Humphries was the first to move to Britain and make a living out of the concept of Australian philistinism.

As long as countries like New Zealand considered themselves provincial and acknowledged Britain as a cultural centre, Britain retained the power to influence the way 'provinces' defined themselves. The power produced the definition, which in turn re-inforced the power, and so on. And on the home front, the equation between prosperity and philistinism colluded with the New Zealand government's concern that higher living standards were maintained only by borrowing from overseas. It would reduce the national debt if New Zealanders could be persuaded to prefer cultural riches to material comfort.

Owls Do Cry plays its part in re-inforcing the proposition that material prosperity and cultural deprivation are general. A significant part of the novel is devoted to attacking the values described by Pearson and Chapman, through a satirical account of Chicks and her middle-class pretensions.

Chicks has all the vices attributed to the New Zealand bourgeoisie in the 1950s: Swedish made furniture, an electric cake-mixer, ambition for her children coupled with shame for her 'odd' brother and sister, and time set aside each day for spiritual and cultural pursuits because these are expected of her. And of course she knows deep down that all of this in inauthentic. 'What if I have no inner life?'

The satire on Chicks links inauthentic living with materialism, a connection unquestioned by the literati of the 50s.

But the portrayal of Bob and Amy suggests that Janet Frame's memories did not conform with the complementary proposition: that if prosperity means inauthenticity, authentic living must derive from poverty. Their problem is not too much materialism but too little. They are deadened by constant toil. Bob 'seemed to get angrier every day, and more frightened and the bills kept coming in one on top of the other.' Amy is withered and old, worn out by a life of work and looking after other people. The 'fixed expression of agreement and comfort and faith that had settled about her mouth (was) belied by the fear and loneliness that flowed round and round, at times, in capture, within her faded blue eyes.'

Amy recalls that when she was in service her employers had a party on her evening off, and having nowhere else to go she came back to the house and looked through a window where the blind had not been pulled right down. 'She could see their hands and the cards, but mostly the big drawing room table with the red velvet cover, thick, like a carpet laid out for a queen, and rich, like a dark rose.' Years later, Amy 'cannot help seeing over and over again the red velvet tablecloth that was her share of the party.'

This perspective on materialism condemns it not for its inauthenticity but for its exclusiveness: Amy did not have a fair share of the party, and her 'fear and loneliness' cannot be caused by her going in the wrong (materialist) direction because she could not afford to. There is no irony in the description of the red velvet tablecloth, no mockery of bourgeois aspirations to finery. It is an image of warmth which Amy needs: in her mind, 'the tablecloth grows bigger and falls upon her bed, and covers her like a blanket and she sleeps.'

In 1954, Janet Frame's memories of poverty were close and her experience of bourgeois materialism limited. A passage in *An Angel at My Table* suggests the influence of Frank Sargeson in her perceptions of the latter.

'I worshipped him and was in awe of him and with my now ingrained fear of authority or those "in charge", I felt in need of his approval . . . He informed me in a tone which said that working class was "good" that I was working class. And once again he described my sister and her husband, with whom I spent most weekends, as bourgeois and once again I marvelled at the use of terms that seemed archaic.'

Janet Frame also recalls Sargeson making it clear that the memory of an over-worked mother was not a valid visionary experience. 'So what?' he apparently asked when she told him her mother had died that morning although later she overheard him being more sympathetic about it.

This is not to say that Sargeson in 1954 shaped perceptions that could be thrown off later. The latest novel, *The Carpathians,* shows no softening towards those who suffer from indiscretions of taste and inauthenticities of living. Janet Frame clearly believes that the false god of consumerism diverts attention from the true treasure.

But the way Bob and Amy are portrayed, and her recollection of Sargeson's attitude to the working and bourgeois classes, are indications that in 1954 she had to adjust memories which associated poverty with inauthentic living, to conform with the more generally accepted view that materialism was the greater enemy. The accepted view wins: Amy fades from the text and through concentration on Chicks, bourgeois attitudes, not poverty, are foregrounded as the cause of inauthentic living.

A result of this tension between private memory and public perception is that authentic living is almost unimaginable—except for the professional artist. [In his essay "Janet Frame: No Cowslip's Bell in Waimaru,"] Lawrence Jones sees it as a flaw in the novel that Janet Frame denies to her characters the freedom through art that she herself found. But if neither poverty nor wealth provide access to the freedom of art, the only way in is to make a full time job of living by the imagination. Janet Frame managed to do that, but having decided that Daphne is not to be released from hospital as an acknowledged artist, there is no hope for her.

Pearson and Chapman both emphasised the 'otherness' of the New Zealand artist. Chapman wrote, 'writers are on the outside, like men clinging to a net which encloses a balloon, unable to live in the gas-filled interior, but in a fine though precarious position to see where the balloon is going and to tell from the whiffs of escaping gas how things are in the interior.'

Writers are on the outside: the rest of us are in the gas-filled interior. In the light of this view of New Zealand society, it is logical that Janet Frame should deny her characters the freedom through art that she herself found. You either get to be a writer, or you might as well give up. ***The Carpathians*** suggests a view of New Zealand basically unaltered: as Patrick Evans notes, [in a review entitled "Alien Land," in *The Listener,* September 24, 1988,] 'By implication Dinny Wheatstone has got it right through the simple act of being a writer, imposter or otherwise.'

The views about New Zealand society held by the literati in the 50s were stultifying. They were contestable at the time, although uncontested, and they confined the writer to a role of perpetually sounding the trumpet of insight (Chapman's metaphor) or trying to awaken the fretful sleepers (Pearson's), increasingly remote from the everyday lives and aspirations of ordinary people. Janet Frame knew more about these in 1954 than her fellow literati. Amy is not entirely obliterated from ***Owls Do Cry,*** and nor is the image of a red velvet tablecloth that was her share of the party.

Elizabeth Alley (interview date June 1991)

SOURCE: "'An Honest Record': An Interview with Janet Frame," in *Landfall,* Vol. 45, No. 2, June, 1991, pp. 154-68.

[*In the interview with Alley below, Frame discusses her thoughts on the genres of autobiography and fiction as well as on the act of writing.*]

What follows is made out of two separate interviews recorded for Radio New Zealand by Elizabeth Alley and broadcast on the Concert Programme. The first was recorded at Wanganui in April 1983. The second was recorded in 1988 when Elizabeth Alley visited Janet Frame at her home, this time near the small North Island town of Shannon, in a valley of rich grasslands fringed by the jagged range of the Tararuas. This is the mountain range that became the Carpathians of her eleventh novel, and her first long fiction since she completed the three volumes of autobiography.

Janet Frame does not enjoy interviews. Nevertheless, at Wanganui and five years later in her Shannon farmhouse with its Rhode Island red chickens, some geese and assorted animals who visit from the neighbouring farm, she submitted with much grace but some discomfort to conversations about her writing. The writer for whom the written word is an instrument of magic, for whom language is in its widest sense 'the hawk suspended above eternity', finds the spoken word, the expression of ideas about herself or her writing, can be undertaken only with effort and cost to her work. 'It's the writing that's important', she says. 'Not the talking about it.' . . .

[*Alley:*] *In the autobiography you seem more willing than in the fiction to open some of the doors about yourself and your life—to correct some of the myths that surround you.*

[Frame:] I wanted to write my story, and you're right of course, it is possible to correct some things which have been taken as fact and are not fact. My fiction is genuinely fiction. And I do invent things. Even in ***The Lagoon*** which has many childhood stories, the children are invented and the episodes are invented, but they are mixed up so much with part of my early childhood. But they're not quite, they're not the *true,* stories. ***To the Is-Land*** was the first time I'd written the true story. For instance, ***Faces in the Water*** was autobiographical in the sense that everything happened, but the central character was invented.

But with the autobiography it was the desire really to make myself a first person. For many years I was a third person—as children are. 'They', 'she' . . . and as probably the oppressed minority has become, 'they'. I mean children are forever 'they' until they grow up.

For a long time you really were quite reluctant to discuss anything that had to do with the genesis or meaning of your work.

Well I *write,* you see. I don't tell about my life. I just write and that is my telling, but in order to set down a few facts and tell my story, *this* is my say.

Tell me about your title, **To the Is-Land.** *Is this something to do with your feeling about the truth of words. And the way that you always prefer to take the very literal meaning of words.*

Yes, and it arose from my meeting with the word 'Is-Land', in an early story I was reading, one of those Whitcombes stories, and my refusal to accept that it was Island, that it really wasn't Is-Land. Of course, looking at it now I chose the title ***To the Is-Land*** for obvious reasons, because of the obvious double/triple meanings. I assumed that words meant what they said, and everyone about me seemed to assume that they did. It was just a gradual process of learning the depths of words, I suppose.

Words were always revered in your house though, weren't they? As 'instruments of magic' I think you described them.

Certainly, I think so. I was thinking of that knowing I was coming here to be interviewed by you. I was having a cup of tea at that little place next door and I took out the bus timetable to read. And I remembered that everyone at home always had something to read.

When did you first discover you could make words work for you?

Oh I've never discovered that . . . I'm still working at that . . .

But it was a conscious search in your life, wasn't it, to make the power of words into . . .

Well yes, as I was writing the autobiography, much was revealed to me about my growth that I hadn't realised. You've referred to my description of words in our family as 'instruments of magic'. Spoken words, in childhood, arrive from 'on high'—as high as the sky—you can't reach out to grasp them and play with them; they travel from room to room and in a magical way come in from outside the house. They can be anything—bombshells, globules of honey or small utilitarian hinges, hooks. . . . You can see how words might become a most desirable property.

Also, in our family the spoken words were far from ordinary—my father's recitation of the places he passed on his daily train journeys; and my mother's reciting of poetry.

Did you perceive this as something missing?

Yes, simply again, no one had told me I had imagination. I think I probably did have. I wasn't even aware of it, but it was something that was valued and I wanted it. It was really in a way like a material possession because I saw that anyone who did have imagination—I wasn't looking outside into the world of New Zealand and its writers because I didn't know about them, —but I perceived that anyone who did have imagination was revered. It was something to be treasured, and anyone at school who had imagination was always spoken of with awe.

I wonder how much the material deprivation that you were exposed to in your childhood caused this search for the imagination. Did you feel that there was something extra that you wanted to look for?

I don't think so; very slightly, I think it was the excitement and importance of the poetry, reading and words, and when I began to write poetry I enjoyed it very much.

Somebody once wrote of you that your art was—I think he called it 'born from a predicament'. Do you think that a different kind of writer would have emerged from a different kind of environment, or is it something that was going to be there regardless of the kind of circumstances in which you lived?

I don't for one thing know what kind of a writer I'm supposed to be. For myself, I think it was inevitable, whether I was materially deprived or not, that I should try to write. Simply because it was part of my background.

Thinking about this aspect of imagination still, do you think the fact that you've chosen to lead a fairly solitary life—that you need that to be able to continue with your writing—means that you need to draw on a more heightened sense of imagination than if you were leading a life full of experiences and activity and crowded with people all the time.

Well, I think a writer needs to lead a solitary life. When I say

that, you have to be in isolation to do your work. After you've done your work, well that's another matter. The work is the response.

*You talk in **To the Is-Land** about the arrival of literature in your life. You describe it as 'the other world's arrival into you world. The literature streaming through it like an array of beautiful ribbons through the branches of a green growing tree'. What precipitated that?*

Well, it was my discovery of poetry and prose. My mother always recited poetry. But then I discovered it for myself, reading for myself, and the discovery was mostly through school books of course. We had a shelf of books, there was *The Last Days of Pompeii, John Halifax Gentleman,* a book which we called God's Book because it was full of swirling Blake-like pictures of heaven and hell. And the dictionary, packed tight with words. And the Bible which in my early years, the Wyndham days, had a special place. Every Sunday (and often on other days) Mother who was a devout Christadelphian insisted we read from the Bible, and when she (who knew many of the passages by heart) began to read I was convinced she had been there, and that impression remained. Her clam belief that Jesus Christ was 'among us', her reminders that any person could be an angel or even Christ in disguise made daily life extraordinary and exciting.

Later, when we lived in Oamaru, the influence of religion diminished, for me, and was replaced, possibly, by the influence of words. I had an abiding memory of Bible-reading days, of the red-letter Bible which I used to pore over, trying to see significance in the lines in red print—'And seeing the multitudes he went up on to the mountain'—certainly that was red print material, but other lines were a mere group of and, went, saw, and verily . . .

*In some of your earlier novels I suppose what the critics call the dark side, the pain prevails. But in **To the Is-Land** it's the joy and humour and the fun that is prevalent. And really, humour and satire have always been very important to you, haven't they?*

In **To the Is-Land** I wrote the story of my life. My story, and this is me which comes out. There is pain, things happen, but whatever comes out is ordinary me without fiction or characters.

How do you react to the critics who so often talk about that dark vision, that's too narrow to share?

Well, a novelist is subjected in reviews to the blurring of the fine distinction between the writer's work and the writer's life. Extreme views based on the content of a book might even pass judgement on what is assumed to be the outlook of the writer herself. In a sense this is agreeable, proving the successful reality of the book. For example, reviewers of ***The***

Adaptable Man referred to my desire to live in another age, the age of St Cuthbert. And also spoke of my interest in gardening and my knowledge of plants.

Which is not true, is it?

Well, I'm interested—I'm not *passionately* interested in gardening, I'm interested in everything—but I'm not a gardener. And there was a character who was a gardener, an intense gardener. When I visited the United States, someone in California took me round Santa Barbara Botanical Gardens and pointed out every plant. Others talk of my pessimistic outlook on life, and my habit of bringing disaster to the characters, this was in *The Adaptable Man*—referring to the close of *The Adaptable Man* where one character is left almost totally paralysed, able to view life only through a mirror.

The critical references to me and my supposed personal views, I think they're simply a failure of the art of literary criticism. Well, they're an impurity of response which I suppose is natural, but who said literary criticism should be natural? The critic reminds me of the film *The Fly*, where the scientist, immersed in his experiment, doesn't realise that a fly has accompanied him to the cabinet. When he emerges, his work finished, he's part-man, part-housefly. I mean the critic has the sort of little impurity, but the writer works within the limitations or framework of her personality although the outlook and the view over the territory of time and space and human endeavour is endless. But writing also is a kind of job. You ask about the dark side, well, if I'm a plumber and I find there is a certain amount of work to be done in a certain street, exclusively with, say, the pressure of the household water supply, then you can't assume that I'm not qualified also to fix your sewer or install a shower, or a swimming pool.

If, as a writer I happen to work in a street where a few disasters occur, this is no foundation for the belief that I'm interested only in disasters. Similarly, if I write of a dark side, it doesn't mean that I'm not interested also in the whole view. You must be.

What about those critics who say that 'the range of emotional experience of your characters is limited.' Is the full emotional range of experience something that you're not really all that interested in expressing amongst your characters, or do you feel in fact that it is expressed adequately?

Well, I wouldn't say that I have successfully expressed many things. I'm still trying, but I wouldn't exclude any experience, any human experience from a book. Sometimes I think what is called the dark vision isn't necessarily so; I'm an optimist. For instance, this man who is totally paralysed in *The Adaptable Man* and views life through a mirror, I think that's a triumph. It sounds a bit twisted perhaps, but it is a triumph. There *are* people who survive. It's a triumph of survival.

How do you see the characters in your fiction. Are you quite objective about them? Is there a quality of detachment, or do you get quite involved with them?

I'm interested in watching how they develop and how they feel and so on.

Because if we can look at another character, in **Living in the Maniototo,** *Mavis says 'the writer knows that his want should fill the world, that to write you have to be at a terrible point of loss and stay there wanting to write, wanting in not out—certainly it's a rat and mouse life.' Now accepting the fact that you say your characters' opinions are not necessarily your own, it would still seem that that could be quite perilously close to your own experiences.*

I would think that—the bit about the rat and mouse life, that's obviously not too well written that bit, but the bit about the point of loss. I think that's good. I think that is right, correct. I think that is important because so many people want to write and just don't have that point of loss. Really, if you want to write you have to be desperate to write. It's no use just spending your life saying I've always wanted to write a book. Still, I know there are circumstances which prevent . . . there are 'mute inglorious Miltons', I think they do happen.

Someone once suggested that you were your own best character. But from what you're saying, you'd totally refute that I would think?

I think so, obviously I am writing the book, so . . . it's all in me. But not necessarily so because there are some surprising, I mean, factual characters about. Even if one didn't invent any. For instance I chose to come on the bus this morning, rather than a taxi, because I like to watch the people on the bus and hear the conversation and it was much more rewarding time spent than if I had got in a taxi and whizzed in to the studio and arrived with nothing sticking to the surface. Whereas when I did arrive, I had all these little events that had happened in the half hour/20 minutes on the bus.

I don't mean I will sit down and write about them. They are there, you see, and they will emerge when the time is ripe and fit into the pattern of things.

Fitting into the pattern of things is quite important for you, isn't it? A lot of your characters seem to be quite concerned with fitting in.

That's quite interesting. I don't mean fitting into the patterns of affairs, but the whole of writing is expressing an emerging pattern and shape. And the satisfaction of when the shape is concluded, although there is the frustration of knowing it may not be quite right, or something is amiss. It's something that emerges and this is for me the real joy of writing. I mean it's not publication or anything else, it's just as one is writing a pattern grows and everything seems to fall into place—very exciting, *very* exciting just to see it. If it's a novel I see it happen. When I say 'see' I sort of perceive it, I can see it from beginning to end and it's there. And so it's the seeing it and seeing it's there which is the motivation to write it. You sort of live through it, it's like playing a record player, I don't mean the sound or anything, but it's like playing a record player and speeding it up like that and it's there. Of course, you have to go through the awful task of sitting down and plodding, plodding, till you get to the end. With your life sustained by the, I suppose you would call it, 'the vision'.

What are the sparks that feed that imagination that are important to you?

It's everything that surrounds me. The thing which prompts you to sit down and write must be something which haunts you. You would savour it even without knowing, then it comes to mind, it comes to mind again, and you look at it and—I would give the example of again *The Adaptable Man*. I wrote that as a result of a visit to the dentist in London. He was very vague. He went to the window and he looked out and there was a patch of blue in the sky. He said 'what wouldn't I give to be in Sussex.' Then he said 'rinse whilst I'm gone.' And I hadn't heard anyone say 'whilst' and it was that word that prompted me to write the whole book. I mean, the book was about a clergyman, and I did put a dentist in, I think. But I never saw that dentist again. It wasn't an invented dentist, but it was the *word*.

So, were you 'haunted' in the same way when it came to writing the autobiography? It must have been rewarding to be able to leave the invention of fiction for a while, for the truth of autobiography?

I was anxious to finish it so I could get on with the novel [*The Carpathians*]. Again I wanted to have my say about my life because I have been rather disconcerted by some details which have been incorrect. I can't escape from this desire to shape. The fact of writing it, and expecting people to read it, is rather an arrogance.

I recall that you once talked about your novels as being explorations and this was really how you liked them to be seen.

Well, I said that because I don't (and it looks as if I'm justified in saying this) think that I'm very successful at creating characters, and my novels are explorations in the sense that I talked about the pattern; it is seeing what pattern emerges. I might have a view of the whole novel, everything that happens, but in the actual writing it's like an exploration. Again, this is for me the enjoyment. It's just the ideas which come. Sometimes they're quite frightening because I know I won't be able to put them down, just because of my lack of skill, you know. One always hopes for improvement.

Were there any problems turning back to fiction after writing the autobiographies? You don't make very strong distinctions between the genres of fiction and autobiography.

Well, I am always in fictional mode, and autobiography is found fiction. I look at everything from the point of view of fiction, and so it wasn't a change to be writing autobiography except the autobiography was more restrictive because it was based in fact, and I wanted to make an honest record of my life. But I was still bound by the choice of words and the shaping of the book, and that is similar to when one is writing fiction. I think that in writing there's no feeling of returning to or leaving a definite form, it's all in the same country, and within view of one's imaginative home so to speak, or in the same town. They are different and each has its own interest.

I wondered if writing your own story, having your own say, as you said at the time, helped to clarify the way people behave. By writing about real people as you did in your autobiography, did that help you to find and to manage the characters of your fiction, in that qualities of their characters and personalities had become clearer to you?

Well, the writing of the autobiography clarified for me things about my own life, and about the people I grew up with. But strangely enough I have always felt I have insight into how people operate, and saying this rather startles, even alarms me. Because I always feel people are so transparent in their behaviour. I suppose the fact is that to be interested in writing novels, you have to have a passion for reading people and their behaviour, and their lives. You are sort of an everlasting observer, and it's not really a conscious decision. From as far back as I can remember, I have spent my time watching and listening, and wondering about what I watched and listened to. It seems a natural way of life. I do acknowledge though, that my insights aren't always accurate. It is just that I have grown so used to watching people and reading people, and reading faces and hearing what people say, and reading their natures; people who write do operate in this way.

I remember an occasion when I was at Yaddo in New York and we used to dine together, at dinner and breakfast. I think it was at dinner, we were all sitting round and there were some very brilliant writers sitting there, and I looked around and I could see everyone was talking, and I could see their faces were absolutely full of knowing what others almost were thinking, and someone made a remark, an observation, and there was a rather shy young novelist, a very good novelist, sitting opposite me. I could see absolutely everything she was feeling just at that moment. But the point is she glanced at me and she could see everything I was feeling. There was a sensitivity; you don't do it consciously, but when you're writing you remember all these things that come to you and you choose what you want to choose.

Have you got a retentive memory for holding that sort of material?

I think so, yes.

So you don't have to write down the store of memories from the past? They just come back naturally in the process of writing?

No, I don't need to write these things down. I have often been rather alarmed that I don't keep notebooks because I always wanted to be a writer, and the ideal writer keeps note-books. Virginia Woolf kept notebooks and she was my hero-ine for a long time. She still is, and Katherine Mansfield kept her diary, her notebooks. But I, since I have been grown up I haven't kept a notebook, but I do write titles of stories, I am always looking, seeing stories, and someday I will write them all down.

Did **The Carpathians** *start that way; did it just start as a title?*

Well, it started as a title, 'Housekeepers of Ancient Spring-time,' which I felt was too much for a title. It became **The Carpathians** as I was writing it. You know, when I was writ-ing it I felt as if I were in a whirlpool, and after I'd written it I wanted those reading it, I felt those reading it, to be sort of within this whirlpool, the whole world with everything bro-ken by the gravity star, but not lost. Everything was to be renewed, rebuilt, selves, thought, language, everything. It was a death but only in the sense that death is a horizon to be travelled beyond, it wasn't hopeless.

You see in the first part of the book Mattina is collecting detail, and her object is to sort of perfect her love, and the second part of the book is where she carries all this detail away, sort of everything reaches this horizon and is sort of broken into pieces like a whirlpool, her identity; she has be-come two-dimensional and three-dimensional, she even has these experiences which are repeated in a kind of so-called novella (the 'imposter' novel), and so she finds herself slid-ing along on, probably going down into, the whirlpool. But there's this sense of unease, I did feel it when I re-read it, I felt this particularly at one point. I felt what on earth's hap-pened, everything's gone, it's like a death, but it's not a death, it's not really gloomy.

There is a wonderful twist at the end of the book, when the structure is revealed, when that enigmatic note from the per-son who signs himself JHB in the frontispiece is revealed. Can you tell me a little about how you arrived at that struc-ture?

It is part of the whirlpool. But I had a basis in real life for the characters. That has been changed of course, and mixed with, on a palette, you know, with other things.

The last part of the book written from New York reads quite differently from the rest of the book.

Yes, well the first book was a collection, Mattina's collection of detail and what happened to her there. Perhaps in a sense I didn't build up enough of her relationship with her husband to make it so desperately important that she sort of achieved this perfect love. I was not directly concerned with my own memories in any part of that. Mattina's memories of New York are not my memories of New York. But obviously they are chosen from a selection of observations that I made, but I didn't have the experiences that Mattina had in New York. I just had to invent her memories, I haven't written of my own memories of New York, and as for returning to New Zealand, I have different memories of returning to New Zealand be-cause I belong here.

Does the way you use memory change at all?

I think so, I use less of my own memories than I did. I wrote the first volume of my autobiography for many reasons, one reason was that I wanted to get rid of the memories of the past up to a certain stage, to the time I was 40. Then I was really freeing myself from memories.

The Gravity Star really exists, doesn't it?

Yes. I wrote about it in the front in the note. The quote is from *The Dominion:* 'A survey of distances to galaxies has revealed something that at first could have seemed implau-sible—a galaxy that appears both relatively close and seven billion light years away'. If that is true (whatever truth is), if one accepts that, then one sort of accepts total impossibilities unreasoned, yet one remains as one is. Well, it's a possibility of something new really.

Did the book grow out of that report?

Yes. That and the idea of The Housekeepers of Ancient Springtime. 'Housekeepers' is my word, but I was reading a poem of Rilke's, 'The Orchard', and he wrote of ancient spring-time. Puamahara of course is not Levin, but I drew on the locality of Levin and the orchards that are out of town just before you reach the Tararuas, the Carpathians. And the coming of the blossom each year, and so on, and the memory flower I invented.

I was fascinated by the way you've used Mattina as the wealthy New Yorker coming to look at small town New Zealand life. And that by bringing her in as an outsider, you really al-lowed us, the readers, to see this through her eyes. It was a total standing-off, an objective way of looking at things.

Well you see, the technique of the stranger's point of view is an old tried technique going way back to fairy tales. The stranger comes in and sees the view, it had been much used in all literature, especially in our literature which is full of journeys. Writing of Mattina and her view, or what I imagine her view to be, I would have betrayed my faith in the process of writing if I'd really given my own view of life in a small town. I wrote what I imagined her view might be. I stress this because novelists are always confronted by a reading public that supposes all views are the writer's views. I meet this constantly with critics who ought to know better, but who suppose that the character's thoughts are my thoughts but in reality of course they are the thoughts of the character.

Imagined thoughts.

Yes.

But is there still a certain amount of interaction between you and the characters before they find their place in the story?

Depending on one's skill. One is full of faults in the writing. Depending on one's skill, one tries to imagine a character who has her own life, her own thoughts and feelings. Naturally, I draw from what I've seen and observed and people I have seen, but it's always a mixture.

You say that your characters don't express your views, but do your characters sometimes say what you would like to say?

Oh, yes. They sometimes do when, after they have spoken, I realise, well I wish, I might like to think that. Fictional characters of course are a mixture of what I have observed and what I've imagined. But often, like other writers, I use characters to exploit the tricks of the trade—novels that feature novelists writing novels, but they are becoming a bit of a bore. Unless there's an urgency in what is being written. I do have a great interest in the actual writing of a novel, in the technique and possibilities, but there are many many ways of doing it. I have allowed myself the fun of putting novelists in because they have so much to say, and of course they can take all points of view, but I do realise that's not the only way to write a novel.

You've mentioned the interior novel, the story within the novel which you call the imposter novel. Is there a sense in which you see the novelist as an imposter?

No, I don't think so, except that the imposter Dinny Wheatstone—her type of imposter demolishes herself and leaves her free to absorb any character which comes along—in *that* sense, the writer is an imposter.

The imposter novelist Dinny Wheatstone says at one stage in her part of the story, 'I have seized control of all points of view'.

Yes, well that happens to a novelist, a novelist must seize control of all points of view.

'And the words take charge of the telling', she goes on to say.

I feel that words take charge of the telling, refers to the delinquencies of language, or rather, the delinquent use we make of language. I refer there to ordinary everyday life, how often it's not that the words are failing us but we fail them. And the extreme words can play executioner. Even the smallest words because they can persuade us, the use of them can persuade us into action that we might not have taken.

And does that apply too to the structure of the story, that you can find that the use of a certain word indicates a path that the story might now take?

Yes, or one tries if one is standing back and writing a novel to take control over the words and not let the words, one has to be watching them, always watching them in case they either escape or in case they go in the wrong direction. You have to have, I think, a writer has to have control over them. But there is a lot of reference here to words in everyday life.

But then language has always been as important as that to you, hasn't it?

Yes, there is so much about language and about a lack of language that I wonder if the answer is music.

Do you ever find that words have taken their own momentum, I mean you talk about needing to have control, but are there ever times when you decide to go on impulse and see what happens?

I think when I'm writing and I write the first version, I don't like to be held back by any wondering about what things are. I just go ahead and get it down, whatever the words are, they are there, but in the second version I find words that have intruded. The imagination however is free to go on, it is always free to, as I'm in the country I'll say, graze. As I said before, I think it is essential to be in control of the writing because the words are the instrument, I mean you are playing a musical instrument, you must be in control of it. There is a comparison with music. In writing the hope is always that the imagination will come home to rest in invisible places. The bee comes home and leaves on each word traces of honey that we've never had before, that sort of thing.

I remember you saying it was Frank Sargeson who gave you advice about using language and peeling down to the dead wood, peeling off the dead wood.

Yes, well it was Frank Sargeson who used the phrase 'dead wood' when he was talking to me about writing a novel. I quote him, he said 'a certain amount of dead wood is necessary', he said it like that you see. But I've never agreed with this. A work of writing must be wholly alive and essential, yet if one pursues a metaphor of the dead wood, one can become convinced that dead wood is necessary and simply be persuaded by a metaphor.

I think that's extraordinary. I thought about that, and I thought, well, dead wood is necessary in trees and so on, and I almost became convinced it was necessary in novels and again that is an example of the way the use of words can control actually our thoughts and our actions. But it made me think since then, I disagreed heartily with him when he said you need a certain amount of dead wood. Possibly because that was the only time I had shown him a story, I showed him a story called **'An Electric Blanket'**. He didn't think much of it, you know. I really think poems are the highest form of literature because you can have no dead wood in a poem. I am not really quite sure what he meant, but when he spoke of it, he said in a novel dead wood is necessary. I had this image of just a hunk of dead wood.

You have asked me before, you know, if writing ever becomes easier. Well, each time it's different, but I always feel that the process of writing is like a reward for my having overcome the many obstacles to writing. I am sure each writer has different obstacles, but you see there are so many before one writes, one has the theme in view and there are distractions and so on. When I had the Sargeson Fellowship, not having to housekeep and so on, I was able just to write out what had been in my mind for some time but hadn't been able to be plucked because of the obstacles. Not only obstacles outside but I make obstacles for myself, of course. You have to have courage to write and I get very scared of what I see the book is going to be about, and I am frightened to face it. So it is rather good for me to be in that position of capture where I've got no excuses.

I would like to come back to this question of the characters of **The Carpathians** *again for a minute. The position of the characters in the novel reminded me of a painting to a certain extent, and the way that characters are placed in a painting. There is this sort of visual sense of the placement of the characters and how they will move.*

Yes, at the preliminary, they are being reduced to destruction, they're being reduced to two dimensions. It quite scared me you know, that.

And did you get over that?

Well I found it very chilling, but I was quite surprised that it had its effect on me. Normally when I write a book, there's usually only, say, I'm lucky if there is one sentence or one paragraph or one short scene that moves me. I read the book and I feel it, but I can usually concentrate on one sentence which I think well, yes, that's alright. But here it wasn't the book, it wasn't what was in the book itself but what sort of surrounded it, like the jagged peak of the paintings of the Tararuas, which I remembered, which I felt after I read it.

You've used surreal elements in your work for a long time, haven't you, and **The Carpathians** *reinforces this theme very strongly. Is surrealism becoming a stronger interest now?*

Well, perhaps it is. I would define it as what is beyond the real, the invisible beyond the real. But I don't really think that that is surrealism. That's my notion of it. It becomes like staring at an x-ray of the real and visible. That's what I'm interested in.

A way of taking the reader into more richly imagined experience?

Possibly yes, yes finding more, as you said, more than meets the eye. I am interested in the crossing of incidents and so on.

Are you saying, do you think, that we basically lack imagination, and that we should all really learn to look much more beneath the surface?

I do feel that while not lacking in imagination we sometimes recoil from using it, or we are denied the opportunity. I think as I said before the proper use of imagination is a form of courage, daring to explore beyond horizons.

And how far does the writer dare? How far can you push that dislocation from reality? Is the writer bound by limits of readers' expectations?

Possibly, but I wouldn't think so. I wouldn't feel bound. I am glad you mentioned readers, because you see readers are so important; if one is going to be published, the reader reads the work. It is a kind of courtesy to readers that I don't think I always indulge in. I just write for myself and in that I possibly agree with some of the critics.

I do my best. It is just the best of my ability and I fail in some ways, and succeed in others. It is the best I can do.

Nancy Potter (essay date 1991)

SOURCE: "Janet Frame," in *International Literature in English: Essays on the Major Writers,* edited by Robert L. Ross, Garland Publishing, 1991, pp. 547-56.

[*Potter is an American educator and short story writer who has lived in New Zealand. In the essay below, she provides a brief synopsis of each of Frame's major works and discusses the literary climate of the eras in which they were published.*]

Janet Frame has characterized the New Zealand society of her youth as a house with neither basement nor attic. This metaphor illuminates only one aspect of her complicated background. More substantial details of Frame's life are treated impressionistically in her three-volume autobiography, particularly the enduring poverty of the Depression, tragic accidents, and a series of misfortunes that haunted her early years.

She was born in Dunedin, in 1924, and grew up in Oamaru, the child of an itinerant railway engineer father and a mother who yearned to be a writer. Of the five children, the one son was early diagnosed as epileptic, and two of the four daughters drowned in coincidentally similar accidents ten years apart. Janet Frame left the University of Otago for a brief teaching career but spent eight years of her early adulthood in mental hospitals, under the mistaken diagnosis of schizophrenia. She endured a series of electric shock treatments and narrowly escaped a lobotomy. Suffering isolation and insecurity, she found comfort in close reading of writers from Shakespeare to Rilke and Virginia Woolf.

After leaving the hospital, she was befriended by the short story writer Frank Sargeson, and her fortunes and confidence began to improve. Although she has lived abroad for periods of time in England, France, and the United States, she has always returned to New Zealand, settling in various towns before resuming her travels. She held the Robert Burns Fellowship at the University of Otago in 1965, the Winn-Menton Scholarship in 1974, and has been a fellow of Yaddo and the MacDowell Colony. She was awarded the 1989 Commonwealth Writers Prize for *The Carpathians.* In 1973, she changed her surname to Clutha, the name of the river that flows south of Oamaru, but she continues to be published as Janet Frame. Since Frame has given almost no lectures and few interviews, her reflections on her work and the influences of reading, childhood, education, family life, and travel are best derived from her three volume autobiography.

For Janet Frame writing has been not only vocation and art but a life- and mind-saving act as well. While not being linked conventionally, her works possess a remarkable organic unity; they retell similar stories with systematic variation in kaleidoscopic patterns. Her fiction continues to investigate ultimate questions: the nature of reality, art, sanity, memory, truth, life, and death.

Born nearly forty years after Katherine Mansfield, Frame began to publish following World War II. Her fictional world bears occasional resemblance to that of Iris Murdoch, Patrick White, Chistina Stead, and Elizabeth Jolley, and her language reveals that, like Lawrence Durrell, she is also a poet. Fundamentally skeptical of institutions and disdainful of the comfortably unexamined life, she creates fiction that extends the traditional limits of genre and form. The discoveries her characters make are not always easily transmitted to a public arena, nor do their discoveries make them happier or more loving human beings. They learn personal courage and inner wisdom by disregarding the world's deceptive order and unity.

Frame remains difficult to categorize as futuristic, experimental, fabulist, illusionist, or trickster. Her reader must practice patience and avoid reaching neat conclusions or rushing to parables. The reader, like some of the characters, may be initially struck by one symbol: a burning snowman, a nightmare garden, the town rubbish dump, a field of toy soldiers, or the legendary Memory Flower. But Frame and her various narrators prefer indirection and enjoy the possibilities of satire and irony. An example of this capacity for wit occurs in *Scented Gardens for the Blind.* Both the title and epigraph of this novel suggest a form of communication: that the sightless might experience their surroundings by smelling the flowers. The initial narrator Vera Glace tries to fulfill the possibility of her name by willing her silent daughter into lucidity and clear speech. But the daughter prefers to take her philosophic instruction from a congenial teacher named Uncle Black Beetle, who discourses from the windowsill on death and the futility of materialism. The reader is instructed (and warned) by a literary cousin of Uncle Black Beetle who dwells in the dictionary between the words *trichotomy* and *trick.*

In selecting names of characters and places and even titles, Frame often sets up one expectation and demolishes it with systematic brilliance. Some of the choices have enduring significance, as in the cases of the Withers, Livingston, and Rainbird families. Others tempt and tease, like Malfred Signal, Ciss Everest, Miss Float, Colin Monk, and Turnlung. Some choices invite association of Frame's story and intention with familiar myths. So it is with Daphne Withers, Thora Pattern, and Istina Mavet. From childhood, Frame read appreciatively from classic mythology through Shakespeare and the Brontës and Hardy; she mixes well-known tales with her characters' private discoveries, as they hold up not a mirror but a prism to experience. The grand sweep of legendary heroes has been reduced in the late twentieth century. Godfrey Rainbird, awakened from his coma and back at his job in the Dunedin Tourist Bureau (in *The Rainbirds*), envies the original Lazarus and thinks his grave could be merchandised as a minor attraction.

Frame employs all the fictional furniture—titles, names, language, climate, and seasons—to enlarge and intensify her theme. In *The Adaptable Man,* one of her most traditional works, she uses (and parodies) the traditional English novel. Later novels suggest more cosmopolitan influences. Although Frame can never be accused of being a conventional realist, she can describe arrestingly much twentieth-century malaise at the edges of her landscapes, from urban squalor to the threat of nuclear disaster. Since Frame has been an intelligent tourist or pilgrim throughout much of her life, the settings of her fiction convey the atmosphere of various places and the sense of dislocation. Many of the first stories of *The Lagoon* and *The Reservoir* are set in a childhood world, threatened by adulthood, a world that can be associated with some of the landscape and situations of Frame's own youth. Her first three novels reflect the disappointments in leaving childhood, in such a town as Waimaru, for the nightmares of mental hospitals like Cliffhaven, Treecroft, and Lawn Lodge, or for the ritual voyage "home" to England undertaken by Toby Withers, afflicted by the Overseas Dream, via the *S.S. Matua* to London.

As Frame has moved around the world, her settings have also: *Scented Gardens for the Blind* links England and New Zealand; *The Adaptable Man* is entirely rooted in the town of Little Burgelstatham deep in the Suffolk countryside; *A State of Siege* is set in the far north of New Zealand; *The Rainbirds* brings an English family to Dunedin. The dominant images of *Intensive Care* derive from the Great War; the action moves between a Recovery Unit in a converted English great house, Culin Hall, and the increasingly surreal Waipori City with its cement factory and slaughterhouse. More recently, Frame's settings have linked the United States and New Zealand. *Daughter Buffalo* moves from such Manhattan scenes as the Natural History Museum and the Central Park Zoo to a geriatric hospital in New Zealand. The protagonist of *Living in the Maniototo* never does visit the desolate Maniototo plains in Otago, but she lives intensely, if briefly, in three contrasting locations: Blenheim, an upscale new Auckland suburb; Baltimore, portrayed as Poe might have experienced it; and Berkeley, California, Blenheim's "sister city." The mountain range for which *The Carpathians* is named appears only during an incidental dream; that novel is set in New York City and on Kawai Street in the North Island town of Puamahara, where the lifelong New Yorker Mattina Brecon settles temporarily.

Of course, Frame is also a poet, and scattered throughout what might be classified as her prose are poetic passages from lyric songs to complex meditations. Centrally concerned as she is with communicating from inside the mind and imagination, she presents characters who inhabit those risky situations at the borders of language, as the title *The Edge of the Alphabet* suggests. Such characters live on this dangerous fringe as Daphne Withers in her "dead room" or the silent Erlene Glace or Decima James, the institutionalized autistic of *The Carpathians*. Even the artist Malfred Signal leaves her home to settle in a lonely storm-battered cottage and finally retreats into a miniature room in her mind. On the other hand, attempted communication can be disappointing; for example, Mattina Brecon, whose career has been spent in publishing, realizes the limits of language in the patter of the astronauts describing their moon walk.

Like many experimental novelists, Frame attempts to test not only the limits of language as communication but the validity of witness and memory. Toward that end, she presents various entertaining and distracting techniques and voices, such as notebook entries, dreams, fantasies, and letters. Tricks and coincidences abound in her work; the supposed dead emerge from coma or earthquake. Others die in bizarre circumstances, under a falling chandelier or in a swirl of household detergent, for example. Often the identity of the narrator is in question. The epilogue of *Daughter Buffalo,* a novel set

exclusively in America, reveals the real author as the geriatric Turnlung, who has never left New Zealand. It is not entirely certain who narrates *Living in the Maniototo*—Mavis Furness Barwell Halleton or her alter egos Alice Thumb, novelist, or Violet Pansy Produlock, ventriloquist. Similarly the conclusions of *Scented Gardens for the Blind* and *The Carpathians* cast doubt on the originally announced narrators.

The internalized and experimental language along with the complex and somewhat ambiguous themes of Frame's fiction may be better understood by considering closely her autobiography. After publishing ten novels and four books of short stories and poems and having reached her sixtieth year, she undertook to interpret her past in three volumes: *To the Is-land, An Angel at My Table,* and *The Envoy from Mirror City.* These three books treat her first forty years—1924 to 1963, that is, her childhood, educations, sickness, recovery, and first trip overseas. Without denying the final relativity of individual observation, the autobiography reveals the process of transforming intense personal experience into art. The first volume, in a chapter called "Imagination," describes Frame's struggle with "true personal history," its dates and years, either stretching out horizontally or arranged in neat vertical piles. She concludes that " . . . the memories do not arrange themselves to be observed and written about, they whirl, propelled by a force beneath, with different memories rising to the surface at different times and thus denying the existence of a 'pure' autobiography". The process of remembering, therefore, creates a sort of whirlpool, " . . . a dance of dust or sunbeams or bacteria".

Few readers had expected a neatly reconstructed chronicle of dates and facts. Several critics have suggested that Frame has reclaimed her own life through the autobiography into an interior mirror city, into which the reader may gaze. She has also provided a personal history of an international English writer from a transitional generation. The New Zealand writers in the generation immediately before hers included Frank Sargeson (1903-1982), Sylvia Ashton-Warner (1908-1984), and Robin Hyde (Iris Wilkinson) (1906-1939). These writers frequently described their struggles against provincialism, conformity, and cultural isolation. Frame is of the generation of the poet James K. Baxter—a generation that broke away from the provincial and was less traumatized by philistinism than disappointed by the failure to attain an ideal society in the Happy Islands.

For Frame it was necessary to measure her national literature (or its absence) in relation to that of the rest of the world. Appropriately, her autobiography is marked, or framed, by journeys: Volume One ends on the Sunday slow train to Dunedin; Volume Two leaves her on the deck of a passenger ship bound from Wellington on her first trip to England; at the end of Volume Three she is returning on another ship to New Zealand. The three volumes are in themselves messengers, intermediaries, between their events—death, disappointment, illness, and exile—and her interior life. As the title of Volume Three indicates, Frame has successfully set out on pilgrimages to Mirror City, an amalgam of those yearned-for, exotic, ever-larger cities from Dunedin to London to New York. She had become a citizen of these places; it was irresponsible to stare passively at them as a tourist: "What use is there in returning only with a mirrorful of me? . . . The self must be the container of the treasures of Mirror City, the Envoy as it were, and when the time comes to arrange and list those treasures for shaping into words, the self must be the worker, the bearer of the burden, the chooser, place and polisher" [*The Envoy from Mirror City*]. She concludes sternly that collecting images is travel writing, not worthy of fiction; her trips to the mirror cities have been apprenticeships in the politics of use. The creative self is an Orpheus or Envoy figure who has taken on some of the traits of Rilke's Angel, the presence invoked by the title of her second volume.

Interestingly, Frame seems less hostile to both environments (New Zealand and the various mirror cities) in her autobiography than in her fiction. She does emphasize consistently her isolation and her perception of the stigma of being poor, then different, and, finally, mentally ill: "It was best for me to escape from a country where, since my student days, a difference which was only myself, and even my ambition to write, had been looked on as evidence of abnormality." All three volumes provide a selection of sharp impressions of a Depression childhood as glimpsed from 56 Eden Street in Oamaru, a place that might have been under other circumstances "a kingdom by the sea." There was the usual mix of Saturday movie matiness and the growing discovery of real literature, balanced by the liabilities of rotting teeth and dirty clothes. The misery was probably more dense than in usual childhoods, although Frame seems to deny her singular experiences, at least originally. Speaking of one sister's death, she says, "Somehow Myrtle's death did not really 'qualify'; it was too much within me and a part of me, and I could not look at it and say *dreamily, poetically,* 'Ah, there's a tragedy. All poets have tragic lives.' My brother's illness did not 'qualify' either; it was too present." Many of the events in *To the Is-land* are described with more distance and cooler emotion than evident in their original appearance in fiction. For example, it is possible to compare the short story **"The Bull Calf"** with the episode as recounted in Chapter 23, "Scrapers and Bluey," of *To the Is-land*. Both describe a child's discovery that the family's bull calf has been castrated. In the autobiography Frame rather casually narrates the incident, concluding with the observation that she was infuriated by the adults' secretive attitude. The story concentrates on the maturation of its heroine, Olive, intensifies her sense of betrayal, and concludes with a tearful scene in which Olive begins to comprehend priorities or compromises in adult life.

Generally the mood of *To the Is-land* is remarkably cheerful, as if the disappointments and tragedies have been distanced. *Owls Do Cry* is a far more terrifying book. The four Withers children fear the complete collapse, not only of their house but of their entire world, as if they had been trapped inside a squirrel cage. The death of Francie Withers in the volcanic fury of the dump fire may be compared with the restrained account of Myrtle's drowning in the town baths. Some aspects of the real story, too coincidental or poignant for fiction—like Myrtle's disappearance from a family photograph, had been excised from *Owls Do Cry*; they were either too painful or too unrealistic for fiction. On the whole, the autobiography in its first volume emphasizes nostalgia, produced by the inevitable loss of innocence. The first chapter of *An Angel at My Table* describes how the future constructs itself over the past. "The future accumulates like a weight upon the past. The weight upon the earliest years is easier to remove to let that time spring up like grass that has been crushed."

> **The most unsettling discovery revealed in the autobiography was Frame learning in the winter of 1957 that she had never been a schizophrenic at all.**
>
> —*Nancy Potter*

From age 24 to 32 Janet Frame moved in and out of mental hospitals, and she has frequently drawn directly and indirectly upon this buried life for her fiction. In *Angel at My Table* she indicates that she put on a mask dissolved herself into a sense of doomed eternity and that, subsequently, in her fiction she deliberately understated the squalor and inhumanity of those years: " . . . were I to rewrite *Faces in the Water* I would include much that I omitted because I did not want a record by a former patient to appear to be over-dramatic." It is not an analytical explanation of her mental collapse that engages her; aside from the strains of poverty and the shock of loss when her sisters drowned, she refused to dwell on causes for her breakdown. Almost from childhood and adolescence she disappeared for about a decade, missing post-war affluence, labor strikes, McCarthyism, and the culture of the times, emerging into a strange world. "I knew only of Prospero, Caliban, King Lear, and Rilke, these for me, being occasions of the past decade." She suggests the difficulty of identifying herself, even in terms of the correct pronoun: "My previous community had been my family. In *To the Is-land,* I constantly use the first person plural—we, not I. My time as a student was an I-time. Now as a Seacliff patient, I was again part of a group. . . . I became 'she,' one of 'them'."

She adopted a classification provided by Frank Sargeson as a "sane, mad person." The autobiography suggests that she accepted this distinction as a protection. From her earliest marking as "so original" by a patronizing teacher, she assumed the "distorted privilege" of mental illness. By the time she reached the university, she was sitting in the Dunedin Public Library reading case histories of Van Gogh, Hugo Wolf, or Schumann and identifying with them. "My place was set, then, at the terrible feast. I had no illusions about 'greatness' but at least I could endow my work and—when necessary—my life with the mark of my schizophrenia." The really remarkable journey of this autobiography into self reclamation is expressed in the second and third volumes as she releases herself from that dubious distinction of such classification:

> Although I was still inclined to cherish the distorted "privilege" of having schizophrenia because it allied me with the great artists more readily than my attempts to produce works of art might have done, I suspected that my published writing might destroy that tenuous alliance, for I could not people, everlastingly, my novels with characters suffering from "the Ophelia syndrome" with details drawn from my observations in hospital. [*The Envoy from Mirror City*]

This identification with that gray and mysterious and private world set her apart. The circumstance qualified her for special consideration and distanced her sharply from her readers. It also provided additional problems in the writing of a candid autobiography. "The fact that, invariably, I was forced to go to such lengths to uncover my 'secret, true' self, to find the answers to questions that, had I the confidence and serenity of being myself 'in the world' could have been asked directly, was evidence to me of a certain unhealthy self-burial."

Her early life was constructed on compensatory strategies. At school she might have been awkward, badly dressed, obviously poor, and socially unacceptable, but she compensated by becoming the prizewinning pupil, the teacher's favorite, the obliging and uncomplaining good girl. In a sad bargain she gave up identity and resigned herself to an apparently lifelong residence in the hospital: "I had woven myself into a trap, remembering that a trap is also a refuge." Freed of the temptations or requirements of so-called "normal" society, she was free to cultivate an interior life seen by nightmare vision, which she repeatedly encapsulated in a literary figure as "the room two inches behind the eyes". This is an identical construction of Malfred Signal's refuge in *A State of Siege.* Even after her release from the hospital, Frame describes herself as maintaining the submissive role; she continues to deliver herself to various protectors. The autobiography allows her to name and describe her behavior: " . . . at its best it is the role of the queen bee surrounded by her attendants; at its worst it is that of a victim without power or possessions, and in both cases there is no ownership of one's self". In selecting a public role that was so circumscribed, she established social and perhaps literary limits. She finds it significant that she refused to explore the second story of a house in which she

lived on the Balearic Islands. She seems to have fled from demanding relationships while accepting the attentions of protectors whom she scorned. These episodes are awkwardly described; it is obviously difficult for a sixty-year-old writer to re-create her clumsy attempts of almost thirty years before to make up for a tragically lost decade.

But the most unsettling discovery revealed in the autobiography was her learning in the winter of 1957 that she had never been a schizophrenic at all. More sophisticated medical evaluation at Maudsley Hospital in London clarified that a tragic error in diagnosis had been made. She was both vindicated and confused; the revelation swept away excuses and explanation. The discovery was what she described as "the official plunder of my self-esteem". Painful as the discovery was, it attended the most intensely productive period of her life. She was able to announce her confirmation as an artist: "I can erase myself completely and live through the feelings of others".

This statement of self confidence did not mark a dramatic change in the tone, techniques, and voice of Frame's work. She has continued to refine her craft consistently and to construct bridges between her complicated retreat in that richly furnished mind and the external world of mirror cities around the globe. She tells us that writing actually saved her life; as in her fiction, the purpose of her writing the autobiography was to connect the events and myths of her two worlds, inner and outer.

Carolyn Bliss (review date Spring 1992)

SOURCE: A review of *An Autobiography,* in *World Literature Today,* Vol. 66, No. 2, Spring, 1992, pp. 408-09.

[*Bliss is an American writer and critic. In the review below, she considers Frame's* An Autobiography *"an illuminating tour" of the author's upbringing in New Zealand.*]

Contemporary theorists of the autobiography are fairly well agreed that the genre's interest and worth lie less in the "facts" it provides about a historically verifiable life than in the nature of the invented self which the autobiographical text constructs and enacts. The New Zealand writer Janet Frame would probably endorse this critical posture, having adopted it as a compositional strategy for her own autobiography. On the book's opening page she alerts us that the "mixture of fact and truths and memories of truths" contained therein tends always toward a state of being for which "the starting point is myth." Very deliberately, then, her text searches for a satisfying myth of self, and finds it in a celebration of the imagining self as emissary to and from a "Mirror City," within which a reaffirmed "real" world is reflected as and projected into fiction.

Frame's three-volume *Autobiography,* published in New

Zealand in 1989 and now available in the U.S. in a paperback edition, gathers the partial accounts of her life which appeared separately earlier in the eighties. The first volume, *To the Is-Land* covers her childhood and youth—mostly spent in Oamaru and shadowed by poverty, the epilepsy of her brother, and the death of a sister—up to the time of her departure for college in Dunedin. *An Angel at My Table* follows her through college, the abrupt abandonment of a teaching career, a suicide attempt, eight years of incarceration as a mental patient due to a mistaken diagnosis of schizophrenia, the deaths of another sister and her mother, and the beginning of her real writing career. This coincided with residence in an army hut provided her by Frank Sargeson and is imaged as a rediscovery of the thread that would draw the unraveled self together again. Volume 2 leaves her on the eve of her departure for Europe, on a trip underwritten by the New Zealand Literary Fund for the purposes of "broaden[ing her] experience."

Volume 3, *The Envoy from Mirror City* (1985), shows her fulfilling the mandate of the Literary Fund: unearthing and reclaiming her sexuality, her sanity, and a surer identity. More important to these processes than the travels she chronicles to London, Paris, the island of Ibiza, or the Basque Country are the trips she makes to and from "Mirror City," the citadel of the imagination whose shining, mirrored palaces re-form life into art. By the time this volume closes, Frame is on intimate terms with the "Envoy" from Mirror City, the imagining self who both supplies material for the transformative acts of art and retrieves the finished products for presentation to an outside world.

The autobiography leaves Frame back in New Zealand, a land with a history less "layered" than that of Europe and therefore still "in an age of mythmakers" which offers her nearly unlimited freedom to make the maps of imagination that will guide and inspire later artists. By now Frame is a much-published author with an "overseas reputation." However, the date is still only 1964; Frame is still only forty years old. At this point, she says, she must resist the temptation to proceed with her memoirs, because the Envoy demands that she "pack" the past for a more arduous and imperative journey back to Mirror City.

The interim self which the text of the autobiography constructs is thus confident, curious, and committed, but well aware that its real work still lies ahead. It is perhaps less aware of the lacunae left in its account of the past. There is a curious flatness to some of this—an emptying out of emotional presence—most evident in her accounts of response to family deaths and in particular the double drownings which claimed her sisters. There is also the avoidance of virtually any reference to her years in mental institutions, an omission explained by her claim to have told that story in *Faces in the Water* but one which leaves the reader feeling that she may have used art to insulate herself from this part of her past, that these rooms in Mirror City have simply been boarded up and con-

demned. Many other rooms, however, have been thrown open to the light of a probing and self-critical imagination. On the whole, Frame's *Autobiography* guides the reader on an illuminating tour through the precincts from which one of New Zealand's finest writers has set out to make the myths of the self and its native land.

FURTHER READING

Bibliography

Beston, John B. "A Bibliography of Janet Frame." *World Literature Written in English* 17, No. 2 (November 1978): 570-85.

> Provides a comprehensive bibliography of work by and about Frame, including unpublished dissertations, translations, and dramatizations.

Biography

Beston, John B. "A Brief Biography of Janet Frame." *World Literature Written in English* 17, No. 2 (November 1978): 565-69.

> Offers an overview of Frame's life and works up to 1978.

Criticism

Brown, Kevin. "Wonder Currencies." *Times Literary Supplement,* No. 4311 (15 November 1983): 1295.

> Finds that Frame's novel *Owls Do Cry* falls short of its potential poignancy.

Buitenhuis, Peter. "Silent Jungle." *New York Times Book Review* (16 August 1964): 5, 20.

> Unfavorable assessment of *Scented Gardens for the Blind.*

Chisholm, Anne. "Needing to Imagine." *Times Literary Supplement,* No. 4188 (8 July 1983): 737.

> Favorably assesses the first volume of Frame's autobiography, *To the Is-Land,* claiming that the author writes with "originality and power."

Delbaere-Garant, Jeanne. "Beyond the Word: Janet Frame's *Secret Gardens for the Blind,*" in *The Commonwealth Writer Overseas: Themes of Exile and Expatriation,* edited by Alastair Niven, pp. 289-300. Liège: Revue des Langues Vivantes, 1976.

> Considers *Secret Gardens for the Blind* Frame's quintessential novel, arguing that the work skillfully expresses the disconnectedness and despair of the modern world.

Evans, Patrick. *Janet Frame.* Boston: Twayne Publishers, 1977, 228 p.

> Offers a comprehensive overview of Frame's life and works up to 1978.

Jones, Lawrence. "No Cowslip's Bell in Waimaru: The Personal Vision of *Owls Do Cry*." *Landfall* 24, No. 3 (September 1970): 280-96.

    Discusses Frame's *Owls Do Cry* as a modern psychological novel, comparing it to works by Virginia Woolf, James Joyce, and William Faulkner.

MacLennan, Carol. "Dichotomous Values in the Novels of Janet Frame." *The Journal of Commonwealth Literature* XXII, No. 1 (1987): 179-89.

    Argues that Frame has repeatedly chosen to write about alternative views of the world, life, and reality.

Muchnick, Laurie. "Up from Down Under." *The Village Voice* XXXVI, No. 33 (13 August 1991): 69.

    Discusses Frame's career, with an emphasis on several of her later literary works, including *The Carpathians, An Autobiography,* and *Living in the Maniototo.*

Williams, Mark. "Janet Frame's Suburban Gothic." In *Leaving the Highway: Six Contemporary New Zealand Novelists,* pp. 30-56. Auckland: Auckland University Press, 1990.

    Provides a bio-critical overview of Frame's work.

Additional coverage of Frame's life and career is contained in the following sources published by Gale Research: *Contemporary Authors,* **Vol. 1-4, rev. ed.;** *Contemporary Authors New Revision Series,* **Vols. 2, 36;** *Contemporary Literary Criticism,* **Vols. 2, 3, 6, 22, 66; and** *Major 20th-Century Writers.*

René Marqués

1919-1979

Puerto Rican playwright, short story writer, novelist, essayist, and poet.

The following entry provides critical discussion of Marques's work through 1992.

INTRODUCTION

Widely recognized as the dominant Puerto Rican literary figure of the 1950s and 1960s, Marqués was a prolific, charismatic advocate of Puerto Rican national sovereignty. He wrote numerous award-winning short stories, essays and two novels, but he is best known for his innovative dramas, exemplified by *La carreta* (1953; *The Oxcart*), *Los soles truncos* (1958; *The Fanlights*), and *Un niño azul para esa sombra* (1960; *A Blue Boy for That Shadow*)—considered by many critics his finest. Associated with the group of nationalistic Latin-American intellectuals known as the "Generation of the Forties," Marqués expressed forceful resistance to Western cultural and political influence, especially as exerted by the United States. His prophetic plays confront the pernicious effects of colonialism, industrialization, and the rapid erosion of traditional, rural island life. Through skillful adaptation of contemporary Western literature and his own experiments with theatrical device, Marqués introduced new standards of excellence to his own national literature and achieved an international reputation.

Biographical Information

Born in Arecibo, Puerto Rico, Marqués received a rural upbringing on his grandparents' haciendas, where he learned the conservative values and agrarian life idealized in his writings. He earned a degree in agronomy at the College of Agriculture and Mechanical Arts in 1942, and two years later resigned a position with the Department of Agriculture to publish *Peregrinación* (1944), his first and only book of poetry. In 1946 he departed for Spain to study literature at the University of Madrid, where he wrote his first drama, *El hombre y sus sueños* (1973; *The Man and His Dreams*). The next year he returned to Puerto Rico, founded a small theater group in Arecibo, and contributed regular literary reviews to several newspapers and journals in San Juan. With the aid of a Rockefeller Foundation scholarship, Marqués left for the United States in 1949 to study drama at Columbia University, where he wrote *Palm Sunday* (1953) in a workshop, his only English-language play. That year he also won the first of many Ateneo awards with his short story "El miedo" ("Fear"), included in the collection *Otro día nuestro* (1955; *Another Day of Ours*). After a brief tour of experimental American theaters, Marqués

returned to Puerto Rico in 1950 to begin his most significant creative period. He established the Experimental Theater of the Atheneum in 1951, then achieved critical acclaim with consecutive performances of *The Oxcart* in New York, San Juan, and Madrid. In 1957 he moved to the United States, this time with a Guggenheim Fellowship, to begin writing his semi-autobiographical first novel, *La víspera del hombre* (1959; *The Eve of Man*). Marqués eventually returned to his native land, where he continued to produce well-received works of fiction, plays, and essays, including his literary manifesto, *Pesimismo literario y optimiso politico: Su coexistencia en el Puerto Rico actual* (1959; *Literary Pessimism and Political Optimism: Their Coexistence in Contemporary Puerto Rico*). He served as editorial director with the Department of Public Instruction from 1953 to 1969, and as a professor of literature at the University of Puerto Rico from 1969 until his retirement in 1976.

Major Works

Marqués's dramas consistently scrutinize the dissipation of Puerto Rican national identity, cultural heritage, and traditional values. Dominated by themes of guilt, betrayal and sacrificial redemption, his socio-political commentary is typically accentuated by complex symbolism and evocative dramatic technique. Such elements are evident in his earliest plays, from the allegorical characters and expressionistic setting of *The Man and His Dreams*, to the patriotic realism of *Palm Sunday* and his initial experiments with temporal juxtaposition in *El sol y los MacDonald* (1950; *The Sun and the MacDonalds*). *The Oxcart* represents his first popular success and marks the beginning of Marqués's artistic maturity. To a large extent this work embodies the salient characteristics of his most effective subsequent productions, especially the integration of lighting, sound effects, and the prominent recurring motif of cultural disorientation. The play traces the fortunes of a Puerto Rican peasant family lured from ancestral lands to seek economic prosperity in the city. Their circular route, suggested by the ominous offstage sound of cart wheels, leads them through the slums of San Juan, New York City, and finally back to their native land to recover from dejection and loss. *The Fanlights* similarly demonstrates the lethal effect of modern progress on an unprepared, agricultural society. Unlike the adventurous family of *The Oxcart*, this work features three reclusive sisters whose voluntary isolation comes to an abrupt end when one of them dies. Impoverished and faced with selling the family mansion, the two surviving sisters set fire to the house and perish inside rather than endure forced exposure to the detested outside world. More overtly political, *La muerte no entrará en palacio* (1959; *Death Shall Not Enter the Palace*) is a satire with tragic pretensions. The work, which is viewed as a denunciation of the American extension of Commonwealth status to Puerto Rico in 1952, features a main character who bears strong resemblance to real-life Puerto Rican governor Muñoz Marín. In this historical reinterpretation, a failed assassination attempt drives the national leader and his family into a fortified palace, where he becomes tyrannical and resorts to brutish self-preservation. His daughter ultimately ends the hopeless situation by murdering him as he is signing away his country's independence. Generally regarded as his consummate work, *A Blue Boy for That Shadow* explores the irreconcilable perception of illusion and reality in the mind of the child protagonist, Michelín. When his father abandons the family to pursue a political cause, the idealistic boy is left to his materialistic mother who comfortably subsists on a family fortune while enjoying effete entertainments. Her poisoning of a tree becomes the complex metaphor for lost security, the death of heroic ideals, and the betrayal of Puerto Rican freedom. As in *The Fanlights*, the convergence of past, present, and future is achieved through flashbacks and daydreams, creating multiple levels of reality and a temporal circularity reminiscent of *The Oxcart*. In the end, disparaged and unable to establish his own identity amid his parents' contradictory values, Michelín commits suicide and becomes a symbol of Puerto Rican sacrifice and self-destruction.

Critical Reception

Consistently praised for his stylistic accomplishment and tire-

less innovation, Marqués was among the most gifted Hispanic writers of his generation. Though he emerged from the relative obscurity of his own country to achieve international recognition during the 1960s, his influence on younger writers had noticeably waned by the end of the decade. The nostalgic, conservative values and tenacious patriotism that once sustained his literary agenda was judged repetitious and anachronistic by some. Even at the height of his influence, Marqués was faulted for his melodramatic theatrics and overly complex symbolism. Despite his opposition to Western cultural hegemony, Marqués was not averse to assimilating the current literary forms of North America and Europe for his own purposes. Many of his dramas and prose works contain studied allusions to Greek mythology and feature existentialist underpinnings. Marqués remains an outstanding figure in Puerto Rican literature for his technical contributions to the theater of that land, his commitment to the writing profession, and his persistent efforts to draw attention to issues concerning Puerto Rican society and independence.

PRINCIPAL WORKS

Peregrinación (poetry) 1944

El sol y los MacDonald [*The Sun and the MacDonalds*] (drama) 1950

La carreta [*The Oxcart*] (drama) 1953

Palm Sunday (drama) 1953

Otro día nuestro [*Another Day of Ours*] (short stories) 1955

Los soles truncos [*The Fanlights*] (drama) 1958

**La muerte no entrará en palacio* [*Death Shall Not Enter the Palace*] (drama) 1959

Pesimismo literario y optimiso politico: Su coexistencia en el Puerto Rico actual [*Literary Pessimism and Political Optimism: Their Coexistence in Contemporary Puerto Rico*] (essay) 1959

Teatro I (drama collection) 1959

La víspera del hombre [*The Eve of Man*] (novel) 1959

En una ciudad llamada San Juan (short stories) 1960

Un niño azul para esa sombra [*A Blue Boy for That Shadow*] (drama) 1960

La casa sin reloj [*The House without a Clock*] (drama) 1961

Carnaval afuera, carnaval adentro (drama) 1962

El apartamiento (drama) 1964

Mariana; o, El alba (drama) 1965

†*Ensayos 1953-1966* (essays) 1966

David y Jonatán / Tito y Bernice: Dos dramas de amor, poder y desamor (drama) 1970

Sacrificio en el Monte Moriah [*Sacrifice at Mount Moriah*] (drama) 1970

Teatro II (drama collection) 1971

Teatro III (drama collection) 1971

El hombre y sus sueños [*The Man and His Dreams*] (drama) 1973

La mirada (novel) 1975

Immersos en el silencio (short stories) 1976

*This work first appeared in *Teatro I* and was never officially staged.

†This collection was subsequently revised and enlarged as *Ensayos 1953-1971* (1972), *El puertorriqueño dócil y otros ensayos 1953-1971* (1977), and translated as *The Docile Puerto Rican: Essays* (1976).

CRITICISM

Frank Dauster (review date September 1960)

SOURCE: "New Plays by René Marqués," in *Hispania,* Vol. XLIII, No. 3, September, 1960, pp. 451-52.

[*In the following review, Dauster provides a concise evaluation of* La muerte no entrará en palacio, Un niño azul para esa sombra, *and* Los soles truncos.]

Under the title *Teatro,* José Luis González' Ediciones Arrecife has just published three plays by the distinguished Puerto Rican playwright, best known as author of *La carreta.* The plays included are *La muerte no entrará en palacio, Un niño azul para esa sombra* (Premio del Certamen de Teatro de 1958 del Ateneo Puertorriqueño) and *Los soles truncos* (included in the volume *Teatro puertorriqueño* published by the Instituto de Cultura Puertorriqueña to commemorate its Primer Festival de Teatro Puertorriqueño). All three are complex works representing the author's concern for the loss of traditional values, and *Los soles truncos,* particularly requires several readings before its various levels of meaning are fully apparent. All three plays make heavy demands on the actors and full use of music and lighting effects, as well as complex staging. The measure of Marqués' skill is his ability to use all these resources without falling into sheer stage trickery and effect.

La muerte no entrará en palacio is an attack on demagoguery, with obvious reference to political situations in Puerto Rico; its first act is strongest, while the second tends toward heavier emphasis on the political and less on the highly interesting personal relationships developed earlier. *Los soles truncos* is a symbolic drama of the clash between the heritage of the past and the realities of the present; it is a technical tour de force which does not lose sight of the individuals involved. For this writer, the best of the three is *Un niño azul para esa sombra,* a drama of a child caught in the struggle between dream and reality. Probably Marqués' best play, it is one of the best in Latin America.

Frank Dauster (essay date Spring 1964)

SOURCE: "The Theater of René Marqués," in *Symposium,* Vol. XVIII, No. 1, Spring, 1964, pp. 35-45.

[*In the following essay, Dauster offers a balanced survey of Marqués's major dramatic works, giving particular attention to the development of theme and theatrical device.*]

Among Puerto Rican dramatists today, René Marqués occupies a unique place. Although widely known for his naturalistic and intensely nationalistic *La carreta,* he has consistently devoted himself to experimenting with dramatic techniques. *La carreta* and *Palm Sunday* are his only dramas in an overtly realistic framework; they are neither his best nor his most typical work, which is characterized by shifting temporal relationships and by extreme use of such devices as flashback, integrated offstage effects, and the extensive use of lighting for dramatic purposes. This characteristic technical orientation is clear in his earliest work, the one-act *El hombre y sus sueños,* which bears the subtitle "Esbozo intrascendente para un drama trascendental." A somewhat diffuse attack on materialism and the rejection of ideals, *El hombre y sus sueños* takes place on a stage bare except for a semicircle of large white columns against a black drop; a four-step platform in the center holds a monumental bed upon which lies the motionless figure of a man. Against this scene a series of characters enters: the three Friends (Poet, Politician, Philosopher), the Son and his Stepmother, the Nurse, the Maid, and the Priest. In various combinations they play out their minuscule dramas of lust and greed, interrupted only by the three Shadows, Red, Blue and Black, who debate the meaning of the dying man's existence. The play is of minor importance except for its anticipation of later themes, particularly *La muerte no entrará en palacio,* and for the author's willingness to use symbolic staging at a time when the theater in Puerto Rico was almost exclusively naturalistic in style.

Marqués' second play, *Palm Sunday,* was written in English in 1949 as an exercise for a playwrighting course at Columbia University. It is a straightforward realistic presentation of events which take place just prior to and during the Palm Sunday Massacre of 1937. The chief characters are the American police commissioner, John Winfield, his Puerto Rican wife Mercedes, and their son Alberto. The play suffers from stereotyping: Winfield is a bigot, and father and son are irrevocably estranged before the curtain rises. Rather than the tragic irony he might have achieved had his characters not been so fixed, Marqués presents in Alberto's death as a result of the massacre ordered by his own father, the wasteful and unnecessary result of blind stubbornness.

In his third play, *El sol y los MacDonald,* Marqués turns to a degenerate remnant of southern American aristocracy. The work is an odd mixture of obvious dislike for everything which the characters represent, with technical elements reminiscent of O'Neill and Faulkner: the long brooding, introspective passages, the desperate balance between semi-awareness of weakness and brassy compensatory flaunting of these weaknesses. A tendency toward rhetoric, the unrelieved degeneracy of the family and a virtual parade of incestuous desires are serious weaknesses, although there are effective moments.

El sol y los MacDonald prefigures the technical apparatus used so successfully in the later plays. Each act begins with a lengthy reflective soliloquy, relieved in the first and last acts by spotlighting of other characters to create double planes of reality. Lighting is also used to heighten tension: during the climactic equivocal embrace of Teresa and her son Ramiro, the focus of lighting shrinks while they are covered with a red spot. During the final commentary by Gustavo, a narrator-actor, the lighting gradually dims, until at the curtain only the garden is dimly lit, allowing the speaker's figure to be perceived vaguely. This is not trickery, but a conscious subordination of external reality to the internal reality which is the real matter of the play. It is also the first major use of these devices in the Puerto Rican theater, the first serious effort to combine the use of narrator-actor, flashback, simultaneous levels of action and monologue as flow of consciousness.

Marqués' dramatic maturity begins with *La carreta,* an unabashedly naturalistic portrait of the *via crucis* of a rural Puerto Rican family. The play has been a success on several occasions in Puerto Rico, and has been staged in New York and in Madrid. Its reception in San Juan is nothing short of apotheosic, and during a recent revival at the Fourth Theater Festival in May, 1961, it played to wildly enthusiastic houses for each of five performances. This success was due to three factors: certain real dramatic values in the play, a virtuoso performance by Lucy Boscana in the lead role, and a definite identification with the play by the audience. The three acts or "estampas," as the author calls them, correspond to three stations of the family's calvary. At each station it becomes morally weaker; at each station it suffers and loses a member. As the play begins, doña Gabriela and her three children, Juanita, Luis, and Chaguito, are preparing to leave their mountain farm driven by Luis' dreams of quick wealth in the city. At the end of the first act, they have left in a cart, whence the title, leaving only the grandfather, don Chago, who refuses to leave the land he loves for a world he no longer understands: "Yo creo en la tierra. Enanteh creía en loh hombreh. Pero ya sólo creo en la tierra." Act Two takes place in San Juan's infamous La Perla slum; Luis' dreams have evaporated. He is able to find only occasional work, Chaguito has become a petty thief, Juanita has been raped, and doña Gabriela lives in a nightmare of stench, filth, and corruption. As the act ends, Juanita has attempted suicide, Chaguito has been arrested, but Luis urges them toward the metropolis, New York. Act Three brings the family full circle. Luis, the apostle of the machine, is killed in an industrial accident, and Gabriela and Juanita vow to return to the island, to work the land and attempt to remake their lives. This is, of course, the key to the entire work. Luis, with his faith in progress and the machine, is the culprit; his failure as a farmer is due less to incompetence than to lack of love for the land.

This socio-economic orientation has contributed largely to the success of *La carreta*. A song of love for the land, emi-nently understandable in view of Marqués' own background in the provinces and his training as an agronomist, it echoes the fears of many Puerto Ricans about their island's future in the face of an increasing industrialization which many of them feel to be economically unsound. Coupled with their longing for political independence and a considerable resentment of the role of the United States in Puerto Rican history, this las led many to take *La carreta* as virtually a national drama, a sort of theatrical cry of independence.

This does not, of course, deny the theatrical excellences of *La carreta,* of which there are many, primarily a brilliantly designed first act which reflects accurately and without sentimentality the misgivings of the family in the face of its abandoning its home and tradition. The uneasiness of doña Gabriela, Chaguito's reluctance to wear shoes and his comic attempt to smuggle his pet rooster with him, Juanita's furtive efforts to bid goodbye to a local peón, all reflect the family's real desire to remain, but they are swayed by Luis' dream of the prosperity awaiting them. Only don Chago retains his perspective, don Chago who represents man's harmony with nature, counterpoised to Luis' blind faith in progress. The oscillation of mood is handled well; there is a moment of profound nostalgia for what each is losing. The act ending is dominated by the distinctive sound of cart wheels, becoming increasingly louder as the spell is broken and the characters rush to finish their preparations. Only when they have gone do we learn of old don Chago's intent; a man out of joint with his time, he plans to live out what life remains him on the land: "Cuando loh sombreh noh patean entoavía quea la tierra pa dejarse querel." This authenticity of dramatic emotion—the characters were conceived while Marqués was in the mountains filming *Una voz en la montaña* in 1951—is enhanced by a series of off-stage sounds and by the use of concrete objects which effectively serve as objective correlatives to the emotion of the characters. Doña Gabriela's wooden figure of a saint and Juanita's model of a cart, given to her by the sweetheart she has left behind, are concrete objects which incarnate their basic unwillingness to leave, and are, at the same time, symbols of the tradition which they are abandoning. Opposed to them is the sound of cart wheels, the inexorable movement of change.

Unfortunately, the last two acts are not up to the same high standard, although there is effective use of the same techniques. Act Two becomes almost a series of individual scenes of degradation, and Act Three's episodic character is even more pronounced, with the intrusion of a series of characters who represent what Marqués regards as elements of modern society detrimental to the essentially Catholic-tropical-agricultural tradition represented by the family.

In *Juan Bobo y la dama de occidente,* he returns to this orientation, although the style is diametrically opposed. Actually, this one-act drama divided into three *cuadros* is not a play at all but a pantomime for a ballet libretto. Its purpose is specific: it is a direct attack on the universalist, cosmopolitan philosophy espoused by the University of Puerto Rico and its rector, Jaime Benítez. In a brilliant display of stage pyrotechnics, Marqués makes very clear his absolute rejection of any attempt to abandon the traditional bases of Puerto Rican culture.

Marqués' maturity as a dramatist is signaled by a remarkable work, *Los soles truncos*. It is, perhaps, his best performance in terms of integration of the technical elements with the theme: the shock of the collision of two cultures. It reflects again his absorption in the question of the reality of Puerto Rico and his rejection of a transplanted culture. After years of voluntary seclusion, three sisters, poverty-stricken, survivors of a wealthy and influential island family, are faced with a final dilemma. One has died, and the two remaining must arrange for her burial and themselves leave their home, which is to be destroyed in the name of progress. Rather than allow the detested outside world to intrude on an existence in which they have never permitted themselves to acknowledge the passage of time, they bedeck themselves and the dead Hortensia in the remaining jewels, which they have refused to sell even at the cost of hunger, and set fire to their home.

This allegory of time functions on three levels: time within the house, a deliberate effort to retain the customs of the past; time without, the real world which intrudes despite their efforts; and memory, a fantasy world which exists differently for each sister. These shifting levels are achieved by means of flashbacks and dream sequences, which are carefully integrated with special lighting effects, and by off-stage effects which are frequently keyed to onstage happenings. The external world is represented by the cries of street vendors and, later, by the deafening knocking of the police, but on a more subtle level, by the light which enters through the blinds. Emilia's constant closing of these blinds and her habit of protecting her eyes from even the slightest external lighting are effective dramatic devices. From this technique comes the play's title, since the three glass half-moons, or truncated suns, as the author calls them, are the three sisters. The doors are kept closed and the halfmoons are obscured by dust and time. Flashbacks are used to establish motives and key actions within the past and at the same time to maintain the illusion of simultaneous levels of time. Thus, through flashbacks we learn of Hortensia's voluntary rejection of the world because of a disappointment in love, we learn of Emilia's frustrated eroticism and Inés' recognition of her guilty love for her sister's fiance. But we learn of these not as incidents in a remote past, but as part of a past which, for the sisters, is present.

Un niño azul para esa sombra is in many respects Marqués' best work to date. Michelín, the child protagonist, is the son of a former university professor, Michel, who has been imprisoned for his political activities. Upon his release, he is placed in the intolerable situation of either renouncing his ideas or depending for employment on his wife's wealthy relatives, since he is too proud a man simply to vegetate while living on his wife's fortune. Unable to resolve the situation, he leaves in order to fight elsewhere for his ideas. Michelín survives only because he is able to keep the past alive. Surrounded by an existence of cocktail parties and brittle, amoral sophistication, the child's dreams become more real than reality, and his mother's blundering attempt to shock him into accepting reality leads to his suicide. Again, as in *Los soles truncos,* Marqués makes use of flashback and daydream sequences to maintain cutaneous levels of time and to translate Michelín's psychological state into dramatic tension. A new device is the regression in time; Act Three, which chronologically follows directly after the action of Act One, is separated from it by Act Two, whose action takes place two years before. This is not, however, disruptive, since the events have already been outlined in Michelín's daydreams, and the temporal regression both develops the dramatic conflict and strengthens the illusion of coetaneity. Marqués again uses the concrete objects with which characters are identified. In this case it is the massive tree in which Michelín had played as a child, a tree which has been destroyed in order to enlarge the garden terrace. Michelín hovers constantly about the fence which has replaced the tree; it has become for him a symbol of his mother's abandoning his father. For the audience, the murder of the tree becomes a complex dramatic metaphor of Michel-Michelín, betrayed by a society which has turned its back on freedom and dignity. Unable to cope any longer with his situation, Michelín drinks poison and slowly climbs the fence, entwining his arms in it. Obviously, his death is not meant to be taken realistically. The deliberate resemblance to a crucified figure, the equation between tree and child, the eerie blue lighting of the final moments, are all designed to remove the meaning from the plane of reality and confer on it various levels of significance. Yet, such is the magic of the play that the extraordinary figure of Michelín continues to dominate it. He is a symbol of a dying culture, of a people sacrificed to a civilization which is not their own, but he never ceases to be a particularly appealing figure, doubly so in his mixture of childish innocence and lost naïveté.

In his next play, *La muerte no entrará en palacio,* Marqués attempted to trace the decay of a political figure who, if not modeled on Governor Muñoz Marín of Puerto Rico, bears some striking resemblances to him. The play is a complex blend of political satire and a conscious effort to create within the tragic form. It begins with a projection of the future in the form of a prologue spoken by Tiresias, the friend and former political associate of the governor, Don José, against the background of the ruined palace. Throughout the first act, Don José is treated with understanding and even some affection, although he is depicted as a man who has led his people along the wrong road. In the second act, he has changed radically; he has become a petty tyrant devoted to calculated histrionics and the preservation of his own power. An attempted assassination has converted the palace into an armed fortress, and the emotional pressures on his family are intolerable. His own daughter recognizes the impossibility of the situation and kills him.

The weakness of the drama lies in the second act, and it is both internal and external. The external weakness is the almost tract-like nature of certain passages, in which the author's sympathies win out over his sense of dramatic necessity. The internal weakness is the abrupt change in Don José during the interval between the two acts. He is transformed into an alternately pompous and terrified figure, without even the momentary grandeur we have previously seen. The ideals in which he seriously believed in the first act have given way before political expediency and immoral political repression. It is not that Don José is a thief or a traitor in the obvious sense; he is a materialist who believes that a full stomach is an end in itself. In this lies his treason; in this, also, lies the play's weakness. It is difficult to believe in the total degradation of a man who, until the end of the first act, has held to a large part of his old ideals, and who even now believes in the welfare of his people, albeit a welfare considerably different from that which he had earlier espoused. In Act I he is the stuff of which tragic figures come. In Act II he is a nervous, irritable, petty dictator.

Despite this weakness, ***La muerte no entrará en palacio*** is a highly theatrical piece, in which the author uses several devices not seen earlier in his work. One is the blackout during which a kaleidoscopic series of sound effects indicate a rapid passage of time while conveying to the audience some sense of what has happened during this time. Although it is employed somewhat excessively, it is very effective at the beginning of Act II where the words of Don Rodrigo, the leader of the independence movement, are contrasted with the tyranny of Don José. Another extremely effective moment is at the end of Act II. Don José, the representative of an obvious Northern power and various functionaries are gathered for the signing of a treaty. The stage is divided into two terraces. On one are Don José and his court of bureaucrats; on the other, their wives. Snatches of conversation and bits of action are used effectively to underline the basic falsity of the entire proceeding, the selfishness and hypocrisy which have collaborated in this act of treachery. The movement comes very close to stylized comic ballet, interrupted abruptly by the entrance of Casandra and the subsequent murder of her father.

Marqués latest play, the recently published ***La casa sin reloj,*** is described in the subtitle as a "Comedia antipoética en dos absurdos y un final razonable." It is Marqués' first comedy and marks a return to the realistic idiom. As the play begins, two detectives force their way into Micaela's home in the absence of her husband Pedro. They are searching for nationalists in the wake of an armed assault on the Fortress (which, by no coincidence, is the name of the residence of the residence of the Governor of Puerto Rico). These are,

however, oddly matched detectives. One is brusque, business-like, obviously delighted with his work, while the other becomes absorbed in a novel and makes comments on Micaela's state of undress. After their departure, the house is again invaded, this time by the object of their search, the nationalist José. The remainder of the first act is devoted to the peculiar and comic relationship which develops between Micaela and the intruder. The act is pervaded by a deliberately out-of-focus absurdity, in which the spectacle of José's housecleaning or the involved discussion of the comic possibilities inherent in the selection by Micaela of furniture for the apartment in which Pedro keeps a mistress are both typical and oddly diverting. The second act, however, rapidly develops a different orientation. Although Micaela continues to amuse and perplex both the audience and José, who is revealed as Pedro's brother, it becomes apparent that she is radically unhappy, disturbed by a lack of any sense of being. She feels herself to be outside the realm of normal existence; with no sense of guilt or deep emotional ties, she exists in an atemporal, rootless world. It is only when she and José recognize that they are in love that she begins the search which leads to both their disaster and her salvation: the search for guilt, for involvement, the guilt which will make her a member of the human race. She finds this guilt in the murder of José. This is not a new theme for Marqués, although it is the first time that it has been given major treatment. It is an important theme of several short stories, notably **"El cuchillo y la piedra," "En una ciudad llamada San Juan,"** and **"La muerte."** The last is of particular note; it is the drama of a minor bureaucrat whose life has withered under the daily barrage of an unimportant job and a conventional marriage. Suddenly, for no logical reason, he takes an action which is incoherent in terms of his entire life: in a student parade upon which the police have opened fire, he seizes the banner of Puerto Rican independence. Even as the police fire on him, he realizes the secret of his action: "Era el acto de actuar lo que le salvaba." **"En una ciudad llamada San Juan"** is even more explicit. A young Puerto Rican kills an American Marine in rage at the latter's contemptuous attitude, but the murder is only the immediate manifestation of the fundamental confusion of the Puerto Rican. He is confused and disturbed by the schizophrenia of his island, unable to determine a course of action which will give his own life some meaning: "¿Cómo dar con el asidero si sus manos se mantenían laxas, impotentes para el gesto salvador de agarrarse a su circunstancia y exprimirla, torturarla, hasta obtener de ella su más íntima autenticidad?" It is in this context that Micaela's action becomes comprehensible. She is searching for her own authenticity; she is, like Michelín of ***Un niño azul para esa sombra*** and the three recluses of ***Los soles truncos,*** a dramatic metaphor of what Marqués regards as his confused nation.

The two themes of time and guilt are of fundamental importance in Marqués' theater. They play shifting roles, but underlying them is the meaning of what he is attempting to do. Repeatedly, time is seen as the destructive force, as the vehicle of change which his characters resist doggedly, if unsuccessfully. The world has gone mad, and man is left to seek some stability. . . .

This change is inevitable in some cases, but frequently it is related to the political content of the works. The decay of the family in *Los soles truncos* is due not only to time but also to the alien civilization which time has forced on them. The disaster of *La carreta* is due to Luis' infatuation with a new mechanistic civilization which he does not really understand, and Marqués makes clear that he feels that the only hope for these people is to return to an older way of life. As María Teresa Babín has pointed out, "El resto de la familia de don Chago vive desvinculado del pasado feliz, agobiado por la miseria, la hipoteca de la tierra, arrastrado a una existencia nómada en una época deslumbrada por el progreso material de la isla." Time has worked its destructive change in *La muerte no entrará en palacio;* the ideals which had led the three dreamers on their magnificent pilgrimage through the mountains have been betrayed. The Philosopher is dead, the Poet is an artifact out of the past, the Politician has been corrupted. *Un niño azul para esa sombra* shows the same lethal effect of time; Michelín's suicide is the direct result of his recognition that the past is irretrievably gone.

> **The two themes of time and guilt are of fundamental importance in Marqués' theater. They play shifting roles, but underlying them is the meaning of what he is attempting to do. Repeatedly, time is seen as the destructive force, as the vehicle of change which his characters resist doggedly, if unsuccessfully. The world has gone mad, and man is left to seek some stability.**
>
> **—*Frank Dauster***

In *La casa sin reloj,* Marqués seems to have evolved toward a somewhat different concept. Where previously he had seemed to say that time is necessarily evil and destructive, in this latest play he has added an element. Even though Micaela was content in her atemporal existence, she was little more than a vegetable—a singularly delightful vegetable, admittedly, but a vegetable nevertheless. Only through the double-edged sword of love and action can she truly live. Only through guilt can she find redemption.

This paradox is an underlying theme of all Marqués' work. It is as though all his characters suffered from a monumental guilt complex, forever in search of the sacrificial death through which alone they may expiate their sins. As early as *El sol y*

los Macdonald, Ramiro is conscious of the incestuous nature of his relationship with his mother, and Gustavo dwells morbidly on his own obvious sexual desire for his sister. Oddly, in *La carreta* only Luis, who is really responsible for the family's disaster, seems impervious to a pervading sense of guilt. *Los soles truncos* is a virtual panorama of the same guilty feelings. Inés' renunciation of the world, while supposedly an act of abnegation in order to accompany her sister, is in fact expiation of her own guilty love, while Emilia is alternately obsessed by and ashamed of her erotic fantasy world. The conflagration which ends the drama is, on one level, their deliberate rejection of an intolerable world. On another plane, however, it is Eliot's fire sermon, purification through sacrifice.

This preoccupation with guilt and sacrifice is at the center of *Un niño azul para esa sombra*. Michelín is the scapegoat; he must bear the full weight of the guilt of family and society. His identification with Christ in the final scene is intentional; he is, for Marqués, a symbol of a guilt-ridden people, at once betrayed by their leaders and conniving at their own betrayal. It is this awareness of his own treachery which lends some degree of humanity to the figure of Don José in the second act of *La muerte no entrará en palacio*. This preoccupation with betrayal and guilt is frequently related to a Christ-figure. Michelín's autocrucifixion is the most obvious example, but there are many others. In *Los soles truncos,* Inés reflects the unspoken desire which haunts the two living sisters: "Inés va lentamente al fondo. Se acerca a una de las puertas cerradas. Apoya la frente sobre la puerta, luego extiende los brazos como si quisiera abrazarse a la puerta, y solloza así, como crucificada sobre las hojas que no han de abrirse jamás." In *La muerte no entrará en palacio,* the disenchanted Alberto, son of the governor's oldest ally, hints at the same obscure wish:

> ALBERTO: ¡Qué Vía Crucis para un conductor de pueblo!
> DON JOSÉ: ¡Basta!
> ALBERTO: ¡Qué calvario!
> DON JOSÉ: ¡Déjame! ¡Vete!
> ALBERTO: Si lo único que le falta es el sacrificio final.
> DON JOSÉ: (a gritos) ¡Cállate!
> ALBERTO: Si casi está usted pidiendo la crucifixión.

This attitude is common in the short stories, as well. In one of the best, **"Otro día nuestro,"** the imprisoned Nationalist leader is repeatedly identified with Christ. As the story develops, however, we realize that the sympathetic old man is himself responsible for this identification. He suffers from an advanced Christ-complex, complete with a strong death wish, and his failure becomes clear to him only when he realizes that he is not of this time, that his entire concept is psychologically unworkable. Interwoven with the basic substance of the stories, the conflict between two cultures, the strange insistence on sacrifice recurs. Even the Judas-figure of **"El delator"** is obscurely pleased by the suffering he causes himself, and in **"En la popa hay un cuerpo reclinado,"** the protagonist resorts to murder and self-mutilation. Furthermore, these attitudes are not unconscious on the author's part. He gives the key to his attitude in his prologue to the anthology, *Cuentos puertorriqueños de hoy*:

> El pesimismo, imperante en nuestra literatura narrativa desde finales del siglo pasado, se acentúa en los jóvenes escritores. La pupila observadora del creador se hace cruelmente incisiva, penetrando más allá del superficial optimismo de la actual vida pública puertorriqueña para descubrir síntomas perturbadores en el cuerpo social. Dentro de esta perspectiva pesimista merece destacarse el impulso de autodestrucción que caracteriza a un buen número de personajes literarios puertorriqueños. Hay en la nueva literatura narrativa una alarmante cantidad de suicidas, bien literales o potenciales. Los amantes de las estadísticas podrían relacionar el hecho literario con una realidad social que les revelan los números: Puerto Rico es el país católico con más alta incidencia de suicidios en el mundo. Ambos fenómenos—el estadístico y el literario—quizás tengan su raíz sicológica en la agudización, durante los últimos años, del complejo de culpa inherente a un pueblo colonial que no ha logrado el hallazgo de una salida airosa a su secular encrucijada.

This, then, lies at the heart of Marqués' work. His theater is a complex and peculiarly suggestive metaphor for a people he regards as guilt-ridden and obsessed with a desire for self-destruction. The measure of his ability as playwright is the fact that out of this material, he has created plays which are not only one of the achievements of the Puerto Rican theater renaissance, but among the most distinguished in Latin America today.

> **Marqués' theater is a complex and peculiarly suggestive metaphor for a people he regards as guilt-ridden and obsessed with a desire for self-destruction.**
>
> —*Frank Dauster*

D. L. Shaw (essay date Fall 1968)

SOURCE: "Rene Marques' *La muerte no entrará en palacio:* An Analysis," in *Latin American Theatre Review,* Vol. II, No. 1, Fall, 1968, pp. 31-38.

[*In the following essay, Shaw examines elements of social protest and tragedy in* La muerte no entrará en palacio.]

Since the origins of the theatre in Latin America, playwrights there have struggled to conciliate two major ideals: to interpret the reality of their native environment and to remain abreast of innovations in the European theatre. Among the works by contemporary dramatists included in Carlos Solórzano's *El teatro hispanoamericano contemporáneo*(1964) is the Puerto Rican René Marqués' fifth play **La muerte no entrará en palacio** (1957) which attempts to do justice to both aspects of this dual imperative. It stands out in consequence from the mass of *teatro de protesta* which, if the recent history of the Latin American novel offers reliable indications, is a genre destined to date very rapidly as social change continues.

Three features of the play call for special comment. First, although this is a play of protest (against threats from abroad to the independence of Latin American countries and against arbitrary presidential power), it avoids oversimplification and even contains an element of analysis. Second, it is not only a play of ideas but aims at being also a drama of basically human conflict. Most striking of all, it is alleged to be something rare in the Latin American theatre of today, a tragedy. In what follows it is proposed to examine by means of an analysis of its structure Marqués' success in coordinating these aspects of the play into a consistent whole.

From the outset it is clear that we are in the presence of a sophisticated example of theatre. The first two scenes already provide an example of Marqués' technical skill. Teresias' speech as the curtain rises is designed to create, through its heavily-emphasized references to time and the universal moral order, a sense of tragic atmosphere. But the impression of portentousness, having served its dramatic purpose, is immediately effaced by Casandra's happy laughter and her appearance, together with her fiancé Alberto, dressed for tennis in the sunny garden. The daring contrast between the two scenes is reflected in the more muted contrast of tone between Alberto's speeches and those of the heroine. Their characters are at once sharply differentiated. He, henceforth, never moves from this initial level of intelligence and idealism. Casandra, on the other hand, presented here as trivial and rather scatterbrained, is allowed margin to develop towards her final decision. Finally, when reference is made to don Rodrigo, the center of opposition to Casandra's father President José, the main counterforce in the action is brought into early prominence. In these brief scenes, then, Marqués very effectively solves the problem of exposition.

They are linked to the principal scene of Act 1, *Cuadro* I, by a sequence of dialogue which has not only the function of introducing doña Isabel, Casandra's mother, and establishing her character, but also that of reemphasizing the significance of don Rodrigo's return from prison and exile. Don

Rodrigo's role in the play is that of the symbol-figure of national dignity and independence. Just as Casandra, in her initial reference to him had associated her mother with his ideal, so now doña Isabel in her turn associates Teresias with it, through his friendship and esteem for the returning exile. Thus don Rodrigo is seen from the beginning as a focal point around which are gathered the forces of resistance to President José within his own close circle of relatives and friends.

Only now does President José himself make his carefully prepared entrance, which is the signal for the main ideological scene of Act 1, *Cuadro* I. In the conversation between him and his wife which follows, Marqués once more achieves a double object. The clash of outlook which emerges not only clarifies the message of the play (Marqués' championship of the superior, if intangible, values of national self-sufficiency and self-realization over the material advantages accruing from dependence on a foreign power) but also, and in a way more importantly, establishes don José as a fundamentally weak and insecure human being. In doing so it introduces the secondary aspect of the play: its human dimension, which turns on the study of the dictatorial mentality in don José, and the evolution of Casandra from her initial superficiality of outlook towards total dedication to the national ideal. It may be noted at this point that don José and Casandra are in fact the only characters whose psychology does actually evolve during the course of the action.

President José's insecurity is suggested by his need of alcohol but more effectively by his dependence on his wife's presence for relief from nervous tension. Marqués, with a subtle touch, makes the scene between the President and his wife both begin and end on this note with José's speeches: "No me dejes solo" and later "Sin ti estoy siempre a solas." In this way the argument between them about don José's political policy, on which the theme of the play is centered, is obliquely correlated with his personal, human inadequacy.

From this contrast stems Marqués' clash of allegiances in the rest of the play. The problem is a common one in literature of social protest and can be readily illustrated by reference both to the novel in Latin America and to other plays in this category. To be effective a work of protest must do one of two things. Either it must attack the oppressors, emphasizing all their negative qualities, while idealizing the oppressed, as for example in Alegría's novel *El mundo es ancho y ajeno,* or (less crudely) it must portray any virtues of the oppressors as less important than their vices, and present the vices of the oppressed as deriving from their oppression, as in Icaza's *Huasipungo.* In this way a balance of sympathy in favor of the oppressed is preserved. Failure to accomplish this may make a work more realistic, since we know that neither oppressors nor oppressed have a monopoly of virtues or vices, but it will seriously endanger the ideological impact. An illustration of this is seen in another well-known play in Solórzano's anthology, the Chilean Egon Wolff's *Los*

invasores (1962). Here the portraiture of the bourgeois exploiters of the poor is conventional enough, though Meyer, their spokesman, makes some shrewd remarks in his own defense; but as the play progresses Wolff, while seeming to realize that there is something crude about idealizing the now insurgent slum-dwellers, is unable to find a suitable alternative. Just at the moment when what is needed to balance the play ideologically is a clear statement of positive policy on behalf of the now triumphant invaders, Alí Babá emerges as the advocate of blind violence and brutality and China, the rebels' moderate leader, can find no better definition of the movement, hitherto presented as childishly destructive than the vague statement that it is "una cruzada de buena fe." In consequence the play is neither a successful piece of propaganda nor a genuine drama of ideas. Failure to present the invaders in a positive light prevents it from achieving the former category while the crudity of its attack on the bourgeois group removes it from the latter.

La muerte no entrará en palacio is open to criticism on similar grounds. From the moment Marqués begins to develop the play not simply as a drama of protest but as a tragedy as well he runs the risk of falling between two stools. Tragedy and straight social or political protest are intrinsically incompatible, for tragedy in so far as it is a protest at all is a protest against the *human* condition and not against specific social or political conditions. Though it is possible to envisage a tragedy which includes social or political criticism, this can only be indirect and balanced against some other force which is not in itself morally superior. For tragedy, as we know, obviously results from the clash of equally justified forces. Thus it would be a critical error to interpret Lorca's depiction in *La casa de Bernada Alba* of narrowness of mentality in an Andalusian *pueblo* as primarily a protest against the conditions which contribute to its formation. The mentality in question is seen rather as a factor in the human situation of Bernada's family which conflicts with another factor: Adela's emotional and sexual frustration. Both are viewed with detachment and the tragedy is born out of the clash between them which is seen as both inevitable and wasteful. No such detachment and balance of dramatic forces are visible in *La muerte no entrará en palacio,* however. In the last part of Act I, *Cuadro* I, the interview between President José and the peasants' delegation, the equilibrium between José's belief in "pan y techo seguros, instrucción, libertades, progreso" and doña Isabel's defense of "algo que vale más que toda la ciencia y todo el progreso del mundo" (i.e., national independence) is shattered. The protest element in the play takes over as Marqués obviously sides with the young spokesman of the peasants against the President. Once this has taken place we are no longer confronted with a momentous choice between two equally defensible principles of public conduct. The tragic possibilities of the play are henceforth severely limited.

Cuadro II of Act I is no less interesting technically than

Cuadro I. It consists basically of four scenes. Three of these are really discussions of the situation; the fourth is a dramatic curtain-scene designed to carry over suspense into Act II. They are separated by quotations from the speeches on the theme of independence by the returned exile don Rodrigo. These provide both a recurrent contrast to the discussions themselves and the context of growing unrest against which the discussions take place. The order in which the three discussion-scenes are presented is significant. The first conveys the reaction of President José himself; the second that of his wife doña Isabel; the third that of his daughter Casandra. The audience is thus confronted successively with an illustration of the dubious political morality on which the President's regime rests; the assertion of the need for a moral choice on the part of the leaders opposed to it; and Casandra's actual choice, which is to sacrifice her happiness with Alberto. Of the three, the first, centering on the President is dramatically the most interesting. Superficially, it is concerned with the fragility of José's regime now under strong attack from don Rodrigo and the doubtful judicial methods by means of which it defends itself. But there is another element; the rebellion of don José himself (or of his better self) against the effects of his own position and policies. Fortunately for the literary quality of the play, don José has nothing in common with Asturias' Señor Presidente. He is seen here to be conscious of the degeneration of his own personality contrasted with that of Alberto's father, who died before their common ideal became tarnished by contact with reality. In his last speech of the scene with its poignant statement "es fácil serlo todo antes de llegar al poder," we are invited momentarily to see president José as the unwilling victim of his position, a man forced to compromise with his ideals by the realities and responsibilities of power. Similarly in his instinctive rejection of the cynical attitudes of his Chief Justice, there is a further element of unhappy self-awareness: "Todavía soy capaz de sentir asco. Pero lo horrible es que cada vez siento menos asco." These flashes of self-insight unquestionably raise don José's character above the level of the stock dictator-figure and recapture for him a great deal of the audience's sympathy. In doing so they at the same time lift the play out of the category of mere protest-drama with its characteristic contrast of black and white, and bring into sight an issue which is far more complex and fundamental than that which is symbolized by the block of stone brought by the peasants to their interview with the President. The question, that is, of a final justification for don José.

Throughout the play don José is assumed to be wrong. But the opposition acts as if his contemptuous view of the people over whom he presides is correct. If what Alberto and Casandra believe is true: that an unscrupulous President can manipulate even democratic methods for his own ends; if the people are incapable of understanding the message of don Rodrigo; if there is no confidence in the triumph of right unaided by force (for as we perceive at the end of Act I even the idealist side is not exempt from violence and bloodshed); then the question arises whether don José is not half-right after all. The real issue in the play, expressed in terms of a direct confrontation between the President and don Rodrigo with the people as arbiter, is avoided. As a consequence some rather worrying interrogations about Marqués ultimate convictions remain.

Meanwhile, in Act I, *Cuadro* II, the President's over-violent treatment of the *Jefe de Justicia* brings with it for the audience the recognition that he is in fact willfully closing his eyes to the consequences of his own regime, and re-emphasizes his basic weakness and insecurity as a human being. A potentially tragic character up to this point, torn between nostalgia for his youthful ideals and the realism of experience, this is for him the key-scene. But his momentary flashes of self-insight lead to no decision, tragic or otherwise. Henceforth he is lost.

The second discussion, between doña Isabel and Teresias, shows the counter-movement against the President gaining ground within his own intimate circle. Both his wife and friend recognize the necessity for a realignment of allegiances. Teresias' "tenemos que escoger—tenemos que ser fieles sólo a una voz" indicates that the issues have crystallized. In the final discussion they are underlined again by Alberto: "Estamos viviendo una crisis y no podemos eludir nuestras responsabilidades." "Hay algo en don José que se ha deteriorado, que se está deteriorando de modo lamentable." But as yet matters have not come to a head. The effect of Alberto's dramatic revelation of don José's plan to turn the country into a foreign protectorate is mitigated by the hope that the better side of the President's nature will yet prevail. The attempted assassination of don José closes the act with an effective curtain-scene.

A significant feature of Act II is that in *Cuadro* I the play marks time: there is no real advance in the action as such. Why is this? To perceive the answer it is necessary to examine the dramatic forces in play at this point. One is obvious: it is the President himself, now a force for evil advancing towards the goal of establishing the protectorate. Which is the other? Here we have a clue as to another weakness of the play. The second dramatic force is composed of all the other major characters: the youth from Altamira, Teresias, Alberto, Isabel and Casandra, with Casandra as the eventual dramatic *agent*. Don Rodrigo hovers behind them in the background but never appears.

This fragmentation of the opposing dramatic force has two important consequences. First, the time that should be devoted to a direct clash of character between anyone of the opposing group (one had hopes of don Rodrigo in this act) and the President is used instead to give each one the possibility of revealing his or her hostility, keeping Casandra in reserve for the final *cuadro*. Second, and more important, it has the effect of restricting the underlying conflict to the external plane. Reconsidering the situation we recognize in don José a fundamentally good man gone wrong and vaguely aware of it: a good start for a tragic figure. But apart from the minor instance already noticed (the scene with the *Jefe de Justica*) and his question to Teresias in this act "¿Qué puedo hacer para escuchar tu voz?" there is little or no evidence of a consistent conflict *within* the President himself. Next we have a situation in which the tragic agent is don José's own daughter Casandra. But, instead of centering the play on her terrible decision, Marqués chooses to range a whole series of characters against the President and only sets her in motion suddenly after a seemingly fortuitous event has caused her to bring about the death of Alberto her fiancé.

Once more, as in the deputation-scene in Act I, Marqués' divided allegiances, driving him now in the direction of straight protest, now back towards more intrinsically literary effects, seem to play him false. What is uppermost here is the ideological aspect: the contrast of the single dictator with the solid phalanx of his nationalist opponents. By wasting time showing them clashing with don José in this *cuadro* (first Teresias, then Isabel, the political and the personal in interesting symmetry) followed by Alberto's exclamation "Tenemos que hacer algo," as if this were not already obvious at the end of Act I, Marqués loses the opportunity to develop adequately a tragic evolution of character in Casandra and the conclusion of the play is reduced to the level of the merely dramatic, not to say novelesque.

The last *cuadro* is by contrast an extremely effective piece of stagecraft. Too late to salvage the tragedy, Marqués makes a good job of ending the drama. Casandra's growing insight had been deliberately indicated as early as Act I, *Cuadro* II ("Oh, Alberto mío, estoy aprendiendo mucho") and re-emphasized by her temporary flight from her father's once-loved Palace at the end of Act II, *Cuadro* I. She is given additional strength for her later action by the interview with her mother which now takes place. Doña Isabel's plea to her "¡No pierdas tu fe, hijita!" marks a decisive point in Casandra's evolution. Next don José is allowed to drop several notches lower in the moral scale: his actions are seen to derive not merely from weakness, from compromise, from false choice between material and ideal values, but from a hidden contempt for "este miserable, estúpido pueblo." His next words, with their reference to *dignidad,* are ironically an unwitting compliment to the ideal of Alberto and the others, which reveals how confused the President's value-system has now become.

The penultimate scene contains, as usual, the moment of pathos before the climax. Normally the last two scenes of a play are deliberately contrasted in tone in order to reinforce the effect of the concluding one. But here this is not the case. For although the scene opens on a moving note of renunciation and parting, it shifts abruptly into high drama as Casandra, struggling to get possession of her fiancé's pistol in order to prevent him from assassinating her father, shoots Alberto.

The usual contrast is thus foreshortened so as to bring Cassandra's evolution rapidly to its peak with her cry of "Cualquier otro, menos tú" and at that precise point to bind together inextricably her private catastrophe and the events which follow. The last two scenes of the play are thereby functionally connected. It is by the breaking of her bond with Alberto that Casandra is freed for and in a sense impelled to her final action. This occurs in a spectacular scene in which Marqués mobilizes every possible resource of scenery, groups of characters, symbolism and dramatic contrast to produce a memorable climax with the President struck down by his daughter as he is in the act of signing away the independence of his country. In all the last *cuadro* there is the mounting intensity characteristic of the work of a highly professionalized dramatist. The only criticism of it is that the last scene and epilogue are possibly a trifle over-written and melodramatic.

But the real criticism of Marqués' play is not this. It is that there is no conflict of ideal with ideal. Ultimately the clash here is between right and wrong as the dramatist sees them. And there is no such thing as a tragedy of thesis. Equally, both don José and Casandra lack authentic tragic stature. Tragic grandeur of character arises from inner conflict or from conscious involvement in a tragic situation disposed by an irony of fate. These are largely absent here.

The play is in fact a compromise. Marqués, with great technical resourcefulness strives to conciliate belief in his duty as a "committed" writer with pressure from his artistic conscience to aim at a work in one of the highest universal categories. *La muerte no entrará en palacio* thus illustrates with particular clarity the dilemma confronting so many contemporary Latin American dramatists. It is for this, rather than for its documentary significance, that it is worthy of note.

Charles M. Tatum (review date Winter 1977)

SOURCE: A review of *The Docile Puerto Rican,* translated by Barbara B. Aponte, in *World Literature Today,* Vol. LI, No. 1, Winter, 1977, p. 72.

[*In the following review of* The Docile Puerto Rican, *Tatum praises the work for its historical and political insight.*]

The Puerto Rican René Marqués is well known as a dramatist and prose fiction writer, but he has received little attention as an essayist. This volume of his essays thus constitutes a valuable contribution to our knowledge of this important Latin American writer as well as to our understanding of the Puerto Rican and his unique relationship to the United States.

In her introduction the translator wastes no time in going to the heart of Marqués's essays: the problem of the US's political, economic and cultural domination of Latin America in general and of Puerto Rico in particular. Throughout his literary career he has addressed himself to this relationship;

in his popular play *La carreta* (1950) Marqués describes the cultural upheaval a *jíbaro* family undergoes when it emigrates from the Puerto Rican countryside to New York City. Long an exponent of Puerto Rican nationalism, in the essays included in this volume he expresses the urgency of retaining the Spanish language, of reviving and supporting interest in Puerto Rican folkways and traditions and, primarily, of resisting American efforts to dominate the island culturally.

Marqués shows himself to be a sensitive interpreter of his people's history, capable of tracing the dominant patterns of thought which reflect themselves in contemporary Puerto Rican politics and literature. A theme running throughout the essays which gives unity to the collection is that of the docile Puerto Rican who has been too quick to accept the official policies of his government, even when these policies clearly would run counter to the island's future best interests. Aponte has carefully chosen the essays to illustrate this idea of the islander's indifference and insensitivity to his own history. The lack of historical consciousness, warns Marqués, can mean the island's demise as a cultural entity and hasten a certain fate as a permanent colony of the United States.

The essays in [*The Docile Puerto Rican*] add to our understanding of how the United States is perceived by many respected Latin American intellectual leaders. We are given a glimpse of the dangers of cultural domination arising from our economic and political policies toward Latin America.

Carlos R. Hortas (essay date Spring-Summer 1980)

SOURCE: "René Marqués' *La mirada:* A Closer Look," in *Latin American Literary Review,* Vol. VIII, No. 16, Spring-Summer, 1980, pp. 196-212.

[*In the following essay, Hortas examines mythological, Christian, and sexual metaphors in* La mirada.]

René Marqués *La mirada* was published in an unexpurgated first edition in Puerto Rico in 1976, two years after Spanish censors had refused to grant it publication unless certain objectionable passages were either deleted or modified. The last major work of the widely acclaimed Puerto Rican writer before his death in 1979, *La mirada* has generally been dismissed by critics as an incoherent, disjointed piece of writing by an author past his prime. In the recent issue of the literary review, *Sin Nombre,* dedicated to René Marqués, *La mirada* commands very little attention and no praise at all. Arcadio Díaz Quiñones states flatly:

> Over the last few years his literary output was a failure. The novel *La mirada* (1976) and some of his recent short stories were but a weak echo of his own work, a worn-out repetition, at times an involuntary parody of himself, or the recapitulation of a well-known literary agenda. The last texts that he published made one think that his creative reserves were prematurely exhausted.

In an essay entitled "René Marqués ¿escritor misógino?", Maria Solá makes passing reference to *La mirada,* calling it and Marqués' short story **"El bastón,"** . . . bitter narratives that bring his literary output to a close." In 1977 Efrain Barradas had already observed: "Marqués' ideological confusion, which reaches its moment of greatest crisis in *La mirada,* leads him to create this anarchic novel, full of clichés, full of structural faults. One must conclude that his last novel is a failure." Eleanor J. Martin's recent monograph on René Marqués compares Marqués' two novels, *La vispera del hombre* and *La mirada:*

> Marqués' novel *The Eve of Manhood,* written just prior to a peak period of drama, reflects the artistic expertise of that moment. Some of these stylistic devices carried over into his much later novel, *The Glance,* are—symbolism, flashback, the presentation of reality through the psyche of a young man, for example. Yet the later novel seems less well realized, because the zig-zag presentation of reality and change in identities, time, and space, although reflecting the flow of consciousness of the protagonist, are at times confusing to the reader.

For the moment, suffice it to say that *La mirada* is much richer, much more suggestive and thought-provoking, and structurally sounder than the opinions just cited would indicate. Ostensibly, the novel narrates a series of incident in which the nameless protagonist interacts with a group of "hippies," and it also relates his incestuous love affair with his niece, Maria. *La mirada* is, however, much more than that. It is, as its title suggests, a novel of vision, a new look at traditional Christian symbols and an irreverent glance at the interplay between sexuality and religion. Some may claim that Marqués hallucinates, yet, though the protagonist of the novel is subject to drug-induced hallucinations, the novel itself is very much in focus.

La mirada opens in the Puerto Rican countryside, where a group of local citizens becomes alarmed when their small, picturesque beach is "invaded" by a group of hippies. Some of the young men of the town, led by the novel's protagonist and his friend, Julito, conclude that the hippies must be driven from the beach, and they formulate a plan to evict them by force. Before their plan can be carried out, however, the young protagonist of *La mirada* feels an irresistible compulsion to go down to the beach and have a first-hand look at the "invaders." He seems to be beckoned there by the bearded leader of the hippies, a green-eyed, long-haired man known as *Sem.* When he reaches the beach, the protagonist is welcomed by the hippies and offered a brown-colored round "cookie" described to him as *nourishment.* A woman whom the protagonist identifies to the reader as *Gaea,* because she reminds him of the mythological Greek deity, distributes these round cookies to all present, then places one on her own tongue, "as if it were a sacred host" (como una hostia).

After the goddess (or priestess) distributes holy communion, she enters a tent and returns with a sword (cimitarra) in her hands, which she offers to the protagonist. The cookies apparently contain a hallucinogenic drug, and he now feels its effects. He takes up the sword and, under the influence of the drug, decapitates *Gaea* and cuts off the hands and genitalia of the leader of the group, *Sem,* now also identified as *Uranus*. The protagonist at this point believes that he is *Cronus,* son of *Gaea* and *Uranus,* and that the sword he is wielding is "the jeweled scythe for the ritual castration." Following the decapitation of Gaea and the mutilation of Sem, the protagonist is incarcerated together with the hippies found on the beach with him, and his friend, Julito, a late arrival at the scene.

Here we must pause briefly to consider a point that is mentioned only in passing but is of crucial importance to the understanding of the novel's symbolism and its metaphorical density. During the protagonist's short visit to the hippie encampment on the beach, he speaks with the woman identified as *Gaea* about a paperback book, "worn-out from much handling" [bastante manoseado], which belongs to the hippie commune. The book is entitled *The Sacred Mushroom and the Cross,* by John Allegro. The woman recommends that he purchase a copy and read it. He asks if it is a religious book and she tells him:

> —In a profound sense, yes. All religions are based from prehistoric times on the adoration of the sacred mushroom. Christianity as well. Had you noticed that the cross with the crucified Christ is in reality a mushroom?
>
> —I had never noticed such a thing. This mushroom on the cover seems rather like something phallic.
>
> ———
>
> —One must eat the sacred mushroom in order to achieve the mystical separation of body and soul.
>
> —Death?
>
> —On the contrary. Life. Eternal unity for a true life.

John Allegro's *The Sacred Mushroom and the Cross* is not mentioned anywhere else in the novel, yet it is central to an understanding of the novel's imagery and its seemingly strange mix of religion, sex, drugs, myth and legend. Allegro, a lecturer in Biblical Studies at the University of Manchester, England, author of several articles on Semitic philology, and an authority on Sumerian and later Middle Eastern lan-

guages, is also a member of an international editing team presently preparing the Dead Sea Scrolls for publication. His book on the Dead Sea Scrolls has sold over 250,000 copies and has been translated into eight languages. In *The Sacred Mushroom and the Cross,* his most recent work, Allegro advances the hypothesis that the Bible, both the Old and the New Testaments, contains hidden, encoded meanings that refer to an ancient cult of the sacred mushroom, *amanita muscaria.* According to Allegro, the New Testament may not be what it seems; the story of Christ may simply be a literary "cloak," a means of disguising and at the same time transmitting secret knowledge about the cult of the sacred mushroom to the faithful, those able to decode the texts.

Allegro maintains that the early Christians may have been members of a sect devoted to the worship and use of the sacred mushroom and that, persecuted and driven underground, they chose to encode their rituals and practices in the New Testament in order to deceive the Roman authorities about their true purpose. As Allegro says:

> The whole point of a mystery cult was that few people knew its secret doctrines. So far as possible, the initiates did not commit their special knowledge to writing ... When such special instruction was committed to writing, care would be taken that it should be read only by the members of the sect. This could be done by using a special code or cypher ... Another way of passing information was to conceal the message, incantations or special names within a document ostensibly concerned with a quite different subject.

Allegro maintains that philogians have never been satisfied with some of the translations of the Bible which do not seem to offer a rendering of the original texts, and that these *Pseudo-translations* are of crucial importance: "They provide us with a clue to the true nature of original Christianity. Concealed within are secret names for the sacred fungus, the sect's 'Christ.'" Allegro also postulates that the early Christians believed in the possibility of achieving a separation of body and soul (a mythical state) by ingesting the sacred mushroom. Thus did man gain knowledge of God. However, when Christians suffered persecution at the hands of the Romans, the cult of the mushroom almost went out of existence and what survived was a sect who took over the name of Christian, but forgot or purged from its rituals the real essence of Christianity—the cult of the sacred mushroom. In fact, these new "Christians" forgot the secret code of cypher which informs the New Testament:

> Christians, hated and despised, were hauled forth and slain in their thousands. The cult well nigh perished. What actually took its place was a travesty of the real thing, a mockery of the power that could raise men to heaven and give them the glimpse of God for which they gladly died. The story of the rabbi cruci-

fied at the instigation of the Jews became an historical peg upon which the new cult's authority was founded. what began as a hoax, became a trap even to those who believed themselves to be the spiritual heirs of the mystery religion and took to themselves the name of "Christian." Above all they forgot or purged from the cult and their memories, the one supreme secret on which their whole religious and ecstatic experience depended: the names and identity of the true source of the drug, the key to heaven—the sacred mushroom.

According to Allegro, other mythologies of the Near East, based on the concept of a god or gods of fertility, (Greek classical mythology and Yahwehism) are also partly based on mushroom mythology. Christianity was then the last manifestation of the cult of the sacred mushroom before it was purged of its drug-takers and:

> . . . eventually so conformed to the will of the State that in the fourth century it became an integral part of the ruling establishment. By then its priests were raising wafers and sweet wine at the altar and trying to convince their followers that the host had miraculously become the flesh and juice of the god.

This introduction to John Allegro's theories is indispensable to an understanding of the richness and interplay of the religious, sexual and mushroom symbolism in *La mirada*. Using Allegro's theories as a point of departure, René Marqués constructs a number of scenes in *La mirada* which utilize as central motifs the sacred mushroom, the rites of Christianity and stories from Greek mythology.

Returning to René Marqués' text, we will take another look at *Sem,* the leader of the hippie commune. During his mutilation Sem is compared to the Greek god Uranus; earlier in the novel he is compared to Christ:

> . . . with his faded blue jeans, purposefully tattered, his face with its long beard, sideburns and drooping mustache, his features showed a clear resemblance to Christ . . . displaying rather muscular biceps and more pronounced nipples than what one would expect from someone with such a thick beard.

In this description Sem's sexual outline, his bodily contours, appear rather ambiguous. His sexuality is further obscured when he is emasculated by the protagonist. At that moment Sem becomes Uranus:

> Ah, Uranus, whose smile and arms extended in the shape of a cross were a sacred mushroom. He brought down the blade and cleanly severed Sem's right hand and, with a howl, the left and, with another howl his

loincloth (el taparrabos) and then the genitals, because he was Cronus.

In this scene a number of images are combined: the crucifix, *brazos en cruz;* the sacred mushroom, and the myth of Uranus and Cronus. The cross and the sacred mushroom have phallic configurations, as does the sword wielded by the protagonist. Thus the protagonist (Cronus, the son) is empowered to emasculate Sem (Uranus, the father) by the ingestion of the sacred mushroom, itself a phallus.

Before emasculating his father, Uranus, the protagonist in his role as Cronus also decapitates his mother, Gaea. The matricide, not part of the original myth of Uranus and Gaea, may be added here by the author to evoke the Clytemnestra-Orestes story, which he alludes to later in the novel. The beach scene ends with the protagonist finally restrained and disarmed and then taken to jail, along with other members of the group who were with him on the beach, including the mutilated Sem.

In jail, we come to that section of the novel considered "objectionable" by Spanish censors. The objectionable material consists of a scene during which a number of prisoners commit homosexual aggression on the person of the protagonist. Particularly objectionable to the censors, no doubt, is the analogy drawn between the sexual violation of the protagonist and the passion of Christ and his crucifixion. In jail the protagonist is befriended by a member of the hippie group, a black man who takes him under his wing for protection: "You'll be under my protection. (Serás mi protegido.) It's worth your while. Don't look at me. Don't let on. It's for your own good". However, the other prisoners soon demand that the two engage in a homosexual act to prove that they are lovers, and the sexual "crucifixion" of the protagonist takes place.

First, the protagonist performs fellatio on his black companion: "The sacred mushroom was immense and it kept on growing and growing in his mouth. . . ." Then, the mutilated Sem-Christ-Uranus lies in front of him:

> And the Christ, that is, Sem, hands and other parts missing, lay down in front of him, between his legs, and began gently sucking and he felt a sudden indescribable pleasure while the mushroom of the black man had come to have the hardness of stone between his teeth and lips.

The protagonist's friend, Julito, who will later say, "I nailed you in jail" (Te clavé en la cárcel), now penetrates him from behind, figuratively *nailing* him to the cross, and his right and left arms are extended in the form of a cross to grasp the *nails* (penises) of the two "guitarists": "And his left hand was made to grasp the nail (el clavo) of the good guitarist and the right hand the nail of the evil guitarist". To complete the crucifixion scene a young man:

. . . frenetically nailed his small pointed lance between his nipple and right side with the intention of
wounding him, but was unable to achieve it, while
the two guards or high priests, with their pants around
their knees, masturbated or seemed to masturbate, in
unified rhythm, at the entrance.

This scene, which Spanish censors wanted to delete, is the
apotheosis of Marqués' fusion of the symbols of the sacred
mushroom, the phallus and the cross. The passion of Christ,
his crucifixion and the sacraments of baptism and holy communion are fused with sexual symbols. As the protagonist is
crucified he is also adoring the sacred mushroom and receiving it into his body. The phallus-mushroom is at the same
time the host which the protagonist receives into his mouth
in the sacrament of holy communion, the agent of his passion
and the instrument by which he is "nailed" to the cross. During his crucifixion the protagonist experiences both pain and
pleasure until finally: "The pain disappeared or became im-
perceptible and pleasure triumphed along his entire body. . . ."
The passion of the protagonist terminates in a moment of
supreme ecstasy. He moves rhythmically with the others,

    . . . until the paroxysm of a tragic chorus arrived in
    an oh! joyously triumphant and, simultaneously, se-
    men in his mouth and over his entire body, baptized
    with the sacred liquid, like a weeping also tragic and
    absolutely final.

    And in the agony, the ultimate anguish of the ritual
    he cried out or thought he cried out: Father, father of
    mine! Why have you forsaken me? And he fainted.

Within this scene we find the constituents of Marqués' metaphoric and symbolic edifice: the sacred mushroom, the phallus, the passion of Christ, the crucifixion, and the reference
to Greek myths, here alluded to in the words *tragic chorus.*

Marqués' words, *baptized with the sacred liquid* suggest that
the protagonist is receiving the sacrament of baptism and also
being "baptized" or initiated into the rituals of the cult of the
sacred mushroom. The *sacred liquid* or semen is also the holy
water of baptism and may be further understood by John
Allegro's observations regarding the ancient sanctity of semen. Allegro claims that the strictures of the Roman Catholic
Church against birth control preserve, in our day, the ancient
regard for the sanctity of semen. As he puts it:

    The real objections to contraception have little to do
    with family morals or, indeed, with morality at all as
    the modern world understands the term; it is simply
    that wasting seed is a religious 'sin': it is a blasphemy
    against the 'word of god,' the 'holy spirit'.

Allegro also observes that "The principal gods of the Greeks
and Hebrews, Zeus and Yahweh (Jehovah), have names derived from Sumerian meaning 'juice of fecundity,' sperma-
tozoa, 'seed of life'." It is with this in mind that we must
interpret the name *Sem* (semen) that Marqués gives to the
Christ-Uranus figure. Halfway through the novel, the black
member of the hippie group is speaking to the protagonist:

    —The leader was Sem.
    —Sam?
    —Sem. Puerto Rican.

Marqués wants to make sure that his readers make no mistake. The name of his character is *Sem,* not Sam. In this character Marqués tries to create a tripartite being, Uranus-
Christ-Sem; Father, Son, and Holy Spirit. Although the protagonist assumes various guises in the novel (Cronus, the crucified Christ, Orestes, and his real identity as an only son), he
is always the son. Sem, on the other hand, encompasses three
different aspects of one divine being and, as *Sem,* he represents semen, the sacred liquid, the holy water, the holy spirit
which endows man with divine powers of creation. As the
leader of the hippie group which worships the sacred mushroom, Sem is also identified with the cult of the phallus, the
sacred mushroom whose juice is the key to heaven.

Within the scene of the sexual crucifixion of the protagonist
there are constant, intricate allusions to sexual, Christian and
mushroom symbols that pile up one on top of the other. For
instance, the black member of the hippie group reveals that,
in his earlier life, he had worked in a nightclub in the nude
while a dancer ". . . made believe that she adored me while
she danced." He tells the protagonist, "I was a black god, in
the nude. . . ." Thus the black man is also a god, adored by the
protagonist during his sexual crucifixion. The black god is
the possessor of the sacred mushroom which grows to its full
size in the mouth of the protagonist. The protagonist receives
the body (sacred mushroom) and blood (semen, sacred liquid) of the god, the black man who has told him: "You will
be under my protection" (Serás mi protegido). The black god,
unable to protect him against the sexual violation to which he
is subjected, is addressed by the protagonist when he exclaims:
"Father, father of mine! Why have you forsaken me?" Like
the crucified Christ, the protagonist feels forsaken by God
the father, his protector, at his hour of greatest need. If, however, we consider the mushroom-phallus as the god being
worshipped in this scene, then the crucified protagonist is
"forsaken" when, after the climatic moment of his "passion",
the mushroom-phalluses are removed from his mouth, hands
and anus.

The crucifixion scene is completed by the presence of the
two *guitarists* to the right and left sides of the crucified Christ-
protagonist, and the prison guards who witness the proceedings. Further identification of mushroom and Christian
symbols is accomplished by the alternate references to the

penises of the *guitarists* as *nails* and to the crosses to which the *guitarists* are nailed as *mushrooms*. The sexual *nailing* of the protagonist is analogous to the eleventh station of the *Via Crucis:* Christ is nailed on the cross. The prison guards are the *high priests* who lasciviously observe the goings-on, "with joyous smiles and occasional tonguings of their dry lips," and masturbate during the adoration of the sacred mushroom. The allusion here is to the Catholic mass and to the mediating role of priests who recreate the passion of Christ upon the altar, for the sake of the faithful who have come to worship. In the prison scene, the "passion" of the guard-priests is shown to be self serving; they are empty beings, cardboard figures capable only of self-love when moved by the passion of the protagonist in his role as the crucified Christ. The prison scene ends with the protagonist fainting, (Y se desmayó), which parallels the end of Christ's passion, his death upon the cross.

After the scene of sexual crucifixion, we are immediately presented with one of the hallucinatory sections of the novel. Now the protagonist finds himself a spectator at the scene of a crucifixion. *Sem* is the one being crucified, ". . . high upon the sacred mushroom. . . ." From on high Sem looks down at the protagonist and at Gaea, who is now cast in the role of the Virgin Mary, and says:

> Woman, behold thy son. Son, behold thy mother. And he looked once more beside him and did not see his mother but a strange and aged woman, horribly wrinkled . . . He raised his head to look at the crucified one and was not surprised. He was the same Christ that he had seen in the classroom, the solitary leader upon the rock, the mutilated one that had taken part in the sexual orgy in jail. . . .

Now Sem is the crucified Christ and the protagonist is cast in the role of Jesus' favorite disciple, present at his crucifixion (John 19: 26, 27). The two "guitarists" appear, crucified to the right and left of Sem. They both speak to Christ-Sem and remind him: "When you have the cookie (la bolita), remember me." *La bolita* refers to the round drugged "cookie" that the protagonist ate when he first visited the hippie encampment on the beach. The words are also a play on the biblical, "Jesus, remember me when you come into your Kingdom" (Luke 23:42). *La bolita* or sacred mushroom is the key or means by which the faithful enter God's kingdom. The hallucination that follows the ingestion of the sacred mushroom is the equivalent of a mystical experience, an experience of God, an entrance into his kingdom.

Within this hallucinatory section the protagonist assumes still another biblical identity:

> Making a superhuman effort, he was able to look away from the increasingly more anguished look of the other, and, turning around, he ran towards a guard dressed in khaki, snatched his lance away from him

and nailed the man, that is he nailed the dull lance into his side. And the liquid flowed.

> Free at last, the other raised his eyes to heaven and seemed to cry out almost inaudibly:

> -It is done

The protagonist now becomes the Roman soldier who pierced Jesus' side with a spear at the crucifixion (John 19: 34). The cross and the sacred mushroom are fused once more at the conclusion of this section:

> And the bolt of lightning fell upon the center *mushroom,* but the fire spread to the two neighboring mushrooms. And it was the *cross* of the man wrapped in flames that came crashing down, making the earth tremble, the whole earth . . .

> (Italics mine).

In *La mirada* there are a number of other references to characters from Greek mythology, particularly those belonging to the accursed house of Atreus. Although exact names of mythological characters are not always used, a long hallucinatory passage in the novel, which begins after the protagonist and his friend, Julito, have each "popped some pills," makes constant reference to the "the last *Atridas*" and "the golden Atridas." This suggest Orestes who, by killing his mother Clytemnestra and her lover (Agamemnon's brother, Aegisthus), avenged the murder of his father, Agamemnon.

In the hallucinatory section based on the Orestes-Clytemnestra matricide, the role of the last *Atridas* is played by the protagonist. He is kidnapped by his friend Julito, a few of the hippies, and Sem. They hold him for ransom and, to prove they have him, send a package to his mother, in which are the protagonist's severed testicles. When the mother opens the package and realizes what it contains, she reels backward from the shock and falls over a low second-floor balcony to her death.

The section which immediately follows this hallucinatory passage is set back at the protagonist's house in the countryside. There, a wake is being held for his mother. We do not know the cause of her death, therefore the preceding hallucination is either a portent of the imminent death of the protagonist's real mother or a narrative device by which the figurative castration of the protagonist leads to the sorrow and death of the mother. Like Orestes, the protagonist is responsible for his mother's death. Earlier in the novel the protagonist's real father, angry and bewildered because of the direction his son's life has taken, and because his son speaks of the sacred mushroom, warns:

> Do we continue to have drugs here? Because I can't

take it anymore. And whenever you talk like a crazy man, you kill your mother. Don't you see how she looks?

He could see. But she reassured him smiling.

-No one is killing me, son.

And he could not contain himself any longer and embraced her and wept uncontrollably, a cry of centuries, for a long, long time, and he could only whisper:

-Forgive me.

Towards the conclusion of the novel, after the death of the protagonist's mother and of his niece, Maria, his father cries: "God, God, what curse have you placed upon this family?" This suggests an identification between the protagonist's family and the accursed house of Atreus. Thus the cryptic message that appears in the author's italics twice in the novel, and comprises its final words: *Justice discharged, Destiny inexorable (Justicia cumplida, Destino implacable)*.

We cannot conclude this study of **La mirada** without a discussion of the novel's title, translatable as either **The Look, The Glance** or **The Gaze**. An important *leit-motif* throughout the novel is the presence of green eyes and the feelings and reactions that the protagonist experiences when gazing into green eyes, or when he is the subject of their gaze. Most of the women in the novel are green-eyed: the protagonist's niece Maria, a university student to whom he feels attracted, Maria's mother (the same dancer who worked in a nightclub and pretended to adore the black god while she danced), a married woman whom the protagonist meets and makes love to during a party at his brother's house, the hippie "priestess" referred to as Gaea, and, finally, Sem, the Christ figure who is devoid of sexual organs and, as we have already mentioned, sexually ambiguous. Green eyes seem to denote intense sexuality or attraction. At times they may also represent exotic or unusual beauty, temptation, depravity, malevolence or evil. In **La mirada,** the green eyes of his niece Maria and Sem have the strongest attraction for the protagonist. Maria is intelligent and sexually precocious; her eyes are provocative and all-knowing. They haunt the protagonist:

He was horror-stricken with the possibility that he had before him a monster, a mythical fire-breathing dragon, instead of the little girl with her questioning, innocent green eyes.

The little girl (la nena), he thought again. I wonder what those innocent green eyes can be hiding?

Sem's green eyes exert a strong influence: in fact Sem can command the protagonist with a look. Early in the novel, in a university classroom, Sem looks fixedly at the protagonist:

He was correcting the passage where Cronus devours his children when he felt the discomfort of a fixed, persistent stare. He raised his eyes and saw him sitting down in the corner across the way, near the door.

The protagonist is irresistibly drawn to the beach where the hippies are encamped, after looking into Sem's eyes from a distance:

He saw him raise his arms slowly, as if in flight or in the shape of a cross, and he looked at him. In spite of the distance separating them, he was sure that the man was looking at him. And he felt an irresistible impulse to go down to him.

The black man who befriends the protagonist in jail says of Sem: "He demanded many things, just like that, without speaking, just with a look." Shortly before the sexual crucifixion of the protagonist, he is asked by the other prisoners to take off his clothes. He wants to refuse, "But he felt Sem's gaze upon him, and he undressed."

One other mention of green eyes is of particular importance; the image is that of a serpent with green eyes. The serpent first appears during the hallucinatory scene in which the protagonist assumes the role of the last male member of the house of Atreus. Before he is castrated, his kidnappers contemplate the possibility of amputating one of his fingers instead. They choose the ring finger of the left hand, on which the protagonist wears a ring ". . . made of gold in the shape of a serpent, with two small emeralds like malignant eyes." The *ring-finger of the left hand* suggests a love bond and the image is repeated later on in the novel, when the incestuous love between the protagonist and his niece is finally consummated.

After he finally admits to himself that his love for his niece Maria is carnal, rather than paternal or fraternal, the protagonist is about to make love to her for the first time when he discovers that she had made love once before, with his friend Julito. Here the green-eyed serpent (jealousy) rears its ugly head. His ego wounded and feeling deceived, the protagonist gets up and kicks Maria brutally:

And he was on his feet adjusting his belt and under him only the golden serpent with the expensive emeralds and he kicked, he kicked the golden ring without pity, until it was purple from blood and bruises. . . .

The serpent with the emerald eyes is Maria, towards whom he experiences feelings of both love and revulsion. The temptation to have an incestuous relationship with her finally culminates in ". . . the only true night of love in his life. . . ." The serpent, a traditional symbol of evil, associated with the temptation of Eve, also suggests that because of woman man has fallen into temptation and sin. Maria is the evil temptress who has lured the protagonist into the sin of incest. John Allegro, discussing the figure of the serpent coiled around the Tree of Knowledge in the Garden of Eden, claims that the Tree of Knowledge was in reality the *amanita muscaria,* the sacred mushroom, that opened man's eyes, ". . . so that when you eat of it your eyes will be opened, and you will be like God, knowing good and evil. (Genesis 3: 5)." Again we see how Marqués utilizes strong, polyvalent symbols which play upon one another to develop and strengthen the novel's central images.

Speaking about the short story (*La mirada* is only 100 pages long), Marqués once mentioned that it lent itself ". . . the fortunate use of the symbol as a means of achieving poetic synthesis." He also said at the time that there should be no sexual taboos in literature, that writers should avoid the use of euphemisms and treat sex openly:

> Another facet which characterizes a substantial part of the new narrative is the bold treatment of sex as a legitimate literary device. Since the traditional taboo that always forced the use of a euphemism or circumlocution when speaking of sex has disappeared from Puerto Rican society, young writers can now utilize sex as a poetic symbol or as a dramatic device in order to illustrate problems and conflicts of modern man.

What René Marqués has achieved in *La mirada* is the creation of poetic correspondences and symbolic parallels which identify some of the basic constituents of the Western world's religions and myths. The serpent, the cross, the sacred mushroom, the phallus, mythological gods of creation, the passion of Christ—all these elements are brought together in a daring poetic synthesis that reveals new insights into the nature and role of man and his gods. As Paul Ricoeur has observed, poetic or metaphorical language, in contrast to ordinary, descriptive language, ". . . suggests, reveals, unconceals—or whatever you say—the deep structures of reality to which we are related as mortals. . . ."

Thus I would disagree with those who view *La mirada* as a critique of Puerto Rico or as a loss of faith in the destiny of the island, and I do not believe that the sexual crucifixion of the protagonist is intended to be merely a treatment of the theme of homosexuality. It is not that Marqués' political views and concerns about the erosion of Puerto Rican identity are not

expressed in *La mirada;* they are at times intrusive and serve to weaken the internal unity of the novel. The novel speaks about ritual, suffering, passion, sin, temptation, the ambiguities of sexual expression, desire, destiny and hallucination.

As for the protagonist's sexual crucifixion, it is not a treatment of the theme of homosexuality, but a poetic if irreverent treatment of the passion of Christ. *La mirada* gives expression to man's doubts about the historicity of tradition and the "revealed" truths of the Christian faith, and it questions the literal accuracy of myth and legend.

> **[*La mirada*] speaks about ritual, suffering, passion, sin, temptation, the ambiguities of sexual expression, desire, destiny and hallucination. As for the protagonist's sexual crucifixion, it is not a treatment of the theme of homosexuality, but a poetic if irreverent treatment of the passion of Christ. *La mirada* gives expression to man's doubts about the historicity of tradition and the "revealed" truths of the Christian faith, and it questions the literal accuracy of myth and legend.**
>
> **—*Carlos R. Hortas***

The thematic and symbolic richness of *La mirada* is deserving of much more than the indifferent or negative reaction that critics have shown it to date. Many of its allusions and symbols need still closer examination. Only Charles Pilditch, to my knowledge, has recognized that *La mirada* demands much more than a superficial reading. At the end of his monograph on René Marqués, Pilditch comments:

> In August 1973, Marqués completed his second novel, *La mirada,* a masterful blend of all his previous themes, styles and symbols, and the veritable summit of his artistic creations as of this writing . . . With its cosmic orientation and multiple interpretations *La mirada* is Marqués most universal work to date.

Perhaps the explanation of the critics' reactions to *La mirada* lies in the profound ambiguities the novel explores. *La mirada* forces us to consider and question the nature of religious experience and the meaning of traditional symbols. The novel provides no answers; it points up the fact that sexual and religious experience and the very nature of man are fundamentally ambiguous. The mistake of the critics is to judge that Marqués' political commitment to Puerto Rican independence means that every work he wrote must be examined, *first of all,* for its political content. Even if Marqués began this novel as a political statement, *La mirada* acquired a life of its own in the writing. A political "reading" of it is indeed possible, but when we read only for its political import, its literary scope and value are significantly diminished.

In the last few years, in the eternal oedipal struggle between older and younger writers, there has been a tendency to find fault with René Marqués. Some consider him *passé,* part of the *old guard,* dated, a writer who repeats himself, whose aims are transparent. Nothing could be further from the truth. Marqués will continue to be read long after much younger authors lose their reading public; his literary experimentation and theatrical innovations continue to insure his modernity. He may repeat certain themes and concerns from one work to another, but then what writer doesn't? And the textual richness of *La mirada* make this novel anything but a rehash of Marqués' earlier works. *La mirada* is not Marqués most finished work, but it is certainly his most suggestive and provocative. It demands a careful, and closer look.

Thomas Feeny (essay date May 1982)

SOURCE: "Woman's Triumph Over Man in René Marqués's Theater," in *Hispania,* Vol. 65, No. 2, May, 1982, pp. 187-93.

[*In the following essay, Feeny examines the portrayal of female superiority in Marqués' drama and several short stories, especially in the context of Puerto Rican social and political subservience.*]

One particularly interesting and rather neglected aspect of the late René Marqués's writing is the unique concept of woman that pervades much of his work. In examining Marqués's dramas, short stories, novels and essays, a literary achievement covering over three decades, we find the author's portrayal of the female consistently presents her as far more capable and effective than the male. Where the latter fails, woman succeeds. And although she at times may provide encouragement for foundering man, often Marqués's forceful woman ultimately causes him shame and even death.

A number of critics have already noted Marqués's insistence upon portraying woman as man's superior. What we have attempted here is a detailed study of the relationship between this particular view of woman and the author's dire concern both with his country's continued political subservience and with its newly emerged matriarchal society. We shall examine the crucial roles of many of the principal female characters in Marqués's dramas, as well as pertinent passages from his other writing. In addition to illustrating the depth of his anguish, this material also indicates that a good measure of Marqués's inevitable tendency to exalt woman's strength appears at least tangentially related to personal experiences.

As early as *El sol y los MacDonald,* one of Marqués's first plays, the author gives an inkling of the role frequently befalling his male protagonist. Fearful of manhood's challenges, Gustavo throws himself at his mother's feet, crying out: "No quiero crecer. Quiero estar a tu lado. Quiero sentirme niño. Es horrible sentirse hombre" Both the young man's words

and his prone position prove significant for, as we shall see, in Marqués's writing it is quite common for man to end up prostrate before woman.

Regarding the strong female characterizations in *La carreta,* María Teresa Babín affords us a lengthy discussion in her introduction to the 1963 edition. She points out that the matriarch, Doña Gabriela, functions as the "centro vital" of the peasant family that falls on hard times first in San Juan and later in New York. This type of good, forceful, country woman whose innate wisdom withstands modern urban society's false values turns up in several of Marqués's early plays. Equally resourceful in *La carreta,* though in a different fashion, is Juanita, Gabriela's daughter, who ultimately manages to rescue herself from life as a New York prostitute. Her strength seems even greater when contrasted with the passiveness of her adopted brother, Luis, whom Marqués offers as a prototype of the Puerto Rican who surrenders to "Yankee" ways. Clearly voicing the author's own beliefs, Juanita condemns as failures those Puerto Rican males who "no saben darle la cara a la vía allá en su propia tierra" and so emigrate, dragging their families into a life of hardship.

A single incident, Juanita's bold participation at a defense rally to help a group of condemned blacks, apparently so appealed to the author's imagination that he made use of the same episode a couple of years later as the basis for his short story, **"Isla en Manhattan."** Both narratives contrast male cowardice with womanly courage. In **"Isla,"** Marqués openly indicts the Puerto Rican male by having Nico, the girl's fiancé, beg her in vain not to sign the petition on behalf of the black men. In *La carreta,* however, the coward is an American black who, with trembling hands, rejects the petition he is asked to sign. Here two major points emerge: (1) Marqués's heroines are far more appealing to him than his men are as possible heroes; and (2), while the author most often chooses one of his countrymen to portray the male weakling, Marqués also depicts men other than Puerto Ricans as cowardly, especially in comparison to women.

Doña Isabel of *La muerte no entrará en palacio* bears considerable resemblance to Doña Gabriela. The wife of a former revolutionary leader turned puppet ruler, Doña Isabel's peasant background enables her to feel the pulse of her people. Sensing their wish to independence, she vainly urges her husband to resist foreign enticements that might preclude the island's autonomy. Here as elsewhere, Marqués selects a woman to represent the voice of Puerto Rican integrity, while her husband symbolizes those who readily sell out to the North. And although Isabel eventually fails to prevent this betrayal, her daughter, significantly named Casandra, denounces the sell-out by assassinating her father.

One of Marqués's most highly acclaimed works, *Los soles truncos,* has as protagonists three ageing sisters who live in seclusion in their ancient San Juan mansion. This is a psychological-poetical drama very different from the starkly re-alistic *La carreta*. Although Inés, the central female charac-ter, comes from an aristocratic background quite unlike that of Gabriela or Isabel, she evinces a force of will similar to theirs as she spares no effort to shield her two more vulner-able sisters from the intrusions of time and changing society. There are no male characters in this work. Yet here, too, Marqués manages to portray woman as man's victor, for through her denunciation of the Spanish officer's infidelity, Inés prevents his marriage to her sister. As in several of Marqués's other plays, *Los soles truncos* ends with an act of violence on the part of the heroine. Aware that she has lost her struggle against life's realities, Inés chooses to immolate herself and her sisters within the family mansion.

The author's other notable success completed in 1958 is *Un niño azul para esa sombra*. Cecilia, a secondary character in this drama, closely resembles Gabriela and Isabel in her un-lettered peasant wisdom. Throughout his writing Marqués shows a special regard for this kind of woman, whose innate perceptiveness owes nothing to education or social polish. In *Un niño azul* he chooses Cecilia to watch over the welfare of the two males, the title character and Michel, his weak, ideal-istic father. The latter's convictions come from his certainty that only full independence can save his country. Introspec-tive, intellectual, an *hombre de pensamiento* rather than *acción,* Michel proves ineffective and so garners a bitter fate: first imprisonment, then exile and early death. We should note that those idealists whom Marqués depicts as failures are always males. Although the author's idealistic females (Casandra in *Muerte,* Juanita in **"Isla en Manhattan,"** and Mariana in *Mariana o el alba*) are not more successful than his males, Marqués inevitably honors the women's idealism and portrays them as heroines.

We also find, particularly in his early works, that it is woman whom Marqués chooses to sustain faltering ideals. In *La carreta,* for example, Doña Gabriela manages to preserve a respect for decency in her household, despite the threats from a corrosive environment. And in *Muerte,* Doña Isabel en-treats Casandra to cling to the nationalistic ideals of her fiancé, to "creer en él ciegamente"; ironically, in heeding her mother's works, Casandra comes to believe in the righteousness of patricide. Similarly, in *Un niño azul,* Cecilia echoes Isabel's plea not to forsake ideals by urging Michel to combat the rumors concerning his wife's infidelities in order to preserve the sanctity of the family.

In *La carreta* and *Muerte,* woman's opposition and humilia-tion of man is generally absent. The author sees his early heroines as principally upholders of traditional Puerto Rican values. Though depicted as stronger than the male charac-ters, these women strive to support rather than belittle their men. We find, however, in *Un niño azul* and the writing that follows, that without ever abandoning his penchant for creat-ing highly laudatory female characterizations, Marqués now

often portrays woman as contributing much to the trials and dishonor of the idealistic male.

In the latter play, for example, Mercedes, Michel's wife, represents the Puerto Rican woman who renounces tradi-tional values for the modern ways of the United States. Although in this respect she differs from the author's ear-lier heroines, Mercedes shares with them a striking *fuerza* or *poder*. Her strength, she boasts, comes from seeing the world as it is, "sin ideales." Mercedes derides what she regards as her husband's idealistically distorted view of reality. By humiliating Michel with her selfish behavior, she eventually causes his death and their young son's sui-cide. Yet despite these tragedies Marqués shows an ap-preciable degree of admiration for Mercedes's forceful nature.

Mercedes is but one of the author's women who are totally callous to their husband's aspirations and beliefs. We find her precursor in the self-centered wife of the short story **"En la popa hay un cuerpo reclinado."** Although she does not have Mercedes's intensity, her effect on her husband, a gentle and idealistic teacher, is significant. Driven to a hatred of all women, he slays his wife and then commits suicide through self-emasculation in order to escape "un mundo de devoradoras." We should not pass over the plurality of *devoradoras,* for throughout the story the hero also reveals a fierce resentment of his mother, whose countless admonitions never cease to echo in his brain.

This domineering female is a frequent character in Marqués's writing. In **"En la popa,"** for example, the mild-mannered teacher quakes before the power of his female superior. Al-though only sketchily delineated, she remains a figure of to-tal authority who calls to mind the woman principal encountered in both **"El juramento"** and the partially auto-biographical *La víspera del hombre*. In each work the woman brutalizes a young Puerto Rican boy for refusing to salute the American flag. The repeated appearance of this character raises the possibility that she might be the product of the author's personal experiences.

These women, with their imposing *virilismo,* either threaten man or exhort him to act. In *Carnaval adentro, carnaval afuera,* Tía Matilde nearly strangles Guillermo-Willie, rep-resentative of the docile Puerto Rican whose readiness to ca-pitulate unnerves her; later Matilde urges the idealistic Angel to action with the stentorian declamation: "No es hora de hacer sonar liras, sino tambores. No es hora de lágrimas, sino de golpes." Angel's response is also noteworthy. The youth feels a new courage until struck by the reality that all has been pure illusion, *farsa*. Realizing this, "se deja caer al piso y, hecho un ovillo, oculta la cabeza entre los brazos." Once again Marqués's male seeks refuge in the fetal position. But Angel's state does not faze Tía Matilde, who cracks her whip and shouts for the carnival to continue.

Even his highly idealized title character of *Mariana o el alba* occasionally evinces "una decision y dureza . . . casi viriles." This play treats the futile Puerto Rican struggle for independence from Spain during the mid-nineteenth century. Making free use of literary license, the author depicts what one character terms "prácticamente una revolución de mujeres." A mere cursory reading of *Cuadro* III shows to what extent Marqués's heroines dominate the action. Though her husband surrenders to "un gesto de cansancio, de impotencia, de derrota." Mariana manages to incite others with exhortations reminiscent of those of Cecilia and Tía Matilde: "¡Nada de lástima . . . Su lucha . . . seguirá! Seguirá siempre."

It is not just Mariana's bravery that has her overshadow all her male allies in the struggle for independence. She alone, strangely enough, has the insight to realize that the new Puerto Rican flag must be more than a mere imitation of the Dominican. So the reader is not surprised eventually to find Reinaldo, the betrayer of the revolution, in front of Mariana, "de rodillas, hecho un ovillo, las manos ocultando el rostro, voz llorosa." She calmly orders him knifed to death. Reinaldo is not the only male in this drama whom Marqués causes to humble himself in this way. Several times we witness Rendición, the young mulatto in love with Mariana's ward, drop to his knees before the two women.

A good part of the author's veneration of woman derives from his scant regard for the potential of the men, Puerto Rican or otherwise, populating his pages. For Marqués, female idealism is always firmly anchored in reality and, most important, leads to action.

—*Thomas Feeny*

Although one critic interprets the death of Mariana's child while she is in prison as symbolic of the revolution's failure, the play's final notes are extremely optimistic. As his heroine, bearing her stillborn baby, emerges from the cell and heads off into an ever brightening sky, Marqués seems to be honoring the triumph of woman over all adversity.

A good part of the author's veneration of woman derives from his scant regard for the potential of the men, Puerto Rican or otherwise, populating his pages. For Marqués, female idealism is always firmly anchored in reality and, most important, leads to action. Not so the vain yearnings of his male protagonists. The early hopes of Luis in *La carreta,* the dreams of Michel in *Un niño azul,* of Alberto in *Muerte,* of Angel in *Carnaval,* do not have sufficient strength to succeed. Michel's fate, in fact, is never in doubt, since early in the play the author has Mercedes cut down the quenepo tree, symbolic of

her husband's traditional Puerto Rican values. In *Casa sin reloj* José appears to find his ideals much of a burden. He acknowledges: "Yo no soy libre, no puedo serlo. Soy prisionero de mi propio ideal." In contrast, rather than pausing to analyze her idealism, Marqués's typical heroine would at once move to act.

Often a notable readiness to acknowledge his deficiencies characterizes Marqués's hero. In *Muerte,* for example, old Teresias, who years before had embodied the hopes of the revolution, has become known as *El Padrino,* for he was best man when Doña Isabel, the woman he loved, married José. The latter has since risen to the island's governorship. Significantly, the idealist, having lost his beloved to the man of action, accepts his failure as part of the natural order of things: "Tú, eres el Hombre, José. Yo, soy sólo el Poeta," the old man admits.

In *Sacrificio en el Monte Moriah,* Marqués's last major drama, the author goes well beyond merely depicting the idealistic male as easy prey for the stronger, more crafty female. Marqués's Sarah, unlike the long-suffering biblical figure, abuses, betrays and finally murders her husband, Abraham. The very choice of subject matter proves most telling. The author himself has pointed out that the story of Sarah and Abraham is "el primer ejemplo . . . de marido débil y subordinado que nos dan los textos del Viejo Testamento." In his introduction to the play, the dramatist relates that his son's preoccupation with the injustices of the Vietnam War drew him to this theme of a father's willingness to sacrifice his offspring. Yet we cannot overlook Marqués's awareness that Abraham's story is the story of the patriarch who "sigue perdiendo patriarcalidad." These same words would describe the author's view of the Puerto Rican male in mid-twentieth century. Marqués repeatedly observes in *Ensayos* that woman has come to dominate present-day Puerto Rican society and, at the same time, man has had to renounce his traditional prerogatives and accept a more passive role.

As in *Mariana o el alba,* the author's use of poetic license is most revealing. According to biblical legend, Sarah gave birth after years of barrenness. Marqués contends that Sarah was not sterile but that Abraham was impotent. Whether or not such was the case is hardly as intriguing as Marqués's decision to revise the age-old legend. His conclusions are obviously in keeping with this penchant for subordinating man to woman. Like most of the author's men with a mission, Abraham is feeble and ineffective. Despite his boasts, he seems little more than a cuckold. In his contention that the patriarch was probably aware of his inferiority to Sarah, Marqués appears to equate sterility with impotency: "El astuto, pero rudo, ignorante y viejo jefe de tribu se sentía inferior (es decir, impotente) ante aquella espléndida e inteligente mujer que él veía y sentía como superior (y que indudablemente lo era)."

From this evaluation it would appear that Marqués's admiration of Sarah, as he portrays her, ought rightly to stem from an appreciation of her intelligence and finer qualities. Yet the Sarah in *Sacrificio* earns the author's esteem and awe above all for her ability to force men to do what she wants them to. Despite the author's allusions to her cultured background, he portrays her as physically abusive to both Abraham and Agar. She plots the seduction of young Ismael, whom Marqués presents as Isaac's father, and later obliges Abraham to banish Agar and Ismael to Egypt. While Sarah dies before Abraham in the legend, Marqués alters this ending. His heroine stabs the old patriarch to death and challenges Jehovah to condemn her soul.

It does not matter that the dramatist did not adhere to the facts of the legend. It is significant, however, that Marqués depicts Sarah as a splendid, intelligent woman far superior to her husband. In his various comments on *Sacrificio,* the author acknowledges that Sarah's challenge to Jehovah would have been most unlikely since during this period there was no conception of life beyond the grave. Nevertheless, Marqués is willing to risk the anachronism. He does so not to show Sarah's skepticism regarding Abraham's God, since she has already made her attitude known, but rather because, totally enthralled by Sarah's strength of will, the author cannot deny her this final act of defiance.

As in earlier works, we find that Marqués indicates the subordination of his males by the physical positions he assigns them. Prior to Sarah's seduction of Ismael, Marqués has him kneel beside her. Later the stage directions read: "Sara sentada en escabel. Abrahán echado a sus pies," and "Sara hila y, sentado a sus pies está Isaac." And as before, Marqués surrenders to the compulsion to depict man in the virtually *de rigueur* fetal position; after having duped her husband into believing he is the cause of her pregnancy, Sarah turns and gazes with scorn upon "el ovillo que es Abrahán."

Marqués asserts that Abraham must have felt an *auto-humillación* after lending his wife to foreign rulers. This shame, the author contends, would only have contributed to the patriarch's "complejo de inferioridad, . . . la causa psicológica de su impotencia." Thus, in keeping with his tendency to present woman as man's oppressor, the playwright ignores advanced age as a plausible cause since he wishes to attribute Abraham's supposed deficiency to an inferiority complex.

Because he has twice sold her favors to foreign potentates to save his own skin, Sarah's scorn for her husband is indeed justified. Marqués has the tables do a complete turn, however, for at the drama's conclusion Sarah reasserts her supposedly royal origins: "*Princesa* (a translation of *Sara*) es mi nombre. Y hoy eres mi siervo," she shouts at Abraham before killing him. In retrospect, we see that all of *Sacrificio en el Monte Moriah* has been moving unwaveringly toward this one end: Sarah's domination and ultimate annihilation of her

husband. The title, in fact, now appears inappropriate since Abraham's would-be sacrifice of Isaac, prevented by Sarah, proves little more than an anticlimax. In short, what the author originally conceived as a protest against adult society's readiness to sacrifice its children to the futility of war becomes essentially a paean to the ferocity of an inordinately forceful woman.

Related to Marqués's tendency to portray his hero as subjugated or defeated is the question of the author's literary pessimism. Tamara Holzapfel finds that in his first play, the existentialistic *El hombre y sus sueños,* true pessimism is absent, for in spite of the grim plot line, in the final analysis man's works always count. This observation, along with her later remark that Marqués rejects the claim of the dramatists of the theater of the absurd "that man is condemned to an existence of futility and purposelessness." might lead the reader to expect some type of optimism in Marqués's writing. But considering his work as a whole, we find that despite the occasional encouraging note detected in the endings of *La carreta* and *Mariana o el alba,* the author shows little hope for his heroes. Although in an early critique of E. S. Belaval's *La muerte,* Marqués claimed that Belaval was unduly gloomy about the New World's possibilities for salvation, Marqués later recognized that the pessimism in the fiction of Puerto Rican writers around mid-century came about precisely because these men were describing "la realidad tal como la encontraron." From all appearances, Marqués included himself within this group. Of the scant optimism the author does show, almost all has to do with the accomplishments of his females. Gabriela and Juanita manage to rescue their family from the hell of their New York slum. Mariana's disappearance into the sunset foretells a better future. But for the most part, the reader is hard put to find Marques's writing encouraging.

The author points out several times the "impulso de autodestrucción" he finds so common in Puerto Rican literature. This impulse is characteristic of a good number of his male protagonists, who commit suicide in **"Otro día nuestro,"** *La carreta, Palm Sunday* (1949), and *Un niño azul.* Marqués is careful to indicate that suicide is not always a part of *autodestrucción,* as this may occur not only "en el plano físico" but also "en el moral y espiritual." Marqués's allusion to moral and spiritual self-destruction refers particularly to self-destruction through self-humiliation. This is the spiritual suicide he finds most closely associated with those Puerto Ricans who have given up hope of their island's independence. Marqués views their "claudicación, humillación, servillismo" as both cause and result of this insistence upon self-denigration.

Since most of his major male characters are Puerto Rican nationalists, the pessimism in Marqués's writing is understandable. Several of his protagonists, however, reveal no political involvement, and one or two are disloyal to Puerto

Rico. Yet regardless of the politics of his heroes, the author nearly always depicts them as ultimately outdistanced and humbled by women.

Marqués usually depicts woman as successful and honors her even when she is not. His female protects man, exerts authority over him, humiliates him and sometimes even destroys him.

—*Thomas Feeny*

Thus far we have presented evidence establishing Marqués's penchant for portraying woman as vastly superior to man. Although the author's idealistic male appears doomed to fail, Marqués usually depicts woman as successful and honors her even when she is not. His female protects man, exerts authority over him, humiliates him and sometimes even destroys him. We shall now examine the author's view of man as sexually subordinate to woman.

In Marqués's theater, allusions to man's sexual inferiority to woman appear primarily in *Sacrificio*. But such references also turn up in his short stories and novels. In **"El cuchillo y la piedra,"** for example, the protagonist is a man cursed with stunted arms who at the moment of sexual climax vainly begs the help of his partner. And the first contact that young Piruelo of *La víspera del hombre* has with female coquetries instantly affects his bowels: "Fue una sola descarga, casi líquida, pero le pareció que se quedaba vacío por dentro." In **"El miedo"** the woman's erect tongue in the male's mouth causes him alarm and vomiting; here fear is the man's constant companion, allowing him reassurance only when lying naked against his wife, as he experiences "la sensación de formar parte del cuerpo de ella; como un niño antes de nacer." This passage brings to mind Professor Holzapfel's suggestion that Luis's death in *La carreta* "is clearly suicidal and symbolizes, ironically 'a return to the womb'."

In two of his most recent works, **"El bastón"** and *La mirada,* Marqués furnishes autobiographical data that might shed additional light on why the author invariably chooses woman as the instrument of man's abasement. The protagonist of **"El bastón"** is, like Marqués, a middle-aged Puerto Rican writer, divorced, with three children. Primarily a dramatist, he decides, as Marqués seems to have done, to abandon the theater and devote himself to other literary forms. The writer sees himself as dominated by women. His frustration at his mother's continued control over his life, his recollections of his grandmother's bitter nature, of his ex-wife's jealousies and his daughter-in-law's deceits, call to mind the sense of domination by female authority that drove the schoolteacher of **"En la popa"** to murder and suicide. It is not known to

what extent the characterizations of **"El bastón"** are autobiographical. We note, however, that although the protagonist in his youth wanted to become a writer, his mother forced him to enroll in El Colegio de Agricultura y Artes Mecánicas de Mayagüez, where Marqués, himself, studied. In his analysis of the relationship between mother and son, Marqués describes the "cordón umbilical interminable. El mismo del cual había él tratado de escapar toda su vida." Feeding on his resentment of his inability to break free, the protagonist delves back into his childhood to recall his mother's past injustices. He remembers the five-tongued belt with which she would "descargar sobre él su furia, sin que él a menudo pudiese entender el porque de aquella furia, pues no había hecho nada que él juzgaba castigable." This picture of the child as innocent victim of maternal arbitrariness pervades both **"El bastón"** and *La mirada*.

We also find in the latter work the appearance of a new type of sexual self-humiliation. While under the influence of drugs, the novel's protagonist imagines he is engaging in the most degrading kinds of homosexual practices. One could obviously interpret this sort of fantasy as merely the result of subconscious desires seeking an outlet. But Marqués does not present the hero of *La mirada* as homosexual and, in fact, has him jeer at his brother for the latter's earlier aberrant behavior. An examination of the fantasies reveals that the protagonist's imagined homosexual involvement is never an active one. Though he does little, he must endure the whole gamut of possible sexual perversions, all in the same scene. His disgust at homosexuality, combined with the passive role forced upon him, serves to increase his self-humiliation. This time, however, the degradation appears unrelated to any sense of inadequacy regarding woman. Since the protagonist is a devoted nationalist who has failed in his mission, quite possibly the humiliation he undergoes in his unconscious state serves as a kind of self-punishment for his failures.

Because Marqués's male protagonists who share his dedication to Puerto Rican autonomy inevitably fail, he inflicts shame upon them as a form of retribution for their inability to gain independence. Similarly, we find that the frequent choice of woman to humble and oppress man stems at least in part from the author's resentment of the emergence of a matriarchy that relegates man to a secondary position and threatens the underpinnings of traditional Puerto Rican culture. Marqués's image of emasculated manhood is a direct allusion to the social-political-cultural dilemma of his country today.

We must also bear in mind that the author's persistent depiction of man, outstripped and humiliated by woman, extends well beyond the framework of modern Puerto Rican society. For Marqués perceives within the female an inherent superiority, pre-dating the Puerto Rican woman's social ascendancy in the middle of the twentieth century. This awesome respect of woman, most evident in his plays and short stories, also surfaces in his nonfiction. Marqués asserts in *Ensayos* that before one can ever truly consider himself a writer, he must first be able to analyze woman and to explore "con fría lucidez" every nook and cranny of the feminine psyche. We find that even in a work like *Sacrificio,* where his characters are not his countrymen and where his acknowledged intent is to comment on universal rather than national concerns, Marqués, as if by compulsion, portrays woman as man's superior in every way.

Bonnie Hildebrand Reynolds (essay date Fall 1983)

SOURCE: "Coetaneity: A Sign of Crisis in *Un niño azul para esa sombra.*" in *Latin American Theater Review,* Vol. 17, No. 1, Fall 1983, pp. 37-45.

[*In the following essay, Reynolds discusses the chronological presentation and psychological effect of* Un niño azul para esa sombra.]

René Marqués' play, *Un niño azul para esa sombra,* written in 1958, won the "Eugenio Fernández Garcia" theatre prize that same year in the Ateneo Puertorriqueño's Christmas Festival. This play, produced two years later during the Third Theatre Festival sponsored by the Instituto de Cultura Puertorriqueña, is, according to Frank Dauster, "probably Marqués' best play" and "one of the best in Latin America." Like several of Marqués' plays, it is thematically based on previously-written short stories—in this case, **"La sala," "El niño en el árbol"** and, perhaps, **"El juramento."**

The play tells the story of the child Michelín, caught between the liberationist ideals of his father and the materialistic, North-Americanized world of his mother. Although the play's various elements can be dichotomized between the two sides, and Michelín undoubtedly belongs on the freedom side, his position is really much more complex than would appear on the surface. The liberty for which Michelín struggles is that of the individual's right to his own unique identity. This child, however, is prevented from exercising that right because of the "shadows" that prevail in his life. His mother, Mercedes, controls his physical world and he lives in the material luxury that has resulted from the choices his mother has made in her life. His emotional, inner world, however, depends on a self-created, false relationship with a non-existent father. This is an illusory relationship originally encouraged by his father's adopted sister, Cecilia, and later developed as an integral part of Michelín's own imagined world. Both sets of values—the mother's and the father's—so dominate Michelín's life that he is constantly torn between them with never an opportunity to develop any meaningful values that are truly his own. In the end, the only freedom which Michelín can exercise is that of choosing to create the circumstances of his own death.

Acts I and III take place on Michelín's tenth birthday as the tension of waiting for the play's *denouement* parallels that of

waiting for the arrival of the birthday party guests. The first act introduces Michelín's solitary world, based on dreams and illusions, in which his own anguish becomes related to his mother's poisoning of a large *quenepo* tree which once shaded the terrace and which had been, for the child, a father-figure and make-believe protector. The retrospective second act takes place two years prior to both Acts I and III. This portion of the play, portrayed as part of Michelín's dream, establishes the tension between the child's past and his imminent future, thus creating his present moment—a present which contains both past and future. In Act II we witness not only the dissolution of the parents' marriage and the total destruction of his father's future, but the beginning of the child's own self-destruction as well. Act III brings the child back to reality and to the moments preceding the party. In this act he is confronted with the reality of his father's death and the falseness of the dream world in which he attempts to survive. This knowledge forces him to act, and suicide becomes a logical and a heroic choice.

The author experiments not only with the chronological presentation of the story, but also with the play's movement toward its own end. Structurally, the present surrounds and contains the past until the suicidal death of the child protagonist in the final moments. At that point, the child's past affirms his identity.

Through a series of interrelated signals transmitted to the audience, the play creates the impression of temporal coetaneity which signifies a life and death crisis for the child protagonist. Michelín, who finds himself trapped between the heroic ideals of his father and the worldly values of his mother, embodies a two-dimensional crisis: that of the anguished individual within the realm of humanity, and that of the island of Puerto Rico under the shadow of a large and powerful nation. Time does not merely "stand still," however, but rather it, like the child, is trapped in a kind of vacuum. In the temporal approach which Marqués takes in this work, the second act is of prime importance. Because the action occurs as part of the child's dream, no time actually passes in the play's story. In addition, although hours and minutes obviously do pass in the playing time of the drama, the audience is swept up by the illusion that time has stopped for a short while. Because of the nature of the second act, past, present and future co-exist in a world of circular, rather than forward movement. This combination of circular movement and temporal coetaneity guides us to an understanding of the present, real anguish which Michelín suffers, and of the symbolic meaning behind his death.

Circularity is apparent in the lineal structure of the work, the stage setting, and the imagery. In the first and third acts, the birthday party motif calls attention to the play's structural ellipsis. The work opens and closes on the protagonist's tenth birthday. Michelín has invited a friend, Andrés, to come earlier than his other party guests, all of whom have been invited by Mercedes. Andrés' presence serves to reinforce the play's temporal circularity:

> ANDRÉS—Oye, ¿a qué hora empieza la fiesta?
> MICHELÍN—A la tarde.
> ANDRÉS—¿Y por qué me hiciste venir tan temprano?

From this moment on we wait, with Andrés, for the celebration to begin. In Act II, the image of the birthday is implicitly present. As Michel, the child's father, re-experiences his eight-year imprisonment for revolutionary activities in an expressionistic scene, the author's stage directions subtly reintroduce the birthday image:

> (. . . Se oye un llanto de un niño de un año de edad. No es el llanto inconsciente y chillón de un bebé, sino el llanto de una criatura que empieza a descubrir con horror la vida. Michel se vuelve bruscamente hacia el fondo. El llanto arrecia),

and he shouts, "Michelín!" Although the cries are not those of a newborn infant, the fact that they *are* associated with the child protagonist as a baby brings to mind for the audience the idea of his birth, and by extension, the party which has yet to take place from Act I. Act III finalizes this image in the last scene as the offstage guests ironically sing "Happy Birthday," in English, to Michelín, who hangs dead on the trellis of the terrace. His birthday anniversary and his birth itself co-exist with his day of death, therefore making the play's physical structure also a temporal one in which beginning and end—or past and present—meet.

The stage setting creates the illusion of entrapment and is a physical representation of Michelín's own feeling of imprisonment. Acts I and III take place on the terrace, while Act II develops in the living room of the luxurious mansion. In both spaces, there are several supposed exits which, in fact, do not connect directly to the world outside. In the terrace scenes, a glass door opens upon the terrace from the living room. The terrace itself is surrounded by a railing which has one opening into the yard and another open space where the *quenepo* once stood, and where the trellis on which Michelín dies now stands. The author carefully describes this latter opening as follows: "En elcentro mismo, fondo de la terraza, la baranda está partida dejando un espacio que hubiera podido ser salida del jardín" This description tells us, as the stage setting would show, that this space is not an exit even though it might seem once to have been. Ironically, it does serve as a way out for Michelín at the play's end when he dies on the trellis.

This living room of Act II has several dimensions of height and depth, as well as several exits from the room. There are the stairway on which we see Michelín as he witnesses the

confrontation between his parents, and the vestibule which connects to a hall, and we assume, finally out of the house. At the very back of this area there hangs a large portrait of Mercedes, seemingly guarding any exits from the house and giving even more depth to the scene. The glass door at stage left is the one that opens onto the terrace, which as we know from the previous act, is also enclosed, thus intensifying the illusion of there being no exit.

In this Marqués play, the accumulating impressions and images of entrapment and death work harmoniously with the structure and the *mise-en-scene* to communicate to the audience Michelín's feeling of anguish and utter helplessness and to further support the creation of the "no exit" concept. Act I integrates many of these images into the dramatic presentation itself while in Act II, they appear expressionistically in the scene depicting Michelín's suffering, as well as in the dialogue between the parents. By the end of the third and final act, Michelín's suicidal death is the logical extension of these accumulated impressions.

The opening scene introduces the idea of imprisonment as well as of death. Michelín enters carrying a caged canary across the terrace into the garden where we suppose he frees the little bird. Immediately following this action, and as the invited guest calls for his host from offstage, Cecilia, also offstage, sings a song about a dead child. This song dramatically associates Michelín with death as it subsequently becomes part of a kind of offstage dialogue between the child protagonist and Cecilia:

> MICHELÍN—(Su voz fuera de escena) ¡Cecilia! ¡Cállate!
> CECILIA—(Su voz más lejana en el interior)
> El niñito muerto
> ya va para el cielo,
> Los ángeles cantan
> en el cementerio.
> MICHELÍN—(Su voz fuera de escena, histérica ahora)
> ¡Cállate! ¡Cállate! No quiero oír esa canción. ¡Cállate!

If the spectator does not, as a normal reaction, associate the song with the child, Michelín's strong, hysterical reaction forces such an association to take place. This act further creates a parallel between the child and death in the dream-like sequence depicting Mercedes' assassination of the *quenepo,* and again in the final dream sequence as the boy's father, closing the child's eyes by placing his hand over them, asks a blessing on his son.

In Act II, both parents bequeath an inheritance of imprisonment to their son. Michel, the father, on a darkened stage from which we hear only his voice, expresses the anguish of his eight-year confinement:

> No es fácil convertir en sonido los pensamientos propios cuando hay tantos años de silencio—o de casi silencio—envolviéndolo todo: la luz matinal y la medianoche, la soledad, el cuerpo, la ventana y la puerta; los pasos, las manos.... Todo en fin! ¡Callado hasta los huesos de silencio! Las palabras circulando en el alma sin salida; prisioneras del tiempo, sin espacio!

These words express not only the physical confinement which reduced Michel's world to a window, a door and his own footsteps as he paced back and forth, but also the silencing of his thoughts and ideas, for which there is no outlet and so, therefore are also trapped, in the prison of his own soul. In this same act, Mercedes reveals that she, too, feels imprisoned: "Y las puertas cerradas. Como si las del presidio al cerrarse dieran la señal a todas las puertas del mundo: 'Ciérrense, puertas, ciérrense bien'" She adds in the same conversation: "sólo quiero que sepas que también yo supe del horror de sentirme prisionera." Ironically, Mercedes' "prison" is that fear of being excluded from the world to which she aspires so that she is, in a sense, trapped outside rather than inside. The legacy, then, that the child Michelín inherits from both father and mother is one of stagnation, and of the frustration of unrealized dreams.

Evidence of death and destruction prevails throughout the play, providing perhaps, the only apparent progression, albeit a negative one, in the work. The assassination of the tree in Act I and the violent acts against the tin Statue of Liberty in Act II culminate in Michelin's suicide in the last act. The depiction of those events in the order in which they are presented, while out of chronological sequence, makes the sacrificial suicide of Michelin the logical ending for the play. In the acting out of the tree's assassination, Michelín feels the pain of death as his tree-friend dies. According to the stage directions: "Michelín, quien observa la escena de espaldas a nosotros, se va encorvando, replegándose en sí mismo, como si sintiera los efectos del veneno, hasta que cae de rodillas mordiéndose los puños." This empathy and self-induced suffering reveal to the audience the boy's psychological state in the play's early stages.

In Act II, we see the motivating factors behind the child's violent tendencies and ultimate self-destruction. This act culminates in Michelín's violent act of aggression against a replica of the Statue of Liberty which stands near his house. His defacing of the statue, which for him represents both his mother as the destroyer of his own personal world, and the United States as the destroyer of his father's deals, makes clear his own preoccupations as well as his violent tendencies.

In Act III, although we do not witness Michelín's ingesting

of the poison, we assume it, by focusing all of these past impressions of death which point towards that logical end. Each successive act of destruction involves Michelín more than the previous one. Although he apparently feels pain as he witnesses the tree's death, he is merely an observer of the ceremony. His mother commits the act. He himself carries out the attack in the second act, but directs it toward someone else. In Act III, as the circle closes in on the child and he cannot escape, he aims his destructiveness at himself.

We further sense the frustration of movement as we detect strong parallels between the young boy of Acts I and III, and his father of Act II. Throughout the second act, in which we seem to enter Michelín's innermost consciousness, we are made aware of the establishment of a very close symbolic relationship between the child and his father. This, in turn, leads us to perceive strong similarities in the life pattern of each one.

One of the strongest relationships develops out of Mercedes' destruction of the large *quenepo* that had once stood on the terrace, and of her similar destruction of Michel's manuscripts which were his only hope of creating a future for himself after his release from prison. Michel's words exemplify the importance of the tree and of the manuscripts in both lives. He says of Michelín's fondness for the *quenepo:* "Pero en su soledad nuestro hijo habia hecho de él un compañero, un confidente, un . . . protector." Of his own manuscripts, he says: "La única esperanza que me quedaba . . . El único asidero . . . ¡Qué destrucción tan total!" In neither case was either father or son capable of preventing the obliteration of his last security. And, in both cases, Mercedes, representative of the materialistic world, is the person responsible for the total destruction of hope.

The accumulation of such parallels leads us to perceive the similar life patterns of Michelín and of his father. The father comes from a past whose history is tied to France and to Puerto Rico during a period when his own father and grandfather were also searching for freedom. Those past worlds were not really Michel's own, however, as he is a man of thoughts, not of action, as Thomas Feeny so aptly points out. His own future lies in the Bowery of New York where he dies an alcoholic. Michelín's past consists of a father who was in prison for most of his son's life, a mother who has adopted foreign values, and of Cecilia—raised a sister to Michel—who offers the child an attractive set of values related to his father's family and to past tradition, but which prove to be false because Michelín, as an individual, has no place in that world. The final correspondence in the similar life patterns comes with death. The father destroys himself with alcohol while the son destroys himself with another liquid—the poison used to kill the tree. Both die a lonely death, the only difference being that the father leaves a son—a sign of optimism for the future—but the son leaves no hope for a future at all.

In the Puerto Rican colonial world, and in the family controlled by Mercedes' materialism, Michelín's father's ideals of individual freedom, though noble ones, are unable to create a meaningful life for either father or son, except in death. Carlos Solórzano generalizes this idea as follows: "El antagonismo entre la civilización actual y el deseo de libertad individual, que constituye el tema central de todo el teatro de la posguerra, cobra en esta obra perfiles de crueldad extrema." In each case—that of father and of son—the anguish resulting from the failure to liberate oneself motivates a painful and a solitary death. Although father and son represent two generations—normally a sign of forward movement in time—, their parallel life patterns in which failures repeat themselves and ideals are lost would indicate the incidents of time to be repetitive and non-progressive.

The play's actual structure in which the present of Acts I and III in fact surrounds the past of Act II provides the key to the definitive establishment of coetaneity within Michelín's world. According to Piri Fernández, the entire second act can be seen as "una continuación técnica del juego de Michelín en escena." That game is what Michelín calls "playing the past," in which he enters into a dream-like realm, conjuring up images and events from an earlier time. The end of Act I and the beginning of Act III find him on the terrace in that dream-like state, implying that all of the events of the second act occur within that same condition. The penetration into the interior of the house in Act II, which takes place in the living room, suggests the invasion of Michelín's innermost consciousness.

The interiorization into Michelín's dream world occurs on two levels: that of the game in which he himself evokes the past, seemingly at will, and that of a deep sleep, in which the audience perceives on stage what supposedly is happening inside of the child's mind. In the former case, Michelín is somewhat in control of his own suffering (for instance, as he painfully feels the tree's death). On this level he consciously elicits the help of Cecilia in playing the game, and even reveals it to his friend Andrés. We understand the latter, however, to be his unshared dream world, of which the game is only a symptom. In the words of Piri Fernández, Michelín "rehace los momentos del pasado a su antojo, trocando así a la realidad en sombras, y, en cambio, convirtiendo a las sombras de su imaginación en sus más preciadas realidades." His game of "playing the past" is, in Michelín's way, a solution to the problems with which he is confronted in Act II, since it is through this pastime on the superficial level that he can transform the present into a world with which he can cope.

Even though Michelín is not visibly present throughout Act II, the author subtly makes his presence known as the past events unfold. As audience, we realize that we are observing simultaneously *with* Michelín those same events that he previously witnessed. In the tense encounter between the parents in which the father accuses the mother of having brought

about his own destruction, physically mistreats her, and then definitively leaves the family, we see Michelín's hand on the staircase. Interspersed throughout the parents' conversation the author's stage directions describe the effect: "(La mano de Michelín aparece en la pared del recodo alto de la escalera.)" —and "(Tras la mano de Michelín empieza a aparecer parte de su cuerpo, de espaldas a nosotros, muy pegado a la pared, como si quisiera incrustarse en ella . . .)." Because of the child's presence, this key scene does not exist primarily to disclose details of the plot to the audience, but rather to reveal the nature of Michelín's past as a part of his inner present.

Michelín's reaction to the scene he has witnessed pulls together the images of circularity and entrapment prevalent throughout the play. He descends the stairs, in the author's words, "como si, de súbito, el buen Dios hubiese puesto una carga de siglos sobre sus espaldas." He then seems to try to leave, but cannot. He goes to the hall by which his father left only to find this exit seemingly guarded by the full-length painting of his mother. He runs to the glass door leading to the terrace but stops as if that exit, too, were closed to him. We see him motivated by all that he has learned from his parents' conversation, trying to escape from that burden of knowledge which he has acquired, but at the same time physically and emotionally trapped. This, then, is the world which exists in the innermost sanctum of the child protagonist as he tries to survive his present exterior world.

The play's coetaneit becomes an indicator of the dual-level crisis which Michelín personifies and points to the child's heroic aspects as he becomes the sacrificial victim of the world of conflicts in which he lives. Caught between the libertarian ideals of his father and the materialistic world of his mother, Michelín's personal conflict involves the suffocation of his own creative potential. Both value systems, at the same time, are intricately tied to the family's past and to Puerto Rico's history as a colony, first of Spain and later of the United States. These historical connections, then, bring in the second level of the crisis, that of political freedom. On this larger scale, Michelín's conflict is that of the Puerto Rican island, caught between a search for individual identity and a materialistic world which gradually destroys the possibility of finding (or of developing) that identity.

In his treatise on human existence, Jean Paul Sartre claimed: "At my limit, at that infinitesimal instant of my death, I shall be no more than my past. It alone will define me." In this same spirit, Michelín's death gives him an indelible identity, as the fusion of past, present and future into one instant invests meaning into the child's suicide. The spectator realizes he is witnessing an approximation of the psychological time and state-of-mind of the protagonist. It is therefore important to reflect on just who this child is and what he signifies in relation to the conflicts dramatized.

Michelín's age, his natural opposition to Andrés, and the ritual with which the protagonist is associated reveal him to be a symbolic representative of the future, a learning experience personified, and an expiatory victim of the present world in which he lives. The fact that this protagonist is a child is significant in itself, inasmuch as children in general, on a symbolic level, represent the future of their own society. Furthermore, this is a child nearing adulthood which in many early societies was achieved at the age of twelve.

The natural opposition which Marqués creates between Michelín and his guest Andrés provides another clue to the protagonist's symbolic nature. Michelín's intelligence, intellectual maturity, sensitivity, and his poetic tendencies contrast with the personal qualities of Andrés, who is of lesser intelligence and lacks sensitivity, and is therefore incapable of understanding Michelín's game of the past. In the author's stage directions he says: "Andrés será, sin duda, en los años por venir, un hombre sabiamente pegado a la tierra; un ciudadano intachable, hasta un funcionario probo, pero jamás un ser humano en quien el género puede experimentar una experiencia heroicamente aleccionadora." In view of the series of contrasts established between the two, this statement would tell us that Michelín *is* a person through whom the human race can experience a "heroic" enlightenment.

Furthermore, nearly every action which Michelín initiates during the course of the play is of a ritualistic nature. Michelín's game of the past in which he forces Cecilia to participate is indicative of the ritual. First of all, he and Cecilia each take specific positions: she, near the door to the house and he, on the trellis itself, looking like a crucified victim. There are next certain words which are uttered to the rhythm of violin music: "El niño estaba en el árbol y dijo: '¡Odiame viento y azótame la cara!' (*Sube suavemente la musica*) Pero el viento estaba lejos, inflando la vela púrpura de un pescador en el mar. Y el árbol estaba inmóvil como si fuese de piedra. Y el niño estaba en la rama pensando en el árbol muerto." The chanted nature and the solitary meaning of his words indicate his isolation and state of helplessness as well as underline the fact that this is no child's game, but rather a most solemn ceremony. He approaches his other actions in a like manner: for example, after the "assassination" of the statue, he explains symbolically each of the designs he painted on the standard bearer of liberty. Likewise, his own act of suicide, paralleling the game of the tree's assassination, is of a symbolic nature, with the exception that this time it is no game, and Michelín himself takes the place of the tree. As a result of these rites with which Michelín is associated, he becomes the "niño-ofrenda," as Professor Juan Villegas so appropriately refers to him.

Michelín is the representative of his own society—a society whose potential is exemplified in that of a child on the verge of manhood. He stands for a society, however, trapped in a state of non-progress, between the conflicting ideals of U.S. materialism and a quest for freedom and individuality—a conflict in which Puerto Rico's own identity and potential might become a victim as do Michelín's, or, might be saved because of the lesson to be learned from his example.

The play's coetaneity defines Michelín's identity which, in turn, symbolizes that of Marqués' Puerto Rico.

All of the play's events co-exist in the present time: Acts I and III are, of course, the actual present; while Act II is Michelín's present inner reality. All together form the child's identity apart from which he does not exist. He performs a heroic act upon choosing suicide as a response to his dilemma because, in this case, the only freedom open to the child is the freedom to make this particular choice. His death is an ironic event (like that of Emilia and Inés in *Los soles truncos*) for while it is heroic and serves as a learning experience for the audience, it implies no future at all for the play's ill-fated protagonist.

Michelín's death is a message which demonstrates the dimensions of the conflict which the play portrays. This is a struggle in which the "status quo" relationship with the United States signals the death of cultural identity and political progress for the island of Puerto Rico, and in which materialistic ideals signal the destruction of artistic creativity and philosophical progress on the level of the individual.

Julia Ortiz Griffin (essay date Fall-Winter 1983)

SOURCE: "The Puerto Rican Woman in René Marqués' Drama," in *Revista Chicano-Riqueña,* Vol. XI, Nos. 3-4, Fall-Winter 1983, pp. 169-76.

[*In the following essay, Griffin explores the female characters in Marqués's major dramatic works, particularly as they relate to the theme of national salvation.*]

René Marqués is probably, after Hostos, the best known of all Puerto Rican authors, and certainly his country's leading playwright. Profoundly concerned with the problems of Puerto Rico, he made them the substance of his dramas. He saw these problems arising from the abandonment of cultural traditions and values, and traced them to the industrialization and modernization that transformed the island under the domination of the United States. His work constantly affirms the need for self-respect and the assertion of identity; no where is this more evident than in the presentation of the Puerto Rican woman in his dramas.

Under "Operation Bootstrap" foreign businesses and investments were attracted to the island during the 1950s and 1960s by tax exemptions and the promise of cheap labor. Hundreds of factories were established, tens of thousands of industrial workers were employed, new roads, housing developments and shopping complexes were created; a tremendous increase in annual production, average income and standard of living were attained. The government thus changed the face of Puerto Rico, and, within little more than a decade, the island was transformed from the "Poorhouse of the Caribbean" into a country with the highest per-capita income in Latin America. But this economic miracle had serious social implications. A people accustomed over many generations to a slow-moving, tradition-bound way of life had been industrialized, urbanized and plunged into the preoccupations of a technological age. Once largely self-sufficient, almost overnight they had become consumers, obsessed with the acquisition of material goods and dependent upon government agencies and foreign investors for the satisfaction of their needs.

The Puerto Ricans, uprooted, restless, grasping at the gaudy novelties of the moment, were in danger of losing their individuality, of becoming mere cogs in the world-wide industrial complex.

This disrupted, disoriented society is the focal point of Marqués' drama. His plays are an exhortation to his people to resist the national and personal corruption of soul-less "progress." Nowhere is this appeal to identity and integrity more evident than in his numerous striking portrayals of women.

For centuries the education and indoctrination of Puerto Rican women had stressed passivity and obedience as the primary virtues, synonymous with femininity. A modern Puerto Rican writer who describes a female character this way: "Camelia . . . dotada de una femeneidad perfecta . . . pasiva, sentimental e intuitiva," is merely expressing an accepted concept. Women eventually accepted this way of thinking. For them, too, femininity which meant passivity became the ultimate perfection of womanhood.

With keen perception Marqués recognized that the national crisis which his country was undergoing affected its women in a particularly acute way. Thus the female characters of his plays, in their efforts to assert their identity and their human dignity, are the most striking embodiments of his persistent theme: the salvation of the nation's soul.

—Julia Ortiz Griffin

These women, of Puerto Rico, bred to be submissive and self-effacing, were even more profoundly threatened than their men by the great change sweeping over the island. Conditioned to a dependent status and an existence centering on the family and the home, they saw their secure way of life crumbling. As their men struggled for survival in a rapidly

shifting economy, the women seemed doomed to the role of onlookers and victims. The land-oriented traditional culture was under assault by a new materialism in which the factory replaced the plantation and the farmer became an urban slum dweller. This alien and hostile environment was particularly traumatic for women, who had to abandon their almost child-like passivity and become mature human beings almost overnight. The insecurity and pain of an accelerated adolescence were the particular burden of Puerto Rican women during this turbulent period of social change.

With keen perception Marqués recognized that the national crisis which his country was undergoing affected its women in a particularly acute way. Thus the female characters of his plays, in their efforts to assert their identity and their human dignity, are the most striking embodiments of his persistent theme: the salvation of the nation's soul.

Marqués' awareness of the Puerto Rican woman's condition and burden inspired him to create very intriguing and intense female characters. They are of three distinct types. To the first belong those who are pillars of strength, sure of themselves and their values. Doña Gabriela of *La carreta (The Oxcart)* and Doña Isabel of *La muerte no entrará en palacio (Death Shall not Enter the Palace)* are such women. To the second belong those who, lacking the strength of the first type, become victims of their surroundings. Juanita of *La carreta* and Mercedes of *Un niño azul para esa sombra (A Blue Child for that Shadow)* are such. To the third belong those who, after being victims themselves, forcefully strike back and eventually prevail because of their will to do so. Casandra of *La muerte no entrará en palacio,* Micaela of *La casa sin reloj (The House Without a Clock),* Sara of *Sacrificio en el monte Moriah (Sacrifice at Mount Moriah)* and the three old women in *Los soles truncos (The Fanlights)* are such women.

Doña Gabriela, the widowed mother in *La carreta,* is strong, the result of a life of hard work and belief in tradition and common sense. She has deep faith in a land-centered culture which eventually saves her and her remaining family. She is also, and above all, a mother. Her moves to the slums in San Juan and ultimately to New York are motivated by her concern for her children's happiness. Her son Luis rejects the rural life and is convinced that salvation lies in industrialization, in the guts of the machine—in which he, ironically, finds death. But his mother cannot defy him, not only because she loves him dearly, but because she lives by the old codes and will not oppose his decisions as head of the family.

Doña Gabriela believes that the land is the only sure and decent source of life. This conviction and her belief in moral values are out of place in the slums of San Juan and New York to which the family's wanderings take them. In San Juan she is beset by noise, stench and dirt. She complains, in the idiom of the *jíbaro:*

¡Tengo un dolor de cabesa . . . ! ¡Lah pehteh! ¡Loh ruido! Ni la mar qué llevárseloh. Condená mar. El aire se encucia y jase daño. Pa qué silve tanta agua si no pué limpiar ehta porquería

She is nostalgic for the clean air of her former home: "Era limpio el aire de la montaña." Dirt is everywhere and even in the lives of all the slum dwellers. This spiritual pollution soon harms her children, victims of forces she can not control or understand—economic disruption, population shifts, unemployment, urban crime. Chaguito becomes a thief and suffers imprisonment. Juanita is raped and endures an abortion that makes her try to commit suicide. Doña Gabriela, who has been concerned about Chaguito's childish pranks and vigilant over Juanita's virtue, has to endure now the sorrow and humiliation of dishonor. Their misfortunes prompt her, in a moment of desperation, to say: "¿Por qué Dioh se está orviando e nojotroh?"

It seems that God has indeed forgotten the poor *jíbaro* family. In New York, the last stop of their journey, tumult and squalor overwhelm Doña Gabriela, who must also endure the near-destruction of her family. Luis has become preoccupied with machines, and, as his sister points out, they have become his friends, his family, his whole life. Doña Gabriela suffers because she sees him become more and more obsessed and unhappy: "Ehtá enfermo por dentro . . . un gusanillo de pena le ehtá royendo el corasón." Moreover, she sees that Juanita has changed. She has seen her wearing make-up, curling her hair and wearing flashy clothes. But more importantly, she has seen her change her values and way of life. Juanita had moved out of their home, and, defying family honor and values, has become a prostitute. Doña Gabriela therefore realizes that the quest for happiness which brought them to a strange place with strange people who speak an incomprehensible language has failed completely. What can she do about it? While Luis is alive there is nothing much she can do. Since she will not defy the head of the family, she is forced to sit both literally and symbolically in the rocking chair the family brought from their old home. As someone says: "De atrah palante. Y de alante patráh. Moviéndose sin moverse. Moviéndose, pero sin llegar a ninguna parte."

But she never loses faith, and her determination gives her strength, and her strength saves her remaining family. Her belief in the life-giving power of the land "La tierra es sagrá" which never left her, now guides her back to where she and her family truly belong.

Doña Isabel, in *La muerte no entrará en palacio* (which is set in an imaginary country clearly based on Puerto Rico) is another strong woman like Doña Gabriela. She is a very levelheaded person who is not deceived by outward appearances of happiness even though they may come accompanied by material prosperity and progress. She is married to a loving husband who also is a leader who has stirred their country to material prosperity and has a daughter who is sweet, affectionate and lively; moreover she lives in a beautiful island which is making tremendous progress in the field of social justice and economic development. But she is neither complacent nor satisfied, because certain values which she holds very dear are being forgotten or disregarded. She is an idealist who believes in freedom, especially freedom to live one's own destiny and use one's own resources. She cannot accept the betrayal of her people by a government, headed by her husband, that has promised bread, land and liberty, only to deliver the first at the expense of the other two. This situation, which was similar to that created by the government of Luis Muñoz Marín in Puerto Rico, confused and changed life for the people. Doña Isabel cannot accept such betrayal, and dares call her husband tyrant. Though she believes in the unquestioned authority of the head of the family, like Doña Gabriela (as proven by her advice to her daughter to follow her man blindly and make his beliefs hers), she also believes that certain values, like "tierra" and "libertad" are worth fighting for. The fact that she does not put her beliefs into action can be explained by her loyalty to her husband or by the fact that her daughter, as will be seen, is driven to act first.

Marqués' female characters of the second type also suffer from the social dislocation and cultural shock caused by the new and alien materialistic spirit of the times, but do not have the strength or nobility of Doña Gabriela or Doña Isabel. They become victims of these new social forces and emerge from the experience profoundly changed. Juanita, Doña Gabriela's daughter, and Mercedes of *Un niño azul* are, though in different ways, examples of such women.

Life in the slums is not to Juanita's liking from the very beginning. Being a sensitive person, she does not adjust to it or accept it. She protests:

> ¿Qué tú te creeh? ¿Que voy a ehtar tó el día viendo y oliendo la porquería en que vivimoh, ah? Pueh no me da la gana bay . . . Aquí to apehta a mierda y a basura.

She seeks escape from this misery and the only kind available to her is the escape of the mind. So she spends all her time listening to soap operas on the radio and then dreams about their heroines—beautiful princesses and countesses with palaces, elegant clothes, expensive perfumes and "jabla fina" (refined speech). She also dreams of a clean and decent life away from the slums, which makes her share at one point Luis' vision of moving to New York, because the snow in that city is pure and clean and it will bring purity and cleanliness to their lives. In her mind cleanliness and snow go together.

In the slums Juanita is brutally raped and has to endure the trauma of an abortion she does not believe in and that is a sin according to her religious and traditional principles. She afterwards tries to commit suicide out of shame and desperation. Though the attempt fails, the old Juanita dies that day. She becomes someone stripped of everything decent, of every dream and every value, and even of memories. Juanita the prostitute who lives in New York has escaped from her misery by means of rebelling against the old Juanita and everything she had believed in.

When at the end of the play she decides to go back with her mother to the land they left and live as the old *jíbora* family was meant to do, she is going back to her own roots. Now she and her mother share once more the same values. The difference between the two women is that Juanita has learned the hard way that true happiness can only be found in being true to oneself and to one's own traditional values and roots.

Mercedes of **Un niño azul,** like Juanita, has been hurt and changed by a hostile and materialistic society. Although her change is not as dramatic or drastic as Juanita's because she had always lacked strong desires or convictions, it is more deadly. Juanita hurts only herself by her actions, while Mercedes destroys her husband and child. Mercedes was young and weak and could not resist society's pressures to repudiate her husband's belief in freedom and way of life. Since he was imprisoned for his political beliefs and was not there to give her the strength and support she needed, she decided to join the rest of the world which for the upper class to which she belonged meant complete rejection of values that cannot be bought or sold or measured. Not only does she forget her absent husband and take a lover, but she destroys her husband's writings, which amounts to destroying his thoughts and his ideas. This is done to appease the forces of materialism represented by her banker brothers. And she destroys her little boy as well, because he adores his father and the idea of freedom for which he sacrificed his life.

Mercedes is callous and selfish, but she is also a victim. One can see that she tries to make her husband and son happy. When her husband returns home from prison, she abandons the lover for whom she still cares; she brings children to play with her little boy. But these attempts fail. She cannot establish a genuine human relationship with either of them because her sensibilities have been blunted by the unfeeling ambience in which she has lived for so long.

Marqués' female characters of the third group are neither mere figures of endurance nor hapless pawns, but women who take strong action against the social forces that beset them. They are prepared to go to great lengths and make great sacrifices in order to survive and be saved. The heroines of **La muerte no entrará en palacio, La casa sin reloj, Sacrificio en el monte Moriah** and **Los soles truncos** must kill in order to save themselves from evil or corruption, to save their values or what is good and just.

Casandra, the true heroine of **La muerte no entrará en palacio,** is at first an average girl. But she is also an intense young woman, not completely frivolous. She is very much in love, and through love she finds both sacrifice and greatness. Her sweetheart's ideal of freedom and his concern over the betrayal of this ideal by her father, the governor, become hers. When she suspects the young man of planning to assassinate her father, she attempts to snatch away his gun and accidentally kills him. Moved by remorse and a new-found idealism, she then assumes his mission and sets out to destroy tyranny and the tyrant, her father. At first a product of her environment, Casandra changes through love to become a woman of high ideals. She is Marqués' model Puerto Rican, who not only believes in a cause, but is willing to sacrifice herself for it.

The same change takes place in Micaela of **La casa sin reloj,** a play whose deliberate absurdity does not deprive its character of significance. At the start of the play, Micaela is living in a sort of moral limbo where her concerns are washing clothes, cleaning the house, listening to the radio and reading romantic novels. She is a product of her environment—no lofty feelings, passions or ideas, and, as she says, "sin remordimientos, conciencia o culpa." She is not moved by the struggle for freedom taking place in her country nor has she felt any guilt over the oppressive conditions which beset it. In order to feel something, to feel guilty at last, she kills her brother-in-law, the only man she has ever truly loved. Whether the killing is intentional or accidental is not clear, but nonetheless, it is evident that only through violent rejection of the status quo and through sacrifice can sensitivity and conscience flourish.

Something similar happens in **Sacrificio en monte Moriah,** a play based, though quite loosely, on the biblical story of Abraham. In Marqués' play, Sara, Abraham's wife, is the central character of the drama. Sara has been forced to live a life without honor. Her husband, a stupid, tyrannical and fanatical man, has forced her to forsake her religion and to prostitute herself so that he can obtain material goods or political advantages. Though he poses as a great leader, it is because of Sara's forced involvement with the Pharaoh and with another leader that Abraham has obtained his advantages. But since Abraham's meanness is accompanied by stupidity, Sara manipulates him in order to thwart tyranny and death. She makes her old husband believe that he has sired two sons, Ismael and Isaac, even though he is really impotent. When Abraham is going to sacrifice Isaac because of what he understands to be a command from his God, Sara, disguised as an angel, stops Abraham as he is about to strike the fatal blow. Finally she kills Abraham in order to free herself and the people from his tyranny. Because of her intervention, evil and superstition have been defeated. She is never afraid to act when action is needed, and therefore she can control her destiny and events.

The three old women in **Los soles truncos** are not afraid to act, either. They see their enemies, time and society, closing in on them, and they take charge of their own fate to prevent these hostile forces from destroying their old, beautiful world. They had grown up in a world where art, music and beauty were appreciated. But after the American invasion, the world that they knew and loved, together with their own youth and wealth, ceased to exist, and they had sought refuge in their own old house in San Juan. In the play, they become aware that the outside world is going to invade their sanctuary; the house is going to be taken away from them for non-payment of taxes. Rather than giving in and have their sanctuary desecrated, and being forced to live in a time and world that is not theirs, they set fire to the house and perish in a glorious suicide.

Casandra, Micaela, Sara and the three old women are brave women who see the need for action and sacrifice to right wrongs. The fact that they resort to crimes in order to accomplish their noble aims is not as important as the message that acquiescence, status quo or complacency are not solutions to the problems of having to live in a materialistic society where virtue and freedom are not valued and where women must accept corruption to survive. The only proper response to the problems is action—true, decisive action for freedom and the ideal.

René Marqués tells us what happens when there is no action or dedication. It is the world of *El apartamiento*. The world of its heroine can become the world of the Puerto Rican woman if she chooses material goods and practical or expedient solutions over virtue and freedom. In this play, Carola does not have to worry about cooking or cleaning—every need has been taken care of. But she is trapped in an apartment with no exit and is not allowed to pursue her beauty and poetry. Instead, she must devote herself to the mindless pastime of measuring over and over a ribbon that never ends. The message is clear: if the Puerto Rican woman chooses a way of life that values material comfort above all else, she will end up like Carola in a hermetically sealed world, pursuing mindless occupations which lead to a life without intellect or sensitivity.

On the basis of some of his short stories, Marqués has earned a reputation as a misogynist. Whatever he may appear to say elsewhere, however, in his dramas he has given ample evidence of his sympathy and admiration for the Puerto Rican woman. Marqués' heroines are bursting with life and energy. Through them Marqués shows the Puerto Rican woman's position in her milieu, her strengths and her weaknesses. Most importantly, he shows how she must act and live if she is to save herself and, in so doing, her homeland.

Bonnie Hildebrand Reynolds (essay date 1985)

SOURCE: "*La carreta*: Virtual Space and Broken Rhythm," in *Crítica Hispánica*, Vol. VII, No. 1, 1985, pp. 75-83.

[*In the following essay, Reynolds examines the temporal movement, tempo, and use of lighting and scenery to create illusory space in* La carreta.]

La carreta was the first of René Marqués' dramatic creations to bring him enthusiastic critical acclaim. Indeed, the well-respected critic María Teresa Babín has said that this play "is worthy of figuring among the best works of all of Latin American theatre." The fact that *La carreta* is one of the most-often performed of Marqués' works, speaks to its dramatic appeal and universality. The three-act play depicts the story of a rural Puerto Rican family, who, at the insistence of the older son, leaves the traditional way of life to search for better social and economic conditions in the mechanized, industrial life of the city. Each act corresponds respectively in time and place to: 1) the poor country shack in the mountains; 2) the makeshift hut in the San Juan district of La Perla; and 3) the sixth-floor walk-up apartment in the Bronx, New York.

The play derives its dynamism from the creation of virtual space which, in combination with the treatment of tempo, rhythm and chronological time, determines the play's forward movement while creating the tension of conflict through which the play communicates to the theatre audience its ultimate message. The theatrical space which any play—and this one in particular—creates is related to the concept of what Susanne Langer calls "virtual space." To explain the concept, she uses the example of the space created in a painting, which is organized by color and shapes. This space does not exist without the arrangement of colors and shapes on a given canvas. In other words, it is a "virtual space." This is very similar to the kind of visible space created by the scenification of a play. The objects, characters, lighting, etc. create an illusory space upon the real place of the stage that ceases to exist at the end of the performance. Because the space which a dramatic work creates is three-dimensional as well as pictorial, virtual space in the theatre also includes the creation of a certain *ambiance* which we can associate to the virtual space created in an architectural structure, such as a house for example. This space is "the created domain of human relations and activities" and, like the pictorial space, is an illusion, since the "atmosphere" disappears when the structure is significantly altered or is destroyed.

The "virtual space" of René Marqués' *La carreta* is both pictorial and architectural. The play carries the subtitle "Tres estampas boricuas" and is, in a figurative sense, an engraving in which each act imprints visually and experientially for the spectator a different scene in the changing life of *this* Puerto Rican family. The specific setting of each act is the family's living quarters, in which objects take on significance past their contribution to the scenification, as they continually serve as a reminder of another life style. The word *boricuas* of the subtitle (meaning literally, Puerto Rican) signifies the vital feeling which dominates the three scenes, each of which offers René Marqués' view of the disintegration of what is Puerto Rican in the life of these particular characters. The diminishing boricuan ambiance from one act to the next transforms the play from being exclusively a *costumrista* work into one with universal subtleties in which two conflicting life styles are embodied in the lives of the characters. This is not the more simply stated conflict between the past and present, nor is it a plea for a return to the past; but rather, it is a conflict which develops from two co-existing ways of approaching life in the face of the particular crises of the period it depicts. As the tension between the two visions grows into open conflict, the characters are forced into a dramatic resolution which creates hope for their own future.

Time in the play interacts with the virtual space to create dramatic movement within each act and within the whole work. Against this spatial background it indicates the destructive direction in which the family is heading as the traditional rhythm of their life is broken, so that each act reflects not only the changing physical conditions and superficial relationships, but the deeper emotional ones as well. First, time manifests itself as part of the theme. This aspect is the chronological ordering that makes up the experience we call past, present and future and whose underlying principle is change. That same principle applies to the linear time in *La carreta* as we see the family at three successive moments, whose juxtaposition simultaneously implies temporal movement, as well as the changes that have occurred between one episode and the next.

Second, the time-related element known as tempo creates an experiential link between the play and the audience. According to J.L. Styan, tempo in a dramatic work is the certain speed in time in which dramatic impressions follow one another in a related sequence, and it tempo "always exists to evoke meaning." In *La carreta,* changing tempo from one act to the next makes the spectator aware of a repeated pattern of disintegration of the traditional life. While linear time indicates change, and tempo conveys the experience of disintegration, physical objects in each act symbolize the transformations that take place from year to year while simultaneously those same objects serve to point out the tempo of life at each stage.

The virtual space and vital feeling, which each stage setting creates, reflect the disintegrating rhythm of the play as well as of the way of life of the rural Puerto Rican who, as presented by Marqués in this play, has abandoned his land. In the first act, the economic and cultural conflict is evident from the beginning, in the stage setting and in the values of the characters, especially of Don Chago and of Luis. The tempo is slow and drawn out, and despite the activity of the moving preparations, not much happens, an indication of the pace of life in the rural setting. The setting of Act One is the interior of a country house made of "buenas maderas del país, como restos de una época de mejor situación económica, remendada con pichipén y retazos de madera barata importada" Thus,

the very appearance of the house, against a background of a more desirable past, tells a story of the worsening economic conditions from which the family is fleeing.

Each of the family members represents a slightly different position on a scale of values, with Don Chago, the patriarch, and Luis, the oldest son, at the two extremes. Don Chago's view of life sees the dollar and "progress" as having taken the place of human dignity. While he does present the past as a better way of life, what Don Chago ultimately stands for is not so much the physical style of living as the spiritual involvement and responsibility of the people in their style of life. Luis, however, has a different opinion of where a person's involvement should lie. He is also concerned about the loss of dignity, but his concern is related to what he sees as a hierarchical social status in which progress has to do with upward mobility. He associates a "better life" with more money, and in turn, having more money with a more highly regarded social status. The play's development moves the family away from Don Chago's side of the scale towards Luis's, and then back again, making a full circle at the work's end.

The tension grows throughout the act but becomes explicit through the image of the oxcart. Near the end of this act, the sound of the oxcart's turning wheels interrupts the nostalgic scene in which the family enjoys their final cup of coffee together, and makes the confrontation with the present problem imminent. At the first sound, the characters become immobile for a short while, giving the audience time to reflect on the meaning contained in this scene. The stage directions describe the play's ambiance as follows: "Sobre ellos pasa una gran sombra de angustia, una muda interrogación al futuro, un miedo al mañana, un deseo de no actuar, de permanecer allí clavados y dejar que pase de largo la fascinación de la carreta." In this manner, the idea of the oxcart (for it never appears on stage) juxtaposed to the long, slow nostalgic scene communicates to the viewer the importance of this moment which represents a crossroad of life for these people.

The second act, taking place one year later, finds the family located in San Juan between the old fortress wall and the ocean, in *La Perla.* Despite Luis' dream of a more comfortable life for the family, the fact that there has been no improvement in their economic status is readily apparent. Moreover, this Puerto Rican family is embroiled in the cultural conflict between the old and the new ways of life at which the first act only hints. The economic and cultural contention is revealed in the stage setting as it contrasts to the house of the past; in the changing values and bitterness of each of the characters; in the now frenzied tempo which creates a sensation of dizziness; and in the tension which the constant presence of a rocking chair brought from the country creates visually. These dramatic elements highlight the development of the play's implicit meaning which the various contrasts and changes, together with the frenetic tempo, create.

The curtain opens onto an empty stage, thus allowing time for the audience to experience the disparities to which the stage setting itself contributes. Because of the arrangement of the house in La Perla, the spectator immediately perceives a clear similarity to the former house in the country. The material of which the house is constructed, however, is in opposition to the country home, which, although it has a run-down appearance due to the attempts at repair, is made of "good wood from the island" and therefore has a strong basic construction. Antithetically, the house in La Perla gives a precarious appearance because it lacks a solid foundation and is nothing more than an accumulation of unmatched, discarded non-durable type materials. In the brief moment at the beginning, when the stage is empty, then, the audience has the opportunity to perceive the obvious economic and cultural changes which have taken place, and to become aware of the growing disillusionment throughout the act which causes the disintegration of the family's intimate relationship with each other as well as that of each individual's personal values.

Throughout this act we see the value system of each family member threatened and while not totally destroyed, at least diminished in the face of the new crises which confront each character and which bring the family to one of the lowest points of morale. Chaguito, the youngest son, is the first to succumb to the city life as he is caught and imprisoned for stealing money from tourists while trying to sell them the San Antonio statue he had stolen from his own mother. Doña Gabriela's daughter, Juanita, is raped and reluctantly agrees to an abortion and then attempts suicide. Luis' plight at first seems to have improved, as he has finally found a job and has many plans for the future. However, he, too, becomes disillusioned as the way of life destroys *his* dreams one by one. Doña Gabriela, through all of her family's tragedies, holds on to her father's ideals of "digniá y vergüensa," but she, too, finally gives up, leaving Luis to make the final decision about the future.

The rhythm of this act that serves as background to these crises, is the final dramatic element that combines with the setting and actual events to convey the characters' experience of desperation to the audience. Various sounds as well as the frenzy of activity and ups and downs in tension convey to the spectator a dizzying tempo. The focus of this act is on the actual experience of the characters, surrounded by a way of life to which they have no means of adapting. Sounds associated rhythmically with the action figure prominently in the experience of vertigo as the characters search for a direction to follow. The first of these sounds is that of a jukebox whose harsh music does not blend with what remains of the vital boricuan feeling within the family home. What the spectator perceives visually is a house resembling the old one. Experientially, the viewer perceives the stark contrast between

the jukebox music and the solitude on stage. Throughout this act, the music penetrates at key moments from the outside until it becomes an intruder over which the family has no control.

The change in the rhythm of life between the first act and the second is most obvious at the moment when Juanita opens a hand-carved replica of the oxcart which her former boyfriend sends to her. The sight of the gift evokes the way of life behind as Juanita lifts up the oxcart and the spectator hears the words as if from Juanita's memories of the oxcart driver. Those words are then drowned out by the sound of an airplane. In this scene, we find Juanita symbolically and emotionally torn between Don Chago's world, which the oxcart evokes, and her brother Luis' world, for which the airplane stands. As the sound of the plane drowns out the sounds of Juanita's memories, we are reminded of the changing pace and of the lost values. Significantly, each of these sounds communicates meaning when examined as an integral part of the whole act. Each sound has a rhythm of its own and the variety of rhythms as well as the quantity of different tempos work with the rapid scene changes and variety of happenings to convey the experience of frenzied movement which seems to bring only negative results.

The presence of a rocking chair, obviously brought from the old house, serves as the focal point, physically and spiritually, of the constant cultural crises which the family undergoes in this act. Because of the contrast it offers to the rest of the furnishings, the chair becomes a constant visual reminder of the life left behind. Moreover, its position in the center of the room makes it symbolic of the central place the former life still maintains within the family nucleus. The back and forth rocking motion contrasts directly to the frenzy of the world revolving around the chair and reflects the differences in values as well as in the pace of life. Throughout this act, then, the rocking chair's central position on stage constantly reminds both audience and characters of the cultural (and personal) tensions at work in this dramatized world.

The last scene of act two brings together the differing life styles and creates a second crossroads revealing to us the further disintegration of family and of its ideals. Here the juxtaposition of the rocking chair itself to the sounds of the jukebox music communicates the downward direction in which the family is heading. Each one in his or her own way tries to escape the problem without really facing it: Chaguito by stealing; Juanita by attempting to end her life; Doña Gabriela by rocking and going nowhere, and all have failed to change or alleviate their worsening situation. Only Luis is left to impose *his* way of escaping, which is to go—by plane—to New York.

The third act shows many changes—both economic and cultural. The absence of the once traditional way of life is evident in the stage setting as well as in the supposed values and in the characters' physical appearance. The stage setting, so totally different from the first two, offers almost no link to the past. The Bronx apartment reveals both poverty and foreignness as we compare this home to the two previous ones. The arrangement of the room has no similarity to the previous stage settings and many aspects suggest isolation and distance, physically as well as culturally, from the original rural setting. Not the least of these is the fact that the apartment is on the sixth floor, vertically adding distance to that between the family and their homeland. In addition, the presence of a steam heater and heavy winter clothing—uncommon sights in the Puerto Rican past—also lend a certain foreign aura to the surroundings.

Changes in the physical appearance of the characters reflect transformations in their personal values as well as in their family relationships. Ironically, the cause of the changes comes from the fact that, although the family's economic condition is much improved over the previous acts, their spiritual and emotional well-being has deteriorated to the point of making them either bitter, as in the case of Juanita, or desperate, as is Luis. Juanita's choice to move away from her family and isolate herself from them reflects the tendency of the Puerto Ricans in this particular play to each go in his or her own direction alone, so that the family, which once moved together, no longer has a unity with which to face the strange new life.

In the first few moments of this act, sounds and rhythms set the tempo as well as reflect the play's direction and *denouement*. Not only is the tempo here syncopated and fragmented, but it is at times a violent and destructive force at work in the lives of these characters. As the curtain opens onto the empty stage, the sounds of a jackhammer and of an elevated train enter through the window. These rhythms, together with that of blues music heard a few minutes later, blend with the various forms of fragmentation prevalent throughout the act as well as within the characters' sense of lack of direction in their lives. However, after this impression, the well-known Puerto Rican danza, "Margarita" replaces the blues music, an indication of Juanita's progressive awareness and definite decision, and a suggestion, in a subliminal way, of the final direction she and her mother will take.

In addition to conflicts within the family group and evidence of the adulteration of their language, which takes on many anglicisms in this act, the most significant relaters of the tempo are the varied events which involve people from outside the family. These events seem to suggest the possible avenues which the Puerto Rican might follow and together form a chaotic world whose roads lead either to unhappiness or to physical destruction. Such incidents indicate the chaos surrounding the protagonist family, while simultaneously, the lives of Luis and Juanita take on specific directions. Luis, motivated by his fascination for the industrialized society's machines, holds stubbornly to his dream of progress. Through-

out the act, and despite his feeling of unrest and disappointment Luis follows the course he has set for himself even before the play begins, a course which costs him his life as the machine that so attracts him, in the end, destroys him. Juanita's own direction begins to take form and it is, finally, through the lesson she recognizes in Luis' death that the play's message becomes clear, unity is restored to the family, and hope for regaining the lost spiritual relationship between man and his homeland once more seems possible.

Just prior to news of Luis' death, Doña Gabriela reveals what the play has clearly suggested from the start—that Luis was neither her nor her husband's son. Although some critics have objected to this relationship, it seems quite relevant when taken as part of the ultimate message hinted at throughout the play. Doña Gabriela reveals this final part of the lesson to her daughter as follows: "Pero Luis siempre ha sio un huéfano. ¿No lo veh perdío en ehte mundo que no eh el dél? ¿No te dah cuenta que se la pasa buhcando, como un cabrito perdío que no encuentra a su madre?" At this point, Luis becomes a symbol of that Puerto Rican who, according to René Marqués, is an orphan because he does not recognize where to look for his parent, but rather, follows blindly the direction set by foreign values and ways of life.

Through Luis' sacrifice then, Juanita, with her new knowledge, imposes the final order on the play as she makes of the oxcart the symbol of the "correct" (according to the playwright) direction one should follow. Juanita's famous words reveal her new knowledge and strength:

> Porque no eh cosa de volver a la tierra pa vivir como muertoh. Ahora sabemos que el mundo no cambia por sí mihmo. Que somoh nosotroh loh que cambiamoh al mundo. Y vamoh a ayudar a cambiarlo. Vamoh a dir como gente con digniá, como desía el abuelo. Con la cabesa muy alta.

Juanita, in her various experiences, and finally in Luis' death, has learned the meaning of what her grandfather said when the family left their home and what Doña Gabriela repeats—that the land has the capacity to nurture and to give dignity and respect to its people, but that those people must recognize their responsibility to return their own love and respect to that land in exchange.

In conclusion, *La carreta* presents three separate visual and experiential impressions which convey the dramatically conceived "vital feeling" of the conflictive Puerto Rican life. The creation of this virtual space upon the stage couples with disintegrating rhythms to communicate to the spectator the spiritual losses within a system that, in the dramatist's view, is attempting to reconcile its cultural heritage with a changing life style. In the work's development, as the family becomes more and more torn apart physically and spiritually, the remaining members come to an awareness that only by accepting the legacy of the Puerto Rican heritage while simultaneously fulfilling their responsibility to their native land can they maintain intact their spiritual integrity.

Richard Callan (essay date Fall 1992)

SOURCE: "Marqués' *La muerte no entrará en palacio* and Dionysianism," in *Latin American Theatre Review,* Vol. 26, No. 1, Fall, 1992, pp. 43-53.

[*In the following essay, Callan analyzes the mytho-psychological theme and symbolism of* La muerte no entrará en palacio, *drawing parallels with elements of Greek religion and drama.*]

The protagonist don José, long-time governor of an island largely dependent on a foreign power, has grown rigid and dictatorial, forsaking his original goal of emancipation for the people. An attempt to overthrow him, inspired by the exiled revolutionary don Rodrigo, fails. The ruler's friend Teresias, José's wife Isabel, their daughter Casandra, and others exhort him in the interest of freedom not to sign a treaty with the northern power which would perpetuate its dominance of their country. The play ends with the governor's death by the hand of his daughter.

La muerte is a *livre a clèf* portraying twentieth-century politics in Puerto Rico. José, idealistic in youth but now domineering, is a substitute for Luis Muñoz Marín, the country's governor from 1948 to 1964, and the treaty to be signed by José suggests the 1952 agreement between the United States and Puerto Rico which established the present Commonwealth status. The revolutionary Rodrigo parallels Pedro Albizu Campos, a Nationalist leader in the '30s who was imprisoned in the United States for subversive efforts to achieve independence from the influence exerted by Washington since 1898. Nationalist opposition to the status quo intensified in the '50s, the decade in which *La muerte* was written and published (1957). Marqués's belief that his small agricultural country should not reach beyond its traditions by pursuing the pattern of industrialization found in the United States is well known, and the play reflects this conviction while also depicting José's tragedy in the context of Greek religion and drama. Eleanor Martin notes such Greek references as the Theban Teresias, the prophet Casandra, and the Chorus, as well as mythological material in other Marquesian plays.

The ensuing mytho-psychological study proposes that José's hubris results from a mental imbalance caused by rejection of his affective side and his concomitant exaltation of reason as the sole factor in determining opinions or actions. Affectivity is the humanizing factor experienced in love, faith, freedom, and nature which unites people in a bond of equality, and the play's mythological background emphasizes this through the figure of Dionysus, perhaps antiquity's profoundest expression of feeling.

> **Marqués's belief that his small agricultural country should not reach beyond its traditions by pursuing the pattern of industrialization found in the United States is well known, and *La muerte no entrará en palacio* reflects this conviction while also depicting José's tragedy in the context of Greek religion and drama.**
>
> **—*Richard Callan***

The mythological content of *La muerte* also raises today's spatio-temporal problem of Puerto Rico to the universal plane, as it did in plays concerned with Athenian problems of the fifth century BC. Dionysus is the god in whose honor tragedians like Aeschylus, Sophocles, and Euripides offered their plays in the spring theatre ritual called the Greater Dionysia, and Marqués continues this religious origin of drama by espousing Dionysianism as the indispensable curb on reason's drift to the extreme of rationalism. Dionysus is that deeply interior world where "the dark must speak to the light, the instinctual to the rational"; he is "freedom and ecstatic joy" with much that is "lovely, good, and freeing." Dionysus personifies "the secret inexhaustible life shown by the new birth of plant and beast in the spring. . . ." In his season the latent egotism of individualism abates and "the individual forgets himself completely"; "all that separated man from man, gave way to an overwhelming sense of unity which led back into the heart of nature."

La muerte's accent on the opposites of reason and feeling will reveal the Dionysian absence in José, and as if to reinforce at once the point that opposite tensions must be integrated for wholeness, the long, dreamlike, philosophical opening describes, in antithetical terms, a mythical representative of equilibrium: Teresias, a Dionysian advocate. He is old and blind but with a complexion of almost youthful freshness and eyes like those of children discovering new worlds beyond them. His voice can be darkly grave or jovially lovable.

Like the androgynous Dionysus, his prophet Teresias had been man and woman. This fusion of sexual opposites, also evident on the spiritual level in the bond between Isabel and him, underscores Dionysus's rapport with women, such as the maenads who personify life, instinct, and feeling. Most Dionysians were women for whom "beauty, sweetness, and charm must combine their rays into the sun of motherliness that warms and nurtures the most delicate life for all eternity," but a Dionysian woman was also a faithful wife as attested to by the permanent and loving marriage between Ariadne and Dionysus. Isabel, friend and ally of Teresias in trying to restrain her husband's hubris, exemplifies these Dionysian values:

> Su verdadero papel es de esposa y madre y a él se dedica en cuerpo y alma. No entiende la política como ciencia. De un modo peculiarmente femenino la intuye, es decir, también ante el pueblo y sus necesidades reacciona como madre o esposa.

Isabel and her friend Teresias speak about faith, an example of the pararational both in *La muerte* and Euripides's play about Dionysus, *The Bacchae*. In the Greek tragedy King Pentheus like Governor José refuses to believe in the God Dionysus whom Marqués portrays through Rodrigo, the proponent of independence against the Governor's design for a Protectorate. Although Isabel wants a reconciliation between the opponents, Teresias maintains that if that does not come to pass they must choose and remain faithful to their choice. Contrary to José's conviction that science and technology alone will bring improvement to the island, she believes in the Dionysian world of love and life: a simple home, an honest husband, and a daughter able to enjoy youth and love. In her strongest plea for the pararational Isabel exhorts Casandra to have faith in Alberto, her intended husband:

> Tienes que creer en él ciegamente . . . irracionalmente, con la misma fe ciega con que creemos en Dios. Cuando la razón haga caer a pedazos todo lo que te habías creído seguro, . . . cuando te veas de pronto en un mundo arrasado, desolado, tendrás el asidero de tu fe que será tu única salvación.

This sentiment and many of its words are repeated through the voice of Isabel in Casandra's prayer soliloquy.

In José's first appearance, the implication that progress and security are achieved only through reason is contrasted with Dionysian feeling and nature, the latter in the sense of both instinct and the physical world. He is rebuking Isabel for her sentimental concern over the upcoming interview with a rural delegation about its grievances, assuring his wife that the time has come for reason to prevail over emotion, and that the technology he will bring is exactly what the people need. She retorts that he should speak to her in the language of the heart, not of science. In the interest of equilibrium she warns against bringing too much progress: "Pero no pases del límite. Ten cuidado de que la dosis no sea excesiva. Porque le puedes matar algo que vale más que toda la ciencia y todo el progreso del mundo." Overvaluation of intellect is the danger here, and her affective side knows that there are things that science cannot prove nor even express; they simply are and are felt. When Gilbert Murray explains the meaning of Dionysus, his words are strikingly similar to Isabel's: "Reason is great, but it is not everything. There are in the world things not of reason, but both below and above it; causes of emotion, which we cannot express, which we

tend to worship, which we feel, perhaps, to be the precious elements in life."

Isabel has another role in the nature-science debate, a subject often discussed by Puerto Ricans because of the enormous contrast between the *jíbaro's* rural life style and the influx of industrialism. After the farm representatives have spoken for greater liberty, José reflects that "la semilla que alguien sembrara aún no ha muerto"; he is referring to the exiled Rodrigo who long ago sowed the seed of freedom. Dionysus, god of liberty, agriculture, and the vine, is a seed. Isabel furthers the agro-political metaphor: "¿Y por qué matarla, mi Joseíto? ¿Por qué no dejarla germinar? . . . ¡Es tan hermoso ayudar a la naturaleza en su empeño de lucha contra la muerte! ¡Es tan hermoso ayudar al triunfo de la vida!" The drama is replete with other allusions to nature and agriculture in keeping with Marqués's concept of Puerto Rican reality, but which are also germane to the god of Nature and vegetation: for example, several references to the *coquí,* the ceiba tree, and nightingales; the stone and its importance to the young man from Altamira, and the customs scene at the airport where an official questions a woman and Rodrigo about carrying seeds and plants.

Opposites are again stressed in the scene where guests and dignitaries gather for the treaty ceremony. It is rumored that Casandra will appear in an expensive evening cape bought by her father, but one of the women present mockingly says that this daughter of a rural mother will not dare to wear it for fear of seeming a peasant playing the role of a princess. Also, the description of the officials suggests a predisposition to rationalism as well as lack of feeling: they are intelligent and skillful but limited to their specialties, without "la nobleza que confiere una auténtica comprensión y sabiduría de la vida y sus problemas, o la mirada encendida por el fuego de una eterna juventud visionaria." Dionysian associations are patent here, particularly to the young god of life and fire whose epithet, Pyrigenes, means "born from fire," and to the wine god with "a fiery nature."

Stage directions for the signing ceremony further stress contrast:

> debe haberse establecido desde el principio cierto sutil contraste entre la 'atmósfera' del grupo de funcionarios al fondo de la terraza circular (más formal, más 'política' y 'oficialesca'), y la 'atmósfera' de la terraza inferior (más 'social', más festiva y frívola, y por ello quizás más humana también).

Another example of opposites are the male and female choruses, a division frequent in Greek drama as in Euripides's *Lysistrata.* They sing twice in *La muerte*: following Casandra's prayer scene and after she has shot José. The repeated words are "Dolor y miseria. ¡Amor!" i. e., grief and want because of hubris exacerbated by rationalism; love and life as the antidote. The word "dolor" (grief) recalls *The Bacchae* where Pentheus's name is defined as "grief".

Music is a major factor in the play, as it was in Greece, with a CORO MASCULINO and a CORO FEMENINO listed in the *dramatis personae,* followed by MUSICA IRREAL, MUSICA DRAMATICA, MUSICA RELIGIOSA, a VALS VIENES, and the "BLUES." It is believed that Greek drama originated with the dithyramb, song and dance by a chorus honoring Dionysus. Since "dithyramb" derives from Dithyrambus, an epithet of the god meaning Child of the Double Door (Dionysus means Twice Born), it is significant that the choruses appear twice. Music was an essential part of the spring dramas in Athens celebrating the agricultural deity's birth. Nietzsche says in *The Birth of Tragedy from the Spirit of Music* that folk songs originate in a Dionysian substratum, a statement in accord with the play's popular waltz, the Blues, and the religious music accompanying Casandra in the death scene of José.

Casandra, young and in love, is the epitome of life and an embodiment of the Dionysian principle, but as her father adamantly continues to oppose the principle, she is led to discharge the negative function of a maenad in the god's ritual of life and death. Maenads and Sibyls were divinely possessed women who ecstatically served their god through ritual or prophecy, and the Greek Cassandra, the prophet whose warnings go unheeded, is of this lineage. In Euripides's *Iphigenia in Aulis* "the wild Cassandra / Will loose her laurelled hair, / Bright hair tossed wide on a wind of dreams, / And cry aloud when God / Cries to men through her." The lines mean for Erwin Rohde that "she wildly shakes her head like the Bacchants," and he adds that in Euripides's *Hecuba* she is the "frenzied prophetess." In *The Bacchae* King Pentheus is killed by his mother Agave during her maenadic rapture while worshipping Dionysus. Pentheus rejected him but out of curiosity he climbed a tree to watch the ceremony. The priests saw him, uprooted the tree, and Agave tore off his head. Casandra has a nightmare in which she cuts down the palace ceiba. The tree represents José and the dream foreshadows her patricide, although she is a daughter maenad and not mother Agave.

A maenad is also described as bloodstained from killing the ritual animal and with eyes that "stare wildly." Marqués's description of Casandra includes both these bacchic specifics: her evening dress is in the style of a Greek tunic, and right after Alberto's accidental death she enters the area where the Protectorate is to be signed with "el cabello . . . semisuelto . . . una mirada alucinada. .. pliegues de la túnica gris manchados de sangre: la mano y parte del brazo . . . están también ensangrentados. . . ." Since this is the only scene with daughter and father together, stage directions state that it must add a special significance to the symbolic encounter, and since the Protectorate itself symbolizes the final affront to the god of freedom, this is the moment for a maenadic assertion of Dionysus. José acknowledges Casandra at once,

but the lighting and strange music lend a mysterious air to her presence, as if she were not his daughter but a voice and force from the beyond censuring a fallen mortal. In keeping with the play's polar structure, she speaks in antithetical terms: "¡José! ¡Devuelve lo que nos has quitado! ¡Limpia lo que has mancillado! ¡Humilla lo que has ensalzado! ¡Resucita lo que has matado!" and her father responds: "¿Quién me habla, Dios Santo? Esa voz. . . ." She then shoots him fatally before he signs the document.

In the last scene her hair is again undone like a devotee of Dionysus, and "su cuerpo se mantiene hierático, su mirada perdida en el misterio de la noche, el brazo derecho en alto . . . la mano abierta como sacerdotisa que derrama dones." With the double reference to priest, Casandra is a maenadic night follower of Dionysus, and the blessing she dispenses is freedom because her murder of José has symbolically prevented a further loss of liberty for the people. Death as symbolized by the stagnation of a Protectorate did not enter the palace, but it had already destroyed the god of love and life in the Governor's soul.

Dionysus is never seen in the play but his voice is heard from afar as in a religious apparition: he is the Voz de don Rodrigo and the Gran Voz with whom Teresias communicates. A voice uttering words is historically the manifestation of spirit, as in the Christian belief that 'the word became Flesh,' and inasmuch as music always accompanies Rodrigo's words, his link with the dithyrambic god is further strengthened. Throughout the drama Rodrigo speaks like a god either with biblical allusions or his own divine-like utterances. For example, with liturgical magnificence and prophetic intensity his voice refers to the parable about a house built on sand that will fall, or Christ's declaration that he had not come to bring peace but a sword. The divine Dionysus too arrives with violence, sweeping away the security which prevails and causing "walls to fall in ruins." He does so because he is that inner force for change which shakes the complacent in order to further life; thus after Rodrigo's arrival there is an armed attempt to assassinate José and a bloody uprising in the countryside. Directly following this violence José says to Teresias that even the blind forces of nature favor the island by having spared it a cyclone for over twenty years. Marqués is using metaphoric and ironic language: José has had political power for over twenty years as had Muñoz Marín but all has not been calm, and Dionysus is now in full rage. As Martin notes [in *Caligula and La Muerte no entrará en palacio: A Study in Characterization*], the Governor is "blind" to the imminent storm which will take his life.

Like Dionysus "whose appearance is far more urgent, far more compelling than that of any other god," Rodrigo comes to his homeland as did Dionysus to Thebes with the message of freedom and change. When questioned at the airport about bringing seeds into the country, the voice of Rodrigo answers that it is the seed of freedom; Dionysus is both seed and freedom with the "highly significant name of the 'liberator'". Rodrigo's importance in the feeling-reason conflict is clear when Alberto marks the treaty as a desperate move by José to counter Rodrigo's influence, i.e., the Governor's rationalism is now reaching the Heraclitian point of enantiodromia where it will convert to its irrational opposite. Subsequent to Rodrigo's return the Governor soliloquizes that his enemy will not vanquish him, and then after the rural rebellion he imprisons Rodrigo as Pentheus did Dionysus. Although jailed, the god's spirit continues to influence others and to bring about the leader's downfall. A political system must favor the free expression of its people and cannot tolerate a status quo which does nothing but solidify the pride and power of its ruler. Such was the reality for Euripides and Marqués. A regime whose axiology depends exclusively on rationalism provokes a Dionysian reaction in order "to transform the ordered, placid world," but due to fear this reaction will be "opposed by established systems of governance."

The confrontation between Teresias and José at the beginning of Act 2 is perhaps the most substantive example of Dionysianism. Curiously it is the only scene with advisor and ruler together, as in *The Bacchae*. Teresias was to deliver lyrics apropos a national hymn for the future Protectorate, and this friend of many years, addressed by José as a visionary, vents his disgust with the leader in his first impassioned words: "¡Estás loco!" He had said to Pentheus: "your mind is most pitifully diseased." Madness is a lack of balance between intellect and emotion with pride and tyrannical power as dire examples of it. The wise man's judgment of Pentheus in *The Bacchae* applies equally to José: "But though you seem . . . to be intelligent, yet your words are foolish. Power and eloquence in a headstrong man can only lead to folly; and such a man is a danger to the state."

The balanced Teresias reminds the ruler of past opportunities to achieve freedom peacefully but which were not taken due to the leader's obsession with perpetuating his power. Alberto will likewise note José's mental deterioration when he criticizes the Governor for chances missed through the desire for control and security. José's decline is further apparent from his scorn of the populace and his arrogant individualism: "¡Al estampar mi firma en ese doumento estaré elevando a este miserable, estúpido pueblo, a un nivel de dignidad que jamás ha conocido!" Such a disrespect for life had earlier led the Governor to think that only he could bring happiness to the land. Teresias then confronts him with the real flaw, fear of change and loss, tantamount to fear of life: "¡Protectorado! Te gusta esa palabra. . . . ¿Sabes por qué? Porque necesitas un 'protector' que te garantice la seguridad que tú mismo no has sabido proporcionarte," and he concludes with the admonition that "protectors" devour the weak. For Carlos Solórzano the Protectorate has all the characteristics "de un infantalismo, de falta de madurez humana que revisten, hoy en día, todas las fuerzas materiales que subyugan al hombre." José cannot find security against change because he cannot accept the

whole of reality which must comprise the Dionysian constants of faith, love, and the furtherance of all life through the practice of human equality. These are Isabel's virtues sorely needed by an insecure José, who, as Shaw observes, depends on "his wife's presence for relief from nervous tension." The governor does turn to his wife because when a man's inner capacity for feeling is inoperative, there is a psychological conflict driving him to seek this energy externally in a feminine figure. [According to Richard Hughes in *The Lively Image: Four Myths in Literature,*] "Dionysus is the daring to leave the security of the commonplace and enter the challenge of the unusual," i.e., to have the healthy abandon of the hero.

José is drinking more and more, not in the celebration of life, but to obliterate the fear of it, and the god of life and wine "destroys his enemies with madness." Teresias is aware of a tragic end when the Dionysian Gran Voz lets him see the future, and the visionary reacts to it, in a psalmodic tone, with words to be repeated by the chorus: "¡Ay dolor, dolor! \?? \Dolor y miseria . . . Porque Tu mano, Señor, caerá sobre el palacio . . . Se ha roto el equilibrio de Tu ley inmutable. Y la sangre de los míos correrá. . . ." Equilibrium between feeling and reason is the divine injunction which Teresias accepts because he reveres the inflexible laws of human nature. Dionysus is that affective half of human wholeness which must be heard, and the divine message to the Josés and Pentheuses who break the law is that blood will flow.

Teresias's words to Pentheus about the danger of power in the hands of a foolish leader parallel those to José: "Cuando se borra el límite entre la farsa y la vida, se tiende a vivir sólo la farsa. Pero no basta entonces vivir la farsa. Se pretende . . . que otros también la vivan." If one does not live for life one exists in a foolish, absurd realm and imposes it on others. When Teresias then refers to himself as a free voice and reproves José for demanding the lyrics, the Governor accuses him of exaggeration: "Te complaces en hacer un drama absurdo de una cosa racional, lógica. . . . Es el himno revolucionario, el himno que surgía del pueblo hace más de cien años." The accusation is both foolish and ironic because the hymn is no product of a true revolution, and Teresias—Marqués is not involved in an absurd drama although the play is about the absurdity of carrying reason and logic to the extreme.

Madness is a persistent theme in the Dionysian myth, and *La muerte* has suggested that the Governor is unbalanced by his denial of the human potential for feeling. Therefore the problem is ultimately psychological. In a section on the Jungian approach to drama, Grínor Rojo alludes to *La muerte* when discussing the subject of "las raíces 'intrahistóricas' de la nacionalidad" and its relation to Jung's concept of the collective unconscious. Similarly William Siemens analyzes Marqués's *El apartamiento* with support from R.D. Laing and Carl Jung, psychologists also referred to in Richard

Hughes's study of Dionysus and rationalism. Hughes finds the psyche a bipartite structure of consciousness and the unconscious with Dionysus as "the unconscious itself." In this context, José's antagonism toward Rodrigo transcends political or ideological motivations and focuses on his disturbed unconscious, i. e., his affective need to embrace life by overcoming the myopic belief in reason as the sole reality. Hughes paraphrases Jung when saying that the psyche is a "complex, self-regulating organism, striving continually for a realization of its whole self." In Jung's words:

> Whenever life proceeds one-sidedly in any given direction, the self-regulation of the organism produces in the unconscious an accumulation of all those factors which play too small a part in the individual's conscious existence. . . . The further we remove ourselves from it [the unconscious] with our enlightenment and our rational superiority, the more it fades into the distance, but is made all the more potent by everything that falls into it, thrust out by our one-sided rationalism. This lost bit of nature seeks revenge . . . .

José is no stereotypical villain, and he is correct in saying that reason should control emotion. There is however the peril that reason will refuse to admit its limitation when faced with loss, change, or a diminished control over events; in effect, José's reason is refusing to accept death, and the living of life is thereby inhibited. A death-like existence ensues—the farce mentioned by Teresias—whether it be called the status quo or insanity. Power then seems to be the godly recourse for permanence and immortality, and, indeed, José wants an entry in the book of immortality written by the gods. For Teresias this is legitimate if one's actions are pure and just, but hubris disqualifies the Governor. The alternative to pride is the Dionysian affirmation of life, all of life, including mortality. Dionysus, the vegetation that dies and is resurrected each year, teaches that human existence is not life against death but "life with death": "He who begets something which is alive must dive into the primeval depths in which the forces of life dwell . . . because in those depths death lives cheek by jowl with life."

It seems likely that René Marqués intended such a mytho-psychological content as presented herein. This highly cultured playwright was surely cognizant of and formed by these elements' long tradition in drama since the fifth century BC through today's Eugene O'Neill, Jean-Paul Sartre, and many others. Be that as it may, in *La muerte* an ancient myth and a modern work of art unite to observe the truth that human affects must temper reason's bent to control life. With Dionysus there is death but also rebirth; without him, only death.

FURTHER READING

Criticism

Giner, Oscar. "Exorcisms." *Theater* 9, No. 3 (Summer 1978): 75-81.
> Examines the impact of colonialism on artistic expression through a comparison of William Butler Yeats's *Purgatory* and Marqués's *The Fanlights*.

Holzapfel, Tamara. "The Theater of René Marqués: In Search of Identity and Form." In *Dramatists in Revolt: The New Latin American Theater*, edited by Leon F. Lyday and George W. Woodyard, pp. 146-66. Austin: University of Texas Press, 1976.
> Surveys Marqués's major dramatic works, focusing on theme, style, and content.

Marquez, Roberto. "The Stuff of Fiction." *The Nation* 223, No. 22 (25 December 1976): 696-8.
> Reviews the English translation of several works by distinguished Latin-American authors, including Marqués's *The Docile Puerto Rican*.

Martin, Eleanor J. "*Caligula* and *La muerte no entrará en palacio*: A Study in Characterization." *Latin American Theatre Review* 9, No. 2 (Spring 1976): 21-30.
> Provides comparative analysis of characterization in Albert Camus's *Caligula* and Marqués's *La muerte no entrará en palacio*.

Additional coverage of Marqués's life and career is contained in the following sources published by Gale Research: *Contemporary Authors*, **Vols. 85-88, 97-100;** *Dictionary of Literary Biography*, **Vol. 113;** *DISCovering Authors Modules: Multicultural Authors;* *Hispanic Literature Criticism;* **and** *Hispanic Writers*.

Okot p'Bitek
1931-1982

Ugandan poet, essayist, novelist, translator, and editor.

The following entry provides an overview of p'Bitek's career.

INTRODUCTION

One of East Africa's best-known poets, p'Bitek helped redefine African literature by emphasizing the oral tradition of the native Acholi people of Uganda. His lengthy prose poems, often categorized as poetic novels, reflect the form of traditional Acholi songs while expressing contemporary political themes. In the preface to his essay collection *Africa's Cultural Revolution* (1973), p'Bitek explained: "Africa must re-examine herself critically. She must discover her true self, and rid herself of all 'apemanship.' For only then she can begin to develop a culture of her own. . . . As she has broken the political bondage of colonialism, she must continue the economic and cultural revolution until she refuses to be led by the nose by foreigners."

Biographical Information

p'Bitek's respect for ancestral art forms began during his childhood in Gulu, Uganda, where his father, a school teacher, was an expressive storyteller, and his mother was considered a great singer of Acholi songs. An outstanding student, p'Bitek composed and produced a full-length opera while still in high school. At the age of twenty-two he published his first literary work, a novel in Acholi entitled *Lak tar miyo kinyero wi lobo?* (1953; *White Teeth*). After studying at King's College in Budo, p'Bitek played on Uganda's national soccer team while maintaining a position as a high school teacher. In the summer of 1956 he participated in the Olympic Games in London and remained in England to study at several institutions, including the Institute of Social Anthropology in Oxford and University College, Wales. He was first recognized as a major new voice in African literature in 1966 when he published *Song of Lawino*. In the same year he was named director of the Uganda National Theater and Cultural Center. In this capacity he founded the highly successful Gulu Arts Festival, which celebrates the traditional oral history, dance, and other arts of the Acholi people. Political pressures, however, forced p'Bitek from his directorship after two years. He moved to Kenya, where, with the exception of frequent visits to universities in the United States, he remained throughout the reign of Ugandan dictator Idi Amin. After founding the Kisumu Arts Festival in Kenya and later serving as a professor in Nigeria, p'Bitek eventually returned to Makerere University in Kampala, Uganda, where he was a professor of creative writing until his death in 1982.

Major Works

Widely regarded as p'Bitek's most famous work, *Song of Lawino* is a plea for the preservation of Acholi cultural tradition from the encroachment of Western influences. The prose poem is narrated by Lawino, an illiterate Ugandan housewife, who complains bitterly that her university-educated husband, Ocol, has rejected her and his own Acholi heritage in favor of a more modern lifestyle. Perceiving his wife as an undesirable impediment to his progress, Ocol devotes his attention to Clementine (Tina), his Westernized mistress. Throughout the work, Lawino condemns her husband's disdain for African ways, describing her native civilization as beautiful, meaningful, and deeply satisfying: "Listen Ocol, my old friend, / The ways of your ancestors / Are good, / Their customs are solid / And not hollow. . . ." She laments her husband's disrespect for his own culture and questions the logic of many Western customs: "At the height of the hot season / The progressive and civilized ones / Put on blanket suits / And woollen socks from Europe. . . ." In an interview, p'Bitek remarked on the protagonist of *Song of Lawino*: "Lawino realizes that we are evolving too rapidly away from our historical and cultural roots. Her song is a challenge for

African leaders and scientists: You learned from white books, but do you link this imported knowledge to Africa? Be aware of your own background." In contrast, *Song of Ocol* (1970) expresses Ocol's disgust for African ways and the destructive force of his self-hatred: "Smash all these mirrors / That I may not see / The blackness of the past / From which I came / Reflected in them." Rather than reflecting the superiority of Western civilization, Ocol's voice has been characterized as an enraged, violent outpouring against Africa and African culture. Bernth Lindfors observed: "His fanatical [Westernization] and rejection of himself have prevented him from developing into a creative human being. He has lost not just his ethnic identity but his humanity." p'Bitek's next major work, *Two Songs* (1971), won the Kenya Publishers Association's Jomo Kenyatta Prize in 1972. Widely praised for its political significance, *Song of Prisoner* describes the anguish of a convicted criminal as he suffers from depression, delusions, and claustrophobia. The specific nature of the prisoner's crime remains unclear: he first claims that he was arrested for loitering in the park but later asserts that he has assassinated a political leader whom he describes as "a murderer / A racist / A tribalist / A clanist / A brotherist." Although he frequently presents himself as a hero, the ambiguous narrator also reveals intense feelings of impotence and anxiety: "I am an insect / Trapped between the toes / Of a bull elephant." In contrast, *Song of Malaya* (which loosely means "Song of Whore") is narrated by a prostitute whose strength and stable personality prevails as she exposes the hypocrisy of those who condemn her. Several critics have interpreted the narrator's voice as symbolizing tolerance for human diversity. Bernth Lindfors described the work's narrator as "the great social equalizer, humanity's most effective democratizer because she mixes with high and low indiscriminately. All who come to her are reduced to the same level." In his later years p'Bitek focused on translating African literature, and in 1974 he published *The Horn of My Love,* a collection of Acholi folk songs about death, ancient Acholi chiefs, love, and courtship. *Hare and Hornbill* (1978) is a collection of folktales presenting both humans and animals as characters. Praising p'Bitek's translation of *The Horn of My Love,* Gerald Moore commented that anyone "familiar with [p'Bitek's] own poetry, especially *Song of Lawino,* will recognize here the indigenous poetic tradition in which that fine work is embedded."

Critical Reception

Critical reaction to p'Bitek's work has centered on the musical qualities of his poetry and his concern with such social and political themes as freedom, justice, and morality. *Song of Malaya,* for instance, attacks society's accepted concepts of good and bad. Bahadur Tejani described the work's composition as "one of the most daring challenges to society from the malaya's own mouth, to see if we can stand up to her rigorous scrutiny of ourselves." Interpreting *Song of a Prisoner* as an allegory for the turbulent political climate in East

Africa during the 1970s, Tanure Ojaide stated: "[p'Bitek's] viewpoint in *Prisoner* is pessimistic about Africa's political future, for there is no positive alternative to the bad leader. The poet sees the need to eradicate a repressive regime, but he fears that the successor could be equally bad or worse." Commentators have also remarked on p'Bitek's concern with the preservation of African culture. In his role as cultural director and author, p'Bitek sought to prevent native African culture, especially that of his native Acholi, from being swallowed up by the influences of Western ideas and arts. While serving as director for the Uganda National Theater and Cultural Center, he proclaimed in an interview: "The major challenge I think is to find what might be Uganda's contribution to world culture. . . . [W]e should, I think, look into the village and see what the Ugandans—the proper Ugandans—not the people who have been to school, have read—and see what they do in the village, and see if we cannot find some root there, and build on this." He further explained his feelings about the influence of Western culture on his own: "I am not against having plays from England, from other parts of the world, we should have this, but I'm very concerned that whatever we do should have a basic starting point, and this should be Uganda, and then, of course, Africa, and then we can expand afterwards."

PRINCIPAL WORKS

Lak tar miyo kinyero wi lobo? [*White Teeth*] (novel) 1953
Song of Lawino: A Lament (prose poem) 1966
African Religions in Western Scholarship (nonfiction) 1970
Song of Ocol (prose poem) 1970
Religion of the Central Luo (nonfiction) 1971
Song of a Prisoner (prose poem) 1971
Two Songs: Song of Prisoner and Song of Malaya (prose poems) 1971
Africa's Cultural Revolution (essays) 1973
The Horn of My Love [translator] (folk songs) 1974
Hare and Hornbill [translator] (folktales) 1978
Acholi Proverbs [translator] (nonfiction) 1985

CRITICISM

Edward Blishen (essay date 1971)

SOURCE: An Introduction, in *Song of a Prisoner* by Okot p'Bitek, The Third Press, 1971, pp. 1-40.

[*Blishen is an English autobiographer, fiction writer, and critic. In the following excerpt, he discusses p'Bitek's* Song of Lawino, Song of Ocol, *and* Song of a Prisoner. *He asserts that p'Bitek's poetry is musical and entertaining even as it expresses the agony of his people.*]

Song of Lawino: A Lament is a poem in thirteen parts. It was translated into English from the Acholi by the author who states that he "has thus clipped a bit of the eagle's wings and rendered the sharp edges of the warrior's sword rusty and blunt, and has also murdered rhythm and rhyme." As to this, I can only say that the eagle's wings must originally have been of quite terrifying span, and the warrior's sword dazzlingly sharp and shining. As to rhyme, the loss of it has led, in English, to a curiously exciting pace which, as we have the poem, might cause any reader to fell that rhyme would act as an unwelcome brake. The rhythm, in English, is most subtle and flowing.

Taban lo Liyong is convinced that **Lawino** is the final form of a poem Okot was working on in 1954, when it had some such title as *Te Okono pe Luputu*—"positively translatable," says lo Liyong, "as: Respect the Ways of Your People, or Stick to Acholi Customs, or Blackman, Be Proud of African Traditions—and Don't Abandon Them for the Whiteman's." Any of these titles certainly sums up the apparent statement the poem makes. The argument is put into the bitter mouth of the wife of Ocol, a chief's son, who has thrown her aside in favour of "a modern girl." The dominant tone of Lawino's comment on her rival can be illustrated from her first discussion of "the beautiful one," whose name is Clementine.

> Brother, when you see Clementine!
> The beautiful one aspires
> To look like a white woman;
>
> Her lips are red-hot
> Like glowing charcoal,
> She resembles the wild cat
> That has dipped its mouth in blood,
> Her mouth is like raw yaws,
> It looks like an open ulcer,
> Like the mouth of a fiend!
> Tina dusts powder on her face
> And it looks so pale . . .

This is the manner, widely throughout the poem. The tone is, on the surface, one of naive astonishment. Lawino is almost tenderly bemused by Tina's makeup, as she is by Ocol's preference for English over his mother tongue, for books over dancing; and, when it comes to dancing, for Western forms rather than Ugandan ones. But there's no tenderness here, of course. In his reading, to Richard Hughes and me, Okot's tone in such a passage had the quality of a kind of surprised purring, but it was not the purring of a domestic cat. Intense

savagery lies under this surface, and never more so than when Lawino is pretending to be reasonable. To me, part of the comic force of the poem lies in the frequent conflict between the tone and the actual words that Lawino speaks: and one of Okot's great skills in writing it, certainly in this translation, lies in his having so laid out the poem that, inevitably, one registers this clash of manner and content.

Setting out her case in the opening section of the poem, Lawino inveighs against her husband's distaste for her, her relatives and his own clansmen. She is, according to Ocol, unlettered, unbaptised (and so no better than a dog), primitive. She is at fault because she cannot play the guitar or count coins. She is silly. Her mother is a witch: her clansmen are fools "because they eat rats." All of them are sorcerers. Indeed, all black people are primitive, and "their ways are utterly harmful."

> Ocol says he is a modern man,
> A progressive and civilised man,
> He says he has read extensively and widely
> And he can no longer live with a thing like me
> Who cannot distinguish between good and bad.

Alongside this report of Ocol's opinions, Lawino chides him, in terms that are to grow stronger as the poem continues. He is not a man any longer—he is a dead fruit! He is behaving like a child! His people, she hints, make up songs of ridicule about him—he who, as son of a Chief, should be the subject of songs of praise.

Then follows the attack on Clementine. This has, at times, a feline hilarity: the claws scratch deep.

> And when she walks
> You hear her bones rattling.
> Her waist resembles that of the hornet.

But suddenly the note changes. There are passages in this poem, whcn Lawino celebrates the customs of her own people, that have a quality of elation—limpid, lyrical—and also of great gravity that are most deeply moving. So here, at the end of her tooth-and-nail attack on her rival, Lawino is made to speak of the Acholi woman's traditional attitude to her husband's need of other women.

> I am not unfair to my husband.
> I do not complain
> Because he wants another woman,
> Whether she is young or aged!
> Who has ever prevented men
> From wanting women?

Jealousy is a weakness—it can only mean that a woman is aware of her own defects. The competition for a man's love is a fair one, conducted according to perfectly reasonable rules.

> You win him with a hot bath
> And sour porridge.
> The wife who brings her meal first,
> Whose food is good to eat . . .
> Such is the woman who becomes
> The head-dress keeper.

She has no fear of competing with Clementine, Lawino claims. What she asks is that her husband should cease insulting her, and should recognise that the ways of his ancestors are good:

> Their customs are solid,
> And not hollow,
> They are not thin, not easily breakable,
> They cannot be blown away
> By the winds
> Because their roots reach deep into the soil.

And Lawino goes on to make an important statement—important, that is, because it has so often been said, carelessly, that *Song of Lawino* is simply an attack on the Western way of life.

> I do not understand
> The ways of foreigners,
> But I do not despise their customs.
> Why should you despise yours?

It is still possible, taking this passage into account, to claim (as lo Liyong does) that the poem is a hopeless plea for the cessation of all cultural borrowing: that the Acholi customs themselves have no particular purity in this respect: and that indeed many of the customs celebrated by Lawino had fallen into disuse by the time the poem was written. But I believe it is essential to note that Lawino is not crying out against imported practices because those practices are in themselves detestable. She is rather trying to preserve a dream of, as it were, coherent cultural habit. The argument, as an argument, is so vulnerable (thus Okumu pa'Lukubo can point out that Acholi women are themselves great users of cosmetics, and that the great Acholi dances have become museum-pieces) that, given so plainly intelligent a poet, we have to look, I believe, below the surface for what is really being said. Given also the lyrical beauty of many of the passages in which Lawino speaks of Acholi customs. In a way, one could say this of the poem: that the litense longing for cultural coher-

ence that arises from such passages is the *point* of the poem. It may be true that we cannot halt the dislocation of cultures that everywhere is occurring; or it may simply be true, as the poem seems often to imply, that the price paid for such dislocation is too high. But in fact it is an apparently impossible thing that is being said in *Song of Lawino:* that perhaps we should pause, or that perhaps we cannot afford to move at such a fantastic pace. This is impossible, as a statement, because we have nowhere in the world really begun to think along such lines. But in the impossible propositions set out by a poet have often lain the seeds of what, belatedly, the world has seen to be necessary kinds of action. *Lawino,* I suspect, is a poem that performs this function. We may swarm critically all over it, and point to all its logical weaknesses, and yet we may still not have robbed it of a fraction of its intrinsic strength. The poet, after all, is only describing his own sense of being himself intolerably divided. You can hardly study in three Western universities without becoming something of an Ocol, and yet we cannot doubt—I do not see how we can—that Lawino's voice is in great measure Okot's. It is in this sense that I mean that the argument may not yet be ready for wholly rational discussion. What appears to be an argument is often, I suggest, a simple statement of the poet's awareness of being divided against himself, and (as I think we shall see plainly when we turn to *Song of a Prisoner*) his awareness that the whole world is, in some such way, intolerably divided. I am often reminded, reading *Lawino,* of the great cry uttered, in so many and powerful ways, by the English poet John Donne as he stood with one foot in the medieval world and the other in the world of early modern science. Donne's arguments do not stand up: he cannot abolish the work of Copernicus: he cannot restore the medieval sense of a coherent chain of being. And yet his cry was essential to the awareness of his time. It was a cry that, under the hopelessness of the surface argument, was an utterly necessary reminder of the permanent human need of coherence, of order. And such a cry, I believe, *Lawino* utters: being, for that reason, a poem important not only to Africa, but to the whole world.

> **It is an apparently impossible thing that is being said in *Song of Lawino*: that perhaps we should pause, or that perhaps we cannot afford to move at such a fantastic pace.**
>
> **—Edward Blishen**

So, throughout much of the poem, a double operation is being conducted. All of Okot p'Bitek's deft and darting sense of mischief is at work when he attacks, in terms of Lawino's carefully wide-eyed and deceptively innocent amazement, the forms of dancing preferred by Ocol and Clementine: their

Westernised taste in dress, their Western attitudes to time and to sickness and death. In much of this there is a marvellous, mischievous comedy. I have known Western readers bereft of all appetite for a while by Lawino's account of their feeding habits:

> The white man's stoves
> Are good for cooking
> White men's food:
> For cooking the tasteless
> Bloodless meat of cows
> That were killed many years ago
> And left in the ice
> To rot!
> For frying an egg
> Which when ready
> Is slimy like mucus,
>
> For boiling hairy chicken
> In saltless water.
> You think you are chewing paper!

Lo Liyong has curiously little patience with this element in the poem. It turns the work, he suggests, into "light literature" (a term which he surely ought to discuss before he uses it merely as a phrase of disparagement). "Too much space and energy," he argues, "is taken up with pointing out the foibles in the Western way of life . . . these foibles that are easily seen." Lo Liyong regards this as "childishness": "Some of it is fun for an Acholi audience: some impudence, some sarcasm, and plenty of 'raw' social anthropology. Juvenility. . . ." To say such things is surely to fail to weigh the pure comic success of these elements in the poem. It is not easy to imagine an Okot p'Bitek entirely or even largely stripped of his wicked and mocking manner. Even when he is most deeply serious, as we shall see when we look at *Song of a Prisoner,* a kind of dark laughter is never far away. And the truth is that much of *Lawino,* much that Okot's old classmate frowns over for its "lightness," has proved to be durable fun for audiences much wider and less special than Acholi ones. There is no wishing away the jester in this poet's work. When his targets are obvious, they are most unobviously teased and taunted.

The second part of the operation that one can see Okot conducting in *Lawino* lies in the account of Acholi customs and ways of life—idealised, no doubt, but not the less lovely and grave for all that. So, opposed to the hilariously mocking descriptions of Western dance is Lawino's celebration of Acholi dancing: to the tendentiously revolting view of the European *cuisine,* Lawino's marvellous tour of the Acholi kitchen:

> Here on your left
> Are the grinding stones:

> The big one
> Ashen and dusty
> And her daughter
> Sitting in her belly
> Are the destroyers of millet
> Mixed with cassava
> And sorghum.

It is all appallingly unfair, as lo Liyong notes—and yet again, one has to say that we are not really concerned with an attempt to be fair, to provide a balanced argument. It is with Western dance and cooking exactly as it was, in that dispute of Okot's with the British Council, with the piano. I remember that Okot made the piano, that patently superb musical instrument, seem an absurdity beneath one's contempt! How ridiculous the piano was! Not for one moment did one believe that Okot truly withheld his admiration from the piano: just as one would not have been surprised to see him dancing the detested rumba. This was not the sort of argument he was conducting. Mockery of the one was necessary to reinforce the idealisation of the other: of the piano, to promote the drum: of the rumba, to intensify the claims made for the get-stuck dance. Lo Liyong asks us to set on one side "all the crocodile tears which Okot made Lawino shed profusely, for Okot is a sceptic on the surface as well as between the lines." But for that sentence really to have meaning, lo Liyong would have had to say that Okot was a *cynic,* not a sceptic: the claim being that he is making an empty show, in order to secure easy laughter and literary honour. Of course the surface of the work sparkles with scepticism, with all the facets of a complex and elusive mind. But I would argue that under this, there is the deepest possible gravity. And again, the test is one that each reader must make for himself, subjectively: it lies in the *tone* of what is written. I cannot doubt the profound seriousness of tone with which Okot addresses himself to the ways of the Acholi world. He may, for his own purpose, have turned that world into a Utopia. But to claim that he wrote these passages, so lyrically celebratory, with his tongue in his cheek, is (on the evidence of my ear) nonsense.

Another quality of Okot's writing to which I want to pay more attention when I come to *Song of a Prisoner* seems also, for what it implies as to the poet's entire intention, an element that can be weighed only by the ear, as it were—by the reader's general sensitiveness. It lies in that habit, so intrinsic to Okot p'Bitek's writing that one almost ceases to notice it, of referring incessantly to life other than human—to the life of animals, insects, plants.

> His eyes grow large,
> Deep black eyes,
> Ocol's eyes resemble those of the Nile Perch!
> He becomes fierce

Like a lioness with cubs,
He begins to behave like a mad hyena . . .

The backs of some books
Are hard like the rocky stem of the *poi* tree . . .

You wish you were lucky
To find someone to assist you
Who does not shout
Like house-flies
When disturbed
From an excreta heap! . . .

This is certainly a habit of Ugandan poetry, a deep part of the oral tradition. It is not an originality, in Okot. And yet it seems to me that his use of it, constant, profuse, is another means by which he roots his vision in Africa, and nowhere else: by which he brings the reader back, time and again, to that profound sense of place that, together with that profound sense of rooted custom he appears endlessly to offer as an alternative to the shallow confusions of half-westernised ways. Again, it is the rootedness he seems to insist upon. Again, under all the imperfections of the surface argument, what he can be felt to be saying is: Let us, before we enter the nowhereness of uniform modern existence, consider desperately the importance of knowing *where* we come from, *where* we live. Let us think generally in terms of roots. Or, to adapt the famous epigraph to the poem: Let us think what we shall be doing before we uproot the pumpkin in the old homestead. Lawino, in fact, is no innocent and naive village girl, at all. She is a poet and anthropologist, mingled, with a profoundly difficult and provocative argument to put forward in whatever ways may offer.

Of course, poets of any quality are mixed creatures! Of course, many of the criticisms that, in his lively way, Taban lo Liyong brings to bear against *Lawino,* and which really stem from his knowledge of Okot the man, are likely to be justified. Into Lawino's attacks on Western forms of religion lo Liyong reads Okot's malice towards the Catholic missions. No one can read this section without suspecting that personal revenges are being exacted. It is in this section and again in the section on politics, which lo Liyong feels to be the best in the poem, that Okot's impersonation of Lawino, the village girl, most obviously slips. The poet steps out from behind the mask. Without being experts on the Ugandan political situation, we can believe that, here and there, the voice that speaks is that of Okot p'Bitek, the disappointed political candidate. Lo Liyong says, from his knowledge of his friend, that if Okot has "an overriding passion beyond living life, it is politics." But when we have accepted that such a section of this poem, from a man so committed and concerned, so clearly and properly anxious to play a part in the developing history of his country, *must* have its moments when the frustrated or ordinarily irritated man speaks, rather than the larger poet, still, and es-

pecially in view of what is to come in *Song of a Prisoner,* one must note, and with proper gravity, what in essence is said in the eleventh part of *Song of Lawino*:

If only the parties
Would fight poverty
With the fury
With which they fight each other,
If diseases and ignorance
Were assaulted
With the deadly vengeance
With which Ocol assaults his mother's son,
The enemies would have been
Greatly reduced by now. . . .

. . . those who have
Fallen into things
Throw themselves into soft beds,
But the hip bones of the voters
Grow painful
Sleeping on the same earth
They slept on
Before Uhuru!

This does not belong to the field of purely personal revenges or irritations or disappointments. It is again a cry of something like panic at the rootless disorder of things—the too sudden and too infatuated plunge into some travesty of national politics.

I cannot leave *Lawino,* such a deviously serious poem, as I claim, and yet such a fiercely comic one, without a word about the twelfth part, called "My Husband's House is a Dark Forest of Books." Here is Okot p'Bitek, nourished on books, producer of books, in a wild extravaganza of disdain attacking Ocol for being a bookman. The section is worth looking at closely by any reader because it is so relevant to the accusation that, in much of the poem, Okot is intent purely on mischief, on appealing to the sense of fun of an Acholi audience. Whatever a reader's view about any argument for or against intellectualism, or bookishness, it would require a reader of some owlishness, and considerable resistance to comedy, not to be vastly entertained by this section.

My husband's house
Is a mighty forest of books,
Dark it is and very damp,
The steam rising from the ground
Hot thick and poisonous
Mingles with the corrosive dew
And the rain drops
That have collected in the leaves . . .

For all our young men
Were finished in the forest,
Their manhood was finished
In the classrooms,
Their testicles
Were smashed
With large books!

Of course, one thinks with that radical academic, this is to put the clock back with a vengeance! Of course, one thinks momentarily with Lo Liyong, here is "Okot the sceptic posing as a champion for dying and dead customs he doesn't believe in." Here is Okot p'Bitek the intellectual pretending to a swinging anti-intellectualism! But one recovers quickly—I speak for myself—and adds two other statements. First: here is fun! Here is the most hilarious delight! If there had to be mockery of book-reading, could it be more amusingly, and more unexpectedly, expressed? in terms of a more grotesque poetry? And second: this cannot, in the nature of the poem and the poet, be merely mischief, or merely fun—or merely perversity! By an unbalanced bookishness, I think Okot is saying, it is possible that the new African is being severely damaged. Books have taken on an undue importance. Books have been resorted to beyond their true virtue. The use and reading of books, too, needs rooting in the African soil. The new man who tries to climb by books alone will climb nowhere at all.

Taban lo Liyong argued, in the essay already quoted, that *Song of Lawino* should be part of a triptych. Ocol should be allowed to state his case: so should Clementine. I don't know if it was in response to this suggestion that Okot wrote *Song of Ocol,* which appeared in 1970. It is a furious, headlong, bewildering poem, far briefer than *Lawino,* without the swarming life of its predecessor. I am indebted to my friend Cosmo Pieterse for the suggestion that, in this poem, Ocol is attempting to defend himself against accusations of which he has forgotten the actual nature. In the first five of its nine parts Ocol simply rages against old Africa. Lawino's song is

the mad bragging
Of a defeated general . . .

The whole past will be swept away. The pumpkin will go early—had already almost gone.

I see a large pumpkin
Rotting
A thousand beetles
In it;
We will plough up
All the valley,

Make compost of the pumpkins
And the other native vegetables,
The fence dividing
Family holdings
Will be torn down,
We will uproot
The trees demarcating
The land of clan from clan,
We will obliterate
Tribal boundaries
And throttle native tongues
To dumb death.

And this is the tone, this the wild and whirling character, of the first half of the poem. It is destructive shout, close to hysteria. Old Africa is blisteringly impugned. All that Lawino celebrated is savaged by this extraordinary song of Ocol's. He cries out against the very fact of his Africanness.

Mother, mother,
Why,
Why was I born
Black?

All will be burned and broken. The whole past will be swept away: all the witches and wizards, the poets, priests, musicians, story tellers, myth makers, glorifiers of the past. There will be an end to

The stupid village anthem of
"Backward ever,
Forwards never."

All the professors of anthropology and teachers of African history shall be hanged. All the anthologies of African literature destroyed. All the schools of African studies closed down. Ocol becomes surely, in these passages, not a character at all, but an extreme part of the tormented African spirit: the part that, in its despair, would turn from the effort of knitting past with present. "Smash all these mirrors," cries Ocol,

Smash all these mirrors
That I may not see
The blackness of the past
From which I came
Reflected in them.

So taboos, customs and traditions must be shattered. The women of Africa must be shown that they have taken pride in what is merely grotesque. The men must be shown how derisory their achievements have been, over the centuries:

> A large arc
> Of semi-desert land
> Strewn with human skeletons . . .
> A monument to five hundred years
> Of cattle theft!

This Ocol—the Ocol of the first half of his song—is driven by a destructive dread and hatred of his African self. And later in the poem, his desire to efface Africa is given a monumental wildness of utterance:

> We will uproot
> Each tree
> From the Ituri forest
> And blow up
> Mount Kilimanjaro,
> The rubble from Ruwenzori
> Will fill the Valleys
> Of the Rift,
> We will divert
> The mighty waters
> Of the Nile
> Into the Indian Ocean.

But from the sixth section of the poem onwards, the whole nature of the statement seems to change. Now Ocol is one of those who have done well out of Uhuru. In the sixth section, with guilty defiance, he taunts the poor and dispossessed with an account of his properties—

> Do you see
> That golden carpet
> Covering the hillside?
> Those are my sheep . . .

and denies his responsibility for the poverty of the peasantry. And from now on, we are not sure how to take the voice of Ocol. He speaks at times in terms of an ironical observer regarding him from outside.

> We sowed,
> We watered
> Acres of Cynicism,
> Planted forests of Laughter,
> Bitter Laughter . . .
> Fat Frustrations

> Flourished fast
> Yielding fruits
> Green as gall . . .

Those who stand aside from this fearful opportunism are "cowardly fools"; they must creep back and hide in their mothers' wombs. And in the eighth section there is another change in the voice—or another note enters briefly and confusingly into it. For a moment Ocol speaks with something like tenderness of the world he once shared with Lawino:

> That shady evergreen *byeyo* tree
> Under which I first met you
> And told you
> I wanted you,
> Do you remember
> The song of the *ogilo* bird
> And the chorus
> Of the grey monkeys
> In the trees nearby?

But from this unexpected wistfulness Ocol turns at once to a fiercer fury than ever. He tells Lawino that there are only two alternatives:

> Either you come in
> Through the City Gate,
> Or take that rope
> And hang yourself!

The City is barely described. It is defined almost entirely by negation—by an account of what must be destroyed to clear the way for it.

And as an end to the poem there is a last storm of wildly ironical self-disgust. The monuments in the modern Africa will be effigies of its founders: Leopold of Belgium, Bismarck. Streets will be named after the European explorers. All the great men of the African past were made nothing by defeat and irrelevance.

> What proud poem
> Can we write
> For the vanquished?

A final question that makes it impossible not to remark to oneself that such a proud poem has certainly been written, and by Okot p'Bitek: and that it was called ***Song of Lawino.***

Song of Ocol, as fierce and powerful as anything Okot has published, seems to me very much a poem in which the author is moving towards a new position. I mean that it begins as a statement that, in the extreme violence of the view it expresses, must make it an expression of the impulse in a modern African to raze his whole world flat and begin again. Ocol, whom we had taken even at Lawino's worst estimation to be a new young African of a fairly characteristic type, turns out to be a sort of super-Tamburlaine, in his destructiveness, driven by an almost hysterical dread of the black past and much of the black present. Clearly, Okot is no more expressing the whole of his self here than he was in *Lawino.* It doesn't begin to be a personal statement: it is the ferociously extreme utterance of something that is in the African air. But the poet cannot keep this up: because the destructive, desperate Ocol is also one of those who have turned Uhuru into an opportunity for their own advancement. So the end of the poem, its second half, is an attack, by ironical implication, on those who have betrayed the hopes that fed the fight for independence. By the end of *Song of Ocol,* it seems to me, Okot p'Bitek has moved into the position that made possible the writing of this new sequence of poems, *Song of a Prisoner.* Certainly, to turn from his first long published poem to these last ones, he had to swivel: from teasing impersonations to impersonations that are deadly serious: from the "lightness" of which Taban lo Liyong has spoken to an unsmiling gravity. The distance between *Lawino* and *Song of a Prisoner* is, I feel, in some respects so great that added force is given to lo Liyong's suspicion that the earlier poem was in essence very early indeed.

"Only rarely," lo Liyong wrote of *Lawino,* "do I see an Okot with tight lips and protracted visage." That a friend who knew him so well should have looked for such an Okot, and should have based so much of his criticism of Lawino's lament on that Okot's absence, does suggest that between the jester and the more serious man an acute struggle may long have been going on. The fact is that *Song of a Prisoner* is throughout a work of the tightest lips, the most protracted visage. The jester has vanished; though not the user of masks. In *Lawino* and *Ocol* Okot spoke—as we have seen, with bafflingly variable degrees of convincingness—through the mouths of his characters. Much of the voice of Lawino must have been his own: and, one feels, even in its desperate extremism, something of the voice of Ocol. In this new sequence, Okot dons several such masks. The prisoner cannot be read as a single character. At times he is a kind of Patrice Lumumba, being beaten to the point of death: a betrayed hero of Uhuru. At other times he seems to be any political detainee, imprisoned for his opinions or his political actions. Again, he is an assassin, who has rid his country of a tyrant: who pretends wildly not to understand why his captors do not form a guard of honour for him.

We see, from the dedication, that the sequence is wide-spread in its reference. It makes two major statements: both familiar to us, though not in such agonised tones, from *Song of*

Lawino. The first is that the hopes of Uhuru have been wrecked, and horribly. The state of a newly independent African country may be even worse than before, since it is worse to be devoured by your own people than by strangers. The second statement is barely a statement at all . . . rather it is a constant reference to a dream. As Lawino looked back at the vision of Acholi order and comeliness of life, so the prisoner constantly sets up a dream of peaceful happiness:

> I have bought
> A farm
> In the fertile valley,
> A thousand acres
> Of heaven
> For you and me
> And our children,
>
> The crested cranes
> Dance love dances
> By the stream
> That flows gently
> Through our garden,
> Our children will play
> And swim in the stream
> And hook fish
> For the afternoon meal . . .

It is the tone of Lawino's celebration of the good things in the Acholi way of life. And added to this is the longing for old prides, old understandings. The assassin yearns to go back to his village, to be received there as one who has killed from a necessity generally understood, to be cleansed and to be marked with the killer mark. It seems to me, I must say here, as widely off the point to claim that, in such passages, Okot is crying for a return to an older Africa as to make such a claim for his arguments in *Song of Lawino.* It is a hearking back, rather, to the past, not as a pleasing mode of life, but as an experience on which some decent order had been laid: when there were recognised ways of setting a limit to the larger tyrannies, the more intolerable greeds. In the light of this sequence, I do not see how one can continue to have any doubt as to the import of Okot's backward looking. It is, in a sense, a metaphor for a kind of forward looking—for a looking, at any rate, in any direction but towards the spectacle of modern Africa as the prisoner experiences it: where

> Black corpses stream
> Along the streets,
> Dead to free Africa
>
> So that they may
> Suffer in
> Freedom!

And to these elements we must add another. There is a great cry, at many points in these poems, but most clearly towards the end of the sequence, for a sort of vast international tolerance—a relaxed international order. The prisoner wants to dance all the dances of the world, to sing all the world's songs. He wants even

> to dance the dances
> Of colonialists and communists . . .

Even, that is, to span the widest gulfs of ideology and political action. There is a great weariness in this sequence of all the waste of human strife.

For all the changeableness of the masks behind which the poet sings his desperate songs, *Song of a Prisoner* seems to me a true sequence, as some series of poems so linked do not succeed in being. It is held together, of course, in the first place, by the pure style of the poet. There is much here that readers of *Lawino* will recognise—given the far grimmer context. There is, above all, and even more cunningly and evocatively used than before, the constant reference back and forth to the life of animals, insects, plants. These references are methodically placed in the sequence, so that no human event is without its gloss drawn from nature. Again, the images may be used to suggest a deceptive simplicity and sweetness, a sort of hopeless happiness: sometimes, as in **"This Stupid Bitch"** and **"Voice of a Dove,"** the references to animals (in both these cases, to birds) give to the opening a soaring pleasantness that makes all the fiercer the descent into the prison, the actual *use* made of the image. I am struck, in many of these passages, by the absence of all strain, the effortlessness, with which Okot modulates into lyricism. He has always been a poet who seems to sing with ease: it is hard to find a phrase in his work behind which you can detect any large pretension. So with:

> The yellow acacia thorn tree
> Lifts up her arms,
> Her clean fingers
> Speak soft invitations
> To the yellow birds . . .

It may even be careless (a purist might object to the obviousness of the three adjectives in those three lines—I mean, to the obviousness with which each noun is given its adjective). But the lyricism seems always to come at the right—that is, usually, the startling—moment: to sustain this curious weaving, so characteristic of the poetry, of violence and sweetness. And once more, the effect of these images drawn from the common scenes of a continent rich in insect, animal and vegetable life is far more than decorative, or descriptive: again,

this is one of Okot's devices for giving the deepest possible roots to his work. And at other times the references to nature are fierce and grim:

> A stone wall
> Of guns
> Surround our village,
> Steel rhinoceroses
> Ruin the crops . . .
>
> I am an insect
> Trapped between the toes
> Of a bull elephant . . .

I am struck always, as I say, by the naturalness of these images, in the sense that they arise in Okot's text with a kind of inevitability. Never behind such images was there less feeling of a mere search for colourfulness. But then, Okot can indeed—and I suppose it is partly the oral tradition that makes this possible for him—employ even a slightly bizarre figure of speech and make it seem natural: as in

> Olympic athletes throw javelins
> Inside my belly.

The sequence is held together, too, by the recurring or echoing themes or passages. So we are constantly in a court of law, or some other place of judgement: so the prisoner, in this of his guises or that, is perpetually being required to plead guilty or not guilty. And always he answers with another plea altogether, until, when the sequence is over, he has pleaded a great range of emotions: fear, helplessness, hopelessness, smallness (how unexpected and telling, that!), hatred . . . It is the entire history of the moods of imprisonment; we are swept through the whole awful landscape of imprisoned despair. And again, a theme to which the earlier poems have accustomed us appears—or perhaps it is rather a note struck than a theme. Lawino spoke so often of the manliness of her clansmen, of the masculinity and athletic pride she felt Ocol had lost. The prisoner's sense of his own fate is made more bitter by the memory of his own virility: he was a footballer and a boxer: he is a man to whom it is natural to compare the pains of hunger with javelins thrown by Olympic athletes. He had teeth that

> were the
> White *okok* birds
> Standing on the back
> Of a buffalo bull.

Beaten by his "uniformed brothers," refused a blessing by

"our black nationalistic bishop," aware of wife raped, of children excluded from school and employment—raging against tribalism, capitalism, diseased nationalism—he thinks constantly, intolerably, of the power there once was in his own beaten body.

I spoke earlier of the dark laughter in *Song of a Prisoner*: and I can understand that a reader might claim that he found no laughter in this sequence, at all. I use the word in its very widest reference. It seems to me, for example, that those two companion poems, **"Bonfire"** and **"This Stupid Bitch"**—in the first of which the prisoner upbraids his dead, rotting father for choosing such a wife, and in the second of which he attacks his mother for marrying such a husband—a very dark humour is at work, using the mirror argument of these two poems to bear his meaning as to the intolerable character of tribalism, and especially of tribalism wedded to modern politics, which may exclude so many of the beneficiaries of Uhuru from all prospects in life.

In the end, when we have read and thought about these latest poems by this remarkable African, we may be left—and particularly non-Africans may be left—with a sense of having, in a dialectical sense, bitten off more than we can chew. I mean this: that we may feel (and many Africans must feel) we do not exactly know how to evaluate this apparently wide-glancing attack on post-Uhuru Africa. This is no issue, especially for an outsider, to comment upon lightly. We cannot attempt to gather up the entire African experience and to say that on it *Song of a Prisoner* is a meaningful general statement. It is certainly no cue for a widespread disillusionment with independent Africa. All an outsider can say is that, given the disorder which colonialism brought to Africa, given the disorder in which it quitted Africa, it will take patience and nerve to rebuild African stability, and to repair what has been broken. Perhaps only a fellow Ugandan can judge Okot p'Bitek's particular case. In all respects in which it is a sequence of personal poems, it must be left to longer and more intimate judgement than we can bring to it. But *Song of a Prisoner* is, clearly enough, not simply a series of poems of personal experience. It is a song, agonisingly felt, most powerfully expressed, vivid and individual, about the universal experience of political imprisonment.

> How can I think freely
> When the very air I breathe
> Has ears larger than
> Those of the elephant
> And keener than the bones
> Of the *ngaga* fish?

More than Africa speaks there, and to an audience larger than Africa.

I am aware of letting Okot p'Bitek down, rather, in those last words. Of course this is a poem of very explicit personal anguish. Of course no one can doubt that Okot feels himself to be the "proud Eagle, shot down by the arrow of Uhuru." He cries out clearly enough to the "pressmen of the world":

> I want to speak to you,
> For the candle
> Of Uhuru
> Has been blown out . . .

I did not wish to evade this direct challenge of the poet's: but only, as (to return to the beginning) a modest early mapmaker, not to plunge into judgements of a kind not strictly necessary to a verdict on a poem or a sequence of poems. As a private reader, I have my own way of reading *Song of a Prisoner.* As a public critic, I can only try to account for my admiration of the poems as poems.

But I feel of them much as I have felt about *Lawino.* As I see it, Okot's power as a poet is of the kind that perpetually raises his work above the particular emotions and experiences—necessarily very tangled in any poet, and in him probably most severely tangled—from which it sprang. This is to be a really good poet. I don't believe anyone could seriously think about modern Africa without trying to weigh the meaning of *Song of Lawino* and *Song of a Prisoner.* I believe *Lawino* has an importance far beyond the boundaries of Uganda: it is, when generalised, a poem about the situation in which we all find ourselves, being dragged away from all our roots at an ever-quickening rate. I believe, as I have said, that beyond the note of alarm and anguish that it strikes as to the condition of some newly independent African countries, *Song of a Prisoner* is full of the despair and anger, fiercely expressed, of anyone anywhere who is politically in chains. But having said all this, one is left with a last—and perhaps, in the end, even more important—thing to say. And that is that Okot p'Bitek is a marvellous poet. I wish I could read him in his own language. But in English he has found a tone, a pattern of verse, a rhythm, that are highly original and inventive. It would not be easy to mistake Okot, in English, for anyone else. Though—and perhaps my friend Taban lo Liyong will note this—his matter is never light, his manner often is, in a sense that any writer must envy. I count him among the few masters I have read of literary mischievousness. He can modulate from one mood to another with a skill that, though startling in its effect, rarely draws attention to itself. He is a master of writing for the human voice—and sometimes, I suspect, for the animal or insect voice, too. Much in his style might be made the basis of an argument for drumming, as a musical accomplishment for a poet, in much the way that one might have said experience of the lute was a formative influence on Elizabethan verse. And finally, Okot p'Bitek, as man and poet, is one of those valuable souls who add manifestly to the gaiety of the nations, at the same time that much of what he expresses is closely concerned with their agony.

Bahadur Tejani (review date 1973)

SOURCE: A review of *Two Songs: 'Song of a Prisoner' and 'Song of Malaya'*, in *African Literature Today*, No. 6, 1973, pp. 160-66.

[*In the following review, Tejani asserts that p'Bitek's* Song of Prisoner *explores a search for justice, while* Song of Malaya *attacks society's concept of morality.*]

Produced in a lovely white and red jacket, with the two faces of the prostitute and the prisoner evoking a harrowing harmony, Okot's latest compositions are a demonstration of the amount of matter a truly creative hand can pack into a very brief space. The publishers have altered their style of publicity as well, to suit the poet's originality. Instead of the usual prosaic piece at the back, there is an evaluating comment with the emphasis on connotative use of language. Eleven enticing illustrations by Trixi Lerbs, in the right places, make this volume compulsory possession. The only major complaint from the reader's point is the price. Who is going to buy Okot's work? One thought he was famous enough now for the publishers to take a risk and produce ten to fifteen thousand copies for the first edition to bring the price down.

Okot's prisoner [in ***Song of Prisoner***] is a vagrant in the city, and his first question as he lies beaten and torn behind bars is:

> Brother,
> How could I . . .
> A young tree
> Burnt out
> By the fierce wild fire
> Of Uhuru . . .
> Inspire you
> To such heights
> Of Brutality.

In section after section, the irresistible, plaintive, rich, hungry voice of mad ecstasy draws us on, pleading for justice. It is the 'cry of his children' with bellies 'drumming the sleep off their eyes'; the 'fiery lips of his sister's song'; the 'helpless ululation of his mother'; the cold body of his wife rocking 'with grief and regrets'; it is the voice of a clan surrounded by 'steel rhinoceroses and roaring kites sneezing molten lead and splitting the skies' with bombardment. It is the call of the common man for justice and for revenge, a defiance of the power-laden bellow of the chief's dog growing fat on people's labour:

> Listen to the Chief's dog

> Barking like a volcano,
> Listen to the echoes
> Playing on the hillsides!
> How many pounds
> Of meat
> Does this dog eat
> In a day?
> How much milk . . . ?

The dog is the perfect symbol to expose the Chief's alienation from society, for only when man wants to barricade himself from his own kind, does he use this savage species as a means of protection. Later in one of the loveliest passages he has composed so far, the poet evokes the image of the Big Chief himself, breaking into the prisoner's home, riding his wife. Our sight, smell, sound and sense of movement combine to form this memorable picture created by a mind always exploring the language for fresh meaning.

> A black Benz
> Slithers smoothly
> Through the black night
> Like the water snake
> Into the Nile,
> Listen to it purring
> Like a hopeful leopard,
> Listen to its
> Love song,
> The soft poem
> That embraces the valleys
> And caresses the hills . . .

> The grasses on
> The pathway
> Hiss in protest
> The shrubs scratch
> Its ribs
> With their nails,
> Foxes hit the windscreens
> With their laughter,
> Dogs whine

> And sharpen their teeth,
> The gods riddle the car
> With yellow arrows
> Of starlight. . . .

The combined efforts of natural, animal, and spiritual life are powerless in preventing the soft caress of the Wabenzi from spreading itself. This theme is not new to East Africa. But the poet's style and rich imagery expresses the contrast between the haves and have-nots in an entirely new manner. Implicit in the lines is the ruthless mercenary power of the politician, his quiet hunting style, his capacity for sacrilege. As the exploiter's fingers reach the very centre of his life, the prisoner demands revenge in words that have the terror of the French guillotine in them.

> I want to drink
> Human blood
> To cool my heart,
> I want to eat
> Human liver
> To quench my boiling thirst,
> I want to smear
> Human fat on my belly
> And on my forehead.

Here Okot speaks for all the wretched of the earth. Indeed in his dream, the prisoner actually imagines himself shooting and destroying 'The sharks of Uhuru that devour their own children'. But in section nine the poet's humanity, while justifying the action of the prisoner, consoles the widow of the Big Chief.

In the last five sections of the poem, Okot tries a complex experiment, of contrasting the inner life of a 'Minister' with that of the prisoner. Somehow this doesn't quite come off, simply because it's difficult to judge who is who. One also feels the Minister's portrait to be a stereotype, though once again, in the description of the prisoner's clan-life, proud and dignified like the 'colourful cattle egret', there is excellence.

In the last two sections, the poem takes another turn. The dream is over. The futility of protest, a voice shouting in the wilderness for justice and revenge, is understood, accepted. The poet's plea seems to suggest that at least if we can't have social and political justice, let's have the freedom of spirit to sing and dance. This is what is claimed in the synthesis, which follows Okot's usual anthropological bent, of combining various cultures:

> I want to dance the dances
> Of our friends and
> The dances of our enemies,
>
> I want to lift their daughters
> To my shoulder
> And elope with them . . .
>
>   . . . Let me dance and forget
> For a small while
> That I am a wretch,
> The reject of my Country,
> A broken branch of a Tree

> Torn down by the whirlwind
> Of Uhuru.

Yet if Okot's verse is to sell here and not in U.K., or U.S.A., if it's African ears who are to feel the twang of the social and political injustice, and not foreign mouths which are to savour the fantasies of his rich imagery, if the poet is to belong to us and not to them, E.A.P.H. had better look into their accounts again. Give us more Okot and give it to all of us, not the big chiefs only.

There is no discipline better suited than anthropology when you want to destroy the reading public's concept of morality.

Okot has given his historical and cultural sense full play in the malaya's song [*Song of Malaya*], which explodes all our sacred notions of good and bad.

The composition is one of the most daring challenges to society from the malaya's own mouth, to see if we can stand up to her rigorous scrutiny of ourselves.

The prudes, the puritans, and the respectable, have always frowned upon the street-walker, the adulteress, the courtesan, the malaya. But the history of sexual deviation, of perversion, seduction, and temptation, it is as old as man himself, embracing, according to the poet, the great names in world history.

Okot has given his historical and cultural sense full play in *Song of Malaya,* which explodes all our sacred notions of good and bad.

—*Bahadur Tejani*

The sly glance and the sensuous laugh is in the shanty of the slum, the royal bed, the appetite of Eve, and in the action of the acolyte near the saint, so claims the malaya:

> Listen, Sister Prostitutes
> In the Hilton suites.
> Fill your glasses
> With champagne . . .
> And you in the slums
> Distilling illegal gin . . .
> Here's to Eve
> With her golden apples.
> And to the Egyptian girl
> Who stole Abraham from Sarah's bed . . .
> We'll drink to the daughter of Sodom

And to the daughter of Gomorrah

Who set the towns ablaze
With their flaming kisses . . .
Let's drink to Rahab
With her two spy boy friends,
To Esther the daughter of Abigail,
To Delilah and her bushy-headed
Jaw bone gangster,
To Magdalena who anointed
The feet of Jesus!
We will remember Theodora
The Queen of Whores . . .
And the unknown prostitute sister
Who fired Saint Augustine
To the clouds.

In the malaya's philosophy, Christianity, that supporter of the sexless, is given special treatment. The poet creates a warm human picture of mother-malaya waiting for the return of her school child. Upon the discovery that the lad has been dubbed a bastard, her wisdom lets itself loose upon our fundamentals.

Now, tell me
Who was the greatest man
That ever lived?
The saviour
Redeemer
The light . . .
King of Kings
The Prince of peace . . .
What was His Father's name?
Was the Carpenter
Really His Father?

And a pertinent question is put to the teacher:

How many teenagers
Have you clubbed
With your large-headed hammer.
Sowing death in their
Innocent fields?

The malaya's song is for everyone. The sailor coming ashore with 'a time bomb pulsating' in his loin, the released detainee with 'granaries full to overflow', the debauching Sikhs at the nightclubs with heads broken open, and the vegetarian Indian 'breeding like a rat'.

The schoolboy lover is given a concession for the 'shy smile on his face' so long as he does not swap tales with the teacher who was there last night!

The bush-teacher, chief, business executive, factory workers and shop assistants, party whips and demagogues, will all line up at her door to quench their thirst.

Okot's merciless satire takes toll of a whole humanity and the political mercenary collects the largest part of the whip-lash on his groin.

Oh-ha-ya-ya!
But you were drunk,
You could not finish . . .
You feigned sleep.
Snoring like a pregnant hippo . . .
Your silly baby tortoise
Withdraw its shrunken skinny neck . . .
Leaving me on fire
The whole night long . . . !

The big chief's impotency is matched only by the dark frustration of the family man. In one of the illustrations we see his pumpkin-bosomed wife, with a waistline like a barn door, ranting while a bunch of skinny children shiver at the hut's entrance.

No wonder the mini-skirted malaya, with breasts arched like the underbelly of the Concorde, is a relief for his soul. Automatically with such pleasure and brightness goes the poet's question: 'How dare you blame the gay-time girl?'

The malaya because of her intricate and wide experience of men, can teach the house-wife a thing or two.

Come on Sister.
Do you think
Your wild screams
And childish sobs
Are sweet music
In the ears of
Our man?

The irony of the last line, of course, works both ways, for the malaya as well as the well-wedded wife.

The total effect of this intimate, seductive voice of the malaya is as illuminating as a thunder-flash in the silent night. Her rancour, her claims, her knowledge of men's ways and movements are unsurpassable. Through her, Okot explores the essence of guilt and shame that we harbour in ourselves.

The malaya is sharp enough to have facts and situations at her fingertips[;] she knows how to silence her brother's sham morality by pointing out who it was that shared a bed with her friend next door two nights ago.

The sergeant who calls her a vagrant carries the 'battleaxe' with which he wounded her last night. For her and her kind, the cycle of the geisha is as natural as the rise of the morning sun and its dip in the west at dusk.

The bouncing vigorous voice of the malaya has enough intelligence and humour for her song to get the listener at one go.

> Black students
> Arriving in Rome,
> In London, in New York
> Arrows ready, bows drawn
> For the first white kid

The imagery is superbly hilarious, as when

> The wife
> In house
> Eats lizard eggs
> To prevent pregnancy!

Or when disease has made some inexperienced fool run mad, the courtesan adjusts her focus kindly for him

> Let the disappointed
> Shout abuses at us.
> Let them groan, sleep
> Their spears vomiting butter,
> Their buttocks swollen
> After the doctor's caning

Gerald Moore (review date 21 February 1975)

SOURCE: "Songs from the Grasslands," in *The Times Literary Supplement,* No. 3807, February 21, 1975, p. 204.

[*In the following review, Moore praises p'Bitek's* The Horn of My Love, *asserting that p'Bitek's translation captures the evolving nature of Acoli culture and the expressiveness of Acoli song.*]

In his preface to **The Horn of My Love,** a collection of Acoli traditional songs, Okot p'Bitek argues the case for African poetry as poetry, as an art to be enjoyed, rather than as ethnographic material to be eviscerated. The latter approach has too often predominated, even among those scholars who have actually troubled to make collections. This book, with Ulli Beier's valuable anthologies, can help to build up the stock of African poetry for enjoyment.

The Acoli (pronounced "Acholi") are a grassland people of the Uganda-Sudan borders whose songs and ceremonial dances are still remarkably alive. Not preserved, with all that this word implies of mustiness and artificiality, but continually changing; continually acquiring new words, new tunes, and in the case of the dances, new steps or instruments. Okot p'Bitek himself describes the many changes of style and title undergone by the Acoli *Orak* (Love Dance) over the past seventy years. Dances do not change in this way unless they are still in the mainstream of the people's cultural experience.

Perhaps the Acoli were relatively lucky in this respect. Their music and poetry were not court products, played by a corps of professional artists. They were the common stock of the whole population, diffused by the communal dances and ceremonies into the knowledge and practice of every member of the group. A young man or girl unable to perform adequately on such occasions could not escape ridicule. There was no question of being "in the audience" when great ceremonial dances like the *Otole* (war dance), *Bwola* (victory dance) or *Guru Lyel* (funeral dance) were performed.

This total cultural involvement lasted until quite recent times. The main occupations for men who left Acoliland were soldiering or policing, both easily assimilated into the traditional concept of the warrior. Indeed, army terms, drilling moves and whistles were often incorporated into the constantly changing dances, which is another example of the response of these popular arts to the changing experience of the people. Add to this the relative inaccessibility of the area, far from the major towns, with few roads and no railway until the 1960s, and with a colonial interlude which really lasted only some forty years. All these factors worked in favour of continued vitality within the traditional arts of the Acoli, and they were assisted by the recent efforts of a small group of educated young men, such as Okot p'Bitek himself, who studied and mastered these arts in order to introduce them in the schools. Thus the schools became the new sphere for acquainting the young with the cultural achievements of their people, instead of the sphere for their estrangement and reorientation towards foreign cultures.

The expressive range of Acoli song is remarkable, extending from the fiercest of war chants to the tenderest of love lyrics or funeral laments. There is no more stirring sight than that of hundreds of men and women, ostrich plumes waving in the sunlight, singing and stamping in unison, so the ground seems literally to shake and the dust rises ever higher. But many of these songs are also sung on small and comparatively private occasions, to the accompaniment of a solo *nanga* (boat-zither) or *adungu* (jaw-harp) played by the singer. Thus the same song may be heard in the moonlit arena of the Love Dance, sung by hundreds of young people to the electric beat of calabashes and the stamp of anklets, or floating in the still night air from the top of an anthill, where a girl is crying the praises of her lover:

> When the chief of youths enters
> 　　the arena
> He is like a waterbuck breaking
> 　　the circle of hunters.

This variety in the modes of presentation is matched by the variety of imagery to be found within even a single genre. In his interesting chapter, "Themes in Acoli Dirges", Okot p'Bitek identifies no fewer than six more or less distinct groups of imagery, all of which might be heard sung in the course of a single night-long *Guru Lyel.* This event might open with an advancing group of warriors entering the arena and fighting the "mock fight" with Death to the accompaniment of words like these:

> If I could reach the homestead of
> 　　Death's mother,
> I would make a long grass torch;
> If I could reach the homestead of
> 　　Death's mother,
> I would destroy everything, utterly,
> 　　utterly,
> Like the fire that rages at Layima.

Yet this cry of anger and aggression may be interrupted by a new chorus, sung perhaps by some of the women mourners, whose words re-evoke the actual agony of a death suffered many months before (since the *Guru Lyel* is performed only in the dry season and only after elaborate preparations):

> Death burned the body of the
> 　　young woman
> Like fire,
> She cried with pain in her chest,
> Beloved of my mother, Oh!
> Death burned your body,
> At last, today, it has taken you.

Among the most interesting, though not among the most moving, of these digres are those in which the dead person is actually attacked, for having in some way disgraced the clan. There is a bitterness in these satirical songs which is conventionally shocking. But they are probably best understood as

having the same basic virtue as the others: they articulate the spite and resentment within the group, just as the others articulate its grief, and thus play something of the same purgative role. Every feeling aroused by this particular death is thus given open but ritualized expression, and the solidarity of the surviving group is actually renewed by this very expressiveness.

Another valuable chapter is devoted to the patterns of relationship between the chiefdom songs (*Bwola*) and certain historical events in the story of each chiefdom. These are not the explicit historical narratives which are found among many African peoples. The references are cryptic and vivid, but they cannot be fully understood without some independent historical instruction. Their very presence within these ceremonial songs, however, serves to keep alive some of the group emotion associated with these, often ancient, events.

There are useful descriptive notes introducing each group of songs but, owing to some vagary of composition, these notes are all placed together, instead of each being set separately before the particular group to which it refers. There is also an occasional visual irritation, where a very short poem, rightly given a page to itself, is set tightly at the very top, crowding the title and leaving an ugly expanse of blank paper beneath it. The book would also benefit from a bibliography, though there are some bibliographical references scattered in the text.

Above all, however, it is a book of poetry to be handled and enjoyed, rather than a ponderous headstone placed on the living body of a popular art. It can be read with equal enjoyment, in these facing texts, by Acolis relishing the felicities of the original languages and by English readers relishing the muscularity of Okot p'Bitek's translations. Those familiar with his own poetry, especially *The Song of Lawino,* will recognize here the indigenous poetic tradition in which that fine work is embedded. The bitterness of Lawino's sense of betrayal is not a personal but a cultural bitterness. And it takes on additional depth and meaning for those who understand, from these songs, why a husband who cannot show his body in the dance arena is an insult to his whole clan, not just to his deserted wife.

> **Those familiar with p'Bitek's own poetry, especially *The Song of Lawino,* will recognize in *The Horn of My Love* the indigenous poetic tradition in which that fine work is embedded. The bitterness of Lawino's sense of betrayal is not a personal but a cultural bitterness.**

> **—Gerald Moore**

These songs must also deliver a fatal blow to those who contend that romantic love is an alien importation, unknown in traditional African cultures. The great love-duets sung by Goya and his wife, in which they jointly ridicule "the rough-skinned man" once destined to be her husband, attack the avarice of her father, and proclaim their intention of running off together without the payment of bridewealth, expose the hollowness of pronouncements based on anthropological norms. And it would be hard to imagine a more romantic lyric than that of this deserted lover, as he watches the hot pathway all day long:

> She has taken the path Nimule:
> Tomorrow she will return.
> As she walked away her buttocks
>   danced.
> Bring Alyeka, let me see her!
> My eyes are fixed on the path,
> my eyes on the path . . .

Robert L. Berner (review date Summer 1979)

SOURCE: A review of *Hare and Hornbill,* in *World Literature Today,* Vol. 53, No. 3, Summer, 1979, p. 550.

[*In the following review of* Hare and Hornbill, *Berner states that p'Bitek is uniquely qualified to translate a collection of East African folktales and comments on the tales' themes and subjects.*]

The ethnographers and missionaries who have produced collections of East African folktales have worked at a disadvantage because of their imperfect understanding of languages, narrative conventions and cultural contexts. Inevitably they have produced collections flawed by artificial texts and extraneous elements. As p'Bitek explains in his introductory note, this oral literature derives from the close relation of the storyteller and "a live, responsive audience, taking up the chorus, laughing and enjoying the jokes." p'Bitek is particularly qualified to deal with these tales; he has already produced a collection of renderings of Acoli oral verse [*The Horn of My Love*]; and his own poetry, such as the *Song of Lawino,* reveals a thorough understanding of African folk materials.

The population of these tales [collected under the title *Hare and Hornbill*] is about evenly divided between human beings and animals, and the plots reveal similarities with motifs which are widely observable in other oral literatures. One tale is a carefully structured parable about the process by which a poor man gives the "gift" of poverty to a rich man. Others have to do with the origins of institutions—for example, of a particular chiefdom. The animal stories often concern ten-eyed Ogres, who are associated with natural forces and who must be subdued by trickery. Several of them account for the

origin of natural phenomena—why Leopard is spotted, why Tsetse is always killed, why Owl flies only at night, and so on. The Trickster figure, which is universal, appears frequently in these stories as Hare, who tricks and is tricked in return and who thus serves to educate the human audience. The moral of one really funny story, for example (about Hare's tricking his mother-in-law into sexual intercourse), is that "Even if you take your mother-in-law under the lake you will be found out."

The field of African folklore is vast, and extensive recording is necessary before the task of comparative study can begin. p'Bitek's collection, though he has made no attempt to exhaust his subject and though this edition lacks scholarly apparatus, is a model for this enormous task.

Annemarie Heywood (essay date August 1980)

SOURCE: "Modes of Freedom: The Songs of Okot p'Bitek," in *The Journal of Commonwealth Literature,* Vol. XV, No. 1, August, 1980, pp. 65-83.

[*In the following essay, Heywood argues that p'Bitek's songs form an "ongoing meditation on Freedom."*]

Seen against the evolving context of historic change, the work of the leading African writers marks phases of ideological radicalization. The process stamps the *oeuvre* of Ngugi, Achebe, Armah, and Soyinka. In Okot's Songs it finds its most poignant voice.

The antinomy Lawino/Ocol utters the phase of hope and assertion: future roles and modes of self-perception are being defined in the positive, active mood of struggle for nationhood, a struggle which is still experienced as a struggle for freedom from colonial exploitation and alienation. With the antinomy Prisoner/Malaya we find ourselves in a later perspective. *Freedom from* has been attained, and what Berdyaev calls "the second freedom", the *freedom to,* is experienced as destructive chaos and painful anarchy. Uhuru has become a prison, the sustaining mother country a punitive, barren nightmare.

> . . . The stone floor
> Lifts her powerful arms
> In cold embrace
> To welcome me
> As I sit on her navel.
> My head rests
> On her flat
> Whitewashed breasts . . .
>   [*Song of Prisoner*]

This chill blankness recalls that "tabula rasa" which Frantz

Fanon says [*The Wretched of the Earth,* 1967] "characterises at the outset all decolonisation." As early as 1961 he pointed out how such a disillusioned, blank phase is a necessary condition in that "total change from the bottom up" without which decolonisation must remain merely a change of masters.

In a way which seems to me fruitful the sequence of four Song cycles can be viewed as an ongoing meditation on Freedom—not a private meditation, to be sure, but an interactive meditation by, and on behalf of, the whole social web which is undergoing change. It is from this angle that I propose to look at Okot's work, and I shall deliberately give less attention to what has already been well described and analysed in the critical literature than to what seems to me to have been neglected, if not misapprehended.

Okot's meditation is from the outset troubled and painfully torn by conflicting loyalties and belief structures. He explores the conflicting claims of the Old and the New by means of complementary personae. Lawino and Ocol confront one another not as fictional 'characters' but as choral presences. They are masks which hold our attention precisely because they are vividly and vitally particularised, but choral masks nevertheless. Soyinka did something similar in *Kongi's Harvest* where Kongi and Danlola confront and mirror one another in dialectical opposition. But Soyinka's approach was still Hegelian: he sketched a proposed third term, a saving synthesis, in Daodu/Segi. Okot's rendering is more penetrating, uncompromising, radical. He presents us with a true antinomy, a confrontation of irreconcilable and equally valid positions, and does not resolve the painful tension between them with even a hinted conciliation. There is something profoundly moving, truly tragic, to the laments and recriminations of these two lovers torn apart by the growth process of liberation. Listen to them both:

> Lawino: . . . But oh! Ocol
> You are *my master and husband,*
> You are the father of my children,
> You are a man,
> You are you!
>
> Do you not feel ashamed
> Behaving like another man's dog
> Before your own wife and children?
>
> My husband, Ocol
> *You are a Prince*
> *Of an ancient chiefdom.*
> Look!
> There in the middle of the homestead
> Stands your grandfather's Shrine,
> Your grandfather was a Bull among men
> And although he died long ago
> His name still blows like a horn,

His name is still heard
Throughout the land . . .

> Has the Fire produced Ash?
> Has the Bull died without a Heart?
> Aaa! A certain man
> Has no millet field,
> He lives on borrowed foods . . .
>   [*Song of Lawino*]

> Ocol: . . . *Sister*
> *Woman of Acoliland*
> Throw down that pot
> With its water,
> Let it break into pieces
> Let the water cool
> The thirsty earth;
>
> It is taboo
> To throw down water pots:
> With water in them,
> But taboos must be broken,
> *Taboos are chains*
> *Around the neck,*
> *Chains of slavery;*
>
> Shatter that pot,
> Shatter taboos, customs,
> Traditions . . .
>
> Listen not
> To the song of the poet
> The blind musician
> Plays for his bread,
> The bread owners
> Are your slavers . . .
>
> *Lift up your head*
> *Walk erect*
> *My love,*
>
> Let me see
> Your beautiful eyes,
> Let me caress
> Your sultry neck,
> Let me kiss your dimples . . .
>
> In Buganda
> They buy you
> With two pots
> Of beer,
> The Luo trade you
> For seven cows . . .
> They purchase you

On hire purchase even,
Like bicycles,

You are furniture,
Mattress for man
Your arm
A pillow
For his head!

Woman of Africa
Whatever you call yourself,
Whatever the bush poets
Call you
You are not
A wife!

        [*Song of Ocol*]

Each addresses the other's freedom, a nobility which is not realised: Lawino addresses the forgotten nobility of the past, Ocol the potential nobility of the future; but for all their passion they no longer meet in the present. The only escape from this painful tension is total change, a radical leap into the undefined, still-to-be-created future. Fanon of course makes the same point. The men who will create the new society have still to create themselves in the struggle to do so (in Armah's words, The Beautyful Ones Are Not Yet Born!).

> . . . this struggle which aims at a fundamentally different set of relations between men cannot leave intact either the form or the content of the people's culture. After the conflict there is not only the disappearance of colonialism but also the disappearance of colonised man. This new humanity cannot do otherwise than define a new humanism both for itself and for others. [Fanon, *The Wretched of the Earth*]

In the same vein, Marcuse speaks of a Nietzschean "radical transvaluation of values" which can, by its very nature, not be programmatic.

> . . . What kind of life? We are still confronted with the demand to state the 'concrete alternative'. The demand is meaningless if it asks for a blueprint of the specific institutions and relationships which would be those of the new society: they cannot be determined *a priori;* they will develop, in trial and error, as the new society develops. [*An Essay on Liberation,* 1969]

Once one perceives the lawfulness of chaos within the radicalisation programme, and one's sympathies are opened to the *"positive and positing effect of negative thinking,"* the Songs of Prisoner and Malaya take on a new colour. "But so long as we insist that disintegration is bad *per se* and that anyone producing it can only wish to 'destroy'," says Charles

Hampden-Turner in *Radical Man,* "we shall fail to understand the growth process itself." The anguish, rage and moral anarchy of these Songs, justly seen, are tokens of radicalisation "oriented towards," in the words of Marcuse, "and comprehending a future which is 'contained' in the present. And in this containment, the future appears as possible liberation." Marcuse's term 'containment' employs the same metaphor as **Prisoner**: as Camus remarked, *à propos* of The Plague, imprisonment is the most suitable metaphor for life in the Absurd which is the expression of radical Freedom. (I am further moved by the correspondence of this metaphor to certain icons which portray the Christ child as contained within the body of the dark Virgin).

It is in this light that I propose to view the progression of the Songs. Okot's greatness lies in the—I think—unique achievement that he leads his reader fully into the human experience of each position. He brings each home to heart and mind as experience, in all its shades and nuances and implications—and then sets it against an opposite developed with equal attention and compassion; and in doing so, avoids all judgemental rancour. His Songs, moreover, are truly popular, truly accessible to every reader. Originally written in Luo and employing, with tremendous success, the conventions of traditional laments, mocking songs and songs of challenge, they have even in the English versions an irresistible authentic life.

But my focus must be on themes rather than form. To summarise the relationship between the four cycles, I shall use a typology proposed by Raymond Williams in Chapter 3 ('Individuals and Society') of *The Long Revolution* which offers a useful shorthand in describing African Literature generally. Williams defines a spectrum of ways in which a given individual may relate to the social structure within which he finds himself. Society and its structures, he says, are by definition oppressive. They impose restraints on the free play of human energy and regulate its expression into controlled forms which permit the greatest possible good for the greatest possible number. This restraint is experienced as anything from benevolent to intolerable according to the degree to which the individual identifies with it, or accommodates to it. Williams proposes six types of stance:

To the MEMBER society is his own community which he endorses unconditionally, and the demands of which he perceives as his own. To the SERVANT society is an establishment within which he finds his place. He is comfortable within it so long as he studiously avoids all friction and consents to serve collective goals loyally; his conscience is in abeyance. To the SUBJECT society is an imposed system in which his place is determined without choice; he must conform or perish. To the REBEL a particular society is a tyranny. He actively opposes it, fights to change it. He exercises his freedom to offer it a new and better future. The EXILE withdraws. He may hope for change, but does not participate in the struggle to attain it. The VAGRANT repudiates the condition of society as such. He is a liminal, radically withdrawn from all collective goals, and serves his individual conscience alone.

Okot's greatness lies in the—I think— unique achievement that he leads his reader fully into the human experience of each position. He brings each home to heart and mind as experience, in all its shades and nuances and implications—and then sets it against an opposite developed with equal attention and compassion.

—Annemarie Heywood

If we apply Williams' typology to Okot's Songs, we find an interesting progression. Lawino is a MEMBER at that unreflecting stage where the question of individual freedom has not yet arisen. She appears politically unawakened; her focus is clannish; she sees only the tribal community. Her political ignorance is the focus of Ocol's impatience. Ocol has been a REBEL as an activist in the liberation struggle; he now is a SERVANT of independent nationhood in its primary form, that established by the departing colonial masters; and striving to become a MEMBER by freely accepting responsibility for the shaping of a new, authentically structured society. One of his most potent accusations against Lawino is that she is blind to her SUBJECT status within the system she so ignorantly seeks to perpetuate. He calls on her to assume the freedom which is her due—but only if she rouses herself to claim it. Ocol's status then is that of REBEL turned SERVANT. (There is an interesting parallel here to the progression in Armah's *Beautyful Ones:* the Man who was REBEL finds himself the impotent SERVANT of a rotting system, and is reborn into VAGRANCY). Later, in *Song of Prisoner,* the Ocol-type again turns to REBELlion. Within Williams' typology the choral personages of *Prisoner* and *Malaya* are both VAGRANTS, with moods of REBELlion. Their rebellion however is anarchic and radical; it is no longer the structured programme which inspired Ocol.

Prisoner and *Malaya* are polar antinomies just like *Lawino* and *Ocol.* Ocol and Lawino polarised the Old and the New. Prisoner and Malaya polarise, if you like, the masculine and the feminine Eros or ethos; or the NO and YES as found in Fanon's *Black Skin, White Masks,* a book which affords a truly remarkable record of the radicalisation process. The conscientious, rational, compassionate SERVANT of humanity undergoes a violent rebirth; an inconceivable sphincter convulses and the VAGRANT is born:

> . . . with all my strength I refuse to accept that amputation. I feel in myself a soul as deep as the deepest

of rivers, my chest has the power to expand without limit. I am master and I am advised to adopt the humanity of a cripple. Yesterday, awakening to the world, I saw the sky turn upon itself utterly and wholly. I wanted to rise, but the disembowelled silence fell back upon me, its wings paralysed. Without responsibility, straddling Nothingness and Infinity, I began to weep.

[In *Minima Moralia,* 1951] Theodor Adorno writes beautifully on this radical conversion:

> Someone who has been offended, slighted, has an illumination as vivid as when agonizing pain lights up one's own body. He becomes aware that in the innermost blindness of love, that must remain oblivious, lives a demand not to be blinded. He was wronged; from this he deduces a claim to right and must at the same time reject it, for what he desires can only be given in freedom. In such distress he who is rebuffed becomes human.

This stripped, liminal human potential knows itself only in its commitments. On a later page, Fanon notes passionately:

> . . . man is a *yes.* I will never stop reiterating that. *Yes* to life. *Yes* to generosity. But man is also a *no. No* to scorn of man. *No* to degradation of man. *No* to exploitation of man. *No* to the butchery of what is most human in man: freedom. [*Black Skin White Masks*]

It is this voice of the primary libido, of Love and Rage, which speaks through the masks of Prisoner and Malaya. In these later Songs Okot gives utterance to moods of bitterness and frustration the only release from which lies in explosive violence and anarchic hedonism. Prisoner's rage has gone beyond structured rebellion. It envisions no social future, puts forward no causes:

> . . . I am intoxicated
> With anger
> My fury
> Is white hot,
> My brain is melting
> My throat is on fire
>
> Fan the fire
> I am engulfed
> By a red whirlwind of pains
> [*Song of Prisoner*]

Malaya's last song is a radiant *Yes* to the fertile chaos of life in its anarchic phase of dissolution. Having defied every institution and authority, she declares her radical freedom:

> . . . Who can command
> The sun
> Not to rise in the morning?
> [*Song of Malaya*]

In order to reach this position of positive commitment Malaya had to become a social nothing and rid herself of all collective restraints and dependencies. The lines preceding her affirmation read like a ritual stripping, or like a formal exorcism. She casts off in succession all familial, social, and societal bonds, defying in turn men and their wives; parents and brothers; church and state; God himself (if he is on their side); and every power of civic law and persecution. We have come a long way indeed from Lawino: these were the very ties, connections, bonds of responsibility and affection which were so precious to her.

They were equally precious, of course, to Okot when he embarked on *Song of Lawino.* He tells about his innocent frame of mind then, in the early 60s, in the Serumaga interview published in *African Writers Talking:*

> When I was doing my work on the oral literature of the people of Northern Uganda, I first got the inspiration. I found that the poetry was rich, the oral literature was full-blooded, the dance was wonderful and the music just inspiring; and I just couldn't stop; I just wanted to go on and on.

From this euphoria of rediscovery sprang *Song of Lawino,* published in 1966 to instant critical and popular acclaim, and much imitated since. The Song projected a base situation with which every African reader could identify in the dilemma of Lawino, the first wife fighting for the loyalty of her Europeanised husband. As a village wife she is at one and the same time highly cultured and accomplished within the tribal context, *and* an incompetent illiterate within that of the new nationhood. She is a daughter of chiefs, the leader of her age group, a celebrated beauty in her youth and in her maturity an accomplished exponent of the treasured arts of song and dance and a repository of skills and lore. She is also obsolete. Illiterate and uninformed, she lacks the flexibility and the drive to adapt to wider horizons. The formula works admirably: form and impulse are perfectly married. Lawino's songs allow Okot to build up an extended lyrical celebration of a coherent dignity of life from which the African intellectual is in danger of being alienated, and at the same time unrestrained mockery of the imitative urban consumer culture of the nascent black bourgeoisie which is replacing it, thus throwing into vivid relief the alienation of the colonised which Fanon analyses so brilliantly. Lawino was the perfect persona for

Okot's mood in the early 1960s, and was a stirring reminder of cultural integrity for his audience in the early days of independence.

She represents that cultural Eden which Fanon [in *The Wretched of the Earth*] tells us the colonial freedom fighter passionately rediscovers only to leave it behind, for

> the desire to attach oneself to tradition or bring abandoned traditions to life again, does not only mean going against the current of history but also opposing one's own people. When a people undertakes an armed struggle, or even a political struggle against a relentless colonialism, the significance of tradition changes. . . .

The "seething pot out of which the learning of the future will emerge," alas, is not to be found with the beautiful clay pots in the orderly homestead of Lawino's mother. The euphoria of rediscovery which Okot spoke of to Serumaga informs every line of this song cycle nevertheless. Lawino speaks direct to the heart and inflames it with affection for, and pleasure in, the tribal ways.

Whereas *Lawino* appeals to the heart, Ocol's reply addresses itself to the head, and the traditional song formula does not support the character and his message in the same way. There is no traditional format adequate to what Ocol has to say. His song is shorter, harsher, more urgent and abrupt. It rarely allows itself the space to build up an argument by iterative persuasion: instead it harangues. The traditional song format is here turned against the very life style from which it sprang.

Fanon remarks, "The task of bringing the people to maturity will be made easier by the thoroughness of the organisation and by the high intellectual level of its leaders," and in Ocol Okot has created the persona of an intellectual leader of this sort whose political acumen is attained at the cost of cultural alienation. For the primary model of organisation is, quite inevitably, that inherited from the departed masters and uncritically adopted by a leadership which has emerged, in Fanon's words, from

> an intellectual elite . . . which will attach a fundamental importance to organisation, so much so that the fetish of organisation will often take precedence over a reasoned study of colonial society. The notion of the party is a notion imported from the mother country . . . and thrown down just as it is upon real life with all its infinite variations and lack of balance.

Ocol is such a party politician who still hopes that the new wine may be contained in old bottles, and thus does not yet perceive the necessity of "total change from the bottom up." Song IX deals with this thorny dilemma direct. But it may be best to summarise the drift of the whole cycle song by song, in order that both the validity and the tragic incompleteness of Ocol's position may reveal itself.

Ocol does recognise of course the hypnotic power of Lawino's Song. To him it is a siren song of the past. Such nostalgia for a golden age in the tribal Eden can only cripple those who are actively engaged in forging a possible future. He therefore sees as falling to him the unpleasant task of demystifying the potencies of the past which paralyse the minds of his people. The fierceness of his Song must be seen, I think, as springing from the strength of his love. He sees the minds of his people— exemplified by Lawino—enslaved by apathy; they must sever the bonds—bonds of habit and of love—which bind them to kin, village, tribe, in order to embrace the new nationhood. Only by assuming this new dignity as responsible citizens and servants of the future can they, he sings, save themselves from degradation and express their freedom. The dream, Ocol sings, is a possibility in the future, not a memory of the past.

In I, he addresses Lawino direct: her Song is ineffectual, of a past already in decay—

It's the dull thud
Of the wooden arrow
As it strikes the concrete
Of a wall
And falls to earth

In turning the clans into a nation there must be destruction—

We will obliterate
Tribal boundaries
And throttle native tongues
To dumb earth

Nostalgia is a waste of energy and vision. Africa as a human reality, he sings in II, is backward and afflicted—

Diseased with a chronic illness,
Choking with black ignorance,
Chained to the rock
Of poverty,

And yet laughing,
Always laughing and dancing,
The chains on its legs
Jangling;

Displaying his white teeth
In bright pink gum,

Loose white teeth
That cannot bite,
Joking, giggling, dancing

III: To this wretchedness Ocol opposes a programme of change and reform which will free the people from superstition and disease. Deliverance must come from science and technology; Negritude offers only a barren pride in ignorance and dread. Song IV is a call to tribal woman to awaken her degradation in poverty and servitude. When Ocol challenges Lawino to prepare to take her place as equal in the new nationhood, he sees with Fanon

the danger of perpetuating the feudal tradition which holds sacred the superiority of the masculine element over the feminine. Women will have exactly the same place as men, not just in the clauses of the constitution but in the life of every day: in the factory, at school and in the parliament.

In seeking to demystify the warrior code, Song V is aimed at the liberation of the masculine element. Cuttingly Ocol asks what has been achieved by all the glorious tribal wars—

A large arc
Of semi desert land
Strewn with human skeleton
Barely covered by the
Hostile thorn bushes
And the flowering cactus,
A monument to five hundred years
Of cattle theft!

He calls on the young warrior to abjure customs which dissipate productive energies and degrade not only his own human dignity but also that of his female partners in love and marriage—

Come brother . . .
Walk into your City
With your head up . . .
Here you do not have
To kill a man or a lion first.

Take that girl
She wants you.

These five songs are harshly iconoclastic; their tone of insulting bitterness springs from their defensive stance. Song V is Ocol's self-justification, and the remaining three songs are increasingly pierced with poignant sorrow. Ocol praises the liberating effect of his education; yet whilst his generation were dedicating their youth to rigorous and painful self-training, the tribes were dancing, hunting, talking—

> We spent years
> In detention
> Suffering without bitterness
> And planning for the revolution;
>
> Tell me
> My friend and comrade,
> Answer me simply and frankly, . . .
> What was your contribution
> In the struggle for uhuru?

He points to his progressive fertile farm and exhorts those who have been left in the wake of progress to help themselves by acquiring the knowledge and the skills required. Uhuru is not a magic privilege; it is a responsibility which each man must grasp for himself. VII offers an interlude, the crippled beggar's song of Uhuru: a lament over the decaying of the dream and its exploitation by cynical selfseekers. Ocol replies with a challenge—

> Out of my way
> You cowardly fool . . .
> Vex me no more
> With your hollow wailings
> And crocodile tears
> Over uhuru!
>
> You pigmy men . . .
> What is uhuru to you?

He asserts that freedom is for the free, those ready to seize it. Uhuru is no mirage, it is progress and transformation achieved through applied knowledge and energy. Ocol's savagery in this song of bravado barely subdues a mood of raging pity for the impotent afflicted whom he scourges. This mood is sublimated in VIII which invites the new nation to celebrate the passing of the old/homestead. It is a formal, elegiac salutation of the old sanctities before passing on, and a controlled purging of grief. (There is a direct parallel to this in the dirge in Soyinka's *Kongi's Harvest*—"This the last / that we shall dance together . . .").

> Weep long
> For the village world
> That you know
> And love so well
> Is gone . . .

> Say Goodbye
> For you will never
> Hunt together again,
> Nor dance the war dance
> Or the *bwola* dance . . .

Song IX starts with salutations to the new rulers, the Courts of Law, and the entire political and civic organisation representing the three estates of democratic government on the European model. Painful perplexities are exposed. Ocol is aware of absurdities implicit in the transplantation into the newborn body politic of institutions developed by the erstwhile oppressors, and of their inadequacy to the social distress. Yet the New cannot be based in the African past either, for that has contributed nothing to human evolution—

> What proud poem
> Can we write
> For the vanquished?

Ocol's Song ends here, abruptly, without harmony. Ocol emerges as a complex, tortured persona aware of his alienation and of the paradoxes inherent in his position, but too proud to whisper. His Song is one of challenge, an arrogant call to action. The way onward lies, he believes and says, away from the social and psychological impotence of the tribal, as well as the colonial, past. In spite of the bravado, however, his Song leaves the impression, at the end, of a mind totally exhausted by awareness of what has had to be left behind, and by the magnitude of the task ahead.

The first two Songs define the aspirations feeding the new nationhood. The second pair deal with Uhuru, actual liberty and chaos. "The truths of a nation are in the first place its realities," says Fanon [in *The Wretched of the Earth*]. In a newly independent state these realities may, he warns, include three major threats to full decolonisation: firstly, the rise of an urban bourgeoisie, "a sort of little greedy caste, avid and voracious, with the mind of a huckster"; secondly, "the heartbreaking return to chauvinism i.e. tribalism, feudalism, regionalism in its most bitter and detestable form"; and thirdly, the automatic "building-up of . . . yet another system of exploitation" through the very mechanics of militancy itself. Fanon thus anticipated the rise of military dictatorships, tribal enmity, and the continuing economic humiliation of the common man, which have been the scourges of African independence. These grinding realities form the background to the second pair of Songs.

Song of Prisoner lacks the mask of a single persona. It is a choral song of those who are trapped by freedom. The reader is taken into the very heart of that "zone of occult instability where the people dwell," which Fanon speaks of as the place where "our souls are crystallised and . . . transfused with light." Different social roles and stances are represented in individual laments, but the Song is of a collective, a corporate bewilderment and despair. Every song speaks of entrapment: disappointment, frustration, rage at the cruelty of man to man. In some cases the trap was sprung on apathy and helplessness, in some on militant partisanship; one prisoner at least is a committed assassin. None are criminals in the ordinary sense: all are victims of either social or political change which has overwhelmed them. Hence the refrain of 'confessions'—

> *I plead* drunkenness
> *I plead* hunger
> *I plead* insanity
> *I plead* smallness
> I plead fear
> I plead helplessness
> I plead hopelessness

"In such distress," Adorno observes, "he who is rebuffed becomes human." The bafflement turns into anarchic outrage—

> *I plead guilty* to hatred
> My anger explodes
> Like a grenade

In some songs this hatred and anger is turned on existence itself, "the foul smell / of the world"; both father and mother are blasphemingly accused for engendering life at all; the malaise is ingrained.

The songs are indictments of social abuses, to be sure. But their bitterness goes much deeper. They rail against the betrayal of life's promise, against the dissolution of human roles and functions, against the denial of hope. There is also a pervasive sense of collusive pollution. Again we turn to Fanon for a clinical description of this contradictory anguish—

> The collective struggle presupposes collective responsibility at the base and collegiate responsibility at the top. Yes; everybody will have to be compromised in the fight for the common good. No one has clean hands; there are no innocents and no onlookers; *we are all soiling them in the swamps of our country and in the terrifying emptiness of our brains.* Every onlooker is either a coward or a traitor.

(This very bitter condition of necessary pollution has been magnificently explored in Ngugi wa Thiong'o's *A Grain of Wheat*).

The predominant mood in **Prisoner** is rage. One example must suffice, that of the outraged prisoner whose wife is betraying him with a member of the new élite. A famous passage describes the adulterous exploiter's Mercedes on his way to the assignation—

> A black Benz
> Slithers smoothly
> Through the black night
> Like the water snake
> Into the Nile,
> Listen to it purring
> Like a hopeful leopard,
> Listen to its
> Love song,
> The soft poem
> That embraces the valleys
> And caresses the hills . . .

The Mercedes is a stunning metaphor of what Fanon calls "the libidinal tie of the second nature"—

> The so-called consumer economy and the politics of corporate capitalism have created a second nature of man which ties him libidinally and aggressively to the commodity form.

The Mercedes, the commodity form at its most ostentatious and recognisable, is here metaphorically exhibited as, literally, the vehicle of this secondary libido and aggression. In this metaphoric process the singer's anguished mind has made the leap into recognition, and is therewith casting off the chains of the second nature—a process which in turn, as Fanon is at pains to demonstrate, leads to a release of "primary aggressiveness on an unprecedented scale." And so we find the singer, the impotent watcher in the grass, exploding into a desire which is wholly and radically destructive—

> I want to drink
> Human blood
> To cool my heart,
> I want to eat
> Human liver
> To quench my boiling thirst

Marcuse says, rightly, that—

> in art, literature and music, insights and truths are expressed which cannot be communicated in ordinary language, and with these truths often an entirely new dimension is opened, which is either repressed or tabooed in reality; namely the image of human existence and of *nature no longer confined within*

the norms of the repressive reality principle, but really striving for their fulfilment and gratification, even at the price of death and catastrophe. ["Herbert Marcuse on the Need for an Open Marxist Mind," *The Listener* (9 February 1978)]

The 'confessions' of weakness and guilt are one strand in *Song of Prisoner;* the other is the irrepressible stirring of primary human energy. From the prisoners' guilt, anguish, and anger breaks a new raw libido, expressed in "I want . . . ." The betrayed husband wants to drink blood. The singer of **'Youthful Air'** wants—

> . . . to drink
> A whole bottle of whisky
> To quench my thirst
> For freedom . . .
> I *want* to drink
> With the peasants
> In the fields
> And with the old women
> In my constituency, (surprised, we recognise Ocol)
> I *want* to suck *lacoi* beer
> And share the sucking tube
> With the old men
> Around the fire . . .
> I *want* to drink
> All the drinks
> Of the world . . .
> I *want* to forget
> That I am a lightless star,
> A proud eagle
> Shot down
> By the arrow
> Of Uhuru

This is the song of an Ocol released from his second nature and waking to his primary freedom—

> I *want* to breathe the air
> Of my own choice

Lawino is here too, in **'Cattle Egret'**—

> Free my hands and feet,
> I *want* to clap my hands
> And sing for my children

Apart from primary rage and aggression, then, there emerges also a dream of universal anarchic hedonism which is the positive expression of the primary libido. It is a dream that is only partly 'escapist'; more importantly it signals what Marcuse calls "the ascendancy of the life instincts over aggressiveness and guilt" [*An Essay on Liberation*], a coming to the senses: *"The revolution would be liberating only if it were carried by the non-repressive forces stirring in the existing society"* [Armah, *The Beautiful Ones Are Not Yet Born*]. **'Oasis'** is blindly escapist (I want to dance all the dances, and I want to dance with all the girls)—

> Let me dance
> And forget my sorrow.

But the singer of the final song **'Undergrowth'** does not seek to forget: he remembers the sorrows of the whole wretched world, and still dances—

> Free my hands and feet
> You uniformed Stone,
> Open the steel gate,
> I *want* to join the dances
> Of the world

"The form of freedom," says Marcuse, "is not merely self-determination and self-realisation, but rather the determination and realisation of goals which enhance, protect and unite life on earth." One dream in the Song does transcend the anarchic hedonism of the primary libido as it breaks its bonds. **'Voice of a Dove'** is a song of love and defiance expressing only transpersonal drives of joy, tenderness and militant courage. The prisoner, a man facing his death, is fully liberated, free of both anger and personal desire. This one song within the choral fever of *Song of Prisoner* anticipates, embodies those goals Marcuse speaks of which "enhance, protect and unite life on earth."

With *Song of Malaya* we find ourselves in Fanon's "seething pot out of which the future will emerge." The fundamental shattering of the old strata of culture has been accomplished. Malaya sings the positive anarchism of the radicalised humane. For the seething

> which aims at a fundamentally different set of relations between men cannot leave intact either the form or the content of the people's culture.

In a review of this Song Behadur Tejani remarks, "There is no discipline better suited than anthropology when you want to destroy the reading public's concept of morality" ["Okot p'Bitek," *African Literature Today* (1973)]. There is also no better anthropologist's persona than the prostitute. Like him, she knows all men both as they present themselves and as they nakedly are; is no respecter of social roles and pretensions; is herself a liminal, a professional outsider, and thus singularly well equipped for the exposure of collusive hypocrisy and cant. The prostitute persona has been so used through the ages, e.g. by Dostoyevski, by the existentialists, and in Blake's poem 'London', which indicts the "mind-forg'd manacles" of social man.

Malaya then is positive, combative, and free. "The token of freedom attained," says Nietzsche in *Die Frönliche Wissenschaft,* "is no longer being ashamed of ourselves." Malaya is not ashamed of anything. She has cast off the manacles of social stricture and browbeating morality—

> Sister Harlots
> Wherever you are,
> The bedcovers of the world
> Have been removed

—and who bugs and parasites, one might ask, need scuttle from the exposure? Her values are radically different, boiled down into "enhancing, protecting, and uniting life on earth." All men come to her—the needy, the debauched, the unfaithful, the timid—and all are welcomed, comfronted and entertained each according to his fantasy. Her knowledge of their ways is unclouded by sentiment, hence expert, and uninhibited by customary restraints and judgments. Husbands are looked after and cherished as by a wife; she advises realistically and shrewdly on hygiene; she solaces those who have no other haven—sailors, soldiers, convicts, travellers; and tenderly initiates the novices. She has no prejudices and very little snobbishness; on the contrary, she shows herself wrily tolerant, wise, shrewd, joyous and humane. To condemn Malaya is to condemn vitality, fecundity, woman, nature herself.

It is also hypocritical. When it comes to hypocrisy, and to the social evils and human suffering caused by authoritarian norms, Malaya's laughing voice becomes harsh. Her humanism is militant, whether she is battling for the dignity of her child (**'Peals of Crying'**) or exhorting her married sister to freedom and solidarity (**'Part-Time'**). She is saltily feminist, and has only scorn for those who purchase comfort by collaboration in a system of mutual bondage—

> Look at the slaves
> Of the world
> Calling themelves
> Wives,
> Penned like goats
> To unwilling pegs.

Malaya's marvellous vigour, humour, and defiance find their fullest expression in the final song **'Flaming Eternity'** which enacts the stripping of the "mind-forg'd manacles" and culminates in a radiant assertion of basic natural freedom—

> Let the disappointed men
> Shout abuses at us . . .
> Let their jealous wives
> Rage and beat them . . .
> Let the bitches
> Pour boiling water on us . . .
> Let their secret
> Schoolgirl wives hiss . . .
> Let our parents
> Spit curses,
> Let our brothers
> Choke with shame and anger
> And run mad
>
> . . . . .
>
> Let the black Bishops
> And priests
> Preach against us . . .
> Let the Lord
> Grant their prayers
> And condemn us all
> To flaming eternity
>
> . . . . .
>
> Let Parliamentarians
> Debate and pass laws
> Against us,
> Let the police arrest us
> And lock us up
> In their cells,
> Let the magistrates
> Sentence us to jails
>
> . . . . .
>
> But
> Who can command
> The sun
> Not to rise in the morning? . . .
> Sister prostitutes
> Wherever you are
> Wealth and health
> To us all . . .

The stance of Malaya is not a final one. Like the others, it is transitional. Malaya is VAGRANT, antisocial. She is, of necessity, a denizen of the unstructured alternative, the liminal underground. But her lively warmth, her awareness, and her militancy are the soundest base for the transvaluation of values, through trial and error, by the radically humane in the process of positing a political future which is worthy of humanity.

Chikwenye Okonjo Ogunyemi (essay date October 1982)

SOURCE: "The Song of the Caged Bird: Contemporary African Prison Poetry," in *Ariel: A Review of International English Literature,* Vol. 13, No. 4, October, 1982, pp. 65-84.

[*In the following excerpt, Ogunyemi discusses the physical and mental deterioration of the prisoner in p'Bitek's* Song of a Prisoner.]

Okot p'Bitek had been writing in the 50's and his memorable works were written in the late 60's and early 70's, a turbulent period in East African politics. It marked the time when progressive Kenyans were disoriented, bitterly disappointed by a Kenyatta leadership that had no relationship with his Mau Mau radicalism. There was instability under Milton Obote's rule in neighbouring Uganda. Political history was being made in Rhodesia, where Ian Smith held Britain to ransom and Zimbabweans bore the brunt of the impasse between the two. With this instability in the background, p'Bitek's political prison poem, *Song of Prisoner* or *Song of a Prisoner,* as he more aptly titled the American edition, was not just timely but was to be prophetic: soon a brutalizing force would sweep through Idi Amin's Uganda. In the tumultuous East African political climate, it was conceptually easy for p'Bitek, though he himself had only had brushes with the authorities, to write about the fate that awaited a political prisoner.

Writing from personal experience, Etheridge Knight had made a memorable statement about prison life [in "Inside These Walls," in *Black Voices from Prison,* 1970]: "The fact is that physical brutality is as nothing compared to the brutality of the soul incurred by years and years of cancerous prison life." p'Bitek would agree with him. In *Song of Prisoner,* he concentrates imaginatively on the nature of a prisoner's mental health and conjures up for the reader the primitive conditions under which the prisoner is detained. The brutal treatment p'Bitek's prisoner has received leaves him physically incapacitated and mentally disoriented. The burden of *Song of Prisoner* is a dramatization of his mental disorientation.

In his private capacity, the prisoner worries about the fate of his family—his children and his wife—and frets about the future of the children of a prisoner. p'Bitek also deals with the prisoner as a public person. This prisoner is severally referred to, from the viewpoint of the government's law enforcement agents, as "A vagrant / A loiterer" and "A foreign bastard." He confesses to the assassination of a public figure, a "capitalist reactionary." The hero thus is established as a political prisoner who claims to have killed to free his people.

Intriguingly, we never know whether to believe him or not. He is mentally deranged and is occasionally given to boasting and delusions of grandeur. Ironically, he insists, like any government, that he is for law and order and Uhuru. From the government's viewpoint, however, the assassination is against law and order and earns him the loss of his freedom. In spite of his heroic act, his "uniformed Brothers" (one is almost tempted to refer to them as uninformed) club him in his cell. Cowed by their brutality, he becomes less belligerent than most political prisoners. Panic stricken, he confesses unabashedly:

> I plead fear,
> I plead helplessness,
> I plead hopelessness,
> . . .
> I am an insect
> Trapped between the toes
> Of a bull elephant.

Earlier he had cried out,

> I plead insanity,
> I am
> Mad,
> Can't you see?

And yet he later insists,

> I am not senseless,
> I am not cowardly,
> Not dastardly,
> I am not a thug,
> I am not insane,
> This is not
> Cold-blooded murder,
> I did not do it
> For the money. . . .

Incidentally he had informed us that he was "hired" to eliminate his victim. His contradictions and shifts in point of view could confuse the reader. However, in the schema they are indicative of the prisoner's deteriorating mental state. He reminds us in vivid, unforgettable images that

> There is a carpenter
> Inside my head,
> He knocks nails
> Into my skull.

We should at this point believe the prisoner since these statements are revealing and might help in our understanding of the poem and prevent us from encountering the difficulties G. A. Heron faced in his interpretation [*The Poetry of Okot p'Bitek,* 1976]. Heron rightly observes that "Section 3 illustrates the way fantasy, the present reality, and memories are confused and intermingled." To cover his interpretive difficulties, however, he blames p'Bitek: "In spite of the importance of this fictional structure, Okot is very careless about the internal fiction of the poem. Much more descriptive detail goes into what are almost certainly fantasies than into information about the past of the prisoners and there are inconsistencies in the information we are given. In Section 7 the vagrant tells his wife to 'Dream about our first meeting / In the forest,' yet in Section 13 the same man talks of 'our first meeting / At the dancing arena'." Heron's mistake is in limiting the confused state of affairs to Section 3 rather than seeing the entire poem as a representation of the prisoner's confusion. The prisoner-singer hallucinates a greater part of the poem. p'Bitek, not writing a memoir, remains detached, a position that enables him to present his prisoner as a creature succumbing to the rigours of prison life, helplessly but steadily moving towards insanity. The incipient madness is graphically captured in the constant, broken thoughts, the scrambled time scheme, and the gross disregard for spatial limitations. His arguments are contradictory: he rebels against his dead father and blames him for marrying somebody unworthy of him—the prisoner's mother. Yet, in an about-face, he sharply criticizes his mother for marrying his father. His self-depreciation demonstrates the depth of his depression. At one point the prisoner threatens to exhume his father's bones in order to hang him by the neck! Rudderless, he desperately attempts to connect with his gaolers who prefer to "communicate" with him by brutalizing him. But, like other schizophrenics, he has moments of sanity, as when he criticizes his country's social conditions. Thinking about the Chief's dog and his own children, in very clever juxtapositioning, he asks

> How many pounds
> Of meat
> Does this dog eat
> In a day?
> How much milk . . . ?
>   . . .
> Have you seen
> The mosquito legs
> Of my children?

He wins us completely to his side by the poignant sarcasm implicit in his phrase "infant pregnancies" to describe the bloated stomachs his children have to bear as a result of malnutrition.

Once we have grasped the true nature of the prisoner's situation and the attendant effect on his health, the poem becomes intelligible as the soliloquy or song of a *schizophrenic* prisoner. The entire poem is sung in the first person. From the text, we have no cause to believe, as Heron proposes, that other prisoners are involved and also lament their plight using the same first person. There is no indication of a change in the singer. The title, ***Song of a Prisoner,*** under which the poem was published in America, is important in grasping the notion of one singer who comes to represent the other singers. The controversial Section II, the section on the minister of state, is by and about the same prisoner. At this point he suffers from delusions of grandeur and believes he is a minister. Since he was a former bodyguard to some dignitary, the sophisticated life of a minister would not be beyond the prisoner's comprehension. His subconscious wishes surface in this section, and he solves in one swoop the problems that have preoccupied him—the fate of his family, their poverty, and his disconcerting relationship with his parents, marked by his confusion about whether his father is dead or alive. He imagines himself writing out "fat cheques." Furthermore, he thinks he will not be absent from his family for too long, which is in keeping with his earlier optimism when, filled with self-importance, he felt the "best lawyers" would defend him and understanding judges would spring him from prison. The minister section thus serves as an exercise in wish-fulfilment fantasies.

> **In *Song of Prisoner,* p'Bitek concentrates imaginatively on the nature of a prisoner's mental health and conjures up for the reader the primitive conditions under which the prisoner is detained.**
>
> **—*Chikwenye Okonjo Ogunyemi***

Suffering from claustrophobia, the prisoner desperately wants connection on a world-wide basis to escape the constrictions of his immediate environment. He wants communion with Russians, South Africans, Indians, the French, and the Chinese. From these global thoughts, his mind drifts closer home, and he feels a need to connect with the Munyoro and the Kikuyu. He is obviously suffering from ideological confusion, or else he is an incorrigible idealist. p'Bitek takes us through "the entire history of the moods of imprisonment; we are swept through the whole awful landscape of imprisoned despair" [Edward Blishen, Introduction to *Song of a Prisoner,* 1971].

I think the prisoner is deluding himself when he says:

> I am intoxicated

With anger,
My fury
Is white hot.

His inability to dramatize his anger beyond mouthing it belies his position. He is clearer about himself when he says, "I am dizzy / With frustration." And a few lines later, "My head is bursting . . . ." What we see in this prisoner then is a human wreck, the living consequence of the brutality of incarceration. Although he complains about his physical discomforts, he has already undergone a metamorphosis mentally without knowing it. He is, tragically for him and for us,

A young tree
Burnt out
By the fierce wild fire
Of Uhuru.

Despite his difficulties he rambles through some thoughts of the outside world. Like the prisoner Soyinka, who writes about air raids in "Flowers for My Land," p'Bitek's prisoner expresses the same anxieties:

Roaring kites
Split the sky
And excrete deadly dungs
On the heads
Of the people,
Pots and skulls
Crack. . . .

Ironically, he still concerns himself with the people's property and lives, as shown in the phrase "pots and skulls," although, as the last two stanzas show, he is in truth a tragic hero, rejected and unacclaimed by the people he fought for. Incarcerated and deprived of meaningful human contact, the closing lines stress his desire for sex and freedom:

Open the door,
Man,
I want to dance
All the dances of the world,
I want to sleep with
All the young dancers
          . . .
Let me dance and forget
For a small while
That I am a wretch,
The reject of my Country.

Detached from the sordidness of prison life, p'Bitek has been able to give us a vivid and penetrating account of the excruciating loneliness that the isolated political prisoner has to endure by showing us the inroads into the mental health and physical condition of a previously happy family man.

K. L. Goodwin (essay date 1982)

SOURCE: "Okot p'Bitek," in *Understanding African Poetry: A Study of Ten Poets,* Heinemann, 1982, pp. 154-72.

[*In the following excerpt, Goodwin describes p'Bitek's work as an effort toward "cultural analysis" and provides an overview of p'Bitek's major poetry, discussing his influences, sources, style, and themes.*]

As a poet Okot p'Bitek has several claims to importance. He was the first major East African poet in English; he has influenced a number of other poets; and he is a maker of abiding satiric myths. *Song of Lawino* (1966) not only showed that East African poetry could achieve more than the nonchalantly slight lyrics or brief graphic situation poems that had earlier appeared in periodicals and anthologies; it established that there was a readership for volumes of poetry in English by a single author, and so made possible the publication of such works as Okello Oculi's *Orphan* (1968), Joseph Buruga's *The Abandoned Hut* (1969)—two volumes heavily influenced by *Song of Lawino*—, John Mbiti's *Poems of Nature and Faith* (1969), Jared Angira's *Juices* (1970), Taban lo Liyong's *Frantz Fanon's Uneven Ribs* (1971) and Richard Ntiru's *Tensions* (1971). The East African literary desert for works in English that Taban lo Liyong [in his *The Last Word: Cultural Synthesism*] had polemically described in 1965 clearly no longer existed; if, indeed, it ever had in Liyong's terms.

Okot p'Bitek has been reticent and even off-handed when questioned about his literary antecedents. Unlike a large number of African poets in English, he did not read English as a university subject and, though he has taught literature at school and university, he seems to have a mild contempt for the formal questions raised by its more earnest practitioners. That, together with his mischievous sense of fun, means that such statements as this comment on *Song of Lawino* and *Song of Ocol* cannot be taken too literally:

> I don't think they are very much influenced by the African oral tradition; they cannot be sung, for instance. Possibly they are influenced by *The Song of Hiawatha* by H. W. Longfellow and also by *Song of Solomon.* These books I enjoyed very much when I was a student and I consider *Song of Solomon* the greatest love song ever.

Hiawatha seems at first an improbable suggestion, but Okot may have been referring to its discursive, repetitive mode of story-telling; its athletic hero ('Swift of foot was Hiawatha');

his love of music and story; and his requirements in a wife ('Feet that run on willing errands'). He may also have remembered its short unrhymed lines, though their trochaic tetrameter measure bears little resemblance to Okot's standard free-verse two- and three-beat lines. *Song of Solomon* is more plausible, for Okot is an expansive, even extravagant, love poet.

The dismissal of orally composed and recited poetry as an influence must be considered playful. *Song of Lawino* was written in Acoli and translated into English. The two Acoli versions (composed in 1956 and 1969) not only draw directly on many Acoli songs, but could themselves be sung. In the English translation, as Okot says in the preliminary matter to the poem, he has 'murdered rhythm and rhyme'; or at least has dispensed with rhyme and settled for a very free rhythm. Even so, one can readily appreciate something of the traditional Acoli songs quoted by Lawino and can appreciate how similar they are to the surrounding context of Lawino's own 'Song' or 'Lament'. So, for instance, the love song of the Acoli man imploring his father to 'Gather the bridewealth' is the first part of the traditional song, *Wora kel lim,* translated in *The Horn of My Love* as 'Father, bring the bridewealth'. Or, in section 8, when Lawino sings the dirge 'Fate has brought troubles', she is quoting part of the traditional dirge, *Woko okelo ayela* (*The Horn of My Love*). Or again, just before the end of the poem, when Lawino sings 'She has taken the road to Nimule', she is quoting from *Okwanyo ger Lumule,* the song about the 'Chief of all women, Alyeka, the brown one' (*The Horn of My Love*).

It is not, however, only in direct quotation that Okot is indebted to the Acoli oral tradition. When, for instance, Lawino says

> My husband's tongue
> Is bitter like the roots of the *lyonno* lily

she is quoting an Acoli proverb referring to the bitterness of a wild lily, the tubers of which are eaten only when nothing else is available. When she ends section 2 with

> The pumpkin in the old homestead
> Must not be uprooted!

she is quoting a proverb much used by old men to make the point that old customs, like the wild pumpkins that grow over abandoned settlements, do no harm and may even be useful.

The point is too obvious to need labouring. *Song of Lawino* is clearly related, in content, tone, and style, to Acoli songs. Its basic three-beat line, with frequent variations, is as close

as one could expect to get in English to the pattern of the Acoli line. It is also very similar to the kind of line being written in English at this time by such East African poets as Taban lo Liyong, John Mbiti, Joseph Mutiga, John Ruganda, Edwin Waiyaki or Walter Bgoya.

What is new is the sustained rhetoric of the complaint, the organized characterization and satire of the dramatic monologue, and the use of translation as a subject to make polemical and satiric points. Of Okot's four major poems, this is the one that lies closest to his own education in traditional culture, for which he was largely indebted to his mother, Lacwaa Cerina, 'who first taught me to sing', as he says in the dedication to *Song of Ocol. Song of Lawino* is, indeed, named after her, for Lawino (meaning born with the umbilical cord wrapped round the neck) was one of his mother's names; and, like the fictional Lawino, his mother had been 'chief of girls'. It is also the poem closest to his academic studies in anthropology and religion; it contains a dramatic summary of some of the main positions taken up in his later study, *African Religions in Western Scholarship.* It has the most detailed characterization of any of his works and, in that Lawino is very much a woman who has been brought up in an identifiably Acoli culture, the narrowest frame of cultural reference. Lawino is, of course, also representative of the values of village life anywhere in Africa, as contrasted with those of European colonialism. She represents, too, the values of the African woman (or at least of a certain kind of African woman) faced with rivalry in love. But her quarrel with Ocol is more personal and more specific than one finds in Okot's later works. They spread out into cultural and political comment on the whole of black Africa in a way that would be quite foreign to the mind of the village-raised Lawino.

The beginning of the poem and the last section are addressed to her husband, Ocol, meaning Son of Black, or Blackman, as Taban lo Liyong points out [in "Lawino is Unedu," in *The Last Word*]. Once, says Lawino, he

> . . . was still a Black man
> The son of the Bull
> The son of Agik

but now—and there is hence a good deal of irony implicit here—

> My husband pours scorn
> On Black People

These two passages, like all the poem[s] between the opening and section 13 (except for a brief passage in section 12), are part of the diatribe addressed to her clansmen as a complaint against her husband.

It is a proud complaint, however, for she was chief of girls and so has a 'Bull name,' a title or nickname given to an outstanding person. This, like so many key concepts, is a literal translation from the Acoli, for in this poem, though not in others, Okot finds the strategy of literal translation a fruitful source of ironic comment. In this instance, however—and it is a fairly rare one—any amusement is immediately neutralized by an explanation of why such names are called 'Bull names' and how they come to be bestowed. Lawino says

> My Bull name is Eliya Alyeker
> I ate the name
> Of the Chief of Payira
> Eliya Aliker,
> Son of Awic.

The Payira, the most populous and most extensive in landholding of the Acoli chiefdoms, had as their chief in the 1940s Eliya Aliker, of whom Okot tells something in *The Horn of My Love.* Lawino was given his name as a tribute to her leadership, but it was assimilated into the word *alyeker,* a term of affection. She is the daughter of a man with the title 'Lengamoi', someone who has killed another man and is probably a respected leader in warfare. She knows that she is neither 'shy' nor 'easily browbeaten'; that she is not 'a fool' and not 'cold'. She is proud of her appearance, of her skin and her hair, of her tattoos, her breasts and eyes and her singing, playing, and dancing. She knows that in fair competition she could hold Ocol's love by her appearance and by her housekeeping.

Ocol, too, has reason to be proud of the place he holds in his own clan, for he is a 'Prince Of an ancient chiefdom', one whose grandfather and father were great men. But he has been so seduced by European ways that he 'abuses all things Acoli', even threatening to cut down the *Okango,* the small sacred tree at his father's shrine.

His change of heart is symbolized in his supplanting of Lawino by Clementine, 'a modern girl . . . Who speaks English'. Lawino at first professes herself not jealous but then admits 'We all suffer from a little jealousy'. Her own common sense tells her, however, that it is impossible to prevent men from wanting women and her pride that 'I do not fear to compete with her'.

Section I is a summary of the insults and arguments her husband has used against her; sections 2 to 5 contrast the ways of the rival, Clementine, with Acoli ways; sections 6 to 12 leave Clementine in order to concentrate on Ocol's other prejudices, all of which are contrasted with Acoli beliefs and customs; section 13 is a final appeal to Ocol. All of this would, of course, be mere raillery if Lawino had no desire or hope of drawing Ocol back. Despite his insults, she is still in love with him, deeply hurt that he treats her 'As if I am no longer a person'. She is concerned that he will be ridiculed by the clan; she recalls his infatuated courtship of her; she imagines herself taunting him with his putative flabbiness and with her accomplished boyfriend who plays the *nanga*; and she ends by asking him to let her dance before him and sing his praises. Her main argument, however, always implicit and sometimes explicit, is that Acoli ways, though not necessarily better than European ways, are the right ones for an Acoli; that he should be true to his lineage, should cease behaving like a woman and behave like the Acoli prince he is, having due respect for his ancestors. The ancestral shrine, the *otole* war dance praising past leaders of the clan, the Stool of the chieftain, the images of prowess with spear and shield in warfare are the outward emblems of large-scale argument in favour of Acoli ways.

Lawino's moderation, exemplified in her admission that talcum powder is 'good on pink skin', that white woman's hair 'Is soft like silk', that Ocol is free to eat 'White men's foods' if he enjoys them is intersected by passages of bitter raillery, not just at Clementine and Ocol for foolishly aping white ways, but also at some of the white ways themselves. The coprologous description of a modern dance-hall in section 3; the description of white man's food as tasteless or repulsive (a fried egg as being 'slimy like mucus'); or the exposition of the idiocies and inconsistencies of Christian catechetical instruction in sections 8 and 9 not only are very funny in themselves, but they also serve to characterize Lawino as passionately biased and sometimes deficient in understanding or judgment.

She is, for instance, a believer in talismans or charms, saying that Ocol once beat her

> For wearing the toe of the edible rat
> And the horn of the rhinoceros
> And the jaw-bone of the alligator.

As she points out, though, the nuns of the Catholic faith to which her husband adheres seem to use the crucifix for similar purposes. In section 7 she says that Ocol is angry because

> I cannot keep time
> And I do not know
> How to count the years.

Her explanation that the Western system of time-keeping is

unnecessary is rhetorically effective as far as it goes. In a rural environment, all events of the day, the year, and the lifetime can be satisfactorily timed by the sun, the cock, the stomach, the climate, the moon, the crops, and unusual events. The notion of a continuum of time ticking away whether anyone notices or needs it, a single linear framework for relating all events to, even to the point where it dictates those events, is a scientific one. It was found necessary in Egypt, Babylon, China, and India originally, it would seem, as a basis for astronomical and astrological calculations. Even thoroughly rural communities have, of course, found some need for a calendar, if only to calculate regular market days. To that extent, Lawino's argument is a bit extreme. But then it is part of her character: she is prone to hyperbole. And to stubborn, almost incorrigible ignorance. She cannot tell the time and seems to refuse to learn; she uses the electric stove, but detests it and refuses to master the controls (section 6); she cannot or will not tune the radio.

[In "The Patriot as An Artist," in *African Writers African Writing,* edited by G. D. Killam, 1973] Ali Mazrui has criticized the poem for making Lawino

> a little too simple. A mind that exaggerates so much
> and in such an obvious way is not simply *culturally*
> distinct from the modernity which enchants Ocol; it
> is also a mind too naïve to stand a chance of saving
> Ocol from that enchantment.

Similarly, in a review of the published Acoli version, **Wer pa Lawino,** Okumo pa'Lukobo objects that Lawino is impossibly backward as a representative of a present-day rural Acoli woman: 'I know of no place in Acoli today where the village girls can't dance at least a sort of rumba'.

This is no doubt true if we assume that the setting of the verse-novel is the 1960s, as the elections of section II and the availability of several sophisticated Western articles clearly indicate. But while this is so for the surface of the novel, the clash of culture-values has to be seen as placed a couple of decades earlier, contemporary, say, with Ngugi's *Weep Not, Child* or even *The River Between.* The gap between the date of the superficial life and the date of the work's more deeply felt cultural life should worry no one who is prepared to see the whole poem as a myth. Okot needed to sharpen the contrast between the traditional village and the Westernized town, even to exaggerate the two sets of *mores* by idealization and caricature. So Lawino is more stubbornly opposed to Western ways despite her assertions of tolerance, and Ocol more intransigent and fervent in his new faith and culture than would be literally credible in the 1960s. Such distortions and anachronisms are inevitable in myth from *Gilgamesh,* the *Mahabharata,* or the *Iliad* on. It is Mazrui's failure to understand that representativeness invariably implies some distortion of individuality in character that vitiates his criticisms of the poem.

The poem does, of course, contain discrepancies, but they can, I think, all be attributed to Lawino's blinding sense of outrage and the hyperbole or distortion that stem from it. When, for instance, in the section on time, she says that among the Acoli

> A person's age
> Is shown by what he or she does
> It depends on what he or she is,
> And on what kind of person
> He or she is

She has forgotten that earlier she implied a different system (one that her clansmen must have known very well) in the wonderfully vindictive jibe at Clementine as 'this age-mate of my mother' and in her reporting of Ocol as using the expression 'age-mate of my grandfather'. While these are very broad categories of age-mateship, it is clear, as Taban lo Liyong points out (*The Last Word*), that the Acoli do in fact use a much narrower age-mate system, rather than relying on categorization 'by what he or she does'. The conclusion to be drawn, though, is simply that Lawino is inconsistent and that this is part of her vehement desire to make as bold a case as she can. To say that she is aware of putting on an act is perhaps going beyond the literary evidence, but certainly Lawino is a performer and has always enjoyed being one.

Okot poured a great many of his own interests into the poem. traditional dancing and singing, rites and ceremonies, education, religion, and other matters of cultural and anthropological interest; the role of the Christian church; and the two-party system of politics that operated early in Uganda's independence are all incorporated into the poem. His treatment of the church runs parallel to the more extended treatment he gives in his academic works. At the heart of his approach is the belief that in trying to relate their own religion to Acoli religion by translation, Christian missionaries misunderstood Acoli religion and distorted their own. They began with the assumption that the Acoli, clearly a polytheistic people, must believe in a Supreme Being or High God. Okot considers this a gross error not just about the Acoli but about all the peoples of the Upper Nile, that is, the Nilotes. Their attitude to a *jok* or god he describes thus:

> When the Nilotes encounter *jok,* it is with a specific
> and named or easily definable *jok,* and not some vague
> 'power' that they communicate with. The proper
> name identifies the *jok,* placing it in a specific category
> and social context, for action. There is no occasion
> when the Nilotes think of all the *jogi* (pl. of
> *jok*) simultaneously. And there is no evidence to show
> that they regard the named *jogi* as refractions or manifestations,
> or hypostases of a so-called High God.
> Each category of *jok* is independent of other *jogi,*

although some are used against others. For the Nilotes there are many deities. Not one. [*African Religions in Western Scholarship*]

The Christian idea of God as omnipotent and as creator, which Okot considers to be a Greek philosophical one applied to Jewish religious experience, thus could not be conveyed in Acoli. But according to Okot the Italian Catholic priests insisted on finding the appropriate words:

> In 1911, Italian Catholic priests put before a group of Acoli elders the question 'Who created you?'; and because the Luo language does not have an independent concept of *create* or *creation,* the question was rendered to mean, 'Who moulded you?'. But this was still meaningless, because human beings are born of their mothers. The elders told the visitors that they did not know. But, we are told that this reply was unsatisfactory, and the missionaries insisted that a satisfactory answer must be given. One of the elders remembered that, although a person may be born normally, when he is afflicted with tuberculosis of the spine, then he loses his normal figure, he gets 'moulded'. So he said '*Rubanga* is the one who moulds people'. This is the name of the hostile spirit which the Acoli believe causes the hunch or hump on the back.

And so 'The name of the Christian God in Lwo is *Rubanga*', as Okot notes [in] . . . *Lawino,* and throughout sections 8 to 10 of the poem he insists on translating the Christian *Rubanga* as 'the Hunchback', making the unstated assumption that the Acoli *jok* responsible for spinal deformation in human beings is himself deformed. Similarly, the Acoli word for the Christian heaven is retranslated literally as 'Skyland', the Holy Ghost is 'the Clean Ghost', angels are 'the beautiful men With birds' wings', the Apostles' Creed is 'the Faith of the Messengers', the Holy Bible 'the Clean Book', and the gospel 'the good word'. None of the amusement of these literal retranslations could of course exist in the Acoli version, for the language has assimilated these meanings and lost the original incongruities. It is a little disingenuous of Okot to ignore the fact that words in any language change their denotations and connotations over a period of time and that even at the one time a single word may have a wide range of connotations, the intended one being indicated by context and purpose. It is, nevertheless, all good fun in English, and serves the wider aim of showing the disparity between the two sets of value-systems. It is not a method used elsewhere in his work.

If Okot is right in believing that the Acoli could not accomodate the Graeco-Christian notion of God, it is difficult to see what he expected proselytizing missionaries to do, except give up and go home. Even if their labour was ultimately vain, it seems a little harsh to blame them for trying,

albeit misguidedly. The important point remains, though, that in Okot's view no accommodation was possible between two such dissimilar religions. It serves to strengthen Lawino's view that the two cultural systems—religious, educational, artistic, aesthetic, medical, culinary, sartorial, architectural, political, and linguistic—should be kept separate alongside each other. Her attitude is

> I do not understand
> The ways of foreigners
> But I do not despise their customs.
> Why should you despise yours?

She is prepared for Ocol to adopt an eclectic attitude to the two cultures, provided he ceases despising his traditional one. But syncretism between the two cultures seems beyond her conceptualization, and is perhaps alien to Okot p'Bitek's own beliefs. She is prepared, though, to admit that her own culture changes, for she takes umbrage at being grouped by Ocol with her grandmother:

> He says there is no difference
> Between me and my grandmother
> Who covers herself with animal skins.

While the Western-educated reader may find goliardic verse, or Skeltonics, or Elizabethan complaints, or Swiftian satire appropriate comparisons for the tone of *Song of Lawino,* there is no need to go beyond what Okot himself says of Acoli oral literature, whether satirical attacks in short stories, or 'songs of bitter laughter', including dirges that include attacks on the living:

> these poems do not cause social strife among the clansmen. On the contrary, they provide a channel through which members of this close-knit group pour out their grievances and jealousies against one another, in public. These attacks, with all the abuse, ridicule and cruel insults, act as a cleansing activity. (*The Horn of My Love*)

Lawino herself represents her society as a competitive one: 'when a girl knocks you You strike back'; a society where all she asks is the chance to compete openly for her husband's favours, eating 'in the open Not in the bed room.' It is a lusty, vigorous community, where absence of noise is characteristic of wizards. If she seems overemphatic and raucous at times, she can also modulate her tone to blandishment and appeal, though she never becomes servile.

In this characterization of her society she is borne out by her husband's retort, *Song of Ocol,* which appeared four years later. He begins by drawing attention to the monotony and stridency of Lawino's song, and it is noticeable that his own is much more flexible and varied, its basic two-beat line (in contrast to *Song of Lawino*'s three beats) creating a general effect less of ululation than of curt bitter vilification. It is not a self-confident assertion of one set of values, as Lawino's song is; on the contrary, it mourns the passing of Lawino's values and their replacement by a dubious and, indeed, already collapsing set of values. It is an ironic lament for what has been lost, interspersed with the hollow face-saving formulae appropriate to an intelligent and self-critical member of the new Westernized élite. It hints constantly at an unstated self-disgust. It can also be seen to contain the seeds of Okot's two later *Songs*.

The tone of *Song of Ocol* has not, I think, been well grasped by most critics. It is not, except in superficial ways that the author intends us to recognize as such and reject, a defence of Westernization. It is certainly not an answer to Lawino. Indeed, except for section 1, it is not addressed to her. It lacks the specific, dramatic setting of Lawino's monologue. Instead, it is addressed, more in Ocol's thinking than in actuality, to various groups of people, not just Acoli, but groups from all over East Africa. For the richly varied tone there are traditional African precedents, but not, I think, for the wide range of (mostly imagined) addressees. Here the analogy might be with some of Léopold Sédar Senghor's or Walt Whitman's poems, particularly those that combine rhetorical address with symbolic visions. Or, as a dramatic monologue, one might relate it to the fantasizing and the imaginary situations of *The Love-Song of J. Alfred Prufrock* rather than to the solidly dramatized situations of Browning; it is largely interior monologue rather than spoken monologue.

Its battery of imagery is not, as one would have expected had it been a reply to Lawino, drawn mainly from Western technology, economics, and social philosophy. It is true that in the first section Ocol refers to the boot of his car and to having the house painted by a professional; in section 5 to putting 'the Maasai in trousers'; in section 6 to the modern party system and his own (probably imaginary) town house, farm, and Mercedes; in section 7 to grandiose engineering works; and in section 9 to Westernized Africans in various professions. Many of these references are, however, ironic, filled with a tone of self-loathing and disgust. But even so they are outweighed by the traditional African images, many of them, it is true, offered in a tone of denigration or repulsion, but others offered with affection or nostalgia. The balance of imagery is, in other words, at least as much in favour of traditional imagery as in *Song of Lawino*.

The extended image of the exiled monarch in section 1 represents not merely Lawino in her irreparable separation from Ocol, but more importantly—for this is a more widely symbolic and less localized poem than *Song of Lawino*—Ocol, the Blackman, irreparably exiled from his kingdom, the in-

heritance of his traditional society. Ocol, the character in the poem, is sympathizing with Lawino's plight, bemoaning his own separation from the clan, and then rising beyond these personal concerns into symbolic mourning for the African's separation from his roots. Even in section 1, the most specifically dramatic part of the poem, the wider symbolic framework is introduced.

It might be objected that he cannot be mourning for acts that he accepts responsibility for. He does, after all, say 'We will plough up . . . We will uproot . . . We will obliterate . . .'. In fact, however, this responsibility for one's own destruction, this plucking up of one's own roots, is what makes the whole process so tragic. Ocol, as a character and as the symbolic African, is deeply divided. He knows he is destroying himself but he does not seem able to help it. He despoils his own culture but he loathes himself for doing so. The futile 'Song of the woman' is not merely the woman Lawino's lament; it is the representative case Lawino has put up for the preservation of African culture. It is a doomed case, represented by the symbol of an already defeated General. The symbol is taken up again at the very end of the poem:

> As for Shaka
> The Zulu General,
> How can we praise him
> When he was utterly defeated
> And killed by his own brothers?

It is not the mere defeat that is bitter and desolate: it is the fact that, after the defeat of the African dream, Africans themselves abrogated their leader and killed him.

Similarly, with the images that follow that of the General in section 1, the emphasis is on something once good that has been neglected or abused and allowed to decay: the song of Lawino is 'rotting buffalo', 'sour sweet', 'pork gone rancid', 'sour milk', 'rotting Pumpkin'. In section 2, affection and ridicule are mingled in a lyrical interior monologue that draws on Négritude images for affection and on white caricatures of Africa ('white teeth in bright pink gum') for ridicule.

The mood of section 3 is more violent as Ocol rouses himself to threats of root-and-branch destruction of African ways. This is much more hysterical than anything in Lawino's song, much nearer neurosis. 'All the village poets Musicians and tribal dancers' are to be put in detention, all the 'schools of African studies' closed down. Ocol expresses frenzied hatred for anything reminding him that he is black.

Section 4 changes from this vituperative tone to one of nostalgia, though not uncritical nostalgia, as Ocol recalls a scene of the blind *nanga* player Adok Too or Omal Lakana singing while an Acoli woman returns from the well. Ocol adjures her and her sisters from elsewhere in East Africa to release themselves from their slavery, ignorance, and unhygienic ways, to revolt against a system that makes them chattels. Lawino had nothing of the feminist in her: she wanted her man to adopt the traditional male rôle while she entertained him and cooked for him; she even used the bridewealth system, which she obviously accepted, as an argument against the plausibility of the Christian story of the birth of Jesus. Ocol here professes concern at the subjection inherent in such a view of wifehood.

The review of traditional ways continues in section 5, though it is now applied to the more masculine pursuits of the peoples of East Africa and it ranges over various historical periods. The nostalgic roll-call of these people is then succeeded by further vicious threats to eliminate such practices and to turn these rural people into urban dwellers. The tone has, in other words, fluctuated between nostalgia and frenetic ideology.

Section 6 is a long piece of self-justification by Ocol addressed to a village man, a constituent who, it appears, has never seen his local-member of parliament before. It can be taken literally, but such is the extravagance of the tone that it seems best to take it as a daydream: Ocol imagining himself to be a member of parliament with a town house, a Mercedes and a farm, and imagining how he would deal with a constituent. If taken literally, then this is not the Ocol of *Song of Lawino,* section 11; it is a wealthier Ocol some years later and he has not got rid of Lawino in the intervening years. It seems better to interpret it as a dream of Ocol projected into the future when he has been elected to parliament and has begun to reap the rewards of his Party loyalty.

---

p'Bitek had written a proud poem for the people he now believes to be vanquished: *Song of Lawino. Song of Ocol* is, by contrast, a poem of despair for the lost culture of the vanquished.

—*K. L. Goodwin*

In section 7 there is another change of mood. Self-doubt is given expression in the prophetic vision attributed to a crippled beggar. Ocol is abusive to the frightened beggar, but quotes the whole of his song. It is about the cynicism and frustration following Uhuru, then their replacement by anger, which results in a purifying explosion or revolution. The beggar's song reflects Ocol's own fear, but he sublimates his fear into vituperation, ending with the absurd hyperbole of the projected schemes to blow up Mount Kilimanjaro, fill in the Rift Valley, and turn the waters of the Nile into the Indian Ocean. Ocol's divided nature and his tenuous hold on reality are again in evidence.

Section 8 similarly balances nostalgia for tradition and brutal abolition of it. It has some lovely reminiscences of a woman once loved—not Lawino as a character, for this is a prophetic vision of the final destruction of traditional Africa, of the absorption of the country into the city.

The visionary strain continues in section 9, as Ocol surveys the roles of the modern intelligentsia. His cynicism has now taken a very sombre hue. The voice of 'United Africa' has been drowned out by guns, Marxism has been assimilated and distorted to make it seem peculiarly African, even though it is expressed in such widely dissimilar modes as Senghor's rhetoric and Nyerere's Arusha Declaration. The fever of Ocol's address reaches the madness it has always been threatening to embrace with the diatribe on

> the founders
> Of modern Africa
> Leopold II of Belgium
> Bismarck . . .

and ends with the sorrowful, tragic plaint:

> What proud poem
> Can we write
> For the vanquished?

Okot p'Bitek had of course written a proud poem for the people he now believes to be vanquished: *Song of Lawino. Song of Ocol* is, by contrast, a poem of despair for the lost culture of the vanquished. It is a poem much more varied in tone, without the long unrelieved stridency of Lawino's complaint. The variety and the deeply troubled subtlety of Ocol's mind have, regrettably, not always been appreciated by readers and critics.

Song of Prisoner arises generally out of the image of corrupt self-justification attributed to successful politicians in *Song of Ocol,* and specifically out of the following passage from section 6:

> Trespassers must be jailed
> For life,
> Thieves and robbers
> Must be hanged,
> Disloyal elements
> Must be detained without trial . . .

The anger and madness of Ocol are now transferred to one of the victims of such a policy of repression, a poor man who is delirious after (and while) being beaten up by sadistic ward-ers in gaol. As Ocol lamented to his mother that he was born black (end of section 2), so Prisoner curses his father (section 4) and his mother (section 6) for his genes. Prisoner puts into words what was implicit in *Song of Ocol*: that 'the cancer of Uhuru' is 'Far worse than The yaws of Colonialism'. In *Song of Ocol*, 'The lamb Uhuru' was a rotting carcase with decep-tively open eyes. In *Song of Prisoner,* the remains of the lamb's carcase are fought over by 'Old hyenas'. Uhuru is also a 'fierce wild fire' that has burnt out the Prisoner, and a 'whirlwind'. Its effects, in the hands of those who pervert and direct it for their own ends, are like a 'shark' devouring its own children, a 'Rhino' prodding its brothers in the back, or an 'arrow' bringing down an eagle.

Song of Prisoner has evoked a good deal of puzzlement and speculation about the dramatic situation in the poem, much of it generated by Edward Blishen's unfortunate remarks in his Introduction to the New York edition about a multiple persona rather than a single characterized speaker. Apart from one or two very minor inconsistencies, the poem makes sense as the more or less delirious dramatic monologue of a poor man who is being held and beaten up in gaol after he has assassinated an important political leader. The poem was be-gun immediately after Okot heard the news of the assassina-tion in Nairobi on 5 July 1969 of Tom Mboya, the cabinet minister widely regarded as the most promising candidate to succeed Jomo Kenyatta as President. According to Okot,

> The killer of Tom Mboya is the prisoner in *Song of Prisoner.* He hadn't been captured yet. I captured him first, in this poem. [Bernth Lindfors, "An Inter-view with Okot p'Bitek," *World Literature Written English* (November 1977)]

In section 11 he overhears another prisoner, a disgraced Min-ister for Police and Justice, being beaten up, and he inter-sperses his own comments. Section 12 is an interior monologue in the mind of the Minister; or, if one insisted on absolute singleness in the point of view, in the mind of the poor Prisoner as he imagines the Minister's thoughts or even overhears them (for the Minister is aware that 'the very air Has ears').

It is not, I think, impossible to work this out from the poem itself, particularly from the clues given at the beginning of section 11, when the Prisoner hears and shushes the 'milli-pede'. If external support were needed, however, it comes from Margaret Marshment, who said of section 11:

> Okot tells me that this is the voice of a man in the next cell, whom the Prisoner overhears. This was not clear to me, and we could wish it were clearer be-cause it is important . . . But we can guess at one reason why he might be in prison: that he was the assassin's employer. ["Song of Prisoner: A Reply to

Atieno-Odhiambo," in *Standpoints on African Lit-erature,* edited by Chris L. Wanjala, 1973]

It is a plausible guess, for the Prisoner at one stage has no doubt that the machinery of the Law will soon set him free, an appropriate theory if his hirer had been the Minister in charge of 'Law and Order', and if this was the same man he had been bodyguard to, political organizer for, and procurer of girls for. But it seems as if the hirer-Minister-employer is unable to protect his assassin-bodyguard-Prisoner, for he him-self has been thrown into gaol and beaten up in the wake of the assassination. In gaol, one of his desires is 'to sleep With experienced prostitutes presumably the type lined up for him previously by the Prisoner.

Filling in further details of the dramatic situation, we can say that the Prisoner has apparently been arrested while sleeping in the 'City Park'; that he has been before a magistrate for a preliminary hearing, charged with vagrancy and asked whether he pleads guilty or not guilty (a recurring refrain); that the police have beaten him up several times, perhaps sa-distically asking him as they do so whether he pleads guilty or not guilty to other offences including the assassination; that he believes the man he killed was a gross political crimi-nal who had wrongfully imprisoned many citizens, that he is so poor that his family is short of food and his children will never go to school, and that during his imprisonment, per-haps in the early stages, he has had visions or hallucinations of being treated as a national hero for his bold action. The height of his euphoria is succeeded by the Minister's mono-logue, and this is a highly dramatic and ironic interruption, for his dreams of adulation could presumably only be real-ized if his employer, the Minister, stood by him and acknowl-edged him as his instrument. But the Minister himself is disgraced. He too has hopes of quick release; he too is beaten; he too has thoughts of his children, though they go to school and should prosper, and of his parents, though unlike the Prisoner's they are comfortably supported; he too has hallu-cinations of wild pleasure (section 12) to contrast against the brutal realities of the cell.

The main bulk of the Prisoner's dreams of pleasure follow the return of the monologue from the Minister to him in sec-tion 13. His pleasures are to be first with his wife, family, and clan, not among the city prostitutes like the Minister's. Then, in sections 14 and 15 his mind takes him beyond his clan, beyond East Africa, to a world survey of music, song, and dancing. It is a visionary expansion comparable to what hap-pens at the end of *Song of Ocol*. There is madness about it all, as there was in *Song of Ocol*. Prisoner has been tortured, he has admitted that his mind is on fire and that he is mad. In his delirium, then, conventional moral attitudes are thrown away, and he can 'want to try the dances Of neo-colonialists and ex-Nazis'. Margaret Marshment saw this as an indica-tion of the Prisoner's unreliability as a moral guide, of his reprehensible denial of responsibility for his own act or, indeed, for anybody's acts. It could, of course, also be seen as evidence of delirium brought about by his action, his imprisonment, the brutal treatment he has received, his fears for himself and his family, and his hunger. Or we may recognize that at the end of the poem (as in *Song of Ocol*) the clear outline of the human protagonist are being expanded and blurred as he is apotheosized into a symbol of the political detainee or political criminal anywhere in the world. Like many such people accused of acts against governments, he sees himself as a world citizen, justified by the euphoric internationalism of his act and condition. But the balance of sympathy still lies, I think, on the side of the Prisoner, whose exposé of the hypocrisy of the independent régime of which he is a citizen has been all too convincing.

In section 15, the examples of international brotherhood narrow down to Africa, and the dancing images are now mingled with images of war, famine, and bloodshed. The last word in the poem is 'Uhuru', and the whole poem has to be seen as a bitter and sorrowful myth of what can happen after so-called Independence, an indictment of African governments and nations as no better than anyone else at establishing a just society. More generally, *Song of Prisoner* can be seen as a myth of the oppressed citizen, deprived of freedom and dignity in the unjust state. Once again Okot p'Bitek has created a memorable myth centred on a representative type. Once again he has begun with a character and turned the character into a symbol.

The myth of *Song of Malaya* concerns African attitudes to sex in contrast to missionary-advocated exclusivity and repression. Once again, the seeds of this poem can be found in the earlier ones. Lawino, accepting that she should share her husband with Clementine, asked

> Who has ever prevented men
> From wanting women?

At the end of *Song of Malaya,* the prostitute (*malaya* in kiSwahili, but used in East Africa even by non-Swahili speakers) asks

> Who can command
> The sun
> Not to rise in the morning?

This is a poem celebrating sex as joyful, good, and liberating. The *malaya* says *karibu* ('come near' in kiSwahili) to all: sailors, soldiers, Sikhs, Hindus, whites, schoolboys, teachers, chiefs, drivers, factory workers, shop assistants, political organizers, doctors, municipal officers, Kaffirs, farmers, policemen, even perhaps the detested 'advisors The experts and mercenaries', the 'one pest' of Africa.

There are, however, detractors and enemies to be combated. The chief who complains of contracting venereal disease is reminded in section 2 of his visit a few nights earlier, when his virility was impaired by drunkenness. But the section ends with some practical advice on sexual manners: the Kaffir is advised to get circumcised and to bring 'Gum boots' or contraceptives next time; and her Sister Prostitutes are similarly advised to have 'boxing gloves' in their handbags. The outraged wife is met in section 3 with the argument that her husband is made happier and more amenable by his visits to the prostitute; and there is also advice to do something about bad breath. The moralizing black bishop in section 4 is reminded that he is himself a bastard and that both chastity and monogamy are alien to nature. It is in this section that the poem (like *Song of Ocol* and *Song of Prisoner*) moves outward in time and space, drawing analogies from Eve, Hagar, the daughters of Sodom and Gomorrah, Rahab, Esther, Delilah (all Old Testament examples, by no means all normally considered as prostitutes), Magdalena, Theodora, and St Augustine's whore (examples from the New Testament, Byzantium, and the Church Fathers). The analogies are continued into section 5 with the illegitimacy of Jesus, used as a comforting example by the prostitute to her son who has been taunted at school by a teacher, himself indiscriminately licentious. The moral disapproval of her own brother is met by the prostitute in section 6 with evidence of his own reliance on prostitutes, his wife's unfaithfulness, and his own illegitimacy. There is also here a diatribe against wives as 'slaves Of the world', 'Married whores', 'Penned like goats To unwilling pegs'. After the harshness of her criticism she demurely offers to help her brother find a suitable partner, but he apparently storms out in affected disgust while she is speaking. Section 7 begins with her arrest by a police sergeant. She reminds him that he had visited her in another capacity only the previous night and then, echoing the words of the Prisoner, she asks

> But how can you now
> Call me
> A vagrant?

Then follows a malediction, summarizing her proud defiant argument in the whole of the poem. She defies all her enemies and detractors to do their worst and consign her to hell,

> But
> Who can command
> The sun
> Not to rise in the morning?

This is a less serious, less gloomy, and less political poem than *Song of Ocol* or *Song of Prisoner.* Its joyous celebration and its relatively unvaried rhetorical tone are more reminiscent of *Song of Lawino*. But like all the other poems it expresses ideas important to Okot p'Bitek through the monologue of a character who rises into symbolism. The *malaya*, however, remains very much an individual to the end: her representative character has been conveyed by the repeated addresses of her song to her sister prostitutes of the world.

Okot's uncollected poems are few in number, and can easily be related to his four major works. **'Return the Bridewealth'** [available in *Poems from East Africa*, edited by David Cook and David Rubadiri, 1971], for instance, fits easily into the world of *Song of Lawino*. The village man wants to marry a second time. Apparently improvident, he shamelessly asks his father for bridewealth, but is ignored. He thinks of borrowing money in the town, but is rejected, apparently as a bad risk. He then has the effrontery to ask his first wife (whose father he says he cannot trace) to return her own bridewealth. And, with a taunt, she does—by cheque. **'Harvest'** and **'Order of the Black Cross'** are political pieces of a slightly sibylline kind, the second marking the end of the war in Biafra. They can be accommodated within the world of *Song of Ocol* and *Song of Prisoner*. They can also be seen as pointing forward to Okot's fifth major poem, which he discussed with Bernth Lindfors in 1976:

> I am now working on *Song of a Soldier,* which examines the destructive role of the military in Africa. It raises the question of just how are we going to get rid of them? The central character is a particular soldier, this great thief, parading all over Africa. I wish he was only a thief! He's much worse than that! He is the one speaking in most of the poem, but the book will have a slightly different structure from most of the others because there is also a narrator who comes in every now and then saying things like, 'He came soon after midnight and sneezed.' Then the soldier will speak, and the narrator will return later. So it's a two-sided sort of thing, the kind of structure you saw in *Song of Prisoner*. Even the corpses, the victims of the soldier, will speak and interact with their murderer, and then the narrator will push the story on to the next phase. It's a very painful thing I'm writing. It's been going on for some time because it's a very tearful thing to do . . . But it is a very terrible book because I lost quite a lot of relatives in the Uganda coup, a lot of friends too, and after I write a few lines, I drop it because it causes a lot of tears. [*World Literature Written in English* (November 1977)]

This dramatic monologue will, then, present the horrific corruption and corrupting influence of the individual agent of destruction. The humorous idiom has now turned very sour indeed, and Okot has moved a long way from the celebratory ebullience of *Song of Lawino* and *Song of Malaya*. The new poem confirms the fact, however, that his strength lies in the extended poem. In his four major published pieces he has created memorable symbols of African culture, the perversion of Westernization, the corruption of independent régimes, and African sexuality. The fifth will bring the cultural analysis even closer to the present time.

Ogo A. Ofuani (essay date December 1985)

SOURCE: "The Traditional and Modern Influences in Okot p'Bitek's Poetry," in *The African Studies Review*, Vol. 28, No. 4, December, 1985, pp. 87-99.

[*In the following essay, Ofuani examines the traditional and modern literary influences in p'Bitek's poetry and the difficulty in separating the specific sources of influence.*]

This article discusses the traditional and modern literary influences in Okot p'Bitek's poetry. It must be borne in mind, however, that the question of influences is very complicated because it is difficult to pin down an influence to a particular source. If those sources have become assimilated into an integral whole, it is difficult to sort them out—to know where the modern ends and the traditional begins, or where the Western ends and the African begins. Therefore, no attempt will be made to show that the modern and traditional influences are mutually exclusive. As with all aspects of life, there are bound to be overlaps, and this kind of overlap cannot be any more expected than in the work of a poet with the diverse kinds of experiences of p'Bitek.

A brief survey of his background is illuminating. Okot p'Bitek is an Acholi from Uganda. His father, Opii Jebedyo, was a teacher from the pa-Cua clan of the Patiko chiefdom and his mother, Lacwaa Cerina, came from the Palaro chiefdom. p'Bitek has repeatedly testified to his early interest in oral literature and his mother's influence in forming that interest:

> . . . my interest in African literature . . . [was] sparked by my mother's songs and the stories that my father performed around the evening fire. [*Africa's Cultural Revolution*]

The title, *Song of Lawino,* is derived from his mother's name and confirms that his mother, as a composer and singer, taught him many of the songs that he enjoyed throughout his life and used in many aspects of his varied career. [In an endnote, Ofuani adds: "In an interview at Aarhus University in 1977, p'Bitek said that *Song of Lawino* has his mother's name and that his mother 'was a very important woman in my life and she taught me a lot. She was talented and composed thirty-four of the songs in *Horn of My Love.*'"] In the several interviews p'Bitek granted, he revealed that the oral literature of the Acoli of Uganda had played a very prominent and significant part in his literary development. Oral literature shaped p'Bitek's imagination in his infancy through the contact with, and the influence of, his mother and was at the center of much of his adult employment in Makerere and Nairobi, where he organized several festivals of dance and song.

It is true that oral literature also shaped his own conception of literature. We are of the opinion that p'Bitek's statements at Syracuse University, New York, in 1970, seemed to have been taken too literally by Heron [in his *The Poetry of p'Bitek,* 1976] when he says that "Okot p'Bitek professes both a contempt and ignorance of the formal study of literature." From our reading of the text of that lecture, it is agreed that p'Bitek professes "contempt" for the formal study of literature because of the strains of examination, but not ignorance of it. As is obvious from his biographies and from numerous interviews, the study of forms of Western literature, if anything, seemed to have merged with traditional literary influences in sparking his own creativity. Thus, it is our contention that for a man who, as Heron points out, "went to a teacher training college immediately after his Advanced Level examinations and thereafter taught English and Religious Knowledge at a secondary school," any claim of complete ignorance of the forms and conventions of modern Western literature would amount to more than "a little exaggeration." Our understanding of that portion of p'Bitek's lecture that is often misinterpreted is that he showed full contempt for the rigors that accompanied the Advanced Level literature examination:

> As a Sixth Former at Budo, near Kampala, I used to take part in the weekly seminar at the Headmaster's house for the final preparation for the Cambridge School Certificate. We dressed up like "ladies" and "gentlemen," and sat on comfortable sofas and were served coffee. Those of use who were smokers were offered cigarettes. The atmosphere was always relaxed and pleasurable. But, halfway through the evening, quite a number of us would be snoring in the corners. When the year ended we made a bonfire of the now useless notebooks and English setbooks. Somehow I managed to pass the literature paper; *but, on leaving school, I never read another novel or book of poetry, and never visited the theatre, until very much later on* (emphasis added).

Though recounted in 1970, this was about an experience that took place in the fifties before p'Bitek went to Government Training College, Mbarara, between 1952 and 1954. In the excerpt above, the crucial elements are those emphasized. p'Bitek did not deny the obvious influence of Western literary tradition on his work. All he said was that he "never read" Western literature of any type "until very much later on." *Song of Lawino* was published in 1966, more than a decade after his A Levels, but his creativity as a writer started in his school days. He published his Acoli novel *Lak Tar* in 1953 and wrote the early version of *Wer pa Lawino* in 1956. Before these, while still a student, he had written and produced an opera in English called *Acan.* There is, therefore, no doubt that those boring seminars and literary sessions at the

headmaster's house must have left their imprint, at least in sparking his own creative instincts. Some of the influences of Western literary traditions, such as the use of verse lines, stanzas, and even writing in English in the first instance, are discussed later in this paper. There is also an unmistakable trace of the influence of such Western literary masters as Robert Browning in his predilection for the long poem and the dramatic monologue. Browning, Coleridge, Donne, Eliot, Milton, Pope, and Shakespeare may have been featured in the Advanced Level English literature syllabuses which in the 1950s ranged from Chaucer to Eliot. African writers and works were hardly featured since most of the prominent African writers today—Achebe, Clark, Ngugi, Okigbo, Soyinka and p'Bitek himself—were still students. One cannot but agree, however, that the place of oral literature in p'Bitek's works "separates him distinctly from many of his fellow African writers," since "all of these writers have been very much involved in the formal study of a European literary tradition." The predominant role of oral literature in shaping the trend of p'Bitek's works is not unconnected with his own conception of literature, a conception which he has been very vocal in defending.

In his article **"What is Literature?"** [*Busara,* Vol. 4, No. 1 (1972)] p'Bitek calls for a redefinition of "literature." According to him, the typical dictionary definition, with its emphasis on writing, implies that literature is the exclusive preserve of literate societies. It excludes the literary activities of the vast majority of mankind, both in terms of history and geography. This definition, he says, should be replaced by a "dynamic and democratic" one, by which:

> . . . literature stands for all the creative works of man expressed in words. Writing . . . is a mere tool for expressing ideas . . . the poet uses words for expressing his feelings. Now words can be spoken, sung or written. The voice of the singer or the speaker and the pen or paper are mere midwives of a pregnant mind. A song is a song whether it is sung, spoken or written down.

He thus emphasizes the importance of a word, the substance, irrespective of its formal realization. This accounts for the overlaps we find in his poetry of traditional oral poetic forms in which the spoken word is supreme and modern conventions dependent on the graphic mode. With this in mind, p'Bitek defines oral literature as follows:

> Literature is the communication and sharing of deeply felt emotions. The vehicle of this communication is *words.* The aim of any literary activity must be to ensure that there is communication between the singer and the audience, between the story-teller and his hearers. There must be full participation by all present (author's emphasis).

In this direction, literature is to be de-emphasized as an examination-bound subject which gives the student little joy but only "pains." Literature is to be made into a "festival" as it is in the countryside. His stand is also reiterated later in the preface to his collection of translated Acoli poetry, **Horn of My Love** and several other interviews. This belief aroused his interest in the literature of the Acoli, especially their poetry and short stories collected in **Horn of My Love** and **Hare and Hornbill** repectively. This interest in Acoli literature also influenced his own creations. It influenced his writing of **Wer pa Lawino** in Acoli language and the translation **Song of Lawino,** a song in which Lawino, the arch-traditionalist, seeks to maintain the Acoli culture from the corrupting Westernizing influence of Ocol, her husband, and Tina, Ocol's mistress. The conflict between traditional African and Western cultural norms and values is thematically central to **Song of Lawino.** The importance of this conflict, which is highlighted in his other songs, is that it reflects the centripetal (traditional and modern) forces which converge in p'Bitek's poetry.

We have so far seen that the main influences on p'Bitek's works are those of his mother, his home, his Acoli background with its tradition of stories, dances and songs. The school influenced his literacy in Acoli and the English language. [In "Aesthetic Dualism and Creative Literature in East Africa," in *Black Aesthetics,* edited by P. Zirimu and A. Gurr, 1973] Mazrui summed up the sources of this kind of dualism as it affects creative writing in East Africa:

> The problem for creative literature in East Africa, as in much colonial Africa, is the problem of what one might call aesthetic dualism. This is the coexistence of two artistic universes drawn from vastly different cultures, which have yet to coalesce or merge into a new distinct phenomenon. In reality each African country has more than two aesthetic worlds since each nation consists of several ethnic groups with their own civilizations. But for each African individual, the dualism is between the foreign and the indigenous, or the modern and the traditional. The dualism which is most pertinent to the crisis of identity within the arts in Africa is the dualism between the pull of western artistic influences and the stability of older modes of creativity.

The major perceptible traditional influences on p'Bitek's poetry are those arising from his interest in and knowledge of Acoli oral literary performance, while the modern are those that arise from his exposure to Western literary art. That these two main areas have influenced p'Bitek's creative development has been affirmed by Heron, Mbise, and Moore. For instance, Moore has indicated [in "Okot p'Bitek," a paper presented at the Fourth Annual Ibadan African Literature Conference in 1979] that "the new educated class in Acoli land contained many who refused to let their English education turn them aside from the language and literature of their own people." p'Bitek is clearly a member of this class of educated Acoli.

Taken as they are, p'Bitek's four Songs (**Lawino, Ocol, Prisoner,** and **Malaya**) are in print, irrespective of mode of initial composition. The impression this therefore creates is that p'Bitek's poems are to be taken, first and foremost, as written. But this does not rule out the fact that poetry conceived and written may have features of oral art. [In "Aspects of Varietie, Differentiation," *Journal at Linguistics,* Vol. 3, No. 2 (1967)] Gregory has distinguished two kinds of poetry: in non-literate and in literate societies. In non-literate societies, poems are recited, technically meaning that they involve the speaking of the poetic texts, non-spontaneously, such texts "written down" in the reciter's memory, as it were. If this subdivision is pursued to its logical conclusion, we find ourselves immersed in the controversy about which medium is primary, speech or writing? The implication of the dual categorization is that, at one level, speech is primary (the written text is secondary and dependent upon speech in writing) and that at another, writing is primary and is aimed at speech.

This kind of dualism is perceptible in p'Bitek's poetry with both influences, the non-literate and verbal, blended with the written to produce a complex and integral whole. But whatever differences exist between the two in p'Bitek's songs, especially as we are presented with their printed texts, our desire to see poetry as primarily either written or spoken derive from our everyday experience of language, or rather from the way we tend to think about it. As Levenston observes [in "Speech and/or Writing: Lyric Poetry and the Media of Language," *PTL,* Vol. 4, No. 3 (1979)], we are accustomed to regarding the two media, speech and writing, as functioning independently. Thus because of the predominantly written form of the poetic texts in literate cultures, the tendency has been for poets and critics to see the written text as primary.

This conventional stereotyped view of the difference between speech and writing is clearly an over simplification. The continuous deliberation of speech and writing supremacy in poetry will not aid a resolution of the debate since it is obvious that poetry has a dual existence, a dual existence which is not sequential, one deriving from the other, but simultaneous. Poetry seems therefore to be essentially both written and spoken, with neither primary, both of equal status. Levenston further observes that this simultaneous duality is seen on examination of the actual process of a poem's composition where it seems that what really happens is the poet's representation in writing of an imagined utterance:

> Neither the transcription nor the utterance itself can be independently completed. We can only say the poem when it is completely written out; we can only write it down when we have heard the end. Only when the poet abandons the act of composition is the poem complete.

This exposition about the process of a poet's composition seems to suit only literate societies. Does the composition of poetry in oral, non-literate situations fit into this scheme? How is the poetry "written down" (or conserved) in this context—in the memory through which it is stored or handed down through generations? According to Levenston again:

> It has been assumed that poetry exists in a world of speech and writing. This assumption is largely justified as far as western tradition is concerned. It only breaks down when we broaden our conception of poetry to include oral performance in non-literate societies.

This observation is valid for the discussion of p'Bitek's poetry because it reveals that the "aesthetic dualism" Mazrui discusses can be exemplified in p'Bitek's work. This dualism has to a large extent become characteristic of East African poets, p'Bitek and lo Liyong included. As has been queried by the present writer in connection with this dualism in discussing lo Liyong's poetic form in *Another Nigger Dead,* especially in relation to the choice of medium:

> What, for instance, is the pattern adopted or to be adopted by the African writer (poet), caught, as he is, in the web of western literate tradition but who is very much part of his immediate background, its poetic forms and devices? . . . Can he not use the graphic form of the Western tradition by putting his poems on paper where his ancestors had depended on memory for record-keeping, and at the same time, modify this alien medium to give the purely phonic substance of his background . . . ?

The discussion here attempts to reveal how p'Bitek has successfully blended the two traditions—the non-literate "orature" of his Acoli background and the literate tradition of English literary art acquired through formal education. As will become obvious, the lines beyond the two are not usually as clear as could be suggested.

p'Bitek's language and imagery are drawn from the whole range of Acoli song. The sources of influence include the satirical songs of the beer party, the victory songs of the *bwola* dance, the war songs, and the praise songs. It has been pointed out that even the narrator's self-praise in *Song of Lawino* is deeply consonant with the Acoli tradition where praising is not merely permitted but required. Moore, for instance, points out that "every male Acoli carries an animal horn around his neck, on which he is expected to blow his own praise-name as he approaches any inhabited compound as a way of announcing himself." Girls too are allowed to praise not only their lovers but their own charms. Lawino does so a lot. The Malaya was especially exultant in praising herself, her kindred, and her profession (*Song of Lawino*). The funeral dirges (*guru lyel*) of the Acoli were also a source of inspiration for

Lawino in her songs of mourning for the culturally dead Ocol, her husband (*Song of Lawino*):

> O my husband
> Let us all cry together;
> Come,
> Let us mourn the death of my husband,
> The death of a Prince
> The ash that was produced
> By a great Fire!

Every phrase, if compared to the dirges in *Horn of My Love,* might be found in many of the dirges which are sung and danced at the second burial ceremonies of the Acoli. But what lends them poignancy and force, contextually, is that they are being sung for a man who is still alive. Her song is a testimony of her rejection of her husband and his ways.

It is also possible to reveal the existence of a communal voice in the Songs, a voice typical of that of oral literary form. This communcal aspect has fundamental and philosophical implications. The communal nature of the narrator's voice is in the use of personal pronouns. For instance, the "I" of *Song of Lawino* is more than the obvious grammatical first person singular. When Lawino speaks, she does so with a collective tone. It is "I" on behalf of the clan, the kinsmen, the whole society. This happens too in the use of the pronoun "you"—a device p'Bitek exploits in using the English language since you is neutral and has both singular (individual) and plural (general, communal) meanings. The collective tone is an important aspect of traditional literature. It is a feature that differentiates oral literature from literature, emanating from modern industrial and technological societies whose poets can afford to be introverted and isolated (or alienated) from the very society they are writing about. The language which p'Bitek uses therefore has communally evolved symbols whose ideas are therefore shared, such as his use of the pumpkin metaphor. In very sense, he seems to speak for his community, its values and its norms.

Part of the background to *Song of Lawino* and the other Songs then is total participation by the poet in the still flourishing and developing culture of his people. It is possible to go on listing the traditional influences exhibited in p'Bitek's poetry. One could mention the use of formulas that initiate stories and aid memory—formulas that act as a mnemonic device, a device favored by the traditional orator, singer and storyteller. The impression that this leaves with a reader is that p'Bitek was merely imitating the literary form of his people by using a new medium. In going back to his tradition, there would seem to be little room for the individual's creativity or originality. p'Bitek has been shown to follow that which is traditional and that which is traditional cannot belong to any one individual. It can only be copied; and then it is transmitted from one generation to another for further imitation and modification. In traditional Africa this is how oral literature survived. But the concept of imitation here is to be defined, especially imitation that is transposed from the oral to the printed word.

A traditional singer is an artist, and his art involves a degree of creativity and originality. Since not everyone can write a novel or a poem or be a singer or composer, it can be concluded logically that an artist is indeed a unique person in society, whether traditional or modern. In traditional society, the originality or creativity of an artist was not necessarily in the material (the corpus) used as such, but in the artist's performance. This mode of operation demanded the use of the traditional aesthetics. Here, then, is where p'Bitek's mastery of traditional techniques elevates him above most of his contemporaries in East Africa. To produce a work of art with traditional artistic qualities like *Song of Lawino,* the poet must be a good listener, a good traditional singer and dancer. The poet has revealed these features in his Songs (the singers all sing; Prisoner even wants to "dance" in *Song of Prisoner*).

p'Bitek also reveals a tremendous zest for teasing, a quality which is really a common, if not essential, part of traditional praise songs and satires. Individuals like Ocol, Tina, the politicians, the general public, are satirized, but in doing so, p'Bitek seems to place more emphasis on ideas than on characters, such that the dramatic monologuers are more of p'Bitek's mouthpieces than fully developed characters. With the exception of Lawino, the characterization of these monologuers yields place to the ideas being developed. Commenting on p'Bitek's art, generally, especially in his relationship with his background, Moore observes that,

> This is no question of plagiarism here [in p'Bitek's poetry], for within such a tradition the artist is judged by his knowledge of it and his ability to manipulate it. The western concept of originality is essentially post-classical in original and has no relevance here.

As traditional as p'Bitek may be shown to be, he is at the same time a modern poet with a personal idea of literature and commitment. He is speaking his own ideas in a way, especially if his Songs are seen as fiction, his own creations. It is in this creative realm that the merger of the traditional and modern features of his poetry becomes obvious. p'Bitek is essentially a poet, and poetry as a genre has certain features which distinguish it from other genres, particularly prose. Such distinguishing features are most prominently formal, though a relationship exists between the form and the language used. As a literate artist, p'Bitek has leaned on the written word rather than the spoken mode for the preservation of his art. (This gives his poems their fixedness.) It is possible, however, to talk of his poems as written to be spoken, performed orally, or sung. The features of his literacy in his work include the typography and the graphological lay out of his

poems, the use of punctuation and the verse line as a feature of the written shape.

But poetry, whether spoken or written, traditional or modern, African or European, is poetry because of certain ways in which language is organically used in the genre to effect rhythm, rhyme, alliteration, metre, the line, enjambment, caesura, assonance, consonance, and other sound effects, metaphors, similes, hyperboles, litotes, and so on—irrespective of the language or the mode of expression. These are the areas where the traditional and modern features merge in p'Bitek's poetry.

One striking instance of this merger worth mentioning is the verse form of p'Bitek's poetry. As is usual in a discussion of p'Bitek's works, his monumental *Song of Lawino* often provides a take-off point since it set the trend for the other songs. Heron has demonstrated in his study of p'Bitek's poetry how the writer, in deviating from the traditional pattern of Acoli poetry which is not rhymed, has produced what he described as Acoli "unsung verse" by developing a new prosody for Acoli in using an a-b-a-b rhyme scheme and a more or less regular metrical beat of some nine or ten syllables per line.

This style was adopted in the Acoli original *Wer pa Lawino* which was later translated into English. p'Bitek was under no illusion about the losses translating would involve, stating in the preface that he must inevitably "clip a bit of the eagle's wings" in the process. He therefore wisely resolved to abandon both rhyme and metrical regularity. To have remained with those features would have forced him to move away from the mainly literal translation which "enabled him to preserve the force and character of the original imagery" (Moore). English is also more prolix than Acoli, which makes abundant use of prefixes and suffixes to modify root words. Okot therefore decided to adopt a short, fast-moving line in the English version, since a line-by-line translation would have been clumsy and long-winded. The result is that *Song of Lawino* has no rhyme and no consistent stress pattern, all combining to make it an irregular free verse song. This form is thereofre not accidental to *Song of Lawino* (having been determined by the translation constraints) since it is adopted for the other Songs.

In oral literature, poetry is mainly oral, chanted, or recited, and so there is the problem of establishing the verse lines when writing the poems down. The chanter or reciter often pauses to take a fresh, audible, breath. It is logical, therefore, to use these pauses to delimit the line in oral poetry. But as Olatunji has pointedly observed in a description of his transcription of Yoruba poetry:

> There are problems arising from this [use of the pause to delimit the line] which cannot be glossed over. There are occasions when the chanter or reciter rushes through a very long utterance without taking any

perceptible breath. Should we regard the utterance as a line? And when the pause occurs in the middle of a syntactic group, especially when the chanter has been struggling for breath, should we write the corpus on different lines? Apart from these two problems, we still need to set up degrees of pauses to know which shall delimit the line and which the period within the line.

His suggestion therefore is that a combination of pauses determined by lexicostructural, lexical, and semantic criteria, should be taken into consideration in determining the nature of the verse line in Yoruba oral poetry. Various questions arise about p'Bitek's poetry. Did he use something similar to Olatunji's prescription in determining his verse line? Did he represent an utterance in lines on the basis of the repetition of lexical items and sentence structure? Or is there any such rule that parts of a sentence or a clause should not be represented in separate lines. For a writer eager to put down all his ideas before he forgets (just as the oral performer who depends on memory and mnemonic devices does), are breath pauses not as useful for deciding his verse lines? Or is his verse so "free" that it has no system? Because he was writing in English, is it not possible that the dictates of English poetry determined his own form?

The answers will not be obvious until we have looked at some of these "dictates" of English poetic form. Such criteria for English verse have already been established. [In his *A Linguistic Guide to English Poetry,* 1969] Leech has suggested the need to consider how to identify and define a line of poetry—"for to function as a phological unit of verse, the line must be distinguishable on some grounds other than mere typography." As Abercombie points out in working out such a guideline, a line of verse is delimited by "various devices which may be called line-end markers, and there seem to be three of these in English verse." The three he specifies which may be used individually or in combination are the following:

1. rhyme, or some other sound scheme;

2. a silent final stress; and

3. a monosyllabic measure, not used anywhere else, coinciding with the last syllable of the line.

If one or more of these markers are present in a poem, even though it may be printed or recited as if it were prose, a person confronted with it for the first time should be able to recognise the line divisions.

As useful as these suggestions may have been about English poets, they do not seem to apply with any exactness to *Song of Lawino* or the other songs. For instance, rhyme is ruled out since all the Songs are free verse. The other two criteria

may apply in different degrees, especially 2 which does not specify line length. The lines have irregular length and rhythm, and rhyme is absent. An examination of the two passages below makes this clear:

> (i) The one who follows Okang
>   Is called Oboi.
>   He is always jealous,
>   He fights with his brother
>   And fights for his brother
>   The third son is called Odai
>   And the last son is Cogo.
>   If you hit his head
>   With your finger
>   His mother will throw
>   Things at you;
>   Because that is the child
>   Of which a mother is most fond.
>   [*Song of Lawino*]

> (ii) I want to drink
>   All the drinks
>   Of the world
>   I want to meet
>   All the drunkards
>   And chat with them . . .
>   [*Song of Prisoner*]

Example (i) has no perceptible rhyme and no specific metre as the lines are of irregular length with an unequal number of syllables. Lines four and five look like a couplet but that is not possible if we start from line one. They are only two parallel structures involving repetition of clause structure, lexical variation in the use of preposition in the prepositional phrase ("with / for his brother") and repetition of "brother"— all for emphasis. Instead of adopting some of the features Abercombie suggests, we instead notice that the lexico-structural, lexical and semantic criteria Olatunji mentions in his work seem applied with some system in the passage. Whether a line is made up of a clause, a group or phrase, none of them is unnecessarily divided into two lines. For instance, line one is a nominal group, line two a predicate clause, line three a full sentence-clause, line 9 an adverbial phrase and so on, with the exception of 10-11 that look truncated.

The comments for (i) also apply to (ii). There is absence of rhyme: irregular line length in terms of syllables. In general, there is no specific rhythmic regularity though lines 4-6 seem regular but with irregular metrical patterning (in terms of stress). The verse here is more condensed than in (i) with the result that they are shorter, faster, with a sense of urgency unlike (i) that is rather slow and ponderous, a feature of the listing which its speaker is engaged in. Passage (ii) also has parallel structures. There are two clauses, each taking three lines (1-3, 4-6), and the structures in lines 1 and 4 ("I want to meet / drink") and in lines 2 and 5 ("All the drinks / drunkards") are repeated with lexical variation in the last word in each structure. This repetition could give these lines parallel rhythms, but the repetition is for emphasis as in the first example.

So it is possible that both traditional and modern influences may have helped in determining the shape of the verse lines in the Songs. It may be difficult to enumerate the degree of both sources of influence since the poet has denied any consistent and prolonged knowledge of Western literary art, but also accepted the influence of the *Songs of Solomon* and Longfellow's *Hiawatha.* He has on occasions said that he does not think that his songs are "very much influenced by the African oral tradition," but he assesses the sources of his imagery in the following words:

> It is based mainly on the traditional, I think, but one
> is bound to be influenced by friends, enemies, school,
> etc., so it becomes all mixed up.

However, as indicated early in this paper, the poet was introduced to some Western authors (poets, novelists, dramatists) through exposure to texts in school syllabuses. The narrative and ballad form of poems is not peculiar to only English or European literary tradition, but it is possible to reveal similarities between p'Bitek's form and that of notable English poets like Browning, Coleridge, Keats, Wordsworth, and Yeats, especially in the predilection for the one-speaker, long, dramatic, monologue poem. Apart from their narrative forms, it is also easy to see how they all exhibit similar qualities of suggestion and concentrated power.

In terms of content or subject matter, in terms of the experiences verbalized, and in terms of the use of the English language, the monologuers in the poems are obviously East Africans of the modern period. The allusions of Lawino, to some extent, stand out from those of Ocol, Malaya, and Prisoner. Lawino is however a village woman living in East Africa. The others are metropolitan in their outlook. The speech of all the narrators, however, retains an unmistakable African flavor in the English they speak. It is as if p'Bitek, having established a kind of confidence between himself and his langage, is able to extend it to cover situations which are not encountered in traditional Acoli poetry. Lawino's comments on the style of independence politics have the same pungency as when she ranges over the familiar life of the village. Thus contemporary issues in modern East African life preoccupy all the monologuers, though they see them from different points of view.

We can sum up this discussion of the traditional and modern influences in p'Bitek's poetry with Mutiso's remarks [in his *Socio-Political Thought in African Literature,* 1974] which,

though about Lawino, also applies to the other Songs and to p'Bitek's art in general and reveals the type of controversy that a compartmentalisation of influences can cause:

> One of the most intriguing women in African literature is Lawino. .. Although p'Bitek has taken a traditional Acoli form, the praise song, and written an extended poem about Lawino's husband, Ocol, who is modern, the poem is not traditional since it is set in the present.

Mutiso agrees that p'Bitek's poetry has traditional form, but that because its content is contemporary, it is modern. This critic is clearly in the minority since most others conclude that because of its traditional form, p'Bitek is a traditional poet. We wish to observe that, often, **Song of Lawino** provides the basis for each conclusion, but an overall assessment of all his poems, including **Song of Ocol, Song of Prisoner,** and **Song of Malaya,** reveals that Lawino is the most traditional of all the personae in her protection of Acoli values. Prisoner, Ocol, and Malaya are products of the modern East African environment. Our interest, however, is not with only thematic influences but also formal influences, and as we have shown, such a discussion deserves utmost restraint. The influences under which a poet writes are often so complicated that they cannot be easily pinned down. These influences are not mutually exclusive, and without contradiction we may choose to label p'Bitek a traditional modern poet.

Charles Okumu (essay date Fall 1992)

SOURCE: "The Form of Okot p'Bitek's Poetry: Literary Borrowing from Acoli Oral Traditions," in *Research in African Literature,* Vol. 23, No. 3, Fall, 1992, pp. 53-66.

[*In the following essay, Okumu asserts that p'Bitek uses the traditional Acoli song in* Song of Lawino *to comment on "the social, political, religious, and economic situation in post-independence Uganda and by extension, in the entire Third World."*]

Acoli traditional culture is a living culture in which folklore contributes to the governing of society. Regularly performed before responsive audiences, Acoli folklore genres are as old as Acoli society itself, but they are also individual creations by means of which people fulfill their psychological needs. Over a period of time, these genres become imprinted on the society's collective consciousness, but each performance is unique in the sense that it takes place at a specific time and place. Highly specialized genres like oral songs are performed by adult professional singers who often accompany themselves on a musical instrument. The proverb is another specialized genre, and it is used by Acoli elders to give weight and authority to arguments, teachings or other forms of discourse.

The Acoli word for proverb is *carolok,* meaning that which

alludes to the real thing or to a fact. The allusive character of proverbs is of course not uniquely Acoli. Ruth Finnegan records similar findings and notes [in *Oral Literature in Africa,* 1970] that "the figurative quality of proverbs is especially striking: one of their most noticeable characteristics is their allusive wording, usually in metaphorical form. This also emerges in many of the native words translated as 'proverb'." As for other peoples, the allusive metaphor is a storehouse of wisdom and philosophy for the Acoli. The form of the proverb and its relative brevity help endow it with the poetic quality of rhythm. The Acoli proverb has two distinct structural units, the topic and comment, and they are often separated by a comma. This construction can be seen in the proverb that forms the basis of Lawino's argument against cultural alienation in Okot's *Song of Lawino "te okono, pe luputu"*—the pumpkin must not be uprooted.

A subgenre closely associated with the proverb is the simile, for which the Acoli term is *calo,* meaning that which looks like or resembles something else. Generally composed of a noun, adjective, preposition, and an article, the simile is defined by Clive Scott [in *A Dictionary of Modern Critical Terms,* 1973] as a "comparison, discoursive, tentative, in which the 'like' or 'as ... as' suggests, from the view point of reason, separateness of compared item. . . . Simile is usually a pointedly rationalised perception whose function is explanatory or illustrative." The simile, like the proverb, is used in ordinary conversation when the speaker wants to make a comparison between two related objects. Acoli similes tend to revolve around behavioral patterns, character, color, size, appearance, intelligence, the five senses, temptation, greed, etc.

Speakers' choices of proverbs and similes are entirely dependent on their creative imagination and their powers of speech. Great orators at clan, family, and chiefdom meetings use proverbs to lend credence to their contentions and they use similes to shorten what they would otherwise describe in detail. Similes enliven conversation and speech, for they often express admiration, abuse, disgust, and sympathy. For example, someone who is said to be "dull like a sheep" is not only being abused; he is also sympathized with. A girl whose neck is long and beautiful might be compared with a giraffe whereas one with a short neck is said to have a "neck like that of a beetle."

Similes are frequently used by poets who, as Scott points out, do not wish, for one reason or another, to use metaphors. For them, similes serve as "the repository for their inventive boldness" and play an "alleviatory role, letting air and whimsy into involved narrative or analysis. . . ." Okot adopts similes for this reason in his *Song of Lawino.* For example, Lawino's clinical and somewhat repugnant description of Tina is achieved through the use of similes. Her intention is clear: she wants to discredit Tina and to prevent her from competing for Ocol's love. Okot also uses similes to describe the

sordid night-club atmosphere which he is contrasting with the beauty of the Acoli Orak dance. If proverbs convey the social and moral norms that govern society, similes communicate the wit, irony, and humor that enliven social intercourse. Unlike proverbs, similes can be used by anyone who desires to employ a comparison to express succinctly what might otherwise require a long narrative description.

The Acoli term for the oral song is *wer.* The texts of these songs do not differ from those of written poetry; the distinction between them lies in the performance. An oral song is meant to be performed to a responsive audience on a particular occasion and for a specific purpose; often it is accompanied by one of several traditional musical instruments. The Acoli song genre is a complex form with sub-genres that are thematically substantive enough to warrant separate occasions for their performances. The sub-genres are intricately linked to the traditional dances from which some derive their generic names. To an Acoli, the generic name of each song indicates the dance during which it is performed and the type of musical instrument that accompanies it. Composer-singers create individual songs, but once they have given public performances, the songs gradually enter the cultural main stream of society. Other singers are then free to give their own renditions (or recreations) of the original songs. [In "Principles of Oral Transmission in Folk Culture," *Acta Ethnographica* (1959)] Gyula Ortutay describes this process as a "continuously changing course of alternate demolition and construction, with recurring intersections where new and transitional types, old and new themes are steadily interlaced, separated and reunited." Simply knowing the text of a song is as useless as knowing a proverb; one needs to know how it is used in context.

In the generic classification of Acoli songs, two factors must be considered: the theme and the dance during which they are performed. The five broad sub-genres that dominate this genre are: children's songs, historical songs, funeral songs, satirical songs, and spirit possession songs. A more detailed classification requires a breakdown of this board classification, and this is precisely what Okot did in his B.Lit thesis at Oxford and in his *Horn of My Love.* Because he listed love and war songs separately, his classification includes seven sub-genres: children's songs and games; love songs; satirical songs; songs of the spirit possession dance; songs of war; historical songs; and the dirges.

The oral literary features that Okot borrowed from Acoli traditional culture gave his poetry the distinctive oral song character that sets it apart from other written poetry. Nevertheless, Okot's songs can neither be sung nor fitted into the thematic classification of Acoli oral songs. Oral songs are composed in response to an immediate event or as a means of reflecting a localized issue within the village or clan. They are ephemeral, and their length is dictated by three factors: the creative ability of the composer-singer, the chosen theme, and the reaction of the audience. Other singers therefore have no obligation to perform the whole composition of any song. Modification of the original song gives it renewed life, and the audience's reaction depends on the quality of the performance.

In contrast, written poetry generally consists of fixed texts that have a certain number of lines per stanza. Its organization cannot be altered by anyone except the original poet. The images, symbols, and other literary qualities in it always remain the same, whereas the oral song can be modified to fit the specific performance situation. Once poetry has been written down, critics can only praise or blame the poet. For example, Okot's mother recognized a creative ability in her son, as Okot recounts during an interview with Bernth Lindfors [in *Mazungumso: Interviews with East African Writers, Publishers, Editors and Scholars,* 1980]:

> She went on and asked, "Is it a love song?" . . . "What kind of song is it?" So I said, "You shut up. Let me read it to you." . . . She was very pleased but kept on saying, "I wish there was some tune to it." You see, it was not really like Acoli song. . . .

Her positive critical appraisal encouraged Okot to imitate the oral poets to the best of his ability; in fact, his extensive borrowing of literary features from oral songs give his written poetry its songlike quality and its originality. These features include symbols, proverbs and similes. The common symbols in Okot's poetry are the spear, the pumpkin, the bull, and the cave. In Acoli traditional society, the spear is a weapon used for hunting and warfare. There are two types of spear: *kaba* and *alwiri.* The difference between them resides in the size of the metal blades and of the handles. *Alwiri* is the ideal weapon for hunting smaller animals and for daily use, whereas *kaba* is only brought out when hunters undertake a long hunting expedition (*dwar*) or when a buffalo or elephant has been sighted in the village. Every male adult has a *kaba* which has been ritually blessed and can only be used by him. It cannot be substituted for another, for the loss of the *kaba* is tantamount to losing one's manhood. In Acoli history, disregard for this sacred rule led to a split in the tribe—an event that was mythified in the story of Labongo and Gipir and later recorded by both Okot and Taban lo Liyong. Oral poets have euphemistically used the kaba in place of the penis. The man who has many wives and children is a man whose spear is sharp and strong. At the clan gathering, he commands respect; his advice is accepted and followed. However hardworking or handsome a man might be, if he is impotent or *lalur* (spearless) he has no place among the elders and will die *labot* (wifeless). A barren woman is also ostracized, and oral singers describe her as "the woman whose womb has been sucked by the leopard."

Okot's euphemistic use of the spear is a direct borrowing from Acoli oral poetry. In *Song of Lawino,* Lawino laments the

sexual starvation of the young men who go to the mission schools in search of foreign names. They, she says:

> Sleep alone
> Cold, like knives
> Without handles
> And the spear
> Of the lone hunters
> The trusted right-hand spears
> Of the young bulls
> Rust in the dewy cold
> Of the night.

The stanza is a direct borrowing and modification of the oral song **"Tong Raa"** in *Horn of My Love:*

> Bull of men, son of my father;
> The people have left the hippopotamus
> spear in the cold
> The hippopotamus spear has been
> eaten by rust.

This dirge is sung at the funeral rites of *Mukamoi,* the great warrior who had killed a man and a boy during a clan war. He is further described in the song as "bull of men." On a symbolic level, he will never use his spear again for procreation, while on a physical level, his rusty spear will be a permanent reminder of the great warrior that he once was. In his poem, Okot transforms the situation from the funeral dance to the cold church hall, which is analogous to the cold and lonely tomb. The written poem appeals directly to an audience which is expected to sympathize with the young bulls and to pass its own judgment on their keepers (the missionaries).

A direct contrast to the imposed sexual death of the young men is the fertility prayer at the ancestral shrine. The prayer is couched in explicitly sexual symbols. While blessing the spears, the old woman chants the traditional prayer, part of which Okot has combined with a Bwola dance song to produce the following stanza in *Song of Lawino:*

> She will spit blessing in their hands,
> So that their spears may be sharp,
> Sharp and hard
> So that their trusted spears
> Should not sleep outside
> But should strike the death spot
> Deep and painful
> Then the young cob
> Will scream

And shed tears of sweet pains.

The stanza is composed of borrowings from lines recorded in *Religion of the Central Luo.* From the Pa-Chua clan fertility prayer that was chanted at the annual feast of the Jok-Lalwak clan, Okot adapted these lines:

> The spears, let them be sharp
> Let them be sharp, sharp, sharp.

From the Bwola dance song performed on the same occasion, he took the following lines:

> The spear sleeps in the cold
> The spear I used to trust
> The spear sleeps in the cold oh!

At the end of her *Song,* Lawino asks Ocol to beg his ancestors, among other things, to restore his manhood so that he can once again consummate their marriage:

> Ask them to give you
> A new spear
> A new spear with a sharp and hard point
> A spear that will crack the rock
> One that does not bend easily
> Like the earth-worm
> Ask them to restore your manhood!
> For I am sick
> Of sharing a bed with a woman!

The image the poet wants to create is that of a socially and sexually powerful man and not the "ash" (impotent) man that Ocol has become. Commenting on the spear symbol, Laura Tanna states: "The image of the spear runs through the text of Lawino, enhancing aspects of physical beauty, stressing prowess in hunting and fighting and finally emerging as the dominant phallic symbol of the poem, a symbol against which Lawino measures Ocol and finds him lacking."

In interpreting the last three lines as Lawino's sexual frustration, Ali Mazrui attributes Ocol's temporary impotence with Lawino to his infatuation with Clementine and to his sexual relationship with her. Whatever caused Ocol's impotence, however, Lawino's position as his first wife is clear: if Ocol cannot consummate their marriage, it must come to an end. The explicit use of the spear and other sexual symbols prompted the Acoli Literary Committee to reject Okot's Acoli draft version of the poem in 1959. Nevertheless, the phallic

connotation of the spear actually derive from its importance in a society where sexual virility and male prowess are highly valued.

Other sexual symbols in the *Song of Lawino* include the hoe, the knife, and the battle-axe. For example, the fertile and rich land, symbolising Mother-Earth, is sexually assaulted by the gardener who comes with his hoe and plants his seeds, as Lawino says when she describes the process of creation:

> And when a gardener comes
> Carrying two bags of *live seeds*
> And a *good strong hoe*
> The rich red soil
> Swells with a new life.

The seeds must be live seeds, and the hoe must be strong not "like the earth-worms"; otherwise, procreation cannot take place. This is the predicament of impotent men whose spears:

> Refuse to stand
> Lazy spears
> That sleep on their bellies
> Like earth-worms.

The image of the crawling earth-worms reduces the impotent men to the lowest social status in a society where male virility is greatly admired.

Another oral literary feature that Okot borrowed from the Acoli tradition and creatively used in his poetry is the proverb—*carolok.* The structural form and allusive metaphor of the proverb appeal to oral compose-singers who easily weave it into songs without being obliged to make radical grammatical changes. J. H. Kwabena Nketia, a Ghanaian musicologist and folklorist, succinctly expresses the artist's feeling for the use of proverbs: "For the poet today or indeed for a speaker who is some sort of an artist in the use of words, the proverb is a model of compressed or forceful language. In addition to drawing on it for its words of wisdom, therefore, he takes interest in its verbal techniques as a method of statement. . ." ["Folklore in Ghara," *The Ghanaian Achimota* (1958)].

The composer singer does not have to use the proverb in its original form. He might paraphrase it to suit his poetic diction while retaining its metaphorical meaning. In his own poetry, Okot follows the same technique as the Acoli composer-singer. Unlike the Yugoslav oral poet in A. B. Lord's *The Singer of Tales,* he does not merely group the proverbs together to form an epigram, for his dramatic monologue technique requires him to paraphrase proverbs and to incorporate them into narrative fragments that fit the poetic diction of a particular stanza. For example, the proverb "Yat ka ogom, dong pe tire" (a tree that is bent cannot be straightened) is paraphrased as:

> A young tree that is bending
> They do not like to straighten.

In the traditional social context, an elder uses this proverb to criticize a child who fails to respond to the corrective measures of society. In Okot's poetic context, however, the same proverb is used to criticize the Catholic missionaries who fail to answer Lawino's deep searching questions about Catholic dogma pertaining to creation and to the Trinity.

The only proverb that Okot does not paraphrase is the central one in *Song of Lawino:* "Do not uproot the pumpkin." At the beginning of the poem, Lawino uses the proverb in an attempt to dissuade Ocol from his emulation of European customs. Her hope is that the proverb will add weight to her argument and open Ocol's eyes to the danger of cultural alienation:

> Listen, my husband,
> You are the son of a chief
> The pumpkin in the old homestead
> Must not be uprooted.

In the land of the Acoli, the pumpkin grows all year round and is therefore an important source of food and life. No sensible person would intentionally uproot a pumpkin because it symbolizes the continuity of Acoli traditional life as represented by Lawino. Okot is generally critical of the educated middle-class Acoli who embrace Western culture and technology, regardless of whether or not they are appropriate in the African environment. R. S. Anywar made the same criticism during the 1950s [in his *Acoli Kiker Megi,* 1953]:

> Perhaps some Acoli believe that all those things that the Europeans brought here are good. This is untrue because some of them are so dangerous that if you mishandle them they will cause you shame at the least and death at the most. So I suggest that before any new thing is accepted, it must be thoroughly examined. We should not forget our customs altogether simply because we are learning those of the Europeans.

Anywar and Okot are advocating the same set of values, and Elizabeth Knight clearly identifies it when she explains: "Okot calls not for the destruction of the village but a recreation of it incorporating modern technical advances, such as electricity but maintaining the basic values. . . ."

The parallel between the poet and the elder historian has been drawn to demonstrate that Okot's voice is not a solitary one and that he was not the only educated Acoli to recognize the danger inherent in the blind acceptance of an alien culture. Yet, **Song of Lawino** transcends the cultural conflict with which Anywar was concerned, for it includes the poet's critical appraisal of the new breed of politicians and their role in post-independence Uganda.

In **Song of Lawino,** Lawino tells us that Ocol's grandfather and father were Bulls among their people. When she is not driven to madness by Ocol's cultural insanity, she respectfully calls him "Son of the Bull." In fact, Ocol's cultural failure can best be measured against his illustrious father's social status as a war leader and Bull. Okot uses the proverb "Mac onywalo buru" (fire has begotten ashes) to highlight the contrast between father and son. Ashes are easily blown away by the wind just as the alienated Ocol has been blown away from Acoli traditional culture by foreign winds and from Lawino by Clementine. Lawino expresses her disappointment in Ocol in the rhetorical proverbial questions:

> Has the Fire produced Ash?
> Has the Bull died without a Head?

In contrast, Lawino's own leadership among her agemates earned her an honorary Bull name:

> My bull name is Eliya Alyeker
> I ate the name
> Of the chief of Payira
> Eliya Alyeker
> Son of Awic.

Typical of a proud Acoli woman, she sings her own praises in the fourth section of the poem, **"My Name Blew Like A Horn Among The Payira."** She also sings the Orak songs in which the composer-singer praises her beauty and her dancing ability. In another variant of the same song, the name changes, and she becomes the daughter of Lengamoi. Taking Acoli traditional society as a standard, Lawino has been more successful than Ocol, and we can understand his bitterness in a society where the man is suppsosed to be the "won gangowner of the home." Lawino's strong-headedness and her pride in her Acoli identity also bring about a confrontation with the Catholic missionaries and eventually lead to her rejection of Catholicism.

Besides his creative borrowing of literary features from Acoli traditional culture, Okot has blended the different modes of Acoli oral songs in the *Song of Lawino.* Satire dominates the early sections of the poem, which ends on a note of lament reminiscent of Acoli dirges. In the rest of the poem, Okot adopts the openly critical mode of the Bwola, Otole and Apiti dance songs in which singers discard their satirical masks and directly confront the people they are satirizing. This approach is particularly appropriate for his criticism of politicians and Catholic missionaries. Although Lawino sometimes sings her own praises, she returns to the lament at the end of her Song. She laments the "death" of Ocol on two levels: the loss of a husband who can no longer consummate their marriage and the loss of a "Son of the Chief" who can longer uphold his people's culture because he has assimilated Western values.

Okot's creative use of satire derives from his knowledge of Acoli satirical songs, which he classified in his thesis as songs of justice. These songs contain open criticisms of those who do not conform to social norms. Okot himself recognizes the wide range of subjects that can be satirized by the oral poet when he says, "Any act, behaviour or spoken, so long as it is a breach of, a divergence from the straight and narrow path of customs, is seized upon as a subject for these poems." In *Song of Lawino,* the traditional social norms provide a standard, and Lawino uses the poetic licence accorded to her by Okot to criticize anyone who departs from this standard. Ocol and Clementine are the principal targets of her satire but she herself does not escape completely unscathed, for she is the member of a community whose social norms she accepts and whose demands "she perceives as her own," but "she is also a Subject who has to conform to the society's norms without choice or perish" [Annemarie Heywood, "Modes of Freedom," *Journal of Commonwealth Literature* (1980)]. Ocol chose to perish rather than be a "Subject" of the traditional society, thereby subjecting himself to the alienation and cultural death that Lawino laments.

Besides his creative borrowing of literary features from Acoli traditional culture, Okot has blended the different modes of Acoli oral songs in the *Song of Lawino.*

—*Charles Okumu*

Lawino's attack on Ocol is two-pronged: she criticizes him as the husband who deserted her for another woman and as the non-conformist who refused to respect the social and cultural norms of her society. According to Lawino, Ocol deserted her because she was an uneducated traditionalist who was inappropriate for his new social status as a university graduate. Thus, she claims, "he has fallen in love" with Clementine, a modern girl whose "apemanship" equals his own; however, Lawino does not maintain this line of argument for long. She soon draws other members of her clan into the affair by telling them that Ocol's insults are directed against them:

> He says Black People are primitive
> And their ways are utterly harmful,
> Their dances are mortal sins
> They are ignorant, poor and diseased. . . .

Lo Liyong erroneously agrees with Ocol and dismisses Lawino as an uneducated village woman who cannot comprehend what Ocol says. In reality, Lawino's selective accounts of Ocol's abuses of her clansmen reflect back on the missionary teachings and prejudices that he absorbed from them. Whereas Lawino admits her limitations with regard to Western culture and technology, Ocol's exaggerated allegiance to the new culture leads him to dismiss traditional culture as irrelevant to modern society. But because he cannot gain full access to this modern society, he remains an alien in both cultures.

In the twelfth section of the *Song of Lawino,* Lawino destroys Ocol's pride by contemptuously describing his newly acquired house and life-style. The section is appropriately titled "My Husband's House is a Dark Forest of Books." Lawino argues that these books have destroyed the Africanness of the educated class and transformed them into mouthpieces for the colonizers' propaganda against Africans. She concludes:

> For all our young men
> Were finished in the forest
> Their manhood was finished
> In the classroom
> Their testicles
> Were smashed
> With large books. . . .

Okot himself describes the university graduate in the following terms: "At the end of the third year he dons his black gown and flat-topped cap. In his hand he carries the piece of paper they give him at graduation—the key to power, money and a big car. Over dressed in his dark suit he walks out of the University gate, out into the world materially comfortable, but culturally castrated, dead" [*Africa's Cultural Revolution*].

In Acoli society, the oral composer-singer wears many masks, just as he plays many different roles. The transition from satirical composition to open critism, reminiscent of the Bwola and Otole dance songs, is a subtle one in the *Song of Lawino.*

Like the composer-singer, the writer discards his mask and plays the role of an angry member of society who has been wronged by another individual or by those in power. His poetic outburst is direct, and it is intended to correct the wrong that has been done, as Okot himself points out: "I really hold that an artist should tease people, should prick needles into everybody so that they do not go to sleep and think everything is fine . . ." [Lee Nicholas, "Conversation with Okot p'Bitek," *Conversation with African Writers,* 1981]. In *Song of Lawino,* Lawino's needles are directed at middle-class, educated Africans who inherited the multi-party system introduced by their colonial masters as a way of sowing discord among Africans. Okot criticizes the politicians primarily because they are more concerned about their own stomachs than about the need to work together to eliminate the three scourges: poverty, disease, and ignorance. The masses never benefited from flag independence and whenever they confront the looters to demand their share of the national wealth, the Ocols of African society have a ready solution:

> Trespassers must be jailed
> For life
> Thieves and robbers
> Must be hanged.

In reality, the opposite is true: the politicians and their collaborators should be hanged for having wronged the masses.

Okot's criticism of Ugandan politicians for the disunity they fostered through their exploitation of the multi-party system cannot be dismissed as a personal vendetta or as an extension of the religious confrontation between Catholics and Protestants, as lo Liyong claims. In *The Acoli of Uganda,* F. K. Girling defines the smallest unit of Acoli society as the family, which joins with other families to form a clan, the most powerful social unit. Lawino laments the death of the family. When two bulls fight in the same kraal, the kraal will be destroyed, and, by implication, when two brothers fight, the family will die. Lawino reports that Ocol (D.P.) and his brother (U.P.C.) are deadly enemies who only share water from the same river:

> I am concerned
> About the well-being of our homestead!
> The women there wear mourning clothes
> The homestead is surely dead
> The enmity, the black-heartedness,
> The quarrels, the jealousies . . .
> When the fiends . . .
> Go through our homestead
> The people will be finished,
> This will be the gift
> That political parties have brought.

Okot's hope is that the pricking of his needles will awaken the politicians and other authorities to the truth about their own crimes.

Commenting on the role of the oral songs as a means of communicating dissatisfaction to those in authority, Finnegan says, "The indirect means of communicating with someone in power through the artistic medium of a song is a way by which the singers hope to influence while at the same time avoiding the open danger of speaking directly." However, in the case of written verse, the poet can neither be indirect nor switch his allegiance to new rulers as easily as can the oral poets.

In the thirteenth section of the poem, Lawino returns to the lament mode which she had used earlier when she was lamenting the death of family unity—a death that had been caused by the introduction of political parties. Her later lament is triggered by two deaths: the cultural death of Ocol and the death of their marriage. She herself feels powerless to halt the changes that have brought about the two deaths. She continues to love Ocol, as evidenced in her desperate attempt to rekindle whatever flame of love may yet be glowing in his heart.

Realizing that her tears are futile she nevertheless performs the traditional *nanga* dance, her final act before bowing out of the love contest between herself and Tina:

> Let me dance before you
> My love
> Let me show you
> The wealth in your house
> Ocol my husband
> Son of the bull
> Let no one uproot the pumpkin.

Her plea is similar to those that commonly appear in Acoli dirges that Okot has classified as "songs of the pathway" (*Horn of My Love*). In these songs, the singer knows that the person being mourned is dead yet there remains a lingering hope that it is not too late or that someone else and not the loved one might be dead. For example, in Ogwang Clipper's song, "Omel, the Great Swimmer," the singer asks:

> Was he (the swimmer) dreaming?
> Am I hearing the news through a dream?

According to Okot, disbelief is the dominant theme in "songs of the pathway" although the shock of the news must, in the end, be accepted by the disbeliever. In *Song of Lawino,* Lawino knows that her pleas cannot change the existing situation. On the cultural level, she is lamenting the "apemanship" which is the root of Ocol's alienation from the culture she represents. The polarization between them reflects the poet's conception of the difference between the two cultures.

While Lawino laments the death of Ocol as her husband and as an alienated modern man, he adopts an arrogant and dismissive attitude towards her and towards the culture she represents. His impatience is evident from what he says:

> Woman,
> Shut up!
> Pack your things
> Go!

This arrogance is characteristic of Ocol's modern attitudes. He is a social type, and [in "Okot p'Bitek, Literature and Cultural Revolution in East Africa," *Journal of African Studies* (1978)] Samuel Asein correctly points out that "p'Bitek's focus on Ocol as a type is a convenient poetic device which enables him to make a thrust at a whole generation of apemen and charlatans, insecure, self-centred politicians and other various institutions which grew in the blind acceptance of Western civilization." Yet Ocol's criticism of Lawino is also partly justified, for she is ignorant of modern politics and university culture, whereas Okot himself had always advocated a balance between African and Western cultures. The satirical and open critical modes that he adopted from Acoli oral traditions enabled him to comment on a broad range of Western assumptions about African culture. Against these assumptions, partly echoed by Western-educated, middle-class Africans, stands traditional African culture as presented by an integrated but uneducated Acoli woman.

The form of Okot's poetry is clearly derived from Acoli oral songs, which in many cases are inseparable from the dances during which they are performed. Viewed from this perspective, *Song of Lawino* falls into three overlapping parts. The satirical criticism in the first nine sections is directly related to the Orak dance songs that Okot classified in his B.Lit. thesis as songs of "poetic justice." In Section Eleven, the mode is that of the political and topical songs that accompany the Bwola, Otole, and Apiti dances. The composer-singers of these songs do not wear the satirical masks of the Orak composer-singers, for their criticisms are collectively expressed by the participants in the dances; therefore, the lead singer cannot be held responsible for criticisms embedded in collectively performed songs. Sections Twelve and Thirteen are characterized by a mixture of modes, but the dominant one is that of lament. Lawino's attempt to dissuade Ocol has failed, and he has therefore died a cultural death. Their marriage has also ended, and her lament echoes the form and themes of an Acoli dirge.

Okot's poetic style is essentially vocal rather than visual; in fact, it is less concerned with the formal pattern on the written page than with breath. The mixture of humor, satire, and lament in *Song of Lawino* reflect Acoli oral poetic forms, which are interwoven with proverbs, similes, metaphors, symbols, and other figures of speech to constitute a powerful personal commentary on the social, political, religious, and economic situation in post-independence Uganda and by extension, in the entire Third World.

FURTHER READING

Bibliography

Ofuani, Ogo A. "Okot p'Bitek: A Checklist of Works and Criticism." *Research in African Literature* 16, No. 3 (Fall 1985): 370-83.
> Presents a brief bibliography of works on p'Bitek.

Criticism

Gathungu, Maina. "Okot p'Bitek: Writer, Singer or Culturizer?" In *Standpoints on African Literature: A Critical Anthology,* edited by Chris L. Wanjala, pp. 52-61. Nairobi: East African Literature Bureau, 1973.
> Discusses point of view in p'Bitek's poetry. Using biographical information, Gathungu attempts to determine if any of the characters or beliefs p'Bitek describes in his writing represent his own beliefs.

Mbughuni, P. "A Grain of Wheat, Song of Lawino, Song of Ocol, and Kongi's Harvest." *UMMA* 5, No. 1 (1975): 64-74.
> Analyzes the literary treatment of political values in East African literature. Mbughuni uses *A Grain of Wheat, Song of Lawino, Song of Ocol,* and *Kongi's Harvest* to discuss the ideals and reality of politics and literature.

Ogunyemi, C.O. "In Praise of Things Black: Langston Hughes and Okot p'Bitek." *Contemporary Poetry* 4, No. 1 (1981): 19-39.
> Discusses how Langston Hughes and p'Bitek have helped to demythicize the image of the black man through their poetry.

"Unfettered, Unfree." *The Times Literary Supplement,* No. 3390 (16 February 1967): 125.
> Praises the sharpness of imagery in p'Bitek's *Song of Lawino.*

wa Thiong'o, Ngugi (James Ngugi). "Okot p'Bitek and Writing in East Africa." In *Homecoming: Essays on African and Caribbean Literature, Culture and Politics,* pp. 67-77. London: Heinemann, 1972.
> Presents an overview of East African literature. Wa Thiong'o discusses p'Bitek's *Song of Lawino* in terms of its place in East African literature.

Ward, Michael R. "Okot p'Bitek and the Rise of East African Writing." In *A Celebration of Black and African Writing,* edited by Bruce King and Kolawole Ogungbesan, pp. 217-31. Oxford: Oxford University Press, 1975.

> Discusses the emergence of East African literature after independence. Ward asserts that p'Bitek's poetry displays a strong sense of East African identity.

Weinstein, Mark. "The Song of Solomon and *Song of Lawino*." *World Literature Written in English* 26, No. 2 (Autumn 1986): 243-44.

> Asserts that "The Song of Solomon" was a source for *Song of Lawino* and analyzes aspects of love poetry found in p'Bitek's work.

Interviews

Serumaga, Robert. "Okot p'Bitek." In *African Writers Talking,* edited by Cosmo Pieterse and Dennis Duerden, pp. 149-55. New York: Africana Publishing Corporation, February, 1967.

> Serumaga and p'Bitek discuss the Uganda National Theatre and its place in Ugandan culture.

Additional coverage of p'Bitek's life and career is contained in the following sources published by Gale Research: *Black Literature Criticism, Black Writers,* **Vol. 2;** *Contemporary Authors,* **Vols. 107, 124;** *Dictionary of Literary Biography,* **Vol. 125;** *DISCovering Authors Modules;* **and** *Major 20th-Century Writers.*

Caryl Phillips
1958-

English novelist, playwright, and essayist.

INTRODUCTION

Phillips is perhaps better known today for his novels, particularly *Cambridge* (1991) and *Crossing the River* (1993), than for his plays, which have been produced for the stage, television, radio, and cinema. In both his drama and awarding-winning fiction, Phillips consistently has related the experiences of the African diaspora in the Caribbean, Europe, and America; his works offer a historical and an international perspective on the themes of immigration (forced and otherwise), cultural and social displacement, and nostalgia for an elusive "home" that often exists in mythical proportions in the minds of his characters. Yet Phillips adamantly has refused the label "black" writer. In the preface to his play *The Shelter* (1983), he said: "In Africa I was not black. In Africa I was a writer. In Europe I am black. In Europe I am a black writer. If the missionaries wish to play the game along these lines then I do not wish to be an honorary white."

Biographical Information

Born March 13, 1958, in St. Kitts, West Indies, Phillips was brought to England when he was only twelve weeks old. He was raised in Leeds and attended The Queen's College, Oxford, from which he received a B.A. with honors in 1979. Phillips's first stage play, *Strange Fruit,* was produced in 1980, followed by *Where There Is Darkness* (1982) and *The Shelter.* He then pursued other media for his dramatic productions. In 1984 he produced the radio play *The Wasted Years,* which was published in *Best Radio Plays of 1984,* and the television plays *The Hope and the Glory* and *The Record.* In 1985 Phillips was awarded the Malcolm X Prize for his first novel, *The Final Passage,* which encouraged him to write another novel, *A State of Independence* (1986), and a collection of three novellas, *Higher Ground* (1986). Upon returning from a European tour during 1986, he wrote *The European Tribe* (1987), a collection of travel essays for which he received the Martin Luther King Memorial Prize. With the publication of his third novel, *Cambridge* (1991), Phillips was recognized by the London *Sunday Times* as "Young Writer of the Year" in 1992 and was listed among *GRANTA'*s "Best of Young British Novelists" of 1993. His latest novel, *Crossing the River* (1993), was nominated for the respected Booker Prize. Phillips was appointed writer-in-residence at Mysore, India, in 1987 and at Stockholm University, Sweden, in 1989. Since 1990 he has been Visiting Professor of English at Amherst College in Massachusetts.

Major Works

The dominant theme in most of Phillips's works is the human displacement and dislocation associated with the migratory experience of blacks in both England and America. His first plays explore the lives of West Indian immigrants pulled between England and their Caribbean homeland; his later dramas focus on historical situations concerning the African slave trade in America and England. Much of Phillips's fiction expands the issues presented in his plays. For instance, *The Final Passage* tells of a West Indian family who gain passage to England during the 1950s, while *A State of Independence* relates the return of a man who had left his native island twenty years earlier for an Oxford scholarship. *Cambridge* juxtaposes the journal of Emily, a nineteenth-century English woman living at her father's West Indian plantation, with the story of Cambridge, an educated slave there; it reflects the situation portrayed in the play *The Shelter*, in which a white widow and a freed slave are shipwrecked on a desert island at the end of the eighteenth century. *Crossing the River*, like Phillips's radio play of the same name, addresses the human cost of the African slave trade, but the novel is narrated by several voices, including a father who sold his children, a slave-ship captain, and an English shopgirl who loves an African-American soldier stationed in England during World War II. *Higher Ground* voices the separate tales of an African operative in the slave trade, an African-American convict during the 1960s, and Irene, a Jewish Pole exiled in London after World War II. Notable among the travel essays in *The European Tribe* are studies of the Shakespearean characters Othello and Shylock, made while the author was in Venice, and reminiscences of a dinner party with James Baldwin and Miles Davis in France.

Critical Reception

Critics almost universally acclaimed Phillips's first novel, *The Final Passage*, which revealed to David Montrose the author's "clear potential as a novelist." But detractors began to appear with the release of *A State of Independence*. According to Adewale Maja-Pearce, the novel suffers from "appalling prose style and indifferent characterisation." *Higher Ground* generated confusion about whether the individual stories were meant to be linked thematically; nonetheless, Charles P. Sarvan called it "a moving and disturbing book." The racial theme in *The European Tribe* made this work "too important a book to be ignored," in the opinion of Charles R. Johnson, but most critics concurred with Merle Rubin, who found the collection "significant but uneven." Phillips reached a considerably larger audience with the publication of *Cambridge*, "a masterfully sustained, exquisitely crafted novel," according to Maya Jaggi. Following the appearance of this work, certain commentators noted Phillips's adept handling of female voices in his fiction, while others detected an undercurrent of pessimism in his novelistic vision. Recently, scholars have started exploring Phillips's texts within the context of postcolonial literary theory. Many critics found significance in the "multi-voiced chorus" of *Crossing the River*; as John Brenkman indicated, "the global awareness of the [black] diaspora has stimulated a writer like Caryl Phillips to find the languages and the stories in which [our] complex fates can be told."

PRINCIPAL WORKS

Strange Fruit (drama) 1980
Where There Is Darkness (drama) 1982
The Shelter (drama) 1983
The Hope and the Glory (television screenplay) 1984
The Record (television screenplay) 1984
The Wasted Years (broadcast drama) 1984
The Final Passage (novel) 1985
Lost in Music (television screenplay) 1985
Crossing the River (broadcast drama) 1986
*Higher Ground (novellas) 1986
Playing Away (screenplay) 1986
A State of Independence (novel) 1986
The European Tribe (travel essays) 1987

The Prince of Africa (broadcast drama) 1987
Cambridge (novel) 1991
Writing Fiction (broadcast drama) 1991
Crossing the River (novel) 1993

*Comprises the novellas "Heartland," "The Cargo Rap," and "Higher Ground."

CRITICISM

Hugh Barnes (review date 7 March 1985)

SOURCE: "Return of the Native," in *London Review of Books*, Vol. 7, No. 4, March 7, 1985, pp. 20-21.

[*In the following excerpt, Barnes discusses the myth of re-settlement in* The Final Passage, *concluding that Phillips "only partially illuminates its theme."*]

Homesickness is fabulous magic. Even as the world shrinks and the epic edge is blunted, the resettlement myth persists. Ulyssean travelogues are few and far between in Caryl Phillips's *The Final Passage* and the novels of Paule Marshall, but families uproot themselves. Their stories correspond, but not in time or place. Phillips's travellers leave their small Caribbean island for Britain in the 1950s, when prospects were cheery. The white folks of the West had never had it so good: too good, or so their masters told them, to settle at menial labours. Since the publication of her first novel, *Brown Girl, Brownstones,* in 1959, Paule Marshall has been weaving a delicate history of the Barbadians who emigrated to America earlier in the century. Stepping off the boats, though not all were so fortunate, the wayfarers arrived in their new homes with nothing to declare but memories and aspirations.

The West Indians who alighted at Southampton and Bristol, wives in cotton dresses, husbands in demob suits and trilbies, were items of unfinished history, dredged up from the bottom of the sea of progress. Perhaps their experience has still not been assimilated. It is appropriate that *The Final Passage* opens at the seafront with the exiles-to-be waiting for the SS *Winston Churchill* to drop anchor. The peanut vendor offers comfort to the greedy. Leila and her baby son Calvin are waiting not only for embarkation orders but also for a third passenger whose valedictory boozing has left him worse for wear. Phillips ruptures the time-scheme of his novel, leading us back from impending departure into the events of the previous year. Michael is an unprepossessing family man. He takes what he likes and abuses the rest, which is sometimes his wife. When her pregnancy entered its advanced stages, she became useless, no longer pleasurable, and he left her for the consolations of his mistress. Nevertheless, for all his shortcomings, he emerges as the avatar of his companions' forebodings: 'Leaving this place going to make me feel old, you know, like leaving the safety of your family to go live with strangers.' Leila would say he was a fine one to talk of his family and its safeties. Phillips's thesis is straightforward and unassuming. *The Final Passage* chronicles loss, not acquisition. The opening section which unveils this small beginning is ominously entitled 'The End'.

Leila is unimpressed by the amenity of Baytown and environs, which she interprets as stasis: 'this small proud island, overburdened with vegetation and complacency'. And not much else, apart from dreams of excellence at sex or cricket or calypso. Bordered by mountains that contain the heat, the island sprawls in dust, its inhabitants for the most part listless and contented. Politics and anger surface intermittently, but they seem to belong to the older generation always, to Leila's mother, who scolds her for loitering with white tourists, or to Michael's grandfather, who tries in vain to prepare him for the ways of the world: 'Too much laughing is bad for the coloured man, too much sadness is bad for the coloured man, but too much hating is the baddest of them all and can destroy a coloured man for true.' Michael listens doubtfully, taking little of it in. His determination to reach England is founded on fantastic rumours about white women, for whose sake he is cultivating a Ronald Coleman moustache. Alphonse Waters tells him it's 'a stupid and bad crazy world' across the sea. Secretly this is what he hopes. During the sea voyage, the men assemble on deck and exchange boastful ignorance, gleaned from random studies of *The History of the English-Speaking Peoples* and the *Encyclopedia Britannica*. There's an industrial revolution raging in England, that much they are agreed on, but who's leading it, and against whom, remain mysteries. Phillips neatly captures the harsh reality of the promised land, its smugness and its outlook of permanent grey, booms and recessions notwithstanding. The notices outside guest-houses and cafés are manifestly hostile, and the faces on the advertising hoardings stare down reprovingly at the strangers. The family move out of a communal slum into a slum of their own, which they cannot pay for. Michael's periods of silence draw out and last for days at a time. Seldom at home, when he is he trains his surliness like a weapon, or returns in the early hours for drunken assaults on his wife and for vomiting. After one particularly ugly ordeal, and dispiriting inquiries from the social work department, Leila abandons Michael and his adopted country for the sufferable hardships of home. Perhaps this is the novel's bleakest moment: it is also one of affirmative self-discovery which unites Leila with the heroines of Paule Marshall's novels. Selina Boyce in *Brown Girl, Brownstones* leaves Brooklyn for Barbados, where her father had inherited a plot of land. And Avey Johnson in *Praisesong for the Widow* digs deep into her past, and that of her ancestors in South Carolina, to replenish it and make it usable. *The Final Passage* is a small story by comparison, and only partially illuminates its theme. There is sadness certainly, and defeat. But as Christmas comes to London, Leila's hopes are exhausted and also just beginning.

David Montrose (review date 8 March 1985)

SOURCE: "Out and Back," in *Times Literary Supplement,* No. 4275, March 8, 1985, p. 266.

[*In the following review, Montrose finds little to fault in* The Final Passage, *noting that Phillips "has clear potential as a novelist."*]

Caryl Phillips's first novel [*The Final Passage*] opens in 1958, with its young black heroine, Leila Preston, queuing on a Caribbean dockside. Along with Michael, her husband of twelve months, and her baby son, she is about to leave the unnamed island of her birth for England. As the voyage begins, a long flashback retails the events which brought her to seek "a new start after the pain of the last year".

The cause of that pain has been Leila's ill-advised marriage. Michael is unreliable, selfish, a drunk and a layabout; a noted philanderer, too. While courting Leila, indeed, he continued his long-standing affair with Beverley, the wife of a man working in America. Michael is the father of her child. Leila knew all this, but accepted him nevertheless, jilting the steady Arthur—also in America, studying—and alienating her invalid mother, who emigrated to England soon afterwards. Obviously, Leila found Michael the more exciting suitor, but an impatience to change her life was a factor as well; it would have been another two years before Arthur qualified and they could marry. Michael has inflicted heartache from their wedding day onwards. After a quarrel at the reception, he walked out and spent the next two nights at Beverley's. Returning, he passed a fortnight with Leila—during which she conceived—then took up with Beverley once again. Leila had already decided to follow her mother when he reappeared, spurned by Beverley, promising to accompany her, to "make it work".

But the new start proves to be a resumption of the old pain. Leila's mother is in hospital, terminally ill; Michael quickly reverts to his familiar ways and virtually fades from the scene (though not before making Leila pregnant a second time). England itself administers further hurts. The weather is unkind even in summer, the people are largely indifferent or hostile. Walls carry racist slogans, landlords' signs stipulate "No coloureds". Finally, her mother now dead, with Christmas icily approaching, Leila determines to return without Michael to her homeland. This resolution is preceded by the symbolic burning of "the objects and garments that reminded her of her five months in England". The novel ends, as it opens, with Leila on the verge of a fresh beginning. Her prospects of serenity remain uncertain, but the outlook at least seems promising.

Despite some shortcomings—notably a rather jumbled structure—*The Final Passage* shows that Phillips, hitherto known as a play-wright, has clear potential as a novelist. The characterization of Leila is a trifle flat, but Michael is admirably portrayed, especially when rationalizing his behaviour. In addition, the author sustains an atmosphere of emotional adversity without ever allowing the book to degenerate into soap opera. (He proves, however, less adept when the gloom lifts: little comes across of the misplaced hope with which Leila contemplates marriage and emigration.) Phillips left his native St Kitts as a baby in 1958; Leila's experience of England is that undergone by many of his parents' generation. One looks forward to a novel drawing on his own past.

Adewale Maja-Pearce (review date February 1986)

SOURCE: "Like a River in Summer," in *Books and Bookmen*, No. 364, February, 1986, pp. 35-36.

[*In the following review, Maja-Pearce pans* A State of Independence, *faulting its "appalling prose style and indifferent characterisation."*]

For some time now writing by 'black' authors has been extremely fashionable. We know this because last year the Greater London Council, giving its seal of approval to current fashion, instituted a number of annual awards exclusively for young 'black' writers. It was a case of never mind the quality, feel the ethnicity. The most lucrative of these prizes, the GLC Malcolm X Prize, was awarded to Caryl Phillips, once upon a time from the West Indian island of St Kitts, for his novel *The Final Passage*. It wasn't a good novel, but who cared? The organisers had been able to pat their little black brother on the head. Now Caryl Phillips has published a second novel, *A State of Independence*. It is as bad as the first and for much the same reasons: an appalling prose style and indifferent characterisation.

The novel opens with the hero, Bertram Francis, returning to the Caribbean island of his birth after a 20-year absence in England. Entering the village in which he had been born and brought up, he is arrested by the following sight: 'Underneath (the) houses played the children and fowls, while the sun-blackened adults tended to the sporadic yam or cassava plants that speckled the yard. Above them towered the stubborn breadfruit trees, pregnant with food, and together with the thick rubbery banana leaves, the wispier leaves of the palm, and the blazing red of the hibiscus, they created a spectacle of foliage through which only the sharpest spokes of light could penetrate.' I'm not quite sure what a 'sun-blackened adult' is, though one must assume that he doesn't mean an adult who was once white. Nor would I have described plants as 'sporadic', however few and far between; in any case, to say that they 'speckled the yard' conjures up the image of small spots or stains, however pleasingly alliterative. Meanwhile the breadfruit trees are made to carry a heavy load: 'stubborn' and 'pregnant' at the same time, like wilful teenage daughters who didn't listen to their mothers. Nothing can be simple or straightforward: the banana leaves must

be 'thick and rubbery' and the hibiscus must be 'blazing red'. This is typical of the level of the prose which, when not buried under the weight of so many adjectives, is deadened by clichés: 'The gate still hung drunkenly from its hinges'; 'Their letters to each other, though never frequent, seemed to have dried up like a river in summer'. Caryl Phillips is obsessed with similes. Nothing can be left to stand on its own. Matters are made worse when he attempts to be original: 'The houses . . . were wooden shacks painted all colours, as though a rainbow had bent down and licked some life into the place'; 'The stillness of the sea in the foreground looked . . . like a mirror set ablaze'. And where he isn't straining for effect the writing is simply bad. People are forever 'peeling' themselves off the sand, 'draping' their arms around each other, 'threading' their way through bars, 'folding' into embraces or over counters, 'winding' themselves round doors. It is all very unconvincing, as unconvincing as the story itself.

Bertram Francis has returned to his island with the idea of perhaps opening a small business and settling down to look after his elderly mother. To this end he seeks out his childhood friend, Jackson Clayton, now a politician and wealthy businessman. But Jackson's business consists of being the local representative of foreign capital. For this reason he is hostile to people like Bertram who want to develop indigenous industries, on however small a scale. Their relationship is further complicated by a long-standing feud over a woman, Patsy, whom Bertram had been on the verge of marrying before he won the scholarship which took him away. This left the way open for Jackson, who has a brief affair with her, but it comes to nothing. Patsy has only ever loved Bertram, and when he returns she is conveniently waiting for him. Bertram discovers this after his final showdown with Jackson, and the novel ends with him back in Patsy's bed. The characters themselves are all crudely drawn. Patsy in particular is a cliché of the woman as symbol for the country which finally embraces our returning hero. Apparently she didn't have anything better to do in the meantime. If she has any inner life the author does not suggest so. But then none of the characters do. All Bertram can remember of England is the fog, which seemed to him 'like a grey-white blanket that would rip as easily as water, yet it was as thick as solidified milk'.

There is even reason to think that such an appalling novel would never have been published if it had been written by a 'white' author, despite the publishers' assurance that Caryl Phillips, in his second novel, 'has given us yet another deftly drawn study of the Caribbean predicament'.

Richard Eder (review date 6 July 1986)

SOURCE: A review of *A State of Independence*, in *Los Angeles Times Book Review*, July 6, 1986, p. 3.

[*In the following review, Eder finds "a singular freshness" in Phillips's characters in* A State of Independence.]

From the time he lands in St. Kitts, the Caribbean island he left 20 years earlier for a scholarship in Britain, Bertram Francis is assaulted by the heat.

He feels it at every moment and in every movement—this native, returned from what was to have been a brilliant future but turned out to be two decades of improvisation in London's West Indian slums.

Now it is independence eve in St. Kitts. Bertram is back, not as the successful lawyer and future judge that scholarship boys hoped to become in the old days of the Queen, but with a little money and vague hopes of finding a place.

But he sweats all the time. He changes his clothes continually, pulling them out of the two English suitcases that take up half the floor space in his mother's hut on the outskirts of the capital. His antiperspirant is flooded out.

It is the sign of a larger estrangement. In Caryl Phillips' acrid and touching novel [*A State of Independence*], the message is both: "You can't go home again" and "You have nowhere else to go." Independence is a party, and a shift of the colonial axis from Britain to the United States. What remains on these Caribbean microdots is a bleak constant.

There is nowhere to seek a fortune, neither at home nor abroad. There is no frontier, or big city; merely a cramped economy with dying sugar mills, a few luxury hotels for the tourists, shadowy administrative facilities made available to shadowy foreign businessmen, and the women in print dresses who sit all morning in a dead marketplace with their tiny piles of wares.

It is a somber message, but *A State of Independence* is far from a somber book. For the most part, Bertram's adventures in attempting a return that resists him are told with dry comedy. Phillips, who comes from St. Kitts and lives in London, adorns a harsh judgment with the gentlest of lampoons. It is calypso, if you like: a moral played out with a lilting absence of moralism.

Bertram left St. Kitts under a halo, having won the prize examination at his village school. The examination scene, told in flashback, is a wondrously colonial affair. A dozen papers arrive in a sealed packet from London; three hours later, a dozen futures are mailed to London to be judged and returned.

Even as he sits there writing, Bertram is visibly set apart from his best friend, Jackson Clayton, who is affable, a prize cricket-player and an indifferent student. And when he wins and goes off, it is clear that nothing will ever be the same between him and his friend.

Nothing *is* the same, and it is the book's hinge. Studying law in London was simply the token pigeonhole provided for

blacks from the islands. If it meant a job once, when the empire was in bloom, it means very little now that the empire has withered. Bertram drifts off from his studies; Clayton, on the other hand, uses his cricket and his affability to make connections, go into politics and flourish.

And so, Bertram comes home counting on his friend, now deputy prime minister as well as minister of agriculture, lands, housing, labor and tourism. But things are not that simple. Bertram is an ebullient miscalculation bobbing in a sea of frigid calculations.

Times have changed, as Clayton makes brutally clear when Bertram finally manages to see him in his lavish office. Surely, Bertram ventures, his London background and his connections will let him "make a contribution" in the new St. Kitts.

London counts for nothing, Clayton tells him. St. Kitts' metropolis is Miami now, along with the money and deals that trickle down from it. As for connections, he intimates with considerable pleasure; none of the deals are for Bertram. There are not, after all, that many to go around.

And there is the old resentment. Bertram's old girlfriend, Patsy, explains it to him. She had favored him over Clayton in the pre-scholarship days.

"I don't see why that can't just fall into the past now. What is done is done," Bertram protests. This is too simple; the author is setting him up for Patsy's reply. But the reply is worth it.

"You really feel so?" said Patsy. "Nothing in this place ever truly falls into the past. It's all here in the present, for we're too small a country to have a past."

Patsy, aging, disillusioned yet welcoming in her skeptical way, provides a lot of the book's life. Neither the theme, the story nor the relationships are particularly new; and toward the end, matters become decidedly forced.

But for much of the time, Phillips provides a singular freshness through the delicacy with which he handles his characters and their feelings. There is an intriguing balance of intimacy and distance. It is as if, as he introduces us to them, he were introducing himself to them as well.

Ashok Bery (review date 10 April 1987)

SOURCE: "Sudden Departures," in *Times Literary Supplement,* No. 4384, April 10, 1987, p. 396.

[*Below, Bery calls* The European Tribe *"an uneven, thin-textured book."*]

Caryl Phillips's novel *A State of Independence* deals with

the dilemma of a man who goes back to the Caribbean after twenty years in England, only to find his assumption that he would be able to settle easily into life on his native island shaken by his experiences. Phillips, who left St Kitts at the age of twelve weeks, also made a journey back, but, as he explains in the introduction to *The European Tribe,* "still felt like a transplanted tree that had failed to take root in foreign soil". He travelled around Europe for nearly a year in an attempt to understand the forces that had helped to shape him; this book comes out of that period.

Phillips finds that "there is one story and one story only": the reality of the racism he sees almost everywhere in Europe. During his travels he encounters responses ranging from insufferable self-satisfaction to outright hostility; his account is rounded off by a polemical conclusion which explores the consequences of European colonialism and angrily attacks the continent for its bigotry and its deficient sense of history.

There are plenty of things to be angry about, incidents of a sort that can be paralleled in the lives of many black people, and Phillips describes some of them powerfully; Norwegian customs officials single him out for interrogation at Oslo airport; a London publishing house editor refers to him as a "jungle bunny". Europe, he concludes, is indivisible, united in its exclusive attitude towards blacks. The anger is real and abundantly justified, but it also seems to shut him off from some of his experiences.

There is a compulsive, driven quality about his actions which he never explicitly acknowledges. Like the Ancient Mariner, Phillips is always leaving places and people, hurriedly passing from land to land, from city to city, sometimes for obvious reasons, sometimes impelled by more obscure urges. After seeing *Rocky II* in a Casablanca cinema (though why he should want to do this in Casablanca remains a mystery), he is so disgusted that he has to leave Morocco. The vulgarity of Torremolinos repels him; there are sudden departures from Dresden and Frankfrut; and a meeting with a drunk, unhappy Trinidadian woman in Tromsö—where Phillips has gone to test his "own sense of negritude", expecting to be the only black person around—is summarily ended when she invites him home.

> **There are plenty of things to be angry about, incidents of a sort that can be paralleled in the lives of many black people, and Phillips describes some of them powerfully.**
>
> —*Ashok Bery*

This kind of abruptness is a symptom of a wider failure: he

engages only intermittently with the people he meets, the countries he passes through, and even with himself. The impression is reinforced by an odd mixture of materials: personal encounters are encased in a doughy mass of statistics, routine descriptions and elementary historical, geographical or social information. Much of the book exudes dutifulness. Spain, for example, is described in lame guidebook fashion as

> a beautiful and large country, second only to the Soviet Union in Europe. Of all its disparate parts Andalucía is probably the best known, the most often written about, and the most romantic. The climate is good, food and drink cheap, so it has always attracted writers. . . .

Later, an account of Dresden-Neustadt railway station is snuffed out by a copywriter's cliché: "The atmosphere was bleak, haunting, and strangely beautiful."

The result is an uneven, thin-textured book, with the second-hand material continually interposing itself between Phillips and his experiences. It could have been different: in his final paragraph, he describes himself standing on the Rialto, unmoved by the culture of which Venice is a symbol, excluded from a Europe which denies part of its history, the part he represents. It is an eloquent image, worth much of the hackneyed description which he has felt obliged to include.

Andrea Lee (review date 9 August 1987)

SOURCE: "Into the White Continent," in *New York Times Book Review,* August 9, 1987, p. 7.

[*In the following review, Lee suggests that the essays in* The European Tribe *are too brief for "sustained analysis" since Phillips's focus is too broad.*]

Part travelogue, part *cri de coeur,* [*The European Tribe,* a] short book of essays, records a year-long odyssey through the multiracial Europe of the 1980's. Caryl Phillips, a young British novelist of African-Caribbean descent, seems ideally suited to explore themes of national and racial identity, exile and cultural disorientation. An Oxford graduate who grew up in white working-class London feeling like "a transplanted tree that had failed to take root in foreign soil," Mr. Phillips embarked on a voyage of self-discovery after a trip back to the Caribbean had convinced him that, willy-nilly, he belonged, at least culturally, to Europe. "I knew," he writes in his introduction, "I would have to explore the European Academy that had shaped my mind. A large part of finding out who I was, and what I was doing here, would inevitably mean having to understand the Europeans."

Mr. Phillips chose a fascinating and topical subject. Present-day Europe percolates with third world influences, and is home to an expanding population of non-whites, born and educated in Britain or on the Continent, who are now struggling to define their relationship to societies that only half accept them. The riots in Brixton and Birmingham are one manifestation of the struggle; new voices raised by-young writers like Mr. Phillips are another. The subject is also curiously elusive. Any discussion of race and nationality touches both irrational emotion and hard social and economic fact. A satisfying approach could be either scholarly or subjective and impressionistic. Mr. Phillips takes neither, which is the chief weakness of *The European Tribe*. Although in a preface he describes the book as nonacademic, a notebook based on personal experience, his brief essays—which are not long enough for any sustained analysis of the countries they address—break with disconcerting frequency into a simplistic didacticism, offering information and figures more appropriate to a magazine article.

What educated reader, of the type likely to be attracted to this book, needs a description, for example, of Anne Frank's diary? Or to be told that there is a housing shortage in the Soviet Union? Throughout these pieces, which, for Mr. Phillips's purposes, need to be quirky and perceptive, banal travel writing obfuscates more important themes. Rarely is there a sense of focus. Moreover, one does not feel that Mr. Phillips has attempted much objective penetration into the national mood of the countries he visits. One of the unintentional ironies of the book is that alongside the author's justifiably scathing condemnation of European racism are included offensive national stereotypes. "East Germans," he writes, passing through Berlin, "love saluting." His final essay, an emotional indictment of Europe for its mistreatment of minorities, suffers from the same irony; the central image of a homogeneous, colonizing "European tribe" seems only a pointless answering of prejudice with prejudice.

Mr. Phillips is a born observer and writer, and when he abandons rhetoric he creates disturbingly powerful images of the cultural, collision between black and white. There is the drunken Trinidadian woman, displaced and desperate, whom Mr. Phillips meets in Tromso, Norway, 200 miles inside the Arctic Circle; the Irish archbishop reminiscing nostalgically about missionary work among the Ibo; the deadend stylishness of African street people in Paris, with their Oxford bags and Burberry coats; James Baldwin and Miles Davis laughing late at night behind the isolating walls of Mr. Baldwin's estate in St.- paul-de-Vence. These and other images convey the disorientation and anguish of minorities in Europe far better than anything that Mr. Phillips can explain. For the American reader, the territory he charts in *The European Tribe* is new and important; had he narrowed his focus, the result, paradoxically, would have covered more ground.

Merle Rubin (review date 19 August 1987)

SOURCE: "Racial Undertones in European Attitudes," in *The*

Christian Science Monitor, Vol. 79, No. 186, August 19, 1987, p. 22.

[*In the following review, Rubin determines that* The European Tribe *"is a significant book, but an uneven one."*]

"As a first-generation migrant, I came to Britain at the portable age of 12 weeks; I grew up riddled with the cultural confusions of being black and British," writes Caryl Phillips. Born in St. Kitts in the West Indies, Phillips spent his formative years in England, living in predominantly white, working-class neighborhoods while attending predominantly white, middle-class schools. Until meeting up with a defiantly black American fellow student at Oxford, so he tells us, he had little idea that a black person might become a writer or that blacks have a long history worthy of study.

In truth, it may be said, young Phillips had almost exactly the same uninformed view of black people as that held by the vast majority of the white "European tribe." The chief difference—though a crucial one—was that where his white neighbors, teachers, classmates, and colleagues saw him at best as a kind of blank, a white man *manqué,* Phillips felt that sense of void within himself.

A trip to America helped inspire him to become a writer. (He has written two novels and several plays in addition to this book.) A trip to his Caribbean birthplace brought him insights about his "roots," but could not explain the cultural forces that had shaped his development. As a product of Europe, Phillips decided to undertake a journey, starting from Casablanca, with stops in Spain, France, Venice, Amsterdam, Belfast, Dublin, Germany, Poland, Norway, and Moscow, in order to explore the culture that seemed at once to have nurtured and rejected him.

The European Tribe is a significant book, but an uneven one. Some parts are thin. Of Casablanca, Phillips has little more to say than that its very real poverty is nothing like the glamorous image dreamed up by Hollywood. In Gibraltar, he is predictably snide about the self-consciousness "Britishness" of this last outpost of empire. Visiting the novelist James Baldwin in the south of France, he tactfully retreats when jazz musician Miles Davis arrives, so as to leave the two old friends alone, which may have been nice for them, but is, to say the least, disappointing for the reader.

Here, and elsewhere throughout [*The European Tribe*], Phillips traces parallels between anti-Semitism and anti-black attitudes.

—Merle Rubin

Describing what he sees, writing at times off the top of his head because he wants to keep this book impressionistic, Phillips is occasionally inaccurate, often naive, and always highly impressionable. Yet, he also has the capacity for making sustained judgments, for putting things in perspective, and for pinpointing the dangerous trends building up throughout a continent whose white "tribe" feels inundated by floods of immigrants from Africa, Asia, the Middle East, and the West Indies.

In France, he takes note of the National Front slogan "2 million immigrants—2 million unemployed." In Amsterdam, at the Anne Frank House, a room documenting the history of fascism contains a photo of a 1924 banner in Berlin: "500,000 unemployed. 400,000 Jews. Solution very simple. National Socialism."

Recoiling from neofascism in Western Europe, Phillips finds no comfort in the East. In Moscow, he finds the official artwork as chilling as the weather and is deeply distressed by the plight of a *refusednik* family. A Polish writer in Warsaw indicates that there are "benefits in being a victim of Western imperialism that those in the Eastern bloc could only dream about."

At Auschwitz, he finds the sheer number of killings beyond comprehension: "At least the Atlantic slave trade had some vestige of logic, however unpalatable. Auschwitz transcended the imagination." Back in England, however, a member of the educated, liberal class dismisses Phillips's reference to the 11 million Africans forced into slavery as "bloody ridiculous."

In Venice, that most scenic of settings, Phillips achieves a striking—and poignant—effect by looking inward instead of outward. Rather than admire the wealth of culture all around him, he ponders the fates of two who were outsiders, aliens in Venice: Shylock and Othello. One is a Jew, scorned by Christian society; the other a black who "makes it" in white society only to discover that he is alone and isolated in a world whose signals he does not know how to interpret.

Here, and elsewhere throughout the book, Phillips traces parallels between anti-Semitism and anti-black attitudes. He rightly resents the fact that in his educational experience, the oppression of colonialism and the scandal of slavery received no attention on television or in text-books.

Brought up in a Europe still sensitive to the Holocaust, he was, however, able to identify with the plight of the Jews. His sense of parallels between the two groups does not blind him to the differences in their situations. But, to his credit perhaps, he remains at a loss to account for the virulent strain of anti-Semitism among some American blacks, beyond echoing the far-from-adequate "explanation" that inner-city blacks felt exploited by Jewish shopkeepers.

The impression one gains from reading this book is that European blacks have only begun in recent decades to face the kinds of prejudice and antipathy that American blacks have known for hundreds of years. Phillips writes calmly, succinctly, at considerable pains not to exaggerate, but alarms go off throughout his European journey and throughout this book, which, for all its flaws, sounds an important warning, a call for a sea change in attitudes that is well worth heeding.

Adam Lively (review date 2-8 June 1989)

SOURCE: "After Slavery," in *Times Literary Supplement,* No. 4496, June 2-8, 1989, p. 619.

[*In the following review, Lively complains that the theme of oppression in* Higher Ground *"sticks out too much."*]

One of the most damaging ways in which to draw and quarter a novel is by plucking out "themes". And conversely, one of the most dangerous traps that a writer can dig and jump into is to take an overly conceptual approach, imposing an idea on the imagination rather than letting it breed there. Something like this may have been the case with Caryl Phillips's *Higher Ground*. He describes it—in what sounds more like an apology than a subtitle—as "a novel in three parts", and in a sense the problem with the book is not that the parts lack connection, but that the connection is too transparent. The "theme" sticks out too much.

This theme is the long history of racial exploitation and oppression that has followed in the wake of the Atlantic slave trade. The first part is set on the West African coast some time in the eighteenth century; the second in a jail in the American South in the 1960s; and the third in London in the late 1950s, where the backlash against post-war immigration is beginning to be felt. The intention, clearly, is to illustrate this dreadful history from a variety of perspectives, each carefully chosen. The last part, for example, is written from the point of view of a Jewess who escaped as a child from Poland just before the Second World War. Here, Phillips is making a connection between the unhappiness and sense of dislocation felt by West Indian immigrants and that felt by other "alien" groups. To make his point absolutely plain, he steers Irina, the Polish woman, towards a lonely one-night stand with Louis, who is about to return in disgust to the Caribbean.

If the overall plan of the book is a little cut-and-dried, much of the writing in the first two parts is powerful and gripping. The opening piece, **"Heartland"**, is a particularly impressive single sweep of narrative, a tale told by a collaborator, an African who acts as an interpreter and general stooge for the British slave traders. It is a vivid evocation of historical time and place, getting inside the web of force and moral corruption through which the business was pursued. Whereas **"Heartland"** owes its immediacy to strength of visual imagination, the second part, **"Cargo Rap,"** is notable for the way it catches and holds up for examination a particular voice—that of the 1960s Black Power movement. The voice—authentic in its puritanical authoritarianism and forthright sexism—is heard in the letters that one Rudi Williams writes from jail, explaining Black history and politics to his family and berating them for their Uncle Tom tendencies. But having set up this character and his situation so brilliantly, Phillips seems unsure what to do with them, and the story slides into bathos. This descent continues in the last part, where the grim emotions tend to lack context and clarity.

The history of the African diaspora is an enormous and complex subject—exploring it could consume an entire creative life. In the first two parts of **Higher Ground,** Caryl Phillips does get inside that complexity, but it was perhaps a mistake to give the impression that he was trying to wrap the whole subject up in one book.

Barbara Smith (review date 24 September 1989)

SOURCE: "The Past Has Fled," in *New York Times Book Review,* September 24, 1989, p. 7.

[*In the following review, Smith laments the lack of "a vision of transformation" in* Higher Ground.]

Caryl Phillips's novel **Higher Ground** recounts a tragically familiar tale three times over. Through his subtle portraits of an African go-between for British slave traders in the 1080's, an African-American prisoner during the late 1960's and a Jewish woman from Poland exiled in London following World War II, Mr. Phillips—the author of **The European Tribe** and two previous novels—creates a complex chronicle of oppression. The focus is not on the politics of those who have used racial, religious and sexual differences as a rationale for hatred and injustice, but instead upon the internal impact of oppression, especially its numbing effect on the individual spirit.

The unnamed narrator of the novel's first section, **"Heartland,"** has been taught English in order to assist the slave traders and has thus avoided being sold. He is expected to act as an interpreter for the Europeans, not only of languages, but of behavior and customs. The whites' objective, of course, is not to communicate with the Africans, but to learn just enough to dominate them, to carry out the trade as safely and efficiently as possible.

Although his position is filled with contradictions, the go-between does not dwell on these, but sees himself as a person caught by events over which he has no control. His emotional and physical survival hinges upon his capacity to obliterate his former life, to forget the very meaning of freedom and what it was to be a respected member of the community he now helps to exploit. He thinks: "I am grateful, and would

thank the Gods (if there were any to thank) that I have finally mastered this art of forgetting—of murdering the memory."

> **Rudi's stark assessment of this country's racial battleground is as applicable to the late 1980's as it is to the late 1960's and "Cargo Rap" contains the novel's most explicitly political writing.**
>
> *—Barbara Smith*

This "murdering of memory"—the destruction of the past and of history—is one of the novel's major themes. For people who are in bondage, the ability to forget may make it possible to survive the terror of the present, but it also undermines the vital core of self.

When the go-between falls in love with a young African woman, whom he originally helped to bring to the fort for the use of one of the brutal officers, his relationship to his past and present alters. Inspired by the woman's courage and independence of spirit, he finds a reason to risk his fragile security. When their relationship is discovered, the two are separated and shackled for shipment to the New World. Just before the ship sails, the go-between begins a chant that his fellow captives join, despite their different languages. He explains that "we are all saying the same thing; we are all promising to one day return."

Despite this dream of freedom, the African's final statement is one of absolute despair: "My present has finally fractured; the past has fled over the horizon and out of sight."

Rudi Williams, the protagonist of **"Cargo Rap,"** the novel's longest section, keeps the dream of African return alive. Centuries later this descendant of slaves and victim of modern-day racism imagines going back to Africa, a place the has never seen. As a black man in a Southern prison, his current reality is intolerable. Logically, he draws sustenance from the possibility of freedom in the future, as well as from the legacy of black political struggle in the past.

The section is composed entirely of letters written by Rudi to his family and to members of his defense committee. Mr. Phillips convincingly captures the voice of a self-educated prisoner—both its incisive originality and its occasional awkwardness. The character's tenacity and faith come through, but so do his arrogance and insensitivity. For example, he constantly plays his parents off against each other, depending on which one of them has most recently offended his revolutionary sensibilities.

Rudi's stark assessment of this country's racial battleground is as applicable to the late 1980's as it is to the late 1960's, and **"Cargo Rap"** contains the novel's most explicitly political writing. The limitations of his hard-line black nationalism become glaringly apparent, however, in the realm of sexual politics. He is a firm believer in male dominance and a supporter of the double standard. When Laverne, his teenage sister, becomes pregnant, he castigates her and cuts off all communication. The fact that he fathered a child, with another teenager nine years earlier does nothing to mitigate his wrath.

In a moment of rare humility, Rudi admits his emotional limitations: "Dr. King used the phrase as the title of one of his books: 'Strength to Love.' I have not the strength. I do not even have the strength to be kind."

But love and kindness may not be particularly useful in the hell that Rudi inhabits. Like the African go-between, he adopts the psychological stance most likely to assure his survival. His haunting last letter to his mother indicates that his captors may have succeeded in breaking his mind and body, but not his spirit. Like his African ancestors, he vows in the end to "return to you a whole, honorable, and clean man. Hold on."

In **"Higher Ground,"** the novel's final section, the theme of forcible separation from one's past is fully crystallized. Although Irina is neither a slave nor a prisoner, she is nevertheless bound. She has survived the Nazi Holocaust because her father managed to send her from Poland to England on a children's transport. Although his decision saved her physical life, the loss of her family has destroyed her sanity. After 10 years in a hospital, she is having trouble living on her own. No matter where she is, she cannot rid herself of her past, nor of her longing for the father, mother and sister she will never see again: "Today was Papa's birthday and Irene began to cry. She could not spend another winter in England staunching memories like blood from a punched nose. She could not afford a memory-haemorrhage, but to not remember hurt." Irina can neither forget her past nor return to the physical place where it occurred. Insanity is a perfectly plausible response to the magnitude of this loss.

The only character in the entire novel who actually gets to return home is a West Indian man whom Irina meets, fleetingly, hours before he leaves London for the Caribbean: "He was going home, for he knew that it was better to return as the defeated traveller than be praised as the absent hero and live a life of spiritual poverty. . . . Louis was going home to where his short, but presently experienced, nightmare would eventually distil down into rum stories of the past. This way he could keep the faith."

Each of the novel's three protagonists tries to keep the faith all of them ultimately fall prey to the bigotry and forced dislocation of the society they inhabit. Perhaps because Caryl Phillips has chosen to depict their struggles in such extreme isolation, the novel conveys an unsettling pessimism about the possibility of freedom for the dispossessed. Oppression and the violence it spawns have destroyed many, but by no means all. The most compelling art about oppression has inherent in it a vision of transformation, a vision that is missing from *Higher Ground*.

Charles P. Sarvan and Hasan Marhama (essay date Winter 1991)

SOURCE: "The Fictional Works of Caryl Phillips: An Introduction," in *World Literature Today*, Vol. 65, No. 1, Winter, 1991, pp. 35-40.

[*In the following essay, Sarvan and Marhama examine the representation of historical violence and its consequences in* The Final Passage, A State of Independence, *and* Higher Ground.]

Caryl Phillips was born in St. Kitts in 1958 and was brought by his parents to England in that year. He grew up in Leeds, studied at the University of Oxford, but returned recently to St. Kitts and the Caribbean. (Of course, there are no real returns but always and only onward journeys.) He has traveled extensively in the United States and Europe and has visited Africa.

The Final Passage (winner of the Malcolm X Prize) is the story of Leila, who comes to England, bringing her husband Michael (more burden than baggage) and infant son Calvin. Left alone by her unfaithful husband, living without hope or happiness in slum conditions, she decides to return to her little Caribbean island. However, by this time Leila has suffered a breakdown, is unemployed, and one wonders if she will be able to give the decision practical, financial expression. It is not that Britain has opened her eyes to previously overlooked positive aspects of her island home; return is merely the lesser of two unattractive alternatives. The author, who himself was taken to England as a baby and who as an adult has made the journey back, writes about "the West Indian wave of immigration" into Britain, the so-called mother country, in the 1960s. Through Leila we gain an inkling of understanding as to why people left the Caribbean and what life was like for those immigrants in Britain, where at that time it was legal and normal to display signs that read, "No coloureds [or 'blacks']. No dogs." (Wole Soyinka records his experiences in the satiric poem "Telephone Conversation.") The novel thus has wider dimensions—of a historical, economic, and cultural nature.

In 1962 V. S. Naipaul published a collection of essays titled *The Middle Passage*. The phrase "the middle passage" comes down from the days of slavery. The "first passage" was when a ship left England for Africa, carrying baubles, cheap industrial products that were bartered for slaves. Then began the dreadful "middle passage," to the American and Caribbean plantations, during which voyage many died and were thrown overboard. (It is estimated that as many as twenty million Africans were abducted from the continent.) The survivors were sold at auction; with the money realized, raw materials were purchased to feed the voracious industrial machines back home, and the ship began "the final passage," so much the richer for the "enterprise." Leila wishes to make her final passage black to the Caribbean, although, as already indicated, she may end up marooned and captive for the rest of her life: a different form of life imprisonment from that experienced by Rudy in **Higher Ground** (more on this later). On the other hand, the first section of the novel bears the subtitle "The End," describing Leila's departure from the Caribbean: the end may also be the beginning of a return after all. Her mother, dying in a London hospital, says, "London is not my home. . . . And I don't want you to forget that either." Naipaul, in *The Middle Passage,* observes with detachment the subdued, bewildered immigrants herding onto the ship for England. Phillips presents us with the case of one out of those anonymous thousands, one from the historical statistics.

In the same collection of essays Naipaul describes St. Kitts as "an overpopulated island of sixty-eight square miles, producing a little sea-island cotton, having trouble to sell its sugar, and no longer growing the tobacco, the first crop of the settlers. . . . We were . . . watching the lights of the toy capital where people took themselves seriously enough to drive cars from one point to another." He records his nightmare, "that I was back in tropical Trinidad," a land indifferent to virtue as well as to vice. History, he argues, is built around achievement and creation, and nothing was created in the West Indies. (The epigraph of **The Final Passage** is from Eliot: "A people without history / Is not redeemed from time.") Slavery has bred self-contempt, and the "West Indian, more than most, needs writers to tell him who he is and where he stands." Phillips undertakes a telling, and absence becomes the essence of the novel: absence of history and achievement, of scope in the present and hope for the future.

The second and longer section of the work is "Home." Michael's grandfather uses a metaphor to convey the island's cultural hybrid: yams from Africa, mangoes from India, and coconuts from the Pacific. The men almost miraculously find money to go drinking day and night, but it is not a glorious riot, a Bacchanalian celebration of life, but rather a drinking through boredom and hopelessness to a state of stupor. The island is a place where the sound of a motorcycle starting up is a sufficient event to attract adult spectators: "There's nothing here for me to do, nothing! . . . Nothing, man!" Michael falls back on physical vanity: great care is taken over the length of his shirt sleeves and trousers; the motorcycle gives him the illusion of power, and he possesses the "freedom" that is a total denial of responsibility. In sleep, with pose and posturing set aside, his tired face crumbles like a bride collapsing into rubble. He gets drunk on his wedding day and spends

the night with Beverley, by whom he already has a son. As Leila's pregnancy advances, he moves into Beverley's shack and sees the baby for the first time when it is six weeks old.

In order to escape from the life in which she was trapped, Leila decides to emigrate to England. Michael's preparation for the challenges of this new life is to wonder whether or not to grow a moustache. Leila does all the packing; Michael drinks—and almost misses the ship. Leila's beauty, discipline, and determination attract Michael, but he feels inferior and, as a consequence, resentful. He has no understanding of himself, of the forces that have shaped him and account for his circumstances and behavior. He is an unthinking victim: his situation is all vague and confused but, nevertheless, real and damaging. His grandfather had advised, "You must hate enough, and you must be angry enough to get just what you want," but disgruntled, destructive Michael is not clear about what he wants, much less how to set about getting it.

Unqualified, unskilled, and unprepared, Michael and Leila move into a depressed part of London, initially to a boardinghouse, where men sleep "head to toe" for want of space. The house they later rent is squalid.

> Two of the upstairs window panes were broken in, and the door looked like it had been put together from the remains of a dozen forgotten doors. . . .
>
> The light switch did not work. The house was dark and smelled of neglect. . . .
>
> Upstairs there was a solitary bedroom. A soiled double mattress lay prostrate in the middle of an otherwise naked floor. . . . The small bathroom consisted of a toilet bowl and a wash basin. . . . There was no bath, and the door to this room hung from its hinges.

Michael's reaction is to walk out (escape), saying he expected to find the house in better shape on his return. Whether describing scene, house, character, or conduct, the narrator impassively, "factually" gives us the details.

> Michael forced his hand down between her legs and prised them open. Then he hauled himself on top of her, unable to take any of the weight himself. . . . But it was no good. He leaned over and vomited beside her head, catching the edge of the pillow and running back some of the vomit into her hair. Then, having emptied his stomach for the third time, he lay unconscious and draped across her. . . . She looked at the side of his head and waited until morning came. . . .

Leila had booked passage on a ship, but a passage is also a path, an initiation, as in Forster's *Passage to India.* Having learned, she would rather retrace her steps and come to terms with life back home: there she has a friend who loves and understands her. Her experience is one that was shared by many: "home" is a plantation economy in dilapidation, with an imported population (the descendants of slaves and indentured laborers) without history or hope. Attempting to fashion a more meaningful life, they leave their stagnant societies and come to Britain, only to find that she can be as cruel as the heartless stepmother in fairy tales. Lacking education, training, and (especially the men) inner resources, encountering racial prejudice, reduced to mean employment, and restricted to certain areas for accommodation, they neither find nor are able to create opportunities. Since individuals like Michael are unaware of the impersonal forces that have damaged their lives, they continue the pattern: irresponsible, violent, fantasizing, trying to find temporary escape from a reality they do not comprehend and cannot combat. It is the reader who reaches an understanding.

The title of Phillips's second novel, *A State of Independence,* recalls Naipaul's *In a Free State.* Bertram Francis returns to his Caribbean home (having lived the last twenty years in Britain) three days before the country gains its independence. The island has turquoise coral and green forests, but outside the capital the houses are small fragile boxes with roofs of corrugated-iron sheets: "People seem just as poor as they always been" (*sic*). In the naïve rhymes there are shades of Naipaul's perception of Caribbean politics: "Forward ever— backward never"; "Proud, Dignified and Black / None Can Take my Freedom Back!" There is a touch of satire in the doctor and the funeral director's joint ownership of a rum distillery, in the fire-brigade station's catching fire and burning down. And, as in most of what is hopefully called the "developing" world, there is exploitation: "Our finest minds . . . who all been overseas [*sic*] . . . are so bored with how easy it is to make money off the back of the people that they are getting drunk for kicks and betting on who can lap up the most sewage water from the gutter."

Much of this is embodied in Jackson Clayton, once a close friend of and almost a brother to Bertram and now deputy prime minister as well as minister of agriculture, lands, housing, labor, *and* tourism. Among the things Clayton proudly claims to have done for his country is the bringing in of the luxury liner *Queen Elizabeth II* (with her affluent tourists), Pan American Airlines, and Hollywood films. In short, this man who once referred to himself as Jackson X, following the example of the radical Malcolm X, is a representative of Western capitalism rather than of the island's people. Made calloused and smug by wealth and power, Jackson now advocates closer ties with the United States, not because of a rejection of Britain and her imperial past but because the United States is commercially more promising to him. (Jackson imports Japanese cars via the U.S.) Independence means that, in addition to economic "clout," complete political power will now pass into such hands. To the people, celebrating independence is a patriotic excuse to drink more and longer

than usual. It is an inefficient, poor, and polluted island, "And what is the response from the people with the money? The Rotary Club decide to donate a dustbin to every village. . . . As a people we come like prostitutes." The people are not angry, not even cynical, but only apathetic. (Cynicism implies understanding.) Enter Bertram Francis.

Francis went on a scholarship to England but, after two years, was asked to leave college. Thereafter he drifted: "My time just slide away from me . . . there's plenty more just like me. . . . People who went there for five years, then one morning they wake up with grey hair and wonder what happened." Bertram returns with guilt and apprehension, after an absence of two decades. The airport runway is his welcome carpet, but otherwise, to adapt the words of Christopher Okigbo, he was the sole witness of his homecoming. It is not that Bertram has been away so long; it is not that he slacked in his studies and returns with nothing to show for all those years, but that during his absence he did not write to anyone—not to his mother, his brother Dominic, his girlfriend Patsy, or his friend Clayton—much less send the odd bit of money to his long and silently struggling mother. Bertram returns unaware that his brother, who had become an alcoholic, was killed by a hit-and-run driver. This failure in human relationships, and the obligations which go with them, is paralleled by our misgivings about his political stance.

Bertram returns because the country is about to become free. He did not help in the hunt and, in fact, showed no interest in it, but has come to see if he can get a share of the meat. He seems to think that the mere fact of his having lived in Europe is qualification enough, something that makes him superior. An obnoxious Clayton demands, "What do you have to offer us? What is it about yourself that you think might be of some benefit to our young country?" All he has is a vague notion of setting up a commercial venture that will not depend on the white man. It is significant that he wants to "seize the opportunity" by going into business: he does not think of a cooperative project, or rural development, or of education, but only of making money for himself. Neither in personal relationships nor in public matters is he any different from Clayton, and his sense of moral superiority is baseless. Most of the time between arrival and independence (three days later) he spends drinking bottle after bottle of beer. The positive characters are the minor ones (and all female): Bertram's mother; Mrs. Sutton, who, though old herself and having no obligation to do so, cares for Bertram's mother; and Patsy, who loves, forgives, is quietly cheerful, and takes back the failed and directionless man.

Bertram has lived "in a free state," one without commitment and duties, but now accepts his "mediocrity," resumes his relationship with Patsy, and begins to wonder what he can do for his bedridden mother. (Perhaps nineteen-year-old Livingstone is his son.) As Bertram moves away from his selfish, sterile "freedom," the country is moving into *its* state of independence under the likes of the Honourable Jackson Clayton. Are the rains which disrupt the celebrations inauspicious or a sign of fertility and promise? A similar enigma is also faced at the end of Ngugi wa Thion o's novel *A Grain of Wheat.*

Higher Ground, subtitled "A Novel in Three Parts," consists of three stories. The first, **"Heartland,"** is told by a "collaborationist" (an anachronistic term), an African who assists in the slave trade: "It is moments such as these . . . marooned between [the European traders and the enslaved Africans] . . . that the magnitude of my fall strikes me." Circumstances have distorted the narrator—"If survival is a crime then I am guilty"—and there is a diminution of human feelings to the point of extinction. Because **"Heartland"** is a first-person narrative, the reader is situated within the consciousness of this man, and contradictory impulses result: between identification and sympathy, on the one hand, and recoil on the other. The reader must constantly remind her- or himself of the appalling wretchedness the slave trade inflicted, of the terror and misery. The brutality is heightened by the neutral tone of the narrator: "In the corner trading equipment is temporarily stored: whips, flails, yokes, branding-irons, metal masks." Women are kept separate because they often attempt, mercifully, to take the lives of their children. The European slavers, who equate literacy, technological (military) superiority, and fine clothes with "civilization," are barbarous in conduct, often perverted and sadistic; but the African chiefs are also guilty of selling their own for baubles and beer.

This holocaust is little remembered because it was visited upon "natives" long ago, at a time when that graphic recorder of human cruelty, the camera, had not yet been invented. In the end the narrator resists and is himself transported to the United States as a slave. Beyond degradation, there is regeneration and moral recovery. He decides to feign ignorance of English, for competence in the language is a liability and has led to his being a tool in the exploitation of his own people. Caliban ostensibly forgoes Prospero's language yet is subversive in that he writes his memoir in it, using the language of the slave masters to indict them, to return, if not to his home across the ocean, then to himself: "We are promising ourselves that we will return to our people. . . . And the promise comes from deep inside of our souls."

"Heartland" is told throughout in the present tense, which accords with the narrator's determination to keep the past alive and thus to "return" to it, yet it is more a memoir than a diary. As with that earlier African novel, *Houseboy,* apart from literary conventions and a willing suspension of disbelief, the impact is such that we do not query how the narrator, given his circumstances, contrived to write, and preserve, his testimony.

Prisons have sometimes proved to be places of education, reflection, writing. At random, one thinks of Pandit Nehru of

India and, from more recent times, of Kenya's Ngugi and Nigeria's Soyinka. The letters that constitute **"The Cargo Rap"** (the longest and the most central of the three stories) are the direct descendants of the prison letters of George Jackson, published in 1970 as *Soledad Brother.* In 1960, at the age of eighteen, Jackson was misadvised to plead guilty to a charge of robbery and was sentenced to an indeterminate prison term of one year to life. In Soledad Prison he was accused of the murder of a white prison guard and transferred to San Quentin, pending trial. He was killed there on 21 August 1971 in circumstances that have never been satisfactorily explained. "Rudy," who writes the letters of **"The Cargo Rap,"** is very similar to Jackson. He did not enter prison because of a politically motivated act, and his consciousness developed while he was in prison. As Jackson wrote, "I have almost arrived but look at the cost."

Both Jackson and the fictional Rudy arrive at an understanding of society and what it has done to them, but too late. Indeed, because of their awareness, consequent stance, and political influence, the system does not release them. Jackson's letters were to his parents, whom he loved (but about whose limitations—their mental shackles and timidity—he remained bitter and upbraiding); to his younger brother (shot dead while attempting to free him); to his lawyer Fay and to Angela Davis, the black activist. Rudy, also serving a "one year to life" sentence for robbery, writes to his parents, his sister, and two female lawyers. However, unlike in Jackson's case, finally it is not Rudy's life but his sanity that is killed. In style too, the letters—in one instance real, in the other fictional—are similar, for Jackson's correspondence ranges from sardonic, terse, and witty to impassioned protests of tremendous rhetorical power. Jackson belongs to history, however, and what is interesting in **"The Cargo Rap"** is the fictional Rudy: the processes by which character is created, the character himself, and his perceptions. Unlike *Soledad Brother: The Prison Letters of George Jackson,* **"The Cargo Rap"** must provide its own context, its own external data, necessary for an understanding of the fictional present.

The narrator of **"Heartland"** lived inside a fort, a stockade; Rudolph Leroy Williams is in prison, and prison becomes the metaphor for an unfree society and for captive lives: "It is only logical that two hundred years of exposure to the idea of a 'natural' (*inferior*) position should have nappied your mind," Rudy writes to his mother. His teacher had told him that he had talent and could, one day, become a clerk: "He did not mention doctor, lawyer, judge, professor, or nuclear physicist. . . . He wanted me to make peace with my mediocrity." Black Americans are released from the womb "only into the greater captivity of American society," and prison brutality is but a reflection of that brutality which is present in society. Rudy describes himself as follows: "Name: Homo Africanus; Occupation: Survivor; Age: 200-300 years; Parents: Africans captured and made slaves; Education: American school of life." The reader wonders whether this survivor will survive.

Will he succeed in being moved from solitary confinement to the main block? Will he win parole? "In the bosom of this country there is a man who is being stretched and tortured for forty dollars."

Rudy's passing references to a broken arm, a concussion, and to spitting blood indicate that the letters do not tell everything; this is an epistolary story, and the letters are all we have to go by: "I am once again down here on Max Row. I apologize to you for the disappointment that this will no doubt cause you." What happened? Why is he back in the "maximum" (solitary) wing of the prison? His struggles are protracted, and there are increasing signs of irrationality. Don't let mother work so hard and physically, he writes, without confronting the reality that the family needs the money, that his mother cannot find other work. Has his sister lost her virginity? Can he pay his lawyers with fruit from Africa, once he is released and "returns" to that continent? And, writing to his father, he asks whether the latter still derives sexual pleasure from sleeping with Mother or whether he masturbates. Rudy's last letter, poignantly, is addressed to his mother, whose death a month earlier represented the proverbial final nail.

Since there is no narrator other than himself and the replies he receives are not included, Rudy is characterized solely through his letters. These can be direct, with a conversational casualness: "Come a Saturday night Mr Charlie likes nothing better than to go out and crack a coon [black man] or two." Rudy educated himself politically, relying on books, and the language of these works enters his vocabulary with incongruous effects, so that in writing to his family we have "I'll amplify upon this in my next communication. . . . She is being malprogrammed in a hostile and alien culture." He uses words and phrases such as "peruse" or "your senescent body" and pellucid disquisitions, but he can be succinct: "For half an hour each day, I breathe fresh, if not free, air." Life in prison is like being inside not a boxing ring but the boxing glove itself: one passively and helplessly encounters pain. Rudy uses irony ("I tried to liberate some money"), puns ("We are trying to make the white Americans change their attitudes but are we getting any change [results]?"), and paradox ("I sit here in the darkness of constant light")—the last phrase also possessing biblical overtones of a people who sat in darkness and then saw a great light. He can be warm and persuasive, as when writing to his mother—"You describe yourself as an invalid. . . . In-valid. . . . You are a very valid part of our world"—or sardonic and bitter: "In the mornings, grandfather would get up, take down his cap and jacket, hang up his dignity and his mind, and slope out to slave and giggle for the white man." He can rise to tremendous verbal power, reminiscent of protest and revivalist rhetoric: "Do you want mustard for your hot dog, flowers for your hair or bullets for your gun?"; "Hang in or hang up." Black women in prison are there "for whoring, not warring." The black man needs "your support, not your scorn. . . . I am a literal and metaphorical

prisoner, Moma. I need you to stand by me, not sit on me." His perceptions and his power point to potential, and thus to the waste.

Rejecting the society in which he is a prisoner, Rudy turns (in order to fill the void) to the original home of his people, to Africa and to a "Negro Zionism": "Is this America, the civilized country of satellites and color television? . . . We must flee and burn bridges behind us as we leave. . . . The dice are loaded, the terms are unacceptable, the American odds too long." It is here that the setting (in terms of time) throws a cruel irony on Rudy: his (fictional) letters were written between January 1967 and August 1968; *Higher Ground* was published in 1989, and, seen from the perspective of the latter date, Rudy's vision of Africa is undercut and mocked. His heroes are Lumumba, Nyerere, and Kenyatta; he wishes to visit Egypt and Ethiopia, and then settle in Ghana. Patrice Lumumba of the Congo was killed before he could implement his policies, but Nyerere's long experiment with village socialism led Tanzania to economic ruin; indirectly admitting his mistakes and failure, he resigned from office. Jomo Kenyatta "hijacked" the Kenyan revolution and created an exploitative society, with his family and supporters being the beneficiaries—the structures Ngugi condemns and opposes. Egypt has grave economic difficulties; so does Ghana, which has the added bane of military coups and violence. As for Ethiopia, it is now associated with extreme poverty, mass starvation, and the attempt to raise money through international music concerts. These are Rudy's ideal leaders and countries: the irony is gained by placing the story two decades back in time. Events and developments of the seventies and eighties subvert and mock Rudy, even as we are moved by his predicament and words, and leave the reader to make her or his own way out: a disturbed character, and a work that is disturbing in more ways than one.

The third story, **"Higher Ground,"** begins with the narrator telling us that Irene did this, Irene did that, Irene, Irene, Irene. It is winter and the trees are naked; when they put on their clothes, so will Irene. We move from an outer observation of Irene to what she thinks and feels, and we realize that she has passed beyond what is termed normality. A headache is an iron handcuff around her head—again, the prison image. "Stop talking to yourself, you crazy Polish bitch," shouts the incontinent old man next door, throwing a shoe at the dividing wall as an added expletive.

We gradually make sense of it all. Rachel and Irina were daughters of a Jewish shopkeeper in Poland: decent, caring parents; a frugal flat but well stocked with books; a close relationship between the sisters; prospects of university studies. Then Nazism reaches out, Rachel is beaten up and takes to her bed, and the sisters no longer attend school. There is talk of mother and daughters escaping while father remains to tidy up and sell the shop. (How can one abruptly abandon a shop slowly built up over the years? And he could not have known the virulence of the evil coming closer.) The ominous minutes of history tick by, and suddenly it is too late. Time only to hustle Irina, clutching the family photographs, to Vienna and so to England. Working in a factory, she meets and goes out with Reg, gets pregnant, and miscarries; relieved of responsibility in this way, he abandons her. She meets Louis from the Caribbean; he has been in London ten days and has already decided to return home, on the reasoning that "it was better to return as the defeated traveller than be praised as the absent hero and live a life of spiritual poverty." There is a strong affinity between them; but Louis is determined to return, and Irene is left to her loneliness. In the face of her alienation and total loss (parents, sister, home, language, and even name, with *Irina* Anglicized into *Irene*), destruction seems inevitable. In his book-length essay *The European Tribe* Phillips writes that the exploitation and sufferings of black people were not in his school curriculum, nor did they find articulation on television and in the media: "As a result I vicariously channelled a part of my hurt and frustration through the Jewish experience."

Joseph Conrad in his "Author's Note" to *Youth* wrote that the three stories "lay no claim to unity of artistic purpose"; *Higher Ground* is described as a novel in three parts. However, one expects a degree of integration within a novel, and if, for example, the work produces new characters, we assume they will be related, however tenuously, to the preceding characters. The three parts of *Higher Ground* take us from Africa and the slave trade, to the United States of the 1960s, and finally to Britain during and shortly after World War II. The characters are an African, a black American, and a Polish-Jewish woman. Therefore, to claim that *Higher Ground* is a novel—not short stories on the same theme—is to urge readers to see the stories as a unity. The work is a triptych, and it is not only that when we place the three parts together they form a unity—of damaged and hurt lives—but that there emerges a significance which no one part by itself can communicate with such clarity and force: "If one takes a piece of banal journalistic prose and sets it down on a page as a lyric poem, surrounded by intimidating margins of silence, the words remain the same but their effects for readers are substantially altered." So too, by the simple device of asserting that *Higher Ground is* a novel, Phillips makes us approach it as a single, unified work, and to respond and draw significance accordingly.

In Phillips's work there is a strong sense of historical violence and its consequences, of resulting journeys and alienation, but also the effort to find (or make for oneself) a little peace.

—Charles P. Sarvan and Hasan Marhama

Can Phillips be described as a British (or a black British) writer? In the bulk of Conrad's work, Poland—in terms of setting—is not significant, yet his Polish life shaped a part of his basic awareness. So too with Phillips, and even if little of his work thus far is set in England, his British years, from infancy to manhood, have given him great advantages. The term *advantages* may surprise, given the degree of racism—covert or overt, suave or crude—that pervades contemporary Britain. Still, I would argue that having grown up in Britain has heightened Phillips's awareness and fine (in the two meanings of *sharp* and *excellent*) sensitivity. This is not to suggest that Phillips is some bruised plant trembling delicately in unkind winds. His difference and exile have positively defined him; they make up his essential being, and, if often a source of hurt or anger, of alienation and loneliness, they also constitute his awareness and strength. It is the turning of what a hostile society and a denigrating culture would impose as misfortune and limitation into advantage and a wonderful broadening out of understanding and sympathy, a turning of prisons into castles (with acknowledgment to George Lamming and his novel *In the Castle of My Skin*), a moving from pain to knowledge and beyond to joy, pride, and thence to celebration.

To return to the question, can Phillips be labeled "British" despite his "return" to the Caribbean? Not to do so would leave our taxonomic lust unsatisfied. If anything, his latest work, *Higher Ground,* shifting from the days of slavery somewhere on the coast of black Africa to a contemporary maximum-security prison cell in the United States and then to a Polish-Jewish woman suffering incomprehension, loneliness, and a breakdown in Britain during World War II, shows a liberated Phillips, a writer who can penetrate the inner being of people vastly different from himself in time, place, and gender, yet people very much like us all in the common and eternal human inheritance of pain and suffering. In a recent essay Phillips writes that his "branches have developed, and to some extent continue to develop and grow, in Britain" but that his "roots are in Caribbean soil." Eluding labels that will seize and fix him, he finally remains Caryl Phillips.

If one were to ask what unifies the fictional works of Phillips, I would turn to the words of the Spaniard Camilo José Cela (winner of the 1989 Nobel Prize in Literature), who said that he is on the side not of those who make History but of those who *suffer* History. In Phillips's work there is a strong sense of historical violence and its consequences, of resulting journeys and alienation, but also the effort to find (or make for oneself) a little peace. As Rudy urged from prison, don't let anyone take away your dreams.

Maya Jaggi (review date 15 March 1991)

SOURCE: "Society and Its Slaves," in *Times Literary Supplement,* No. 4589, March 15, 1991, p. 10.

[In the following review, Jaggi finds Cambridge *to be "a masterfully sustained, exquisitely crafted novel."]*

Caryl Phillips's first two novels skilfully probed the link between Britain and the Caribbean after the Second World War. The common theme was migration, whether viewed through Leila's hopeful journey to the metropolis in *The Final Passage* (1985) or Bertram's tentative return to a de-colonized island following a twenty-year absence in *A State of Independence* (1986). In his fourth novel, Phillips resumes this Anglo-Caribbean exploration but in a nineteenth-century setting, where the nexus is not migration but slavery.

A young Englishwoman, Emily Cartwright, is despatched by her father, an absentee plantation-owner, to visit his sugar estate in the West Indies. Most of the novel (following a third-person prologue signalling her departure) consists of Emily's journal, in which her impressions of the voyage and plantation life are described in genteel, if convoluted, Austenian prose. Elements of gothic mystery unfold through her eyes, around the puzzling presence in the Great House of a slave woman, Christiana, who dabbles in *obeah,* and the repeated chastisement of Cambridge, a literate, Christian slave, by the enigmatic overseer, Mr Brown.

In Part Two, the perspective shifts to Cambridge. His account of his life echoes the late-eighteenth-century autobiographies of freed African slaves such as Olaudah Equiano (Cambridge's Guinea name is Olumide), Ignatius Sancho, Ottobah Cugoano and Ukawsaw Gronniosaw, whose eloquent testimonies lent fuel to the Abolition movement. Part Three is a brief official record of the events leading to Brown's death and the hanging of Cambridge for his murder.

Through this triple perspective, Phillips builds on the ambitious experiments with structure and style of his last novel, *Higher Ground* (1989), where the reader was left to discern links between three disparate narratives set in different times and locations. In *Cambridge,* the unity is more compelling, and the novel achieves a profound marriage of stylistic virtuosity and artistic purpose.

Cambridge is set at a time when the slave trade has been outlawed (after 1807) but slavery continues and, as plantation profits decline, debate rages in England over the merits of the "institution". The "open mind" which Emily professes reveals itself through her journal to be blinkered. In the manner of contemporary travel writers, Emily transforms the harshness of plantation life into a pastoral in which slaves are viewed as a contented part of the local fauna. Africans are not heard to speak, but to "bray", "jabber", "bellow", "drawl", and "slobber", as they "gawp", "slink", "squat" and "teem". Compounding this insistence on the animality of the "sable stock" is a litany of their putative vices: indolence, uncleanliness, dishonesty, promiscuity. Even the perceived attribute of "loyalty" becomes "the virtuous animal fidelity of the dog".

While at times the narrative approaches parody (as when Emily dreads her dreams being invaded by "dark incubae"), Phillips skilfully steers away from facile laughter or deflating ridicule.

Cambridge's testimony provides relief from the relentless insularity of Emily's vision. He describes his capture and passage to England where he received an education and became a Christian, lobbying against slavery until he was betrayed into re-enslavement in the West Indies. His narrative inverts notions of African "otherness" (the European slavers were first viewed as "men of no colour, with their loose hair and decayed teeth") while exposing the hypocrisies of English society, where slavery was illegal but "human flesh merchants" plied their trade. In condemning slavery, Cambridge appeals, in the manner of his day, both to self-interest and to the Christian conscience.

Yet Phillips's primary concern appears not to be to re-write history from the standpoint of the enslaved, in the established African-American literary tradition. (The horrors of the middle passage are scarcely dwelt on.) Rather the novel sets out to explore through its shifting perspective the psychological nature of the society which upheld slavery, and the moral contradictions which it endeavoured not to see.

The prejudices rife in Emily's perception are attributable not merely to ignorance, but to a self-serving system of deliberately nurtured and forcibly sustained myths. Emily's rival suitors, McDonald and the clergyman, Rogers, insist that education and Christianity be denied to slaves, lest they view themselves as "equal to the white man in the eyes of the Lord", and rebel. More to the point, since the moral justification of slavery rested on the "self-evident inferiority" of Africans, to acknowledge their equality would be to undermine the consensus in England favouring the continuation of the institution. And, as Brown puts it, "if negroes do not labour, then who will?"

Cambridge's very existence poses a challenge to this system of myths, raising a red rag to the bullish Mr Brown. Nor can the coarse overseer feel particularly at ease with a slave who possesses a "firmer grasp of the English language than . . . Mr Brown might ever conceive of achieving". Cambridge's account confirms Brown to be a bullying, swaggering brute who sees in Cambridge's "wife" Christiana a perverse means of subjugating him.

Yet part of Phillips's considerable achievement in *Cambridge* is to situate this central conflict within a wider social context. The distinctions of colour emerge as part of an obsessively hierarchical society where a "correct degree of deference" from the lower orders is deemed crucial to keeping "anarchy" at bay. Sexual inequality is also rigorously enforced. In the prologue and epilogue, the author evokes the pathos of Emily's circumscribed life in England. Subject to a father's imperious commands and the "horse-trading" of the marriage market, the woman who haughtily assumes the privileged role of "massa's daughter" is herself in flight from an oppressive powerlessness.

Nor is Cambridge's narrative free from authorial irony, since he, too, is a product of his age. In endeavouring to rule Christiana, Cambridge asserts that "a Christian man possesses his wife, and the dutiful wife must obey her Christian husband", oblivious of the fact that in rendering her a "possession", he is also enslaving her. It is the "mad" Christiana, clinging to her "pagan" beliefs, who mocks Cambridge for disdaining his "uncivilized" African past, "a history I had cast aside" in order to become "an Englishman". Christiana's story remains one of the lingering mysteries of these partial accounts. *Cambridge* is a masterfully sustained, exquisitely crafted novel. Through its multiple ironies and fertile ambiguity, if offers a startling anatomy of the age of slavery, and of the prejudices that were necessary to sustain it.

Caryl Phillips with Graham Swift (interview date 1991)

SOURCE: "Caryl Phillips Interviewed by Graham Swift," in *Kunapipi,* Vol. XIII, No. 3, 1991, pp. 96-103.

[In the following interview, Phillips discusses the genesis of Cambridge *and comments on the different cultural influences at work in his writings.]*

I first met Caryl, or Caz as I've come to know him, a few years ago at a literary jamboree in Toronto. I think we fulfilled all our official duties, but we spent a lot of time in a place in downtown Toronto called the Bamboo Club—one of those places which has acquired since a sort of metaphysical status, because whenever Caz and I have met again in some far-flung corner of the globe, it seems our first instinct has been to find out where the 'Bamboo Club' is. Caz, I confess, is a little bit better at finding it than I am.

Caz was born in 1958 in St. Kitts, one of the Leeward Islands in the Caribbean. He came to England when still a babe in arms and was brought up and educated here. In more recent years, he has travelled extensively and has made his temporary home in many parts of the world, including his native St. Kitts. In keeping with his nomadic inclination, it could be said that one of the main themes of his work is that of the journey or, put rather differently, of human displacement and dislocation in a variety of forms. The journey behind his first novel, *The Final Passage* (1985), was the one Caz himself took part in, albeit unwittingly—the emigration of the postwar years from the Caribbean to this country. The journey that lies behind both Caz's last novel, *Higher Ground* (1989), and his new novel, *Cambridge,* is a more historic, more primal and more terrible journey, the journey of the slave trade westwards from Africa.

Caz has maintained, however, a keen interest in Europe or, to be more precise, in Europe's pretensions and delusions about the place of European civilization in the world. His book of essays, *The European Tribe* (1987), was devoted to the subject. In *Higher Ground,* a novel in three parts, we travel from Africa in the slave trade days to North America at the time of the Black Power movement, only to end up in a Europe still nursing its wounds from the last war. In *Cambridge,* Caz has reversed the direction of this journey to bring a European consciousness face to face with Europe's global perpetrations. He does this through the person of Emily, a woman of the early nineteenth century who escapes an arranged marriage by travelling to her father's estate in the West Indies (her father being an absentee landlord), where she is exposed to and, indeed, exposed by the effects of slavery and colonialisation.

Like its predecessor, *Cambridge* is a novel in three distinct parts, the first and longest of which is Emily's own account of her journey and her observations when she arrives. From what seems at first to be an inquisitive, self-consoling travelogue there emerges a drama revolving around a handful of characters: Emily herself; Brown, an Englishman whom we understand has somehow ousted the previous manager of the estate; the Cambridge of the title, a negro slave who has suffered the singular and equivocal fate of having lived in England and having been converted to Christianity; and another slave, Christiania, who, despite her name, indulges in decidedly un-Christian rites and appears to be on the verge of madness.

The second part of the book is Cambridge's own account of how he came to be Anglicized and Christianized. The third, written in the form of a report (which we guess to be far from reliable), describes how Cambridge comes to be executed for the murder of Brown. And the brief epilogue of the novel tells us the effect of all this on Emily. These last few pages are particularly astonishing. Coming at the end of a novel of enormous accumulative power, they pack a tremendous punch and, written in a prose of tense intimacy, they show how facile it is to assess either Caz's work as a whole, or his heroine, by any crude cultural or racial analysis. Caz is interested in human beings. Emily's plight at the end of the novel plainly has its cultural and racial dimension, but it's essentially one of personal trauma—psychological, sexual, moral and (a word Caz will no doubt love) existential.

[Swift:] How did **Cambridge** *arise? What was the germ, the idea behind it?*

[Phillips:] You know that period when you've finished a book and you don't know what to do? We generally have lunch during these periods in that place around the corner from the British Library, as one of us is pretending to be 'working' in there. Well true to form, I was doing little more than scrambling around in the British Library, having just finished *Higher*

Ground, and having a month and a half on my hands before I was due to go down to St. Kitts. It was during this period that I happened upon some journals in the North Library. One in particular caught my eye. It was entitled *Journal of a Lady of Quality,* and written by a Scotswoman, named Janet Schaw, who at the beginning of the 19th century travelled from Edinburgh to the Caribbean. What attracted me to this story was the fact that she visited St. Kitts. Right beside what was once my brother's place, up in the mountains in St. Kitts, is a broken-down Great House. Janet Schaw described going to a dinner there when it was the centrepiece of one of the grandest plantations in the Eastern Caribbean. I began to realize then that there was a whole literature of personal narratives written primarily by women who had travelled to the Caribbean in that weird phase of English history between the abolition of slavery in 1807 and the emancipation of the slaves in 1834. Individuals who inherited these Caribbean estates from their families were curious to find out what this property was, what it would entail to maintain it, whether they would get any money. The subject matter began to speak, but that's never enough, for there's another and formidable hurdle to leap; that of encouraging a character to speak to you. At the back of '88 when we used to meet, I was concerned with the subject matter and the research, but as yet no character had begun to speak.

And how did the character of Cambridge evolve?

Actually, he came second. Emily, the woman's voice, came first, partly because for the last ten years I'd been looking for a way of writing the story of a Yorkshire woman. I'd grown up in Yorkshire and I had also read and reread *Wuthering Heights,* so I'd this name in my head, Emily. Emily, who wasn't anybody at the moment.

The novel's called **Cambridge,** *but Emily certainly has more prominence in terms of pages. I wondered whether you'd ever thought of Cambridge as the main character, or indeed if you'd still think of him as the main character?*

No. Emily was always going to be the main character, but Cambridge was conceived of as a character who would be ever-present. He doesn't appear often in her narrative, in terms of time, but he's always in the background of what she's doing, and what she's saying, and what she's thinking. And then, of course, in the second section of the novel, he has his own narrative.

There's a lovely irony to **Cambridge***'s narrative. We've had many pages of Emily and then we get Cambridge's account: Emily figures in Cambridge's mind merely as that Englishwoman on the periphery—scarcely at all, in fact.*

There is a corrective in having Cambridge's perspective. Cambridge's voice is politically very important because it is only through painful application that he has acquired the skills

of literacy. There are so few African accounts of what it was like to go through slavery, because African people were generally denied access to the skills of reading and writing. Reading and writing equals power. Once you have a language, you are dangerous. Cambridge actually makes the effort to acquire a language. He makes the effort to acquire the skills of literacy and uses them to sit in judgement on himself and the societies he passes through.

Did your feelings about Cambridge change as you wrote the novel? He is a very ambiguous character.

You know you cannot be too judgmental about your characters. Novels are an incredibly democratic medium. Everyone has a right to be understood. I have a lot of problems swallowing most of what Emily says and feels. Similarly, I have difficulties with many of Cambridge's ideas and opinions, because in modern parlance he would be regarded as an Uncle Tom. But I don't feel I have the right to judge them.

Emily seems to be a mixture of tentative liberal instincts and blind prejudice. And it could be easy for us, with our 20th century complacent hindsight, to judge her quite harshly, but you are very sympathetic—and we can't do anything but sympathize with her, pity her. I wonder if your feelings about her changed as you wrote her long narrative?

(pause) Maybe.

Did you have the end even as you wrote the narrative?

No. No. I think she grows. She has to make a journey which begins from the periphery of English society. I could not have told this story from the point of view of a man. She was regarded, as most women of that time were regarded, as a 'child of lesser growth' when placed alongside her male contemporaries. She was on the margin of English society, and I suspect that one of the reasons I was able to key into her, and to listen to what she had to say, was the fact that, like her, I also grew up in England feeling very marginalized. She also made a journey to the Caribbean for the purpose of keeping body and soul together, which is a journey I made ten years ago. So in that sense, looking at it coldly now, through the prism of time, I can understand why I would have listened to somebody like her and why she would have entrusted me with her story. And through the process of writing . . . you are right, I did begin to feel a little warmer towards her. She rose up above her racist attitudes.

She became alive in her own right.

Because she was courageous. It may be a small and somewhat unpleasant thing in the context of 1991 to find a woman expressing some warmth and affection for her black maid, but in the early nineteenth-century it was remarkable that a woman, and particularly this woman, was able to confess to such emotions. A nineteenth century man couldn't have done this, for men have a larger capacity for bullshit and for self-deception, even when they are talking only to themselves. I am not sure that I would have trusted the narrative of a nineteenth century man engaged in the slave trade. The only time I read men's narratives which seem to me be lyrical is when the men, nineteenth century or otherwise, are in prison.

Emily, in a way, is about to be sold into a kind of slavery— her arranged marriage—which gives her a perspective on what she sees. Is that how you saw it?

Yes. I don't want to push it too hard, for the two things are obviously only analogous on a minor key. However, an arranged marriage to a widower who possessed three kids and a guaranteed income was a form of bondage. Emily finds the strength, the wit, and the way out of this. I admire her for this. What makes her grow are a series of events which are particularly painful and distressing for her. As I have already stated, part of the magic of writing is that you cannot be too judgmental about a character. You have to find some kind of trust, some form of engagement. You attempt to breathe life into these people and if you're lucky they breathe life into you. You love them with passion; then, at the end of two or three or four years, you abandon them and try and write another book.

You said a moment ago that men could only become lyrical when they are in prison. The second part of **Higher Ground** *actually consists of letters from prison in a very distinct male voice. In that novel generally, you seemed to depart from your previous work in using strong first person voices. In* **Cambridge** *again, there is an emphasis on first person narrative. Was that a conscious decision or did that just happen?*

It was conscious. There are any number of stories that you can tell. You are populated with the potential for telling stories from now until doomsday, for these things are circling around in your head. But it seems to me that the real test of a writer's ability is the degree to which that writer applies him or herself to the conundrum of form, to the task of imposing a form upon these undisciplined stories. I had written two novels in the form of the third person and somehow I couldn't address myself again to such a manner of telling a story. It was as though I had to find some way of expanding my repertoire. So the first part of **Higher Ground** is written in first person present tense, the second part as a series of letters and the third part is in the third person but with these rather strange flashbacks. Each segment of the novel demanded a different point of attack. It was a way of breaking out of what was becoming, to me, the straightjacket of the third person. We used to talk about this when you were writing *Out of This World.* I remember you saying that there was an intimacy about the first person which you found attractive. Well, me too. And like you, I am interested in history, in memory, in time, and in the failure of these three things. It seems to me,

at this stage anyhow, that the first person gives me an intimate flexibility which I can't find in the third person.

Nine-tenths of **Cambridge** *is written in a pastiche of 19th century language. Certainly, the final few pages of it are your language, the language of the 20th century. This sense of a language that can talk about certain things suddenly bursting through Emily's own language in which she can't, is very volcanic. It is a brilliant conclusion to a novel. I wonder if we could broaden things out and talk more generally about your writing. You say in* **The European Tribe** *that you wanted to be a writer while sitting by the Pacific in California with the waves lapping around your ankles . . .*

All right, all right! The summer of my second year in college, I travelled around America on a bus until my money ran out in California. And I went into this bookshop and bought this book, *Native Son,* by Richard Wright. There weren't many black people writing in England. So it never occurred to me that writing as a profession was a possibility. But when I was in the States, I discovered such people as Jimmy Baldwin and Richard Wright and Toni Morrison.

Do you think it was necessary to go to America to become a writer?

I was slouching towards a writing career. Being in the States shifted me into high gear and out of the very slovenly third that I was stuck in.

How old were you when you first went back to St Kitts?

Twenty-two. I had written a play, **Strange Fruit,** in 1980, which was done at the Crucible Theatre in Sheffield. And with the royalties from that, I went back to St. Kitts with my mother, who had left in 1958 when she was twenty. It was strange, because I had grown up without an overbearing sense of curiosity about the Caribbean. My mother hadn't been back either. She held it in her memory. But when we arrived in St. Kitts, many of the things that she remembered were no longer there: her school had burnt down, people that she knew had died, and someone she dearly wanted me to meet had long since emigrated to America. For her it was like discovering a ghost town. But for me, it fired my curiosity about myself, about England, about the Caribbean. Naturally, the 'rediscovery' confused and confounded me, but that was no bad thing for, after all, writers are basically just people who are trying to organize their confusion.

Your first two novels were very much about the Caribbean, coming from and going back to. How much was that actually paralleling your life and exorcising your own feelings about the Caribbean?

My first novel, **The Final Passage,** was published in 1985. I had started it some five years earlier, on the inter-island ferry between St. Kitts and Nevis. I looked back at St. Kitts and began to write some sentences down. I wanted to try and tell the story of the journey from the Caribbean to England, which seemed to me to be, in terms of fiction in this country, an untold story. People had written novels and stories about this journey, but not people of my generation. The second novel, *A State of Independence* (1986), although not autobiographical, followed the emotional contours of my life, in that it dealt with the problems of returning to the Caribbean and thinking, they are not sure if I am one of them, and yet feeling that I am not sure if I am one of them either. However, I have certainly not exorcised my feelings about the Caribbean. I have no desire to do so. The reason I write about the Caribbean is that the Caribbean contains both Europe and Africa, as I do. The Caribbean belongs to both Europe and Africa. The Caribbean is an artificial society created by the massacre of its inhabitants, the Carib and Arawak Indians. It is where Africa met Europe on somebody else's soil. This history of the Caribbean is a bloody history. It is a history which is older than the history of the United States of America. Columbus didn't arrive in the United States. He arrived in the Caribbean. The Caribbean is Marquez' territory. He always describes himself as a Caribbean writer. It's Octavio Paz' territory. It's Fuentes' territory. The Caribbean for many French and Spanish-speaking writers has provided more than enough material for a whole career. For me, that juxtaposition of Africa and Europe in the Americas is very important.

But now it's not just Europe, America has moved in. How do you feel about that? You are living in America now, teaching there.

The reason I am living in America is because, like yourself, like many people, business occasionally takes me to the United States. When I'm not there all I have to do is turn on the TV, or open up the papers, and I am bombarded with images of America. In other words, over the years I have come to think of myself as somebody who knows America because I have some kind of a relationship with it. However, I'm not sure that anybody

---

> I really want to understand a bit more about American people rather than simply imagining them all to be characters out of *Dallas,* or a nation whose soul is reflected in the studio audience and guests of *The Oprah Winfrey Show.*
>
> —*Caryl Phillips*

---

can seriously claim to 'know' a country as large and as diverse as the United States. It seemed important, given the opportunity of spending a year or maybe two years in the United States, to make a concerted effort to get to know a part of the country more intimately. That's really why I'm living there. Furthermore, the Caribbean is now, to some extent, culturally an extension of the Florida Keys, and I really want to understand a bit more about American people rather than simply imagining them all to be characters out of *Dallas,* or a nation whose soul is reflected in the studio audience and guests of *The Oprah Winfrey Show.*

I've one last question and it's quite a big one. We always have a lot of fun together, whenever we meet we have some laughs. Yet your work doesn't really glow with optimism. You are very hard on your characters; most of your central characters are lost people, they suffer. Pessimism seems to win through. Is that ultimately your view of the world?

I am always surprised that people think I am a pessimist. *Cambridge* is to some extent optimistic. Emily grows. Okay, she suffers greatly, but she still grows. It's the price of the ticket, isn't it? The displacement ticket. Displacement engenders a great deal of suffering, a great deal of confusion, a great deal of soul-searching. It would be hard for me to write a comedy about displacement. But there is courage. Emily has a great amount of courage. As does Cambridge. And in *Higher Ground* there is faith. I don't necessarily mean faith with a religious gloss on it. I mean the ability to actually acknowledge the existence of something that you believe in, something that helps you to make sense of your life. You are right when you say that the characters are often lost, and that they suffer. But I would like to claim that the spirit and tenacity with which my characters fight to try and make a sense of their often helplessly fated lives is in itself optimistic. Nobody rolls over and dies. If they are to 'go under', it is only after a struggle in which they have hopefully won our respect.

Caryl Phillips with C. Rosalind Bell (interview date Summer 1991)

SOURCE: "Worlds Within: An Interview with Caryl Phillips," in *Callaloo,* Vol. 14, No. 3, Summer, 1991, pp. 578-606.

[*In the following excerpt from an interview conducted in St. Kitts, West Indies, Phillips speaks to his identity as a writer, relates various literary and cultural influences in his work, and discusses his writing process.*]

[*Bell:*] *When did you start to allow yourself to be introduced as a writer? Was it at the point of your first sale or while you were actually in the middle of some work?*

[Phillips:] I still don't like to be introduced as a writer.

Really? Why is that?

Well . . . I think it takes a long time to earn the title. A lot of people are interested in being called writers, but not a lot of people are interested in writing. So to me I am very wary about that title. I think it is sort of debased by a lot of people. I just prefer not to be a part of that. Eventually, maybe.

What's eventually? You already have three novels, four plays.

Yeah, but I am still learning.

How would I introduce you?

I am a writer. That's what I do, but I don't like to be presumptuous.

So you haven't come to terms with the term.

No, it's still a dream. I suppose, when you know that there is so much more to be done and more that you can do, you don't want people to judge you quite yet. You don't want them to give you the label before you have actually earned it. I feel uncomfortable a lot of the time when people ask me what I do. I don't usually say "writer." I usually say that I work for the BBC, or I say journalist, because "writer" just. . . .

Conjures up too many stereotypes?

Yeah. People say, "Ah. Um Hmm."

They want to tell you what they've written.

I have written some things, and no doubt I will write some more things. And eventually one day I will feel comfortable. When that day arrives, I might stop writing. But then again I might not. Who knows.

At the time that you're talking about, ten years ago, when **Strange Fruit** was about to be produced, when there was the possibility of my TV play being produced, I certainly didn't think of myself as a writer. I felt like someone who wanted to be a writer, still. But just because I got a contract, I couldn't figure myself as part of the club.

So every day or nearly every day, you were going home and doing nothing but pen and paper?

Yes, and right now I would say to anyone who is doing what I was doing ten years ago, "Yes, you're a writer. You must think of yourself as a writer." But, I don't know. It's just a label I have always been uncomfortable with. I'm less uncomfortable with it now than I was. It is just something that is easily appropriated by a lot of people. It's actually a hard title to earn.

Were there times that you wondered, "What am I doing here?" Or times that you wanted to give up?

No, never. I never wanted to give up. I got a lot of rejection and met a lot of people who were not interested in the ideas that I had or the proposals I put forth. I must have very thick skin, because I cannot think of a single moment when I thought that I would go get a job as a banker or go be a lawyer or a teacher. It never occurred to me to do that. But it was a curious period. At the same time I had no evidence that I could write except my own self belief. I was convinced that the subject area that I was dealing with, irrespective of my talent (or lack of it), was vitally important. I was writing mainly about—in a few short stories, in **Strange Fruit,** and certainly in the television play—the dilemma of being a West Indian in Britain, both in my parents' generation, the sacrifices they had to make and the contradictions that this created in them, and in their ambivalence towards their children, (i.e. us, the second generation not knowing how to relate to the Caribbean, not knowing how to relate to Britain, and not knowing how to relate to our parents). I was convinced, you see, that people ought to know about this debate and this area of confusion in British social history which was pressing, urgent, and needed to be talked about. I think if I'd been writing some sort of high faluting, airy-fairy kind of fantasy that wasn't rooted in contemporary reality, I would have been much more likely to have thrown the towel in. It was the importance of what I was writing.

It was virgin territory for the most part.

I hadn't seen stuff which had tackled the same area, you see. It was an area which I knew from friends and family. My own life was as important and, at least, as dramatic and real as anyone else's. I didn't see why on earth I could not be given a hearing.

The BBC did, in fact, produce the play?

No. They paid for it. I wrote the play; I can't remember the title. I can't remember what it was about! I did write a play, a 50-minute play for the BBC, which they never made.

Subsequent to that, did they?

They made other plays, but you see the thing with the BBC or any television company is that they commission far more material than they need.

You were in London, and you had an agent; you were bolstered by the fact that you've sold things. What next?

I went around Europe for a month. I got a Eurail Pass. I just travelled around on my own because I had never been to the continent. I had been to America, but had never been to France and Germany and Holland.

You were interested?

No, never. I didn't know anything about Europe, so I figured

I needed to do something about my ignorance in that depart-ment. It was so close. All the kids at college had been to France and Spain on holiday. I had never seen anything like this, and I wanted to go. I had a month before we started rehearsing at Sheffield, and I wasn't going to be living in Edinburgh any-more. I was going to be living in London. I tried for a couple of weeks to find somewhere to live in London, but I couldn't get that together at all. So I thought, I'll go around Europe for the month, come back and go to Sheffield where the play was being produced and then try again to live in London at the end of the year. So that's what I did.

When I travelled around in Europe, I took a lot of notes and determined then that one day I would write a book about trav-elling around in Europe as a black person. So many weird things happened to me as I was travelling around in Europe in 1980. I knew that there was a great travel book in this, and I knew that there was something there. That was the note in the back of my head—do it properly.

And you did.

Yes, four years later.

That was **The European Tribe**. *Did you find an outlet for publishing?*

I already had a publisher. **The European Tribe** was written after **The Final Passage**.

I read in the biography . . . the criticism leveled at **The Euro-pean Tribe** *was sort of barbed.*

Some. **The European Tribe** is the book that has created the most . . . .

Controversy.

Yes. A hell of a lot. It deals with Europe from a point of view from which Europe has never had to deal with itself. It deals with Europe from the point of view of somebody who has had the benefit (or however anyone wants to put it) of a European education. I grew up in Europe; I was schooled in Europe. I didn't buy the hype. I see what I see. I refuse to buy the notion of a Europe which is holding at bay the "barbarism" of the rest of the world, particularly America. I've seen what Europe is. I've seen what Europe can be. I have visited Auschwitz and Dachau. If you want to talk about tribal warfare in Africa, check out Northern Ire-land. You want to talk about imperialist double-speak, check out Gibraltar. I went around with the view of just relating what I saw and how I felt to who I am. The word "tribe" upset some people. But if it's a word that's applicable to black people and red people and yellow people, it's applicable to white people too. If you deal me that card, I deal it back to you.

It got a couple of particularly vicious reviews, but it doesn't really bother me because you have to look at who is judging you. The people that judged me were, in the main, second-rate and utterly dismissable. I have received more letters and more commentary on that book than anything I have ever written. I still do get mail. White and black people alike say that they are glad somebody said it. The criticism just washes by. I don't think that there is any single black writer who hasn't been subjected at one time or another to racist reviews. It is how you deal with them that will tell you something about what type of writer you are. If you write just to be praised, you're in the wrong business. I think it is just part of the territory. You are going to be abused. People are going to get personal about you; people are going to misunderstand what you intended. In the case of that book, because it was written from the first person, it was non-fiction and it was me; I put myself on the line. I am bound to feel it more than a play. The criticism was bound to be more extreme. It is hard to really get at a writer who has written a play or has written a novel. You have to put yourself down the line as a critic. You have to make it clear that you are not actually criticizing the play; you are being small enough to criticize the man who wrote the play.

That was the harshest criticism you've received. With that was there a lesson on how to deal with criticism?

Yes. Very much so. The lesson is this: I really don't read reviews. I don't read anything that is written about me. I don't read interviews.

You have not read a review of **Higher Ground***?*

No. I have not read a review of anything for three and a half years.

Because of that experience?

Not directly related to that because I didn't read half the re-views for **The European Tribe**. I couldn't avoid them be-cause people kept telling me, "Have you seen this?" But I had already made up my mind that I was not interested in reviews. I have to stress that most of the reviews were great. There were just a couple that were a mite personal. But they of themselves would not be enough to make me want to say I don't want to read reviews. I was already very loathe to read them. But now I just can't be bothered. I think it is a total waste of time. I don't have any curiosity, to be honest, about what's written.

In terms of your sphere of influence, what has influenced you as a writer? Personal experience is influential but apart from that . . . .

Let me see. I don't know how to answer that properly. I'll just run off a list of names as they occur to me: Ibsen, Baldwin,

Richard Wright, Toni Morrison, Faulkner—those are the principal people. Some for the same reason. Ibsen because he was the first writer whom I ever read where I detected passion. I detected real, absolute passion. The domestic conflicts of these plays reminded me of black families—people tearing strips off each other, completely at odds with society, parents and kids in conflict. I read something in this thing you gave me about one of the actors in the "Cosby Show": Ed Hyman, one of the old black actors who learned Norwegian because he loves Ibsen so much. I was like that, you know. I just loved it. That's why I went to Norway. I've been to Norway a few times. This actor was saying that when he first saw a production of Ibsen, it made him want to be an actor, and he took it to the extreme that George Bernard Shaw did and actually wanted to learn Norwegian so he could read it from the original. It was quite interesting that he as an older actor is talking about it in this way and about the experience of going to Norway and doing Ibsen in Norwegian. Ibsen was so much at odds with the mainstream Norwegian life. He also wrote really great women's parts. So there's Ibsen.

What's your favorite of his?

Ghosts, maybe closely followed by *Hedda Gabbler.*

A Doll's House*?*

I love it! *Nora*—I think Ibsen is a truly great writer. Richard Wright because he was a man who really made me feel like I wanted to write after reading *Native Son.* And if I had to be marooned with one book, I think I'd take *Black Boy.* It just made me laugh, and it made me feel desperate at the same time. It made me run the gamut of my emotions. It's a work of great, consummate genius. It is so funny in places, very, very funny. Yet, at other times it is so sad and so desperate. I love the prose.

Baldwin, because he's a monumental intellect. . . .

If you were marooned on that same island, could you choose just one?

I think I would take "Strangers in the Village." It's about him going to a small village in Switzerland. These people, not having seen a black person before, keep following him around. He went there to write in the 1950s. I think it's in *Notes of a Native Son.* I like his fiction, too, but it's his essays where the prose is unbelievable. Also, knowing him as I did, I learned in a paradoxical way about how not to be a writer.

How so?

Well, because he got seduced into becoming a personality, and he didn't spend enough time at his desk. It's a lot easier to talk about writing and to be the writer, than it is to write. And Jimmy had such a magnetic personality. I mean, he al-

ways wanted to be an actor. You could see that whenever you talked to him. He was a great, huge personality. But having a personality and having personal magnetism can be a very bad thing for you as a writer, because you develop a social life which is more preferable to writing. Jimmy spent too much time entertaining and being generous with his time, and not enough time writing. That's why I say there is a paradox in Jimmy teaching me a lot about how not to go about being a writer.

To guard jealously your time.

Yes. You have to. And I asked him several times why he surrounded himself with these idiots. Anybody who knew him well will tell you the same thing—Jimmy always had a bunch of complete fools that were always around him, and he tolerated it. One half of you admired the fact that he was so tolerant and generous and open; the other half wanted to say, "You're being had." You wanted him to get on to doing what he did best. I got very angry with him one night about six years ago. We had both drunk too much. I asked him why he was pissing about. He was 60, and he had written six novels. He had written his last novel nearly eight years before, and he had done nothing since. Jimmy Baldwin giving a talk on such and such a chat show is all well, but it wasn't his job. Maybe I was a bit insensitive, and maybe I was talking out of place, but we'd drunk a lot. I felt I knew him well enough to tell him. I was telling him out of frustration, because I'd had enough of trying to get to Jimmy through conventional means. It didn't work. I wouldn't say that he wasted his talent. He did not. I wouldn't say that he'd have necessarily written better. I think he could have written *more,* and I think he had more to say. He dissipated his talent in a way (I think that even he acknowledged this) that was perhaps self-defeating. There's umpteen Baldwin interviews; there's umpteen lectures and chat shows. In 1972, he wrote *If Beale Street Could Talk,* which is a bad, bad novel. It is a terrible novel, I don't care what anybody says. It is a thin vapid piece of work. He then wrote a novel, *Just Above My Head,* and this was his last novel, a novel which needed editing. It needed someone to run a line through some of it, and it needed to be sharpened up. Between then and the nine years that he had to live— nothing. I just felt that a lot of time had been taken up "being a writer" but not writing. I admire Faulkner because I think that he did something with form in twentieth-century American fiction. He wrestled with questions of form and structure that others haven't even come anywhere near exploring. I find some of his work rather self-indulgent and a bit, quite frankly, boring because of his whole thing about the genealogy of the South; but the peculiar thing about Faulkner is that even though I might think his story is a bit so-so, I will like the way he tried to tell it. That is what I like about him.

Toni Morrison, I think, is a consummate artist.

You met her?

Briefly, at Jimmy's funeral. I just admire her so much. I think she's a master in subject, she's a master in form. She's very adept at managing her time and public appearances. When she does appear in public, she speaks sensibly and incisively. I think she's a great, great novelist.

Are there any Caribbean writers?

Derek Walcott, he's my favorite. I admire him; and although I am not a poet (and I don't feel qualified to criticize poetry), I admire his struggle to reconcile being of the Caribbean but not submitting to the parochialism that the Caribbean can impose upon your work. Many poets of Derek's generation have, if you like, wings that they can spread; they have learned how to fly, but few have soared like Derek. He has gone from strength, taking whatever influences he finds: be it Greek mythology or whatever interest he has in Eastern Europe from knowing Brodsky; be it from being among Black Americans and witnessing things in Black America. He has managed to take all of these various influences and graft them back into the Caribbean experience and make it more resonant. In his work I admire that he has never lost sight of the Caribbean. He has never closed his eyes to other ways of viewing the Caribbean and using other experiences to feed back in. On the physical side there is the determination to actually maintain a link with the Caribbean. That is something that I have only recently begun to try to do. The fact that he has been trying to do it for many, many years and succeeded, gave me, in a sense, the confidence to come here. It made me realize, when I looked at the quality of his work, how important it was that I did so.

To keep the link.

To keep the link. To try to not be afraid of the disorientation and the feeling of displacement, both here and there. To consciously be aware of this and to know the price that he's paid is a very important thing. He's had to hope that the work could justify the personal discomfort, in a sense. When I look at a lot of his contemporaries, other West Indian writers in fact, very few have had the courage to attempt to pay the price of some degree of personal discomfort that comes with living the life of the itinerate and the toll that takes on one's personal life, the domestic life. He's done it.

You're in it; you're not of it. You're of it; you're not in it.

Exactly. Derek, more so than any writer I know, is a great exiled writer. But he's not in exile. I admire him for not having taken up American citizenship.

When people question you about where you are from or where you are now, do you find inherent in that a question of your loyalty?

Absolutely. All the time. Whenever I go to a conference, par-ticularly if it is in Britain, Germany, Canada, wherever, people always want to find a label for me. They may see me as somebody born in St. Kitts, and they say I live half the time in St. Kitts. Then I open my mouth, and they hear this English accent coming out. So they want to know what my story is. What's my game? What they are trying to do is make me choose. People have tried to make Caribbean writers do that all the time. I think that is what Derek has resisted. I'm sure that Derek and many other writers have had to pay a heavy price for refusing to be pigeon-holed. My own small experience with it is quite straight-forward. I hold a British passport, and I hold a St. Kitts passport. I see no reason why, for the sake of any idle gesture, I should toss one in the fire. I have them both, and I will use them both as I deem fit. I write about both places.

Do the mechanics of writing seem to be as enjoyable as the creative parts of it?

Eventually . . . you see, it's how you tell the story that seems to me to be most important. There are endless numbers of stories. When I look at the subject matter that I would like to deal with or that I have dealt with, it is a matter of telling a story about . . . let's take "Heartland," the first part of ***Higher Ground***. You're telling a story about someone who collaborated. Now what was interesting to me was not just the story, but how to tell the story and the technique and the challenge of telling in the first person and in the present tense. That was something that gave it a little added relish when I sat down to write. It was. . . .

A novelty.

A technique. How you tell the story . . . well, I think Wallace Stevens said that it's a real test of your seriousness. That may be a bit of an exaggeration, but there is something in it. Grappling with form is very important. We talked about this before: Ibsen changed the form of the theatre. It wasn't further developed until you got to people like Tennessee Williams or Arthur Miller, who introduced the notion of magic and poetry, flashbacks and techniques of the cinema. You look at people like William Faulkner: he changed the form of the novel. There are many writers who are fine writers but who are not obsessed with technique or form. But, to me personally, it is one of the things that I feel is one of the distinguishing features between English Caribbean literature and Spanish Caribbean literature. You can look at Spanish literature like Marquez or Carpentier and actually see a different form or technique from English Caribbean literature. English Caribbean literature tends to be much more imitative of European forms. I think that we have a lot to learn in English speaking zones in the Caribbean. We are always in danger of becoming an exotic imitation of what is being done in London or New York.

For some writers, the whole aspect of writing it may not be a chore, but it is, however, a hard thing to do. It is hard to be alone and to devote the amount of time that it requires. Do you feel that way?

One thing that James Baldwin said about six years ago about writing—this was when I was working on what turned out to be *The Final Passage*—he basically told me that if I thought it was "hard to write a novel now, just you wait. It gets harder." He was right. It gets harder. First of all, I think you can work on a certain degree of ambition and desire the first time, even the second time, because you want to have the evidence of this thing. You want to have a novel; you want to get a novel out. The second or third time you are concerned about imitating yourself and writing the same book again. You have a different story, but you have to find a new way of telling it. Otherwise, you will fall into the trap of just repeating a well-worn narrative. It becomes more difficult, because you want to find a new way to tell a new story. You have to find a new vehicle for it to travel on, a new narrative form, a new narrative technique.

It doesn't matter how interesting the story.

Well, you hope that the story is at least as interesting as the one you told before. In fact, you hope it is much more interesting, but you don't want to travel on the same rickety wheels. You want to transport your story. You want to further sharpen the narrative blades at your disposal so that you can thrust into the heart of the reader with even more precision.

Is writing for you wrapped up in great mystery? Do you find that you have to go to certain places in your imagination before you come to terms with what it is you want to write?

I think what happens is that you have to learn patience. To get the idea for a novel, for me, isn't that difficult, but, the idea isn't enough. What I have to have is characters that speak to me. An idea suggests that it might turn out as some kind of socio-historical bullshit. I am a firm believer in character. If a character doesn't speak to me, no matter how strong an idea I have, if I don't feel I can engage him or her to some extent and arrest that character and be their guardian, then I won't pursue it. I might try to pursue it in a different form, maybe a play or a film, but certainly not in prose. . . .

The character comes first.

Sometimes the idea comes first. To me, it remains merely an idea until I've got a character. When I have a character, then it becomes a reality. It is easy to say that I want to write something about a slave from the South who joined up and fought with the North, because it's an interesting phenomenon—the black troops in the war. But it's not enough to have the idea. It's a good idea and very little fiction has been written about it. But I need to know who this slave is. He has to have a

name, or she has to have a name. I might read a book about that period and see if anything happens. Then I wait a bit. Eventually, what I hope is that the character will speak back to me. That's when I know something is happening, when the character starts to talk back to me. That waiting period is incredibly frustrating, and what you need is patience. I was talking to Jimmy [James Baldwin] once, and he said, "What are you doing?" I said, "Well, I am working on this novel, and I'm looking for my characters." He fell about laughing [sic]. And then he said, "You don't look for them. You have to wait for them." And he was right. He told me that as I got more mileage on me as an author that I would learn to wait.

Have you leapt out of the bed?

Yeah. I know when something is right. I can always tell. It happened in the novel I'm finishing now. I just knew almost immediately. I knew this character had a voice that was so insistent that all I had to be was this conduit through which this voice was going to come. It's a bit like when Alice Walker talks about how *The Color Purple* happened. She was a vehicle. I think the same thing when I read Toni Morrison. Her work is so magical and brilliant. You can't imagine how come this book didn't exist before. It's like the book should have existed. How come *Beloved* wasn't there before? It's because these people's voices were real and resonant and inside somewhere. It was as if Toni Morrison was the chosen one. She was able to be patient enough to listen and receive. She had the discipline to put this stuff down. That's more or less the voices from the past demanding that you tell their story. There are a few imposters running around to whom you have to say, "Well, actually, brother, your story . . . maybe I'll just hold off." But there are voices that are around that demand that their story be told. If you think that you're honest enough to tell the story, then tell it. That's what I mean when I say you have to wait. Particularly for a black person, there are so many avenues of our history that remain untold. That's why *Glory* was such a revelation. I could not believe that they'd actually gotten Hollywood money to make this film about our history. But somehow somebody had gone in there and realized that it was a part of American history which needed to be dealt with. There are any number of stories which need to be told. I don't think the subject area is a problem. If you are interested in history, even a superficial interest in history, every page you turn there are stories. You go back to Harriet Tubman, then forward a bit to Frederick Douglass. There are all the people who don't have a profile right now. There's all this. Langston Hughes wrote a great essay about subject matters for black writers. Although it was a bit prescriptive, what he was saying was basically correct: all writers mark their characters, like dogs. I think for a black writer who is interested in himself or herself and his or her history, it is a tremendously privileged and responsible position. It's how you tell the story that's the real struggle.

Black authors are in the process of constructing a literary tradition. It is a wonderfully exciting and dynamic process.

—Caryl Phillips

My white contemporaries, particularly in England, I see what they are writing about and some of them are less sure than black writers, black American writers in particular, about their area. In a way, English history is much travelled territory. You're in a tradition that's pretty goddamn deep. There's Chaucer, Milton, Shakespeare, Dickens—that's heavy, heavy tradition. Black authors are in the process of constructing a literary tradition. It is a wonderfully exciting and dynamic process.

It's uncharted.

It's dangerous. You can hit those "rocks"; you can go down. But because it's uncharted, it gives you a certain freedom.

Is there anything that you fear when you write?

Good question. No. The only thing I ask when I've finished anything is "Could I do better today?" If the answer is "no," then it's done properly. Maybe tomorrow it could be done better, but you finished yesterday, so . . . There's no fear because there is a great surge of power that comes with creativity. You feel very confident when it's going well. A fear, not at that time, but a later fear is that you may be pulling the punch or you are just not being as honest as possible for fear of hurting someone.

When that thought comes to mind, I guess that it's like an indicator.

You have to go back and look again. Don't give up. The revising process that I am doing right now is painful and slow, word by word. I'm changing quite a lot. But the reason I have to do this is—even though it is really uphill, having spent two years working on it—this is the most crucial phase: It's now that you have to find the energy to go up again. Now, when you're out of gas.

Having scaled once.

You have to go back again. You know in your heart that there are a few things that are wrong. You know you could get away with it because the book is sold, the deal is done, it's going to be published. Probably not many people would notice this odd word or sentence or sentiment that was slightly out of key. You could just watch TV. Yesterday, I wanted to watch a Magic Johnson all-star game, but I couldn't. I just thought, "NO."

You could become a slave to something. . . .

You know why you've gotta go back there? It's not only for yourself. You actually make the commitment early on to your characters, and you are prepared to be a clean and proper conduit for them. They're going to haunt you if you mess with them now . . . .

The last things you published have been novels. Are you going specifically to write more novels, or do you still have an interest in plays?

I still have an interest in plays. I am going to work on a play this autumn which I wrote four years ago.

Can you do this simultaneously, or do you, when writing a novel just devote time to that novel?

I can do them simultaneously. I can, but I think that a play can reach a critical stage or a novel can reach a critical stage where it just demands . . . there's a point where you can see the end of the thing and you just have to go. While I am in the earliest first draft stages, I can actually fiddle with one and then go and fiddle on another. I'm in the sort of, hopefully, home run stage of this play, and I want to finish it when I'm in Amherst.

You started it four years ago?

I wrote it in London for the Hampstead Theatre Club. I wrote it originally for nobody. Then a guy at Hampstead saw a draft of it. And they commissioned a second draft, and they worked with me on it. We worked hard on it. Michael Attenborough wanted to go in one direction, and I wanted to go in another. So, gentlemen's agreement, we just figured it wasn't going to work. I left for about one and a half years while I wrote **Higher Ground**. It's only now that I've come back to it that I can see a way of finishing it.

During those four years, did the play nibble at your brain?

Again, it is not the play, but the characters. There are three characters, and I can't leave them without the final reel. All three of them are strong, insistent individuals. Their way of speaking is in that play. I can't condemn them. Anything that I have ever done which hasn't been produced, I can't remember the names of the characters. I sort of vaguely remember what went on. But whenever there is a strong character, they will always find a way.

In the books I've read, the things of home seem to be pervasive: looking for an identity, looking to belong.

My feeling is that anybody who grew up with the sort of background in which I did, and that is not an insignificant percentage of the population of England, will question their identity. In other words, we grew up not quite knowing if this was home. Being told to go back to where we came from. The question of home is a very serious thing because you don't feel at home in this place which is the only thing you know. The other alternative smacks of idealism, because you don't have any notion of it. You probably couldn't even pinpoint it on a map. It just reflects my generation's continuing struggle.

I think that members of the emerging third generation feel much more comfortable describing themselves as black Britons, which is something my generation always had some difficulty with because they didn't even want to deal with the term "Briton." At the same time, they couldn't really deal with the term "West Indian" either.

—Caryl Phillips

What about the comfort level?

I think that members of the emerging third generation feel much more comfortable describing themselves as black Britons, which is something my generation always had some difficulty with because they didn't even want to deal with the term "Briton." At the same time, they couldn't really deal with the term "West Indian" either. So I think that what will happen in this generation is that more barriers will be broken down. You see this when you turn on the TV set; you see black people on the TV and heading the news. They are doing things that they weren't doing ten years ago. I think people today feel a lot more comfortable describing themselves as British and black. Whereas, when I was a teenager, there was a real confusion with color and nationalism. I think that it has straightened itself out slowly, thankfully.

This relationship to Africa—in the U.S. there was a movement in the late 1960s to relate to the search for roots to find "home." Has a similar thing happened in the Caribbean?

Yes. It's been happening for a long time. Well, there was Marcus Garvey, and the whole philosophy of Rastafarianism is rooted in the notion that Africa, Ethiopia in particular, is the homeland and that we will go back to Ethiopia for redemption. I mean, it was strong even before its development in the United States.

Has it done a 360 degree turn?

I think so.

Away from Africa. I tend to feel that.

To be perfectly honest.

I haven't seen one Mandela t-shirt.

I've got a lot of Mandela cups and t-shirts in my house! The focus of identification is the United States of America. The aspiration is not to be a Black African. It's to be a black success. They want to be somebody who's got something going for them. Michael has—Jackson or Jordan. Like the rest of the world, this place is becoming more culturally identifiable with the United States rather than with Africa.

The only identity the U.S. can provide is a megalomanic one.

But that's powerful. It's much more interesting than identifying with a bunch of people who are still, if you switch on the TV, presented as barbaric. People bought the hype pre-Haley. Some of them continued to buy it post-Haley.

*I think about **State of Independence** or the last few pages in it about cable TV being introduced at the same time independence is being introduced to the island. Is there some kind of correlation between them?*

It is saying basically that there is no independence. They've become nominally independent from Britain, but what do they do in the cultural and economic dependency? That's symbolized by cable television. The whole notion of independence for a place as small as St. Kitts or for islands generally as small as these in the Caribbean is a non-starter. You have to be dependent on somebody, given the world economy. So it's just a matter of what comes with your dependency, and what comes with the dependency with the new Caribbean is a sort of cultural imperialism which is, perhaps, inevitable. Africa, of course, is closer historically, but the price of developing cultural and economic links with Africa is just too high. It's not practical given the realities of the world in which we live. So the politicians and the people naturally gravitate toward the power, which is the United States.

Riding around the island with you, I've been struck by the beauty on the left and just as awestruck by the absolute poverty on the right. The roads are lined with shanties and people without running water or things that we tend to take for granted in the U.S.A. I know the island's history includes slavery, for the purpose of harvesting sugar cane. Today, 140 years removed from slavery, there seems to be some link to that past.

I think you notice that more in the Caribbean than you would in the U.S.A., because the Caribbean remains principally a set of islands based on agriculture, upon tilling of the soil. That has changed slightly, but people essentially remained close to the domestic patterns of slavery in the villages: seasonal labor for the cane and then getting work wherever they can.

What strikes most for me, especially in **The Final Passage,** *is the lyricism. It is evident throughout your work, but in* **The Final Passage** *I seem to denote it more than anything. I was finding myself in your character's future and in the next paragraph being in their past without losing any of the logic. Is that something you strove for, a new way of telling a story, or was it something that just grew?*

I think it grew out of telling that particular story. I think most people when they set out to write a first novel are just desperate to get the damn thing done. For me, I think, a type of lyricism comes from the environment here. I was most powerfully struck when I came here 10 years ago, by the trees, by the landscape. Having grown up as a kind of concrete jungle kid in England, it had never occurred to me to describe things. Your environment was not something you described; it was something you endured. I knew that when I got back to England I would have to describe what it was like going back to the land of my birth and with that came a particular vocabulary. Because of the nature of the visions here—the visual feast—you have to be lyrical. In terms of the characters, I was trying to tell a story about some people who were looking forward. So there was inevitably this time dislocation between the narrator, the characters, and what the characters were hoping for.

In **Higher Ground,** *you tackled three very different issues. The first one, "Heartland," you told me the impetus was Sophie's Choice.*

Partly, I wouldn't say it was an impetus, but it was something that was at the back of my mind: the notion of the disruption, perhaps even the destruction of the family base, the family unit, in the people who eventually become slaves. That had always interested me, that and the choices they had to make. It was not as neat as *Sophie's Choice.* You could be wrenched from your mother, father or brother, or your wife or daughter in a very vicious way. You weren't given a choice. I was aware of some parallels to the great twentieth-century crime against the Jews. It had some parallels and echoes for me as a black kid growing up in Europe. I felt that if white people can do that to themselves, what the hell are they going to do to me? I became interested in Jewish history, and I subsequently visited Auschwitz and Dachau and Anne Frank's house. I was interested in these places as monuments, for they existed. From reading I knew that physical edifices of the slave trade also existed. I started putting together this notion of the family unit breaking down. The idea of the lack of choice. Out of this mish-mash of things emerged a story about the captivity of Africans and one man who collaborated in this.

You did this story before actually journeying to Africa. You just recently journeyed there and saw these things. How close do you think you came to. . . .

It is really for the Africans to say. The ones that I spoke to when I gave readings seem to think that it was pretty close. When I got there, I was kind of surprised. I think the historical memory is deeper and a lot more powerful than some of us recognize. And perhaps writing about it exorcised some of the horror of actually seeing. I got there, and I understood it. I understood instinctively what was going on because I had written about it. I don't think that I made any factual or emotional errors. I felt I had already imagined what it was like, and so being there was like a journey back to something that I already knew about.

The second story basically attends to a "soul brother" in the 1960s becoming aware of politics in the U.S.A. at that time and how black people were apart from the politics in the nation and excluded from "main stream" society opportunities. How did that come about?

That came about because I was in Alabama making a film in 1982-83. I was doing a documentary film in Birmingham, nearly 20 years after the bombings in that city. Obviously, I had an interest before that in civil rights, but in Birmingham, I came face to face with the realities of the movement. I went to Birmingham City Jail where King was incarcerated. I went to Jefferson Country Jail which is where a lot of black people were held and continue to be held for a variety of reasons. I really am quite interested in the whole process of the psychology of the 1960s in America. A combination of exposing myself to reading about the 1960s, being aware of the martyrdom that many Black Americans went through in the 1960s, their struggles and misunderstandings, the difficulties of Vietnam and the hippie movement, and the actual physical horror, for the first time in my life, of being in a couple of prisons which had huge black populations and were primarily staffed by bigoted, Southern red-necks—I had to write something about all of this.

The third one seems to be a story of ultimate desperation and disillusionment, by not belonging to any place or anyone.

Well, it is on the one hand about two displaced ships passing in the night, so to speak. It's about two people, neither of whom belong in this big city, both of whom feel, "What the hell am I doing here?" One character is a Jewish woman who is a refugee from Poland. The other is a West Indian who is newly arrived in Britain. The story is set in the late 1950s, and they don't know what is going on. It's really about one of them who is too far gone because she's been in the country for nearly twenty years now. She's been sucked up into a vacuum of the nightmare of trying to survive as a displaced person. She knows no other way of surviving. The other can actually see, although he's only been there a few weeks, that if he stays how things are going to turn out: he is actually going to become mentally damaged by the experience of environment, feeling like an exotic but unwanted appendage to the larger British culture. There's a lack of despair, in that the black man, the West Indian, decides that he doesn't want to know. Most circumstances, as one might expect—and this has happened with lots of West Indian migrants in Britain—forced them to throw in the towel and take the path of least resistance, which would (in this case) have been to stay in her flat and just figure, "what the hell."

I've arrived. . . .

"I've met a friend, somebody I can talk to. She's good looking and a bit strange, but hell. I suppose I look a bit strange at the moment, too." He found the strength, the real strength not to do it. He has the strength to insist that he was going back to where he came from. From her point of view, yes, there is a terrible despair. Her despair is qualified by the twenty years of experiences that she's had. It is also qualified by her life before she left: how close the family was. It was a very tight Jewish family. When she walks outside of that framework, she is likely to fall apart anyway. When he talks about his family life in the Caribbean, he only does it very briefly. But it is a lot cooler, a lot more loose and fluid.

Claudia Roth Pierpont (review date 10 August 1992)

SOURCE: "English Lessons," in *The New Yorker,* Vol. 68, No. 25, August 10, 1992, pp. 76-9.

[*In the following excerpt, Pierpont analyzes* Cambridge *in the context of Phillips's other works.*]

In the introduction to his play *The Shelter,* produced in 1983, when he was twenty-five, the British writer Caryl Phillips described a postcard photograph that he had kept pinned to the wall above his desk for over a year: "A white woman's face, probably that of a woman of thirty or thirty-five, who had probably just cried, or who would cry; and curled around her forehead, with just enough pressure to cause a line of folds in the skin above her eyes, were two black hands; obviously power and strength slept somewhere within them but at this moment they were infinitely gentle, describing with eight fingers that moment when a grip of iron weakens to a caress of love." The story of the relationship between this white woman and this black man—"perhaps the most explosive of all relationships, seldom written about, seldom explained, feared, observed, hated"—seemed to the author impossible to get down on paper, and many times, Phillips tells us, he wanted to quit: "The responsibility was too big, I would say, to myself only; and I would wait until I was more mature." It was with what he thought to be a final, regretful glance at the image that he experienced at last a clearing of the mind and with it the knowledge that "the postcard was a part of me and if I did not acknowledge it I would be haunted

. . . . I clearly saw in it, perhaps for the first time, something that had made me what I was."

What Phillips was at the time—besides a budding playwright—was a recent Oxford graduate, brought up in Leeds, who was born in the West Indies and taken to England before his first birthday. He was just moving toward the discovery of his voice—the voice of an England not often heard, far from sweeping lawns and university quadrangles. Phillips has written elsewhere of the depths of exclusionism and ignorance which continually challenged his right to feel himself English, from the deliberate humiliations of boyhood to the questions of a BBC television producer as to "what African languages I spoke, and if I spoke them when I'm with other West Indians." At Oxford, he envied the African students for having "a home to which they could return"; he implies almost as much about black Americans. Two years after *The Shelter,* which dealt with the impossible relations of a black man and a flesh-and-blood Britannia, Phillips began writing novels on the subject of West Indian rootlessness—of in-betweenness, of pained unacceptance and categorically enforced un-Englishness—set forth in the measured and evocative prose of a natural master of the language.

Both Phillips' insistent early theme and his developing virtuosity of style are brought to an extreme pitch in his most recent novel, *Cambridge*. Set in the British West Indies before the victory of abolitionism, under a system of slavery carried out half a world away from its masters and beneficiaries, the story concerns the voyage of an Englishwoman, a near-perfect representative of the formative conventions of her class—"I am simply a lady of polite status with little talent, artistic or otherwise"—directly into the heat and confrontation of an island where her countrymen have painstakingly raised up a hell in the bower of paradise. Miss Emily Cartwright, come to inspect the running of her father's sugar plantation, is the proverbial drawing-room mirror, silvered and polished and transported over an ocean in order to capture in reflection the unthinkable English beast of slavery. Caryl Phillips, like Pat Barker, approaches the evils of history through the trials of individual conscience. His book, too, seems to set up a challenge of will against will, and a promise of transformation—in this case, through the presence on the plantation of a highly educated and articulate slave, called Cambridge. Yet as the story progresses these apparent promises grow dimmer and dimmer, until Phillips fatally reverses every prospect, every expectation. He leads where no one could expect who does not know his painfully divided earlier work.

Phillips' first novels centered on the physical beauty and social squalor of the Caribbean, the tiny islands of sizzling tin roofs and sleep and beer, "overburdened with vegetation and complacency," offering nothing, without future. This splendorous desolation he set against the cold, gray refusal of the great mother island, where what is offered is always out of reach, and where the past is all the comfort left. His people sailed away from their homes with a pity for all those "satisfied enough to stay," and they inevitably returned, defeated—in *The Final Passage* after several months; in *A State of Independence* after twenty years—and at once grateful and unfitted for the slow, eventless life they had thought to abandon.

In 1989, Phillips published a collection of three novellas under the title *Higher Ground,* in which he seemed not only to have become a new writer but to have become several writers. The growth and the range were remarkable, and the command of voice—with narrators belonging to different sexes, races, countries, and times—was uncanny. The strongest of the stories was a dramatic monologue in letters called **"The Cargo Rap,"** which records a black American's seventh year in prison during the nineteen-sixties. Here Phillips captures an era and a way of thinking and speaking with line-for-line precision, and renders a particular human personality with almost unbearable penetration: a young man of mental complexity and blanketing self-deception, whose belligerence and naïve schemes slowly give way to a seeping, cracking desperation. All of this hundred-page story is told in the singular and ever-recognizable voice of one Rudolph Leroy Williams, although Phillips manages to create—over the teller's shoulder, as it were—an array of other characters. And it is characteristic of the author's temperament that the tale begins in prison, with his narrator's crime obscured in the past, barely relevant, and all his actions cut off at the level of thought. Even rage is something that the reflective and rather gentle Phillips explores rather than releases.

The narrator of Phillips' third novella is an educated and privileged slave employed by the British military at an African trading post, whose job it is to translate between English and the dialects of captured tribes. The story, again, is delivered as a monologue, but eighteenth-century speech is alluded to rather than reproduced; something other than historical accuracy is intended. This nameless figure is marooned between his two peoples, "knowing that neither fully trusts me, that neither wants to be close to me, neither recognizes my smell or my posture." In the end, despite his Christianized learning and civility, he is turned upon by his masters and shackled to the latest group of captives; in a vortex of self-realization and terror, he is sold, in a distant country, on the block. This is a potent nightmare, as hard and irreducible as myth. In varied forms, it is at least as old as Stowe's Uncle Tom. For Phillips, its gospel seems to be especially urgent, and it reappears, elaborated in detail and consequence, at the ambitions and inscrutable heart of *Cambridge.*

The familiar Phillips gifts are much in evidence in the new novel, and its early sections have an intoxicating vocal grace. Here is the Englishwoman's story, told in her own steady voice, a brief prelude of dishevelled memory quickly bound up into the ordered form of a journal: "I shall have a record of all I have passed through, so that I might better recount for

the use of my father what pains and pleasures are endured by those whose labour enables him to continue to indulge himself in the heavy-pocketed manner to which he has become accustomed."

A great part of the delight of these early pages lies in the secret of high and risky artifice shared between author and reader—the perfect balance with which Phillips has summoned up this nineteenth-century Emily. But there is also the simple appeal of the woman herself, with her dartings of bitter knowledge and need beneath the dutiful pose of the lady, with her wry intelligence and her distinctive way of trying out a new thought or expression—restyling the conventional inflections of an even earlier period—as though pressing the taste of it up against her palate, as when she notes of a seasick cabin boy: "Merely a few years hence he will have *sea legs* as opposed to *land legs,* and find it difficult to reside in a world that is devoid of motion." One believes in this Emily, and cares for her, as she broods and italicizes her way across the ocean.

Confusion sets in soon after her arrival, however, and slowly expands throughout the book. At first, we lose our hold on who Emily is or might be. Simultaneously appalled and seduced by tropical languor, the woman who left England with the bold hope that she might one day "encourage Father to accept the increasingly common, though abstract, English belief in the iniquity of slavery" is converted with startling immediacy—through plainly expressed disgust with black features and habits, with violations of "laws of taste"—to a stony conviction of the natural rightness of the slave system. The character closes up, becomes merely priggish, loses the Brontë-like sense of mettle beneath apparent mildness; even in giving herself over to island delicacies and sensualities, she is reduced to the hard and casually abusive England she had so recently sought to escape.

While there is no requirement, of course, that the heroine of a novel be also a political or moral heroine, and while the brutalization of this woman's mind is as potentially valid and perhaps more devastating a subject than its liberation, the reversal here is carried out without struggle or question, or even transition. More, the tight airlessness of that diminishing mind becomes stifling for the reader, who is, after all, trapped inside it, craning to locate a clear fact or another human face, to escape a monologue that turns into a drone long before its hundred and twenty-plus pages are out. Phillips' extraordinary control of tone never wavers, but the cost is great.

It was perhaps part of the author's rhythmic plan to have the plot rush in so late and so wild: a love affair, a baby, a murder. Emily's lover is the cruel plantation foreman, whose killer is the "black Hercules" called Cambridge, the sole slave who would not back down, who sought justice. We have seen the two men facing off in the fields—the result is the first whipping that Emily witnesses—and have seen Cambridge sitting outside Emily's sickroom reading his Bible:

> I asked if this was his common form of recreation, to which he replied in highly fanciful English, that indeed it was. You might imagine my surprise when he then broached the conversational lead and enquired after my family origins, and my opinions pertaining to slavery. I properly declined to share these with him, instead counter-quizzing with enquiries as to the origins of his knowledge.

Learning nothing of these origins, Emily "quickly closed in the door, for I feared this negro was truly ignorant of the correct degree of deference that a lady might reasonably expect from a base slave."

The history of this "base slave" is given at last by his own testimony, some thirty pages written out on the eve of hanging. Cambridge, born Olumide, was captured and taken to England, and there renamed, reclothed, reëducated, and eventually freed—"Truly I was now an Englishman, albeit a little smudgy of complexion!"—before the final and irrevocable betrayal back into slavery, aboard a ship travelling to Africa to convert the heathen. But his tale resolves the plot in only the most cursory way, and the book not at all. Where is Cambridge's voice? Far from sounding particularly fanciful, as Emily hears him, he sounds to us hardly different from Emily herself. It is soon apparent that Cambridge is less a man than an archetype, as isolated from sources of life as, finally, Emily is—or as she comes to be, it seems, once she has chosen, in the fields, in some mysterious and unexplored way, to set her heart toward the whip-wielding foreman rather than his steadfast opponent.

It is presumptuous to claim that an author should have stayed true to intentions that he may not, after all, have possessed. But everything that goes wrong with *Cambridge*—the sudden moral reduction of the heroine, the plot too sketchy and immaterial to contain, or even occupy, the characters, and the lack of conviction in the presentation of Cambridge himself—suggests a change of direction, the uprooting of a vital motivation: the meeting of this complex woman, white and free, and this complex man, black and enslaved, in a world set apart. Such is the magnetism of these twin poles of the narrative that just the anticipation of their mutual discovery is sufficiently charged to hold the story in tension, until the prospect is, chance by chance, eliminated. That there will be no connection made between these two people, no recognition, is emphasized more than once, as a kind of refutation, a warding off. ("That I might have conversed with her at ease, perhaps even discussed acquaintances in common, undoubtedly never occurred to her," Cambridge muses near the story's end.) This is not to say that these characters need to have become lovers but that the reader feels led inexorably toward some greater awareness, some eruption of sympathy, or of

any emotion that would fertilize the sterile grounds in which the pair have been planted.

It is difficult to know whether this negative choice reflects technical restrictions or philosophical ones. On the simplest level, Phillips has chosen to retain his monologue form, his passive and dissociated poise, his tight control. But the choice encompasses, too, a backing away from the assailable cliché of black man and white woman—that "most explosive of all relationships," the exploration of which Phillips once regarded as part of his "inevitable task" and the responsibility for which he had feared. The image on the postcard that so obsessed the young writer remains one of essential division. Phillips' insistence that we are forever separate in our skins, that every voyage out is a foundering, is manifest in *Cambridge*—which begins by promising so much more—through the cutting back of dimension in the characters and of freedom in the author. Yet if *Cambridge* is a smaller book than it might have been, and more self-protective, it leaves one with the conviction that Phillips has it in him to write books that are larger and bolder. One would not require of the artist a different conclusion, or a feigned optimism—or, for that matter, a real optimism—but only the breath of possibility, without which the most meticulous creation is stillborn.

Evelyn O'Callaghan (essay date 1993)

SOURCE: "Historical Fiction and Fictional History: Caryl Phillips's *Cambridge*," in *Journal of Commonwealth Literature,* Vol. XXIX, No. 2, 1993, p. 34-47.

[*In the following essay, O'Callaghan treats the intertextual aspects of* Cambridge *by examining the novel's relation to slave narratives and travel journals or diaries.*]

> Post-modernism maintains that everything is fiction. Post-modernists say that there is no such thing as reality, only versions of reality. History is fiction, science is fiction, psychology is fiction.
>
> So what about fiction itself? What is it supposed to do now? Plot and character are done for. If there is nothing to reveal but fiction, then fiction, some writers believe, can't tell us about anything but itself. So they give us metafiction: self-conscious fiction which draws attention to the fact that it's fiction. It's no longer enough for the conjurer to perform the trick without declaring that it *is* a trick.

Despite the rather peevish tone of this reflection on postmodernist literary theory, it raises certain issues which I find useful in approaching Caryl Phillips's latest narrative, *Cambridge* (1991). Firstly, this work does constitute self-conscious fiction: to a great extent, it is a pastiche of other narratives and, it seems to me, deliberately calls attention to its intertextuality. Secondly, the source narratives for *Cam-*

bridge have long been considered the proper domain of West Indian historians and have been read as historical reconstructions. However, the particular nature of most of these documents—the slave narrative and the travel journal/diary, with their first-person narrators, their conventions of rhetoric and structure—emphasizes their fictionality. Finally, *Cambridge* itself is a "novel" that attempts historical reconstruction in order to interrogate and, possibly, rewrite the European record of the West Indies. In a sense, then, *Cambridge* wears the mask of fiction (as the term is commonly used), but reveals its matrix in historical narratives, which are in turn unmasked by the text's process and shown to be rather insidiously fictional in their claim to "the truth".

If my logic is tortured, this results from attempting to come to terms with a text that does declare itself "as a trick". The title, for example, refers to the eponymous character, whose real name turns out *not* to be Cambridge after all; neither does he recount the majority of the narrative. Rather, this centres around the experiences of an Englishwoman (Emily Cartwright) in the Caribbean, some time between the abolition of the slave trade and full emancipation. *Cambridge* consists of three "stories", sandwiched between a prologue and epilogue which foreshadow and echo each other. These latter combine omniscient narration with representation of Emily's thoughts and memories prior to and after the central events of the whole.

The bulk of *Cambridge* is the travel-journal of Emily, a thirty-year-old spinster sent by her father to survey his plantation in an unnamed West Indian island (obviously based on Phillips's native St. Kitts) before facing her fate, a loveless marriage to an elderly suitor in England. During the course of her stay on the estate and her growing intimacy with the overseer, Mr. Brown, she comes into contact with the Bible-reading slave Cambridge whose grasp of English impresses her. Her account ends with the murder of Brown by Cambridge, and "the negro . . . hanged from a tree, no longer able to explain or defend his treacherous act". Emily is mysteriously ill, the estate threatened with ruin and her father sent for.

Part Two gives Cambridge the chance to "explain or defend" himself. It purports to be the written testimony of the African Cambridge ("true Guinea name, Olumide"), enslaved as a youth, who, surviving the middle passage, enters into domestic service (as Black Tom) in the household of a retired English captain in London. Here he learns to adopt the English language, dress, customs, Calvinism and his latest appellation, David Henderson. He marries an English servant and after the death of his employer, lectures on the anti-slavery circuit around the country until his wife passes away. Subsequently, en route to Africa as a missionary, he is robbed, re-enslaved and finally, rechristened Cambridge, sold to the West Indian estate where he suffers the bullying of Mr. Brown and Brown's power over his "wife" (the strange Christiania who so threatened Emily in her account). He finally approaches Brown,

determined to state his grievances, but a violent confrontation ensues in which Brown's "life left his body" and, as Cambridge understands, his own death will soon follow by law.

Part Three takes the form of another historical document: perhaps an anecdotal account in a report or a newspaper story, judging from the inclusion of rhetorical flourishes and sensationalizing details. It records the premeditated murder of Brown by the "insane" slave Cambridge because of an "innocent amour" between Mr. Brown and Christiania, whom Cambridge held "in bondage, his mind destroyed by fanciful notions of a Christian life of moral and domestic responsibility". Details of the actual ambush and murder are supplied by a "faithful black boy" accompanying Mr. Brown, who hid and observed the event. Emily is not mentioned in this narrative, which concludes with Cambridge's trial, hanging and gibbeting.

And so to the Epilogue, which ties up the loose ends: so much for the absence of plot and character in the postmodernist text! Emily, having lost Brown's child, lives in dereliction off the estate with her faithful slave Stella, supported by the charity of neighbouring blacks, and looks forward to death.

For those who have a nodding acquaintance with West Indian history, this brief summary will no doubt evoke similar "historical" accounts on which Phillips has drawn. In effect, Emily's (fictional) travel journal is a pastiche of similar writings by Monk Lewis, Lady Nugent, Mrs. Carmichael *et al*. I do not refer simply to the narrative's conventional form and use of nineteenth-century "polite" English, but to specific incidents, phrases, even whole passages in the novel which are deliberately "lifted" from the source documents. Compare, for example, the following passages in (a) *Cambridge* and (b) Monk Lewis's *Journal of a West Indian Proprietor*:

> a) Sea terms: WINDWARD, whence the wind blows; LEE-WARD, to which it blows; STARBOARD, the right of the stern; LARBOARD, the left . . .

> b) Sea Terms. —*Windward, from* whence the wind blows; *leeward, to* which it blows; *starboard, the right* of the stern; *larboard,* the *left* . . .

This shipboard observation is shortly followed in both narratives by an account of a little cabin boy, his friendship with a dog, and his seasickness on this, his debut voyage. Emily's account of her ill-fated maid's illness ("she complained of feeling the motion sickness, of throbbing temples, burning head, freezing limbs, feverish mouth and a nauseous stomach") echoes that of Lewis: "My temples throbbing, my head burning, my limbs freezing, my mouth all fever, my stomach all nausea, my mind all disgust".

Then there is the obligatory storm at sea, and once again, Emily's narrative and that of Lewis are almost word for word:

> I was . . . consulting with the captain, who took the precaution of snuffing out one of his candles and readying himself to affix the other to the table. However . . . the sudden lurch of the ship throw it from the table-top and for a moment we were plunged into complete darkness. And then the noise! . . . The cracking of bulkheads! The sawing of ropes! The screeching of the wood! The trampling of the sailors! The clattering of crockery! Everything above and below all in motion at once! Chairs, writing-desks, boxes, books, fire-irons, flying all about . . . (**Cambridge**).

> The captain snuffed out one of the candles, and both being tied to the table, could not relight it with the other . . . when a sudden heel of the ship made him extinguish the second candle . . . and thus we were all left in the dark. Then the intolerable noise! the cracking of bulkheads! the sawing of ropes! the screeching of the tiller! the trampling of the sailors! the clattering of the crockery! Everything above deck and below deck, all in motion at once! Chairs, writing-desks, books, boxes, bundles, fire-irons and fenders, flying to one end of the room . . . (*Journal of a West Indian Proprietor*).

Emily's leaking cabin roof mirrors that reported by Monk Lewis; the approaching tropical weather is described as "excessively close" and "sultry" in **Cambridge** and in Lewis's *Journal*; the captain of the ship in both narratives becomes "out of patience with the tortoisepace" of progress, and so the voyage and arrival in the Caribbean proceed intertextually, as it were. Once ashore, Emily is warned to beware of the very dangers that Lewis itemizes:

> There were three things against which I was particularly cautioned, and which three things I was determined *not* to do: to take exercise after ten in the day; to be exposed to the dews after sun-down; and to sleep at a Jamaica lodging house. (*Journal*)

Compare, also, reactions to the extravagance of the planter's table in Lady Nugent's *Journal* and Emily's account:

> Such loads of all sorts of high, rich, and seasoned things, and really gallons of wine and mixed liquors as they drink! . . . a dish of tea, another of coffee, a bumper of claret, another large one of hocknegus; then Madeira, sangaree, hot and cold meats, stews and fries . . . [*Lady Nugent's Journal of her Residence in Jamaica from 1801 to 1805*] I have never seen such rich and heavily seasoned food: land-and-

sea turtles, quails, snipes and pigeons . . . Dishes of tea, coffee, bumpers of claret, Madeira, *sangaree*, were all to be followed . . . (**Cambridge**).

Emily's reportage of the hypochondria of the slaves ("a tropical doctor's life is squandered on the bizarre imaginary diseases with which the negro claims to be suffering. Monday morning is a great time for the lazy or ill-disposed . . .") sounds very much like Mrs. Carmichael's assertion, in *Domestic Manners,* that "Negroes have more imaginary diseases than any set of people I ever was amongst . . . Monday morning is always a great day for the sick". Consider also the similarity of the following comments on theft among the slaves in (a) **Cambridge** and (b) *Domestic Manners:*

> a) His thievishness is more than a match for all the laws that can emanate from any parliament, and even when apprehended in the act the black will invariably fly into a passion if you refuse him the honour of being able to take up the book and swear to the truth of what he knows to be false.

> b) Negroes will steal, cheat and deceive in every possible way . . . what is worse, they invariably get into a passion if you refuse to let them take the book and swear to the truth of what you know to be false.

In the case of Cambridge's story, the echoes are largely from *Equiano's Travels*. Equiano tells of being captured at the age of ten in Nigeria, enslaved (under various names), schooled in England, freed and converted to Calvinism, travelling as part of the anti-slavery lobby throughout England, married to an Englishwoman and involved in a projected trip to Sierra Leone, where he wished to go as a missionary; Cambridge's narrative, like Emily's, deliberately draws on the earlier autobiography. Equiano's fear that his captors will kill and eat him on the journey to the New World also haunts Olumide/Cambridge. The descriptions of conditions on the slave ship are similar in both texts:

> we were to be lodged below deck . . . Once below our bodies received a salutation of supreme loathsomeness in the form of a fetor (**Cambridge**)

> I was soon put down under the decks, and there I received such a salutation in my nostrils as I had never experienced in my life; so that with the loathsomeness of the stench and crying together, . . . I was not able to eat, nor had I the least desire to taste anything. (*Equiano's Travels*)

Similar treatment is meted out to Olumide/Cambridge ("The white men came below with eatables. Those who found the strength to refuse were lashed, often to death") as to Equiano ("two of the white men offered me eatables, and on my refusing to eat . . . flogged me severely", p. 26). The two narratives illustrate the brutality of whites, even to each other, with the same example of a sailor being flogged to death with a "mass of rope" and then tossed overboard. Olumide/Cambridge receives instruction aboard ship "to help me smatter a little imperfect English", echoing Equiano's experience: "By this time however I could smatter a little imperfect English". At the sight of England, Equiano relates that "Every heart on board seemed gladdened", in *Cambridge,* the phrase recurs: "every heart was gladdened when sight of merry England was announced". Compare also the despair of both (a) Cambridge and (b) Equiano at being deceitfully re-enslaved, and at the prospect of another middle passage:

> a) I very much feared the horrors that lay ahead. My former passage rose in dreadful review and showed only misery, stripes and chains. In one moment of weakness I called upon God's thunderous avenging power to direct the sudden state of death to myself, rather than permit me to become a slave and be passed from the hand of one man to another . . .

> b) At the sight of this land of bondage, a fresh horror ran through all my frame . . . My former slavery now rose in dreadful review to my mind, and displayed nothing but misery, stripes, and chains; and, in the first paroxysm of my grief, I called upon God's thunder and his avenging power to direct the stroke of death to me rather than permit me to become a slave, and be sold from lord to lord.

One could continue such collation, but the textual strategy in the first two sections—one which research would doubtless expose in Part Three also—has been sufficiently illustrated. Phillips has gone to great pains to establish the historical "authenticity" of his fiction. Furthermore, the deliberate, even ostentatious, borrowing from and echoing of source material ("the conjurer declaring it is a trick") focuses attention on the *connection* between the fictional and historical narratives. For what purpose? I will return to this issue shortly, but it is important to note that while the reading of *Cambridge* is a disconcertingly echoic experience—one constantly, and correctly, feels "I've read this before!" —there is no sense of a stylistic patchwork. Each of its narratives is relatively consistent and suited to its presumed author. At the same time, what Phillips has achieved is a sense of their *representative* natures, their combined impressions of place and time evoke the feel of the place and period.

Nonetheless, one can empathize with the response of a historian colleague asked to check the novel's historical verisimilitude: "But what *is* it?" The answer, of course, is a hybrid, a syncretic fabrication. As such, the text conforms to one definition of post-colonial literature, which sees its perspective as having "given explicit confirmation to the perception that genres cannot be described by essential characteristics, but by an interweaving of features, a 'family resemblance'

which denies the possibility of either essentialism or limitation" (*The Empire Writes Back,*) as do the cultures such literature grows out of.

Elsewhere in *The Empire Writes Back,* the authors postulate that "much of post-colonial literature . . . is 'about' a void, a psychological abyss between cultures". Certainly, this permeates the structural arrangement of *Cambridge*. The novel also treats of "gaps" within cultures, significantly between male and female on both sides of the Sargasso Sea. For all the "bond" felt by Cambridge for his "wife" Christiania (whom, even he accepts, is a "heathen"), he tells her nothing about his past for fear of tainting "my Anna's memory by association" and his attempts to convert her fail because "her undeniably spiritual nature was absorbed in an entirely different direction", a direction that finally leads her to mock his Christian beliefs. This angers Cambridge "for, as is well known, a Christian man possesses his wife, and the dutiful wife must obey her Christian husband".

The same perception of woman as innately subservient pervades Emily's world, and the "void" between cold male authority and resentful female obeisance is introduced in the Prologue to *Cambridge*: "A woman might play upon a delicate keyboard, paint water-colours, or sing. Her father conducted himself as a stern audience"; "she had once overheard her father insisting that sensible men should only trifle with these children of a larger growth. And then he laughed. To reside under the auspices of a 'petticoat government'!" Both Christiania and Emily have "buried feelings", unarticulated thoughts which "unspool in silence". The metropolitan *and* plantation societies of the nineteenth century confined and silenced women.

To an extent, *Cambridge* gives them voice. One may ask what prompts a black male West Indian writer—the author's photograph is prominent on the dust-jacket—to reflect on his country's past through the memoirs of a white female English persona? Again, *The Empire Writes Back* suggests an answer: "In writing out of the condition of 'Otherness' post-colonial texts assert the complex of intersecting 'peripheries' as the actual substance of experience". So, of course, do female-authored texts. In attempting to shed light on the past, Phillips has chosen to explore the voids, gaps between cultures, races and sexes. In terms of gender, then, Emily's account is a useful perspective from the periphery. On the one hand, she does read the West Indian island and its inhabitants according to imperialist and racist discourse; on the other hand, her place within this discourse is clearly established as marginal. The text stresses her ignorance (had not "Stella informed me" on numerous occasions, she would be lost), her frequent mystification ("By now I was so confused that my feverish head had begun to spin anew"), her false conclusions and, above all, her powerlessness at home and in the Caribbean (the estate overseer has her bodily carried off the field by a slave when she annoys him).

> **I am suggesting, then, that rather than utilize a symmetrical white male account to balance that of the slave, Cambridge, Phillips's choice of a "mistress" rather than a master-narrative far more tellingly exposes the "complex of intersecting peripheries" that informed nineteenth-century plantation life.**
>
> —*Evelyn O'Callaghan*

So one can perceive, through her narrative, some of the cracks in the edifice of colonialism: its contradictions and inconsistencies, the holes in its "logic" are inadvertently exposed. For example, in the Epilogue, Emily reflects on her position: "They were kind, they journeyed up the hill and brought her food. Cassava bread and bush tea mixed with milk. The mistress. Six months, six weeks, six days, it mattered little for her status was secure". Yet her own narrative has demonstrated the insecurity of her status, the indeterminacy of the title "mistress": the deposed estate manager acknowledged that "the mistress" "lacked the power of either censure or discipline" on her father's estate. Indeed, the irony of the term and her assertion of the identity it confers is explicit in her situation at the end of her tale: deserted by the man whose "mistress" she had become, shunned by white society for her illegitimate pregnancy, alone in a derelict cottage and dependent on her servant and the charity of strange blacks. Even as she has come to recognize the truth of Mr. Brown's assurance that "when I had spent more time among them I might come to understand that everything is not as in England", she clings to the imperialist myth of the natural supremacy of white and English. But her own narrative has exposed this, as it has so many other "truths".

I am suggesting, then, that rather than utilize a symmetrical white male account to balance that of the slave, Cambridge, Phillips's choice of a "mistress" rather than a master-narrative far more tellingly exposes the "complex of intersecting peripheries" that informed nineteenth-century plantation life.

At this point, I would like to return to my earlier suggestion that *Cambridge* calls attention to its intertextuality, the connection between its fictional narratives and its "historical" source documents. As stated earlier, travel-diaries and planter journals and slave narratives, some of which *Cambridge* draws upon, have long been used by historians as sources for the reconstruction of social relations in Caribbean plantation societies. Of course, historians have been aware of the danger of bias in such narratives. Witness Elsa Goveia's general warning:

> Among the historians of the British West Indies, most

of the earlier writers tend to claim authenticity, while the later ones usually lay claim to impartiality as well. The need for a narrative which should be true to the facts was well established as an essential element of historical writing. What varied was the judgement of the nature of the facts . . .

But what must also be taken into consideration is the essentially "fictional" nature of these texts, particularly in terms of the way conventional formal structures shape the manner in which the "objective" narrator shapes and judges the "facts". Again Goveia's study notes this conventionality:

> The diversity of subject and method in British West Indian historical writing is comprehended under a certain regularity of form . . . the diversity of temperaments, motives and opinions among the historians, was, to a significant extent, overlaid by a regularity of interpretation. (Goveia).

Henry Louis Gates, Jr. has written about the similarity of content and structure across slave narratives; of the influence on each new writer of "other slave authors who preceded them"; of the apprenticeship in rhetoric and oratory many writers served while on the anti-slavery lecture circuit (evidence of this is explicit in *Cambridge*); of common rhetorical features such as metaphor, irony, apostrophe, chiasmus and—in the case of Equiano *and* Cambridge—"the use of two distinct voices". In addition, Gates touches on both the appropriation by the slave narrative of other literary forms (the popular sentimental novel, for example) and the appropriation of the slave narrative by novels such as Ishmael Reed's *Flight to Canada* (1976). In so far as the printed texts of the slave narratives were often "formal revisions of their spoken words organized and promoted by antislavery organizations" (Gates) and that such lectures were organized according to some of the conventions and rhetorical strategies mentioned above, we have come a long way from a perception of the slave narrative as a bald account of historical facts. The narratives were, rather, highly crafted and self-conscious works (sharing many features with other fictional genres) that filter, as it were, "facts".

The same can be said of the travel-journal. Eve-Marie Kröller has recently catalogued some rhetorical strategies in travel-writing by Victorian women, including the use of the "poetic" and "objective" modes to shore each other up, the use of set-pieces of natural description to familiarize the exotic environment, the use of servants' explanations to translate "a foreign epistemology", the advertisement of the *partial* nature of the account and the mixture of genres (the account may incorporate lyric rhapsody, botanical information, cookery recipes, missionary story and adventure tale!) .

My point in emphasizing the constructed, fictional nature of the "source narratives" in *Cambridge* is that in both Emily's and Cambridge's accounts, the narrating "I" is evasive, as is the "truth" of her/his relation. As Kröller points out, the travel-diarist is doubly self-conscious as protagonist in both an alien geographical environment and a potentially unsettling, even embarrassing narrative environment. Emily's account is self-referential because she must make herself, as narrator/protagonist, an object of consciousness; like Cambridge, her self-consciousness accounts for certain gaps, ambiguities, discreet omissions and self-protective explanations in her text. Thus our attention is drawn to both the fictive nature of the narratives in the novel and, by their faithfulness to the conventions and discursive strategies of the originals, to the *story-like* quality of these originals.

At the same time, even as we discover that history is yet another fiction, Phillips's deliberate echoing of his "parent narratives" forcibly reminds us of their historical nature: to borrow a term from deconstruction, the fact that the appellation "historical" is "under erasure" does not eliminate the concept of "historical" when we approach the fiction. Accordingly, the informed reader will judge *Cambridge,* at least in part, according to its faithfulness to the form and tone of the originals, to the "facts" of history. It must be said that the tone of the novel's language *is* accurate and deftly manipulated to specific purposes. One may query whether any planter-class West Indian newspaper or anecdotal account (the form suggested in Part Three) would consider it necessary to mention that Mr. Brown was a Christian; on the other hand, narrative irony—and symmetry—is facilitated by the adjective, which nicely contrasts with "the *Christian* Cambridge" later in the account. Again, the apparently random italicization of the earlier nineteenth century lends a "period tone" in this instance as well as serving to underscore the irony of contrasting "Christian" behaviours.

I referred earlier to the sense of familiarity, of *déjà vu* which the informed reader experiences in *Cambridge*. This, as noted, is largely due to the deliberate incorporation into the novel of certain conventional narrative and attitudinal features proper to the "parent documents", and results in an acceptance of Emily's and Cambridge's accounts as historically representative. Yet, in drawing attention to the several discursive strategies through which past "facts" have been filtered, and to the evasive, even enigmatic, nature of the first-person narrators of the tale, Phillips lulls us into a sense of familiarity only to jolt us out of it.

As I also suggested earlier, the self-conscious artificiality of the slave narrative and travel diary-forms helps to account for certain holes and silences, certain contradictions and ambiguities in this novel which draws on them. For example, the deliberate evocation of Equiano's classic slave narrative underscores the public, rhetorical, missionary quality of the testimony of black Tom turned free David Henderson: "Truly I was now an Englishman, albeit a little smudgy of complexion! Africa spoke to me only of a history I had cast aside". But, in the next breath—well, paragraph—the narrative is

coloured by the voices of the effaced Olumide and the disillusioned, re-enslaved Cambridge, with devastatingly ironic effect: "We who are kidnapped [by Englishmen] from the coast of Africa, and bartered [by Englishmen] on the shores of America, enjoy a superior and free status in England". Likewise, the sentiments of the Christianized Cambridge who thanks God "for granting me powers of self-expression in the English language" are undercut by his reportage of Olumide's fate in the hands of "so-called Christian customers" whose English "resembled nothing more civilized than the manic chatter of baboons"; of course, this also qualifies Emily's reference to "the incoherent slobber of negro speech".

As for Emily's narrative, contradictions and revisions abound. At one moment, she salutes the tropical climate and foliage; at the next, she rails against its strangeness, the heat, the insects. The dualities of England and the unfamiliar Caribbean estate are sometimes reversed, so that their opposition in terms of "home" is dismantled: for example, the creole menu soon becomes one that

> gave so much pleasure to the palate that I began to wonder if I should ever again adjust to the fare of England. Was I doomed to become an exotic for the rest of my days? This, it now seemed to me, would be no bad thing . . .

The slave she admires as "Hercules" is revalued when she discovers that "this Cambridge is lettered, can read his Bible, and even endeavours to teach it to his fellow blacks. which leads me to conclude that . . . [he] is no ordinary negro"; later he is a "treacherous" villain. And in Part Three, he is an "insane" murderer. Emily's repulsion at the brutal whipping of a slave is followed by her trite assertion, on viewing a negro village, that

> If I were to be asked if I should enter life anew as an English labourer or a West Indian slave I should have no hesitation in opting for the latter. It seems to me manifestly worth abandoning the propriety and civility of English life for the pleasant clime of this island and the joyous spirit which abounds upon it.

No wonder a recent review of the novel cites Emily as "one of the most skilfully created unreliable narrators in contemporary fiction"!

The texture of the novel as a whole is that of a web. One can easily identify links (between Christiania and Emily; between Cambridge and Brown, who both lose a "wife", a child and finally their lives) and parallels (the sea voyages of sickness and death, the two arrivals on the island and journeys to the estate, of Emily and Cambridge) and contrasts (Brown's view of Cambridge as a thief, liar and troublemaker, against Cambridge's view of Brown as "a bullying brute of an overseer", a violent rapist determined to crush all spirit in the slaves). Such an interconnected network is fertile ground for irony: Emily comments on the blacks' promiscuity and their difference "from us in their disregard of marriage vows"; ironically, Cambridge's account informs us that "Mr. Brown had taken no interest in . . . Miss Emily once the details of the latter's condition had been discovered by the physician". Emily mentally admonishes her father's laxity ("Does he have no conception of what would claim us all in the tropics were we to slip an inch below the surface of respectability?") and feels only contempt for the poor whites, "these pale-fleshed niggers"; she ends up in a similar predicament as a result of her own moral turpitude. Throughout, the narrative challenges first impressions: the stock "mammy" figure of Stella turns out to have been Brown's mistress and the mysterious Christiania, his supposed mistress, as only a pawn in his humiliation of Cambridge. The "safe" society of doctor and reverend with whom Emily surrounds herself in fact masks a "clown and his oafish friend . . . engaged in some manner of feud for my favours".

Without further catalogue, it should be clear that the text's apparent familiarity (of form, of known "facts") is subtly destabilized by strategies such as those outlined above so as to shock the reader into awareness of incongruities and discordance below the conventional surface. In this, of course, Phillips is being true to the dualities of plantation culture. Expectations are frustrated—the virtuous lady becomes a shunned sinner; her "romance" ends in degradation; Cambridge's history of moral upliftment and Christian missionary zeal ends in murder, madness and execution - just as the brutality, debasement and self-deceit hidden behind imperial truisms about plantation life are unmasked. All the facts, the statistics and the explanations are given but the whole "story" of the enigmatic Cambridge remains a mystery.

The incidental image of "Two sorry horses, one perhaps of fourteen hands and white in colour, the other a rough brown beast resembling a Shetland pony, . . . often to be observed shackled incongruously together" may serve as a metaphor for this text. Incongruity and discordance arise from the "shackling together" of unlike races, genders, cultures, economic and philosophical systems, narratives. And yet, as in Rhys's *Wide Sargasso Sea,* the insistence on giving "the other side"—not simply as a mirroring of opposites, but as a demonstration of how the same horror corrupts in different ways—is perhaps the least imperfect methodology a writer can adopt in delivering a glimpse of our chaotic and puzzling past.

Finally, as noted earlier, it is worth situating *Cambridge* within certain concepts of post-colonial literary theory. In *The Empire Writes Back,* such theory—of the type practised by Bhabha, Spivak, JanMohammed etc.—is seen as offering "ways of dismantling colonialism's signifying system and exposing its operation in the silencing and oppressing of the

colonial subject". According to Bhabha, the authors explain, "the colonized is constructed within a disabling master discourse of colonialism which specifies a degenerate native population to justify its conquest and subsequent rule". Such a "signifying system" or "master discourse" informs most of Parts One and Three of *Cambridge* and, indeed, a sizable portion of Cambridge's own narrative, particularly after he acknowledges that "Africa spoke to me of a barbarity I had unfortunately fled".

At the same time, in calling attention to the "parent narratives" that inform these sections, texts which intend a particular (Eurocentric) historical construction of the colonized Other; *and* simultaneously exposing the "fictionality" of such accounts; *and* enabling both colonized Other (Cambridge) and colonizing Other (the woman, Emily) to speak through such discourses while evading reductive labelling (objectification) by the retention of incongruity, discordance, contradictions, silences in their narratives, *Cambridge* casts doubt on the very possibility of definitive historical construction. As such, the novel fulfils another criterion of post-colonial literature:

> it has been the project of post-colonial writing to interrogate European discourse and discursive strategies from its position within and between two worlds; to investigate the means by which Europe imposed and maintained its codes in its colonial domination of so much of the rest of the world. Thus the rereading and the rewriting of the European historical and fictional record is a vital and inescapable task at the heart of the post-colonial enterprise.

Cambridge enables us to see, with Foucault, that there are no "true" discourses only more or less powerful ones. And while I recognize that the discovery of fictional elements in the type of source narratives utilized in *Cambridge* does not essentially alter the *power* of the tradition to which they belong, I would maintain that after careful reading of *Cambridge* one will never read the other versions (Lewis, Carmichael, Long and the rest) in the same way again.

Oliver Reynolds (review date 14 May 1993)

SOURCE: "Sold into Slavery," in *Times Literary Supplement,* No. 4702, May 14, 1993, p. 22.

[*In the following review, Reynolds likens the structure of* Crossing the River *to "a consciousness of the burdens of slavery."*]

Crossing the River, Caryl Phillips's fifth novel, returns to the structure of his third, *Higher Ground* (1989), by juxtaposing stories from the past and near-present. It is divided into four main parts and two of its four stories overlap. In the first part, Edward Williams, an American tobacco planter and a solid

Christian, sets off for West Africa in 1841 in search of a former slave of his, Nash, who is now a missionary.

A substantial pleasure of *Cambridge,* Phillips's last book, was the way it enjoyed making obeisance to the orotundities of nineteenth-century prose. Whereas *Cambridge* encouraged the luxury of slow reading, the prose here is plain to the point of worthiness, and when Nash's story is told through his letters to Williams, it is hard not to look ahead to see when normal narrative service will be resumed. The story proceeds by juxtaposition and compression. The drawbacks to this are evident in the second section, which has the lurid jumpiness of a Western. A slave-auction, a gunfight in Dodge, circled waggons, passing buffalo—these all whizz round an image (used at the end of two previous novels) of a lone woman in falling snow. However, the book's narrative methods are superbly borne out by its second half.

The third part consists of the journal of a slave-ship in West Africa in 1752. These are crowded literary waters—the same coastline and the same year were used in Barry Unsworth's *Sacred Hunger.* Where that, though, was ponderously detailed, this journal is incisively selective, a flying-fish to Unsworth's great whale. The horror of slaving, left to the imagination, is ever-present. "Carpenter began to raise the gratings of the women's room. . . ." This entry like many others, sails very close to the actual *Journal* of John Newton (author of "Amazing Grace", friend of William Cowper, who is glimpsed in *The Prelude* as the castaway who teaches himself geometry "With a long stick upon the sand"). Phillips acknowledges his "particular obligation" to Newton for "invaluable research material". His use of this source is direct, if a little abashed (a thermometer reading, for example, is changed from 74 to 78). Technically, it is a fine piece of editing, of seizing potential; in the context of the novel, it is just right.

One of Phillips's gifts is his ability to transform his sources into the felt life of fiction. The last part of *Crossing the River,* mostly set in Yorkshire during the Second World War, is a triumphant piece of writing, equally confident in evoking the exact sound of bombers, "all out of tune", and the compelling presence of Joyce, the first-person narrator. Joyce falls in love with an American GI who is both emblematic and singular: sharing a name with one of the children sold at the novel's beginning. The colour of his skin is referred to once; the book is often beautifully tacit and brief. Joyce, presumably, is white. At the close of the novel she is at one with the children sold into slavery and mourned at the start. Mourning, though, is now to be transformed.

Phillips's novels derive their structure from the forced relocations of the slave trade and their moral power from a depiction of human goodness surviving degradation. A presiding consciousness, and conscience, found at the beginning and at the end of *Crossing the River,* takes up one of the burdens of slavery in a repeated sentence: "I sold my children." How can one be virtuous in a world which treats children as goods?

Maya Jaggi (review date 30 May 1993)

SOURCE: "Tracking the African Diaspora," in *Manchester Guardian Weekly,* Vol. 148, No. 22, May 30, 1993, p. 29.

[*In the following review, Jaggi relates Phillips's own comments on* Crossing the River.]

Graham Greene once said childhood was the bank balance of the writer. For Caryl Phillips, the source goes deeper: "For writers who are black, and working against an undertow of historical ignorance, it's our history that's our bank balance."

Phillips's novel *Cambridge* (1991) exposed the lasting psychological legacy of slavery through layers of irony in the twin accounts of Emily, a 19th century Englishwoman visiting her father's plantation in the West Indies, and the eponymous slave she encounters there. It won him last year's Sunday *Times* Young Writer of the Year award, and has been a huge seller in the United States, where the author is Visiting Professor of English at Amherst College, Massachusetts.

His new novel, *Crossing the River,* spans 250 years of the African diaspora. It tracks two brothers and a sister on their separate journeys through different epochs and continents—as a missionary to Liberia in the 1830s, a pioneer on a wagon trail to the American Wild West later that century, and a GI posted to a Yorkshire village in the second world war. Their stories are framed within a haunting "dialogue" between the guilt-wracked African father who, in "a desperate foolishness", sold them into slavery, and the 18th century English captain who traded him "gold coins for warm flesh".

The germ of the novel was an 11-minute radio play, performed on Radio 3 eight years ago, about the anguish of a father who sold his children.

There were black cowboys, settlements in Colorado and California, pioneers. It's seeing history from another angle, from the point of view of people normally written out of it.

—Caryl Phillips

Frankness and a gently dry humour are among the author's salient traits. As is a propensity to keep on the move. When I spoke to him at his house in Shepherd's Bush, he had run the London Marathon the day before, and was set to take off for Cuba. An interest in history is evident on his walls. Alongside old prints is an antiquarian map of St Kitts, the island where Phillips was born 35 years ago, before being brought to the north of England at the "portable age" of 12 weeks.

Billed among the 1993 Best of Young British Novelists, Phillips has been prolific. Much of his output—five novels, a travel book (*The European Tribe,* 1987), stage and radio plays, screenplays—charts the spectral triangle of Europe, Africa and the Americas. But the focus is on England and the Caribbean—whether linked in the novels by migration (*The Final Passage,* 1985), the vexed return to West Indian "roots" (*A State Of Independence,* 1986), or the "peculiar institution" (*Cambridge*).

With *Crossing the River,* the axis shifts towards the US, where he has taught since 1990. "You take a period people presume they know about—like the Wild West of John Wayne and Sergio Leone—and make them look again," he says. Many former southern slaves headed west, rather than to the industrial north. "There were black cowboys, settlements in Colorado and California, pioneers. It's seeing history from another angle, from the point of view of people normally written out of it."

In the section set in Liberia, Nash, a black missionary grateful for his Christian upbringing, can only stop disparaging his "pagan" ancestors when freed from an insidious dependency on his former master—and lover—Edward.

Curiously, the tale of the brother Travis is told through the eyes of the Yorkshire woman, Joyce, who falls in love with the GI. Called a "traitor" in England, she is barred from going to the US as Travis's wife by the Jim Crow segregation laws. Yet only half way through her account do we learn the soldier she has fallen for is black.

Her creator is ambivalent. "Joyce is a natural. She has an admirably non-racist view of the world," he says. "But she scares the shit out of me. She's vulnerable in her absolute naivety, because the world isn't like that. You want to hug her and shake her by the shoulders at the same time." Phillips believes there were possibly many Joyces among the English in the 1940s. "When the US army arrived, it was the first time many Britons outside the slaving ports had come into contact with black people."

Phillips had driven around the Deep South "looking" for Travis. "But I couldn't find his voice, and if it's not working, I don't care about balance for its own sake. You simply cut through to whatever gives you the truth, as you understand it."

He hesitates, when asked why he found the truth in the Englishwoman's voice. "The undercurrents that feed your writing can take time to become clear. . . . Joyce speaks a Yorkshire dialect I grew up speaking. But it's probably the most painful thing I've ever written." In the final pages, Joyce is embraced by the African father as one of his children. "It seemed emotionally correct. She grew up without a dad, and what binds her to the others is that lack."

Phillips was eight when his own parents divorced. While he grew up in Leeds, his father had "shall we say, an on-and-off relationship with the household". The diasporan experience in his work is largely one of painful dislocation, fracture and abandonment. But the final pages of *Crossing the River* are suffused with a moving, almost jubilant, sense of redemptive love. The children, "hurt but determined", reach the far bank of the river buoyed by their own "many-tongued chorus" and by a father's healing embrace.

"There is an annealing force," Phillips agrees. "I didn't want only to explore the fissures and crevices of migration. There's an underlying passion that informs people's ability to do more than just survive—a love and faith present everywhere I look among the children of the African diaspora, from Jimmy Baldwin to Miles Davis, to Marvin Gaye, that's both triumphant and celebratory."

Janet Burroway (review date 30 January 1994)

SOURCE: "Slaves to Fate," in *New York Times Book Review,* January 30, 1994, p. 10.

[*In the following review, Burroway considers* Crossing the River *"a brilliant coherent vision" and "a book with an agenda."*]

"The past is never dead," William Faulkner observed. "It's not even past." This perception is brought home in Caryl Phillips's fifth novel, *Crossing the River*—which, although it plays with disjunctive time, presents a brilliantly coherent vision of two and a half centuries of the African diaspora.

The main body of Mr. Phillips's novel consists of four taut narratives—two white voices, two black; two male, two female. But its structure is poetic, built on a single refrain: "Why have you forsaken me?" The voices are richly counterpointed, and the forsakings are as various as the author's extraordinary imagination can make them.

In the prologue, a nameless' African father, his crops having failed, sells his children to the master of a slave ship. Haunted for 250 years by "the chorus of a common memory," he discovers "among the sundry restless voices" those of his lost children: "My Nash. My Martha. My Travis." Gradually, as the stories in the main text unfold, we realize that this father has taken on the mythic proportions of the continent of Africa, that his abandonment represents the irreversible history of entire peoples.

In the first section, set in the early 1840's, we follow Nash

Williams, the gifted freed slave of an abolitionist Virginia tobacco planter. Having undergone "a rigorous program of Christian education," Nash is sent as a missionary to the west coast of Africa, under the auspices of the American Colonization Society. His letters back to Virginia, a mélange of stoicism and plaint, are interleaved with narrative concerning his adoptive white father and onetime master, Edward Williams. A bitter former favorite makes his way into the story; it also appears that Edward's prudish wife, now dead, intercepted Nash's letters. Such information comes piecemeal and aslant, but when the sources of the bitterness and the interference reveal themselves the events seem inevitable.

Nash disappears, "lost somewhere on the dismal coastline of Africa," and Edward sets out to find him. In the sort of paradox that persists throughout the book, Nash—who has been "bettered" by his Christian education and thereby become a leader among a group of Liberians—is ultimately demoralized by his life in Africa and in turn demoralizes his new community. When paternalistic Edward appears among them, the Liberians see only a purposeless and strange old man, an emblem of abasement.

Skip to the end of the century. In the next section, an old black woman named Martha Randolph, hired on as a cook but now too weak to travel, is abandoned by a wagon train in the snowy streets of Denver. Sold away from her husband and daughter in Virginia, her second man and her business in Colorado lost to white violence, worn out by long days of washing and ironing, Martha has spent her life creeping westward. She entertains fantasies of her daughter, Eliza Mae, in finery on the California coast.

As she draws toward death, Martha is befriended by a local white woman who takes her home. Martha has throughout her life been "unable to sympathize with the sufferings of the son of God when set against her own private misery," and has fought the arbitrary imposition of identity. Now, ironically, when Martha dies without disclosing who she is, her benefactor reflects that "they would have to choose a name for her if she was going to receive a Christian burial."

Reel back a century. In the most spectacular accomplishment of the novel, Mr. Phillips produces the journal and letters home of one James Hamilton, captain of the slave ship Duke of York on its voyage from Liverpool to "the Windward Coast of Africa" and thence across "the river" that is the Atlantic.

Like Edward Williams, the 26-year-old Hamilton has reason to go searching in Africa: his father died there, and the death is shrouded in mystery. The elder Hamilton was without religion, perceiving that his profession of slave ship captain was incompatible with a profession of faith. There are hints that he "traded not wisely" and that he "cultivated a passionate hatred, instead of a commercial detachment," toward his slaves.

> **One of the values of fiction is that it can tell the story anew, can go back and include a neglected truth. *Crossing the River* does this and is therefore a book with an agenda.**
>
> —*Janet Burroway*

The young Hamilton's log is terse, businesslike, admirably controlled. His letters to his wife are tender and full of delicate devotion, longing. He suffers the intransigence of his first mate and the death of his second; he faces insurrection, rats, rising prices, raging fevers. He is resilient and honorable; he absorbs recurrent hardship with fortitude and grace. But in that stunning myopia that can attend such honorable men, he buys, feeds, punishes, worries about, loses to sickness and washes down the walls after his load of black flesh: "This day buried 2 fine men slaves, Nos. 27 and 43, having been ailing for some time, but not thought in danger. Taken suddenly with a lethargic disorder from which they generally recover."

Throughout, Hamilton is perplexed by the mood of his cargo, who "appeared gloomy and sullen, their heads full of mischief." Just before departing from Africa, he is "approached by a quiet fellow" from whom he buys the "2 strong man-boys, and a proud girl," of the prologue.

Fast-forward two centuries. In the book's final section, a working-class Yorkshire woman named Joyce, whose father died in World War I, makes a bad marriage with a black-lung lager lout on the eve of World War II. He is safe from the draft, but that damages his manhood, which he bolsters by punching her. He is jailed for trafficking in the black market—"a vulture picking at the carcass of his wounded country," as the judge puts it—and Joyce drags through her war, her life, until an invasion of Yank defenders sets in her path a shy black soldier with hair like fine wool, combed shiny from a razor part. Joyce is an image of possibility in the novel. But when her lover, Travis, like her father, abandons her by dying, she in turn forsakes their child, giving him up for adoption in the great machine of British do-goodery.

Identity, in both individuals and peoples, is composed of the story that we tell ourselves of the past. That story is necessarily partial and selective, but if it deliberately omits significant events the resultant self is inauthentic. One of the values of fiction is that it can tell the story anew, can go back and include a neglected truth. *Crossing the River* does this and is therefore a book with an agenda. Mr. Phillips proposes that the diaspora is permanent, and that blacks throughout the world who look to Africa as a benevolent fatherland tell themselves a stunted story. They need not to trace but to put down roots. The message, however, is neither simply nor stridently conveyed. Mr. Phillips's prologue strikes it as a stately note, and its resonance continues to deepen; only in the epilogue does it become uncomfortably literal. Mr. Phillips's theme sounds throughout, perhaps most poignantly in the laconic notation of Captain Hamilton:

"We have lost sight of Africa."

Caryl Phillips with Carol Margaret Davison (interview date 14 February 1994)

SOURCE: "Crisscrossing the River: An Interview with Caryl Phillips," in *Ariel*, Vol. 25, No. 4, October, 1994, pp. 91-99.

[In the following interview, Phillips talks about his literary success and his responsibilities as a writer.]

Taken to England at the "portable" age of 12 weeks from St. Kitts, one of the Leeward Islands in the Caribbean, 35-year-old Caryl Phillips grew up in Leeds, was educated at Oxford, and has spent his literary career probing the ramifications of displacement, a complex condition that he claims characterizes the twentieth century and "engenders a great deal of suffering, a great deal of confusion, a great deal of soul searching." Describing writers as "basically just people who are trying to organize their confusion," he has opted, it would seem, for the right calling. The rapidly growing list of honours for his prolific output certainly validates his choice. The author of five novels, Phillips was the recipient of the Malcolm X Award for his first novel, *The Final Passage* (1985), and the Martin Luther King Memorial Prize for his travel-commentary *The European Tribe* (1987). While *The Final Passage* and *A State of Independence* (1986) were "written out of a sense of great elation at having 're-discovered' the Caribbean," his third novel, *Higher Ground* (1989), encompasses everything from Africa in the days of slave trading to post-World War II Europe and the Black Power Movement. With the publication in 1991 of his fourth novel, *Cambridge,* which chronicles the story of Emily, a nineteenth-century woman who escapes an arranged marriage by travelling to her father's West Indian plantation where she is exposed to the effects of slavery and colonialism, Phillips garnered more serious attention in North America. Back "home" in England, he was subsequently named *(London) Sunday Times'* Young Writer of the Year in 1992 and listed among GRANTA's Best of Young British Novelists of 1993. He is also a well-established playwright and currently is Visiting Professor of English at Amherst College in Massachusetts, USA.

Phillips's fifth novel, *Crossing the River,* shortlisted for Britain's prestigious Booker Prize in 1993 and published in January 1994 by Knopf, Canada, is a sophisticated, sometimes-sorrowful meditation upon the painful dislocations, longings, and "weird" relationships borne of the aptly named "peculiar institution" of slavery. Three years in the making and spanning 250 years of the African diaspora, *Crossing the River* is a fragmented work plagued by questions of iden-

tity, paternalism, and spiritual growth. The novel is framed by an African father's melancholic reflections on his desperate act of selling his three children into slavery following his crop's failure and relates their life stories. In each instance, Phillips conjures up largely unchronicled moments in black history: Nash becomes a Christian missionary repatriated to the new land of Liberia in the 1830s; Martha, at the end of the nineteenth century, accompanies some black pioneers west in search of her beloved daughter; and Travis is stationed as an American GI in a small Yorkshire village during the Second World War.

This interview was conducted by telephone on 14 February 1994, when Phillips was engaged to read from *Crossing the River* at Harbourtfront, in Toronto, Canada.

[Davison:] **Crossing the River** *has been called your most ambitious work to date. Do you think that's an accurate description?*

[Phillips:] Not really. I think they're all pretty ambitious. When you sit down with an idea—to turn it into a novel, it's always a big risk, it's always a danger. So there's an element of ambition always. In the formal sense, however, it probably is my most ambitious work. But it's not in the more specific way of looking at the desire to write a book and the ambition. They're all as hard as each other.

What was the seed of this book?

Originally, I had lots of ideas in my mind, including doing a piece about something in the Second World War. That was the idea to start with and then it just got out of control.

The novel reminded me somewhat of your 1983 play **The Shelter***. You span a great deal of time there too, moving from Act One, set in the eighteenth century, to Act Two in the 1950s. You also deal there with interracial relationships.*

That's interesting. Most people haven't made any references to *The Shelter,* a play I wrote back in 1982-83, because they don't know of it. It's not as easily accessible as most of the novels, but if I were to look at one piece of work of mine which has the beginning of this structural paranoia and schizophrenia, that would be it. You could say that I've been writing or exploring the way of writing and connecting across centuries for ten years.

What was your principal aim in writing **Crossing the River***? What did you feel you wanted to do here that you hadn't done in your earlier work?*

Well, I wanted to make a connection between the African world which was left behind and the diasporan world which people had entered once they crossed the water. I wanted to make an affirmative connection, not a connection based upon exploitation or suffering or misery, but a connection based upon a kind of survival. This is an unusually optimistic book for me. I don't have a deliberately downbeat feel, but there's never been a redemptive spirit to the things that I've written. There's always been a sense that things have been rough and people have just about managed to limp by and survive, but I don't think there's any reason why one should be "positive." I have never really had a very optimistic view of things.

In some of your earlier interviews, however, you have expressed surprise about being pegged as a pessimist.

I have been surprised because I've never really considered myself to be a pessimist, but I've never really given people any good reason to think otherwise.

As your wonderful portraits of the elderly Western pioneer, Martha, and the restrained British housewife, Joyce, attest in **Crossing the River,** *you have a tremendous ability to do cross-gender writing. By that I am referring to the ability to enter the consciousness of a woman—and in the case of Joyce, here, and Emily in* **Cambridge,** *you have the added difficulty of traversing racial difference too. Do you have any thoughts about assuming a female voice? Do you think this involves a special ability at all?*

I don't feel it requires any particular strengths. The deal is really that we all play to our own strings, and you find out where you feel most comfortable. Women's position on the edge of society—both central in society, but also marginalized by men—seems to me, in some way, to mirror the rather tenuous and oscillating relationship that all sorts of people, in this case, specifically, black people, have in society, and maybe there is some kind of undercurrent of communicable empathy that's going on. Again, I don't want to make too much of anything because I don't really see it as that much of a mystery. It doesn't appear to be that way to me, and I don't want to find a logical reason in case the ability to do so somehow goes away. I do think that to write only from the point of view of a male is to exclude half of the world and I obviously want to include as many different points of view as I can, so I'm very pleased that I've never really felt a problem doing that.

There are certainly many different literary influences in **Crossing the River.** *Several critics mention the echoes of Toni Morrison's* Beloved *in the Martha Section. It also seems to me that the father figure here whose voice frames the four narrative segments encompasses the voices of the African diaspora just as Saleem Sinai encompasses the whole of India in Salman Rushdie's* Midnight's Children. *Could you speak a bit about the various literary influences at work here?*

I haven't sat down and thought too clearly about what books have perhaps influenced me in putting this novel together, but you have certainly named some authors who are big influences. *Beloved* has been particularly influential. It's al-

ways easier for an author to see these things in retrospect and, looking back, yes, I can see the influences of all of these people. It's a novel which is fragmentary in form and structure, polyphonic in its voices, which means that a lot of my reading and a lot of the people whose work I've enjoyed have made their way in. Obviously there's ample room for echoes of all sorts of people. It's great for me as a writer because it allows me to switch gear or switch direction, shift perspective, and at each new turn I'm able to employ something else which, obviously, I have learned by reading other people's work.

Another book that kept coming to mind while I was reading **Crossing the River** *was Edward Brathwaite's jazzy Caribbean poem-trilogy,* The Arrivants. *I decided finally to pull it off the shelf and, lo and behold, I discovered that Chapter Five is entitled "Crossing the River."*

Is it? I know him. He's going to murder me. Is it really? I'm going to write that down. That's probably where I got the original title because I first thought of this title 10 or 11 years ago.

There is a haunting, reiterated Biblical question throughout this novel, namely, "Father, why hast thou forsaken me?" Nash mentions this about his white "father" Edward; Martha seems to be addressing God when she repeats the same phrase in Section Two. In the larger picture, of course, they are addressing their flesh-and-blood father who has sold them to the slave traders. The connected issues of paternalism and responsibility are often mediated upon here. What exactly fascinates you about these subjects?

It seems to me that the very nature of the relationship between the master and the slave, the colonizer and the colony, Britain and the Caribbean, is paternalistic. The whole question of relationships between black and white historically has tended to be paternalistic and perhaps enshrouded in some air of patronage at times, and so I've always been interested in those kinds of power relationships. It has such Biblical overtones as well because it is also a reference to religious

> There tends to be a preponderance of single mothers. I'm very interested in the whole question of how, on the personal level, that has emerged out of the larger development of slavery and all of those kinds of diasporan movements. There is a very commonly held theory that one of the reasons there is such a preponderance of single mothers is *because* of slavery, an institution which greatly disrupted the black family.
>
> *—Caryl Phillips*

themes. In the immigrant experience in Britain, the father was often pretty absent from the home. There are so many broken families in the black community in general, not just in the migrant community. There tends to be a preponderance of single mothers. I'm very interested in the whole question of how, on the personal level, that has emerged out of the larger development of slavery and all of those kinds of diasporan movements. There is a very commonly held theory that one of the reasons there is such a preponderance of single mothers is *because* of slavery, an institution which greatly disrupted the black family. There is an idea that if you take away a man's responsibility for his children, which is what happened in slavery when the man was replaced by the master as head of the family, it does something to the psyche of the man of African origin. It induces an irresponsibility. I don't know whether this is true or not. I'm not a sociologist or an anthropologist, but all of these issues make me interested in that whole power-father-paternalistic-patronage issue. They all seem to be pretty linked.

I want to ask you about your changing ideas about the writer's responsibilities. In the introduction to your play **The Shelter,** *you speak of the various burdens on the writer; in particular, you state that you were then motivated by the luxury of inexperience and felt that your "only responsibility was to locate the truth in whatever piece I was working on, live with it, sleep with it, and be responsible to that truth, and that truth alone." In* **The European Tribe** *[1987], written a few years later, you seem to be more aware of the power the writer has along political lines. You state towards the end of that book: "I had learnt that in a situation in which history is distorted, the literature of a people often becomes its history, its writers the keepers of the past, present, and future. In this situation a writer can infuse a people with their own unique identity and spiritually kindle the fire of resistance." What do you feel today about your responsibility as a writer?*

I think that the second piece from **The European Tribe** is a development from what I thought earlier. It doesn't displace what I thought earlier, because I do think that that remains true—your first responsibility is to locate the truth and to deal with the truth, particularly as it relates specifically to the characters—but I think that by travelling and writing a bit more and becoming hopefully a bit more knowledgeable about writing and the world and about other writers' lives in other communities, I did realize—and I think that I already knew it, but I wasn't able to articulate it—that there is a particular responsibility in *certain* situations for the writer to take up. He doesn't have to become a politician, but the writer has to be aware of the writer's power, his capacity for good as well as his ability to duck larger social responsibility. I agree with the position I had in **The European Tribe,** but I would go further than that and say that it seems to me increasingly important since then that one, as a writer, does try to locate the truth in one's work. You do become aware of the possibility of being somebody who can identify a history and perhaps

do something about redressing the imbalance of some of the ills and falsehoods that have been perpetrated by others about your own history. But beyond that, I think a writer really has a responsibility to at least acknowledge that he was produced by very specific social circumstances. We weren't, any of us—male, female, black, white, whatever—immaculate conceptions dropped out of nowhere without a history. One shouldn't feel a guilt for one's history and one shouldn't feel ashamed of one's history, one should just take responsibility for it.

Do you ever feel, though, that you have to compromise conveying your own personal "truths" because they clash with your responsibilities as a writer, or is it your primary responsibility to tell the truth, the whole truth, and nothing but the truth, so help you God?

The latter. I don't think I could actually write properly if I felt that in any way, even in any small way, that I was somehow in my life as well as in my writing, not tackling issues of injustice and speaking up when they appear. I just don't think I could do it, because I think that eventually those kinds of lies and that kind of self-deception do seep into your work. It has honestly never occurred to me to pull a punch a little bit or change gears. I don't think you can do that. I mean I just don't see how you can. You just have to continually risk coming up against irate people.

As you are certainly aware, today is not only Valentine's Day. Today marks the fifth anniversary of the fatwa *declared against Salman Rushdie. Do you have any comments about Rushdie's situation and the issue of censorship and writing in general?*

I just got off the phone with him. He and I speak a lot. To tell you the truth, I don't think that I have got anything to say that hasn't already been said and maybe said better by others, but I was talking to somebody earlier today about his situation. It seems to me clearly that one of the most unfortunate things in the *fatwa* is the way a lot of people in the West have taken it as a convenient excuse to hammer Islam, and it's not Islam that needs to be hammered. It's a particular extreme branch of Islam. It really is like judging the whole of Christianity on the actions of the Spanish Inquisition. It doesn't really make any sense. That has nothing to do with Salman personally. That is just my own discomfort at watching writers and other people, including a lot of people who should know better, who claim to be defending Salman Rushdie making incredibly sweeping and stupid comments about Islam, but not taking into consideration that this isn't Islam. There are many Muslims all over the world who think this is an outrage.

What were your feelings about being nominated for the Booker Prize? Were you surprised?

That's a good question. Was I surprised? Well, I suppose I

was a little bit. To tell you the truth, I was more surprised that *Cambridge* wasn't nominated because everyone kept telling me it would be. So by the time this came around, I was pleased but I just didn't care because I realized how much of a lottery it was. I wondered about it in the days leading up to it when it was *Cambridge*. This time I didn't even know that it was the day of the announcements or anything. I came into my office and there was a message from Salman on the machine. I was pleased because of the sales.

What were your feelings when Roddy Doyle received it?

Oh, that was fine. I know Roddy. I was sitting right at the next table. I didn't mind you see because it wasn't really about winning it. I was just pleased to be on the shortlist. After a while, you need to get sales because the more sales you get, the more money you get. The more money you get, the more time you have, and that's the deal. I'm not sure that I would want to be like Miss World for a year, which is what you would be if you won. I was pleased that Roddy won because he is a nice guy. At the Booker Prize dinner everybody talked to everybody. The person that I knew the best was David Malouf and, in some ways, I would have liked David Malouf to have won simply because he's 25 years older than Roddy and I who are both 35. I'll get another chance as will Roddy, even though he doesn't really need another chance, but I would have liked David Malouf, whose work I really admire, to have won it and gained this recognition at this stage of his career. As Kazuo Ishiguro, who called me up the morning of it, said: "Just remember, it's an exercise in public humiliation."

Speaking of influences, taking into consideration both their life and their work, who stands out as the most important single literary influence on you?

I would probably have to say, if it's a combination of their life and their work, James Baldwin. I hesitated because there's no other person who I've ever met who is a writer who has been as important to me. I think that this is partly because at the time when I met him I was a sort of "wanna-be" writer. To meet a real and a great writer, I was incredibly lucky. He was also incredibly generous with his time.

The novel seems to have a firm hold on you. Would you ever consider writing another play?

Oh yes, I'm probably going to write another play next year or later this year. I prefer the theatre to film. There are just too many people involved in television and film. I have worked in both mediums, and I don't particularly enjoy them that much.

Have you ever been approached by anyone about adapting one of your novels for the screen?

I have often been approached by people who have wanted to do that. I'm afraid that I'm not usually very good at replying. I get my agent to speak to them, but it's not a world that I feel particularly comfortable in anymore. A number of my friends have had bad experiences having their novels adapted or even adapting them themselves. I'll tell you the truth. I look upon adaptations of my work for the screen as something that I would like to be involved in and I would like to see happen at a time when I don't feel quite so fertile about producing original work. There may be a time down the line, whether it's in 5 or 25 years' time, when I just feel I don't have anything else to say, or I dry up, then it would be fun to go back and look at some of the early work and try to find new ways of saying that stuff and working on the screen. But right now, I'm too keen and eager and hungry to write prose, so I don't want to waste time on screen work.

Farah Jasmine Griffin (review date June-September 1994)

SOURCE: A review of *Crossing the River*, in *Boston Review*, Vol. XIX, Nos. 3-4, June-September, 1994, pp. 45-46.

[*In the following review, Griffin gives a favorable assessment of* Crossing the River, *concluding that "the book's final pages [are] surely among the most powerful and beautiful pages written in contemporary literature."*]

Caryl Phillips's stunning novel [*Crossing the River*] begins in a painful act of abandonment: the anonymous narrator, a father on West Africa's Pagan Coast, sells his three children into slavery. Through this desperate act, he unwittingly initiates a "many-tongued . . . chorus of common memory" that extends from the Middle Passage, through Liberia, across the United States to Colorado, and to World War II Britain. The voices that comprise this chorus bear eloquent witness to the disruption, displacement, and loss of Diaspora—and to the common humanity of the enslaved, the enslavers, and their common descendants.

James Hamilton, slave trader and captain of the *Duke of York,* records the mundane details of his life in a captain's log: "Thursday 27th August . . . All day fair weather. A brig informed us of variable winds"; "Monday 5th October . . . Caught a small dolphin"; "Monday 16th November . . . Was shown 11 slaves, of whom I picked 5, viz., 4 men, 1 woman." On January 10th he writes to his wife, "My affection for you goes beyond any words I can find or use, and I simply wish that it were possible for you to travel with me, and strengthen my purpose in fatigue and difficulty, without actually suffering them." Twelve days later he notes in the ship's log, "Bought a pair of man-boys from an African *prince*." Such juxtapositions underscore the horror of Hamilton's trade. His actions are so frightening because his sensibilities—his concern for the weather, his inexpressible love for his wife, and his sense that "a continued indulgence in this trade and a keen faith cannot reside in one breast"—are so familiar.

Edward Williams, too, is guilt-ridden. At age 29, he inherits his father's estate, including 300 slaves. Concerned to still his conscience, Williams educates them and trains the best and brightest to become missionaries. He also displays an "excess of affection" for his young male slaves, especially Nash Williams who calls Edward "Father," signing letters from Liberia, "Your son."

Nash Williams is the ambivalent diasporic subject in search of "home." His seven years of unanswered letters to Edward—letters intercepted by Edward's jealous wife—trace his growth from a westernized Christian missionary, grateful for his master's benevolence, into the embittered man who has "freely [chosen] to live the life of the African." In a letter dated September 11, 1834, Williams writes, "Liberia, the beautiful land of my forefathers, is a place where persons of color may enjoy their freedom. It is the home for our race, and a country in which industry and perseverance are required to make a man happy and wealthy. Its laws are founded upon justice and equality, and here we may sit under the palm tree and enjoy the same privileges as our white brethren in America. Liberia is the star in the East for the free colored man. It is truly our only home." Nash's final letter to Edward Williams crystallizes his growing distance from his former master and from his role as missionary: "We, the colored man, have been oppressed long enough. We need to contend for our rights, stand our ground, and feel the love of liberty that can never be found in your America. Far from corrupting my soul, this Commonwealth of Liberia has provided me with the opportunity to open up my eyes and cast off the garb of ignorance which has encompassed me all too securely the whole course of my life." Nash Williams emerges from his letters as an assured and defiant descendant of the anonymous African, finally recognizing the need to resist white supremacy, even when it appears in the garb of benevolent paternalism.

While Phillips reveals Hamilton and Williams through the subtle linearity of their own voices, in journal entries and letters, we learn about Martha, the only black woman of the novel, through interior monologue and the observations of an omniscient narrator. An elderly former slave, Martha joins a band of black pioneers traveling west. Having lost first her daughter and then her lover, she is abandoned on the streets of Denver when she becomes too much of a burden on the other travellers. Huddled in a doorway, "curling herself into a tight fist against the cold," Martha resembles the street people of our day, lost and abandoned souls who garner our pity or our wrath. Wondering whether a passerby will spit on her, she finally asks, *"Father, why hast thou forsaken me?"*

Martha's story is rich, nuanced and unfamiliar. She is an elderly black woman, tired, not strong or invincible: victimized but not victim. Both blacks and whites abandon her. And, she is not religious: "Martha could find no solace in religion, and was unable to sympathize with the sufferings of the son of God when set against her own private misery." Her ques-

tion, "Father, why hast thou forsaken me?" is not a momentary lapse but an emblem of her crisis of faith. Moreover, her story takes place in an unfamiliar territory, the west. Few African American writers have mapped the terrain of those black pioneers who trekked west in search of "a place where things were a little better than bad, and where you weren't always looking over your shoulder and wondering when somebody was going to do you wrong." Although Martha's body moves in a freer space, that tired, broken body cannot take advantage of this freedom, and its mind remains enslaved by memory.

Through Martha we learn the subtle differences between slavery and freedom: life doesn't get easier, one just has the right to claim a momentary happiness. "I was free now, but it was difficult to tell what difference being free was making in my life. I was just doing the same things like before, only I was more contented, not on account of no emancipation proclamation, but on account of my Chester." This freedom is a tenuous thing. When white men kill her independent black lover, the man who "has made [her] happy . . . made [her] forget—and that's a gift from above," Martha wonders "if love was possible without somebody taking it from her." A daughter of the despondent African father, Martha dies alone, anonymous, on the far bank of the river.

The final section of the novel brings the progeny of slave and enslaver together in an act of passion and love. Travis is an American GI stationed "somewhere in England." His beloved Joyce is a married, white, working-class, English woman. Joyce's sensitive, if cynical, voice dominates her tale. Speaking of Churchill and the war, she says, "I was getting good at learning the difference between the official stories and the evidence before my eyes." She is able, in particular, to see through an American officer's warnings about the black GIs stationed in her town, and she falls in love with Travis. Her defiance and independence allow her to be open to Travis, while distancing her from her provincial and abusive mother and husband. The clear-eyed, unsentimental Joyce speaks one of the major truths of the novel. Looking at her coffee-colored son, Greer, she thinks, "I almost said make yourself at home, but I didn't. At least I avoided that."

Through her love for Travis and the child they share, Joyce joins the Diaspora, and she pays a price for this alliance. In loving Travis, she boldly resists the color line, but she is forced to give up their child—yet another brown baby given away by a loving but desperate parent.

Caryl Phillips gives us a world of abandoned souls, of resistance, and of desperate, momentary love—the world of the African Diaspora and the new culture that is born from it. In the book's final pages, surely among the most powerful and beautiful pages written in contemporary literature, we hear this culture's own song. Phillips's culture of diaspora is not romanticized, rooted in a mythological African past, and the culminating chorus is correspondingly inharmonious. It sounds the voices of all the novel's characters, including that prophetic anonymous narrator who, having initiated the chorus, maps the contours of the African Diaspora in its complex, multicolored pathos and its human beauty.

FURTHER READING

Criticism

Campbell, James. "Answering Back." *London Review of Books* 13, No. 13 (11 July 1991): 20.
>   Praises *Cambridge* for revealing the consequences of the slave trade from an African's perspective.

Campbell, Peter. "Pictures." *London Review of Books* 11, No. 10 (18 May 1989): 16-17.
>   Comments on the "colonial impulse" in *Higher Ground.*

Chambers, Veronica. "A Father's Lament." *Los Angeles Times Book Review* (6 February 1994): 3, 10.
>   Claims *Crossing the River* is more than a historical novel about slavery: it is also "about parenting, about bad decisions, and remorse."

Davis, Clive. "Noble Black Suffering." *New Statesman & Society* 2, No. 46 (21 April 1989): 36.
>   Derides the theme of "noble black suffering" in *Higher Ground.*

Delbanco, Nicholas. "Themes of Lament." *Chicago Tribune Books* (23 January 1994): 5.
>   Mixed assessment of *Crossing the River,* concluding that "we focus on the teller not the tale."

Forbes, Calvin. "Slavery's Cruel Web." *Chicago Tribune Books* (1 March 1992): 6.
>   Examines *Cambridge* in the context of both American and West Indian slavery.

Friedman, Melvin J. Review of *Cambridge,* by Caryl Phillips. *Review of Contemporary Fiction* 12, No. 3 (Fall 1992): 195-6.
>   Compares *Cambridge* to William Styron's *The Confessions of Nat Turner.*

Garrett, George. "Separate Prisons." *New York Times Book Review* (16 February 1992): 1, 24-25.
>   Positive review of *Cambridge,* focusing on Phillips's characterization and narrative style.

Holmstrom, David. "Triple Mirror Images in Black and White." *Christian Science Monitor* (10 February 1994): 11.
>   Discusses racial relations in *Crossing the River.*

Johnson, Charles R. Review of *The European Tribe,* by Caryl Phillips. *Los Angeles Times Book Review* (19 July 1987): 3, 11.
>   Concludes that *The European Tribe* "is too important a book to be ignored."

———. "Slaves and Slavers, Then and Now." *Los Angeles Times Book Review* (1 October 1989): 2, 11.
>   Summarizes the novellas comprising *Higher Ground.*

Review of *The European Tribe,* by Caryl Phillips. *Journal of Black Studies* 20, No. 1 (September 1989): 113.
>   Praises *The European Tribe* for its "penetrating insights" into the social and cultural isolation of blacks in white societies.

Ledbetter, James. "Victorian's Secret." *Village Voice* 37, No. 17 (28 April 1992): 67.
>   Glowing review of *Cambridge* in terms of its "sterling and lyrical" language.

Lehmann-Haupt, Christopher. Review of *The European Tribe,* by Caryl Phillips. *The New York Times* (27 July 1987): C20.
>   Examines Phillips reasons for writing *The European Tribe.*

Lezard, Nicholas. "Facing It." *London Review of Books* 15, No. 18 (23 September 1993): 21.
>   Likens Phillips's prose in *Crossing the River* to "a mirror and a level surface on which the superficial differences between black and white can be smoothed out."

MacErlean, Neasa. "Tales of Fortune." *Books and Bookmen,* No. 353 (February 1985): 27.
>   Calls *The Final Passage* "a finely written and intelligent first novel."

Miller, Lucasta. "Passages." *New Statesman & Society* 6, No. 253 (21 May 1993): 34-35.
>   Considers *Crossing the River* "a nuanced, humane, and sympathetic" work.

Nixon, Rob. "Home Truths." *Village Voice* (16 August 1988): 51.
>   Reviews *A State of Independence* in the context of West Indian literature.

Pritchard, William H. Review of *Cambridge,* by Caryl Phillips. *Hudson Review* XLV, No. 3 (Autumn 1992): 489-90.
>   Favorable review of *Cambridge,* comparing it to Jonathan Swift's *Gulliver's Travels*

Sarvan, Charles P. Review of *Higher Ground,* by Caryl Phillips. *World Literature Today* 64, No. 3 (Summer 1990): 518.
>   Observes that *Higher Ground* "is a moving and disturbing book."

Sarvan, Charles P., and Bulaila, Abdul Aziz. Review of *Crossing the River,* by Caryl Phillips. *World Literature Today* 68, No. 3 (Summer 1994): 624-5.
> Treats *Crossing the River* in terms of postmodern, postcolonial discourse.

Spurling, John. "But Not the Passions of the Slaves." *Spectator* 270, No. 8603 (29 May 1993): 30-31.
> Finds *Crossing the River* "too imaginatively timid."

Sutherland, John. "Carre on Spying." *London Review of Books* 8, No. 6 (3 April 1986): 5-6.
> Briefly considers *A State of Independence,* calling it "an accomplished work."

Washington, Laura. "Still Invisible." *Chicago Tribune Books* (5 July 1987): 5, 9.
> Praises *The European Tribe,* but notes that Phillips is "sometimes an uneven and disjointed writer."

Additional coverage of Phillips's life and career is contained in the following sources published by Gale Research: *Black Writers; Contemporary Authors,* **Vol. 141;** *Dictionary of Literary Biography,* **Vol. 157; and** *DISCovering Authors Modules.*

Paul West

1930-

English-born American novelist, critic, short story writer, essayist, poet, and autobiographer.

The following entry provides coverage of West's career from 1987 to 1996. For further information on his life and works, see *CLC,* Volumes 7 and 14.

INTRODUCTION

Though West's publications range from poetry to literary criticism and autobiography, he is perhaps best known for his fiction, written in an intricate and ornate style that is frequently concerned with the psychological lives of minor historical figures. A French war refugee in *Rat Man of Paris* (1986) and the Romantic artist Walter Sickert in *The Women of Whitechapel and Jack the Ripper* (1992) are two examples of minor real-life figures who become key players in West's prose. These and other novels explore the complex motivations of various characters, with West's writing providing a window on their actions and life choices. West acknowledges influences on his writing as diverse as Samuel Beckett, Juan Goytisolo, and Marcel Proust, and he identifies more strongly with the writing of South Americans than North Americans. West's nonfiction has also been well received, especially his two-volume set of literary criticism, *The Modern Novel* (1963), a collection of essays that put forth his philosophy of fiction writing.

Biographical Information

West was born in Derbyshire, England, to a working class father partially blinded during combat in World War I and a middle-class mother whose career as a pianist was deferred to care for the family. The couple's relationship is the topic of West's autobiographical novel, *Love's Mansion* (1992), in which two people from differing backgrounds overcome obstacles of class and politics to form a lifelong bond that manages to transcend even boredom and familiarity. West received his Masters degree at Columbia University in 1953 and shortly afterwards relocated to the United States to teach, spending most of his career at Pennsylvania State University. West has one daughter, Mandy, born brain-damaged and mostly deaf, who is the subject of two of his books: *Words for a Deaf Daughter* (1969) and *Gala* (1976), in which he attempts to explain his daughter's place in an imperfect and random universe. West himself has suffered from various illnesses, including heart disease, diabetes, and migraine; in *A Stroke of Genius* (1995) he chronicles his experiences as a stroke victim.

Major Works

Most critical attention is focused on West's novels. Though his first novel, *A Quality of Mercy,* was published in 1961, his fiction did not gain wide critical reception until *The Very Rich Hours of Count von Stauffenberg* (1980). This historical rendering of the plot to kill Adolf Hitler is similar to West's other novels in that it presents a highly personal history of someone on the periphery of public history. This was followed by *Ratman of Paris,* a story about a real-life eccentric who roamed the streets of post-war Paris exposing passersby to a "rat"—a fox stole—which was one of his few remaining possessions from before the war. West gives the Rat Man a history and describes the chain of events that may have eventually led to his notoriety. In *Lord Byron's Doctor* (1989), West travels further back in time to fictionalize the events of Lord Byron's elite circle of writers and friends in the early eighteenth century. Though much is known of Percy and Mary Shelley, and even Mary's half sister Claire Clairmont, a more obscure figure is Byron's doctor, John William Polidori, who travelled with the group and was accepted at least in part into their literary parlors. West describes the doctor as a character filled with self-importance and second-rate prose, who eventually bored his companions and fell from their favor. One of West's most popular novels is *The Women of Whitechapel and Jack the Ripper,* in which he expounds upon the previously-published theory of a sinister plot in eighteenth-century London to keep scandal at a safe distance from the throne—a task that involved murdering several prostitutes who knew too much about Prince Edward's dealings in the city's underworld.

Critical Reception

While West has not enjoyed the widespread popular success of many well-received novelists, his reputation among critics is secure. Most have regarded his novels as well-crafted and consistent, even if some have taken issue with his meticulous prose style, marked by frequent and lengthy passages in which characters contemplate their motives and thoughts. These criticisms have prompted West to write an essay entitled "In Defense of Purple Prose," in which he lambasts the current preference of critics for a more minimalist style and staunchly defends his ornate prose as being richer and more colorful than a novel constructed with as few words as possible. Conversely, some critics admire this style. Of *The Very Rich Hours of Count von Stauffenberg, Partisan Review* critic Ronald Christ noted that "the richness of West's prose is the real wealth here and it is, like Stauffenberg's hours, loaded with all the treasures of a 'truant mind.'"

PRINCIPAL WORKS

The Fantasy Poets: Number Seven (poetry) 1952
The Growth of the Novel (nonfiction) 1959
Byron and the Spoiler's Art (nonfiction) 1960
The Spellbound Horses (poetry) 1960
A Quality of Mercy (novel) 1961
Byron: A Collection of Critical Essays [editor] (nonfiction) 1963
I, Said the Sparrow (memoir) 1963
The Modern Novel [two volumes] (nonfiction) 1963; revised edition, 1965
Alley Jaggers (novel) 1964
Robert Penn Warren (criticism) 1964
The Snow Leopard (poetry) 1964
Tenement of Clay (novel) 1965
The Wine of Absurdity: Essays on Literature and Consolation (nonfiction) 1966
I'm Expecting to Live Quite Soon (novel) 1969
Words for a Deaf Daughter (biography) 1969
Caliban's Filibuster (novel) 1971
Bela Lugosi's White Christmas (novel) 1972
Colonel Mint (novel) 1973
Gala (novel; sequel to *Words for a Deaf Daughter*) 1976
The Very Rich Hours of Count von Stauffenberg (historical novel) 1980

Out of My Depths: A Swimmer in the Universe (autobiography) 1983
Rat Man of Paris (novel) 1986
Sheer Fiction (criticism) 1987
The Place in Flowers Where Pollen Rests (novel) 1988
The Universe, and Other Fictions (short stories) 1988
Lord Byron's Doctor (historical novel) 1989
Portable People (nonfiction) 1990
Sheer Fiction, Volume 2 (nonfiction) 1991
Love's Mansion (memoir) 1992
The Women of Whitechapel and Jack the Ripper (historical novel) 1992
A Stroke of Genius: Illness and Self-Discovery (memoir) 1995
The Tent of Orange Mist (novel) 1995
My Mother's Music (memoir) 1996
Sporting with Amaryllis (novel) 1997

*These novels form the "Alley Jaggers" trilogy.

CRITICISM

David Lehman (review date 2 August 1987)

SOURCE: "Uncommonly Good Common Readers," in *Book World The Washington Post,* Vol. XVII, No. 31, August 2, 1987, p. 10-11.

[*In the following review of* Sheer Fiction, *a collection of essays explaining West's love of elaborate, colorful prose, Lehman praises the author's style in an era typified by minimalist writing.*]

In *Sheer Fiction,* Paul West votes for verbal gigantism, a high-caloric linguistic pleasure principle. West, whose 10 published novels include *Rat Man of Paris* and *The Very Rich Hours of Count von Stauffenberg,* is an unabashed proponent and practitioner of purple prose. He is for pageantry, against austerity; for prose that is "revved up, ample, intense, incandescent, or flamboyant"; against any sensibility that would regard "taut, clean, crisp, tight, terse, lean" as virtues; for baroque elaboration and sheer invention, against naturalism in any narrow sense. The foremost enemy is trendy "minimalism," a dandy punching bag. Minimalism, West writes, is "the ponderous ho-hum of the gull who thinks fiction somehow photographs life instead of mimicking life's creative ways. Minimalism to me is what there cannot be too little of."

The essays in *Sheer Fiction* rely on digressions, deviations, and bravura displays of associative logic to enact their themes. Take, for example, **"A Rocking Horse on Mars"** (one of several marvelous titles), which begins as an autobiographical memoir ("I was born in Lady Chatterley's village"). When we arrive at the author's discovery of William Faulkner ("Sometimes there were four pages of narrative to one word of dialogue—an act of sublime defiance"), we seem to be in familiar Wordsworthian territory, charting the growth of the writer's mind. Suddenly, the essay makes a sharp right turn—or, rather, it signals right and proceeds to turn left. Reminiscence breaks off; what we get instead are scientific wonders and metaphysical speculations. By the close of the piece, the argument (for there remains the structure of an argument, even if it eludes paraphrase) has transformed itself not once but several times, with the freedom of a poetic equation, the freedom of "sensuous opportunism."

"Sometimes," West writes, "the game we play with literature interests us more than literature itself." This is often the case with West himself. There is something compulsive in his procedures, as if he cannot ask a rhetorical question without needing to exfoliate it into five others. The result occasionally resembles a feast of words that go down smoothly but leave us feeling a little hungry again a half hour later. There is also the tendency to overstate the case, as when West asserts that "sheer consumerism has always kept the novel back, making it into a commodity rather than an art form." Didn't Dickens prove it was possible for the novel to be both?

It's impossible, however, to stay mad for very long with anyone who writes so well, and with such evident zest, about a time when minimalism will have breathed its last, when novelists will feel as "technically" free as abstract expressionists, and when "literary art may never offer a beginning, a middle, and an end, in that order, again, except out of nostalgia." An extreme statement? To be sure, but sometimes those are the most effective kind.

Gregory Feeley (review date 31 July 1988)

SOURCE: "Fragments and Fancy," in *Book World The Washington Post,* Vol. XVIII, No. 31, July 31, 1988, p. 9.

[*In the following mixed review of West's collection of short stories entitled* The Universe, and Other Fictions, *Feeley comments that the author's narrative voice fluctuates little over the series of stories.*]

The stories in Paul West's ***The Universe, and Other Fictions*** are [short, dense] and so learned as to seem often gnomic. More shapely as fictions, they take on themes familiar from West's earlier books but here greatly compressed, like a sauce boiled down to daunting richness. **"Life With Atlas"** is more récit or meditation than dramatic narrative, in which the Atlas of myth speaks about his endless burden, how he misses his daughters the Pléiades, and the hydrogen whisper of the universe. "Atlas is coming out in words," his interlocutor remarks,

> and I'm in the near-fatuous position of transposing a voice-in-the-head, but spoken into the tape by myself, into yet another medium, of which not even my

best friend, Etna, would call me master . . . When the Voice of Ages (or whatever) deigns to favor you with some friendly gab, you don't make picayune cracks about the quality of reception, the speed or slowness of the transmission, the timbre of his vowels, and you certainly don't mind that occasionally you get lost in him, he in you, the pair of you in the maze of triply-transposed transcription.

It must be said that a little of this goes a long way. West's narrative voice in these monologues, a kind of bardic breath that ranges over questions of consciousness, astrophysics, and the birth and death of galaxies, ends up sounding very similar whether the narrator is Atlas, one of Shakespeare's brain cells, or the sun. About half the stories consist of such starstruck, anachronism-ridden ("Such poachings or previsions are part of cranial voxology, take my word for it") discourse, the rest more traditional narratives, which also tend to concern yearnings toward the ineffable. In one a physicist stares too long at a solar eclipse and finds his sight burned into intolerable clarity, while in another a Jamaican tour guide dreams of finding fleshly transcendence by breaking through his glass-bottomed boat.

Both volumes show a narrower range than the author's novels do; and each seems likelier to interest its author's present readers than gain him new ones—less a gallery opening than a peep into the workshop, though nonetheless welcome enough for that.

Hartman H. Lomawaima (review date 9 October 1988)

SOURCE: "The Moment in Fiction When Truth Flees," in *The Los Angeles Times Book Review,* October 9, 1988, pp. 2, 15.

[*In the following review, Lomawaima faults* The Place in Flowers Where Pollen Rests *for its simplistic portrayal of Hopi life and accuses West of imposing his own meaning on Native American culture.*]

The title of this novel is also the surname of its protagonist. George The Place In Flowers Where Pollen Rests is a Hopi man who has lived his entire life among the majestic high mesas of northeastern Arizona. The Hopi people have lived here for more than a thousand years, and among their villages is the oldest settlement in all of North America.

The story that unfolds is not in all ways unique. It is about a small-scale society, a small village, a small family and small minds. The author could have selected from an infinite number of backdrops where *small* was the operative word. In this work, he has selected to project his story against a Hopi screen. Does it work? In a word (the favorite word of George's nephew Oswald Beautiful Badger Going Over the Hill), *Negatorio:* an unequivocal no.

The story is set in our time, and the place names used are easy to locate in any Rand McNally guide. George The Place In Flowers Where Pollen Rests is not an old man, but he is beset with heart trouble and on-coming blindness, which will permanently curtail his lifelong activity as an artist. George is a carver of wooden figurines Hopis call *Tihu,* also known as kachina dolls. According to Hopi belief, kachinas are guardian spirits that possess supernatural powers.

In Hopi culture, artistry has many definitions. The farmer who dares to plant in an almost impossible environment yet manages successfully to provide for his family year after year, is an artist. The composer of songs, who is counted upon by fellow villagers to create poetic prayers for ceremonial occasions knowing that once his or her song is used, it will never be uttered in ritual again, is an artist. The sculptor who transforms driftwood and mineral pigments into likenesses of spiritual friends, kachinas for his maternal nieces, is also an artist. In actuality, Hopi who dedicate themselves to the "life of the short ear of corn" realizing both hardship and prosperity are all these things and more. They are truly artists.

George The Place In Flowers Where Pollen Rests, however, has become an artist in the narrower European sense. He is a full-time kachina doll carver, supporting himself by selling his wares. Having tried all the other Hopi "stuff," he is happiest with a piece of seasoned cottonwood root in one hand and a carving tool in the other. He is also driven by an American market that has endowed kachina dolls with a monetary value too tempting to pass up. George has resigned himself to producing dolls solely for the outside market. The market, it seems, helps George justify and sustain the solitary path he has taken.

Everyone in George's family lives on or near the Hopi homeland except for one paternal nephew, Oswald Beautiful Badger Going Over The Hill. Oswald is seeking his place among the big stars of Hollywood, paying his dues not on the old casting couch but on a set in full view of producers, directors, camera people and cameras. He thinks that pornographic movies are the avenue to bigger and better opportunities. But Oswald's part in the accidental death of a porn starlet makes him decide to return to his people.

At first glance, Oswald sees that little has changed on the Hopi mesas. He is happy to see his family, and Uncle George, in particular. After considering all the options available to him, Oswald decides he wants to learn to be a doll carver. He spends almost all his waking hours with George, who by now is completely blind but still making dolls. We become privy to the relationship that was always there between uncle and nephew, reawakened by a mutual need. We learn a little about daily reservation life. We learn something of the attitudes that government-sponsored professionals, teachers, physicians, etc., bring with them and something of how Hopis cope with their presence. But this jousting is only superficial. The

author's mind can only see what his eyes tell him to see and his inability to see beyond the obvious runs throughout the work.

Oswald enlists in the military and is sent to Vietnam. Through his eyes, we see and experience action that is all too familiar by now. After his tour of duty in Southeast Asia, he returns home again, still searching for a niche in Hopi society or any society, for that matter. In the end, he commits a most heinous act in the presence of his family, fellow villagers and guardian spirits. At last, we realize that his niche is simply to be outrageous on principle and by any society's terms.

This is the clearest indictment of Oswald's *kahopi* or non-Hopi-ness. To be a nonconformist, to act out, to disregard family, clan and village—to be *kahopi*—is the ultimate transgression of Hopi life.

West's own *kahopi* has to do with his abuse of actual Hopi people. At the opening of the book, I expected to find some disclaimer like "the names herein are fictitious . . . any resemblance to individuals living or dead is purely coincidental." But no: Thomas, Fermina, Abbott, Emory, Oswald, Dextra and, yes, even George are names of well-known contemporary Hopis.

West may object that since these first names are not *unique* to the Hopi and since he uses no Hopi last names, no actual Hopis appear in his novel. What he seems not to know or chooses to ignore is that a Hopi may have many different "last" names given to him or her by different relatives. The anchoring Hopi name—the nearest functional equivalent of a European family name—is the first name. The Place In Flowers Where Pollen Rests is not a Hopi name. Beautiful Badger Going Over The Hill is not a Hopi name. These names are the author's fantasy. But in the tiny Hopi community, the names Thomas, Fermina, George, Oswald, etc., are like Ron, Nancy, George, Barbara. Their references are inescapable. Thus making "Oswald" a porn star is like making "Ron" a porn star: It is at once eerie and outrageously vulgar.

West's Hopis, in their shallowness, one-dimensionality and simple-mindedness, owe nothing to Hopi culture. Perhaps this is inevitable, given West's incomplete knowledge of Hopi religion and the spirituality that permeates and informs all aspects of Hopi life. But to say this is scarcely to excuse him.

The italicized forms for Hopi place names, personal names and sacred names, which he scatters throughout his book, are such gross linguistic nonsense that they are almost beneath comment. Suffice it to say that assembling make-believe words from randomly selected, "Hopi-sounding" syllables does not add up to Hopi. West's pretense that they do is offensive, but, alas, this is the least of his offenses.

The principal narrator, Sotuqnangu, is identified as a kind of great spirit to the Hopi. From time to time, we find George in communication with this deity. Their interactions are likely to appeal to those who would seek refuge in Native American spirituality. But, neither the name of the deity nor the ideals Sotuqnangu is imbued with have any relationship to Hopi theology.

A high point in the book comes when the kachina doll carvings are given the opportunity to speak. They tell us how it feels to be fashioned from slabs of cottonwood root. They speak endearingly of George The Place In Flowers Where Pollen Rests and praise his skillfulness: "You always know who's boss, he works so hard his knife and chisel never cool down. He works so fast, once he knows where he's headed, you have to get used in a hurry to what you're going to be. Here I was, a slab, and I'm fast turning into *Guts in the Snow* after several hundred cuts, all of them certain as the sun coming up." This section may make delightful reading for artists, perhaps even for some Hopis. Unfortunately, it is also emblematic of the author's confusion of intent.

If he wants to write about a Hopi artist, drawing on specifically Hopi strengths for his novel, then he must not write yet another stereotypical account of a provincial artist rebelling against his benighted home community. Whatever strength that kind of story may have, it is a quintessentially European or "Western" strength, not a Hopi strength. One suspects, reading this novel, that for West, any artist in any small, isolated community would have served. The Hopi were there: Why not use them?

This is regrettable because the return of a Native American youth to his birthright is a legitimate theme. A wealth of available real-life material could have made this novel a truly human and genuinely instructive experience for its readers. What went wrong? Perhaps at some point the author realized he was overmatched in trying to understand Hopi systems of belief and artistry. At this juncture he decided to substitute his own free-form ideas for Hopi conventions and knowledge. At that point, his kachina doll turned back into a slab of wood.

Lee Lescaze (review date 1 November 1988)

SOURCE: "Mayhem on the Mesa," in *The Wall Street Journal,* November 1, 1988, p. A26.

[*In the following review, Lescaze criticizes some of the passages in* The Place in Flowers Where Pollen Rests, *suggesting that much of the narrative long-windedness dulls the characters' actions.*]

Paul West is much concerned with the pathetic puniness of man. He also has a liking for grotesques. In his previous novel, *Rat Man of Paris,* his protagonist wraps his body in filthy rags, his head in infantile dreams, and walks the streets of

Paris, alarming people by brandishing rats. In the end, he finds love, fatherhood and peace.

Oswald Beautiful Badger Going Over the Hill (it's shorter in Hopi), Mr. West's new protagonist, has an even harder time of things before reaching the level of self-discovery. We first meet him at the instant he realizes he has accidentally strangled Trudy Blue while performing in a pornographic movie.

That ends his porn career and sends him back to the Arizona mesa where he was born—and where death by suffocation is something of a motif, being ritually administered to baby eagles and to foxes. He is aimless and feeling bad, for himself at least. "Life cost more than a man ever earned," he says.

The most compelling man on the mesa is Oswald's uncle (really father, but that comes later), George the Place in Flowers Where Pollen Rests, a carver of the Hopi dolls representing gods and spirits called kachinas. Not just a carver, a compulsive carver, perhaps also the greatest of carvers.

Oswald tells us: "Suffering, joy, grief, love. He turns them into contours of the wood, turning his entire world into cottonwood root, where others turn it into conversation, fast driving, lost sleep, food uneaten." Oswald isn't entirely right. Whatever part of his world George turns into dolls, he has plenty left over to turn into conversation and monologue. While George carves, he talks. On and on. Mr. West once defined fiction as "hallucination made to behave." In *The Place in Flowers Where Pollen Rests,* Mr. West's 11th work of fiction, the hallucination is abundant, but it's out of control.

Most of the novel is in the voices of Oswald and George. Their tale is a mixture of Hopi myth, porn film making, accidental killings, Vietnam combat, village idiots, idiot-savants and long, long musings about life, art, gods, the cosmos.

Sometimes they grow lyrical. Sometimes their storytelling achieves the power of the oral tradition Mr. West is emulating. Here, for example, George imagines himself on the edge of death:

"His heart is hard as leather. His face has begun to shine like polished corn. His toes do a little scamper as if running away. His hands, too big for any human, have locked into fists. When he becomes calm, he is very close. It is like the solstice when the sun stands still and you hope the world is not going to end. He is between places."

Too often the voices grow tiresome. George speaks of modern tools, a device to take blood pressure for example, with a long-winded childlike wonder. Oswald is given an astronomy book and we get pages and pages on the movements of stars.

Always, the voices are icy cold. George is an egomaniac who

takes what he wants and let others pick up the pieces. Oswald must be one of the most unsympathetic young men ever to wander through a novel seeking to find himself.

For all Mr. West's skill, and there are pages when the incantatory tone of his prose captures the reader like a wave lifting a surfboard, *The Place in Flowers Where Pollen Rests* falls in its almost impossible mission of making a compelling story out of an almost plotless tale of two men on a mesa musing on their lives and man's fate.

Crucial events are recalled again and again. Each time the reader learns a bit more about the death of Trudy Blue (baseball fans will remember when Oakland A's former owner Charles Finley offered to pay pitcher Vida Blue to change his first name to "True"), or is fed another scrap of speculation about what really happened when Bessie went swimming with the idiots who share one name, BertandAnna.

It is a relief from mesa-musing when Oswald gets sent to Vietnam in mid-novel. At least war will provide some action. And it does. Oswald's war is wildly grotesque, far more exaggerated than such stylized killing as the battle scenes in the movie *Full Metal Jacket.* Blood spurts. Soldiers hallucinate. GIs mutilate dead enemies. In a crescendo of horror, Oswald becomes buried under the dead bodies of his comrades, safe but suffocating.

Mr. West makes the scene vivid even if not literally credible: "He threw up into his mouth, but his teeth were jammed shut against the ground with his lips hauled out of shape sideways. Again and again he heaved, longing to pass out and let history have its way with him, but he didn't, he didn't even have one of those low blood-sugar swoons he'd had before in Vietnam. The wump-wump of the rockets he now heard through his stomach."

In Vietnam, Oswald, nephew/son of the great kachina carver who tries and fails to carve kachinas himself, finds a depraved new way to carve dolls. He builds himself a companion with body parts cut from dead Vietcong. And he names it for his uncle.

Oswald's psyche, hung out to dry by his plunges into pornographic acting and Vietnam soldiering, never gets much more interesting than this. Finally, the mesa misfit finds a role for himself. He turns himself into a kachina, the "death fly" kachina from Hopi ritual.

David W. Madden (interview date 15-17 June 1989)

SOURCE: "An Interview with Paul West," in *The Review of Contemporary Fiction,* Vol. 11, No. 1, Spring, 1991, pp. 154-76.

[*In the following interview, Madden and West discuss major themes and influences in West's fiction.*]

The following interview was conducted in the front room of Paul West's home in Ithaca, New York, 15-17 June 1989. The discussion was memorable for many reasons, not the least of which were the torrential downpour outside, a temperamental fluorescent light that hummed and buzzed on and off, and a persistent groundhog determined to drown itself in West's pool. Each day West would greet me at noon with lunch, and throughout our conversations he was patient with the questions and eager to respond. He has been equally gracious in answering further questions through the mail. In all my dealings with Paul West I have found him to be delightful witty, considerate, solicitous, and extremely generous. In all ways, this project has been a genuine pleasure.

[*Madden:*] *Will you describe the importance Samuel Beckett has had for you? Much that you write has direct references, allusions, mentions of Beckett.*

[West:] Nearly everybody you talk to about fiction seems to think there's a fundamental incompatibility between writing fiction and having a good mind. Beckett struck me as somebody with a good mind who is also able to write fiction, thus demonstrating that there is no paradox at all. On the level of sheer intellectual entertainment, he gives you nonstop fodder, and I like that about him. He is adroit and sophisticated, not showing off, but actually inventing things, in an almost Nabokovian way. When I did my Beckett seminar, we did the fiction; we didn't do the plays, and the students responded to the arc of a career. There is a real trajectory in Beckett, and you can see his complexes developing. His books like *Watt* are difficult reading, but they repay you enormously if you stay with them. They're funny; they're profound; they're poignant in the extreme, more poignant than anything. When I first read him in the early sixties, I thought: Here's a man who believes, as few do, that fiction can evolve, can mutate, can become different things at different times. It's not fixed for all times ever, by anyone. I think *The Lost Ones* and *Texts for Nothing* are marvelous. He did something with fiction nobody else wanted to do. He shredded it and distilled it, but it's not minimalist. Beckett is not a minimalist; he has a maximal mind distilled and shrunken almost to a breaking, snapping point. That's a very different predicament from the vacancy paraded in minimalist writing.

What about Byron? Lately you've been returning to Byron.

Byron, by and large, is a bad poet, but fascinating nonetheless. Byron is a bit like Beckett. He has a good mind, a shrewd, adroit, concise, analytical mind, and I think the real Byron is in the letters, which are marvelous. The journals are even better, at least those we've got. If you go from them to some of the poetry, there's a tremendous intellectual lapse.

In **Lord Byron's Doctor,** *this is the Byron you're giving free play to.*

That's a well-taken point, that this Byron who is I suppose vestigially there (some of the journals were actually destroyed) is worth thinking about. A human being leaves, really, a very paltry record behind, no matter how much he/she has written when you compare that with all the thinking that went on nonstop every day of that person's life. Nathalie Sarraute calls it sub-conversation.

Sub-conversation, that's a great coinage.

Sub-conversation. Krishnamurti said, "How the mind chatters to itself." The whole idea of the mind's chattering to itself without being spoken, printed, published, or recorded fascinates me. The sub-conversation isn't available; therefore, the fiction writer has to do it. In bulk.

You've spoken elsewhere about your admiration for Sartre's Existentialism and Humanism; *could you talk about its effects on you?*

When I first read this man at seventeen, I thought: He understands. He knows what *I* want to do. From an early age I knew I wanted to get out of the mining village of my youth and had intimations from reading of different ways of living, but it did not occur to me that I wanted to be a novelist. I just wanted to get out of there to some university and think about it again. That was a reasonably big shift for a kid from a mediocre grammar school. Except that I had three amazing women who taught English, French, and Latin and Greek. They were marvelous to me. They encouraged me because they felt I had some gift for languages and should pursue that, and they groomed me. The one who taught Latin, her favorite reading was Proust, and I remember when I was about fifteen, she said here's something you really ought to read, and she gave me some of *A la recherche*. I don't think I did. I was reading Faulkner on my own, but I thought my god, this is wonderful; I've got Proust to come after Faulkner.

Could you discuss what you do when you write? How do your novels start; is each a new, unique experience?

There are two answers to that. All the time, whatever I'm doing, I hear this noise in my head that really never goes away. It's permanent. I mean I'm out there throwing a ball around. I'm swimming. I'm cooking. I'm talking. It's always there. I wish it weren't because sometimes it's a damn nuisance. Like a squeaky conveyor belt. There's always something on it, and perhaps that something isn't very useful all the time. When a novel begins, there's just more on the belt, just images and phrases, really quite obsessive things start coming along, and I ask, "What's this? Is this worth pursuing?" It's very concrete and specific when I get to the point of thinking maybe I can write a book. **Stauffenberg** began with an image, and I didn't know whose, but it was actually an image from a war magazine. The thing began haunting me. My father was half-blinded in the war, and he wore an

eye-patch sometimes; but it wasn't my father. Finally I ran it down in a very systematic way, then went and researched it and figured out who he was. But not before having already written twenty or twenty-five pages predicated on the vignette of the face and sheer ignorance. I wrote a trial piece with him being hanged. Of course he wasn't hanged. He was shot. I must have had some subliminal record of what happened to him. Then I thought, "It's the man who tried to kill Hitler." I began using third person, wrote fifty pages and stopped. It sounded like John Toland or William Shirer, so I junked it, went back and put it in first person and immediately took off and felt right. Though I had problems because he was this German whose English was fluent. In what language did he think? I mean he thought in German. He wasn't thinking in English, so there was a certain fraudulence to the whole thing. But I learned to live with that; whereas, writing in third person, I was less responsible for the chatter of his mind and could tell things from the outside quite responsibly.

But what about a book like **Tenement of Clay**? *Did that too have some vague inspiration? I know you have mentioned Kaspar Hauser; was the novel a conscious attempt to produce a twentieth-century Kaspar Hauser? Or did it come about in some fluky, inadvertent way?*

Not really. Papa Nick, who runs the brownstone tenement, actually existed, and I found him in a news magazine with a picture. Somebody had discovered him running this place. I unwisely told Harper & Row it had come from a news magazine, and they immediately installed in the contract an indemnification clause in case this guy brought any kind of legal action. But he died soon after the book came out, so there were never any problems. Much later on, I realized I was doing another Kaspar Hauser, who in the novel is John Lacland.

While the focus of attention is on Papa Nick, I found Pee Wee Lazarus incredibly hypnotic and compelling with his verbal hesitation and perverse motivation.

He just came. He was not a construct. He sprang fully formed. He was fun to work with. He was fun to write. I enjoyed doing that. I remember very distinctly writing it to Prokofiev's *Fourth Symphony*.

This sounds very much like writing **Place** *to Busoni.*

Yes, exactly the same. I just happened to have that record and began to associate it with the act of writing a book and eventually couldn't split them apart.

Was this in your mind before you began writing and you put the thing on and . . .

It's actually serendipity. But once it's happened about fifty-sixty times the engrams are saturated. I guess if I had dropped the bloody record I would have had to buy another. I wouldn't have been able to continue.

The entry in World Authors *describes* **Tenement of Clay** *as "a cruel but also extremely funny novel." As you look back on it, how do you see* **Tenement**?

I see it as neither: not cruel and not funny. It's poignant and mythic. I haven't read it in a long time, but I'm still fond of it, even if only for the music I listened to while writing it.

This is very complex. I think that because I enjoy words as much as I do, I sometimes find it hard to see beyond the words to simplistic, visual external of a human being. I sometimes need to see them in a different way, as if they were commonplace, as if on the street or in the toilet. Maybe that's why I do it. It's a way of curbing the expansive verbal element in the performance. I have to pin things down.

—Paul West

At one point in **Tenement** *Pee Wee Lazarus writes, "I know now at the least in my moments of repose that the secret of life is to learn to exclude, to achieve fullness we must achieve a shutout." Do you agree with Lazarus? Much of your writing celebrates the embrace, the inclusion of fullness.*

I don't agree with him at all. He's wrong, and I never did believe that.

It seems so antithetical to everything else you've said.

He's antithetical in every way. His resurrection is a tiny one, hence, Pee Wee Lazarus. The name, I think, was meant to be allegorical. Pee Wee is not PW.

That's not the next question by the way. Lacland reminds me very much of Bartleby, especially when he begins to revert to his former self. Knowing that you appreciate Melville, was he any inspiration for this?

No way. I hadn't read it when the work was written. To me it's my first novel. The one I repudiated is not my first novel. I had a totally different feeling writing **Tenement** than I had writing *A Quality of Mercy*.

Can you explain what that feeling was? Did you know you were on to something, this was more the real thing?

Writing the first novel was hard work. In writing the second, there was something compulsive. It wanted to be written. It came naturally. I wasn't straining for effects. I wasn't running out of characters.

It sounds as if this is where you discovered your own voice.

I think so. The first novel was very much an attempt to write in the manner of other writers, like Hemingway and Faulkner, and then never write like that again and to find my voice. I think *Tenement* plays the beginnings of the voice, though maybe not the complete register.

You've commented that with **Rat Man** *you learned of a boulevardier from friends who returned from Paris and told you about the fellow. All that sounds very neat and logical. Did it come at all from your seeing mutilés de guerre or any other people, or was it actually this one particular person who worked his way into your head?*

That seed burgeoned fast, but only because I had a book on the massacre of Oradour which I immediately linked with Rat Man's possible past. All of this is vision. It's not just music; it's visual too. Once I get the right visual image, I know where I am; I know what I'm doing. But until I get it, I don't think I'm in the mood.

This reminds me of the watercolor illustrations you made of Stauffenberg standing before the firing squad.

Yes, they helped me a great deal because I kept getting them wrong, which eye and which arm he'd lost.

Were these focusing agents for you? Did they center you?

This is very complex. I think that because I enjoy words as much as I do, I sometimes find it hard to see beyond the words to the simplistic, visual external of a human being. I sometimes need to see them in a different way, as if they were commonplace, as if on the street or in the toilet. Maybe that's why I do it. It's a way of curbing the expansive verbal element in the performance. I have to pin things down.

With **Gala** *you include all these illustrations of the Milky Way. Is this another of your attempts to give shape to something largely intangible?*

Yes. The missing piece here is that I began as a painter, before writing poetry. I especially enjoyed collages. Some of them are all right and won prizes. And there's a link, I think, between collages and comparative literature and indeed between disparate objects linked together in the style. There's a deliberate attempt to synthesize. I can see it in all aspects of things.

One can see this in the manuscript version of **Rat Man,** *which features collages and illustrations that appear and then re-appear in slightly altered form.*

That was deliberate. I'd been thinking about Breton's *Nadja,* and how wonderful the photographs are in that book. If I could only do a kind of flick-book novel; it didn't work, but I made up twenty-thirty collages and spread them throughout.

Yes, up to the Nice section, when it stops. Why did you abandon these? Was it your choice or the publisher's?

My choice. I looked at it and found the collages useful for these same reasons while writing the book, even though they were distortions, grotesque distortions in some cases. I took pieces of the novel and put them under the collages as captions. At some point I simply thought: The words are good enough on their own. This is scaffolding. I don't need it.

The dust jacket of the Doubleday edition preserves one of the collages. Who are these people?

Klaus Barbie. I don't know who the other is. I got that from *Paris Match,* I think. This is uncontaminated, unmessed with—the real thing.

When writing, how consciously do you think of an audience? What is this audience? Nabokov, for instance, once said his primary audience is himself, and then only his wife Vera and a few select readers who know his work. But he says he never writes to the "general" reader. Who's your audience?

The same. You can't. I go most of all with the first one. I write for me. And perhaps for nobody else. I'm not aware of trying to please anyone.

Do you ever think, "Oh, this friend will like this"?

Oh, I play games. I do indeed incorporate things. In the sequel to **Rat Man of Paris,** which is set in New York, there is an American novelist with an eye-patch, who happens to be Walter Abish, who is an echo of the Spanish novelist in **Rat Man of Paris** who is Juan Goytisolo. And Goytisolo picked up on that so fast and was vastly amused. So there are times when I think, Bill Gass will like this section, or he will like that phrase. There are little jokes and references. In **The Women of Whitechapel,** my Jack the Ripper novel, there is a deliberate parody towards the end, about ten lines long, in the prose style of Maurice Blanchot, and anybody who's read Blanchot is going to laugh because it's a tribute. When the writing is going full steam, I'm not even aware of being anybody at all. That's not to say it's orgasmic or anything, or that I'm the conduit for anything. But I have a tremendous sense not of its writing itself but of almost being along for the ride. I'm still in charge, but it's not an audience mode at all.

Yes, Nabokov utterly rejects the notion of a book just writing itself. Somewhere he says something about being the perfect creator of his little world.

You've got to be in charge. You are in charge of keeping a team of wild horses on track. Writing depresses some people. It doesn't depress me. I love to be doing it two or three hours a day. And that's quite enough. It's draining and fatiguing, but when I go back and revise, I'm in a very different frame of mind, calculating, very deliberate. And quite savage, willing to slash anything out that doesn't seem right. You have to be ringmaster. You have to be transcriber, translator, eavesdropper; you're all of those things. You are still responsible. If you're a good existentialist, it's still your fault, whatever happens. It's not the fault of the prose; it's not the typewriter; it's you. You're the only one who's getting it wrong, and I think that's a big responsibility. It never goes away.

Is there anything more you want to say about influence or appreciation of the Mexican, Latin American, or South American writers whom you have talked about in so many places? Do you want to say anything about why you have such strong feelings of affinity with them?

I think they reminded other people than me as well that it was possible to write the "total novel." I think the phrase is Mario Vargas Llosa's. In other words, the novel is not a form of exclusion. Anything can fall into the novel, including unrespectable things like superstition. There is no taboo. In other words we can move into history and move it around. History can be imagery, and theology can be a matter of miracles and textures and impromptu discoveries. It's all available, ransackable material. I think that the Latin Americans in their sophisticatedly innocent way remind us of that. I guess I knew it all along because I was always zooming off, thinking Europeans have a much wider horizon than the English writers I was supposed to be reading in my student days.

Did it provide a shock like that of finding unknown kin?

Yes, I felt less lonely all of a sudden. Reading Sartre I felt less lonely and reading the Latin Americans made me feel there are people who are doing the kind of thing I want to do and they have different reasons than I. An enormous door swung open and I thought I'd come to the wrong country. I should have gone south of the border, down Mexico way. That's where I really belonged. You see, I don't want the arts to linger behind. It's not so much a matter of experiment; you can experiment in the dark or you can be deliberate about it, but I think there is an energy in a given art form that propels it. There is a potential in both the doer and in the product, the book that implies further development. There is no full-fledged or consummate form of the novel or poem. Things have to evolve just as human beings have to evolve. It's defeatist and defeating to think that back in 1927 they discovered for all time the perfect way to have the novel and everything else after that is redundant or repetitious.

Don DeLillo has said that our best writers "feel that the novel's vitality requires risks not only by them [the writers] but by readers as well." He goes on to say, "Maybe it's not writers alone who keep the novel alive, but a more serious kind of reader." What do you think the reader's role is or should be?

Accomplice. I think the reader has to be willing to work hard, has to be willing to do some work. No worthwhile book is going to go through them like a laxative. It's not as if fiction were a recipe. If you followed it, you got a perfect meal within those parameters. It's not. It's a hit-or-miss game and the reader brings a subjectivity to another subjectivity. A very chancy game. It's like the thing they make you sign in hospitals. Medicine is not an exact science, and I always wanted to write under it, "Nor is it an exact art," and fiction is not an exact art. What you try to reproduce is a subjective microcosm you then try to introduce to other subjective microcosms. It's an undulating process, and I am always heartened to find readers who are willing to try. In teaching you always have to figure out: does the book you're dealing with in any way teach you how to read it? And sometimes the answer is no, and you fall on your face; whereas a book like *Remembrance of Things Past* does teach you how to read it because you begin it by thinking it will never end, and you end up wondering if it will ever begin.

You recently wrote a review of Katherine Dunn's Geek Love, *and you were taken to task by a feminist critic. Do you think her reaction, small though it may be, reveals in a broader sense an increasing, almost ideological intolerance of literature, whether that ideology—if that is the best word—is feminist, deconstructionist, or religious (as in the case of the Salman Rushdie controversy)?*

Literature is here to disturb us and make us more aware. If you're disturbed, you're probably more aware anyway. I've always believed that education (and I think that reading novels is a part of your education) exists primarily to unfit people for society; society has so many means of steamrolling people down, trimming them until they fit exactly. Education goes on after college in the form of reading books—if that doesn't protect them and save them from society, then nothing else will.

You've written book reviews for many years and still continue to write them. Why? What's in it for you? Why do it?

I used to do many more. In the old days I did it for the money because I wasn't being paid very well, and if you did enough of it, you could actually double your income. I thought it a good discipline; I learned a lot about being concise. Why do

I do it now? It keeps me up-to-date. It brings books my way which I might never read. And it's good for me, especially when I'm not writing a novel or something. I don't get rusty, and I think I learn something. I find writing reviews much more difficult than writing novels. The amount of work that goes into reading a novel, thinking about it; writing a satisfactory comment on it in a thousand words or so, that's a real discipline.

In the preface to **Stauffenberg,** *you mention medieval books of hours influencing your writing of that novel. Could you comment a bit more on the nature of the influence? Were books of hours a serendipitous kick in the pants?*

Those books offer a way of looking at people that is heraldic and I think expressionistic. Those drawings are extraordinary.

Given what we were saying earlier about existentialism and the idea of responsibility, can't **Stauffenberg,** *in one way, be seen as the story of a man who comes to assume a responsibility, an awesome, arduous, terrible responsibility?*

Yes.

But he is absolutely compelled, and books of hours are all about responsibility—who we should be and how we should live.

Good point.

I'm wondering if there isn't a connection there.

There probably was. I don't remember being specific about it. I know while writing I had King René's book on my desk. I wasn't using it as any kind of stimulus, but it was there, and I distinctly remember seeing people with their faces painted gold. No doubt about it, Stauffenberg was a prince deprived of his inheritance by the Nazis, and he could get it back only by walking back into the deadly enclosure. What he didn't realize was that in order to prevail he had to lose his life. I think that's in several of the pictures in King René's book; people are removing their hearts from their bodies and handing them to somebody else. I regard the book of hours as part of the nobleman's duty. It's all part and parcel of his responsibility to his tribe, to his people, I guess to his destiny.

Stauffenberg was a Catholic, and I wonder if this suggests another connection with the notion of responsibility, what one must do?

Oh, I think so. That's the pitch he made to his friends to get them to come in with him, that to kill Hitler was the Christian thing to do, though not the Catholic thing. Lots of them had trouble with murder, and lots of them had trouble with suicide. I find it fascinating, this Hamletizing. He wants it both ways. He wants to kill the man, and he wants to inherit Germany, be one of the people who are going to run it. It seems to me almost like the core of a Greek tragedy. In order to get things back, he had to lose his life, which is a very Christian notion.

Early in **The Place in Flowers** *George thinks of those who admire his kachina dolls. And at one point we have this passage: "and one is a guy from Pennsylvania who flies in once a year, to see what he can pick up." I assume this is a reference to yourself.*

I like to fly in occasionally and see what I can pick up. You know it's nice to have a walk-on part in your own book, especially when one is that one.

And I think we're back to something we talked about earlier, the jokes, the asides, the things . . .

Little indices to me; pretty overt, I guess. Little signs of the author playing games as he's telling you the story.

In many ways **Place** *strikes me as a very religious book. It deals with faith for those who have and for those who don't have it. Could you comment on this aspect of the novel and any research you did on Hopi religion?*

It's a religious book in a wide sense, not sectarian though. I really saw something in what they were doing.

Did you make a study of their religion?

I got into it, and I still am into it to a certain extent. They revere everything around them, never mind how paltry-looking it is. When they kill something, they actually commune with it before they kill it, and after they kill it, they see a blank where it was. They are very remarkable people. I didn't, however, learn the Hopi language. It would take a long time to do that. But it struck me that they were almost into this I/thou thing which Buber used to talk about, which was fashionable twenty years ago. They have an ecumenical, holistic sense of everything they do. Nothing's trivial. Everything is consequential. Everything is universal. I found that reassuring. My other research consisted of talking to some Hopi and to some experts on the Hopi as well. I found the Hopi fascinating. I began collecting kachina dolls. These are personifications, at least to the Hopi. Rehearsals and ways of getting to know their rituals and masks and images that show up in the tribal dances.

Since we were talking about religion, what was your religious training, if any, and how lasting was its influence? Sectarian or not?

Virtually nil. Oh, I was obliged to go to Sunday school, and that was what you would call Episcopalian until I was about ten. And then I rebelled. I was bored and used to hide out.

One of the places I used to hide out was an outdoor toilet, and I used to sit in there and couldn't wait until Sunday school was over and then come back. I did this for a year, and then was found out. My father said, "Why should he have to go to Sunday school? To hell with it." *He* didn't go, and my mother said, "Fine, if he doesn't go, he'll be a liberal." They never were really, my father especially, devout people, so I never absorbed much of that. I have very distinct memories of being in church watching all the rituals, thinking: this is splendid, but I can't connect it with God. This was as a kid. I didn't really know why I was there. I used to love to go to the theater and the movies, but I couldn't see why this particular movie theater was so special. It was obligatory. I was getting something that would improve me as a human being. I forgot it, and I've had very little contact with any kind of organized religion since. Several students or people who have written about my stuff have said, "You're a real Hindu, an actual Hindu," which surprised me. Several other people said, "You're really a natural mystic," and since the Hopi novel several other people have said it too.

But the way you talk about the universe, as a beloved thing which you come to with almost reverential speculation, is almost a religious response to the all and the everything.

Probably so, but it's not sentimental. And it's not programmatic. The universe is a hostile place, and stars are not gentle entities. Some planets are not gentle. Venus is ungentle; it'll fry you and dissolve you. I think there's an equal measure of revulsion and delight. It's magnificent, but it has no brain. It has no intellect. It's matter. It's violent, destructive matter. Some people think the universe is a gentle, accommodating place. I don't see how you can. Fission, fusion, quasars, novas and supernovas, red giants—ultimately the Earth will be fried by the sun, turned into a red giant. It's benign enough now, but it won't be. I don't think there's any program-creating, presiding intellect watching over it. It wouldn't make sense to me that it was like that, which I guess is to say that it's not there to cater to human beings, and that's probably a stupid point of view. The universe is not cut to the human scale. It's not there to please human beings. It's its own project. I got into all this thinking about the absurd because there's nothing absurd about the universe. The only absurd thing in the universe is the human being, who wants the universe not to seem "absurd," and absurd means in defiance of human desire. Camus said the absurd is the gap between the mind that desires and the world that disappoints. I don't think the universe is going to change to please us. It's always going to disappoint.

Could you comment on the sense of time in **The Place in Flowers**? *It seems to me an almost atemporal book.*

The Hopi sense of time is incredibly universe-ridden. Time gets abolished in certain sections, mainly via Uncle George who has absolutely no sense of where he is. He doesn't even know if death comes after life, he's not sure, and that was deliberate.

And isn't that what Oswald is received into when he dresses up as Mastop, the death fly kachina, at the end? His entree there is to George's time which is no time, atemporality.

Oswald has nowhere to go; essentially time swallows him, provided he puts on the garb of Mastop. As long as he is willing to make that concession to local mysticism, he can disappear from time into a universe as old as Hopi myth, which goes back to Spider Woman, rolling a bit of clay in her hands, creating the world and people in it. Originally the book had a very long pseudo-epigraph, like seven pages, from a totally bogus astronomy primer that I had broken up into various sections.

And all this is spurious now?

I took the epigraph out. What I was trying to do was indicate a cosmic cloud or a galaxy winding among the sections; you can't do this in words. It doesn't work. It's the wrong shape. It looks like print. So I was playing with a group of galaxies called Stephan's Quintet: five galaxies, I think of different kinds, all traveling at different speeds. Four of them coming toward us and one going away. Four red-shifted, one blue—this has always intrigued me. I wanted five sections. I still do. One of which was *really* going away. If I were making a mobile, I could do it. If I were painting, I could probably do it. How do you do this in words, other than sort of feeble puns about recession and distance and smaller print? So I abandoned it.

But you're talking about how to do it stylistically, linguistically, rather than referentially.

Yes, absolutely. If you had enough money you could do it. If the book didn't look like a book, but like one of those children's books. Everything pops up and amplifies. Origami novel.

Do you think that the presence of Sotuqnangu amounts to a voice from the other side and reinforces the sense of atemporality?

Yes; he's the narrator and he's protean. He's sometimes a god, sometimes a narrator, sometimes a malicious eavesdropper. And I think there are other incarnations.

He's the bane of George's existence. George can't decide where he stands with him, invokes him, at other times profanes him.

He overhears everything, and rarely intervenes. I think in the original version, I mean the manuscript of this thing was gigantic, it was 1400 pages, I thought what a wonderful thing it would be if on one page only he said one word in his own right, but I threw that idea out too. I found him fascinating because he was a repersonification of the omniscient narrator, but omniscient in a very different way. He was omniscient in about everything else as well, not just about the novel. I hope that comes through. He is interested in more than people. He's vaguely tending his creation and saying, "Why do they make models of me; it's stupid." He was fun to play with. He didn't come easily. It took me three versions to realize his role.

What kind of historical research did you conduct to prepare for **Stauffenberg***?*

The university I was teaching at had a rather splendid collection of some five hundred books on the German Resistance. I went up there one day, when I had finally realized who this guy was, that he had been shot and not hanged, and I wanted more details, and there were masses of books with photographs and everything. I read all, or skimmed most of them.

How long did this take?

About two years. It's a lot quicker than you might think because you get to know what you're looking for with good use of indexes and so on. I would sit up there every afternoon and evening making my notes, Xeroxes, sketches, etc., actually trying to read some of the stuff that was in German. I don't know German. There's one book, a little red book that didn't seem very significant, *Death in Plötzensee,* and it was nothing but an account for all the executions that had ever been done in that particular jail and how they were conducted and what the technique was and what they did after the execution. They either drew a line through the person's name in pen or they drew a cross alongside.

I also noticed that you began doing a clutch of reviews dealing with things related to the Third Reich. Did these stoke the fires?

They provided me with other books to read, other images, and I also discovered what I guess is no discovery to most people: that history is really fiction, and that the most reliable names in history actually lie and embellish, and I would perhaps find fifteen to twenty accounts of one event. I would type them out and look at them, and ultimately give what really happened, what was true.

How much variance could you find sometimes?

Gigantic. Enormous. Unthinkable. And my feeling was, hey, I'm the fiction writer. Leave me alone. Leave me something to do. For instance, a number of historians contend that some of the plotters were hanged with piano wire on hooks. It wasn't piano wire. It was cord made of hemp. Some of them went beyond even that and said Admiral Canaris was hanged seven times and lifted down six. The truth is they hanged him and hanged him just once.

How free did you feel to take liberties with history?

I thought I was absolutely free. I didn't take many liberties at all. There was no need to intensify or rearrange. The whole design of the plot had an eerie symmetry. It was ready-made. And the image I was groping for earlier was, we don't use it anymore, people *buying* people's souls. He bought their souls, meaning he didn't buy them; he redeemed them. Stauffenberg was trying to buy people's, at least young people's, souls. I am glad I wrote the book. It got through to a lot of people.

This next question deals with the area in which I think you take the greatest liberties. Both the novels **Stauffenberg** *and* **The Place in Flowers,** *some of the stories in* **Universe,** *and even the final section of* **Lord Byron's Doctor** *revolve around voices from the other side, dead figures who people the world with language, shadowy but nonetheless palpable presences. Could you comment on this tendency?*

Nicely said. I agree. I hear voices. Do *they* hear *me?*

And in that whole last section Stauffenberg is dead, yet he tells us of the rest of the executions.

Since becoming a novelist, I've heard many more voices more irresistibly coming through, sometimes when I don't want them. I think I hear a character's voice before I see his or her face or anything else. Fiction can sometimes get close to opera, recitative, and it's tied into what I said about the mind chattering to itself. In a way human beings, while living their lives, are singing to themselves, as if they all had a Bach cantata inside their heads. It's involuntary. It's not something they think about. It's a keening noise. It's the noise of being human, even though you don't express it overtly in language. And I think sometimes those voices, which appear to be voices of the characters, are their covert, clandestine, underground, interior voices, not the voices they use to talk to people with, and they tend to merge sometimes; it's a chorus, a fact or phenomenon I find very interesting and don't quite understand. Not quite Greek chorus, not quite symphonic, operatic chorus, but voices, you know, rising out of the mud. I think Beckett is the person with the most voices, voices rising out of the mud, soaring above the mud, moving through the galaxy.

Look at Molloy talking and talking, especially about the sucking stones. The major point there is the exercise of a voice. One of my friends has a phrase for this. He says it's talking in tones. It's not what you're saying; it's how you're saying it.

I believe that. And it's rhythm too. Maybe voice is the wrong word for it; maybe that sounds too external. It's a kind of soft, communing evocation. It's powerful to me, and novels that I have finished still make noises as do characters that I

no longer deal with. I think the sound of *Stauffenberg* will never go from my ears, whether it's his mind I'm overhearing or his actual voice. Ah, the vox pox.

In her rollicking soliloquy in **Gala,** *Milk makes the following remark . . .*

A rollicking soliloquy?

That's the way I see it.

Well, that's nice.

She says, "After all, to miss a trick such as AUG and have your protagonist remind you of it through [centrifugal] ventriloquism, isn't that a bit thick?" What exactly is the lesson she's trying to teach her father?

A good question. He is providing her with a thought that perhaps she already has but which she cannot voice. This is her interior voice talking.

And his presumed ideas.

Presumptions, of what her interior voice might be like although he doesn't know and he never will. And that in a sense is another of these damned voices. It's also an example of how in words, and maybe not in any other medium, you can do an impossibility. This is unique to words. I don't think you can do this in music or in painting. I think that you can use the language against itself. Here is an example of nonlanguage being done in a very articulate, almost pedantic, scholarly way, and the joke is that it's unverifiable. You make a very good point. If somebody had said to me, "Can you give an example from your work of the De Quinceyan involute, in other words, a compound experience incapable of being disentangled, something very close to what Beckett has said and Keats's negative capability?" I would pick that. One is entitled to confront the reader with responses to the universe every bit as baffling as the universe itself. I do, and that is one version of it. Not a typical version. A fairly uplift version. You said "rollicking." I think that's a good word.

In your collected papers I found something, it probably means nothing to you, in a file on deafness. On a piece of notepaper there's one line in your handwriting that reads, "assault on the reader—ice axe." Does this fragment suggest an approach you think is consistent in most of your writing, especially in your novels?

You've rung a bell. All I can think of is Kafka; it has something to do with Kafka.

That image of the ice axe is particularly compelling.

The quote, as I recall it, is something like using an ice axe on a frozen sea. I think that's Kafka. It's a phrase I found in a review I'd written. The image has to do with getting through to the reader, which was as difficult as going out to a frozen sea with an ice axe and hammering your way through.

Do you see fiction as a kind of assault on the reader in the demands it makes?

Mine sometimes, a lot of fiction, no. Much fiction is like mustard spread over the belly, take it or leave it, who cares. Some fiction has intentions on the reader and wants to inflict grievous bodily harm. My Hopi novel inflicts grievous bodily harm on the reader as does some of Beckett, and some Kafka. They create disturbances in the well-tempered harmony of everyday life. I think perhaps one novelist in twenty-five does it. Thomas Bernhard certainly inflicts something upon the reader, and Max Frisch in that very short book, *The Man in the Holocene,* is trying to injure the reader. De Quincey was trying to do it. And Carlyle. Joyce certainly.

I think Nabokov also destabilizes the reader.

A lot. What's that dreadful phrase? Reader-friendly? It isn't reader-friendly; it's saying to the reader, "I bet you can't take this, and if you can you're the kind of reader I want and you'll stay with me. If you can't take it, I don't want you to read me anyway." It's a power play, I guess, and I do some of that. Some of that is in my Ripper novel, not half as much as you might think. There is very little of it in ***Byron's Doctor,*** very little indeed, but it's in the Hopi novel.

I think another novel in which you do that is **Colonel Mint**. *I'm curious about your reaction to the critic who objected to the "detectable relish with which sadism is elaborated in that novel."*

That reviewer thought I enjoyed my character's sufferings. I didn't. This is complicated. I gave a reading, and somebody said, "How did you manage to bring yourself to write about all these people being hanged and mutilated and so on," and I gave a flip answer—I thought about some heads of departments, some deans, etc., and it became easier. This was flip. As I said to somebody who had written about me, this isn't sadism, this isn't gloating. I have to dump my mind in this kind of thing, and the reader's mind, to persuade at least me that this kind of thing actually goes on. I don't believe how badly human beings behave to human beings. It's easy to forget because it's so unpalatable and loathsome. Nothing to do with sadism. I see it as a kind of incessant reminder . . . we should not be treating one another as if we had all the license of stars.

Colonel Mint *presents one with this quasi-scientific deprogramming which turns into something out of control.*

They don't know what he's seen; he tells them he's seen an

angel. Harold Brodkey wrote a long story about an angel appearing in Harvard Yard, and I think one is entitled to produce the preposterous and say to the reader what would you do? How would you verify this? Would you go through these maneuvers? I think this kind of writing is not popular among American novelists. Few do it. Extremely popular in Europe. It's not quite absurd; it's on the verge of it. It happens in the theater. It would be a very strange planet without violence. There would be nothing on the news. Wouldn't it be wonderful if you switched on the news, and these vastly overpaid anchor-fatheads came on and said the top story of the night was Virgil Copland had just finished a new symphony? And things of that ilk for thirty minutes: peaceful, creative news? It perturbs me and sometimes you get the feeling it's no good writing novels about such things.

It should be the novelist's place to speculate.

I think so, even if you can't achieve anything, at least you can remind yourself what life's really like. And if anyone wants to tune in, it can remind them too. I don't think the serious novelist's place is to cozy up to the reader. Matisse said that he painted so that the tired businessman coming home at night could look at one of his paintings and feel refreshed. Certain kinds of writers have that in mind and want to do it. I don't think that's me; what I tend to write is much harsher and less generous and gentle, although there are pacific sections. In other words, he painted in order to entertain, but I get bothered when I think of the serious art form like the novel or the symphony or the elegiac poem as entertainment. It may be incidentally, but primarily it's not. It's something much more aggressive and monumental.

In a recent interview you say that you now regard **Colonel Mint** *as "a little superficial and flip." Many critical responses saw a great deal more in the novel than you apparently do now. Why do you feel a little off of that work?*

I haven't read it in a long time, but when I last looked at it, it seemed to me too allegorical. I'm not sure allegory is a sufficiently complex form or genre for me to be writing. It seems to me a diagrammatic book, a book with an overt message about the military, a doctrinaire book.

I don't see it that way at all.

Nobody does. Only *I* am this critical of it. I think it should have been more a book of symbolism, more a book of myth, not so much an apparently political allegory. I'll have to reread it. It has a following. People read it and can understand it. I won't quarrel with anybody who thinks he/she understands.

Is there any chance that you'll produce a fourth installment to the Alley Jaggers saga?

No, done with him, done in by him. I'm grateful he soared

through my life, but I'm through with him. I've come a long way. *Alley Jaggers,* the first one, was turned into an opera I never saw. Students at Manchester University put it on. Apparently it was a big success, a rock opera. They sent me photos and so on, but I never heard the music. I wonder why.

How do you feel about **Caliban's Filibuster***?*

I like the title and the idea of a journey across the spectrum, and I wanted the publisher to print it on different colors of paper. The book would have been priced at $75. I still think it would be nice to have five hundred handcrafted copies with the color changing. I enjoyed writing *Caliban*. It was a completely self-indulgent binge, and I enjoyed doing the drawings in *Gala*. Actually there's a file of them somewhere and they're all in color. They're very pretty. Each one is on a separate page done in all kinds of colors, almost like an illuminated manuscript. Of course, none of that got into the book. Both *Gala* and *Caliban* are books of color whose color's been denied them.

Could you talk a little about **Portable People***? What provoked you to work in such a restricted form beyond the convenience of being able to read these pieces at different functions?*

I did one short-short, **"The Paganini Break,"** for *Tri-Quarterly,* who brought out a special issue called *The Minute Story*. Then about ten years ago I wrote a long story that appeared in the *Cornell Review* called **"Captain Ahab, A Novel by the White Whale."** I read it and said there's another way to do this thing and did the very short version. It was an interesting form to work with. Not quite like the sonnet and not quite like a prose form. But mainly either ventriloquial or narrative, spoken by people still alive, but mainly by people who are dead, either looking back on their careers or just sounding off in general, such as Count Basie, George Gershwin, Madame Curie, Nixon, Pele. Virginia Woolf drowning herself, Nabokov revisiting Cayuga Heights and his favorite liquor store, Goebbels, Göring, Amy Johnson, the aviatrix who crashed into the Thames and was never seen again, a lost soul in every sense. Churchill in Marrakesh. One of them is the Baba of Rai Bouba, the potentate of some weird little kingdom who, whenever he travels outside this tiny country, has two guys walk in front of him with a sack of soil and sprinkle some in front of him, so wherever he walks, he's walking on home soil. They're almost like stained glass windows, looking through into history. I collect such things as specimens of human behavior, and I am amazed at the originality and the vitality of people's responses. It's a kind of *Canterbury Tales*. I wanted a lot of people together, but not to send them on a pilgrimage. I just want a prologue, a permanent prologue as in Chaucer.

Earlier you mentioned about **The Place** *that you wanted this five-part structure but settled on four, and that fit there. In*

other books it's the spectrum or the DNA chain. Is there a sense of forms that is always there and seeking expression and which precedes character or plot or anything else?*

I think maybe I'm some sort of composer and really want to design symphonies or sonatas or operas. I do have a strong compulsion to shape, design found-form, ready-made form. I used to look in the table of elements, among other things, and the spectrum, and Stephan's Quintet. These were givens that I was fascinated by; I thought nobody's used these as artificial structures in art, why not do it?

Would you care to comment further on your Jack the Ripper novel?

It's a complex story, almost bloodcurdling. Long and deceptive because it begins as a romance.

Who's the protagonist?

It struck me that nobody had ever written about the *victims* or regarded them as anything more than pawns, and that was worth doing. At least it was really worth doing until I had to kill them off. The Ripper's victims are the romance interest.

In your novels, some characters achieve a kind of muted triumph Rat Man at the end holding up his thumb, Alley in the nuthouse retaining his individuality, Oswald in **The Place in Flowers** *finding a place in the Hopi community and in the world at large. In the Ripper novel, though, it doesn't sound like anyone is able to triumph over the forces of conformity. True?*

You sent me in so many different directions with that question. Let me interject one thing. I'm not sure that Rat Man's holding up his thumb signifies any kind of triumph. It's conceivable that he means let it all come down, let it happen all over again. It may be a gesture of supreme apathy or stoicism perhaps. Now what did you ask about conformity?

In some of your novels there's a qualified victory in the sense that the character continues, carries on. In this novel it sounds like all the people who either want to or try to pit themselves against conformity are annihilated or taken over?

They are. There were no survivors. Sickert, for instance, is marked for life, and although he goes on and has a fairly successful career, he can't shed the burden until the very end when he tells his son. What interests me most, though, are the women. They don't really have anywhere they can hide, and nobody gave a damn. Retrospectively, it would be nice to have them give their account.

Sickert, the painter, witnesses these murders. Is it your design to present a divided guy who on the one hand wants to find a way to save the women and get out of the whole thing, and at the same time is driven to see how awful all this can be?

Absolutely right. He has this double emotion. He wants to be rid of it. He wants to get the women out of harm's way, but another part of him wants to see it happen so he can paint it. He can't resist. An alternative title was "The Eye of the Beholder" [since changed to ***The Women of Whitechapel***]. He's a voyeur, your friendly neighborhood voyeur who gets in too deep, and can't get out and witnesses the murders.

"The Eye of the Beholder" is an interesting title because it suggests that this eye is also that of the novelist who from a different perspective writes this from a point of view of Sickert's son, who eventually learns of his father's role in the atrocities. Just as the father has to carry this awful burden, here's the son who one day discovers a new father and now he carries this burden.

You're absolutely right. The son doesn't appear much, but I make the novelist into a voyeur too. It's a third-person novel, and the voice of Sotuqnangu is heard again in the land. First I thought I'd write it in first person with Sickert looking back from all of this, but it didn't give me enough range and perspective. I wanted to get away from him, had to get away from him because of the little things he wouldn't allow himself to see.

Whether it is landscape or the inner recesses of the mind or whatever, I'm concerned with your notion of setting in the broadest sense.

Whitechapel was a slum. I read a powerful essay on conditions of life in Whitechapel in 1888. Apparently when children died, as they often did, they just put them under the table and left them there to rot and this brought the rats.

So life here was completely expendable, especially for the most powerless women and children.

Yes, it says a great deal about the status or nonstatus of women at that time. There weren't five hundred men being killed. Women were a lower order. Nobody cared what happened to them. They themselves had a sort of, to take your word, "rollicking" stoicism about it because they were mostly walking about blind, easy, easy prey. I thought it was interesting to look at them as the lowest of the low, sort of fighting back against the massive establishment and getting nowhere and being wiped out.

In one of our conversations you mentioned that you felt any writer has a finite number of deeply held ideas to which he or she returns frequently. Without being hopelessly reductive, can you share some of those that you're consciously aware of?

That applied to other people, but one of them is the holistic idea that anything belongs next to anything else. I think the notion of decorum has stunted a lot of fiction. It has somehow stopped people from combining things which could at least be put next door to each other. I think it's ultimately a failure of spontaneity and availability. Fiction can afford to be at least as openminded as a good essay, and often it's not. A novel is made of prose and prose is an enormous liberty. I mean the latitude you have when you say I'm a prose writer is gigantic. I don't see why the novelist shouldn't exploit the liberties of the prose writer. If there's a principle in this it's that the fiction writer should not be intimidated or blinkered. Too much American fiction for too long has been very blinkered indeed, whereas, much of that written in Europe and Latin America is not.

The theme that I've noticed repeatedly in your work is that of the isolated individual confronting forces sometimes hostile, at other times appealing, which demand conformity. Care to respond to that?

Deep down you know it's you, not so much versus them, but you in the context of this enormous, successful universe, that doesn't give a damn about your writing or your reputation or your books or your prose rhythms or anything. I'm always being daunted or fazed. I think the brutality of human beings, the impersonality and the vastness of the cosmos these are things almost incredible, and that's why I come back to them, as if some day I'll get the point, or come to terms.

As you review your career as a novelist, how would you describe the development of your fiction and your thinking about fiction?

Good question. Seems to me there was a steady movement away from realism, and realism is photographic, documentary writing. I think realism fizzles out in the second volume of the Alley Jaggers books because the third volume is not realistic at all. It's hallucinatory, and I feel happy with hallucination. I know people whose account of the world—whose expressionistic deformation of it—is more interesting than what's actually out there. Fiction is, to a very large extent, about emotion, though I don't think you can have a convincing novel without emotion, or a series of emotions, that will saturate the reader. I've become much happier with my fiction. I don't think I was that happy with the first four or five books.

What book or books do you think you took the most chances in?

I took enormous chances in ***The Place in Flowers***. A risky book. Very, very long and much of it slow. I'm flattered by the number of people who stayed through it. There are, however, one or two friends whom I've put on notice that, in the summer of 1991, there will be a short, three-hour examination on the text, questions in Hopi, answers in English. Penalty for failing grade: no more gifts of autographed novels. I guess the **Stauffenberg** novel is also a risky book because some people have an immediate reflex and say, "Oh, he's found a nice Nazi, and we don't like books about nice Nazis. He actually sees virtue in this Nazi officer, how dare he?"

I was thinking too of **Caliban;** *that's a challenge to the reader.*

Caliban is a verbal orgy. If you have a willing reader, it's fine, but if you have the wrong reader, then that's definitely the wrong book. What amazes me, I really haven't quite gotten used to this, is that you write a risky, dangerous book that could be slammed, and by and large it isn't. The few books that get querulous reviews are not the risky ones; they're the ones a little bit closer to the predictable line. I've never understood that. I don't have complaints. I'm fortunate with critics and reviewers. I know how hard reviewing is, and I know there are people who actually pride themselves on the caliber of their reviews.

You have commented elsewhere about being attracted to writers like Bernanos, Saint-Exupéry, Gide, Malraux, and T. E. Lawrence, whom you describe as having "a more urgent sense of life." Could you define what that urgent sense of life is, especially for you as a writer of fiction?

Life is not dependable. Life can be snuffed out fast, soon, easily; it's a gift. Almost a fluke. If you have it, you have to make as much of it as you can. I'm saying that part of the obligation, if there is one, of being alive is to realize it, to relish it. I think this is what the urgency comes from. A severe illness taught me that; it changed my way of looking at things. There's a permanent, perpetual wake as soon as you're born. The urgency comes when you recognize that death is not an alternative. Death is a nothing, and you have to think of life almost as an absolute. I'm not just saying you have to be grateful for life. You have to be indignant about it. In other words, I never have an emotion about it that isn't undercut by its opposite.

You've spoken or written about literary influences frequently, but are there other specific influences you'd care to mention, like science, cinema, art, religion? I'm speaking here quite broadly of inspiration, influence.

I might have been influenced by science but not to write something scientific. I do have certain abiding obsessions like with planes and astronomy; I'm always looking for structures out there.

What about cinema? Has that played any part?

I watch a lot of movies. If, as I'm told, I have a strong visual imagination, that has been fed by movies. I like to look at Kurosawa a great deal, and I have a book about him, a good, detailed book. I don't have books about any other movie-makers. I think it's significant he's the only one; some of his work is magnificent. I like best *Dodesukaden.* Kurosawa and Bergman matter most.

What about music?

Music is my favorite art. All art aspires to its condition. I think my novels, as they have developed, have aspired to some such condition, in which you try for naked emotion. You can't do it because words have meanings, you're always running into trouble but you can try, and I think that the fact that I tend to listen to music while writing is revealing.

There is a very strong Aristotelian tendency in people who can't write, and people who can write well don't need the Aristotelian; it gets in the way. People who want to dominate literature wheel up almost any kind of incomprehensible machinery to sap or castrate it. Literature frightens people. And it should.

—Paul West

You talked about Prokofiev and elsewhere about Busoni; was there anyone you were listening to while writing **Rat Man***?*

No one in particular.

What about **Stauffenberg***?*

I always listen to some kind of classical music while writing. During a lot of these books I've listened to the same music, the music of Frank Bridge, for example. I spend a lot of time listening to ragas, believe it or not. It provides me with a level on which I feel free; it's a childhood thing. It takes me back, it liberates me because when I did my homework as a kid I was accustomed to hearing my mother's piano, and it became essential to have that kind of music. I like being in the presence of a superior art form. I also like total silence. I have extremely sensitive ears. So I don't play the radio very loud, barely audible, but it cuts me off and puts me in a third dimension.

To what extent if any does dreaming play a role in the creation of your novels? I'm reminded of your remark that after hearing about the Rat Man you "dreamed on" him for a while. I'm using the word loosely here; do you dream?

Until I got sick I don't think dreams played much part in my writing at all. Since then, being on various drugs, and one in particular, propranolol, gives me dreams of incredible technicolor. For the last five years I've had technicolor dreams of enviable precision and length very often about what I've been writing, so if I remember them I get whole sequences that come unbidden.

Do these feed the muse?

Yes, they do. They sometimes choke her. Sometimes I don't use them, but I think they remind me what I should be doing and I get ideas from them. I don't think people should take drugs to get hallucinations, but, if you have to take the drug anyway, it's good that you get an aesthetic benefit. I also like to daydream, just mentally float. Very often I brood on what won't go right in a novel, and that can take hours and hours of wondering and shuffling images around. On planes I go into this semidream state and make some notes, but they're cryptic, concise, a few words only after several hours' thinking. I got the structure of the Ripper novel on a jet from Pittsburgh to Ithaca, and I hadn't intended doing anything. That was not a dream, but it wasn't a waking function either.

In an interview Raymond Federman complains that many readers and writers aren't interested in ideas but in stories. Can these be so easily divided? And where do you stand on this issue?

It's a clear mind indeed that knows how to sever these things. I could never do it. People often ask me, "How do you know when you're writing nonfiction or fiction?" I don't know. My nonfiction is full of fiction and my fiction is full of nonfiction.

There's the clichéd term reviewers invoke to codify something—the novel of *ideas, as if novels don't have ideas. Can one legitimately say that?*

Well, what about a poem of ideas? It's preposterous. How about the drama of ideas or the sermon of ideas? It seems to me utterly natural that the novel should be full of ideas, and if it isn't then it's a stupid novel.

Is this part of the sacrifice in minimalism, not just a sacrifice in style, or a "monofilamental style" as you've described it, but a sacrifice of intellect?

It doesn't matter how little the thing you write about is *if* your imagination, your prose style, can conquer the vacancy. If you can't write and you don't have ideas and perhaps you're not very observant, you're not going to be very good. At that level, codification becomes a substitute for the imaginary. If people would go and read Coleridge's *Biographia Literaria,* they would stop using what you call codifications or categories or compartments. There is a very strong Aristotelian tendency in people who can't write, and people who can write well don't need the Aristotelian; it gets in the way. People who want to dominate literature wheel up almost any kind of incomprehensible machinery to sap or castrate it. Literature frightens people. And it should.

Could you talk about your revision practices?

I write on a typewriter and early in my career never changed anything. And then, I don't remember when it was, I started revising, and now I revise like a maniac, slowly and laboriously, by hand, and very often throw whole pages away. This for me was a departure. As I've mentioned, *The Place* I revised enormously. Large lumps thrown out, 250 pages one time. I find revision utterly fascinating, because I can see that it's not quite automatic, but the bell goes off pretty swiftly—this is wrong, expand this, etc. I usually know what to do because I'm in a different frame of mind from when I'm composing. In the heat of composition you have almost no judgment, but if you come back cold it's easy to see what's wrong.

What do you have planned for the future; are you working on anything you can talk about at this point?

Work planned some time ago and in part accomplished includes the long story "Banquo and the Black Banana" for the *Random House Gothic Anthology;* a novel about two American reconnaissance pilots who get shot down over the Danakili desert in Ethiopia (some fifty or sixty pages done); and the first volume of a fresco devoted to the childhood, courtship, and marriage of my parents (some two hundred pages written of *Pianos Don't Explode*). I am going to collect my remaining short stories and my essays on poetry; maybe my general essays as well. There are many poems uncollected too. Perhaps I'm tidying up, clearing the decks, razing the ground. I certainly have enough in mind to keep me busy until the year 2000, by which time I may decide just to listen to music while my agent and publishers sort out what to do; by then I will have decided which books of mine should stay out of print, which not. It won't be an agonizing decision. I know already, I think, which I'd like to be judged on, even by the astoundingly obsolete criteria prevalent in English-speaking countries. By then, my blood will be so thin that I'll be able to live somewhere without air-conditioning, like Paris, and not feel suffocated. See you on the rue Sainte-Beuve, near the drugstore with the green cross that shrinks and swells.

Angeline Goreau (review date 3 September 1989)

SOURCE: "Physician, Behave Thyself," in *The New York Times Book Review,* September 3, 1989, pp. 2, 16.

[*In the following mixed review, Goreau criticizes West's portrayal of the poet George Byron in* Lord Byron's Doctor, *claiming that in an effort to elevate the importance of the poet's bumbling doctor, he renders Byron himself a caricature.*]

"Mad—bad—and dangerous to know," Lady Caroline Lamb wrote in her journal on the evening she first set eyes on Lord Byron. She was, like most of London in the latter part of March 1812, fresh from an impassioned reading of the first two cantos of "Childe Harold's Pilgrimage" and wild to know its author. Disregarding her own warning, Lady Caroline threw herself into a love affair whose notorious course shocked even Regency morals and launched Byron on the series of scandals whose accumulated force finally propelled him into exile from England four years later.

Byron did not leave scandal behind, however, nor did the extraordinary phenomenon of Byronmania abate in the slightest with the hero's expatriation. On the contrary, no detail of his sayings or doings was too insignificant to arouse the interest of his admirers—or his detractors, for that matter. A swarm of self-appointed biographers was busy recording the particulars of the poet's famous exile.

Among the aspiring Boswells was J. W. Polidori, the hero of Paul West's 12th novel, *Lord Byron's Doctor*. On the recommendation of his friend Sir Henry Halford, Byron hired Polidori as his traveling physician shortly before leaving England. Polidori, who was only 20, had taken his medical degree at Edinburgh the year before.

The young doctor nursed extravagant literary ambitions and saw in his new position a great opportunity. John Murray, Byron's publisher, had offered £500 for a diary of his author's travels on the Continent. Polidori also, it seems, had hopes of enlisting Byron's support in the world of letters: even before they took ship at Dover, he had pressed a play of his own composition on the great poet. Byron had to pass the last evening he was ever to spend in England perusing Polidori's drama. He read, Polidori's diary smugly records, "with so much attention that the others [Byron's friends] declared he had never been so attentive before."

For the next few months, Polidori continued to obtrude himself on Byron's attention in every possible way—popping into every conversation, sulking when he was ignored, challenging Percy Bysshe Shelley to a duel, attacking an apothecary and getting arrested, "accidentally" banging his employer on the knee with an oar and saying he wasn't sorry—until finally Byron dismissed him. Mary Wollstonecraft Shelley—who with her future husband and her half-sister, Claire Clairmont, formed Byron's intimate circle in Switzerland—thought Polidori an irritating, vain, pompous fool, a monster of insensitivity who took advantage of Byron's natural generosity. But Byron, in the beginning at least, was kinder: "I know no great harm of him," he wrote to Murray, "but he had an alacrity of getting into scrapes—& was too young and heedless—and having enough to attend to in my own concerns—without time to become his tutor—I thought it much better to give him his Congé." They parted on good terms: Byron continued to correspond with Polidori, furnished him with numerous letters of introduction, helped find patients for him and later on in Milan did his best to extricate him from yet another "scrape."

Byron's essentially charitable feelings toward Polidori be-

gan to sour, however, when he discovered that his former doctor had purloined a fragment of a ghost story Byron had begun one evening as part of a game. Polidori had added his own ending and published the whole as "The Vampyre" in 1819—under Byron's name. From Venice, Byron wrote indignantly to deny authorship. Polidori disclaimed responsibility, protesting that a third party, with whom he had left the manuscript, had given it to the publisher. But the affair rankled.

Losing Byron's good will was only the beginning of Polidori's reversals. In Italy three patients (his *only* patients) died under his care, damaging his medical reputation. And the Gothic novel and volume of poems for which he finally managed to find a publisher were disappointingly received. Gambling debts accumulated. In 1821, at the age of 26, Polidori committed suicide.

The historical Polidori is a pathetic figure who haunts the pages of Byron biography as a minor character, mainly because his diary fills in a few details for which there is no other authority. But Polidori was a failure even in his role as Boswell. A privileged observer of one of the most dramatic interludes in literary history, he records details of landscape and costume, hours of rising, slights to himself, events of little importance. There is, remarkably enough, hardly any mention of Lord Byron. Instead, for example, we read: "*May 8.*—Went to see the Cathedral; full of people, lower ranks, hearing Mass. Miserable painting, architecture, etc." Not surprisingly, Murray never published the diary. Polidori's sister, Charlotte, censored it, but in the preface to the 1911 edition his nephew William Michael Rossetti (who had read the original) tells us that her excisions amounted to little more than a few relatively harmless references "related without any verbal impropriety."

Lord Byron's Doctor rescues Polidori from his status as minor character and gives him the center stage for which he so passionately yearned in life. Beneath the deadly dull surface of the diary, Mr. West imagines a complex character roiling with envy, spite, fury and, most of all, the desire to *be* Lord Byron—so much so that Polidori imagines Lord Byron "wanted to *be me*."

The novel takes the Polidori of record (quoting directly) and fleshes out around him a Polidori who knows he's behaving like a fool, but can't help himself; a Polidori who knows he's writing a diary so boring no one will want to read it, but can't make himself write what he thinks he ought to; a Polidori who knows (or comes to realize) that Byron is dangerous to know, but can't resist the fatal attraction. He is a hero profoundly at work against himself, a worthy successor to the brilliantly conceived Rat Man of Paris, the central character in one of Mr. West's recent novels.

But Mr. West's Polidori differs from the Rat Man in one important respect: whereas the latter has suffered horrors at the hands of the Nazis, the former's wounds are largely self-inflicted. Polidori knows this himself, but nevertheless lays responsibility for his downfall at Byron's door. "I began as a calm individual," he tells us, "not given to sudden uproars, but being close to milord set the appetitive side of my nature running." And later: "Left to my own devices away from the shadow of Lord B., I might have come out normally."

The young doctor, in the first chapter of Mr. West's narrative, is a befuddled innocent who bears appalled witness to Byron's methods of seduction: the great poet tears off a chambermaid's clothes with his hands and teeth, setting out to "prime" her with a "hard dunt in the belly," then "cuffing the girl hard about the face and breast" while he completes the act. Polidori, compelled to watch the whole performance, then has to listen to this fatuous lecture: "'Work it,' he told me, 'always work it, Polly, and naught will go amiss. The same with our brain. Even when there is nothing to think, work the brain. Fret it to an indecent fever. Never leave anything alone, my dear.'"

The Byron that Mr. West conjures in *Lord Byron's Doctor* is a cynical exploiter who sees "other people as eye baths, receptacles, towels, blotting-paper, chamber pots, jakeses, finger-bowls, thimbles." Sententiously, he tells Polidori that "people were there for the plucking." This Byron is indeed "mad—bad—dangerous to know," but he's also a bore. He doesn't sound like the clever, witty, naughty Byron whose voice we have infallibly come to know in the 11 volumes of letters he left behind. Filtered through the belittling whine of Polidori, Mr. West's version of Byron talking is allowable, but when Mr. West gives Byron dialogue of his own, credibility wanes. It seems a shame that in order to elevate Polidori to the status of hero—albeit failed hero—Mr. West had to reduce Byron to a caricature of himself.

The exceedingly repulsive Byron that Mr. West draws raises difficulties in the narrative's logic as well: one can't imagine how anyone would find him attractive. Can this be the Byron Lady Caroline Lamb threw herself at, not to mention countless other women? Without Byron's stupendous power to attract, the Byronic myth doesn't make sense—and Mr. West's whole premise crumbles.

The language of *Lord Byron's Doctor* may also prove an annoyance for some readers. In general, Mr. West makes a concerted effort to give Polidori, who is writing in the first person, vocabulary proper to the Regency era (although some of it misses by half a century or more). But every once in a while words like "thought processes" or "life-style" creep in. The rhythm, too, seems wrong for 1816: "I was on tour with a self-defiling snowman suffocating in an oven full of gingerbread men swelling and bulging as the heat grew high," writes Polidori. Even allowing for the fact that the doctor is going out of his mind, it seems a bit much. The miscellany of

language, period and style may be a deliberate strategy, but if it is, Mr. West doesn't give us enough clues to clearly discern what that strategy is.

Nevertheless, readers who can ignore these impediments will find in *Lord Byron's Doctor* a powerful book, a disturbing and memorable evocation of the pernicious consequences that Byronism could have: a whole century awash with victims of its heady influence. One thinks of the tragic Branwell Brontë, whose story—fascination with the demonic hero, large ambition, smaller talent, opium, debts, suicide—uncannily resembles that of the Polidori Mr. West has invented.

R. Z. Sheppard (review date 11 September 1989)

SOURCE: "The Cruelty of Genius," in *Time*, Vol. 134, No. 11, September 11, 1989, p. 82.

[*In the following excerpt, Sheppard favorably reviews* Lord Byron's Doctor, *calling it a successful portrayal of the "passionately entwined" Romanticism and egoism of Byron and his colleagues.*]

Doubleday assures editors and reviewers that *Lord Byron's Doctor* is Paul West's "most accessible novel to date." What does this suggest about the writer's previous work? That it is less accessible, or even impenetrable? With a publisher like that, who needs critics? Far better to have readers willing to discover for themselves that, if anything, West, 59, is one of the most vigorous and inviting literary talents still punching away in semiobscurity. West wants to bowl over his audience and usually does, in virtuoso performances like *Alley Jaggers, Bela Lugosi's White Christmas* and *The Very Rich Hours of Count von Stauffenberg,* the last a fictionalization of the failed 1944 plot by German officers to assassinate Hitler.

The author's twelfth novel is an equally successful imagining of a historical event, the 1816 European tour of Romanticism's Rolling Stones, George Gordon (Lord Byron) and Percy Bysshe Shelley. Their entourage had its own claim to notoriety. Shelley's wife Mary was the daughter of the radical philosopher William Godwin and Mary Wollstonecraft, author of the basic feminist text *Vindication of the Rights of Woman,* Mary, 18, would soon write *Frankenstein.* Her step-sister and an intimate of both Byron's and Shelley's, Claire Clairmont, was also part of the group, which swapped stories and much more at a rented villa overlooking Switzerland's Lake Leman.

Lesser known but indispensable to West's enterprise was John William Polidori, a young physician traveling as the club-footed Byron's secretary and medical adviser. He also had a £500 commission from a London publisher to report on the poet's adventures. Impatient for death's sting, Polidori was 25 when he drank a fatal concoction of opium, arsenic and prussic acid in 1821. His journal was eventually published, but not before his sister removed the naughty parts.

West puts them back, or rather reconceives and embellishes them in his fecund imagination. One of his accomplishments is Polidori's "lyrical forensic way" of describing the crippled Byron: "Lord B.'s habitual gait was more of a rapid, sliding slither than anything, and I had noticed how quickly he entered a room, almost at the run, as if simulating precipitate eagerness . . . Out of doors he had none of the indolent lounge, both languid and effete, of the fashionable *flâneur,* but rather a lubricated-looking traipse, exactly what you would expect of someone trying to walk on just the toes and balls of his feet."

Through Polidori, West compiles a lurid case history on the cruelty of genius. Shelley may have been "polite to God and pious towards women," but Byron was arrogant about both. His disdain toward lesser literary figures was godlike, and his venery demonic. "The sexes were all one to him," notes Polidori, "the main thing being to *spend* and thus clear the mind for matters more important: the next canto, the new play."

Romanticism and egoism normally go hand in hand. Here they are passionately entwined. Rocking and rolling in Byron's carriage, sailing through storms, discussing the uses of opium or exchanging ghost stories at the Villa Diodati, the group is principally concerned with who will be favored by the muse. Even Polidori is bitten by the literary bug or, in his case, bat. His story *The Vampyre* is inspired by an idea of Byron's, thus suggesting that His Lordship has power to damn with a pathetic immortality.

West concludes that Polidori killed himself because of disappointment: to be an artist was to be fully alive, but not to make the grade was a living death. His friend Mary Shelley succeeded with *Frankenstein.* Subtitled "The Modern Prometheus," the gothic classic comes alive by galvanizing the divine and the tragic in human nature. In its own way so does West's tour de force—a grand tour sparked by an irresistible force.

C. S. Schreiner (review date Summer 1990)

SOURCE: A review of *The Place in Flowers Where Pollen Rests,* in *Prairie Schooner,* Vol. 64, No. 2, Summer, 1990, pp. 135-36.

[*In the following review of* The Place in Flowers Where Pollen Rests, *Schreiner interprets the book as a demonstration of West's philosophy of artistic necessity.*]

[*The Place in Flowers Where Pollen Rests* is a] teeming, propulsive book with the spirit and substance of butterflies clinging to a moving locomotive. Although Paul West's new novel is about Hopi life animated to a large extent by the perversities of American culture, these phenomena are not depicted with any concern for empirical accuracy but are taken in terms of their verbal energies, which are staggered across time in some attempt at narrative development. The writing produces the effect of shifting radio bands or a phased array radar system where one used to expect a consciousness. What one hears, West would say, are the sounds of the universe pollinating itself. Such sounds will scare the average consumer. *The Place In Flowers Where Pollen Rests* is not necessarily a crowd pleaser in spite of all its gore and libido. It is as if Rabelais, Conrad Aiken, and Natalie Sarraute had succeeded in trying to make something artistically redeemable out of Rambo. West delivers pure artifice, yet with more *brio* and detail than most realistic writing around today.

The inner necessity of this narrative is apparently personal. Paul West on his back in the hospital after visiting Arizona and suffering near-fatal heart failure conjures precious life through a couple of Hopi Indians, life of "enormous scope beyond blame and accuracy." As West was (and remains) on the brink, so are his Indians, one near death in old age, the other virile and diffuse, on the brink of a life that only becomes salient in brushes with death in Hollywood and Vietnam. The older Hopi, George The Place In Flowers Where Pollen Rests, his eyesight gone, has no time but has the gift of focus, of being preoccupied, having one's own craft—carving Kachina dolls. George's young nephew, Oswald Beautiful Badger Going Over The Hill, has the gift of time but no craft, no concrete activity to direct him. The narrative follows Oswald from Hollywood to the mesa in Arizona where he was born, then to Vietnam and back, the viewpoints (or voiceprints) alternating between Oswald and George and some Hopi relatives at the mesa. Almost everything is generated by this very alteration, which seems to transcribe Virginia Woolf's notion of "unity, dispersity" into a sort of genetic law for writing and the constitution of character.

It would be misleading, however, to suggest Oswald is anything other than an artist—the world being his Kachina doll to carve into shape, the novel being (as West has said) our Kachina doll to make of it what we will. The artistic propensity undercuts the totality of extant shapes and enterprises, and the phrases uttered by a half-crazed soldier can create the atmosphere of a planet. Thus West's novel does not only arise out of personal exigency, for artistic necessity and actual circumstance are here, as in most of his work, utterly indistinguishable. One of his strengths—very rare today among American writers—is his exteriority, the easy conversion of his kitchen into a Nasa observation post, that is, his ability to let language show us how thought is already outside carousing among things. Thus when West says in his recent *Conjunctions* interview, "Lying in intensive care, I thought about the feisty egolessness of the Hopis in their extraordinary bleak, vivid, other-directed world," we are to take this as a therapeutic reaffirmation of his own artistic impulses. In this Paul

West is to be commended for his rigor. One could predict that an author near death might throw together a ribald story in a fit of nostalgia for the transgressions of youth. Yet this novel does not sing an anthem of liberation, especially when it is most explicitly a portrait of the artist(s). Its commotion allows such an anthem, but does not allow it to become the basic theme. The novel is more about engagement than anything else. And genuine engagement, often myopic, may be judged cruel and freewheeling in its disregard of the codes and duties of the average citizen. But such engagement is not an enviable freedom. Here, as in West's **Rat Man of Paris** (1986), adversity and the demands of commitment (ethnic, moral, emotional) translate the narrative of freedom into one about the risks of exposure, "being in the open too much."

David W. Madden (review date Fall 1990)

SOURCE: A review of *The Very Rich Hours of Count von Stauffenberg,* in *The Review of Contemporary Fiction,* Vol. 10, No. 3, Fall, 1990, pp. 192-94.

[*In the following review, Madden applauds the reprinting of* The Very Rich Hours of Count von Stauffenberg, *calling it a "major work" that explores the moral subtleties involved in the rise of Nazi power and the motives of those involved with the unsuccessful attempt to assassinate Adolf Hitler.*]

The republication (here in reduced print with the original pagination) of Paul West's novel from 1980 is cause for genuine celebration. The fact that the book has been out of print for so many years is both inexplicable and deplorable, and one can only hope that Overlook Press intends to rectify that mistake keeping it in print for many years to come.

Of course the publication of any Paul West novel should be welcome news, and any consideration of his canon quickly reveals an embarrassment of riches. But **The Very Rich Hours of Count von Stauffenberg** may well represent the pinnacle of a truly prodigious, distinguished career. Put simply, the novel is a *major* work, and the nine intervening years since its first publication have done nothing to diminish the novel's brilliance.

In so many ways this is an extremely daring book—in subject, scope, method, and linguistic inventiveness. Anyone looking at the Third Reich and finding some glimmer of heroism runs the risk of denunciation, and in examining the life and motives of Hitler's nearly successful assassin, Claus von Stauffenberg, West might appear to have surrendered to the worst revisionist history—that the Nazis really were guys with consciences. However his purposes are far more subtle.

In the figure of his Count von Stauffenberg, West creates an intricately complex, often decidedly contradictory figure, a man, for instance, who came to literally despise Hitler yet kept a large portrait of him in his office, for Stauffenberg a

talisman of all he chose to obliterate. In showing so many facets of Stauffenberg's personality, West conveys not only the chaos of one man's consciousness and motives but also the pandemonium and haphazardness of the whole assassination plot. As the hero says near the novel's end, in one of his most guilt-ridden moments, "My own poorest hours . . . belonged to others, whose lives I stole and brutally cut off. The thousands of the dead had millions of hours to come, all of which, like some butchering pawnbroker, I made miserably cheap."

What the novel manages to capture, which very few histories can come close to rivaling, is the tangled nexus of conflicting personalities and motives of the conspirators. Especially fascinating is the role the German aristocracy played in the abortive attempt. Impelled as much by feudal notions of the responsibility of the nobility as by pure class chauvinism, this faction of the Nazi war machine was always uneasy with the Führer's authority. For Stauffenberg, a latent sense of Roman Catholic duty as well as a personal conviction that he must serve others compelled not only his role but his willingness at a makeshift court-martial to assume all guilt.

West filters everything through Stauffenberg's tortured consciousness, yet this is hardly another typical first-person narration but an experiment in narrative ventriloquism. The novel opens with a gorgeously evocative first line ("Only kneelers find wild strawberries"), and just as one realizes the passage refers to Stauffenberg and his wife, before their marriage, the reader is quickly thrown into the blinding heat of the Tunisian desert as the hero recalls these more halcyon days.

At times the audience is with the hero in the hospital after a disfiguring war injury, training his favorite horse in his youth, or in some cases shuttling back to the thirteenth century to briefly inhabit the days of his ancestors. All is told, somewhat elliptically, in the past tense, but only after one has read two-thirds of the narrative does he realize why—Stauffenberg is dead, executed for his role in the conspiracy and looking back through the mist of time to reorder otherwise disjointed events. Thus, Stauffenberg emerges as a kind of conscience of an era, both reviewing the past and previewing the future for a ravaged world.

The one disappointment with this edition comes from the inexplicable exclusion of the preface to the original edition. Here West offers a privileged glimpse into the novel's origins—personal (his father was an injured veteran of World War I), scholarly (the massive research he conducted), literary (the influence of Stefan George of Stauffenberg, the conspirators, and West himself as he plotted the novel), and religious (the influence of medieval books of hours, hence the novel's title). Still present, however, are appendices of character names and maps of key locations.

The Very Rich Hours of Count von Stauffenberg continues

to stand as a triumph in a brilliant career. With this novel West reaffirms his primary place in contemporary fiction and reveals he is anything but another novelist. Instead, West stands as a literary *provocateur,* forcing readers to see the world in ever new and challenging ways, as this fiction so richly demonstrates.

Robert Lima (essay date Spring 1991)

SOURCE: "Words of Power: Openings to the Universe of Paul West," in *The Review of Contemporary Fiction,* Vol. 11, No. 1, Spring, 1991, pp. 212-18.

[*In the following essay, Lima studies the language of West's novels, which he compares to that of Dante's* Inferno, *as well as his characters, some of whom he refers to as "grotesques."*]

Many years ago, nearly twenty-three in fact, I received a request from a Spanish priest stationed in the Philippines for an essay by Paul West. Knowing that the author and I taught at the same university, he had taken it for granted that I would have access to the piece. I didn't. Since I was at a campus other than University Park, where Paul West taught, I didn't know the author either (nor, to my chagrin, even his name). Checking the meager holdings of my small campus library for a book of his that might contain the piece, I drew the proverbial blank. But since collegiality is the hallmark in the best of all possible worlds, the academic, I wrote the author a note explaining my friend's pressing need for the essay (he was working on his doctoral dissertation) and his offer to pay for it (I don't recall if in Spanish *pesetas* or Philippine *pesos*).

Sometime thereafter, I received a letter from the author explaining that the essay would reach me as soon as the English Department secretary got around to Xeroxing it. I guess she never did for I received instead a package via intercampus mail that contained not one but two copies of Paul West's *The Wine of Absurdity,* in which the desired essay on Graham Greene appeared. And the books were gifts from the author, one for the needy priest and one for me! It was my first opening to Paul West.

The largesse of my newly discovered colleague toward two strangers not only impressed me as a humanitarian (or should I say, humanistic?) sort of thing, but also verified my Panglossian belief in the utopic nature of collegiality. Over the years, where others have caused deep erosion of my naïveté, Paul West has continued to uphold its veracity by periodically bestowing upon me many and sundry titles—novels, essays, stories, memoirs, poetry. These works have made manifest to me what a reviewer writing in the *New York Times Book Review* has termed "his ability to make language behave the way he wants it to."

And, indeed, in his writing Paul West's words are impressive in their virtuosity and power. They open venues and vistas for the one who accompanies him, the reader, much like Virgil's statements rendered openings for Dante's entry into the uncharted geography encountered in his journey through the inner depth that is the first part of *The Divine Comedy.*

Having led Dante through the gate of Hell into the infernal vestibule, Virgil sought passage for both of them across the river Acheron. But Charon refused to ferry the living body of the Florentine. It was then that Virgil used the first Word of Power in the *Inferno:* "Thus it is willed where Power / and Will are one; enough; ask thou no more" (canto 3). The hellish oarsman wilted before the authority behind Virgil's commanding words and gave safe passage across the infernal river to the petitioners. Again, on encountering opposition from Minos, the judge of Hell, Virgil uttered similar formulaic words that would guarantee the continuance of his and Dante's journey (canto 5). Yet another incident, this time with Pluto, caused Virgil to use the Word of Power a third time, with equal efficacy (canto 7).

Just as the reader accompanies Dante on his personal journey, proceeding through levels that spiral in or out of the depths of the Florentine's fertile mind, so too is the follower of Paul West led to the gates of the complex edifice that is his creative work; and, just as Dante the author has granted his character Virgil the wherewithal to permit passage, Paul West opens the structure of each piece and helps the visitor to ford the stream of his poetry and fiction through Words of Power uttered by an omniscient narrator, an eloquent character, or both. Potent words powerfully stated open the pathways to the author's highly charged, often chilling imagination, as selected examples from his poetry and prose will illustrate.

The journey could well begin in *The Snow Leopard,* the 1964 collection of poetry, which opens with **"Avila"** where the poet observes that in the evening "black pigs are driven in through dark stone gates," there to encounter "a splutter and fury of oil frying" which "Says, pigs, oil, people, accept their conditions" perhaps like the reluctant denizens of Dante's *Inferno,* for West sees that "Neither meaning / Nor bafflement fits this place" where Saint Teresa was born and lived out her mystic existence, "her nose / Upturning from the sealike stench of frying oils." Nonetheless, access to the esoteric city of Ávila is seen as gratifying by the poet because "There, the walking is privileged, the light indulgent," as in the place of Dante's unique perambulation.

The image of pigs driven into the walled city through its "dark stone gates" is indeed reminiscent of Dante's *Inferno* since these unfortunate beings, like those in the Florentine's work, must abandon all hope upon entering their own infernal world. Not only does Paul West's image make a powerful impact upon the reader with its implacable promise of destruction, the nonchalant, reportorial nature of the statement itself underscores the terrible stoicism in the lives of both pigs and humans. Like Dante before the tribulations of the denizens of his Inferno, West finds that both sense and perplexity are inadequate where the harshness of life culminates in the frying fires of Ávila. Perhaps it is their glowing embers that make it possible for the poet to see the intertwined fate of two types of beings, one wholly a beast and the other, a pretender to superior laurels, concealing its bestial nature under human guise. Dante too could see in Hell despite the utter darkness there.

Journeys through the insanity and absurdity of the human condition are the stuff of West's locutions. But why not, for as his first collection of short fiction, *The Universe, and Other Fictions* (1988), suggests via its Borgesian title, the very cosmos is unreal; furthermore, in West's expansive perspective, it is a *situ* fraught with supernatural inanities. The opening piece, **"Life with Atlas,"** initiates the reader into West's particular cosmic vision through the narrative voice of one Thor, a writer with apparent (*read* hallucinatory) deific connections:

> I no sooner thought than I began to withdraw from the consequences; understand, if you will, the embarrassments of being a vicarious voice: I, hearing Atlas, uttered him, but in no way managing to reproduce the intonations, nuances, or even the tart symphonic thrust of the voice I heard. And now, thanks be Fortune, Atlas is coming out as words, and I'm in the near-fatuous position of transposing a voice-in-the-head, but spoken into the tape by myself, into yet another medium, of which not even my best friend, Etna, would call me master.

The Atlas who speaks through the mediumship of Thor is less than a Titan in tone, sounding at times like a vulgar page out of London's *News of the World* as he trivializes mythology: Maia becomes Ma; Mercury, Merc or Herm; Zeus is diminutized into Zeusy-Boy. At other times, he apologizes for being "downright sentimental" in recalling how his daughter Maia rubbed his massive back to soothe the aches brought on by his punishing and eternal task. Thor first observes that "Atlas sounds like he's cracking up," and later, as the Titan's voice dwindles, that the sound is "Atlas groaning in the hoosegow of his mind." Like Nimrod, one of the Giants whom Dante (and others) confused with the Titans, Atlas speaks randomly and makes sense only part of the time. When he ceases talking altogether, his interviewer-medium, practical man that he is, prepares for a potential second exchange of cosmic words with the Titan: "I need my wits about me, peace of mind, some extra supplies of sherry, and, above all, some fresh tapes, *tabulae rasae* for him to deface."

And in the ironic dark humor of Paul West, here as elsewhere, lies another entry into the power of his words to startle first and then to embroil the reader in the discord between fantasy and reason, somewhat like Calvino in his outlandish cosmogonic mode. In an interview appended to *Caliban's Filibus-*

ter, West says of the mind that it "is *in* the world, *at* the world, yet only contingently attached to it, and is often in outright opposition to it, to its predominantly bourgeois or square quality. God's the square pig in the round hell." The mind's position in West's world is akin to that of the soul in the Gnostic universe, "a stranger in a strange place," except that here literature is the concern, not religion; that contrast can also be made with *The Divine Comedy.*

But there is also the more down-to-earth perspective of other novels. The "three feet five inches high" Pee Wee Lazarus, narrator of *Tenement of Clay* (1965), introduces himself to the reader directly: "Pardon me for interrupting whatever it is that you might better be doing just now. Having got this far, I hope to grow on you." That he can deal with not having grown normally is evident in his cavalier, if self-deprecating, way of describing his physical condition: "It's all a matter of perspective: for toilet basins and washbowls I am lower, and to whatever they contain and diffuse . . . . Call me navel-high if you like, or buttock-low: it's true." But he is not only stunted in size, for as he says of himself: "It is not the nicest person who is telling all this." And yet, he does grow on the reader because, as he states with a leer, "you are all easy to involve, even at my level."

Another lowlife type with aspirations to creativity is Alley Jaggers, protagonist first of the 1966 novel that bears his name. On the first page, he questions his own strange thoughts: "Ee, what the hell's wrong wi' me? I get some funny ideas; real daft." Shortly before this autopsychoanalysis, he enters into the reader's view riding a phallic symbol à la Freud: "Coasting home fed-up, a spluttering engine below his knees, Alley Jaggers falls out of love with his motor-bike. Revving, he shuts out the engine noise and tunes in to himself with both ears, as he always does when he is miserable." Those ears are "heavily lobed and face forward as if to measure the wind or brake the bike." They are the best features of a head with very odd mouth and jaw and nose rather ill-suited to each other: "The over-all effect is not pleasing . . . He leers, scowls, squints, and even inflates his cheeks, hoping to become so abominable that lightning will kill him out of sympathy."

Living grotesques were very much in Paul West's ken from the beginning of his novelistic career, as pervasive therein as the exotically distorted dead-existing beings in the *Inferno.* In their physical deformity and inner depravity, Pee Wee Lazarus and Alley Jaggers seem to have crawled into modern times out of a phantasmagoric canvas by Breughel or Bosch or, closer yet to our era, out of the human follies etched by Goya. West, the contemporary writer once thought of largely as one of the new realists in British fiction, is better thought of as being in the line of the Spaniards Quevedo, Valle-Inclán, and Cela, maestros who pursued the aesthetic of the grotesque by going beyond the limitations of the world around them. For Paul West too, as he says in the interview-afterword to *Caliban's Filibuster,* reality is a springboard for imagination—the faculty we were given for the express purpose of flying in the face of the First Cause. What a gratuitous universe it is, anyway; what a bloody surd; Bela Lugosi's White Christmas—as I found out in some depth while writing *Words for a Deaf Daughter,* what with such defectives as waltzing mice, axolotls that should become salamanders but don't, children born without one of the human senses. Not that I'm harping on the universe's lapses rather than its norms; no, what impresses me finally is the scope for error within the constancy of the general setup contrasted with our power to imagine things as otherwise—to rectify, to deform.

That power is what ultimately makes Alley Jaggers a dreamer; in that metamorphosis lies the rectification of and compensation for the character's physical deformity.

The protagonist of *Rat Man of Paris* (1986) is another of the odd fellows in this line of strange, quirky beings, a human figure avenging his personal hell on earth by "tweaking" the sensibilities of the bourgeoisie with the rat he carries inside his coat.

In the old, postwar days, before his rage mellowed, he worked the streets of the city with a squad of kids, flashed his live rat at the diners and Pernod sippers on the boulevards while the kids picked pockets. . . . Poulsifer, alias Rat Man, seemed to be everywhere, a postwar apparition both harsh and playful, reminding the world of what it had recently gone through, but also making fun of the trauma too. A Rat Man could amuse. . . . He still hunts the perfect demeanor for what he does with his rats. He envisions the correct degree of limp, the just-so pouncing movement as he reveals the off-color pink of the nose. He dreams of the perfect accost. . .

West presents his antihero with Rabelaisian gusto, meaning as well to tweak the societal sensibility that finds Poulsifer (and indeed Lazarus and Jaggers) repugnant at first and ultimately ludicrous. Yet, like the last human in Ionesco's *Rhinoceros,* Poulsifer will join the throng, becoming Poussif, "the ordinary chap." Once again the author has called upon the imagination to recast a lost soul through the magical power of his words. Paul West, Redeemer, is yet another facet that opens itself to the reader of his exotic fictions. Again, like Dante, he faces the death of body or of spirit around him and carries on, but he does so without truculence, his words underscored instead by his sardonic glee over the curious state of things.

The stuff of his writing is at the juncture of the ridiculous and the sublime. The opening to *The Place in Flowers Where Pollen Rests* is through death, the seemingly peaceful death of a beautiful woman who, had a wake been held, "would still have been the best-looking person present." It is a death that came about "because of a fluke" rather than through the premeditation of the perpetrator, who can behold her inert form with detachment.

Her eyes in the final spasm had this far-beyond-it-all and happy look: well, if not exactly happy, then at least resigned, as if she was glad it was over and done with for this lifetime anyway, all because of a fluke. . . . She looked as if she had seen a familiar ghost and was just on the point of greeting it, her eyes wide with gentle surprise. . . . She looked every inch in contact with her life . . .

The power of this gentle opening is that it instigates the reader to pursue the rest of the paragraph, which runs to more than three pages, in order to learn more about the dead beauty and the "fluke" that caused her demise. But in the process of reading on, the reader is confronted with the implacability that turns the beauty of her stillness into the clinical reality of death's toll:

Nothing but that first faint reek of baby napkin, coming from below where the muscles had begun to relent a little. She was only being normal. Her body, where she had recently been, was behaving like a body. . . . He [Oswald] could see how she had begun to sag, all slack and quite rested-looking. . . . She was naked, of course, but nobody had thought of covering her up. She worked naked and naked she had died. It was as if her breasts and thatch were all of a sudden invisible, which was what happened when he looked at those ghastly pictures from the death camps. . . . It was so quiet, though he could hear some gurgling from deep inside her. The vital processes were still going on.

Through the skillful rendering of his words, West has turned the beautifully evocative Sleeping Beauty, albeit a naked one, into a sexless corpse ready for disposal at the hands of the other two men present: "There was a flurry of newspapers and plastic bags, ropes and sticky tape, as if Stu and Clu had been ready for this all along, and all he could think to do was dress and go wash his hands over and over." The blood on his hands leaves indelible marks, like those that haunted Lady Macbeth and that Pontius Pilate thought he could wash out of history; like them, they had others to dispose of the victims.

Such friends-in-need as in West's novel (first voyeurs to Oswald's passion, then witnesses to his inadvertent crime, now co-conspirators in the coverup) "kept you fresh to keep them off the hook. You became a kind of trophy, a souvenir, to keep their eyes on." And when the time came for them to get him, "they would find all the fight gone out of him, his throat arched in soft welcome to the razor, her image on fire in his vacant eyes."

The *New York Times* reviewer of *The Place in Flowers* addressed the verbal virtuosity of the author as displayed in the novel: "Paul West is fascinated by what language tries to hide from us in its deep pleats and pockets, and he's good at loosening its folds just enough to glimpse what may be inside." This is exactly what Jewish mystics sought through the esoteric exegesis of the Pentateuch, the Torah. In another age West most assuredly would have joined the company of the cabalists to work with letters and numbers toward the decipherment of the secret meaning of the universe. In his time, he has opened hermetic seals on his own, decoding a broad spectrum of things on the terrestrial and astral planes of the universe. In this he has followed Dante's path.

On reading that first of his many books to come my way, I had become a fan of Paul West the critic; subsequently, I began to seek out other of his works and so read his poetry, novels, and memoirs. A year or so after the initial contact, I became his colleague at the main campus of Penn State and took the occasion to have him autograph *The Wine of Absurdity*. More importantly, I became his friend, so I began to know the man as well and, in the process, came to an appreciation of him which has increased over the years of partaking in conversation and banter on subjects high and low. It's all a matter of words, as he said in the *Caliban's Filibuster* interview:

> When we die, our bodies fit back into nature in predictable ways, but what our minds put into print or paint, or whatever, affects people in ways that aren't predictable at all. If it isn't put into print or paint, or whatever, though, it vanishes. Ah, the miracle of words! Life's one long filibuster, killing of time with talk.

Paul West's is a language which opens those who encounter it, be it in its vocal or its written states, to new perceptions of the universe. As with Dante's Virgilian locutions, his language is composed of powerful verbal signs powerfully stated which open hearer or reader to the torrents of imaginative filibustering that gush forth out of Paul West's mighty ken. His are, as these samplings from openings to his works verify in their verbal diversity, Words of Power.

John Clute (review date 28 April 1991)

SOURCE: "In the Service of Empire," in *Book World The Washington Post,* Vol. XXI, No. 17, April 28, 1991.

[*In the following review, Clute gives a negative assessment of* The Women of Whitechapel and Jack the Ripper, *claiming that it is weighed down by too much verbalizing and too little urgency on the part of the characters.*]

Jack the Ripper is a bit like the Boojum. Like that most invisible and most threatening of all the varieties of Snark in Lewis Carroll's famous poem, he lurks blank and ravenous at the end of the hunt, and it is an unlucky Bellman who runs across

his likeness in the flesh. The most famous murderer in the world, he remains unexposed, a phantom of the London fog, and it may be just as well that the many writers who continue to search for his true identity will, almost certainly, never prove that they have found it. The stench of the Ripper's crimes is perhaps more salutary when the banality of evil behind them remains unplumbed.

Certainly the lessons Paul West hopes to impart in his new novel, *The Women of Whitechapel and Jack the Ripper,* have little or nothing to do with any attempt to come up with a new candidate for the murderer. In his short preface he acknowledges several sources for the choice he has made, chief among them Stephen Knight's *Jack the Ripper* (1976), a rather breathless nonfiction attempt to pin the role mainly upon Dr. William Gull, physician and lobotomist at Guy's Hospital, with assists from the painter Walter Sickert (1860-1942); the choice of Gull as Jack the Ripper also impels Iain Sinclair's fine, dark, surreal, London-obsessed *White Chappell: Scarlet Tracings* (1987), a novel West may not have come across, as he does not acknowledge it.

Following Knight, West places the beginning of the whole tragedy several years before 1888. The young Duke of Clarence, second in line to the throne, falls in love with a Catholic working-class woman, marries her, has a child by her. In all of this he is aided and abetted by Sickert, a painter long since famous for his louring brown palette, for his interest in the stews and brothels of East London, and for his obsession with the violent deaths of prostitutes. But the 1880s are a decade of social upheaval, the vast empire has finally begun to show signs of wear; and for Queen Victoria and the prime minister, Lord Salisbury, her grandson Eddie's sexual fling in the slums dangerously weakens the fabric of an established order already under threat. So the young lovers are forcibly separated. The duke's young wife is lobotomized by Salisbury's fellow Mason, William Gull. The daughter is abducted. Sickert observes all, with loathing and vicarious arousal.

But the whore who has been nursing the duke's daughter will not stay quiet. Her name is Marie Kelly. Along with three cronies, she signs a blackmailing letter to the Queen. Salisbury asks Gull to deal with the problem, not guessing that Gull will himself, along with a vicious coachman and the protesting but fascinated Sickert, seek the four whores out and kill them, terribly mutilating their bodies. And the Ripper is born. He is not a man but a gang, whose members represent the gilded ceremonial facade of the Victorian age at its height, but whose actions demonstrate, in the most graphic way possible, the terrible cost of maintaining that facade. And Sickert— the central character of this extremely long novel— spends the rest of his life nursing the obscenity he has become.

That this story is in general a piece of historical nonsense— and that it calumniates Walter Sickert in particular—seems not to bother West in the slightest. Nor should it, perhaps. Nonsense or not, Stephen Knight's was, after all, a scintillating version of the Ripper myth. Lurid and comprehensive, it was a prism through which an entire world could be seen to expose itself. If West had been able to retell this tale with anything of the urgency of his source, then *The Women of Whitechapel and Jack the Ripper* might have been a classic elegy for a dying world, a classic analysis of obsession and evil, a classic celebration of the green shoot of life.

Unfortunately, it is nothing of the sort. West recounts the terrible events at the heart of his book with a tangible twice-told ennui, concentrating his creative energy instead on a series of internal monologues meant to recreate the protagonists' minds in a flow of humanizing prose poetry. Some of these passages are clever, many are sensitive, but all exhibit a self-regarding expertise of verbalizing that drowns the cast in words; despite the occasional brilliant page of dialogue, the unrelenting sonorous gush of the book becomes, in the end, nearly unbearable.

To no avail is James Joyce's Molly Bloom evoked in Marie Kelly's flow of unspoken thoughts, for Molly Bloom was the words she dreamed, and Marie Kelly sounds very much more like Paul West than any East End whore in 1886. And after hundreds of pages of soft-edged pudgy-minded "impressionist" matter, Sickert himself seems no more than doleful. In the banality of daylight, the Ripper turns into a sentimental bore. Drowning Sickert and *The Women of Whitechapel* in regrets, West has fatally domesticated the dark fable of the Ripper, and in doing so has ignored a central lesson. If you think you've found the Boojum, what you've found is no longer the Boojum.

An excerpt from *The Women of Whitechapel and Jack the Ripper*

Never again did Sickert want a woman to come and discuss her intimate life with him; he would rather wonder about how they got the poor drowned sluts or princesses out of the paddle wheels in the Thames, first running the wheel to dislodge the corpse but only managing to tear it into large chunks, then setting convicts to cut the remains away smaller, passing piece after piece up to another convict with a sack. That was the place to be for such a realist as himself, as unafraid to peer as to sniff. . . . He always wanted extremes, even if only to paint what was middling and middle-of-the-road. "Otherwise, gentlemen," he'd always say, "we have no north, no south. I am groping for directions. I keep looking for the horizon, trying to reach it." They would never see. He doted on the prospect of green marrow-fat remnants—human sirloins afloat on the river as toiling convicts dropped them and watched them settle to a suitable floating depth, their eyes on what they now had to fish out of the water.

Paul West, in his The Women of Whitechapel and Jack the Ripper, *Random House, 1991.*

Josh Rubins (review date 12 May 1991)

SOURCE: "Serial Murder by Gaslight," in *The New York Times Book Review,* May 12, 1991, pp. 11-12.

[*In the following review, Rubins praises* The Women of Whitechapel and Jack the Ripper, *saying that the characters emerge as distinct personalities and the book vividly portrays the seediness of Victorian London with a fresh sense of horror.*]

Admirers of Paul West's recent fiction probably won't be surprised to learn that this new novel, despite its title, begins not as a tale of crime or horror but as a quirky, almost dreamy love story—complete with a plucky shopgirl, a real-life prince and a soon-to-be-famous artist as matchmaker. After all, in such books as *Lord Byron's Doctor* and *The Very Rich Hours of Count von Stauffenberg,* Mr. West burrowed his way into history from the oddest angles, weaving in and around factual episodes (Byron and Shelley on vacation, the von Stauffenberg plot to assassinate Hitler) with nervy imagination. His specialty is filling in the missing details—psychological and otherwise—through verbally exquisite interior monologues or provocatively vivid evocations of unfamiliar milieus.

This time, of course, it isn't just the details that need fictional filling in. It's virtually the whole story, since no one has ever proved whodunit, let alone offered a convincing explanation of the motive behind the savage murders of five East End prostitutes in the autumn of 1888. Indeed, although speculations abound, the Ripper remains true crime's most enduring unsolved mystery. So there's special fascination and suspense as Mr. West's narrative, whimsically expansive yet also firmly paced, demonstrates how that illiterate shopgirl's 1884 romance supposedly led to the mayhem in Whitechapel four years later.

The smitten prince is none other than Queen Victoria's slow-witted grandson Eddy, the future Duke of Clarence, who, bored with Cambridge secretly escapes whenever possible to Cleveland Street—the Montmartre of London. The prince's guide to the bohemian life there is his surrogate older brother, the English Impressionist Walter Richard Sickert (1860-1942), then a 24-year-old "painter *maudit*" in the French tradition, "dabbling in all kinds of unspeakable experiences just to see what would come out at the other end in works of art." And it's Sickert who introduces Prince Eddy (a voracious bisexual) to the cheerful shopgirl-model Annie Crook, a poor Catholic lass from up north. The two far-from-innocent waifs instantly fasten upon each other with "sloppy-lipped adoration," produce a baby girl named Alice and carry on their clandestine affair over the next few years in near-perfect bliss (Eddy sometimes prefers the company at Cleveland Street's male brothel).

This idyll soon comes to an abrupt halt, however. The old

Queen, having got wind of her grandson's indiscretions, wants the whole disgusting thing ended, hushed up. Her patrician Prime Minister, Lord Salisbury, afraid that a Prince Eddy scandal would fuel antimonarchist, revolutionary rumblings, couldn't agree more. He arranges for thugs to abduct Annie Crook and drag her off to Guy's Hospital, where she's lobotomized and put under permanent wraps by jovial Sir William Gull (1816-90), the personal physician to the royal family as well as "the most famous vivisectionist of his day."

Won't anyone act or speak out against such an outrage? Not Sickert: he's far too fearful (for himself and Annie's child), far too ambitious, for heroism. But Annie's best chum, a breezy, confident young prostitute named Marie Kelly (Sickert's sometime mistress), *does* dare to strike back. Fortified by anger and alcohol, egged on by three of her colleagues, Marie writes audacious blackmail notes to the powers that be—and all four women of Whitechapel sign the letters, which threaten a public airing of the dirty linen unless Annie is freed and the women's silence paid for. So it's not long before Sir William, the Queen's "silencer," begins touring the East End by night in a horse-drawn carriage, offering rides to a very select group of prostitutes. His highly reluctant accomplice: Walter Sickert, who can identify most of the would-be blackmailers by sight. The killings, assumed to be the random attacks of a sex-crazed maniac, are in fact death sentences carried out against enemies of the state—with no less tacit approval than Becket's murders received from Henry II.

Unfortunately, Mr. West can't be given credit for this gloriously farfetched, deeply beguiling plot. His prefatory note—acknowledging that Stephen Knight's *Jack the Ripper: The Final Solution* "fed me some usefully preposterous *données*"—doesn't suggest, perhaps, the extent to which **The Women of Whitechapel and Jack the Ripper** follows Knight's elaborate theory of the case. The Eddy/Annie liaison, the abduction, the blackmail attempt, the *modus operandi* of the killings, the roles played by Gull and Sickert and others—all these basic elements, along with a few surprising twists and dozens of details, are derived from Knight's 1976 book, which was itself largely based on interviews with Joseph Sickert, the painter's natural son, who claimed to have heard the story from his Ripper-obsessed father.

Knight's theory, like earlier speculation that Prince Eddy himself was the Ripper, has since been discredited by Donald Rumbelow and other "Ripperologists." Joseph Sickert confessed in 1978 that most of his account was "a whopping fib," although he stuck to his claim that his mother was Alice, the Prince's illegitimate daughter.

Still, whoever originated the tale, and whatever its iffy relationship to historical fact, Mr. West has generally made the most of it as fiction. The late Victorian period, with all its charm and filth and wretchedness, is delivered up in dazzling

set pieces—from frolics with a bathing machine at Yarmouth to a plague of flies descending on London—that never interfere with the story's grimly steady momentum. Mr. West's lyrical, clever prose, now and then too ostentatiously paraded in his previous novels, remains under shrewd control here.

Each of the victimized prostitutes registers as a distinct, warm-blooded personality—especially the bumptious, unapologetically lewd Marie Kelly. Whether playing nanny to little Alice, hawking condoms, composing a letter to the Queen ("was it *behoves* or *behooves*?"), or fantasizing about group sex with the Prince of Wales and a whip-lashing William Gladstone, Marie commands the stage—a great character out of some alternative, X-rated Dickens—without becoming a scatological cartoon. She also emerges as a bona fide radical feminist hero of sorts, making Mr. West's sporadic attempts at explicit political statement (the exploitation of women, the sins of capitalism) seem redundant.

Sickert, the novel's central figure, is more problematic. At first his depiction as the experience-hungry artist—an "addict of the seamy," the "muse of the unsavory"—verges on mere bohemian stereotype, although Mr. West does shade in the portrait with a few fetching, idiosyncratic touches. In moments of great stress Sickert dresses up in assorted costumes; in moments of private glee he does his "Affable Arthur walk," a comical music-hall strut. Eventually, however, as events force Sickert into ever more ghastly situations, his confrontations with the evil within do take on poignant, if not quite tragic, dimensions.

Witnessing the Ripper's brutal mutilations, he finds himself "reluctantly stimulated, insufficiently repelled, secretly enthralled." The fine line between amorality and monstrosity is fiercely illuminated: "One wrong step was all it took, and down the gradient you went screaming, lapsed from being what your headmaster called A Boy of Ability Who Does Not Concentrate or Work Hard to a slobbering demon."

Throughout, in fact, no matter how literary and bawdy and ironic Mr. West's treatment of this melodramatic material may become, he continually rediscovers—and summons up fresh for us—the genuine horror in heinous deeds. No small achievement, not in these low-affect days of teen-age slasher movies, the corpse-strewn *6 O'Clock News* and *American Psycho*.

Paul West (excerpt date Fall 1991)

SOURCE: "Deep-Sixed into the Atlantic," in *The Review of Contemporary Fiction*, Vol. 11, No. 3, Fall, 1991, pp. 260-62.

[*In the following excerpt, West annotates a letter he wrote to* The Atlantic *on July 4, 1991, after the magazine refused to publish a positive review of his novel,* The Women of Whitechapel and Jack the Ripper.]

When word came that the *Atlantic,* enthusiastic about my work, had commissioned a long review of **The Women of Whitechapel and Jack the Ripper,** I was impressed; middlebrow America was getting to grips at last. Some time later I heard from the reviewer, Bill Marx, editor of the *Boston Phoenix*'s Literary Supplement, that he had indeed written the review but that Jack Beatty, senior editor at the *Atlantic,* had killed it: he could not print an enthusiastic review, he said, of a novel devoted to the chopping up of women. In the meantime, other reviews had pointed out the novel's severe feminism, most recently applauded by Andrea Dworkin in *Ms.* It was clear that Beatty and his colleagues hadn't read the novel, but were treating it as if it were by Brett Easton Ellis. The *New York Times* picked up the tale and published a story in my favor that many other newspapers printed in its entirety. Mr. Marx's phone began to ring, and it became clear that, although he might have no future at the *Atlantic,* he had a solid one elsewhere. In his letter of rejection, Beatty had actually told him his review was *not dull enough* for the *Atlantic.* Meanwhile the novel's author was wondering if they would have printed a negative review. My editor at Random House had told me, with some chagrin, early in May that a short nasty review would be forthcoming in the *Atlantic.* It seemed that this dull glossy was determined to get me at all costs, either long nasty or short nasty, and dull. Surely they wouldn't print both. In an early conversation with Marx, Beatty had said how much he admired my work; thereafter, presumably, word came down from above, or from outside, and my novel was beyond the pale. About the same time, *Time* killed a favorable review by R. Z. Sheppard, for reasons unknown.

Being deep-sixed by the *Atlantic* isn't as useful as being banned in Boston, but it will serve; the book has been selling at a good clip. I am left to wonder at the presence in American culture of the huge backside called puritanism. Trapped between the enervated matrons of National Public Radio, which is as out of touch with modern fiction as you can get, and the newfound hypocrisy of the *Atlantic,* we lash back as hard as we can. The country is drowning in dullness, cant, and flatulent pietism. The glossies go on printing the pale prose of the warhorses, conning their readers that they are reading the best in American culture, and the readers are too dumb to know to what an extent they're being taken. We shouldn't be surprised, then, if a supposedly respectable magazine pretends to a bogus feminism in order to suppress stylish prose. The age of minimalism is over, it seems, but that of timidity has only just begun.

I append my unpublished letter to the *New York Times;* declining to publish it, the *Times* behaved oddly, for some reason samizdating my letter, with my signature painted out, to (I presume) carefully selected people, one of whom sent my letter back to me, with enthusiastic comments in the margin. He thought *I* had sent it to him, but I hadn't sent copies to anyone. I suppose that's one way of tasting a scandal without getting your tongue burned. One of these days, I gather, all

the relevant letters in this disgraceful episode will be gathered up and published. The sad thing is that a proscribed review attracted the attention of only one radio station, in Santa Monica (I discussed with Digby Diehl, literary editor of *Playboy*), and no TV stations at all. Restriction of freedom to praise (or to damn) is not news, evidently. If that is not the thin end of a pernicious wedge, I don't know wedges. Being beastly to the Ripper is one thing; being beastly to free opinion is quite another, closer to Naziism than to bestiality.

4 July 1991

The Editor

The New York Times

Sir:

In Book Notes (July 3, 1991) Roger Cohen reveals why the *Atlantic Monthly* decided not to print a review it had commissioned of my recent novel **The Women of Whitechapel and Jack the Ripper**. The review was enthusiastic, as Mr. Cohen says, but the magazine's senior editor, Jack Beatty, vetoed it because, he said, obviously not having looked at the book, it was "about chopping women up." Since my novel is about an historical event, and not something I trumped up, then I have to conclude that the *Atlantic* is against reviewing—favorably—any book about a piece of history it finds unpalatable. According to this criterion, it would not allow itself to review favorably any book about, say, Hitler, the Gulag, or the Thirty Years War. In other words, the *Atlantic* wants a cozy world to deal with, and certainly not serious thinking about the atrocities of our own times, or times previous. This isn't merely schizophrenic, but daffy. I can only think that the magazine would have printed an *un*favorable review of my novel because that is what, in the end, it did, commissioning the review from someone else, who, among assorted infelicities and inaccuracies, said that the novel was about two lesbians on a rug.

The *Atlantic* and its minions stand revealed in all their triviality and pollyanna nastiness. It is amazing to find a magazine that thinks it has to protect readers from the world. What it was really protecting its readers from in this instance was what several reviewers called the book's extreme feminism. When I was a student, the word we applied to such as Beatty was "prig," which we enunciated very carefully, lest in the shuffle of consonants it sounded like a term of abuse less precise. It is astounding to be told that the *Atlantic*'s initial impulse had been to review a book by someone whose work it admired, only to kill the review according to criteria that would not hold up in a kindergarten. So-called political correctness as practiced by Beatty is only bigotry in a new guise; we do not need it and we should denounce it wherever we find it.

Yours,

Paul West

Gerald Mangan (review date 8 November 1991)

SOURCE: "A London Dunghill," in *The Times Literary Supplement*, No. 4623, November 8, 1991, p. 31.

[*In the following review of* The Women of Whitechapel and Jack the Ripper, *Mangan focuses on the sexual and scatalogical tone of the novel, passages of which he declares "rhetorical flights" and "sheer nonsense."*]

Paul West is an Englishman now in his early sixties, who emigrated to the United States in 1962 and now lives in New York State. His thirteenth novel is the first to be published in Britain, and it arrives surrounded by an honour-laden reputation which has also spread to France, by way of his two previous novels **Rat Man of Paris** and **Lord Byron's Doctor**. The territory he inhabits as novelist, poet and polemicist has recently been plotted in colourful detail by the French press, which traces his ancestry to Rabelais by way of the Elizabethans, and notes the significance of his professorial chair as a successor to Nabokov. His pugnacious critical position, as a scourge of the Carver-inspired school of "minimalist" fiction, has apparently earned him the nickname "Maximalist Rex".

The Women of Whitechapel purports to be the inside story of Jack the Ripper, and his victims; and it is based on the theory, explored in recent books and films, which attributes the murders to an Establishment conspiracy. It proceeds from the supposition that Queen Victoria's son, the young Prince Edward, has fathered an illegitimate daughter by a Catholic shopgirl, who is bundled off to a madhouse to keep the matter quiet. Four of the murdered prostitutes were co-signatories of a letter demanding hush-money from the Palace, and the royal physician William Gull is called on to silence the would-be blackmailers. His methodical eviscerations, by surgical razor, conform to masonic ritual.

Readers unfamiliar with Ripper theory may be intrigued enough to persevere with it, as a melodramatic thriller. But we are warned in a preface that the story appeals to West mainly as "a true merchant of the untrue"; and the element that seems to be his main criminological contribution is probably the most preposterous. The lynch-pin of his version proves to be the painter Walter Sickert, who appears as a pimp to the bi-sexual brothel-cruisings of his chum Prince "Eddy", and an accomplice to murder.

The pigments of the novel are more grimy and lurid than any Sickert canvas. "London was a dunghill and the royal family stood atop it crowing" is the radical *aperçu* behind the swarming tableau of eminent and obscure Victorians whose bodily functions and secret perversions are continually made to stand for waste and corruption in the body politic. The most loquacious of the prostitutes is Marie Kelly, an Irish sex-aid vendor modelled shamelessly on Molly Bloom whose wet-daydreams issue in a macaronic Cockney packed with synonyms for her *funnel, gutter pie, oyster, muffin, holster snatch* or *rabbit-hole*.

The artist's reluctant partnership with the ice-hearted doctor allows West to revive some dusty *fin-de-siècle* arguments between art and science and ethics; and he shows some insight into the psychology of guilt. But the themes soon turn to mush in a witches' brew of ribaldry and horripilation, that betrays more than a *soupçon* of misogyny; and its fluid is a very curious brand of mock-Gothic prose that churns out puns, conceits and quotations, with scant regard for register. ("I want something good period" muses Kelly, "By gum I want my period. Where does the comma go, then?") It would be easy to take it all as self-conscious pastiche, if it were at least competent; but the felicities lose out heavily to the preciosities, which often sound like a translator's howlers' ("beds enveloped him in cuddly mummery"); and the rhetorical flights too often collapse into bathos, or sheer nonsense.

Jonathan Yardley (review date 27 September 1992)

SOURCE: "When Harry Met Hilly," in *Book World The Washington Post*, Vol. XXII, No. 39, September 27, 1992, p. 3.

[*In the following review, Yardley proclaims the autobiographical nature of* Love's Mansion, *West's fictionalized biography of his parents' marriage, of less importance than his successful contemplation of love and marriage.*]

Paul West takes the title of this, his 14th work of fiction, from a line by Diane Ackerman: "Love's mansion has so many rooms." It is an image that persists throughout the novel, the subject of which is the strangely affecting romance of a man and woman closely modeled upon West's own parents: The houses in which they meet, court, marry, live and die have many rooms, all of them consecrated to different purposes, yet all of them containing a love that somehow survives the years.

That the novel is autobiographical is interesting but in the end unimportant; what West makes of his material matters more than where he found it. No doubt he could have told his parents' story in a memoir or joint biography or family history, had he so chosen, but in making a novel out of that story he liberates his imagination and is thus able to reflect upon questions to which a child is not customarily privy.

Reflect is precisely what West does. *Love's Mansion* is a leisurely, meditative book, the pace of which may not be to all readers' tastes. Though scarcely devoid of incident, it is primarily an interior drama in which the state of the two central characters' hearts and minds is always of greater moment than what they do or what is done to them. This, West understands, is how love and marriage proceed.

The partners in this marriage are Hildred Fitzalan, called Hilly, and Hereword Moxon, called Harry. Their story is narrated, after their deaths, by their son Clive, who—like West himself—has left Derbyshire for America: "He was a novelist, perhaps not a busy enough one, and in some peculiar zone of his brain, an anachronistic nursery no doubt, he longed to have his mother's and father's childhood to set alongside his own: three lost children regained against the heave of time that had taken his father, allowed him his mother as far as ninety-four, and pushed himself well into middle age."

Hilly and Harry are children of the last Victorian years, born into an England that now seems impossibly innocent and remote. Each is a dreamer, though their dreams are very different. Hilly, member of a prosperous butcher's family, hears "music in the air," literally and figuratively; she plays the piano, and quite well, but she also believes that music penetrates "beyond things they could see and hear." She is "music's daughter, warmed by an arc-light powered by self-esteem as much as by electricity"; over the years she matures into "a romantic, a woman who was prelude, fugue and enigma variation all in one; a volcano inside a Dresden shepherdess."

Harry is no volcano; "he would for ever, in both this life and the next, be a listener, a dreamer at the keyboard, lifted or lofted to that abyss called music, though it deserved a better name, one that told of its coming-from-within quality." He is "tenderhearted, shy, wincing, easily hurt, never to be trusted not to cry," yet his dreams are not of music but of war: "He yearned to flee—to his books of war, of all things, perhaps because the din and smoke and blood were shut off from him; he had never been to a zoo, but had heard about zoos, and he thought his picture books were a bit like that: stirring but not sickening. Besides, above the chromatics of the martial inferno flew the colors of honor."

So when World War I comes, Harry goes off "to shoot the Boche and fight a manly war." Hilly stays at home, waiting for him, utterly oblivious to the horror he must confront:

> He tried to imagine Hilly imagining how the war was: the noise, the flashes, the rats, the bully beef, the mud, the sandbags . . . and the executions for cowardice, the incessant curse words and the filled latrines beginning to leak into the main trenches during rain. No, she was not thinking of such things; she had the gift of wholesome loneliness and no doubt envisioned

war as cherry orchards, chiming bells and soft paintable sunsets. Were there warm baths in Hilly's imagination? There was music, martial perhaps, but slithering out of the top of the universe to grace and sway the men in tin helmets, urging them to gentleness: always to surrender, to turn the other cheek . . .

Somehow Harry manages to survive, but at an awful price: He is blinded in both eyes and sent to military hospital. There two miraculous things occur: He is introduced to the pleasures of the flesh by a nurse who apparently makes it her mission to do so for many wounded men, and he is given the gift of restored sight in one eye by an American surgeon. So he comes home a different man: "It was as if he had lived his life already and his remaining years were a pseudoblissful charade, himself a caricature somewhere between war hero and water pistol . . . Hilly knew there was something broken in him somewhere, but not exactly what; she knew only that he had flamed and died in the same moment and had to be dealt with gently."

They marry; it is a marriage, in West's lovely image, "that had the dry fragrance of a bouquet thrown to them decades ago, caught, then made permanent by talcum powder, kept in a high cupboard with cracked basins, dead clocks, wobbly candlesticks and defunct letter racks." And: "So dear and close they were, so tenderly mutual, they had shared and lost dogs, seen all their friends married and breeding, and yet had gone on and on in their interruptible sublime conversation, less a marriage of minds than an alliance of whispers."

In time marriages seems "an enormous barrier to what used to be their affection," yet they soldier on. Hilly, determined over Harry's objections to have a child, at last becomes pregnant with Clive and then with a daughter, Kotch. However improbable a family they may be, a family is what they are: a small mansion with four rooms, but a mansion all the same. Not until age and death have caused that mansion to crumble does Clive comprehend the truth about his parents' lives: "It would be a long time before he saw that his parents had come into the world to use life a lot, not to make a little glancing contact, and, as such, were bulk users, helping themselves with both hands in spite of vicissitudes and injuries, until they had enough, and cried bravely aloud for a full stop."

Love's Mansion is at once an expression of filial love and a bold work of imagination. Nothing on earth is more secret than the inner life of a marriage; West has managed to invent his way into the innermost heart of this one, and to do so plausibly, charmingly and unsentimentally. His book moves at a slow and steady pace, but then so too does life.

Joseph Coates (review date 18 October 1992)

SOURCE: "Creating Your Creators: The Protean Paul West

Tackles His Toughest Inventions: Mom and Dad," in *Chicago Tribune—Books,* October 18, 1992, p. 5.

[*In the following review of* Love's Mansion, *Coates theorizes that West's portrayal of his parents' lives is in line with his fictionalization of other historical figures in such novels as* Lord Byron's Doctor *and* The Rat Man of Paris.]

Love's Mansion is either Paul West's consummate novel or his most atypical—if, come to think of it, a "typical" Paul West novel can be imagined. Prolific, protean in impersonation, gamy and yet uncannily tender in sensibility and subject matter, he relishes inhabiting "real" historical people we thought we knew, as well as many we didn't, as some of his titles indicate: *Lord Byron's Doctor, The Very Rich Hours of Count von Stauffenberg, The Women of Whitechapel and Jack the Ripper.*

In last year's tour de force, *Portable People,* there spring to amazing life and sometimes grim death 85 personages from Nixon in China, Simone Weil and the author himself to Rudolf Schwarzkogler, "sonneteer of meat"—his own, an Austrian avant-gardist who in 1940 sculpted himself away from himself, the "patron saint of minimalists" who used razor blades on his own body as a way of "beseeching us to stick together or else."

A biographical note at the end of *Love's Mansion* says that the author is "at work on a nonfiction book about living with illness," so perhaps what West said of John Keats in *Portable People* applies to West himself: "He is the perfect image of the compulsive maker who, burning away with a sickness he could not defeat, exploited it for his own purposes. Increasingly consumed, he consumed life itself." Similarly, in *Love's Mansion* West's thinly fictionalized "parents had come into the world to use life a lot, not to make a little glancing contact, and, as such, were bulk users, helping themselves with both hands in spite of vicissitudes and injuries, until they had had enough, and cried bravely aloud for a full stop."

In *Love's Mansion* West takes on the supreme challenge of inhabiting those historic, even mythic, personages most important to each of us, our parents, whom we never quite outlive or outgrow or really comprehend; and in his hands they become as astonishing as his other "real" subjects. On the one hand, they are ordinary people with a touch of the grotesque, the heroic and the transcendent; on the other, they are heroic figures who remain transcendent despite their feet of clay.

Hilly and Harry Moxon, born in the "Byron-D.H. Lawrence country"—tough northern land of mines and moors—begin life heroically named Hildreth Fitzalan, on her part, and Hereward on his, "after Hereward the Wake, who defended the Fen country against Norman invaders." But, village-wise, they are soon cut down to a size they rebel against all their lives.

She, petit-bourgeoise daughter of a rich butcher, is very likely a concert pianist and composer of genius who fails a Royal Academy exam in London out of pure cussedness by playing her pieces brilliantly but out of sequence, instinctively rebelling against arbitrary authority; he, like Lawrence a miner's son, passes the crucial essay test for grammar-school entrance that would raise his status but can't afford the school's requisite blazer, tie and cap, and so reads and dreams of military glory, becoming early in life at an inferior school the "superfluous boy, a nuisance man" he would be all his days.

All this is being recollected in agitation by their son, the novelist Clive, at age 55, as he feels his way into the early lives of his dead father and live mother, still vital and challenging at 94. She amazes him during a visit to her nursing home with a rousing version of King Porter Stomp a la Jelly Roll Morton—music he thought she'd always said was "not music"—thus changing his novelist's re-imagination of her within days of her death.

Lying about his age to enter the Great War, Harry becomes at 15 a machine-gunner with a reputation for killing thousands of the enemy and at least three of his own officers, the first part true and the second part mostly a macabre myth manufactured by circumstances. It was customary for a subaltern to take a newly minted sergeant out on night patrol in no-man's-land to draw a little fire and see enough action—"with a lot of bangs, eh, and some blood splashed about," as young Lt. Clive Hastilow puts it—for the officer to recommend a decoration for his sergeant's bravery.

Instead, Harry drags back the dead Hastilow, hit in the back of the head by a random rifle shot. His second officer-patron drowns in a shell-hole, after which a major decides Harry is "some type of anarchist feller having his own private war in the middle of the Great one" and is killed by Harry in self-defense on the mission that is meant to trap him.

This Westian comic interlude—"'He's wiped out half my staff,' the colonel whined"—occurs amidst the most barbaric atrocities against civilians by both sides, and ends with Harry being half-blinded by a random artillery round and, at age 16, introduced to oral sex by a lascivious Belgian nurse named Sister Binche, an "angel of satiety" whose nightly ministrations ruin Harry for the blander Hilly when at last, in 1928, they fulfill the troth they plighted decades before as children.

Both of them know it's a misalliance, each having "made a new demand of life" that excludes the other without having the resources to enforce it. Harry is an existentialist before his time, wanting nothing better than a life of continental vagrancy and sensuality; Hilly wanting a life in art, as Clive their novelist son, (named for Harry's first slain officer), sees things from half a century later: "Clive writhed, loving his father as a young man, wanting to kill those who had killed him without killing him."

For a while Clive the viewer disappears, "doomed by powers beyond his control to take a back seat, so as to have a preamble to his own birth, lest he interrupt it in a bout of irascible fellow-feeling predicated upon the trashing of his father," who most intensely does not want a child. Hilly, however, having reached her creative limits by teaching piano to keep them alive when Harry is laid off in the Depression, puts all her artistic eggs in the basket of conceiving the artist Clive would become.

Clive, once born, tells us that this tempestuous failed marriage is largely his fault: "Had they at this point decided against children, they might have thrived," but, as conventional people, "both Hilly and Harry felt their lives being designed by conspicuous failures in the shops, the pubs, and at the bus stops," where they are told that children are their raison d'etre.

Here, it seems, West gives us a perhaps inadvertent glimpse into the sources of his own creativity, the compulsion to keep creating new beings to inhabit in order to maintain his own sense of existence, since he came so close to not being born. (He has even gone so far as to "revise" lives that are known —for example, implicating the Victorian painter Walter Sickert in the murders of *Jack the Ripper*.) The reader is impressed both by the vividness of the life rendered and the eerie feeling that it is being lived on the page, as necessary as breath to its author.

By whatever means, West the author also constantly impresses us with his gravely cheerful acceptance of mortality, as in the remarkable scene where Harry and Clive find the hanged body of a man whom his father had bested in a dispute only a few days earlier. And in *Love's Mansion* he seems to have gratefully tracked his talent to its source in this fully imagined valentine to his tumultuously romantic, disappointed but somehow fulfilled mother, who went on "manufacturing the life she had made up" until her death, which closes the book:

"By Monday she had died in her sleep and been revived with paddles long enough to whisper . . . 'I think I'm dying, I'm sorry,' as if unable to quell some final cosmic prejudice, and Clive knew he was not in her class at all."

David Sacks (review date 4 November 1992)

SOURCE: "Hilly and Harry, an Enduring Love Story," in *The Wall Street Journal,* Vol. CCXX, No. 90, November 4, 1992, p. A12.

[*In the following review, Sacks offers a favorable assessment of* Love's Mansion.]

Any marriage lasting 50 years deserves to be written up. In his moving and highly enjoyable novel *Love's Mansion* Paul West presents a thinly fictionalized memoir of his parents, starting with their shared childhood in an English Midlands village in the early 1900s and ending with his widowed mother's recent death at age 94.

Giving them new names—Hilly and Harry Moxton—Mr. West treats them with candor, sympathy and (for the reader) merciful selectivity, focusing on certain episodes but flying through whole decades in between. In its unpretentious way, *Love's Mansion* is a tale of the 20th century, and a tribute to the aspiring human spirit (symbolized, in this novel, by music). "To live amidst the universe without thinking about it— why, that is to have Beethoven on the player and be afraid to turn it on," we are told at the story's end.

Nearly half the book is devoted, in marvelous detail, to Harry's hellish experiences in World War I. After enlisting by faking his age, 16-year-old Harry becomes an expert machine-gunner, rising to sergeant's rank before a German shell blast leaves him blind. He eventually recovers sight in one eye, and the steadfast Hilly marries him as planned, despite his handicap and despite the class difference between them (her father is a butcher, his a mere miner). The marriage weathers sexual disappointments, the Depression, a second World War and Harry's experiment with adultery; by the 1930s their union has been blessed with two children, the elder of whom, named Clive, is the author's alter ego.

A naturalized American citizen, 62-year-old Mr. West is one of our esteemed men of letters. His numerous books include the novel *Rat Man of Paris* (about a Parisian derelict haunted by the Nazis' obliteration of his boyhood village) and the nonfiction memoir *Words for a Deaf Daughter*. His trademark has been verbal panache—one of his essays is titled **"In Defense of Purple Prose"**—but his erudition has been known to intimidate readers. In *Love's Mansion,* however, the author wisely keeps the flame on low; despite occasional overwriting and some precious dialogue, he tells his story simply and touchingly, from the heart.

He sketches well his parents' complementary personalities, starting with the scene of their first meeting in their Derbyshire village, circa 1905—two children barely older than the century. Hilly (Hildreth) is high-strung and intellectual, a talented pianist but practical-minded and sharp-tongued. Quieter and sweeter is Harry, a small boy with black hair and "large, flushed, Irish ears." Harry is grandly named for the Anglo-Saxon leader Hereward the Wake, but his sensitive, brainy side is shown to go undeveloped amid the British class system.

Mr. West excels at long-range narrative passages, with their need for summary and choice detail. In describing Harry and Hilly's wedded life, he captures the calm slide toward middle age, the change from urgent intimacy to politeness and routine: "A pattern of living had begun to exert itself, and it was not one of communication. They had begun to veer apart." Here we comprehend the ambiguity of the novel's title.

The couple's problems are inflamed by Hilly's distaste for sex—she participates mainly in order to get pregnant—and by Harry's new, *faux*-gentlemanly vice of gambling. But their partnership reknits with the arrival of (first) children and (then) Hitler, as World War II makes for common cause at home. Mr. West devotes a gloriously lyric and sad four pages to Clive's impressions of the Blitz, when German bombers nightly pound the nearby city of Sheffield.

Clive's presence dominates the story's final quarter, and this is sometimes a distraction, although the precocious lad does remind us of his parents' legacy: Their values shaped the man who has written this novel to commemorate them. It is the ambitious Hilly who motivates her adolescent son to think big. Similarly, Clive's future choice of the U.S. as home is suggested by Harry's anger at the British class system and his love for America, dating from his wartime hospitalization (a visiting surgeon from Baltimore had saved his one eye).

Love's Mansion opens with an epigraph, a verse from American writer Diane Ackerman: "Love's mansion has so many rooms." In fact, both that quote and the book title seem to derive from another poet, W.B. Yeats, who wrote approvingly, "But Love has pitched his mansion in / The place of excrement . . ." Appropriate to a story of love and decay, Mr. West's novel contains many references to beauty and squalor combined: Young Hilly's elegant music room, for example, was paid for by her family's slaughterhouse. To strive for grace amid destruction is the human condition, in Mr. West's view. As he writes of his task in *Love's Mansion*: "The temptation was to give them a lovelier life than they had had, but the chore was to record their happiness, between body soil and intelligent anguish."

Vicki Weissman (review date February-March 1993)

SOURCE: A review of *Sheer Fiction II,* in *The American Book Review,* Vol. 14, No. 16, February-March, 1993, p. 30-1.

[*In the following review of* Sheer Fiction II, *Weissman finds that the essays in the collection require considerable contemplation and knowledge to understand.*]

Paul West has been keeping the written word alive and well for a good long time. Nine nonfiction and twelve fiction titles are listed at the beginning of [*Sheer Fiction II*], his tenth work of nonfiction and follow-up to *Sheer Fiction*. Yet, endearingly, he opens by writing, "Doing these pieces reminds me of different calisthenics from those of novel-writing; I find them difficult to do, so presumably I must keep on trying my hand at them till I improve," and he concludes, "I try to be accurate." Statements of genuine literary humility, to be sure, but these are signals too. Reader, beware. You too are going to have to do a little work here. This is a writer who takes his craft seriously, who can quite unself-consciously give us Djuna Barnes, Gombrowicz, Frisch, Goytisolo, and

Dante in a four-paragraph introductory note and who feels that "an avid reader should strive for some sense of the international main."

With that brief hint of effort in store, we are plunged straight into the literary world of one of fiction's brighter and better-stocked minds. The first piece in the book deals with the Broadway production of *Les Miserables*. And away goes West, with Inspector Javert, the SS, Milton, Solzhenitsyn, and Aeschylus—all combining, not only to give a vivid sense of what the production is like, but also to tie "the prettily sung rather vapid lyrics" into the true tragic tradition of good and evil, to show how they conjured Artaud's "little breath of . . . metaphysical fear."

If all this sounds like incredibly pretentious heavy going, it is not. West's next piece is a wild riff in the persona of Djuna Barnes, and the collection provides plenty more fun and games. Nor is it devoid of personal feeling. The first section ends with a memorial to one of his students, Maria Thomas, perhaps best known for her first novel, *Antonia Saw the Oryx First*. The sense of loss is almost tangible—loss of a friend and of a genuinely fresh novelistic voice, which West knows the world of American letters needed. This piece is perhaps the key to the book as a whole. Literature is all-pervasive. Dickens, Dostoevsky, and Faulkner are brothers under the skin, the world of the imagination is universal, "a small part of even the most fantastic writing is realistic, founded on experience held by humans." No national boundaries here, just the human race as inspiration's source.

If Part I is credo, then Part II is application of the same. A dazzling run of fifty pieces ranges across the world of modern fiction, from South America to the Antipodes, trying always to get at the core, the mysterious nugget of what makes a writer's work something out-of-the-ordinary, special, to be treasured. Not all of his judgments are what you might expect. Of George MacDonald Fraser's *Royal Flash* he writes, "A blue and humorous vein is open; let it pour," whereas for J.R.R. Tolkien's *The Hobbit* he has little time: "the cult is an unweening quest for the unmeaning." I happen to agree, but it's nonetheless a refreshing surprise to have one English professor so firmly wiping the floor with another. It is while discussing Tolkien that West writes, "One thing about this world: if you want something outlandish, you don't ever have to invent it; just look around a bit"— . . . .

As he pursues his search West ranges across a wide panorama, including the works of writers with whom I am not at all familiar. But he has some pretty accurate words on the current British literary scene. His piece on Anthony Burgess's *MF* opens with a flourish, "Literary puritanism still prevails in Britain" and segues into two paragraphs of wonderfully exact tartness—for example, "The lady novelists appear on TV, invoking George Eliot." The day after I read that, an interview with British woman writer A. S. Byatt appeared in

New York Newsday. I quote: "Byatt herself claims that she knows George Eliot as well as her own husband. 'Well, I do!' she says earnestly. 'I've read what she has written, we have spent long hours together—it's a very intimate relationship.'" Spot on, Mr. West. Interestingly enough, in *Sheer Fiction II* the Burgess piece is followed by a discussion of A. S. Byatt's work, which West admires, but still he urges her "to strike out and make what she's best at the mainstay of things," rather than "trying to toe the lines of the orthodox English novel (nothing too much, too inward and certainly not too much 'existential passion')." I say this at some length simply because knowing him to be so accurate in one case makes me happy to follow him into previously uncharted waters. Petru Dumitriu, Claudio Magris, Eca de Queiroz, Philippe Jullian—new names to me, but written about with enthusiasm by a critic who has shown elsewhere that he knows his onions. That makes one want to try out the writers he names. Such provocation to extend oneself should surely be criticism's prime function.

It is finally West's zest that gets you. I have not liked all his novels, though *Lord Byron's Doctor* was a real jeu d'esprit, and in this current volume I would not always agree with him. But he revels in the world of literature—even such byways as Thomas Mann's widow's gossip, or Jules Verne's insomniac obsession with crossword puzzles—he is informed, he is painstaking, and he loves what he does.

Sheer Fiction II is full of pleasures. Whether or not the whole is as good as the sum of its parts is another question. All the pieces in the book have appeared previously, the earliest dated being **"The Eskimo Motor in the Detention Cell,"** 1979. That is getting on for fifteen years back. Someone as erudite and witty as West, with an evidently ranging mind, has presumably moved on a long way since then, has new perceptions to share. One slightly gets the feeling of the publisher's urging West to go through the back files and come up with something to fill out the first section.

Again, reading through the review pieces, reprinted from *The New York Times, The Washington Post, The Gettysburg Review, The Southern Review,* and various other leading periodicals, this reader for one became in the end irked by an ever-present sense of the restrictions imposed by a word-limit. Some of the pieces were simply too short—a quick toe dipped in the water on Chuang Hua, René-Victor Pilhes, or Chaim Potok does not sit well with the eight-page piece on Djuna Barnes's *Ryder*. But the latter is the afterword to a new edition of the novel, whereas the snippets I've listed were all reviews. It's not that what we get is no good, it's that it's not enough, especially from a critic with West's vision. Anyone who has had to write a brief review knows how frustrating such pieces are, how inevitably one paints in the broadest strokes. What's more, these are restraints imposed by an editor, not by the writer. The fact that we have six pages on the letters of Thomas Mann and Hesse and only three on Kafka's

correspondence with Felice reflects not the shape of West's interest, but the shape of a page.

It may seem ungracious to complain, but when the writer's professed aim is to widen our scope, to give us a "sense of things European, South American or ancient," perhaps fewer pieces in greater depth would be a better idea. Such a plethora of newness can give the mind a touch of the glacial skid after a while. *Sheer Fiction II* is a travelogue, opening new frontiers and signposting new vistas. Perhaps we might do better to sit and look at fewer views for longer. This is a small caveat.

Gary Davenport (essay date Spring 1993)

SOURCE: "True Merchants of the Untrue," in *The Sewanee Review,* Vol. CI, No. 2, Spring, 1993, pp. 300-03.

[*In the following excerpt, Davenport examines how* The Women of Whitechapel and Jack the Ripper *fits the conventions of the historical novel and the political novel, and pronounces the book "a considerable achievement." He also comments briefly on* Love's Mansion.]

In 1850 Alessandro Manzoni published an essay called *Del romanzo storico* (it first appeared in English in 1984 as *On the Historical Novel*). Nineteenth-century admirers of historical fiction who read that essay must have been disheartened when the author of *I promessi sposi* declared the genre hopelessly unworkable, declaring that faithfulness to history and freedom of invention are inherently contradictory principles. Naive as this judgment might sound to a poststructuralist critic, Manzoni nonetheless correctly assumes that even a sophisticated reader expects a historical novel to be faithful to the past—just as he expects a novel with a contemporary setting to be faithful to the present. (Ian Watt and others have even defined the novel—as distinct from romance, fantasy, fable, and the like—in terms of such empirical faithfulness.)

The real difficulty here may well lie in determining what the past was—and this is not a problem that is any closer to solution today than it was in 1850. On the contrary, at the end of a century of R. G. Coolingwoods and New Historicists, we are more skeptical about the truth of history than ever. We find ourselves unable to consider even such a relatively recent, well-documented, and compact set of events as the Whitechapel murders of 1888 without observing that those events were given disproportionate importance (for there have been many more heinous crimes) by the new tabloid journalism of late Victorian England—or that the persistent notion of Jack the Ripper as a member of the upper (perhaps even royal) classes is only a mythologized protest against what the Haves were doing to the Have-Nots.

Such an atmosphere of relativity would be a nightmare to a Rankean historian, or to a naive historical novelist. (By naive

I do not simply mean premodern: Manzoni knew that the most objective historical record often merely left "the credulous deceived and the more reflective in doubt.") But it may be one of the salient characteristics of the historical novelists of our time that they can regard the uncertainty of history as liberating rather than disabling—and that they consciously accept the responsibility of making something essentially true out of what they know to be actually untrue or at best uncertain.

In his prefatory remarks to *The Women of Whitechapel and Jack the Ripper* Paul West makes it clear that he sees his role much in these terms: "Although I based this novel on facts, I based it on few enough of them, having discovered that one Ripper specialist's fact is another's fiction. Each denounces the other's work as ballyhoo, which is an ideal starting point for a true merchant of the untrue."

West may sound flippant here, but even an amateur Ripper specialist will quickly see that the research for this novel has been thorough and meticulous. And for the most part I find this high standard upheld in a number of contemporary historical novels—which, taken as a group, strike me as superior to the general run of postmodern fiction with contemporary settings. History may not be finally "true," but it is still being taken seriously.

Georg Lukács rightly maintained that without "a felt relationship to the present, a portrayal of history is impossible," but his Hegelian and Marxist background caused him to see historical fiction primarily as enabling the reader to reexperience the past as "a phase of mankind's development which concerns and moves us" in an obviously political sense. In my judgment the best contemporary historical novelists are not merely political animals: it would be closer to the truth to say that the imagined past gives them access to a fictional universe that transcends the unprecedentedly standardized language, thought, and behavior that characterize, even at the most exalted levels, our cheerfully post-Everything society.

And yet *The Women of Whitechapel* would delight a Marxist critic. It is among other things a political novel and can even be strident at times about the gulf between the "two nations" of Victorian England the world of the Duke of Clarence who is free to "attend house parties, go shooting, contemplate an excursion to India or the West Indies, trot off to join his regiment" vis-à-vis the squalid world of Whitechapel, "where a child might lie untended, dead, on the floor of a room that slept ten people." Such a novel could be set in modern New York, and in this sense it evinces Lukács' "felt relationship with the present": ruthless power and abject poverty are not conditions that a modern novelist needs to research.

The class tensions of the novel stem from the bohemian dalliances of the Duke of Clarence, "Prince Eddy." One of the

Whitechapel prostitutes bears his daughter and the government quickly erases this indiscretion by having the daughter sequestered and the mother lobotomized and confined by William Withey Gull, the queen's physician. The prime minister (acting with the queen's approval) responds to the inquiries of the other prostitutes and their threats to publicize the scandal by authorizing Gull to "go and dissolve the noxious mixture" as he sees fit. It is the only encouragement the unbalanced Gull requires to become Jack the Ripper. And it is thus that West makes concrete in the simplest and most horrifying way imaginable the class warfare that constitutes the political element of the novel.

But a political inclination, correct or incorrect, does not make a novel, and it is certainly not what makes *The Women of Whitechapel* the considerable achievement that it is. Its worth lies in its persuasive creation of a world (West assimilates and uses his research without any sense of strain), and above all in its development of characters whose significance is first of all neither contemporary nor historical but human. The main such character is the Victorian painter Walter Sickert, who was in reality one of the many proposed Rippers, but who here is only a reluctant accomplice. Gull makes use of Sickert, who is a well-known and trusted figure among the victims, as a sort of scout.

It may seem implausible that the Sickert of the novel—who is on the best terms with the women of Whitechapel and is thoroughly alienated from respectable society—would allow himself to be thus used; but this is the paradox of his character that makes him interesting to us. For there is an element of Sickert that wants "to see life at its worst and help to bring the worst into being," that reaches out "across the centuries to Catullus and Propertius, to Juvenal and Ovid, ah yes, to the Inquisition, the Terror, and the compulsive exoticist Lord Byron." This depravity—at first only a bohemian artist's game—is what allows him to participate, although with disgust and self-loathing, in the brutal murders of his models and lovers. Sickert's remarkable psychology requires the political context for its realization, but that context is finally the means and the psychology the end.

Paul West is not always able to do so much with his characters: in fact, with the occasional exception of one or two of the victims (the novel is not so much centered on them as the title implies), most of the characters don't matter to the reader as they might. For West sometimes has too much cool virtuosity for his own good. And, although this tendency is certainly present in *The Women of Whitechapel,* it is rampant in the novel that quickly followed it. Set in rural England between the two world wars, *Love's Mansion* is West's most personal novel to date, being based on the lives of his own parents from their childhood forward. The father, Harry Moxon, is socially a cut below his sweetheart Hilly, so West's political consciousness is once again exercised, though in a more genial way than in *The Women of Whitechapel.*

The subject may well have been too close to the author, but rather than falling into self-indulgent sentimentality he seems to overcompensate by verbal acrobatics that lower the emotional temperature all too effectively. Of Clive Moxon, who is presumably West's alter ego, we learn that his mother "taught him grammar from the age of four onward, with the result that he became a perfect monster, with nothing to say but a precisian's way of saying it." If this is intended as a self-criticism of the author, I must say in his defense that it is overstated—but on the other hand the arch, self-conscious diction of such a passage as the following makes it hard to think or feel very deeply about the character described (Hilly, who is a music teacher): "The other three in the family soon became aware that they were living with a romantic, a woman who was prelude, fugue, and enigma variation all in one; a volcano inside a Dresden shepherdess. If any one of them winked wrong, or sniggered, or misintoned, the steeplechase wrath reserved for erring music pupils came their way instead, a shower of darts and brick-bats, a ready-aim-fire onslaught of the complete denouncer, full of hysterical crescendos, tympanic accusations, jangling triangular rebuffs."

Yet, despite the problems with this novel, Paul West at the top of his form is a talented writer who demonstrates the continuing possibilities for the historical novel and deserves a wide audience—more so I think than the Doctorows and other better known practitioners of the genre.

Dwight Garner (review date 20 March 1995)

SOURCE: "Do Not Go Gentle," in *The Nation,* March 20, 1995, p. 394.

[*In the following excerpt, Garner describes* A Stroke of Genius *as "a brave and lovely book" which "quickly moves well beyond being a survivor's celebration."*]

In the case of the upstate New York novelist Paul West, who in *A Stroke of Genius* recounts the various illnesses that have besieged him in recent years—heart disease, diabetes, debilitating migraines—"the sheer majesty of salt" was among the active agents in his physical decline. "Nothing tasted right unless it had been fried," West writes about his restless appetite, but it wasn't until quite late in life, after suffering a serious stroke, that he found that he'd been a "slow suicide whose corroded emblem was the frying pan."

Told that he was likely to die quickly without a pacemaker implant to regulate his faltering heartbeat, West reluctantly agreed. "It was not just a patch applied, a decal, but an incubus," he writes, that would "send me stumbling back out into the world as a well-wired freak at the mercy of microwave ovens and thunderstorms, insect-repelling wave-emitter boxes and airport security barriers."

While *A Stroke of Genius* brims with exacting accounts of

West's post-implant life ("I have been mortified into becoming some *Homo adaptus,* a modified man") and of what he calls the "panjandrum hubris" of arrogant doctors, this memoir is more diffuse and philosophical than either [Reynolds Price's *A Whole New Life* or Wilfrid Sheed's *In Love with Daylight*]. Like his contemporaries, West is fascinated by the links between illness and creativity, and goes so far as to call disease "the supreme art form." But one of the rewards of this brave and lovely book is that it quickly moves well beyond being a survivor's celebration.

West writes convincingly about his generation's ingrained existentialism, a world view that has "argued against passivity, telling us to push, to take the blame, to be—above all—energetic in designing ourselves." That "puritanical message" has carried over, he notes, into his generation's contemplation of not only the good life, but the good death. And happily, one of the signal messages that *A Stroke of Genius* imparts . . . is that there does indeed seem to be, as West perceives, a simple dignity in being a "critic, fighter, and perfectionist to the end."

Richard Eder (review date 10 September 1995)

SOURCE: "The Smashing of a Child's World," in *Los Angeles Times Book Review,* September 10, 1995, pp. 3, 10.

[*In the following mixed review, Eder finds* The Tent of Orange Mist *to be "in some ways a small masterpiece," yet identifies several qualities of West's writing that he finds "irritating."*]

Like J. G. Ballard's *Empire of the Sun,* the agony in Paul West's *The Tent of Orange Mist* lies in a drowning of what Yeats called the ceremony of innocence. In both books the ceremony belongs to children who must face, by themselves, the savagery of modern war. In both books the terror comes with the Japanese invasion of China; at the start of World War II in one case, and just before it in the other.

In *Empire* a 12-year-old English boy, separated from his family by the chaos of the Japanese attack on Shanghai, makes his way home to find that his parents have been violently abducted. Alone, he finds himself in a prison camp for foreign families, a gentle child turned feral, and scavenging to stay alive. It is an atrocity, but in the boy's survival there is something of the picaresque freedom of other displaced children, Kim or Huck Finn, for instance, and of their growth—although here it is growth into a world turned hallucinogenic by Hiroshima's mushroom. Ballard's novel, a masterpiece of the '80s, opens mysteriously outward.

West's book, on the other hand, closes inward. The lives of its two innocents, a girl and her father, are crushed, though one survives deformed in spirit. They are caught in the 1937 Rape of Nanking (Nanjing), whose toll the Chinese have estimated at 300,000. The accuracy of the figure is uncertain

—here as in other parts of its war Japan has yet to confront its past—but it was a terrible one.

Tent is claustrophobic, deliberately and brilliantly so. War comes to Scald Ibis, 16 years old and delicately reared, when the Japanese burst into her house. She does not know that they have just beheaded her younger brother and thrown him into the garden well, or dropped the raped, bayoneted body of her mother in the Yangtze River. Her father, a wealthy scholar and calligrapher—his daughter's odd name stems from two of his whimsical allusions—is not there and she is alone.

A precocious student of art and poetry, Ibis lacks brute images and language to understand what is happening to her. All she has available is the refined reasoning that has served her in her sheltered life.

West is an original and daring writer whose books have been both made and marred by the chances he takes. He has never written anything so risky and triumphant as the terrible evolution of Ibis' perceptions when a half-dozen Japanese officers, led by Col. Hayashi, rape her, interrogate her and turn her house into a brothel. Her immediate reaction is to grasp at the vestiges of civilization that they retain while brutalizing her—it is what she has been conditioned to see.

"Scald Ibis found herself being questioned by weary, sedate men of discernible cultivation," West writes. She fixes on the illogic of the interrogation—which she can cope with—not its horror. "Surely hordes of invaders should not be asking such questions of a 16-year-old. If they upset a country they should know where the pieces landed." She could be prim Alice in a nightmare Wonderland.

Desperately, she registers demeanors. After the officers assault her, they "kept looking at her as if they had shared a good joke together, as if her ravishment had been a prelude to good-humored reverie, a whiff of opium, a bite into succulent plums." Then, insinuating itself through her shock, comes the feeling that she is "transformed, somehow distorted, no longer eligible for the finer things." The pain grows more specific but still partly figurative: "Men pummeled her as if ramming home an inferior argument."

Eventually, in this awful ascent from innocence—by this time Hayashi has become both her protector and abuser—we hear a howl all the more terrible for the literate metaphors that Ibis can no more relinquish than her own odor:

> Hayashi remained a morose and tricky man with a feral cry deep inside him; when he climaxed, he let it out like someone being disemboweled. That was it, she decided: He needs it out of him and therefore inflicts upon himself a repetitious pain. One day the pain will fall silent and he will leave me alone for-

ever. I am a hutch and he is trying to take up residence within me. I am a kennel and he is the dog. I am a coffin in which he wants to die.

Worse than the smashing of a child's world is the rebuilding. The violence of the first days gives way to a deadly order. Hayashi, an ambitious bureaucrat, hopes to win a medal for setting up the finest military "comfort" house in Nanking. Other women will serve as house prostitutes; Ibis will be a geisha. He keeps his fellow officers at a distance, virtually giving up having sex with her himself, and imports two geishas to train her.

She sings, recites, learns the gestures and the rituals and, at the same time, the odd authority that a geisha exercises. The same officers who unhesitatingly rape a helpless Chinese girl submit, as they do to other ritual hierarchies, to the ceremonies that the geisha is mistress of. Ibis makes them babble in French and English; she tells herself that it is they who are being humiliated, not she. If she can survive she will return, someday, to her old life and innocence.

West lets her believe it for a while, the more so when her father, Hong, sneaks into the house disguised as a servant. She now has two to protect. And just as the daughter's cultivation leads Hayashi not so much to favor her as to confine her in a higher humiliation, the same happens to Hong. He is given a uniform and made an interpreter. Both are saving themselves; both are losing themselves.

It is too much for the wonderfully fiery and complex Hong to bear. Seeing Ibis perform a geisha act so grotesquely vile that it cannot be described here—it is the Japanese spectators, she insists, who are degraded—he breaks out in macabre violence and meets a macabre end.

Ibis survives, and lives on after the war in a prosperous, savagely ironic exile from the childhood she thought to reclaim.

West has written what in some ways is a small masterpiece. His portraits of an innocent in the breakers of Yeats' blood-dimmed tide, and of the fierce and civilized passions of Hong, her father, burn in the imagination and the heart. His Japanese officers, brutal, comical and banal, are not without compunction, but it is a compunction so devoid of any awareness of their Chinese victims that it becomes monstrous: the monstrosity we suffer from those who don't see us.

Some of the book's strength is clouded by an excessive stylistic elaborateness that can seem arbitrary. A series of brief interpolations from what purport to be the journals of an early Jesuit missionary take on a didactic irrelevance; irrelevant because they interrupt and because it is unclear what light they are meant to cast.

Notably, there are a number of passages in which the

missionary describes in repulsive detail the hygienic difficulties he experiences owing to the fact that he is not circumcised.

These things are irritating—at least I find them so—but perhaps not terribly important. A more serious objection comes, paradoxically, from the book's extraordinary qualities. Caught in their trap between survival and soul, Ibis and Hong are truly caught. Hong breaks out, terribly; Ibis' unique light hardens into gray. West is delivering judgement, which he has a right to do, and it is a mordantly just one. Only, he has raised two such winged characters that judgement seems to fall short; what is wanted is transfiguration.

David W. Madden (review date Spring 1996)

SOURCE: A review of *The Tent of Orange Mist,* in *Review of Contemporary Fiction,* Spring, 1996, p. 145.

[*In the following positive review, Madden asserts that* The Tent of Orange Mist *is "a gorgeous assertion of the dignity of the human spirit" and should elevate West to the position of "premier practitioner of historical fiction in America."*]

With the publication of **The Tent of Orange Mist,** Paul West takes his place as the premier practitioner of historical fiction in America. In each of his novels since **The Very Rich Hours of Count von Stauffenberg,** West has consistently explored the possibilities of reimagined historical events and personages ranging from a Parisian mutilé de guerre, to his own parents, to an eccentric kachina carver, and in each case he presents history as deeply personal and highly individual and for some a nightmare from which they cannot awaken.

His new novel takes place in Nanking in 1937 when the Japanese invaded China. The protagonist is a sixteen-year-old girl named Scald Ibis who is abruptly divorced from all that is familiar and nurturing. Her father is away from home serving in the army, and unbeknownst to her, her brother has been beheaded and his body thrown into a well and her mother raped and her body tossed into the Yangtze. The family home becomes the base of operations for Colonel Hayashi, who chooses the girl as his personal concubine. Hayashi is a diffident commander and imagines himself an aesthete treasuring the finer pleasures of the world. He gathers a group of teenage girls and transforms Scald Ibis's home into a bordello called The Tent of Orange Mist. Scald Ibis remains his private pleasure whom he tutors to become a geisha. In time the girl's father, Hong, returns to the family home after going AWOL and poses as a houseboy. He ingratiates himself with Hayashi and soon becomes the colonel's official translator. After discovering his son's body and the defilement of his daughter, he garrotes Hayashi and is himself executed. The novel then hurdles ahead fifty-five years when an aged Scald Ibis reflects back upon her chaotic existence.

With *The Tent of Orange Mist* West once more uses the novel as a means of moving beyond the veil of historical incident to investigate its emotional and psychological dimensions. In each of his novels history is filtered through the experiences of a single, alienated figure trying to make his or her way through a chaotic maelstrom. Like other West heroes, Scald Ibis yearns to make sense of her new circumstances: "If only she had been able to live outside history, able in a country so vast as China to face away from headlong invaders; alone and aloof in western mountains, accessible only by bomber, and devoting herself all over again to art, literature, and the other kind of history: the one somebody else had lived before her, in distant pain."

In her pain and confusion the girl is forced to construct an entirely new sense of self, an identity that is repugnant and foreign to her, as prostitute and entertainer of men, yet an identity that is also born of her severed past. As in so many of his other novels, West manipulates a horrifying subject to fashion a staunchly affirmative assertion of the primacy of life itself. Scald Ibis is continually attuned to the miraculous in the mundane: "A born transcendentalist, she excelled at seeing the good in things. . . . She seemed indiscriminately grateful," and she freely recognizes that there is always something of value in anyone, even in her captors. At the conclusion of *Rat Man of Paris* the protagonist, imagining a return of the Nazis who slaughtered his parents, resolves to face his tormentors one day with a thumb held aloft. After watching her father's homicidal response to oppression, Scald Ibis lifts her own thumb of assent to life when she questions, "If life's worth having, worth keeping, then who's to say what you should or shouldn't do?" *The Tent of Orange Mist* is a gorgeous assertion of the dignity of the human spirit in spite of its most depraved dreams of destruction.

David Sacks (review date 12 May 1996)

SOURCE: "A Volcano in a Dresden Shepherdess," in *The New York Times Book Review,* May 12, 1996, p. 11.

[*In the following review, Sacks praises West's ability to write skillfully and convincingly about his adoration of his mother in* My Mother's Music.]

It takes guts for a grown man, in America today, to write adoringly about his mom. Love of mother, tainted by pop psychology, is one of our favorite movie and novel cliches, signaling male sexual confusion, blocked development or psychosis. In real life a man may honor the woman who nurtured and sacrificed for him. But speak or write earnestly about her and you risk sounding ridiculous.

That's a challenge too good for the eminent author and literary critic Paul West to pass up. "I'm afraid I belong to those who cannot resist a verbal opportunity, whatever the cost," he confides in [*My Mother's Music,* a] poignant memoir about his devoted, high-strung British mother, who died a few years ago at age 94.

Mildred Noden West more or less saved her teen-age son's life—urging him up and out of "the bottom social class" of an exhausted postwar England—and Mr. West minces no words about his feelings: "I hero-worshiped her." "I dote on that face of hers." "We had held hands at all ages, un-self-conscious."

The reader soon falls into step, without embarrassment, won over by the story's candor, telling detail and deft prose.

A naturalized American citizen, the 66-year-old Mr. West has written over two dozen books, including the memoir *Words for a Deaf Daughter* and the novel *Rat Man of Paris.* His best novel is *Love's Mansion* (1992), a thinly fictionalized biography of his parents, from their shared turn-of-the-century childhood to the widowed wife's death nine decades later. *My Mother's Music* revisits that territory, in nonfictional form.

Although the memoir goes so far as to repeat a few phrases from *Love's Mansion,* it tracks a far different tale. This time Mr. West hardly mentions his father, a gentle foundry worker left half blind and spiritually stunted by service in World War I. Instead, the narrator and his mother are the only important characters, shown mostly during Paul's adolescence in the grim, dramatic years of World War II, at the family's home in a Derbyshire mining village.

Paul is an awkward kid—sickly, dreamy, "hypersensitive and neurotic," bullied at school, cowed by the savage German bombings of the nearby city of Sheffield. Yearning for some spiritual-cerebral escape, Paul finds in "Mommy" a haven, a soul mate and (eventually) an exacting mentor, who plies him with good books and high standards and goads him toward scholarships and success. With verbal finesse, Mr. West captures the birdlike mannerisms but manic energy of this frail, high-toned woman—"a volcano inside a Dresden shepherdess." As a girl, Mildred had been a brilliant pianist aiming at a concert career, but her parents had pushed her into piano teaching. "A performer denied," she channels anger into improving her two children's future.

To supplement her husband's meager wages, she gives piano lessons at home nine hours a day; her music is associated with spiritual beauty, hard work and a decent income. Paul in 1947 wins a coveted scholarship to Oxford. Later he emigrates, pursuing "an addiction to literature and a subsidiary role as a teacher." Referring to his sister, the author writes, "We were both in vastly differing ways our mother's satellites . . . birds launched from an Alcatraz of class, history, and self-denial, yet one full of music too."

There are some flaws in the storytelling here. The tight focus on son and mother can become monotonous. We get page after page about teen-age Paul's erudite love of literature and music, yet less than a paragraph on his growing attraction to girls—omitted because not inspired by his mother, perhaps, but Mr. West leaves the impression that she somehow monopolized his feelings. Similarly, Paul's final decision to emigrate is left unexplored: Was it painful to move so far from her? Was it a relief?

Still, *My Mother's Music* stands as a bold, touching, entertaining work. Asked by Mildred to describe heaven, Paul replied that "it was here and now, *being with her*." Mr. West makes clear that his happiest hours have been spent alone with his mother. In composing this gallant tribute, he has found a way to be alone with her again.

FURTHER READING

Bibliography

Mann, Charles. "The Man Who Breaks Typewriters." *The Review of Contemporary Fiction* 11, No. 1 (Spring 1991): 298-303.

> Short explanation of West's collected papers, including their contents and locations. Includes appendix listing the items at Pennsylvania State University, which has to date the largest collection of West's manuscripts.

Criticism

McWilliam, Candia. "Miner's Son, Butcher's Daughter." *The New York Times Book Review* (20 September 1992): 16.

> Favorable review of *Love's Mansion,* in which McWilliam applauds West for portraying something as "unfashionable" as the relationship of a "long-married couple."

Additional coverage of West's life and career is contained in the following sources published by Gale Research: *Contemporary Authors,* Vols. 13-16, rev. ed.; *Contemporary Authors Autobiography Series,* Vol. 7; *Contemporary Authors New Revision Series,* Vols. 22, 53; *Contemporary Literary Criticism,* Vols. 7, 14; and *Dictionary of Literary Biography,* Vol. 14.

□ Contemporary Literary Criticism

Indexes

Literary Criticism Series
Cumulative Author Index
Cumulative Topic Index
Cumulative Nationality Index
Title Index, Volume 96

How to Use This Index

The main references

Camus, Albert
1913-1960 ...... **CLC 1, 2, 4, 9, 11, 14,
32, 69; DA; DAB; DAC; DAM DRAM,
MST, NOV; DC2; SSC 9; WLC**

list all author entries in the following Gale Literary Criticism series:

BLC = *Black Literature Criticism*
CLC = *Contemporary Literary Criticism*
CLR = *Children's Literature Review*
CMLC = *Classical and Medieval Literature Criticism*
DA = *DISCovering Authors*
DAB = *DISCovering Authors: British*
DAC = *DISCovering Authors: Canadian*
DAM = *DISCovering Authors Modules*
  DRAM = *dramatists;* **MST** = *most-studied*
  authors; **MULT** = *multicultural authors;* **NOV** =
  novelists; **POET** = *poets;* **POP** = *popular/genre*
  writers; **DC** = *Drama Criticism*
HLC = *Hispanic Literature Criticism*
LC = *Literature Criticism from 1400 to 1800*
NCLC = *Nineteenth-Century Literature Criticism*
PC = *Poetry Criticism*
SSC = *Short Story Criticism*
TCLC = *Twentieth-Century Literary Criticism*
WLC = *World Literature Criticism, 1500 to the Present*

The cross-references

See also CA 89-92; DLB 72; MTCW

list all author entries in the following Gale biographical and literary sources:

AAYA = *Authors & Artists for Young Adults*
AITN = *Authors in the News*
BEST = *Bestsellers*
BW = *Black Writers*
CA = *Contemporary Authors*
CAAS = *Contemporary Authors Autobiography Series*
CABS = *Contemporary Authors Bibliographical Series*
CANR = *Contemporary Authors New Revision Series*
CAP = *Contemporary Authors Permanent Series*
CDALB = *Concise Dictionary of American Literary Biography*
CDBLB = *Concise Dictionary of British Literary Biography*

DLB = *Dictionary of Literary Biography*
DLBD = *Dictionary of Literary Biography Documentary Series*
DLBY = *Dictionary of Literary Biography Yearbook*
HW = *Hispanic Writers*
JRDA = *Junior DISCovering Authors*
MAICYA = *Major Authors and Illustrators for Children and Young Adults*
MTCW = *Major 20th-Century Writers*
NNAL = *Native North American Literature*
SAAS = *Something about the Author Autobiography Series*
SATA = *Something about the Author*
YABC = *Yesterday's Authors of Books for Children*

A. E. .... TCLC 3, 10
See also Russell, George William

Abasiyanik, Sait Faik 1906-1954
See Sait Faik
See also CA 123

Abbey, Edward 1927-1989 ...... CLC 36, 59
See also CA 45-48; 128; CANR 2, 41

Abbott, Lee K(ittredge) 1947- ...... CLC 48
See also CA 124; CANR 51; DLB 130

Abe, Kobo
1924-1993 .... CLC 8, 22, 53, 81;
DAM NOV
See also CA 65-68; 140; CANR 24; MTCW

Abelard, Peter c. 1079-c. 1142 ... CMLC 11
See also DLB 115

Abell, Kjeld 1901-1961 .... CLC 15
See also CA 111

Abish, Walter 1931- .... CLC 22
See also CA 101; CANR 37; DLB 130

Abrahams, Peter (Henry) 1919- ..... CLC 4
See also BW 1; CA 57-60; CANR 26;
DLB 117; MTCW

Abrams, M(eyer) H(oward) 1912-... CLC 24
See also CA 57-60; CANR 13, 33; DLB 67

Abse, Dannie
1923- ... CLC 7, 29; DAB; DAM POET
See also CA 53-56; CAAS 1; CANR 4, 46;
DLB 27

Achebe, (Albert) Chinua(lumogu)
1930- ..... CLC 1, 3, 5, 7, 11, 26, 51, 75;
BLC; DA; DAB; DAC; DAM MST,
MULT, NOV; WLC
See also AAYA 15; BW 2; CA 1-4R;
CANR 6, 26, 47; CLR 20; DLB 117;
MAICYA; MTCW; SATA 40;
SATA-Brief 38

Acker, Kathy 1948- .... CLC 45
See also CA 117; 122

Ackroyd, Peter 1949- .... CLC 34, 52
See also CA 123; 127; CANR 51; DLB 155;
INT 127

Acorn, Milton 1923- .... CLC 15; DAC
See also CA 103; DLB 53; INT 103

Adamov, Arthur
1908-1970 .... CLC 4, 25; DAM DRAM
See also CA 17-18; 25-28R; CAP 2; MTCW

Adams, Alice (Boyd) 1926- ... CLC 6, 13, 46
See also CA 81-84; CANR 26, 53;
DLBY 86; INT CANR-26; MTCW

Adams, Andy 1859-1935 .... TCLC 56
See also YABC 1

Adams, Douglas (Noel)
1952- .... CLC 27, 60; DAM POP
See also AAYA 4; BEST 89:3; CA 106;
CANR 34; DLBY 83; JRDA

Adams, Francis 1862-1893 .... NCLC 33

Adams, Henry (Brooks)
1838-1918 ...... TCLC 4, 52; DA; DAB;
DAC; DAM MST
See also CA 104; 133; DLB 12, 47

Adams, Richard (George)
1920- .... CLC 4, 5, 18; DAM NOV
See also AAYA 16; AITN 1, 2; CA 49-52;
CANR 3, 35; CLR 20; JRDA; MAICYA;
MTCW; SATA 7, 69

Adamson, Joy(-Friederike Victoria)
1910-1980 .... CLC 17
See also CA 69-72; 93-96; CANR 22;
MTCW; SATA 11; SATA-Obit 22

Adcock, Fleur 1934- .... CLC 41
See also CA 25-28R; CAAS 23; CANR 11,
34; DLB 40

Addams, Charles (Samuel)
1912-1988 .... CLC 30
See also CA 61-64; 126; CANR 12

Addison, Joseph 1672-1719 .... LC 18
See also CDBLB 1660-1789; DLB 101

Adler, Alfred (F.) 1870-1937 ...... TCLC 61
See also CA 119

Adler, C(arole) S(chwerdtfeger)
1932- .... CLC 35
See also AAYA 4; CA 89-92; CANR 19,
40; JRDA; MAICYA; SAAS 15;
SATA 26, 63

Adler, Renata 1938- .... CLC 8, 31
See also CA 49-52; CANR 5, 22, 52;
MTCW

Ady, Endre 1877-1919 .... TCLC 11
See also CA 107

Aeschylus
525B.C.-456B.C. .... CMLC 11; DA;
DAB; DAC; DAM DRAM, MST

Afton, Effie
See Harper, Frances Ellen Watkins

Agapida, Fray Antonio
See Irving, Washington

Agee, James (Rufus)
1909-1955 .... TCLC 1, 19; DAM NOV
See also AITN 1; CA 108; 148;
CDALB 1941-1968; DLB 2, 26, 152

Aghill, Gordon
See Silverberg, Robert

Agnon, S(hmuel) Y(osef Halevi)
1888-1970 .... CLC 4, 8, 14
See also CA 17-18; 25-28R; CAP 2; MTCW

Agrippa von Nettesheim, Henry Cornelius
1486-1535 .... LC 27

Aherne, Owen
See Cassill, R(onald) V(erlin)

Ai 1947- .... CLC 4, 14, 69
See also CA 85-88; CAAS 13; DLB 120

Aickman, Robert (Fordyce)
1914-1981 .... CLC 57
See also CA 5-8R; CANR 3

Aiken, Conrad (Potter)
1889-1973 .... CLC 1, 3, 5, 10, 52;
DAM NOV, POET; SSC 9
See also CA 5-8R; 45-48; CANR 4;
CDALB 1929-1941; DLB 9, 45, 102;
MTCW; SATA 3, 30

Aiken, Joan (Delano) 1924- .... CLC 35
See also AAYA 1; CA 9-12R; CANR 4, 23,
34; CLR 1, 19; DLB 161; JRDA;
MAICYA; MTCW; SAAS 1; SATA 2,
30, 73

Ainsworth, William Harrison
1805-1882 .... NCLC 13
See also DLB 21; SATA 24

Aitmatov, Chingiz (Torekulovich)
1928- .... CLC 71
See also CA 103; CANR 38; MTCW;
SATA 56

Akers, Floyd
See Baum, L(yman) Frank

Akhmadulina, Bella Akhatovna
1937- .... CLC 53; DAM POET
See also CA 65-68

Akhmatova, Anna
1888-1966 .... CLC 11, 25, 64;
DAM POET; PC 2
See also CA 19-20; 25-28R; CANR 35;
CAP 1; MTCW

Aksakov, Sergei Timofeyvich
1791-1859 .... NCLC 2

Aksenov, Vassily
See Aksyonov, Vassily (Pavlovich)

Aksyonov, Vassily (Pavlovich)
1932- .... CLC 22, 37
See also CA 53-56; CANR 12, 48

Akutagawa Ryunosuke
1892-1927 .... TCLC 16
See also CA 117

Alain 1868-1951 .... TCLC 41

Alain-Fournier .... TCLC 6
See also Fournier, Henri Alban
See also DLB 65

Alarcon, Pedro Antonio de
1833-1891 .... NCLC 1

Alas (y Urena), Leopoldo (Enrique Garcia)
1852-1901 .... TCLC 29
See also CA 113; 131; HW

Albee, Edward (Franklin III)
1928- ...... CLC 1, 2, 3, 5, 9, 11, 13, 25,
53, 86; DA; DAB; DAC; DAM DRAM,
MST; WLC
See also AITN 1; CA 5-8R; CABS 3;
CANR 8; CDALB 1941-1968; DLB 7;
INT CANR-8; MTCW

Alberti, Rafael 1902- .... CLC 7
See also CA 85-88; DLB 108

Albert the Great 1200(?)-1280 .... CMLC 16
See also DLB 115

Author Index

Andouard
See Giraudoux, (Hippolyte) Jean

Andrade, Carlos Drummond de . . . . . . **CLC 18**
See also Drummond de Andrade, Carlos

Andrade, Mario de   1893-1945 . . . . . **TCLC 43**

Andreae, Johann V(alentin)
     1586-1654 . . . . **LC 32**
See also DLB 164

Andreas-Salome, Lou   1861-1937 . . . **TCLC 56**
See also DLB 66

Andrewes, Lancelot   1555-1626 . . . . **LC 5**
See also DLB 151

Andrews, Cicily Fairfield
See West, Rebecca

Andrews, Elton V.
See Pohl, Frederik

Andreyev, Leonid (Nikolaevich)
     1871-1919 . . . . **TCLC 3**
See also CA 104

Andric, Ivo   1892-1975 . . . . **CLC 8**
See also CA 81-84; 57-60; CANR 43;
     DLB 147; MTCW

Angelique, Pierre
See Bataille, Georges

Angell, Roger   1920- . . . . **CLC 26**
See also CA 57-60; CANR 13, 44

Angelou, Maya
     1928- . . . . **CLC 12, 35, 64, 77; BLC; DA;**
     DAB; DAC; DAM MST, MULT, POET,
                          POP
See also AAYA 7; BW 2; CA 65-68;
     CANR 19, 42; DLB 38; MTCW;
     SATA 49

Annensky, Innokenty Fyodorovich
     1856-1909 . . . . **TCLC 14**
See also CA 110

Anon, Charles Robert
See Pessoa, Fernando (Antonio Nogueira)

Anouilh, Jean (Marie Lucien Pierre)
     1910-1987 . . . . . . **CLC 1, 3, 8, 13, 40, 50;**
                          DAM DRAM
See also CA 17-20R; 123; CANR 32;
     MTCW

Anthony, Florence
See Ai

Anthony, John
See Ciardi, John (Anthony)

Anthony, Peter
See Shaffer, Anthony (Joshua); Shaffer,
     Peter (Levin)

Anthony, Piers   1934- . . **CLC 35; DAM POP**
See also AAYA 11; CA 21-24R; CANR 28;
     DLB 8; MTCW; SAAS 22; SATA 84

Antoine, Marc
See Proust, (Valentin-Louis-George-Eugene-)
     Marcel

Antoninus, Brother
See Everson, William (Oliver)

Antonioni, Michelangelo   1912- . . . . . **CLC 20**
See also CA 73-76; CANR 45

Antschel, Paul   1920-1970
See Celan, Paul
See also CA 85-88; CANR 33; MTCW

Anwar, Chairil   1922-1949 . . . . **TCLC 22**
See also CA 121

Apollinaire, Guillaume
     1880-1918 . . . . **TCLC 3, 8, 51;**
                   DAM POET; PC 7
See also Kostrowitzki, Wilhelm Apollinaris
     de
See also CA 152

Appelfeld, Aharon   1932- . . . . **CLC 23, 47**
See also CA 112; 133

Apple, Max (Isaac)   1941- . . . . **CLC 9, 33**
See also CA 81-84; CANR 19; DLB 130

Appleman, Philip (Dean)   1926- . . . . . **CLC 51**
See also CA 13-16R; CAAS 18; CANR 6,
     29

Appleton, Lawrence
See Lovecraft, H(oward) P(hillips)

Apteryx
See Eliot, T(homas) S(tearns)

Apuleius, (Lucius Madaurensis)
     125(?)-175(?) . . . . **CMLC 1**

Aquin, Hubert   1929-1977 . . . . **CLC 15**
See also CA 105; DLB 53

Aragon, Louis
     1897-1982 . . . . . **CLC 3, 22; DAM NOV,**
                             POET
See also CA 69-72; 108; CANR 28;
     DLB 72; MTCW

Arany, Janos   1817-1882 . . . . **NCLC 34**

Arbuthnot, John   1667-1735 . . . . **LC 1**
See also DLB 101

Archer, Herbert Winslow
See Mencken, H(enry) L(ouis)

Archer, Jeffrey (Howard)
     1940- . . . . **CLC 28; DAM POP**
See also AAYA 16; BEST 89:3; CA 77-80;
     CANR 22, 52; INT CANR-22

Archer, Jules   1915- . . . . **CLC 12**
See also CA 9-12R; CANR 6; SAAS 5;
     SATA 4, 85

Archer, Lee
See Ellison, Harlan (Jay)

Arden, John
     1930- . . . . . **CLC 6, 13, 15; DAM DRAM**
See also CA 13-16R; CAAS 4; CANR 31;
     DLB 13; MTCW

Arenas, Reinaldo
     1943-1990 . . . . . . **CLC 41; DAM MULT;**
                              HLC
See also CA 124; 128; 133; DLB 145; HW

Arendt, Hannah   1906-1975 . . . . **CLC 66**
See also CA 17-20R; 61-64; CANR 26;
     MTCW

Aretino, Pietro   1492-1556 . . . . **LC 12**

Arghezi, Tudor . . . . **CLC 80**
See also Theodorescu, Ion N.

Arguedas, Jose Maria
     1911-1969 . . . . **CLC 10, 18**
See also CA 89-92; DLB 113; HW

Argueta, Manlio   1936- . . . . **CLC 31**
See also CA 131; DLB 145; HW

Ariosto, Ludovico   1474-1533 . . . . **LC 6**

Aristides
See Epstein, Joseph

Aristophanes
     450B.C.-385B.C. . . . . **CMLC 4; DA;**
         DAB; DAC; DAM DRAM, MST; DC 2

Arlt, Roberto (Godofredo Christophersen)
     1900-1942 . . . . . **TCLC 29; DAM MULT;**
                             HLC
See also CA 123; 131; HW

Armah, Ayi Kwei
     1939- . . . . **CLC 5, 33; BLC;**
                    DAM MULT, POET
See also BW 1; CA 61-64; CANR 21;
     DLB 117; MTCW

Armatrading, Joan   1950- . . . . **CLC 17**
See also CA 114

Arnette, Robert
See Silverberg, Robert

Arnim, Achim von (Ludwig Joachim von
     Arnim)   1781-1831 . . . . **NCLC 5**
See also DLB 90

Arnim, Bettina von   1785-1859 . . . . **NCLC 38**
See also DLB 90

Arnold, Matthew
     1822-1888 . . . . . **NCLC 6, 29; DA; DAB;**
     DAC; DAM MST, POET; PC 5; WLC
See also CDBLB 1832-1890; DLB 32, 57

Arnold, Thomas   1795-1842 . . . . . . **NCLC 18**
See also DLB 55

Arnow, Harriette (Louisa) Simpson
     1908-1986 . . . . **CLC 2, 7, 18**
See also CA 9-12R; 118; CANR 14; DLB 6;
     MTCW; SATA 42; SATA-Obit 47

Arp, Hans
See Arp, Jean

Arp, Jean   1887-1966 . . . . **CLC 5**
See also CA 81-84; 25-28R; CANR 42

Arrabal
See Arrabal, Fernando

Arrabal, Fernando   1932- . . . **CLC 2, 9, 18, 58**
See also CA 9-12R; CANR 15

Arrick, Fran . . . . **CLC 30**
See also Gaberman, Judie Angell

Artaud, Antonin (Marie Joseph)
     1896-1948 . . . **TCLC 3, 36; DAM DRAM**
See also CA 104; 149

Arthur, Ruth M(abel)   1905-1979 . . . . **CLC 12**
See also CA 9-12R; 85-88; CANR 4;
     SATA 7, 26

Artsybashev, Mikhail (Petrovich)
     1878-1927 . . . . **TCLC 31**

Arundel, Honor (Morfydd)
     1919-1973 . . . . **CLC 17**
See also CA 21-22; 41-44R; CAP 2;
     CLR 35; SATA 4; SATA-Obit 24

Asch, Sholem   1880-1957 . . . . **TCLC 3**
See also CA 105

Ash, Shalom
See Asch, Sholem

Ashbery, John (Lawrence)
     1927- . . . . . . **CLC 2, 3, 4, 6, 9, 13, 15, 25,**
                 41, 77; DAM POET
See also CA 5-8R; CANR 9, 37; DLB 5,
     165; DLBY 81; INT CANR-9; MTCW

Ashdown, Clifford
See Freeman, R(ichard) Austin

Ashe, Gordon
See Creasey, John

Ashton-Warner, Sylvia (Constance)
1908-1984 . . . . **CLC 19**
See also CA 69-72; 112; CANR 29; MTCW

Asimov, Isaac
1920-1992 . . . . . . **CLC 1, 3, 9, 19, 26, 76,**
92; DAM POP
See also AAYA 13; BEST 90:2; CA 1-4R;
137; CANR 2, 19, 36; CLR 12; DLB 8;
DLBY 92; INT CANR-19; JRDA;
MAICYA; MTCW; SATA 1, 26, 74

Astley, Thea (Beatrice May)
1925- . . . . **CLC 41**
See also CA 65-68; CANR 11, 43

Aston, James
See White, T(erence) H(anbury)

Asturias, Miguel Angel
1899-1974 . . . . **CLC 3, 8, 13;**
DAM MULT, NOV; HLC
See also CA 25-28; 49-52; CANR 32;
CAP 2; DLB 113; HW; MTCW

Atares, Carlos Saura
See Saura (Atares), Carlos

Atheling, William
See Pound, Ezra (Weston Loomis)

Atheling, William, Jr.
See Blish, James (Benjamin)

Atherton, Gertrude (Franklin Horn)
1857-1948 . . . . **TCLC 2**
See also CA 104; DLB 9, 78

Atherton, Lucius
See Masters, Edgar Lee

Atkins, Jack
See Harris, Mark

Attaway, William (Alexander)
1911-1986 . . . . **CLC 92; BLC;**
DAM MULT
See also BW 2; CA 143; DLB 76

Atticus
See Fleming, Ian (Lancaster)

Atwood, Margaret (Eleanor)
1939- . . . . . **CLC 2, 3, 4, 8, 13, 15, 25, 44,**
84; DA; DAB; DAC; DAM MST, NOV,
POET; PC 8; SSC 2; WLC
See also AAYA 12; BEST 89:2; CA 49-52;
CANR 3, 24, 33; DLB 53;
INT CANR-24; MTCW; SATA 50

Aubigny, Pierre d'
See Mencken, H(enry) L(ouis)

Aubin, Penelope 1685-1731(?) . . . . **LC 9**
See also DLB 39

Auchincloss, Louis (Stanton)
1917- . . . . **CLC 4, 6, 9, 18, 45;**
DAM NOV; SSC 22
See also CA 1-4R; CANR 6, 29; DLB 2;
DLBY 80; INT CANR-29; MTCW

Auden, W(ystan) H(ugh)
1907-1973 . . . . . . **CLC 1, 2, 3, 4, 6, 9, 11,**
14, 43; DA; DAB; DAC; DAM DRAM,
MST, POET; PC 1; WLC
See also AAYA 18; CA 9-12R; 45-48;
CANR 5; CDBLB 1914-1945; DLB 10,
20; MTCW

Audiberti, Jacques
1900-1965 . . . . . . **CLC 38; DAM DRAM**
See also CA 25-28R

Audubon, John James
1785-1851 . . . . **NCLC 47**

Auel, Jean M(arie)
1936- . . . . **CLC 31; DAM POP**
See also AAYA 7; BEST 90:4; CA 103;
CANR 21; INT CANR-21

Auerbach, Erich 1892-1957 . . . . . . **TCLC 43**
See also CA 118

Augier, Emile 1820-1889 . . . . **NCLC 31**

August, John
See De Voto, Bernard (Augustine)

Augustine, St. 354-430 . . . . . . **CMLC 6; DAB**

Aurelius
See Bourne, Randolph S(illiman)

Aurobindo, Sri 1872-1950 . . . . **TCLC 63**

Austen, Jane
1775-1817 . . . . . **NCLC 1, 13, 19, 33, 51;**
DA; DAB; DAC; DAM MST, NOV;
WLC
See also CDBLB 1789-1832; DLB 116

Auster, Paul 1947- . . . . **CLC 47**
See also CA 69-72; CANR 23, 52

Austin, Frank
See Faust, Frederick (Schiller)

Austin, Mary (Hunter)
1868-1934 . . . . **TCLC 25**
See also CA 109; DLB 9, 78

Autran Dourado, Waldomiro
See Dourado, (Waldomiro Freitas) Autran

Averroes 1126-1198 . . . . **CMLC 7**
See also DLB 115

Avicenna 980-1037 . . . . **CMLC 16**
See also DLB 115

Avison, Margaret
1918- . . . . **CLC 2, 4; DAC; DAM POET**
See also CA 17-20R; DLB 53; MTCW

Axton, David
See Koontz, Dean R(ay)

Ayckbourn, Alan
1939- . . . . . . **CLC 5, 8, 18, 33, 74; DAB;**
DAM DRAM
See also CA 21-24R; CANR 31; DLB 13;
MTCW

Aydy, Catherine
See Tennant, Emma (Christina)

Ayme, Marcel (Andre) 1902-1967 . . . **CLC 11**
See also CA 89-92; CLR 25; DLB 72

Ayrton, Michael 1921-1975 . . . . **CLC 7**
See also CA 5-8R; 61-64; CANR 9, 21

Azorin . . . . **CLC 11**
See also Martinez Ruiz, Jose

Azuela, Mariano
1873-1952 . . . . . **TCLC 3; DAM MULT;**
HLC
See also CA 104; 131; HW; MTCW

Baastad, Babbis Friis
See Friis-Baastad, Babbis Ellinor

Bab
See Gilbert, W(illiam) S(chwenck)

Babbis, Eleanor
See Friis-Baastad, Babbis Ellinor

Babel, Isaak (Emmanuilovich)
1894-1941(?) . . . . . . **TCLC 2, 13; SSC 16**
See also CA 104

Babits, Mihaly 1883-1941 . . . . **TCLC 14**
See also CA 114

Babur 1483-1530 . . . . **LC 18**

Bacchelli, Riccardo 1891-1985 . . . . . **CLC 19**
See also CA 29-32R; 117

Bach, Richard (David)
1936- . . . . . . **CLC 14; DAM NOV, POP**
See also AITN 1; BEST 89:2; CA 9-12R;
CANR 18; MTCW; SATA 13

Bachman, Richard
See King, Stephen (Edwin)

Bachmann, Ingeborg 1926-1973 . . . . . **CLC 69**
See also CA 93-96; 45-48; DLB 85

Bacon, Francis 1561-1626 . . . . **LC 18, 32**
See also CDBLB Before 1660; DLB 151

Bacon, Roger 1214(?)-1292 . . . . . . **CMLC 14**
See also DLB 115

Bacovia, George . . . . **TCLC 24**
See also Vasiliu, Gheorghe

Badanes, Jerome 1937- . . . . **CLC 59**

Bagehot, Walter 1826-1877 . . . . . . **NCLC 10**
See also DLB 55

Bagnold, Enid
1889-1981 . . . . . . **CLC 25; DAM DRAM**
See also CA 5-8R; 103; CANR 5, 40;
DLB 13, 160; MAICYA; SATA 1, 25

Bagritsky, Eduard 1895-1934 . . . . . **TCLC 60**

Bagrjana, Elisaveta
See Belcheva, Elisaveta

Bagryana, Elisaveta . . . . **CLC 10**
See also Belcheva, Elisaveta
See also DLB 147

Bailey, Paul 1937- . . . . **CLC 45**
See also CA 21-24R; CANR 16; DLB 14

Baillie, Joanna 1762-1851 . . . . **NCLC 2**
See also DLB 93

Bainbridge, Beryl (Margaret)
1933- . . . . **CLC 4, 5, 8, 10, 14, 18, 22, 62;**
DAM NOV
See also CA 21-24R; CANR 24; DLB 14;
MTCW

Baker, Elliott 1922- . . . . **CLC 8**
See also CA 45-48; CANR 2

Baker, Nicholson
1957- . . . . **CLC 61; DAM POP**
See also CA 135

Baker, Ray Stannard 1870-1946 . . . **TCLC 47**
See also CA 118

Baker, Russell (Wayne) 1925- . . . . . . **CLC 31**
See also BEST 89:4; CA 57-60; CANR 11,
41; MTCW

Bakhtin, M.
See Bakhtin, Mikhail Mikhailovich

Bakhtin, M. M.
See Bakhtin, Mikhail Mikhailovich

Bakhtin, Mikhail
See Bakhtin, Mikhail Mikhailovich

Bakhtin, Mikhail Mikhailovich
1895-1975 . . . . **CLC 83**
See also CA 128; 113

Bauchart
See Camus, Albert

Baudelaire, Charles
1821-1867 .... NCLC 6, 29, 55; DA;
DAB; DAC; DAM MST, POET; PC 1;
SSC 18; WLC

Baudrillard, Jean 1929- .... CLC 60

Baum, L(yman) Frank 1856-1919 ... TCLC 7
See also CA 108; 133; CLR 15; DLB 22;
JRDA; MAICYA; MTCW; SATA 18

Baum, Louis F.
See Baum, L(yman) Frank

Baumbach, Jonathan 1933- ...... CLC 6, 23
See also CA 13-16R; CAAS 5; CANR 12;
DLBY 80; INT CANR-12; MTCW

Bausch, Richard (Carl) 1945- ...... CLC 51
See also CA 101; CAAS 14; CANR 43;
DLB 130

Baxter, Charles
1947- .... CLC 45, 78; DAM POP
See also CA 57-60; CANR 40; DLB 130

Baxter, George Owen
See Faust, Frederick (Schiller)

Baxter, James K(eir) 1926-1972 .... CLC 14
See also CA 77-80

Baxter, John
See Hunt, E(verette) Howard, (Jr.)

Bayer, Sylvia
See Glassco, John

Baynton, Barbara 1857-1929 ...... TCLC 57

Beagle, Peter S(oyer) 1939- .... CLC 7
See also CA 9-12R; CANR 4, 51;
DLBY 80; INT CANR-4; SATA 60

Bean, Normal
See Burroughs, Edgar Rice

Beard, Charles A(ustin)
1874-1948 .... TCLC 15
See also CA 115; DLB 17; SATA 18

Beardsley, Aubrey 1872-1898 ..... NCLC 6

Beattie, Ann
1947- .... CLC 8, 13, 18, 40, 63;
DAM NOV, POP; SSC 11
See also BEST 90:2; CA 81-84; CANR 53;
DLBY 82; MTCW

Beattie, James 1735-1803 .... NCLC 25
See also DLB 109

Beauchamp, Kathleen Mansfield 1888-1923
See Mansfield, Katherine
See also CA 104; 134; DA; DAC;
DAM MST

Beaumarchais, Pierre-Augustin Caron de
1732-1799 .... DC 4
See also DAM DRAM

Beaumont, Francis
1584(?)-1616 .... LC 33; DC 6
See also CDBLB Before 1660; DLB 58, 121

Beauvoir, Simone (Lucie Ernestine Marie
Bertrand) de
1908-1986 .... CLC 1, 2, 4, 8, 14, 31, 44,
50, 71; DA; DAB; DAC; DAM MST,
NOV; WLC
See also CA 9-12R; 118; CANR 28;
DLB 72; DLBY 86; MTCW

Becker, Carl 1873-1945 .... TCLC 63:
See also DLB 17

Becker, Jurek 1937- .... CLC 7, 19
See also CA 85-88; DLB 75

Becker, Walter 1950- .... CLC 26

Beckett, Samuel (Barclay)
1906-1989 ...... CLC 1, 2, 3, 4, 6, 9, 10,
11, 14, 18, 29, 57, 59, 83; DA; DAB;
DAC; DAM DRAM, MST, NOV;
SSC 16; WLC
See also CA 5-8R; 130; CANR 33;
CDBLB 1945-1960; DLB 13, 15;
DLBY 90; MTCW

Beckford, William 1760-1844 .... NCLC 16
See also DLB 39

Beckman, Gunnel 1910- .... CLC 26
See also CA 33-36R; CANR 15; CLR 25;
MAICYA; SAAS 9; SATA 6

Becque, Henri 1837-1899 .... NCLC 3

Beddoes, Thomas Lovell
1803-1849 .... NCLC 3
See also DLB 96

Bedford, Donald F.
See Fearing, Kenneth (Flexner)

Beecher, Catharine Esther
1800-1878 .... NCLC 30
See also DLB 1

Beecher, John 1904-1980 .... CLC 6
See also AITN 1; CA 5-8R; 105; CANR 8

Beer, Johann 1655-1700 .... LC 5
See also DLB 168

Beer, Patricia 1924- .... CLC 58
See also CA 61-64; CANR 13, 46; DLB 40

Beerbohm, Henry Maximilian
1872-1956 .... TCLC 1, 24
See also CA 104; DLB 34, 100

Beerbohm, Max
See Beerbohm, Henry Maximilian

Beer-Hofmann, Richard
1866-1945 .... TCLC 60
See also DLB 81

Begiebing, Robert J(ohn) 1946- ..... CLC 70
See also CA 122; CANR 40

Behan, Brendan
1923-1964 .... CLC 1, 8, 11, 15, 79;
DAM DRAM
See also CA 73-76; CANR 33;
CDBLB 1945-1960; DLB 13; MTCW

Behn, Aphra
1640(?)-1689 ...... LC 1, 30; DA; DAB;
DAC; DAM DRAM, MST, NOV,
POET; DC 4; PC 13; WLC
See also DLB 39, 80, 131

Behrman, S(amuel) N(athaniel)
1893-1973 .... CLC 40
See also CA 13-16; 45-48; CAP 1; DLB 7,
44

Belasco, David 1853-1931 .... TCLC 3
See also CA 104; DLB 7

Belcheva, Elisaveta 1893- .... CLC 10
See also Bagryana, Elisaveta

Beldone, Phil "Cheech"
See Ellison, Harlan (Jay)

Beleno
See Azuela, Mariano

Belinski, Vissarion Grigoryevich
1811-1848 .... NCLC 5

Belitt, Ben 1911- .... CLC 22
See also CA 13-16R; CAAS 4; CANR 7;
DLB 5

Bell, James Madison
1826-1902 .... TCLC 43; BLC;
DAM MULT
See also BW 1; CA 122; 124; DLB 50

Bell, Madison (Smartt) 1957- ...... CLC 41
See also CA 111; CANR 28

Bell, Marvin (Hartley)
1937- .... CLC 8, 31; DAM POET
See also CA 21-24R; CAAS 14; DLB 5;
MTCW

Bell, W. L. D.
See Mencken, H(enry) L(ouis)

Bellamy, Atwood C.
See Mencken, H(enry) L(ouis)

Bellamy, Edward 1850-1898 ...... NCLC 4
See also DLB 12

Bellin, Edward J.
See Kuttner, Henry

Belloc, (Joseph) Hilaire (Pierre)
1870-1953 ... TCLC 7, 18; DAM POET
See also CA 106; 152; DLB 19, 100, 141;
YABC 1

Belloc, Joseph Peter Rene Hilaire
See Belloc, (Joseph) Hilaire (Pierre)

Belloc, Joseph Pierre Hilaire
See Belloc, (Joseph) Hilaire (Pierre)

Belloc, M. A.
See Lowndes, Marie Adelaide (Belloc)

Bellow, Saul
1915- ...... CLC 1, 2, 3, 6, 8, 10, 13, 15,
25, 33, 34, 63, 79; DA; DAB; DAC;
DAM MST, NOV, POP; SSC 14; WLC
See also AITN 2; BEST 89:3; CA 5-8R;
CABS 1; CANR 29, 53;
CDALB 1941-1968; DLB 2, 28; DLBD 3;
DLBY 82; MTCW

Belser, Reimond Karel Maria de 1929-
See Ruyslinck, Ward
See also CA 152

Bely, Andrey .... TCLC 7; PC 11
See also Bugayev, Boris Nikolayevich

Benary, Margot
See Benary-Isbert, Margot

Benary-Isbert, Margot 1889-1979 ... CLC 12
See also CA 5-8R; 89-92; CANR 4;
CLR 12; MAICYA; SATA 2;
SATA-Obit 21

Benavente (y Martinez), Jacinto
1866-1954 ..... TCLC 3; DAM DRAM,
MULT
See also CA 106; 131; HW; MTCW

Benchley, Peter (Bradford)
1940- ..... CLC 4, 8; DAM NOV, POP
See also AAYA 14; AITN 2; CA 17-20R;
CANR 12, 35; MTCW; SATA 3, 89

Benchley, Robert (Charles)
1889-1945 .... TCLC 1, 55
See also CA 105; DLB 11

Benda, Julien 1867-1956 .... TCLC 60
See also CA 120

Benedict, Ruth 1887-1948 .... TCLC 60

Benedikt, Michael 1935- . . . . **CLC 4, 14**
See also CA 13-16R; CANR 7; DLB 5

Benet, Juan 1927- . . . . **CLC 28**
See also CA 143

Benet, Stephen Vincent
1898-1943 . . . . . **TCLC 7; DAM POET;**
SSC 10
See also CA 104; 152; DLB 4, 48, 102;
YABC 1

Benet, William Rose
1886-1950 . . . . . . **TCLC 28; DAM POET**
See also CA 118; 152; DLB 45

Benford, Gregory (Albert) 1941- . . . . **CLC 52**
See also CA 69-72; CANR 12, 24, 49;
DLBY 82

Bengtsson, Frans (Gunnar)
1894-1954 . . . . **TCLC 48**

Benjamin, David
See Slavitt, David R(ytman)

Benjamin, Lois
See Gould, Lois

Benjamin, Walter 1892-1940 . . . . . . **TCLC 39**

Benn, Gottfried 1886-1956 . . . . **TCLC 3**
See also CA 106; DLB 56

Bennett, Alan
1934- . . . **CLC 45, 77; DAB; DAM MST**
See also CA 103; CANR 35; MTCW

Bennett, (Enoch) Arnold
1867-1931 . . . . **TCLC 5, 20**
See also CA 106; CDBLB 1890-1914;
DLB 10, 34, 98, 135

Bennett, Elizabeth
See Mitchell, Margaret (Munnerlyn)

Bennett, George Harold 1930-
See Bennett, Hal
See also BW 1; CA 97-100

Bennett, Hal . . . . **CLC 5**
See also Bennett, George Harold
See also DLB 33

Bennett, Jay 1912- . . . . **CLC 35**
See also AAYA 10; CA 69-72; CANR 11,
42; JRDA; SAAS 4; SATA 41, 87;
SATA-Brief 27

Bennett, Louise (Simone)
1919- . . . . . **CLC 28; BLC; DAM MULT**
See also BW 2; CA 151; DLB 117

Benson, E(dward) F(rederic)
1867-1940 . . . . **TCLC 27**
See also CA 114; DLB 135, 153

Benson, Jackson J. 1930- . . . . **CLC 34**
See also CA 25-28R; DLB 111

Benson, Sally 1900-1972 . . . . **CLC 17**
See also CA 19-20; 37-40R; CAP 1;
SATA 1, 35; SATA-Obit 27

Benson, Stella 1892-1933 . . . . **TCLC 17**
See also CA 117; DLB 36, 162

Bentham, Jeremy 1748-1832 . . . . . **NCLC 38**
See also DLB 107, 158

Bentley, E(dmund) C(lerihew)
1875-1956 . . . . **TCLC 12**
See also CA 108; DLB 70

Bentley, Eric (Russell) 1916- . . . . **CLC 24**
See also CA 5-8R; CANR 6; INT CANR-6

Beranger, Pierre Jean de
1780-1857 . . . . **NCLC 34**

Berendt, John (Lawrence) 1939- . . . . **CLC 86**
See also CA 146

Berger, Colonel
See Malraux, (Georges-)Andre

Berger, John (Peter) 1926- . . . . . . **CLC 2, 19**
See also CA 81-84; CANR 51; DLB 14

Berger, Melvin H. 1927- . . . . **CLC 12**
See also CA 5-8R; CANR 4; CLR 32;
SAAS 2; SATA 5, 88

Berger, Thomas (Louis)
1924- . . . . **CLC 3, 5, 8, 11, 18, 38;**
DAM NOV
See also CA 1-4R; CANR 5, 28, 51; DLB 2;
DLBY 80; INT CANR-28; MTCW

Bergman, (Ernst) Ingmar
1918- . . . . **CLC 16, 72**
See also CA 81-84; CANR 33

Bergson, Henri 1859-1941 . . . . **TCLC 32**

Bergstein, Eleanor 1938- . . . . **CLC 4**
See also CA 53-56; CANR 5

Berkoff, Steven 1937- . . . . **CLC 56**
See also CA 104

Bermant, Chaim (Icyk) 1929- . . . . . . **CLC 40**
See also CA 57-60; CANR 6, 31

Bern, Victoria
See Fisher, M(ary) F(rances) K(ennedy)

Bernanos, (Paul Louis) Georges
1888-1948 . . . . **TCLC 3**
See also CA 104; 130; DLB 72

Bernard, April 1956- . . . . **CLC 59**
See also CA 131

Berne, Victoria
See Fisher, M(ary) F(rances) K(ennedy)

Bernhard, Thomas
1931-1989 . . . . **CLC 3, 32, 61**
See also CA 85-88; 127; CANR 32;
DLB 85, 124; MTCW

Berriault, Gina 1926- . . . . **CLC 54**
See also CA 116; 129; DLB 130

Berrigan, Daniel 1921- . . . . **CLC 4**
See also CA 33-36R; CAAS 1; CANR 11,
43; DLB 5

Berrigan, Edmund Joseph Michael, Jr.
1934-1983
See Berrigan, Ted
See also CA 61-64; 110; CANR 14

Berrigan, Ted . . . . **CLC 37**
See also Berrigan, Edmund Joseph Michael,
Jr.
See also DLB 5

Berry, Charles Edward Anderson 1931-
See Berry, Chuck
See also CA 115

Berry, Chuck . . . . **CLC 17**
See also Berry, Charles Edward Anderson

Berry, Jonas
See Ashbery, John (Lawrence)

Berry, Wendell (Erdman)
1934- . . . . **CLC 4, 6, 8, 27, 46;**
DAM POET
See also AITN 1; CA 73-76; CANR 50;
DLB 5, 6

Berryman, John
1914-1972 . . . . . . **CLC 1, 2, 3, 4, 6, 8, 10,**
13, 25, 62; DAM POET
See also CA 13-16; 33-36R; CABS 2;
CANR 35; CAP 1; CDALB 1941-1968;
DLB 48; MTCW

Bertolucci, Bernardo 1940- . . . . **CLC 16**
See also CA 106

Bertrand, Aloysius 1807-1841 . . . . **NCLC 31**

Bertran de Born c. 1140-1215 . . . . . **CMLC 5**

Besant, Annie (Wood) 1847-1933 . . . **TCLC 9**
See also CA 105

Bessie, Alvah 1904-1985 . . . . **CLC 23**
See also CA 5-8R; 116; CANR 2; DLB 26

Bethlen, T. D.
See Silverberg, Robert

Beti, Mongo . . . . **CLC 27; BLC; DAM MULT**
See also Biyidi, Alexandre

Betjeman, John
1906-1984 . . . . **CLC 2, 6, 10, 34, 43;**
DAB; DAM MST, POET
See also CA 9-12R; 112; CANR 33;
CDBLB 1945-1960; DLB 20; DLBY 84;
MTCW

Bettelheim, Bruno 1903-1990 . . . . . . **CLC 79**
See also CA 81-84; 131; CANR 23; MTCW

Betti, Ugo 1892-1953 . . . . **TCLC 5**
See also CA 104

Betts, Doris (Waugh) 1932- . . . . **CLC 3, 6, 28**
See also CA 13-16R; CANR 9; DLBY 82;
INT CANR-9

Bevan, Alistair
See Roberts, Keith (John Kingston)

Bialik, Chaim Nachman
1873-1934 . . . . **TCLC 25**

Bickerstaff, Isaac
See Swift, Jonathan

Bidart, Frank 1939- . . . . **CLC 33**
See also CA 140

Bienek, Horst 1930- . . . . **CLC 7, 11**
See also CA 73-76; DLB 75

Bierce, Ambrose (Gwinett)
1842-1914(?) . . . . **TCLC 1, 7, 44; DA;**
DAC; DAM MST; SSC 9; WLC
See also CA 104; 139; CDALB 1865-1917;
DLB 11, 12, 23, 71, 74

Biggers, Earl Derr 1884-1933 . . . . . **TCLC 65**
See also CA 108

Billings, Josh
See Shaw, Henry Wheeler

Billington, (Lady) Rachel (Mary)
1942- . . . . **CLC 43**
See also AITN 2; CA 33-36R; CANR 44

Binyon, T(imothy) J(ohn) 1936- . . . . **CLC 34**
See also CA 111; CANR 28

Bioy Casares, Adolfo
1914- . . . . **CLC 4, 8, 13, 88;**
DAM MULT; HLC; SSC 17
See also CA 29-32R; CANR 19, 43;
DLB 113; HW; MTCW

Bird, Cordwainer
See Ellison, Harlan (Jay)

Bird, Robert Montgomery
1806-1854 . . . . **NCLC 1**

Bonnefoy, Yves
    1923- ...... **CLC 9, 15, 58; DAM MST,**
                                    POET
    See also CA 85-88; CANR 33; MTCW

Bontemps, Arna(ud Wendell)
    1902-1973 .... **CLC 1, 18; BLC;**
               DAM MULT, NOV, POET
    See also BW 1; CA 1-4R; 41-44R; CANR 4,
    35; CLR 6; DLB 48, 51; JRDA;
    MAICYA; MTCW; SATA 2, 44;
    SATA-Obit 24

Booth, Martin 1944-.............. **CLC 13**
    See also CA 93-96; CAAS 2

Booth, Philip 1925-.............. **CLC 23**
    See also CA 5-8R; CANR 5; DLBY 82

Booth, Wayne C(layson) 1921- ..... **CLC 24**
    See also CA 1-4R; CAAS 5; CANR 3, 43;
    DLB 67

Borchert, Wolfgang 1921-1947 ..... **TCLC 5**
    See also CA 104; DLB 69, 124

Borel, Petrus 1809-1859......... **NCLC 41**

Borges, Jorge Luis
    1899-1986 ... **CLC 1, 2, 3, 4, 6, 8, 9, 10,**
         13, 19, 44, 48, 83; DA; DAB; DAC;
         DAM MST, MULT; HLC; SSC 4; WLC
    See also CA 21-24R; CANR 19, 33;
    DLB 113; DLBY 86; HW; MTCW

Borowski, Tadeusz 1922-1951...... **TCLC 9**
    See also CA 106

Borrow, George (Henry)
    1803-1881 .... **NCLC 9**
    See also DLB 21, 55, 166

Bosman, Herman Charles
    1905-1951 .... **TCLC 49**

Bosschere, Jean de 1878(?)-1953... **TCLC 19**
    See also CA 115

Boswell, James
    1740-1795 ...... **LC 4; DA; DAB; DAC;**
                         DAM MST; WLC
    See also CDBLB 1660-1789; DLB 104, 142

Bottoms, David 1949-............. **CLC 53**
    See also CA 105; CANR 22; DLB 120;
    DLBY 83

Boucicault, Dion 1820-1890...... **NCLC 41**

Boucolon, Maryse 1937(?)-
    See Conde, Maryse
    See also CA 110; CANR 30, 53

Bourget, Paul (Charles Joseph)
    1852-1935 .... **TCLC 12**
    See also CA 107; DLB 123

Bourjaily, Vance (Nye) 1922- .... **CLC 8, 62**
    See also CA 1-4R; CAAS 1; CANR 2;
    DLB 2, 143

Bourne, Randolph S(illiman)
    1886-1918 .... **TCLC 16**
    See also CA 117; DLB 63

Bova, Ben(jamin William) 1932-.... **CLC 45**
    See also AAYA 16; CA 5-8R; CAAS 18;
    CANR 11; CLR 3; DLBY 81;
    INT CANR-11; MAICYA; MTCW;
    SATA 6, 68

Bowen, Elizabeth (Dorothea Cole)
    1899-1973 ..... **CLC 1, 3, 6, 11, 15, 22;**
                      DAM NOV; SSC 3
    See also CA 17-18; 41-44R; CANR 35;
    CAP 2; CDBLB 1945-1960; DLB 15, 162;
    MTCW

Bowering, George 1935-........ **CLC 15, 47**
    See also CA 21-24R; CAAS 16; CANR 10;
    DLB 53

Bowering, Marilyn R(uthe) 1949-... **CLC 32**
    See also CA 101; CANR 49

Bowers, Edgar 1924- .... **CLC 9**
    See also CA 5-8R; CANR 24; DLB 5

Bowie, David .... **CLC 17**
    See also Jones, David Robert

Bowles, Jane (Sydney)
    1917-1973 .... **CLC 3, 68**
    See also CA 19-20; 41-44R; CAP 2

Bowles, Paul (Frederick)
    1910- .... **CLC 1, 2, 19, 53; SSC 3**
    See also CA 1-4R; CAAS 1; CANR 1, 19,
    50; DLB 5, 6; MTCW

Box, Edgar
    See Vidal, Gore

Boyd, Nancy
    See Millay, Edna St. Vincent

Boyd, William 1952-........ **CLC 28, 53, 70**
    See also CA 114; 120; CANR 51

Boyle, Kay
    1902-1992 ..... **CLC 1, 5, 19, 58; SSC 5**
    See also CA 13-16R; 140; CAAS 1;
    CANR 29; DLB 4, 9, 48, 86; DLBY 93;
    MTCW

Boyle, Mark
    See Kienzle, William X(avier)

Boyle, Patrick 1905-1982......... **CLC 19**
    See also CA 127

Boyle, T. C. 1948-
    See Boyle, T(homas) Coraghessan

Boyle, T(homas) Coraghessan
    1948- ..... **CLC 36, 55, 90; DAM POP;**
                                    SSC 16
    See also BEST 90:4; CA 120; CANR 44;
    DLBY 86

Boz
    See Dickens, Charles (John Huffam)

Brackenridge, Hugh Henry
    1748-1816 .... **NCLC 7**
    See also DLB 11, 37

Bradbury, Edward P.
    See Moorcock, Michael (John)

Bradbury, Malcolm (Stanley)
    1932- .... **CLC 32, 61; DAM NOV**
    See also CA 1-4R; CANR 1, 33; DLB 14;
    MTCW

Bradbury, Ray (Douglas)
    1920- .... **CLC 1, 3, 10, 15, 42; DA;**
         DAB; DAC; DAM MST, NOV, POP;
                                    WLC
    See also AAYA 15; AITN 1, 2; CA 1-4R;
    CANR 2, 30; CDALB 1968-1988; DLB 2,
    8; INT CANR-30; MTCW; SATA 11, 64

Bradford, Gamaliel 1863-1932..... **TCLC 36**
    See also DLB 17

Bradley, David (Henry, Jr.)
    1950- ...... **CLC 23; BLC; DAM MULT**
    See also BW 1; CA 104; CANR 26; DLB 33

Bradley, John Ed(mund, Jr.)
    1958- .... **CLC 55**
    See also CA 139

Bradley, Marion Zimmer
    1930- .... **CLC 30; DAM POP**
    See also AAYA 9; CA 57-60; CAAS 10;
    CANR 7, 31, 51; DLB 8; MTCW

Bradstreet, Anne
    1612(?)-1672 ...... **LC 4, 30; DA; DAC;**
                      DAM MST, POET; PC 10
    See also CDALB 1640-1865; DLB 24

Brady, Joan 1939- .... **CLC 86**
    See also CA 141

Bragg, Melvyn 1939- .... **CLC 10**
    See also BEST 89:3; CA 57-60; CANR 10,
    48; DLB 14

Braine, John (Gerard)
    1922-1986 .... **CLC 1, 3, 41**
    See also CA 1-4R; 120; CANR 1, 33;
    CDBLB 1945-1960; DLB 15; DLBY 86;
    MTCW

Brammer, William 1930(?)-1978 .... **CLC 31**
    See also CA 77-80

Brancati, Vitaliano 1907-1954..... **TCLC 12**
    See also CA 109

Brancato, Robin F(idler) 1936-..... **CLC 35**
    See also AAYA 9; CA 69-72; CANR 11,
    45; CLR 32; JRDA; SAAS 9; SATA 23

Brand, Max
    See Faust, Frederick (Schiller)

Brand, Millen 1906-1980.......... **CLC 7**
    See also CA 21-24R; 97-100

Branden, Barbara .... **CLC 44**
    See also CA 148

Brandes, Georg (Morris Cohen)
    1842-1927 .... **TCLC 10**
    See also CA 105

Brandys, Kazimierz 1916- .... **CLC 62**

Branley, Franklyn M(ansfield)
    1915- .... **CLC 21**
    See also CA 33-36R; CANR 14, 39;
    CLR 13; MAICYA; SAAS 16; SATA 4,
    68

Brathwaite, Edward Kamau
    1930- .... **CLC 11; DAM POET**
    See also BW 2; CA 25-28R; CANR 11, 26,
    47; DLB 125

Brautigan, Richard (Gary)
    1935-1984 .... **CLC 1, 3, 5, 9, 12, 34, 42;**
                                    DAM NOV
    See also CA 53-56; 113; CANR 34; DLB 2,
    5; DLBY 80, 84; MTCW; SATA 56

Brave Bird, Mary 1953-
    See Crow Dog, Mary
    See also NNAL

Braverman, Kate 1950- .... **CLC 67**
    See also CA 89-92

Brecht, Bertolt
    1898-1956 ...... **TCLC 1, 6, 13, 35; DA;**
         DAB; DAC; DAM DRAM, MST; DC 3;
                                    WLC
    See also CA 104; 133; DLB 56, 124; MTCW

Brown, William Wells
    1813-1884 . . . . NCLC 2; BLC;
                  DAM MULT; DC 1
  See also DLB 3, 50

Browne, (Clyde) Jackson   1948(?)-. . . CLC 21
  See also CA 120

Browning, Elizabeth Barrett
    1806-1861 . . . . . NCLC 1, 16; DA; DAB;
      DAC; DAM MST, POET; PC 6; WLC
  See also CDBLB 1832-1890; DLB 32

Browning, Robert
    1812-1889 . . . . NCLC 19; DA; DAB;
          DAC; DAM MST, POET; PC 2
  See also CDBLB 1832-1890; DLB 32, 163;
    YABC 1

Browning, Tod   1882-1962 . . . . CLC 16
  See also CA 141; 117

Brownson, Orestes (Augustus)
    1803-1876 . . . . NCLC 50

Bruccoli, Matthew J(oseph)   1931- . . CLC 34
  See also CA 9-12R; CANR 7; DLB 103

Bruce, Lenny . . . . CLC 21
  See also Schneider, Leonard Alfred

Bruin, John
  See Brutus, Dennis

Brulard, Henri
  See Stendhal

Brulls, Christian
  See Simenon, Georges (Jacques Christian)

Brunner, John (Kilian Houston)
    1934-1995 . . . . . . CLC 8, 10; DAM POP
  See also CA 1-4R; 149; CAAS 8; CANR 2,
    37; MTCW

Bruno, Giordano   1548-1600 . . . . LC 27

Brutus, Dennis
    1924- . . . . . CLC 43; BLC; DAM MULT,
                      POET
  See also BW 2; CA 49-52; CAAS 14;
    CANR 2, 27, 42; DLB 117

Bryan, C(ourtlandt) D(ixon) B(arnes)
    1936- . . . . CLC 29
  See also CA 73-76; CANR 13;
    INT CANR-13

Bryan, Michael
  See Moore, Brian

Bryant, William Cullen
    1794-1878 . . . . . NCLC 6, 46; DA; DAB;
           DAC; DAM MST, POET
  See also CDALB 1640-1865; DLB 3, 43, 59

Bryusov, Valery Yakovlevich
    1873-1924 . . . . TCLC 10
  See also CA 107

Buchan, John
    1875-1940 . . . . TCLC 41; DAB;
                   DAM POP
  See also CA 108; 145; DLB 34, 70, 156;
    YABC 2

Buchanan, George   1506-1582 . . . . LC 4

Buchheim, Lothar-Guenther   1918- . . . CLC 6
  See also CA 85-88

Buchner, (Karl) Georg
    1813-1837 . . . . NCLC 26

Buchwald, Art(hur)   1925-. . . . . CLC 33
  See also AITN 1; CA 5-8R; CANR 21;
    MTCW; SATA 10

Buck, Pearl S(ydenstricker)
    1892-1973 . . . . CLC 7, 11, 18; DA; DAB;
            DAC; DAM MST, NOV
  See also AITN 1; CA 1-4R; 41-44R;
    CANR 1, 34; DLB 9, 102; MTCW;
    SATA 1, 25

Buckler, Ernest
    1908-1984 . . CLC 13; DAC; DAM MST
  See also CA 11-12; 114; CAP 1; DLB 68;
    SATA 47

Buckley, Vincent (Thomas)
    1925-1988 . . . . CLC 57
  See also CA 101

Buckley, William F(rank), Jr.
    1925- . . . . CLC 7, 18, 37; DAM POP
  See also AITN 1; CA 1-4R; CANR 1, 24,
    53; DLB 137; DLBY 80; INT CANR-24;
    MTCW

Buechner, (Carl) Frederick
    1926- . . . . . . CLC 2, 4, 6, 9; DAM NOV
  See also CA 13-16R; CANR 11, 39;
    DLBY 80; INT CANR-11; MTCW

Buell, John (Edward)   1927-. . . . . CLC 10
  See also CA 1-4R; DLB 53

Buero Vallejo, Antonio   1916- . . . CLC 15, 46
  See also CA 106; CANR 24, 49; HW;
    MTCW

Bufalino, Gesualdo   1920(?)-. . . . . CLC 74

Bugayev, Boris Nikolayevich   1880-1934
  See Bely, Andrey
  See also CA 104

Bukowski, Charles
    1920-1994 . . . . CLC 2, 5, 9, 41, 82;
               DAM NOV, POET
  See also CA 17-20R; 144; CANR 40;
    DLB 5, 130; MTCW

Bulgakov, Mikhail (Afanas'evich)
    1891-1940 . . . . TCLC 2, 16;
          DAM DRAM, NOV; SSC 18
  See also CA 105; 152

Bulgya, Alexander Alexandrovich
    1901-1956 . . . . TCLC 53
  See also Fadeyev, Alexander
  See also CA 117

Bullins, Ed
    1935- . . . . CLC 1, 5, 7; BLC;
          DAM DRAM, MULT; DC 6
  See also BW 2; CA 49-52; CAAS 16;
    CANR 24, 46; DLB 7, 38; MTCW

Bulwer-Lytton, Edward (George Earle Lytton)
    1803-1873 . . . . NCLC 1, 45
  See also DLB 21

Bunin, Ivan Alexeyevich
    1870-1953 . . . . TCLC 6; SSC 5
  See also CA 104

Bunting, Basil
    1900-1985 . . . . CLC 10, 39, 47;
                   DAM POET
  See also CA 53-56; 115; CANR 7; DLB 20

Bunuel, Luis
    1900-1983 . . . . CLC 16, 80;
                DAM MULT; HLC
  See also CA 101; 110; CANR 32; HW

Bunyan, John
    1628-1688 . . . . . . LC 4; DA; DAB; DAC;
              DAM MST; WLC
  See also CDBLB 1660-1789; DLB 39

Burckhardt, Jacob (Christoph)
    1818-1897 . . . . NCLC 49

Burford, Eleanor
  See Hibbert, Eleanor Alice Burford

Burgess, Anthony
    . CLC 1, 2, 4, 5, 8, 10, 13, 15, 22, 40, 62,
                  81, 94; DAB
  See also Wilson, John (Anthony) Burgess
  See also AITN 1; CDBLB 1960 to Present;
    DLB 14

Burke, Edmund
    1729(?)-1797 . . . . LC 7; DA; DAB; DAC;
               DAM MST; WLC
  See also DLB 104

Burke, Kenneth (Duva)
    1897-1993 . . . . CLC 2, 24
  See also CA 5-8R; 143; CANR 39; DLB 45,
    63; MTCW

Burke, Leda
  See Garnett, David

Burke, Ralph
  See Silverberg, Robert

Burke, Thomas   1886-1945 . . . . TCLC 63
  See also CA 113

Burney, Fanny   1752-1840 . . . . NCLC 12, 54
  See also DLB 39

Burns, Robert   1759-1796. . . . . PC 6
  See also CDBLB 1789-1832; DA; DAB;
    DAC; DAM MST, POET; DLB 109;
    WLC

Burns, Tex
  See L'Amour, Louis (Dearborn)

Burnshaw, Stanley   1906-. . . . . CLC 3, 13, 44
  See also CA 9-12R; DLB 48

Burr, Anne   1937- . . . . CLC 6
  See also CA 25-28R

Burroughs, Edgar Rice
    1875-1950 . . . . TCLC 2, 32; DAM NOV
  See also AAYA 11; CA 104; 132; DLB 8;
    MTCW; SATA 41

Burroughs, William S(eward)
    1914- . . . . CLC 1, 2, 5, 15, 22, 42, 75;
      DA; DAB; DAC; DAM MST, NOV,
               POP; WLC
  See also AITN 2; CA 9-12R; CANR 20, 52;
    DLB 2, 8, 16, 152; DLBY 81; MTCW

Burton, Richard F.   1821-1890. . . . NCLC 42
  See also DLB 55

Busch, Frederick   1941- . . . CLC 7, 10, 18, 47
  See also CA 33-36R; CAAS 1; CANR 45;
    DLB 6

Bush, Ronald   1946- . . . . CLC 34
  See also CA 136

Bustos, F(rancisco)
  See Borges, Jorge Luis

Bustos Domecq, H(onorio)
  See Bioy Casares, Adolfo; Borges, Jorge
  Luis

Butler, Octavia E(stelle)
    1947- . . . . . CLC 38; DAM MULT, POP
  See also AAYA 18; BW 2; CA 73-76;
    CANR 12, 24, 38; DLB 33; MTCW;
    SATA 84

Butler, Robert Olen (Jr.)
1945- . . . . **CLC 81; DAM POP**
See also CA 112; INT 112

Butler, Samuel 1612-1680 . . . . **LC 16**
See also DLB 101, 126

Butler, Samuel
1835-1902 . . . . . . **TCLC 1, 33; DA; DAB;**
DAC; DAM MST, NOV; WLC
See also CA 143; CDBLB 1890-1914;
DLB 18, 57

Butler, Walter C.
See Faust, Frederick (Schiller)

Butor, Michel (Marie Francois)
1926- . . . . **CLC 1, 3, 8, 11, 15**
See also CA 9-12R; CANR 33; DLB 83;
MTCW

Buzo, Alexander (John) 1944- . . . . . . **CLC 61**
See also CA 97-100; CANR 17, 39

Buzzati, Dino 1906-1972 . . . . **CLC 36**
See also CA 33-36R

Byars, Betsy (Cromer) 1928- . . . . **CLC 35**
See also CA 33-36R; CANR 18, 36; CLR 1,
16; DLB 52; INT CANR-18; JRDA;
MAICYA; MTCW; SAAS 1; SATA 4,
46, 80

Byatt, A(ntonia) S(usan Drabble)
1936- . . . **CLC 19, 65; DAM NOV, POP**
See also CA 13-16R; CANR 13, 33, 50;
DLB 14; MTCW

Byrne, David 1952- . . . . **CLC 26**
See also CA 127

Byrne, John Keyes 1926-
See Leonard, Hugh
See also CA 102; INT 102

Byron, George Gordon (Noel)
1788-1824 . . . . . **NCLC 2, 12; DA; DAB;**
DAC; DAM MST, POET; PC 16; WLC
See also CDBLB 1789-1832; DLB 96, 110

C. 3. 3.
See Wilde, Oscar (Fingal O'Flahertie Wills)

Caballero, Fernan 1796-1877 . . . . . **NCLC 10**

Cabell, Branch
See Cabell, James Branch

Cabell, James Branch 1879-1958 . . . **TCLC 6**
See also CA 105; 152; DLB 9, 78

Cable, George Washington
1844-1925 . . . . **TCLC 4; SSC 4**
See also CA 104; DLB 12, 74; DLBD 13

Cabral de Melo Neto, Joao
1920- . . . . **CLC 76; DAM MULT**
See also CA 151

Cabrera Infante, G(uillermo)
1929- . . . . . **CLC 5, 25, 45; DAM MULT;**
HLC
See also CA 85-88; CANR 29; DLB 113;
HW; MTCW

Cade, Toni
See Bambara, Toni Cade

Cadmus and Harmonia
See Buchan, John

Caedmon fl. 658-680 . . . . **CMLC 7**
See also DLB 146

Caeiro, Alberto
See Pessoa, Fernando (Antonio Nogueira)

Cage, John (Milton, Jr.) 1912- . . . . . **CLC 41**
See also CA 13-16R; CANR 9;
INT CANR-9

Cain, G.
See Cabrera Infante, G(uillermo)

Cain, Guillermo
See Cabrera Infante, G(uillermo)

Cain, James M(allahan)
1892-1977 . . . . **CLC 3, 11, 28**
See also AITN 1; CA 17-20R; 73-76;
CANR 8, 34; MTCW

Caine, Mark
See Raphael, Frederic (Michael)

Calasso, Roberto 1941- . . . . **CLC 81**
See also CA 143

Calderon de la Barca, Pedro
1600-1681 . . . . **LC 23; DC 3**

Caldwell, Erskine (Preston)
1903-1987 . . . . **CLC 1, 8, 14, 50, 60;**
DAM NOV; SSC 19
See also AITN 1; CA 1-4R; 121; CAAS 1;
CANR 2, 33; DLB 9, 86; MTCW

Caldwell, (Janet Miriam) Taylor (Holland)
1900-1985 . . . . **CLC 2, 28, 39;**
DAM NOV, POP
See also CA 5-8R; 116; CANR 5

Calhoun, John Caldwell
1782-1850 . . . . **NCLC 15**
See also DLB 3

Calisher, Hortense
1911- . . . . . **CLC 2, 4, 8, 38; DAM NOV;**
SSC 15
See also CA 1-4R; CANR 1, 22; DLB 2;
INT CANR-22; MTCW

Callaghan, Morley Edward
1903-1990 . . . . . **CLC 3, 14, 41, 65; DAC;**
DAM MST
See also CA 9-12R; 132; CANR 33;
DLB 68; MTCW

Callimachus
c. 305B.C.-c. 240B.C. . . . . **CMLC 18**

Calvino, Italo
1923-1985 . . . . . **CLC 5, 8, 11, 22, 33, 39,**
73; DAM NOV; SSC 3
See also CA 85-88; 116; CANR 23; MTCW

Cameron, Carey 1952- . . . . **CLC 59**
See also CA 135

Cameron, Peter 1959- . . . . **CLC 44**
See also CA 125; CANR 50

Campana, Dino 1885-1932 . . . . **TCLC 20**
See also CA 117; DLB 114

Campanella, Tommaso 1568-1639 . . . . **LC 32**

Campbell, John W(ood, Jr.)
1910-1971 . . . . **CLC 32**
See also CA 21-22; 29-32R; CANR 34;
CAP 2; DLB 8; MTCW

Campbell, Joseph 1904-1987 . . . . **CLC 69**
See also AAYA 3; BEST 89:2; CA 1-4R;
124; CANR 3, 28; MTCW

Campbell, Maria 1940- . . . . . . **CLC 85; DAC**
See also CA 102; NNAL

Campbell, (John) Ramsey
1946- . . . . **CLC 42; SSC 19**
See also CA 57-60; CANR 7; INT CANR-7

Campbell, (Ignatius) Roy (Dunnachie)
1901-1957 . . . . **TCLC 5**
See also CA 104; DLB 20

Campbell, Thomas 1777-1844 . . . . **NCLC 19**
See also DLB 93; 144

Campbell, Wilfred . . . . **TCLC 9**
See also Campbell, William

Campbell, William 1858(?)-1918
See Campbell, Wilfred
See also CA 106; DLB 92

Campion, Jane . . . . **CLC 95**
See also CA 138

Campos, Alvaro de
See Pessoa, Fernando (Antonio Nogueira)

Camus, Albert
1913-1960 . . . . **CLC 1, 2, 4, 9, 11, 14, 32,**
63, 69; DA; DAB; DAC; DAM DRAM,
MST, NOV; DC 2; SSC 9; WLC
See also CA 89-92; DLB 72; MTCW

Canby, Vincent 1924- . . . . **CLC 13**
See also CA 81-84

Cancale
See Desnos, Robert

Canetti, Elias
1905-1994 . . . . . . **CLC 3, 14, 25, 75, 86**
See also CA 21-24R; 146; CANR 23;
DLB 85, 124; MTCW

Canin, Ethan 1960- . . . . **CLC 55**
See also CA 131; 135

Cannon, Curt
See Hunter, Evan

Cape, Judith
See Page, P(atricia) K(athleen)

Capek, Karel
1890-1938 . . . . . . **TCLC 6, 37; DA; DAB;**
DAC; DAM DRAM, MST, NOV; DC 1;
WLC
See also CA 104; 140

Capote, Truman
1924-1984 . . . . . . **CLC 1, 3, 8, 13, 19, 34,**
38, 58; DA; DAB; DAC; DAM MST,
NOV, POP; SSC 2; WLC
See also CA 5-8R; 113; CANR 18;
CDALB 1941-1968; DLB 2; DLBY 80,
84; MTCW

Capra, Frank 1897-1991 . . . . **CLC 16**
See also CA 61-64; 135

Caputo, Philip 1941- . . . . **CLC 32**
See also CA 73-76; CANR 40

Card, Orson Scott
1951- . . . . . . **CLC 44, 47, 50; DAM POP**
See also AAYA 11; CA 102; CANR 27, 47;
INT CANR-27; MTCW; SATA 83

Cardenal, Ernesto
1925- . . . . **CLC 31; DAM MULT,**
POET; HLC
See also CA 49-52; CANR 2, 32; HW;
MTCW

Cardozo, Benjamin N(athan)
1870-1938 . . . . **TCLC 65**
See also CA 117

Carducci, Giosue 1835-1907 . . . . **TCLC 32**

Carew, Thomas 1595(?)-1640 . . . . **LC 13**
See also DLB 126

Christie
See Ichikawa, Kon

Christie, Agatha (Mary Clarissa)
1890-1976 . . . . . . **CLC 1, 6, 8, 12, 39, 48;
DAB; DAC; DAM NOV**
See also AAYA 9; AITN 1, 2; CA 17-20R;
61-64; CANR 10, 37; CDBLB 1914-1945;
DLB 13, 77; MTCW; SATA 36

Christie, (Ann) Philippa
See Pearce, Philippa
See also CA 5-8R; CANR 4

Christine de Pizan 1365(?)-1431(?) . . . . **LC 9**

Chubb, Elmer
See Masters, Edgar Lee

Chulkov, Mikhail Dmitrievich
1743-1792 . . . . **LC 2**
See also DLB 150

Churchill, Caryl 1938- . . . **CLC 31, 55; DC 5**
See also CA 102; CANR 22, 46; DLB 13;
MTCW

Churchill, Charles 1731-1764 . . . . **LC 3**
See also DLB 109

Chute, Carolyn 1947- . . . . **CLC 39**
See also CA 123

Ciardi, John (Anthony)
1916-1986 . . . . **CLC 10, 40, 44;
DAM POET**
See also CA 5-8R; 118; CAAS 2; CANR 5,
33; CLR 19; DLB 5; DLBY 86;
INT CANR-5; MAICYA; MTCW;
SATA 1, 65; SATA-Obit 46

Cicero, Marcus Tullius
106B.C.-43B.C. . . . . **CMLC 3**

Cimino, Michael 1943- . . . . **CLC 16**
See also CA 105

Cioran, E(mil) M. 1911-1995 . . . . **CLC 64**
See also CA 25-28R; 149

Cisneros, Sandra
1954- . . . . . **CLC 69; DAM MULT; HLC**
See also AAYA 9; CA 131; DLB 122, 152;
HW

Cixous, Helene 1937- . . . . **CLC 92**
See also CA 126; DLB 83; MTCW

Clair, Rene . . . . **CLC 20**
See also Chomette, Rene Lucien

Clampitt, Amy 1920-1994 . . . . **CLC 32**
See also CA 110; 146; CANR 29; DLB 105

Clancy, Thomas L., Jr. 1947-
See Clancy, Tom
See also CA 125; 131; INT 131; MTCW

Clancy, Tom . . . . . **CLC 45; DAM NOV, POP**
See also Clancy, Thomas L., Jr.
See also AAYA 9; BEST 89:1, 90:1

Clare, John
1793-1864 . . . . **NCLC 9; DAB;
DAM POET**
See also DLB 55, 96

Clarin
See Alas (y Urena), Leopoldo (Enrique
Garcia)

Clark, Al C.
See Goines, Donald

Clark, (Robert) Brian 1932- . . . . **CLC 29**
See also CA 41-44R

Clark, Curt
See Westlake, Donald E(dwin)

Clark, Eleanor 1913-1996 . . . . . . **CLC 5, 19**
See also CA 9-12R; 151; CANR 41; DLB 6

Clark, J. P.
See Clark, John Pepper
See also DLB 117

Clark, John Pepper
1935- . . . . **CLC 38; BLC; DAM DRAM,
MULT; DC 5**
See also Clark, J. P.
See also BW 1; CA 65-68; CANR 16

Clark, M. R.
See Clark, Mavis Thorpe

Clark, Mavis Thorpe 1909- . . . . **CLC 12**
See also CA 57-60; CANR 8, 37; CLR 30;
MAICYA; SAAS 5; SATA 8, 74

Clark, Walter Van Tilburg
1909-1971 . . . . **CLC 28**
See also CA 9-12R; 33-36R; DLB 9;
SATA 8

Clarke, Arthur C(harles)
1917- . . . . **CLC 1, 4, 13, 18, 35;
DAM POP; SSC 3**
See also AAYA 4; CA 1-4R; CANR 2, 28;
JRDA; MAICYA; MTCW; SATA 13, 70

Clarke, Austin
1896-1974 . . . . . . **CLC 6, 9; DAM POET**
See also CA 29-32; 49-52; CAP 2; DLB 10,
20

Clarke, Austin C(hesterfield)
1934- . . . . **CLC 8, 53; BLC; DAC;
DAM MULT**
See also BW 1; CA 25-28R; CAAS 16;
CANR 14, 32; DLB 53, 125

Clarke, Gillian 1937- . . . . **CLC 61**
See also CA 106; DLB 40

Clarke, Marcus (Andrew Hislop)
1846-1881 . . . . **NCLC 19**

Clarke, Shirley 1925- . . . . **CLC 16**

Clash, The
See Headon, (Nicky) Topper; Jones, Mick;
Simonon, Paul; Strummer, Joe

Claudel, Paul (Louis Charles Marie)
1868-1955 . . . . **TCLC 2, 10**
See also CA 104

Clavell, James (duMaresq)
1925-1994 . . . . **CLC 6, 25, 87;
DAM NOV, POP**
See also CA 25-28R; 146; CANR 26, 48;
MTCW

Cleaver, (Leroy) Eldridge
1935- . . . . . **CLC 30; BLC; DAM MULT**
See also BW 1; CA 21-24R; CANR 16

Cleese, John (Marwood) 1939- . . . . . **CLC 21**
See also Monty Python
See also CA 112; 116; CANR 35; MTCW

Cleishbotham, Jebediah
See Scott, Walter

Cleland, John 1710-1789 . . . . **LC 2**
See also DLB 39

Clemens, Samuel Langhorne 1835-1910
See Twain, Mark
See also CA 104; 135; CDALB 1865-1917;
DA; DAB; DAC; DAM MST, NOV;
DLB 11, 12, 23, 64, 74; JRDA;
MAICYA; YABC 2

Cleophil
See Congreve, William

Clerihew, E.
See Bentley, E(dmund) C(lerihew)

Clerk, N. W.
See Lewis, C(live) S(taples)

Cliff, Jimmy . . . . **CLC 21**
See also Chambers, James

Clifton, (Thelma) Lucille
1936- . . . . **CLC 19, 66; BLC;
DAM MULT, POET**
See also BW 2; CA 49-52; CANR 2, 24, 42;
CLR 5; DLB 5, 41; MAICYA; MTCW;
SATA 20, 69

Clinton, Dirk
See Silverberg, Robert

Clough, Arthur Hugh 1819-1861 . . **NCLC 27**
See also DLB 32

Clutha, Janet Paterson Frame 1924-
See Frame, Janet
See also CA 1-4R; CANR 2, 36; MTCW

Clyne, Terence
See Blatty, William Peter

Cobalt, Martin
See Mayne, William (James Carter)

Cobbett, William 1763-1835 . . . . . **NCLC 49**
See also DLB 43, 107, 158

Coburn, D(onald) L(ee) 1938- . . . . . . **CLC 10**
See also CA 89-92

Cocteau, Jean (Maurice Eugene Clement)
1889-1963 . . . . **CLC 1, 8, 15, 16, 43; DA;
DAB; DAC; DAM DRAM, MST, NOV;
WLC**
See also CA 25-28; CANR 40; CAP 2;
DLB 65; MTCW

Codrescu, Andrei
1946- . . . . **CLC 46; DAM POET**
See also CA 33-36R; CAAS 19; CANR 13,
34, 53

Coe, Max
See Bourne, Randolph S(illiman)

Coe, Tucker
See Westlake, Donald E(dwin)

Coetzee, J(ohn) M(ichael)
1940- . . . . . . **CLC 23, 33, 66; DAM NOV**
See also CA 77-80; CANR 41; MTCW

Coffey, Brian
See Koontz, Dean R(ay)

Cohan, George M. 1878-1942 . . . . . **TCLC 60**

Cohen, Arthur A(llen)
1928-1986 . . . . **CLC 7, 31**
See also CA 1-4R; 120; CANR 1, 17, 42;
DLB 28

Cohen, Leonard (Norman)
1934- . . . . **CLC 3, 38; DAC; DAM MST**
See also CA 21-24R; CANR 14; DLB 53;
MTCW

Cormier, Robert (Edmund)
  1925- .... **CLC 12, 30; DA; DAB; DAC;
          DAM MST, NOV**
  See also AAYA 3; CA 1-4R; CANR 5, 23;
  CDALB 1968-1988; CLR 12; DLB 52;
  INT CANR-23; JRDA; MAICYA;
  MTCW; SATA 10, 45, 83

Corn, Alfred (DeWitt III) 1943- .... **CLC 33**
  See also CA 104; CANR 44; DLB 120;
  DLBY 80

Corneille, Pierre
  1606-1684 .... **LC 28; DAB; DAM MST**

Cornwell, David (John Moore)
  1931- .... **CLC 9, 15; DAM POP**
  See also le Carre, John
  See also CA 5-8R; CANR 13, 33; MTCW

Corso, (Nunzio) Gregory 1930- ... **CLC 1, 11**
  See also CA 5-8R; CANR 41; DLB 5, 16;
  MTCW

Cortazar, Julio
  1914-1984 ...... **CLC 2, 3, 5, 10, 13, 15,
      33, 34, 92; DAM MULT, NOV; HLC;
                                    SSC 7**
  See also CA 21-24R; CANR 12, 32;
  DLB 113; HW; MTCW

CORTES, HERNAN 1484-1547..... **LC 31**

Corwin, Cecil
  See Kornbluth, C(yril) M.

Cosic, Dobrica 1921- .... **CLC 14**
  See also CA 122; 138

Costain, Thomas B(ertram)
  1885-1965 .... **CLC 30**
  See also CA 5-8R; 25-28R; DLB 9

Costantini, Humberto
  1924(?)-1987 .... **CLC 49**
  See also CA 131; 122; HW

Costello, Elvis 1955-.............. **CLC 21**

Cotter, Joseph Seamon Sr.
  1861-1949 .... **TCLC 28; BLC;
                                DAM MULT**
  See also BW 1; CA 124; DLB 50

Couch, Arthur Thomas Quiller
  See Quiller-Couch, Arthur Thomas

Coulton, James
  See Hansen, Joseph

Couperus, Louis (Marie Anne)
  1863-1923 .... **TCLC 15**
  See also CA 115

Coupland, Douglas
  1961- .... **CLC 85; DAC; DAM POP**
  See also CA 142

Court, Wesli
  See Turco, Lewis (Putnam)

Courtenay, Bryce 1933-........... **CLC 59**
  See also CA 138

Courtney, Robert
  See Ellison, Harlan (Jay)

Cousteau, Jacques-Yves 1910-...... **CLC 30**
  See also CA 65-68; CANR 15; MTCW;
  SATA 38

Coward, Noel (Peirce)
  1899-1973 .... **CLC 1, 9, 29, 51;
                                DAM DRAM**
  See also AITN 1; CA 17-18; 41-44R;
  CANR 35; CAP 2; CDBLB 1914-1945;
  DLB 10; MTCW

Cowley, Malcolm 1898-1989 ...... **CLC 39**
  See also CA 5-8R; 128; CANR 3; DLB 4,
  48; DLBY 81, 89; MTCW

Cowper, William
  1731-1800 ...... **NCLC 8; DAM POET**
  See also DLB 104, 109

Cox, William Trevor
  1928-....... **CLC 9, 14, 71; DAM NOV**
  See also Trevor, William
  See also CA 9-12R; CANR 4, 37; DLB 14;
  INT CANR-37; MTCW

Coyne, P. J.
  See Masters, Hilary

Cozzens, James Gould
  1903-1978 .... **CLC 1, 4, 11, 92**
  See also CA 9-12R; 81-84; CANR 19;
  CDALB 1941-1968; DLB 9; DLBD 2;
  DLBY 84; MTCW

Crabbe, George 1754-1832....... **NCLC 26**
  See also DLB 93

Craddock, Charles Egbert
  See Murfree, Mary Noailles

Craig, A. A.
  See Anderson, Poul (William)

Craik, Dinah Maria (Mulock)
  1826-1887 .... **NCLC 38**
  See also DLB 35, 163; MAICYA; SATA 34

Cram, Ralph Adams 1863-1942.... **TCLC 45**

Crane, (Harold) Hart
  1899-1932 .... **TCLC 2, 5; DA; DAB;
      DAC; DAM MST, POET; PC 3; WLC**
  See also CA 104; 127; CDALB 1917-1929;
  DLB 4, 48; MTCW

Crane, R(onald) S(almon)
  1886-1967 .... **CLC 27**
  See also CA 85-88; DLB 63

Crane, Stephen (Townley)
  1871-1900 .... **TCLC 11, 17, 32; DA;
      DAB; DAC; DAM MST, NOV, POET;
                                SSC 7; WLC**
  See also CA 109; 140; CDALB 1865-1917;
  DLB 12, 54, 78; YABC 2

Crase, Douglas 1944-............. **CLC 58**
  See also CA 106

Crashaw, Richard 1612(?)-1649...... **LC 24**
  See also DLB 126

Craven, Margaret
  1901-1980 .... **CLC 17; DAC**
  See also CA 103

Crawford, F(rancis) Marion
  1854-1909 .... **TCLC 10**
  See also CA 107; DLB 71

Crawford, Isabella Valancy
  1850-1887 .... **NCLC 12**
  See also DLB 92

Crayon, Geoffrey
  See Irving, Washington

Creasey, John 1908-1973.......... **CLC 11**
  See also CA 5-8R; 41-44R; CANR 8;
  DLB 77; MTCW

Crebillon, Claude Prosper Jolyot de (fils)
  1707-1777 .... **LC 28**

Credo
  See Creasey, John

Creeley, Robert (White)
  1926- ..... **CLC 1, 2, 4, 8, 11, 15, 36, 78;
                                DAM POET**
  See also CA 1-4R; CAAS 10; CANR 23, 43;
  DLB 5, 16; MTCW

Crews, Harry (Eugene)
  1935- .... **CLC 6, 23, 49**
  See also AITN 1; CA 25-28R; CANR 20;
  DLB 6, 143; MTCW

Crichton, (John) Michael
  1942- .... **CLC 2, 6, 54, 90; DAM NOV,
                                    POP**
  See also AAYA 10; AITN 2; CA 25-28R;
  CANR 13, 40; DLBY 81; INT CANR-13;
  JRDA; MTCW; SATA 9, 88

Crispin, Edmund .... **CLC 22**
  See also Montgomery, (Robert) Bruce
  See also DLB 87

Cristofer, Michael
  1945(?)- .... **CLC 28; DAM DRAM**
  See also CA 110; 152; DLB 7

Croce, Benedetto 1866-1952 ...... **TCLC 37**
  See also CA 120

Crockett, David 1786-1836 .... **NCLC 8**
  See also DLB 3, 11

Crockett, Davy
  See Crockett, David

Crofts, Freeman Wills
  1879-1957 .... **TCLC 55**
  See also CA 115; DLB 77

Croker, John Wilson 1780-1857 .. **NCLC 10**
  See also DLB 110

Crommelynck, Fernand 1885-1970 .. **CLC 75**
  See also CA 89-92

Cronin, A(rchibald) J(oseph)
  1896-1981 .... **CLC 32**
  See also CA 1-4R; 102; CANR 5; SATA 47;
  SATA-Obit 25

Cross, Amanda
  See Heilbrun, Carolyn G(old)

Crothers, Rachel 1878(?)-1958..... **TCLC 19**
  See also CA 113; DLB 7

Croves, Hal
  See Traven, B.

Crow Dog, Mary.................. **CLC 93**
  See also Brave Bird, Mary

Crowfield, Christopher
  See Stowe, Harriet (Elizabeth) Beecher

Crowley, Aleister.................. **TCLC 7**
  See also Crowley, Edward Alexander

Crowley, Edward Alexander 1875-1947
  See Crowley, Aleister
  See also CA 104

Crowley, John 1942-.............. **CLC 57**
  See also CA 61-64; CANR 43; DLBY 82;
  SATA 65

Crud
  See Crumb, R(obert)

Crumarums
  See Crumb, R(obert)

Davis, Richard Harding
1864-1916 . . . . **TCLC 24**
See also CA 114; DLB 12, 23, 78, 79;
DLBD 13

Davison, Frank Dalby 1893-1970 . . . **CLC 15**
See also CA 116

Davison, Lawrence H.
See Lawrence, D(avid) H(erbert Richards)

Davison, Peter (Hubert) 1928- . . . . . **CLC 28**
See also CA 9-12R; CAAS 4; CANR 3, 43;
DLB 5

Davys, Mary 1674-1732 . . . . **LC 1**
See also DLB 39

Dawson, Fielding 1930- . . . . **CLC 6**
See also CA 85-88; DLB 130

Dawson, Peter
See Faust, Frederick (Schiller)

Day, Clarence (Shepard, Jr.)
1874-1935 . . . . **TCLC 25**
See also CA 108; DLB 11

Day, Thomas 1748-1789 . . . . **LC 1**
See also DLB 39; YABC 1

Day Lewis, C(ecil)
1904-1972 . . . . **CLC 1, 6, 10;**
DAM POET; PC 11
See also Blake, Nicholas
See also CA 13-16; 33-36R; CANR 34;
CAP 1; DLB 15, 20; MTCW

Dazai, Osamu . . . . **TCLC 11**
See also Tsushima, Shuji

de Andrade, Carlos Drummond
See Drummond de Andrade, Carlos

Deane, Norman
See Creasey, John

de Beauvoir, Simone (Lucie Ernestine Marie Bertrand)
See Beauvoir, Simone (Lucie Ernestine
Marie Bertrand) de

de Brissac, Malcolm
See Dickinson, Peter (Malcolm)

de Chardin, Pierre Teilhard
See Teilhard de Chardin, (Marie Joseph)
Pierre

Dee, John 1527-1608 . . . . **LC 20**

Deer, Sandra 1940- . . . . **CLC 45**

De Ferrari, Gabriella 1941- . . . . **CLC 65**
See also CA 146

Defoe, Daniel
1660(?)-1731 . . . . **LC 1; DA; DAB; DAC;**
DAM MST, NOV; WLC
See also CDBLB 1660-1789; DLB 39, 95,
101; JRDA; MAICYA; SATA 22

de Gourmont, Remy(-Marie-Charles)
See Gourmont, Remy (-Marie-Charles) de

de Hartog, Jan 1914- . . . . **CLC 19**
See also CA 1-4R; CANR 1

de Hostos, E. M.
See Hostos (y Bonilla), Eugenio Maria de

de Hostos, Eugenio M.
See Hostos (y Bonilla), Eugenio Maria de

Deighton, Len . . . . **CLC 4, 7, 22, 46**
See also Deighton, Leonard Cyril
See also AAYA 6; BEST 89:2;
CDBLB 1960 to Present; DLB 87

Deighton, Leonard Cyril 1929-
See Deighton, Len
See also CA 9-12R; CANR 19, 33;
DAM NOV, POP; MTCW

Dekker, Thomas
1572(?)-1632 . . . . . **LC 22; DAM DRAM**
See also CDBLB Before 1660; DLB 62

Delafield, E. M. 1890-1943 . . . . . . **TCLC 61**
See also Dashwood, Edmee Elizabeth
Monica de la Pasture
See also DLB 34

de la Mare, Walter (John)
1873-1956 . . . . **TCLC 4, 53; DAB; DAC;**
DAM MST, POET; SSC 14; WLC
See also CDBLB 1914-1945; CLR 23;
DLB 162; SATA 16

Delaney, Franey
See O'Hara, John (Henry)

Delaney, Shelagh
1939- . . . . **CLC 29; DAM DRAM**
See also CA 17-20R; CANR 30;
CDBLB 1960 to Present; DLB 13;
MTCW

Delany, Mary (Granville Pendarves)
1700-1788 . . . . **LC 12**

Delany, Samuel R(ay, Jr.)
1942- . . . . **CLC 8, 14, 38; BLC;**
DAM MULT
See also BW 2; CA 81-84; CANR 27, 43;
DLB 8, 33; MTCW

De La Ramee, (Marie) Louise 1839-1908
See Ouida
See also SATA 20

de la Roche, Mazo 1879-1961 . . . . . . **CLC 14**
See also CA 85-88; CANR 30; DLB 68;
SATA 64

Delbanco, Nicholas (Franklin)
1942- . . . . **CLC 6, 13**
See also CA 17-20R; CAAS 2; CANR 29;
DLB 6

del Castillo, Michel 1933- . . . . **CLC 38**
See also CA 109

Deledda, Grazia (Cosima)
1875(?)-1936 . . . . **TCLC 23**
See also CA 123

Delibes, Miguel . . . . **CLC 8, 18**
See also Delibes Setien, Miguel

Delibes Setien, Miguel 1920-
See Delibes, Miguel
See also CA 45-48; CANR 1, 32; HW;
MTCW

DeLillo, Don
1936- . . . . . **CLC 8, 10, 13, 27, 39, 54, 76;**
DAM NOV, POP
See also BEST 89:1; CA 81-84; CANR 21;
DLB 6; MTCW

de Lisser, H. G.
See De Lisser, Herbert George
See also DLB 117

De Lisser, Herbert George
1878-1944 . . . . **TCLC 12**
See also de Lisser, H. G.
See also BW 2; CA 109; 152

Deloria, Vine (Victor), Jr.
1933- . . . . **CLC 21; DAM MULT**
See also CA 53-56; CANR 5, 20, 48;
MTCW; NNAL; SATA 21

Del Vecchio, John M(ichael)
1947- . . . . **CLC 29**
See also CA 110; DLBD 9

de Man, Paul (Adolph Michel)
1919-1983 . . . . **CLC 55**
See also CA 128; 111; DLB 67; MTCW

De Marinis, Rick 1934- . . . . **CLC 54**
See also CA 57-60; CAAS 24; CANR 9, 25,
50

Dembry, R. Emmet
See Murfree, Mary Noailles

Demby, William
1922- . . . . . **CLC 53; BLC; DAM MULT**
See also BW 1; CA 81-84; DLB 33

Demijohn, Thom
See Disch, Thomas M(ichael)

de Montherlant, Henry (Milon)
See Montherlant, Henry (Milon) de

Demosthenes 384B.C.-322B.C. . . . **CMLC 13**

de Natale, Francine
See Malzberg, Barry N(athaniel)

Denby, Edwin (Orr) 1903-1983 . . . . . **CLC 48**
See also CA 138; 110

Denis, Julio
See Cortazar, Julio

Denmark, Harrison
See Zelazny, Roger (Joseph)

Dennis, John 1658-1734 . . . . **LC 11**
See also DLB 101

Dennis, Nigel (Forbes) 1912-1989 . . . . **CLC 8**
See also CA 25-28R; 129; DLB 13, 15;
MTCW

De Palma, Brian (Russell) 1940- . . . . **CLC 20**
See also CA 109

De Quincey, Thomas 1785-1859 . . . **NCLC 4**
See also CDBLB 1789-1832; DLB 110; 144

Deren, Eleanora 1908(?)-1961
See Deren, Maya
See also CA 111

Deren, Maya . . . . **CLC 16**
See also Deren, Eleanora

Derleth, August (William)
1909-1971 . . . . **CLC 31**
See also CA 1-4R; 29-32R; CANR 4;
DLB 9; SATA 5

Der Nister 1884-1950 . . . . **TCLC 56**

de Routisie, Albert
See Aragon, Louis

Derrida, Jacques 1930- . . . . **CLC 24, 87**
See also CA 124; 127

Derry Down Derry
See Lear, Edward

Dersonnes, Jacques
See Simenon, Georges (Jacques Christian)

Desai, Anita
1937- . . . **CLC 19, 37; DAB; DAM NOV**
See also CA 81-84; CANR 33, 53; MTCW;
SATA 63

de Saint-Luc, Jean
See Glassco, John

de Saint Roman, Arnaud
See Aragon, Louis

Descartes, Rene 1596-1650 . . . . . . LC 20, 35

De Sica, Vittorio 1901(?)-1974 . . . . . CLC 20
See also CA 117

Desnos, Robert 1900-1945 . . . . TCLC 22
See also CA 121; 151

Destouches, Louis-Ferdinand
1894-1961 . . . . CLC 9, 15
See also Celine, Louis-Ferdinand
See also CA 85-88; CANR 28; MTCW

Deutsch, Babette 1895-1982 . . . . CLC 18
See also CA 1-4R; 108; CANR 4; DLB 45;
SATA 1; SATA-Obit 33

Devenant, William 1606-1649 . . . . LC 13

Devkota, Laxmiprasad
1909-1959 . . . . TCLC 23
See also CA 123

De Voto, Bernard (Augustine)
1897-1955 . . . . TCLC 29
See also CA 113; DLB 9

De Vries, Peter
1910-1993 . . . . CLC 1, 2, 3, 7, 10, 28, 46;
DAM NOV
See also CA 17-20R; 142; CANR 41;
DLB 6; DLBY 82; MTCW

Dexter, John
See Bradley, Marion Zimmer

Dexter, Martin
See Faust, Frederick (Schiller)

Dexter, Pete
1943- . . . . CLC 34, 55; DAM POP
See also BEST 89:2; CA 127; 131; INT 131;
MTCW

Diamano, Silmang
See Senghor, Leopold Sedar

Diamond, Neil 1941- . . . . CLC 30
See also CA 108

Diaz del Castillo, Bernal 1496-1584 . . LC 31

di Bassetto, Corno
See Shaw, George Bernard

Dick, Philip K(indred)
1928-1982 . . . . CLC 10, 30, 72;
DAM NOV, POP
See also CA 49-52; 106; CANR 2, 16;
DLB 8; MTCW

Dickens, Charles (John Huffam)
1812-1870 . . . . . . NCLC 3, 8, 18, 26, 37,
50; DA; DAB; DAC; DAM MST, NOV;
SSC 17; WLC
See also CDBLB 1832-1890; DLB 21, 55,
70, 159, 166; JRDA; MAICYA; SATA 15

Dickey, James (Lafayette)
1923- . . . . CLC 1, 2, 4, 7, 10, 15, 47;
DAM NOV, POET, POP
See also AITN 1, 2; CA 9-12R; CABS 2;
CANR 10, 48; CDALB 1968-1988;
DLB 5; DLBD 7; DLBY 82, 93;
INT CANR-10; MTCW

Dickey, William 1928-1994 . . . . . CLC 3, 28
See also CA 9-12R; 145; CANR 24; DLB 5

Dickinson, Charles 1951- . . . . CLC 49
See also CA 128

Dickinson, Emily (Elizabeth)
1830-1886 . . . . NCLC 21; DA; DAB;
DAC; DAM MST, POET; PC 1; WLC
See also CDALB 1865-1917; DLB 1;
SATA 29

Dickinson, Peter (Malcolm)
1927- . . . . CLC 12, 35
See also AAYA 9; CA 41-44R; CANR 31;
CLR 29; DLB 87, 161; JRDA; MAICYA;
SATA 5, 62

Dickson, Carr
See Carr, John Dickson

Dickson, Carter
See Carr, John Dickson

Diderot, Denis 1713-1784 . . . . LC 26

Didion, Joan
1934- . . CLC 1, 3, 8, 14, 32; DAM NOV
See also AITN 1; CA 5-8R; CANR 14, 52;
CDALB 1968-1988; DLB 2; DLBY 81,
86; MTCW

Dietrich, Robert
See Hunt, E(verette) Howard, (Jr.)

Dillard, Annie
1945- . . . . CLC 9, 60; DAM NOV
See also AAYA 6; CA 49-52; CANR 3, 43;
DLBY 80; MTCW; SATA 10

Dillard, R(ichard) H(enry) W(ilde)
1937- . . . . CLC 5
See also CA 21-24R; CAAS 7; CANR 10;
DLB 5

Dillon, Eilis 1920-1994 . . . . CLC 17
See also CA 9-12R; 147; CAAS 3; CANR 4,
38; CLR 26; MAICYA; SATA 2, 74;
SATA-Obit 83

Dimont, Penelope
See Mortimer, Penelope (Ruth)

Dinesen, Isak . . . . CLC 10, 29, 95; SSC 7
See also Blixen, Karen (Christentze
Dinesen)

Ding Ling . . . . CLC 68
See also Chiang Pin-chin

Disch, Thomas M(ichael) 1940- . . . CLC 7, 36
See also AAYA 17; CA 21-24R; CAAS 4;
CANR 17, 36; CLR 18; DLB 8;
MAICYA; MTCW; SAAS 15; SATA 54

Disch, Tom
See Disch, Thomas M(ichael)

d'Isly, Georges
See Simenon, Georges (Jacques Christian)

Disraeli, Benjamin 1804-1881 . . NCLC 2, 39
See also DLB 21, 55

Ditcum, Steve
See Crumb, R(obert)

Dixon, Paige
See Corcoran, Barbara

Dixon, Stephen 1936- . . . . . CLC 52; SSC 16
See also CA 89-92; CANR 17, 40; DLB 130

Dobell, Sydney Thompson
1824-1874 . . . . NCLC 43
See also DLB 32

Doblin, Alfred . . . . TCLC 13
See also Doeblin, Alfred

Dobrolyubov, Nikolai Alexandrovich
1836-1861 . . . . NCLC 5

Dobyns, Stephen 1941- . . . . CLC 37
See also CA 45-48; CANR 2, 18

Doctorow, E(dgar) L(aurence)
1931- . . . . . CLC 6, 11, 15, 18, 37, 44, 65;
DAM NOV, POP
See also AITN 2; BEST 89:3; CA 45-48;
CANR 2, 33, 51; CDALB 1968-1988;
DLB 2, 28; DLBY 80; MTCW

Dodgson, Charles Lutwidge 1832-1898
See Carroll, Lewis
See also CLR 2; DA; DAB; DAC;
DAM MST, NOV, POET; MAICYA;
YABC 2

Dodson, Owen (Vincent)
1914-1983 . . . . CLC 79; BLC;
DAM MULT
See also BW 1; CA 65-68; 110; CANR 24;
DLB 76

Doeblin, Alfred 1878-1957 . . . . TCLC 13
See also Doblin, Alfred
See also CA 110; 141; DLB 66

Doerr, Harriet 1910- . . . . CLC 34
See also CA 117; 122; CANR 47; INT 122

Domecq, H(onorio) Bustos
See Bioy Casares, Adolfo; Borges, Jorge
Luis

Domini, Rey
See Lorde, Audre (Geraldine)

Dominique
See Proust, (Valentin-Louis-George-Eugene-)
Marcel

Don, A
See Stephen, Leslie

Donaldson, Stephen R.
1947- . . . . CLC 46; DAM POP
See also CA 89-92; CANR 13;
INT CANR-13

Donleavy, J(ames) P(atrick)
1926- . . . . CLC 1, 4, 6, 10, 45
See also AITN 2; CA 9-12R; CANR 24, 49;
DLB 6; INT CANR-24; MTCW

Donne, John
1572-1631 . . . . LC 10, 24; DA; DAB;
DAC; DAM MST, POET; PC 1
See also CDBLB Before 1660; DLB 121,
151

Donnell, David 1939(?)- . . . . CLC 34

Donoghue, P. S.
See Hunt, E(verette) Howard, (Jr.)

Donoso (Yanez), Jose
1924- . . . . CLC 4, 8, 11, 32;
DAM MULT; HLC
See also CA 81-84; CANR 32; DLB 113;
HW; MTCW

Donovan, John 1928-1992 . . . . CLC 35
See also CA 97-100; 137; CLR 3;
MAICYA; SATA 72; SATA-Brief 29

Don Roberto
See Cunninghame Graham, R(obert)
B(ontine)

Doolittle, Hilda
1886-1961 ..... **CLC 3, 8, 14, 31, 34, 73;
DA; DAC; DAM MST, POET; PC 5;
WLC**
See also H. D.
See also CA 97-100; CANR 35; DLB 4, 45;
MTCW

Dorfman, Ariel
1942- .... **CLC 48, 77; DAM MULT;
HLC**
See also CA 124; 130; HW; INT 130

Dorn, Edward (Merton) 1929-... **CLC 10, 18**
See also CA 93-96; CANR 42; DLB 5;
INT 93-96

Dorsan, Luc
See Simenon, Georges (Jacques Christian)

Dorsange, Jean
See Simenon, Georges (Jacques Christian)

Dos Passos, John (Roderigo)
1896-1970 ..... **CLC 1, 4, 8, 11, 15, 25,
34, 82; DA; DAB; DAC; DAM MST,
NOV; WLC**
See also CA 1-4R; 29-32R; CANR 3;
CDALB 1929-1941; DLB 4, 9; DLBD 1;
MTCW

Dossage, Jean
See Simenon, Georges (Jacques Christian)

Dostoevsky, Fedor Mikhailovich
1821-1881 ...... **NCLC 2, 7, 21, 33, 43;
DA; DAB; DAC; DAM MST, NOV;
SSC 2; WLC**

Doughty, Charles M(ontagu)
1843-1926 .... **TCLC 27**
See also CA 115; DLB 19, 57

Douglas, Ellen .... **CLC 73**
See also Haxton, Josephine Ayres;
Williamson, Ellen Douglas

Douglas, Gavin 1475(?)-1522........ **LC 20**

Douglas, Keith 1920-1944 .... **TCLC 40**
See also DLB 27

Douglas, Leonard
See Bradbury, Ray (Douglas)

Douglas, Michael
See Crichton, (John) Michael

Douglass, Frederick
1817(?)-1895 .... **NCLC 7, 55; BLC; DA;
DAC; DAM MST, MULT; WLC**
See also CDALB 1640-1865; DLB 1, 43, 50,
79; SATA 29

Dourado, (Waldomiro Freitas) Autran
1926- .... **CLC 23, 60**
See also CA 25-28R; CANR 34

Dourado, Waldomiro Autran
See Dourado, (Waldomiro Freitas) Autran

Dove, Rita (Frances)
1952- .... **CLC 50, 81; DAM MULT,
POET; PC 6**
See also BW 2; CA 109; CAAS 19;
CANR 27, 42; DLB 120

Dowell, Coleman 1925-1985........ **CLC 60**
See also CA 25-28R; 117; CANR 10;
DLB 130

Dowson, Ernest (Christopher)
1867-1900 .... **TCLC 4**
See also CA 105; 150; DLB 19, 135

Doyle, A. Conan
See Doyle, Arthur Conan

Doyle, Arthur Conan
1859-1930 .... **TCLC 7; DA; DAB;
DAC; DAM MST, NOV; SSC 12; WLC**
See also AAYA 14; CA 104; 122;
CDBLB 1890-1914; DLB 18, 70, 156;
MTCW; SATA 24

Doyle, Conan
See Doyle, Arthur Conan

Doyle, John
See Graves, Robert (von Ranke)

Doyle, Roddy 1958(?)- .... **CLC 81**
See also AAYA 14; CA 143

Doyle, Sir A. Conan
See Doyle, Arthur Conan

Doyle, Sir Arthur Conan
See Doyle, Arthur Conan

Dr. A
See Asimov, Isaac; Silverstein, Alvin

Drabble, Margaret
1939- .... **CLC 2, 3, 5, 8, 10, 22, 53;
DAB; DAC; DAM MST, NOV, POP**
See also CA 13-16R; CANR 18, 35;
CDBLB 1960 to Present; DLB 14, 155;
MTCW; SATA 48

Drapier, M. B.
See Swift, Jonathan

Drayham, James
See Mencken, H(enry) L(ouis)

Drayton, Michael 1563-1631........ **LC 8**

Dreadstone, Carl
See Campbell, (John) Ramsey

Dreiser, Theodore (Herman Albert)
1871-1945 ...... **TCLC 10, 18, 35; DA;
DAC; DAM MST, NOV; WLC**
See also CA 106; 132; CDALB 1865-1917;
DLB 9, 12, 102, 137; DLBD 1; MTCW

Drexler, Rosalyn 1926- .... **CLC 2, 6**
See also CA 81-84

Dreyer, Carl Theodor 1889-1968.... **CLC 16**
See also CA 116

Drieu la Rochelle, Pierre(-Eugene)
1893-1945 .... **TCLC 21**
See also CA 117; DLB 72

Drinkwater, John 1882-1937 ...... **TCLC 57**
See also CA 109; 149; DLB 10, 19, 149

Drop Shot
See Cable, George Washington

Droste-Hulshoff, Annette Freiin von
1797-1848 .... **NCLC 3**
See also DLB 133

Drummond, Walter
See Silverberg, Robert

Drummond, William Henry
1854-1907 .... **TCLC 25**
See also DLB 92

Drummond de Andrade, Carlos
1902-1987 .... **CLC 18**
See also Andrade, Carlos Drummond de
See also CA 132; 123

Drury, Allen (Stuart) 1918- .... **CLC 37**
See also CA 57-60; CANR 18, 52;
INT CANR-18

Dryden, John
1631-1700 .... **LC 3, 21; DA; DAB;
DAC; DAM DRAM, MST, POET;
DC 3; WLC**
See also CDBLB 1660-1789; DLB 80, 101,
131

Duberman, Martin 1930- .... **CLC 8**
See also CA 1-4R; CANR 2

Dubie, Norman (Evans) 1945- ...... **CLC 36**
See also CA 69-72; CANR 12; DLB 120

Du Bois, W(illiam) E(dward) B(urghardt)
1868-1963 .... **CLC 1, 2, 13, 64, 96;
BLC; DA; DAC; DAM MST, MULT,
NOV; WLC**
See also BW 1; CA 85-88; CANR 34;
CDALB 1865-1917; DLB 47, 50, 91;
MTCW; SATA 42

Dubus, Andre 1936-... **CLC 13, 36; SSC 15**
See also CA 21-24R; CANR 17; DLB 130;
INT CANR-17

Duca Minimo
See D'Annunzio, Gabriele

Ducharme, Rejean 1941- .... **CLC 74**
See also DLB 60

Duclos, Charles Pinot 1704-1772 ..... **LC 1**

Dudek, Louis 1918- .... **CLC 11, 19**
See also CA 45-48; CAAS 14; CANR 1;
DLB 88

Duerrenmatt, Friedrich
1921-1990 ...... **CLC 1, 4, 8, 11, 15, 43;
DAM DRAM**
See also CA 17-20R; CANR 33; DLB 69,
124; MTCW

Duffy, Bruce (?)-................. **CLC 50**

Duffy, Maureen 1933- .... **CLC 37**
See also CA 25-28R; CANR 33; DLB 14;
MTCW

Dugan, Alan 1923- .... **CLC 2, 6**
See also CA 81-84; DLB 5

du Gard, Roger Martin
See Martin du Gard, Roger

Duhamel, Georges 1884-1966 .... **CLC 8**
See also CA 81-84; 25-28R; CANR 35;
DLB 65; MTCW

Dujardin, Edouard (Emile Louis)
1861-1949 .... **TCLC 13**
See also CA 109; DLB 123

Dumas, Alexandre (Davy de la Pailleterie)
1802-1870 .... **NCLC 11; DA; DAB;
DAC; DAM MST, NOV; WLC**
See also DLB 119; SATA 18

Dumas, Alexandre
1824-1895 .... **NCLC 9; DC 1**

Dumas, Claudine
See Malzberg, Barry N(athaniel)

Dumas, Henry L. 1934-1968 ..... **CLC 6, 62**
See also BW 1; CA 85-88; DLB 41

du Maurier, Daphne
1907-1989 .... **CLC 6, 11, 59; DAB;
DAC; DAM MST, POP; SSC 18**
See also CA 5-8R; 128; CANR 6; MTCW;
SATA 27; SATA-Obit 60

Ekeloef, (Bengt) Gunnar
1907-1968 . . . . **CLC 27; DAM POET**
See also CA 123; 25-28R

Ekelof, (Bengt) Gunnar
See Ekeloef, (Bengt) Gunnar

Ekwensi, C. O. D.
See Ekwensi, Cyprian (Odiatu Duaka)

Ekwensi, Cyprian (Odiatu Duaka)
1921- . . . . . . **CLC 4; BLC; DAM MULT**
See also BW 2; CA 29-32R; CANR 18, 42;
DLB 117; MTCW; SATA 66

Elaine . . . . **TCLC 18**
See also Leverson, Ada

El Crummo
See Crumb, R(obert)

Elia
See Lamb, Charles

Eliade, Mircea 1907-1986 . . . . **CLC 19**
See also CA 65-68; 119; CANR 30; MTCW

Eliot, A. D.
See Jewett, (Theodora) Sarah Orne

Eliot, Alice
See Jewett, (Theodora) Sarah Orne

Eliot, Dan
See Silverberg, Robert

Eliot, George
1819-1880 . . . . . **NCLC 4, 13, 23, 41, 49;**
DA; DAB; DAC; DAM MST, NOV;
WLC
See also CDBLB 1832-1890; DLB 21, 35, 55

Eliot, John 1604-1690 . . . . **LC 5**
See also DLB 24

Eliot, T(homas) S(tearns)
1888-1965 . . . . . **CLC 1, 2, 3, 6, 9, 10, 13,**
15, 24, 34, 41, 55, 57; DA; DAB; DAC;
DAM DRAM, MST, POET; PC 5;
WLC 2
See also CA 5-8R; 25-28R; CANR 41;
CDALB 1929-1941; DLB 7, 10, 45, 63;
DLBY 88; MTCW

Elizabeth 1866-1941 . . . . **TCLC 41**

Elkin, Stanley L(awrence)
1930-1995 . . . . . . **CLC 4, 6, 9, 14, 27, 51,**
91; DAM NOV, POP; SSC 12
See also CA 9-12R; 148; CANR 8, 46;
DLB 2, 28; DLBY 80; INT CANR-8;
MTCW

Elledge, Scott . . . . **CLC 34**

Elliott, Don
See Silverberg, Robert

Elliott, George P(aul) 1918-1980 . . . . . **CLC 2**
See also CA 1-4R; 97-100; CANR 2

Elliott, Janice 1931- . . . . **CLC 47**
See also CA 13-16R; CANR 8, 29; DLB 14

Elliott, Sumner Locke 1917-1991 . . . **CLC 38**
See also CA 5-8R; 134; CANR 2, 21

Elliott, William
See Bradbury, Ray (Douglas)

Ellis, A. E. . . . . **CLC 7**

Ellis, Alice Thomas . . . . **CLC 40**
See also Haycraft, Anna

Ellis, Bret Easton
1964- . . . . **CLC 39, 71; DAM POP**
See also AAYA 2; CA 118; 123; CANR 51;
INT 123

Ellis, (Henry) Havelock
1859-1939 . . . . **TCLC 14**
See also CA 109

Ellis, Landon
See Ellison, Harlan (Jay)

Ellis, Trey 1962- . . . . **CLC 55**
See also CA 146

Ellison, Harlan (Jay)
1934- . . . . . . **CLC 1, 13, 42; DAM POP;**
SSC 14
See also CA 5-8R; CANR 5, 46; DLB 8;
INT CANR-5; MTCW

Ellison, Ralph (Waldo)
1914-1994 . . . . **CLC 1, 3, 11, 54, 86;**
BLC; DA; DAB; DAC; DAM MST,
MULT, NOV; WLC
See also BW 1; CA 9-12R; 145; CANR 24,
53; CDALB 1941-1968; DLB 2, 76;
DLBY 94; MTCW

Ellmann, Lucy (Elizabeth) 1956- . . . . **CLC 61**
See also CA 128

Ellmann, Richard (David)
1918-1987 . . . . **CLC 50**
See also BEST 89:2; CA 1-4R; 122;
CANR 2, 28; DLB 103; DLBY 87;
MTCW

Elman, Richard 1934- . . . . **CLC 19**
See also CA 17-20R; CAAS 3; CANR 47

Elron
See Hubbard, L(afayette) Ron(ald)

Eluard, Paul . . . . **TCLC 7, 41**
See also Grindel, Eugene

Elyot, Sir Thomas 1490(?)-1546 . . . . . **LC 11**

Elytis, Odysseus
1911-1996 . . . . **CLC 15, 49; DAM POET**
See also CA 102; 151; MTCW

Emecheta, (Florence Onye) Buchi
1944- . . **CLC 14, 48; BLC; DAM MULT**
See also BW 2; CA 81-84; CANR 27;
DLB 117; MTCW; SATA 66

Emerson, Ralph Waldo
1803-1882 . . . . . **NCLC 1, 38; DA; DAB;**
DAC; DAM MST, POET; WLC
See also CDALB 1640-1865; DLB 1, 59, 73

Eminescu, Mihail 1850-1889 . . . . . **NCLC 33**

Empson, William
1906-1984 . . . . **CLC 3, 8, 19, 33, 34**
See also CA 17-20R; 112; CANR 31;
DLB 20; MTCW

Enchi Fumiko (Ueda) 1905-1986 . . . . **CLC 31**
See also CA 129; 121

Ende, Michael (Andreas Helmuth)
1929-1995 . . . . **CLC 31**
See also CA 118; 124; 149; CANR 36;
CLR 14; DLB 75; MAICYA; SATA 61;
SATA-Brief 42; SATA-Obit 86

Endo, Shusaku
1923- . . . **CLC 7, 14, 19, 54; DAM NOV**
See also CA 29-32R; CANR 21; MTCW

Engel, Marian 1933-1985 . . . . **CLC 36**
See also CA 25-28R; CANR 12; DLB 53;
INT CANR-12

Engelhardt, Frederick
See Hubbard, L(afayette) Ron(ald)

Enright, D(ennis) J(oseph)
1920- . . . . **CLC 4, 8, 31**
See also CA 1-4R; CANR 1, 42; DLB 27;
SATA 25

Enzensberger, Hans Magnus
1929- . . . . **CLC 43**
See also CA 116; 119

Ephron, Nora 1941- . . . . **CLC 17, 31**
See also AITN 2; CA 65-68; CANR 12, 39

Epsilon
See Betjeman, John

Epstein, Daniel Mark 1948- . . . . **CLC 7**
See also CA 49-52; CANR 2, 53

Epstein, Jacob 1956- . . . . **CLC 19**
See also CA 114

Epstein, Joseph 1937- . . . . **CLC 39**
See also CA 112; 119; CANR 50

Epstein, Leslie 1938- . . . . **CLC 27**
See also CA 73-76; CAAS 12; CANR 23

Equiano, Olaudah
1745(?)-1797 . . . . **LC 16; BLC;**
DAM MULT
See also DLB 37, 50

Erasmus, Desiderius 1469(?)-1536 . . . . **LC 16**

Erdman, Paul E(mil) 1932- . . . . **CLC 25**
See also AITN 1; CA 61-64; CANR 13, 43

Erdrich, Louise
1954- . . . . **CLC 39, 54; DAM MULT,**
NOV, POP
See also AAYA 10; BEST 89:1; CA 114;
CANR 41; DLB 152; MTCW; NNAL

Erenburg, Ilya (Grigoryevich)
See Ehrenburg, Ilya (Grigoryevich)

Erickson, Stephen Michael 1950-
See Erickson, Steve
See also CA 129

Erickson, Steve . . . . **CLC 64**
See also Erickson, Stephen Michael

Ericson, Walter
See Fast, Howard (Melvin)

Eriksson, Buntel
See Bergman, (Ernst) Ingmar

Ernaux, Annie 1940- . . . . **CLC 88**
See also CA 147

Eschenbach, Wolfram von
See Wolfram von Eschenbach

Eseki, Bruno
See Mphahlele, Ezekiel

Esenin, Sergei (Alexandrovich)
1895-1925 . . . . **TCLC 4**
See also CA 104

Eshleman, Clayton 1935- . . . . **CLC 7**
See also CA 33-36R; CAAS 6; DLB 5

Espriella, Don Manuel Alvarez
See Southey, Robert

Espriu, Salvador 1913-1985 . . . . **CLC 9**
See also CA 115; DLB 134

Espronceda, Jose de 1808-1842 . . . **NCLC 39**

Esse, James
See Stephens, James

Esterbrook, Tom
    See Hubbard, L(afayette) Ron(ald)

Estleman, Loren D.
    1952- ...... CLC 48; DAM NOV, POP
    See also CA 85-88; CANR 27;
    INT CANR-27; MTCW

Eugenides, Jeffrey 1960(?)- .... CLC 81
    See also CA 144

Euripides c. 485B.C.-406B.C. .... DC 4
    See also DA; DAB; DAC; DAM DRAM,
    MST

Evan, Evin
    See Faust, Frederick (Schiller)

Evans, Evan
    See Faust, Frederick (Schiller)

Evans, Marian
    See Eliot, George

Evans, Mary Ann
    See Eliot, George

Evarts, Esther
    See Benson, Sally

Everett, Percival L. 1956- .... CLC 57
    See also BW 2; CA 129

Everson, R(onald) G(ilmour)
    1903- .... CLC 27
    See also CA 17-20R; DLB 88

Everson, William (Oliver)
    1912-1994 .... CLC 1, 5, 14
    See also CA 9-12R; 145; CANR 20; DLB 5,
    16; MTCW

Evtushenko, Evgenii Aleksandrovich
    See Yevtushenko, Yevgeny (Alexandrovich)

Ewart, Gavin (Buchanan)
    1916-1995 .... CLC 13, 46
    See also CA 89-92; 150; CANR 17, 46;
    DLB 40; MTCW

Ewers, Hanns Heinz 1871-1943 ... TCLC 12
    See also CA 109; 149

Ewing, Frederick R.
    See Sturgeon, Theodore (Hamilton)

Exley, Frederick (Earl)
    1929-1992 .... CLC 6, 11
    See also AITN 2; CA 81-84; 138; DLB 143;
    DLBY 81

Eynhardt, Guillermo
    See Quiroga, Horacio (Sylvestre)

Ezekiel, Nissim 1924- .... CLC 61
    See also CA 61-64

Ezekiel, Tish O'Dowd 1943- .... CLC 34
    See also CA 129

Fadeyev, A.
    See Bulgya, Alexander Alexandrovich

Fadeyev, Alexander .... TCLC 53
    See also Bulgya, Alexander Alexandrovich

Fagen, Donald 1948- .... CLC 26

Fainzilberg, Ilya Arnoldovich 1897-1937
    See Ilf, Ilya
    See also CA 120

Fair, Ronald L. 1932- .... CLC 18
    See also BW 1; CA 69-72; CANR 25;
    DLB 33

Fairbairns, Zoe (Ann) 1948- .... CLC 32
    See also CA 103; CANR 21

Falco, Gian
    See Papini, Giovanni

Falconer, James
    See Kirkup, James

Falconer, Kenneth
    See Kornbluth, C(yril) M.

Falkland, Samuel
    See Heijermans, Herman

Fallaci, Oriana 1930- .... CLC 11
    See also CA 77-80; CANR 15; MTCW

Faludy, George 1913- .... CLC 42
    See also CA 21-24R

Faludy, Gyoergy
    See Faludy, George

Fanon, Frantz
    1925-1961 .... CLC 74; BLC;
                                   DAM MULT
    See also BW 1; CA 116; 89-92

Fanshawe, Ann 1625-1680 .... LC 11

Fante, John (Thomas) 1911-1983 ... CLC 60
    See also CA 69-72; 109; CANR 23;
    DLB 130; DLBY 83

Farah, Nuruddin
    1945- ..... CLC 53; BLC; DAM MULT
    See also BW 2; CA 106; DLB 125

Fargue, Leon-Paul 1876(?)-1947 ... TCLC 11
    See also CA 109

Farigoule, Louis
    See Romains, Jules

Farina, Richard 1936(?)-1966 .... CLC 9
    See also CA 81-84; 25-28R

Farley, Walter (Lorimer)
    1915-1989 .... CLC 17
    See also CA 17-20R; CANR 8, 29; DLB 22;
    JRDA; MAICYA; SATA 2, 43

Farmer, Philip Jose 1918- .... CLC 1, 19
    See also CA 1-4R; CANR 4, 35; DLB 8;
    MTCW

Farquhar, George
    1677-1707 .... LC 21; DAM DRAM
    See also DLB 84

Farrell, J(ames) G(ordon)
    1935-1979 .... CLC 6
    See also CA 73-76; 89-92; CANR 36;
    DLB 14; MTCW

Farrell, James T(homas)
    1904-1979 .... CLC 1, 4, 8, 11, 66
    See also CA 5-8R; 89-92; CANR 9; DLB 4,
    9, 86; DLBD 2; MTCW

Farren, Richard J.
    See Betjeman, John

Farren, Richard M.
    See Betjeman, John

Fassbinder, Rainer Werner
    1946-1982 .... CLC 20
    See also CA 93-96; 106; CANR 31

Fast, Howard (Melvin)
    1914- .... CLC 23; DAM NOV
    See also AAYA 16; CA 1-4R; CAAS 18;
    CANR 1, 33; DLB 9; INT CANR-33;
    SATA 7

Faulcon, Robert
    See Holdstock, Robert P.

Faulkner, William (Cuthbert)
    1897-1962 ..... CLC 1, 3, 6, 8, 9, 11, 14,
            18, 28, 52, 68; DA; DAB; DAC;
            DAM MST, NOV; SSC 1; WLC
    See also AAYA 7; CA 81-84; CANR 33;
    CDALB 1929-1941; DLB 9, 11, 44, 102;
    DLBD 2; DLBY 86; MTCW

Fauset, Jessie Redmon
    1884(?)-1961 .... CLC 19, 54; BLC;
                                   DAM MULT
    See also BW 1; CA 109; DLB 51

Faust, Frederick (Schiller)
    1892-1944(?) ..... TCLC 49; DAM POP
    See also CA 108; 152

Faust, Irvin 1924- .... CLC 8
    See also CA 33-36R; CANR 28; DLB 2, 28;
    DLBY 80

Fawkes, Guy
    See Benchley, Robert (Charles)

Fearing, Kenneth (Flexner)
    1902-1961 .... CLC 51
    See also CA 93-96; DLB 9

Fecamps, Elise
    See Creasey, John

Federman, Raymond 1928- ...... CLC 6, 47
    See also CA 17-20R; CAAS 8; CANR 10,
    43; DLBY 80

Federspiel, J(uerg) F. 1931- .... CLC 42
    See also CA 146

Feiffer, Jules (Ralph)
    1929- ...... CLC 2, 8, 64; DAM DRAM
    See also AAYA 3; CA 17-20R; CANR 30;
    DLB 7, 44; INT CANR-30; MTCW;
    SATA 8, 61

Feige, Hermann Albert Otto Maximilian
    See Traven, B.

Feinberg, David B. 1956-1994 ...... CLC 59
    See also CA 135; 147

Feinstein, Elaine 1930- .... CLC 36
    See also CA 69-72; CAAS 1; CANR 31;
    DLB 14, 40; MTCW

Feldman, Irving (Mordecai) 1928- .... CLC 7
    See also CA 1-4R; CANR 1

Fellini, Federico 1920-1993 ..... CLC 16, 85
    See also CA 65-68; 143; CANR 33

Felsen, Henry Gregor 1916- .... CLC 17
    See also CA 1-4R; CANR 1; SAAS 2;
    SATA 1

Fenton, James Martin 1949- .... CLC 32
    See also CA 102; DLB 40

Ferber, Edna 1887-1968 .... CLC 18, 93
    See also AITN 1; CA 5-8R; 25-28R; DLB 9,
    28, 86; MTCW; SATA 7

Ferguson, Helen
    See Kavan, Anna

Ferguson, Samuel 1810-1886 ..... NCLC 33
    See also DLB 32

Fergusson, Robert 1750-1774 .... LC 29
    See also DLB 109

Ferling, Lawrence
    See Ferlinghetti, Lawrence (Monsanto)

Ferlinghetti, Lawrence (Monsanto)
1919(?)- . . . . **CLC 2, 6, 10, 27;**
DAM POET; PC 1
See also CA 5-8R; CANR 3, 41;
CDALB 1941-1968; DLB 5, 16; MTCW

Fernandez, Vicente Garcia Huidobro
See Huidobro Fernandez, Vicente Garcia

Ferrer, Gabriel (Francisco Victor) Miro
See Miro (Ferrer), Gabriel (Francisco
Victor)

Ferrier, Susan (Edmonstone)
1782-1854 . . . . **NCLC 8**
See also DLB 116

Ferrigno, Robert 1948(?)- . . . . **CLC 65**
See also CA 140

Ferron, Jacques 1921-1985 . . . **CLC 94; DAC**
See also CA 117; 129; DLB 60

Feuchtwanger, Lion 1884-1958 . . . . . **TCLC 3**
See also CA 104; DLB 66

Feuillet, Octave 1821-1890 . . . . . . **NCLC 45**

Feydeau, Georges (Leon Jules Marie)
1862-1921 . . . . . **TCLC 22; DAM DRAM**
See also CA 113; 152

Ficino, Marsilio 1433-1499 . . . . **LC 12**

Fiedeler, Hans
See Doeblin, Alfred

Fiedler, Leslie A(aron)
1917- . . . . **CLC 4, 13, 24**
See also CA 9-12R; CANR 7; DLB 28, 67;
MTCW

Field, Andrew 1938- . . . . **CLC 44**
See also CA 97-100; CANR 25

Field, Eugene 1850-1895 . . . . **NCLC 3**
See also DLB 23, 42, 140; DLBD 13;
MAICYA; SATA 16

Field, Gans T.
See Wellman, Manly Wade

Field, Michael . . . . **TCLC 43**

Field, Peter
See Hobson, Laura Z(ametkin)

Fielding, Henry
1707-1754 . . . . . . **LC 1; DA; DAB; DAC;**
DAM DRAM, MST, NOV; WLC
See also CDBLB 1660-1789; DLB 39, 84,
101

Fielding, Sarah 1710-1768 . . . . **LC 1**
See also DLB 39

Fierstein, Harvey (Forbes)
1954- . . . . . **CLC 33; DAM DRAM, POP**
See also CA 123; 129

Figes, Eva 1932- . . . . **CLC 31**
See also CA 53-56; CANR 4, 44; DLB 14

Finch, Robert (Duer Claydon)
1900- . . . . **CLC 18**
See also CA 57-60; CANR 9, 24, 49;
DLB 88

Findley, Timothy
1930- . . . . . . **CLC 27; DAC; DAM MST**
See also CA 25-28R; CANR 12, 42;
DLB 53

Fink, William
See Mencken, H(enry) L(ouis)

Firbank, Louis 1942-
See Reed, Lou
See also CA 117

Firbank, (Arthur Annesley) Ronald
1886-1926 . . . . **TCLC 1**
See also CA 104; DLB 36

Fisher, M(ary) F(rances) K(ennedy)
1908-1992 . . . . **CLC 76, 87**
See also CA 77-80; 138; CANR 44

Fisher, Roy 1930- . . . . **CLC 25**
See also CA 81-84; CAAS 10; CANR 16;
DLB 40

Fisher, Rudolph
1897-1934 . . . . **TCLC 11; BLC;**
DAM MULT
See also BW 1; CA 107; 124; DLB 51, 102

Fisher, Vardis (Alvero) 1895-1968 . . . . **CLC 7**
See also CA 5-8R; 25-28R; DLB 9

Fiske, Tarleton
See Bloch, Robert (Albert)

Fitch, Clarke
See Sinclair, Upton (Beall)

Fitch, John IV
See Cormier, Robert (Edmund)

Fitzgerald, Captain Hugh
See Baum, L(yman) Frank

FitzGerald, Edward 1809-1883 . . . . **NCLC 9**
See also DLB 32

Fitzgerald, F(rancis) Scott (Key)
1896-1940 . . . . . . **TCLC 1, 6, 14, 28, 55;**
DA; DAB; DAC; DAM MST, NOV;
SSC 6; WLC
See also AITN 1; CA 110; 123;
CDALB 1917-1929; DLB 4, 9, 86;
DLBD 1; DLBY 81; MTCW

Fitzgerald, Penelope 1916- . . . **CLC 19, 51, 61**
See also CA 85-88; CAAS 10; DLB 14

Fitzgerald, Robert (Stuart)
1910-1985 . . . . **CLC 39**
See also CA 1-4R; 114; CANR 1; DLBY 80

FitzGerald, Robert D(avid)
1902-1987 . . . . **CLC 19**
See also CA 17-20R

Fitzgerald, Zelda (Sayre)
1900-1948 . . . . **TCLC 52**
See also CA 117; 126; DLBY 84

Flanagan, Thomas (James Bonner)
1923- . . . . **CLC 25, 52**
See also CA 108; DLBY 80; INT 108;
MTCW

Flaubert, Gustave
1821-1880 . . . . **NCLC 2, 10, 19; DA;**
DAB; DAC; DAM MST, NOV; SSC 11;
WLC
See also DLB 119

Flecker, Herman Elroy
See Flecker, (Herman) James Elroy

Flecker, (Herman) James Elroy
1884-1915 . . . . **TCLC 43**
See also CA 109; 150; DLB 10, 19

Fleming, Ian (Lancaster)
1908-1964 . . . . . . **CLC 3, 30; DAM POP**
See also CA 5-8R; CDBLB 1945-1960;
DLB 87; MTCW; SATA 9

Fleming, Thomas (James) 1927- . . . . **CLC 37**
See also CA 5-8R; CANR 10;
INT CANR-10; SATA 8

Fletcher, John 1579-1625 . . . . . . **LC 33; DC 6**
See also CDBLB Before 1660; DLB 58

Fletcher, John Gould 1886-1950 . . . **TCLC 35**
See also CA 107; DLB 4, 45

Fleur, Paul
See Pohl, Frederik

Flooglebuckle, Al
See Spiegelman, Art

Flying Officer X
See Bates, H(erbert) E(rnest)

Fo, Dario 1926- . . . . . **CLC 32; DAM DRAM**
See also CA 116; 128; MTCW

Fogarty, Jonathan Titulescu Esq.
See Farrell, James T(homas)

Folke, Will
See Bloch, Robert (Albert)

Follett, Ken(neth Martin)
1949- . . . . . . **CLC 18; DAM NOV, POP**
See also AAYA 6; BEST 89:4; CA 81-84;
CANR 13, 33; DLB 87; DLBY 81;
INT CANR-33; MTCW

Fontane, Theodor 1819-1898 . . . . . **NCLC 26**
See also DLB 129

Foote, Horton
1916- . . . . **CLC 51, 91; DAM DRAM**
See also CA 73-76; CANR 34, 51; DLB 26;
INT CANR-34

Foote, Shelby
1916- . . . . **CLC 75; DAM NOV, POP**
See also CA 5-8R; CANR 3, 45; DLB 2, 17

Forbes, Esther 1891-1967 . . . . **CLC 12**
See also AAYA 17; CA 13-14; 25-28R;
CAP 1; CLR 27; DLB 22; JRDA;
MAICYA; SATA 2

Forche, Carolyn (Louise)
1950- . . . . **CLC 25, 83, 86; DAM POET;**
PC 10
See also CA 109; 117; CANR 50; DLB 5;
INT 117

Ford, Elbur
See Hibbert, Eleanor Alice Burford

Ford, Ford Madox
1873-1939 . . . . **TCLC 1, 15, 39, 57;**
DAM NOV
See also CA 104; 132; CDBLB 1914-1945;
DLB 162; MTCW

Ford, John 1895-1973 . . . . **CLC 16**
See also CA 45-48

Ford, Richard 1944- . . . . **CLC 46**
See also CA 69-72; CANR 11, 47

Ford, Webster
See Masters, Edgar Lee

Foreman, Richard 1937- . . . . **CLC 50**
See also CA 65-68; CANR 32

Forester, C(ecil) S(cott)
1899-1966 . . . . **CLC 35**
See also CA 73-76; 25-28R; SATA 13

Forez
See Mauriac, Francois (Charles)

Forman, James Douglas 1932- . . . . . . **CLC 21**
See also AAYA 17; CA 9-12R; CANR 4,
19, 42; JRDA; MAICYA; SATA 8, 70

Fuchs, Daniel 1909-1993 . . . . **CLC 8, 22**
See also CA 81-84; 142; CAAS 5;
CANR 40; DLB 9, 26, 28; DLBY 93

Fuchs, Daniel 1934- . . . . **CLC 34**
See also CA 37-40R; CANR 14, 48

Fuentes, Carlos
1928- . . . . . . **CLC 3, 8, 10, 13, 22, 41, 60;**
DA; DAB; DAC; DAM MST, MULT,
NOV; HLC; WLC
See also AAYA 4; AITN 2; CA 69-72;
CANR 10, 32; DLB 113; HW; MTCW

Fuentes, Gregorio Lopez y
See Lopez y Fuentes, Gregorio

Fugard, (Harold) Athol
1932- . . . . **CLC 5, 9, 14, 25, 40, 80;**
DAM DRAM; DC 3
See also AAYA 17; CA 85-88; CANR 32;
MTCW

Fugard, Sheila 1932- . . . . **CLC 48**
See also CA 125

Fuller, Charles (H., Jr.)
1939- . . . . **CLC 25; BLC; DAM DRAM,**
MULT; DC 1
See also BW 2; CA 108; 112; DLB 38;
INT 112; MTCW

Fuller, John (Leopold) 1937- . . . . **CLC 62**
See also CA 21-24R; CANR 9, 44; DLB 40

Fuller, Margaret . . . . **NCLC 5, 50**
See also Ossoli, Sarah Margaret (Fuller
marchesa d')

Fuller, Roy (Broadbent)
1912-1991 . . . . **CLC 4, 28**
See also CA 5-8R; 135; CAAS 10;
CANR 53; DLB 15, 20; SATA 87

Fulton, Alice 1952- . . . . **CLC 52**
See also CA 116

Furphy, Joseph 1843-1912 . . . . **TCLC 25**

Fussell, Paul 1924- . . . . **CLC 74**
See also BEST 90:1; CA 17-20R; CANR 8,
21, 35; INT CANR-21; MTCW

Futabatei, Shimei 1864-1909 . . . . . . **TCLC 44**

Futrelle, Jacques 1875-1912 . . . . . . **TCLC 19**
See also CA 113

Gaboriau, Emile 1835-1873 . . . . . . **NCLC 14**

Gadda, Carlo Emilio 1893-1973 . . . . **CLC 11**
See also CA 89-92

Gaddis, William
1922- . . . . . **CLC 1, 3, 6, 8, 10, 19, 43, 86**
See also CA 17-20R; CANR 21, 48; DLB 2;
MTCW

Gaines, Ernest J(ames)
1933- . . . . **CLC 3, 11, 18, 86; BLC;**
DAM MULT
See also AAYA 18; AITN 1; BW 2;
CA 9-12R; CANR 6, 24, 42;
CDALB 1968-1988; DLB 2, 33, 152;
DLBY 80; MTCW; SATA 86

Gaitskill, Mary 1954- . . . . **CLC 69**
See also CA 128

Galdos, Benito Perez
See Perez Galdos, Benito

Gale, Zona
1874-1938 . . . . . . **TCLC 7; DAM DRAM**
See also CA 105; DLB 9, 78

Galeano, Eduardo (Hughes) 1940- . . . **CLC 72**
See also CA 29-32R; CANR 13, 32; HW

Galiano, Juan Valera y Alcala
See Valera y Alcala-Galiano, Juan

Gallagher, Tess
1943- . . **CLC 18, 63; DAM POET; PC 9**
See also CA 106; DLB 120

Gallant, Mavis
1922- . . . . **CLC 7, 18, 38; DAC;**
DAM MST; SSC 5
See also CA 69-72; CANR 29; DLB 53;
MTCW

Gallant, Roy A(rthur) 1924- . . . . **CLC 17**
See also CA 5-8R; CANR 4, 29; CLR 30;
MAICYA; SATA 4, 68

Gallico, Paul (William) 1897-1976 . . . **CLC 2**
See also AITN 1; CA 5-8R; 69-72;
CANR 23; DLB 9; MAICYA; SATA 13

Gallo, Max Louis 1932- . . . . **CLC 95**
See also CA 85-88

Gallois, Lucien
See Desnos, Robert

Gallup, Ralph
See Whitemore, Hugh (John)

Galsworthy, John
1867-1933 . . . . . . **TCLC 1, 45; DA; DAB;**
DAC; DAM DRAM, MST, NOV;
SSC 22; WLC 2
See also CA 104; 141; CDBLB 1890-1914;
DLB 10, 34, 98, 162

Galt, John 1779-1839 . . . . **NCLC 1**
See also DLB 99, 116, 159

Galvin, James 1951- . . . . **CLC 38**
See also CA 108; CANR 26

Gamboa, Federico 1864-1939 . . . . . . **TCLC 36**

Gandhi, M. K.
See Gandhi, Mohandas Karamchand

Gandhi, Mahatma
See Gandhi, Mohandas Karamchand

Gandhi, Mohandas Karamchand
1869-1948 . . . . . **TCLC 59; DAM MULT**
See also CA 121; 132; MTCW

Gann, Ernest Kellogg 1910-1991 . . . . **CLC 23**
See also AITN 1; CA 1-4R; 136; CANR 1

Garcia, Cristina 1958- . . . . **CLC 76**
See also CA 141

Garcia Lorca, Federico
1898-1936 . . . **TCLC 1, 7, 49; DA; DAB;**
DAC; DAM DRAM, MST, MULT,
POET; DC 2; HLC; PC 3; WLC
See also CA 104; 131; DLB 108; HW;
MTCW

Garcia Marquez, Gabriel (Jose)
1928- . . . . **CLC 2, 3, 8, 10, 15, 27, 47, 55,**
68; DA; DAB; DAC; DAM MST,
MULT, NOV, POP; HLC; SSC 8; WLC
See also AAYA 3; BEST 89:1, 90:4;
CA 33-36R; CANR 10, 28, 50; DLB 113;
HW; MTCW

Gard, Janice
See Latham, Jean Lee

Gard, Roger Martin du
See Martin du Gard, Roger

Gardam, Jane 1928- . . . . **CLC 43**
See also CA 49-52; CANR 2, 18, 33;
CLR 12; DLB 14, 161; MAICYA;
MTCW; SAAS 9; SATA 39, 76;
SATA-Brief 28

Gardner, Herb(ert) 1934- . . . . **CLC 44**
See also CA 149

Gardner, John (Champlin), Jr.
1933-1982 . . . . . **CLC 2, 3, 5, 7, 8, 10, 18,**
28, 34; DAM NOV, POP; SSC 7
See also AITN 1; CA 65-68; 107;
CANR 33; DLB 2; DLBY 82; MTCW;
SATA 40; SATA-Obit 31

Gardner, John (Edmund)
1926- . . . . **CLC 30; DAM POP**
See also CA 103; CANR 15; MTCW

Gardner, Miriam
See Bradley, Marion Zimmer

Gardner, Noel
See Kuttner, Henry

Gardons, S. S.
See Snodgrass, W(illiam) D(e Witt)

Garfield, Leon 1921-1996 . . . . **CLC 12**
See also AAYA 8; CA 17-20R; 152;
CANR 38, 41; CLR 21; DLB 161; JRDA;
MAICYA; SATA 1, 32, 76

Garland, (Hannibal) Hamlin
1860-1940 . . . . **TCLC 3; SSC 18**
See also CA 104; DLB 12, 71, 78

Garneau, (Hector de) Saint-Denys
1912-1943 . . . . **TCLC 13**
See also CA 111; DLB 88

Garner, Alan
1934- . . . . **CLC 17; DAB; DAM POP**
See also AAYA 18; CA 73-76; CANR 15;
CLR 20; DLB 161; MAICYA; MTCW;
SATA 18, 69

Garner, Hugh 1913-1979 . . . . **CLC 13**
See also CA 69-72; CANR 31; DLB 68

Garnett, David 1892-1981 . . . . **CLC 3**
See also CA 5-8R; 103; CANR 17; DLB 34

Garos, Stephanie
See Katz, Steve

Garrett, George (Palmer)
1929- . . . . **CLC 3, 11, 51**
See also CA 1-4R; CAAS 5; CANR 1, 42;
DLB 2, 5, 130, 152; DLBY 83

Garrick, David
1717-1779 . . . . **LC 15; DAM DRAM**
See also DLB 84

Garrigue, Jean 1914-1972 . . . . **CLC 2, 8**
See also CA 5-8R; 37-40R; CANR 20

Garrison, Frederick
See Sinclair, Upton (Beall)

Garth, Will
See Hamilton, Edmond; Kuttner, Henry

Garvey, Marcus (Moziah, Jr.)
1887-1940 . . . . **TCLC 41; BLC;**
DAM MULT
See also BW 1; CA 120; 124

Gary, Romain . . . . **CLC 25**
See also Kacew, Romain
See also DLB 83

Gascar, Pierre . . . . **CLC 11**
See also Fournier, Pierre

Gascoyne, David (Emery) 1916- .... **CLC 45**
See also CA 65-68; CANR 10, 28; DLB 20;
MTCW

Gaskell, Elizabeth Cleghorn
1810-1865 .. **NCLC 5; DAB; DAM MST**
See also CDBLB 1832-1890; DLB 21, 144,
159

Gass, William H(oward)
1924- ... **CLC 1, 2, 8, 11, 15, 39; SSC 12**
See also CA 17-20R; CANR 30; DLB 2;
MTCW

Gasset, Jose Ortega y
See Ortega y Gasset, Jose

Gates, Henry Louis, Jr.
1950- .... **CLC 65; DAM MULT**
See also BW 2; CA 109; CANR 25, 53;
DLB 67

Gautier, Theophile
1811-1872 ...... **NCLC 1; DAM POET;
SSC 20**
See also DLB 119

Gawsworth, John
See Bates, H(erbert) E(rnest)

Gay, Oliver
See Gogarty, Oliver St. John

Gaye, Marvin (Penze) 1939-1984 ... **CLC 26**
See also CA 112

Gebler, Carlo (Ernest) 1954- .... **CLC 39**
See also CA 119; 133

Gee, Maggie (Mary) 1948- .... **CLC 57**
See also CA 130

Gee, Maurice (Gough) 1931- .... **CLC 29**
See also CA 97-100; SATA 46

Gelbart, Larry (Simon) 1923- ... **CLC 21, 61**
See also CA 73-76; CANR 45

Gelber, Jack 1932- .... **CLC 1, 6, 14, 79**
See also CA 1-4R; CANR 2; DLB 7

Gellhorn, Martha (Ellis) 1908- .. **CLC 14, 60**
See also CA 77-80; CANR 44; DLBY 82

Genet, Jean
1910-1986 ...... **CLC 1, 2, 5, 10, 14, 44,
46; DAM DRAM**
See also CA 13-16R; CANR 18; DLB 72;
DLBY 86; MTCW

Gent, Peter 1942- .... **CLC 29**
See also AITN 1; CA 89-92; DLBY 82

Gentlewoman in New England, A
See Bradstreet, Anne

Gentlewoman in Those Parts, A
See Bradstreet, Anne

George, Jean Craighead 1919- ...... **CLC 35**
See also AAYA 8; CA 5-8R; CANR 25;
CLR 1; DLB 52; JRDA; MAICYA;
SATA 2, 68

George, Stefan (Anton)
1868-1933 .... **TCLC 2, 14**
See also CA 104

Georges, Georges Martin
See Simenon, Georges (Jacques Christian)

Gerhardi, William Alexander
See Gerhardie, William Alexander

Gerhardie, William Alexander
1895-1977 .... **CLC 5**
See also CA 25-28R; 73-76; CANR 18;
DLB 36

Gerstler, Amy 1956- .... **CLC 70**
See also CA 146

Gertler, T. .... **CLC 34**
See also CA 116; 121; INT 121

gfgg......................... **CLC XvXzc**

Ghalib...................... **NCLC 39**
See also Ghalib, Hsadullah Khan

Ghalib, Hsadullah Khan 1797-1869
See Ghalib
See also DAM POET

Ghelderode, Michel de
1898-1962 .... **CLC 6, 11; DAM DRAM**
See also CA 85-88; CANR 40

Ghiselin, Brewster 1903- .... **CLC 23**
See also CA 13-16R; CAAS 10; CANR 13

Ghose, Zulfikar 1935-............. **CLC 42**
See also CA 65-68

Ghosh, Amitav 1956- .... **CLC 44**
See also CA 147

Giacosa, Giuseppe 1847-1906 ...... **TCLC 7**
See also CA 104

Gibb, Lee
See Waterhouse, Keith (Spencer)

Gibbon, Lewis Grassic .... **TCLC 4**
See also Mitchell, James Leslie

Gibbons, Kaye
1960- .... **CLC 50, 88; DAM POP**
See also CA 151

Gibran, Kahlil
1883-1931 .... **TCLC 1, 9; DAM POET,
POP; PC 9**
See also CA 104; 150

Gibran, Khalil
See Gibran, Kahlil

Gibson, William
1914- .... **CLC 23; DA; DAB; DAC;
DAM DRAM, MST**
See also CA 9-12R; CANR 9, 42; DLB 7;
SATA 66

Gibson, William (Ford)
1948- .... **CLC 39, 63; DAM POP**
See also AAYA 12; CA 126; 133; CANR 52

Gide, Andre (Paul Guillaume)
1869-1951 .... **TCLC 5, 12, 36; DA;
DAB; DAC; DAM MST, NOV; SSC 13;
WLC**
See also CA 104; 124; DLB 65; MTCW

Gifford, Barry (Colby) 1946-....... **CLC 34**
See also CA 65-68; CANR 9, 30, 40

Gilbert, W(illiam) S(chwenck)
1836-1911 ..... **TCLC 3; DAM DRAM,
POET**
See also CA 104; SATA 36

Gilbreth, Frank B., Jr. 1911-....... **CLC 17**
See also CA 9-12R; SATA 2

Gilchrist, Ellen
1935- .... **CLC 34, 48; DAM POP;
SSC 14**
See also CA 113; 116; CANR 41; DLB 130;
MTCW

Giles, Molly 1942- .... **CLC 39**
See also CA 126

Gill, Patrick
See Creasey, John

Gilliam, Terry (Vance) 1940-...... **CLC 21**
See also Monty Python
See also CA 108; 113; CANR 35; INT 113

Gillian, Jerry
See Gilliam, Terry (Vance)

Gilliatt, Penelope (Ann Douglass)
1932-1993 .... **CLC 2, 10, 13, 53**
See also AITN 2; CA 13-16R; 141;
CANR 49; DLB 14

Gilman, Charlotte (Anna) Perkins (Stetson)
1860-1935 .... **TCLC 9, 37; SSC 13**
See also CA 106; 150

Gilmour, David 1949-............. **CLC 35**
See also CA 138, 147

Gilpin, William 1724-1804....... **NCLC 30**

Gilray, J. D.
See Mencken, H(enry) L(ouis)

Gilroy, Frank D(aniel) 1925-........ **CLC 2**
See also CA 81-84; CANR 32; DLB 7

Ginsberg, Allen
1926- ...... **CLC 1, 2, 3, 4, 6, 13, 36, 69;
DA; DAB; DAC; DAM MST, POET;
PC 4; WLC 3**
See also AITN 1; CA 1-4R; CANR 2, 41;
CDALB 1941-1968; DLB 5, 16; MTCW

Ginzburg, Natalia
1916-1991 .... **CLC 5, 11, 54, 70**
See also CA 85-88; 135; CANR 33; MTCW

Giono, Jean 1895-1970.......... **CLC 4, 11**
See also CA 45-48; 29-32R; CANR 2, 35;
DLB 72; MTCW

Giovanni, Nikki
1943- ...... **CLC 2, 4, 19, 64; BLC; DA;
DAB; DAC; DAM MST, MULT, POET**
See also AITN 1; BW 2; CA 29-32R;
CAAS 6; CANR 18, 41; CLR 6; DLB 5,
41; INT CANR-18; MAICYA; MTCW;
SATA 24

Giovene, Andrea 1904-............. **CLC 7**
See also CA 85-88

Gippius, Zinaida (Nikolayevna) 1869-1945
See Hippius, Zinaida
See also CA 106

Giraudoux, (Hippolyte) Jean
1882-1944 .... **TCLC 2, 7; DAM DRAM**
See also CA 104; DLB 65

Gironella, Jose Maria 1917- .... **CLC 11**
See also CA 101

Gissing, George (Robert)
1857-1903 .... **TCLC 3, 24, 47**
See also CA 105; DLB 18, 135

Giurlani, Aldo
See Palazzeschi, Aldo

Gladkov, Fyodor (Vasilyevich)
1883-1958 .... **TCLC 27**

Glanville, Brian (Lester) 1931- ...... **CLC 6**
See also CA 5-8R; CAAS 9; CANR 3;
DLB 15, 139; SATA 42

Glasgow, Ellen (Anderson Gholson)
1873(?)-1945 .... **TCLC 2, 7**
See also CA 104; DLB 9, 12

Glaspell, Susan (Keating)
1882(?)-1948 .... **TCLC 55**
See also CA 110; DLB 7, 9, 78; YABC 2

Glassco, John 1909-1981 . . . . **CLC 9**
See also CA 13-16R; 102; CANR 15;
DLB 68

Glasscock, Amnesia
See Steinbeck, John (Ernst)

Glasser, Ronald J. 1940(?)- . . . . **CLC 37**

Glassman, Joyce
See Johnson, Joyce

Glendinning, Victoria 1937- . . . . **CLC 50**
See also CA 120; 127; DLB 155

Glissant, Edouard
1928- . . . . **CLC 10, 68; DAM MULT**

Gloag, Julian 1930- . . . . **CLC 40**
See also AITN 1; CA 65-68; CANR 10

Glowacki, Aleksander
See Prus, Boleslaw

Gluck, Louise (Elisabeth)
1943- . . . . **CLC 7, 22, 44, 81;
DAM POET; PC 16**
See also CA 33-36R; CANR 40; DLB 5

Gobineau, Joseph Arthur (Comte) de
1816-1882 . . . . **NCLC 17**
See also DLB 123

Godard, Jean-Luc 1930- . . . . **CLC 20**
See also CA 93-96

Godden, (Margaret) Rumer 1907- . . . **CLC 53**
See also AAYA 6; CA 5-8R; CANR 4, 27,
36; CLR 20; DLB 161; MAICYA;
SAAS 12; SATA 3, 36

Godoy Alcayaga, Lucila 1889-1957
See Mistral, Gabriela
See also BW 2; CA 104; 131; DAM MULT;
HW; MTCW

Godwin, Gail (Kathleen)
1937- . . . . **CLC 5, 8, 22, 31, 69;
DAM POP**
See also CA 29-32R; CANR 15, 43; DLB 6;
INT CANR-15; MTCW

Godwin, William 1756-1836 . . . . . . **NCLC 14**
See also CDBLB 1789-1832; DLB 39, 104,
142, 158, 163

Goethe, Johann Wolfgang von
1749-1832 . . . . **NCLC 4, 22, 34; DA;
DAB; DAC; DAM DRAM, MST,
POET; PC 5; WLC 3**
See also DLB 94

Gogarty, Oliver St. John
1878-1957 . . . . **TCLC 15**
See also CA 109; 150; DLB 15, 19

Gogol, Nikolai (Vasilyevich)
1809-1852 . . . . **NCLC 5, 15, 31; DA;
DAB; DAC; DAM DRAM, MST; DC 1;
SSC 4; WLC**

Goines, Donald
1937(?)-1974 . . . . **CLC 80; BLC;
DAM MULT, POP**
See also AITN 1; BW 1; CA 124; 114;
DLB 33

Gold, Herbert 1924- . . . . **CLC 4, 7, 14, 42**
See also CA 9-12R; CANR 17, 45; DLB 2;
DLBY 81

Goldbarth, Albert 1948- . . . . **CLC 5, 38**
See also CA 53-56; CANR 6, 40; DLB 120

Goldberg, Anatol 1910-1982 . . . . **CLC 34**
See also CA 131; 117

Goldemberg, Isaac 1945- . . . . **CLC 52**
See also CA 69-72; CAAS 12; CANR 11,
32; HW

Golding, William (Gerald)
1911-1993 . . . . **CLC 1, 2, 3, 8, 10, 17, 27,
58, 81; DA; DAB; DAC; DAM MST,
NOV; WLC**
See also AAYA 5; CA 5-8R; 141;
CANR 13, 33; CDBLB 1945-1960;
DLB 15, 100; MTCW

Goldman, Emma 1869-1940 . . . . . . **TCLC 13**
See also CA 110; 150

Goldman, Francisco 1955- . . . . **CLC 76**

Goldman, William (W.) 1931- . . . . **CLC 1, 48**
See also CA 9-12R; CANR 29; DLB 44

Goldmann, Lucien 1913-1970 . . . . . . **CLC 24**
See also CA 25-28; CAP 2

Goldoni, Carlo
1707-1793 . . . . **LC 4; DAM DRAM**

Goldsberry, Steven 1949- . . . . **CLC 34**
See also CA 131

Goldsmith, Oliver
1728-1774 . . . . . . **LC 2; DA; DAB; DAC;
DAM DRAM, MST, NOV, POET;
WLC**
See also CDBLB 1660-1789; DLB 39, 89,
104, 109, 142; SATA 26

Goldsmith, Peter
See Priestley, J(ohn) B(oynton)

Gombrowicz, Witold
1904-1969 . . . . **CLC 4, 7, 11, 49;
DAM DRAM**
See also CA 19-20; 25-28R; CAP 2

Gomez de la Serna, Ramon
1888-1963 . . . . **CLC 9**
See also CA 116; HW

Goncharov, Ivan Alexandrovich
1812-1891 . . . . **NCLC 1**

Goncourt, Edmond (Louis Antoine Huot) de
1822-1896 . . . . **NCLC 7**
See also DLB 123

Goncourt, Jules (Alfred Huot) de
1830-1870 . . . . **NCLC 7**
See also DLB 123

Gontier, Fernande 19(?)- . . . . **CLC 50**

Goodman, Paul 1911-1972 . . . . **CLC 1, 2, 4, 7**
See also CA 19-20; 37-40R; CANR 34;
CAP 2; DLB 130; MTCW

Gordimer, Nadine
1923- . . . . **CLC 3, 5, 7, 10, 18, 33, 51, 70;
DA; DAB; DAC; DAM MST, NOV;
SSC 17**
See also CA 5-8R; CANR 3, 28;
INT CANR-28; MTCW

Gordon, Adam Lindsay
1833-1870 . . . . **NCLC 21**

Gordon, Caroline
1895-1981 . . . **CLC 6, 13, 29, 83; SSC 15**
See also CA 11-12; 103; CANR 36; CAP 1;
DLB 4, 9, 102; DLBY 81; MTCW

Gordon, Charles William 1860-1937
See Connor, Ralph
See also CA 109

Gordon, Mary (Catherine)
1949- . . . . **CLC 13, 22**
See also CA 102; CANR 44; DLB 6;
DLBY 81; INT 102; MTCW

Gordon, Sol 1923- . . . . **CLC 26**
See also CA 53-56; CANR 4; SATA 11

Gordone, Charles
1925-1995 . . . . . **CLC 1, 4; DAM DRAM**
See also BW 1; CA 93-96; 150; DLB 7;
INT 93-96; MTCW

Gorenko, Anna Andreevna
See Akhmatova, Anna

Gorky, Maxim . . . . **TCLC 8; DAB; WLC**
See also Peshkov, Alexei Maximovich

Goryan, Sirak
See Saroyan, William

Gosse, Edmund (William)
1849-1928 . . . . **TCLC 28**
See also CA 117; DLB 57, 144

Gotlieb, Phyllis Fay (Bloom)
1926- . . . . **CLC 18**
See also CA 13-16R; CANR 7; DLB 88

Gottesman, S. D.
See Kornbluth, C(yril) M.; Pohl, Frederik

Gottfried von Strassburg
fl. c. 1210- . . . . **CMLC 10**
See also DLB 138

Gould, Lois . . . . **CLC 4, 10**
See also CA 77-80; CANR 29; MTCW

Gourmont, Remy (-Marie-Charles) de
1858-1915 . . . . **TCLC 17**
See also CA 109; 150

Govier, Katherine 1948- . . . . **CLC 51**
See also CA 101; CANR 18, 40

Goyen, (Charles) William
1915-1983 . . . . **CLC 5, 8, 14, 40**
See also AITN 2; CA 5-8R; 110; CANR 6;
DLB 2; DLBY 83; INT CANR-6

Goytisolo, Juan
1931- . . . . . **CLC 5, 10, 23; DAM MULT;
HLC**
See also CA 85-88; CANR 32; HW; MTCW

Gozzano, Guido 1883-1916 . . . . **PC 10**
See also DLB 114

Gozzi, (Conte) Carlo 1720-1806 . . **NCLC 23**

Grabbe, Christian Dietrich
1801-1836 . . . . **NCLC 2**
See also DLB 133

Grace, Patricia 1937- . . . . **CLC 56**

Gracian y Morales, Baltasar
1601-1658 . . . . **LC 15**

Gracq, Julien . . . . **CLC 11, 48**
See also Poirier, Louis
See also DLB 83

Grade, Chaim 1910-1982 . . . . **CLC 10**
See also CA 93-96; 107

Graduate of Oxford, A
See Ruskin, John

Graham, John
See Phillips, David Graham

Graham, Jorie 1951- . . . . **CLC 48**
See also CA 111; DLB 120

Graham, R(obert) B(ontine) Cunninghame
See Cunninghame Graham, R(obert)
B(ontine)
See also DLB 98, 135

Graham, Robert
See Haldeman, Joe (William)

Graham, Tom
See Lewis, (Harry) Sinclair

Graham, W(illiam) S(ydney)
1918-1986 . . . . CLC 29
See also CA 73-76; 118; DLB 20

Graham, Winston (Mawdsley)
1910- . . . . CLC 23
See also CA 49-52; CANR 2, 22, 45;
DLB 77

Grahame, Kenneth
1859-1932 . . . . TCLC 64; DAB
See also CA 108; 136; CLR 5; DLB 34, 141;
MAICYA; YABC 1

Grant, Skeeter
See Spiegelman, Art

Granville-Barker, Harley
1877-1946 . . . . . . TCLC 2; DAM DRAM
See also Barker, Harley Granville
See also CA 104

Grass, Guenter (Wilhelm)
1927- . . . . . CLC 1, 2, 4, 6, 11, 15, 22, 32,
49, 88; DA; DAB; DAC; DAM MST,
NOV; WLC
See also CA 13-16R; CANR 20; DLB 75,
124; MTCW

Gratton, Thomas
See Hulme, T(homas) E(rnest)

Grau, Shirley Ann
1929- . . . . CLC 4, 9; SSC 15
See also CA 89-92; CANR 22; DLB 2;
INT CANR-22; MTCW

Gravel, Fern
See Hall, James Norman

Graver, Elizabeth 1964- . . . . CLC 70
See also CA 135

Graves, Richard Perceval 1945- . . . . CLC 44
See also CA 65-68; CANR 9, 26, 51

Graves, Robert (von Ranke)
1895-1985 . . . . . . CLC 1, 2, 6, 11, 39, 44,
45; DAB; DAC; DAM MST, POET;
PC 6
See also CA 5-8R; 117; CANR 5, 36;
CDBLB 1914-1945, DLB 20, 100;
DLBY 85; MTCW; SATA 45

Graves, Valerie
See Bradley, Marion Zimmer

Gray, Alasdair (James) 1934- . . . . . . CLC 41
See also CA 126; CANR 47; INT 126;
MTCW

Gray, Amlin 1946 . . . . CLC 29
See also CA 138

Gray, Francine du Plessix
1930- . . . . CLC 22; DAM NOV
See also BEST 90:3; CA 61-64; CAAS 2;
CANR 11, 33; INT CANR-11; MTCW

Gray, John (Henry) 1866-1934 . . . . TCLC 19
See also CA 119

Gray, Simon (James Holliday)
1936- . . . . CLC 9, 14, 36
See also AITN 1; CA 21-24R; CAAS 3;
CANR 32; DLB 13; MTCW

Gray, Spalding 1941- . . CLC 49; DAM POP
See also CA 128

Gray, Thomas
1716-1771 . . . . . . LC 4; DA; DAB; DAC;
DAM MST; PC 2; WLC
See also CDBLB 1660-1789; DLB 109

Grayson, David
See Baker, Ray Stannard

Grayson, Richard (A.) 1951- . . . . CLC 38
See also CA 85-88; CANR 14, 31

Greeley, Andrew M(oran)
1928- . . . . CLC 28; DAM POP
See also CA 5-8R; CAAS 7; CANR 7, 43;
MTCW

Green, Anna Katharine
1846-1935 . . . . TCLC 63
See also CA 112

Green, Brian
See Card, Orson Scott

Green, Hannah
See Greenberg, Joanne (Goldenberg)

Green, Hannah . . . . CLC 3
See also CA 73-76

Green, Henry . . . . CLC 2, 13
See also Yorke, Henry Vincent
See also DLB 15

Green, Julian (Hartridge) 1900-
See Green, Julien
See also CA 21-24R; CANR 33; DLB 4, 72;
MTCW

Green, Julien . . . . CLC 3, 11, 77
See also Green, Julian (Hartridge)

Green, Paul (Eliot)
1894-1981 . . . . . . CLC 25; DAM DRAM
See also AITN 1; CA 5-8R; 103; CANR 3;
DLB 7, 9; DLBY 81

Greenberg, Ivan 1908-1973
See Rahv, Philip
See also CA 85-88

Greenberg, Joanne (Goldenberg)
1932- . . . . CLC 7, 30
See also AAYA 12; CA 5-8R; CANR 14,
32; SATA 25

Greenberg, Richard 1959(?)- . . . . CLC 57
See also CA 138

Greene, Bette 1934- . . . . CLC 30
See also AAYA 7; CA 53-56; CANR 4;
CLR 2; JRDA; MAICYA; SAAS 16;
SATA 8

Greene, Gael . . . . CLC 8
See also CA 13-16R; CANR 10

Greene, Graham
1904-1991 . . . . CLC 1, 3, 6, 9, 14, 18, 27,
37, 70, 72; DA; DAB; DAC; DAM MST,
NOV; WLC
See also AITN 2; CA 13-16R; 133;
CANR 35; CDBLB 1945-1960; DLB 13,
15, 77, 100, 162; DLBY 91; MTCW;
SATA 20

Greer, Richard
See Silverberg, Robert

Gregor, Arthur 1923- . . . . CLC 9
See also CA 25-28R; CAAS 10; CANR 11;
SATA 36

Gregor, Lee
See Pohl, Frederik

Gregory, Isabella Augusta (Persse)
1852-1932 . . . . TCLC 1
See also CA 104; DLB 10

Gregory, J. Dennis
See Williams, John A(lfred)

Grendon, Stephen
See Derleth, August (William)

Grenville, Kate 1950- . . . . CLC 61
See also CA 118; CANR 53

Grenville, Pelham
See Wodehouse, P(elham) G(renville)

Greve, Felix Paul (Berthold Friedrich)
1879-1948
See Grove, Frederick Philip
See also CA 104; 141; DAC; DAM MST

Grey, Zane
1872-1939 . . . . TCLC 6; DAM POP
See also CA 104; 132; DLB 9; MTCW

Grieg, (Johan) Nordahl (Brun)
1902-1943 . . . . TCLC 10
See also CA 107

Grieve, C(hristopher) M(urray)
1892-1978 . . . . CLC 11, 19; DAM POET
See also MacDiarmid, Hugh; Pteleon
See also CA 5-8R; 85-88; CANR 33;
MTCW

Griffin, Gerald 1803-1840 . . . . NCLC 7
See also DLB 159

Griffin, John Howard 1920-1980 . . . . CLC 68
See also AITN 1; CA 1-4R; 101; CANR 2

Griffin, Peter 1942- . . . . CLC 39
See also CA 136

Griffiths, Trevor 1935- . . . . CLC 13, 52
See also CA 97-100; CANR 45; DLB 13

Grigson, Geoffrey (Edward Harvey)
1905-1985 . . . . CLC 7, 39
See also CA 25-28R; 118; CANR 20, 33;
DLB 27; MTCW

Grillparzer, Franz 1791-1872 . . . . . . NCLC 1
See also DLB 133

Grimble, Reverend Charles James
See Eliot, T(homas) S(tearns)

Grimke, Charlotte L(ottie) Forten
1837(?)-1914
See Forten, Charlotte L.
See also BW 1; CA 117; 124; DAM MULT,
POET

Grimm, Jacob Ludwig Karl
1785-1863 . . . . NCLC 3
See also DLB 90; MAICYA; SATA 22

Grimm, Wilhelm Karl 1786-1859 . . NCLC 3
See also DLB 90; MAICYA; SATA 22

Grimmelshausen, Johann Jakob Christoffel
von 1621-1676 . . . . LC 6
See also DLB 168

Grindel, Eugene 1895-1952
See Eluard, Paul
See also CA 104

Grisham, John 1955- . . CLC 84; DAM POP
See also AAYA 14; CA 138; CANR 47

Grossman, David 1954- . . . . CLC 67
See also CA 138

Grossman, Vasily (Semenovich)
1905-1964 . . . . CLC 41
See also CA 124; 130; MTCW

Grove, Frederick Philip . . . . TCLC 4
See also Greve, Felix Paul (Berthold
Friedrich)
See also DLB 92

Grubb
See Crumb, R(obert)

Grumbach, Doris (Isaac)
1918- . . . . CLC 13, 22, 64
See also CA 5-8R; CAAS 2; CANR 9, 42;
INT CANR-9

Grundtvig, Nicolai Frederik Severin
1783-1872 . . . . NCLC 1

Grunge
See Crumb, R(obert)

Grunwald, Lisa 1959- . . . . CLC 44
See also CA 120

Guare, John
1938- . . . . CLC 8, 14, 29, 67;
DAM DRAM
See also CA 73-76; CANR 21; DLB 7;
MTCW

Gudjonsson, Halldor Kiljan 1902-
See Laxness, Halldor
See also CA 103

Guenter, Erich
See Eich, Guenter

Guest, Barbara 1920- . . . . CLC 34
See also CA 25-28R; CANR 11, 44; DLB 5

Guest, Judith (Ann)
1936- . . . . CLC 8, 30; DAM NOV, POP
See also AAYA 7; CA 77-80; CANR 15;
INT CANR-15; MTCW

Guevara, Che . . . . CLC 87; HLC
See also Guevara (Serna), Ernesto

Guevara (Serna), Ernesto 1928-1967
See Guevara, Che
See also CA 127; 111; DAM MULT; HW

Guild, Nicholas M. 1944- . . . . CLC 33
See also CA 93-96

Guillemin, Jacques
See Sartre, Jean-Paul

Guillen, Jorge
1893-1984 . . . . . . CLC 11; DAM MULT,
POET
See also CA 89-92; 112; DLB 108; HW

Guillen, Nicolas (Cristobal)
1902-1989 . . . . CLC 48, 79; BLC;
DAM MST, MULT, POET; HLC
See also BW 2; CA 116; 125; 129; HW

Guillevic, (Eugene) 1907- . . . . CLC 33
See also CA 93-96

Guillois
See Desnos, Robert

Guillois, Valentin
See Desnos, Robert

Guiney, Louise Imogen
1861-1920 . . . . TCLC 41
See also DLB 54

Guiraldes, Ricardo (Guillermo)
1886-1927 . . . . TCLC 39
See also CA 131; HW; MTCW

Gumilev, Nikolai Stephanovich
1886-1921 . . . . TCLC 60

Gunesekera, Romesh . . . . CLC 91

Gunn, Bill . . . . CLC 5
See also Gunn, William Harrison
See also DLB 38

Gunn, Thom(son William)
1929- . . . . CLC 3, 6, 18, 32, 81;
DAM POET
See also CA 17-20R; CANR 9, 33;
CDBLB 1960 to Present; DLB 27;
INT CANR-33; MTCW

Gunn, William Harrison 1934(?)-1989
See Gunn, Bill
See also AITN 1; BW 1; CA 13-16R; 128;
CANR 12, 25

Gunnars, Kristjana 1948- . . . . CLC 69
See also CA 113; DLB 60

Gurganus, Allan
1947- . . . . CLC 70; DAM POP
See also BEST 90:1; CA 135

Gurney, A(lbert) R(amsdell), Jr.
1930- . . . . CLC 32, 50, 54; DAM DRAM
See also CA 77-80; CANR 32

Gurney, Ivor (Bertie) 1890-1937 . . . TCLC 33

Gurney, Peter
See Gurney, A(lbert) R(amsdell), Jr.

Guro, Elena 1877-1913 . . . . TCLC 56

Gustafson, Ralph (Barker) 1909- . . . . CLC 36
See also CA 21-24R; CANR 8, 45; DLB 88

Gut, Gom
See Simenon, Georges (Jacques Christian)

Guterson, David 1956- . . . . CLC 91
See also CA 132

Guthrie, A(lfred) B(ertram), Jr.
1901-1991 . . . . CLC 23
See also CA 57-60; 134; CANR 24; DLB 6;
SATA 62; SATA-Obit 67

Guthrie, Isobel
See Grieve, C(hristopher) M(urray)

Guthrie, Woodrow Wilson 1912-1967
See Guthrie, Woody
See also CA 113; 93-96

Guthrie, Woody . . . . CLC 35
See also Guthrie, Woodrow Wilson

Guy, Rosa (Cuthbert) 1928- . . . . CLC 26
See also AAYA 4; BW 2; CA 17-20R;
CANR 14, 34; CLR 13; DLB 33; JRDA;
MAICYA; SATA 14, 62

Gwendolyn
See Bennett, (Enoch) Arnold

H. D. . . . . CLC 3, 8, 14, 31, 34, 73; PC 5
See also Doolittle, Hilda

H. de V.
See Buchan, John

Haavikko, Paavo Juhani
1931- . . . . CLC 18, 34
See also CA 106

Habbema, Koos
See Heijermans, Herman

Hacker, Marilyn
1942- . . . . CLC 5, 9, 23, 72, 91;
DAM POET
See also CA 77-80; DLB 120

Haggard, H(enry) Rider
1856-1925 . . . . TCLC 11
See also CA 108; 148; DLB 70, 156;
SATA 16

Hagiosy, L.
See Larbaud, Valery (Nicolas)

Hagiwara Sakutaro 1886-1942 . . . . TCLC 60

Haig, Fenil
See Ford, Ford Madox

Haig-Brown, Roderick (Langmere)
1908-1976 . . . . CLC 21
See also CA 5-8R; 69-72; CANR 4, 38;
CLR 31; DLB 88; MAICYA; SATA 12

Hailey, Arthur
1920- . . . . CLC 5; DAM NOV, POP
See also AITN 2; BEST 90:3; CA 1-4R;
CANR 2, 36; DLB 88; DLBY 82; MTCW

Hailey, Elizabeth Forsythe 1938- . . . CLC 40
See also CA 93-96; CAAS 1; CANR 15, 48;
INT CANR-15

Haines, John (Meade) 1924- . . . . CLC 58
See also CA 17-20R; CANR 13, 34; DLB 5

Hakluyt, Richard 1552-1616 . . . . LC 31

Haldeman, Joe (William) 1943- . . . . . CLC 61
See also CA 53-56; CANR 6; DLB 8;
INT CANR-6

Haley, Alex(ander Murray Palmer)
1921-1992 . . . . CLC 8, 12, 76; BLC; DA;
DAB; DAC; DAM MST, MULT, POP
See also BW 2; CA 77-80; 136; DLB 38;
MTCW

Haliburton, Thomas Chandler
1796-1865 . . . . NCLC 15
See also DLB 11, 99

Hall, Donald (Andrew, Jr.)
1928- . . CLC 1, 13, 37, 59; DAM POET
See also CA 5-8R; CAAS 7; CANR 2, 44;
DLB 5; SATA 23

Hall, Frederic Sauser
See Sauser-Hall, Frederic

Hall, James
See Kuttner, Henry

Hall, James Norman 1887-1951 . . . TCLC 23
See also CA 123; SATA 21

Hall, (Marguerite) Radclyffe
1886-1943 . . . . TCLC 12
See also CA 110; 150

Hall, Rodney 1935- . . . . CLC 51
See also CA 109

Halleck, Fitz-Greene 1790-1867 . . NCLC 47
See also DLB 3

Halliday, Michael
See Creasey, John

Halpern, Daniel 1945- . . . . CLC 14
See also CA 33-36R

Hamburger, Michael (Peter Leopold)
1924- . . . . CLC 5, 14
See also CA 5-8R; CAAS 4; CANR 2, 47;
DLB 27

Hamill, Pete 1935- . . . . CLC 10
See also CA 25-28R; CANR 18

Hamilton, Alexander
1755(?)-1804 . . . . NCLC 49
See also DLB 37

Hamilton, Clive
See Lewis, C(live) S(taples)

Hamilton, Edmond 1904-1977 . . . . . . CLC 1
See also CA 1-4R; CANR 3; DLB 8

Hamilton, Eugene (Jacob) Lee
See Lee-Hamilton, Eugene (Jacob)

Hamilton, Franklin
See Silverberg, Robert

Hamilton, Gail
See Corcoran, Barbara

Hamilton, Mollie
See Kaye, M(ary) M(argaret)

Hamilton, (Anthony Walter) Patrick
1904-1962 . . . . CLC 51
See also CA 113; DLB 10

Hamilton, Virginia
1936- . . . . CLC 26; DAM MULT
See also AAYA 2; BW 2; CA 25-28R;
CANR 20, 37; CLR 1, 11, 40; DLB 33,
52; INT CANR-20; JRDA; MAICYA;
MTCW; SATA 4, 56, 79

Hammett, (Samuel) Dashiell
1894-1961 . . . . CLC 3, 5, 10, 19, 47;
SSC 17
See also AITN 1; CA 81-84; CANR 42;
CDALB 1929-1941; DLBD 6; MTCW

Hammon, Jupiter
1711(?)-1800(?) . . . . NCLC 5; BLC;
DAM MULT, POET; PC 16
See also DLB 31, 50

Hammond, Keith
See Kuttner, Henry

Hamner, Earl (Henry), Jr. 1923- . . . CLC 12
See also AITN 2; CA 73-76; DLB 6

Hampton, Christopher (James)
1946- . . . . CLC 4
See also CA 25-28R; DLB 13; MTCW

Hamsun, Knut . . . . TCLC 2, 14, 49
See also Pedersen, Knut

Handke, Peter
1942- . . . . CLC 5, 8, 10, 15, 38;
DAM DRAM, NOV
See also CA 77-80; CANR 33; DLB 85,
124; MTCW

Hanley, James 1901-1985 . . . CLC 3, 5, 8, 13
See also CA 73-76; 117; CANR 36; MTCW

Hannah, Barry 1942- . . . . CLC 23, 38, 90
See also CA 108; 110; CANR 43; DLB 6;
INT 110; MTCW

Hannon, Ezra
See Hunter, Evan

Hansberry, Lorraine (Vivian)
1930-1965 . . . . . . CLC 17, 62; BLC; DA;
DAB; DAC; DAM DRAM, MST,
MULT; DC 2
See also BW 1; CA 109; 25-28R; CABS 3;
CDALB 1941-1968; DLB 7, 38; MTCW

Hansen, Joseph 1923- . . . . CLC 38
See also CA 29-32R; CAAS 17; CANR 16,
44; INT CANR-16

Hansen, Martin A. 1909-1955 . . . . . TCLC 32

Hanson, Kenneth O(stlin) 1922- . . . . CLC 13
See also CA 53-56; CANR 7

Hardwick, Elizabeth
1916- . . . . CLC 13; DAM NOV
See also CA 5-8R; CANR 3, 32; DLB 6;
MTCW

Hardy, Thomas
1840-1928 . . . . . . TCLC 4, 10, 18, 32, 48,
53; DA; DAB; DAC; DAM MST, NOV,
POET; PC 8; SSC 2; WLC
See also CA 104; 123; CDBLB 1890-1914;
DLB 18, 19, 135; MTCW

Hare, David 1947- . . . . CLC 29, 58
See also CA 97-100; CANR 39; DLB 13;
MTCW

Harford, Henry
See Hudson, W(illiam) H(enry)

Hargrave, Leonie
See Disch, Thomas M(ichael)

Harjo, Joy 1951- . . . CLC 83; DAM MULT
See also CA 114; CANR 35; DLB 120;
NNAL

Harlan, Louis R(udolph) 1922- . . . . . CLC 34
See also CA 21-24R; CANR 25

Harling, Robert 1951(?)- . . . . CLC 53
See also CA 147

Harmon, William (Ruth) 1938- . . . . . CLC 38
See also CA 33-36R; CANR 14, 32, 35;
SATA 65

Harper, F. E. W.
See Harper, Frances Ellen Watkins

Harper, Frances E. W.
See Harper, Frances Ellen Watkins

Harper, Frances E. Watkins
See Harper, Frances Ellen Watkins

Harper, Frances Ellen
See Harper, Frances Ellen Watkins

Harper, Frances Ellen Watkins
1825-1911 . . . . TCLC 14; BLC;
DAM MULT, POET
See also BW 1; CA 111; 125; DLB 50

Harper, Michael S(teven) 1938- . . CLC 7, 22
See also BW 1; CA 33-36R; CANR 24;
DLB 41

Harper, Mrs. F. E. W.
See Harper, Frances Ellen Watkins

Harris, Christie (Lucy) Irwin
1907- . . . . CLC 12
See also CA 5-8R; CANR 6; DLB 88;
JRDA; MAICYA; SAAS 10; SATA 6, 74

Harris, Frank 1856-1931 . . . . TCLC 24
See also CA 109; 150; DLB 156

Harris, George Washington
1814-1869 . . . . NCLC 23
See also DLB 3, 11

Harris, Joel Chandler
1848-1908 . . . . TCLC 2; SSC 19
See also CA 104; 137; DLB 11, 23, 42, 78,
91; MAICYA; YABC 1

Harris, John (Wyndham Parkes Lucas)
Beynon 1903-1969
See Wyndham, John
See also CA 102; 89-92

Harris, MacDonald . . . . CLC 9
See also Heiney, Donald (William)

Harris, Mark 1922- . . . . CLC 19
See also CA 5-8R; CAAS 3; CANR 2;
DLB 2; DLBY 80

Harris, (Theodore) Wilson 1921- . . . . CLC 25
See also BW 2; CA 65-68; CAAS 16;
CANR 11, 27; DLB 117; MTCW

Harrison, Elizabeth Cavanna 1909-
See Cavanna, Betty
See also CA 9-12R; CANR 6, 27

Harrison, Harry (Max) 1925- . . . . . . CLC 42
See also CA 1-4R; CANR 5, 21; DLB 8;
SATA 4

Harrison, James (Thomas)
1937- . . . . CLC 6, 14, 33, 66; SSC 19
See also CA 13-16R; CANR 8, 51;
DLBY 82; INT CANR-8

Harrison, Jim
See Harrison, James (Thomas)

Harrison, Kathryn 1961- . . . . CLC 70
See also CA 144

Harrison, Tony 1937- . . . . CLC 43
See also CA 65-68; CANR 44; DLB 40;
MTCW

Harriss, Will(ard Irvin) 1922- . . . . . . CLC 34
See also CA 111

Harson, Sley
See Ellison, Harlan (Jay)

Hart, Ellis
See Ellison, Harlan (Jay)

Hart, Josephine
1942(?)- . . . . CLC 70; DAM POP
See also CA 138

Hart, Moss
1904-1961 . . . . . . CLC 66; DAM DRAM
See also CA 109; 89-92; DLB 7

Harte, (Francis) Bret(t)
1836(?)-1902 . . . . TCLC 1, 25; DA; DAC;
DAM MST; SSC 8; WLC
See also CA 104; 140; CDALB 1865-1917;
DLB 12, 64, 74, 79; SATA 26

Hartley, L(eslie) P(oles)
1895-1972 . . . . CLC 2, 22
See also CA 45-48; 37-40R; CANR 33;
DLB 15, 139; MTCW

Hartman, Geoffrey H. 1929- . . . . CLC 27
See also CA 117; 125; DLB 67

Hartmann von Aue
c. 1160-c. 1205 . . . . CMLC 15
See also DLB 138

Hartmann von Aue 1170-1210 . . . . CMLC 15

Haruf, Kent 1943- . . . . CLC 34
See also CA 149

Harwood, Ronald
1934- . . . . CLC 32; DAM DRAM, MST
See also CA 1-4R; CANR 4; DLB 13

Hasek, Jaroslav (Matej Frantisek)
1883-1923 . . . . TCLC 4
See also CA 104; 129; MTCW

Hass, Robert 1941- . . . . . CLC 18, 39; PC 16
See also CA 111; CANR 30, 50; DLB 105

Hastings, Hudson
See Kuttner, Henry

Hastings, Selina . . . . CLC 44

Housman, Laurence 1865-1959 . . . . . **TCLC 7**
See also CA 106; DLB 10; SATA 25

Howard, Elizabeth Jane 1923- . . . **CLC 7, 29**
See also CA 5-8R; CANR 8

Howard, Maureen 1930- . . . . . **CLC 5, 14, 46**
See also CA 53-56; CANR 31; DLBY 83;
INT CANR-31; MTCW

Howard, Richard 1929- . . . . . . **CLC 7, 10, 47**
See also AITN 1; CA 85-88; CANR 25;
DLB 5; INT CANR-25

Howard, Robert Ervin 1906-1936 . . . **TCLC 8**
See also CA 105

Howard, Warren F.
See Pohl, Frederik

Howe, Fanny 1940- . . . . **CLC 47**
See also CA 117; SATA-Brief 52

Howe, Irving 1920-1993 . . . . **CLC 85**
See also CA 9-12R; 141; CANR 21, 50;
DLB 67; MTCW

Howe, Julia Ward 1819-1910 . . . . . **TCLC 21**
See also CA 117; DLB 1

Howe, Susan 1937- . . . . **CLC 72**
See also DLB 120

Howe, Tina 1937- . . . . **CLC 48**
See also CA 109

Howell, James 1594(?)-1666 . . . . **LC 13**
See also DLB 151

Howells, W. D.
See Howells, William Dean

Howells, William D.
See Howells, William Dean

Howells, William Dean
1837-1920 . . . . **TCLC 7, 17, 41**
See also CA 104; 134; CDALB 1865-1917;
DLB 12, 64, 74, 79

Howes, Barbara 1914-1996 . . . . **CLC 15**
See also CA 9-12R; 151; CAAS 3;
CANR 53; SATA 5

Hrabal, Bohumil 1914- . . . . **CLC 13, 67**
See also CA 106; CAAS 12

Hsun, Lu
See Lu Hsun

Hubbard, L(afayette) Ron(ald)
1911-1986 . . . . **CLC 43; DAM POP**
See also CA 77-80; 118; CANR 52

Huch, Ricarda (Octavia)
1864-1947 . . . . **TCLC 13**
See also CA 111; DLB 66

Huddle, David 1942- . . . . **CLC 49**
See also CA 57-60; CAAS 20; DLB 130

Hudson, Jeffrey
See Crichton, (John) Michael

Hudson, W(illiam) H(enry)
1841-1922 . . . . **TCLC 29**
See also CA 115; DLB 98, 153; SATA 35

Hueffer, Ford Madox
See Ford, Ford Madox

Hughart, Barry 1934- . . . . **CLC 39**
See also CA 137

Hughes, Colin
See Creasey, John

Hughes, David (John) 1930- . . . . **CLC 48**
See also CA 116; 129; DLB 14

Hughes, Edward James
See Hughes, Ted
See also DAM MST, POET

Hughes, (James) Langston
1902-1967 . . . . . **CLC 1, 5, 10, 15, 35, 44;
BLC; DA; DAB; DAC; DAM DRAM,
MST, MULT, POET; DC 3; PC 1;
SSC 6; WLC**
See also AAYA 12; BW 1; CA 1-4R;
25-28R; CANR 1, 34; CDALB 1929-1941;
CLR 17; DLB 4, 7, 48, 51, 86; JRDA;
MAICYA; MTCW; SATA 4, 33

Hughes, Richard (Arthur Warren)
1900-1976 . . . . . . **CLC 1, 11; DAM NOV**
See also CA 5-8R; 65-68; CANR 4;
DLB 15, 161; MTCW; SATA 8;
SATA-Obit 25

Hughes, Ted
1930- . . . . **CLC 2, 4, 9, 14, 37; DAB;
DAC; PC 7**
See also Hughes, Edward James
See also CA 1-4R; CANR 1, 33; CLR 3;
DLB 40, 161; MAICYA; MTCW;
SATA 49; SATA-Brief 27

Hugo, Richard F(ranklin)
1923-1982 . . . . **CLC 6, 18, 32;
DAM POET**
See also CA 49-52; 108; CANR 3; DLB 5

Hugo, Victor (Marie)
1802-1885 . . . . **NCLC 3, 10, 21; DA;
DAB; DAC; DAM DRAM, MST, NOV,
POET; WLC**
See also DLB 119; SATA 47

Huidobro, Vicente
See Huidobro Fernandez, Vicente Garcia

Huidobro Fernandez, Vicente Garcia
1893-1948 . . . . **TCLC 31**
See also CA 131; HW

Hulme, Keri 1947- . . . . **CLC 39**
See also CA 125; INT 125

Hulme, T(homas) E(rnest)
1883-1917 . . . . **TCLC 21**
See also CA 117; DLB 19

Hume, David 1711-1776 . . . . **LC 7**
See also DLB 104

Humphrey, William 1924- . . . . **CLC 45**
See also CA 77-80; DLB 6

Humphreys, Emyr Owen 1919- . . . . . **CLC 47**
See also CA 5-8R; CANR 3, 24; DLB 15

Humphreys, Josephine 1945- . . . . **CLC 34, 57**
See also CA 121; 127; INT 127

Huneker, James Gibbons
1857-1921 . . . . **TCLC 65**
See also DLB 71

Hungerford, Pixie
See Brinsmead, H(esba) F(ay)

Hunt, E(verette) Howard, (Jr.)
1918- . . . . **CLC 3**
See also AITN 1; CA 45-48; CANR 2, 47

Hunt, Kyle
See Creasey, John

Hunt, (James Henry) Leigh
1784-1859 . . . . . . **NCLC 1; DAM POET**

Hunt, Marsha 1946- . . . . **CLC 70**
See also BW 2; CA 143

Hunt, Violet 1866-1942 . . . . **TCLC 53**
See also DLB 162

Hunter, E. Waldo
See Sturgeon, Theodore (Hamilton)

Hunter, Evan
1926- . . . . **CLC 11, 31; DAM POP**
See also CA 5-8R; CANR 5, 38; DLBY 82;
INT CANR-5; MTCW; SATA 25

Hunter, Kristin (Eggleston) 1931- . . . **CLC 35**
See also AITN 1; BW 1; CA 13-16R;
CANR 13; CLR 3; DLB 33;
INT CANR-13; MAICYA; SAAS 10;
SATA 12

Hunter, Mollie 1922- . . . . **CLC 21**
See also McIlwraith, Maureen Mollie
Hunter
See also AAYA 13; CANR 37; CLR 25;
DLB 161; JRDA; MAICYA; SAAS 7;
SATA 54

Hunter, Robert (?)-1734 . . . . **LC 7**

Hurston, Zora Neale
1903-1960 . . . . **CLC 7, 30, 61; BLC; DA;
DAC; DAM MST, MULT, NOV; SSC 4**
See also AAYA 15; BW 1; CA 85-88;
DLB 51, 86; MTCW

Huston, John (Marcellus)
1906-1987 . . . . **CLC 20**
See also CA 73-76; 123; CANR 34; DLB 26

Hustvedt, Siri 1955- . . . . **CLC 76**
See also CA 137

Hutten, Ulrich von 1488-1523 . . . . **LC 16**

Huxley, Aldous (Leonard)
1894-1963 . . . . . **CLC 1, 3, 4, 5, 8, 11, 18,
35, 79; DA; DAB; DAC; DAM MST,
NOV; WLC**
See also AAYA 11; CA 85-88; CANR 44;
CDBLB 1914-1945; DLB 36, 100, 162;
MTCW; SATA 63

Huysmans, Charles Marie Georges
1848-1907
See Huysmans, Joris-Karl
See also CA 104

Huysmans, Joris-Karl . . . . **TCLC 7**
See also Huysmans, Charles Marie Georges
See also DLB 123

Hwang, David Henry
1957- . . . . **CLC 55; DAM DRAM; DC 4**
See also CA 127; 132; INT 132

Hyde, Anthony 1946- . . . . **CLC 42**
See also CA 136

Hyde, Margaret O(ldroyd) 1917- . . . **CLC 21**
See also CA 1-4R; CANR 1, 36; CLR 23;
JRDA; MAICYA; SAAS 8; SATA 1, 42,
76

Hynes, James 1956(?)- . . . . **CLC 65**

Ian, Janis 1951- . . . . **CLC 21**
See also CA 105

Ibanez, Vicente Blasco
See Blasco Ibanez, Vicente

Ibarguengoitia, Jorge 1928-1983 . . . . **CLC 37**
See also CA 124; 113; HW

Ibsen, Henrik (Johan)
1828-1906 . . . . **TCLC 2, 8, 16, 37, 52;
DA; DAB; DAC; DAM DRAM, MST;
DC 2; WLC**
See also CA 104; 141

Ibuse Masuji 1898-1993 . . . . **CLC 22**
See also CA 127; 141

Ichikawa, Kon 1915- . . . . **CLC 20**
See also CA 121

Idle, Eric 1943- . . . . **CLC 21**
See also Monty Python
See also CA 116; CANR 35

Ignatow, David 1914- . . . . . . **CLC 4, 7, 14, 40**
See also CA 9-12R; CAAS 3; CANR 31;
DLB 5

Ihimaera, Witi 1944- . . . . **CLC 46**
See also CA 77-80

Ilf, Ilya . . . . **TCLC 21**
See also Fainzilberg, Ilya Arnoldovich

Illyes, Gyula 1902-1983 . . . . **PC 16**
See also CA 114; 109

Immermann, Karl (Lebrecht)
1796-1840 . . . . **NCLC 4, 49**
See also DLB 133

Inclan, Ramon (Maria) del Valle
See Valle-Inclan, Ramon (Maria) del

Infante, G(uillermo) Cabrera
See Cabrera Infante, G(uillermo)

Ingalls, Rachel (Holmes) 1940- . . . . . **CLC 42**
See also CA 123; 127

Ingamells, Rex 1913-1955 . . . . **TCLC 35**

Inge, William Motter
1913-1973 . . **CLC 1, 8, 19; DAM DRAM**
See also CA 9-12R; CDALB 1941-1968;
DLB 7; MTCW

Ingelow, Jean 1820-1897 . . . . **NCLC 39**
See also DLB 35, 163; SATA 33

Ingram, Willis J.
See Harris, Mark

Innaurato, Albert (F.) 1948(?)- . . **CLC 21, 60**
See also CA 115; 122; INT 122

Innes, Michael
See Stewart, J(ohn) I(nnes) M(ackintosh)

Ionesco, Eugene
1909-1994 . . . . **CLC 1, 4, 6, 9, 11, 15, 41,
86; DA; DAB; DAC; DAM DRAM,
MST; WLC**
See also CA 9-12R; 144; MTCW; SATA 7;
SATA-Obit 79

Iqbal, Muhammad 1873-1938 . . . . . **TCLC 28**

Ireland, Patrick
See O'Doherty, Brian

Iron, Ralph
See Schreiner, Olive (Emilie Albertina)

Irving, John (Winslow)
1942- . . . . . **CLC 13, 23, 38; DAM NOV,
POP**
See also AAYA 8; BEST 89:3; CA 25-28R;
CANR 28; DLB 6; DLBY 82; MTCW

Irving, Washington
1783-1859 . . . . . **NCLC 2, 19; DA; DAB;
DAM MST; SSC 2; WLC**
See also CDALB 1640-1865; DLB 3, 11, 30,
59, 73, 74; YABC 2

Irwin, P. K.
See Page, P(atricia) K(athleen)

Isaacs, Susan 1943- . . . **CLC 32; DAM POP**
See also BEST 89:1; CA 89-92; CANR 20,
41; INT CANR-20; MTCW

Isherwood, Christopher (William Bradshaw)
1904-1986 . . . . **CLC 1, 9, 11, 14, 44;
DAM DRAM, NOV**
See also CA 13-16R; 117; CANR 35;
DLB 15; DLBY 86; MTCW

Ishiguro, Kazuo
1954- . . . . . . **CLC 27, 56, 59; DAM NOV**
See also BEST 90:2; CA 120; CANR 49;
MTCW

Ishikawa, Takuboku
1886(?)-1912 . . . . **TCLC 15;
DAM POET; PC 10**
See also CA 113

Iskander, Fazil 1929- . . . . **CLC 47**
See also CA 102

Isler, Alan . . . . **CLC 91**

Ivan IV 1530-1584 . . . . **LC 17**

Ivanov, Vyacheslav Ivanovich
1866-1949 . . . . **TCLC 33**
See also CA 122

Ivask, Ivar Vidrik 1927-1992 . . . . **CLC 14**
See also CA 37-40R; 139; CANR 24

Ives, Morgan
See Bradley, Marion Zimmer

J. R. S.
See Gogarty, Oliver St. John

Jabran, Kahlil
See Gibran, Kahlil

Jabran, Khalil
See Gibran, Kahlil

Jackson, Daniel
See Wingrove, David (John)

Jackson, Jesse 1908-1983 . . . . **CLC 12**
See also BW 1; CA 25-28R; 109; CANR 27;
CLR 28; MAICYA; SATA 2, 29;
SATA-Obit 48

Jackson, Laura (Riding) 1901-1991
See Riding, Laura
See also CA 65-68; 135; CANR 28; DLB 48

Jackson, Sam
See Trumbo, Dalton

Jackson, Sara
See Wingrove, David (John)

Jackson, Shirley
1919-1965 . . . . **CLC 11, 60, 87; DA;
DAC; DAM MST; SSC 9; WLC**
See also AAYA 9; CA 1-4R; 25-28R;
CANR 4, 52; CDALB 1941-1968; DLB 6;
SATA 2

Jacob, (Cyprien-)Max 1876-1944 . . . **TCLC 6**
See also CA 104

Jacobs, Jim 1942- . . . . **CLC 12**
See also CA 97-100; INT 97-100

Jacobs, W(illiam) W(ymark)
1863-1943 . . . . **TCLC 22**
See also CA 121; DLB 135

Jacobsen, Jens Peter 1847-1885 . . **NCLC 34**

Jacobsen, Josephine 1908- . . . . **CLC 48**
See also CA 33-36R; CAAS 18; CANR 23,
48

Jacobson, Dan 1929- . . . . **CLC 4, 14**
See also CA 1-4R; CANR 2, 25; DLB 14;
MTCW

Jacqueline
See Carpentier (y Valmont), Alejo

Jagger, Mick 1944- . . . . **CLC 17**

Jakes, John (William)
1932- . . . . . . **CLC 29; DAM NOV, POP**
See also BEST 89:4; CA 57-60; CANR 10,
43; DLBY 83; INT CANR-10; MTCW;
SATA 62

James, Andrew
See Kirkup, James

James, C(yril) L(ionel) R(obert)
1901-1989 . . . . **CLC 33**
See also BW 2; CA 117; 125; 128; DLB 125;
MTCW

James, Daniel (Lewis) 1911-1988
See Santiago, Danny
See also CA 125

James, Dynely
See Mayne, William (James Carter)

James, Henry Sr. 1811-1882 . . . . . **NCLC 53**

James, Henry
1843-1916 . . . . . . **TCLC 2, 11, 24, 40, 47,
64; DA; DAB; DAC; DAM MST, NOV;
SSC 8; WLC**
See also CA 104; 132; CDALB 1865-1917;
DLB 12, 71, 74; DLBD 13; MTCW

James, M. R.
See James, Montague (Rhodes)
See also DLB 156

James, Montague (Rhodes)
1862-1936 . . . . **TCLC 6; SSC 16**
See also CA 104

James, P. D. . . . . **CLC 18, 46**
See also White, Phyllis Dorothy James
See also BEST 90:2; CDBLB 1960 to
Present; DLB 87

James, Philip
See Moorcock, Michael (John)

James, William 1842-1910 . . . . . **TCLC 15, 32**
See also CA 109

James I 1394-1437 . . . . **LC 20**

Jameson, Anna 1794-1860 . . . . **NCLC 43**
See also DLB 99, 166

Jami, Nur al-Din 'Abd al-Rahman
1414-1492 . . . . **LC 9**

Jandl, Ernst 1925- . . . . **CLC 34**

Janowitz, Tama
1957- . . . . **CLC 43; DAM POP**
See also CA 106; CANR 52

Japrisot, Sebastien 1931- . . . . **CLC 90**

Jarrell, Randall
1914-1965 . . . . **CLC 1, 2, 6, 9, 13, 49;
DAM POET**
See also CA 5-8R; 25-28R; CABS 2;
CANR 6, 34; CDALB 1941-1968; CLR 6;
DLB 48, 52; MAICYA; MTCW; SATA 7

Jarry, Alfred
1873-1907 . . . . **TCLC 2, 14;
DAM DRAM; SSC 20**
See also CA 104

Jarvis, E. K.
See Bloch, Robert (Albert); Ellison, Harlan
(Jay); Silverberg, Robert

Jeake, Samuel, Jr.
See Aiken, Conrad (Potter)

Jonson, Ben(jamin)
1572(?)-1637 ..... **LC 6, 33; DA; DAB;**
DAC; DAM DRAM, MST, POET;
DC 4; WLC
See also CDBLB Before 1660; DLB 62, 121

Jordan, June
1936- ..... **CLC 5, 11, 23; DAM MULT,**
POET
See also AAYA 2; BW 2; CA 33-36R;
CANR 25; CLR 10; DLB 38; MAICYA;
MTCW; SATA 4

Jordan, Pat(rick M.) 1941- .... **CLC 37**
See also CA 33-36R

Jorgensen, Ivar
See Ellison, Harlan (Jay)

Jorgenson, Ivar
See Silverberg, Robert

Josephus, Flavius c. 37-100 ..... **CMLC 13**

Josipovici, Gabriel 1940- .... **CLC 6, 43**
See also CA 37-40R; CAAS 8; CANR 47;
DLB 14

Joubert, Joseph 1754-1824 .... **NCLC 9**

Jouve, Pierre Jean 1887-1976 ..... **CLC 47**
See also CA 65-68

Joyce, James (Augustine Aloysius)
1882-1941 .... **TCLC 3, 8, 16, 35, 52;**
DA; DAB; DAC; DAM MST, NOV,
POET; SSC 3; WLC
See also CA 104; 126; CDBLB 1914-1945;
DLB 10, 19, 36, 162; MTCW

Jozsef, Attila 1905-1937 .... **TCLC 22**
See also CA 116

Juana Ines de la Cruz 1651(?)-1695 ... **LC 5**

Judd, Cyril
See Kornbluth, C(yril) M.; Pohl, Frederik

Julian of Norwich 1342(?)-1416(?) .... **LC 6**
See also DLB 146

Juniper, Alex
See Hospital, Janette Turner

Junius
See Luxemburg, Rosa

Just, Ward (Swift) 1935- .... **CLC 4, 27**
See also CA 25-28R; CANR 32;
INT CANR-32

Justice, Donald (Rodney)
1925- .... **CLC 6, 19; DAM POET**
See also CA 5-8R; CANR 26; DLBY 83;
INT CANR-26

Juvenal c. 55-c. 127 .... **CMLC 8**

Juvenis
See Bourne, Randolph S(illiman)

Kacew, Romain 1914-1980
See Gary, Romain
See also CA 108; 102

Kadare, Ismail 1936- .... **CLC 52**

Kadohata, Cynthia .... **CLC 59**
See also CA 140

Kafka, Franz
1883-1924 .... **TCLC 2, 6, 13, 29, 47, 53;**
DA; DAB; DAC; DAM MST, NOV;
SSC 5; WLC
See also CA 105; 126; DLB 81; MTCW

Kahanovitsch, Pinkhes
See Der Nister

Kahn, Roger 1927- .... **CLC 30**
See also CA 25-28R; CANR 44; SATA 37

Kain, Saul
See Sassoon, Siegfried (Lorraine)

Kaiser, Georg 1878-1945 .... **TCLC 9**
See also CA 106; DLB 124

Kaletski, Alexander 1946- .... **CLC 39**
See also CA 118; 143

Kalidasa fl. c. 400- .... **CMLC 9**

Kallman, Chester (Simon)
1921-1975 .... **CLC 2**
See also CA 45-48; 53-56; CANR 3

Kaminsky, Melvin 1926-
See Brooks, Mel
See also CA 65-68; CANR 16

Kaminsky, Stuart M(elvin) 1934- ... **CLC 59**
See also CA 73-76; CANR 29, 53

Kane, Paul
See Simon, Paul

Kane, Wilson
See Bloch, Robert (Albert)

Kanin, Garson 1912- .... **CLC 22**
See also AITN 1; CA 5-8R; CANR 7;
DLB 7

Kaniuk, Yoram 1930- .... **CLC 19**
See also CA 134

Kant, Immanuel 1724-1804 ...... **NCLC 27**
See also DLB 94

Kantor, MacKinlay 1904-1977 ...... **CLC 7**
See also CA 61-64; 73-76; DLB 9, 102

Kaplan, David Michael 1946- ...... **CLC 50**

Kaplan, James 1951- .... **CLC 59**
See also CA 135

Karageorge, Michael
See Anderson, Poul (William)

Karamzin, Nikolai Mikhailovich
1766-1826 .... **NCLC 3**
See also DLB 150

Karapanou, Margarita 1946- .... **CLC 13**
See also CA 101

Karinthy, Frigyes 1887-1938 ...... **TCLC 47**

Karl, Frederick R(obert) 1927- ..... **CLC 34**
See also CA 5-8R; CANR 3, 44

Kastel, Warren
See Silverberg, Robert

Kataev, Evgeny Petrovich 1903-1942
See Petrov, Evgeny
See also CA 120

Kataphusin
See Ruskin, John

Katz, Steve 1935- .... **CLC 47**
See also CA 25-28R; CAAS 14; CANR 12;
DLBY 83

Kauffman, Janet 1945- .... **CLC 42**
See also CA 117; CANR 43; DLBY 86

Kaufman, Bob (Garnell)
1925-1986 .... **CLC 49**
See also BW 1; CA 41-44R; 118; CANR 22;
DLB 16, 41

Kaufman, George S.
1889-1961 ...... **CLC 38; DAM DRAM**
See also CA 108; 93-96; DLB 7; INT 108

Kaufman, Sue .... **CLC 3, 8**
See also Barondess, Sue K(aufman)

Kavafis, Konstantinos Petrou 1863-1933
See Cavafy, C(onstantine) P(eter)
See also CA 104

Kavan, Anna 1901-1968 ...... **CLC 5, 13, 82**
See also CA 5-8R; CANR 6; MTCW

Kavanagh, Dan
See Barnes, Julian

Kavanagh, Patrick (Joseph)
1904-1967 .... **CLC 22**
See also CA 123; 25-28R; DLB 15, 20;
MTCW

Kawabata, Yasunari
1899-1972 .... **CLC 2, 5, 9, 18;**
DAM MULT; SSC 17
See also CA 93-96; 33-36R

Kaye, M(ary) M(argaret) 1909- ..... **CLC 28**
See also CA 89-92; CANR 24; MTCW;
SATA 62

Kaye, Mollie
See Kaye, M(ary) M(argaret)

Kaye-Smith, Sheila 1887-1956 ..... **TCLC 20**
See also CA 118; DLB 36

Kaymor, Patrice Maguilene
See Senghor, Leopold Sedar

Kazan, Elia 1909- .... **CLC 6, 16, 63**
See also CA 21-24R; CANR 32

Kazantzakis, Nikos
1883(?)-1957 .... **TCLC 2, 5, 33**
See also CA 105; 132; MTCW

Kazin, Alfred 1915- .... **CLC 34, 38**
See also CA 1-4R; CAAS 7; CANR 1, 45;
DLB 67

Keane, Mary Nesta (Skrine) 1904-1996
See Keane, Molly
See also CA 108; 114; 151

Keane, Molly .... **CLC 31**
See also Keane, Mary Nesta (Skrine)
See also INT 114

Keates, Jonathan 19(?)- .... **CLC 34**

Keaton, Buster 1895-1966 .... **CLC 20**

Keats, John
1795-1821 .... **NCLC 8; DA; DAB;**
DAC; DAM MST, POET; PC 1; WLC
See also CDBLB 1789-1832; DLB 96, 110

Keene, Donald 1922- .... **CLC 34**
See also CA 1-4R; CANR 5

Keillor, Garrison .... **CLC 40**
See also Keillor, Gary (Edward)
See also AAYA 2; BEST 89:3; DLBY 87;
SATA 58

Keillor, Gary (Edward) 1942-
See Keillor, Garrison
See also CA 111; 117; CANR 36;
DAM POP; MTCW

Keith, Michael
See Hubbard, L(afayette) Ron(ald)

Keller, Gottfried 1819-1890 .... **NCLC 2**
See also DLB 129

Kellerman, Jonathan
1949- .... **CLC 44; DAM POP**
See also BEST 90:1; CA 106; CANR 29, 51;
INT CANR-29

Kipling, (Joseph) Rudyard
1865-1936 ...... **TCLC 8, 17; DA; DAB;**
DAC; DAM MST, POET; PC 3; SSC 5;
WLC
See also CA 105; 120; CANR 33;
CDBLB 1890-1914; CLR 39; DLB 19, 34,
141, 156; MAICYA; MTCW; YABC 2

Kirkup, James 1918- .... **CLC 1**
See also CA 1-4R; CAAS 4; CANR 2;
DLB 27; SATA 12

Kirkwood, James 1930(?)-1989 ...... **CLC 9**
See also AITN 2; CA 1-4R; 128; CANR 6,
40

Kirshner, Sidney
See Kingsley, Sidney

Kis, Danilo 1935-1989 .... **CLC 57**
See also CA 109; 118; 129; MTCW

Kivi, Aleksis 1834-1872 .... **NCLC 30**

Kizer, Carolyn (Ashley)
1925- ..... **CLC 15, 39, 80; DAM POET**
See also CA 65-68; CAAS 5; CANR 24;
DLB 5

Klabund 1890-1928.............. **TCLC 44**
See also DLB 66

Klappert, Peter 1942-............. **CLC 57**
See also CA 33-36R; DLB 5

Klein, A(braham) M(oses)
1909-1972 .... **CLC 19; DAB; DAC;**
DAM MST
See also CA 101; 37-40R; DLB 68

Klein, Norma 1938-1989 .... **CLC 30**
See also AAYA 2; CA 41-44R; 128;
CANR 15, 37; CLR 2, 19;
INT CANR-15; JRDA; MAICYA;
SAAS 1; SATA 7, 57

Klein, T(heodore) E(ibon) D(onald)
1947- .... **CLC 34**
See also CA 119; CANR 44

Kleist, Heinrich von
1777-1811 .... **NCLC 2, 37;**
DAM DRAM; SSC 22
See also DLB 90

Klima, Ivan 1931-..... **CLC 56; DAM NOV**
See also CA 25-28R; CANR 17, 50

Klimentov, Andrei Platonovich 1899-1951
See Platonov, Andrei
See also CA 108

Klinger, Friedrich Maximilian von
1752-1831 .... **NCLC 1**
See also DLB 94

Klopstock, Friedrich Gottlieb
1724-1803 .... **NCLC 11**
See also DLB 97

Knebel, Fletcher 1911-1993........ **CLC 14**
See also AITN 1; CA 1-4R; 140; CAAS 3;
CANR 1, 36; SATA 36; SATA-Obit 75

Knickerbocker, Diedrich
See Irving, Washington

Knight, Etheridge
1931-1991 .... **CLC 40; BLC;**
DAM POET; PC 14
See also BW 1; CA 21-24R; 133; CANR 23;
DLB 41

Knight, Sarah Kemble 1666-1727 ..... **LC 7**
See also DLB 24

Knister, Raymond 1899-1932...... **TCLC 56**
See also DLB 68

Knowles, John
1926- ...... **CLC 1, 4, 10, 26; DA; DAC;**
DAM MST, NOV
See also AAYA 10; CA 17-20R; CANR 40;
CDALB 1968-1988; DLB 6; MTCW;
SATA 8, 89

Knox, Calvin M.
See Silverberg, Robert

Knye, Cassandra
See Disch, Thomas M(ichael)

Koch, C(hristopher) J(ohn) 1932- ... **CLC 42**
See also CA 127

Koch, Christopher
See Koch, C(hristopher) J(ohn)

Koch, Kenneth
1925-....... **CLC 5, 8, 44; DAM POET**
See also CA 1-4R; CANR 6, 36; DLB 5;
INT CANR-36; SATA 65

Kochanowski, Jan 1530-1584....... **LC 10**

Kock, Charles Paul de
1794-1871 .... **NCLC 16**

Koda Shigeyuki 1867-1947
See Rohan, Koda
See also CA 121

Koestler, Arthur
1905-1983 .... **CLC 1, 3, 6, 8, 15, 33**
See also CA 1-4R; 109; CANR 1, 33;
CDBLB 1945-1960; DLBY 83; MTCW

Kogawa, Joy Nozomi
1935- ...... **CLC 78; DAC; DAM MST,**
MULT
See also CA 101; CANR 19

Kohout, Pavel 1928-.............. **CLC 13**
See also CA 45-48; CANR 3

Koizumi, Yakumo
See Hearn, (Patricio) Lafcadio (Tessima
Carlos)

Kolmar, Gertrud 1894-1943....... **TCLC 40**

Komunyakaa, Yusef 1947-...... **CLC 86, 94**
See also CA 147; DLB 120

Konrad, George
See Konrad, Gyoergy

Konrad, Gyoergy 1933- ...... **CLC 4, 10, 73**
See also CA 85-88

Konwicki, Tadeusz 1926-..... **CLC 8, 28, 54**
See also CA 101; CAAS 9; CANR 39;
MTCW

Koontz, Dean R(ay)
1945- ...... **CLC 78; DAM NOV, POP**
See also AAYA 9; BEST 89:3, 90:2;
CA 108; CANR 19, 36, 52; MTCW

Kopit, Arthur (Lee)
1937- ..... **CLC 1, 18, 33; DAM DRAM**
See also AITN 1; CA 81-84; CABS 3;
DLB 7; MTCW

Kops, Bernard 1926-.............. **CLC 4**
See also CA 5-8R; DLB 13

Kornbluth, C(yril) M. 1923-1958.... **TCLC 8**
See also CA 105; DLB 8

Korolenko, V. G.
See Korolenko, Vladimir Galaktionovich

Korolenko, Vladimir
See Korolenko, Vladimir Galaktionovich

Korolenko, Vladimir G.
See Korolenko, Vladimir Galaktionovich

Korolenko, Vladimir Galaktionovich
1853-1921 .... **TCLC 22**
See also CA 121

Korzybski, Alfred (Habdank Skarbek)
1879-1950 .... **TCLC 61**
See also CA 123

Kosinski, Jerzy (Nikodem)
1933-1991 .... **CLC 1, 2, 3, 6, 10, 15, 53,**
70; DAM NOV
See also CA 17-20R; 134; CANR 9, 46;
DLB 2; DLBY 82; MTCW

Kostelanetz, Richard (Cory) 1940- .. **CLC 28**
See also CA 13-16R; CAAS 8; CANR 38

Kostrowitzki, Wilhelm Apollinaris de
1880-1918
See Apollinaire, Guillaume
See also CA 104

Kotlowitz, Robert 1924-........... **CLC 4**
See also CA 33-36R; CANR 36

Kotzebue, August (Friedrich Ferdinand) von
1761-1819 .... **NCLC 25**
See also DLB 94

Kotzwinkle, William 1938- ... **CLC 5, 14, 35**
See also CA 45-48; CANR 3, 44; CLR 6;
MAICYA; SATA 24, 70

Kozol, Jonathan 1936-............ **CLC 17**
See also CA 61-64; CANR 16, 45

Kozoll, Michael 1940(?)-.......... **CLC 35**

Kramer, Kathryn 19(?)-........... **CLC 34**

Kramer, Larry 1935- .. **CLC 42; DAM POP**
See also CA 124; 126

Krasicki, Ignacy 1735-1801....... **NCLC 8**

Krasinski, Zygmunt 1812-1859 .... **NCLC 4**

Kraus, Karl 1874-1936............ **TCLC 5**
See also CA 104; DLB 118

Kreve (Mickevicius), Vincas
1882-1954 .... **TCLC 27**

Kristeva, Julia 1941- .... **CLC 77**

Kristofferson, Kris 1936-.......... **CLC 26**
See also CA 104

Krizanc, John 1956-.............. **CLC 57**

Krleza, Miroslav 1893-1981......... **CLC 8**
See also CA 97-100; 105; CANR 50;
DLB 147

Kroetsch, Robert
1927- .... **CLC 5, 23, 57; DAC;**
DAM POET
See also CA 17-20R; CANR 8, 38; DLB 53;
MTCW

Kroetz, Franz
See Kroetz, Franz Xaver

Kroetz, Franz Xaver 1946- .... **CLC 41**
See also CA 130

Kroker, Arthur 1945-............. **CLC 77**

Kropotkin, Peter (Aleksieevich)
1842-1921 .... **TCLC 36**
See also CA 119

Krotkov, Yuri 1917-.............. **CLC 19**
See also CA 102

Lardner, Ring(gold) W(ilmer)
1885-1933 . . . . **TCLC 2, 14**
See also CA 104; 131; CDALB 1917-1929;
DLB 11, 25, 86; MTCW

Laredo, Betty
See Codrescu, Andrei

Larkin, Maia
See Wojciechowska, Maia (Teresa)

Larkin, Philip (Arthur)
1922-1985 . . . . **CLC 3, 5, 8, 9, 13, 18, 33,**
39, 64; DAB; DAM MST, POET
See also CA 5-8R; 117; CANR 24;
CDBLB 1960 to Present; DLB 27;
MTCW

Larra (y Sanchez de Castro), Mariano Jose de
1809-1837 . . . . **NCLC 17**

Larsen, Eric 1941- . . . . **CLC 55**
See also CA 132

Larsen, Nella
1891-1964 . . . . **CLC 37; BLC;**
DAM MULT
See also BW 1; CA 125; DLB 51

Larson, Charles R(aymond) 1938- . . . **CLC 31**
See also CA 53-56; CANR 4

Las Casas, Bartolome de 1474-1566 . . **LC 31**

Lasker-Schueler, Else 1869-1945 . . **TCLC 57**
See also DLB 66, 124

Latham, Jean Lee 1902- . . . . **CLC 12**
See also AITN 1; CA 5-8R; CANR 7;
MAICYA; SATA 2, 68

Latham, Mavis
See Clark, Mavis Thorpe

Lathen, Emma . . . . **CLC 2**
See also Hennissart, Martha; Latsis, Mary
J(ane)

Lathrop, Francis
See Leiber, Fritz (Reuter, Jr.)

Latsis, Mary J(ane)
See Lathen, Emma
See also CA 85-88

Lattimore, Richmond (Alexander)
1906-1984 . . . . **CLC 3**
See also CA 1-4R; 112; CANR 1

Laughlin, James 1914- . . . . **CLC 49**
See also CA 21-24R; CAAS 22; CANR 9,
47; DLB 48

Laurence, (Jean) Margaret (Wemyss)
1926-1987 . . . . **CLC 3, 6, 13, 50, 62;**
DAC; DAM MST; SSC 7
See also CA 5-8R; 121; CANR 33; DLB 53;
MTCW; SATA-Obit 50

Laurent, Antoine 1952- . . . . **CLC 50**

Lauscher, Hermann
See Hesse, Hermann

Lautreamont, Comte de
1846-1870 . . . . **NCLC 12; SSC 14**

Laverty, Donald
See Blish, James (Benjamin)

Lavin, Mary 1912-1996 . . **CLC 4, 18; SSC 4**
See also CA 9-12R; 151; CANR 33;
DLB 15; MTCW

Lavond, Paul Dennis
See Kornbluth, C(yril) M.; Pohl, Frederik

Lawler, Raymond Evenor 1922- . . . . **CLC 58**
See also CA 103

Lawrence, D(avid) H(erbert Richards)
1885-1930 . . . . **TCLC 2, 9, 16, 33, 48, 61;**
DA; DAB; DAC; DAM MST, NOV,
POET; SSC 4, 19; WLC
See also CA 104; 121; CDBLB 1914-1945;
DLB 10, 19, 36, 98, 162; MTCW

Lawrence, T(homas) E(dward)
1888-1935 . . . . **TCLC 18**
See also Dale, Colin
See also CA 115

Lawrence of Arabia
See Lawrence, T(homas) E(dward)

Lawson, Henry (Archibald Hertzberg)
1867-1922 . . . . **TCLC 27; SSC 18**
See also CA 120

Lawton, Dennis
See Faust, Frederick (Schiller)

Laxness, Halldor . . . . **CLC 25**
See also Gudjonsson, Halldor Kiljan

Layamon fl. c. 1200- . . . . **CMLC 10**
See also DLB 146

Laye, Camara
1928-1980 . . . . **CLC 4, 38; BLC;**
DAM MULT
See also BW 1; CA 85-88; 97-100;
CANR 25; MTCW

Layton, Irving (Peter)
1912- . . . . **CLC 2, 15; DAC; DAM MST,**
POET
See also CA 1-4R; CANR 2, 33, 43;
DLB 88; MTCW

Lazarus, Emma 1849-1887 . . . . **NCLC 8**

Lazarus, Felix
See Cable, George Washington

Lazarus, Henry
See Slavitt, David R(ytman)

Lea, Joan
See Neufeld, John (Arthur)

Leacock, Stephen (Butler)
1869-1944 . . **TCLC 2; DAC; DAM MST**
See also CA 104; 141; DLB 92

Lear, Edward 1812-1888 . . . . **NCLC 3**
See also CLR 1; DLB 32, 163, 166;
MAICYA; SATA 18

Lear, Norman (Milton) 1922- . . . . . . **CLC 12**
See also CA 73-76

Leavis, F(rank) R(aymond)
1895-1978 . . . . **CLC 24**
See also CA 21-24R; 77-80; CANR 44;
MTCW

Leavitt, David 1961- . . . **CLC 34; DAM POP**
See also CA 116; 122; CANR 50; DLB 130;
INT 122

Leblanc, Maurice (Marie Emile)
1864-1941 . . . . **TCLC 49**
See also CA 110

Lebowitz, Fran(ces Ann)
1951(?)- . . . . **CLC 11, 36**
See also CA 81-84; CANR 14;
INT CANR-14; MTCW

Lebrecht, Peter
See Tieck, (Johann) Ludwig

le Carre, John . . . . **CLC 3, 5, 9, 15, 28**
See also Cornwell, David (John Moore)
See also BEST 89:4; CDBLB 1960 to
Present; DLB 87

Le Clezio, J(ean) M(arie) G(ustave)
1940- . . . . **CLC 31**
See also CA 116; 128; DLB 83

Leconte de Lisle, Charles-Marie-Rene
1818-1894 . . . . **NCLC 29**

Le Coq, Monsieur
See Simenon, Georges (Jacques Christian)

Leduc, Violette 1907-1972 . . . . **CLC 22**
See also CA 13-14; 33-36R; CAP 1

Ledwidge, Francis 1887(?)-1917 . . . **TCLC 23**
See also CA 123; DLB 20

Lee, Andrea
1953- . . . . . **CLC 36; BLC; DAM MULT**
See also BW 1; CA 125

Lee, Andrew
See Auchincloss, Louis (Stanton)

Lee, Chang-rae 1965- . . . . **CLC 91**
See also CA 148

Lee, Don L. . . . . **CLC 2**
See also Madhubuti, Haki R.

Lee, George W(ashington)
1894-1976 . . . . **CLC 52; BLC;**
DAM MULT
See also BW 1; CA 125; DLB 51

Lee, (Nelle) Harper
1926- . . . . **CLC 12, 60; DA; DAB; DAC;**
DAM MST, NOV; WLC
See also AAYA 13; CA 13-16R; CANR 51;
CDALB 1941-1968; DLB 6; MTCW;
SATA 11

Lee, Helen Elaine 1959(?)- . . . . **CLC 86**
See also CA 148

Lee, Julian
See Latham, Jean Lee

Lee, Larry
See Lee, Lawrence

Lee, Laurie
1914- . . . . **CLC 90; DAB; DAM POP**
See also CA 77-80; CANR 33; DLB 27;
MTCW

Lee, Lawrence 1941-1990 . . . . **CLC 34**
See also CA 131; CANR 43

Lee, Manfred B(ennington)
1905-1971 . . . . **CLC 11**
See also Queen, Ellery
See also CA 1-4R; 29-32R; CANR 2;
DLB 137

Lee, Stan 1922- . . . . **CLC 17**
See also AAYA 5; CA 108; 111; INT 111

Lee, Tanith 1947- . . . . **CLC 46**
See also AAYA 15; CA 37-40R; CANR 53;
SATA 8, 88

Lee, Vernon . . . . **TCLC 5**
See also Paget, Violet
See also DLB 57, 153, 156

Lee, William
See Burroughs, William S(eward)

Lee, Willy
See Burroughs, William S(eward)

Lewis, (Percy) Wyndham
1884(?)-1957 . . . . TCLC 2, 9
See also CA 104; DLB 15

Lewisohn, Ludwig 1883-1955 . . . . . . TCLC 19
See also CA 107; DLB 4, 9, 28, 102

Leyner, Mark 1956- . . . . CLC 92
See also CA 110; CANR 28, 53

Lezama Lima, Jose
1910-1976 . . . . CLC 4, 10; DAM MULT
See also CA 77-80; DLB 113; HW

L'Heureux, John (Clarke) 1934- . . . . CLC 52
See also CA 13-16R; CANR 23, 45

Liddell, C. H.
See Kuttner, Henry

Lie, Jonas (Lauritz Idemil)
1833-1908(?) . . . . TCLC 5
See also CA 115

Lieber, Joel 1937-1971 . . . . CLC 6
See also CA 73-76; 29-32R

Lieber, Stanley Martin
See Lee, Stan

Lieberman, Laurence (James)
1935- . . . . CLC 4, 36
See also CA 17-20R; CANR 8, 36

Lieksman, Anders
See Haavikko, Paavo Juhani

Li Fei-kan 1904-
See Pa Chin
See also CA 105

Lifton, Robert Jay 1926- . . . . CLC 67
See also CA 17-20R; CANR 27;
INT CANR-27; SATA 66

Lightfoot, Gordon 1938- . . . . CLC 26
See also CA 109

Lightman, Alan P. 1948- . . . . CLC 81
See also CA 141

Ligotti, Thomas (Robert)
1953- . . . . CLC 44; SSC 16
See also CA 123; CANR 49

Li Ho 791-817 . . . . PC 13

Liliencron, (Friedrich Adolf Axel) Detlev von
1844-1909 . . . . TCLC 18
See also CA 117

Lilly, William 1602-1681 . . . . LC 27

Lima, Jose Lezama
See Lezama Lima, Jose

Lima Barreto, Afonso Henrique de
1881-1922 . . . . TCLC 23
See also CA 117

Limonov, Edward 1944- . . . . CLC 67
See also CA 137

Lin, Frank
See Atherton, Gertrude (Franklin Horn)

Lincoln, Abraham 1809-1865 . . . . . NCLC 18

Lind, Jakov . . . . CLC 1, 2, 4, 27, 82
See also Landwirth, Heinz
See also CAAS 4

Lindbergh, Anne (Spencer) Morrow
1906- . . . . CLC 82; DAM NOV
See also CA 17-20R; CANR 16; MTCW;
SATA 33

Lindsay, David 1878-1945 . . . . TCLC 15
See also CA 113

Lindsay, (Nicholas) Vachel
1879-1931 . . . . TCLC 17; DA; DAC;
DAM MST, POET; WLC
See also CA 114; 135; CDALB 1865-1917;
DLB 54; SATA 40

Linke-Poot
See Doeblin, Alfred

Linney, Romulus 1930- . . . . CLC 51
See also CA 1-4R; CANR 40, 44

Linton, Eliza Lynn 1822-1898 . . . . NCLC 41
See also DLB 18

Li Po 701-763 . . . . CMLC 2

Lipsius, Justus 1547-1606 . . . . LC 16

Lipsyte, Robert (Michael)
1938- . . . . CLC 21; DA; DAC;
DAM MST, NOV
See also AAYA 7; CA 17-20R; CANR 8;
CLR 23; JRDA; MAICYA; SATA 5, 68

Lish, Gordon (Jay) 1934- . . CLC 45; SSC 18
See also CA 113; 117; DLB 130; INT 117

Lispector, Clarice 1925-1977 . . . . . . CLC 43
See also CA 139; 116; DLB 113

Littell, Robert 1935(?)- . . . . CLC 42
See also CA 109; 112

Little, Malcolm 1925-1965
See Malcolm X
See also BW 1; CA 125; 111; DA; DAB;
DAC; DAM MST, MULT; MTCW

Littlewit, Humphrey Gent.
See Lovecraft, H(oward) P(hillips)

Litwos
See Sienkiewicz, Henryk (Adam Alexander
Pius)

Liu E 1857-1909 . . . . TCLC 15
See also CA 115

Lively, Penelope (Margaret)
1933- . . . . CLC 32, 50; DAM NOV
See also CA 41-44R; CANR 29; CLR 7;
DLB 14, 161; JRDA; MAICYA; MTCW;
SATA 7, 60

Livesay, Dorothy (Kathleen)
1909- . . . . CLC 4, 15, 79; DAC;
DAM MST, POET
See also AITN 2; CA 25-28R; CAAS 8;
CANR 36; DLB 68; MTCW

Livy c. 59B.C.-c. 17 . . . . CMLC 11

Lizardi, Jose Joaquin Fernandez de
1776-1827 . . . . NCLC 30

Llewellyn, Richard
See Llewellyn Lloyd, Richard Dafydd
Vivian
See also DLB 15

Llewellyn Lloyd, Richard Dafydd Vivian
1906-1983 . . . . CLC 7, 80
See also Llewellyn, Richard
See also CA 53-56; 111; CANR 7;
SATA 11; SATA-Obit 37

Llosa, (Jorge) Mario (Pedro) Vargas
See Vargas Llosa, (Jorge) Mario (Pedro)

Lloyd Webber, Andrew 1948-
See Webber, Andrew Lloyd
See also AAYA 1; CA 116; 149;
DAM DRAM; SATA 56

Llull, Ramon c. 1235-c. 1316 . . . . . CMLC 12

Locke, Alain (Le Roy)
1886-1954 . . . . TCLC 43
See also BW 1; CA 106; 124; DLB 51

Locke, John 1632-1704 . . . . LC 7, 35
See also DLB 101

Locke-Elliott, Sumner
See Elliott, Sumner Locke

Lockhart, John Gibson
1794-1854 . . . . NCLC 6
See also DLB 110, 116, 144

Lodge, David (John)
1935- . . . . CLC 36; DAM POP
See also BEST 90:1; CA 17-20R; CANR 19,
53; DLB 14; INT CANR-19; MTCW

Loennbohm, Armas Eino Leopold 1878-1926
See Leino, Eino
See also CA 123

Loewinsohn, Ron(ald William)
1937- . . . . CLC 52
See also CA 25-28R

Logan, Jake
See Smith, Martin Cruz

Logan, John (Burton) 1923-1987 . . . . . CLC 5
See also CA 77-80; 124; CANR 45; DLB 5

Lo Kuan-chung 1330(?)-1400(?) . . . . . . LC 12

Lombard, Nap
See Johnson, Pamela Hansford

London, Jack . . TCLC 9, 15, 39; SSC 4; WLC
See also London, John Griffith
See also AAYA 13; AITN 2;
CDALB 1865-1917; DLB 8, 12, 78;
SATA 18

London, John Griffith 1876-1916
See London, Jack
See also CA 110; 119; DA; DAB; DAC;
DAM MST, NOV; JRDA; MAICYA;
MTCW

Long, Emmett
See Leonard, Elmore (John, Jr.)

Longbaugh, Harry
See Goldman, William (W.)

Longfellow, Henry Wadsworth
1807-1882 . . . . . NCLC 2, 45; DA; DAB;
DAC; DAM MST, POET
See also CDALB 1640-1865; DLB 1, 59;
SATA 19

Longley, Michael 1939- . . . . CLC 29
See also CA 102; DLB 40

Longus fl. c. 2nd cent. - . . . . CMLC 7

Longway, A. Hugh
See Lang, Andrew

Lonnrot, Elias 1802-1884 . . . . NCLC 53

Lopate, Phillip 1943- . . . . CLC 29
See also CA 97-100; DLBY 80; INT 97-100

Lopez Portillo (y Pacheco), Jose
1920- . . . . CLC 46
See also CA 129; HW

Lopez y Fuentes, Gregorio
1897(?)-1966 . . . . CLC 32
See also CA 131; HW

Lorca, Federico Garcia
See Garcia Lorca, Federico

Machiavelli, Niccolo
1469-1527 ..... **LC 8; DA; DAB; DAC;
DAM MST**

MacInnes, Colin 1914-1976..... **CLC 4, 23**
See also CA 69-72; 65-68; CANR 21;
DLB 14; MTCW

MacInnes, Helen (Clark)
1907-1985 ..... **CLC 27, 39; DAM POP**
See also CA 1-4R; 117; CANR 1, 28;
DLB 87; MTCW; SATA 22;
SATA-Obit 44

Mackay, Mary 1855-1924
See Corelli, Marie
See also CA 118

Mackenzie, Compton (Edward Montague)
1883-1972 .... **CLC 18**
See also CA 21-22; 37-40R; CAP 2;
DLB 34, 100

Mackenzie, Henry 1745-1831 .... **NCLC 41**
See also DLB 39

Mackintosh, Elizabeth 1896(?)-1952
See Tey, Josephine
See also CA 110

MacLaren, James
See Grieve, C(hristopher) M(urray)

Mac Laverty, Bernard 1942-....... **CLC 31**
See also CA 116; 118; CANR 43; INT 118

MacLean, Alistair (Stuart)
1922-1987 .... **CLC 3, 13, 50, 63;
DAM POP**
See also CA 57-60; 121; CANR 28; MTCW;
SATA 23; SATA-Obit 50

Maclean, Norman (Fitzroy)
1902-1990 .... **CLC 78; DAM POP;
SSC 13**
See also CA 102; 132; CANR 49

MacLeish, Archibald
1892-1982 .... **CLC 3, 8, 14, 68;
DAM POET**
See also CA 9-12R; 106; CANR 33; DLB 4,
7, 45; DLBY 82; MTCW

MacLennan, (John) Hugh
1907-1990 .... **CLC 2, 14, 92; DAC;
DAM MST**
See also CA 5-8R; 142; CANR 33; DLB 68;
MTCW

MacLeod, Alistair
1936- ...... **CLC 56; DAC; DAM MST**
See also CA 123; DLB 60

MacNeice, (Frederick) Louis
1907-1963 ...... **CLC 1, 4, 10, 53; DAB;
DAM POET**
See also CA 85-88; DLB 10, 20; MTCW

MacNeill, Dand
See Fraser, George MacDonald

Macpherson, James 1736-1796 ...... **LC 29**
See also DLB 109

Macpherson, (Jean) Jay 1931-..... **CLC 14**
See also CA 5-8R; DLB 53

MacShane, Frank 1927-........... **CLC 39**
See also CA 9-12R; CANR 3, 33; DLB 111

Macumber, Mari
See Sandoz, Mari(e Susette)

Madach, Imre 1823-1864....... **NCLC 19**

Madden, (Jerry) David 1933- .... **CLC 5, 15**
See also CA 1-4R; CAAS 3; CANR 4, 45;
DLB 6; MTCW

Maddern, Al(an)
See Ellison, Harlan (Jay)

Madhubuti, Haki R.
1942- .... **CLC 6, 73; BLC;
DAM MULT, POET; PC 5**
See also Lee, Don L.
See also BW 2; CA 73-76; CANR 24, 51;
DLB 5, 41; DLBD 8

Maepenn, Hugh
See Kuttner, Henry

Maepenn, K. H.
See Kuttner, Henry

Maeterlinck, Maurice
1862-1949 ...... **TCLC 3; DAM DRAM**
See also CA 104; 136; SATA 66

Maginn, William 1794-1842....... **NCLC 8**
See also DLB 110, 159

Mahapatra, Jayanta
1928- .... **CLC 33; DAM MULT**
See also CA 73-76; CAAS 9; CANR 15, 33

Mahfouz, Naguib (Abdel Aziz Al-Sabilgi)
1911(?)-
See Mahfuz, Najib
See also BEST 89:2; CA 128; DAM NOV;
MTCW

Mahfuz, Najib .... **CLC 52, 55**
See also Mahfouz, Naguib (Abdel Aziz
Al-Sabilgi)
See also DLBY 88

Mahon, Derek 1941-.............. **CLC 27**
See also CA 113; 128; DLB 40

Mailer, Norman
1923- ...... **CLC 1, 2, 3, 4, 5, 8, 11, 14,
28, 39, 74; DA; DAB; DAC; DAM MST,
NOV, POP**
See also AITN 2; CA 9-12R; CABS 1;
CANR 28; CDALB 1968-1988; DLB 2,
16, 28; DLBD 3; DLBY 80, 83; MTCW

Maillet, Antonine 1929-...... **CLC 54; DAC**
See also CA 115; 120; CANR 46; DLB 60;
INT 120

Mais, Roger 1905-1955 .... **TCLC 8**
See also BW 1; CA 105; 124; DLB 125;
MTCW

Maistre, Joseph de 1753-1821 .... **NCLC 37**

Maitland, Frederic 1850-1906 ..... **TCLC 65**

Maitland, Sara (Louise) 1950-...... **CLC 49**
See also CA 69-72; CANR 13

Major, Clarence
1936- .... **CLC 3, 19, 48; BLC;
DAM MULT**
See also BW 2; CA 21-24R; CAAS 6;
CANR 13, 25, 53; DLB 33

Major, Kevin (Gerald)
1949- .... **CLC 26; DAC**
See also AAYA 16; CA 97-100; CANR 21,
38; CLR 11; DLB 60; INT CANR-21;
JRDA; MAICYA; SATA 32, 82

Maki, James
See Ozu, Yasujiro

Malabaila, Damiano
See Levi, Primo

Malamud, Bernard
1914-1986 ...... **CLC 1, 2, 3, 5, 8, 9, 11,
18, 27, 44, 78, 85; DA; DAB; DAC;
DAM MST, NOV, POP; SSC 15; WLC**
See also AAYA 16; CA 5-8R; 118; CABS 1;
CANR 28; CDALB 1941-1968; DLB 2,
28, 152; DLBY 80, 86; MTCW

Malaparte, Curzio 1898-1957 ..... **TCLC 52**

Malcolm, Dan
See Silverberg, Robert

Malcolm X .... **CLC 82; BLC**
See also Little, Malcolm

Malherbe, Francois de 1555-1628..... **LC 5**

Mallarme, Stephane
1842-1898 .... **NCLC 4, 41;
DAM POET; PC 4**

Mallet-Joris, Francoise 1930-...... **CLC 11**
See also CA 65-68; CANR 17; DLB 83

Malley, Ern
See McAuley, James Phillip

Mallowan, Agatha Christie
See Christie, Agatha (Mary Clarissa)

Maloff, Saul 1922-................. **CLC 5**
See also CA 33-36R

Malone, Louis
See MacNeice, (Frederick) Louis

Malone, Michael (Christopher)
1942- .... **CLC 43**
See also CA 77-80; CANR 14, 32

Malory, (Sir) Thomas
1410(?)-1471(?) ...... **LC 11; DA; DAB;
DAC; DAM MST**
See also CDBLB Before 1660; DLB 146;
SATA 59; SATA-Brief 33

Malouf, (George Joseph) David
1934- .... **CLC 28, 86**
See also CA 124; CANR 50

Malraux, (Georges-)Andre
1901-1976 ...... **CLC 1, 4, 9, 13, 15, 57;
DAM NOV**
See also CA 21-22; 69-72; CANR 34;
CAP 2; DLB 72; MTCW

Malzberg, Barry N(athaniel) 1939-... **CLC 7**
See also CA 61-64; CAAS 4; CANR 16;
DLB 8

Mamet, David (Alan)
1947- .... **CLC 9, 15, 34, 46, 91;
DAM DRAM; DC 4**
See also AAYA 3; CA 81-84; CABS 3;
CANR 15, 41; DLB 7; MTCW

Mamoulian, Rouben (Zachary)
1897-1987 .... **CLC 16**
See also CA 25-28R; 124

Mandelstam, Osip (Emilievich)
1891(?)-1938(?) ...... **TCLC 2, 6; PC 14**
See also CA 104; 150

Mander, (Mary) Jane 1877-1949... **TCLC 31**

Mandiargues, Andre Pieyre de....... **CLC 41**
See also Pieyre de Mandiargues, Andre
See also DLB 83

Mandrake, Ethel Belle
See Thurman, Wallace (Henry)

Mangan, James Clarence
1803-1849 .... **NCLC 27**

Maniere, J.-E.
See Giraudoux, (Hippolyte) Jean

Manley, (Mary) Delariviere
1672(?)-1724 . . . . LC 1
See also DLB 39, 80

Mann, Abel
See Creasey, John

Mann, (Luiz) Heinrich 1871-1950 . . . TCLC 9
See also CA 106; DLB 66

Mann, (Paul) Thomas
1875-1955 . . . . TCLC 2, 8, 14, 21, 35, 44,
60; DA; DAB; DAC; DAM MST, NOV;
SSC 5; WLC
See also CA 104; 128; DLB 66; MTCW

Mannheim, Karl 1893-1947 . . . . . . TCLC 65

Manning, David
See Faust, Frederick (Schiller)

Manning, Frederic 1887(?)-1935 . . . TCLC 25
See also CA 124

Manning, Olivia 1915-1980 . . . . . . CLC 5, 19
See also CA 5-8R; 101; CANR 29; MTCW

Mano, D. Keith 1942- . . . . CLC 2, 10
See also CA 25-28R; CAAS 6; CANR 26;
DLB 6

Mansfield, Katherine
. . TCLC 2, 8, 39; DAB; SSC 9, 23; WLC
See also Beauchamp, Kathleen Mansfield
See also DLB 162

Manso, Peter 1940- . . . . CLC 39
See also CA 29-32R; CANR 44

Mantecon, Juan Jimenez
See Jimenez (Mantecon), Juan Ramon

Manton, Peter
See Creasey, John

Man Without a Spleen, A
See Chekhov, Anton (Pavlovich)

Manzoni, Alessandro 1785-1873 . . NCLC 29

Mapu, Abraham (ben Jekutiel)
1808-1867 . . . . NCLC 18

Mara, Sally
See Queneau, Raymond

Marat, Jean Paul 1743-1793 . . . . LC 10

Marcel, Gabriel Honore
1889-1973 . . . . CLC 15
See also CA 102; 45-48; MTCW

Marchbanks, Samuel
See Davies, (William) Robertson

Marchi, Giacomo
See Bassani, Giorgio

Margulies, Donald . . . . CLC 76

Marie de France c. 12th cent. - . . . . CMLC 8

Marie de l'Incarnation 1599-1672 . . . . LC 10

Mariner, Scott
See Pohl, Frederik

Marinetti, Filippo Tommaso
1876-1944 . . . . TCLC 10
See also CA 107; DLB 114

Marivaux, Pierre Carlet de Chamblain de
1688-1763 . . . . LC 4

Markandaya, Kamala . . . . CLC 8, 38
See also Taylor, Kamala (Purnaiya)

Markfield, Wallace 1926- . . . . CLC 8
See also CA 69-72; CAAS 3; DLB 2, 28

Markham, Edwin 1852-1940 . . . . . TCLC 47
See also DLB 54

Markham, Robert
See Amis, Kingsley (William)

Marks, J
See Highwater, Jamake (Mamake)

Marks-Highwater, J
See Highwater, Jamake (Mamake)

Markson, David M(errill) 1927- . . . . CLC 67
See also CA 49-52; CANR 1

Marley, Bob . . . . CLC 17
See also Marley, Robert Nesta

Marley, Robert Nesta 1945-1981
See Marley, Bob
See also CA 107; 103

Marlowe, Christopher
1564-1593 . . . . . LC 22; DA; DAB; DAC;
DAM DRAM, MST; DC 1; WLC
See also CDBLB Before 1660; DLB 62

Marmontel, Jean-Francois
1723-1799 . . . . LC 2

Marquand, John P(hillips)
1893-1960 . . . . CLC 2, 10
See also CA 85-88; DLB 9, 102

Marques, Rene
1919-1979 . . . . . . CLC 96; DAM MULT;
HLC
See also CA 97-100; 85-88; DLB 113; HW

Marquez, Gabriel (Jose) Garcia
See Garcia Marquez, Gabriel (Jose)

Marquis, Don(ald Robert Perry)
1878-1937 . . . . TCLC 7
See also CA 104; DLB 11, 25

Marric, J. J.
See Creasey, John

Marrow, Bernard
See Moore, Brian

Marryat, Frederick 1792-1848 . . . . NCLC 3
See also DLB 21, 163

Marsden, James
See Creasey, John

Marsh, (Edith) Ngaio
1899-1982 . . . . . . CLC 7, 53; DAM POP
See also CA 9-12R; CANR 6; DLB 77;
MTCW

Marshall, Garry 1934- . . . . CLC 17
See also AAYA 3; CA 111; SATA 60

Marshall, Paule
1929- . . . . CLC 27, 72; BLC;
DAM MULT; SSC 3
See also BW 2; CA 77-80; CANR 25;
DLB 157; MTCW

Marsten, Richard
See Hunter, Evan

Marston, John
1576-1634 . . . . LC 33; DAM DRAM
See also DLB 58

Martha, Henry
See Harris, Mark

Martial c. 40-c. 104 . . . . PC 10

Martin, Ken
See Hubbard, L(afayette) Ron(ald)

Martin, Richard
See Creasey, John

Martin, Steve 1945- . . . . CLC 30
See also CA 97-100; CANR 30; MTCW

Martin, Valerie 1948- . . . . CLC 89
See also BEST 90:2; CA 85-88; CANR 49

Martin, Violet Florence
1862-1915 . . . . TCLC 51

Martin, Webber
See Silverberg, Robert

Martindale, Patrick Victor
See White, Patrick (Victor Martindale)

Martin du Gard, Roger
1881-1958 . . . . TCLC 24
See also CA 118; DLB 65

Martineau, Harriet 1802-1876 . . . . NCLC 26
See also DLB 21, 55, 159, 163, 166;
YABC 2

Martines, Julia
See O'Faolain, Julia

Martinez, Jacinto Benavente y
See Benavente (y Martinez), Jacinto

Martinez Ruiz, Jose 1873-1967
See Azorin; Ruiz, Jose Martinez
See also CA 93-96; HW

Martinez Sierra, Gregorio
1881-1947 . . . . TCLC 6
See also CA 115

Martinez Sierra, Maria (de la O'LeJarraga)
1874-1974 . . . . TCLC 6
See also CA 115

Martinsen, Martin
See Follett, Ken(neth Martin)

Martinson, Harry (Edmund)
1904-1978 . . . . CLC 14
See also CA 77-80; CANR 34

Marut, Ret
See Traven, B.

Marut, Robert
See Traven, B.

Marvell, Andrew
1621-1678 . . . . . . LC 4; DA; DAB; DAC;
DAM MST, POET; PC 10; WLC
See also CDBLB 1660-1789; DLB 131

Marx, Karl (Heinrich)
1818-1883 . . . . NCLC 17
See also DLB 129

Masaoka Shiki . . . . TCLC 18
See also Masaoka Tsunenori

Masaoka Tsunenori 1867-1902
See Masaoka Shiki
See also CA 117

Masefield, John (Edward)
1878-1967 . . . . CLC 11, 47; DAM POET
See also CA 19-20; 25-28R; CANR 33;
CAP 2; CDBLB 1890-1914; DLB 10, 19,
153, 160; MTCW; SATA 19

Maso, Carole 19(?)- . . . . CLC 44

Mason, Bobbie Ann
1940- . . . . CLC 28, 43, 82; SSC 4
See also AAYA 5; CA 53-56; CANR 11,
31; DLBY 87; INT CANR-31; MTCW

Mason, Ernst
See Pohl, Frederik

Mason, Lee W.
See Malzberg, Barry N(athaniel)

Mason, Nick 1945-.............. CLC 35

Mason, Tally
See Derleth, August (William)

Mass, William
See Gibson, William

Masters, Edgar Lee
1868-1950 ..... TCLC 2, 25; DA; DAC;
DAM MST, POET; PC 1
See also CA 104; 133; CDALB 1865-1917;
DLB 54; MTCW

Masters, Hilary 1928-............ CLC 48
See also CA 25-28R; CANR 13, 47

Mastrosimone, William 19(?)-...... CLC 36

Mathe, Albert
See Camus, Albert

Matheson, Richard Burton 1926- ... CLC 37
See also CA 97-100; DLB 8, 44; INT 97-100

Mathews, Harry 1930-.......... CLC 6, 52
See also CA 21-24R; CAAS 6; CANR 18,
40

Mathews, John Joseph
1894-1979 ...... CLC 84; DAM MULT
See also CA 19-20; 142; CANR 45; CAP 2;
NNAL

Mathias, Roland (Glyn) 1915-...... CLC 45
See also CA 97-100; CANR 19, 41; DLB 27

Matsuo Basho 1644-1694........... PC 3
See also DAM POET

Mattheson, Rodney
See Creasey, John

Matthews, Greg 1949- .... CLC 45
See also CA 135

Matthews, William 1942-.......... CLC 40
See also CA 29-32R; CAAS 18; CANR 12;
DLB 5

Matthias, John (Edward) 1941-...... CLC 9
See also CA 33-36R

Matthiessen, Peter
1927- .... CLC 5, 7, 11, 32, 64;
DAM NOV
See also AAYA 6; BEST 90:4; CA 9-12R;
CANR 21, 50; DLB 6; MTCW; SATA 27

Maturin, Charles Robert
1780(?)-1824 .... NCLC 6

Matute (Ausejo), Ana Maria
1925- .... CLC 11
See also CA 89-92; MTCW

Maugham, W. S.
See Maugham, W(illiam) Somerset

Maugham, W(illiam) Somerset
1874-1965 ...... CLC 1, 11, 15, 67, 93;
DA; DAB; DAC; DAM DRAM, MST,
NOV; SSC 8; WLC
See also CA 5-8R; 25-28R; CANR 40;
CDBLB 1914-1945; DLB 10, 36, 77, 100,
162; MTCW; SATA 54

Maugham, William Somerset
See Maugham, W(illiam) Somerset

Maupassant, (Henri Rene Albert) Guy de
1850-1893 ..... NCLC 1, 42; DA; DAB;
DAC; DAM MST; SSC 1; WLC
See also DLB 123

Maupin, Armistead
1944- .... CLC 95; DAM POP
See also CA 125; 130; INT 130

Maurhut, Richard
See Traven, B.

Mauriac, Claude 1914-1996........ CLC 9
See also CA 89-92; 152; DLB 83

Mauriac, Francois (Charles)
1885-1970 .... CLC 4, 9, 56
See also CA 25-28; CAP 2; DLB 65;
MTCW

Mavor, Osborne Henry 1888-1951
See Bridie, James
See also CA 104

Maxwell, William (Keepers, Jr.)
1908- .... CLC 19
See also CA 93-96; DLBY 80; INT 93-96

May, Elaine 1932- .... CLC 16
See also CA 124; 142; DLB 44

Mayakovski, Vladimir (Vladimirovich)
1893-1930 .... TCLC 4, 18
See also CA 104

Mayhew, Henry 1812-1887 ...... NCLC 31
See also DLB 18, 55

Mayle, Peter 1939(?)-............. CLC 89
See also CA 139

Maynard, Joyce 1953-............ CLC 23
See also CA 111; 129

Mayne, William (James Carter)
1928- .... CLC 12
See also CA 9-12R; CANR 37; CLR 25;
JRDA; MAICYA; SAAS 11; SATA 6, 68

Mayo, Jim
See L'Amour, Louis (Dearborn)

Maysles, Albert 1926- .... CLC 16
See also CA 29-32R

Maysles, David 1932-............. CLC 16

Mazer, Norma Fox 1931- .... CLC 26
See also AAYA 5; CA 69-72; CANR 12,
32; CLR 23; JRDA; MAICYA; SAAS 1;
SATA 24, 67

Mazzini, Guiseppe 1805-1872 .... NCLC 34

McAuley, James Phillip
1917-1976 .... CLC 45
See also CA 97-100

McBain, Ed
See Hunter, Evan

McBrien, William Augustine
1930- .... CLC 44
See also CA 107

McCaffrey, Anne (Inez)
1926- ...... CLC 17; DAM NOV, POP
See also AAYA 6; AITN 2; BEST 89:2;
CA 25-28R; CANR 15, 35; DLB 8;
JRDA; MAICYA; MTCW; SAAS 11;
SATA 8, 70

McCall, Nathan 1955(?)-.......... CLC 86
See also CA 146

McCann, Arthur
See Campbell, John W(ood, Jr.)

McCann, Edson
See Pohl, Frederik

McCarthy, Charles, Jr. 1933-
See McCarthy, Cormac
See also CANR 42; DAM POP

McCarthy, Cormac 1933-..... CLC 4, 57, 59
See also McCarthy, Charles, Jr.
See also DLB 6, 143

McCarthy, Mary (Therese)
1912-1989 ... CLC 1, 3, 5, 14, 24, 39, 59
See also CA 5-8R; 129; CANR 16, 50;
DLB 2; DLBY 81; INT CANR-16;
MTCW

McCartney, (James) Paul
1942-..................... CLC 12, 35
See also CA 146

McCauley, Stephen (D.) 1955- ..... CLC 50
See also CA 141

McClure, Michael (Thomas)
1932-..................... CLC 6, 10
See also CA 21-24R; CANR 17, 46;
DLB 16

McCorkle, Jill (Collins) 1958-...... CLC 51
See also CA 121; DLBY 87

McCourt, James 1941-............. CLC 5
See also CA 57-60

McCoy, Horace (Stanley)
1897-1955 .... TCLC 28
See also CA 108; DLB 9

McCrae, John 1872-1918........ TCLC 12
See also CA 109; DLB 92

McCreigh, James
See Pohl, Frederik

McCullers, (Lula) Carson (Smith)
1917-1967 .... CLC 1, 4, 10, 12, 48; DA;
DAB; DAC; DAM MST, NOV; SSC 9;
WLC
See also CA 5-8R; 25-28R; CABS 1, 3;
CANR 18; CDALB 1941-1968; DLB 2, 7;
MTCW; SATA 27

McCulloch, John Tyler
See Burroughs, Edgar Rice

McCullough, Colleen
1938(?)-.... CLC 27; DAM NOV, POP
See also CA 81-84; CANR 17, 46; MTCW

McDermott, Alice 1953- .... CLC 90
See also CA 109; CANR 40

McElroy, Joseph 1930- .... CLC 5, 47
See also CA 17-20R

McEwan, Ian (Russell)
1948- .... CLC 13, 66; DAM NOV
See also BEST 90:4; CA 61-64; CANR 14,
41; DLB 14; MTCW

McFadden, David 1940-.......... CLC 48
See also CA 104; DLB 60; INT 104

McFarland, Dennis 1950- .... CLC 65

McGahern, John
1934- .... CLC 5, 9, 48; SSC 17
See also CA 17-20R; CANR 29; DLB 14;
MTCW

McGinley, Patrick (Anthony)
1937-...................... CLC 41
See also CA 120; 127; INT 127

McGinley, Phyllis 1905-1978 ...... CLC 14
See also CA 9-12R; 77-80; CANR 19;
DLB 11, 48; SATA 2, 44; SATA-Obit 24

McGinniss, Joe 1942-............. CLC 32
See also AITN 2; BEST 89:2; CA 25-28R;
CANR 26; INT CANR-26

Michaux, Henri 1899-1984 ...... **CLC 8, 19**
See also CA 85-88; 114

Michelangelo 1475-1564 .... **LC 12**

Michelet, Jules 1798-1874 ...... **NCLC 31**

Michener, James A(lbert)
1907(?)- .... **CLC 1, 5, 11, 29, 60;**
DAM NOV, POP
See also AITN 1; BEST 90:1; CA 5-8R;
CANR 21, 45; DLB 6; MTCW

Mickiewicz, Adam 1798-1855 ..... **NCLC 3**

Middleton, Christopher 1926- ...... **CLC 13**
See also CA 13-16R; CANR 29; DLB 40

Middleton, Richard (Barham)
1882-1911 .... **TCLC 56**
See also DLB 156

Middleton, Stanley 1919- .... **CLC 7, 38**
See also CA 25-28R; CAAS 23; CANR 21,
46; DLB 14

Middleton, Thomas
1580-1627 .... **LC 33; DAM DRAM,**
MST; DC 5
See also DLB 58

Migueis, Jose Rodrigues 1901- ..... **CLC 10**

Mikszath, Kalman 1847-1910 ..... **TCLC 31**

Miles, Josephine
1911-1985 .... **CLC 1, 2, 14, 34, 39;**
DAM POET
See also CA 1-4R; 116; CANR 2; DLB 48

Militant
See Sandburg, Carl (August)

Mill, John Stuart 1806-1873 ..... **NCLC 11**
See also CDBLB 1832-1890; DLB 55

Millar, Kenneth
1915-1983 .... **CLC 14; DAM POP**
See also Macdonald, Ross
See also CA 9-12R; 110; CANR 16; DLB 2;
DLBD 6; DLBY 83; MTCW

Millay, E. Vincent
See Millay, Edna St. Vincent

Millay, Edna St. Vincent
1892-1950 ..... **TCLC 4, 49; DA; DAB;**
DAC; DAM MST, POET; PC 6
See also CA 104; 130; CDALB 1917-1929;
DLB 45; MTCW

Miller, Arthur
1915- .... **CLC 1, 2, 6, 10, 15, 26, 47, 78;**
DA; DAB; DAC; DAM DRAM, MST;
DC 1; WLC
See also AAYA 15; AITN 1; CA 1-4R;
CABS 3; CANR 2, 30;
CDALB 1941-1968; DLB 7; MTCW

Miller, Henry (Valentine)
1891-1980 .... **CLC 1, 2, 4, 9, 14, 43, 84;**
DA; DAB; DAC; DAM MST, NOV;
WLC
See also CA 9-12R; 97-100; CANR 33;
CDALB 1929-1941; DLB 4, 9; DLBY 80;
MTCW

Miller, Jason 1939(?)- .... **CLC 2**
See also AITN 1; CA 73-76; DLB 7

Miller, Sue 1943- ..... **CLC 44; DAM POP**
See also BEST 90:3; CA 139; DLB 143

Miller, Walter M(ichael, Jr.)
1923- .... **CLC 4, 30**
See also CA 85-88; DLB 8

Millett, Kate 1934- .... **CLC 67**
See also AITN 1; CA 73-76; CANR 32, 53;
MTCW

Millhauser, Steven 1943- .... **CLC 21, 54**
See also CA 110; 111; DLB 2; INT 111

Millin, Sarah Gertrude 1889-1968 .. **CLC 49**
See also CA 102; 93-96

Milne, A(lan) A(lexander)
1882-1956 .... **TCLC 6; DAB; DAC;**
DAM MST
See also CA 104; 133; CLR 1, 26; DLB 10,
77, 100, 160; MAICYA; MTCW;
YABC 1

Milner, Ron(ald)
1938- ..... **CLC 56; BLC; DAM MULT**
See also AITN 1; BW 1; CA 73-76;
CANR 24; DLB 38; MTCW

Milosz, Czeslaw
1911- .... **CLC 5, 11, 22, 31, 56, 82;**
DAM MST, POET; PC 8
See also CA 81-84; CANR 23, 51; MTCW

Milton, John
1608-1674 ...... **LC 9; DA; DAB; DAC;**
DAM MST, POET; WLC
See also CDBLB 1660-1789; DLB 131, 151

Min, Anchee 1957- .... **CLC 86**
See also CA 146

Minehaha, Cornelius
See Wedekind, (Benjamin) Frank(lin)

Miner, Valerie 1947- .... **CLC 40**
See also CA 97-100

Minimo, Duca
See D'Annunzio, Gabriele

Minot, Susan 1956- .... **CLC 44**
See also CA 134

Minus, Ed 1938- .... **CLC 39**

Miranda, Javier
See Bioy Casares, Adolfo

Mirbeau, Octave 1848-1917 ...... **TCLC 55**
See also DLB 123

Miro (Ferrer), Gabriel (Francisco Victor)
1879-1930 .... **TCLC 5**
See also CA 104

Mishima, Yukio
.... **CLC 2, 4, 6, 9, 27; DC 1; SSC 4**
See also Hiraoka, Kimitake

Mistral, Frederic 1830-1914 ...... **TCLC 51**
See also CA 122

Mistral, Gabriela .... **TCLC 2; HLC**
See also Godoy Alcayaga, Lucila

Mistry, Rohinton 1952- ...... **CLC 71; DAC**
See also CA 141

Mitchell, Clyde
See Ellison, Harlan (Jay); Silverberg, Robert

Mitchell, James Leslie 1901-1935
See Gibbon, Lewis Grassic
See also CA 104; DLB 15

Mitchell, Joni 1943- .... **CLC 12**
See also CA 112

Mitchell, Margaret (Munnerlyn)
1900-1949 ...... **TCLC 11; DAM NOV,**
POP
See also CA 109; 125; DLB 9; MTCW

Mitchell, Peggy
See Mitchell, Margaret (Munnerlyn)

Mitchell, S(ilas) Weir 1829-1914 .. **TCLC 36**

Mitchell, W(illiam) O(rmond)
1914- ...... **CLC 25; DAC; DAM MST**
See also CA 77-80; CANR 15, 43; DLB 88

Mitford, Mary Russell 1787-1855 .. **NCLC 4**
See also DLB 110, 116

Mitford, Nancy 1904-1973 .... **CLC 44**
See also CA 9-12R

Miyamoto, Yuriko 1899-1951 ..... **TCLC 37**

Mo, Timothy (Peter) 1950(?)- ...... **CLC 46**
See also CA 117; MTCW

Modarressi, Taghi (M.) 1931- ...... **CLC 44**
See also CA 121; 134; INT 134

Modiano, Patrick (Jean) 1945- ..... **CLC 18**
See also CA 85-88; CANR 17, 40; DLB 83

Moerck, Paal
See Roelvaag, O(le) E(dvart)

Mofolo, Thomas (Mokopu)
1875(?)-1948 .... **TCLC 22; BLC;**
DAM MULT
See also CA 121

Mohr, Nicholasa
1935- ..... **CLC 12; DAM MULT; HLC**
See also AAYA 8; CA 49-52; CANR 1, 32;
CLR 22; DLB 145; HW; JRDA; SAAS 8;
SATA 8

Mojtabai, A(nn) G(race)
1938- .... **CLC 5, 9, 15, 29**
See also CA 85-88

Moliere
1622-1673 ..... **LC 28; DA; DAB; DAC;**
DAM DRAM, MST; WLC

Molin, Charles
See Mayne, William (James Carter)

Molnar, Ferenc
1878-1952 ..... **TCLC 20; DAM DRAM**
See also CA 109

Momaday, N(avarre) Scott
1934- ..... **CLC 2, 19, 85, 95; DA; DAB;**
DAC; DAM MST, MULT, NOV, POP
See also AAYA 11; CA 25-28R; CANR 14,
34; DLB 143; INT CANR-14; MTCW;
NNAL; SATA 48; SATA-Brief 30

Monette, Paul 1945-1995 .... **CLC 82**
See also CA 139; 147

Monroe, Harriet 1860-1936 .... **TCLC 12**
See also CA 109; DLB 54, 91

Monroe, Lyle
See Heinlein, Robert A(nson)

Montagu, Elizabeth 1917- .... **NCLC 7**
See also CA 9-12R

Montagu, Mary (Pierrepont) Wortley
1689-1762 .... **LC 9; PC 16**
See also DLB 95, 101

Montagu, W. H.
See Coleridge, Samuel Taylor

Montague, John (Patrick)
1929- .... **CLC 13, 46**
See also CA 9-12R; CANR 9; DLB 40;
MTCW

Montaigne, Michel (Eyquem) de
1533-1592 ...... **LC 8; DA; DAB; DAC;
DAM MST; WLC**

Montale, Eugenio
1896-1981 .... **CLC 7, 9, 18; PC 13**
See also CA 17-20R; 104; CANR 30;
DLB 114; MTCW

Montesquieu, Charles-Louis de Secondat
1689-1755 .... **LC 7**

Montgomery, (Robert) Bruce 1921-1978
See Crispin, Edmund
See also CA 104

Montgomery, L(ucy) M(aud)
1874-1942 .... **TCLC 51; DAC;
DAM MST**
See also AAYA 12; CA 108; 137; CLR 8;
DLB 92; DLBD 14; JRDA; MAICYA;
YABC 1

Montgomery, Marion H., Jr. 1925- .. **CLC 7**
See also AITN 1; CA 1-4R; CANR 3, 48;
DLB 6

Montgomery, Max
See Davenport, Guy (Mattison, Jr.)

Montherlant, Henry (Milon) de
1896-1972 .... **CLC 8, 19; DAM DRAM**
See also CA 85-88; 37-40R; DLB 72;
MTCW

Monty Python
See Chapman, Graham; Cleese, John
(Marwood); Gilliam, Terry (Vance); Idle,
Eric; Jones, Terence Graham Parry; Palin,
Michael (Edward)
See also AAYA 7

Moodie, Susanna (Strickland)
1803-1885 .... **NCLC 14**
See also DLB 99

Mooney, Edward 1951-
See Mooney, Ted
See also CA 130

Mooney, Ted .... **CLC 25**
See also Mooney, Edward

Moorcock, Michael (John)
1939- .... **CLC 5, 27, 58**
See also CA 45-48; CAAS 5; CANR 2, 17,
38; DLB 14; MTCW

Moore, Brian
1921- ...... **CLC 1, 3, 5, 7, 8, 19, 32, 90;
DAB; DAC; DAM MST**
See also CA 1-4R; CANR 1, 25, 42; MTCW

Moore, Edward
See Muir, Edwin

Moore, George Augustus
1852-1933 .... **TCLC 7; SSC 19**
See also CA 104; DLB 10, 18, 57, 135

Moore, Lorrie .... **CLC 39, 45, 68**
See also Moore, Marie Lorena

Moore, Marianne (Craig)
1887-1972 .... **CLC 1, 2, 4, 8, 10, 13, 19,
47; DA; DAB; DAC; DAM MST, POET;
PC 4**
See also CA 1-4R; 33-36R; CANR 3;
CDALB 1929-1941; DLB 45; DLBD 7;
MTCW; SATA 20

Moore, Marie Lorena 1957-
See Moore, Lorrie
See also CA 116; CANR 39

Moore, Thomas 1779-1852....... **NCLC 6**
See also DLB 96, 144

Morand, Paul 1888-1976 .. **CLC 41; SSC 22**
See also CA 69-72; DLB 65

Morante, Elsa 1918-1985....... **CLC 8, 47**
See also CA 85-88; 117; CANR 35; MTCW

Moravia, Alberto....... **CLC 2, 7, 11, 27, 46**
See also Pincherle, Alberto

More, Hannah 1745-1833 .... **NCLC 27**
See also DLB 107, 109, 116, 158

More, Henry 1614-1687............. **LC 9**
See also DLB 126

More, Sir Thomas 1478-1535 .... **LC 10, 32**

Moreas, Jean .... **TCLC 18**
See also Papadiamantopoulos, Johannes

Morgan, Berry 1919- .... **CLC 6**
See also CA 49-52; DLB 6

Morgan, Claire
See Highsmith, (Mary) Patricia

Morgan, Edwin (George) 1920- ..... **CLC 31**
See also CA 5-8R; CANR 3, 43; DLB 27

Morgan, (George) Frederick
1922- .... **CLC 23**
See also CA 17-20R; CANR 21

Morgan, Harriet
See Mencken, H(enry) L(ouis)

Morgan, Jane
See Cooper, James Fenimore

Morgan, Janet 1945- .... **CLC 39**
See also CA 65-68

Morgan, Lady 1776(?)-1859...... **NCLC 29**
See also DLB 116, 158

Morgan, Robin 1941-............. **CLC 2**
See also CA 69-72; CANR 29; MTCW;
SATA 80

Morgan, Scott
See Kuttner, Henry

Morgan, Seth 1949(?)-1990 .... **CLC 65**
See also CA 132

Morgenstern, Christian
1871-1914 .... **TCLC 8**
See also CA 105

Morgenstern, S.
See Goldman, William (W.)

Moricz, Zsigmond 1879-1942 ..... **TCLC 33**

Morike, Eduard (Friedrich)
1804-1875 .... **NCLC 10**
See also DLB 133

Mori Ogai .... **TCLC 14**
See also Mori Rintaro

Mori Rintaro 1862-1922
See Mori Ogai
See also CA 110

Moritz, Karl Philipp 1756-1793 ...... **LC 2**
See also DLB 94

Morland, Peter Henry
See Faust, Frederick (Schiller)

Morren, Theophil
See Hofmannsthal, Hugo von

Morris, Bill 1952-............... **CLC 76**

Morris, Julian
See West, Morris L(anglo)

Morris, Steveland Judkins 1950(?)-
See Wonder, Stevie
See also CA 111

Morris, William 1834-1896 .... **NCLC 4**
See also CDBLB 1832-1890; DLB 18, 35,
57, 156

Morris, Wright 1910-.... **CLC 1, 3, 7, 18, 37**
See also CA 9-12R; CANR 21; DLB 2;
DLBY 81; MTCW

Morrison, Chloe Anthony Wofford
See Morrison, Toni

Morrison, James Douglas 1943-1971
See Morrison, Jim
See also CA 73-76; CANR 40

Morrison, Jim .... **CLC 17**
See also Morrison, James Douglas

Morrison, Toni
1931- .... **CLC 4, 10, 22, 55, 81, 87;
BLC; DA; DAB; DAC; DAM MST,
MULT, NOV, POP**
See also AAYA 1; BW 2; CA 29-32R;
CANR 27, 42; CDALB 1968-1988;
DLB 6, 33, 143; DLBY 81; MTCW;
SATA 57

Morrison, Van 1945- .... **CLC 21**
See also CA 116

Mortimer, John (Clifford)
1923- ...... **CLC 28, 43; DAM DRAM,
POP**
See also CA 13-16R; CANR 21;
CDBLB 1960 to Present; DLB 13;
INT CANR-21; MTCW

Mortimer, Penelope (Ruth) 1918-.... **CLC 5**
See also CA 57-60; CANR 45

Morton, Anthony
See Creasey, John

Mosher, Howard Frank 1943-...... **CLC 62**
See also CA 139

Mosley, Nicholas 1923-........ **CLC 43, 70**
See also CA 69-72; CANR 41; DLB 14

Moss, Howard
1922-1987 .... **CLC 7, 14, 45, 50;
DAM POET**
See also CA 1-4R; 123; CANR 1, 44;
DLB 5

Mossgiel, Rab
See Burns, Robert

Motion, Andrew (Peter) 1952-...... **CLC 47**
See also CA 146; DLB 40

Motley, Willard (Francis)
1909-1965 .... **CLC 18**
See also BW 1; CA 117; 106; DLB 76, 143

Motoori, Norinaga 1730-1801 .... **NCLC 45**

Mott, Michael (Charles Alston)
1930-.................... **CLC 15, 34**
See also CA 5-8R; CAAS 7; CANR 7, 29

Mountain Wolf Woman
1884-1960 .... **CLC 92**
See also CA 144; NNAL

Moure, Erin 1955- .... **CLC 88**
See also CA 113; DLB 60

Mowat, Farley (McGill)
1921- . . . . . . **CLC 26; DAC; DAM MST**
See also AAYA 1; CA 1-4R; CANR 4, 24,
42; CLR 20; DLB 68; INT CANAR-24;
JRDA; MAICYA; MTCW; SATA 3, 55

Moyers, Bill 1934- . . . . **CLC 74**
See also AITN 2; CA 61-64; CANR 31, 52

Mphahlele, Es'kia
See Mphahlele, Ezekiel
See also DLB 125

Mphahlele, Ezekiel
1919- . . . . . **CLC 25; BLC; DAM MULT**
See also Mphahlele, Es'kia
See also BW 2; CA 81-84; CANR 26

Mqhayi, S(amuel) E(dward) K(rune Loliwe)
1875-1945 . . . . **TCLC 25; BLC;
DAM MULT**

Mrozek, Slawomir 1930- . . . . **CLC 3, 13**
See also CA 13-16R; CAAS 10; CANR 29;
MTCW

Mrs. Belloc-Lowndes
See Lowndes, Marie Adelaide (Belloc)

Mtwa, Percy (?)- . . . . **CLC 47**

Mueller, Lisel 1924- . . . . **CLC 13, 51**
See also CA 93-96; DLB 105

Muir, Edwin 1887-1959 . . . . **TCLC 2**
See also CA 104; DLB 20, 100

Muir, John 1838-1914 . . . . **TCLC 28**

Mujica Lainez, Manuel
1910-1984 . . . . **CLC 31**
See also Lainez, Manuel Mujica
See also CA 81-84; 112; CANR 32; HW

Mukherjee, Bharati
1940- . . . . **CLC 53; DAM NOV**
See also BEST 89:2; CA 107; CANR 45;
DLB 60; MTCW

Muldoon, Paul
1951- . . . . **CLC 32, 72; DAM POET**
See also CA 113; 129; CANR 52; DLB 40;
INT 129

Mulisch, Harry 1927- . . . . **CLC 42**
See also CA 9-12R; CANR 6, 26

Mull, Martin 1943- . . . . **CLC 17**
See also CA 105

Mulock, Dinah Maria
See Craik, Dinah Maria (Mulock)

Munford, Robert 1737(?)-1783 . . . . **LC 5**
See also DLB 31

Mungo, Raymond 1946- . . . . **CLC 72**
See also CA 49-52; CANR 2

Munro, Alice
1931- . . . . . . **CLC 6, 10, 19, 50, 95; DAC;
DAM MST, NOV; SSC 3**
See also AITN 2; CA 33-36R; CANR 33,
53; DLB 53; MTCW; SATA 29

Munro, H(ector) H(ugh) 1870-1916
See Saki
See also CA 104; 130; CDBLB 1890-1914;
DA; DAB; DAC; DAM MST, NOV;
DLB 34, 162; MTCW; WLC

Murasaki, Lady . . . . **CMLC 1**

Murdoch, (Jean) Iris
1919- . . . . . . **CLC 1, 2, 3, 4, 6, 8, 11, 15,
22, 31, 51; DAB; DAC; DAM MST,
NOV**
See also CA 13-16R; CANR 8, 43;
CDBLB 1960 to Present; DLB 14;
INT CANR-8; MTCW

Murfree, Mary Noailles
1850-1922 . . . . **SSC 22**
See also CA 122; DLB 12, 74

Murnau, Friedrich Wilhelm
See Plumpe, Friedrich Wilhelm

Murphy, Richard 1927- . . . . **CLC 41**
See also CA 29-32R; DLB 40

Murphy, Sylvia 1937- . . . . **CLC 34**
See also CA 121

Murphy, Thomas (Bernard) 1935- . . . **CLC 51**
See also CA 101

Murray, Albert L. 1916- . . . . **CLC 73**
See also BW 2; CA 49-52; CANR 26, 52;
DLB 38

Murray, Les(lie) A(llan)
1938- . . . . **CLC 40; DAM POET**
See also CA 21-24R; CANR 11, 27

Murry, J. Middleton
See Murry, John Middleton

Murry, John Middleton
1889-1957 . . . . **TCLC 16**
See also CA 118; DLB 149

Musgrave, Susan 1951- . . . . **CLC 13, 54**
See also CA 69-72; CANR 45

Musil, Robert (Edler von)
1880-1942 . . . . **TCLC 12; SSC 18**
See also CA 109; DLB 81, 124

Muske, Carol 1945- . . . . **CLC 90**
See also Muske-Dukes, Carol (Anne)

Muske-Dukes, Carol (Anne) 1945-
See Muske, Carol
See also CA 65-68; CANR 32

Musset, (Louis Charles) Alfred de
1810-1857 . . . . **NCLC 7**

My Brother's Brother
See Chekhov, Anton (Pavlovich)

Myers, L. H. 1881-1944 . . . . **TCLC 59**
See also DLB 15

Myers, Walter Dean
1937- . . . . . **CLC 35; BLC; DAM MULT,
NOV**
See also AAYA 4; BW 2; CA 33-36R;
CANR 20, 42; CLR 4, 16, 35; DLB 33;
INT CANR-20; JRDA; MAICYA;
SAAS 2; SATA 41, 71; SATA-Brief 27

Myers, Walter M.
See Myers, Walter Dean

Myles, Symon
See Follett, Ken(neth Martin)

Nabokov, Vladimir (Vladimirovich)
1899-1977 . . . . . **CLC 1, 2, 3, 6, 8, 11, 15,
23, 44, 46, 64; DA; DAB; DAC;
DAM MST, NOV; SSC 11; WLC**
See also CA 5-8R; 69-72; CANR 20;
CDALB 1941-1968; DLB 2; DLBD 3;
DLBY 80, 91; MTCW

Nagai Kafu . . . . **TCLC 51**
See also Nagai Sokichi

Nagai Sokichi 1879-1959
See Nagai Kafu
See also CA 117

Nagy, Laszlo 1925-1978 . . . . **CLC 7**
See also CA 129; 112

Naipaul, Shiva(dhar Srinivasa)
1945-1985 . . . . . **CLC 32, 39; DAM NOV**
See also CA 110; 112; 116; CANR 33;
DLB 157; DLBY 85; MTCW

Naipaul, V(idiadhar) S(urajprasad)
1932- . . . . **CLC 4, 7, 9, 13, 18, 37; DAB;
DAC; DAM MST, NOV**
See also CA 1-4R; CANR 1, 33, 51;
CDBLB 1960 to Present; DLB 125;
DLBY 85; MTCW

Nakos, Lilika 1899(?)- . . . . **CLC 29**

Narayan, R(asipuram) K(rishnaswami)
1906- . . . . **CLC 7, 28, 47; DAM NOV**
See also CA 81-84; CANR 33; MTCW;
SATA 62

Nash, (Frediric) Ogden
1902-1971 . . . . **CLC 23; DAM POET**
See also CA 13-14; 29-32R; CANR 34;
CAP 1; DLB 11; MAICYA; MTCW;
SATA 2, 46

Nathan, Daniel
See Dannay, Frederic

Nathan, George Jean 1882-1958 . . . **TCLC 18**
See also Hatteras, Owen
See also CA 114; DLB 137

Natsume, Kinnosuke 1867-1916
See Natsume, Soseki
See also CA 104

Natsume, Soseki . . . . **TCLC 2, 10**
See also Natsume, Kinnosuke

Natti, (Mary) Lee 1919-
See Kingman, Lee
See also CA 5-8R; CANR 2

Naylor, Gloria
1950- . . . . . . **CLC 28, 52; BLC; DA; DAC;
DAM MST, MULT, NOV, POP**
See also AAYA 6; BW 2; CA 107;
CANR 27, 51; MTCW

Neihardt, John Gneisenau
1881-1973 . . . . **CLC 32**
See also CA 13-14; CAP 1; DLB 9, 54

Nekrasov, Nikolai Alekseevich
1821-1878 . . . . **NCLC 11**

Nelligan, Emile 1879-1941 . . . . **TCLC 14**
See also CA 114; DLB 92

Nelson, Willie 1933- . . . . **CLC 17**
See also CA 107

Nemerov, Howard (Stanley)
1920-1991 . . . . **CLC 2, 6, 9, 36;
DAM POET**
See also CA 1-4R; 134; CABS 2; CANR 1,
27, 53; DLB 5, 6; DLBY 83;
INT CANR-27; MTCW

Neruda, Pablo
1904-1973 . . . . . **CLC 1, 2, 5, 7, 9, 28, 62;
DA; DAB; DAC; DAM MST, MULT,
POET; HLC; PC 4; WLC**
See also CA 19-20; 45-48; CAP 2; HW;
MTCW

Nerval, Gerard de
1808-1855 . . . . . **NCLC 1; PC 13; SSC 18**

Nervo, (Jose) Amado (Ruiz de)
1870-1919 . . . . **TCLC 11**
See also CA 109; 131; HW

Nessi, Pio Baroja y
See Baroja (y Nessi), Pio

Nestroy, Johann 1801-1862 . . . . . . **NCLC 42**
See also DLB 133

Neufeld, John (Arthur) 1938- . . . . . . **CLC 17**
See also AAYA 11; CA 25-28R; CANR 11,
37; MAICYA; SAAS 3; SATA 6, 81

Neville, Emily Cheney 1919- . . . . **CLC 12**
See also CA 5-8R; CANR 3, 37; JRDA;
MAICYA; SAAS 2; SATA 1

Newbound, Bernard Slade 1930-
See Slade, Bernard
See also CA 81-84; CANR 49;
DAM DRAM

Newby, P(ercy) H(oward)
1918- . . . . **CLC 2, 13; DAM NOV**
See also CA 5-8R; CANR 32; DLB 15;
MTCW

Newlove, Donald 1928- . . . . **CLC 6**
See also CA 29-32R; CANR 25

Newlove, John (Herbert) 1938- . . . . . **CLC 14**
See also CA 21-24R; CANR 9, 25

Newman, Charles 1938- . . . . **CLC 2, 8**
See also CA 21-24R

Newman, Edwin (Harold) 1919- . . . . **CLC 14**
See also AITN 1; CA 69-72; CANR 5

Newman, John Henry
1801-1890 . . . . **NCLC 38**
See also DLB 18, 32, 55

Newton, Suzanne 1936- . . . . **CLC 35**
See also CA 41-44R; CANR 14; JRDA;
SATA 5, 77

Nexo, Martin Andersen
1869-1954 . . . . **TCLC 43**

Nezval, Vitezslav 1900-1958 . . . . . . **TCLC 44**
See also CA 123

Ng, Fae Myenne 1957(?)- . . . . **CLC 81**
See also CA 146

Ngema, Mbongeni 1955- . . . . **CLC 57**
See also BW 2; CA 143

Ngugi, James T(hiong'o) . . . . **CLC 3, 7, 13**
See also Ngugi wa Thiong'o

Ngugi wa Thiong'o
1938- . . . . . **CLC 36; BLC; DAM MULT,
NOV**
See also Ngugi, James T(hiong'o)
See also BW 2; CA 81-84; CANR 27;
DLB 125; MTCW

Nichol, B(arrie) P(hillip)
1944-1988 . . . . **CLC 18**
See also CA 53-56; DLB 53; SATA 66

Nichols, John (Treadwell) 1940- . . . . **CLC 38**
See also CA 9-12R; CAAS 2; CANR 6;
DLBY 82

Nichols, Leigh
See Koontz, Dean R(ay)

Nichols, Peter (Richard)
1927- . . . . **CLC 5, 36, 65**
See also CA 104; CANR 33; DLB 13;
MTCW

Nicolas, F. R. E.
See Freeling, Nicolas

Niedecker, Lorine
1903-1970 . . . . **CLC 10, 42; DAM POET**
See also CA 25-28; CAP 2; DLB 48

Nietzsche, Friedrich (Wilhelm)
1844-1900 . . . . **TCLC 10, 18, 55**
See also CA 107; 121; DLB 129

Nievo, Ippolito 1831-1861 . . . . **NCLC 22**

Nightingale, Anne Redmon 1943-
See Redmon, Anne
See also CA 103

Nik. T. O.
See Annensky, Innokenty Fyodorovich

Nin, Anais
1903-1977 . . . . . . **CLC 1, 4, 8, 11, 14, 60;
DAM NOV, POP; SSC 10**
See also AITN 2; CA 13-16R; 69-72;
CANR 22, 53; DLB 2, 4, 152; MTCW

Nishiwaki, Junzaburo 1894-1982 . . . . **PC 15**
See also CA 107

Nissenson, Hugh 1933- . . . . **CLC 4, 9**
See also CA 17-20R; CANR 27; DLB 28

Niven, Larry . . . . **CLC 8**
See also Niven, Laurence Van Cott
See also DLB 8

Niven, Laurence Van Cott 1938-
See Niven, Larry
See also CA 21-24R; CAAS 12; CANR 14,
44; DAM POP; MTCW

Nixon, Agnes Eckhardt 1927- . . . . . . **CLC 21**
See also CA 110

Nizan, Paul 1905-1940 . . . . **TCLC 40**
See also DLB 72

Nkosi, Lewis
1936- . . . . . **CLC 45; BLC; DAM MULT**
See also BW 1; CA 65-68; CANR 27;
DLB 157

Nodier, (Jean) Charles (Emmanuel)
1780-1844 . . . . **NCLC 19**
See also DLB 119

Nolan, Christopher 1965- . . . . **CLC 58**
See also CA 111

Noon, Jeff 1957- . . . . **CLC 91**
See also CA 148

Norden, Charles
See Durrell, Lawrence (George)

Nordhoff, Charles (Bernard)
1887-1947 . . . . **TCLC 23**
See also CA 108; DLB 9; SATA 23

Norfolk, Lawrence 1963- . . . . **CLC 76**
See also CA 144

Norman, Marsha
1947- . . . . **CLC 28; DAM DRAM**
See also CA 105; CABS 3; CANR 41;
DLBY 84

Norris, Benjamin Franklin, Jr.
1870-1902 . . . . **TCLC 24**
See also Norris, Frank
See also CA 110

Norris, Frank
See Norris, Benjamin Franklin, Jr.
See also CDALB 1865-1917; DLB 12, 71

Norris, Leslie 1921- . . . . **CLC 14**
See also CA 11-12; CANR 14; CAP 1;
DLB 27

North, Andrew
See Norton, Andre

North, Anthony
See Koontz, Dean R(ay)

North, Captain George
See Stevenson, Robert Louis (Balfour)

North, Milou
See Erdrich, Louise

Northrup, B. A.
See Hubbard, L(afayette) Ron(ald)

North Staffs
See Hulme, T(homas) E(rnest)

Norton, Alice Mary
See Norton, Andre
See also MAICYA; SATA 1, 43

Norton, Andre 1912- . . . . **CLC 12**
See also Norton, Alice Mary
See also AAYA 14; CA 1-4R; CANR 2, 31;
DLB 8, 52; JRDA; MTCW

Norton, Caroline 1808-1877 . . . . . . **NCLC 47**
See also DLB 21, 159

Norway, Nevil Shute 1899-1960
See Shute, Nevil
See also CA 102; 93-96

Norwid, Cyprian Kamil
1821-1883 . . . . **NCLC 17**

Nosille, Nabrah
See Ellison, Harlan (Jay)

Nossack, Hans Erich 1901-1978 . . . . . **CLC 6**
See also CA 93-96; 85-88; DLB 69

Nostradamus 1503-1566 . . . . **LC 27**

Nosu, Chuji
See Ozu, Yasujiro

Notenburg, Eleanora (Genrikhovna) von
See Guro, Elena

Nova, Craig 1945- . . . . **CLC 7, 31**
See also CA 45-48; CANR 2, 53

Novak, Joseph
See Kosinski, Jerzy (Nikodem)

Novalis 1772-1801 . . . . **NCLC 13**
See also DLB 90

Nowlan, Alden (Albert)
1933-1983 . . **CLC 15; DAC; DAM MST**
See also CA 9-12R; CANR 5; DLB 53

Noyes, Alfred 1880-1958 . . . . **TCLC 7**
See also CA 104; DLB 20

Nunn, Kem 19(?)- . . . . **CLC 34**

Nye, Robert
1939- . . . . **CLC 13, 42; DAM NOV**
See also CA 33-36R; CANR 29; DLB 14;
MTCW; SATA 6

Nyro, Laura 1947- . . . . **CLC 17**

Oates, Joyce Carol
1938- . . . . . . **CLC 1, 2, 3, 6, 9, 11, 15, 19,
33, 52; DA; DAB; DAC; DAM MST,
NOV, POP; SSC 6; WLC**
See also AAYA 15; AITN 1; BEST 89:2;
CA 5-8R; CANR 25, 45;
CDALB 1968-1988; DLB 2, 5, 130;
DLBY 81; INT CANR-25; MTCW

O'Brien, Darcy 1939- . . . . **CLC 11**
See also CA 21-24R; CANR 8

O'Brien, E. G.
See Clarke, Arthur C(harles)

O'Brien, Edna
   1936- .... CLC 3, 5, 8, 13, 36, 65;
                              DAM NOV; SSC 10
   See also CA 1-4R; CANR 6, 41;
      CDBLB 1960 to Present; DLB 14;
      MTCW

O'Brien, Fitz-James 1828-1862... NCLC 21
   See also DLB 74

O'Brien, Flann .... CLC 1, 4, 5, 7, 10, 47
   See also O Nuallain, Brian

O'Brien, Richard 1942- .... CLC 17
   See also CA 124

O'Brien, Tim
   1946- .... CLC 7, 19, 40; DAM POP
   See also AAYA 16; CA 85-88; CANR 40;
      DLB 152; DLBD 9; DLBY 80

Obstfelder, Sigbjoern 1866-1900... TCLC 23
   See also CA 123

O'Casey, Sean
   1880-1964 ...... CLC 1, 5, 9, 11, 15, 88;
                    DAB; DAC; DAM DRAM, MST
   See also CA 89-92; CDBLB 1914-1945;
      DLB 10; MTCW

O'Cathasaigh, Sean
   See O'Casey, Sean

Ochs, Phil 1940-1976 .... CLC 17
   See also CA 65-68

O'Connor, Edwin (Greene)
   1918-1968 .... CLC 14
   See also CA 93-96; 25-28R

O'Connor, (Mary) Flannery
   1925-1964 .... CLC 1, 2, 3, 6, 10, 13, 15,
      21, 66; DA; DAB; DAC; DAM MST,
                         NOV; SSC 1, 23; WLC
   See also AAYA 7; CA 1-4R; CANR 3, 41;
      CDALB 1941-1968; DLB 2, 152;
      DLBD 12; DLBY 80; MTCW

O'Connor, Frank .... CLC 23; SSC 5
   See also O'Donovan, Michael John
   See also DLB 162

O'Dell, Scott 1898-1989 .... CLC 30
   See also AAYA 3; CA 61-64; 129;
      CANR 12, 30; CLR 1, 16; DLB 52;
      JRDA; MAICYA; SATA 12, 60

Odets, Clifford
   1906-1963 ... CLC 2, 28; DAM DRAM;
                                         DC 6
   See also CA 85-88; DLB 7, 26; MTCW

O'Doherty, Brian 1934- .... CLC 76
   See also CA 105

O'Donnell, K. M.
   See Malzberg, Barry N(athaniel)

O'Donnell, Lawrence
   See Kuttner, Henry

O'Donovan, Michael John
   1903-1966 .... CLC 14
   See also O'Connor, Frank
   See also CA 93-96

Oe, Kenzaburo
   1935- ..... CLC 10, 36, 86; DAM NOV;
                                      SSC 20
   See also CA 97-100; CANR 36, 50;
      DLBY 94; MTCW

O'Faolain, Julia 1932- .... CLC 6, 19, 47
   See also CA 81-84; CAAS 2; CANR 12;
      DLB 14; MTCW

O'Faolain, Sean
   1900-1991 .... CLC 1, 7, 14, 32, 70;
                                      SSC 13
   See also CA 61-64; 134; CANR 12;
      DLB 15, 162; MTCW

O'Flaherty, Liam
   1896-1984 .... CLC 5, 34; SSC 6
   See also CA 101; 113; CANR 35; DLB 36,
      162; DLBY 84; MTCW

Ogilvy, Gavin
   See Barrie, J(ames) M(atthew)

O'Grady, Standish James
   1846-1928 .... TCLC 5
   See also CA 104

O'Grady, Timothy 1951- .... CLC 59
   See also CA 138

O'Hara, Frank
   1926-1966 .... CLC 2, 5, 13, 78;
                                  DAM POET
   See also CA 9-12R; 25-28R; CANR 33;
      DLB 5, 16; MTCW

O'Hara, John (Henry)
   1905-1970 .... CLC 1, 2, 3, 6, 11, 42;
                           DAM NOV; SSC 15
   See also CA 5-8R; 25-28R; CANR 31;
      CDALB 1929-1941; DLB 9, 86; DLBD 2;
      MTCW

O Hehir, Diana 1922- .... CLC 41
   See also CA 93-96

Okigbo, Christopher (Ifenayichukwu)
   1932-1967 .... CLC 25, 84; BLC;
                    DAM MULT, POET; PC 7
   See also BW 1; CA 77-80; DLB 125;
      MTCW

Okri, Ben 1959- .... CLC 87
   See also BW 2; CA 130; 138; DLB 157;
      INT 138

Olds, Sharon
   1942- ..... CLC 32, 39, 85; DAM POET
   See also CA 101; CANR 18, 41; DLB 120

Oldstyle, Jonathan
   See Irving, Washington

Olesha, Yuri (Karlovich)
   1899-1960 .... CLC 8
   See also CA 85-88

Oliphant, Laurence
   1829(?)-1888 .... NCLC 47
   See also DLB 18, 166

Oliphant, Margaret (Oliphant Wilson)
   1828-1897 .... NCLC 11
   See also DLB 18, 159

Oliver, Mary 1935- .... CLC 19, 34
   See also CA 21-24R; CANR 9, 43; DLB 5

Olivier, Laurence (Kerr)
   1907-1989 .... CLC 20
   See also CA 111; 150; 129

Olsen, Tillie
   1913- ..... CLC 4, 13; DA; DAB; DAC;
                           DAM MST; SSC 11
   See also CA 1-4R; CANR 1, 43; DLB 28;
      DLBY 80; MTCW

Olson, Charles (John)
   1910-1970 ..... CLC 1, 2, 5, 6, 9, 11, 29;
                                  DAM POET
   See also CA 13-16; 25-28R; CABS 2;
      CANR 35; CAP 1; DLB 5, 16; MTCW

Olson, Toby 1937- .... CLC 28
   See also CA 65-68; CANR 9, 31

Olyesha, Yuri
   See Olesha, Yuri (Karlovich)

Ondaatje, (Philip) Michael
   1943- .... CLC 14, 29, 51, 76; DAB;
                              DAC; DAM MST
   See also CA 77-80; CANR 42; DLB 60

Oneal, Elizabeth 1934-
   See Oneal, Zibby
   See also CA 106; CANR 28; MAICYA;
      SATA 30, 82

Oneal, Zibby .... CLC 30
   See also Oneal, Elizabeth
   See also AAYA 5; CLR 13; JRDA

O'Neill, Eugene (Gladstone)
   1888-1953 ...... TCLC 1, 6, 27, 49; DA;
      DAB; DAC; DAM DRAM, MST; WLC
   See also AITN 1; CA 110; 132;
      CDALB 1929-1941; DLB 7; MTCW

Onetti, Juan Carlos
   1909-1994 .... CLC 7, 10; DAM MULT,
                              NOV; SSC 23
   See also CA 85-88; 145; CANR 32;
      DLB 113; HW; MTCW

O Nuallain, Brian 1911-1966
   See O'Brien, Flann
   See also CA 21-22; 25-28R; CAP 2

Oppen, George 1908-1984 .... CLC 7, 13, 34
   See also CA 13-16R; 113; CANR 8; DLB 5,
      165

Oppenheim, E(dward) Phillips
   1866-1946 .... TCLC 45
   See also CA 111; DLB 70

Orlovitz, Gil 1918-1973 .... CLC 22
   See also CA 77-80; 45-48; DLB 2, 5

Orris
   See Ingelow, Jean

Ortega y Gasset, Jose
   1883-1955 ..... TCLC 9; DAM MULT;
                                         HLC
   See also CA 106; 130; HW; MTCW

Ortese, Anna Maria 1914- .... CLC 89

Ortiz, Simon J(oseph)
   1941- .... CLC 45; DAM MULT, POET
   See also CA 134; DLB 120; NNAL

Orton, Joe .... CLC 4, 13, 43; DC 3
   See also Orton, John Kingsley
   See also CDBLB 1960 to Present; DLB 13

Orton, John Kingsley 1933-1967
   See Orton, Joe
   See also CA 85-88; CANR 35;
      DAM DRAM; MTCW

Orwell, George
   .... TCLC 2, 6, 15, 31, 51; DAB; WLC
   See also Blair, Eric (Arthur)
   See also CDBLB 1945-1960; DLB 15, 98

Osborne, David
   See Silverberg, Robert

Osborne, George
   See Silverberg, Robert

Osborne, John (James)
   1929-1994 ..... CLC 1, 2, 5, 11, 45; DA;
      DAB; DAC; DAM DRAM, MST; WLC
   See also CA 13-16R; 147; CANR 21;
      CDBLB 1945-1960; DLB 13; MTCW

Osborne, Lawrence 1958- .... **CLC 50**

Oshima, Nagisa 1932- .... **CLC 20**
See also CA 116; 121

Oskison, John Milton
1874-1947 ..... **TCLC 35; DAM MULT**
See also CA 144; NNAL

Ossoli, Sarah Margaret (Fuller marchesa d')
1810-1850
See Fuller, Margaret
See also SATA 25

Ostrovsky, Alexander
1823-1886 .... **NCLC 30, 57**

Otero, Blas de 1916-1979......... **CLC 11**
See also CA 89-92; DLB 134

Otto, Whitney 1955-.............. **CLC 70**
See also CA 140

Ouida .... **TCLC 43**
See also De La Ramee, (Marie) Louise
See also DLB 18, 156

Ousmane, Sembene 1923- .... **CLC 66; BLC**
See also BW 1; CA 117; 125; MTCW

Ovid
43B.C.-18(?) ... **CMLC 7; DAM POET;**
PC 2

Owen, Hugh
See Faust, Frederick (Schiller)

Owen, Wilfred (Edward Salter)
1893-1918 ...... **TCLC 5, 27; DA; DAB;**
DAC; DAM MST, POET; WLC
See also CA 104; 141; CDBLB 1914-1945;
DLB 20

Owens, Rochelle 1936-............. **CLC 8**
See also CA 17-20R; CAAS 2; CANR 39

Oz, Amos
1939- .... **CLC 5, 8, 11, 27, 33, 54;**
DAM NOV
See also CA 53-56; CANR 27, 47; MTCW

Ozick, Cynthia
1928- .... **CLC 3, 7, 28, 62; DAM NOV,**
POP; SSC 15
See also BEST 90:1; CA 17-20R; CANR 23;
DLB 28, 152; DLBY 82; INT CANR-23;
MTCW

Ozu, Yasujiro 1903-1963.......... **CLC 16**
See also CA 112

Pacheco, C.
See Pessoa, Fernando (Antonio Nogueira)

Pa Chin .... **CLC 18**
See also Li Fei-kan

Pack, Robert 1929-.............. **CLC 13**
See also CA 1-4R; CANR 3, 44; DLB 5

Padgett, Lewis
See Kuttner, Henry

Padilla (Lorenzo), Heberto 1932- ... **CLC 38**
See also AITN 1; CA 123; 131; HW

Page, Jimmy 1944-.............. **CLC 12**

Page, Louise 1955-.............. **CLC 40**
See also CA 140

Page, P(atricia) K(athleen)
1916- .... **CLC 7, 18; DAC; DAM MST;**
PC 12
See also CA 53-56; CANR 4, 22; DLB 68;
MTCW

Page, Thomas Nelson 1853-1922.... **SSC 23**
See also CA 118; DLB 12, 78; DLBD 13

Paget, Violet 1856-1935
See Lee, Vernon
See also CA 104

Paget-Lowe, Henry
See Lovecraft, H(oward) P(hillips)

Paglia, Camille (Anna) 1947-....... **CLC 68**
See also CA 140

Paige, Richard
See Koontz, Dean R(ay)

Pakenham, Antonia
See Fraser, (Lady) Antonia (Pakenham)

Palamas, Kostes 1859-1943 .... **TCLC 5**
See also CA 105

Palazzeschi, Aldo 1885-1974...... **CLC 11**
See also CA 89-92; 53-56; DLB 114

Paley, Grace
1922- .... **CLC 4, 6, 37; DAM POP;**
SSC 8
See also CA 25-28R; CANR 13, 46;
DLB 28; INT CANR-13; MTCW

Palin, Michael (Edward) 1943-..... **CLC 21**
See also Monty Python
See also CA 107; CANR 35; SATA 67

Palliser, Charles 1947-........... **CLC 65**
See also CA 136

Palma, Ricardo 1833-1919....... **TCLC 29**

Pancake, Breece Dexter 1952-1979
See Pancake, Breece D'J
See also CA 123; 109

Pancake, Breece D'J.............. **CLC 29**
See also Pancake, Breece Dexter
See also DLB 130

Panko, Rudy
See Gogol, Nikolai (Vasilyevich)

Papadiamantis, Alexandros
1851-1911 .... **TCLC 29**

Papadiamantopoulos, Johannes 1856-1910
See Moreas, Jean
See also CA 117

Papini, Giovanni 1881-1956....... **TCLC 22**
See also CA 121

Paracelsus 1493-1541.............. **LC 14**

Parasol, Peter
See Stevens, Wallace

Parfenie, Maria
See Codrescu, Andrei

Parini, Jay (Lee) 1948- .... **CLC 54**
See also CA 97-100; CAAS 16; CANR 32

Park, Jordan
See Kornbluth, C(yril) M.; Pohl, Frederik

Parker, Bert
See Ellison, Harlan (Jay)

Parker, Dorothy (Rothschild)
1893-1967 .... **CLC 15, 68;**
DAM POET; SSC 2
See also CA 19-20; 25-28R; CAP 2;
DLB 11, 45, 86; MTCW

Parker, Robert B(rown)
1932- .... **CLC 27; DAM NOV, POP**
See also BEST 89:4; CA 49-52; CANR 1,
26, 52; INT CANR-26; MTCW

Parkin, Frank 1940-.............. **CLC 43**
See also CA 147

Parkman, Francis, Jr.
1823-1893 .... **NCLC 12**
See also DLB 1, 30

Parks, Gordon (Alexander Buchanan)
1912- ... **CLC 1, 16; BLC; DAM MULT**
See also AITN 2; BW 2; CA 41-44R;
CANR 26; DLB 33; SATA 8

Parnell, Thomas 1679-1718 .... **LC 3**
See also DLB 94

Parra, Nicanor
1914- ...... **CLC 2; DAM MULT; HLC**
See also CA 85-88; CANR 32; HW; MTCW

Parrish, Mary Frances
See Fisher, M(ary) F(rances) K(ennedy)

Parson
See Coleridge, Samuel Taylor

Parson Lot
See Kingsley, Charles

Partridge, Anthony
See Oppenheim, E(dward) Phillips

Pascal, Blaise 1623-1662 .... **LC 35**

Pascoli, Giovanni 1855-1912 ...... **TCLC 45**

Pasolini, Pier Paolo
1922-1975 .... **CLC 20, 37**
See also CA 93-96; 61-64; DLB 128;
MTCW

Pasquini
See Silone, Ignazio

Pastan, Linda (Olenik)
1932- .... **CLC 27; DAM POET**
See also CA 61-64; CANR 18, 40; DLB 5

Pasternak, Boris (Leonidovich)
1890-1960 ...... **CLC 7, 10, 18, 63; DA;**
DAB; DAC; DAM MST, NOV, POET;
PC 6; WLC
See also CA 127; 116; MTCW

Patchen, Kenneth
1911-1972 ... **CLC 1, 2, 18; DAM POET**
See also CA 1-4R; 33-36R; CANR 3, 35;
DLB 16, 48; MTCW

Pater, Walter (Horatio)
1839-1894 .... **NCLC 7**
See also CDBLB 1832-1890; DLB 57, 156

Paterson, A(ndrew) B(arton)
1864-1941 .... **TCLC 32**

Paterson, Katherine (Womeldorf)
1932- .... **CLC 12, 30**
See also AAYA 1; CA 21-24R; CANR 28;
CLR 7; DLB 52; JRDA; MAICYA;
MTCW; SATA 13, 53

Patmore, Coventry Kersey Dighton
1823-1896 .... **NCLC 9**
See also DLB 35, 98

Paton, Alan (Stewart)
1903-1988 ...... **CLC 4, 10, 25, 55; DA;**
DAB; DAC; DAM MST, NOV; WLC
See also CA 13-16; 125; CANR 22; CAP 1;
MTCW; SATA 11; SATA-Obit 56

Paton Walsh, Gillian 1937-
See Walsh, Jill Paton
See also CANR 38; JRDA; MAICYA;
SAAS 3; SATA 4, 72

Paulding, James Kirke 1778-1860. . **NCLC 2**
See also DLB 3, 59, 74

Paulin, Thomas Neilson 1949-
See Paulin, Tom
See also CA 123; 128

Paulin, Tom . . . . **CLC 37**
See also Paulin, Thomas Neilson
See also DLB 40

Paustovsky, Konstantin (Georgievich)
1892-1968 . . . . **CLC 40**
See also CA 93-96; 25-28R

Pavese, Cesare
1908-1950 . . . . . **TCLC 3; PC 13; SSC 19**
See also CA 104; DLB 128

Pavic, Milorad 1929- . . . . **CLC 60**
See also CA 136

Payne, Alan
See Jakes, John (William)

Paz, Gil
See Lugones, Leopoldo

Paz, Octavio
1914- . . . . **CLC 3, 4, 6, 10, 19, 51, 65;**
DA; DAB; DAC; DAM MST, MULT,
POET; HLC; PC 1; WLC
See also CA 73-76; CANR 32; DLBY 90;
HW; MTCW

p'Bitek, Okot
1931-1982 . . . . **CLC 96; BLC;**
DAM MULT
See also BW 2; CA 124; 107; DLB 125;
MTCW

Peacock, Molly 1947- . . . . **CLC 60**
See also CA 103; CAAS 21; CANR 52;
DLB 120

Peacock, Thomas Love
1785-1866 . . . . **NCLC 22**
See also DLB 96, 116

Peake, Mervyn 1911-1968 . . . . **CLC 7, 54**
See also CA 5-8R; 25-28R; CANR 3;
DLB 15, 160; MTCW; SATA 23

Pearce, Philippa . . . . **CLC 21**
See also Christie, (Ann) Philippa
See also CLR 9; DLB 161; MAICYA;
SATA 1, 67

Pearl, Eric
See Elman, Richard

Pearson, T(homas) R(eid) 1956- . . . . **CLC 39**
See also CA 120; 130; INT 130

Peck, Dale 1967- . . . . **CLC 81**
See also CA 146

Peck, John 1941- . . . . **CLC 3**
See also CA 49-52; CANR 3

Peck, Richard (Wayne) 1934- . . . . . . **CLC 21**
See also AAYA 1; CA 85-88; CANR 19,
38; CLR 15; INT CANR-19; JRDA;
MAICYA; SAAS 2; SATA 18, 55

Peck, Robert Newton
1928- . . **CLC 17; DA; DAC; DAM MST**
See also AAYA 3; CA 81-84; CANR 31;
JRDA; MAICYA; SAAS 1; SATA 21, 62

Peckinpah, (David) Sam(uel)
1925-1984 . . . . **CLC 20**
See also CA 109; 114

Pedersen, Knut 1859-1952
See Hamsun, Knut
See also CA 104; 119; MTCW

Peeslake, Gaffer
See Durrell, Lawrence (George)

Peguy, Charles Pierre
1873-1914 . . . . **TCLC 10**
See also CA 107

Pena, Ramon del Valle y
See Valle-Inclan, Ramon (Maria) del

Pendennis, Arthur Esquir
See Thackeray, William Makepeace

Penn, William 1644-1718 . . . . **LC 25**
See also DLB 24

Pepys, Samuel
1633-1703 . . . . . **LC 11; DA; DAB; DAC;**
DAM MST; WLC
See also CDBLB 1660-1789; DLB 101

Percy, Walker
1916-1990 . . . . **CLC 2, 3, 6, 8, 14, 18, 47,**
65; DAM NOV, POP
See also CA 1-4R; 131; CANR 1, 23;
DLB 2; DLBY 80, 90; MTCW

Perec, Georges 1936-1982 . . . . **CLC 56**
See also CA 141; DLB 83

Pereda (y Sanchez de Porrua), Jose Maria de
1833-1906 . . . . **TCLC 16**
See also CA 117

Pereda y Porrua, Jose Maria de
See Pereda (y Sanchez de Porrua), Jose
Maria de

Peregoy, George Weems
See Mencken, H(enry) L(ouis)

Perelman, S(idney) J(oseph)
1904-1979 . . . . . . **CLC 3, 5, 9, 15, 23, 44,**
49; DAM DRAM
See also AITN 1, 2; CA 73-76; 89-92;
CANR 18; DLB 11, 44; MTCW

Peret, Benjamin 1899-1959 . . . . **TCLC 20**
See also CA 117

Peretz, Isaac Loeb 1851(?)-1915 . . . **TCLC 16**
See also CA 109

Peretz, Yitzkhok Leibush
See Peretz, Isaac Loeb

Perez Galdos, Benito 1843-1920 . . . **TCLC 27**
See also CA 125; HW

Perrault, Charles 1628-1703 . . . . **LC 2**
See also MAICYA; SATA 25

Perry, Brighton
See Sherwood, Robert E(mmet)

Perse, St.-John . . . . **CLC 4, 11, 46**
See also Leger, (Marie-Rene Auguste) Alexis
Saint-Leger

Perutz, Leo 1882-1957 . . . . **TCLC 60**
See also DLB 81

Peseenz, Tulio F.
See Lopez y Fuentes, Gregorio

Pesetsky, Bette 1932- . . . . **CLC 28**
See also CA 133; DLB 130

Peshkov, Alexei Maximovich 1868-1936
See Gorky, Maxim
See also CA 105; 141; DA; DAC;
DAM DRAM, MST, NOV

Pessoa, Fernando (Antonio Nogueira)
1888-1935 . . . . **TCLC 27; HLC**
See also CA 125

Peterkin, Julia Mood 1880-1961 . . . . **CLC 31**
See also CA 102; DLB 9

Peters, Joan K. 1945- . . . . **CLC 39**

Peters, Robert L(ouis) 1924- . . . . **CLC 7**
See also CA 13-16R; CAAS 8; DLB 105

Petofi, Sandor 1823-1849 . . . . **NCLC 21**

Petrakis, Harry Mark 1923- . . . . **CLC 3**
See also CA 9-12R; CANR 4, 30

Petrarch 1304-1374 . . . . **PC 8**
See also DAM POET

Petrov, Evgeny . . . . **TCLC 21**
See also Kataev, Evgeny Petrovich

Petry, Ann (Lane) 1908- . . . . . . **CLC 1, 7, 18**
See also BW 1; CA 5-8R; CAAS 6;
CANR 4, 46; CLR 12; DLB 76; JRDA;
MAICYA; MTCW; SATA 5

Petursson, Halligrimur 1614-1674 . . . . **LC 8**

Philips, Katherine 1632-1664 . . . . **LC 30**
See also DLB 131

Philipson, Morris H. 1926- . . . . **CLC 53**
See also CA 1-4R; CANR 4

Phillips, Caryl
1958- . . . . **CLC 96; DAM MULT**
See also BW 2; CA 141; DLB 157

Phillips, David Graham
1867-1911 . . . . **TCLC 44**
See also CA 108; DLB 9, 12

Phillips, Jack
See Sandburg, Carl (August)

Phillips, Jayne Anne
1952- . . . . **CLC 15, 33; SSC 16**
See also CA 101; CANR 24, 50; DLBY 80;
INT CANR-24; MTCW

Phillips, Richard
See Dick, Philip K(indred)

Phillips, Robert (Schaeffer) 1938- . . . **CLC 28**
See also CA 17-20R; CAAS 13; CANR 8;
DLB 105

Phillips, Ward
See Lovecraft, H(oward) P(hillips)

Piccolo, Lucio 1901-1969 . . . . **CLC 13**
See also CA 97-100; DLB 114

Pickthall, Marjorie L(owry) C(hristie)
1883-1922 . . . . **TCLC 21**
See also CA 107; DLB 92

Pico della Mirandola, Giovanni
1463-1494 . . . . **LC 15**

Piercy, Marge
1936- . . . . **CLC 3, 6, 14, 18, 27, 62**
See also CA 21-24R; CAAS 1; CANR 13,
43; DLB 120; MTCW

Piers, Robert
See Anthony, Piers

Pieyre de Mandiargues, Andre 1909-1991
See Mandiargues, Andre Pieyre de
See also CA 103; 136; CANR 22

Pilnyak, Boris . . . . **TCLC 23**
See also Vogau, Boris Andreyevich

Pincherle, Alberto
1907-1990 . . . . . CLC 11, 18; DAM NOV
See also Moravia, Alberto
See also CA 25-28R; 132; CANR 33;
MTCW

Pinckney, Darryl 1953- . . . . CLC 76
See also BW 2; CA 143

Pindar 518B.C.-446B.C. . . . . CMLC 12

Pineda, Cecile 1942- . . . . CLC 39
See also CA 118

Pinero, Arthur Wing
1855-1934 . . . . . TCLC 32; DAM DRAM
See also CA 110; DLB 10

Pinero, Miguel (Antonio Gomez)
1946-1988 . . . . CLC 4, 55
See also CA 61-64; 125; CANR 29; HW

Pinget, Robert 1919- . . . . CLC 7, 13, 37
See also CA 85-88; DLB 83

Pink Floyd
See Barrett, (Roger) Syd; Gilmour, David;
Mason, Nick; Waters, Roger; Wright,
Rick

Pinkney, Edward 1802-1828 . . . . . NCLC 31

Pinkwater, Daniel Manus 1941- . . . . CLC 35
See also Pinkwater, Manus
See also AAYA 1; CA 29-32R; CANR 12,
38; CLR 4; JRDA; MAICYA; SAAS 3;
SATA 46, 76

Pinkwater, Manus
See Pinkwater, Daniel Manus
See also SATA 8

Pinsky, Robert
1940- . . CLC 9, 19, 38, 94; DAM POET
See also CA 29-32R; CAAS 4; DLBY 82

Pinta, Harold
See Pinter, Harold

Pinter, Harold
1930- . . . . . CLC 1, 3, 6, 9, 11, 15, 27, 58,
73; DA; DAB; DAC; DAM DRAM,
MST; WLC
See also CA 5-8R; CANR 33; CDBLB 1960
to Present; DLB 13; MTCW

Piozzi, Hester Lynch (Thrale)
1741-1821 . . . . NCLC 57
See also DLB 104, 142

Pirandello, Luigi
1867-1936 . . . . . . TCLC 4, 29; DA; DAB;
DAC; DAM DRAM, MST; DC 5;
SSC 22; WLC
See also CA 104

Pirsig, Robert M(aynard)
1928- . . . . CLC 4, 6, 73; DAM POP
See also CA 53-56; CANR 42; MTCW;
SATA 39

Pisarev, Dmitry Ivanovich
1840-1868 . . . . NCLC 25

Pix, Mary (Griffith) 1666-1709 . . . . . . LC 8
See also DLB 80

Pixerecourt, Guilbert de
1773-1844 . . . . NCLC 39

Plaidy, Jean
See Hibbert, Eleanor Alice Burford

Planche, James Robinson
1796-1880 . . . . NCLC 42

Plant, Robert 1948- . . . . CLC 12

Plante, David (Robert)
1940- . . . . CLC 7, 23, 38; DAM NOV
See also CA 37-40R; CANR 12, 36;
DLBY 83; INT CANR-12; MTCW

Plath, Sylvia
1932-1963 . . . . . CLC 1, 2, 3, 5, 9, 11, 14,
17, 50, 51, 62; DA; DAB; DAC;
DAM MST, POET; PC 1; WLC
See also AAYA 13; CA 19-20; CANR 34;
CAP 2; CDALB 1941-1968; DLB 5, 6,
152; MTCW

Plato
428(?)B.C.-348(?)B.C. . . . . CMLC 8; DA;
DAB; DAC; DAM MST

Platonov, Andrei . . . . TCLC 14
See also Klimentov, Andrei Platonovich

Platt, Kin 1911- . . . . CLC 26
See also AAYA 11; CA 17-20R; CANR 11;
JRDA; SAAS 17; SATA 21, 86

Plautus c. 251B.C.-184B.C. . . . . DC 6

Plick et Plock
See Simenon, Georges (Jacques Christian)

Plimpton, George (Ames) 1927- . . . . . CLC 36
See also AITN 1; CA 21-24R; CANR 32;
MTCW; SATA 10

Plomer, William Charles Franklin
1903-1973 . . . . CLC 4, 8
See also CA 21-22; CANR 34; CAP 2;
DLB 20, 162; MTCW; SATA 24

Plowman, Piers
See Kavanagh, Patrick (Joseph)

Plum, J.
See Wodehouse, P(elham) G(renville)

Plumly, Stanley (Ross) 1939- . . . . . . CLC 33
See also CA 108; 110; DLB 5; INT 110

Plumpe, Friedrich Wilhelm
1888-1931 . . . . TCLC 53
See also CA 112

Poe, Edgar Allan
1809-1849 . . . . NCLC 1, 16, 55; DA;
DAB; DAC; DAM MST, POET; PC 1;
SSC 1, 22; WLC
See also AAYA 14; CDALB 1640-1865;
DLB 3, 59, 73, 74; SATA 23

Poet of Titchfield Street, The
See Pound, Ezra (Weston Loomis)

Pohl, Frederik 1919- . . . . CLC 18
See also CA 61-64; CAAS 1; CANR 11, 37;
DLB 8; INT CANR-11; MTCW;
SATA 24

Poirier, Louis 1910-
See Gracq, Julien
See also CA 122; 126

Poitier, Sidney 1927- . . . . CLC 26
See also BW 1; CA 117

Polanski, Roman 1933- . . . . CLC 16
See also CA 77-80

Poliakoff, Stephen 1952- . . . . CLC 38
See also CA 106; DLB 13

Police, The
See Copeland, Stewart (Armstrong);
Summers, Andrew James; Sumner,
Gordon Matthew

Polidori, John William
1795-1821 . . . . NCLC 51
See also DLB 116

Pollitt, Katha 1949- . . . . CLC 28
See also CA 120; 122; MTCW

Pollock, (Mary) Sharon
1936- . . . . CLC 50; DAC; DAM DRAM,
MST
See also CA 141; DLB 60

Polo, Marco 1254-1324 . . . . CMLC 15

Polonsky, Abraham (Lincoln)
1910- . . . . CLC 92
See also CA 104; DLB 26; INT 104

Polybius c. 200B.C.-c. 118B.C. . . . . CMLC 17

Pomerance, Bernard
1940- . . . . CLC 13; DAM DRAM
See also CA 101; CANR 49

Ponge, Francis (Jean Gaston Alfred)
1899-1988 . . . . . CLC 6, 18; DAM POET
See also CA 85-88; 126; CANR 40

Pontoppidan, Henrik 1857-1943 . . . TCLC 29

Poole, Josephine . . . . CLC 17
See also Helyar, Jane Penelope Josephine
See also SAAS 2; SATA 5

Popa, Vasko 1922-1991 . . . . CLC 19
See also CA 112; 148

Pope, Alexander
1688-1744 . . . . . . LC 3; DA; DAB; DAC;
DAM MST, POET; WLC
See also CDBLB 1660-1789; DLB 95, 101

Porter, Connie (Rose) 1959(?)- . . . . . CLC 70
See also BW 2; CA 142; SATA 81

Porter, Gene(va Grace) Stratton
1863(?)-1924 . . . . TCLC 21
See also CA 112

Porter, Katherine Anne
1890-1980 . . . . . . CLC 1, 3, 7, 10, 13, 15,
27; DA; DAB; DAC; DAM MST, NOV;
SSC 4
See also AITN 2; CA 1-4R; 101; CANR 1;
DLB 4, 9, 102; DLBD 12; DLBY 80;
MTCW; SATA 39; SATA-Obit 23

Porter, Peter (Neville Frederick)
1929- . . . . CLC 5, 13, 33
See also CA 85-88; DLB 40

Porter, William Sydney 1862-1910
See Henry, O.
See also CA 104; 131; CDALB 1865-1917;
DA; DAB; DAC; DAM MST; DLB 12,
78, 79; MTCW; YABC 2

Portillo (y Pacheco), Jose Lopez
See Lopez Portillo (y Pacheco), Jose

Post, Melville Davisson
1869-1930 . . . . TCLC 39
See also CA 110

Potok, Chaim
1929- . . . . CLC 2, 7, 14, 26; DAM NOV
See also AAYA 15; AITN 1, 2; CA 17-20R;
CANR 19, 35; DLB 28, 152;
INT CANR-19; MTCW; SATA 33

Potter, Beatrice
See Webb, (Martha) Beatrice (Potter)
See also MAICYA

Potter, Dennis (Christopher George)
1935-1994 .... CLC **58, 86**
See also CA 107; 145; CANR 33; MTCW

Pound, Ezra (Weston Loomis)
1885-1972 ...... CLC **1, 2, 3, 4, 5, 7, 10,**
13, 18, 34, 48, 50; DA; DAB; DAC;
DAM MST, POET; PC 4; WLC
See also CA 5-8R; 37-40R; CANR 40;
CDALB 1917-1929; DLB 4, 45, 63;
MTCW

Povod, Reinaldo 1959-1994 .... CLC **44**
See also CA 136; 146

Powell, Adam Clayton, Jr.
1908-1972 .... CLC **89; BLC;**
DAM MULT
See also BW 1; CA 102; 33-36R

Powell, Anthony (Dymoke)
1905- .... CLC **1, 3, 7, 9, 10, 31**
See also CA 1-4R; CANR 1, 32;
CDBLB 1945-1960; DLB 15; MTCW

Powell, Dawn 1897-1965 .... CLC **66**
See also CA 5-8R

Powell, Padgett 1952-............ CLC **34**
See also CA 126

Power, Susan .... CLC **91**

Powers, J(ames) F(arl)
1917- .... CLC **1, 4, 8, 57; SSC 4**
See also CA 1-4R; CANR 2; DLB 130;
MTCW

Powers, John J(ames) 1945-
See Powers, John R.
See also CA 69-72

Powers, John R. .... CLC **66**
See also Powers, John J(ames)

Powers, Richard (S.) 1957- .... CLC **93**
See also CA 148

Pownall, David 1938-............. CLC **10**
See also CA 89-92; CAAS 18; CANR 49;
DLB 14

Powys, John Cowper
1872-1963 .... CLC **7, 9, 15, 46**
See also CA 85-88; DLB 15; MTCW

Powys, T(heodore) F(rancis)
1875-1953 .... TCLC **9**
See also CA 106; DLB 36, 162

Prager, Emily 1952-.............. CLC **56**

Pratt, E(dwin) J(ohn)
1883(?)-1964 .... CLC **19; DAC;**
DAM POET
See also CA 141; 93-96; DLB 92

Premchand .... TCLC **21**
See also Srivastava, Dhanpat Rai

Preussler, Otfried 1923-.......... CLC **17**
See also CA 77-80; SATA 24

Prevert, Jacques (Henri Marie)
1900-1977 .... CLC **15**
See also CA 77-80; 69-72; CANR 29;
MTCW; SATA-Obit 30

Prevost, Abbe (Antoine Francois)
1697-1763 .... LC **1**

Price, (Edward) Reynolds
1933- .... CLC **3, 6, 13, 43, 50, 63;**
DAM NOV; SSC 22
See also CA 1-4R; CANR 1, 37; DLB 2;
INT CANR-37

Price, Richard 1949- .... CLC **6, 12**
See also CA 49-52; CANR 3; DLBY 81

Prichard, Katharine Susannah
1883-1969 .... CLC **46**
See also CA 11-12; CANR 33; CAP 1;
MTCW; SATA 66

Priestley, J(ohn) B(oynton)
1894-1984 .... CLC **2, 5, 9, 34;**
DAM DRAM, NOV
See also CA 9-12R; 113; CANR 33;
CDBLB 1914-1945; DLB 10, 34, 77, 100,
139; DLBY 84; MTCW

Prince 1958(?)- .... CLC **35**

Prince, F(rank) T(empleton) 1912-.. CLC **22**
See also CA 101; CANR 43; DLB 20

Prince Kropotkin
See Kropotkin, Peter (Alekseievich)

Prior, Matthew 1664-1721.......... LC **4**
See also DLB 95

Pritchard, William H(arrison)
1932-...................... CLC **34**
See also CA 65-68; CANR 23; DLB 111

Pritchett, V(ictor) S(awdon)
1900- .... CLC **5, 13, 15, 41;**
DAM NOV; SSC 14
See also CA 61-64; CANR 31; DLB 15,
139; MTCW

Private 19022
See Manning, Frederic

Probst, Mark 1925-.............. CLC **59**
See also CA 130

Prokosch, Frederic 1908-1989.... CLC **4, 48**
See also CA 73-76; 128; DLB 48

Prophet, The
See Dreiser, Theodore (Herman Albert)

Prose, Francine 1947-............. CLC **45**
See also CA 109; 112; CANR 46

Proudhon
See Cunha, Euclides (Rodrigues Pimenta) da

Proulx, E. Annie 1935- .... CLC **81**

Proust, (Valentin-Louis-George-Eugene-)
Marcel
1871-1922 .... TCLC **7, 13, 33; DA;**
DAB; DAC; DAM MST, NOV; WLC
See also CA 104; 120; DLB 65; MTCW

Prowler, Harley
See Masters, Edgar Lee

Prus, Boleslaw 1845-1912 .... TCLC **48**

Pryor, Richard (Franklin Lenox Thomas)
1940- .... CLC **26**
See also CA 122

Przybyszewski, Stanislaw
1868-1927 .... TCLC **36**
See also DLB 66

Pteleon
See Grieve, C(hristopher) M(urray)
See also DAM POET

Puckett, Lute
See Masters, Edgar Lee

Puig, Manuel
1932-1990 .... CLC **3, 5, 10, 28, 65;**
DAM MULT; HLC
See also CA 45-48; CANR 2, 32; DLB 113;
HW; MTCW

Purdy, Al(fred Wellington)
1918- .... CLC **3, 6, 14, 50; DAC;**
DAM MST, POET
See also CA 81-84; CAAS 17; CANR 42;
DLB 88

Purdy, James (Amos)
1923- .... CLC **2, 4, 10, 28, 52**
See also CA 33-36R; CAAS 1; CANR 19,
51; DLB 2; INT CANR-19; MTCW

Pure, Simon
See Swinnerton, Frank Arthur

Pushkin, Alexander (Sergeyevich)
1799-1837 ..... NCLC **3, 27; DA; DAB;**
DAC; DAM DRAM, MST, POET;
PC 10; WLC
See also SATA 61

P'u Sung-ling 1640-1715 .... LC **3**

Putnam, Arthur Lee
See Alger, Horatio, Jr.

Puzo, Mario
1920- ..... CLC **1, 2, 6, 36; DAM NOV,**
POP
See also CA 65-68; CANR 4, 42; DLB 6;
MTCW

Pym, Barbara (Mary Crampton)
1913-1980 .... CLC **13, 19, 37**
See also CA 13-14; 97-100; CANR 13, 34;
CAP 1; DLB 14; DLBY 87; MTCW

Pynchon, Thomas (Ruggles, Jr.)
1937- ..... CLC **2, 3, 6, 9, 11, 18, 33, 62,**
72; DA; DAB; DAC; DAM MST, NOV,
POP; SSC 14; WLC
See also BEST 90:2; CA 17-20R; CANR 22,
46; DLB 2; MTCW

Qian Zhongshu
See Ch'ien Chung-shu

Qroll
See Dagerman, Stig (Halvard)

Quarrington, Paul (Lewis) 1953-.... CLC **65**
See also CA 129

Quasimodo, Salvatore 1901-1968 ... CLC **10**
See also CA 13-16; 25-28R; CAP 1;
DLB 114; MTCW

Quay, Stephen 1947- .... CLC **95**

Quay, The Brothers
See Quay, Stephen; Quay, Timothy

Quay, Timothy 1947- .... CLC **95**

Queen, Ellery.................... CLC **3, 11**
See also Dannay, Frederic; Davidson,
Avram; Lee, Manfred B(ennington);
Sturgeon, Theodore (Hamilton); Vance,
John Holbrook

Queen, Ellery, Jr.
See Dannay, Frederic; Lee, Manfred
B(ennington)

Queneau, Raymond
1903-1976 .... CLC **2, 5, 10, 42**
See also CA 77-80; 69-72; CANR 32;
DLB 72; MTCW

Quevedo, Francisco de 1580-1645.... LC **23**

Quiller-Couch, Arthur Thomas
1863-1944 .... TCLC **53**
See also CA 118; DLB 135, 153

Quin, Ann (Marie) 1936-1973....... CLC **6**
See also CA 9-12R; 45-48; DLB 14

Quinn, Martin
    See Smith, Martin Cruz

Quinn, Peter 1947-.............. CLC 91

Quinn, Simon
    See Smith, Martin Cruz

Quiroga, Horacio (Sylvestre)
        1878-1937 ..... TCLC 20; DAM MULT;
                                        HLC
    See also CA 117; 131; HW; MTCW

Quoirez, Francoise 1935-........... CLC 9
    See also Sagan, Francoise
    See also CA 49-52; CANR 6, 39; MTCW

Raabe, Wilhelm 1831-1910 ...... TCLC 45
    See also DLB 129

Rabe, David (William)
        1940- ...... CLC 4, 8, 33; DAM DRAM
    See also CA 85-88; CABS 3; DLB 7

Rabelais, Francois
        1483-1553 ...... LC 5; DA; DAB; DAC;
                                DAM MST; WLC

Rabinovitch, Sholem 1859-1916
    See Aleichem, Sholem
    See also CA 104

Racine, Jean
        1639-1699 .... LC 28; DAB; DAM MST

Radcliffe, Ann (Ward)
        1764-1823 .... NCLC 6, 55
    See also DLB 39

Radiguet, Raymond 1903-1923 .... TCLC 29
    See also DLB 65

Radnoti, Miklos 1909-1944 ...... TCLC 16
    See also CA 118

Rado, James 1939-............... CLC 17
    See also CA 105

Radvanyi, Netty 1900-1983
    See Seghers, Anna
    See also CA 85-88; 110

Rae, Ben
    See Griffiths, Trevor

Raeburn, John (Hay) 1941-........ CLC 34
    See also CA 57-60

Ragni, Gerome 1942-1991 .... CLC 17
    See also CA 105; 134

Rahv, Philip 1908-1973 .... CLC 24
    See also Greenberg, Ivan
    See also DLB 137

Raine, Craig 1944-............... CLC 32
    See also CA 108; CANR 29, 51; DLB 40

Raine, Kathleen (Jessie) 1908- ... CLC 7, 45
    See also CA 85-88; CANR 46; DLB 20;
        MTCW

Rainis, Janis 1865-1929......... TCLC 29

Rakosi, Carl...................... CLC 47
    See also Rawley, Callman
    See also CAAS 5

Raleigh, Richard
    See Lovecraft, H(oward) P(hillips)

Raleigh, Sir Walter 1554(?)-1618 .... LC 31
    See also CDBLB Before 1660

Rallentando, H. P.
    See Sayers, Dorothy L(eigh)

Ramal, Walter
    See de la Mare, Walter (John)

Ramon, Juan
    See Jimenez (Mantecon), Juan Ramon

Ramos, Graciliano 1892-1953 ..... TCLC 32

Rampersad, Arnold 1941-.......... CLC 44
    See also BW 2; CA 127; 133; DLB 111;
        INT 133

Rampling, Anne
    See Rice, Anne

Ramsay, Allan 1684(?)-1758 .... LC 29
    See also DLB 95

Ramuz, Charles-Ferdinand
        1878-1947 .... TCLC 33

Rand, Ayn
        1905-1982 ...... CLC 3, 30, 44, 79; DA;
            DAC; DAM MST, NOV, POP; WLC
    See also AAYA 10; CA 13-16R; 105;
        CANR 27; MTCW

Randall, Dudley (Felker)
        1914- ...... CLC 1; BLC; DAM MULT
    See also BW 1; CA 25-28R; CANR 23;
        DLB 41

Randall, Robert
    See Silverberg, Robert

Ranger, Ken
    See Creasey, John

Ransom, John Crowe
        1888-1974 .... CLC 2, 4, 5, 11, 24;
                                        DAM POET
    See also CA 5-8R; 49-52; CANR 6, 34;
        DLB 45, 63; MTCW

Rao, Raja 1909- ... CLC 25, 56; DAM NOV
    See also CA 73-76; CANR 51; MTCW

Raphael, Frederic (Michael)
        1931-.................... CLC 2, 14
    See also CA 1-4R; CANR 1; DLB 14

Ratcliffe, James P.
    See Mencken, H(enry) L(ouis)

Rathbone, Julian 1935-........... CLC 41
    See also CA 101; CANR 34

Rattigan, Terence (Mervyn)
        1911-1977 .... CLC 7; DAM DRAM
    See also CA 85-88; 73-76;
        CDBLB 1945-1960; DLB 13; MTCW

Ratushinskaya, Irina 1954-........ CLC 54
    See also CA 129

Raven, Simon (Arthur Noel)
        1927-.................... CLC 14
    See also CA 81-84

Rawley, Callman 1903-
    See Rakosi, Carl
    See also CA 21-24R; CANR 12, 32

Rawlings, Marjorie Kinnan
        1896-1953 .... TCLC 4
    See also CA 104; 137; DLB 9, 22, 102;
        JRDA; MAICYA; YABC 1

Ray, Satyajit
        1921-1992 ... CLC 16, 76; DAM MULT
    See also CA 114; 137

Read, Herbert Edward 1893-1968.... CLC 4
    See also CA 85-88; 25-28R; DLB 20, 149

Read, Piers Paul 1941- ...... CLC 4, 10, 25
    See also CA 21-24R; CANR 38; DLB 14;
        SATA 21

Reade, Charles 1814-1884 .... NCLC 2
    See also DLB 21

Reade, Hamish
    See Gray, Simon (James Holliday)

Reading, Peter 1946-............. CLC 47
    See also CA 103; CANR 46; DLB 40

Reaney, James
        1926-...... CLC 13; DAC; DAM MST
    See also CA 41-44R; CAAS 15; CANR 42;
        DLB 68; SATA 43

Rebreanu, Liviu 1885-1944 .... TCLC 28

Rechy, John (Francisco)
        1934-............... CLC 1, 7, 14, 18;
                                DAM MULT; HLC
    See also CA 5-8R; CAAS 4; CANR 6, 32;
        DLB 122; DLBY 82; HW; INT CANR-6

Redcam, Tom 1870-1933 .... TCLC 25

Reddin, Keith..................... CLC 67

Redgrove, Peter (William)
        1932-..................... CLC 6, 41
    See also CA 1-4R; CANR 3, 39; DLB 40

Redmon, Anne.................... CLC 22
    See also Nightingale, Anne Redmon
    See also DLBY 86

Reed, Eliot
    See Ambler, Eric

Reed, Ishmael
        1938-........ CLC 2, 3, 5, 6, 13, 32, 60;
                                BLC; DAM MULT
    See also BW 2; CA 21-24R; CANR 25, 48;
        DLB 2, 5, 33; DLBD 8; MTCW

Reed, John (Silas) 1887-1920 ...... TCLC 9
    See also CA 106

Reed, Lou........................ CLC 21
    See also Firbank, Louis

Reeve, Clara 1729-1807 .... NCLC 19
    See also DLB 39

Reich, Wilhelm 1897-1957........ TCLC 57

Reid, Christopher (John) 1949-..... CLC 33
    See also CA 140; DLB 40

Reid, Desmond
    See Moorcock, Michael (John)

Reid Banks, Lynne 1929-
    See Banks, Lynne Reid
    See also CA 1-4R; CANR 6, 22, 38;
        CLR 24; JRDA; MAICYA; SATA 22, 75

Reilly, William K.
    See Creasey, John

Reiner, Max
    See Caldwell, (Janet Miriam) Taylor
        (Holland)

Reis, Ricardo
    See Pessoa, Fernando (Antonio Nogueira)

Remarque, Erich Maria
        1898-1970 .... CLC 21; DA; DAB; DAC;
                                DAM MST, NOV
    See also CA 77-80; 29-32R; DLB 56;
        MTCW

Remizov, A.
    See Remizov, Aleksei (Mikhailovich)

Remizov, A. M.
    See Remizov, Aleksei (Mikhailovich)

Remizov, Aleksei (Mikhailovich)
        1877-1957 .... TCLC 27
    See also CA 125; 133

Renan, Joseph Ernest
1823-1892 . . . . **NCLC 26**

Renard, Jules 1864-1910 . . . . **TCLC 17**
See also CA 117

Renault, Mary . . . . **CLC 3, 11, 17**
See also Challans, Mary
See also DLBY 83

Rendell, Ruth (Barbara)
1930- . . . . **CLC 28, 48; DAM POP**
See also Vine, Barbara
See also CA 109; CANR 32, 52; DLB 87;
INT CANR-32; MTCW

Renoir, Jean 1894-1979 . . . . **CLC 20**
See also CA 129; 85-88

Resnais, Alain 1922- . . . . **CLC 16**

Reverdy, Pierre 1889-1960 . . . . **CLC 53**
See also CA 97-100; 89-92

Rexroth, Kenneth
1905-1982 . . . . . . **CLC 1, 2, 6, 11, 22, 49;**
DAM POET
See also CA 5-8R; 107; CANR 14, 34;
CDALB 1941-1968; DLB 16, 48, 165;
DLBY 82; INT CANR-14; MTCW

Reyes, Alfonso 1889-1959 . . . . **TCLC 33**
See also CA 131; HW

Reyes y Basoalto, Ricardo Eliecer Neftali
See Neruda, Pablo

Reymont, Wladyslaw (Stanislaw)
1868(?)-1925 . . . . **TCLC 5**
See also CA 104

Reynolds, Jonathan 1942- . . . . **CLC 6, 38**
See also CA 65-68; CANR 28

Reynolds, Joshua 1723-1792 . . . . **LC 15**
See also DLB 104

Reynolds, Michael Shane 1937- . . . . **CLC 44**
See also CA 65-68; CANR 9

Reznikoff, Charles 1894-1976 . . . . **CLC 9**
See also CA 33-36; 61-64; CAP 2; DLB 28,
45

Rezzori (d'Arezzo), Gregor von
1914- . . . . **CLC 25**
See also CA 122; 136

Rhine, Richard
See Silverstein, Alvin

Rhodes, Eugene Manlove
1869-1934 . . . . **TCLC 53**

R'hoone
See Balzac, Honore de

Rhys, Jean
1890(?)-1979 . . . . **CLC 2, 4, 6, 14, 19, 51;**
DAM NOV; SSC 21
See also CA 25-28R; 85-88; CANR 35;
CDBLB 1945-1960; DLB 36, 117, 162;
MTCW

Ribeiro, Darcy 1922- . . . . **CLC 34**
See also CA 33-36R

Ribeiro, Joao Ubaldo (Osorio Pimentel)
1941- . . . . **CLC 10, 67**
See also CA 81-84

Ribman, Ronald (Burt) 1932- . . . . **CLC 7**
See also CA 21-24R; CANR 46

Ricci, Nino 1959- . . . . **CLC 70**
See also CA 137

Rice, Anne 1941- . . . . . **CLC 41; DAM POP**
See also AAYA 9; BEST 89:2; CA 65-68;
CANR 12, 36, 53

Rice, Elmer (Leopold)
1892-1967 . . . . **CLC 7, 49; DAM DRAM**
See also CA 21-22; 25-28R; CAP 2; DLB 4,
7; MTCW

Rice, Tim(othy Miles Bindon)
1944- . . . . **CLC 21**
See also CA 103; CANR 46

Rich, Adrienne (Cecile)
1929- . . . . **CLC 3, 6, 7, 11, 18, 36, 73, 76;**
DAM POET; PC 5
See also CA 9-12R; CANR 20, 53; DLB 5,
67; MTCW

Rich, Barbara
See Graves, Robert (von Ranke)

Rich, Robert
See Trumbo, Dalton

Richard, Keith . . . . **CLC 17**
See also Richards, Keith

Richards, David Adams
1950- . . . . **CLC 59; DAC**
See also CA 93-96; DLB 53

Richards, I(vor) A(rmstrong)
1893-1979 . . . . **CLC 14, 24**
See also CA 41-44R; 89-92; CANR 34;
DLB 27

Richards, Keith 1943-
See Richard, Keith
See also CA 107

Richardson, Anne
See Roiphe, Anne (Richardson)

Richardson, Dorothy Miller
1873-1957 . . . . **TCLC 3**
See also CA 104; DLB 36

Richardson, Ethel Florence (Lindesay)
1870-1946
See Richardson, Henry Handel
See also CA 105

Richardson, Henry Handel . . . . **TCLC 4**
See also Richardson, Ethel Florence
(Lindesay)

Richardson, John
1796-1852 . . . . **NCLC 55; DAC**
See also DLB 99

Richardson, Samuel
1689-1761 . . . . . . **LC 1; DA; DAB; DAC;**
DAM MST, NOV; WLC
See also CDBLB 1660-1789; DLB 39

Richler, Mordecai
1931- . . . . **CLC 3, 5, 9, 13, 18, 46, 70;**
DAC; DAM MST, NOV
See also AITN 1; CA 65-68; CANR 31;
CLR 17; DLB 53; MAICYA; MTCW;
SATA 44; SATA-Brief 27

Richter, Conrad (Michael)
1890-1968 . . . . **CLC 30**
See also CA 5-8R; 25-28R; CANR 23;
DLB 9; MTCW; SATA 3

Ricostranza, Tom
See Ellis, Trey

Riddell, J. H. 1832-1906 . . . . **TCLC 40**

Riding, Laura . . . . **CLC 3, 7**
See also Jackson, Laura (Riding)

Riefenstahl, Berta Helene Amalia 1902-
See Riefenstahl, Leni
See also CA 108

Riefenstahl, Leni . . . . **CLC 16**
See also Riefenstahl, Berta Helene Amalia

Riffe, Ernest
See Bergman, (Ernst) Ingmar

Riggs, (Rolla) Lynn
1899-1954 . . . . . **TCLC 56; DAM MULT**
See also CA 144; NNAL

Riley, James Whitcomb
1849-1916 . . . . . . **TCLC 51; DAM POET**
See also CA 118; 137; MAICYA; SATA 17

Riley, Tex
See Creasey, John

Rilke, Rainer Maria
1875-1926 . . . . **TCLC 1, 6, 19;**
DAM POET; PC 2
See also CA 104; 132; DLB 81; MTCW

Rimbaud, (Jean Nicolas) Arthur
1854-1891 . . . . . **NCLC 4, 35; DA; DAB;**
DAC; DAM MST, POET; PC 3; WLC

Rinehart, Mary Roberts
1876-1958 . . . . **TCLC 52**
See also CA 108

Ringmaster, The
See Mencken, H(enry) L(ouis)

Ringwood, Gwen(dolyn Margaret) Pharis
1910-1984 . . . . **CLC 48**
See also CA 148; 112; DLB 88

Rio, Michel 19(?)- . . . . **CLC 43**

Ritsos, Giannes
See Ritsos, Yannis

Ritsos, Yannis 1909-1990 . . . . . **CLC 6, 13, 31**
See also CA 77-80; 133; CANR 39; MTCW

Ritter, Erika 1948(?)- . . . . **CLC 52**

Rivera, Jose Eustasio 1889-1928 . . . **TCLC 35**
See also HW

Rivers, Conrad Kent 1933-1968 . . . . . . **CLC 1**
See also BW 1; CA 85-88; DLB 41

Rivers, Elfrida
See Bradley, Marion Zimmer

Riverside, John
See Heinlein, Robert A(nson)

Rizal, Jose 1861-1896 . . . . **NCLC 27**

Roa Bastos, Augusto (Antonio)
1917- . . . . . **CLC 45; DAM MULT; HLC**
See also CA 131; DLB 113; HW

Robbe-Grillet, Alain
1922- . . . . . . **CLC 1, 2, 4, 6, 8, 10, 14, 43**
See also CA 9-12R; CANR 33; DLB 83;
MTCW

Robbins, Harold
1916- . . . . **CLC 5; DAM NOV**
See also CA 73-76; CANR 26; MTCW

Robbins, Thomas Eugene 1936-
See Robbins, Tom
See also CA 81-84; CANR 29; DAM NOV,
POP; MTCW

Robbins, Tom . . . . **CLC 9, 32, 64**
See also Robbins, Thomas Eugene
See also BEST 90:3; DLBY 80

Robbins, Trina 1938- . . . . **CLC 21**
See also CA 128

Roberts, Charles G(eorge) D(ouglas)
1860-1943 .... TCLC 8
See also CA 105; CLR 33; DLB 92;
SATA 88; SATA-Brief 29

Roberts, Kate 1891-1985 .... CLC 15
See also CA 107; 116

Roberts, Keith (John Kingston)
1935- .... CLC 14
See also CA 25-28R; CANR 46

Roberts, Kenneth (Lewis)
1885-1957 .... TCLC 23
See also CA 109; DLB 9

Roberts, Michele (B.) 1949-........ CLC 48
See also CA 115

Robertson, Ellis
See Ellison, Harlan (Jay); Silverberg, Robert

Robertson, Thomas William
1829-1871 .... NCLC 35; DAM DRAM

Robinson, Edwin Arlington
1869-1935 .... TCLC 5; DA; DAC;
DAM MST, POET; PC 1
See also CA 104; 133; CDALB 1865-1917;
DLB 54; MTCW

Robinson, Henry Crabb
1775-1867 .... NCLC 15
See also DLB 107

Robinson, Jill 1936-.............. CLC 10
See also CA 102; INT 102

Robinson, Kim Stanley 1952- ...... CLC 34
See also CA 126

Robinson, Lloyd
See Silverberg, Robert

Robinson, Marilynne 1944-........ CLC 25
See also CA 116

Robinson, Smokey................. CLC 21
See also Robinson, William, Jr.

Robinson, William, Jr. 1940-
See Robinson, Smokey
See also CA 116

Robison, Mary 1949- .... CLC 42
See also CA 113; 116; DLB 130; INT 116

Rod, Edouard 1857-1910 .... TCLC 52

Roddenberry, Eugene Wesley 1921-1991
See Roddenberry, Gene
See also CA 110; 135; CANR 37; SATA 45;
SATA-Obit 69

Roddenberry, Gene .... CLC 17
See also Roddenberry, Eugene Wesley
See also AAYA 5; SATA-Obit 69

Rodgers, Mary 1931-............. CLC 12
See also CA 49-52; CANR 8; CLR 20;
INT CANR-8; JRDA; MAICYA;
SATA 8

Rodgers, W(illiam) R(obert)
1909-1969 .... CLC 7
See also CA 85-88; DLB 20

Rodman, Eric
See Silverberg, Robert

Rodman, Howard 1920(?)-1985..... CLC 65
See also CA 118

Rodman, Maia
See Wojciechowska, Maia (Teresa)

Rodriguez, Claudio 1934-.......... CLC 10
See also DLB 134

Roelvaag, O(le) E(dvart)
1876-1931 .... TCLC 17
See also CA 117; DLB 9

Roethke, Theodore (Huebner)
1908-1963 ...... CLC 1, 3, 8, 11, 19, 46;
DAM POET; PC 15
See also CA 81-84; CABS 2;
CDALB 1941-1968; DLB 5; MTCW

Rogers, Thomas Hunton 1927- ..... CLC 57
See also CA 89-92; INT 89-92

Rogers, Will(iam Penn Adair)
1879-1935 ...... TCLC 8; DAM MULT
See also CA 105; 144; DLB 11; NNAL

Rogin, Gilbert 1929-.............. CLC 18
See also CA 65-68; CANR 15

Rohan, Koda .... TCLC 22
See also Koda Shigeyuki

Rohmer, Eric..................... CLC 16
See also Scherer, Jean-Marie Maurice

Rohmer, Sax .... TCLC 28
See also Ward, Arthur Henry Sarsfield
See also DLB 70

Roiphe, Anne (Richardson)
1935- .... CLC 3, 9
See also CA 89-92; CANR 45; DLBY 80;
INT 89-92

Rojas, Fernando de 1465-1541 ...... LC 23

Rolfe, Frederick (William Serafino Austin
Lewis Mary) 1860-1913...... TCLC 12
See also CA 107; DLB 34, 156

Rolland, Romain 1866-1944...... TCLC 23
See also CA 118; DLB 65

Rolvaag, O(le) E(dvart)
See Roelvaag, O(le) E(dvart)

Romain Arnaud, Saint
See Aragon, Louis

Romains, Jules 1885-1972.......... CLC 7
See also CA 85-88; CANR 34; DLB 65;
MTCW

Romero, Jose Ruben 1890-1952 ... TCLC 14
See also CA 114; 131; HW

Ronsard, Pierre de
1524-1585 .... LC 6; PC 11

Rooke, Leon
1934- .... CLC 25, 34; DAM POP
See also CA 25-28R; CANR 23, 53

Roper, William 1498-1578 .... LC 10

Roquelaure, A. N.
See Rice, Anne

Rosa, Joao Guimaraes 1908-1967 ... CLC 23
See also CA 89-92; DLB 113

Rose, Wendy
1948- .... CLC 85; DAM MULT; PC 13
See also CA 53-56; CANR 5, 51; NNAL;
SATA 12

Rosen, Richard (Dean) 1949-....... CLC 39
See also CA 77-80; INT CANR-30

Rosenberg, Isaac 1890-1918....... TCLC 12
See also CA 107; DLB 20

Rosenblatt, Joe .... CLC 15
See also Rosenblatt, Joseph

Rosenblatt, Joseph 1933-
See Rosenblatt, Joe
See also CA 89-92; INT 89-92

Rosenfeld, Samuel 1896-1963
See Tzara, Tristan
See also CA 89-92

Rosenthal, M(acha) L(ouis)
1917-1996 .... CLC 28
See also CA 1-4R; 152; CAAS 6; CANR 4,
51; DLB 5; SATA 59

Ross, Barnaby
See Dannay, Frederic

Ross, Bernard L.
See Follett, Ken(neth Martin)

Ross, J. H.
See Lawrence, T(homas) E(dward)

Ross, Martin
See Martin, Violet Florence
See also DLB 135

Ross, (James) Sinclair
1908- ...... CLC 13; DAC; DAM MST
See also CA 73-76; DLB 88

Rossetti, Christina (Georgina)
1830-1894 ..... NCLC 2, 50; DA; DAB;
DAC; DAM MST, POET; PC 7; WLC
See also DLB 35, 163; MAICYA; SATA 20

Rossetti, Dante Gabriel
1828-1882 .... NCLC 4; DA; DAB;
DAC; DAM MST, POET; WLC
See also CDBLB 1832-1890; DLB 35

Rossner, Judith (Perelman)
1935- .... CLC 6, 9, 29
See also AITN 2; BEST 90:3; CA 17-20R;
CANR 18, 51; DLB 6; INT CANR-18;
MTCW

Rostand, Edmond (Eugene Alexis)
1868-1918 ...... TCLC 6, 37; DA; DAB;
DAC; DAM DRAM, MST
See also CA 104; 126; MTCW

Roth, Henry 1906-1995 .... CLC 2, 6, 11
See also CA 11-12; 149; CANR 38; CAP 1;
DLB 28; MTCW

Roth, Joseph 1894-1939.......... TCLC 33
See also DLB 85

Roth, Philip (Milton)
1933- ...... CLC 1, 2, 3, 4, 6, 9, 15, 22,
31, 47, 66, 86; DA; DAB; DAC;
DAM MST, NOV, POP; WLC
See also BEST 90:3; CA 1-4R; CANR 1, 22,
36; CDALB 1968-1988; DLB 2, 28;
DLBY 82; MTCW

Rothenberg, Jerome 1931-....... CLC 6, 57
See also CA 45-48; CANR 1; DLB 5

Roumain, Jacques (Jean Baptiste)
1907-1944 .... TCLC 19; BLC;
DAM MULT
See also BW 1; CA 117; 125

Rourke, Constance (Mayfield)
1885-1941 .... TCLC 12
See also CA 107; YABC 1

Rousseau, Jean-Baptiste 1671-1741 ... LC 9

Rousseau, Jean-Jacques
1712-1778 ..... LC 14; DA; DAB; DAC;
DAM MST; WLC

Roussel, Raymond 1877-1933 ..... TCLC 20
See also CA 117

Rovit, Earl (Herbert) 1927-........ CLC 7
See also CA 5-8R; CANR 12

Rowe, Nicholas 1674-1718 .... **LC 8**
See also DLB 84

Rowley, Ames Dorrance
See Lovecraft, H(oward) P(hillips)

Rowson, Susanna Haswell
1762(?)-1824 .... **NCLC 5**
See also DLB 37

Roy, Gabrielle
1909-1983 .... **CLC 10, 14; DAB; DAC;**
DAM MST
See also CA 53-56; 110; CANR 5; DLB 68;
MTCW

Rozewicz, Tadeusz
1921- .... **CLC 9, 23; DAM POET**
See also CA 108; CANR 36; MTCW

Ruark, Gibbons 1941- .... **CLC 3**
See also CA 33-36R; CAAS 23; CANR 14,
31; DLB 120

Rubens, Bernice (Ruth) 1923- ... **CLC 19, 31**
See also CA 25-28R; CANR 33; DLB 14;
MTCW

Rudkin, (James) David 1936- ...... **CLC 14**
See also CA 89-92; DLB 13

Rudnik, Raphael 1933- .... **CLC 7**
See also CA 29-32R

Ruffian, M.
See Hasek, Jaroslav (Matej Frantisek)

Ruiz, Jose Martinez .... **CLC 11**
See also Martinez Ruiz, Jose

Rukeyser, Muriel
1913-1980 .... **CLC 6, 10, 15, 27;**
DAM POET; PC 12
See also CA 5-8R; 93-96; CANR 26;
DLB 48; MTCW; SATA-Obit 22

Rule, Jane (Vance) 1931- .... **CLC 27**
See also CA 25-28R; CAAS 18; CANR 12;
DLB 60

Rulfo, Juan
1918-1986 .... **CLC 8, 80; DAM MULT;**
HLC
See also CA 85-88; 118; CANR 26;
DLB 113; HW; MTCW

Runeberg, Johan 1804-1877 ...... **NCLC 41**

Runyon, (Alfred) Damon
1884(?)-1946 .... **TCLC 10**
See also CA 107; DLB 11, 86

Rush, Norman 1933- .... **CLC 44**
See also CA 121; 126; INT 126

Rushdie, (Ahmed) Salman
1947- ..... **CLC 23, 31, 55; DAB; DAC;**
DAM MST, NOV, POP
See also BEST 89:3; CA 108; 111;
CANR 33; INT 111; MTCW

Rushforth, Peter (Scott) 1945- ..... **CLC 19**
See also CA 101

Ruskin, John 1819-1900 .... **TCLC 63**
See also CA 114; 129; CDBLB 1832-1890;
DLB 55, 163; SATA 24

Russ, Joanna 1937- .... **CLC 15**
See also CA 25-28R; CANR 11, 31; DLB 8;
MTCW

Russell, George William 1867-1935
See A. E.
See also CA 104; CDBLB 1890-1914;
DAM POET

Russell, (Henry) Ken(neth Alfred)
1927- .... **CLC 16**
See also CA 105

Russell, Willy 1947- .... **CLC 60**

Rutherford, Mark .... **TCLC 25**
See also White, William Hale
See also DLB 18

Ruyslinck, Ward 1929- .... **CLC 14**
See also Belser, Reimond Karel Maria de

Ryan, Cornelius (John) 1920-1974 ... **CLC 7**
See also CA 69-72; 53-56; CANR 38

Ryan, Michael 1946- .... **CLC 65**
See also CA 49-52; DLBY 82

Rybakov, Anatoli (Naumovich)
1911- .... **CLC 23, 53**
See also CA 126; 135; SATA 79

Ryder, Jonathan
See Ludlum, Robert

Ryga, George
1932-1987 .. **CLC 14; DAC; DAM MST**
See also CA 101; 124; CANR 43; DLB 60

S. S.
See Sassoon, Siegfried (Lorraine)

Saba, Umberto 1883-1957 .... **TCLC 33**
See also CA 144; DLB 114

Sabatini, Rafael 1875-1950 ...... **TCLC 47**

Sabato, Ernesto (R.)
1911- .... **CLC 10, 23; DAM MULT;**
HLC
See also CA 97-100; CANR 32; DLB 145;
HW; MTCW

Sacastru, Martin
See Bioy Casares, Adolfo

Sacher-Masoch, Leopold von
1836(?)-1895 .... **NCLC 31**

Sachs, Marilyn (Stickle) 1927- ..... **CLC 35**
See also AAYA 2; CA 17-20R; CANR 13,
47; CLR 2; JRDA; MAICYA; SAAS 2;
SATA 3, 68

Sachs, Nelly 1891-1970 .... **CLC 14**
See also CA 17-18; 25-28R; CAP 2

Sackler, Howard (Oliver)
1929-1982 .... **CLC 14**
See also CA 61-64; 108; CANR 30; DLB 7

Sacks, Oliver (Wolf) 1933- .... **CLC 67**
See also CA 53-56; CANR 28, 50;
INT CANR-28; MTCW

Sade, Donatien Alphonse Francois Comte
1740-1814 .... **NCLC 47**

Sadoff, Ira 1945- .... **CLC 9**
See also CA 53-56; CANR 5, 21; DLB 120

Saetone
See Camus, Albert

Safire, William 1929- .... **CLC 10**
See also CA 17-20R; CANR 31

Sagan, Carl (Edward) 1934- .... **CLC 30**
See also AAYA 2; CA 25-28R; CANR 11,
36; MTCW; SATA 58

Sagan, Francoise .... **CLC 3, 6, 9, 17, 36**
See also Quoirez, Francoise
See also DLB 83

Sahgal, Nayantara (Pandit) 1927- ... **CLC 41**
See also CA 9-12R; CANR 11

Saint, H(arry) F. 1941- .... **CLC 50**
See also CA 127

St. Aubin de Teran, Lisa 1953-
See Teran, Lisa St. Aubin de
See also CA 118; 126; INT 126

Sainte-Beuve, Charles Augustin
1804-1869 .... **NCLC 5**

Saint-Exupery, Antoine (Jean Baptiste Marie
Roger) de
1900-1944 .... **TCLC 2, 56; DAM NOV;**
WLC
See also CA 108; 132; CLR 10; DLB 72;
MAICYA; MTCW; SATA 20

St. John, David
See Hunt, E(verette) Howard, (Jr.)

Saint-John Perse
See Leger, (Marie-Rene Auguste) Alexis
Saint-Leger

Saintsbury, George (Edward Bateman)
1845-1933 .... **TCLC 31**
See also DLB 57, 149

Sait Faik .... **TCLC 23**
See also Abasiyanik, Sait Faik

Saki .... **TCLC 3; SSC 12**
See also Munro, H(ector) H(ugh)

Sala, George Augustus .... **NCLC 46**

Salama, Hannu 1936- .... **CLC 18**

Salamanca, J(ack) R(ichard)
1922- .... **CLC 4, 15**
See also CA 25-28R

Sale, J. Kirkpatrick
See Sale, Kirkpatrick

Sale, Kirkpatrick 1937- .... **CLC 68**
See also CA 13-16R; CANR 10

Salinas, Luis Omar
1937- ..... **CLC 90; DAM MULT; HLC**
See also CA 131; DLB 82; HW

Salinas (y Serrano), Pedro
1891(?)-1951 .... **TCLC 17**
See also CA 117; DLB 134

Salinger, J(erome) D(avid)
1919- ...... **CLC 1, 3, 8, 12, 55, 56; DA;**
DAB; DAC; DAM MST, NOV, POP;
SSC 2; WLC
See also AAYA 2; CA 5-8R; CANR 39;
CDALB 1941-1968; CLR 18; DLB 2, 102;
MAICYA; MTCW; SATA 67

Salisbury, John
See Caute, David

Salter, James 1925- .... **CLC 7, 52, 59**
See also CA 73-76; DLB 130

Saltus, Edgar (Everton)
1855-1921 .... **TCLC 8**
See also CA 105

Saltykov, Mikhail Evgrafovich
1826-1889 .... **NCLC 16**

Samarakis, Antonis 1919- .... **CLC 5**
See also CA 25-28R; CAAS 16; CANR 36

Sanchez, Florencio 1875-1910 ..... **TCLC 37**
See also HW

Sanchez, Luis Rafael 1936- .... **CLC 23**
See also CA 128; DLB 145; HW

Sanchez, Sonia
1934- ...... **CLC 5; BLC; DAM MULT;
PC 9**
See also BW 2; CA 33-36R; CANR 24, 49;
CLR 18; DLB 41; DLBD 8; MAICYA;
MTCW; SATA 22

Sand, George
1804-1876 .... **NCLC 2, 42, 57; DA;
DAB; DAC; DAM MST, NOV; WLC**
See also DLB 119

Sandburg, Carl (August)
1878-1967 .... **CLC 1, 4, 10, 15, 35; DA;
DAB; DAC; DAM MST, POET; PC 2;
WLC**
See also CA 5-8R; 25-28R; CANR 35;
CDALB 1865-1917; DLB 17, 54;
MAICYA; MTCW; SATA 8

Sandburg, Charles
See Sandburg, Carl (August)

Sandburg, Charles A.
See Sandburg, Carl (August)

Sanders, (James) Ed(ward) 1939- ... **CLC 53**
See also CA 13-16R; CAAS 21; CANR 13,
44; DLB 16

Sanders, Lawrence
1920- .... **CLC 41; DAM POP**
See also BEST 89:4; CA 81-84; CANR 33;
MTCW

Sanders, Noah
See Blount, Roy (Alton), Jr.

Sanders, Winston P.
See Anderson, Poul (William)

Sandoz, Mari(e Susette)
1896-1966 .... **CLC 28**
See also CA 1-4R; 25-28R; CANR 17;
DLB 9; MTCW; SATA 5

Saner, Reg(inald Anthony) 1931- .... **CLC 9**
See also CA 65-68

Sannazaro, Jacopo 1456(?)-1530 ...... **LC 8**

Sansom, William
1912-1976 ...... **CLC 2, 6; DAM NOV;
SSC 21**
See also CA 5-8R; 65-68; CANR 42;
DLB 139; MTCW

Santayana, George 1863-1952 ..... **TCLC 40**
See also CA 115; DLB 54, 71; DLBD 13

Santiago, Danny .... **CLC 33**
See also James, Daniel (Lewis)
See also DLB 122

Santmyer, Helen Hoover
1895-1986 .... **CLC 33**
See also CA 1-4R; 118; CANR 15, 33;
DLBY 84; MTCW

Santos, Bienvenido N(uqui)
1911-1996 ...... **CLC 22; DAM MULT**
See also CA 101; 151; CANR 19, 46

Sapper .... **TCLC 44**
See also McNeile, Herman Cyril

Sappho
fl. 6th cent. B.C.- .... **CMLC 3;
DAM POET; PC 5**

Sarduy, Severo 1937-1993 .... **CLC 6**
See also CA 89-92; 142; DLB 113; HW

Sargeson, Frank 1903-1982 .... **CLC 31**
See also CA 25-28R; 106; CANR 38

Sarmiento, Felix Ruben Garcia
See Dario, Ruben

Saroyan, William
1908-1981 ..... **CLC 1, 8, 10, 29, 34, 56;
DA; DAB; DAC; DAM DRAM, MST,
NOV; SSC 21; WLC**
See also CA 5-8R; 103; CANR 30; DLB 7,
9, 86; DLBY 81; MTCW; SATA 23;
SATA-Obit 24

Sarraute, Nathalie
1900- .... **CLC 1, 2, 4, 8, 10, 31, 80**
See also CA 9-12R; CANR 23; DLB 83;
MTCW

Sarton, (Eleanor) May
1912-1995 .... **CLC 4, 14, 49, 91;
DAM POET**
See also CA 1-4R; 149; CANR 1, 34;
DLB 48; DLBY 81; INT CANR-34;
MTCW; SATA 36; SATA-Obit 86

Sartre, Jean-Paul
1905-1980 .... **CLC 1, 4, 7, 9, 13, 18, 24,
44, 50, 52; DA; DAB; DAC;
DAM DRAM, MST, NOV; DC 3; WLC**
See also CA 9-12R; 97-100; CANR 21;
DLB 72; MTCW

Sassoon, Siegfried (Lorraine)
1886-1967 .... **CLC 36; DAB;
DAM MST, NOV, POET; PC 12**
See also CA 104; 25-28R; CANR 36;
DLB 20; MTCW

Satterfield, Charles
See Pohl, Frederik

Saul, John (W. III)
1942- ...... **CLC 46; DAM NOV, POP**
See also AAYA 10; BEST 90:4; CA 81-84;
CANR 16, 40

Saunders, Caleb
See Heinlein, Robert A(nson)

Saura (Atares), Carlos 1932- .... **CLC 20**
See also CA 114; 131; HW

Sauser-Hall, Frederic 1887-1961.... **CLC 18**
See also Cendrars, Blaise
See also CA 102; 93-96; CANR 36; MTCW

Saussure, Ferdinand de
1857-1913 .... **TCLC 49**

Savage, Catharine
See Brosman, Catharine Savage

Savage, Thomas 1915- .... **CLC 40**
See also CA 126; 132; CAAS 15; INT 132

Savan, Glenn 19(?)- .... **CLC 50**

Sayers, Dorothy L(eigh)
1893-1957 ..... **TCLC 2, 15; DAM POP**
See also CA 104; 119; CDBLB 1914-1945;
DLB 10, 36, 77, 100; MTCW

Sayers, Valerie 1952- .... **CLC 50**
See also CA 134

Sayles, John (Thomas)
1950- .... **CLC 7, 10, 14**
See also CA 57-60; CANR 41; DLB 44

Scammell, Michael .... **CLC 34**

Scannell, Vernon 1922- .... **CLC 49**
See also CA 5-8R; CANR 8, 24; DLB 27;
SATA 59

Scarlett, Susan
See Streatfeild, (Mary) Noel

Schaeffer, Susan Fromberg
1941- .... **CLC 6, 11, 22**
See also CA 49-52; CANR 18; DLB 28;
MTCW; SATA 22

Schary, Jill
See Robinson, Jill

Schell, Jonathan 1943- .... **CLC 35**
See also CA 73-76; CANR 12

Schelling, Friedrich Wilhelm Joseph von
1775-1854 .... **NCLC 30**
See also DLB 90

Schendel, Arthur van 1874-1946 ... **TCLC 56**

Scherer, Jean-Marie Maurice 1920-
See Rohmer, Eric
See also CA 110

Schevill, James (Erwin) 1920-....... **CLC 7**
See also CA 5-8R; CAAS 12

Schiller, Friedrich
1759-1805 .... **NCLC 39; DAM DRAM**
See also DLB 94

Schisgal, Murray (Joseph) 1926-..... **CLC 6**
See also CA 21-24R; CANR 48

Schlee, Ann 1934-................ **CLC 35**
See also CA 101; CANR 29; SATA 44;
SATA-Brief 36

Schlegel, August Wilhelm von
1767-1845 .... **NCLC 15**
See also DLB 94

Schlegel, Friedrich 1772-1829 .... **NCLC 45**
See also DLB 90

Schlegel, Johann Elias (von)
1719(?)-1749 .... **LC 5**

Schlesinger, Arthur M(eier), Jr.
1917- .... **CLC 84**
See also AITN 1; CA 1-4R; CANR 1, 28;
DLB 17; INT CANR-28; MTCW;
SATA 61

Schmidt, Arno (Otto) 1914-1979.... **CLC 56**
See also CA 128; 109; DLB 69

Schmitz, Aron Hector 1861-1928
See Svevo, Italo
See also CA 104; 122; MTCW

Schnackenberg, Gjertrud 1953-..... **CLC 40**
See also CA 116; DLB 120

Schneider, Leonard Alfred 1925-1966
See Bruce, Lenny
See also CA 89-92

Schnitzler, Arthur
1862-1931 .... **TCLC 4; SSC 15**
See also CA 104; DLB 81, 118

Schopenhauer, Arthur
1788-1860 .... **NCLC 51**
See also DLB 90

Schor, Sandra (M.) 1932(?)-1990 ... **CLC 65**
See also CA 132

Schorer, Mark 1908-1977 .... **CLC 9**
See also CA 5-8R; 73-76; CANR 7;
DLB 103

Schrader, Paul (Joseph) 1946-...... **CLC 26**
See also CA 37-40R; CANR 41; DLB 44

Schreiner, Olive (Emilie Albertina)
1855-1920 .... **TCLC 9**
See also CA 105; DLB 18, 156

Schulberg, Budd (Wilson)
1914- . . . . CLC 7, 48
See also CA 25-28R; CANR 19; DLB 6, 26, 28; DLBY 81

Schulz, Bruno
1892-1942 . . . . TCLC 5, 51; SSC 13
See also CA 115; 123

Schulz, Charles M(onroe) 1922- . . . . CLC 12
See also CA 9-12R; CANR 6;
INT CANR-6; SATA 10

Schumacher, E(rnst) F(riedrich)
1911-1977 . . . . CLC 80
See also CA 81-84; 73-76; CANR 34

Schuyler, James Marcus
1923-1991 . . . . . CLC 5, 23; DAM POET
See also CA 101; 134; DLB 5; INT 101

Schwartz, Delmore (David)
1913-1966 . . . CLC 2, 4, 10, 45, 87; PC 8
See also CA 17-18; 25-28R; CANR 35;
CAP 2; DLB 28, 48; MTCW

Schwartz, Ernst
See Ozu, Yasujiro

Schwartz, John Burnham 1965- . . . . CLC 59
See also CA 132

Schwartz, Lynne Sharon 1939- . . . . . CLC 31
See also CA 103; CANR 44

Schwartz, Muriel A.
See Eliot, T(homas) S(tearns)

Schwarz-Bart, Andre 1928- . . . . CLC 2, 4
See also CA 89-92

Schwarz-Bart, Simone 1938- . . . . CLC 7
See also BW 2; CA 97-100

Schwob, (Mayer Andre) Marcel
1867-1905 . . . . TCLC 20
See also CA 117; DLB 123

Sciascia, Leonardo
1921-1989 . . . . CLC 8, 9, 41
See also CA 85-88; 130; CANR 35; MTCW

Scoppettone, Sandra 1936- . . . . CLC 26
See also AAYA 11; CA 5-8R; CANR 41;
SATA 9

Scorsese, Martin 1942- . . . . CLC 20, 89
See also CA 110; 114; CANR 46

Scotland, Jay
See Jakes, John (William)

Scott, Duncan Campbell
1862-1947 . . . . TCLC 6; DAC
See also CA 104; DLB 92

Scott, Evelyn 1893-1963 . . . . CLC 43
See also CA 104; 112; DLB 9, 48

Scott, F(rancis) R(eginald)
1899-1985 . . . . CLC 22
See also CA 101; 114; DLB 88; INT 101

Scott, Frank
See Scott, F(rancis) R(eginald)

Scott, Joanna 1960- . . . . CLC 50
See also CA 126; CANR 53

Scott, Paul (Mark) 1920-1978 . . . . CLC 9, 60
See also CA 81-84; 77-80; CANR 33;
DLB 14; MTCW

Scott, Walter
1771-1832 . . . . NCLC 15; DA; DAB;
DAC; DAM MST, NOV, POET; PC 13;
WLC
See also CDBLB 1789-1832; DLB 93, 107,
116, 144, 159; YABC 2

Scribe, (Augustin) Eugene
1791-1861 . . . . NCLC 16; DAM DRAM;
DC 5

Scrum, R.
See Crumb, R(obert)

Scudery, Madeleine de 1607-1701 . . . . . LC 2

Scum
See Crumb, R(obert)

Scumbag, Little Bobby
See Crumb, R(obert)

Seabrook, John
See Hubbard, L(afayette) Ron(ald)

Sealy, I. Allan 1951- . . . . CLC 55

Search, Alexander
See Pessoa, Fernando (Antonio Nogueira)

Sebastian, Lee
See Silverberg, Robert

Sebastian Owl
See Thompson, Hunter S(tockton)

Sebestyen, Ouida 1924- . . . . CLC 30
See also AAYA 8; CA 107; CANR 40;
CLR 17; JRDA; MAICYA; SAAS 10;
SATA 39

Secundus, H. Scriblerus
See Fielding, Henry

Sedges, John
See Buck, Pearl S(ydenstricker)

Sedgwick, Catharine Maria
1789-1867 . . . . NCLC 19
See also DLB 1, 74

Seelye, John 1931- . . . . CLC 7

Seferiades, Giorgos Stylianou 1900-1971
See Seferis, George
See also CA 5-8R; 33-36R; CANR 5, 36;
MTCW

Seferis, George . . . . CLC 5, 11
See also Seferiades, Giorgos Stylianou

Segal, Erich (Wolf)
1937- . . . . CLC 3, 10; DAM POP
See also BEST 89:1; CA 25-28R; CANR 20,
36; DLBY 86; INT CANR-20; MTCW

Seger, Bob 1945- . . . . CLC 35

Seghers, Anna . . . . CLC 7
See also Radvanyi, Netty
See also DLB 69

Seidel, Frederick (Lewis) 1936- . . . . . CLC 18
See also CA 13-16R; CANR 8; DLBY 84

Seifert, Jaroslav
1901-1986 . . . . CLC 34, 44, 93
See also CA 127; MTCW

Sei Shonagon c. 966-1017(?) . . . . . . CMLC 6

Selby, Hubert, Jr.
1928- . . . . CLC 1, 2, 4, 8; SSC 20
See also CA 13-16R; CANR 33; DLB 2

Selzer, Richard 1928- . . . . CLC 74
See also CA 65-68; CANR 14

Sembene, Ousmane
See Ousmane, Sembene

Senancour, Etienne Pivert de
1770-1846 . . . . NCLC 16
See also DLB 119

Sender, Ramon (Jose)
1902-1982 . . CLC 8; DAM MULT; HLC
See also CA 5-8R; 105; CANR 8; HW;
MTCW

Seneca, Lucius Annaeus
4B.C.-65 . . . . . . CMLC 6; DAM DRAM;
DC 5

Senghor, Leopold Sedar
1906- . . . . . CLC 54; BLC; DAM MULT,
POET
See also BW 2; CA 116; 125; CANR 47;
MTCW

Serling, (Edward) Rod(man)
1924-1975 . . . . CLC 30
See also AAYA 14; AITN 1; CA 65-68;
57-60; DLB 26

Serna, Ramon Gomez de la
See Gomez de la Serna, Ramon

Serpieres
See Guillevic, (Eugene)

Service, Robert
See Service, Robert W(illiam)
See also DAB; DLB 92

Service, Robert W(illiam)
1874(?)-1958 . . . . . . TCLC 15; DA; DAC;
DAM MST, POET; WLC
See also Service, Robert
See also CA 115; 140; SATA 20

Seth, Vikram
1952- . . . . CLC 43, 90; DAM MULT
See also CA 121; 127; CANR 50; DLB 120;
INT 127

Seton, Cynthia Propper
1926-1982 . . . . CLC 27
See also CA 5-8R; 108; CANR 7

Seton, Ernest (Evan) Thompson
1860-1946 . . . . TCLC 31
See also CA 109; DLB 92; DLBD 13;
JRDA; SATA 18

Seton-Thompson, Ernest
See Seton, Ernest (Evan) Thompson

Settle, Mary Lee 1918- . . . . CLC 19, 61
See also CA 89-92; CAAS 1; CANR 44;
DLB 6; INT 89-92

Seuphor, Michel
See Arp, Jean

Sevigne, Marie (de Rabutin-Chantal) Marquise
de 1626-1696 . . . . LC 11

Sexton, Anne (Harvey)
1928-1974 . . . CLC 2, 4, 6, 8, 10, 15, 53;
DA; DAB; DAC; DAM MST, POET;
PC 2; WLC
See also CA 1-4R; 53-56; CABS 2;
CANR 3, 36; CDALB 1941-1968; DLB 5;
MTCW; SATA 10

Shaara, Michael (Joseph, Jr.)
1929-1988 . . . . CLC 15; DAM POP
See also AITN 1; CA 102; 125; CANR 52;
DLBY 83

Shackleton, C. C.
See Aldiss, Brian W(ilson)

Shacochis, Bob . . . . CLC 39
See also Shacochis, Robert G.

Sillanpaa, Frans Eemil 1888-1964... **CLC 19**
See also CA 129; 93-96; MTCW

Sillitoe, Alan
1928-......... **CLC 1, 3, 6, 10, 19, 57**
See also AITN 1; CA 9-12R; CAAS 2;
CANR 8, 26; CDBLB 1960 to Present;
DLB 14, 139; MTCW; SATA 61

Silone, Ignazio 1900-1978.......... **CLC 4**
See also CA 25-28; 81-84; CANR 34;
CAP 2; MTCW

Silver, Joan Micklin 1935-........ **CLC 20**
See also CA 114; 121; INT 121

Silver, Nicholas
See Faust, Frederick (Schiller)

Silverberg, Robert
1935-............ **CLC 7; DAM POP**
See also CA 1-4R; CAAS 3; CANR 1, 20,
36; DLB 8; INT CANR-20; MAICYA;
MTCW; SATA 13

Silverstein, Alvin 1933-........... **CLC 17**
See also CA 49-52; CANR 2; CLR 25;
JRDA; MAICYA; SATA 8, 69

Silverstein, Virginia B(arbara Opshelor)
1937-....................... **CLC 17**
See also CA 49-52; CANR 2; CLR 25;
JRDA; MAICYA; SATA 8, 69

Sim, Georges
See Simenon, Georges (Jacques Christian)

Simak, Clifford D(onald)
1904-1988................. **CLC 1, 55**
See also CA 1-4R; 125; CANR 1, 35;
DLB 8; MTCW; SATA-Obit 56

Simenon, Georges (Jacques Christian)
1903-1989....... **CLC 1, 2, 3, 8, 18, 47;**
DAM POP
See also CA 85-88; 129; CANR 35;
DLB 72; DLBY 89; MTCW

Simic, Charles
1938-............ **CLC 6, 9, 22, 49, 68;**
DAM POET
See also CA 29-32R; CAAS 4; CANR 12,
33, 52; DLB 105

Simmel, Georg 1858-1918........ **TCLC 64**

Simmons, Charles (Paul) 1924-..... **CLC 57**
See also CA 89-92; INT 89-92

Simmons, Dan 1948-... **CLC 44; DAM POP**
See also AAYA 16; CA 138; CANR 53

Simmons, James (Stewart Alexander)
1933-....................... **CLC 43**
See also CA 105; CAAS 21; DLB 40

Simms, William Gilmore
1806-1870.................. **NCLC 3**
See also DLB 3, 30, 59, 73

Simon, Carly 1945-............... **CLC 26**
See also CA 105

Simon, Claude
1913-.... **CLC 4, 9, 15, 39; DAM NOV**
See also CA 89-92; CANR 33; DLB 83;
MTCW

Simon, (Marvin) Neil
1927-.......... **CLC 6, 11, 31, 39, 70;**
DAM DRAM
See also AITN 1; CA 21-24R; CANR 26;
DLB 7; MTCW

Simon, Paul 1942(?)-.............. **CLC 17**
See also CA 116

Simonon, Paul 1956(?)-........... **CLC 30**

Simpson, Harriette
See Arnow, Harriette (Louisa) Simpson

Simpson, Louis (Aston Marantz)
1923-.... **CLC 4, 7, 9, 32; DAM POET**
See also CA 1-4R; CAAS 4; CANR 1;
DLB 5; MTCW

Simpson, Mona (Elizabeth) 1957-... **CLC 44**
See also CA 122; 135

Simpson, N(orman) F(rederick)
1919-....................... **CLC 29**
See also CA 13-16R; DLB 13

Sinclair, Andrew (Annandale)
1935-...................... **CLC 2, 14**
See also CA 9-12R; CAAS 5; CANR 14, 38;
DLB 14; MTCW

Sinclair, Emil
See Hesse, Hermann

Sinclair, Iain 1943-............... **CLC 76**
See also CA 132

Sinclair, Iain MacGregor
See Sinclair, Iain

Sinclair, Mary Amelia St. Clair 1865(?)-1946
See Sinclair, May
See also CA 104

Sinclair, May.................. **TCLC 3, 11**
See also Sinclair, Mary Amelia St. Clair
See also DLB 36, 135

Sinclair, Upton (Beall)
1878-1968...... **CLC 1, 11, 15, 63; DA;**
DAB; DAC; DAM MST, NOV; WLC
See also CA 5-8R; 25-28R; CANR 7;
CDALB 1929-1941; DLB 9;
INT CANR-7; MTCW; SATA 9

Singer, Isaac
See Singer, Isaac Bashevis

Singer, Isaac Bashevis
1904-1991.... **CLC 1, 3, 6, 9, 11, 15, 23,**
38, 69; DA; DAB; DAC; DAM MST,
NOV; SSC 3; WLC
See also AITN 1, 2; CA 1-4R; 134;
CANR 1, 39; CDALB 1941-1968; CLR 1;
DLB 6, 28, 52; DLBY 91; JRDA;
MAICYA; MTCW; SATA 3, 27;
SATA-Obit 68

Singer, Israel Joshua 1893-1944... **TCLC 33**

Singh, Khushwant 1915-.......... **CLC 11**
See also CA 9-12R; CAAS 9; CANR 6

Sinjohn, John
See Galsworthy, John

Sinyavsky, Andrei (Donatevich)
1925-....................... **CLC 8**
See also CA 85-88

Sirin, V.
See Nabokov, Vladimir (Vladimirovich)

Sissman, L(ouis) E(dward)
1928-1976................. **CLC 9, 18**
See also CA 21-24R; 65-68; CANR 13;
DLB 5

Sisson, C(harles) H(ubert) 1914-..... **CLC 8**
See also CA 1-4R; CAAS 3; CANR 3, 48;
DLB 27

Sitwell, Dame Edith
1887-1964............. **CLC 2, 9, 67;**
DAM POET; PC 3
See also CA 9-12R; CANR 35;
CDBLB 1945-1960; DLB 20; MTCW

Sjoewall, Maj 1935-.............. **CLC 7**
See also CA 65-68

Sjowall, Maj
See Sjoewall, Maj

Skelton, Robin 1925-.............. **CLC 13**
See also AITN 2; CA 5-8R; CAAS 5;
CANR 28; DLB 27, 53

Skolimowski, Jerzy 1938-......... **CLC 20**
See also CA 128

Skram, Amalie (Bertha)
1847-1905................. **TCLC 25**

Skvorecky, Josef (Vaclav)
1924-.......... **CLC 15, 39, 69; DAC;**
DAM NOV
See also CA 61-64; CAAS 1; CANR 10, 34;
MTCW

Slade, Bernard................. **CLC 11, 46**
See also Newbound, Bernard Slade
See also CAAS 9; DLB 53

Slaughter, Carolyn 1946-.......... **CLC 56**
See also CA 85-88

Slaughter, Frank G(ill) 1908-...... **CLC 29**
See also AITN 2; CA 5-8R; CANR 5;
INT CANR-5

Slavitt, David R(ytman) 1935-.... **CLC 5, 14**
See also CA 21-24R; CAAS 3; CANR 41;
DLB 5, 6

Slesinger, Tess 1905-1945........ **TCLC 10**
See also CA 107; DLB 102

Slessor, Kenneth 1901-1971....... **CLC 14**
See also CA 102; 89-92

Slowacki, Juliusz 1809-1849..... **NCLC 15**

Smart, Christopher
1722-1771... **LC 3; DAM POET; PC 13**
See also DLB 109

Smart, Elizabeth 1913-1986........ **CLC 54**
See also CA 81-84; 118; DLB 88

Smiley, Jane (Graves)
1949-......... **CLC 53, 76; DAM POP**
See also CA 104; CANR 30, 50;
INT CANR-30

Smith, A(rthur) J(ames) M(arshall)
1902-1980............CLC 15; DAC
See also CA 1-4R; 102; CANR 4; DLB 88

Smith, Anna Deavere 1950-........ **CLC 86**
See also CA 133

Smith, Betty (Wehner) 1896-1972... **CLC 19**
See also CA 5-8R; 33-36R; DLBY 82;
SATA 6

Smith, Charlotte (Turner)
1749-1806................. **NCLC 23**
See also DLB 39, 109

Smith, Clark Ashton 1893-1961.... **CLC 43**
See also CA 143

Smith, Dave.................. **CLC 22, 42**
See also Smith, David (Jeddie)
See also CAAS 7; DLB 5

Smith, David (Jeddie) 1942-
See Smith, Dave
See also CA 49-52; CANR 1; DAM POET

Smith, Florence Margaret 1902-1971
See Smith, Stevie
See also CA 17-18; 29-32R; CANR 35;
CAP 2; DAM POET; MTCW

Smith, Iain Crichton 1928- .... CLC 64
See also CA 21-24R; DLB 40, 139

Smith, John 1580(?)-1631 .... LC 9

Smith, Johnston
See Crane, Stephen (Townley)

Smith, Joseph, Jr. 1805-1844 .... NCLC 53

Smith, Lee 1944-.............. CLC 25, 73
See also CA 114; 119; CANR 46; DLB 143;
DLBY 83; INT 119

Smith, Martin
See Smith, Martin Cruz

Smith, Martin Cruz
1942- ..... CLC 25; DAM MULT, POP
See also BEST 89:4; CA 85-88; CANR 6,
23, 43; INT CANR-23; NNAL

Smith, Mary-Ann Tirone 1944-..... CLC 39
See also CA 118; 136

Smith, Patti 1946- .... CLC 12
See also CA 93-96

Smith, Pauline (Urmson)
1882-1959 .... TCLC 25

Smith, Rosamond
See Oates, Joyce Carol

Smith, Sheila Kaye
See Kaye-Smith, Sheila

Smith, Stevie .... CLC 3, 8, 25, 44; PC 12
See also Smith, Florence Margaret
See also DLB 20

Smith, Wilbur (Addison) 1933-..... CLC 33
See also CA 13-16R; CANR 7, 46; MTCW

Smith, William Jay 1918- .... CLC 6
See also CA 5-8R; CANR 44; DLB 5;
MAICYA; SAAS 22; SATA 2, 68

Smith, Woodrow Wilson
See Kuttner, Henry

Smolenskin, Peretz 1842-1885.... NCLC 30

Smollett, Tobias (George) 1721-1771 .. LC 2
See also CDBLB 1660-1789; DLB 39, 104

Snodgrass, W(illiam) D(e Witt)
1926- .... CLC 2, 6, 10, 18, 68;
DAM POET
See also CA 1-4R; CANR 6, 36; DLB 5;
MTCW

Snow, C(harles) P(ercy)
1905-1980 .... CLC 1, 4, 6, 9, 13, 19;
DAM NOV
See also CA 5-8R; 101; CANR 28;
CDBLB 1945-1960; DLB 15, 77; MTCW

Snow, Frances Compton
See Adams, Henry (Brooks)

Snyder, Gary (Sherman)
1930- .. CLC 1, 2, 5, 9, 32; DAM POET
See also CA 17-20R; CANR 30; DLB 5, 16,
165

Snyder, Zilpha Keatley 1927- ...... CLC 17
See also AAYA 15; CA 9-12R; CANR 38;
CLR 31; JRDA; MAICYA; SAAS 2;
SATA 1, 28, 75

Soares, Bernardo
See Pessoa, Fernando (Antonio Nogueira)

Sobh, A.
See Shamlu, Ahmad

Sobol, Joshua. .... CLC 60

Soderberg, Hjalmar 1869-1941 .... TCLC 39

Sodergran, Edith (Irene)
See Soedergran, Edith (Irene)

Soedergran, Edith (Irene)
1892-1923 .... TCLC 31

Softly, Edgar
See Lovecraft, H(oward) P(hillips)

Softly, Edward
See Lovecraft, H(oward) P(hillips)

Sokolov, Raymond 1941-........... CLC 7
See also CA 85-88

Solo, Jay
See Ellison, Harlan (Jay)

Sologub, Fyodor .... TCLC 9
See also Teternikov, Fyodor Kuzmich

Solomons, Ikey Esquir
See Thackeray, William Makepeace

Solomos, Dionysios 1798-1857 ... NCLC 15

Solwoska, Mara
See French, Marilyn

Solzhenitsyn, Aleksandr I(sayevich)
1918- ...... CLC 1, 2, 4, 7, 9, 10, 18, 26,
34, 78; DA; DAB; DAC; DAM MST,
NOV; WLC
See also AITN 1; CA 69-72; CANR 40;
MTCW

Somers, Jane
See Lessing, Doris (May)

Somerville, Edith 1858-1949 ...... TCLC 51
See also DLB 135

Somerville & Ross
See Martin, Violet Florence; Somerville,
Edith

Sommer, Scott 1951- .... CLC 25
See also CA 106

Sondheim, Stephen (Joshua)
1930- .... CLC 30, 39; DAM DRAM
See also AAYA 11; CA 103; CANR 47

Sontag, Susan
1933- .... CLC 1, 2, 10, 13, 31;
DAM POP
See also CA 17-20R; CANR 25, 51; DLB 2,
67; MTCW

Sophocles
496(?)B.C.-406(?)B.C..... CMLC 2; DA;
DAB; DAC; DAM DRAM, MST; DC 1

Sordello 1189-1269............. CMLC 15

Sorel, Julia
See Drexler, Rosalyn

Sorrentino, Gilbert
1929- .... CLC 3, 7, 14, 22, 40
See also CA 77-80; CANR 14, 33; DLB 5;
DLBY 80; INT CANR-14

Soto, Gary
1952- .... CLC 32, 80; DAM MULT;
HLC
See also AAYA 10; CA 119; 125;
CANR 50; CLR 38; DLB 82; HW;
INT 125; JRDA; SATA 80

Soupault, Philippe 1897-1990 ...... CLC 68
See also CA 116; 147; 131

Souster, (Holmes) Raymond
1921- ... CLC 5, 14; DAC; DAM POET
See also CA 13-16R; CAAS 14; CANR 13,
29, 53; DLB 88; SATA 63

Southern, Terry 1924(?)-1995 .... CLC 7
See also CA 1-4R; 150; CANR 1; DLB 2

Southey, Robert 1774-1843 .... NCLC 8
See also DLB 93, 107, 142; SATA 54

Southworth, Emma Dorothy Eliza Nevitte
1819-1899 .... NCLC 26

Souza, Ernest
See Scott, Evelyn

Soyinka, Wole
1934- .... CLC 3, 5, 14, 36, 44; BLC;
DA; DAB; DAC; DAM DRAM, MST,
MULT; DC 2; WLC
See also BW 2; CA 13-16R; CANR 27, 39;
DLB 125; MTCW

Spackman, W(illiam) M(ode)
1905-1990 .... CLC 46
See also CA 81-84; 132

Spacks, Barry 1931-.............. CLC 14
See also CA 29-32R; CANR 33; DLB 105

Spanidou, Irini 1946-............. CLC 44

Spark, Muriel (Sarah)
1918- ..... CLC 2, 3, 5, 8, 13, 18, 40, 94;
DAB; DAC; DAM MST, NOV; SSC 10
See also CA 5-8R; CANR 12, 36;
CDBLB 1945-1960; DLB 15, 139;
INT CANR-12; MTCW

Spaulding, Douglas
See Bradbury, Ray (Douglas)

Spaulding, Leonard
See Bradbury, Ray (Douglas)

Spence, J. A. D.
See Eliot, T(homas) S(tearns)

Spencer, Elizabeth 1921-........... CLC 22
See also CA 13-16R; CANR 32; DLB 6;
MTCW; SATA 14

Spencer, Leonard G.
See Silverberg, Robert

Spencer, Scott 1945-.............. CLC 30
See also CA 113; CANR 51; DLBY 86

Spender, Stephen (Harold)
1909-1995 ...... CLC 1, 2, 5, 10, 41, 91;
DAM POET
See also CA 9-12R; 149; CANR 31;
CDBLB 1945-1960; DLB 20; MTCW

Spengler, Oswald (Arnold Gottfried)
1880-1936 .... TCLC 25
See also CA 118

Spenser, Edmund
1552(?)-1599 .... LC 5; DA; DAB; DAC;
DAM MST, POET; PC 8; WLC
See also CDBLB Before 1660; DLB 167

Spicer, Jack
1925-1965 .... CLC 8, 18, 72;
DAM POET
See also CA 85-88; DLB 5, 16

Spiegelman, Art 1948-............ CLC 76
See also AAYA 10; CA 125; CANR 41

Spielberg, Peter 1929-............ CLC 6
See also CA 5-8R; CANR 4, 48; DLBY 81

Spielberg, Steven 1947- . . . . **CLC 20**
See also AAYA 8; CA 77-80; CANR 32;
SATA 32

Spillane, Frank Morrison 1918-
See Spillane, Mickey
See also CA 25-28R; CANR 28; MTCW;
SATA 66

Spillane, Mickey . . . . **CLC 3, 13**
See also Spillane, Frank Morrison

Spinoza, Benedictus de 1632-1677 . . . . **LC 9**

Spinrad, Norman (Richard) 1940- . . . **CLC 46**
See also CA 37-40R; CAAS 19; CANR 20;
DLB 8; INT CANR-20

Spitteler, Carl (Friedrich Georg)
1845-1924 . . . . **TCLC 12**
See also CA 109; DLB 129

Spivack, Kathleen (Romola Drucker)
1938- . . . . **CLC 6**
See also CA 49-52

Spoto, Donald 1941- . . . . **CLC 39**
See also CA 65-68; CANR 11

Springsteen, Bruce (F.) 1949- . . . . . . **CLC 17**
See also CA 111

Spurling, Hilary 1940- . . . . **CLC 34**
See also CA 104; CANR 25, 52

Spyker, John Howland
See Elman, Richard

Squires, (James) Radcliffe
1917-1993 . . . . **CLC 51**
See also CA 1-4R; 140; CANR 6, 21

Srivastava, Dhanpat Rai 1880(?)-1936
See Premchand
See also CA 118

Stacy, Donald
See Pohl, Frederik

Stael, Germaine de
See Stael-Holstein, Anne Louise Germaine
Necker Baronn
See also DLB 119

Stael-Holstein, Anne Louise Germaine Necker
Baronn 1766-1817 . . . . **NCLC 3**
See also Stael, Germaine de

Stafford, Jean 1915-1979 . . . **CLC 4, 7, 19, 68**
See also CA 1-4R; 85-88; CANR 3; DLB 2;
MTCW; SATA-Obit 22

Stafford, William (Edgar)
1914-1993 . . . **CLC 4, 7, 29; DAM POET**
See also CA 5-8R; 142; CAAS 3; CANR 5,
22; DLB 5; INT CANR-22

Staines, Trevor
See Brunner, John (Kilian Houston)

Stairs, Gordon
See Austin, Mary (Hunter)

Stannard, Martin 1947- . . . . **CLC 44**
See also CA 142; DLB 155

Stanton, Maura 1946- . . . . **CLC 9**
See also CA 89-92; CANR 15; DLB 120

Stanton, Schuyler
See Baum, L(yman) Frank

Stapledon, (William) Olaf
1886-1950 . . . . **TCLC 22**
See also CA 111; DLB 15

Starbuck, George (Edwin)
1931- . . . . **CLC 53; DAM POET**
See also CA 21-24R; CANR 23

Stark, Richard
See Westlake, Donald E(dwin)

Staunton, Schuyler
See Baum, L(yman) Frank

Stead, Christina (Ellen)
1902-1983 . . . . **CLC 2, 5, 8, 32, 80**
See also CA 13-16R; 109; CANR 33, 40;
MTCW

Stead, William Thomas
1849-1912 . . . . **TCLC 48**

Steele, Richard 1672-1729 . . . . **LC 18**
See also CDBLB 1660-1789; DLB 84, 101

Steele, Timothy (Reid) 1948- . . . . **CLC 45**
See also CA 93-96; CANR 16, 50; DLB 120

Steffens, (Joseph) Lincoln
1866-1936 . . . . **TCLC 20**
See also CA 117

Stegner, Wallace (Earle)
1909-1993 . . . **CLC 9, 49, 81; DAM NOV**
See also AITN 1; BEST 90:3; CA 1-4R;
141; CAAS 9; CANR 1, 21, 46; DLB 9;
DLBY 93; MTCW

Stein, Gertrude
1874-1946 . . . . . . **TCLC 1, 6, 28, 48; DA;**
DAB; DAC; DAM MST, NOV, POET;
WLC
See also CA 104; 132; CDALB 1917-1929;
DLB 4, 54, 86; MTCW

Steinbeck, John (Ernst)
1902-1968 . . . . . . **CLC 1, 5, 9, 13, 21, 34,**
45, 75; DA; DAB; DAC; DAM DRAM,
MST, NOV; SSC 11; WLC
See also AAYA 12; CA 1-4R; 25-28R;
CANR 1, 35; CDALB 1929-1941; DLB 7,
9; DLBD 2; MTCW; SATA 9

Steinem, Gloria 1934- . . . . **CLC 63**
See also CA 53-56; CANR 28, 51; MTCW

Steiner, George
1929- . . . . **CLC 24; DAM NOV**
See also CA 73-76; CANR 31; DLB 67;
MTCW; SATA 62

Steiner, K. Leslie
See Delany, Samuel R(ay, Jr.)

Steiner, Rudolf 1861-1925 . . . . **TCLC 13**
See also CA 107

Stendhal
1783-1842 . . . . **NCLC 23, 46; DA; DAB;**
DAC; DAM MST, NOV; WLC
See also DLB 119

Stephen, Leslie 1832-1904 . . . . **TCLC 23**
See also CA 123; DLB 57, 144

Stephen, Sir Leslie
See Stephen, Leslie

Stephen, Virginia
See Woolf, (Adeline) Virginia

Stephens, James 1882(?)-1950 . . . . . . **TCLC 4**
See also CA 104; DLB 19, 153, 162

Stephens, Reed
See Donaldson, Stephen R.

Steptoe, Lydia
See Barnes, Djuna

Sterchi, Beat 1949- . . . . **CLC 65**

Sterling, Brett
See Bradbury, Ray (Douglas); Hamilton,
Edmond

Sterling, Bruce 1954- . . . . **CLC 72**
See also CA 119; CANR 44

Sterling, George 1869-1926 . . . . **TCLC 20**
See also CA 117; DLB 54

Stern, Gerald 1925- . . . . **CLC 40**
See also CA 81-84; CANR 28; DLB 105

Stern, Richard (Gustave) 1928- . . . . **CLC 4, 39**
See also CA 1-4R; CANR 1, 25, 52;
DLBY 87; INT CANR-25

Sternberg, Josef von 1894-1969 . . . . . **CLC 20**
See also CA 81-84

Sterne, Laurence
1713-1768 . . . . . . **LC 2; DA; DAB; DAC;**
DAM MST, NOV; WLC
See also CDBLB 1660-1789; DLB 39

Sternheim, (William Adolf) Carl
1878-1942 . . . . **TCLC 8**
See also CA 105; DLB 56, 118

Stevens, Mark 1951- . . . . **CLC 34**
See also CA 122

Stevens, Wallace
1879-1955 . . . . **TCLC 3, 12, 45; DA;**
DAB; DAC; DAM MST, POET; PC 6;
WLC
See also CA 104; 124; CDALB 1929-1941;
DLB 54; MTCW

Stevenson, Anne (Katharine)
1933- . . . . **CLC 7, 33**
See also CA 17-20R; CAAS 9; CANR 9, 33;
DLB 40; MTCW

Stevenson, Robert Louis (Balfour)
1850-1894 . . . . . **NCLC 5, 14; DA; DAB;**
DAC; DAM MST, NOV; SSC 11; WLC
See also CDBLB 1890-1914; CLR 10, 11;
DLB 18, 57, 141, 156; DLBD 13; JRDA;
MAICYA; YABC 2

Stewart, J(ohn) I(nnes) M(ackintosh)
1906-1994 . . . . **CLC 7, 14, 32**
See also CA 85-88; 147; CAAS 3;
CANR 47; MTCW

Stewart, Mary (Florence Elinor)
1916- . . . . **CLC 7, 35; DAB**
See also CA 1-4R; CANR 1; SATA 12

Stewart, Mary Rainbow
See Stewart, Mary (Florence Elinor)

Stifle, June
See Campbell, Maria

Stifter, Adalbert 1805-1868 . . . . . . **NCLC 41**
See also DLB 133

Still, James 1906- . . . . **CLC 49**
See also CA 65-68; CAAS 17; CANR 10,
26; DLB 9; SATA 29

Sting
See Sumner, Gordon Matthew

Stirling, Arthur
See Sinclair, Upton (Beall)

Stitt, Milan 1941- . . . . **CLC 29**
See also CA 69-72

Stockton, Francis Richard 1834-1902
See Stockton, Frank R.
See also CA 108; 137; MAICYA; SATA 44

Author Index

Swenson, May
    1919-1989 .... **CLC 4, 14, 61; DA; DAB;**
        DAC; DAM MST, POET; PC 14
    See also CA 5-8R; 130; CANR 36; DLB 5;
    MTCW; SATA 15

Swift, Augustus
    See Lovecraft, H(oward) P(hillips)

Swift, Graham (Colin) 1949- .... **CLC 41, 88**
    See also CA 117; 122; CANR 46

Swift, Jonathan
    1667-1745 ...... **LC 1; DA; DAB; DAC;**
        DAM MST, NOV, POET; PC 9; WLC
    See also CDBLB 1660-1789; DLB 39, 95,
    101; SATA 19

Swinburne, Algernon Charles
    1837-1909 ...... **TCLC 8, 36; DA; DAB;**
        DAC; DAM MST, POET; WLC
    See also CA 105; 140; CDBLB 1832-1890;
    DLB 35, 57

Swinfen, Ann .... **CLC 34**

Swinnerton, Frank Arthur
    1884-1982 .... **CLC 31**
    See also CA 108; DLB 34

Swithen, John
    See King, Stephen (Edwin)

Sylvia
    See Ashton-Warner, Sylvia (Constance)

Symmes, Robert Edward
    See Duncan, Robert (Edward)

Symonds, John Addington
    1840-1893 .... **NCLC 34**
    See also DLB 57, 144

Symons, Arthur 1865-1945 .... **TCLC 11**
    See also CA 107; DLB 19, 57, 149

Symons, Julian (Gustave)
    1912-1994 .... **CLC 2, 14, 32**
    See also CA 49-52; 147; CAAS 3; CANR 3,
    33; DLB 87, 155; DLBY 92; MTCW

Synge, (Edmund) J(ohn) M(illington)
    1871-1909 .... **TCLC 6, 37;**
        DAM DRAM; DC 2
    See also CA 104; 141; CDBLB 1890-1914;
    DLB 10, 19

Syruc, J.
    See Milosz, Czeslaw

Szirtes, George 1948- .... **CLC 46**
    See also CA 109; CANR 27

Tabori, George 1914- .... **CLC 19**
    See also CA 49-52; CANR 4

Tagore, Rabindranath
    1861-1941 .... **TCLC 3, 53;**
        DAM DRAM, POET; PC 8
    See also CA 104; 120; MTCW

Taine, Hippolyte Adolphe
    1828-1893 .... **NCLC 15**

Talese, Gay 1932- .... **CLC 37**
    See also AITN 1; CA 1-4R; CANR 9;
    INT CANR-9; MTCW

Tallent, Elizabeth (Ann) 1954- ..... **CLC 45**
    See also CA 117; DLB 130

Tally, Ted 1952- .... **CLC 42**
    See also CA 120; 124; INT 124

Tamayo y Baus, Manuel
    1829-1898 .... **NCLC 1**

Tammsaare, A(nton) H(ansen)
    1878-1940 .... **TCLC 27**

Tan, Amy
    1952- .... **CLC 59; DAM MULT, NOV,**
        POP
    See also AAYA 9; BEST 89:3; CA 136;
    SATA 75

Tandem, Felix
    See Spitteler, Carl (Friedrich Georg)

Tanizaki, Jun'ichiro
    1886-1965 ...... **CLC 8, 14, 28; SSC 21**
    See also CA 93-96; 25-28R

Tanner, William
    See Amis, Kingsley (William)

Tao Lao
    See Storni, Alfonsina

Tarassoff, Lev
    See Troyat, Henri

Tarbell, Ida M(inerva)
    1857-1944 .... **TCLC 40**
    See also CA 122; DLB 47

Tarkington, (Newton) Booth
    1869-1946 .... **TCLC 9**
    See also CA 110; 143; DLB 9, 102;
    SATA 17

Tarkovsky, Andrei (Arsenyevich)
    1932-1986 .... **CLC 75**
    See also CA 127

Tartt, Donna 1964(?)- .... **CLC 76**
    See also CA 142

Tasso, Torquato 1544-1595 .... **LC 5**

Tate, (John Orley) Allen
    1899-1979 .... **CLC 2, 4, 6, 9, 11, 14, 24**
    See also CA 5-8R; 85-88; CANR 32;
    DLB 4, 45, 63; MTCW

Tate, Ellalice
    See Hibbert, Eleanor Alice Burford

Tate, James (Vincent) 1943- ... **CLC 2, 6, 25**
    See also CA 21-24R; CANR 29; DLB 5

Tavel, Ronald 1940- .... **CLC 6**
    See also CA 21-24R; CANR 33

Taylor, C(ecil) P(hilip) 1929-1981... **CLC 27**
    See also CA 25-28R; 105; CANR 47

Taylor, Edward
    1642(?)-1729 .... **LC 11; DA; DAB;**
        DAC; DAM MST, POET
    See also DLB 24

Taylor, Eleanor Ross 1920- .... **CLC 5**
    See also CA 81-84

Taylor, Elizabeth 1912-1975 ... **CLC 2, 4, 29**
    See also CA 13-16R; CANR 9; DLB 139;
    MTCW; SATA 13

Taylor, Henry (Splawn) 1942- ...... **CLC 44**
    See also CA 33-36R; CAAS 7; CANR 31;
    DLB 5

Taylor, Kamala (Purnaiya) 1924-
    See Markandaya, Kamala
    See also CA 77-80

Taylor, Mildred D. .... **CLC 21**
    See also AAYA 10; BW 1; CA 85-88;
    CANR 25; CLR 9; DLB 52; JRDA;
    MAICYA; SAAS 5; SATA 15, 70

Taylor, Peter (Hillsman)
    1917-1994 ..... **CLC 1, 4, 18, 37, 44, 50,**
        71; SSC 10
    See also CA 13-16R; 147; CANR 9, 50;
    DLBY 81, 94; INT CANR-9; MTCW

Taylor, Robert Lewis 1912- .... **CLC 14**
    See also CA 1-4R; CANR 3; SATA 10

Tchekhov, Anton
    See Chekhov, Anton (Pavlovich)

Teasdale, Sara 1884-1933 .... **TCLC 4**
    See also CA 104; DLB 45; SATA 32

Tegner, Esaias 1782-1846 .... **NCLC 2**

Teilhard de Chardin, (Marie Joseph) Pierre
    1881-1955 .... **TCLC 9**
    See also CA 105

Temple, Ann
    See Mortimer, Penelope (Ruth)

Tennant, Emma (Christina)
    1937- .... **CLC 13, 52**
    See also CA 65-68; CAAS 9; CANR 10, 38;
    DLB 14

Tenneshaw, S. M.
    See Silverberg, Robert

Tennyson, Alfred
    1809-1892 .... **NCLC 30; DA; DAB;**
        DAC; DAM MST, POET; PC 6; WLC
    See also CDBLB 1832-1890; DLB 32

Teran, Lisa St. Aubin de .... **CLC 36**
    See also St. Aubin de Teran, Lisa

Terence 195(?)B.C.-159B.C...... **CMLC 14**

Teresa de Jesus, St. 1515-1582 ...... **LC 18**

Terkel, Louis 1912-
    See Terkel, Studs
    See also CA 57-60; CANR 18, 45; MTCW

Terkel, Studs .... **CLC 38**
    See also Terkel, Louis
    See also AITN 1

Terry, C. V.
    See Slaughter, Frank G(ill)

Terry, Megan 1932- .... **CLC 19**
    See also CA 77-80; CABS 3; CANR 43;
    DLB 7

Tertz, Abram
    See Sinyavsky, Andrei (Donatevich)

Tesich, Steve 1943(?)-1996...... **CLC 40, 69**
    See also CA 105; 152; DLBY 83

Teternikov, Fyodor Kuzmich 1863-1927
    See Sologub, Fyodor
    See also CA 104

Tevis, Walter 1928-1984 .... **CLC 42**
    See also CA 113

Tey, Josephine .... **TCLC 14**
    See also Mackintosh, Elizabeth
    See also DLB 77

Thackeray, William Makepeace
    1811-1863 .... **NCLC 5, 14, 22, 43; DA;**
        DAB; DAC; DAM MST, NOV; WLC
    See also CDBLB 1832-1890; DLB 21, 55,
    159, 163; SATA 23

Thakura, Ravindranatha
    See Tagore, Rabindranath

Tharoor, Shashi 1956- .... **CLC 70**
    See also CA 141

Thelwell, Michael Miles 1939- ..... **CLC 22**
See also BW 2; CA 101

Theobald, Lewis, Jr.
See Lovecraft, H(oward) P(hillips)

Theodorescu, Ion N. 1880-1967
See Arghezi, Tudor
See also CA 116

Theriault, Yves
1915-1983 .. **CLC 79; DAC; DAM MST**
See also CA 102; DLB 88

Theroux, Alexander (Louis)
1939- .... **CLC 2, 25**
See also CA 85-88; CANR 20

Theroux, Paul (Edward)
1941- .... **CLC 5, 8, 11, 15, 28, 46;**
DAM POP
See also BEST 89:4; CA 33-36R; CANR 20,
45; DLB 2; MTCW; SATA 44

Thesen, Sharon 1946-............ **CLC 56**

Thevenin, Denis
See Duhamel, Georges

Thibault, Jacques Anatole Francois
1844-1924
See France, Anatole
See also CA 106; 127; DAM NOV; MTCW

Thiele, Colin (Milton) 1920- .... **CLC 17**
See also CA 29-32R; CANR 12, 28, 53;
CLR 27; MAICYA; SAAS 2; SATA 14,
72

Thomas, Audrey (Callahan)
1935- .... **CLC 7, 13, 37; SSC 20**
See also AITN 2; CA 21-24R; CAAS 19;
CANR 36; DLB 60; MTCW

Thomas, D(onald) M(ichael)
1935- .... **CLC 13, 22, 31**
See also CA 61-64; CAAS 11; CANR 17,
45; CDBLB 1960 to Present; DLB 40;
INT CANR-17; MTCW

Thomas, Dylan (Marlais)
1914-1953 ... **TCLC 1, 8, 45; DA; DAB;**
DAC; DAM DRAM, MST, POET;
PC 2; SSC 3; WLC
See also CA 104; 120; CDBLB 1945-1960;
DLB 13, 20, 139; MTCW; SATA 60

Thomas, (Philip) Edward
1878-1917 ...... **TCLC 10; DAM POET**
See also CA 106; DLB 19

Thomas, Joyce Carol 1938-........ **CLC 35**
See also AAYA 12; BW 2; CA 113; 116;
CANR 48; CLR 19; DLB 33; INT 116;
JRDA; MAICYA; MTCW; SAAS 7;
SATA 40, 78

Thomas, Lewis 1913-1993 .... **CLC 35**
See also CA 85-88; 143; CANR 38; MTCW

Thomas, Paul
See Mann, (Paul) Thomas

Thomas, Piri 1928-............... **CLC 17**
See also CA 73-76; HW

Thomas, R(onald) S(tuart)
1913- .... **CLC 6, 13, 48; DAB;**
DAM POET
See also CA 89-92; CAAS 4; CANR 30;
CDBLB 1960 to Present; DLB 27;
MTCW

Thomas, Ross (Elmore) 1926-1995 .. **CLC 39**
See also CA 33-36R; 150; CANR 22

Thompson, Francis Clegg
See Mencken, H(enry) L(ouis)

Thompson, Francis Joseph
1859-1907 .... **TCLC 4**
See also CA 104; CDBLB 1890-1914;
DLB 19

Thompson, Hunter S(tockton)
1939- .... **CLC 9, 17, 40; DAM POP**
See also BEST 89:1; CA 17-20R; CANR 23,
46; MTCW

Thompson, James Myers
See Thompson, Jim (Myers)

Thompson, Jim (Myers)
1906-1977(?) .... **CLC 69**
See also CA 140

Thompson, Judith .... **CLC 39**

Thomson, James
1700-1748 ..... **LC 16, 29; DAM POET**
See also DLB 95

Thomson, James
1834-1882 ..... **NCLC 18; DAM POET**
See also DLB 35

Thoreau, Henry David
1817-1862 ..... **NCLC 7, 21; DA; DAB;**
DAC; DAM MST; WLC
See also CDALB 1640-1865; DLB 1

Thornton, Hall
See Silverberg, Robert

Thucydides c. 455B.C.-399B.C. .... **CMLC 17**

Thurber, James (Grover)
1894-1961 .... **CLC 5, 11, 25; DA; DAB;**
DAC; DAM DRAM, MST, NOV; SSC 1
See also CA 73-76; CANR 17, 39;
CDALB 1929-1941; DLB 4, 11, 22, 102;
MAICYA; MTCW; SATA 13

Thurman, Wallace (Henry)
1902-1934 .... **TCLC 6; BLC;**
DAM MULT
See also BW 1; CA 104; 124; DLB 51

Ticheburn, Cheviot
See Ainsworth, William Harrison

Tieck, (Johann) Ludwig
1773-1853 .... **NCLC 5, 46**
See also DLB 90

Tiger, Derry
See Ellison, Harlan (Jay)

Tilghman, Christopher 1948(?)-..... **CLC 65**

Tillinghast, Richard (Williford)
1940- .... **CLC 29**
See also CA 29-32R; CAAS 23; CANR 26,
51

Timrod, Henry 1828-1867 .... **NCLC 25**
See also DLB 3

Tindall, Gillian 1938-............. **CLC 7**
See also CA 21-24R; CANR 11

Tiptree, James, Jr. .... **CLC 48, 50**
See also Sheldon, Alice Hastings Bradley
See also DLB 8

Titmarsh, Michael Angelo
See Thackeray, William Makepeace

Tocqueville, Alexis (Charles Henri Maurice
Clerel Comte) 1805-1859..... **NCLC 7**

Tolkien, J(ohn) R(onald) R(euel)
1892-1973 .... **CLC 1, 2, 3, 8, 12, 38;**
DA; DAB; DAC; DAM MST, NOV,
POP; WLC
See also AAYA 10; AITN 1; CA 17-18;
45-48; CANR 36; CAP 2;
CDBLB 1914-1945; DLB 15, 160; JRDA;
MAICYA; MTCW; SATA 2, 32;
SATA-Obit 24

Toller, Ernst 1893-1939 .... **TCLC 10**
See also CA 107; DLB 124

Tolson, M. B.
See Tolson, Melvin B(eaunorus)

Tolson, Melvin B(eaunorus)
1898(?)-1966 .... **CLC 36; BLC;**
DAM MULT, POET
See also BW 1; CA 124; 89-92; DLB 48, 76

Tolstoi, Aleksei Nikolaevich
See Tolstoy, Alexey Nikolaevich

Tolstoy, Alexey Nikolaevich
1882-1945 .... **TCLC 18**
See also CA 107

Tolstoy, Count Leo
See Tolstoy, Leo (Nikolaevich)

Tolstoy, Leo (Nikolaevich)
1828-1910 ...... **TCLC 4, 11, 17, 28, 44;**
DA; DAB; DAC; DAM MST, NOV;
SSC 9; WLC
See also CA 104; 123; SATA 26

Tomasi di Lampedusa, Giuseppe 1896-1957
See Lampedusa, Giuseppe (Tomasi) di
See also CA 111

Tomlin, Lily .... **CLC 17**
See also Tomlin, Mary Jean

Tomlin, Mary Jean 1939(?)-
See Tomlin, Lily
See also CA 117

Tomlinson, (Alfred) Charles
1927- .... **CLC 2, 4, 6, 13, 45;**
DAM POET
See also CA 5-8R; CANR 33; DLB 40

Tonson, Jacob
See Bennett, (Enoch) Arnold

Toole, John Kennedy
1937-1969 .... **CLC 19, 64**
See also CA 104; DLBY 81

Toomer, Jean
1894-1967 ...... **CLC 1, 4, 13, 22; BLC;**
DAM MULT; PC 7; SSC 1
See also BW 1; CA 85-88;
CDALB 1917-1929; DLB 45, 51; MTCW

Torley, Luke
See Blish, James (Benjamin)

Tornimparte, Alessandra
See Ginzburg, Natalia

Torre, Raoul della
See Mencken, H(enry) L(ouis)

Torrey, E(dwin) Fuller 1937-....... **CLC 34**
See also CA 119

Torsvan, Ben Traven
See Traven, B.

Torsvan, Benno Traven
See Traven, B.

Torsvan, Berick Traven
See Traven, B.

Torsvan, Berwick Traven
See Traven, B.

Torsvan, Bruno Traven
See Traven, B.

Torsvan, Traven
See Traven, B.

Tournier, Michel (Edouard)
1924- . . . . **CLC 6, 23, 36, 95**
See also CA 49-52; CANR 3, 36; DLB 83;
MTCW; SATA 23

Tournimparte, Alessandra
See Ginzburg, Natalia

Towers, Ivar
See Kornbluth, C(yril) M.

Towne, Robert (Burton) 1936(?)-. . . . **CLC 87**
See also CA 108; DLB 44

Townsend, Sue 1946- . . **CLC 61; DAB; DAC**
See also CA 119; 127; INT 127; MTCW;
SATA 55; SATA-Brief 48

Townshend, Peter (Dennis Blandford)
1945- . . . . **CLC 17, 42**
See also CA 107

Tozzi, Federigo 1883-1920. . . . . . . **TCLC 31**

Traill, Catharine Parr
1802-1899 . . . . **NCLC 31**
See also DLB 99

Trakl, Georg 1887-1914. . . . . **TCLC 5**
See also CA 104

Transtroemer, Tomas (Goesta)
1931- . . . . **CLC 52, 65; DAM POET**
See also CA 117; 129; CAAS 17

Transtromer, Tomas Gosta
See Transtroemer, Tomas (Goesta)

Traven, B. (?)-1969. . . . . **CLC 8, 11**
See also CA 19-20; 25-28R; CAP 2; DLB 9,
56; MTCW

Treitel, Jonathan 1959- . . . . **CLC 70**

Tremain, Rose 1943-. . . . . **CLC 42**
See also CA 97-100; CANR 44; DLB 14

Tremblay, Michel
1942- . . . . . . **CLC 29; DAC; DAM MST**
See also CA 116; 128; DLB 60; MTCW

Trevanian. . . . . **CLC 29**
See also Whitaker, Rod(ney)

Trevor, Glen
See Hilton, James

Trevor, William
1928- . . . . . **CLC 7, 9, 14, 25, 71; SSC 21**
See also Cox, William Trevor
See also DLB 14, 139

Trifonov, Yuri (Valentinovich)
1925-1981 . . . . **CLC 45**
See also CA 126; 103; MTCW

Trilling, Lionel 1905-1975 . . . . **CLC 9, 11, 24**
See also CA 9-12R; 61-64; CANR 10;
DLB 28, 63; INT CANR-10; MTCW

Trimball, W. H.
See Mencken, H(enry) L(ouis)

Tristan
See Gomez de la Serna, Ramon

Tristram
See Housman, A(lfred) E(dward)

Trogdon, William (Lewis) 1939-
See Heat-Moon, William Least
See also CA 115; 119; CANR 47; INT 119

Trollope, Anthony
1815-1882 . . . . . **NCLC 6, 33; DA; DAB;
DAC; DAM MST, NOV; WLC**
See also CDBLB 1832-1890; DLB 21, 57,
159; SATA 22

Trollope, Frances 1779-1863 . . . . . **NCLC 30**
See also DLB 21, 166

Trotsky, Leon 1879-1940. . . . . **TCLC 22**
See also CA 118

Trotter (Cockburn), Catharine
1679-1749 . . . . **LC 8**
See also DLB 84

Trout, Kilgore
See Farmer, Philip Jose

Trow, George W. S. 1943-. . . . . **CLC 52**
See also CA 126

Troyat, Henri 1911-. . . . . **CLC 23**
See also CA 45-48; CANR 2, 33; MTCW

Trudeau, G(arretson) B(eekman) 1948-
See Trudeau, Garry B.
See also CA 81-84; CANR 31; SATA 35

Trudeau, Garry B.. . . . . **CLC 12**
See also Trudeau, G(arretson) B(eekman)
See also AAYA 10; AITN 2

Truffaut, Francois 1932-1984. . . . . . **CLC 20**
See also CA 81-84; 113; CANR 34

Trumbo, Dalton 1905-1976 . . . . **CLC 19**
See also CA 21-24R; 69-72; CANR 10;
DLB 26

Trumbull, John 1750-1831. . . . . . . **NCLC 30**
See also DLB 31

Trundlett, Helen B.
See Eliot, T(homas) S(tearns)

Tryon, Thomas
1926-1991 . . . . . **CLC 3, 11; DAM POP**
See also AITN 1; CA 29-32R; 135;
CANR 32; MTCW

Tryon, Tom
See Tryon, Thomas

Ts'ao Hsueh-ch'in 1715(?)-1763. . . . . . **LC 1**

Tsushima, Shuji 1909-1948
See Dazai, Osamu
See also CA 107

Tsvetaeva (Efron), Marina (Ivanovna)
1892-1941 . . . . **TCLC 7, 35; PC 14**
See also CA 104; 128; MTCW

Tuck, Lily 1938-. . . . . **CLC 70**
See also CA 139

Tu Fu 712-770. . . . . **PC 9**
See also DAM MULT

Tunis, John R(oberts) 1889-1975 . . . **CLC 12**
See also CA 61-64; DLB 22; JRDA;
MAICYA; SATA 37; SATA-Brief 30

Tuohy, Frank. . . . . **CLC 37**
See also Tuohy, John Francis
See also DLB 14, 139

Tuohy, John Francis 1925-
See Tuohy, Frank
See also CA 5-8R; CANR 3, 47

Turco, Lewis (Putnam) 1934- . . . **CLC 11, 63**
See also CA 13-16R; CAAS 22; CANR 24,
51; DLBY 84

Turgenev, Ivan
1818-1883 . . . . **NCLC 21; DA; DAB;
DAC; DAM MST, NOV; SSC 7; WLC**

Turgot, Anne-Robert-Jacques
1727-1781 . . . . **LC 26**

Turner, Frederick 1943-. . . . . **CLC 48**
See also CA 73-76; CAAS 10; CANR 12,
30; DLB 40

Tutu, Desmond M(pilo)
1931- . . . . . **CLC 80; BLC; DAM MULT**
See also BW 1; CA 125

Tutuola, Amos
1920- . . . . **CLC 5, 14, 29; BLC;
DAM MULT**
See also BW 2; CA 9-12R; CANR 27;
DLB 125; MTCW

Twain, Mark
. . . . . **TCLC 6, 12, 19, 36, 48, 59; SSC 6;
WLC**
See also Clemens, Samuel Langhorne
See also DLB 11, 12, 23, 64, 74

Tyler, Anne
1941- . . . . **CLC 7, 11, 18, 28, 44, 59;
DAM NOV, POP**
See also AAYA 18; BEST 89:1; CA 9-12R;
CANR 11, 33, 53; DLB 6, 143; DLBY 82;
MTCW; SATA 7

Tyler, Royall 1757-1826. . . . . **NCLC 3**
See also DLB 37

Tynan, Katharine 1861-1931. . . . . . . **TCLC 3**
See also CA 104; DLB 153

Tyutchev, Fyodor 1803-1873 . . . . . **NCLC 34**

Tzara, Tristan . . . . **CLC 47; DAM POET**
See also Rosenfeld, Samuel

Uhry, Alfred
1936- . . . . . **CLC 55; DAM DRAM, POP**
See also CA 127; 133; INT 133

Ulf, Haerved
See Strindberg, (Johan) August

Ulf, Harved
See Strindberg, (Johan) August

Ulibarri, Sabine R(eyes)
1919- . . . . **CLC 83; DAM MULT**
See also CA 131; DLB 82; HW

Unamuno (y Jugo), Miguel de
1864-1936 . . . **TCLC 2, 9; DAM MULT,
NOV; HLC; SSC 11**
See also CA 104; 131; DLB 108; HW;
MTCW

Undercliffe, Errol
See Campbell, (John) Ramsey

Underwood, Miles
See Glassco, John

Undset, Sigrid
1882-1949 . . . . **TCLC 3; DA; DAB;
DAC; DAM MST, NOV; WLC**
See also CA 104; 129; MTCW

Ungaretti, Giuseppe
1888-1970 . . . . **CLC 7, 11, 15**
See also CA 19-20; 25-28R; CAP 2;
DLB 114

Villiers de l'Isle Adam, Jean Marie Mathias
    Philippe Auguste Comte
    1838-1889 . . . . NCLC 3; SSC 14
See also DLB 123

Villon, Francois   1431-1463(?) . . . . PC 13

Vinci, Leonardo da   1452-1519. . . . . . LC 12

Vine, Barbara . . . . CLC 50
See also Rendell, Ruth (Barbara)
See also BEST 90:4

Vinge, Joan D(ennison)   1948- . . . . . . CLC 30
See also CA 93-96; SATA 36

Violis, G.
See Simenon, Georges (Jacques Christian)

Visconti, Luchino   1906-1976 . . . . CLC 16
See also CA 81-84; 65-68; CANR 39

Vittorini, Elio   1908-1966 . . . . . . CLC 6, 9, 14
See also CA 133; 25-28R

Vizinczey, Stephen   1933- . . . . CLC 40
See also CA 128; INT 128

Vliet, R(ussell) G(ordon)
    1929-1984 . . . . CLC 22
See also CA 37-40R; 112; CANR 18

Vogau, Boris Andreyevich   1894-1937(?)
See Pilnyak, Boris
See also CA 123

Vogel, Paula A(nne)   1951- . . . . CLC 76
See also CA 108

Voight, Ellen Bryant   1943- . . . . CLC 54
See also CA 69-72; CANR 11, 29; DLB 120

Voigt, Cynthia   1942- . . . . CLC 30
See also AAYA 3; CA 106; CANR 18, 37,
    40; CLR 13; INT CANR-18; JRDA;
    MAICYA; SATA 48, 79; SATA-Brief 33

Voinovich, Vladimir (Nikolaevich)
    1932- . . . . CLC 10, 49
See also CA 81-84; CAAS 12; CANR 33;
    MTCW

Vollmann, William T.
    1959- . . . . . . CLC 89; DAM NOV, POP
See also CA 134

Voloshinov, V. N.
See Bakhtin, Mikhail Mikhailovich

Voltaire
    1694-1778 . . . . . LC 14; DA; DAB; DAC;
        DAM DRAM, MST; SSC 12; WLC

von Daeniken, Erich   1935- . . . . CLC 30
See also AITN 1; CA 37-40R; CANR 17,
    44

von Daniken, Erich
See von Daeniken, Erich

von Heidenstam, (Carl Gustaf) Verner
See Heidenstam, (Carl Gustaf) Verner von

von Heyse, Paul (Johann Ludwig)
See Heyse, Paul (Johann Ludwig von)

von Hofmannsthal, Hugo
See Hofmannsthal, Hugo von

von Horvath, Odon
See Horvath, Oedoen von

von Horvath, Oedoen
See Horvath, Oedoen von

von Liliencron, (Friedrich Adolf Axel) Detlev
See Liliencron, (Friedrich Adolf Axel)
    Detlev von

Vonnegut, Kurt, Jr.
    1922- . . . . . . CLC 1, 2, 3, 4, 5, 8, 12, 22,
        40, 60; DA; DAB; DAC; DAM MST,
        NOV, POP; SSC 8; WLC
See also AAYA 6; AITN 1; BEST 90:4;
    CA 1-4R; CANR 1, 25, 49;
    CDALB 1968-1988; DLB 2, 8, 152;
    DLBD 3; DLBY 80; MTCW

Von Rachen, Kurt
See Hubbard, L(afayette) Ron(ald)

von Rezzori (d'Arezzo), Gregor
See Rezzori (d'Arezzo), Gregor von

von Sternberg, Josef
See Sternberg, Josef von

Vorster, Gordon   1924- . . . . CLC 34
See also CA 133

Vosce, Trudie
See Ozick, Cynthia

Voznesensky, Andrei (Andreievich)
    1933- . . . . . . CLC 1, 15, 57; DAM POET
See also CA 89-92; CANR 37; MTCW

Waddington, Miriam   1917- . . . . CLC 28
See also CA 21-24R; CANR 12, 30;
    DLB 68

Wagman, Fredrica   1937- . . . . CLC 7
See also CA 97-100; INT 97-100

Wagner, Richard   1813-1883. . . . . . . NCLC 9
See also DLB 129

Wagner-Martin, Linda   1936- . . . . CLC 50

Wagoner, David (Russell)
    1926- . . . . CLC 3, 5, 15
See also CA 1-4R; CAAS 3; CANR 2;
    DLB 5; SATA 14

Wah, Fred(erick James)   1939- . . . . . . CLC 44
See also CA 107; 141; DLB 60

Wahloo, Per   1926-1975 . . . . CLC 7
See also CA 61-64

Wahloo, Peter
See Wahloo, Per

Wain, John (Barrington)
    1925-1994 . . . . CLC 2, 11, 15, 46
See also CA 5-8R; 145; CAAS 4; CANR 23;
    CDBLB 1960 to Present; DLB 15, 27,
    139, 155; MTCW

Wajda, Andrzej   1926- . . . . CLC 16
See also CA 102

Wakefield, Dan   1932- . . . . CLC 7
See also CA 21-24R; CAAS 7

Wakoski, Diane
    1937- . . . . CLC 2, 4, 7, 9, 11, 40;
        DAM POET; PC 15
See also CA 13-16R; CAAS 1; CANR 9;
    DLB 5; INT CANR-9

Wakoski-Sherbell, Diane
See Wakoski, Diane

Walcott, Derek (Alton)
    1930- . . . . . CLC 2, 4, 9, 14, 25, 42, 67, 76;
        BLC; DAB; DAC; DAM MST, MULT,
            POET
See also BW 2; CA 89-92; CANR 26, 47;
    DLB 117; DLBY 81; MTCW

Waldman, Anne   1945- . . . . CLC 7
See also CA 37-40R; CAAS 17; CANR 34;
    DLB 16

Waldo, E. Hunter
See Sturgeon, Theodore (Hamilton)

Waldo, Edward Hamilton
See Sturgeon, Theodore (Hamilton)

Walker, Alice (Malsenior)
    1944- . . . . CLC 5, 6, 9, 19, 27, 46, 58;
        BLC; DA; DAB; DAC; DAM MST,
        MULT, NOV, POET, POP; SSC 5
See also AAYA 3; BEST 89:4; BW 2;
    CA 37-40R; CANR 9, 27, 49;
    CDALB 1968-1988; DLB 6, 33, 143;
    INT CANR-27; MTCW; SATA 31

Walker, David Harry   1911-1992. . . . CLC 14
See also CA 1-4R; 137; CANR 1; SATA 8;
    SATA-Obit 71

Walker, Edward Joseph   1934-
See Walker, Ted
See also CA 21-24R; CANR 12, 28, 53

Walker, George F.
    1947- . . . . CLC 44, 61; DAB; DAC;
        DAM MST
See also CA 103; CANR 21, 43; DLB 60

Walker, Joseph A.
    1935- . . . . CLC 19; DAM DRAM, MST
See also BW 1; CA 89-92; CANR 26;
    DLB 38

Walker, Margaret (Abigail)
    1915- . . . . CLC 1, 6; BLC; DAM MULT
See also BW 2; CA 73-76; CANR 26;
    DLB 76, 152; MTCW

Walker, Ted. . . . . CLC 13
See also Walker, Edward Joseph
See also DLB 40

Wallace, David Foster   1962- . . . . CLC 50
See also CA 132

Wallace, Dexter
See Masters, Edgar Lee

Wallace, (Richard Horatio) Edgar
    1875-1932 . . . . TCLC 57
See also CA 115; DLB 70

Wallace, Irving
    1916-1990 . . . . . CLC 7, 13; DAM NOV,
        POP
See also AITN 1; CA 1-4R; 132; CAAS 1;
    CANR 1, 27; INT CANR-27; MTCW

Wallant, Edward Lewis
    1926-1962 . . . . CLC 5, 10
See also CA 1-4R; CANR 22; DLB 2, 28,
    143; MTCW

Walley, Byron
See Card, Orson Scott

Walpole, Horace   1717-1797. . . . . LC 2
See also DLB 39, 104

Walpole, Hugh (Seymour)
    1884-1941. . . . . TCLC 5
See also CA 104; DLB 34

Walser, Martin   1927- . . . . CLC 27
See also CA 57-60; CANR 8, 46; DLB 75,
    124

Walser, Robert
    1878-1956 . . . . TCLC 18; SSC 20
See also CA 118; DLB 66

Walsh, Jill Paton. . . . . CLC 35
See also Paton Walsh, Gillian
See also AAYA 11; CLR 2; DLB 161;
    SAAS 3

Walter, Villiam Christian
See Andersen, Hans Christian

Wambaugh, Joseph (Aloysius, Jr.)
1937- .... **CLC 3, 18; DAM NOV, POP**
See also AITN 1; BEST 89:3; CA 33-36R;
CANR 42; DLB 6; DLBY 83; MTCW

Ward, Arthur Henry Sarsfield 1883-1959
See Rohmer, Sax
See also CA 108

Ward, Douglas Turner 1930-....... **CLC 19**
See also BW 1; CA 81-84; CANR 27;
DLB 7, 38

Ward, Mary Augusta
See Ward, Mrs. Humphry

Ward, Mrs. Humphry
1851-1920 .... **TCLC 55**
See also DLB 18

Ward, Peter
See Faust, Frederick (Schiller)

Warhol, Andy 1928(?)-1987........ **CLC 20**
See also AAYA 12; BEST 89:4; CA 89-92;
121; CANR 34

Warner, Francis (Robert le Plastrier)
1937-....................... **CLC 14**
See also CA 53-56; CANR 11

Warner, Marina 1946-............ **CLC 59**
See also CA 65-68; CANR 21

Warner, Rex (Ernest) 1905-1986.... **CLC 45**
See also CA 89-92; 119; DLB 15

Warner, Susan (Bogert)
1819-1885 .... **NCLC 31**
See also DLB 3, 42

Warner, Sylvia (Constance) Ashton
See Ashton-Warner, Sylvia (Constance)

Warner, Sylvia Townsend
1893-1978 .... **CLC 7, 19; SSC 23**
See also CA 61-64; 77-80; CANR 16;
DLB 34, 139; MTCW

Warren, Mercy Otis 1728-1814... **NCLC 13**
See also DLB 31

Warren, Robert Penn
1905-1989 .... **CLC 1, 4, 6, 8, 10, 13, 18,
39, 53, 59; DA; DAB; DAC; DAM MST,
NOV, POET; SSC 4; WLC**
See also AITN 1; CA 13-16R; 129;
CANR 10, 47; CDALB 1968-1988;
DLB 2, 48, 152; DLBY 80, 89;
INT CANR-10; MTCW; SATA 46;
SATA-Obit 63

Warshofsky, Isaac
See Singer, Isaac Bashevis

Warton, Thomas
1728-1790 .... **LC 15; DAM POET**
See also DLB 104, 109

Waruk, Kona
See Harris, (Theodore) Wilson

Warung, Price 1855-1911........ **TCLC 45**

Warwick, Jarvis
See Garner, Hugh

Washington, Alex
See Harris, Mark

Washington, Booker T(aliaferro)
1856-1915 .... **TCLC 10; BLC;
DAM MULT**
See also BW 1; CA 114; 125; SATA 28

Washington, George 1732-1799...... **LC 25**
See also DLB 31

Wassermann, (Karl) Jakob
1873-1934 .... **TCLC 6**
See also CA 104; DLB 66

Wasserstein, Wendy
1950-................ **CLC 32, 59, 90;
DAM DRAM; DC 4**
See also CA 121; 129; CABS 3; CANR 53;
INT 129

Waterhouse, Keith (Spencer)
1929-....................... **CLC 47**
See also CA 5-8R; CANR 38; DLB 13, 15;
MTCW

Waters, Frank (Joseph)
1902-1995 .... **CLC 88**
See also CA 5-8R; 149; CAAS 13; CANR 3,
18; DLBY 86

Waters, Roger 1944-.............. **CLC 35**

Watkins, Frances Ellen
See Harper, Frances Ellen Watkins

Watkins, Gerrold
See Malzberg, Barry N(athaniel)

Watkins, Gloria 1955(?)-
See hooks, bell
See also BW 2; CA 143

Watkins, Paul 1964-.............. **CLC 55**
See also CA 132

Watkins, Vernon Phillips
1906-1967 .... **CLC 43**
See also CA 9-10; 25-28R; CAP 1; DLB 20

Watson, Irving S.
See Mencken, H(enry) L(ouis)

Watson, John H.
See Farmer, Philip Jose

Watson, Richard F.
See Silverberg, Robert

Waugh, Auberon (Alexander) 1939-.. **CLC 7**
See also CA 45-48; CANR 6, 22; DLB 14

Waugh, Evelyn (Arthur St. John)
1903-1966 ...... **CLC 1, 3, 8, 13, 19, 27,
44; DA; DAB; DAC; DAM MST, NOV,
POP; WLC**
See also CA 85-88; 25-28R; CANR 22;
CDBLB 1914-1945; DLB 15, 162; MTCW

Waugh, Harriet 1944- .... **CLC 6**
See also CA 85-88; CANR 22

Ways, C. R.
See Blount, Roy (Alton), Jr.

Waystaff, Simon
See Swift, Jonathan

Webb, (Martha) Beatrice (Potter)
1858-1943 .... **TCLC 22**
See also Potter, Beatrice
See also CA 117

Webb, Charles (Richard) 1939-...... **CLC 7**
See also CA 25-28R

Webb, James H(enry), Jr. 1946-.... **CLC 22**
See also CA 81-84

Webb, Mary (Gladys Meredith)
1881-1927 .... **TCLC 24**
See also CA 123; DLB 34

Webb, Mrs. Sidney
See Webb, (Martha) Beatrice (Potter)

Webb, Phyllis 1927-.............. **CLC 18**
See also CA 104; CANR 23; DLB 53

Webb, Sidney (James)
1859-1947 .... **TCLC 22**
See also CA 117

Webber, Andrew Lloyd.............. **CLC 21**
See also Lloyd Webber, Andrew

Weber, Lenora Mattingly
1895-1971 .... **CLC 12**
See also CA 19-20; 29-32R; CAP 1;
SATA 2; SATA-Obit 26

Webster, John
1579(?)-1634(?) ...... **LC 33; DA; DAB;
DAC; DAM DRAM, MST; DC 2; WLC**
See also CDBLB Before 1660; DLB 58

Webster, Noah 1758-1843 .... **NCLC 30**

Wedekind, (Benjamin) Frank(lin)
1864-1918 ...... **TCLC 7; DAM DRAM**
See also CA 104; DLB 118

Weidman, Jerome 1913-............ **CLC 7**
See also AITN 2; CA 1-4R; CANR 1;
DLB 28

Weil, Simone (Adolphine)
1909-1943 .... **TCLC 23**
See also CA 117

Weinstein, Nathan
See West, Nathanael

Weinstein, Nathan von Wallenstein
See West, Nathanael

Weir, Peter (Lindsay) 1944- .... **CLC 20**
See also CA 113; 123

Weiss, Peter (Ulrich)
1916-1982 .... **CLC 3, 15, 51;
DAM DRAM**
See also CA 45-48; 106; CANR 3; DLB 69,
124

Weiss, Theodore (Russell)
1916-.................**CLC 3, 8, 14**
See also CA 9-12R; CAAS 2; CANR 46;
DLB 5

Welch, (Maurice) Denton
1915-1948 .... **TCLC 22**
See also CA 121; 148

Welch, James
1940-..... **CLC 6, 14, 52; DAM MULT,
POP**
See also CA 85-88; CANR 42; NNAL

Weldon, Fay
1933-......... **CLC 6, 9, 11, 19, 36, 59;
DAM POP**
See also CA 21-24R; CANR 16, 46;
CDBLB 1960 to Present; DLB 14;
INT CANR-16; MTCW

Wellek, Rene 1903-1995........... **CLC 28**
See also CA 5-8R; 150; CAAS 7; CANR 8;
DLB 63; INT CANR-8

Weller, Michael 1942-......... **CLC 10, 53**
See also CA 85-88

Weller, Paul 1958-............... **CLC 26**

Wellershoff, Dieter 1925-.......... **CLC 46**
See also CA 89-92; CANR 16, 37

Welles, (George) Orson
1915-1985 .... **CLC 20, 80**
See also CA 93-96; 117

Wellman, Mac 1945- .... **CLC 65**

Wellman, Manly Wade 1903-1986 .. **CLC 49**
See also CA 1-4R; 118; CANR 6, 16, 44;
SATA 6; SATA-Obit 47

Wells, Carolyn 1869(?)-1942 ...... **TCLC 35**
See also CA 113; DLB 11

Wells, H(erbert) G(eorge)
1866-1946 .... **TCLC 6, 12, 19; DA;**
DAB; DAC; DAM MST, NOV; SSC 6;
WLC
See also AAYA 18; CA 110; 121;
CDBLB 1914-1945; DLB 34, 70, 156;
MTCW; SATA 20

Wells, Rosemary 1943-............ **CLC 12**
See also AAYA 13; CA 85-88; CANR 48;
CLR 16; MAICYA; SAAS 1; SATA 18,
69

Welty, Eudora
1909- ...... **CLC 1, 2, 5, 14, 22, 33; DA;**
DAB; DAC; DAM MST, NOV; SSC 1;
WLC
See also CA 9-12R; CABS 1; CANR 32;
CDALB 1941-1968; DLB 2, 102, 143;
DLBD 12; DLBY 87; MTCW

Wen I-to 1899-1946 .... **TCLC 28**

Wentworth, Robert
See Hamilton, Edmond

Werfel, Franz (V.) 1890-1945 ...... **TCLC 8**
See also CA 104; DLB 81, 124

Wergeland, Henrik Arnold
1808-1845 .... **NCLC 5**

Wersba, Barbara 1932-............ **CLC 30**
See also AAYA 2; CA 29-32R; CANR 16,
38; CLR 3; DLB 52; JRDA; MAICYA;
SAAS 2; SATA 1, 58

Wertmueller, Lina 1928- .... **CLC 16**
See also CA 97-100; CANR 39

Wescott, Glenway 1901-1987....... **CLC 13**
See also CA 13-16R; 121; CANR 23;
DLB 4, 9, 102

Wesker, Arnold
1932- .... **CLC 3, 5, 42; DAB;**
DAM DRAM
See also CA 1-4R; CAAS 7; CANR 1, 33;
CDBLB 1960 to Present; DLB 13;
MTCW

Wesley, Richard (Errol) 1945-....... **CLC 7**
See also BW 1; CA 57-60; CANR 27;
DLB 38

Wessel, Johan Herman 1742-1785 .... **LC 7**

West, Anthony (Panther)
1914-1987 .... **CLC 50**
See also CA 45-48; 124; CANR 3, 19;
DLB 15

West, C. P.
See Wodehouse, P(elham) G(renville)

West, (Mary) Jessamyn
1902-1984 .... **CLC 7, 17**
See also CA 9-12R; 112; CANR 27; DLB 6;
DLBY 84; MTCW; SATA-Obit 37

West, Morris L(anglo) 1916-..... **CLC 6, 33**
See also CA 5-8R; CANR 24, 49; MTCW

West, Nathanael
1903-1940 ..... **TCLC 1, 14, 44; SSC 16**
See also CA 104; 125; CDALB 1929-1941;
DLB 4, 9, 28; MTCW

West, Owen
See Koontz, Dean R(ay)

West, Paul 1930- .... **CLC 7, 14, 96**
See also CA 13-16R; CAAS 7; CANR 22,
53; DLB 14; INT CANR-22

West, Rebecca 1892-1983 .. **CLC 7, 9, 31, 50**
See also CA 5-8R; 109; CANR 19; DLB 36;
DLBY 83; MTCW

Westall, Robert (Atkinson)
1929-1993 .... **CLC 17**
See also AAYA 12; CA 69-72; 141;
CANR 18; CLR 13; JRDA; MAICYA;
SAAS 2; SATA 23, 69; SATA-Obit 75

Westlake, Donald E(dwin)
1933- .... **CLC 7, 33; DAM POP**
See also CA 17-20R; CAAS 13; CANR 16,
44; INT CANR-16

Westmacott, Mary
See Christie, Agatha (Mary Clarissa)

Weston, Allen
See Norton, Andre

Wetcheek, J. L.
See Feuchtwanger, Lion

Wetering, Janwillem van de
See van de Wetering, Janwillem

Wetherell, Elizabeth
See Warner, Susan (Bogert)

Whale, James 1889-1957 .... **TCLC 63**

Whalen, Philip 1923-........... **CLC 6, 29**
See also CA 9-12R; CANR 5, 39; DLB 16

Wharton, Edith (Newbold Jones)
1862-1937 ...... **TCLC 3, 9, 27, 53; DA;**
DAB; DAC; DAM MST, NOV; SSC 6;
WLC
See also CA 104; 132; CDALB 1865-1917;
DLB 4, 9, 12, 78; DLBD 13; MTCW

Wharton, James
See Mencken, H(enry) L(ouis)

Wharton, William (a pseudonym)
.... **CLC 18, 37**
See also CA 93-96; DLBY 80; INT 93-96

Wheatley (Peters), Phillis
1754(?)-1784 .... **LC 3; BLC; DA; DAC;**
DAM MST, MULT, POET; PC 3; WLC
See also CDALB 1640-1865; DLB 31, 50

Wheelock, John Hall 1886-1978.... **CLC 14**
See also CA 13-16R; 77-80; CANR 14;
DLB 45

White, E(lwyn) B(rooks)
1899-1985 .. **CLC 10, 34, 39; DAM POP**
See also AITN 2; CA 13-16R; 116;
CANR 16, 37; CLR 1, 21; DLB 11, 22;
MAICYA; MTCW; SATA 2, 29;
SATA-Obit 44

White, Edmund (Valentine III)
1940- .... **CLC 27; DAM POP**
See also AAYA 7; CA 45-48; CANR 3, 19,
36; MTCW

White, Patrick (Victor Martindale)
1912-1990 .. **CLC 3, 4, 5, 7, 9, 18, 65, 69**
See also CA 81-84; 132; CANR 43; MTCW

White, Phyllis Dorothy James 1920-
See James, P. D.
See also CA 21-24R; CANR 17, 43;
DAM POP; MTCW

White, T(erence) H(anbury)
1906-1964 .... **CLC 30**
See also CA 73-76; CANR 37; DLB 160;
JRDA; MAICYA; SATA 12

White, Terence de Vere
1912-1994 .... **CLC 49**
See also CA 49-52; 145; CANR 3

White, Walter F(rancis)
1893-1955 .... **TCLC 15**
See also White, Walter
See also BW 1; CA 115; 124; DLB 51

White, William Hale 1831-1913
See Rutherford, Mark
See also CA 121

Whitehead, E(dward) A(nthony)
1933- .... **CLC 5**
See also CA 65-68

Whitemore, Hugh (John) 1936-..... **CLC 37**
See also CA 132; INT 132

Whitman, Sarah Helen (Power)
1803-1878 .... **NCLC 19**
See also DLB 1

Whitman, Walt(er)
1819-1892 ..... **NCLC 4, 31; DA; DAB;**
DAC; DAM MST, POET; PC 3; WLC
See also CDALB 1640-1865; DLB 3, 64;
SATA 20

Whitney, Phyllis A(yame)
1903- .... **CLC 42; DAM POP**
See also AITN 2; BEST 90:3; CA 1-4R;
CANR 3, 25, 38; JRDA; MAICYA;
SATA 1, 30

Whittemore, (Edward) Reed (Jr.)
1919- .... **CLC 4**
See also CA 9-12R; CAAS 8; CANR 4;
DLB 5

Whittier, John Greenleaf
1807-1892 .... **NCLC 8**
See also DLB 1

Whittlebot, Hernia
See Coward, Noel (Peirce)

Wicker, Thomas Grey 1926-
See Wicker, Tom
See also CA 65-68; CANR 21, 46

Wicker, Tom .... **CLC 7**
See also Wicker, Thomas Grey

Wideman, John Edgar
1941- .... **CLC 5, 34, 36, 67; BLC;**
DAM MULT
See also BW 2; CA 85-88; CANR 14, 42;
DLB 33, 143

Wiebe, Rudy (Henry)
1934- .... **CLC 6, 11, 14; DAC;**
DAM MST
See also CA 37-40R; CANR 42; DLB 60

Wieland, Christoph Martin
1733-1813 .... **NCLC 17**
See also DLB 97

Wiene, Robert 1881-1938........ **TCLC 56**

Wieners, John 1934-.............. **CLC 7**
See also CA 13-16R; DLB 16

Wister, Owen 1860-1938 . . . . **TCLC 21**
See also CA 108; DLB 9, 78; SATA 62

Witkacy
See Witkiewicz, Stanislaw Ignacy

Witkiewicz, Stanislaw Ignacy
1885-1939 . . . . **TCLC 8**
See also CA 105

Wittgenstein, Ludwig (Josef Johann)
1889-1951 . . . . **TCLC 59**
See also CA 113

Wittig, Monique 1935(?)- . . . . **CLC 22**
See also CA 116; 135; DLB 83

Wittlin, Jozef 1896-1976 . . . . **CLC 25**
See also CA 49-52; 65-68; CANR 3

Wodehouse, P(elham) G(renville)
1881-1975 . . . **CLC 1, 2, 5, 10, 22; DAB;**
DAC; DAM NOV; SSC 2
See also AITN 2; CA 45-48; 57-60;
CANR 3, 33; CDBLB 1914-1945;
DLB 34, 162; MTCW; SATA 22

Woiwode, L.
See Woiwode, Larry (Alfred)

Woiwode, Larry (Alfred) 1941- . . . **CLC 6, 10**
See also CA 73-76; CANR 16; DLB 6;
INT CANR-16

Wojciechowska, Maia (Teresa)
1927- . . . . **CLC 26**
See also AAYA 8; CA 9-12R; CANR 4, 41;
CLR 1; JRDA; MAICYA; SAAS 1;
SATA 1, 28, 83

Wolf, Christa 1929- . . . . **CLC 14, 29, 58**
See also CA 85-88; CANR 45; DLB 75;
MTCW

Wolfe, Gene (Rodman)
1931- . . . . **CLC 25; DAM POP**
See also CA 57-60; CAAS 9; CANR 6, 32;
DLB 8

Wolfe, George C. 1954- . . . . **CLC 49**
See also CA 149

Wolfe, Thomas (Clayton)
1900-1938 . . . . . **TCLC 4, 13, 29, 61; DA;**
DAB; DAC; DAM MST, NOV; WLC
See also CA 104; 132; CDALB 1929-1941;
DLB 9, 102; DLBD 2; DLBY 85; MTCW

Wolfe, Thomas Kennerly, Jr. 1931-
See Wolfe, Tom
See also CA 13-16R; CANR 9, 33;
DAM POP; INT CANR-9; MTCW

Wolfe, Tom . . . . **CLC 1, 2, 9, 15, 35, 51**
See also Wolfe, Thomas Kennerly, Jr.
See also AAYA 8; AITN 2; BEST 89:1;
DLB 152

Wolff, Geoffrey (Ansell) 1937- . . . . . **CLC 41**
See also CA 29-32R; CANR 29, 43

Wolff, Sonia
See Levitin, Sonia (Wolff)

Wolff, Tobias (Jonathan Ansell)
1945- . . . . **CLC 39, 64**
See also AAYA 16; BEST 90:2; CA 114;
117; CAAS 22; DLB 130; INT 117

Wolfram von Eschenbach
c. 1170-c. 1220 . . . . **CMLC 5**
See also DLB 138

Wolitzer, Hilma 1930- . . . . **CLC 17**
See also CA 65-68; CANR 18, 40;
INT CANR-18; SATA 31

Wollstonecraft, Mary 1759-1797 . . . . . . **LC 5**
See also CDBLB 1789-1832; DLB 39, 104,
158

Wonder, Stevie . . . . **CLC 12**
See also Morris, Steveland Judkins

Wong, Jade Snow 1922- . . . . **CLC 17**
See also CA 109

Woodcott, Keith
See Brunner, John (Kilian Houston)

Woodruff, Robert W.
See Mencken, H(enry) L(ouis)

Woolf, (Adeline) Virginia
1882-1941 . . . . **TCLC 1, 5, 20, 43, 56;**
DA; DAB; DAC; DAM MST, NOV;
SSC 7; WLC
See also CA 104; 130; CDBLB 1914-1945;
DLB 36, 100, 162; DLBD 10; MTCW

Woollcott, Alexander (Humphreys)
1887-1943 . . . . **TCLC 5**
See also CA 105; DLB 29

Woolrich, Cornell 1903-1968 . . . . **CLC 77**
See also Hopley-Woolrich, Cornell George

Wordsworth, Dorothy
1771-1855 . . . . **NCLC 25**
See also DLB 107

Wordsworth, William
1770-1850 . . . . **NCLC 12, 38; DA; DAB;**
DAC; DAM MST, POET; PC 4; WLC
See also CDBLB 1789-1832; DLB 93, 107

Wouk, Herman
1915- . . **CLC 1, 9, 38; DAM NOV, POP**
See also CA 5-8R; CANR 6, 33; DLBY 82;
INT CANR-6; MTCW

Wright, Charles (Penzel, Jr.)
1935- . . . . **CLC 6, 13, 28**
See also CA 29-32R; CAAS 7; CANR 23,
36; DLB 165; DLBY 82; MTCW

Wright, Charles Stevenson
1932- . . . . **CLC 49; BLC 3;**
DAM MULT, POET
See also BW 1; CA 9-12R; CANR 26;
DLB 33

Wright, Jack R.
See Harris, Mark

Wright, James (Arlington)
1927-1980 . . . . **CLC 3, 5, 10, 28;**
DAM POET
See also AITN 2; CA 49-52; 97-100;
CANR 4, 34; DLB 5; MTCW

Wright, Judith (Arundell)
1915- . . . . **CLC 11, 53; PC 14**
See also CA 13-16R; CANR 31; MTCW;
SATA 14

Wright, L(aurali) R. 1939- . . . . **CLC 44**
See also CA 138

Wright, Richard (Nathaniel)
1908-1960 . . . . **CLC 1, 3, 4, 9, 14, 21, 48,**
74; BLC; DA; DAB; DAC; DAM MST,
MULT, NOV; SSC 2; WLC
See also AAYA 5; BW 1; CA 108;
CDALB 1929-1941; DLB 76, 102;
DLBD 2; MTCW

Wright, Richard B(ruce) 1937- . . . . . . **CLC 6**
See also CA 85-88; DLB 53

Wright, Rick 1945- . . . . **CLC 35**

Wright, Rowland
See Wells, Carolyn

Wright, Stephen Caldwell 1946- . . . . **CLC 33**
See also BW 2

Wright, Willard Huntington 1888-1939
See Van Dine, S. S.
See also CA 115

Wright, William 1930- . . . . **CLC 44**
See also CA 53-56; CANR 7, 23

Wroth, LadyMary 1587-1653(?) . . . . . **LC 30**
See also DLB 121

Wu Ch'eng-en 1500(?)-1582(?) . . . . **LC 7**

Wu Ching-tzu 1701-1754 . . . . **LC 2**

Wurlitzer, Rudolph 1938(?)- . . . **CLC 2, 4, 15**
See also CA 85-88

Wycherley, William
1641-1715 . . . . . **LC 8, 21; DAM DRAM**
See also CDBLB 1660-1789; DLB 80

Wylie, Elinor (Morton Hoyt)
1885-1928 . . . . **TCLC 8**
See also CA 105; DLB 9, 45

Wylie, Philip (Gordon) 1902-1971 . . . **CLC 43**
See also CA 21-22; 33-36R; CAP 2; DLB 9

Wyndham, John . . . . **CLC 19**
See also Harris, John (Wyndham Parkes
Lucas) Beynon

Wyss, Johann David Von
1743-1818 . . . . **NCLC 10**
See also JRDA; MAICYA; SATA 29;
SATA-Brief 27

Xenophon
c. 430B.C.-c. 354B.C. . . . . **CMLC 17**

Yakumo Koizumi
See Hearn, (Patricio) Lafcadio (Tessima
Carlos)

Yanez, Jose Donoso
See Donoso (Yanez), Jose

Yanovsky, Basile S.
See Yanovsky, V(assily) S(emenovich)

Yanovsky, V(assily) S(emenovich)
1906-1989 . . . . **CLC 2, 18**
See also CA 97-100; 129

Yates, Richard 1926-1992 . . . . . **CLC 7, 8, 23**
See also CA 5-8R; 139; CANR 10, 43;
DLB 2; DLBY 81, 92; INT CANR-10

Yeats, W. B.
See Yeats, William Butler

Yeats, William Butler
1865-1939 . . . . . **TCLC 1, 11, 18, 31; DA;**
DAB; DAC; DAM DRAM, MST,
POET; WLC
See also CA 104; 127; CANR 45;
CDBLB 1890-1914; DLB 10, 19, 98, 156;
MTCW

Yehoshua, A(braham) B.
1936- . . . . **CLC 13, 31**
See also CA 33-36R; CANR 43

Yep, Laurence Michael 1948- . . . . . . **CLC 35**
See also AAYA 5; CA 49-52; CANR 1, 46;
CLR 3, 17; DLB 52; JRDA; MAICYA;
SATA 7, 69

Literary Criticism Series
Cumulative Topic Index

This index lists all topic entries in Gale's *Classical and Medieval Literature Criticism, Contemporary Literary Criticism, Literature Criticism from 1400 to 1800, Nineteenth-Century Literature Criticism,* and *Twentieth-Century Literary Criticism.*

Topic Index

Topic Index

CLC Cumulative Nationality Index

Nationality Index

Dorfman, Ariel **48, 77**
Guevara, Che **87**
Mujica Lainez, Manuel **31**
Puig, Manuel **3, 5, 10, 28, 65**
Sabato, Ernesto (R.) **10, 23**
Valenzuela, Luisa **31**

ARMENIAN
Mamoulian, Rouben (Zachary) **16**

AUSTRALIAN
Anderson, Jessica (Margaret) Queale **37**
Astley, Thea (Beatrice May) **41**
Brinsmead, H(esba) F(ay) **21**
Buckley, Vincent (Thomas) **57**
Buzo, Alexander (John) **61**
Carey, Peter **40, 55, 96**
Clark, Mavis Thorpe **12**
Clavell, James (duMaresq) **6, 25, 87**
Courtenay, Bryce **59**
Davison, Frank Dalby **15**
Elliott, Sumner Locke **38**
FitzGerald, Robert D(avid) **19**
Grenville, Kate **61**
Hall, Rodney **51**
Hazzard, Shirley **18**
Hope, A(lec) D(erwent) **3, 51**
Hospital, Janette Turner **42**
Jolley, (Monica) Elizabeth **46**
Jones, Rod **50**
Keneally, Thomas (Michael) **5, 8, 10, 14, 19, 27, 43**
Koch, C(hristopher) J(ohn) **42**
Lawler, Raymond Evenor **58**
Malouf, (George Joseph) David **28, 86**
Matthews, Greg **45**
McAuley, James Phillip **45**
McCullough, Colleen **27**
Murray, Les(lie) A(llan) **40**
Porter, Peter (Neville Frederick) **5, 13, 33**
Prichard, Katharine Susannah **46**
Shapcott, Thomas W(illiam) **38**
Slessor, Kenneth **14**
Stead, Christina (Ellen) **2, 5, 8, 32, 80**
Stow, (Julian) Randolph **23, 48**
Thiele, Colin (Milton) **17**
Weir, Peter (Lindsay) **20**
West, Morris L(anglo) **6, 33**
White, Patrick (Victor Martindale) **3, 4, 5, 7, 9, 18, 65, 69**
Wilding, Michael **73**
Williamson, David (Keith) **56**
Wright, Judith (Arandell) **11, 53**

AUSTRIAN
Adamson, Joy(-Friederike Victoria) **17**
Bachmann, Ingeborg **69**
Bernhard, Thomas **3, 32, 61**
Bettelheim, Bruno **79**
Frankl, Viktor E(mil) **93**
Gregor, Arthur **9**
Handke, Peter **5, 8, 10, 15, 38**
Hochwaelder, Fritz **36**
Jandl, Ernst **34**
Lang, Fritz **20**
Lind, Jakov **1, 2, 4, 27, 82**
Sternberg, Josef von **20**
Wellek, Rene **28**
Wilder, Billy **20**

BARBADIAN
Brathwaite, Edward Kamau **11**

Clarke, Austin C(hesterfield) **8, 53**
Kennedy, Adrienne (Lita) **66**
Lamming, George (William) **2, 4, 66**

BELGIAN
Crommelynck, Fernand **75**
Ghelderode, Michel de **6, 11**
Levi-Strauss, Claude **38**
Mallet-Joris, Francoise **11**
Michaux, Henri **8, 19**
Sarton, (Eleanor) May **4, 14, 49, 91**
Simenon, Georges (Jacques Christian) **1, 2, 3, 8, 18, 47**
van Itallie, Jean-Claude **3**
Yourcenar, Marguerite **19, 38, 50, 87**

BOTSWANAN
Head, Bessie **25, 67**

BRAZILIAN
Amado, Jorge **13, 40**
Andrade, Carlos Drummond de **18**
Cabral de Melo Neto, Joao **76**
Dourado, (Waldomiro Freitas) Autran **23, 60**
Drummond de Andrade, Carlos **18**
Lispector, Clarice **43**
Ribeiro, Darcy **34**
Ribeiro, Joao Ubaldo (Osorio Pimentel) **10, 67**
Rosa, Joao Guimaraes **23**

BULGARIAN
Bagryana, Elisaveta **10**
Belcheva, Elisaveta **10**
Canetti, Elias **3, 14, 25, 75, 86**
Kristeva, Julia **77**

CAMEROONIAN
Beti, Mongo **27**

CANADIAN
Acorn, Milton **15**
Aquin, Hubert **15**
Atwood, Margaret (Eleanor) **2, 3, 4, 8, 13, 15, 25, 44, 84**
Avison, Margaret **2, 4**
Barfoot, Joan **18**
Bellow, Saul **1, 2, 3, 6, 8, 10, 13, 15, 25, 33, 34, 63, 79**
Birney, (Alfred) Earle **1, 4, 6, 11**
Bissett, Bill **18**
Blais, Marie-Claire **2, 4, 6, 13, 22**
Blaise, Clark **29**
Bowering, George **15, 47**
Bowering, Marilyn R(uthe) **32**
Buckler, Ernest **13**
Buell, John (Edward) **10**
Callaghan, Morley Edward **3, 14, 41, 65**
Campbell, Maria **85**
Carrier, Roch **13, 78**
Child, Philip **19, 68**
Chislett, (Margaret) Anne **34**
Clarke, Austin C(hesterfield) **8, 53**
Cohen, Leonard (Norman) **3, 38**
Cohen, Matt **19**
Coles, Don **46**
Cook, Michael **58**
Cooper, Douglas **86**
Coupland, Douglas **85**
Craven, Margaret **17**

Davies, (William) Robertson **2, 7, 13, 25, 42, 75, 91**
de la Roche, Mazo **14**
Donnell, David **34**
Ducharme, Rejean **74**
Dudek, Louis **11, 19**
Engel, Marian **36**
Everson, R(onald) G(ilmour) **27**
Faludy, George **42**
Ferron, Jacques **94**
Finch, Robert (Duer Claydon) **18**
Findley, Timothy **27**
Fraser, Sylvia **64**
Frye, (Herman) Northrop **24, 70**
Gallant, Mavis **7, 18, 38**
Garner, Hugh **13**
Gilmour, David **35**
Glassco, John **9**
Gotlieb, Phyllis Fay (Bloom) **18**
Govier, Katherine **51**
Gunnars, Kristjana **69**
Gustafson, Ralph (Barker) **36**
Haig-Brown, Roderick (Langmere) **21**
Hailey, Arthur **5**
Harris, Christie (Lucy) Irwin **12**
Hebert, Anne **4, 13, 29**
Highway, Tomson **92**
Hillis, Rick **66**
Hine, (William) Daryl **15**
Hodgins, Jack **23**
Hood, Hugh (John Blagdon) **15, 28**
Hospital, Janette Turner **42**
Hyde, Anthony **42**
Jacobsen, Josephine **48**
Jiles, Paulette **13, 58**
Johnston, George (Benson) **51**
Jones, D(ouglas) G(ordon) **10**
Kelly, M(ilton) T(erry) **55**
King, Thomas **89**
Kinsella, W(illiam) P(atrick) **27, 43**
Klein, A(braham) M(oses) **19**
Kogawa, Joy Nozomi **78**
Krizanc, John **57**
Kroetsch, Robert **5, 23, 57**
Kroker, Arthur **77**
Lane, Patrick **25**
Laurence, (Jean) Margaret (Wemyss) **3, 6, 13, 50, 62**
Layton, Irving (Peter) **2, 15**
Levine, Norman **54**
Lightfoot, Gordon **26**
Livesay, Dorothy (Kathleen) **4, 15, 79**
MacEwen, Gwendolyn (Margaret) **13, 55**
MacLennan, (John) Hugh **2, 14, 92**
MacLeod, Alistair **56**
Macpherson, (Jean) Jay **14**
Maillet, Antonine **54**
Major, Kevin (Gerald) **26**
McFadden, David **48**
McLuhan, (Herbert) Marshall **37, 83**
Metcalf, John **37**
Mitchell, Joni **12**
Mitchell, W(illiam) O(rmond) **25**
Moore, Brian **1, 3, 5, 7, 8, 19, 32, 90**
Morgan, Janet **39**
Moure, Erin **88**
Mowat, Farley (McGill) **26**
Munro, Alice **6, 10, 19, 50, 95**
Musgrave, Susan **13, 54**
Newlove, John (Herbert) **14**
Nichol, B(arrie) P(hillip) **18**
Nowlan, Alden (Albert) **15**

Nationality Index

Nationality Index

Nationality Index

CLC-96 Title Index

Title Index

ISBN 0-8103-1060-7

90000